Fodor's

ESSENTIAL
ENGLAND

Welcome to England

From medieval cathedrals to postmodern towers, from prehistoric stones to one-pub villages, England is a tribute to the strength—and flexibility—of tradition. Visitors can explore grand manors and royal castles and also discover cutting-edge art, innovative cultural scenes, and trendy shops. English treasures like the Georgian town of Bath, academic Oxford, and eccentric Brighton remain vibrant, and silvery lakes and green hills provide enduring grace notes. This book was produced during the COVID-19 pandemic. As you plan your travels to England, please confirm that places are still open and let us know when we need to make updates by writing to us at editors@fodors.com.

TOP REASONS TO GO

★ **London:** Landmarks, top theater, museums, village-like neighborhoods—it's all here.

★ **Idyllic Towns:** The Cotswolds' stone cottages, Cornwall's seaside charmers, and more invite leisurely exploration.

★ **Pubs:** For a pint or a chat, a visit to one of "England's living rooms" is essential.

★ **History:** Sights from Stonehenge to Windsor Castle bring the country's past to life.

★ **Great Walks:** Classic trails await in the Lake District and Yorkshire's dales and moors.

★ **Gardens:** Roses, flower borders, and sculpted landscapes flaunt a national talent.

Contents

Fodor's Features

Chapter 1

EXPERIENCE ENGLAND

26 ULTIMATE EXPERIENCES

England offers terrific experiences that should be on every traveler's list. Here are Fodor's top picks for a memorable trip.

1 Oxford and Cambridge

England is home to these two prestigious universities, where you'll find centuries of English history among ancient buildings and museums. Tour the accompanying towns via punting boats on local waterways. (Ch. 4, 12)

2 London

London is the beating heart of England, home to some of the country's most iconic sights including world-class museums and picture-perfect palaces. *(Ch. 3)*

3 Football Matches

Whether you're rooting for Liverpool or Man U, attending a game or watching at a pub, a football match is a great way to observe locals at their most passionate. *(Ch. 10)*

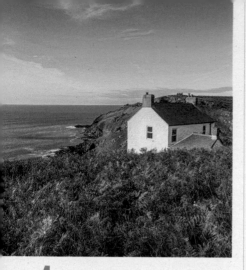

4 The Cornish Coast

Quaint Cornish seaside towns like St. Ives and Padstow offer fresh seafood, charming harbor views, and sandy beaches. *(Ch. 7)*

5 Yorkshire

The stunning natural landscape of Yorkshire's moors and dales inspired the Brontës and continues to attract hikers, cyclists, and nature-lovers. *(Ch. 13)*

6 English Gardens

The English know how to garden, so there's no shortage of bucolic splendor here, from the landscaped wonders of Stourhead to the roses of Sissinghurst Castle Garden. *(Ch. 5, 6)*

7 Wimbledon

Every summer, the world's oldest (and many say most prestigious) tennis tournament takes place in London to much fanfare and with much tradition. *(Ch. 3)*

8 Hadrian's Wall

This ancient wall, parts of which date back to AD 142, once marked the edges of Roman rule and remains one of the last great Roman ruins in England. *(Ch. 14)*

9 Bath

One of the most beautiful cities in Europe, Bath is a testament to both the architectural skills of the Georgians and the Roman love of thermal spas. *(Ch. 8)*

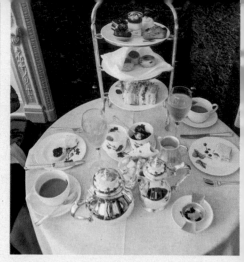

10 Literary England

From Jane Austen and Beatrix Potter to Wordsworth and the Brontë sisters, the homes of famous authors and the inspirations for their works are found all over England. *(Ch. 6, 11, 13)*

11 Afternoon Tea

For a quintessential English ritual, enjoy a pot of tea served in bone china alongside finger sandwiches, fruit scones, and cakes. *(Ch. 3)*

12 Brighton

With its grand architecture, seaside charm, and vast array of music venues and art galleries, it's easy to see why Brighton is often labeled London-by-the-Sea. *(Ch. 5)*

13 Historic Homes and Castles

From Windsor Castle and Blenheim Palace to Highclere Castle and Charlecote House, the manors, castles, and palaces in England will fulfill any Downton Abbey fantasy. *(Ch. 4, 6, 9)*

14 Art Museums

Art museums here hold both historic treasures and contemporary delights. London's Tate Britain and Tate Modern in particular have some of the most celebrated collections in the world. *(Ch. 3)*

15 Stratford-Upon-Avon

The birthplace of William Shakespeare offers plenty for fans of the Bard, including performances of his plays at the Royal Shakespeare Company. *(Ch. 9)*

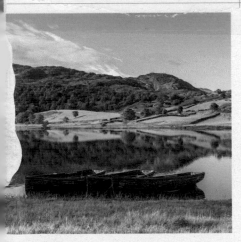

16 The Lake District

Lake District National Park covers over 880 square miles of picturesque wilderness, complete with lovely villages, England's highest mountain, and, of course, lakes galore. *(Ch. 11)*

17 Fish-and-Chips

Whether it's from a small seaside town or a rowdy city pub, fried fish-and-chips are the ultimate British comfort food (don't forget the malt vinegar and mushy peas). *(Ch. 7, 13)*

18 Steam Trains

Once the main mode of transportation for the upper class, today a trip on one of England's few remaining steam railways is a unique way to see the countryside. *(Ch. 7)*

19 Stonehenge

Awe-inspiring and mystical, Stonehenge is one of the most famous prehistoric sites in England, as well as one of history's most enduring mysteries. *(Ch. 6)*

20 The Jurassic Coast

Not only is Dorset's 95-mile Jurassic Coast the most beautiful stretch of coastline in England, but it's also an ancient geological wonder teeming with fossils. *(Ch. 6)*

21 Manchester

England's true second city, Manchester has transformed from a gritty birthplace of industry to a cutting-edge source of excellent music, culture, and cuisine. *(Ch. 10)*

22 Culinary London

London is one of the world's great foodie cities, offering everything from authentic Indian cuisine to smoky Jamaican jerk chicken, from lip-smacking street food to acclaimed fine-dining restaurants. *(Ch. 3)*

23 Grand Cathedrals

The majestic cathedrals of Canterbury, Salisbury, and York Minster, among many others, are essential parts of England's urban landscapes and its history. *(Ch. 5, 6, 13)*

24 Historic Pubs

The history of England's taverns and pubs is the history of the country itself. Grab a pint or a gin cocktail and get to know how the locals live. *(Ch. 3)*

25 The Cotswolds

Full of quaint English villages, the Cotswolds is one of the prettiest regions of the country, thanks to its stone cottages, manicured gardens, and rural charm. *(Ch. 8)*

26 The Beatles in Liverpool

A former merchant city, Liverpool is also the birthplace of the Beatles, and fans can trace the musical history here, from John Lennon's childhood home to Penny Lane. *(Ch. 10)*

WHAT'S WHERE

1 London. Not only Britain's financial and governmental center but also one of the world's great cities, London has mammoth museums, posh palaces, double-decker buses, and iconic sights—from Buckingham Palace to Tower Bridge.

2 Oxford and the Thames Valley. London's commuter belt takes in the charming spires of university city Oxford, as well as Windsor, where the Queen spends most weekends, and Eton, home to the prestigious private school. There are also peaceful river towns such as Henley and Marlow that offer relaxing river excursions, as well as a host of stately homes, from Blenheim Palace to Waddesdon Manor.

3 Canterbury and the Southeast. This compact green and pleasant region within day-trip distance of London takes in Canterbury and its famous cathedral. Other regional highlights include funky seaside resort Brighton, the appealing towns of Rye and Lewes, and Dover's iconic white cliffs.

4 Stonehenge and the South. Hampshire, Dorset, and Wiltshire have quintessential English countryside, with gentle hills and green pastures. Explore the stone circles at Stonehenge and Avebury, take in Winchester (Jane Austen country) and Salisbury, and discover Highclere Castle and Lyme Regis.

5 Cornwall and the West Country. Somerset, Devon, and Cornwall are sunnier and warmer than the rest of the country, with inviting sandy beaches. Cornwall is famed for its stunning coastline and lush gardens. Of the cities, Bristol is the largest and most vibrant, while Wells and Exeter are attractive and compact. Take in the brooding heaths and moors of Exmoor, Dartmoor, and Bodmin, too.

6 Bath and the Cotswolds. The grand Georgian town of Bath is one of England's highlights, with the Roman baths and golden-stone 18th- and 19th-century architecture. Nearby, the Cotswolds region is justly famous for tranquil, stone-built villages, such as Chipping Campden, Stow-on-the-Wold, and Tetbury.

WHAT'S WHERE

7 Stratford-upon-Avon and the Heart of England. About 100 miles northwest of London, Stratford-upon-Avon is the place to see Shakespeare's childhood home and watch his plays. Nearby Warwickshire has Warwick and Kenilworth castles while Birmingham offers a modern urban experience.

8 Manchester, Liverpool, and the Peak District. Liverpool rides the Beatles' coattails but, like Manchester, has transformed its warehouses and docks into sleek hotels, restaurants, and shops. The surrounding Peak District has great opportunities for walking and visiting stately homes such as Chatsworth and Haddon Hall.

9 The Lake District. Home to a popular national park, this startlingly beautiful area has craggy hills, wild moorland, stone cottages, and glittering silvery lakes. Nature lovers and hikers crowd the region in summer. Among the literary high points are the homes of Wordsworth and Beatrix Potter.

10 Cambridge and East Anglia. The biggest lure in this green, flat, low-key region is Cambridge, with its medieval halls of learning. The countryside is dominated by the cathedrals of Ely and Norwich, as well as by time-warp towns such as Lavenham and coastal spots like Aldeburgh.

11 Yorkshire. This wilder part of England has great appeal for lovers of the outdoors, but the ancient walled city of York is also a center of attention. To York's west are the moors and dales that inspired the Brontës, and in east Yorkshire the moors collide with the sea at towns such as Whitby.

12 Hadrian's Wall and the Northeast. Walk in the footsteps of Roman soldiers along atmospheric Hadrian's Wall. Bamburgh and Dunstanburgh castles guard the coast while Alnwick Castle has stunning gardens. The small city of Durham is a medieval gem and a real contrast to modern, cosmopolitan Newcastle.

England Today

England is the biggest region in the United Kingdom (or the U.K.), the nation that also includes Scotland, Wales, Northern Ireland, and the Channel Islands (Guernsey and Jersey). England, Scotland, and Wales form what is referred to as Great Britain (or just Britain). Despite being given the opportunity in a 2014 referendum to become an independent nation, Scottish voters chose to remain part of the United Kingdom. It's worth noting that, while England, Scotland, and Wales are all part of Britain and the U.K., Wales and Scotland aren't part of England, and vice versa. Get that one wrong at your peril—you haven't seen angry until you've seen a Scot referred to as English.

Although it's about the size of Louisiana, England has a population 12 times as large: 56 million people find space to live on its green rolling hills and in its shallow valleys and crowded cities.

POLITICS

Since the general election of 2015, the United Kingdom's government has been in the hands of the Conservative Party. But the unexpected result of a June 2016 referendum, in which the country voted to leave the European Union (a decision known commonly as Brexit), led to the resignation of prime minister David Cameron, who was replaced by Theresa May. Following three turbulent years—which were dominated by Brexit negotiations and marked by the loss of a parliamentary majority, cabinet resignations, tragic terrorist attacks in London and Manchester, the horrific Grenfell Tower fire disaster, and a crisis in the National Health Service (NHS)—May was replaced by Boris Johnson in July 2019. Despite being seen as a deeply divisive figure, Johnson secured an overall parliamentary majority for the Conservatives at the December 2019 general election, and, in

January 2020, proceeded to finally take the U.K. out of the European Union under the terms of his Brexit withdrawal agreement. But in March 2020, the COVID-19 pandemic turned the world upside down, and Britain's official exit from the E.U. has been overshadowed by the safety measures instilled on British citizens as the world waits for a vaccine.

BREXIT

The United Kingdom officially began to leave the European Union in January 2020, but despite this and Boris Johnson's election slogan of "Get Brexit Done," most experts agree that this issue is set to dominate British politics (and newspaper column inches) for years to come. The transition period, during which the U.K. remains in the single market, applies until December 31, 2020, and negotiations are ongoing to finalize a long-term agreement on the future relationship between Britain and the E.U. If no agreement is reached by December 2020, and there is no extension, there will be a "no-deal" Brexit. While visitors to England shouldn't feel the effects of Brexit on their travel plans until the end of the transition period, it is still a topic discussed nearly everywhere. Many major openings and tourism projects have been put on hold until after the official exit, and there have been regular exchange rate fluctuations. Following the end of the transition period, new immigration policies will be introduced, which may mean changes to entry requirements and visa validity.

THE ROYAL FAMILY

Essentially a figurehead monarchy with a symbolic political role, the Royal Family and each member of its four generations continue to exercise the public's fascination, both at home and abroad. Although taxpayer cost for supporting the family is estimated at £67 million (around $85 million) a year, many consider the tourists they bring worth the cost (tourism numbers have been helped along in recent years with the success of television shows like *Downton Abbey* and *The Crown*). The Queen, now the world's longest reigning monarch, celebrated her Sapphire Jubilee (65 years on the throne) in February 2017 and still maintains a full working schedule, although her husband, Prince Philip, has now retired from public life. Both are in their 90s.

Prince Charles remains in the wing, while his son, Prince William, is second in the line of succession. William's personal life has generated plenty of buzz in recent years, from his 2011 wedding to Kate Middleton (now known publicly as Catherine, Duchess of Cambridge) to the births of their three children: future king Prince George, Princess Charlotte, and Prince Louis. However, in the last few years, most of the headlines have gone to his younger brother Harry, first for his wedding to American actress Meghan Markle in May 2018, then for the birth of their son Archie in May 2019, and most recently for the announcement that the couple intend to step back as senior members of the Royal Family and split their time between the United Kingdom and the United States.

HOUSING AND DEVELOPMENT

As one of the most crowded countries in Europe with an ever-expanding population, England has a growing housing crisis on its hands. Consequently, the government has relaxed planning policies, given financial help to first-time home buyers, and pledged to build at least a million new homes over the next five years. The goal is to combat rising house prices and to alleviate a reliance on family inheritance as the only way to set a foot on the housing ladder.

The problem of housing inequality was highlighted by the devastating Grenfell Tower fire in June 2017, which resulted in a staggering 72 deaths. Ironically, this 24-story tower block of affordable housing was situated in Kensington and Chelsea, the wealthiest borough in London. Its charred wreckage serves as a potent reminder of societal unconcern for those less affluent and a government failure to implement adequate fire regulations despite residents' repeated warnings (the focus was instead on cost-cutting measures during recent renovations). A government inquiry was initiated in September 2017 and is currently in its second phase.

SPORTS

Many of the world's most popular sports, including soccer (aka football), cricket, and tennis, were codified in England during the 19th century, and sport continues to play a prominent role in everyday life here. While the United Kingdom sends a combined team to the Olympics (colloqially known as "Team GB"), England has individual national representation for most team sports. The England soccer team is a particular obsession, with its performances at major tournaments affecting the mood of the nation. England is also home to the Premier League, the world's most watched sports league, with globally popular soccer teams like Manchester United, Liverpool, and Chelsea. When the locals aren't watching soccer, you'll find them at rugby games, cricket matches, tennis tournaments, athletics meets, or Formula One races instead. England is also currently home to all four of heavyweight boxing's major belts (shared between Anthony Joshua and Tyson Fury). Don't worry if you prefer less adrenaline-filled sports; England is the spiritual home of darts and snooker (a variation on pool), too.

What to Eat and Drink in England

PIMM'S CUP

Best enjoyed while outside in the sun, Pimm's is a gin-based liqueur typically mixed with lemonade and ice, then filled with sliced strawberries, cucumber, and mint. Popular at weddings, regattas, and Wimbledon, it's the British version of the Aperol Spritz.

FISH-AND-CHIPS

England's most famous dish is available throughout the country and comes in many shapes and sizes. Best enjoyed out of a hot paper wrap from a typical fish-and-chip shop, or *chippy* (and generally takeaway only), the meal should be eaten with a miniature wooden fork for extra authenticity. The fish is usually cod (but haddock, skate, and rock are not uncommon) covered in a crispy deep-fried batter. Chips are thick-cut fried potatoes and sides can include anything from pickled eggs to mushy peas. You can also opt for a sauce, with regional variations including tartare, curry sauce, and gravy.

AFTERNOON TEA

Typically enjoyed between an early lunch and late dinner, afternoon tea is a very British way to spend a few hours. A true afternoon tea consists of cakes, pastries, finger sandwiches, and scones with jam and clotted cream displayed on a tiered stand and served with steaming pots of loose-leaf tea. In many establishments, you can expect a tea menu (and the fanciest might even have a tea sommelier) where you can consider the likes of Earl Grey, Assam (the Queen's favorite teas), Darjeeling, and Ceylon.

CURRY

The 1970s saw a wave of South Asian immigrants arriving in England and setting up restaurants in big urban centers like London, Birmingham, and Manchester. These days, almost every major village has a mix of Indian, Bangladeshi, and Pakistani restaurants serving some of the finest curry anywhere outside of Asia. Aside from classics like vindaloo (super hot!), madras, and tandoori meats, the range of sweet, salty, spicy, and sour curries makes it one of the country's best-loved cuisines.

SUNDAY ROAST

Roasted meat (chicken, beef, pork, or lamb), roast potatoes, assorted vegetables, cauliflower cheese, Yorkshire puddings, and various condiments (mint sauce, bread sauce, English mustard, horseradish, cranberry jelly) make up some of the most important elements of a traditional Sunday roast—a meal that should leave you ready to sleep within 30 minutes of eating it. Almost every pub and restaurant in England serves a roast on Sunday, and the quality ranges dramatically depending on the establishment. You'll also find "carveries" serving buffet-style roasts every day of the week.

CASK ALES

The increased interest in the provenance of food and drink throughout England extends to beer, encouraging microbreweries to develop real or cask ales: beer that's unfiltered and unpasteurized, and that contains live brewer's yeast.

Full English breakfast

The ales can be from kegs, bottles, or casks, and they range from pale amber to full-bodied. The Casque Mark outside pubs signals their availability.

CHEESE

The stalwart cheddar, Cheshire, Double Gloucester, and Stilton cheeses are complemented by traditional and experimental cheeses from small, local makers. Some cheeses come wrapped in nettles or vine leaves, others stuffed with apricots, cranberries, or herbs. Dairies are also producing more sheep and goat cheeses, yogurts, and ice creams.

ETON MESS

Named after the famous boarding school near Windsor, this traditional dessert consists of meringue, whipped cream, and strawberries (or other summer fruits). As the name suggests, it looks a little messy, but it tastes divine.

FULL ENGLISH BREAKFAST

Consisting of eggs (usually fried or scrambled), sausages, bacon, fried tomatoes, black pudding, black beans, mushrooms, and toast, the classic Full English breakfast is best enjoyed with a classic builder's tea on the side to cut through the greasy, calorific mess.

ENGLISH CIDER

Sweet and refreshing, traditional English cider is made from pure apple juice and twice fermented. The drink is usually carbonated, though some variations—like the West Country specialty *scrumpy*—can be still. Perry is a similar drink made from pear juice.

BANGERS AND MASH

Simple but effective, this pub grub staple comprises sausages served on a bed of mashed potatoes and topped with onion gravy. The "bangers" are usually Cumberlands—long, coiled, and particularly meaty pork sausages—but they can also be made from lamb or beef.

CORNISH PASTIES

This traditional, semicircular pastry, which looks similar to an empanada, is filled with minced beef, onion, potato, and rutabaga and seasoned with pepper. As they are easily carried, eaten without cutlery, and stay warm for hours, the pasties were a staple of Cornish tin miners, who subsequently spread the concept everywhere from Australia to Mexico.

What to Buy in England

Gin

LONDON DRY GIN
Gin has had a big resurgence in recent years, and today you'll find a huge selection of gins available in pubs, clubs, and supermarkets across England. Opt for a stylishly packaged, 21st-century gin like Curio, Sipsmith, or Whitley Neill, or choose a classic, centuries-old spirit like Beefeater, Bloom, or Plymouth.

ENGLISH BREAKFAST TEA
Tea is the quintessential souvenir from any England trip, and English Breakfast is probably the country's most popular blend. It's a full-bodied, robust black tea that goes well with a splash of milk and a spoonful of sugar. You can pick up common brands like Twinings and PG Tips from any supermarket or treat yourself to superior blends

from the likes of Harrods and Fortnum and Mason.

CADBURY CHOCOLATE
England's best-selling chocolate bar is Cadbury Dairy Milk, which you'll find in every corner shop (and airport duty-free store) in the land. Along with Dairy Milk, Cadbury makes dozens of other popular chocolate bars, from the biscuit-filled Boost to the

Stuffed Paddington Bear

honeycomb-toffee Crunchie. If you're visiting between New Year and Easter, pick up a Creme Egg, a distinctive egg-shaped confection with a sweet white and yellow filling encased in a thick chocolate shell.

HP SAUCE

A true icon of British culture, this "brown sauce" has a tomato base, blended with malt vinegar, sugars, dates, and tamarind. HP stands for Houses of Parliament, which explains the Westminster illustration on the front of the bottle.

BISCUITS

"Biscuits" here are hard, sweet, baked treats that are akin to cookies or crackers in North America—and they're a cornerstone of English life. For a true local experience, pick up a packet of chocolate digestives, bourbons, or custard creams to take home and dunk in your cup of tea.

A UNION JACK ITEM

More than just a national flag, the Union Jack (well, technically the Union Flag, but we won't get into that) is also a global style icon. Don't think England's souvenir shops haven't noticed; you'll find them packed to the rafters with Union Jack items, from key rings and cushions to handbags and dresses. You'll also find more upscale designs incorporating the Union Jack in department stores like John Lewis.

STUFFED PADDINGTON BEAR

First appearing in the Michael Bond children's book *A Bear Called Paddington* in 1958, the friendly Peruvian bear has had a new lease on life in recent years thanks to two hugely successful and critically acclaimed movies, with a third currently in development. You can pick up a "cuddly toy" version of Paddington in souvenir shops around London and elsewhere.

FOOTBALL GEAR

Football (that's soccer in the States) is England's favorite sport, and probably it's second-favorite topic of conversation (after the weather), so a soccer jersey—or any other item of football merchandise—makes the perfect souvenir or gift. Take your pick from big-name clubs like Liverpool, Manchester United, and Chelsea, or opt for some national England team merch.

Best Museums in England

INTERNATIONAL SLAVERY MUSEUM, LIVERPOOL

Tracing the shameful history and legacy of the transatlantic slave trade, in which the city of Liverpool played a significant role, this important dockside museum recreates what life was like in West African compounds and aboard crammed slave ships bound for the Americas. There's also a focus on today's African diaspora in England, as well as moving exhibits on modern slavery, human trafficking, and child labor.

ROMAN BATHS AND THE PUMP ROOM, BATH

The hot springs of Bath have drawn visitors for thousands of years. This museum displays relics from the Roman bath complex that used to stand on the site, as well as the Pump Room, a hangout for 19th-century society members.

TATE MODERN, LONDON

This spectacular contemporary art gallery starts with a bang, thanks to its entrance, Turbine Hall, filled with gigantic temporary installations from artists including Ai Weiwei, Abraham Cruzvillegas, and Kara Walker. Venture farther inside for the Tate Modern's impressive permanent collection of works by the likes of Warhol, Picasso, Dalí, Rothko, and Gormley, then head to the roof terrace for a gorgeous view of the city.

THE BRITISH MUSEUM, LONDON

Established in 1753, the British Museum has long been one of the world's most famous national museums. Today, the London landmark is home to a permanent collection of eight million works, including the Rosetta Stone and the Elgin Marbles.

NATIONAL MUSEUM OF THE ROYAL NAVY, PORTSMOUTH

Part of the Portsmouth Historic Dockyard, this fascinating maritime museum showcases treasures from the last 350 years of Royal Navy history. Highlights include exhibits related to national hero Horatio Nelson and the Battle of Trafalgar.

ASHMOLEAN MUSEUM, OXFORD

Known to locals simply as "The Ash," this extraordinary Oxford University museum was founded in 1683 (the first public museum in the United Kingdom). With a focus on art and archaeology, the collection spans everything from Egyptian mummies and Saxon jewelry to Renaissance artworks and the world's last remaining dodo skull.

International Slavery Museum

SCIENCE AND INDUSTRY MUSEUM, MANCHESTER

Housed within five buildings, all set around the world's first passenger railway station (built in 1830), the Science and Industry Museum brings Manchester's industrial past, present, and future to life through several fascinating and interactive artifacts, including some focusing on steam engines, cotton looms, and Victorian sewers.

IRONBRIDGE GORGE MUSEUM, TELFORD

Billed as "the birthplace of the Industrial Revolution," the deep canyon known as Ironbridge Gorge was home to an abundance of coal, iron ore, and limestone, fueling the region's 18th-century industry. It also resulted in the building of the world's first iron bridge, a gorgeous river-spanning arch that's the highlight of the UNESCO-listed site.

VICTORIA AND ALBERT MUSEUM, LONDON

With millions of applied arts and design artifacts, the V&A is one of London's big-hitting museums. It's best known for its eclectic fashion collections—expect 18th-century court dresses and royal bridal gowns alongside modern Alexander McQueen designs and David Bowie outfits—but you'll also find everything from ornate Tudor furniture to Japanese samurai armor behind the museum's grand Edwardian facade.

TATE ST. IVES, ST. IVES

Set within a quirky, modernist building, the contemporary Tate St. Ives art gallery displays the work of the artists who lived and worked in Cornwall in the 20th century, as well as influences like Picasso, Braque, and Mondrian.

Best Royal Sites in England

THE ROYAL PAVILION, BRIGHTON
Built as a pleasure palace for King George IV and one of England's most eccentric feats of architecture, the Royal Pavilion is an exotic, Eastern-influenced classical building that has more in common with the Taj Mahal than with Buckingham Palace.

THE TOWER OF LONDON, LONDON
Dating back almost a millennium, the world-famous Tower of London has at times been a fortress, a mint, a palace, a zoo, and a prison. Today, it welcomes tourists to explore its historic attractions, from the Bloody Tower to the Crown Jewels.

WESTMINSTER ABBEY, LONDON
One of England's most famous buildings, Westminster Abbey has hosted 38 coronations (beginning with William the Conqueror in 1066) and 16 royal weddings. Fascinating royal sights include the Coronation Chair (used since 1308), Henry VII's Lady Chapel, and the tombs of Elizabeth I and her sister "Bloody" Mary I.

SANDRINGHAM HOUSE, SANDRINGHAM
The Royal Family traditionally spends Christmas at Sandringham, a vast, redbrick Victorian mansion and estate near the coast in East Anglia. But for most of the rest of year, it's open to visitors. Along with the opulent Edwardian interiors and pretty formal gardens, you'll also find a superb transport museum.

SUDELEY CASTLE, WINCHCOMBE
It may officially be called a castle, but this Cotswolds icon is more akin to a Tudor palace. Once the home of Catherine Parr, Henry VIII's sixth and final wife (the only one who "survived"), it was used as a refuge by Charles I and besieged by Cromwell's army, reducing it to ruins.

BUCKINGHAM PALACE, LONDON
Probably the world's most famous royal residence, Buckingham Palace is the Queen's main home, and as such it is closed to the public for most of the year. However, every summer, when Her Majesty heads up to Balmoral Castle in Scotland, the palace's 19 State Rooms are open to visitors.

WINDSOR CASTLE, WINDSOR
Visible for miles around, this enormous fortification-cum-royal residence (the largest inhabited castle in the world) has been used by the Royal Family since the Middle Ages.

Hever Castle, Hever

HEVER CASTLE, HEVER
Arguably England's most picture-perfect castle, Hever Castle is a 700-year-old mass of romantic turrets, battlements, and manicured gardens, all enveloped by a moat. It was the ancestral home of Henry VIII's second wife Anne Boleyn until her 1536 execution, after which Henry gave it to new wife Anne of Cleves.

HIGHGROVE HOUSE, TETBURY
The personal home and estate of Prince Charles and Camilla, Duchess of Cornwall, Highgrove House is located 20 miles north of Bath. It's renowned for its exquisite gardens, orchards, and woodlands, which showcase Charles's enduring commitment to organic produce.

HAMPTON COURT PALACE, LONDON
This spectacular Tudor residence is one of England's most iconic royal buildings. Begun in 1515 by Cardinal Wolsey in order to curry favor with a young Henry VIII, Hampton Court's Great Hall and State Apartments provide a real insight into the lives of Tudor monarchs.

Best Literary Experiences in England

WILLIAM SHAKESPEARE

While visitors to London can pop into Shakespeare's Globe for a live performance, true theater fans should travel north to Stratford-upon-Avon. Along with Shakespeare's Birthplace, Stratford is home to the Royal Shakespeare Theatre, where the world-renowned Royal Shakespeare Company regularly performs the Bard's plays.

SHERLOCK HOLMES

The London address of Sherlock Holmes (221B Baker Street, London) is as familiar to audiences today as it was when Arthur Conan Doyle first wrote his detective stories in the 19th century. In fact, the address was the real-life home of the author, and today it houses the Sherlock Holmes Museum.

OXFORD UNIVERSITY

C. S. Lewis, Oscar Wilde, and Lewis Carroll all roamed the streets of Oxford, but if there's one writer who is "Mister Oxford," it's J. R. R. Tolkien. After attending Oxford University, he worked at the Oxford English Dictionary, then returned as a professor. And it was there that he wrote his seminal fantasy novels *The Hobbit* and *Lord of the Rings*.

THOMAS HARDY

The market town of Dorchester in Dorset was immortalized in Thomas Hardy's 1886 novel *The Mayor of Casterbridge*. Today, the town and the area surrounding it (known as "Hardy country") is packed with Hardy-related sites, including the author's birthplace.

THE LAKE DISTRICT

For many, the Lake District is forever associated with William Wordsworth, where he "Wandered Lonely as a Cloud." But this bucolic English landscape has also given us other literary greats like Lord Alfred Tennyson, John Ruskin, and—best of all for lovers of children's literature—Beatrix Potter.

HARRY POTTER

Fans of the books and movies can visit the Harry Potter Studio Tour and Platform 9¾ at King's Cross station. In addition, the dramatic exterior of imposing Alnwick Castle in Northeast England is immediately recognizable as the Hogwarts School of Witchcraft and Wizardry in the films.

The Sherlock Holmes Museum, London

JANE AUSTEN

Hampshire in the South of England is known as "Jane Austen country," and for good reason: the *Pride and Prejudice* author's connections span the county, from her House Museum in Chawton to her grave in Winchester Cathedral. However, she is also celebrated farther west in Bath, where she moved at the age of 25. The city is home to the Jane Austen Centre, as well as an annual festival celebrating all things Austen.

CHARLES DICKENS

The Charles Dickens Museum may be in London, but the nearby town of Broadstairs has the strongest connections to the author. This seaside town in Southeast England is where the author lived for several years while writing works like *David Copperfield* and *Oliver Twist*, and you can visit his House Museum there. You'll also find Dickens' famous Bleak House in town, and there's a Dickens Festival each June.

THE BRONTË SISTERS

The little village of Haworth in Yorkshire was once the residence of three titans of English literature: the Brontë sisters. The writer siblings—Emily (the author of *Wuthering Heights*), Charlotte (the author of *Jane Eyre*), and Anne (the author of *The Tenant of Wildfell Hall*)—lived in Haworth Parsonage, now the Brontë Parsonage Museum, and were influenced by the dramatic landscapes of the region when writing their novels.

London's Royal Legacy

THE ROCKY MONARCHY

From medieval castles and keeps, to Royal Parks, palaces, pageants, ceremonies, and processions, London has had a tumultuous and sometimes bloody royal history, which can still be encountered at practically every turn. London has been the royal capital of England since 1066, when the Norman king William the Conqueror began the tradition of royal coronations at Westminster Abbey. All but two reigning monarchs since then—from Richard I (the "Coeur de Lion") in 1189 to the current Queen Elizabeth II in 1953—have been crowned at the Abbey. Many of England's illustrious—and sometimes downright notorious—kings and queens have left a legacy or their majestic mark on the city. You'll find many of the finest places have royal associations: William I subjugated London with the imposing Tower of London; Henry VIII hunted deer at Hampton Court; Elizabeth I enjoyed bear baiting in Southwark; and Charles I was publicly executed on Whitehall. Tyrannical but weak monarchs like King John (1199–1216) granted the City of London extra power under the Magna Carta, while the first "Parliament" sat at the royal Palace of Westminster in 1265 under Henry III. The late medieval Tudors, however, rarely brooked dissent: Elizabeth I's half-sister, "Bloody" Mary I (1553–58), burned heretic Protestant bishops at the stake, and traitors were hung, drawn, and quartered, with their heads stuck on pikes on London Bridge.

A CULTURAL RENAISSANCE

From 1558 to 1601, peace under Elizabeth I ("the Virgin Queen") led to a cultural renaissance and the great flowering of English theater, poetry, letters, music, and drama, centered on Shakespeare's Globe and the open-air playhouses of Southwark. Charles I was later captured by the formidable Puritan Oliver Cromwell during the English Civil War and beheaded on a freezing day outside Banqueting House in Westminster in 1649. Although the Interregnum lasted only 16 years (outlawing simple pleasures, such as dancing and theater), the Restoration of Charles II in 1660 and subsequent monarchs saw London grow and transform into a teeming metropolis. These monarchs included the Dutch Protestant William III and Mary II—who moved into Kensington Palace, now the current home of the Duke and Duchess of Cambridge—and the House of Hanover's four Georgian kings and later Queen Victoria.

THE MODERN ROYALS

These days you might spot the Duke and Duchess of Cambridge (Prince William and Kate Middleton) walking in Kensington Gardens with their three young children. Besides the color, pageantry, and marching bands of the Changing of the Guard ceremony at Buckingham Palace, there's also a rich calendar of royal ceremonies. The Ceremony of the Keys to lock up the Tower of London has taken place at 9:53 pm each night for more than 700 years (bar the odd bombing during the Blitz), and you can see the Monarch take the Royal Salute from the Household Division at the annual Trooping the Colour march from Horse Guards Parade to St. James's Park. The Queen is also drawn by four horses in the dazzling Irish State Coach from Buckingham Palace to the Palace of Westminster in a huge royal procession for the State Opening of Parliament each autumn, and you can see her pay homage to the war dead at the Cenotaph on Remembrance Sunday.

ENGLAND THROUGH THE AGES

English unflappability can cover up a multitude of dark deeds. A landscape, village scene, or ruined castle may present itself as a serene, untroubled canvas, but this is mere show. Trauma and passion are the underlying reality of history; dynastic ambitions, religious strife, and sedition are the subtext. Dig deeper, and what might appear to be a vast, nation-wide museum turns out to be a complex tapestry of narratives and personalities.

On a far-flung corner of Europe, England's geographical position can account for many things: its slowness in absorbing technological and cultural influences from the great Mediterranean civilizations, its speedy adaptation to the global explosion of trade in the early modern era, and its separate, rather aloof identity. But other factors have molded English history too, not least the waves of immigration, settlement and conquest, by Celts, Romans, Danes, and Normans among numerous others. Perhaps the greatest factor of all has been the unforeseen events, accidental meetings, and random coincidences that history delights in throwing up. The careful—sometimes over-zealous—custodianship of England's heritage may pretend otherwise, but behind every object and beneath every ruin lies a tangle of interconnected events. With some context, history is lifted out of the realm of show and into biting reality.

—by Robert Andrews

On stage at Shakespeare's Globe Theatre, London

TIMELINE	**3000 BC** First building of Stonehenge (later building 2400–1600 BC)	**55–54 BC** Julius Caesar's exploratory expeditions to England	**AD 410** Roman rule of Britain ends

| 3000 BC | 1000 BC | 0 | AD 900 |

(clockwise from top left) Avebury Stone Circles in Wiltshire; Roman Baths, Bath; Illuminated manuscript, Liber Vitae, 1031; Iron Age coins from Yorkshire

Early Arrivals

5000 BC–55 BC

The British Isles had already assumed their current shape by 5000 BC, after the final thawing of the last ice age had resulted in a substantial northwestern promontory being detached from the rest of mainland Europe. However, the influx of different peoples and cultures from the east continued as before. It may have been one of these waves of immigrants that brought agriculture to the islands. Numerous burial sites, hill forts, and stone circles have survived from these early societies, notably in the soft chalk downs of southern England.

Roman Britain

55 BC–AD 450

The emperor Claudius declared Colchester Rome's first British colony soon after the invasion of AD 43, and legionary fortresses in the north were established by AD 75. Resistance included Queen Boudicca's uprising and the razing of Londinium (London). However, a Romano-British culture was forged with its northern limit at Hadrian's Wall, built in AD 128. To the south, Celtic Britain became integrated into the Roman Empire with the construction of villas, baths, fortifications, and roads.

Anglo-Saxons

450–1066

Following the withdrawal of the Roman legions, Britain fell prey to invasions by Jutes, Angles, and Saxons from the mainland. The native Celts were pushed back to the fringes of Britain: Cornwall, Wales, northern England, and Scotland. Eventually seven Anglo-Saxon kingdoms emerged, all of which had adopted Christianity by 650. In the 8th century, the Anglo-Saxon kingdoms faced aggressive incomers from Scandinavia, halted only when Alfred the Great, king of Wessex, unified the English against the Viking invaders.

597 St. Augustine arrives in Canterbury to Christianize Britain

1066 William of Normandy defeats King Harold at the Battle of Hastings

1086 Domesday Book completed, a survey of all taxpayers in England

1215 King John signs Magna Carta at Runnymede

AD **1000** AD **1100** AD **1200** AD **1300**

In Focus | ENGLAND THROUGH THE AGES

(clockwise from top left) Tower of London; Bayeux Tapestry, scene where the English flee from Normans; Stone carvings on Litchfield Cathedral; Reliquary of St. Thomas à Becket, 12th century

1066–1381
Middle Ages: Normans and Plantagenets

The course of England's history altered radically when William, duke of Normandy, invaded and became king of England in 1066. A Norman military and feudal hierarchy was established, French became the language of government, and the country became more centralized. Trading and dynastic links with Europe meant that military campaigns abroad consumed resources, while artistic innovations were more easily absorbed at home—for example, the introduction of Gothic architecture in England's churches and cathedrals. The Plantagenet dynasty came to power in 1154 with the accession of Henry II. A power struggle with the church led to the murder of Henry's archbishop Thomas à Becket in Canterbury Cathedral, which became a center for pilgrimage. The autocratic ambitions of Henry's son John were similarly stymied when he was forced to sign the Magna Carta, promulgating basic principles of English law: no taxation except through Parliament, trial by jury, and property guarantees. In 1348–49, the Black Death (bubonic plague) reduced Britain's population from 4.25 million to 2.5 million.

1381–1485
Twilight of the Middle Ages

English kings invested resources in the Hundred Years War, a struggle to increase their territories in France, but Henry V's gains at Agincourt in 1415 were reversed following the succession of the infant Henry VI. In the domestic Wars of the Roses, the House of York, with a white rose as emblem, triumphed over the House of Lancaster (red rose as emblem), when Edward IV seized the crown. But Edward's brother Richard III was defeated by Henry Tudor, who became Henry VII.

TIMELINE | **1485** Henry Tudor (Henry VII) defeats Richard III at the Battle of Bosworth | **1530s** Dissolution of the monasteries under Henry VIII | **1588** Spanish Armada fails to invade England

AD **1450**   **1500**   **1550**   **1600**

(clockwise from top left) Hampton Court Palace; Elizabeth I; English ships and the Spanish Armada; Queen Mary I; Henry VIII

Tudor Renaissance

1485–1603

The Tudor era saw the political consolidation of the kingdom but a deep religious divide. Henry VIII's break with Rome in order to obtain a divorce from Catherine of Aragon coincided with the Reformation, and he pursued his attack on the church with the dissolution of the monasteries. Protestantism became further entrenched under the short reign of Henry's son, Edward VI, but Catholicism was again in the ascendant under Mary. Elizabeth I strove to heal the sectarian divisions while upholding the supremacy of a Protestant Church of England. Her position was further imperiled by the threat of invasion by Spain, which abated with the defeat of the Spanish Armada in 1588. Elizabeth encouraged piratical attacks on the Spaniards throughout the Atlantic, as well as voyages to the New World, with Walter Raleigh leading expeditions to Virginia in the 1580s. A major flourishing of arts and letters took place during the reign of Good Queen Bess, with such figures as Edmund Spenser and William Shakespeare. When Elizabeth died without an heir, her chief minister, Robert Cecil, invited the Stuart James VI of Scotland to occupy the throne as James I of England.

Stuart England

1603–1660

The Stuarts' attempts to rule independently of Parliament led to disaster. Religious tensions persisted, and Puritans and other dissenters began to seek refuge in the New World. Those who stayed were persecuted under James's son Charles I, who alienated the gentry and merchant classes until war was declared between king and Parliament. The Civil War ended with Charles's trial and execution in 1649 and an interregnum in which Oliver Cromwell, the general who became Parliamentarian leader, was declared Lord Protector.

(clockwise from top left) The Great Fire of London by Turner; George III; West front entrance of St. Paul's Cathedral; Charles II; Chippendale mahogany bonnet-top highboy, 1770s

Restoration

1660–1714

In an uneasy pact with Parliament, Charles I's son was invited back from exile to reign as Charles II. The Restoration led to a revival of the arts, especially in the fields of theater and literature, and a wave of church building. Old divisions resurfaced when Charles was succeeded by James II, whose conversion to Catholicism led to the Glorious Revolution (1688), when Parliament offered the English crown to William of Orange and Mary Stuart, James II's daughter. The thrones of England and Scotland were united in the Act of Union (1707).

Georgian England

1714–1837

With the death of Queen Anne, the Stuart monarchy came to an end and the succession of the new kingdom of Great Britain passed to the Protestant German House of Hanover. But real power now lay with Parliament. George I spent most of his reign in Germany; George II leaned heavily on Robert Walpole (the first "prime minister"); George III was intermittently mad; and George IV's life was marked by dissipation. However, despite losing the Thirteen Colonies in the American Revolution, Britain had by now become the leading European power in the Indian subcontinent. It demonstrated martial supremacy over France in the wars that simmered throughout this period, finally ending in Britain's two victories against Napoleon at Trafalgar and Waterloo. The growing empire, combined with engineering and technical advances at home, helped bring about an early Industrial Revolution in Britain. The process accelerated urbanization, especially in the Midlands and north, and created an urban working class. Partly in response, a new sentimental view of rural England emerged, reflected in the building of stately homes with landscaped estates.

(clockwise from top left) Queen Victoria in characteristic mourning clothes; Edward VII in coronation robes; Trellis wallpaper Arts and Crafts design by William Morris, 1862; British troops in France, World War I

Victorian Age of Empire

1837–1901

Victoria's reign coincided with the high-water mark of the British Empire, expanding into Africa and consolidating in India. Two parties dominated politics: the Liberals and the Conservatives. These parties supplied such prime ministers as Benjamin Disraeli (Conservative) and William Gladstone (Liberal), who left their mark in reformist measures relating to working conditions, policing, education, health, welfare provision, and the extension of suffrage—all areas highlighted in the literature of the time, notably in the works of Charles Dickens. A network of railways and a nationwide postal service enhanced infrastructure and the growth of industry. In other spheres, the Victorian age harked back to the past, whether in art, as in the Arts and Crafts and Pre-Raphaelite movements, or in architecture, which revived old forms of building from classical to Gothic and Tudor. After Prince Albert's death in 1861, Victoria became a recluse in her Isle of Wight palace, Osborne House, though her golden and diamond jubilees restored her popularity while glorifying the achievements of her long reign.

Edwardian England and World War I

1901–1918

Edward VII, Victoria's son, was a keen sportsman, gambler, and society figure who embodied the blinkered spirit of the country in the aftermath of the Victorian age. The election to Parliament of 29 members of the newly formed Labour Party in 1906 signaled a realignment of politics, though the eruption of World War I sidetracked domestic concerns. The intense fighting across Europe brought about huge loss of life and economic meltdown.

1939–45 World War II	1952 Queen Elizabeth II accedes to the throne	1994 Channel Tunnel opened	2012 Olympics in London
1940	1965	1990	2015

In Focus | ENGLAND THROUGH THE AGES

(clockwise from bottom left) Winston Churchill; London Aquatics Centre for the 2012 Olympics; The Beatles; The wedding of Prince William and Catherine Middleton, April 2011 (their son, Prince Georgie, future heir to the throne, was born in 2013)

1918–1945

Depression and World War II

The interwar period was one of social upheaval, and the unemployment caused by the Great Depression rose to 70% in some areas. At the start of World War II, Hitler's forces pushed the British army into the sea at Dunkirk. The aerial Blitz that followed devastated cities. Winston Churchill's rousing leadership and the support of United States and Commonwealth forces helped turn the tide, with Britain emerging triumphant—but bankrupt.

1945–PRESENT

To Present Day

Elected in 1945, the new Labour government introduced important reforms in welfare and healthcare and initiated the dismantling of the British empire, starting with independence for India and Pakistan in 1947. The years of austerity lasted until the late 1950s, but the following decade saw a cultural explosion that covered every field, from art to music to fashion. British industry had never recovered its former, prewar strength, however, and inflation and industrial strife marked the 1970s. Britain's entry into the European Economic Community (later to become the European Union) in 1973 did not immediately slow the economic decline. Manufacturing was largely forsaken by Margaret Thatcher (Conservative) and Tony Blair (Labour) in favor of service industries, but Britain's heavy reliance on finance meant that the economy was hit hard by the crash of 2008. While an economic recovery finally began in 2010, the 2016 referendum to leave the E.U. brought chaos and uncertainty. Controversial leader Boris Johnson became PM in 2019, with the United Kingdom finally beginning the leaving process in January 2020. But the country and its economy entered a new era of uncertainty when the COVID-19 pandemic began in spring 2020, which will no doubt continue to change the world well into the new decade.

What to Watch and Read Before You Go

THE CROWN

Since it debuted on Netflix in November 2016, this historical drama about the reign of Queen Elizabeth II has picked up a host of accolades and awards, from Emmys to Golden Globes. While you're unlikely to bump into Liz on your visit to England, you might well visit some of the many palaces, castles, and other locations featured in the show.

FLEABAG

Probably the most talked-about TV show of the late 2010s, this award-winning comedy-drama follows creator Phoebe Waller-Bridge's titular character as she attempts to cope with life and love in London, all while coming to terms with a recent tragedy.

DOWNTON ABBEY

The hugely popular television series, which ran between 2010 and 2015, is one of England's most successful TV exports of recent years, while a movie adaptation was released in 2019. Most of the filming for the show takes place at Highclere Castle in the South of England; it's available to visit throughout the summer.

CALL THE MIDWIFE

This BBC period drama, which follows a group of nurse midwives working in the East End of London in the 1950s and '60s, has been widely praised for tackling subjects like miscarriage, abortion, and female genital mutilation. Nine seasons have been shown since 2012, with two more scheduled for 2021 and 2022.

CHEWING GUM

Written by and starring Michaela Coel, this cult British sitcom (which has since reached a larger international audience through Netflix) features 24-year-old shop assistant Tracey Gordon, who wants to break free of her strict religious upbringing and learn more about the modern world.

THE GREAT BRITISH BAKE OFF

A quaint television baking competition has became an international phenomenon. Every season, a fresh-faced group of 10 amateur bakers is given a series of baking challenges over several weeks to determine the ultimate winner. The Bake Off has spawned dozens of international versions all over the world, including The Great American Baking Show on ABC, but the original—now 10 seasons in— remains the best.

POLDARK

Based on a series of historical novels by Winston Graham, this BBC drama series follows Captain Ross Poldark after his return to Cornwall following the 1783 American War of Independence. Poldark's developing romance with scullery maid Demelza, combined with regular shots of lead actor Aidan Turner's toned torso, sustained the show for 43 episodes over five seasons.

A HARD DAY'S NIGHT

This 1964 musical comedy film, which stars John Lennon, Paul McCartney, George Harrison, and Ringo Starr as themselves, portrays a fictionalized 36 hours in the life of the band at the very height of Beatlemania. Time magazine rated it one of the 100 greatest films of all time.

BEND IT LIKE BECKHAM

Offering insight into England's society-wide obsession with soccer—and with its prodigal son David Beckham— this 2002 romantic comedy sports film follows 18-year-old Jess as she defies her conservative Sikh parents to play for her local women's football team.

LOVE ACTUALLY

Since it was released in 2003, this romantic comedy has become a staple of Christmases all over the world. The movie follows the loosely interconnected love stories of several characters in London, played by a who's who of British acting royalty, including Colin Firth, Kiera Knightley, Chiwetel Ejiofor, Emma Thompson, and Hugh Grant.

HARRY POTTER SERIES BY J. K. ROWLING

The best-selling book series in history, J. K. Rowling's epic fantasy novels chronicle the lives of young wizard Harry Potter, along with his friends Hermione and Ron, as they attend the Hogwarts School of Witchcraft and Wizardry. Visitors to the Northeast can explore the real-life Hogwarts at Alnwick Castle.

PRIDE AND PREJUDICE BY JANE AUSTEN

This romantic, Regency-era novel is one of the world's most enduring love stories. It follows 20-year-old Elizabeth Bennet and the course of her relationship with the older Mr. Darcy. There have been several film and television adaptations of the book, but perhaps the most loved is the BBC's 1995 adaptation starring Jennifer Ehle and Colin Firth.

THE ADVENTURES OF SHERLOCK HOLMES BY ARTHUR CONAN DOYLE

First published in the 1890s, these short stories about fictional private detective Sherlock Holmes, who uses observation, deduction, and logical reasoning to crack seemingly unsolvable cases, have fascinated audiences ever since. The recent BBC series *Sherlock,* based on the stories and starring Benedict Cumberbatch and Martin Freeman as modern versions of Sherlock and his assistant Watson, has breathed new life into the character.

OLIVER TWIST BY CHARLES DICKENS

Charles Dickens's second novel is perhaps his most famous, recounting the story of orphan Oliver Twist and his life as a juvenile pickpocket for the criminal Fagin. It offers a fascinating, unflinching insight into the criminal gangs and cruel treatment of orphans in London during the mid-19th century.

WILLIAM SHAKESPEARE'S HISTORIES

The Bard's series of historical plays chronicle the lives of four centuries of English monarchs, including King John, Henry V, and Richard III. Although widely regarded as Tudor propaganda (Shakespeare lived during the reign of Elizabeth I, the last Tudor monarch), the histories are hugely entertaining and informative, too.

WHITE TEETH BY ZADIE SMITH

This award-winning 2000 novel focuses on the lives of two best friends—Samad Iqbal and Archie Jones—and their families in North London. The novel, which was Zadie Smith's debut, deftly explores themes of cultural identity, faith, race, and gender in modern England.

THE REMAINS OF THE DAY BY KAZUO ISHIGURO

This Man Booker Prize–winning novel by British author Ishiguro tells the story of an English butler who reflects on a life of service and the sacrifices he has made. A 1993 film adaptation, starring Anthony Hopkins and Emma Thompson, was nominated for eight Academy Awards.

WUTHERING HEIGHTS BY EMILY BRONTË

Originally published under the pen name Ellis Bell, this English literature classic from the third-eldest Brontë sibling was groundbreaking and controversial for its stark depiction of mental and physical cruelty, gender inequality, and religious hypocrisy.

MIDDLEMARCH BY GEORGE ELIOT

Set in a provincial Midlands town in the 1830s, Middlemarch centers on the lives of several local residents, including the pious, 19-year-old Dorothea Brooke, who decides to marry the pompous 45-year-old scholar Edward Casaubon (with disastrous consequences).

BRICK LANE BY MONICA ALI

Set on the eponymous Brick Lane, the heart of London's Bangladeshi community, this novel follows the life of Nazneen, an 18-year-old Bangladeshi woman who struggles to adapt to life in England after marrying an older man.

Chapter 2

TRAVEL SMART

Updated by
Ellin Stein

★ **CAPITAL:**
London

👫 **POPULATION:**
67,886,011

💬 **LANGUAGE:**
English

$ **CURRENCY:**
Pound

📟 **COUNTRY CODE:**
44

⚠ **EMERGENCIES:**
999 or 112

🚗 **DRIVING:**
On the left

⚡ **ELECTRICITY:**
240v/50 cycles; plugs have
three rectangular blades

🕐 **TIME:**
Five hours ahead of New
York

🌐 **WEB RESOURCES:**
www.visitbritain.com
www.visitengland.com
www.visitlondon.com

Know Before You Go

England is a big country, with several distinct regions, cultures, and landscapes. Here are a few tips that will help your trip go as smoothly as possible no matter where you're going.

THE WEATHER IN ENGLAND IS ALWAYS TRICKY.

The summer months of June, July, and August give the best chance of good weather, although the crowds are at their largest. The start of August can be very busy for major tourist attractions, and hot weather can make traveling on the non-air-conditioned Tube uncomfortable. November through March is when you'll find England's best flight and hotel deals. Winter, while not generally frigid, can be dismal; the sun sets at 4, and it's pitch-dark by 5. Late spring is the time to see the countryside and the royal parks and gardens at their loveliest, while fall brings autumnal beauty and smaller crowds. Temperatures are usually mild at both times.

BREXIT IS STILL ON EVERYONE'S MINDS.

Although Britain voted to leave the European Union in 2016 and separated politically in 2019, what this means in practice is still being worked out. Border arrangements, trade agreements, and participation in multinational organizations (including aviation safety regulation) all are still under discussion, and the country remains nearly as intractably divided on the issue, so approach with caution.

DESPITE ALL THE BREXIT TALK, ENGLAND IS STILL A MULTICULTURAL PLACE.

The Brexit debate did indeed raise the specter of populist nationalism, and there has been an increase in xenophobic talk and, occasionally, action. Nevertheless, England is still a diverse country made up of people from different cultural traditions, especially in the cities, who generally get along well together.

LEARNING SOME BRITISH IDIOMS CAN BE HELPFUL.

Nearly everyone knows that Britain and America are, in the phrase usually attributed to playwright George Bernard Shaw, "two countries separated by a common language," so you'll find some knowledge of British idiom very helpful for communicating with locals. An elevator is a lift; instead of waiting in line, you queue; the bathroom is known as the toilet, the loo, or the WC (for water-closet) so in public spaces you may see a W/C sign instead of a restroom sign; pants are trousers; underpants are pants or knickers; french fries are chips; potato chips are crisps; and soccer is football. Say "cheers" while clinking glasses or to say good-bye or thank you. The list is extensive, so if something a local is saying doesn't quite make sense to you, it's probably a matter of slang.

CHECK TO SEE IF YOUR TRIP FALLS DURING A BANK HOLIDAY.

Several national "bank" holidays are celebrated throughout the year in the U.K.: May Day (first Monday in May), the last Monday in May, the last Monday in August, and Boxing Day (December 26). Many stores and some attractions might be closed, and some restaurants and museums might be much busier than usual.

THE PUB IS STILL CENTRAL TO BRITISH LIFE, THOUGH LESS SO THAN BEFORE.

The drinking age in England is 18, and pub life is a huge part of local culture throughout the country. Expect rowdy after-work crowds, especially on days of soccer or rugby matches. While not explicitly legal everywhere, alcohol can be consumed in public areas within reason (though not on the Tube), so don't be afraid to bring a gin-based Pimms (just add lemonade) to your picnic. Smoking is banned in all indoor public spaces in England, although you will see that quite a few Brits still smoke cigarettes, especially as you move north. Marijuana is not currently legal in the United Kingdom.

FOOTBALL FEVER IS REAL.

The Brits may not be known for their inclination to make small talk with strangers, but you can always strike up a conversation about football (aka soccer), especially in a pub. One word of warning: tribal loyalties run deep, so make sure you know what you're talking about. Otherwise, ask intelligent questions—fans love to express their opinions on a team's performance.

TO SAVE MONEY, TRY A PASS.

If you plan to visit castles, gardens, and historic houses during your stay in England, look into discount passes or memberships that offer significant savings. Just be sure to match what the pass or membership offers against your itinerary to see if it's worthwhile.

The National Trust, English Heritage, and the Historic Houses Association each encompass hundreds of properties. English Heritage's Overseas Visitors Pass costs £35 for a nine-day pass and £42 for a 16-day pass for one adult. You can order it in advance by phone or online, or purchase it at a participating property in England. The National Trust Touring Pass, for overseas visitors, must be purchased in advance, either by phone or online. A seven-day pass is £33; a 14-day pass is £38.

The London Pass gets you into more than 80 attractions and tours in the capital at considerable savings, and it can help you bypass some lines. Packages range from one day (£75) to ten days (£199). A similar pass for Yorkshire, the York Pass, enables discounted entrance to 30 attractions and costs from £45 for one day to £130 for six days. Annual membership in the National Trust (through the Royal Oak Foundation, the U.S. affiliate) is $80 a year. English Heritage membership is £60, and that for the Historic Houses Association is £56. Memberships entitle you to free entry to properties.

ENGLAND IS QUITE FRIENDLY TO LGBTQ TRAVELERS.

As a country that is predominately secular and historically friendly to unconventional lifestyles (although homosexuality was illegal here until 1967), England welcomes same-sex couples. Same-sex marriage has been legal here since 2014. As in most places in the world, cities like London and Manchester are the most gay-friendly and have plenty to offer in regard to LGBTQ bars, festivals, and events.

IT'S SMART TO KNOW WHEN PLACES ARE OPEN.

In big cities, most banks are open weekdays from 9 until 4 or 5. Some are open until 7, and many are open Saturday morning until 1 and some until 4. In smaller towns, hours are 9:30 to 3:30. Saturday hours are 10 to 2, if they're open at all. However, bank branches are being replaced by ATMs and are harder to find. Normal office hours for most businesses are weekdays 9 to 5.

The major national museums and galleries are open daily 9–6, including lunchtime, but have shorter hours on Sunday. Regional museums are usually closed Monday and have shorter hours in winter. In London, many museums are open late one evening a week.

Independently owned pharmacies are generally open Monday through Saturday 9:30–5:30, although in larger cities some stay open until 10 pm. Local newspapers and websites list which pharmacies are open late.

Usual retail business hours are Monday through Saturday 9–5:30 or 10–6:30, Sunday noon–4. In some small villages, shops may close at 1 pm once a week, often Wednesday or Thursday. They may also close for lunch and not open on Sunday at all. In large cities—especially London—department stores stay open late (usually until 7:30 or 8) one night a week, usually Thursday. On national holidays most stores are closed, and over the Christmas holidays most restaurants are closed as well.

Getting Here and Around

Air

The least expensive airfares to England are often priced for round-trip travel and usually must be purchased in advance. Airlines generally allow you to change your return date for a fee; most low-fare tickets, however, are nonrefundable.

Flying time to London is about 7½ hours from New York, 7¾ hours from Chicago, 9 hours from Dallas, 10½ hours from Los Angeles, and 23 hours from Sydney. From London, flights take 1¼ hours to Paris, Amsterdam, or Luxembourg; 1¾ hours to cities in Switzerland; and 2½ hours to Rome.

AIRPORTS

Most international flights to London arrive at either Heathrow Airport (LHR), 15 miles west of London, or at Gatwick Airport (LGW), 27 miles south of the capital. Most flights from the United States go to Heathrow, with Terminals 3, 4, and 5 handling transatlantic flights (British Airways uses Terminal 5). Gatwick is London's second gateway, serving many U.S. destinations. A third, much smaller airport, Stansted (STN), is 40 miles northeast of the city. It handles mainly European and domestic traffic.

London City Airport (LCY), a small airport inside the city near Canary Wharf, has four flights daily to New York, including a business-class-only flight on British Airways, as well as flights to European destinations. Luton Airport (LLA), 32 miles north of the city, is also quite small and serves British and European destinations. Luton is the hub for low-cost easyJet. Manchester (MAN) in northwest England handles some flights from the United States, as does Birmingham (BHX).

Heathrow and Gatwick are enormous and can seem like shopping malls (Heathrow even offers a personal shopping service). Both airports have several bars and eateries. Several hotels are connected to each airport, and both Gatwick and Heathrow are near dozens of hotels that run free shuttles to the airports. Heathrow has a Hotel Hoppa service that runs shuttles between the airport and around 39 nearby hotels for £5.50 (online) or £6 (on bus) each way. You can find out more at the Central Bus Station or at the Transport for London (TfL) Information Centre in the Underground station serving Terminals 2 and 3. Yotel has budget pod hotels in both Heathrow and Gatwick with cabin-size rooms to be booked in advance in four-hour blocks or overnight. Prices begin at about £45, depending on how long you stay and the time of day.

In comparison, other British airports have much more limited shopping, hotel, and dining options; a delay of a few hours can feel like years.

GROUND TRANSPORTATION

London has excellent bus and train connections between its airports and downtown. Train service can be the fastest, but the downside is that you must get yourself and your luggage to the terminal, often via a series of escalators and connecting trams. Airport buses (generally run by National Express) may be located nearer to the terminals and drop you closer to central hotels, but they're subject to London traffic, which can be horrendous. Taxis can be more convenient than buses, but prices can go through the roof. Minicabs are more economical, but stick to recommended companies. Uber is currently not allowed to operate in London, but it can take you to other destinations, and you can use alternative ride-hailing companies like Bolt, Ola, Kabbee, and Kapten. Expected to open in summer 2022 (only four years late), the Crossrail (aka Elizabeth) Underground line will provide high-speed service between Heathrow Terminals 2, 3, 4, and 5 and central London, while the Heathrow Express train runs a 15-minute nonstop service between Heathrow and Paddington Station. Alternatively, the slightly slower (25-minute) TfL Rail runs between Heathrow Central and Paddington Station.

The Transport for London website has helpful information, as does Airport Travel Line. The official sites for Gatwick, Heathrow, and Stansted are useful resources for transportation options.

Heathrow by Bus: National Express buses take around one hour (longer at peak time) to reach the city center (Victoria Coach Station) and cost £6–£7.50 one way and £15 round-trip. Buses leave every 5 to 75 minutes from 4:20 am to 10 pm. The National Express Hotel Hoppa service runs from all terminals to around 25 hotels near the airport (£6). Alternatively, nearly every hotel in London is served by the Heathrow Airport Hotel Shuttle service. Fares to Central London begin at £21.30. The N9 night bus runs every 15 minutes from 11:35 pm to 4:55 am to Kensington, Hyde Park Corner, Piccadilly Circus, Trafalgar Square, and Aldwych; it takes about 75 minutes and costs £1.50. ■TIP→ **Like all London buses, the N9 takes cash, Visitor Oyster cards, Oyster cards, or contactless "tap and go" debit cards only.**

Heathrow by Train: The cheap, direct route into London is via the Piccadilly line of the Underground (London's extensive subway system, or "Tube"). Trains normally run every three to seven minutes from all terminals from around 5 am until just before midnight (a 24-hour service runs every 10 minutes to Terminals 2, 3, and 5 on Friday and Saturday). The 50-minute trip into central London costs £6 (cash), £5.10 (Oyster card peak times),

From Heathrow to Central London

Travel Mode	Time	Cost
Taxi	40–90 minutes	£50–£90
Heathrow Express Train	15 minutes	£22–£25 one way
Underground	50 minutes	£6 one way
National Express Bus	45–80 minutes	£5–£7.50 one way

or £3.10 (Oyster card off-peak). The Heathrow Express train is comfortable and very convenient, if costly, speeding into London's Paddington Station in 15 minutes. Standard one-way tickets cost £22 (off-peak), £25 (peak), or £32 for first class. All fares are substantially discounted if booked in advance online. If you arrive without tickets you should purchase them at a kiosk before you board, as they're more expensive on the train. There's daily service from 5:10 am (6:10 am on Sunday) to 11:25 pm, with departures every 15 minutes. TfL Rail runs a slightly slower (25 minutes) non-express train service along the same route approximately every 15 minutes from 5:22 am (6 am on Sunday) to just after midnight. Tickets are £10.20.

Gatwick by Bus: Hourly bus service runs from Gatwick's north and south terminals to Victoria Coach Station with 11 stops along the way. The journey takes 80–120 minutes and costs from £10 one way. Make sure you get on a direct bus not requiring a change; otherwise the journey could take much longer. The easyBus service runs to West Brompton Underground Station in west London from as little as £4; to get to Victoria Coach station, the price is as low as £1.99. The later the ticket is booked online, the higher the price (up to £12 on board).

Getting Here and Around

Gatwick by Train: There are three train services to Gatwick. The fast, nonstop Gatwick Express leaves for Victoria Station every 15 minutes 5:41 am–11:11pm. The 30-minute trip costs £17.80 one way online. Tickets cost more on board. The Southern rail company's nonexpress services are cheaper. Trains run regularly throughout the day until midnight to London Victoria, London Bridge, and Blackfriars Stations. Daytime departures are every 15 minutes from 5:44 am to 12:41 am (plus a 4:40 am departure), and the journey to London Victoria takes about 40 minutes. Tickets are from £10.70 one way, and you can pay by Oyster card. You can also reach Gatwick by Southern trains coming from Brighton in the opposite direction. Thameslink offers a service similar to Southern but terminating at St. Pancras International instead of Victoria. The Thameslink and Southern services are on commuter trains, and during rush hour trains can be crowded, with little room for baggage and seats at a premium.

Stansted by Bus: National Express Airport bus A7 (24 hours a day) to Victoria Coach Station via Waterloo Station and Southwark costs from £12 one way, leaves every 15 minutes (hourly 2:40 am–5 am, then half-hourly until 7:50 am), and takes 90–120 minutes. The A6 National Express bus serving west London goes to Portman Square, with stops including Golders Green, Finchley Road, St. John's Wood, Baker Street, Paddington Station, and Marble Arch. It leaves every 20–40 minutes, and the journey time is 90–180 minutes, with fares from £12. The east London A8 service leaves every 30–40 minutes before 11:50 pm and after 6 am (hourly otherwise), terminating at King's Cross and stopping at Farringdon, Liverpool Street Station, Shoreditch High Street, Bethnal Green, and South Hackney. Fares are from £8, and the journey time is 67–77 minutes.

Stansted by Train: The Stansted Express to Liverpool Street Station (with a stop at Tottenham Hale) runs every 15 minutes (every 30 minutes early morning and late evening) 5:30 am–12:30 am daily. The 45-minute trip costs £19.40 each way if booked online. Tickets cost more on board.

Luton by Bus and Train: A free airport shuttle runs every 10 minutes from Luton Airport to the nearby Luton Airport Parkway Station, where you can take a train or bus into London. From there, the Thameslink train service runs to St. Pancras, Farringdon, Blackfriars, and London Bridge. The journey takes 25–50 minutes. Trains leave every 10 minutes or so from 6 am until 12:40 pm, 20–60 minutes at other times. One-way tickets begin at £18.80. The Green Line 757 bus service from Luton to Victoria Station runs every 30 minutes between 7 am and 12:35 am (hourly other times), takes 60 to 100 minutes, and costs from £11.50, while an easyBus shuttle has tickets starting from £2. National Express runs coaches from Victoria Coach Station to Luton from £5 one way.

Heathrow, Gatwick, Stansted, and Luton by Taxi: This is an expensive and time-consuming option. If your destination is within the city's congestion zone, £11.50 will be added to the bill during charging hours. If you get stuck in traffic, a taxi from the stand will be even more expensive; a cab booked ahead is a set price. A taxi trip from Heathrow to Victoria, for example, can take more than an hour and cost between £48 and £90. Private-hire cars may be the same price or even less—at this writing, the fee to Victoria Station is about £50 from Heathrow and £70 from Gatwick and Stansted, not including the congestion charge. Another option, if you have friends in the London area, is to have them book a reputable minicab firm to pick you up, or you can book one yourself via the Kabee app. The cost of a minicab from Heathrow to central London is approximately £47. The Uber fare from Heathrow is currently £28–£37, from Gatwick £60–£75, and from Stansted £55–£71, but Uber's ability to operate in the London area is the subject of ongoing legal proceedings. Your hotel may also be able to recommend a car service.

TRANSFERS BETWEEN AIRPORTS

Allow at least three to four hours for transferring between airports. The National Express Airport bus is the most direct option between Gatwick and Heathrow. Buses depart from Gatwick every 5–35 minutes between 6:45 am and 11:45 pm (25–120 minutes from 3:05 am to 5:50 am) and from Heathrow every 5–35 minutes. The trip takes 75 to 120 minutes, and the fare is £27 one way. Book tickets in advance. National Express buses between Stansted and Gatwick depart every 15 to 100 minutes and take between 3 and 4½ hours. The one-way fare is from £20 to £52. The National Express bus between Stansted and Heathrow takes about 90 minutes on a direct route, runs every 20–100 minutes, and costs from £22.50. Some airlines may offer shuttle services as well—check with your airline before your journey.

The cheapest option—but most complicated—is public transportation: from Gatwick to Stansted, for instance, catch the Gatwick Express train to Victoria Station, then take the National Express bus to Stanstead, or from Victoria take the Tube to Liverpool Street Station and hop on the train to Stansted. Alternatively, take the Thameslink train to Farringdon and transfer to the Tube bound for Liverpool Street. From Heathrow to Gatwick, take the Heathrow Express to Paddington, transfer to the Metropolitan/Circle line to King's Cross/St. Pancras, then take the Thameslink train to Gatwick.

All this should get much easier when the Crossrail (Elizabeth line) service becomes fully operational in summer 2022 (the latest estimate). It will travel directly from Heathrow to Liverpool Street Station for Stansted connections and directly to Farringdon for the Thameslink to Gatwick.

■TIP➜ Check the Transport for London website (www.tfl.gov.uk) to make sure trains and Tube lines are running, especially on weekends when service may be suspended for engineering works.

FLIGHTS

British Airways offers mostly nonstop flights from 24 U.S. cities to Heathrow, along with flights to Manchester, Leeds, and Newcastle and a vast program of discount airfare–hotel packages. Britain-based Virgin Atlantic is a strong competitor in terms of packages. Norwegian Air offers low-cost flights on A380s to New York, Boston, Chicago, Denver, Austin, Los Angeles, Seattle, San Francisco, Orlando, Miami, Tampa, and Fort Lauderdale. London is a very popular destination, so many U.S. carriers have flights and packages, too.

Because England is such a small country, internal air travel is much less important than it is in the United States. For trips of less than 200 miles, trains are often quicker because rail stations are more centrally located. Getting to and from airports can be expensive and complicated compared to train stations, but for longer trips air travel has a considerable time advantage (you need to factor in time for those airport transfers, though).

British Airways operates services between Heathrow or London City (Friday and Sunday only) and Manchester, and frequent daily flights between Heathrow or Gatwick and Edinburgh. Low-cost airlines such as easyJet and Ryanair offer

Getting Here and Around

flights within the United Kingdom as well as to cities in Ireland and continental Europe. Prices are low, but these airlines usually fly out of smaller British airports such as Stansted and Luton, both near London. Check ⊕ *www.cheapflights.com* for price comparisons.

⦿ Boat

Ferries and other boats travel regular routes to France, Spain, Ireland, and Scandinavia. P&O runs ferries to Belgium, France, Ireland, and the Netherlands. DFDS Seaways serves France, Spain, Belgium, Guernsey, and the Netherlands, and Stena Line serves Ireland, Northern Ireland, France, and the Netherlands.

Low-cost airlines and Eurotunnel (which lets you take a car to France on the train) have cut into ferry travel, but companies have responded by cutting fares and upgrading equipment.

Prices vary; booking early ensures cheaper fares, but also ask about special deals. Seaview is a comprehensive online ferry- and cruise-booking portal for Britain and continental Europe. Ferry Cheap is a discount website.

TRANSATLANTIC AND OTHER CRUISES

Most cruise ships leave from southern England—particularly Southampton and Portsmouth. Some ships leave from Liverpool and Dover, or from Harwich, near Cambridge.

⊟ Bus

Britain has a comprehensive bus (short-haul, multistop public transportation) and coach (more direct, plusher long-distance buses) network that offers an inexpensive way of seeing England. National Express is the major coach operator, and Victoria Coach Station, near Victoria Station in central London, is its hub in the region. The company serves more than 1,000 destinations within Britain (and, via Eurolines, 500 more in continental Europe). There are 2,000 ticket agents nationwide, including offices at London's Heathrow and Gatwick airport coach stations.

Green Line is the second-largest national service, serving airports and major tourist towns. A budget option for long-distance travel, Megabus has double-decker buses that serve cities across Britain, with seats that turn into bunk beds on routes to Scotland. In London, Megabus departs from Victoria Coach Station as well as other stops, while Green Line buses also stop at Baker Street and Hyde Park Corner.

Bus tickets can be much less than the price of a train ticket (even lower if you take advantage of special deals). For example, an Oxford Tube bus ticket from London to Oxford is £9, whereas a rush-hour train ticket may be £34.50. Buses are also just as comfortable as trains. However, buses often take twice as long to reach their destinations. The Oxford Tube has onboard Wi-Fi. All bus services forbid smoking.

Double-decker buses, run by private companies, offer local bus service in cities and regions. Check with the local bus station or tourist information center for routes and schedules. Most companies offer daylong or weeklong unlimited-travel tickets, and those in popular tourist areas operate special scenic tours in summer. The top deck of a double-decker bus is a great place from which to view the countryside.

DISCOUNTS AND DEALS

National Express's Young Persons' CoachCard for students age 16 to 26 costs £12.50 annually and gets you 10% to 30% discounts off many fares. Most companies also offer a discount for children under 15. A Senior CoachCard for the over-60s cuts many fares by a third. Apex tickets (advance-purchase tickets) save money on standard fares, and traveling midweek is cheaper than over weekends and holidays.

FARES AND SCHEDULES

You can find schedules online, pick them up from tourist information offices, or get them by phone from the bus companies. Fares vary based on how close to the time of travel you book—Megabus tickets, for example, are cheaper if ordered in advance online.

PAYING

Tickets for National Express can be bought from the Victoria, Heathrow, and Gatwick coach stations; by phone; online; or from most British travel agencies and post offices. Reservations are advised. Tickets for Megabus must be purchased online or by phone (avoid calling, as there's a surcharge).

Most companies accept credit cards for advance purchases, but some companies require cash for onboard transactions.

RESERVATIONS

Book in advance, as buses on busy routes fill up quickly. With most companies (National Express, Megabus, Green Line), advance payment means you receive an email receipt and your name is placed on a list given to the driver.

Car

Many visitors find driving in Britain challenging, considering that people drive on the left side of the often disconcertingly narrow roads, many rental cars have standard transmissions, and the gearshift is on the "wrong" side entirely.

There's no reason to rent a car for a stay in London because the city and its suburbs are well served by public transportation and traffic is desperately congested. Here and in other major cities it's best to rely on public transportation.

Outside the cities, a car can be very handy. Many sights aren't easily reached without one—castles, for example, are rarely connected to any public transportation system. Small villages might have only one or two buses a day pass through them. If you're comfortable on the road, driving between the tall hedgerows on a country road is a truly English experience.

Your own driver's license is acceptable in England. However, you may choose to get an International Driving Permit (IDP), which can only be used in conjunction with a valid driver's license and is valid in 175 countries. Check the Automobile Association of America website for more info as well as to apply for an IDP ($20). These permits are universally recognized, and having one in your wallet may save you a problem with the local authorities.

GASOLINE

Gasoline is called petrol in England and is sold by the liter. The price you see posted at a petrol station is the price of a liter, and there are about 4 liters in a U.S. gallon. Petrol is expensive; it was around £1.27 per liter, or $2 per liter, at the time of this writing. Supermarket pumps just outside city centers frequently offer the best prices. Premium and superpremium are the two varieties, and most cars run

Getting Here and Around

on premium. Diesel has been widely used although it is now being phased out; be sure not to use it by mistake. Electric charging stations are still few and far between outside of cities, but the infrastructure is being boosted. Along busy motorways, most large stations are open 24 hours a day, 7 days a week. In rural areas, hours can vary. Most service stations accept major credit cards, and most are self-service.

PARKING
Parking regulations are strictly enforced, and fines are high. If there are no signs on a street, you can park there, but be sure to check carefully—signs may be far from the actual space. Some streets still have centralized "pay and display" machines, in which you deposit the required money and get a ticket allowing you to park for a set period of time, although these are increasingly being replaced by a pay-by-phone plan, enabling you to pay by cell phone if you've preregistered. In town centers your best bet is to park in a public lot marked with a square blue sign with a white "P" in the center.

If you park on the street, follow these basic rules: Do not park within 15 yards of an intersection. Never park in bus lanes or on double yellow lines, and do not park on single yellow lines when parking meters are in effect. On busy roads with red lines painted on the street you cannot park or stop to let a passenger out of the car.

RENTALS
Rental rates are generally reasonable, and insurance costs are lower than in the United States. If you are renting the car for a trip to the countryside, consider picking up outside London. Rates are cheaper, and you avoid having to navigate London's notoriously complex road system. Rental rates vary widely, beginning at £44 a day and £82 a week for a mid-size car, usually with manual transmission. As in the United States, prices rise in summer and during holidays. Car seats for children cost £8 per day, and GPS is usually around £10 per day. You can also arrange for cell phone hire or a portable Wi-Fi hot spot with your rental.

Major car-rental agencies are much the same in Britain as in the United States: Alamo, Avis, Budget, Enterprise, Hertz, Thrifty, and Dollar all have offices in Britain. Europcar and Sixt are other large companies. Companies may not rent cars to people who are under 23. Some have an upper age limit of 75.

ROAD CONDITIONS
There's a good network of major highways (motorways) and divided highways (dual carriageways) throughout most of England. Motorways (with the prefix "M"), shown in blue on most maps, are mainly two or three lanes in each direction. Other major roads (with the prefix "A") are shown on maps in green and red. Sections of fast dual carriageways (with black-edged, thick outlines on maps) have both traffic lights and traffic circles. Turnoffs are often marked by highway exit numbers, rather than place names. An exit is called a junction in Britain.

The vast network of lesser roads, for the most part old coach and turnpike roads, might make your trip twice as long but show you twice as much. Minor roads are drawn in yellow or white on maps, the former prefixed by "B," the latter unlettered and unnumbered. Should you take one of these, be prepared to back up into a passing place if you meet an oncoming car.

ROADSIDE EMERGENCIES

If you run into trouble, contact your car-rental company or call the police. You can also call the British Automobile Association (AA) toll-free. You can join and receive assistance from the AA on the spot, but the charge is higher than a simple membership fee. If you're a member of the American Automobile Association, check before you travel; reciprocal agreements may give you free roadside aid.

Some British highways are experimenting with a concept called "smart motorways" where the hard shoulder is used as an extra driving lane to absorb traffic and which can supposedly be closed off as soon as CCTV cameras notice a car stopped on one. If you break down on the motorway, you should try to get to an emergency area equipped with a free SOS phone and call for help. If you can't make it to an emergency area, stop on the hard shoulder but be aware it may be a working lane, so move away from the vehicle and call emergency services immediately. The experiment has not been a success and the policy is under review. If you have to stop on a mixed-use hard shoulder, use extreme caution.

🚆 Train

Operated by several different private companies, the train system in Britain is extensive and useful, though often confusing and less than reliable (some privately run lines have recently been taken back into state ownership to salvage performance). Some regional train services use older cars, and virtually all lines suffer from occasional delays, schedule changes, and periodic repair work that runs over schedule. The pricing structure is complex, and prices tend to be high compared to the rest of Europe. Nevertheless, all major cities and many small towns are served by trains, and, despite the difficulties, rail travel is the most pleasant way to cover long distances.

On long-distance runs, some rail lines offer buffet cars while others provide mobile snack carts that pass through all the cars. Most train companies also now have "quiet cars" where mobile phone use is forbidden (in theory if not always in practice).

CLASSES

Most rail lines have first-class and second-class cars. In virtually all cases, second class is perfectly comfortable. First class is quieter and less crowded, has better furnishings, and marginally larger seats. It also usually costs two to three times the price of second class, but not always, so it's worth comparing prices. Most train operators offer a Weekend First ticket. Available on weekends and holidays, these tickets allow you to upgrade for as little as £10. ■ TIP→ Some train lines only let you buy Weekend First tickets on board.

FARES AND SCHEDULES

National Rail Enquiries is a helpful, comprehensive, and free service that covers all the country's rail lines. National Rail will help you choose the best train, and then connect you with the right ticket office. You can also book tickets online. A similar service is offered by the Trainline, which provides online train information and ticket booking for all rail services. The Man in Seat 61, a website, offers objective information along with booking facilities.

Ticket prices are more expensive during rush hour, so plan accordingly. For long-distance travel, tickets cost more the longer you wait. Book in advance and tickets can be half of what you'd pay on the day of departure.

Getting Here and Around

■TIP→ **Ask the local tourist board about hotel and local transportation packages that include tickets to major events.**

PASSES

National Rail Enquiries has information about rail passes such as All Line Rovers, which offers unlimited travel on National Rail services for a week, with some restrictions, for £540. Children, seniors, and disabled Rovers are one-half to one-third less.

If you plan to travel a lot by train in England, consider purchasing a BritRail Pass, which gives unlimited travel over the entire British rail network and can save you money. If you don't plan to cover many miles, you may come out ahead by buying individual tickets. Buy your BritRail Pass before you leave home, as they are not sold in Britain. The passes are available from most U.S. travel agents or from ACP Rail International, Flight Centre, International Rail, RailEurope, Trainline, or VisitBritain. Note that Eurail Passes aren't honored in Britain.

BritRail passes come in two basic varieties: the Consecutive Pass and the England FlexiPass. You can get a Consecutive Pass good for 3, 4, 8, 15, or 22 consecutive days or one month starting at $164 standard and $247 first class for 3 days. The FlexiPass for 3, 4, or 8 days of travel in one month or 15 days in two months costs from $207 standard and $306 first class for 3 days. If you're based in London, the BritRail London Plus pass offers access to southern England destinations such as Oxford, Cambridge, Bath, or Stratford-upon-Avon from $159 for standard class, $223 for first class. Tickets can be used for 3, 4, or 8 days of travel within one month.

Don't assume that a rail pass guarantees you a seat on a particular train. You need to book seats even if you're using a rail pass, especially on trains that may be crowded, particularly in summer on popular routes.

RESERVATIONS

Reserving your ticket in advance is recommended. Even a reservation 24 hours in advance can provide a substantial discount. Look into cheap day returns if you plan to travel a round-trip in one day.

CHANNEL TUNNEL

Short of flying, taking the Eurostar through the Channel Tunnel is the fastest way to cross the English Channel (and perhaps faster after factoring in airport travel time and security). Travel time is 2½ hours from London's St. Pancras Station to Paris's Gare du Nord. Trains also travel to Brussels (2 hours), Lille (1½ hours), and Disneyland Paris (2¾ hours), and to Lyon (5¾ hours), Avignon (6½ hours), and Marseille (7¼ hours), Friday, Saturday, and Monday from May through mid-September (plus Sunday in July and August). On Friday (night train) and Saturday (day train) from late December through March, ski trains go to Moûtiers (9 hours) and four other nearby Alpine ski resorts.

Early risers can easily take a day trip to Paris if time is short. Book ahead, as Eurostar ticket prices increase as the departure date approaches. If purchased in advance, round-trip tickets to Paris start at £58 Monday through Thursday, £78 Friday through Sunday. The SnapEurostar site has last-minute tickets from £25 one way, but although you can specify the general time of day, the exact time of departure is potluck.

Essentials

🛏 Lodging

Hotels, bed-and-breakfasts, rural inns, or luxurious country houses—there's a style and price to suit most travelers. Wherever you stay, make reservations well in advance.

APARTMENT AND HOUSE RENTALS

If you deal directly with local agents, get a recommendation from someone who's used the company. Unlike with hotels, there's no accredited system for apartment-rental standards.

BED-AND-BREAKFASTS

B&Bs can be a good budget option, and will also help you meet the locals. Cottages, unlike B&Bs, usually do not provide breakfast.

HOTELS

Most hotels have rooms with private bathrooms —or "ensuites" as the British call them—although some B&Bs may have only washbasins in the actual room, with showers and toilets down the hall. Rooms and bathrooms, especially in London, may be smaller than those you find in the United States.

Besides the familiar international chains, England has some local chains that are worth a look. These range from the basic (the bargain Travelodge and the slightly more upscale Premier Inn are the most widespread, with the latter and Jurys Inns offering good value in city centers) to the boutique (ABode, Hotel du Vin, Malmaison).

HOTEL GRADING SYSTEM

Hotels, guesthouses, inns, and B&Bs in the United Kingdom are all graded from one to five stars by the tourism board, VisitBritain. Basically, the more stars a property has, the more amenities it has, and the facilities will be of a higher standard. It's a fairly good reflection of lodging from small B&Bs up to palatial hotels. The most luxurious hotels will have five stars; a simple, clean, acceptable hostelry will have one star.

DISCOUNTS AND DEALS

Hotel rates in major cities tend to be cheapest on weekends, whereas rural hotels are cheapest on weeknights. The lowest occupancy is between November and April, so hotels lower their prices substantially during these months.

🍽 Dining

The stereotypical notion of English meals as a dull parade of roast beef, overcooked vegetables, and stodgy desserts has largely been replaced—particularly in London, other major cities, and some country hot spots—with an evolving reputation for innovative, creative cuisine. From trendy gastro-pubs to interesting fusion restaurants to see-and-be-seen fine dining, English food is now known for innovative takes on traditional dishes, with an emphasis on the local and seasonal. In less cosmopolitan areas, though, you're still looking at lots of offerings that are either stodgy, fried, sausages, or curries.

DISCOUNTS AND DEALS

Eating out in England—big cities in particular—can be expensive, but it can be done cheaply. Try local cafés, more popularly known as "caffs," which specialize in heaping plates of English comfort food (bacon sandwiches and stuffed baked potatoes, for example). England has plenty of the big fast food chains, as well as independent outlets selling sandwiches, fish-and-chips, burgers, falafels, kebabs, and the like. For a local touch, check out Indian restaurants, which are found almost everywhere. Marks & Spencer (aka M&S), Sainsbury's, Morrison's, Tesco, Lidl, Aldi, and Waitrose are chain supermarkets

Essentials

with outlets throughout the country. They're good choices for groceries, pre-made sandwiches, or picnic fixings.

MEALS AND MEALTIMES

Cafés serving the traditional English breakfast (called a "fry-up") of eggs, bacon, sausage, beans, mushrooms, half a grilled tomato, toast, and strong tea are often the cheapest—and most authentic—places for breakfast. For lighter morning fare (or for real brewed coffee), try the Continental-style sandwich bars and coffee shops—the Pret-a-Manger chain being one of the largest—offering croissants and other pastries. In London, the Leon chain offers healthy alternatives.

At lunch you can grab a sandwich between sights, pop into the local pub, or sit down in a restaurant. Dinner, too, has no set rules, but a three-course meal is standard in most midrange or high-end restaurants. Pre- or post-theater menus, offering two or three courses for a set price, are usually a good value.

Note that most traditional pubs don't have any waitstaff, and you're expected to go to the bar to order a beverage and your meal. Also, in cities many pubs don't serve food after 3 pm, so they're usually better for lunch than dinner, unless they're gastro-pubs. In rural areas it's not uncommon for pubs to stop serving lunch after 2:30 and dinner after 9 pm.

Breakfast is generally served between 7:30 and 9, lunch between noon and 2, and dinner or supper between 7:30 and 9:30—sometimes earlier and seldom later except in large cities and tourist areas. These days, high tea is rarely a proper meal anymore. It was once served between 4:30 and 6, but tearooms are often open all day in touristy areas (they're not found at all in nontouristy places), so you can have a cuppa and pastry or sandwich whenever you feel you need it. Sunday roast lunches at pubs last from 11 am or noon to 3 pm.

PAYING

Credit cards are widely accepted in restaurants and pubs, though some require a minimum charge of around £10. Be sure that you don't double-pay a service charge. Many restaurants exclude service charges from the printed menu (which the law obliges them to display outside), and then add 10% to 15% to the check. Others will stamp "Service not included" along the bottom of the bill, in which case you should add 10% to 15%. You can also add to the included charge if the service was particularly good. Cash is always appreciated, as it's more likely to go to the specific waiter.

PUBS

A common misconception among visitors to England is that pubs are simply bars. They are also restaurants and community gathering places where people go to relax after work or meet their friends and where the social interaction is as important as the alcohol. In small towns, pubs act almost as town halls. Traditionally pub hours are 11–11, with last orders called about 20 minutes before closing time, but pubs can apply for a license to stay open until midnight or later. Many pubs in larger cities have taken advantage of this.

Though to travelers it may appear that there's a pub on almost every corner, in fact pubs are something of an endangered species, closing at a rate of 2.2 a day (as of 2019), with independent, nonchain pubs in smaller localities at particular risk.

Most pubs tend to be child-friendly, but others have restricted hours for children. If a pub serves food, it'll generally allow children in during the day with adults. Some pubs are stricter than others, though, and won't admit anyone younger than 18. Some will allow children in during the day, but only until 6 pm.

RESERVATIONS AND DRESS

Regardless of where you are, it's a good idea to make a reservation if you can. We mention them specifically only when reservations are essential or when they're not accepted. For popular restaurants, book as far ahead as you can (often 30 days), and reconfirm as soon as you arrive. (Large parties should always call ahead to check the reservations policy.) We mention dress only when men are required to wear a jacket or a jacket and tie.

Online reservation services aren't as popular in England as in the United States, but Open Table and Square Meal have a fair number of listings in England.

WINES, BEER, AND SPIRITS

Although hundreds of varieties of beer are brewed around the country, the traditional brew is known as bitter and isn't carbonated; it's usually served at room temperature. Fizzy American-style beer is called lager. There are also plenty of other alternatives: stouts like Guinness and Murphy's are thick, pitch-black brews you'll either love or hate; ciders, made from apples, are alcoholic in Britain (Bulmer's and Strongbow are the big names, but look out for local microbrews); shandies are a low-alcohol mix of lager and lemon soda. Real ales, which have a natural second fermentation in the cask, have a shorter shelf life (so many are brewed locally) but special flavor; many are worth seeking out. Craft beers are also taking off, especially in cities. Generally, the selection and quality of cocktails is higher in a wine bar or café than in a pub.

🏃 Activities

VisitBritain and local Tourist Information Centres can recommend places to enjoy your favorite sport.

BIKING

The national body promoting cycle touring is the Cycling UK (£48 a year), which can organize cycling vacations. Members get free advice and route information and a magazine. Transport for London publishes maps of recommended routes across the capital, and British Cycling has online route maps of the United Kingdom.

BOATING

Boating—whether on bucolic rivers or former industrial canals—can be a leisurely way to explore the English landscape. For boat-rental operators along Britain's several hundred miles of historic canals and waterways ranging from the Norfolk Broads to the Lake District, contact British Marine Inland Boating or Waterways Holidays. The Canal and River Trust has maps and other information. Waterways Holidays arranges boat accommodations from traditional narrow boats to wide-beam canal boats, motorboats, and sailboats.

GOLF

Invented in Scotland, golf is a popular pastime all over England. Some courses take advantage of spectacular natural settings, with backdrops ranging from beaches to mountains. Most courses are reserved for club members and adhere to strict rules of protocol and dress. However, many famous courses can be used by visiting golfers reserving well in advance. In addition, numerous public courses are open to anyone, though advance reservations are advised. Package tours with companies such as Golf International and Owenoak International Golf Travel allow you into exclusive clubs. For further information on courses, fees, and locations, try the website English Golf Courses.

Essentials

WALKING

Walking and hiking, whether a slow ramble or a challenging mountain climb, are enormously popular in England. National Trails, funded by Natural England, has great resources online. The Ramblers, a well-known charitable organization promoting hiking and footpath preservation, has helpful information like a list of B&Bs close to selected long-distance footpaths. The Ordnance Survey Explorer Maps, available both in hard copy and online, are very useful for walkers.

⊕ Customs and Duties

You're always allowed to bring goods of a certain value back home without having to pay any duty or import tax. But there's a limit on the amount of tobacco and liquor you can bring back duty-free, and some countries have separate limits for perfumes; for exact figures, check with your customs department. The values of so-called duty-free goods are included in these amounts. When you shop abroad, save all your receipts, as customs inspectors may ask to see them as well as the items you purchased. If the total value of your goods is more than the duty-free limit, you'll have to pay a tax (most often a flat percentage) on the value of everything beyond that limit.

Fresh meats, plants and vegetables, controlled drugs, and firearms (including replicas) and ammunition may not be brought into the United Kingdom, nor can dairy products from non-EU countries. Pets from the United States with the proper documentation may be brought into the country without quarantine under the U.K. Pet Travel Scheme (PETS). The process takes about four months to complete and involves detailed steps.

⊙ Media

NEWSPAPERS AND MAGAZINES

The main serious national newspapers in England, known as "broadsheets," are the *Times,* the *Telegraph,* the *Independent,* and the *Guardian* (the *Observer* is the *Guardian*'s Sunday paper). Each has a political viewpoint in both its news coverage and its opinion pages. The *Times* and *Telegraph* are more conservative, whereas the *Independent* and *Guardian* take a more left-wing approach. Tabloids, such as the *Sun* and the *Mirror,* present a notably livelier version of the news, with an emphasis on celebrities, sports, and scandal, while the mid-market *Daily Mail* and *Daily Express* sit between the broadsheets and the tabloids. They, too, have political agendas: the *Sun,* the *Express,* and *Daily Mail* are all conservative, whereas the *Mirror* is more centrist.

For detailed information about what's going on in London, pick up a copy—or check the website or app—of *Time Out* magazine, *Metro,* the *Evening Standard,* or the *Londonist* (⊕ www.londonist. com). For countrywide information about shops, restaurants, and art events, take a look at glossy monthly magazines like *Tatler, Harpers Bazaar, Vogue, or Wallpaper;* the weekend editions of the national newspapers; or regional glossy magazines such as *Cheshire Life.*

TELEVISION

There are five main broadcast television channels: BBC1 and BBC2 from the British Broadcasting Corporation (BBC2 is somewhat more eclectic, with a higher proportion of alternative humor, drama, and documentaries), ITV1 (mainstream commercial programming), Channel 4 (a mix of mainstream and off-the-wall programming), and Channel 5 (big on true-crime dramas, animal-related programs, and nonfiction). Cable and satellite channels increase the diet of entertainment.

Safety

England has a low incidence of violent crime, except for the incidence of gang-related knife crime among young men. However, petty crime, mostly in urban areas, is on the rise, and tourists can be the targets. Use common sense: when in a city center, if you're paying at a shop or a restaurant, never put your wallet down or let your bag out of your hand. When sitting on a chair in a public place, keep your purse on your lap or between your feet. Don't wear expensive jewelry or watches, and don't flash fancy smart phones on the street in London, where there have been snatchings by moped or bicycle-riding thieves. Store your passport in the hotel safe, and keep a copy with you. Don't leave anything in your car.

Although scams do occur in Britain, they aren't pervasive. If you're getting money out of an ATM, beware of someone bumping into you to distract you. You may want to use ATMs inside banks rather than those outside them. In London, scams are most common at ATMs near tourist meccas like Oxford Street and Piccadilly Circus. Watch out for pickpockets, particularly in London. They often work in pairs, one distracting you in some way.

Always take a licensed black taxi or call a car service (sometimes called minicabs) recommended by your hotel. Avoid drivers who approach you on the street, as in most cases they'll overcharge you. Always buy theater tickets from a reputable dealer. If you're driving in from a British port, beware of thieves posing as customs officials who try to "confiscate illegal goods."

While traveling, don't leave any bags unattended, as they may be viewed as a security risk and destroyed by the authorities. If you see an unattended bag on the train, bus, or Tube, find a worker and report it. Never hesitate to get off a Tube, train, or bus if you feel unsafe.

COVID-19

A new novel coronavirus brought all travel to a virtual standstill in the first half of 2020. Although the illness is mild in most people, some experience severe and even life-threatening complications. Once travel started up again, albeit slowly and cautiously, travelers were asked to be particularly careful about hygiene and to avoid any unnecessary travel, especially if they are sick.

Older adults, especially those over 65, have a greater chance of having severe complications from COVID-19. The same is true for people with weaker immune systems or those living with some types of medical conditions, including diabetes, asthma, heart disease, cancer, HIV/AIDS, kidney disease, and liver disease.

Starting two weeks before a trip, anyone planning to travel should be on the lookout for some of the following symptoms: cough, fever, chills, trouble breathing, muscle pain, sore throat, new loss of smell or taste. If you experience any of these symptoms, you should not travel at all.

And to protect yourself during travel, do your best to avoid contact with people showing symptoms. Wash your hands often with soap and water. Limit your time in public places, and, when you are out and about, wear a cloth face mask that covers your nose and mouth. Indeed, a mask may be required in some places, such as on an airplane or in a confined space like a theater, where you share the space with a lot of people.

You may wish to bring extra supplies, such as disinfecting wipes, hand sanitizer (12-ounce bottles were allowed in carry-on luggage at this writing), and a first-aid kit with a thermometer.

Essentials

Given how abruptly travel was curtailed in March 2020, it is wise to consider protecting yourself by purchasing a travel insurance policy that will reimburse you for any costs related to COVID-19 related cancellations. Not all travel insurance policies protect against pandemic-related cancellations, so always read the fine print.

Tipping

You tip in Britain just as you do in the United States, though the amounts are lower, generally 12.5% to 15%. You can tip more if service was exceptional. The server is likely to get more if you leave cash (employers can deduct administrative costs if it's left as a service charge or on a credit card). Tip your bartender £1–£2 per round of drinks, depending on the number of drinks, but don't tip bar staff in pubs—although you can always offer to buy them a drink. In most other cases, rounding up to the nearest pound or 50p is appreciated. For hotel housekeeping, be sure to leave at least £2 per day.

Visitor Information

ONLINE TRAVEL TOOLS

ALL ABOUT ENGLAND

All of England's regions, along with their major towns and cities, have their own dedicated tourism websites that provide helpful information. VisitBritain (⊕ *www.visitbritain.com*), the official visitor

Tipping Guidelines for England

Bartender	£1–£2 per round of drinks, depending on the number of drinks, except in pubs, where tipping isn't the custom
Bellhop	£1 per bag, depending on the level of the hotel
Hotel Concierge	£5 or more, if they perform a service for you
Hotel Doorman	£1 if they help you get a cab
Hotel Housekeeping	£2 per day
Hotel Room-Service	Same as a server, unless a service charge has been added to the bill
Porter at Airport or Train Station	£1 per bag
Taxi Driver	10p per pound of the fare, then round up to nearest pound
Tour Guide	Tipping optional: £1 or £2 is generous
Server	12.5%–15%, with 15% being the norm at high-end London restaurants; nothing additional if a service charge is added to the bill, unless you want to reward particularly good service. Tips in cash preferred

website, focuses on information most helpful to England-bound U.S. travelers, from practical tips to money-saving deals; you can even find out about where your favorite UK-set movie was shot. The London visitor website (⊕ *www. visitlondon.com*) can help you book your accommodations.

GARDENS
The National Gardens Scheme opens exceptional gardens attached to private houses and private garden squares to the public on selected weekends.

HISTORIC SITES
The Royal Family has an official website with information about visiting royal residences and more. English Heritage, the National Trust, and VisitBritain all offer discount passes.

MUSEUMS AND THE ARTS
The London Theatre Guide, created by the Society of London Theatre, lists information about what's on and sells tickets. Its half-price ticket booth, tkts, is located in London's Leicester Square and offers same-day bargains. Museum Crush is a nonprofit site with information about publicly funded museums, art galleries, and historic sights. Theatre Tokens sells gift vouchers for theater tickets.

VISITOR INFORMATION OFFICES
In some towns there are local and regional tourist information centers; many have websites. Offices offer services ranging from discounts for local attractions to visitor guides, maps, parking information, and accommodation advice.

Seven visitor information centers operated by Transport for London can be found at travel hubs like King's Cross-Station, Pancras International, Victoria Station, Liverpool Street Station, and Piccadilly Circus Underground Station, plus Heathrow and Gatwick airports. They offer guides, advice, and tickets for tours and attractions, as well as Oyster cards and other public transportation passes.

Great Itineraries

London Itineraries

LONDON IN 1 DAY

Do a giant best-of loop of the city by open-top boat and bus through six key districts, with a stop at the 953-year-old Tower of London and fun in Soho at the end. Start early, with the first ride of the London Eye at 10 am; you'll have the rest of the day to explore at whatever pace you wish, but be sure to get to Buckingham Palace before the sun sets or you'll miss out on some great photo opportunities.

On your morning ride on the **London Eye,** you'll be able to get an unrivaled bird's-eye view of the city. Then launch from the Eye's namesake pier for a swivel-eyed Thames River cruise past four famous bridges and Traitors' Gate before landing in front of the iconic **Tower of London.**

Once inside the Tower, take in the Crown Jewels and gory royal history on a Yeoman Warder's tour, before jumping on a double-decker bus over **Tower Bridge,** past Monument, the Embankment, Park Lane, Oxford, and Piccadilly circuses and stopping at **Trafalgar Square,** where you can glimpse **Big Ben** and the **Houses of Parliament,** before stopping for lunch at a historic Westminster pub. Then take a walk over to **Westminster Abbey,** where a self-guided tour will take you through centuries of British history within one awe-inspiring building (note that the Abbey closes early on Saturday). Then take another short stroll through **St. James's Park** to **Buckingham Palace;** you'll have missed the daily Changing of the Guard, but that means the palace grounds will be less crowded, with more photo ops. End the day by meandering over to the hip Soho neighborhood, where foodies will find endless eclectic restaurants for dinner, and partygoers will find some of the city's best nightlife.

LONDON IN 5 DAYS
DAY 1: BUCKINGHAM PALACE, TRAFALGAR SQUARE, AND THE NATIONAL PORTRAIT GALLERY

Start day one with coffee in a Dickensian alleyway just north of **St. James's Palace,** before being first into the 19 impossibly grand State Rooms at **Buckingham Palace.** Afterward, join the crowds outside the palace to watch a sea of bearskin Foot Guards perform the **Changing of the Guard** ceremony, held 11:30 am most days. Some Palace tickets include tours of the **Queen's Gallery,** which showcases top Old Masters art from the Royal Collection. Then take a stroll through **St. James's Park** before lunch at a historic Pall Mall pub. It's a short walk to the **National Gallery** at **Trafalgar Square.** Hit its quieter Sainsbury Wing, pick up an audio guide, and hunt down a few choice early Renaissance masterpieces. Enjoy stern portraits of Tudor monarchs at the **National Portrait Gallery** next door, before browsing the antiquarian booksellers on Charing Cross Road or Cecil Court and enjoying fresh handmade dim sum in **Chinatown.**

DAY 2: WESTMINSTER ABBEY, HOUSES OF PARLIAMENT, AND THE EAST END

Devote the early morning of day two to a 90-minute verger guided tour of solemn **Westminster Abbey.** Then investigate the **Houses of Parliament.** If in session, you can attend debate in the Public Galleries or take a 75-minute tour of both houses. The stately **Members' and Strangers' Dining Rooms** in the House of Commons are occasionally open to the public for lunch; otherwise have a ploughman's lunch at a historic pub. Take pics of **Big Ben** and walk up Whitehall to the gates of **No. 10 Downing Street,** the Prime Minister's residence. For a complete change of tune, take the Tube over to the gritty yet hip East End and Bangladeshi-influenced Brick Lane, where you can stroll along the art galleries and have a classic Indian curry for dinner.

DAY 3: THE SOUTH BANK

Start with a ride on the **London Eye** for eye-popping city panoramas. Take a long walk along the Thames, popping into any galleries, cinemas, or shops that catch your eye, like the excellent **Hayward Gallery.** Eventually meander along to **Tate Modern** for a modern art fix, stopping for lunch nearby. Then enjoy a Shakespeare hit with tours of the replica Elizabethan **Shakespeare's Globe.** Wiggle along for venison burgers and foodie stall heaven at **Borough Market** before backtracking over the pedestrian **Millennium Bridge** for a stunning approach to **St. Paul's Cathedral.** Hopefully you'll catch Choral Evensong there at 5 pm, then head east toward Bow Lane alleyway for a customary City pub fish-and-chips dinner.

DAY 4: THE BRITISH MUSEUM AND SOHO

On day four, start early at the **British Museum** in Bloomsbury and leave a few hours to explore hits like the Egyptian mummies, Rosetta Stone, and 7th-century Anglo-Saxon Sutton Hoo treasures. Afterward, Tube it to restaurant-mad **Soho** where you can stop for Sri Lankan rice-and-curry at Hoppers, before browsing **Carnaby Street** and the surrounding indie fashion boutiques. Cut across Regent Street via the dapper gentlemen's tailors of **Savile Row** and head south for **Fortnum & Mason** and the old-world gentlemen's outfitters and bespoke shoe shops on Jermyn Street. Work back through the twinkly Regency red-carpet **Burlington Arcade** and pop into the **Royal Academy** gallery before taking Afternoon Tea at the cozy Brown's Hotel in Mayfair.

DAY 5: KENSINGTON'S MUSEUMS, PICCADILLY, AND THE WEST END

Finally on day five, start with a one-hour tour of the **V&A Museum** of decorative arts and design, whose collection ranges from rare Persian rugs to Tudor chalices. Once out, refuel with a crêpe on pedestrianized Exhibition Road near the South Kensington Tube, then choose either all things science at the **Science Museum,** or the *T. rex* dinosaur trail at the **Natural History Museum.** Then stroll up Knightsbridge to **Harrods'** famous Food Hall, where you can drool over salamis and people-watch to your heart's content. Either duck in for the ace fashion at **Harvey Nichols** or sip early cocktails at **The Ritz** at Green Park. Then enjoy the giant neon lights of **Piccadilly Circus** and **Leicester Square** before having a pretheater dinner in **Covent Garden** and then catching a West End play or musical.

Great Itineraries

Highlights of England: 12 Days

DAY 1: LONDON

The capital is just the jumping-off point for this trip, so choose a few highlights for one day here. If it's the Changing of the Guard at Buckingham Palace, check the ceremony time to be sure you catch the pageantry. If Westminster Abbey appeals to your sense of history, arrive as early as you can. Pick a museum (many are free, so you needn't linger if you don't want to), whether it's the National Gallery in Trafalgar Square, the British Museum in Bloomsbury, or Tate Modern on the South Bank. Stroll through Hyde Park or take a boat ride on the Thames before you find a pub or Indian restaurant for dinner. End with a play; London's theater scene is world-renowned.

DAY 2: WINDSOR

Resplendent with centuries of treasures, Windsor Castle is the Queen's favorite residence, and has been home to many of her ancestors. A tour will give you an appreciation of the monarchy's history and power. The State Apartments are open if the Queen isn't in residence, and 10 kings and queens are buried in the magnificent St. George's Chapel on the grounds. Time permitting, take a walk in the adjacent Great Park. If you can splurge for a luxurious stay (as opposed to taking a day trip from London), head to Cliveden, the Thames Valley's most upscale hotel.

Logistics: Trains from Paddington and Waterloo stations leave about twice hourly and take less than one hour. Green Line buses depart from the Colonnades opposite London's Victoria Coach Station.

DAY 3: SALISBURY AND STONEHENGE OR STOURHEAD

The soaring spire of Salisbury Cathedral is visible for miles around and is a marvel of medieval engineering. The cathedral itself contains one of the original copies of the Magna Carta in its Chapter House. Walk through the town to the water meadows to see the view John Constable immortalized in his painting. While here, you shouldn't miss the opportunity to visit nearby Stonehenge (reachable by car or tour bus). Entry is by timed ticket, so make sure to book in advance to guarantee seeing this extraordinarily fascinating and evocative site. It's usually at its least crowded early or late in the day. If Stonehenge isn't your thing, visit the gardens of Stourhead instead, a superb example of the romantic, naturalistic 18th-century landscaping for which England is famous. Save some time to tour the grand Palladian mansion on the site as well.

Logistics: For trains to Salisbury from Windsor and Eton Riverside, head back to London's Waterloo to catch a train on the West of England line.

DAY 4: BATH

Bath's immaculately preserved, golden-stone Georgian architecture transports you back to the world of the late 18th century. Take time to explore the city on foot; check out the harmonious Royal Crescent (and the period interiors of No. 1) and sample the Pump Room's sulfuric "curative" water, just like Jane Austen's contemporaries would have. Originally established by the Romans when the city was an outpost of empire, the baths have been restored and expanded as the Thermae Bath Spa and today you can relax in the mineral waters fed by hot springs much like the Romans did. There's plenty to do here in the way of museums, shopping, and theater.

Logistics: Trains and buses leave hourly from Salisbury to Bath.

DAY 5: THE COTSWOLDS

Beloved for its mellow stone villages and dreamy green landscapes, the Cotswolds have much to offer a visitor, whether you're after antiques (try charming Stow-on-the-Wold) or just feeding ducks in a picturesque setting (the brook in Lower Slaughter). Choose a rainy or off-season day to visit lovely Broadway or risk being stuck in jams of tourist traffic. To really experience the bucolic landscape, take a walk on the Cotswold Way or any local path.

Logistics: You'll need a car to explore the beautiful countryside. Alternatively, opt for a guided tour bus.

DAY 6: OXFORD AND BLENHEIM PALACE

Join a guided tour to get the best access to Oxford's glorious, centuries-old quadrangles, chapels, and gardens. This leaves time for an excursion to Blenheim, a unique combination of baroque opulence and naturalistic parkland, the work of the great 18th-century landscape designer Capability Brown. For other classic Oxford experiences, rent a punt or go on a pub crawl around town.

Logistics: Hourly trains depart from Bath for Oxford. Buses frequently depart from Oxford's Gloucester Green for Blenheim Palace.

DAY 7: STRATFORD-UPON-AVON

A place of pilgrimage for Shakespeare enthusiasts, in Startford-upon-Avon you can visit the Bard's birthplace, Anne Hathaway's Cottage where the future Mrs. S grew up (walking there is a delight), and then finish by taking in a memorable performance at the Royal Shakespeare Company's magnificently renovated main stage. Start the day early and be prepared for crowds.

Logistics: From Oxford, trains involve one or two changes; there is less-frequent Stagecoach bus service.

DAY 8: SHREWSBURY TO CHESTER

Head north to see the half-timber buildings of Shrewsbury, one of the best preserved of England's Tudor towns, best experienced on foot. The architecture in Chester is very similar (if not always authentic), but don't miss the impressive city walls or the Rows, a terrace of two-story shops with medieval crypts beneath. You can walk part or all of the city walls for views of the town and surrounding area.

Great Itineraries

Logistics: For Shrewsbury, change trains at Birmingham. The train ride to Chester is less than an hour.

DAYS 9 AND 10: THE LAKE DISTRICT

The lakes and surrounding mountains extending north beyond Kendal and Windermere in the area known as the Lake District are renowned for their beauty and peacefulness despite the crowds of hikers in summer and on weekends; rent a car so you can seek out the more isolated destinations. Take a cruise on Lake Windermere or Coniston Water, or rent a boat for another classic Lakeland experience. If you have time for one Wordsworth-linked site, head for Dove Cottage, where you can have afternoon tea, too.

Logistics: Take the train to Oxenholme with a change at Warrington Bank Quay. At Oxenholme you can switch to Windermere.

DAY 11: YORK

The highlight of this historic cathedral city crammed with 15th- and 16th-century buildings (especially in the Shambles) is York Minster with its stunning stained glass and soaring Gothic architecture. Explore the city's Viking past in one of the many museums or unwind with afternoon tea at Betty's or a pint at a pub. A walk along the top of the medieval walls offers excellent views.

Logistics: By train from Oxenholme, switch at Manchester Piccadilly, or from Carlisle change at Newcastle or Leeds.

DAY 12: CAMBRIDGE

Spend the afternoon touring King's College Chapel and the gardens and sprawling meadows of the Backs, then refine your punting skills on the River

Cam. A visit to the excellent Fitzwilliam Museum, full of art and antiquities, is another option, as is the Polar Museum.

Logistics: For train service, switch at Peterborough. Trains leave Cambridge for London frequently.

Tips

■ Train travelers should keep in mind that regional "Rovers" and "Rangers" offer unlimited train travel in one-day, three-day, or weeklong increments. See ⊕ *www.nationalrail.co.uk* for details. Also check out BritRail passes, which must be purchased before your trip.

■ Bus travel is time-consuming, but more scenic and cheaper than train travel. National Express offers discounts including fun fares—return fares from London to various cities (including Cambridge) for as low as £5 if booked more than 24 hours in advance. Or check out the low-cost Megabus.

■ To cut the tour short, consider skipping Chester and Shrewsbury and go directly to the Lake District from Stratford-upon-Avon on day eight. Likewise, you consider passing up a visit to Cambridge if you opt for Oxford. You can add the time to your London stay or anyplace else you'd like to linger.

■ Buy theater tickets well in advance for the Royal Shakespeare Company performances in Stratford-upon-Avon.

On the Calendar

Spring

British Antique Dealers' Association Fair. This large and prestigious antiques fair is England's most popular, with many affordable pieces for sale. It takes place over seven days in mid-March. ⊠ *Duke of York Square, Chelsea* ☎ *020/7589–4128* ⊕ *www.badafair.com.*

Chelsea Flower Show. Tickets usually sell out well in advance for this prestigious five-day, 22-acre extravaganza of garden design held in May on the grounds of London's Royal Hospital in the Chelsea neighborhood. ⊠ *Royal Horticultural Society, Royal Hospital Rd., London* ☎ *0871/338–7501 tickets, 0203/176–5800 inquiries* ⊕ *www.rhs.org.uk/chelsea.*

Head of the River Boat Race. Taking place over a weekend in mid-March, the Head of the River Boat Race offers the spectacle of about 430 eight-man crews speeding down the Thames past southwest London as they race from Mortlake to Putney. The best view is from Surrey Bank above Chiswick Bridge (Tube to Chiswick); the starting time depends on the tide. ⊕ *www.horr.co.uk.*

Oxford and Cambridge University Boat Race. The Oxford versus Cambridge Boat Race between crews from two of Britain's most prestigious universities takes place a week or so after the Head of the River Boat Race. It travels over the same 4½-mile course through southwest London but in the opposite direction, carrying on a rivalry that goes back to 1829. Around a quarter of a million people watch from the banks of the river. ⊕ *www.theboatrace.org.*

The Queen's Birthday. The Queen gets two birthday celebrations: her actual one on April 21, marked by a booming 41-gun salute in London's Hyde Park, and on a Saturday in mid-June, the purely ceremonial Trooping the Colour, a public display of precision military marching, horsemanship, and bands playing.

Summer

Glastonbury Festival. The biggest music festival in England sprawls across Somerset farmland in late June, when hundreds of bands (rock, pop, folk, and world music) perform on a half-dozen stages for three days and nights. Registration is required before tickets go on sale each October, when they then sell out almost immediately. ☎ *0115/896–0073* ⊕ *www.glastonburyfestivals.co.uk.*

Hampton Court Palace Flower Show. Held on the grounds of one of two surviving palaces built by Henry VIII, the six-day Hampton Court Palace Flower Show is a more grow-your-own, environmentally minded version of the Chelsea Flower Show. ⊠ *Hampton Court Palace, East Molesey* ☎ *0844/338–7501 tickets, 0203/176–5800 general inquiries* ⊕ *www.rhs.org.uk/hamptoncourt.*

Henley Royal Regatta. A highlight of the social season with a dress code to match, rowers from around the world compete during this five-day event held over the first weekend in July, cheered on by champagne-fueled crowds lining the banks of the Thames. ⊠ *Henley on Thames* ☎ *01491/571900 inquiries, 01491/572153 tickets* ⊕ *www.hrr.co.uk.*

On the Calendar

International Beatleweek. Held at the end of August, International Beatleweek sees hundreds of Beatles tribute bands descend on Liverpool to stage performances. Biographers and associates of the band add to the memorabilia-fest. ✉ *Liverpool* ☎ *0151/236–9091* ⊕ *www. internationalbeatleweek.com.*

The Proms. Held July through September, this distinguished series of orchestral concerts ranges from classical standards to *Harry Potter* film scores. The main venue is London's Royal Albert Hall, but venues across the country also host some concerts. ✉ *Royal Albert Hall, Kensington Gore, London* ☎ *0207/070– 4441* ⊕ *www.bbc.co.uk/proms.*

Royal Ascot. The most prestigious and glamorous event in British horse racing is usually held over four days during the third week of June in the Thames Valley. An ardent racing fan and thoroughbred owner, the Queen invariably attends. Reserve months in advance for tickets. ✉ *Ascot Racecourse, Ascot* ☎ *0844/346– 3000* ⊕ *www.ascot.co.uk.*

Trooping the Colour. This colorful martial ceremony to mark the Queen's official birthday (her real one is in April) takes place in June at the Horse Guards Parade in London. Seated tickets can be booked for two rehearsals—the Colonel's Review (one week before, £10) and the Major General's Review (two weeks before, £5)—held on the two Saturdays prior to the actual parade; tickets (£40) are only allocated by ballot. Online ticket purchases and ballot entry starts in mid-January and are available through the end of February. Standing tickets for the Trooping the Colour are available for purchase starting in March. ⊕ *www. householddivision.org.uk.*

Wimbledon Lawn Tennis Championships. The crowning event of the world tennis circuit, the Wimbledon Lawn Tennis Championships is a two-week tournament that takes place annually from late June to mid-July in southwest London. Admission is by ticket lottery only, and applications are available from August through mid-December of the preceding year. You can also arrive (very) early to line-up for the very few same-day tickets available. ☎ *020/8971–2473 tickets, 020/8944– 1066 general inquiries* ⊕ *www.wimbledon.com.*

Fall

Bonfire Night. A foiled attempt in 1605 to blow up Parliament is commemorated every November 5 by small bonfires, countrywide municipal and neighborhood fireworks, and, among traditionalists, the burning of an effigy of chief plotter Guy Fawkes. Lewes and York stage some of the biggest festivities.

Winter

New Year's Eve Firework Display. The chimes of Big Ben striking midnight on New Year's Eve herald a magnificent array of fireworks centered around the London Eye. Admission by ticket (on sale in September) gives you a view from the Victoria Embankment opposite, but wherever you are, if you can see the Eye, you'll be able to glimpse at least some of the fireworks. ⊕ *www.london.gov.uk/nye.*

Best Tours in England

Beatles Liverpool Magical Mystery Tour. This two-hour bus tour through the native city of the world's most famous band takes you to iconic locations like the childhood homes of Lennon and McCartney, the schools where they met, and places that inspired songs like the original Penny Lane and Strawberry Fields. Tours end at the Cavern Club where the band paid their dues before hitting it big. Tours leave daily at 10 am from the Albert Dock. ☎ 0151/703–9100 ⊕ www.cavernclub.com/the-magical-mystery-tour ✉ From £19.95.

City Guides. The City Guides (or, to give them their full name, The City of London Guide Lecturers' Association) are the official guides to the City of London, the "City" being not the entire metropolis but the "Square Mile" historic financial district. They offer two highly informed daily walks at 11 am and 2 pm—some bookable but others just turn up on the day—that cover essential sights like Guildhall (the City's town hall), Mansion House, the Bank of England, and the Royal Exchange. More specialized walks offered by the Museum of London focus on topics like Samuel Johnson's London, the gardens of The City, the Great Fire of London, Roman London, or the churches of Christopher Wren, most notably his magnificent St. Paul's Cathedral. ☎ 0207/606–3030 ⊕ www.cityoflondonguides.com ✉ From £7.

English Lakeland Ramblers. This subset of the Ramblers organizes guided hiking tours of the Cotswolds, the Lake District, Wales, and England's coast-to-coast hiking trail, which runs from the Irish Sea to the North Sea. They also provide self-guided walking tours of these and other areas. ☎ 800/724–8801 in U.S. ⊕ www.ramblers.com ✉ From $2,300.

Harry Potter Walking Tour of London. J. K. Rowling's legion of fans won't want to miss these walking tours, which reveal the places that portrayed Potterverse locations in the films based on the books, including Diagon Alley (Cecil Court), the Ministry of Magic entrance (Scotland Yard Place), and the entrance to the Leaky Cauldron (Leadenhall Market). The 2½ hour tours leave Wednesday, Friday, and Saturday at 2 pm and Monday night at 7 pm from the statute of Winston Churchill in Parliament Square. You can pay what you wish. ⊕ www.freetoursbyfoot.com/harry-potter-tour-london ✉ Free; tips encouraged.

Jack the Ripper Tour of London. Retrace the dark journey of Victorian England's most notorious serial killer. This tour of the East London neighborhoods of Spitalfields and Whitechapel takes you down the atmospheric alleys and cobbled streets where he murdered his victims. The guides are experts and often authors of books on the subject; you're presented with evidence to help you solve the long-standing mystery of who the killer really was. Tours leave every night at 7 pm from outside Exit 1 of Aldgate East Tube station. ☎ 0208/530–8443 ⊕ www.jack-the-ripper-tour.com ✉ £10.

The Original Ghost Walk of York. York is allegedly Britain's most haunted city, and on this tour, guides utlilize their backgrounds in history and storytelling to make York's history, legends, and ghost sightings come alive on a walk through the city's medieval streets. The 75 to 90 minute tour leaves from the King's Arms Pub on the Ouse Bridge at 8 pm every night. ☎ 01759/373090 ⊕ www.theoriginalghostwalkofyork.co.uk ✉ £6.

Best Tours in England

The Original London Sightseeing Tour. This one-day, hop-on-hop-off, open-top bus tour with over 80 stops along six different routes takes in major landmarks like the Houses of Parliament, Westminster Abbey, Trafalgar Square, the British Museum, the Tower of London, and, of course, Buckingham Palace, as well as more off-the-beaten-path sites like Lambeth Palace (home of the Bishop of London). Tickets are good for the entire day and for all routes. ⊠ *London* ☎ *020/8877–1722* ⊕ *www.theoriginaltour.com* ✉ *From £29.*

Oxford Walking Tour. This free, two-hour tour is led by current Oxford University students who can give you the skinny on insider topics like Oxford ceremonies, unusual traditions, student life, and college rivalries, as well as the history of beautiful, historic buildings like the Radcliffe Camera, the Bodelian Library, and medieval colleges including Christ Church, Oriel, Trinity, and All Souls. Tours leave from 5 Broad Street at 11 am, 12:30 pm, and 2 pm on weekdays, with additional tours at 10 am and 3:30 pm on weekends. There is a similar tour of Cambridge led by its own students. ☎ *0207/558–8706* ⊕ *www.footprints-tours.com/oxford* ✉ *Free.*

The Stonehenge Tour. This hop-on, hop-off bus tour operated by Salisbury Reds runs from the town center of Salisbury through the beautiful Wiltshire countryside to the Neolithic monuments of Stonehenge, taking in Old Sarum, an Iron Age earthwork fort later occupied by Romans, Saxons, and Normans. The all-inclusive ticket offers you priority entrance to Stonehenge as well as the magnificently Gothic Salisbury Cathedral with its copy of the Magna Carta. ☎ *01202/338420* ⊕ *www.thestonehengetour.info* ✉ *£35.*

Stratford-Upon-Avon Self-Guided Tour. As you might imagine, Shakespeare's birthplace draws hordes of tourists, but a self-guided tour will let you take in the sights at your own pace and avoid the crowds. The one-day Shakespeare's England Explorer Pass (£39) gives you admission to some 18 Bard-related or notable regional locations—including Shakespeare's Birthplace, Anne Hathaway's Cottage, Mary Arden's Farm, and Warwick Castle—saving you as much as 45% on admission prices. ⊕ *www.shakespeares-england.co.uk/explorer-pass.*

Contacts

⚡ Activities

BIKING British Cycling.
☎ 0161/274–2000 ⊕ www.
britishcycling.org.uk.
Cycling UK. ☎ 01483/238–
300 ⊕ www.cyclinguk.org.

**BOATING British
Marine Inland Boating.** ☎ 01784/473377
⊕ www.britishmarine.
co.uk. **Canal and River
Trust.** ☎ 0303/040–4040
⊕ www.canalrivertrust.
org.uk. **Waterways Holidays.** ☎ 01252/796400
⊕ www.waterwaysholidays.com.

GOLF English Golf Courses.
☎ 0141/353–2222 ⊕ www.
englishgolf-courses.
co.uk. **Golf International.**
☎ 212/986–9176 ⊕ www.
golfinternational.com.
**Owenoak International
Golf Travel.** ☎ 203/854–
9000, 800/426 4498
⊕ owenoak.com. **UK Golf
Guide.** ⊕ www.ukgolf-
guide.com.

WALKING National Trails.
⊕ www.nationaltrail.
co.uk. **Ordnance Survey.** ☎ 03456/050–505
⊕ www.ordnancesurvey.
co.uk. **The Ramblers.**
☎ 0203/961–3232
⊕ www.ramblers.org.uk.

✈ Air

AIRPORTS Birmingham Airport. (*BHX*).
☎ 0871/222–0072
⊕ www.birminghamair-
port.co.uk. **Gatwick Airport.**
(*LGW*). ☎ 0844/892–0322
⊕ www.gatwickairport.
com. **Heathrow Airport.**
(*LHR*). ☎ 0844/335–1801
⊕ www.heathrowairport.
com. **London City Airport.**
(*LCY*). ☎ 0207/646–0000
⊕ www.londoncityair-
port.com. **Luton Airport.**
(*LLA*). ☎ 01582/405100
⊕ www.london-luton.
co.uk. **Manchester Airport.**
(*MAN*). ☎ 0800/169–7030
⊕ www.manchesterair-
port.co.uk. **Stansted Airport.**
(*STN*). ☎ 0844/355–1803
⊕ www.stanstedairport.
com.

GROUND TRANSPORTATION Crossrail.
☎ 0345/602–3813
⊕ www.crossrail.co.uk.
easyBus. ⊕ www.easybus.
com. **Gatwick Express.**
☎ 0345/850–1530,
0845/850–1530 from
U.S. ⊕ www.gatwickex-
press.com. **Green Line.**
☎ 0344/801–7261 ⊕ www.
greenline.co.uk. **Heathrow
Express.** ☎ 0845/600–1515
⊕ www.heathrowexpress.
com. **National Express.**
☎ 0871/781–8181
⊕ www.nationalexpress.
com. **Stansted Express.**

☎ 0345/600–7245
⊕ www.stanstedex-
press.com. **Transport for
London.** ☎ 0343/222–1234
⊕ www.tfl.gov.uk. **Traveline.** ☎ 0871/200–2233
⊕ www.traveline.info.

⛴ Boat

**INFORMATION DFDS
Seaways.** ☎ 0871/522–
9955 ⊕ www.dfds.
com. **Direct Ferries.**
☎ 0333/300–0128 ⊕ www.
directferries.co.uk. **P&O.**
☎ 0130/444–8888 ⊕ www.
poferries.com. **Seaview.**
☎ 01442/843050 ⊕ www.
seaviewferries.co.uk. **Stena Line.** ☎ 0844/770–7070
⊕ www.stenaline.co.uk.

🚌 Bus

INFORMATION Green Line.
☎ 0344/801–7261 ⊕ www.
greenline.co.uk. **Megabus.**
☎ 0141/352–4444 ⊕ uk.
megabus.com. **National
Express.** ☎ 0871/781–8181
⊕ www.nationalex-
press.com. **Oxford Tube.**
☎ 01865/772250 ⊕ www.
oxfordtube.com. **Traveline.** ☎ 0871/200–2233
⊕ www.traveline.info. **Victoria Coach Station.** ✉ 164
Buckingham Palace Rd.,
London ☎ 020/7222–5600
⊕ www.tfl.gov.uk.

Contacts

🛏 Lodging

RESERVATION SERVICES Bed & Breakfast. com. ☎ 0208/827–1971 ⊕ www.bedandbreakfast. com. **Wolsey Lodges.** ☎ 01473/822058 ⊕ www. wolseylodges.com.

COTTAGES Classic Cottages. ☎ 01326/555555 ⊕ www.classic.co.uk. **Cool Places UK.** ☎ 0207/820–9333 ⊕ www.coolplaces. co.uk/self-catering/uk. **National Trust Cottages.** ☎ 0344/800–2070 booking ⊕ www.nationaltrust. org.uk. **Rural Retreats.** ☎ 01386/701177 ⊕ www. ruralretreats.co.uk. **VisitBritain.** ☎ 020/757–81000 ⊕ www.visitbritain.org.

FARMHOUSES Farm & Cottage Holidays UK. ☎ 01237/459888 ⊕ www.holidaycottages.co.uk. **Farm Stay UK.** ☎ 02476/696909 ⊕ www. farmstayuk.co.uk.

HISTORIC HOMES Celtic Castles. ☎ 01422/323200 ⊕ www.celticcastles.com. **English Heritage Holiday Cottages.** ☎ 0370/333–1181 ⊕ www.english-heritage. org.uk/visit/holiday-cottages. **The Folly Fellowship.** ⊕ follies.org.uk. **Landmark Trust.** ☎ 01628/825925 ⊕ www.landmarktrust. org.uk. **National Trust Cottages.** ☎ 0344/800–2070 ⊕ www.nationaltrustorg. uk. **Unique Home Stays.**

☎ 01637/881183 ⊕ www. uniquehomestays.com.

LOCAL CHAINS ABode. ☎ 01244/347000 ⊕ www. abodehotels.co.uk. **Hotel du Vin.** ☎ 0330/016–0390 ⊕ www.hotelduvin.com. **Jurys Inn.** ☎ 0870/410–0800 ⊕ www.jurysinn. com. **Malmaison.** ☎ 0330/016–0380 ⊕ www. malmaison.com. **Premier Inn.** ☎ 033/003–8101 ⊕ www.premierinn.com. **Travelodge.** ☎ 0871/984–8484 ⊕ www.travelodge. co.uk.

🚆 Train Travel

INFORMATION The Man in Seat 61. ⊕ www.seat61. com. **National Rail Enquiries.** ☎ 0345/711–4141 ⊕ www.nationalrail.co.uk. **Trainline.** ☎ 033/202–2222 ⊕ www.thetrainline.com.

DISCOUNT PASSES ACP Rail International. ☎ 866/938–7245 in U.S. ⊕ www.acprail.com. **BritRail.** ☎ 866/938–7245 in U.S. ⊕ www.britrail.net. **Flight Centre.** ☎ 0203/056–7993 in U.K., 866/605–7422 in U.S. (known as Liberty Travel) ⊕ www.flight-centre.co.uk. **VisitBritain.** ☎ 0207/578–1000 ⊕ www. visitbritainshop.com.

CHANNEL TUNNEL CAR TRANSPORT Eurotunnel. ☎ 0844/335–3535 in U.K. ⊕ www.eurotunnel.com.

CHANNEL TUNNEL PASSENGER SERVICE Eurostar. ☎ 0343/218–6186 in U.K. ⊕ www.eurostar.com. **Rail Europe.** ☎ 800/622–8600 in U.S., 0847/916–1028 in U.K. ⊕ www.raileurope.com.

📍 Visitor Information

GARDENS National Gardens Scheme. ☎ 01483/211535 ⊕ www.ngs.org.uk.

GENERAL London TfL Information Centres. ☎ 0343/222–1234 ⊕ www.tfl.gov.uk.

HISTORIC HOMES English Heritage. ☎ 0370/333–1181 ⊕ www.english-heritage.org.uk. **National Trust.** ☎ 0344/800–1895 ⊕ www.nationaltrust. org.uk. **The Royal Family.** ☎ 0207/766–7300 for booking tours ⊕ www. royal.uk.

MUSEUMS AND CULTURE Museum Crush. ☎ 01273/623266 ⊕ www. museumcrush.org.. **Official London Theatre.** ☎ 0207/557–6700 ⊕ www.officiallondontheatre.com. **Theatre Tokens.** ☎ 0203/011–0755 ⊕ www. theatretokens.com.

IN THE U.S. VisitBritain. ☎ 212/850–0336 in U.S., 0207/578–1000 in U.K. ⊕ www.visitbritain.com.

Chapter 3

LONDON

Updated by
Jo Caird, James O'Neill,
Toby Orton, Ellin Stein,
and Alex Wijeratna

👁 **Sights**
★★★★★

🍴 **Restaurants**
★★★★★

🏨 **Hotels**
★★★★★

🛍 **Shopping**
★★★★★

🌟 **Nightlife**
★★★★★

WELCOME TO LONDON

TOP REASONS TO GO

★ **The abbey and the cathedral:** That Gothic splendor, Westminster Abbey, soars above the final resting place of several of Britain's most distinguished figures. To the east is St. Paul's, the beautiful English baroque cathedral.

★ **Buckingham Palace:** Although not the prettiest royal residence, this is the public face of the monarchy and the place to watch the culmination of the Changing the Guard ceremony.

★ **Tower of London:** Parts of this complex date back 11 centuries. The tower has been a prison, an armory, and a mint—now it houses the Crown Jewels.

★ **Majestic museums:** Discover the Old Masters at the National Gallery, the cutting-edge works at the Tate Modern, and the historical artifacts of the British Museum.

★ **A city of villages:** Each of London's dozens of neighborhoods has its own personality. Parks, shops, pubs: walk around and discover them for yourself.

1 Westminster and St. James's. Embrace your inner tourist. Take pictures of the mounted Horse Guards, and visit stacks of world-class art in the fantastic national galleries. It's well worth braving the crowds to visit historic Westminster Abbey.

2 Mayfair and Marylebone. You may not have the wallet for London's most prestigious shops, but remember window-shopping in historic Mayfair and chic Marylebone is free.

3 Soho and Covent Garden. More sophisticated than seedy these days, the heart of London puts Theatreland, strip joints, Chinatown, and notable restaurants side by side.

4 Bloomsbury and Holborn. The University of London dominates the city's historical intellectual center, Bloomsbury. Allow for long visits to the incomparable British Museum.

5 The City. London's Wall Street might be the oldest part of the capital, but thanks to the futuristic skyscrapers and a sleek Millennium Bridge, it looks like the newest. There's plenty for period architecture buffs as well, like St. Paul's Cathedral and the Tower of London.

6 East London. Once known for its slums immortalized by Charles Dickens and Jack the Ripper, today the area is home to London's contemporary art scene, along with Brick Lane's curry houses and Spitalfields Market.

7 South of the Thames. The National Theatre, Royal Festival Hall, BFI Southbank, Shakespeare's Globe, and the Tate Modern make this area a cultural hub. Get a bird's-eye view of the whole city from the Shard or the London Eye.

8 Kensington, Chelsea, Knightsbridge, and Notting Hill. Although the many boutiques of King's Road have lost much of their heady '60s swagger, the free musuems are as inspiring as ever, as are nearby Kensington Gardens and Hyde Park. Around Portobello Road, Notting Hill Gate is a trendsetting couple of square miles of galleries, bookshops, boutiques, and restaurants.

9 Regent's Park and Hampstead. London becomes noticeably calmer and greener as you head north from Euston Road. Come here to experience just how laid-back moneyed Londoners can be.

10 Up and Down the Thames. Maritime Greenwich boasts the Royal Observatory and the Prime Meridian. Other river excursions take you to Kew Gardens and Hampton Court Palace.

If London's only attractions were its famous landmarks, it would still be unmissable. But London is so much more. Though its long history is evident at every turn, it's also one of the world's most modern and vibrant cities.

London beckons with great museums, royal pageantry, and historically significant buildings. Unique Georgian terraces perch next to cutting-edge modern skyscrapers, and parks and squares provide unexpected oases of greenery amid the dense urban landscape. Modern central London still largely follows its winding medieval street pattern.

As well as visiting landmarks like St. Paul's Cathedral and the Tower of London, set aside time for random wandering; the city repays every moment spent exploring its backstreets and mews on foot. Go to lesser-known but thoroughly rewarding sites such as Kensington Palace and the unique home of 19th-century architect Sir John Soane, which houses his outstanding collection of antiquities and art.

Today the city's art, style, fashion, and restaurant scenes make headlines around the world. London's chefs have become internationally influential, its fashion designers and art stars set global trends, its nightlife continues to produce exciting new acts, and its theater remains celebrated for superb classical and innovative productions.

Then there's that greatest living link with the past—the Royal Family. Don't let fear of looking like a tourist stop you from enjoying the pageantry of the Changing the Guard at Buckingham Palace, one of the greatest free shows in the world.

As the eminent 18th-century man of letters Samuel Johnson said, "When a man is tired of London, he is tired of life, for there is in London all that life can afford." Armed with energy and curiosity, you can discover its riches.

Planning

When to Go

The heaviest tourist season runs April through September, with another peak around Christmas. Late spring is the time to see the Royal Parks and gardens at their freshest; fall brings autumnal beauty and fewer people. Summer gives the best chance of good weather, although the crowds are intense. Winter can be dismal—it's dark by 5—but all the theaters, concerts, and exhibitions go full-speed ahead, and Christmas lights bring a major touch of festive magic. Weather-wise, winter is cold and wet with occasional light snow, and spring is colorful and fair. June through August can range from a total washout to a long hot summer and anything in between. Autumn ranges from warm to cool to mild. It's impossible to forecast London weather, but you can be certain that it will not be what you expect.

Getting Here and Around

AIR

Most international flights to London arrive at either Heathrow Airport (LHR), 15 miles west of London, or at Gatwick Airport (LGW), 27 miles south of the capital. Most flights from the United States go to Heathrow, which is divided into five terminals, with Terminals 3–5 handling transatlantic flights. Gatwick is London's second gateway. It has grown from a European airport into an airport that also serves dozens of U.S. destinations. A third airport, Stansted (STN), is 35 miles northeast of the city; it handles European and domestic traffic. Three smaller airports, Luton (LTN), 30 miles north of town, Southend (SEN), 40 miles to the east, and business-oriented London City (in east London E16) mainly handle flights to Europe.

BIKE

Nicknamed "Boris bikes" after the former mayor, dedicated cyclist, and current Prime Minister Boris Johnson, a 24-hour bike-rental program called Santander Cycles enables Londoners to pick up a bicycle at one of more than 750 docking stations and return it at another. The first 30 minutes are free, then it's £2 for every 30-minute period thereafter. There is also a £2-per-day access charge. You pay at the docking station, using credit or debit cards only (cash is not accepted)—simply follow the instructions on the touch screen and away you go.

BUS

Although London is famous for its double-decker buses, the old beloved rattletrap Routemasters, with the jump-on, jump-off back platforms, now only serve a single "heritage" route (No. 15H) and only on summer weekends and bank holidays. That route takes you from Trafalgar Square down Fleet Street and on to St. Paul's Cathedral and the Tower of London. Modernized Routemaster buses have taken to the streets on other routes.

Bus stops are clearly indicated; signs at bus stops feature a red TfL symbol on a plain white background. You must flag the bus down at some stops. Each numbered route is listed on the main stop, and buses have a large number on the front with their end destination. Not all buses run the full route at all times; check with the driver to be sure. You can pick up a free bus guide at a TfL Travel Information Centre (at Euston, Liverpool Street, Piccadilly Circus, King's Cross, and Victoria Tube stations, as well as at Heathrow Airport).

Buses are a good way of seeing the town, particularly if you plan to hop on and off to cover many sights, but don't take a bus if you're in a hurry, as traffic can really slow them down. To get off, press the red "Stop" buttons mounted on poles near the doors. You will usually see a "Bus Stopping" sign light up. Expect to get sardined during rush hours, 8–9:30 am and 4:30–6:30 pm.

Night buses, denoted by an "N" before their route numbers, run midnight–5 am on a more restricted route than day buses. However, some night-bus routes should be approached with caution, and the top deck avoided (the danger is that muggings are most likely to occur there, since it's farthest from both the exit doors and the driver). All night buses run by request stop, so flag them down if you're waiting, or push the button if you want to alight.

All London buses are now cash-free, which means you must buy your ticket *before* you board the bus. There are a number of ways to do this. One-day paper bus passes are available at Underground and rail stations as well as London Transport Visitor Centres and cost £5. An easier, and cheaper, option is to pay by prepaid Oyster card or "contactless" bank card. Visitor Oyster cards must be purchased before you arrive; they cost £5 (plus postage), but a day's bus travel is capped at £4.40. Normal Oyster cards (also £5) are available from ticket desks at all major airports or at any Tube station and are transferable if you have money left over. Contactless cards are increasingly being used for London travel: you touch a compatible debit or credit card on a bus or Tube station's reader, and the fare is automatically debited from your bank account.

One alternative is to buy a one- or seven-day Travelcard, which is good for both Tube and bus travel. Travelcards can be bought at Tube stations, rail stations, and travel information centers. However, note that seven-day Travelcards bought in London *must be loaded onto an Oyster card.* Although using a Travelcard may save you some money, it might be easier to just add additional money to your Oyster card as needed, since there are machines at all Tube stations and at lots of London newsagents. A seven-day paper Travelcard can only be purchased in advance, online. However you buy your ticket, just make sure you have one: traveling without a valid ticket makes you liable for a significant fine (£80). Buses are supposed to swing by most stops every five or six minutes, but in reality you often end up waiting a bit longer, although those in the city center are quite reliable.

CONTACTS Transport for London. ☎ *0343/222–1234* ⊕ *www.tfl.gov.uk.*

CAR

The best advice on driving in London is this: don't. London's streets are a winding mass of chaos, made worse by one-way roads. Parking is also restrictive and expensive, and traffic is tediously slow at most times of the day. During rush hours (8–9:30 am and 4:30–6:30 pm) it often grinds to a standstill, particularly on Friday, when everyone wants to leave town. Avoid city-center shopping areas, including the roads feeding Oxford Street, Kensington, and Knightsbridge. Other main roads into the city center are also busy, such as King's Cross and

Euston in the north. Watch out also for cyclists and motorcycle couriers, who weave between cars and pedestrians that seem to come out of nowhere, and you may get a heavy fine for straying into a bus lane during its operating hours—check the signs.

If you are staying in London for the duration of your trip, there's virtually no reason to rent a car, because the city and its suburbs are widely covered by public transportation. However, you may want a car for day trips to castles or stately homes out in the countryside. Consider renting your car in a medium-size town in the area where you'll be traveling, and then journeying there by train and picking up the car once you arrive. Rental rates are generally reasonable, and insurance costs are lower than in comparable U.S. cities. Rates generally begin at £20 per day for a small economy car (such as a subcompact General Motors Vauxhall Corsa or a Renault Clio), usually with manual transmission. Air-conditioning and unlimited mileage generally come with the larger-size automatic cars.

Designed to reduce traffic through central London, a congestion charge has been instituted. Vehicles (with some exemptions) entering central London on weekdays 7 am–6 pm (excluding public holidays) have to pay £11.50 per day; it can be paid up to 90 days in advance, on the day of travel, or on the following "charging day," when the fee goes up to £14. Day-, month-, and yearlong passes are available on the Congestion Charging page of the Transport for London website, at gas stations, parking lots (car parks), by mail, by phone, and by SMS text message. Traffic signs designate the entrance to congestion areas, and cameras read car license plates and send the information to a database. Drivers who don't pay the congestion charge by midnight of the next charging day following the day of driving are penalized £160, which is reduced to £80 if paid within 14 days. On top of the congestion charge, the entire Greater London area has been designated a Low Emissions Zone, which means that all older and pollution-heavy vehicles will be levied with an extra daily charge of £12.50. However, this will almost certainly not apply to rented cars (which tend to be newer and therefore greener), but it's smart to check with the rental company first.

TAXI

Universally known as "black cabs" (even though many of them now come in other colors), the traditional big black London taxicabs are as much a part of the city's streetscape as red double-decker buses, and for good reason: the unique, spacious taxis easily hold five people, plus luggage. To earn a taxi license, drivers must undergo intensive training on the history and geography of London. The course, and all that the drivers have learned in it, is known simply as "the Knowledge." There's almost nothing your taxi driver won't know about the city. Partly because of lobbying efforts by the black cab industry, companies such as Uber have yet to make significant inroads into the London market, although the battle is ongoing.

TRAIN

London has eight major train stations, each serving a different area of the country, and all are accessible by Underground or bus. Various private companies operate trains, but National Rail Enquiries acts as a central rail information number.

CONTACTS National Rail Enquiries.
☎ 0345/748–4950 ⊕ www.nationalrail. co.uk.

UNDERGROUND (TUBE)

London's extensive Underground train system (the Tube) has color-coded routes, clear signage, and many connections. Trains run out into the suburbs, and all stations are marked with the London Underground circular symbol. (Do not be confused by similar-looking signs reading "subway," which is British for "pedestrian underpass.") Trains are all one class; smoking isn't allowed on board or in the stations. There is also an Overground network serving the farther reaches of Inner London.

Some lines have multiple branches (Central, Circle, District, Northern, Metropolitan, and Piccadilly), so be sure to note which branch is needed for your particular destination. Do this by noting the end destination on the lighted sign on the platform, which also tells you how long you'll have to wait until the train arrives. Compare that with the end destination of the branch you want. When the two match, that's your train.

London is divided into six concentric zones (ask at Underground ticket booths for a map and booklet, which give details of the ticket options), so be sure to buy a ticket for the correct zone, or you may be liable for an on-the-spot fine of £80. Don't panic if you do forget to buy a ticket for the right zone: just tell a station attendant that you need to buy an "extension" to your ticket. Although you're meant to do that in advance, if you're an out-of-towner, they generally don't give you a hard time. You also can pay your fare using an Oyster card or a contactless debit or credit card.

Oyster cards are "smart cards" that can be charged with a cash value and then used for discounted travel throughout the city. A Visitor Oyster card, which you must buy before arriving in the United Kingdom, costs £5. Normal Oyster cards also cost £5 and you can open an Oyster account online or pick up an Oyster card at any London Underground station, and then prepay any amount you wish for your expected travel while in the city. Each time you take the Tube or bus, you place the blue card on the yellow readers at the entrance and the amount of your fare is deducted.

Passengers using Oyster cards pay lower rates. For one-way Tube fares paid in cash, a flat £4.90 price per journey now applies across all central zones (1–2), whether you're traveling 1 stop or 12. However, the corresponding Oyster card fare is £2.40 off-peak, £2.90 peak. One-day Travelcards used to be a good value for the money, but now, costing from £12.70 per card, they're a much less attractive option. If you're planning several trips in one day, it's much cheaper to buy an Oyster card: because of the system's daily "cap," you can make as many journeys as you want in Zones 1–2 for just £7 (or, in Zones 1–3 for £8.20). If you're going to be in town for several days, a seven-day Travelcard gives you the same value as an Oyster card (£35.10 for Zones 1–2, £64.20 for Zones 1–6). Children aged 11–15 can travel at discounted rates on the Tube and travel free on buses and trams with an Oyster photocard (must be ordered online at least four weeks before date of travel), while those under 11 travel free on all buses and on the Tube if accompanied by an adult or with an Oyster photocard. Young people aged 16–18 and students over 18 get discounted Tube fares with an Oyster photocard. Oyster card Tube fares start at £2 and go up depending on the number of zones you're covering, the time of day, and whether you're traveling into Zone 1.

However, although Oyster cards sound like the way of the future, they will soon be a thing of the past. Moves are underway to gradually phase out Oyster cards and to encourage passengers to move to a system of direct payments using their bank debit or credit cards instead. In practice, this means swiping a "contactless" bank card instead of your Oyster card at ticket barriers. The cheaper fares available to Oyster card holders are the same as those who pay by contactless cards.

Tube trains now run for 24 hours a day on weekends on five major lines: Piccadilly, Victoria, Northern, Central, and Jubilee. On all other lines the usual timetable still applies, with trains running from just after 5 am Monday to Saturday and with the last services leaving central London between midnight and 12:30 am. On Sunday, trains start an hour later and finish about an hour earlier. The frequency of trains depends on the route and the time of day, but normally you should not have to wait more than 10 minutes in central areas.

Tours

BOAT TOURS
★ City Cruises
BOAT TOURS | FAMILY | In nice weather, an open top-deck ride from Westminster, the London Eye, or Tower Piers to the ancient royal romping ground of Greenwich along the Thames River is one of the best ways to get acquainted with the city. You'll pass sights like Tower Bridge, the Tower of London, and St. Paul's Cathedral, all with a chirpy Cockney boatman running commentary. Lunch, Afternoon Tea, and nighttime cruises are also available. ✉ *Cherry Garden Pier, Cherry Garden St.* ☎ *020/7740–0400* ⊕ *www.citycruises.com* ✆ *From £11.*

BUS TOURS
The Original London Sightseeing Tour
BUS TOURS | FAMILY | This one-day, hop-on-hop-off, open-top bus tour with over 80 stops along six different routes takes in major landmarks like the Houses of Parliament, Westminster Abbey, Trafalgar Square, the British Museum, the Tower of London, and, of course, Buckingham Palace, as well as more off-the-beaten-path sites like Lambeth Palace (home of the Bishop of London). Tickets are good for the entire day and for all routes. ✉ *London* ☎ *020/8877–1722* ⊕ *www. theoriginaltour.com* ✆ *From £29.*

WALKING TOURS
City Guides
WALKING TOURS | The City Guides (or, to give them their full name, The City of London Guide Lecturers' Association) are the official guides to the City of London, the "City" being not the entire metropolis but the "Square Mile" historic financial district. They offer two highly informed daily walks at 11 am and 2 pm—some bookable but others just turn up on the day—that cover essential sights like Guildhall (the City's town hall), Mansion House, the Bank of England, and the Royal Exchange. More specialized walks offered by the Museum of London focus on topics like Samuel Johnson's London, the gardens of The City, the Great Fire of London, Roman London, or the churches of Christopher Wren, most notably his magnificent St. Paul's Cathedral. ☎ 0207/606–3030 ⊕ www.cityoflondonguides.com ➦ From £7.

★ London Food Lovers Food Tours
GUIDED TOURS | **FAMILY** | London's a top global foodie city now, and the London Food Lovers walking tour of Soho is a fascinating way to explore the capital's gastro delights. Well-led and synchronized throughout, the four-hour walk kicks off with Hawaiian blueberry pancakes at burger bar Kua'Aina and takes in offbeat stops for truffle pumpkin ravioli at Soho's retro Italian delicatessen Lina Stores, a hot chocolate tasting at SAID artisanal Roman chocolatiers, and a sit-down lunch of fish-and-chips and Indian pale ale in quaint Soho pub the Dog and Duck. You'll also stop in Chinatown to sample steamed prawn dim sum at Beijing Dumpling and spot celebrities amid the Afternoon Tea crowds at the Maison Bertaux French patisserie and tearoom. The tour ends with a dessert and wine pairing in the Dickensian underground cellar vaults of the 1890s Gordon's Wine Bar. There are various versions of the Soho tour, as well as a Jack the Ripper Happy Hour Tasting Tour and a Borough Market tour. ✉ Islington ☎ 0777/4099–306 ⊕ www.londonfoodlovers.com ➦ £60.

★ London Walks
WALKING TOURS | **FAMILY** | With London's oldest established walking tours, there's no need to book ahead; instead, just turn up at the meeting point at the allotted hour and pay £10 for a first-rate, guided two-hour walk with themes like Secret London, Literary London, Harry Potter film locations, Haunted London, and much more. Top crime historian and leading Ripper authority Donald Rumbelow often leads the 7:30 pm Jack the Ripper walk in Whitechapel. As a bonus bargain, kids can come along for free. ☎ 020/7624–3978 ⊕ www.walks.com ➦ From £10.

Restaurants

For many years English food was a joke, especially to England's near neighbors, the French. But the days of steamed suet puddings and over-boiled brussels sprouts are long gone. For a good two decades London's restaurant scene has been booming, with world-class chefs— Jamie Oliver, Gordon Ramsay, Heston Blumenthal, and Jason Atherton among them—pioneering concepts that quickly spread overseas. Whether you're looking for bistros that rival their Parisian counterparts, five-star fine dining establishments, fantastic fried-chicken and burger joints (American diner food is a current trend), gastro-pubs serving "Modern British," or places serving Peruvian–Japanese fusion, gourmet Indian, or nouveau greasy spoon, you'll be spoiled for choice. And that's just as well because you'll be spending, on average, 25% of your travel budget on dining out.

The British now take pride in the best of authentic homegrown food—local, seasonal, regional, and foraged are the buzzwords of the day. But beyond reinterpretations of native dishes, London's dining revolution is built on its incredible ethnic diversity, with virtually every international cuisine represented.

Hotels

If your invitation from Queen Elizabeth still hasn't shown up in the mail, no worries London's grande-dame hotels are the next best thing—and possibly better. If your budget won't stretch to five-star luxury, don't worry. There are plenty of comfortable, clean, friendly options available for a relatively reasonable price. The key word is relatively. In recent years, London has seen a welcome growth in the value-for-money sector, but overall, accommodations here still remain on the costly side.

If money is no object, London has some of the world's most luxurious hotels. Even these high-end places have deals, and you can sometimes find a bargain, particularly during January and February. Meanwhile, several mid-range hotels have dropped their average prices, which has made some desirable options more affordable. Large business-oriented hotels frequently offer weekend packages as well. Those on a budget should check out the stylish and supercheap hotels that have shaken up the lodging scene of late. The downside is that these places tend to be a little out of the way, but you may find this a price worth paying. Another attractive alternative includes hotels in the Premier and Millennium chains, which offer sleek, modern rooms, many up-to-date conveniences, and discount prices that sometimes fall below £100 a night.

Restaurant and hotel reviews have been shortened. For full information, visit Fodors.com. Restaurant prices are the average cost of a main course at dinner or, if dinner is not served, at lunch.

WHAT IT COSTS in Pounds

	$	$$	$$$	$$$$
RESTAURANTS				
	under £16	£16–£23	£24–£30	over £30
HOTELS				
	under £125	£125–£225	£226–£350	over £350

Visitor Information

You can get good information at the Travel Information Centres at Victoria Station and St. Pancras International train station. These are helpful if you're looking for brochures for London sights and if you need a hotel. Travel Information Centres can also be found at the Euston and Liverpool Street train stations, Heathrow Airport, St. Paul's Cathedral churchyard, and Piccadilly Circus, as well as in Greenwich and some other Outer London locations.

CONTACTS Visit London. ⊕ *www.visitlondon.com.*

Westminster and St. James's

This is postcard London at its best. Crammed with historic churches, grand state buildings, and some of the world's best art collections, the area unites politics and high culture. (Oh, and the Queen lives here, too.) World-class monuments such as Buckingham Palace, the Houses of Parliament, Westminster Abbey, and the National Gallery sit alongside lesser-known but lovingly curated museums redolent of British history. If you only have time to visit one part of London, this is it. This is concentrated sightseeing, so pace yourself.

GETTING HERE

Trafalgar Square—easy to access and in the center of the action—is a good place to start. Take the Tube to Embankment (District, Circle, Bakerloo, and Northern lines) and walk north until you cross the Strand, or exit to Northumberland Avenue at Charing Cross (Bakerloo and Northern lines). Buses are another great option, as almost all roads lead to Trafalgar Square.

◉ Sights

★ Buckingham Palace

CASTLE/PALACE | When the Queen heads off to Scotland on her annual summer holiday (you can tell because the Union Jack flies above the palace instead of the Royal Standard), the 19 State Rooms of her official residence, which was begun in 1702, plus the sprawling palace gardens, open up to visitors. However, the north wing's private apartments always remain behind closed doors. With fabulous gilt moldings and walls adorned with masterpieces by Rembrandt, Rubens, and other Old Masters, the State Rooms are the grandest of the palace's 775 rooms. Admission is by timed ticket with entry every 15 minutes throughout the day. Allow up to two hours. ■ TIP→ Get there by 10:30 to grab a spot in the best viewing section for the ceremonial Changing the Guard—one of London's best free shows—that happens daily at 11 from May until the end of July (varies according to troop deployment requirements) and on alternate days for the rest of the year, weather permitting. ⊠ Buckingham Palace Rd., St. James's ☎ 030/3123–7300 ⊕ www.royalcollection.org.uk/visit 🎟 From £25 ⊗ Closed Oct.–July except on selected dates Ⓜ Victoria, St. James's Park, Green Park.

★ Churchill War Rooms

MUSEUM | FAMILY | It was from this small warren of underground rooms—beneath the vast government buildings of the Treasury—that Winston Churchill and his team directed troops in World War II.

Designed to be bombproof, the whole complex has been preserved almost exactly as it was when the last light was turned off at the end of the war. Every clock shows almost 5 pm, and the furniture, fittings, and paraphernalia of a busy, round-the-clock war office are still in situ, down to the colored map pins.

During air raids, the leading government ministers met here, and the Cabinet Room is arranged as if a meeting were about to convene. In the Map Room, the Allied campaign is charted on wall-to-wall maps with a rash of pinholes showing the movements of convoys. In the hub of the room, a bank of differently colored phones known as the "Beauty Chorus" linked the War Rooms to control rooms around the nation. The Prime Minister's Room holds the desk from which Churchill made his morale-boosting broadcasts; the Telephone Room (a converted broom cupboard) has his hotline to FDR. You can also see the restored rooms that the PM used for dining and sleeping. Telephonists (switchboard operators) and clerks who worked 16-hour shifts slept in lesser quarters in unenviable conditions.

An excellent addition to the War Rooms is the Churchill Museum, a tribute to the great wartime leader himself. ⊠ Clive Steps, King Charles St., Westminster ☎ 020/7416–5000 ⊕ www.iwm.org.uk/visits/churchill-war-rooms 🎟 £22 Ⓜ Westminster.

Downing Street

GOVERNMENT BUILDING | Were it not for the wrought-iron gates and armed guards that block the entrance, you'd probably miss this otherwise unassuming Georgian side street off Whitehall—but this is the location of the famous No. 10, London's modest equivalent of the White House. The Georgian entrance to the mid-17th-century mansion is deceptive; it's actually a huge complex of discreetly linked buildings. Since 1732 it has been the official home and office of the prime minister—the last private

Sights ▼

1 Buckingham Palace..... **C5**
2 Churchill War Rooms... **G4**
3 Downing Street **G4**
4 Houses of Parliament .. **H5**
5 National Gallery......... **G2**
6 National Portrait
  Gallery **G1**
7 St. James's Palace **D3**
8 St. James's Park **E4**
9 Tate Britain **G9**
10 Trafalgar Square........ **G2**
11 Westminster Abbey **G5**

Restaurants ▼

1 Le Caprice **C3**
2 The Ritz Restaurant...... **C2**
3 Wiltons................... **D2**
4 The Wolseley............. **C2**

Hotels ▼

1 Artist Residence **B9**
2 The Corinthia **H2**
3 Hotel 41 .... **C6**
4 The Ritz **C2**
5 The Stafford London.... **D3**
6 Windermere Hotel...... **B9**

A classic photo op: don't miss the cavalry from the Queen's Life Guard at Buckingham Palace.

resident was the magnificently named Mr. Chicken (the current prime minister actually lives in the private apartments above No. 11, traditionally the residence of the Chancellor of the Exchequer, the head of the Treasury). There are no public tours, but the famous black front door to No. 10 is clearly visible from Whitehall. Keep your eyes peeled for Larry the cat, whose official title is Chief Mouser to the Cabinet Office. Just south of Downing Street, in the middle of Whitehall, is the **Cenotaph,** a stark white monolith built to commemorate the 1918 armistice. On Remembrance Day (the Sunday nearest November 11), it's strewn with red poppy wreaths to honor the dead of both world wars and all British and Commonwealth soldiers killed in action since; the first wreath is always laid by the Queen. A hundred yards farther, toward Parliament, is the **Monument to the Women of World War II.** The prominent black marble sculpture uses a string of empty uniforms to symbolize the vital service of women in then-traditionally male jobs during the war, as well as in frontline roles, such as medics and auxiliary officers. ⊠ *Whitehall* Ⓜ *Westminster.*

★ **Houses of Parliament**
GOVERNMENT BUILDING | The Palace of Westminster, as the complex is called, was first established on this site by Edward the Confessor in the 11th century. William II built a new palace in 1097, and this became the seat of English power. Fire destroyed most of the palace in 1834; the current complex dates largely from the mid-19th century. The Clock Tower—renamed Elizabeth Tower in 2012—dates from 1858 and contains the 13-ton bell known as Big Ben. The Visitors' Galleries of the House of Commons are particularly popular during the Prime Minister's Questions at 12 pm every Wednesday when Parliament is sitting (tickets are free, but noncitizens can only line up and hope for no-shows). Westminster Hall, with its remarkable hammer-beam roof, was the work of William the Conqueror's son William Rufus and is one of the largest remaining Norman halls. ⊠ *St. Stephen's Entrance, St.*

Margaret St., Westminster ☎ 020/7219–4114 for public tours ⊕ www.parliament.uk/visiting ✉ Free; tours from £20 ⊘ Closed Sun. Ⓜ Westminster.

★ National Gallery

MUSEUM | FAMILY | Standing proudly on the north side of Trafalgar Square is truly one of the world's supreme art museums, with more than 2,300 works on show. The collection includes masterpieces by Michelangelo, Leonardo, Turner, Monet, van Gogh, Picasso, and more—all for free. Watch out for outstanding temporary exhibitions, too, both free and ticketed. While you could allow a handful of paintings to fill your visit, there are hundreds of other paintings to see, enough to fill a full day, including important works by Van Eyck, Holbein, Velázquez, Caravaggio, and Seurat. One-hour, free, guided tours start at the Sainsbury Wing every weekday at 2 pm. If you are eager for even more insight into the art, pick up a themed audio guide. ✉ Trafalgar Sq., Westminster ☎ 020/7747–2885 ⊕ www.nationalgallery.org.uk ✉ Free; special exhibitions from £7; audio guide £5 Ⓜ Charing Cross, Embankment, Leicester Sq.

★ National Portrait Gallery

MUSEUM | FAMILY | The National Portrait Gallery was founded in 1856 with a single aim: to gather together portraits of famous (and infamous) Britons throughout history. More than 150 years and 200,000 portraits later, it is an essential stop for all history and literature buffs. If you visit with kids, ask at the desk about the excellent Family Trails, which make exploring the galleries with children much more fun. Galleries are arranged clearly and chronologically, from Tudor Times to the present. The huge permanent collections include portraits of all the British monarchs, Shakespeare, the Brontë sisters, and Jane Austen. Temporary exhibitions can be explored on the first three floors, particularly in the Wolfson and Porter galleries, on the ground floor. ⚠ **The National Portrait Gallery is currently closed for renovations until spring 2023.** ✉ St. Martin's Pl., Westminster ☎ 020/7306–0055 ⊕ www.npg.org.uk ✉ Free; special exhibitions from £6; audiovisual guide £3 Ⓜ Charing Cross, Leicester Sq.

St. James's Palace

CASTLE/PALACE | Commissioned by Henry VIII, this Tudor brick palace was the residence of kings and queens for more than 300 years; indeed, while all monarchs have actually lived at Buckingham Palace since Queen Victoria's day, it is still one of the official residences of the Royal Family. (This is why foreign ambassadors are received by the "Court of St. James.") Today it contains various royal apartments and offices, including the working office of Prince Charles. The palace is not open to the public, but the surprisingly low-key Tudor exterior is well worth the short detour from the Mall. Friary Court out front is a splendid setting for Trooping the Colour, part of the Queen's official birthday celebrations. Everyone loves to take a snapshot of the scarlet-coated guardsman standing sentry outside the imposing Tudor gateway. Note the Changing the Guard ceremony at St. James's Palace occurs only on days when the guard at Buckingham Palace is changed. ✉ Friary Ct., St. James's Ⓜ Green Park.

★ St. James's Park

CITY PARK | FAMILY | There is a story that, many years ago, a royal once inquired of a courtier how much it would cost to close St. James's Park to the public. "Only your crown, ma'am", came the reply. Bordered by three palaces—Buckingham, St. James's, and the governmental complex of the Palace of Westminster—this is one of London's loveliest public parks. It's also the oldest; the former marshland was acquired by Henry VIII in 1532 as a nursery for his deer. Later, James I drained the land and installed an aviary, which gave Birdcage Walk its name, and a zoo (complete with crocodiles, camels, and an elephant). When Charles II returned from exile in France, where he had been hugely impressed by the splendor of the gardens at the Palace of Versailles, he transformed the park into formal gardens, with avenues, fruit orchards, and a canal. Lawns were grazed by goats, sheep, and deer, and, in the 18th century, the park became a different kind of hunting ground, for wealthy lotharios looking to pick up nighttime escorts. A century later, John Nash redesigned the landscape in a more naturalistic, romantic style, and if you gaze down the lake toward Buckingham Palace, you could easily believe yourself to be on a country estate.

A large population of waterfowl—including pelicans, geese, ducks, and swans (which belong to the Queen)—breed on and around Duck Island at the east end of the lake. The pelicans are fed at 2:30 daily. From March to October, the deck chairs (charge levied) come out, crammed with office workers at midday, eating lunch while being serenaded by music from the bandstands. One of the best times to stroll the leafy walkways is after dark, with Westminster Abbey and the Houses of Parliament rising above the floodlit lake. ⊠ *The Mall or Horse Guards approach or Birdcage Walk, St. James's* ⊕ *www.royalparks.org.uk* Ⓜ *St. James's Park, Westminster.*

★ Tate Britain

MUSEUM | FAMILY | First opened in 1897, and funded by the sugar magnate Sir Henry Tate, this stately neoclassical institution is a great place to explore British art from 1500 to the present. The museum includes the Linbury Galleries on the lower floors, which stage temporary exhibitions, and a permanent collection on the upper floors. And what a collection it is—classic works by John Constable, Thomas Gainsborough, Francis Bacon, Duncan Grant, Barbara Hepworth, and Vanessa Bell, and an outstanding display from J. M. W. Turner in the Clore Gallery. Sumptuous Pre-Raphaelite pieces are a major draw, while more recent art historical periods are represented with works by artists such as Rachel Whiteread, L.S. Lowry, Vanessa Bell, and David Hockney. There's a good little café, and the excellent Rex Whistler Restaurant has been something of an institution since it first opened in 1927. ■**TIP→ The Tate Boat (£8.60 one-way) offers a direct trip to the Tate Modern every 40 minutes.** ⊠ *Millbank, Westminster* ☎ *020/7887–8888* ⊕ *www. tate.org.uk/britain* ⊠ *Free; special exhibitions from £13; audio guide £5* Ⓜ *Pimlico.*

★ Trafalgar Square

PLAZA | This square is the official center of London: a plaque on the corner of the Strand and Charing Cross Road marks the spot from which distances on U.K. signposts are measured. (London's actual geographic center, as measured in 2014, is a rather dull bench on the Victoria Embankment.) Medieval kings once kept their aviaries of hawks and falcons here; today the humbler grey pigeons flock en masse to the open spaces around the ornate fountains (feeding them is banned). The square was designed in 1830 by John Nash, who envisaged a new public space with striking views of the Thames, the Houses of Parliament, and Buckingham Palace. It remains a magnet for open-air concerts, political demonstrations, and national celebrations. Dominating the square is the 168-foot **Nelson's Column**, erected as a monument to the great admiral in 1843. ⊠ *Westminster* Ⓜ *Charing Cross.*

★ Westminster Abbey

RELIGIOUS SITE | Steeped in hundreds of years of rich and occasionally bloody history, Westminster Abbey is one of England's most iconic buildings, most of which dates from the 1240s. It has hosted 38 coronations and no fewer than 16 royal weddings, but it is equally well known for its permanent residents, from kings to writers, who are buried here—and many more who are memorialized. Highlights include the world's largest rose window, the Coronation Chair (dating from 1301), Grave of the Unknown Warrior, and the Poet's Corner. The adjoining medieval Chapter House is adorned with 14th-century frescoes and a magnificent 13th-century tiled floor. The **College Garden** of medicinal herbs is a delightful diversion. Climb the Weston Tower for historical artifacts and remarkable views from the Queen's Diamond Jubilee Galleries. Exact hours are long and complex (and can change), so it's important to check before setting out. ⚠ **Beware: lines can be long during peak hours.** ⊠ *Broad Sanctuary, Westminster* ☎ *020/7222–5152* ⊕ *www.westminster-abbey.org* ⊠ *£22* ⊙ *Closed Sun., except for worship* Ⓜ *Westminster, St. James's Park.*

Restaurants

Le Caprice
$$$ | **MODERN EUROPEAN** | **FAMILY** | Celebrity hot spot Le Caprice commands the deepest loyalty of any restaurant in London. It must be the 40-odd-year history of famous diners (think Liz Taylor, Joan Collins, Lady Di, and Victoria Beckham), the pitch-perfect service, and the long-standing menu that sits somewhere between Euro peasant and trendy fashion plate. **Known for:** celebrity sightings galore; classic fish-and-chips with minted pea puree; live jazz on Sunday night. Ⓢ *Average main: £26* ⊠ *Arlington House, 20 Arlington St., St. James's* ☎ *020/7629–2239* ⊕ *www.le-caprice.co.uk* Ⓜ *Green Park.*

The Ritz Restaurant
$$$$ | **BRITISH** | **FAMILY** | London's most opulent dining salon here at the Ritz would impress even Marie Antoinette with its sumptuous Gilded Age Rocco Revival trompe-l'oeil frescoes, tasseled silk drapery, and towering marble columns. Sit at the late Margaret Thatcher's favorite seat overlooking Green Park (Table 1) and luxuriate in unreconstructed British haute cuisine such as Bresse chicken with black Périgord truffles or beef Wellington carved table-side. **Known for:** luxurious dining made for the British elite; possibly London's best beef Wellington; legendary traditional Afternoon Tea in the Palm Court. Ⓢ *Average main: £47* ⊠ *The Ritz, 150 Piccadilly, St. James's* ☎ *020/7493–8181* ⊕ *www.theritzlondon.com* ⓜ *Jacket and tie* Ⓜ *Green Park.*

Wiltons
$$$$ | **BRITISH** | Lords, ladies, and other assorted aristocrats blow the family bank at this Edwardian bastion of traditional English fine dining on Jermyn Street (the place first opened near the Haymarket as a shellfish stall in 1742). Posh patrons tend to order half a dozen oysters, followed by grilled Dover sole, Blythburgh pork from the carving trolley, or fabulous native game, such as roast partridge, grouse, or teal. **Known for:** traditional English dining focused on shellfish and game; waiter service that would put Jeeves to shame; Bordeaux-heavy wine menu. Ⓢ *Average main: £38* ⊠ *55 Jermyn St., St. James's* ☎ *020/7629–9955* ⊕ *www.wiltons.co.uk* ⊙ *Closed Sun. and bank holidays. No lunch Sat.* ⓜ *Jacket required* Ⓜ *Green Park.*

The Wolseley
$$$ | **AUSTRIAN** | **FAMILY** | A glitzy procession of famous faces, media moguls, and hedge-funders comes for the spectacle, swish service, and soaring elegance at this bustling Viennese-style grand café on Piccadilly. Located in a former Wolseley Motors luxury-car showroom, this brasserie begins its long decadent days with breakfast at 7 am (8 am at weekends) and serves Dual Monarchy delights until 11:30 pm. **Known for:** old-country Austrian and Hungarian delights; Afternoon Tea with a Viennese twist; classic grand café ambience. Ⓢ *Average main: £25* ⊠ *160 Piccadilly, St. James's* ☎ *020/7499–6996* ⊕ *www.thewolseley.com* Ⓜ *Green Park.*

🏨 Hotels

★ Artist Residence

$$ | HOTEL | As packed with bohemian character as they come, this small boutique hotel, more in Pimlico than Belgravia, oozes retro charm. **Pros:** quirky charm; excellent breakfasts; great staff. **Cons:** some rooms on the small side; stairs to upper floors; most rooms have a shower only. *⑤ Rooms from: £200 ⊠ 52 Cambridge St., Pimlico ☎ 020/7931–8946 ⊕ www.artistresidencelondon.co.uk ⇆ 10 rooms ⦿l Free breakfast Ⓜ Victoria, Pimlico.*

★ The Corinthia

$$$$ | HOTEL | The London outpost of the exclusive Corinthia chain is design heaven-on-earth, with levels of service that make anyone feel like a VIP. **Pros:** so much luxury and elegance you'll feel like royalty; exceptional spa with indoor pool; excellent fine dining options. **Cons:** prices jump to the stratosphere once the least expensive rooms sell out; not many special offers; air-conditioning and lighting is difficult to use. *⑤ Rooms from: £540 ⊠ Whitehall Pl., Westminster ☎ 020/7930–8181 ⊕ www.corinthia.com ⇆ 283 rooms ⦿l No meals Ⓜ Embankment.*

★ Hotel 41

$$$$ | HOTEL | With faultless service, sumptuous designer furnishings, and a sense of fun to boot, this impeccable hotel breathes new life into the cliché "thinks of everything," yet the epithet is really quite apt. **Pros:** impeccable service; beautiful and stylish; Buckingham Palace is on your doorstep. **Cons:** unusual design is not for everyone; expensive; the private bar can feel stuffy. *⑤ Rooms from: £497 ⊠ 41 Buckingham Palace Rd., Westminster ☎ 020/7300–0041 ⊕ www.41hotel.com ⇆ 30 rooms ⦿l No meals Ⓜ Victoria.*

The Ritz

$$$$ | HOTEL | If you're wondering if the *Downton Abbey*–style world of the old British upper class still exists, look no further than here; the Ritz is as synonymous with London's high society and decadence today as it was when it opened in 1906. **Pros:** historic luxury hotel; service at every turn; iconic restaurant and bar. **Cons:** sometimes snooty service; tediously old-fashioned dress code; located on a congested road. *⑤ Rooms from: £555 ⊠ 150 Piccadilly, St. James's ☎ 020/7493–8181 ⊕ www.theritzlondon.com ⇆ 136 rooms ⦿l No meals Ⓜ Piccadilly Circus.*

★ The Stafford London

$$$$ | HOTEL | This is a rare find: a posh hotel that's equal parts elegance and friendliness, and located in one of the few peaceful spots in the area, down a small lane behind Piccadilly. **Pros:** great staff; home to one of London's original "American Bars"; quiet location. **Cons:** traditional style of most rooms may not be to all tastes; perks in the more expensive rooms could be more generous (free airport transfer, but one-way only; free clothes pressing, but only one item per day); some rooms can feel small. *⑤ Rooms from: £450 ⊠ 16–18 St. James's Pl., St. James's ☎ 020/7493–0111 ⊕ www.thestaffordlondon.com ⇆ 107 rooms ⦿l No meals Ⓜ Green Park.*

Windermere Hotel

$$ | HOTEL | FAMILY | This sweet and rather elegant old hotel, on the premises of one of London's first B&Bs (1881), is a decent, well-situated option. **Pros:** good location close to Victoria Station; free Wi-Fi; good amenities for an old hotel of this size, including air-conditioning and an elevator. **Cons:** rooms and bathrooms are tiny; traditional decor might not suit all tastes; many major attractions are a 20-minute walk away. *⑤ Rooms from: £185 ⊠ 142–144 Warwick Way, Pimlico ☎ 020/7834–5163 ⊕ www.windermere-hotel.co.uk ⇆ 19 rooms ⦿l Free breakfast Ⓜ Victoria.*

Nightlife

BARS

★ American Bar

BARS/PUBS | FAMILY | Festooned with a chin-dropping array of old club ties, vintage signed celebrity photographs, sporting mementos, model airplanes, and baseball caps, this sensational hotel cocktail bar has superb martinis and Manhattans. The name dates from the 1930s, when hotel bars in London started to cater to growing numbers of Americans crossing the Atlantic in ocean liners. The collection of paraphernalia was started in the 1970s when a customer left a small carved wooden eagle. ⊠ *The Stafford, 16–18 St. James's Pl., St. James's* ☎ *020/7493–0111* ⊕ *www. thestaffordlondon.com* Ⓜ *Green Park.*

★ Gordon's Wine Bar

BARS/PUBS | Nab a rickety candlelit table in the atmospheric, 1890s, low-slung, brick vaulted cellar interior of what claims to be the oldest wine bar in London, or fight for standing room in the long pedestrian-only alley garden that runs alongside it. Either way, the mood is always cheery as a diverse crowd sips on more than 60 different wines, ports, and sherries. Tempting cheese and meat plates are great for sharing. ⊠ *47 Villiers St., Westminster* ☎ *020/7930–1408* ⊕ *gordonswinebar.com* Ⓜ *Charing Cross, Embankment.*

Performing Arts

Institute of Contemporary Arts (*ICA*)
ARTS VENUE | You would never suspect that behind the stately white John Nash–designed stucco facade in the heart of Establishment London, you'll find a champion of the avant-garde. Since 1947, the ICA has been pushing boundaries in visual arts, performance, theater, dance, and music. There are two movie theaters, a performance theater, three galleries, a high-brow bookstore, a reading room, a restaurant run by top chef Margot Henderson, and a café-bar. ⊠ *The Mall, St. James's* ☎ *020/7930–3647* ⊕ *www. ica.org.uk* ✉ *Exhibitions £3, cinema tickets from £8* Ⓜ *Charing Cross, Piccadilly Circus.*

Shopping

ANTIQUES

The Armoury of St. James's

ANTIQUES/COLLECTIBLES | Besides fine toy soldiers in lead or tin representing conflicts ranging from the Crusades through World War II with prices starting at £15 and going into four figures, the shop has regimental brooches and drums, historic orders and medals, royal memorabilia, and military antiques. ⊠ *17 Piccadilly Arcade, St. James's* ☎ *020/7493–5082* ⊕ *www.armoury.co.uk* ⊙ *Closed Sun.* Ⓜ *Piccadilly Circus.*

BEAUTY

Floris

PERFUME/COSMETICS | What did Queen Victoria, Mary Shelley, and Marilyn Monroe have in common? They all used products from Floris, one of the most beautiful shops in London, with gleaming glass-and-Spanish-mahogany showcases salvaged from the Great Exhibition of 1851. In addition to scents for both men and women (including the current queen), Floris has been making its own shaving products—plus combs, brushes, and fragrances—since 1730 (and is still owned by the same family), reflecting its origins as a barbershop. Other gift possibilities include a famous rose-scented mouthwash and beautifully packaged soaps and bath essences. ⊠ *89 Jermyn St., St. James's* ☎ *0330/134–0180* ⊕ *www.florislondon.com* Ⓜ *Piccadilly Circus, Green Park.*

BOOKS

★ Hatchards

BOOKS/STATIONERY | This is the United Kingdom's oldest bookshop, open since 1797 and beloved by writers themselves—customers have included Oscar

Wilde, Rudyard Kipling, and Lord Byron. Despite its wood-paneled, "gentleman's library" atmosphere and eclectic selection of books, Hatchards is now owned by the large Waterstone's chain. Nevertheless, the shop still retains its period charm, aided by the staff's old-fashioned helpfulness and expertise. Look for the substantial number of books signed by notable contemporary authors on the well-stocked shelves. There's another branch in the St. Pancras International train station. ⊠ *187 Piccadilly, St. James's* ☎ *020/7439–9921* ⊕ *www.hatchards. co.uk* Ⓜ *Piccadilly Circus.*

CLOTHING
Turnbull & Asser

CLOTHING | The Jermyn Street store sells luxurious jackets, cashmere sweaters, suits, ties, pajamas, ready-to-wear shirts, and accessories perfect for the billionaire who has everything. The brand is best known for its superb custom-made shirts—worn by Prince Charles and every James Bond to appear in film, to name a few. These can be ordered at the nearby Bury Street or Davies Street branches, which are devoted to bespoke wear. At least 18 separate measurements are taken, and the cloth, woven to the company's specifications, comes in 1,000 different patterns—the cottons feel as good as silk. The first order must be for a minimum of four shirts, which start at £275 each. ⊠ *71–72 Jermyn St., St. James's* ☎ *020/7808–3000* ⊕ *www. turnbullandasser.co.uk* ⊗ *Closed Sun.* Ⓜ *Green Park.*

FOOD
★ Berry Bros. & Rudd

WINE/SPIRITS | Nothing matches Berry Bros. & Rudd for rare offerings and a unique shopping experience. A family-run wine business since 1698 (Lord Byron was a customer), BBR stores more than 4,000 vintage bottles and casks in vaulted cellars that are more than 300 years old. The in-house wine school offers educational tasting sessions, while the dedicated spirits room also has an excellent selection of whiskeys, cognacs, rums, and more. The shop has a quirky charm, and the staff are extremely knowledgeable—and not snooty if you're on a budget. ⊠ *63 Pall Mall, St. James's* ☎ *800/280–2440* ⊕ *www.bbr.com* ⊗ *Closed Sun.* Ⓜ *Green Park.*

★ Fortnum & Mason

DEPARTMENT STORES | Although F&M is jokingly known as "the Queen's grocer" and the impeccably mannered staff still wear traditional tailcoats, its celebrated food hall stocks gifts for all budgets, including irresistibly packaged luxury foods stamped with the gold "By Appointment" crest for under £5. Try the teas, preserves (including the unusual rose-petal jelly), condiments, or Gentleman's Relish (anchovy paste). The store's famous hampers are always a welcome gift. The gleaming food hall spans two floors and incorporates a sleek wine bar, with the rest of the store devoted to upscale housewares, men's and women's accessories and toiletries, a dedicated candle room, and a jewelry department featuring exclusive designs by breakthrough talent. If you start to flag, take a break in the tea salon, the Gallery café offering tastes of the food hall, the contemporary 45 Jermyn St. restaurant (the three-course set menu is good value), or an indulgent ice-cream parlor, where you can find decadent treats like a banana split or a less-traditional gin-and-tonic float. Gentlemen also can kick back at the traditional barbershop on the fourth floor. There's another branch at St. Pancras International train station. ⊠ *181 Piccadilly, St. James's* ☎ *020/7734– 8040* ⊕ *www.fortnumandmason.com* Ⓜ *Green Park, Piccadilly Circus.*

Mayfair and Marylebone

Mayfair forms the core of London's West End, the city's stylish central area. This neighborhood oozes class and old-school style. The sense of being in one of the world's most wealthy and powerful cities is palpable as you wander along its grand and graceful streets. Scoot across the district's one exception to all this elegance—Oxford Street—and you'll discover the pleasant thoroughfares of Marylebone, the most central of London's many "villages".

GETTING HERE

Three tube stations on the Central Line are handy for reaching these neighborhoods: Marble Arch, Bond Street (also on the Jubilee Line), and Oxford Circus (also on the Victoria and Bakerloo lines). The best buses are the 22, which takes in Green Park, Berkeley Square, and New Bond Street, and the 9—London's oldest existing bus route—which runs along Piccadilly.

Sights

Grosvenor Square

PLAZA | Pronounced "*Grove*-na," this leafy square was laid out in 1721–31 and is as desirable an address today as it was then. Americans have certainly always thought so—from John Adams, the second president, who as ambassador lived at No. 38, to Dwight D. Eisenhower, whose wartime headquarters was at No. 20. The entire west side of the square was home to the U.S. Embassy for more than 50 years until its relocation south of the river. In the square itself stand memorials to Franklin D. Roosevelt and those who died on September 11, 2001. Grosvenor Chapel, completed in 1730 and used by Eisenhower's men during World War II, stands a couple of blocks

south of the square on South Audley Street, with the entrance to pretty **St. George's Gardens** to its left. ⊠ *Mayfair* ⊕ *www.royalparks.org.uk* Ⓜ *Bond St.*

★ Royal Academy of Arts

MUSEUM | Burlington House was built in 1664, with later Palladian additions for the 3rd Earl of Burlington in 1720. The piazza in front dates from 1873, when the Renaissance-style buildings around the courtyard were designed by Banks and Barry to house a gaggle of noble scientific societies, including the Royal Society of Chemistry and the Royal Astronomical Society.

The house itself is home to the Royal Academy of Arts and an ambitious redevelopment for the academy's 250th anniversary in 2018 has meant that even more of its 46,000 treasures are now on display. The statue of the academy's first president, Sir Joshua Reynolds, palette in hand, stands prominently in the piazza. Free tours show off part of the collection and the excellent temporary exhibitions. Every June through August, the RA puts on its Summer Exhibition, a huge and eclectic collection of art by living Royal Academicians and many other contemporary artists. ⊠ *Burlington House, Piccadilly, Mayfair* ☎ *020/7300–8000* ⊕ *www.royalacademy.org.uk* 🎟 *Free –£18* Ⓜ *Piccadilly Circus, Green Park.*

Sherlock Holmes Museum

MUSEUM | FAMILY | Outside Baker Street Station, by the Marylebone Road exit, is a 9-foot-high bronze statue of Arthur Conan Doyle's celebrated detective, who "lived" around the corner at number 221B Baker Street—now a museum to all things Sherlock. Inside, Mrs. Hudson, Holmes's housekeeper, guides you into a series of Victorian rooms where the great man lived, worked, and played the violin. It's all carried off with such genuine enthusiasm and attention to detail that you could

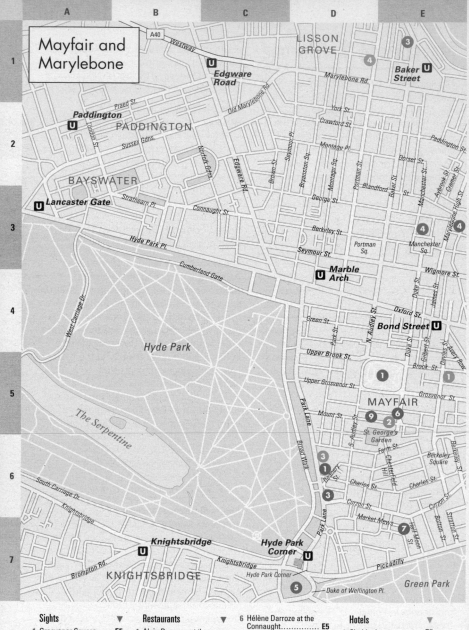

Mayfair and Marylebone

A40 Westway

LISSON GROVE

Edgware Road Ⓤ

Paddington Ⓤ

PADDINGTON

BAYSWATER

Lancaster Gate Ⓤ

Praed St.
Sussex Gdns.
Stratheam Pl.
Connaught St.
Hyde Park Pl.
Cumberland Gate

Hyde Park

The Serpentine

West Carriage Dr.
South Carriage Dr.
Knightsbridge

Knightsbridge Ⓤ
Brompton Rd.
Knightsbridge

KNIGHTSBRIDGE

Old Marylebone Rd.
Edgware Rd.
Marylebone Rd.

Baker Street Ⓤ

York St.
Crawford St.
Montagu Pl.
George St.
Berkeley St.
Seymour St.

Brown St.
Seymour Pl.
Bryanston St.
Montagu St.
Gloucester Pl.
Blandford
Baker St.
Manchester St.

Portman St.
Dorset St.
Ashcroft St.
Cramer St.
Paddington St.
Marylebone High St.

Portman Sq.
Manchester Sq.
Wigmore St.

Marble Arch Ⓤ

Green St.
Upper Brook St.
Upper Grosvenor St.

Bond Street Ⓤ
Oxford St.

Duke St.
James St.
Gilbert St.
Davies St.
S. Audley St.
N. Audley St.
Park St.
Park Lane

Brook St.
Avery Row

MAYFAIR

⑨ ⑥
② ⑧
St. George's Garden
Farm St.
Mount St.

Chesterfield Hill
Charles St.
Berkeley Square
Berkeley St.
Curzon St.

③
①
Deanery St.
③

Charles St.
Curzon St.
Market Mews
⑦
Half Moon St.
Stratton St.
Bolton St.

Broad Walk
Park Lane

Hyde Park Corner Ⓤ
Knightsbridge
Hyde Park Corner
⑤
Duke of Wellington Pl.
Piccadilly

Green Park

Sights ▼

1 Grosvenor Square **E5**
2 Royal Academy of Arts **F6**
3 Sherlock Holmes Museum **E1**
4 Wallace Collection **E3**
5 Wellington Arch **D7**

Restaurants ▼

1 Alain Ducasse at the Dorchester **D6**
2 Cecconi's **F6**
3 CUT at 45 Park Lane **D6**
4 The Golden Hind **E3**
5 Gymkhana **F6**

6 Hélène Darroze at the Connaught **E5**
7 Kitty Fisher's **E7**
8 Pollen Street Social **F5**
9 Scott's **E5**

Hotels ▼

1 Claridge's **E5**
2 The Connaught **E5**
3 The Dorchester **D6**
4 Dorset Square Hotel.... **D1**
5 The Langham **G4**

be forgiven for thinking that Mr. Holmes actually *did* exist. ⊠ *221B Baker St., Regent's Park* ☎ *020/7224–3688* ⊕ *www.sherlock-holmes.co.uk* 🎫 *£15* Ⓜ *Baker St.*

★ **Wallace Collection**

MUSEUM | FAMILY | With its Great Gallery stunningly refurbished, there's even more reason to visit this exquisite gem of an art gallery—although housing one of the world's finest collections of Old Master paintings is reason enough. This glorious collection and the 18th-century mansion in which it's located were bequeathed to the nation by Lady Julie-Amélie-Charlotte Wallace, the widow of Sir Richard Wallace (1818–90). Wallace's father, the 4th Marquess of Hertford, took a house in Paris after the French Revolution and set about snapping up paintings by what were then dangerously unpopular artists. Frans Hals's *Laughing Cavalier* is probably the most famous painting here, or perhaps Jean-Honoré Fragonard's *The Swing*. The full list of painters in the collection reads like a "who's who" of classical European art—from Rubens, Rembrandt, and Van Dyck to Canaletto, Titian, and Velázquez. English works include paintings by Gainsborough and Turner. There are also fine collections of furniture, porcelain, Renaissance gold, and *majolica* (15th- and 16th-century Italian tin-glazed pottery). With craft activities, hands-on sessions, and the "Little Draw" drawing workshops, as well as the chance to try on a suit of armor in the "Arms and Armour" collection, there's plenty to keep kids occupied, too. The conditions of the bequest mean that no part of the collection can leave the building; this is the only place in the world you'll ever be able to see these works. ⊠ *Hertford House, Manchester Sq., Marylebone* ☎ *020/7563–9500* ⊕ *www.wallacecollection.org* 🎫 *Free* Ⓜ *Bond St.*

Wellington Arch

BUILDING | Opposite the Duke of Wellington's mansion, Apsley House, this majestic stone arch surveys the traffic rushing around Hyde Park Corner. Designed by Decimus Burton and completed in 1828, it was created as a grand entrance to the west side of London and echoes the design of that other landmark gate, Marble Arch. Both were triumphal arches commemorating Britain's victory against France in the Napoleonic Wars. Atop the building, the Angel of Peace descends on the *quadriga,* or four-horse chariot of war. Inside the arch, three floors of permanent and temporary exhibits reveal the monument's history. From the balconies at the top of the arch you can peek into the Queen's back garden at across-the-road Buckingham Palace. ⊠ *Hyde Park Corner, Mayfair* ☎ *020/7930–2726* ⊕ *www.english-heritage.org.uk* 🎫 *From £6* Ⓜ *Hyde Park Corner.*

🍴 Restaurants

★ **Alain Ducasse at the Dorchester**

$$$$ | FRENCH | One of only three three-Michelin-starred restaurants in the city, Alain Ducasse at the Dorchester achieves the pinnacle of classical French haute cuisine in a surprisingly fun, lively, and unstuffy salon. Diners feast on a blizzard of beautifully choreographed dishes including classic rum baba with Chantilly cream, sliced open and served in a silver domed tureen. **Known for:** impeccable five-star service; surprisingly unstarchy vibe; signature sautéed lobster with chicken quenelles. 🖇 *Average main: £45* ⊠ *The Dorchester, 53 Park La., Mayfair* ☎ *020/7629–8866 for reservations only* ⊕ *www.alainducasse-dorchester.com* ☉ *Closed Sun. and Mon. No lunch Sat.* Ⓜ *Marble Arch, Green Park.*

Cecconi's

$$$ | **MODERN ITALIAN** | Revel with the A-listers in the glamorous buzz at this upscale Italian brasserie wedged between Cork Street, Savile Row, and the Royal Academy of Arts. It's perfect for a pit stop during a West End shopping spree or after browsing the nearby Mayfair galleries and auction houses, with diners spilling out onto pavement tables for breakfast, brunch, and *cicchetti* (Italian tapas)—and then returning later in the day for something more substantial. **Known for:** favorite of nearby Vogue House staff and Sotheby's clientele; popular veal Milanese; all-day jet-setter hangout. ⑤ *Average main: £29* ✉ *5A Burlington Gardens, Mayfair* ☏ *020/7434–1500* ⊕ *www.cecconis.co.uk* Ⓜ *Green Park, Piccadilly Circus.*

CUT at 45 Park Lane

$$$$ | **STEAKHOUSE** | Austrian-born star chef Wolfgang Puck amps up the stakes at this ultraexpensive steak house on Park Lane. Set against a luxe backdrop of Damien Hirst artwork and globe lights, carnivores go crazy for the pricey prime cuts from England, Australia, Japan, and the United States. **Known for:** rare Kagoshima Wagyu beef steaks; celebrity chef hot spot; art gallery–like interior. ⑤ *Average main: £50* ✉ *45 Park La., Mayfair* ☏ *020/7493–4545 for reservations only* ⊕ *www.dorchestercollection.com* Ⓜ *Marble Arch, Hyde Park Corner.*

The Golden Hind

$ | **SEAFOOD | FAMILY** | You'll land some of the best fish-and-chips in town at this British chippy in a retro 1914 art deco café. Marylebone locals and satisfied tourists alike hunker down for the neatly prepared and decidedly nongreasy deep-fried or steamed battered cod, haddock, and plaice; the classic hand-cut Maris Piper chips; and the traditional mushy peas and homemade tartare sauce. **Known for:** some of the city's best deep-fried battered cod and chips; hard-to-find traditional mushy peas; huge portions. ⑤ *Average main: £14*

✉ *71A–73 Marylebone La., Marylebone* ☏ *020/7486–3644* ⊕ *www.goldenhindrestaurant.com* ⊘ *Closed Sun. No lunch Sat.* Ⓜ *Bond St.*

★ Gymkhana

$$$ | **MODERN INDIAN** | The last days of the Raj are invoked here at one of London's finest Indian curry emporiums, where top choices include dosas with fennel-rich Chettinad duck or the famed suckling pig vindaloo. Diners admire the whirring ceiling fans, rattan chairs, and other decor inspired by the colonial-era gymkhana sporting clubs of yesteryear. **Known for:** unusual game curries; Indian punches in the basement private dining booths; signature kid goat methi keema. ⑤ *Average main: £28* ✉ *42 Albemarle St., Mayfair* ☏ *020/3011–5900* ⊕ *www.gymkhanalondon.com* ⊘ *Closed Sun.* Ⓜ *Green Park.*

Hélène Darroze at the Connaught

$$$$ | **FRENCH** | The city's wealthy flock to French virtuoso Hélène Darroze's restaurant at the Connaught for her dazzling regional French haute cuisine, served up in a stylish Edwardian wood-paneled dining salon. Taking inspiration from Les Landes in southwestern France, Darroze sallies forth with a procession of magnificent dishes, like Robert Dupérier foie gras with fig and port or Limousin sweetbreads with Jerusalem artichokes. **Known for:** sumptuous dining salon; classy French haute dishes; relatively affordable three-course set lunch. ⑤ *Average main: £38* ✉ *The Connaught, Carlos Pl., Mayfair* ☏ *020/3147–7200 for reservations only* ⊕ *www.the-connaught.co.uk* 🍴 *Jacket required* Ⓜ *Green Park.*

Kitty Fisher's

$$$ | **MODERN BRITISH** | Named after an infamous 18th-century courtesan, Kitty Fisher's is situated in a tiny, creaky Georgian town house in Mayfair's Shepherd Market. Crammed with antique prints, portraits, and silver candelabras, here you can sample some of the finest wood-grill and smokehouse fare around. **Known for:** cozy and candlelit town-house setting;

incredible steaks from the grill; high-end showbiz and politico diners. $ *Average main: £29* ✉ *10 Shepherd Market, Mayfair* ☎ *020/3302–1661* ⊕ *www.kittyfishers.com* ⊘ *Closed Sun.* Ⓜ *Green Park.*

Pollen Street Social

$$$$ | MODERN EUROPEAN | Gastro god Jason Atherton may not man the stoves here anymore, but his flagship in a cute Dickensian alleyway off Regent Street still knocks the London dining scene for a loop. Fans can enjoy refined small and large dishes ranging from a "Fruite of the Sea" appetizer to sublime suckling pig belly with Spanish peach. **Known for:** Michelin-star riffs on classic British dishes; dedicated dessert bar; vegan and vegetarian tasting menus. $ *Average main: £35* ✉ *8–10 Pollen St., Mayfair* ☎ *020/7290–7600* ⊕ *www.pollenstreetsocial.com* ⊘ *Closed Sun.* Ⓜ *Oxford Circus, Piccadilly Circus.*

Scott's

$$$$ | SEAFOOD | Imposing doormen in bowler hats greet visitors with a wee nod at this ever-fashionable seafood haven on Mount Street in Mayfair. Originally founded in 1851 in the Haymarket, and a former haunt of James Bond author Ian Fleming (he apparently enjoyed the potted shrimps), Scott's draws the wealthiest of London, who enjoy the fresh Lindisfarne oysters, Dover sole, and tasty shrimp burgers. **Known for:** possibly London's most magnificent crustacean bar; huge platters of fresh fruits de mer; extravagant prices. $ *Average main: £37* ✉ *20 Mount St., Mayfair* ☎ *020/7495–7309 for reservations only* ⊕ *www.scotts-restaurant.com* Ⓜ *Green Park, Bond St.*

🛏 Hotels

★ Claridge's

$$$$ | HOTEL | FAMILY | The well-heeled have been meeting—and eating—at Claridge's for generations, and the tradition continues in the original art deco public spaces of this super-glamorous London institution. **Pros:**

see-and-be-seen dining and drinking; serious luxury everywhere—this is an old-money hotel; famed history. **Cons:** better pack your designer wardrobe if you want to fit in with the locals; all that luxury means an expensive price tag; to protect the privacy of guests, photographs are prohibited in some areas. $ *Rooms from: £650* ✉ *Brook St., Mayfair* ☎ *020/7629–8860, 866/599–6991 in U.S.* ⊕ *www.claridges.co.uk* 🛏 *203 rooms* ❌ *No meals* Ⓜ *Bond St.*

★ The Connaught

$$$$ | HOTEL | FAMILY | A huge favorite of the "we wouldn't dream of staying anywhere else" monied set since its opening in 1917, the Connaught has many dazzlingly modern compliments to its famously historic delights. **Pros:** legendary hotel; great for star-spotting; Michelin-starred dining. **Cons:** history comes at a price; bathrooms are small; the superior king room is small for the price. $ *Rooms from: £650* ✉ *Carlos Pl., Mayfair* ☎ *020/7499–7070, 866/599–6991 in U.S.* ⊕ *www.the-connaught.co.uk* 🛏 *121 rooms* ❌ *No meals* Ⓜ *Bond St.*

★ The Dorchester

$$$$ | HOTEL | Few hotels this opulent manage to be as personable as the Dorchester, which opened in 1939 and boasts a prime Park Lane location with unparalleled glamour; gold leaf and marble adorn the public spaces, and guest quarters are awash in English country house–meets–art deco style. **Pros:** historic luxury in 1930s building; lovely views of Hyde Park; excellent spa. **Cons:** traditional look is not to all tastes; prices are sky-high; some rooms are disappointingly small. $ *Rooms from: £640* ✉ *53 Park La., Mayfair* ☎ *020/7629–8888* ⊕ *www.dorchestercollection.com* 🛏 *250 rooms* ❌ *No meals* Ⓜ *Marble Arch, Hyde Park Corner.*

★ **Dorset Square Hotel**

$$$ | HOTEL | This fashionable boutique hotel occupies a charming old town house in one of London's most upscale neighborhoods. **Pros:** ideal location; lovely design; good afternoon tea. **Cons:** some rooms are small; no bathtub in some rooms; no gym. S *Rooms from: £252* ⊠ *39 Dorset Sq., Marylebone* ☎ *020/7723-7874* ⊕ *www.firmdale-hotels.com* ↪ *38 rooms* ⊧⊙⊦ *No meals* Ⓜ *Baker St.*

★ **The Langham**

$$$$ | HOTEL | Hotel pedigrees don't come much greater than this one: built in 1865, the Langham was *the* original luxury hotel in the city, all but inventing the very image of what a great London hotel looked like. **Pros:** beautiful historic building; gorgeous and peaceful pool; great restaurant and bar. **Cons:** price rises considerably once cheapest rooms sell out; need to book ahead for the wildly popular Artesian Bar; some modernized rooms don't share the building's historic charm. S *Rooms from: £475* ⊠ *1C Portland Pl., Mayfair* ☎ *020/7636-1000* ⊕ *www.langhamhotels.co.uk* ↪ *380 rooms* ⊧⊙⊦ *No meals* Ⓜ *Oxford Circus.*

 Nightlife

Claridge's Bar

BARS/PUBS | This elegant Mayfair meeting place remains unpretentious even when it brims with beautiful people. The bar has an art deco heritage made hip by the sophisticated touch of designer David Collins. A library of rare Champagnes and brandies as well as a delicious choice of traditional and exotic cocktails—try the Flapper or the Black Pearl—will occupy your taste buds. Request a glass of vintage Cristal in the darkly moody, leather-walled, 36-seat Fumoir. ⊠ *Claridge's, 55 Brook St., Mayfair* ☎ *020/7629-8860* ⊕ *www.claridges.co.uk* Ⓜ *Bond St.*

★ **Mr Fogg's Residence**

BARS/PUBS | Explorers of all stripes will be captivated by this Jules Verne–inspired cocktail parlor, which is chock-full of the weathered maps, hunting trophies, taxidermy, suspended penny-farthings, and *Around the World in 80 Days* globe-trotting items of eccentric fictional Victorian British adventurer, Phileas J Fogg. Expect Victorian tipples and gin-based Afternoon "Tipsy teas" from staff in bow ties and other old-fashioned get-ups. ⊠ *15 Bruton La., Mayfair* ☎ *020/7036-0608* ⊕ *www.mr-foggs.com* Ⓜ *Green Park, Oxford Circus.*

Performing Arts

★ **Wigmore Hall**

CONCERTS | FAMILY | London's most beautiful venue for chamber music also happens to boast near-perfect acoustics. The hall has a rich history, including hosting the premieres of a number of works by the British composer Benjamin Britten, and today attracts leading ensembles from all over the world. The varied program contains lunchtime and Sunday morning concerts, plus workshops and concerts for babies and toddlers. ⊠ *36 Wigmore St., Marylebone* ☎ *020/7935-2141* ⊕ *www.wigmore-hall.org.uk* ⊠ *From £18* Ⓜ *Bond St.*

Shopping

ACCESSORIES

Mulberry

CLOTHING | Staying true to its rural Somerset roots, this luxury goods company epitomizes *le style anglais*, a sophisticated take on the earth tones and practicality of English country style. Best known for highly desirable luxury handbags—such as the Lily, Chiltern, and Bayswater models—the company also produces gorgeous leather accessories, from wallets to luggage, as well as shoes and clothing for men and women. Aside from the New Bond Street flagship, there are branches in Knightsbridge, Covent Garden, Heathrow, and the Westfield centers, along with Mulberry concessions in most of the major upscale department stores. The small store on St. Christopher's Place in Marylebone stocks accessories only. ⊠ *50 New Bond St., Mayfair* ☎ *020/7491–3900* ⊕ *www.mulberry.com* Ⓜ *Bond St.*

★ Philip Treacy

JEWELRY/ACCESSORIES | Magnificent hats by Treacy are annual showstoppers on Ladies' Day at the Royal Ascot races and regularly grace the glossy magazines' party and catwalk pages. Part Mad Hatter, part Cecil Beaton, Treacy's creations always guarantee a grand entrance and are favorites with everyone from Lady Gaga to Kate Middleton. In addition to the extravagant, haute couture hats handmade in the atelier, less flamboyant ready-to-wear hats are also for sale, as are some bags. ⊠ *69 Elizabeth St., Belgravia* ☎ *020/7730–3992* ⊕ *www. philiptreacy.co.uk* Ⓜ *Sloane Sq.*

ANTIQUES
Alfies Antique Market

ANTIQUES/COLLECTIBLES | This four-story, bohemian-chic labyrinth is London's largest indoor antiques market, housing more than 75 dealers specializing in art, lighting, glassware, textiles, jewelry, furniture, and collectibles, with a particular strength in vintage clothing and 20th-century design. Come here to pick up vintage (1900–70) clothing, accessories, and luggage from Tin Tin Collectables; antique and vintage glassware and vases at Robinson Antiques; or a spectacular mid-20th-century Italian lighting fixture at Vincenzo Caffarella. The atmosphere may be funky, but the prices are not. There's also a rooftop café with free Wi-Fi if you need a coffee break. In addition to the market, this end of Church Street is lined with excellent antiques shops. ⊠ *13–25 Church St., Marylebone* ☎ *020/7723–6066* ⊕ *www. alfiesantiques.com* ⊙ *Closed Sun. and Mon.* Ⓜ *Marylebone.*

BOOKS
★ Heywood Hill

BOOKS/STATIONERY | Open since 1936, this is considered by some to be the best small bookstore in the English-speaking world—John Le Carré, who set a scene in *Tinker Tailor Soldier Spy* here, is a long-standing customer. Browse for a leather-bound volume on architecture, gardening, natural history, or topography—just some of the topics in which the antiquarian collection specializes. The contemporary selection emphasizes literature, history, biography, travel, architecture, and children's books, and the knowledgeable staff is happy to provide advice. During World War II, author Nancy Mitford helped keep the bookstore going. Today, the 12th Duke of Devonshire, a descendant of her brother-in-law, the 11th Duke, is the owner. ⊠ *10 Curzon St., Mayfair* ☎ *020/7629–0647* ⊕ *www.heywoodhill.com* ⊙ *Closed weekends.* Ⓜ *Green Park.*

Smythson of Bond Street

BOOKS/STATIONERY | No hostess of any standing would consider having a leather-bound guest book made by anyone besides this elegant stationer, and the shop's social stationery and distinctive diaries with their pale-blue pages are the epitome of British good taste. These, along with other made-in-Britain leather goods including a small line of handbags, backpacks, and luggage tags, can be personalized. There are branches in Chelsea, Notting Hill, and Heathrow, plus concessions in leading department stores. ⊠ *131–132 New Bond St., Mayfair* ☎ *020/3535–8009* ⊕ *www.smythson. com* Ⓜ *Bond St., Oxford Circus.*

Waterstone's

BOOKS/STATIONERY | At this megabookshop (Europe's largest, with more than 8 miles of bookshelves) in a former art deco department store near Piccadilly Circus, browse for your latest purchase, attend one of the frequent meet-the-author events, or admire the view with a glass of wine at the 5th View Bar and

Restaurant (open until 9.30); there's also a café in the basement. Waterstone's is the country's leading book chain, and it's pulled out all the stops to make its flagship as welcoming as a bookstore can be. There are several smaller branches throughout the city. ⊠ *203–206 Piccadilly, Mayfair* ☎ *0207/851–2400* ⊕ *www.waterstones.com* Ⓜ *Piccadilly Circus.*

CLOTHING
Browns

CLOTHING | A trendsetting boutique since it opened in the 1970s, this shop occupying interconnecting town houses has been reinvigorated after a purchase by luxury e-tailer Farfetch.com. Browns focuses on well-established international luxury designers such as Vetements, Valentino, Marques Almeida, or Saint Laurent. The menswear, footwear, and accessories collections are equally well chosen. A new Shoreditch branch showcases new design talent, and if you're about to go down the aisle, check out the appointment-only bridal boutique at 12 Hinde Street in Marylebone. ⊠ *23–27 S. Molton St., Mayfair* ☎ *020/7514–0016* ⊕ *www.brownsfashion.com* Ⓜ *Bond St.*

Ozwald Boateng

CLOTHING | The dapper menswear by Ozwald Boateng (pronounced "Bwa-teng") combines contemporary funky style with traditional Savile Row quality. His made-to-measure suits have been worn by the dandyish likes of Jamie Foxx, Mick Jagger, and Laurence Fishburne, who appreciate the sharp cuts, luxurious fabrics, and occasionally vibrant colors (even the more conservative choices have jacket linings in bright silk). ⊠ *30 Savile Row, Mayfair* ☎ *020/7437–2030* ⊕ *www.ozwaldboateng.co.uk* ⊙ *Closed Sun.* Ⓜ *Piccadilly Circus.*

Vivienne Westwood

CLOTHING | From her beginnings as the most shocking and outré designer around, Westwood (now Dame Vivienne) has become a standard-bearer for high-style British couture. At the Chelsea boutique where she first sold the lavish corseted ball gowns, dandified nipped-waist jackets, and tartan-meets-punk daywear that formed the core of her signature look, you can still buy ready-to-wear—mainly items from the more casual Anglomania diffusion line and the exclusive Worlds End label, which draws from her archives. The small Davies Street boutique is devoted to couture (plus bridal), while the flagship Conduit Street store carries all of the above. There's also a men's collection at 18 Conduit Street. ⊠ *44 Conduit St., Mayfair* ☎ *020/7439–1109* ⊕ *www.viviennewestwood.com* Ⓜ *Oxford Circus.*

DEPARTMENT STORES
★ Selfridges

DEPARTMENT STORES | This giant bustling store (the second largest in the United Kingdom after Harrods) gives Harvey Nichols a run for its money as London's most fashionable department store. Packed to the rafters with clothes ranging from mid-price lines to the latest catwalk names, the store continues to break ground with its innovative retail schemes, especially the ground-floor Wonder Room (for extravagant jewelry and luxury watches), a dedicated Denim Studio, a Fragrance Bar where you can create custom perfume, an array of pop-ups ranging from spaces for designers such as Jil Sander to a healthy shot bar (if you need some colloidal silver to keep you going) or a collaboration with boutique boxing club BXR. The giant accessories hall has miniboutiques dedicated to top-end designers such as Chanel, Gucci, and Vuitton while the new Corner Shop offers U.K.-themed gifts and souvenirs at all price points. There are so many zones that merge into one another—from youth-oriented Miss Selfridge to audio equipment to the large, comprehensive cosmetics department—that you practically need a map. Don't miss the Shoe Galleries, the world's largest shoe department, which is filled with more than 5,000 pairs from 120 brands, displayed like works of art under spotlights.

Take a break with a glass of wine at the rooftop restaurant or pick up some tea in the Food Hall as a gift. ⊠ *400 Oxford St., Marylebone* ☎ *0800/123400* ⊕ *www. selfridges.com* Ⓜ *Bond St.*

JEWELRY
Asprey

JEWELRY/ACCESSORIES | The company's "global flagship" store displays exquisite jewelry—as well as silver and leather goods, watches, china, and crystal—in a discreet, very British setting that oozes quality, expensive good taste, and hushed comfort. If you're in the market for an immaculate 1930s cigarette case, a silver cocktail shaker, a pair of pavé diamond and sapphire earrings, or a ladylike handbag, you won't likely be disappointed. And, for the really well-heeled, there's custom service available as well (Ringo Starr had a chess set made here). This store has occupied the premises since 1847, some 66 years after Asprey was established in 1781. ⊠ *167 New Bond St., Mayfair* ☎ *020/7493–6767* ⊕ *www.asprey.com* Ⓜ *Green Park.*

Kabiri

JEWELRY/ACCESSORIES | A carefully curated array of exciting contemporary jewelry by emerging and established designers from around the world is packed into this small shop. There is something to suit most budgets and tastes, though understated minimalism predominates. You can score an elegant, one-of-a-kind piece here for a very reasonable price. ⊠ *94 Marylebone La., Marylebone* ☎ *020/7317–2150* ⊕ *www.kabiri.co.uk* Ⓜ *Baker St.*

Soho and Covent Garden

A red-light district no more, today SoHo is more stylish than seedy and offers some of London's best bars, live music venues, restaurants, and theaters. By day, this hotbed of media production reverts to the business side of its late-night scene. If SoHo is all about showbiz, neighboring Covent Garden is devoted to culture. Both districts offer an abundance of narrow streets packed with one-of-a-kind shops and lots of antique character.

GETTING HERE

Almost all Tube lines cross the Covent Garden and Soho areas, so it's easy to hop off for a dinner or show in this lively part of London. For Soho, take any train to Piccadilly Circus, Leicester Square, Oxford Circus, or Tottenham Court Road. For Covent Garden, get off at the Covent Garden Station on the Piccadilly Line. It might be easier to exit the Tube at Leicester Square or Holborn and walk. Thirty buses connect to the Covent Garden area from all over London.

◉ Sights

★ Covent Garden Piazza

HISTORIC SITE | FAMILY | Once home to London's main flower market, where *My Fair Lady's* Eliza Doolittle peddled her blooms, the square around which Covent Garden pivots is known as the Piazza. In the center, the fine old market building now houses stalls and shops selling expensive clothing, plus several restaurants and cafés, and knickknack stores that are good for gifts. One particular gem is Benjamin Pollock's Toyshop at No. 44 in the market. Established in the 1880s, it sells delightful toy theaters. The superior **Apple Market** has good crafts stalls on most days, too. On the south side of the Piazza, the indoor **Jubilee Market,** with its stalls of clothing, army-surplus gear, and more crafts and knickknacks, feels a bit like a flea market. In summer it may seem that everyone in the huge crowds around you in the Piazza is a fellow tourist, but there's still plenty of office life in the area. Londoners who shop here tend to head for Neal Street and the area to the north of Covent Garden Tube station, rather than the market itself. In the Piazza, street performers—from global musicians to jugglers and mimes—play to the crowds, as they have done since the first English

Punch and Judy Show, staged here in the 17th century. ⊠ *Covent Garden* ⊕ *www.coventgarden.london* Ⓜ *Covent Garden.*

Leicester Square

PLAZA | FAMILY | Looking at the neon of the major movie houses, the fast-food outlets, and the casino and disco entrances, you'd never guess that this square (pronounced "Lester") was a model of formality and refinement when it was first laid out around 1670. By the 19th century, the square was already bustling and disreputable, and although it's not a threatening place, you should still be on your guard, especially at night—any space so full of people is bound to attract pickpockets, and Leicester Square certainly does. Although there's a bit of residual glamour (major red-carpet film premieres often happen here), Londoners generally tend to avoid the place, though it's worth a visit for its hustle and bustle, its mime artists, and the pleasant modern fountain at its center. Also in the middle is a famous statue of a sulking Shakespeare, perhaps remembering the days when the movie houses were live theaters—burlesque houses, but live all the same. On the northeast corner, in Leicester Place, stands the church of **Notre Dame de France,** with a wonderful mural by Jean Cocteau in one of its side chapels. For more in the way of atmosphere, head north and west from here, through Chinatown and the narrow streets of Soho. ⊠ *Covent Garden* Ⓜ *Leicester Sq.*

London Transport Museum

MUSEUM | FAMILY | Housed in the old flower market at the southeast corner of Covent Garden, this stimulating museum is filled with impressive vehicle, poster, and photograph collections. As you watch the crowds drive a Tube-train simulation and gawk at the early Victorian steam locomotives and horse-drawn trams (and the piles of detritus that remained behind), it's unclear who's enjoying it more: children or adults. Best of all, the kid-friendly museum (under 18 admitted free, and there's a play area) has a multilevel approach to education, including information for the youngest visitor and the most advanced transit aficionado alike. Food and drink are available at the Upper Deck café, and the shop has lots of good options for gift-buying: ■ **TIP→ Tickets are valid for unlimited entry for 12 months.** ⊠ *Covent Garden Piazza, Covent Garden* ☎ *0343/222–5000* ⊕ *www.ltmuseum.co.uk* 🖾 *£18* Ⓜ *Covent Garden, Leicester Sq.*

★ Newburgh Quarter

PEDESTRIAN MALL | Want to see the hip style of today's London? Find it one block east of Carnaby Street—where the look of the '60s "Swinging London" was born—in an adorable warren of cobblestone streets now lined with specialty boutiques, edgy stores, and young indie upstarts. A check of the ingredients reveals one part '60s London, one part futuristic fetishism, one part steampunk, and one part British street swagger. The new-bohemian look best flourishes in shops like Peckham Rye, a tiny boutique crowded with rockers and fashionistas who adore its grunge–meets– *Brideshead Revisited* vibe. Quality coffee shops abound—take a break at Department of Coffee and Social Affairs, where you can also browse for home coffee-making equipment. ⊠ *Newburgh St., Foubert's Pl., Ganton St., and Carnaby St., Soho* ⊕ *www.carnaby.co.uk.*

★ The Photographers' Gallery

MUSEUM | Britain's first and foremost public photography gallery programs cutting-edge and provocative exhibitions. The prestigious Deutsche Börse Photography Prize is exhibited and awarded here annually. The gallery also has a print sales room, a bookstore, an archive, and a café-bar—a great spot to escape the bustle of nearby Oxford Street. ⊠ *16–18 Ramillies St., Soho* ☎ *020/7087–9300* ⊕ *www.thephotographersgallery.org.uk* 🖾 *£5 for exhibitions* Ⓜ *Oxford Circus.*

Soho and Covent Garden

FITZROVIA

Wells St.

Oxford St.

Poland St.

Noel St.

Wardour St.

Benwick St.

Gt. Marlborough St.

Foubert's Pl.

Marshall St.

Newburgh Quarter

Carnaby St.

Broadwick St.

Ganton St.

Newburgh St.

Lexington St.

Regent St.

Beak St.

Golden Sq.

Brewer St.

Warwick St.

Sherwood St.

Glasshouse St.

Denman St.

Saville Row

Old Burlington St.

Vigo St.

Regent St.

Cork St.

Sackville St.

Old Bond St.

Piccadilly

Jermyn St.

Duke of York St.

Duke St.

ST JAMES'S

St James's Sq.

Charles II St.

Dean St.

Carlisle St.

Soho Sq.

Frith St.

Greek St.

Sutton Row

Tottenham Court Road U

Charing Cross Rd.

SOHO

Old Compton St.

Romilly St.

Shaftesbury Ave.

Gerrard St.

CHINATOWN

Lisle St.

Rupert St.

Coventry St.

Whitcomb St.

Leicester Sq.

St Martin's

Piccadilly Circus

U Piccadilly Circus

Regent St.

Haymarket

Pall Mall

Cockspur St.

0 1/8 mi

0 200 m

Covent Garden is home to a charming variety of markets, shops, and cafés.

★ Somerset House

MUSEUM | FAMILY | This huge complex—the work of Sir William Chambers (1723–96) and built during the reign of George III to house offices of the Navy Board—has been transformed from dusty government offices to one of the capital's most buzzing centers of culture and the arts, often hosting several interesting exhibitions at one time. The cobblestone Italianate courtyard, where Admiral Nelson used to walk, makes a great setting for 55 playful fountains and is transformed into a romantic ice rink in winter; the grand space is the venue for music and outdoor movie screenings in summer. **The Courtauld Gallery** (currently closed for renovations) occupies most of the north building, facing the busy Strand. Across the courtyard are the barrell-vaulted Embankment Galleries, with a vibrant calendar of design, fashion, architecture, and photography exhibitions. The East Wing has another fine exhibition space, and events are sometimes also held in the atmospherically gloomy cellars below the Fountain Court. Fernandez & Wells is a great spot for an informal meal or snack. In summer, eating and drinking spills out onto the large terrace next to the Thames. ⊠ *Strand, Covent Garden* ☎ *020/7845–4600* ⊕ *www.somersethouse.org.uk* ✉ *Embankment Galleries price varies, other areas free* Ⓜ *Charing Cross, Covent Garden, Holborn, Temple.*

🍴 Restaurants

Andrew Edmunds

$$ | MEDITERRANEAN | Candlelit at night, with a haunting Dickensian vibe, Andrew Edmunds is a permanently packed, old-school dining institution. Tucked away behind Carnaby Street in an 18th-century Soho town house, it's a cozy favorite whose unpretentious and keenly priced dishes draw on the tastes of Ireland, the Mediterranean, and Middle East. **Known for:** deeply romantic, Georgian-era town-house setting; unpretentious daily changing handwritten menus; bargains

galore on the acclaimed wine list.
$ *Average main: £18* ✉ *46 Lexington St., Soho* ☎ *020/7437–5708* ⊕ *www.andrewedmunds.com* Ⓜ *Oxford Circus, Piccadilly Circus.*

Balthazar

$$$ | **BRASSERIE** | **FAMILY** | British restaurateur Keith McNally re-creates his famed New York Parisian brasserie at this busy corner spot just off Covent Garden. The decor creates an enchanting backdrop to enjoy a classic French brasserie menu of few surprises, including flavor-packed dishes like macaroni and Gruyère cheese or ox cheek bourguignon. **Known for:** Parisian-style grand café; handy prix fixe, brunch, children's, and Afternoon Tea menus; vegan and vegetarian options. $ *Average main: £24* ✉ *4–7 Russell St., Covent Garden* ☎ *020/3301–1155* ⊕ *www.balthazarlondon.com* Ⓜ *Covent Garden, Charing Cross, Holborn.*

★ Bancone

$ | **ITALIAN** | London's awash with New Wave, affordable, and fresh pasta joints, but Bancone in Covent Garden is one of the best options. Diners regularly pitch up at the white marble, porcelain, and bronze bar counter and marvel at the silkiness of the pastas and the outstandingly low prices. **Known for:** high-end pasta at cheap prices; slick urban Italian setting of olive greens, earth tones, and natural stones; location close to the National Portrait Gallery. $ *Average main: £12* ✉ *39 William IV St., Covent Garden* ☎ *020/7240–8786* ⊕ *www.bancone.co.uk* Ⓜ *Charing Cross, Covent Garden, Leicester Sq.*

Blacklock

$ | **STEAKHOUSE** | **FAMILY** | Set in a former basement brothel, this Soho meatopia cranks out £20 platters of delectable char-grilled lamb, beef, and pork skinny chops and juice-soaked flat bread, all served on retro antique pearlware. Supplied by master butchers Philip Warren from Cornwall, Blacklock's killer chops are charcoal-grilled under heavy antique blacklock irons from Tennessee. **Known**

for: young and bubbly service with top '80s tunes; huge platters of skinny chops and flat bread; £18 Sunday roasts with all the trimmings. $ *Average main: £12* ✉ *The Basement, 24 Great Windmill St., Soho* ☎ *020/3441–6996* ⊕ *www.theblacklock.com* ◔ *No dinner Sun.* Ⓜ *Piccadilly Circus, Oxford Circus.*

Dean Street Townhouse

$$$ | **BRITISH** | Everyone feels 10 times more glamorous just stepping inside this candlelit restaurant attached to the swanky Georgian-era hotel of the same name. Straightforward retro-British favorites include pea and ham soup, old-school mince and potatoes, smoked haddock soufflé, and tasty sherry trifle. **Known for:** classy candlelit dining salon with British art on the walls; super professional service; cheery High Tea and Afternoon Tea. $ *Average main: £24* ✉ *69–70 Dean St., Soho* ☎ *020/7434–1775* ⊕ *www.deanstreettownhouse.com* Ⓜ *Oxford Circus, Tottenham Court Rd.*

★ Hoppers

$ | **SRI LANKAN** | Sri Lankan curry fans have gone mad for the fermented rice-flour egg pancakes (a Sri Lankan specialty known as hoppers) and paper-thin griddled dosas at this highly spiced Frith Street snuggery. Diners gorge on chili mutton rolls, curried duck hearts, bone marrow curry, and piles of steamed string hoppers dipped in spicy broth, coconut chutney, or onion-and-Maldives-fish-flakes relish. **Known for:** crispy egg hopper pancakes with coconut sambol; authentic Colombo-style cabin atmosphere; signature goat or black pork kari curry. $ *Average main: £9* ✉ *49 Frith St., Soho* ⊕ *www.hopperslondon.com* ◔ *Closed Sun.* Ⓜ *Oxford Circus, Tottenham Court Rd.*

★ The Ivy

$$$ | **MODERN BRITISH** | London's onetime most famous celebrity haunt and West End landmark is still so popular it receives over a thousand calls a day. Established as an Italian café in 1917, today it's still where London's wealthiest dine on haddock and chips, Thai-baked sea bass, and good ol' English classics like Shepherd's pie and sticky toffee pudding. **Known for:** celebrity-filled history; famed house staples like grilled calf's liver; great people-watching. ⑤ *Average main: £26* ✉ *1–5 West St., Covent Garden* ☎ *020/7836–4751* ⊕ *www.the-ivy.co.uk* Ⓜ *Covent Garden, Tottenham Court Rd.*

J Sheekey

$$$ | **SEAFOOD** | This timelessly chic, 1896, seafood haven is a discreet alternative to the more celebrity-focused eateries in the neighborhood. J Sheekey charms with an inviting menu of snappingly fresh Atlantic prawns, pickled Arctic herring, scallop, shrimp, and salmon burgers, or the famous Sheekey fish pie. Better yet, sip Gaston Chiquet Champagne and down half a dozen Fine de Claire rock oysters at the antique mirrored oyster bar for the ultimate in true romance. **Known for:** low-key celebrity hideaway; old-school seafood menu and discreet service; glamorous art deco oyster bar. ⑤ *Average main: £27* ✉ *28–35 St. Martin's Ct., Covent Garden* ☎ *020/7240–2565* ⊕ *www.j-sheekey.co.uk* Ⓜ *Charing Cross, Leicester Sq.*

Kiln

$ | **THAI** | Earthy northern Thai cuisine bursts out of the charcoal-fired kiln and clay pots at this barbecue-focused wonderland in Soho. Overlook the open kitchen and you'll see sizzling cumin-dusted hogget skewers and charcoal-grilled chicken thigh bites, along with other village-style dishes that show influences from Laos, Myanmar, and the Yunnan province of China. **Known for:** open kitchen counter setup with charcoal grill and hot clay pots; array of Cornish grown Thai, Burmese, and other Asian herbs and spices; popular cumin-dusted aged hogget skewers. ⑤ *Average main: £10* ✉ *58 Brewer St., Soho* ⊕ *www.kilnsoho.com* Ⓜ *Oxford Circus, Piccadilly Circus.*

★ Rules

$$$ | **BRITISH** | Opened by Thomas Rule in 1798, London's oldest restaurant is still arguably its most beautiful. Resembling a High Victoriana bordello, here you can dig into classic traditional British fare like jugged hare, steak-and-kidney pie, or roast beef and Yorkshire pudding. **Known for:** the oldest restaurant in London; fancy, high-class game-focused menu; famous diners from Charles Dickens to the Prince of Wales. ⑤ *Average main: £30* ✉ *35 Maiden La., Covent Garden* ☎ *020/7836–5314* ⊕ *www.rules.co.uk* ⋔ *Jacket required* Ⓜ *Covent Garden.*

Savoy Grill

$$$$ | **BRITISH** | You can feel the history at this 1889, art deco, hotel-dining powerhouse, which has wined and dined everyone from Oscar Wilde and Sir Winston Churchill to Elizabeth Taylor and Marilyn Monroe. Nowadays it caters to CEOs and wealthy West End tourists who come for the Grill's famed table-side serving trolley, which might trundle up laden with hulking great roasts like beef Wellington, Suffolk rack of pork, or saddle of lamb. **Known for:** ravishing old-school dining salon; beef Wellington from the daily carvery trolley service; signature glazed omelet Arnold Bennett. ⑤ *Average main: £40* ✉ *The Savoy, 100 Strand, Covent Garden* ☎ *020/7592–1600 for reservations only* ⊕ *www.gordonramsay-restaurants.com/savoy-grill* Ⓜ *Charing Cross, Covent Garden.*

Simpson's in the Strand

$$$ | **BRITISH** | Head straight for the 30-day roast rib of Scottish beef and Yorkshire puddings carved table-side at this magnificent 1828 dining institution. Originally a cigar lounge, coffeehouse, and later a famed chess venue, it was once frequented by the likes of Sir Arthur Conan Doyle, Charles Dickens, and Vincent van Gogh. **Known for:** one of the city's most grand and historic taverns; traditional Sunday roast dinner; roast

beef and Welsh lamb served from the silver domed carving trolley. $ *Average main: £28* ✉ *100 Strand, Charing Cross* ☎ *020/7420–2111 restaurant reservations only* ⊕ *www.simpsonsinthestrand.co.uk* Ⓜ *Charing Cross.*

Social Eating House

$$$ | FRENCH | At Jason Atherton's under-rated but brilliant French *bistronomie* Soho hangout, witty dishes like smoked duck's ham (made from cured duck's breast) and Scotch egg-and-chips are served alongside complex classics like charred Cumbrian pork with mustard jelly. The moodily lit bare-brick salon is decorated with dark parquet floors, antique mirrored ceilings, and red leath-er banquettes. **Known for:** extravagant tasting menus at the open chef's table; popular set lunch menu; vintage cock-tails at the speakeasy lounge upstairs. $ *Average main: £29* ✉ *58 Poland St., Soho* ☎ *020/7993–3251* ⊕ *www. socialeatinghouse.com* ☾ *Closed Sun.* Ⓜ *Oxford Circus, Tottenham Court Rd.*

★ Spring

$$$ | ITALIAN | Australian chef Skye Gyn-gell worships the four seasons at her wildflower-filled dining salon in majestic Somerset House off the Strand. Housed in the building's 1865 neoclas-sical New Wing, Spring offers healthy, root-to-stem, produce-driven, Italian dishes in a light-drenched room. **Known for:** homemade bread, butter, and ice cream; highly seasonal, sustainable, and ingredient-driven dishes; biodynam-ic Fern Verrow Farm salads. $ *Average main: £30* ✉ *Somerset House, New Wing, Lancaster Pl., Covent Garden* ⌖ *Turn right on entering courtyard at Somerset House from the Strand* ☎ *020/3011–0115* ⊕ *www.springres-taurant.co.uk* ☾ *Closed Sun.* Ⓜ *Charing Cross, Holborn.*

🛏 Hotels

★ Covent Garden Hotel

$$$$ | HOTEL | It's little wonder this is now the London home-away-from-home for off-duty celebrities, actors, and style mavens, with its Covent Garden location and guest rooms that are design-maga-zine stylish, using mix-and-match couture fabrics to stunning effect. **Pros:** great for star-spotting; supertrendy; basement cin-ema for movie buffs. **Cons:** you can feel you don't matter if you're not famous; location in Covent Garden can be a bit boisterous; only some rooms come with balcony views. $ *Rooms from: £320* ✉ *10 Monmouth St., Covent Garden* ☎ *020/7806–1000, 888/559–5508 in U.S.* ⊕ *www.firmdalehotels.com/hotels/ london/covent-garden-hotel* ⟿ *58 rooms* ❌ *No meals* Ⓜ *Covent Garden.*

Dean Street Townhouse

$$$ | HOTEL | Discreet and unpretentious—and right in the heart of Soho—this oh-so-stylish Georgian town house has a bohemian vibe and an excellent Modern British restaurant, hung with pieces by renowned artists like Peter Blake and Tra-cy Emin. **Pros:** ultracool vibe; resembles an upper-class pied-à-terre; great location in the heart of Soho. **Cons:** some rooms are extremely small; rooms at the front of the building can be noisy, especially on weekends; the crowd can often feel cooler-than-thou. $ *Rooms from: £330* ✉ *69–71 Dean St., Soho* ☎ *020/7434–1775* ⊕ *www.deanstreettownhouse.com* ⟿ *39 rooms* ❌ *Free breakfast* Ⓜ *Leices-ter Sq., Tottenham Court Rd.*

★ Hazlitt's

$$$$ | HOTEL | This disarmingly friendly place, full of personality, robust antiques, Old Masters portraits, and claw-foot tubs, occupies three connected early 18th-cen-tury town houses, one of which was the last home of critic and essayist William Hazlitt (1778–1830). **Pros:** great for lovers of antiques and Old Masters art; historic atmosphere with lots of small sitting

rooms and wooden staircases; truly beautiful and relaxed. **Cons:** no in-house restaurant; breakfast costs extra; no elevators. $ *Rooms from: £255* ✉ *6 Frith St., Soho* ☎ *020/7434–1771* ⊕ *www. hazlittshotel.com* ⤴ *30 rooms* ◉ *No meals* Ⓜ *Tottenham Court Rd.*

★ ME London

$$$ | HOTEL | A shiny fortress of luxury, the ME brings a splash of modern cool to a rather stuffy patch of the Strand. **Pros:** sleek and fashionable; full of high-tech comforts; stunning views from rooftop bar. **Cons:** design can sometimes verge on form over function; very small closets and in-room storage areas; rooftop bar can get uncomfortably busy. $ *Rooms from: £280* ✉ *336–337 The Strand, Covent Garden* ☎ *020/7395–3400* ⊕ *www.melia. com* ⤴ *157 rooms* ◉ *No meals* Ⓜ *Covent Garden, Charing Cross, Holborn.*

★ The Savoy

$$$$ | HOTEL | One of London's most iconic hotels maintains its status at the top with winning attributes of impeccable service, stunning decor, and a desirable location on the Strand. **Pros:** one of the top hotels in Europe; iconic pedigree; Thames-side location. **Cons:** everything comes with a price tag; street noise is surprisingly problematic, particularly on lower floors; street can be too busy for some. $ *Rooms from: £504* ✉ *The Strand, Covent Garden* ☎ *020/7836–4343, 888/265–0533 in U.S.* ⊕ *www.thesavoylondon. com* ⤴ *268 rooms* ◉ *Free breakfast* Ⓜ *Covent Garden, Charing Cross.*

▼ Nightlife

BARS

★ The Blind Pig

BARS/PUBS | Chances are you won't have heard of half the ingredients on the cocktail menu at this dark and sultry bar above Jason Atherton's smart casual restaurant, Social Eating House in Soho, but the sense of mystery only adds to the experience. So, too, do the antique mirrored ceilings and copper-topped bar, the delectable small plates (like black pepper prawn crackers and macaroni and cheese with shaved mushroom)—and the knowledge that you've nabbed a seat at one of the coolest spots in Soho. ✉ *58 Poland St., Soho* ☎ *020/7993–3251* ⊕ *www.socialeatinghouse.com* Ⓜ *Oxford Circus, Tottenham Court Rd.*

The Dog and Duck

BARS/PUBS | FAMILY | A beautiful example of a late-19th-century London pub, the Dog and Duck has a well-preserved Heritage-listed interior furnished with glazed tiles, cut glass mirrors, and polished wood, though it's often so packed that it's hard to get a good look. There's a decent selection of real ales at the bar and a restaurant serving outstanding pale ale-battered fish-and-chips with mushy peas. Originally built in 1734 and patronized by artists John Constable and Dante Rossetti, the cozy upstairs dining room is named for writer George Orwell, who also frequented this spot. ✉ *18 Bateman St., Soho* ☎ *020/7494–0697* ⊕ *www.nicholsonspubs.co.uk* Ⓜ *Oxford Circus, Tottenham Court Rd.*

Heaven

MUSIC CLUBS | With the best light show on any London dance floor, Heaven is unpretentious, loud, and huge, with a labyrinth of rooms, bars, and live-music parlors. Thursday through Saturday nights it's all about the G-A-Y club and comedy nights. Check in advance about live performances—they can take place any night of the week. If you go to just one gay club in London, Heaven should be it. ✉ *Under the Arches, Villiers St., Covent Garden* ☎ *0844/847–2351 24-hr ticket line* ⊕ *www.heavenlive.co.uk* ⌫ *From £15* Ⓜ *Charing Cross, Embankment.*

Terroirs

WINE BARS—NIGHTLIFE | Specializing in low-intervention "natural wines" (organic, unfiltered, biodynamic, and sustainably produced with minimal added ingredients), Terroirs wine bar has an unusually

The Royal Opera House is simply dazzling inside and out.

large selection of 290 wines from small French and artisan winemakers. Red, white, sparkling and macerated orange and amber wines are served along with delicious, relatively simple wine-friendly dishes—charcuterie, tapas, cheese, and more substantial French-inspired dishes—at a bar and bare oak tables surrounded by whitewashed walls and wooden floors. ⊠ *5 William IV St., Covent Garden* ☎ *020/7036–0660* ⊕ *www.terroir-swinebar.com* Ⓜ *Charing Cross.*

COMEDY AND CABARET

★ The Comedy Store

COMEDY CLUBS | Before heading off to prime time, some of the United Kingdom's funniest stand-ups cut their teeth here, at what's considered the birthplace of alternative comedy. The Comedy Store Players, a team with six comedians doing improvisation with audience suggestions, entertain on Wednesday and Sunday; The Cutting Edge steps in with a topical take every Tuesday; Thursday, Friday, and Saturday have the best stand-up acts. There's also a bar with food. Note you must be over 18 to enter. ⊠ *1A Oxendon St., Soho* ☎ *020/7024–2060 for tickets and booking* ⊕ *www.thecomedystore. co.uk* ✉ *From £12* Ⓜ *Leicester Sq., Piccadilly Circus.*

LIVE MUSIC

Pizza Express Jazz Club

MUSIC CLUBS | One of the United Kingdom's most ubiquitous pizza chains also runs a leading Soho jazz venue. Established in 1976, the dimly lit restaurant hosts both established and emerging top-quality international jazz acts every night, with food available in the downstairs venue (as opposed to the upstairs restaurant) around 90 minutes before stage time. The Italian-style thin-crust pizzas are popular, but they are about what you'd expect from a major chain. ⊠ *10 Dean St., Soho* ☎ *020/7439–4962 for jazz club, 020/7437–9595 for restaurant* ⊕ *www.pizzaexpresslive.com* ✉ *From £16* Ⓜ *Tottenham Court Rd.*

🎭 Performing Arts

★ Royal Opera House

DANCE | Along with Milan's La Scala, New York's Metropolitan, and the Palais Garnier in Paris, this is one of the world's great opera houses. The resident troupe has mounted spectacular productions in the past, while recent productions have tended toward more contemporary operas. Whatever the style of the performance, the extravagant theater delivers a full dose of opulence. The famed Royal Ballet performs classical and contemporary repertoire here, too, and smaller-scale works of both opera and dance are presented in the Linbury Theatre and Clore Studio Upstairs. A small allocation of tickets for each performance of main stage productions for the week ahead—even those that are sold out—goes on sale online at 1 pm every Friday. ■TIP➜ If you wish to see the famed auditorium but are not able to procure a ticket, you can join a backstage tour or one of the less frequent tours of the auditorium; they book up several weeks in advance. BP Big Screens is the ROH's summer series of live relays of its opera and ballet productions. Screenings are free and take place outdoors in public spaces all over the country, including Trafalgar Square. ⊠ Bow St., Covent Garden ☎ 020/7304–4000 ⊕ www.roh.org.uk ⊠ Performances from £4; tours from £10 Ⓜ Covent Garden.

👜 Shopping

BOOKS

★ Foyles

BOOKS/STATIONERY | FAMILY | Founded in 1903 by the Foyle brothers after they failed the Civil Service exams, this family-owned bookstore is in a 1930s art deco building, once the home of the renowned art college Central Saint Martins. One of London's best sources for textbooks and the United Kingdom's largest retailer of foreign language books, with more than 200,000 titles on its four miles of bookshelves, Foyles also stocks everything from popular fiction to military history, sheet music, medical tomes, graphic novels, and handsome, illustrated fine arts books. It also offers the store-within-a-store Ray's Jazz (one of London's better outlets for music) and a cool café. Foyles also has branches in the Royal Festival Hall at the Southbank Centre and at Waterloo Station. ⊠ 107 Charing Cross Rd., Soho ☎ 020/7437–5660 ⊕ www.foyles.co.uk Ⓜ Leicester Sq., Tottenham Court Rd.

CLOTHING

Covent Garden Market

OUTDOOR/FLEA/GREEN MARKETS | FAMILY | This popular destination includes three separate market areas: the Apple Market, the East Colonnade Market, and the Jubilee Market. In the covered area originally designed by Inigo Jones and known as the Apple Market, 40 stalls sell handcrafted jewelry, prints, clothes (such as hand-painted dancewear), ceramics, and crafts Tuesday through Sunday, while Monday is given over to antiques, curios, and collectables. The East Colonnade Market has stalls with mostly handmade specialty items that include soaps and jewelry, as well as housewares, accessories, and magic tricks. The Jubilee Market, in Jubilee Hall toward Southampton Street, tends toward the more pedestrian (kitschy T-shirts, unremarkable household goods, and the like) Tuesday through Friday, but has vintage collectibles and antiques on Monday and worthwhile handmade goods on weekends. Largely aimed at the tourist trade in the past, Covent Garden Market continues its ascent, introducing a more sophisticated image (and correspondingly higher prices) with the opening of upscale restaurants and chains in the surrounding arcades, including the world's second largest Apple Store; beauty outlets for Chanel, M.A.C., and Dior; and boutiques for brands like Tumi, Mulberry, and N. Peal. ■TIP➜ Don't miss the magicians, musicians, jugglers, and escape artists who perform in the open-air piazza; the performances are free (though contributions are welcome). ⊠ *The Piazza, off Wellington St., Covent Garden* ⊕ *www.coventgarden.london* Ⓜ *Covent Garden.*

★ Paul Smith

CLOTHING | British classics with an irreverent twist define Paul Smith's collections for women, men, and children. Beautifully tailored suits for men and women take hallmarks of traditional British style and turn them on their heads with humor and color, combining exceptional fabrics with flamboyant linings or unusual detailing. Gift ideas abound—wallets, scarves, phone cases, and distinctive belts and socks—all in Smith's signature rainbow stripes. There are several branches throughout London, in Notting Hill, Soho, Marylebone, Southwark, and Canary Wharf, plus a Mayfair shop that includes vintage furniture. ⊠ *40–44 Floral St., Covent Garden* ☎ *020/7379–7133* ⊕ *www.paulsmith.com* Ⓜ *Covent Garden.*

DEPARTMENT STORES
★ Liberty

DEPARTMENT STORES | **FAMILY** | The wonderful, black-and-white, mock-Tudor facade, created from the timbers of two Royal Navy ships, reflects this store's origins in the late-19th-century Arts and Crafts movement. Leading designers were recruited to create the classic art nouveau Liberty prints that are still a centerpiece of the brand, gracing everything from cushions and silk kimonos to embossed leather bags and photo albums. Inside, Liberty is a labyrinth of nooks and crannies stuffed with thoughtfully chosen merchandise, including niche beauty, perfume, footwear, and housewares lines such as Soho Home, which features furniture and textiles from the membership clubs. Clothes for both men and women focus on high quality and high fashion, with labels like Rixo and Roland Mouret. The store regularly commissions new prints from contemporary designers, and it

sells both these and its classic patterns by the yard. If you're not so handy with a needle, an interior design service will create soft furnishings for you. There's also a florist, a hair salon, a traditional men's barber, branded beauty treatment rooms, a brow bar, a piercing studio, and a foot spa. ⊠ *Regent St., Soho* ☎ *020/7734–1234* ⊕ *www.libertylondon.com* Ⓜ *Oxford Circus.*

TOYS
★ Benjamin Pollock's Toyshop

TOYS | **FAMILY** | This landmark shop still carries on the tradition of its founder, who sold miniature theater stages made from richly detailed paper from the late 19th century until his death in 1937. Among his admirers was Robert Louis Stevenson, who wrote, "If you love art, folly, or the bright eyes of children, speed to Pollock's." Today the antique model theaters are expensive, but there are plenty of magical reproductions for less than £10. There's also an extensive selection of new but nostalgic puppets, marionettes, teddy bears, spinning tops, jack-in-the-boxes, and similar traditional children's toys from the days before batteries were required (or toys were even run on them). ⊠ *44 The Market Bldg., Covent Garden* ☎ *020/7379–7866* ⊕ *www.pollocks-coventgarden.co.uk* Ⓜ *Covent Garden.*

Bloomsbury and Holborn

With the British Library, the British Museum, and countless colleges of the University of London, Bloomsbury might appear all bookish and cerebral, but fear not, it's much more than that. There's a youthfulness about its buzzing thoroughfares, and this vitality extends from down-by-the-Thames Holborn—once Dickens territory, now the heartbeat of legal London—way up to the revamped King's Cross and classy Islington to the north, and cool Clerkenwell out east.

The massive, glass-roofed Great Court in the British Museum has a couple of cafés.

GETTING HERE

The Russell Square Tube stop on the Piccadilly Line leaves you right at the corner of Russell Square. Tottenham Court Road on the Northern and Central lines is best for the British Museum.

⊙ Sights

British Library

LIBRARY | FAMILY | With a collection totaling more than 150 million items, plus 3 million new additions every year, the British Library is a world-class repository of knowledge. Its greatest treasures are on view to the general public in the Sir John Ritblat Gallery: the Magna Carta, the Codex Sinaiticus (an ancient bible containing the oldest complete copy of the New Testament), Jane Austen's writings, and Shakespeare's First Folio, as well as musical manuscripts by Handel and Beethoven and original handwritten lyrics by the Beatles. ⊠ *96 Euston Rd., Bloomsbury* ☎ *0330/333–1144* ⊕ *www.bl.uk* ⊠ *Free, donations appreciated;*

charge for special exhibitions Ⓜ *Euston, Euston Sq., King's Cross St. Pancras.*

★ British Museum

MUSEUM | FAMILY | The sheer scale and importance of the British Museum's many treasures is impossible to overstate or exaggerate; it truly is one of the world's great repositories of human civilization. Established in 1753 and initially based on the library and "cabinet of curiosities" of the Royal Physician Sir Hans Sloane, the collection grew exponentially over the following decades, partly due to bequests and acquisitions, but also as a result of plundering by the burgeoning British Empire. Inside are some of the greatest relics of humankind: the Parthenon Sculptures (Elgin Marbles), the Rosetta Stone, the Sutton Hoo Treasure, Egyptian mummies, a colossal statue of Ramesses II, fragments of the Seven Wonders of the Ancient World—almost everything, it seems, but the original Ten Commandments. The museum's focal point is the **Great Court**, a brilliant modern design with a vast glass roof atop the museum's covered courtyard. The elegant **Reading Room**, with its gorgeous blue-and-gold dome, hosts temporary exhibitions. ■**TIP**➔ **Free tours cover the highlights in an economical 30 or 40 minutes.** ✉ *Great Russell St., Bloomsbury* ☎ *020/7323–8000* ⊕ *www. britishmuseum.org* ✉ *Free; donations encouraged* Ⓜ *Russell Sq., Holborn, Tottenham Court Rd.*

Charles Dickens Museum

MUSEUM | This is one of the few London houses Charles Dickens (1812–70) inhabited that is still standing, and it's the place where he wrote *Oliver Twist* and *Nicholas Nickleby.* The house looks exactly as it would have in Dickens's day, complete with first editions, letters, and a tall clerk's desk (Dickens wrote standing up). Catch the fascinating Housemaid's Tour (£15) in which you're taken back in time to 1839 by Dickens's housemaid who reveals the private lives of the great author and his family; note that it's only available select Sunday mornings and must be booked in advance. ✉ *48 Doughty St., Bloomsbury* ☎ *020/7405–2127* ⊕ *www.dickensmuseum.com* ✉ *£10* ۞ *Closed Mon.* Ⓜ *Chancery La., Russell Sq.*

Lincoln's Inn

BUILDING | There's plenty to see at one of the oldest, best preserved, and most attractive of the Inns of Court—from the Chancery Lane Tudor brick gatehouse to the wide-open, tree-lined, atmospheric Lincoln's Inn Fields and the 15th-century chapel remodeled by Inigo Jones in 1620. The chapel and the gardens are open to the public, but to see more you must reserve a place on one of the official tours. But be warned: they tend to prefer group bookings of 15 or more, so it's best to check the website or call for details. ✉ *Chancery La., Holborn* ☎ *020/7405–1393* ⊕ *www.lincolnsinn.org.uk* ✉ *Free* ۞ *Closed weekends* Ⓜ *Chancery La.*

★ Sir John Soane's Museum

HOUSE | Sir John (1753–1837), architect of the Bank of England, bequeathed his eccentric house to the nation on one condition: that nothing be changed. It's a house full of surprises. In the Picture Room, two of Hogarth's famous *Rake's Progress* paintings swing away to reveal secret gallery recesses where you can find works by Canaletto and Turner. Everywhere, mirrors play tricks with light and space, and split-level floors worthy of a fairground fun house disorient you. Soane's lovingly restored private apartments are also open to the public, but they can only be viewed as part of a first-come, first-served tour at 1:15 pm and 2 pm daily. While entry to the house is free (with a suggested donation), you must book timed tickets at least a day in advance online or over the phone. ✉ *13 Lincoln's Inn Fields, Bloomsbury* ☎ *020/7405–2107* ⊕ *www.soane.org* ✉ *Free; guided tours £15* ۞ *Closed Mon. and Tues.* Ⓜ *Holborn.*

🍴 Restaurants

Berners Tavern

$$$ | **MODERN BRITISH** | **FAMILY** | All the cool cats swing by this grand brasserie at Ian Schrager's insanely trendy London Edition hotel near Tottenham Court Road. Enter the monumental Edwardian dining salon, where you might swoon over a light lunch of hot smoked Loch Duart salmon or an evening dinner of Herdwick lamb rump with maitake mushrooms and salsa verde. **Known for:** knock-out dining salon; cool back-lit cocktail bar; legendary Buccleuch Estate beef tartare. ⑤ *Average main: £30* ✉ *The London Edition, 10 Berners St., Fitzrovia* ☎ *020/7908–7979* ⊕ *www. bernerstavern.com* Ⓜ *Oxford Circus, Tottenham Court Rd.*

Bloomsbury and Holborn

SOMERS TOWN

Ⓤ **Mornington Crescent**

Regent's Park

King's Cross Station

St. Pancras Station

The British Library ①

King's Cross St. Pancras Ⓤ ⑥

Euston Station

Euston Square Ⓤ

Warren Street Ⓤ

Ⓤ **Great Portland Street**

Regent's Park Ⓤ

University College London

②

Russell Square Ⓤ

BLOOMSBURY

University of London

Russell Sq.

② ②

British Museum

FITZROVIA

Holborn Ⓤ

① ③ ①

Tottenham Court Rd Ⓤ

Ⓤ **Oxford Circus**

Oxford St.

Covent Garden Ⓤ

Covent Garden

KEY
- ① Sights
- ① Restaurants
- ① Hotels

★ Clipstone

$$$ | **FRENCH** | Flavorful, inventive dishes elevate this hipster casual joint to the top rank of London's mid-range gastro titans. With a focus on in-house curing, pickling, smoked meats, and heritage vegetables, expect a cavalcade of unlikely combinations and classic gastronomy specialties. **Known for:** fine dining without the fuss; lots of house-made, pickled, fermented, or cured extras; good value set lunches. ⑤ *Average main: £28* ⊠ *5 Clipstone St., Fitzrovia* ☎ *020/7637–0871* ⊕ *www. clipstonerestaurant.co.uk* ⊙ *Closed Sun.* Ⓜ *Great Portland St., Warren St.*

★ The Delaunay

$$$ | **AUSTRIAN** | **FAMILY** | It's all *fin de siècle* Vienna at this evocative art deco–style grand café on the Aldwych near Covent Garden. Dishes on the majestic 60-item menu would do the Austro-Hungarian Empire proud—think Wiener schnitzel, Hungarian goulash, beef Stroganoff, and wonderful *würstchen* (frankfurters and hot dogs) served with sauerkraut and onions. **Known for:** elegant old-world Austro-Hungarian haunt; proper Holstein schnitzel and frankfurters; excellent wine list. ⑤ *Average main: £25* ⊠ *55 Aldwych, Holborn* ☎ *020/7499–8558* ⊕ *www.thedelaunay.com* Ⓜ *Covent Garden, Holborn.*

Noble Rot

$$$ | **BRITISH** | There's an old Amsterdam coffeehouse vibe at this dark and creaky wine bar and restaurant on historic Lamb's Conduit Street in Bloomsbury. Run by two wine buffs and cult wine magazine publishers, you'll find deceptively simple ingredient-driven British dishes like Whitstable oyster and Cornish turbot braised in oxidized 1998 Bâtard-Montrachet Grand Cru. **Known for:** paradise for oenophiles; unpretentious seasonal British and French wine-friendly fare; neat combos like leeks vinaigrette and Brixham crab. ⑤ *Average main: £26* ⊠ *51 Lamb's Conduit St., Bloomsbury* ☎ *020/7242–8963* ⊕ *www.noblerot.co.uk* ⊙ *Closed Sun.* Ⓜ *Holborn.*

★ St. John

$$ | **MODERN BRITISH** | **FAMILY** | Global foodie fanatics join Clerkenwell locals for the pioneering nose-to-tail cuisine at this high-ceilinged, converted smokehouse near Smithfield Market. Here the chef uses all scraps of a carcass—from tongue and cheeks to tail and trotters—so brace for radically stark signatures like bone-marrow-and-parsley salad. **Known for:** ground zero of influential Modern British nose-to-tail dining; great wine list; crispy pig's-skin appetizer. ⑤ *Average main: £23* ⊠ *26 St. John St., Clerkenwell* ☎ *020/7251–0848* ⊕ *www. stjohnrestaurant.com* ⊙ *No dinner Sun.* Ⓜ *Farringdon, Barbican.*

🛏 Hotels

★ Charlotte Street Hotel

$$$ | **HOTEL** | Superstar London hotel designer Kit Kemp has taken the fabled Bloomsbury Group as her inspiration for this super stylish boutique hotel, which, if anything, feels more like a private members' club. **Pros:** elegant and luxurious; great attention to detail; excellent, lively location. **Cons:** the popular bar can be noisy; reservations essential for the restaurant; some rooms are small considering the price. ⑤ *Rooms from: £320* ⊠ *15–17 Charlotte St., Fitzrovia* ☎ *020/7806–2000, 888/559–5508 in U.S.* ⊕ *www.firmdalehotels.com* ⌐ *52 rooms* ⑩ *No meals* Ⓜ *Goodge St.*

Harlingford Hotel

$$ | **HOTEL** | The most contemporary of the hotels around Bloomsbury's Cartwright Gardens offers sleek, quiet, and comfortable bedrooms and perfectly appointed public rooms. **Pros:** good location; free Wi-Fi; private garden. **Cons:** rooms are small; no air-conditioning; no elevator. ⑤ *Rooms from: £140* ⊠ *61–63 Cartwright Gardens, Bloomsbury* ☎ *020/7387–1551* ⊕ *www.harlingfordhotel.com* ⌐ *43 rooms* ⑩ *Free breakfast* Ⓜ *Russell Sq.*

★ The London Edition

$$$ | HOTEL | Style and image are the draw at the London Edition Hotel, where Michelin-starred chefs and hip bars complement the boutique property's sleek, contemporary design. **Pros:** very trendy; great bars; beautifully designed bedrooms. **Cons:** rooms may feel small to some; lobby can get crowded with trendsetters descending upon the bars; can at times feel more like an events space than a hotel. $ *Rooms from: £333 ⊠ 10 Berners St., Fitzrovia ☏ 020/7781– 0000 ⊕ edition-hotels.marriott.com/ london ⇄ 173 rooms* ⎮○⎮ *Free breakfast* Ⓜ *Oxford Circus.*

★ The Rookery

$$ | HOTEL | A stylish period masterpiece in the heart of laid-back Clerkenwell, the Rookery is a luxury boutique hotel with a hefty dollop of *Downton Abbey* charm. **Pros:** charming decor; free Wi-Fi; good deals in the off-season. **Cons:** breakfast costs extra; no restaurant in the hotel; the resident cat might put off guests with allergies. $ *Rooms from: £240 ⊠ 12 Peter's La., at Cowcross St., Clerkenwell ☏ 020/7336–0931 ⊕ www.rookery-hotel.com ⇄ 33 rooms* ⎮○⎮ *No meals* Ⓜ *Farringdon.*

Rosewood London

$$$$ | HOTEL | So striking it was featured in the movie *Howards End,* this landmark structure (originally built by the Pearl Assurance Company in 1914) now houses a luxurious hotel with a clubby atmosphere, elegant decor and furnishings, and huge comfortable beds. **Pros:** gorgeous romantic space; excellent restaurant; great spa. **Cons:** luxury comes at a price; the area can be quiet on weekends; the rooms can't quite match the splendor of the public areas. $ *Rooms from: £500 ⊠ 252 High Holborn, Holborn ☏ 020/7781–8888, 888/767–3966 in U.S. ⊕ www.rosewoodhotels.com/en/london ⇄ 306 rooms* ⎮○⎮ *No meals* Ⓜ *Holborn.*

★ St. Pancras Renaissance

$$$$ | HOTEL | This stunningly restored Victorian landmark—replete with gingerbread turrets and neo-Gothic flourishes—started as a love letter to the golden age of railways, and now it's one of London's most sophisticated places to stay. **Pros:** unique and beautiful; faultless service; close to the train station. **Cons:** very crowded bar and restaurant; streets outside are busy 24/7; free Wi-Fi only in the lobby and public areas. $ *Rooms from: £270 ⊠ Euston Rd., King's Cross ☏ 020/7841–3540 ⊕ www.marriott.com/ hotels/travel/lonpr-st-pancras-renaissance-hotel-london ⇄ 245 rooms* ⎮○⎮ *No meals* Ⓜ *King's Cross St. Pancras. National Rail: Kings Cross, St. Pancras.*

★ The Zetter

$$ | HOTEL | The five-story atrium, art deco staircase, and slick European restaurant hint at the delights to come in this converted warehouse—a breath of fresh air with its playful color schemes, elegant wallpapers, and wonderful views of the city from the higher floors. **Pros:** huge amounts of character; big rooms; free Wi-Fi. **Cons:** rooms with good views cost more; the contemporary style won't appeal to everyone; the property's best bar is across the street at the Zetter Townhouse. $ *Rooms from: £140 ⊠ 86–88 Clerkenwell Rd., Clerkenwell ☏ 020/7324– 4444 ⊕ www.thezetter.com ⇄ 59 rooms* ⎮○⎮ *Free breakfast* Ⓜ *Farringdon.*

▼ Nightlife

BARS

The Lamb

BARS/PUBS | FAMILY | Charles Dickens and his contemporaries drank here, but today's enthusiastic clientele make sure this intimate and eternally popular pub avoids the pitfalls of feeling too old-timey. One interesting feature: for private chats at the bar, you can close a delicate etched-glass "snob screen" to the bar

124

staff, opening it only when you fancy another pint. ⊠ *94 Lamb's Conduit St., Bloomsbury* ☎ *020/7405-0713* ⊕ *www. thelamblondon.com* Ⓜ *Russell Sq.*

Princess Louise

BARS/PUBS | FAMILY | This fine popular pub is an exquisite museum piece of a Victorian interior, with glazed tiles and intricately engraved glass screens that divide the bar area into cozy little annexes. It's not all show, either. There's a good selection of excellent-value Yorkshire real ales from Samuel Smith's brewery. ⊠ *208 High Holborn, Holborn* ☎ *020/7405-8816* ⊕ *www. princesslouisepub.co.uk* Ⓜ *Holborn.*

🎭 Performing Arts

Almeida Theatre

THEATER | This Off West End venue, helmed by director Rupert Goold, premiers excellent new plays and exciting twists on the classics, often featuring high-profile actors. There's a good café and a licensed bar that serves "sharing dishes," as well as tasty main courses. ⊠ *Almeida St., Islington* ☎ *020/7359-4404* ⊕ *www.almeida.co.uk* 🎫 *From £10* Ⓜ *Angel, Highbury & Islington.*

Little Angel Theatre

PUPPET SHOWS | FAMILY | Innovative puppetry performances for children and adults have been taking place in this adorable former temperance hall since 1961. ⊠ *14 Dagmar Passage, Islington* ☎ *020/7226-1787* ⊕ *www.littleangeltheatre.com* 🎫 *From £7* Ⓜ *Angel, Highbury & Islington.*

The Place

DANCE | This is London's only theater dedicated solely to contemporary dance, and with tickets often under £20, it's good value, too. The Resolution Festival, held in January and February, is the United Kingdom's biggest platform event for new choreographers. There's also an excellent bar and café. ⊠ *17 Duke's Rd., Bloomsbury* ☎ *020/7121-1100* ⊕ *www. theplace.org.uk* 🎫 *From £10* Ⓜ *Euston.*

★ Sadler's Wells

DANCE | FAMILY | If you're into leading classical and contemporary dance companies, head to this purpose-built complex, which opened in 1998 and is the sixth theater on this site in its 300 year history. Choreographers like Matthew Bourne and Hofesh Shechter often bring their work here. The little Lilian Baylis Studio hosts avant-garde work. ⊠ *Rosebery Ave., Islington* ☎ *020/7863-8000* ⊕ *www.sadlerswells.com* 🎫 *From £12* Ⓜ *Angel.*

🛍 Shopping

ACCESSORIES

★ **James Smith & Sons Ltd.**

JEWELRY/ACCESSORIES | This has to be the world's ultimate umbrella shop (it is definitely Europe's oldest), and it's a must for anyone interested in real Victorian London. The family-owned shop has been in this location on a corner of New Oxford Street since 1857 and sells every kind of umbrella, parasol, cane, and walking stick imaginable (including some containing a small flask or a corkscrew or that fold out into a seat). The interior is unchanged since the 19th century; you will feel as if you have stepped back in time. Prices range from about £40 for a folding umbrella to more than £400 for a classic blackthorn root-knob solid stick umbrella to thousands for bespoke items. If the umbrella prices are too steep, smaller accessories like an oxhorn shoehorn or salt spoonmake perfect gifts. ⊠ *Hazelwood House, 53 New Oxford St., Bloomsbury* ☎ *020/7836-4731* ⊕ *www. james-smith.co.uk* ✪ *Closed Sun.* Ⓜ *Tottenham Court Rd., Holborn.*

ANTIQUES

London Silver Vaults

ANTIQUES/COLLECTIBLES | Originally built in 1876 as Britain's first safe deposit building, this extraordinary space five floors beneath ground level has been converted to more than 30 small shops housing silver (plus a few jewelry) dealers, the majority of which are family businesses. Products range from 16th-century items to contemporary pieces (with everything in between), and from the spectacularly over-the-top costing thousands to smaller items—like teaspoons, candlesticks, or a set of Victorian cake forks—at £25. ⊠ *53–64 Chancery La., Holborn* ☎ *020/7242–3844* ⊕ *www.silvervaultslondon.com* ⊘ *Closed Sun.* Ⓜ *Chancery La.*

The City

The capital's fast-beating financial heart, the City is associated with power and pomp, embodied in the three institutions at its epicenter: the Bank of England, the Royal Exchange, and Mansion House. The site of the original Roman settlement from which all of London grew, the "Square Mile" has statement skyscrapers cheek-by-jowl with some of London's most iconic historic buildings, from Wren's uplifting St. Paul's Cathdral to the Tower of London, a royal fortress, prison, and jewel house surrounded by a moat.

GETTING HERE

The City is well served by a concentration of Tube stations—St. Paul's and Bank on the Central Line, and Mansion House, Cannon Street and Monument on the District and Circle lines. Liverpool Street and Aldgate border the City's eastern edge, while Chancery Lane and Farringdon lie to the west. Barbican and Moorgate provide easy access to the theaters and galleries of the Barbican, and Blackfriars, to the south, leads to Ludgate Circus and Fleet Street.

◉ Sights

★ Museum of London

MUSEUM | FAMILY | If there's one place to absorb the history of London, from 450,000 BC to the present day, it's here. There are 7,000 objects to wonder at in all, including Oliver Cromwell's death mask, Queen Victoria's crinolines, Selfridges's art deco elevators, and an original door from the infamous Newgate Prison. The collection devoted to Roman London contains some extraordinary gems, including an astonishingly well-preserved floor mosaic uncovered just a few streets away. Innovative interactive displays abound, and there's also a fine schedule of temporary exhibitions. Don't miss the extraordinary Bronze Age and Roman artifacts unearthed during construction of the new Crossrail underground railway. ⊠ *150 London Wall, City of London* ☎ *020/7001–9844* ⊕ *www.museumoflondon.org.uk* ⊡ *Free* Ⓜ *Barbican, St. Paul's.*

★ St. Paul's Cathedral

RELIGIOUS SITE | For centuries, this iconic structure has represented London's spirit of survival and renewal, and it remains breathtaking, inside and out. The structure is Sir Christopher Wren's masterpiece, completed in 1710 after 35 years of building, and, much later, miraculously spared (mostly) by World War II bombs. It was actually Wren's third plan for the cathedral that was accepted, though he added the distinctive dome later. Up 163 spiral steps is the **Whispering Gallery**, with its incredible acoustic phenomenon; you whisper something to the wall on one side, and a second later it transmits clearly to the other side, 112 feet away. From the upper galleries you can walk outside for a spectacular panorama of London. As in Westminster Abbey, prominent people are buried inside the cathedral, including Wren himself, as well as the poet John Donne, the Duke of Wellington, and Admiral Lord Nelson.

The City

FARRINGDON

BARBICAN

THE CITY

HOLBORN

BLACKFRIARS

KEY
- **1** Sights
- **1** Restaurants
- **1** Hotels

Sights ▼	Restaurants ▼	Hotels ▼
1 Museum of London..... **D3**	1 City Social **G3**	1 The Ned.................. **F4**
2 St. Paul's Cathedral..... **D5**	2 Duck & Waffle **H3**	2 Vintry and Mercer **E5**
3 Tower Bridge............. **J7**	3 Simpson's Tavern **G4**	
4 Tower of London **I6**	4 Sweetings **E5**	

Free, 90-minute, guided tours take place Monday to Saturday at 10, 11, 1, and 2; book a place at the welcome desk (on the day of only). ⊠ *St. Paul's Churchyard, City of London* ☎ *020/7246–8350* ⊕ *www.stpauls.co.uk* ✉ *£20* ⊘ *Closed Sun. except for services* Ⓜ *St. Paul's.*

Tower Bridge

BRIDGE/TUNNEL | Despite its medieval appearance, Britain's most iconic bridge was actually built at the tail end of the Victorian age, first opening to traffic in 1894. Constructed of steel, then clothed in Portland stone, the Horace Jones masterpiece was built in the Gothic style that was highly popular at the time (and it nicely complements the Tower of London, next door). The bridge is famous for its enormous bascules—the 1,200-ton "arms" that open to allow large ships to glide beneath. This still happens several times per month (the website lists upcoming times), but when river traffic was dense, the bascules were raised up to 30 times a day. The **Tower Bridge Exhibition** is a family-friendly tour where you can discover how the bridge actually works before heading out onto the walkways for wonderful city views. ⊠ *Tower Bridge Rd., City of London* ☎ *020/7403–3761* ⊕ *www.towerbridge. org.uk* ✉ *From £10* Ⓜ *Tower Hill.*

★ Tower of London

CASTLE/PALACE | **FAMILY** | Nowhere else does London's history come to life so vividly as it does in this minicity of 20 towers that have housed a palace, barracks, the Royal Mint, archives, an armory, and even the Royal Menagerie. Conceived in 1078 by William the Conqueror, the Tower has been a place of imprisonment, torture, and execution for the realm's most notorious traitors and a few innocents as well. Allow at least three hours for exploring, and take time to stroll along the battlements. Highlights include the **Crown Jewels**, the **White Tower** (the oldest structure here, which includes the Armouries), the Medieval Palace, and **Bloody Tower**. Free

tours by the Yeoman Warders, better known as the Beefeaters (who also mind the Tower's ravens), depart every half hour from the main entrance. ■**TIP**→ **Buy tickets in advance whenever possible; write several months in advance to get free tickets to the 700-year-old Ceremony of the Keys (the nightly locking of main gates).** ⊠ *Tower Hill, City of London* ☎ *020/3166–6000* ⊕ *www.hrp.org.uk* ✉ *£28 (£25 online)* Ⓜ *Tower Hill.*

🍴 Restaurants

City Social

$$$$ | **MODERN BRITISH** | A largely corporate crowd comes here for the Manhattan-esque views of the City and chef Jason Atherton's masterful but straightforward cuisine. Impressed diners look out from level 24 of Tower 42 on a majestic panorama that takes in iconic buildings like the Gherkin and the Walkie Talkie. **Known for:** majestic panoramas of the City; gutsy steak and fish standards; suited financiers and corporate deal-maker crowd. $ *Average main: £34* ⊠ *Tower 42, 25 Old Broad St., City of London* ☎ *020/7877–7703* ⊕ *www.citysociallondon.com* ⊘ *Closed Sun. No lunch Sat.* Ⓜ *Liverpool St.*

Duck & Waffle

$$ | **MODERN BRITISH** | **FAMILY** | Zoom up to the 40th floor of 110 Bishopsgate and head straight for the cult signature dish of confit duck leg, Belgium waffle, fried duck egg, and mustard maple syrup for a taste of foodie bliss. Open 24/7, with spectacular panoramas of The City, you might satisfy the munchies with a foie gras breakfast, served all day, alongside streaky bacon and homemade Nutella or an Elvis PB&J waffle with banana brûlée. **Known for:** rare-to-London 24-hour service; awe-inspiring panoramas of London's skyline; eponymous duck-and-waffle dish. $ *Average main: £19* ⊠ *Heron Tower, 110 Bishopsgate, City of London* ☎ *020/3640–7310* ⊕ *www.duckandwaffle.com* Ⓜ *Liverpool St.*

Continued on page 136

THE TOWER OF LONDON

The Tower is a microcosm of the city itself—a sprawling, organic hodgepodge of buildings that inspires reverence and terror in equal measure. See the block on which Anne Boleyn was beheaded, marvel at the Crown Jewels, and pay homage to the ravens who keep the monarchy safe.

An architectural patchwork of time, the oldest building of the complex is the fairytale White Tower, conceived by William the Conqueror in 1078 as both a royal residence and a show of power to the troublesome Anglo-Saxons he had subdued at the Battle of Hastings. Today's Tower has seen everything, as a palace, barracks, a mint for producing coins, an armoury, and the Royal menagerie (home of the country's first elephant). The big draw is the stunning opulence of the Crown Jewels, kept on-site in the heavily fortified Jewel House. Most of all, though, the Tower is known for death: it's been a place of imprisonment, torture, and execution for the realm's most notorious traitors as well as its martyrs. These days, unless you count the killer admission fees, there are far less morbid activities taking place in the Tower, but it still breathes London's history and pageantry from its every brick and offers hours of exploration.

TOURING THE TOWER

Ticket Office

Outer Wall
Outer Ward

Dry Moat

Martin Tower

Waterloo Barracks

Chapel Royal of St. Peter ad Vincula

Jewel House

Inner Ward

The Fusillier Museum

Dry Moat

Tower Hill Rd

Tower Bridge Road

A100

Lower Thames St.

Beauchamp Tower

White Tower

Broad Arrow Tower

The Wall Walk

Western Entrance

Middle Tower

Bell Tower

Tower Green

Inmost Ward

New Armories Café

Bloody Tower

Wakefield Tower

Salt Tower

Tower Pier

Outer Wall

Water Lane

Lanthorn Tower

Traitors' Gate

Tower Wharf

Tower Bridge

River Thames

0 ── 75 yards

0 ── 75 meters

Entry to the Tower is via the **Western Entrance** and the **Middle Tower,** which feed into the outermost ring of the Tower's defenses.

Water Lane leads past the dread-inducing **Traitors' Gate,** the final point of entry for many Tower prisoners.

Toward the end of Water Lane, the **Lanthorn Tower** houses by night the ravens rumored to keep the kingdom safe, and by day a timely high-tech reconstruction of the Catholic Guy Fawkes's plot to blow up the Houses of Parliament in 1605.

The **Bloody Tower** earned its name as the apocryphal site of the murder of two young princes, Edward and Richard, who disappeared from the Tower after being put there in 1483 by their uncle, Richard III. Two little skeletons (now in Westminster Abbey) were found buried close to the White Tower in 1674 and are thought to be theirs.

The **Beauchamp Tower** housed upper-class miscreants: Latin graffiti about Lady Jane Grey can be glimpsed today on its walls.

GOLD DIGGER?

Keep your eyes peeled as you tour the Tower: according to one story, Sir John Barkstead, goldsmith and Lieutenant of the Tower under Cromwell, hid £20,000 in gold coins here before his arrest and execution at the Restoration of Charles II.

Like a prize gem set at the head of a royal crown, the **White Tower** is the centerpiece of the complex. Its four towers dominate the Inner Ward, a fitting and forbidding reminder of Norman strength at the time of the conquest of England.

Tower of London exterior

ROYAL BLING

The Crown of Queen Elizabeth, the Queen Mother, from 1937, contains the exotic 105-carat Koh-i-Noor (mountain of light) diamond.

Once inside the White Tower, head upstairs for the **Armouries,** where the biggest attraction, quite literally, is the suit of armor worn by a well-endowed Henry VIII. There is a matching outfit for his horse.

Other fascinating exhibits include the set of Samurai armor presented to James I in 1613 by the emperor of Japan, and the tiny set of armor worn by Henry VIII's young son Edward.

The **Jewel House** in **Waterloo Block** is the Tower's biggest draw, perfect for playing pick-your-favorite-crown from the wrong side of bulletproof glass. Not only are these crowns, staffs, and orbs encrusted with heavy-duty gems, they are invested with the authority of monarchical power in England, dating back to the 1300s.

Outside, pause at **Tower Green,** permanent departure point for those of noble birth. The hoi polloi were dispatched at nearby Tower Hill. The Tower's most famous female victims—Anne Boleyn, Margaret Countess of Salisbury, Catherine Howard, and Lady Jane Grey—all went this "priviledged" way.

Behind a well-kept square of grass stands the **Chapel Royal of St. Peter ad Vincula**, a delightful Tudor church and final resting place of six beheaded Tudor bodies. ■TIP➜ **Visitors are welcome for services and can also enter after 4:30 pm daily.**

The **Salt Tower**, reputedly the most haunted corner of the complex, marks the start of the **Wall Walk**, a bracing promenade along the stone spiral steps and battlements of the Tower that looks down on the trucks, taxis, and shimmer-

TIME KILLERS

Some prisoners managed to keep themselves plenty amused: Sir Walter Raleigh grew tobacco on Tower Green, and in 1561 suspected sorcerer Hugh Draper carved an intricate astronomical clock on the walls of his Salt Tower cell.

ing high-rises of modern London.

The Wall Walk ends at the **Martin Tower**, former home of the Crown Jewels and now host to the crowns and diamonds exhibition that explains the art of fashioning royal headwear and tells the story of some of the most famous stones.

On leaving the Tower, browse the **gift shop,** and wander the wharf that overlooks the Thames, leading to a picture-postcard view of Tower Bridge.

WHO ARE THE BEEFEATERS?

First of all, they're Yeoman Warders, but probably got the nickname "beefeater" from their position as Royal Bodyguards which entitled them to eat as much beef as they liked. Part of the "Yeoman of the Guard," started in the reign of Edmund IV, the warders have formed the Royal Bodyguard as far back as 1509 when Henry VIII left a dozen of the Yeoman of the Guard at the Tower to protect it.

Originally, the Yeoman Warders also served as jailers of the Tower, doubling as torturers when necessary. (So it would have been a Beefeater tightening the thumb screws, or ratchetting the rack another notch on some unfortunate prisoner. Smile nicely.) Today 36 Yeoman Warders (men and women since 2007), along with the Chief Yeoman Warder and the Yeoman Gaoler, live within the walls of the Tower with their families, in accommodations in the Outer Ward. They stand guard over the Tower, conduct tours, and lock up at 9:53 pm every night with the Ceremony of the Keys.

■ TIP→ **Free tickets to the Ceremony of the Keys are available by writing several months in advance; check the Tower Web site for details.**

HARK THE RAVENS!

Legend has it that should the hulking black ravens ever leave, the White Tower will crumble and the kingdom fall. Charles II, no doubt jumpy after his father's execution and the monarchy's short-term fall from grace, made a royal decree in 1662 that there should be at least six of the carrion-eating nasties present at all times. There have been some close calls. During World War II, numbers dropped to one, echoing the precarious fate of the war-wracked country. In 2005, two (of eight) died over Christmas when Thor—the most intelligent but also the largest bully of the bunch—killed new recruit Gundolf, named after the Tower's 1070 designer. Pneumonia put an end to Bran, leaving lifelong partner Branwen without her mate.

■ **DID YOU KNOW?** In 1981 a raven named Grog, perhaps seduced by his alcoholic moniker, escaped after 21 years at the Tower. Others have been banished for "conduct unbecoming."

The six that remain, each one identified by a colored band around a claw, are much loved for their fidelity (they mate for life) and their cheek (capable of 440 noises, they are witty and scolding mimics). It's not only the diet of blood-soaked biscuits, rabbit, and scraps from the mess kitchen that keeps them coming back. Their lifting feathers on one wing are trimmed, meaning they can manage the equivalent of a lop-sided airbound hobble but not much more. In situ they are a territorial lot, sticking to Tower Green and the White Tower, and lodging nightly by Wakefield Tower. They've had free front-row seats at all the most grisly moments in Tower history—Anne Boleyn's execution included.

■ TIP→ **Don't get too close to the ravens: they are prone to pecking and not particularly fond of humans, unless you are the Tower's Raven Master.**

AND WHAT ARE THEY WEARING?

A **pike** (or halberd), also known as a partisan, is the Yeoman Warder's weapon of choice. The Chief Warder carries a staff topped with a miniature silver model of the White Tower.

Anyone who refers to this as a costume will be lucky to leave the Tower with head still attached to body: this is the ceremonial uniform of the Yeoman Warders, and it comes at a cool £13,000 a throw.

This **Tudor-style ruff** helps date the ceremonial uniform, which was first worn in 1552.

The black Tudor **bonnet** is made of velvet; the blue undress consists of a felt top hat, with a single Tudor rose in the middle.

Insignia on a Yeoman Warder's upper right arm denote the rank he carried in the military.

The **medals** on a Yeoman Warder's chest are more than mere show: all of the men and women have served for at least 22 years in the armed forces.

This version of the **royal livery** bears the insignia of the current Queen ("E" for Elizabeth) but originally dates from Tudor times. The first letter changes according to the reigning monarch's Christian name; the second letter is always an "R" for *rex* (king) or *regina* (queen).

Slits in the **tunic** date from the times when Beefeaters were expected to ride a horse.

Red socks and **black patent shoes** are worn on special occasions. Visitors are more likely to see the regular blue undress, introduced in 1858 as the regular working dress of the Yeoman Warders.

The **red lines down the trousers** are a sign of the blood from the swords of the Yeoman Warders in their defense of the realm.

(IN)FAMOUS PRISONERS OF THE TOWER

Anne Boleyn   Lady Jane Grey   Sir Walter Raleigh

Sir Thomas More. A Catholic and Henry VIII's friend and chancellor, Sir Thomas refused to attend the coronation of Anne Boleyn (Henry VIII's second wife) or to recognize the multi-marrying king as head of the Church. Sent to the Tower for treason, More was beheaded in 1535.

Anne Boleyn. The first of Henry VIII's wives to be beheaded, Anne, who failed to provide the king with a son, was accused of sleeping with five men, including her own brother. All six got the chop in 1536. Her severed head was held up to the crowd, and her lips were said to be mouthing prayer.

Margaret, Countess of Salisbury. Not the best-known prisoner in her lifetime, she has a reputation today for haunting the Tower. And no wonder: the elderly 70-year-old was condemned by Henry VIII in 1541 for a potentially treacherous bloodline (she was the last Plantagenet princess) and hacked to death by the executioner after she refused to put her head on the block like a common traitor and attempted to run away.

Queen Catherine Howard. Henry VIII's fifth wife was locked up for high treason and infidelity and beheaded in 1542 at age 20. Ever eager to please, she spent her final night practicing how to lay her head on the block.

Lady Jane Grey. The nine-days-queen lost her head in 1554 at age 16. Her death was the result of sibling rivalry gone seriously wrong, when Protestant Edward VI slighted his Catholic sister Mary in favor of Lady Jane as heir, and Mary decided to have none of it.

Guy Fawkes. The Roman Catholic soldier who tried to blow up the Houses of Parliament and kill the king in the 1605 Gunpowder plot was first incarcerated in the chambers of the Tower, where King James I requested he be tortured in ever-worsening ways. Perhaps unsurprisingly, he confessed. He met his seriously grisly end in the Old Palace Yard at Westminster, where he was hung, drawn, and quartered in 1607.

Sir Walter Raleigh. Once a favorite of Elizabeth I, he offended her by secretly marrying her Maid of Honor and was chucked in the Tower. Later, as a conspirator against James I, he paid with his life. A frequent visitor to the Tower (he spent 13 years there in three stints), he managed to get the Bloody Tower enlarged on account of his wife and growing family. He was finally executed in 1618 in Old Palace Yard, Westminster.

Josef Jakobs. The last man to be executed in the Tower was caught as a spy when parachuting in from Germany and executed by firing squad in 1941. The chair he sat in when he was shot is preserved in the Royal Armouries' artifacts store.

FOR FURTHER EVIDENCE . . .

A trio of buildings in the Inner Ward, the **Bloody Tower, Beauchamp Tower,** and **Queen's House,** all with excellent views of the execution scaffold in Tower Green, are the heart of the Tower's prison accommodations and home to a permanent exhibition about notable inmates.

TACKLING THE TOWER (WITHOUT LOSING YOUR HEAD)

MAKING THE MOST OF YOUR TIME: Without doubt, the Tower is worth two to three hours. A full hour of that would be well spent by joining one of the Yeoman Warders' tours (included in admission). It's hard to better their insight, vitality, and humor—they are knights of the realm living their very own fairytale castle existence.

The Crown Jewels are worth the wait, the White Tower is essential, and the Medieval Palace and Bloody Tower should at least be breezed through.

■ TIP→ **It's best to visit on weekdays, when the crowds are smaller.**

WITH KIDS: The Tower's centuries-old cobblestones are not exactly stroller-friendly, but strollers are permitted inside most of the buildings. If you do bring one, be prepared to leave it temporarily unsupervised (the stroller, that is—not your child) outside the White Tower, which has no access. There are baby-changing facilities in the Brick Tower restrooms behind the Jewel House. Look for regular free children's events such as the Knight's school where children can have a go at jousting, sword-fighting, and archery.

■ TIP→ **Tell your child to find one of the Yeoman Warders if he or she should get lost; they will in turn lead him or her to the Byward Tower, which is where you should meet.**

IN A HURRY? If you have less than an hour, head down Wall Walk, through a succession of towers, which eventually spit you out at the Martin Tower. The view over modern London is quite a contrast.

TOURS: Tours given by a Yeoman Warder leave from the main entrance near Middle Tower every half-hour from 10–4, and last about an hour. Beefeaters give occasional 30-minute talks in the Lanthorn Tower about their daily lives. Both tours are free. Check website for talks and workshops.

Simpson's Tavern

$ | BRITISH | FAMILY | The City's oldest tavern and chop house was founded in 1757 and undoubtedly is every bit as raucous now as the day it opened. Approached via a cobbled alleyway, it draws diners who revel in the old boarding school surroundings and are eager to down oodles of claret and English tavern-style grub. **Known for:** lots of history, with past diners from diarist Samuel Pepys to Charles Dickens; signature stewed cheese on toast; charming but old-fashioned service. $ *Average main: £12* ✉ *Ball Court, 38½ Cornhill, City of London* ☎ *020/7626–9985* ⊕ *www.simpsonstavern.co.uk* ⊘ *Closed weekends. No dinner* Ⓜ *Bank.*

Sweetings

$$$ | SEAFOOD | Established in 1889 not far from St. Paul's Cathedral, little seems to have changed since the height of the British Empire at this quirky eatery. Although there are some things Sweetings doesn't do (dinner, reservations, coffee, or weekends), it does, mercifully, do great seafood. **Known for:** fresh Billingsgate fish served at raised linen-covered counters; tankards of "Black Velvet" Guinness and champagne; popular potted shrimp and Dover sole. $ *Average main: £30* ✉ *39 Queen Victoria St., City of London* ☎ *020/7248–3062* ⊕ *www.sweetingsrestaurant.co.uk* ⊘ *Closed weekends. No dinner* Ⓜ *Mansion House.*

🛏 Hotels

★ The Ned

$$ | HOTEL | Bursting with eye-catching art deco design and achingly hip interiors, the Ned is as close to the glamour of the 1920s Jazz Age as you'll find in contemporary London. **Pros:** amazing variety of bars and restaurants, all of high quality; rooftop pool with views of St. Paul's Cathedral; beautiful interiors in all rooms. **Cons:** location in the City means public spaces get very busy after work; neighborhood is deserted on weekends; also doubles as a private members' clubs, so the vibe can get snooty. $ *Rooms from: £195* ✉ *27 Poultry, City of London* ☎ *020/3828–2000* ⊕ *www.thened.com* ⇨ *252 rooms* ❍❘ *No meals* Ⓜ *Bank.*

Vintry and Mercer

$$ | HOTEL | Located close to the London Stock Exchange, merchant banks, hedgefunds, and the City's oldest guilds, the luxury boutique hotel Vintry and Mercer offers a nod to tradition then proceeds to deliver a chic, colorful, and contemporary experience that stands out in this neighborhood. **Pros:** rooms with gorgeous fabrics and chic wallpapers; excellent on-site izakaya restaurant; some rooms have stunning views of the City. **Cons:** predominantly business crowd dominates the bar and restaurant; neighborhood is extremely quiet on weekends; slightly removed from the sights of the West End. $ *Rooms from: £191* ✉ *19–20 Garlick Hill, City of London* ☎ *020/3908–8088* ⊕ *www.vintryandmercer.com* ⇨ *92 rooms* ❍❘ *No meals* Ⓜ *Monument.*

▼ Nightlife

BARS

★ The Blackfriar

BARS/PUBS | FAMILY | A step from Blackfriars Tube station, this spectacular pub has an Arts and Crafts interior that is entertainingly, satirically ecclesiastical, with inlaid mother-of-pearl, wood carvings, stained glass, and marble pillars all over the place. Under finely lettered temperance tracts on view just below the reliefs of monks, fairies, and friars, there is a nice group of ales on tap from independent brewers. The 20th-century poet Sir John Betjeman once led a successful campaign to save the pub from demolition. ✉ *174 Queen Victoria St., City of London* ☎ *020/7236–5474* ⊕ *www.nicholsons-pubs.co.uk* Ⓜ *Blackfriars.*

★ Jerusalem Tavern
BARS/PUBS | FAMILY | Loved by Londoners and owned by the well-respected St. Peter's Brewery in Suffolk, the Jerusalem Tavern is one-of-a-kind: small, historic, atmospheric, and endearingly eccentric. Antique Delft-style tiles meld with wood and concrete in a converted watchmaker and jeweler's shop dating back to the 18th century. The beer, both bottled and on tap, is some of the best available anywhere in London. It's often busy, especially after work, but it's closed on weekends. ⌂ *55 Britton St., Clerkenwell* ☎ *020/7490–4281* ⊕ *www.stpetersbrewery.co.uk/london-pub* ⌕ *Closed weekends* Ⓜ *Farringdon.*

Ye Olde Mitre
BARS/PUBS | FAMILY | Hidden off the side of 8 Hatton Gardens (and notoriously hard to find), this cozy pub's roots go back to 1546, though it was rebuilt around 1782. Originally built for the staff of the Bishop of Ely, whose London residence was next door, it remained officially part of Cambridgeshire until the 20th century. Elizabeth I was once spotted dancing round a cherry tree here with a dashing young beau. Now it's a friendly little labyrinthine place, with a fireplace, well-kept ales, wooden beams, and traditional bar snacks. ⌂ *1 Ely Ct., City of London* ⌖ *Off 8 Hatton Gardens* ☎ *020/7405–4751* ⊕ *www.yeoldemitreholborn.co.uk* ⊙ *Closed weekends* Ⓜ *Chancery La.*

⦿ Performing Arts

★ Barbican Centre
ART GALLERIES—ARTS | FAMILY | Opened in 1982, the Barbican is an enormous Brutalist concrete maze that Londoners either love or hate—but its importance to the cultural life of the capital is beyond dispute. At the largest performing arts center in Europe, you could listen to Elgar, see 1960s photography, and catch German animation with live accompaniment, all in one day. The main concert hall, known for its acoustics, is most famous as the home of the London

Symphony Orchestra. The Barbican is also a frequent host to the BBC Symphony Orchestra. Architecture tours take place several times a week. ⌂ *Silk St., City of London* ☎ *020/7638–8891* ⊕ *www.barbican.org.uk* ⌑ *Art exhibits free–£15, cinema from £6, theater and music from £10, tours £13* Ⓜ *Barbican.*

East London

Made famous by Dickens and infamous by Jack the Ripper, East London is one of London's most enduringly evocative neighborhoods, rich in popular history, architectural gems, and artists' studios. Since the early 1990s, hip gallerists, designers, and new-media entrepreneurs have colonized its handsome Georgian buildings and converted industrial lofts. Today, this collection of neighborhoods lays claim to being the city's hippest area.

GETTING HERE
The London Overground, with stops at Shoreditch High Street, Hoxton, Whitechapel, Dalston Junction, Dalston Kingsland, London Fields, Hackney Central, and Hackney Wick is the easiest way to reach East London. Alternatively, the best Tube stations to use are Old Street on the Northern Line, Bethnal Green on the Central Line, and Liverpool Street on the Metropolitan and Circle lines.

⦿ Sights

★ Christ Church, Spitalfields
RELIGIOUS SITE | This is the 1729 masterpiece of Sir Christopher Wren's associate Nicholas Hawksmoor, one of his six London churches and an example of English baroque at its finest. It was commissioned as part of Parliament's 1711 "Fifty New Churches" Act, passed in response to the influx of immigrants with the idea of providing for the religious needs of the "godless thousands"—and to help ensure they joined the Church of England, as opposed to such nonconformist

East London

Sights ▼

1 Christ Church,
Spitalfields.................**C5**

2 Dennis Severs'
House **B5**

3 Queen Elizabeth
Olympic Park............**E1**

4 Regent's Canal **A2**

5 Whitechapel Gallery **C6**

Restaurants ▼

1 E. Pellicci **D4**

2 Gunpowder................**C6**

3 Lyle's **C4**

Hotels ▼

1 Andaz **D7**

2 The Hoxton
Shoreditch...............**B4**

3 Town Hall Hotel
and Apartments..........**E3**

denominations as the Protestant Huguenots. (It must have worked; you can still see gravestones with epitaphs in French in the crypt.) As the local silk industry declined, the church fell into disrepair, and by 1958 the structure was crumbling, with the looming prospect of demolition. But after 25 years—longer than it took to build the church—and a huge local fund-raising effort, the structure was meticulously restored and is a joy to behold, from the colonnaded Doric portico and tall spire to its soaring, heavily ornamented plaster ceiling. Its excellent acoustics make it a superb concert venue. Tours that take you "backstage" to the many hidden rooms and passages, from the tower to the vaults, are offered by appointment. There's also a café in the crypt. ⊠ *Commercial St., Spitalfields* ☎ *020/7377–2440* ⊕ *www.ccspits.org* ✉ *Free, tours £50 per hr* ⊘ *Closed Sat.* Ⓜ *Overground: Shoreditch High St.*

★ Dennis Severs' House

HOUSE | The remarkable interiors of this extraordinary time machine of a house are the creation of Dennis Severs (1948–99), a performer-designer-scholar from Escondido, California, who dedicated his life to restoring this Georgian terraced house. More than that, he created "still-life dramas" using sight, sound, and smell to evoke the world of a fictitious family of Huguenot silk weavers, the Jervises, who might have inhabited the house between 1728 and 1914. Each of the 10 rooms has a distinctive compelling atmosphere that encourages visitors to become lost in another time, deploying evocative design details like rose-laden Victorian wallpaper, Jacobean paneling, Georgian wing-back chairs, baroque carved ornaments, rich "Catholic" wall colors downstairs, and more sedate "Protestant" shades upstairs. The Silent Night candlelight tour offered Monday, Wednesday, and Friday evenings, a stroll through the rooms with no talking allowed, is the most theatrical and memorable way to experience the house. The Exclusive Silent Night visits, which conclude with champagne or mulled wine by the fire and a chat with the curators, are available one night per month (more frequently near the Christmas holiday), and private group visits can also be arranged. ⊠ *18 Folgate St., Shoreditch* ☎ *020/7247–4013* ⊕ *www.dennissevershouse.co.uk* ✉ *£10 Sun. and Mon., £15 Mon., Wed., and Fri. evenings* ⊘ *Closed Tues., Thurs., and Sat.* Ⓜ *Overground: Shoreditch High St.*

★ Queen Elizabeth Olympic Park

CITY PARK | **FAMILY** | Built for the London 2012 Olympic and Paralympic games, this 560-acre parkland still boasts some of the city's best sporting arenas. The Stadium, site of the London 2012 athletics competitions, is now home to local soccer team Westham United; it also hosts major athletic events. In addition, it's open for behind-the-scenes tours; check the website for dates. You can try four types of cycling (track, road-racing, BMX, and mountain-biking) at the Lee Valley VeloPark or go for a swim in the magnificent pool within the London Aquatics Centre. The ArcelorMittal Orbit, an enormous sculpture, is well worth a visit—the views across London from the top are terrific. Thrill-seekers have a couple of options when it comes to getting back down: a gasp-inducing slide that twists its way around the outside of the structure (art buffs might recognize it as the work of Belgian artist Carsten Höller) or via vertical rappelling (available on selected dates, advance booking essential). ⊠ *East End* ☎ *080/0072–2110* ⊕ *www.queenelizabetholympicpark.co.uk* ✉ *From £13, stadium tours £19* Ⓜ *Stratford, Hackney Wick, Pudding Mill Lane, Leyton.*

★ Regent's Canal

BODY OF WATER | The 19th-century waterway known as Regent's Canal officially starts in Little Venice in West London, but you'll find this quirky section east of City Road Basin. Join the towpath, where horses once walked as they pulled barges carrying all manner of cargo, at Wharf Road in Islington (N1) then head east on foot or by bike to experience the East End from an unusual perspective. What was once a no-go area is now a route lined with trendy cafés, floating bookshops, and a distinct community of water-dwelling Londoners. The Regent's Canal runs through Hackney, before heading south through Bethnal Green and Mile End, ending up at Limehouse Basin and the River Thames. Or you can continue eastward by turning off along the Hertford Union Canal at Victoria Park, a route that eventually leads to the Queen Elizabeth Olympic Park. ⊠ *East End.*

★ Whitechapel Gallery

MUSEUM | Founded in 1901, this internationally renowned gallery mounts exhibitions that rediscover overlooked masters and showcase tomorrow's legends. Painter and leading exponent of abstract expressionism Jackson Pollock was exhibited here in the 1950s as was pop artist Robert Rauschenberg in the 1960s; the 1970s saw a young David Hockney's first solo show. The exhibitions continue to be on the cutting edge of contemporary art. The gallery also hosts talks, film screenings, workshops, and other events; tours of local galleries take place on the first Thursday of every month. Pick up a free East London art map to help you plan your visit to the area. ⊠ *77–82 Whitechapel High St., Whitechapel* ☎ *020/7522–7888* ⊕ *www. whitechapelgallery.org* ☉ *Closed Mon.* Ⓜ *Aldgate East.*

🍴 Restaurants

E. Pellicci

$ | **CAFÉ** | **FAMILY** | It's all Cockney banter and full English breakfasts at this tiny family-run café and onetime gangsters' lair near Brick Lane and Columbia Road markets. A rowdy hole-in-the-wall, it serves the greasy fry-ups Londoners still adore, like copious scrambled eggs, bacon, sausages, baked beans, toast, tomatoes, fried mushrooms, black pudding, cabbage 'n' mash, and scorching hot tea. **Known for:** full cast of East End Cockney characters; copious full English breakfasts and builders' brew tea; cash-only cheap dishes. ⑤ *Average main: £8* ⊠ *332 Bethnal Green Rd., Bethnal Green* ☎ *020/7739–4873* ⊕ *www.epellicci.com* ▭ *No credit cards* ☉ *Closed Sun. and Aug. No dinner* Ⓜ *Bethnal Green.*

Gunpowder

$ | **INDIAN** | Eschew the myriad copy-and-paste curry houses of Brick Lane and opt instead for this broom cupboard–size Spitalfields restaurant serving flawless small plate Indian cuisine. The charming waitstaff is happy to offer guidance when it comes to the menu, with its highly original takes on authentic flavor combinations from the subcontinent. **Known for:** ingredients not normally found on Indian menus, such as duck or seabass; lines out the door, thanks to the no-reservations policy; rasam ke bomb snack, a puff of spiced potato served atop a flavorful Bloody Mary–style shot. ⑤ *Average main: £11* ⊠ *11 White's Row, Spitalfields* ⊕ *www.gunpowderlondon.com* ☉ *Closed Sun.* Ⓜ *Liverpool St.*

★ Lyle's

$$ | **MODERN BRITISH** | Globally acclaimed Brit chef and co-owner James Lowe forsakes heavy sauces and sorcery at this stripped-back, informal British dining mecca in Shoreditch. Stark but highly inventive locally sourced dishes may include house-cured cod with radiant nasturtium flowers or 24-hour Cornish Helford Estuary monkfish with wood sorrel and pick-your-own East Sussex greengages. **Known for:** highly modern and airy dining space; serious new-wave British neo-bistronomy; excellent cheese plates and wines by the glass. ⑤ *Average main: £19* ⊠ *Tea Bldg., 56 Shoreditch High St., East End* ⊹ *Entrance on Bethnal Green Rd.* ☎ *020/3011–5911* ⊕ *www. lyleslondon.com* ☉ *Closed Sun. and bank holiday Mon.* Ⓜ *Shoreditch High St.*

Afternoon Tea in London

So, what is Afternoon Tea, exactly? Well, it means real loose-leaf tea—Earl Grey, English Breakfast, Ceylon, Darjeeling, or Assam—brewed in a fine bone china or porcelain pot, and served with fine bone cups and saucers, milk or lemon, and silver spoons, taken between noon and 6 pm. Tea goers dress smartly (though not ostentatiously), and conversation by tradition should avoid politics and religion. Here are some top places in town to head:

Hands-down, the superglam **Savoy** on the Strand offers one of the most beautiful settings for tea. The Thames Foyer, a symphony of grays and golds centered around a winter garden wrought-iron gazebo, is just the place for the house pianist to accompany you as you enjoy the award-winning house teas along with finger sandwiches, homemade scones, and *yumptious* pastries.

Setting the standard in its English Tea Room for some of London's best-known traditional teas, **Brown's Hotel**, at 33 Albermarle Street—charmingly set in a classic Mayfair town house—offers Afternoon Tea for £55 or, if you wish to splash out, Champagne Tea for £65.

Moving west, you can sit looking out onto fab lawns amid mini potted orange trees at **The Orangery** in Prince William and Kate's London pad, Kensington Palace, inside resplendent Kensington Gardens. Afternoon Tea is £28 and a suitably Royal Afternoon Tea (with a glass of Laurent-Perrier) is £38.

Alternatively, add spice to your experience by trying a popular Moroccan-style Afternoon Tea at the souk-chic tearoom at **Momo** off Regent Street, where you'll enjoy sweet mint tea in colorful glass cups plus scones with fig jam, Maghrebian pastries, Moroccan chicken wraps, and honey-and-nut-rich Berber-style crêpes.

Finally, for frilly trompe l'oeil grandeur, few can compete with Afternoon Tea at **The Ritz** on Piccadilly. It's served in the impressive Palm Court, replete with marble tables, Louis XVI chaises, resplendent bouquets, and musical accompaniment: a true taste of Edwardian London in the 21st century. Afternoon Tea is £54 and Champagne Tea £81. Reserve a few months ahead and remember to wear a jacket and tie.

3

London EAST LONDON

Hotels

Andaz

$$ | **HOTEL** | Swanky and upscale, this hotel sports a modern masculine design, and novel check-in procedure—instead of standing at a desk, guests sit in a lounge while a staff member with a tablet takes their information. **Pros:** nice attention to detail; no standing in line to check in; complimentary "healthy minibars" are stocked with nuts, fruit, and yogurt. **Cons:** sparse interior design is not for all; rates rise significantly for midweek stays; busy, sometimes hectic neighborhood. ⑤ *Rooms from: £240* ✉ *40 Liverpool St., East End* ☎ *020/7961–1234, 800/492–8804 in U.S.* ⊕ *www.andaz.hyatt.com* 🛏 *282 rooms* ⦿ *No meals* Ⓜ *Liverpool St.*

★ The Hoxton Shoreditch

$$ | HOTEL | The design throughout this trendy East London lodging is contemporary—but not so modern as to be absurd; in keeping with a claim to combine a country-lodge lifestyle with true urban living, a fire crackles in the lobby. **Pros:** cool vibe; neighborhood known for funky galleries and boutiques; huge weekend discounts. **Cons:** price skyrockets during the week; away from major tourist sights; cheapest rooms are called "shoeboxes" for a reason. Ⓢ *Rooms from: £149* ✉ *81 Great Eastern St., East End* ☎ *020/7550–1000* ⊕ *www.thehoxton.com* ⇌ *210 rooms* ❍ *Free breakfast* Ⓜ *Shoreditch High St.*

Town Hall Hotel and Apartments

$$$ | HOTEL | An art deco town hall, abandoned in the early 1980s and turned into a chic hotel 30 years later, is now a lively and stylish place, with the best of the building's elegant original features intact. **Pros:** beautifully designed; lovely staff; big discounts on weekends. **Cons:** the area is far from the major sights; a 15-minute Tube ride from central London; some rooms choose style over function. Ⓢ *Rooms from: £198* ✉ *Patriot Sq., Bethnal Green, East End* ☎ *020/7871–0460* ⊕ *www.townhallhotel.com* ⇌ *98 rooms* ❍ *Free breakfast* Ⓜ *Bethnal Green, Overground: Cambridge Heath.*

▼ Nightlife

BARS

Callooh Callay

BARS/PUBS | Cocktails are tasty, well-executed classics, and there's also a selection of unique instant-classics at this eccentric Hoxton bar where the bells and whistles are left to the decor. ✉ *65 Rivington St., Hoxton* ☎ *020/7739–4781* ⊕ *www.calloohcallaybar.com* Ⓜ *Old St.*

The Ten Bells

BARS/PUBS | FAMILY | Although the number of bells in its name has varied between 8 and 12, depending on how many bells were used by neighboring Christ Church, Spitalfields, this pub retains it original mid-Victorian interior and original tiles, including a frieze depicting the area's French Huguenot silk weaving tradition on the north wall and particularly fine floral tiling on two others. Urban legend says that Jack the Ripper's third victim, Annie Chapman, had a drink here before meeting her gory end. The pub is also depicted in Alan Moore's acclaimed graphic novel *From Hell*. ✉ *84 Commercial St., Spitalfields* ☎ *020/7247–7532* ⊕ *www.tenbells.com* Ⓜ *Liverpool St.*

DANCE CLUBS

★ Cafe Oto

MUSIC CLUBS | A relaxed café by day, and London's leading venue for experimental music by night, Cafe Oto is a Dalston institution. Its programming of free jazz, avant-garde electronica, and much more is enough of a draw that it regularly sells out, with music fans steaming up the windows and spilling out onto the pavement and road outside to smoke during breaks. Healthy Persian-inspired food is served in the daytime, before customers are kicked out at 5 pm to make way for sound checks. It's open as a bar (no cover) on nights when no concerts are taking place. ✉ *18–22 Ashwin St., Dalston* ⊕ *www.cafeoto.co.uk* Ⓜ *Overground: Dalston Junction.*

🛍 Shopping

CLOTHING

★ Blue Mountain School

CLOTHING | It's hard to think of somewhere more East London than Blue Mountain School, a building that comprises a fashion, furniture, and accessories archive (the focus at the boutique is slow fashion and homewares by the likes of Anecho, Geoffrey B. Small, and Amy Revier); a gallery with changing contemporary exhibits; a listening room; and a tiny chef's table restaurant from Nuno Mendes, of Chiltern Firehouse fame. Around the corner at 28 Old Nichol Street is Hostem, a more traditional format boutique selling men's and women's garments and footwear by brands such as P.R. Patterson, Casey Casey, and Visvim. This might all sound offputtingly hip, but give it a chance; it's a beautifully curated shopping experience, albeit one that will make considerable demands on your wallet. The store also operates a three-bedroom guesthouse in a converted Georgian town house in Whitechapel. ✉ *9 Chance St., Shoreditch* ☎ *020/7739–9733* ⊕ *www.bluemountain.school* Ⓜ *Overground: Shoreditch High St.*

Rokit

CLOTHING | Magazine and music stylists love these two premises along Brick Lane that carry everything from handbags and ball gowns to jeans, military garb, and Western wear. The ever-changing stock spans the 1930s to the 1990s. There are also branches in Camden and Covent Garden. ✉ *101 and 107 Brick La., Spitalfields* ☎ *020/7375–3864* ⊕ *www.rokit.co.uk* Ⓜ *Overground: Shoreditch High St.*

HOUSEHOLD GOODS

Labour & Wait

HOUSEHOLD ITEMS/FURNITURE | Although mundane items like colanders and clothespins may not sound like ideal souvenirs, this shop (something of a hipster heaven selling both new and vintage items) will make you reconsider. The owners are on a mission to revive retro, functional British household goods, such as enamel kitchenware, genuine feather dusters, bread bins, bottle brushes, and traditional Welsh blankets. ✉ *85 Redchurch St., Shoreditch* ☎ *020/7729–6253* ⊕ *www.labourandwait.co.uk* ⊘ *Closed Mon.* Ⓜ *Overground: Shoreditch High St.*

MUSIC

Rough Trade East

MUSIC STORES | Although many London record stores are struggling, this veteran indie-music specialist in the Old Truman Brewery seems to have gotten the formula right. The spacious surroundings are as much a hangout as a shop, complete with a stage for live gigs and a café. There's another branch on Talbot Road in Notting Hill. ✉ *Dray Walk, Old Truman Brewery, 91 Brick La., Spitalfields* ☎ *020/7392–7788* ⊕ *www.roughtrade.com* Ⓜ *Liverpool St. Overground: Shoreditch High St.*

STREET MARKETS

★ Broadway Market

SHOPPING NEIGHBORHOODS | This parade of shops in hipster-centric Hackney (north of Regent's Canal) is worth visiting for the specialty bookshops, independent boutiques, organic cafés, neighborhood restaurants, and even a traditional (but now rare) pie-and-mash shop. But wait for Saturday (9–5), when it really comes into its own with a farmers' market and more than 100 street-food and produce stalls rivaling those of south London's famed Borough Market. Artisanal breads, cheeses, pastries, organic meats, waffles, fruit and vegetables, seafood, and international food offerings: this is foodie heaven. There are also stalls selling vintage clothes, crafts, jewelry, and more. ✉ *Broadway Market, Hackney* ⊕ *www.broadwaymarket.co.uk* Ⓜ *London Fields.*

★ Columbia Road Flower Market

OUTDOOR/FLEA/GREEN MARKETS | London's premier flower market is about as pretty and photogenic as they come, with more than 50 stalls selling flowers, shrubs, bulbs, and trees—everything from bedding plants to 10-foot banana trees—as well as garden tools, pots, and accessories at competitive prices. The stallholders' patter is part of the fun. It's on Sunday only, and it's all over by 3 pm. Columbia Road itself is lined with 60 interesting independent shops purveying art, fashion, furnishings (most of which are only open on weekends), and the local cafés are superb. ✉ *Columbia Rd., Hoxton* ⊕ *www.columbiaroad.info* ⊘ *Market closed Mon.–Sat.* Ⓜ *Old St. Overground: Hoxton.*

Old Spitalfields Market

OUTDOOR/FLEA/GREEN MARKETS | Once the East End's wholesale fruit and vegetable market and now restored to its original architectural splendor, this fine example of a Victorian market hall is at the center of the area's gentrified revival. The original building is largely occupied by shops (mostly upscale brands like Rag & Bone, Lululemon, and Superga, but some independents like trendy homeware-and-fashion purveyor the Mercantile), with traders' stalls in the courtyard. A modern shopping precinct under a Norman Foster–designed glass canopy adjoins the old building and holds approximately 70 traders' stalls. You may have to wade through a certain number of stalls selling cheap imports and tacky T-shirts to find the good stuff, which includes vintage and new clothing, handmade rugs and jewelry, hand-carved toy trains, vintage maps, unique baby clothes, rare vinyl, and cakes. Thursday is for antiques; Friday for a biweekly record fair; while weekends offer a little of everything. The Kitchens, 10 central dining venues showcasing small, independent chefs and restaurants, provide fresh takes on Mexican, Japanese, and other world cuisines. There are also indie street food stalls and some superior chain outlets. ⊠ *16 Horner Sq., Brushfield St., Spitalfields* ⊕ *www. oldspitalfieldsmarket.com* Ⓜ *Liverpool St. Overground: Shoreditch High St.*

South of the Thames

This area is a magnet for tourists and residents alike, with attractions that include the IWM London, the Southbank Centre (Europe's largest arts center), and the gastronomic delight that is Borough Market.

A borough of the City of London since 1327, Southwark first became well known for its inns (the pilgrims in Chaucer's *A Canterbury Tale* set off from one), theaters, prisons, tanneries, and brothels, as well as entertainments such as cockfighting. For four centuries, this was a sort of border town outside the city walls (and jurisdiction) where Londoners went to let their hair down and behave badly. Originally, you were just as likely to see a few bouts of bearbaiting at the Globe as you were Shakespeare's most recent work. But now that south London encompasses a world-class museum, high-caliber art, music, film, and theater venues, as well as an aquarium, a historic warship, two popular food markets, and greatly improved transportation links, this neighborhood has become one of London's leading destinations.

GETTING HERE

For the South Bank, use Embankment on the District, Circle, Northern, and Bakerloo lines and walk across the Golden Jubilee Bridges; or Waterloo on the Northern, Jubilee, and Bakerloo lines, from where it's a 10-minute walk. London Bridge on the Northern and Jubilee lines is five minutes from Borough Market and Southwark Cathedral. The station also serves Bermondsey Street, although, confusingly, the next stop on the Jubilee Line is called Bermondsey. Brixton has its own stop on the Victoria Line.

◉ Sights

★ Borough Market

MARKET | There's been a market in Borough since Roman times, and this latest incarnation, spread under the arches and railroad tracks leading to London Bridge Station, is where some of the city's best artisanal food producers set up stalls. Fresh coffees, gorgeous cheeses, chocolates, and baked goods complement the organically farmed meats, fresh fish, condiments, fruits, and vegetables.

Don't make any other lunch plans for the day; this is where celebrity chef Jamie Oliver's scallop man cooks them up fresh at Shellseekers, and Ginger Pig's rare-breed sausages sizzle on grills, while for the sweets lover there are chocolates, preserves, and Whirld's artisanal confectionery, as well as 18 restaurants and cafés, most above average. The Market Hall hosts workshops, tastings, and demonstrations, and also acts as a greenhouse. The market is open Wednesday and Thursday 10–5, Friday 10–6, and Saturday 8–5, with only stalls for hot food and produce on Monday and Tuesday 10–5.

On weekends, a separate, highly regarded market specializing in produce and street food operates on nearby Maltby Street. It was originally established by eight breakaway Borough Market traders. Stalls include African Volcano, purveyors of Mozambique-style hot sauces and marinades, and Raclette Brothers' superb melted cheese. ⊠ *8 Southwark St., Borough* ☎ *020/7402–1002* ⊕ *www.boroughmarket.org.uk* ⊗ *Closed Sun.* Ⓜ *London Bridge.*

★ **IWM London**

MUSEUM | **FAMILY** | Despite its name, the cultural venue formerly known as the Imperial War Museum (one of five IWM branches around the country) does not glorify either Empire or bloodshed but emphasizes understanding through conveying the impact of 20th- and 21st-century warfare on citizens and soldiers alike. A dramatic six-story atrium at the main entrance encloses an impressive amount of hardware—including a Battle of Britain Spitfire, a German V2 rocket, the remains of a car blown up in post-invasion Iraq, tanks, guns, and submarines—along with accompanying interactive material and a café. The First World War galleries explore the wartime experience on both the home and fighting fronts, with the most comprehensive collection on the subject in the world—some 1,300 objects ranging from uniforms, equipment, and weapons to letters and diaries. Three permanent exhibitions in the Second World War galleries shed light on that conflict: an extensive and haunting Holocaust exhibition; *A Family In Wartime,* which documents the story of one London family living through

the Blitz; and *Turning Points 1934–1945,* which relates key moments in the conflict to objects on display. *Peace and Security 1945–2015* looks at more contemporary hostilities, including the Cold War, Iraq, Afghanistan, and Kosovo. Other galleries are devoted to works relating to conflicts from World War I to the present day by painters, poets, documentary filmmakers, and photographers. James Bond fans won't want to miss the intriguing Secret War Gallery, which charts the work of secret agents. ⊠ *Lambeth Rd., South Bank* ☎ *020/7416–5000* ⊕ *www.iwm.org.uk* ⊠ *Free (charge for special exhibitions)* Ⓜ *Lambeth North.*

★ **London Eye**

VIEWPOINT | **FAMILY** | To mark the start of the new millennium, architects David Marks and Julia Barfield devised an instant icon that allows Londoners and visitors alike to see the city from a completely new perspective. The giant Ferris wheel was the largest cantilevered observation wheel ever built at the time, and remains one of the city's tallest structures. The 25-minute slow-motion ride inside one of the enclosed passenger capsules is so smooth you'd hardly know you were suspended over the Thames. On a clear day you can see up to 25 miles, with a bird's-eye view of London's most famous landmarks as you circle 360 degrees. For an extra £10, you can save even more time with a Fast Track flight (check in 15 minutes before your "departure"). ■**TIP→ Buy your ticket online to avoid the long lines and get a 15% discount.** ⊠ *Jubilee Gardens, South Bank* ☎ *0871/781–3000* ⊕ *www.londoneye.com* ⊠ *From £27; cruise package from £39 (online only)* Ⓜ *Waterloo.*

★ **Shakespeare's Globe**

ARTS VENUE | **FAMILY** | This spectacular theater is a replica of Shakespeare's open-roof, wood-and-thatch Globe Playhouse (built in 1599 and burned down in 1613), where most of the Bard's greatest works premiered. American

South of the Thames

A | **B** | **C** | **D** | **E**

Temple Ⓤ · Victoria Embankment
River Thames
Northumberland Ave.
Charing Cross Station
Ⓤ Embankment
Golden Jubilee Bridges
Southbank Centre
Royal National Theatre
Bernie Spain Gdns.
②
Upper Ground
Cornwall Rd.
Stamford St.
Hayward Gallery
Royal Festival Hall
The Queen's Walk
Jubilee Gdns.
Belvedere Rd.
Victoria Embankment
Hatfields
Roupell St.
③
York Rd.
Waterloo Ⓤ
Ⓤ Westminster
Waterloo Station
Southwark Ⓤ
Big Ben
Westminster Br.
The Cut
Houses of Parliament
NEWINGTON
Pocack St.
Lambeth Palace Rd.
Royal St.
Westminster Br. Rd.
Baylis Rd.
Waterloo Rd.
Webber St.
Blackfriars Rd.
Ⓤ Lambeth North
Archbishop's Park
Hercules Rd.
Borough Rd.
Lambeth Palace
Lambeth Rd.
London Rd.
LAMBETH
Old Paradise St.
Lambeth Walk
Walnut Tree Walk
Kennington Rd.
Brook Dr.
St. George's Rd.
②
ELEPHANT & CASTLE
Walcott Sq.
Hayles St.
Elephant & Castle Ⓤ
Monkton St.
Lambeth Walk Open Space

KEY
① Sights
① Restaurants
① Hotels

Sights ▼
1 Borough Market **H4**
2 IWM London **C6**
3 London Eye **B3**
4 Shakespeare's Globe... **G2**
5 Southwark Cathedral... **H4**
6 Tate Modern............. **F3**
7 The View from
The Shard................ **H4**

Restaurants ▼
1 Casse-Croûte............. **I6**
2 José **I6**
3 Padella **H4**

Hotels ▼
1 Church Street Hotel **G7**
2 Sea Containers
London................... **E2**
3 The Shangri-La
Hotel at the Shard **H4**

At Shakespeare's Globe theater, you can watch the works of the Bard performed like they would've been in his day.

actor and director Sam Wanamaker worked ceaselessly for several decades to raise funds for the theater's reconstruction 200 yards from its original site, using authentic materials and techniques, a dream that was realized in 1997. "Groundlings"—patrons with £5 standing-only tickets—are not allowed to sit during the performance. Fortunately, you can reserve an actual seat on any one of the theater's three levels, but you will want to rent a cushion for £2 (or bring your own) to soften the backless wooden benches. Forty-minute tours of the theater are offered every half-hour most days until 5 pm (unless there's a matinee performance or other major event, when they're offered until noon). ✉ 21 New Globe Walk, Bankside ☎ 020/7401–9919 general info ⊕ www.shakespearesglobe.com ✉ Globe Theatre tour £17; Bankside tour £14; Wanamaker tour £14; Globe performances £5 (standing), from £19 (seated); Wanamaker performances £10 (standing), from £20 (seated) ☙ No Globe performances mid-Oct.–mid-Apr.; no Wanamaker Playhouse performances mid-Apr.–mid.-Oct. Ⓜ London Bridge; Mansion House, then cross Southwark Bridge.

Southwark Cathedral

RELIGIOUS SITE | Pronounced "Suthuck," this is the oldest Gothic church in London, parts of it dating back to the 12th century. It remains off-the-beaten track, despite being the site of some remarkable memorials and a concert program that offers free half-hour organ recitals at 1:10 pm every Monday (except in August and December) and classical music at 3:15 pm every Tuesday during the school year. Originally the priory church of St. Mary Overie (as in "over the water," on the South Bank), it became a palace church under Henry VIII (when it became known as St Saviour's) until some merchant parishioners bought it from James I in 1611. It was only promoted to cathedral status in 1905. Look for the vivid 15th-century roof bosses (small ornamental wood carvings); the gaudily renovated 1408 tomb of John Gower,

Richard II's poet laureate and a friend of Chaucer's; and the Harvard Chapel, where John Harvard, a local butcher's son who went on to found the American university, was baptized. Another notable buried here (between the choir stalls) is Edmund Shakespeare, brother of William. Free 45-minute tours are offered on Tuesday at 2 and 3 pm, Wednesday at 3 pm, Thursday at 11:30 am, and Friday at 11 am and 3 pm. ⊠ *London Bridge, Bankside* ☎ *020/7367–6700* ⊕ *cathedral. southwark.anglican.org* ⊠ *Free (suggested donation £4)* Ⓜ *London Bridge.*

★ Tate Modern

MUSEUM | This spectacular renovation of a mid-20th-century power station is one of the most-visited museums of modern art in the world. Its great permanent collection, which starts in 1900 and ranges from Modern masters like Matisse to the most cutting-edge contemporary artists, is arranged thematically (from In the Studio and Artist and Society to Materials and Society and Media Networks). Its blockbuster temporary exhibitions have showcased the work of such disparate artists as Gaugin, Roy Lichtenstein, and Dorothea Tanning. The vast **Turbine Hall** is a dramatic entrance point used to showcase big audacious installations that tend to generate a lot of publicity. Past highlights include Olafur Eliasson's massive glowing sun and Carsten Holler's huge metal slides. ⊠ *Bankside* ☎ *020/7887–8888* ⊕ *www.tate.org.uk/modern* ⊠ *Free (charge for special exhibitions)* Ⓜ *Southwark, Blackfriars, St. Paul's.*

The View from the Shard

BUILDING | At 800 feet, this addition to the London skyline currently offers the highest vantage point in Western Europe. Designed by the noted architect Renzo Piano, it has attracted both admiration and disdain. While the building itself is generally highly regarded, many felt it would have been better sited in Canary Wharf (or perhaps Dubai), as it spoils views of St. Paul's Cathedral from traditional vantage points such as Hampstead's Parliament Hill. No matter how you feel about the building, there's no denying that it offers a spectacular 360-degree view over London (extending 40 miles on a clear day) from viewing platforms on level 69, and the open-air skydeck on level 72—almost twice as high as any other viewpoint in the city. Digital telescopes provide information about 200 points of interest. There's a weather guarantee that lets you return on a more clement day if visibility is seriously impeded, and various themed events like silent discos or early morning yoga classes are offered at an extra charge. Admission is by timed ticket only. If you find the price as eye-wateringly high as the viewing platforms, there's a less dramatic but still very impressive (and free) view from the lobby of the Shangri-La hotel on the 35th floor, or, in the evenings, the hotel's chic Gong bar on the 52nd floor (over-18s only). ⊠ *Railway Approach, Borough* ☎ *0344/499–7222* ⊕ *www.theviewfromtheshard.com* ⊠ *From £32* Ⓜ *London Bridge.*

🍴 Restaurants

★ Casse-Croûte

$$ | **BISTRO** | This bistro on Bermondsey Street near the Shard is as French as a pack of Gauloises, from the yellow walls and red-and-white checked tablecloths to the perfectly executed classics like *lapin à la moutarde* (rabbit in a creamy mustard sauce), *suprême de volaille aux mousserons* (chicken breast stuffed with mushrooms), quiche Lorraine, and Paris-Brest (decadent choux pastry stuffed with praline and whipped cream). The daily changing menu offers three reasonably-priced options per course, and the wine list (French, of course) goes off-the-beaten path with discoveries from small local producers. **Known for:** beautifully prepared bistro classics; authentic French atmosphere in tight quarters; reservations necessary for dinner.

$ *Average main: £20* ✉ *109 Bermondsey St., Bermondsey* ☎ *020/7407–2140* ⊕ *www.cassecroute.co.uk* ⊘ *No dinner Sun.* Ⓜ *London Bridge.*

José

$$ | **TAPAS** | Renowned chef José Pizarro has managed to re-create an authentic, slightly rustic Spanish tapas-and-sherry bar. With just 30 seats and no reservations, it's always packed after 6 pm, but it's worth the wait for remarkably fresh, perfectly prepared classic tapas plates like *patatas bravas, croquetas,* flash-fried prawns with chili and garlic, and razor clams with chorizo. **Known for:** notoriously long waits and large crowds; daily changing menu of authentic tapas; unique sherry menu. $ *Average main: £20* ✉ *104 Bermondsey St., Southwark* ☎ *020/7403–4902* ⊕ *www.josepizarro.com/jose-tapas-bar* Ⓜ *Borough¸ London Bridge.*

★ Padella

$ | **ITALIAN** | Sit at the galley kitchen counter and you can watch the chefs toss hot pans of authentic handmade Italian pasta, generally considered among the best in London. The acclaimed but amazingly affordable dishes include a ravioli with Neal's Yard ricotta and sage butter, burrata with Puglian olive oil, papardelle with a slow-cooked beef-shin ragù, or Dorset crab tagliarini with chili and lemon. **Known for:** low priced, high-quality handmade Italian pasta; papardelle with eight-hour beef-shin ragù; no reservations and long waits. $ *Average main: £7* ✉ *6 Southwark St., Borough* ⊕ *www.padella.co* Ⓜ *Borough, London Bridge.*

🛏 Hotels

★ Church Street Hotel

$$ | **HOTEL** | Like rays of sunshine in gritty south London, the rooms at this Camberwell hotel are decorated in rich colors that evoke Mexico, a theme enhanced by authentic touches like elaborately painted crucifixes, tiles handmade in Guadalajara, and homemade iron bed frames. **Pros:** individual and fun vibe; great breakfasts; closer to central London than it might appear. **Cons:** location very urban and busy; a mile from a Tube station (though bus connections are handier); some rooms have shared bathrooms. $ *Rooms from: £115* ✉ *29–33 Camberwell Church St., Camberwell, South East London* ☎ *020/7703–5984* ⊕ *www.churchstreethotel.com* ⇘ *31 rooms* ⦿ *Free breakfast* Ⓜ *Oval St.*

Sea Containers London

$$$ | **HOTEL** | The achingly hip Sea Containers started life as part of London's docklands, and is now a fun callback to the area's history. **Pros:** excellent bars and restaurants; beautiful river views; short riverside walk to Tate Modern and Shakespeare's Globe. **Cons:** river-view rooms are pricey (of course); public areas can be noisy; standard rooms are small. $ *Rooms from: £256* ✉ *Sea Containers House, 20 Upper Ground, Southwark* ☎ *020/3747–1000* ⊕ *www.seacontainerslondon.com* ⇘ *359 rooms* ⦿ *No meals* Ⓜ *Blackfriars, Southwark.*

★ The Shangri-La Hotel at the Shard

$$$$ | **HOTEL** | With its floor-to-ceiling windows, the city's highest cocktail bar and infinity pool, and unrivaled views of the London skyline from 1,016 feet above the South Bank of the Thames, the Shangri-La has become one of London's chicest addresses. **Pros:** perhaps the best views in the city; great infinity pool and spa; superb restaurants and cocktail bar. **Cons:** design flaw allows some guests to see into neighboring rooms at night; decor may be too understated for some; restaurant, bar, and elevator can be crowded due to popularity of the view. $ *Rooms from: £468* ✉ *31 St. Thomas St., South Bank* ☎ *0207/234–8000* ⊕ *www.theshard.com/shangri-la* ⇘ *202 rooms* ⦿ *No meals* Ⓜ *London Bridge Station.*

London's Spectator Sports

Sport in the capital comes into its own when it's watched, rather than participated in. You'll most easily witness London's fervent sporting passions in front of a screen in a pub with a pint in hand. And those passions run deep.

Football

London's top teams—Chelsea, Arsenal, Tottenham Hotspur—are world-class (especially the first two) and often progress in the European Champions League. It's unlikely you'll be able to get tickets for anything except the least popular Premier League games during the August–May season, despite absurdly high ticket prices—as much as £41 for a standard, walk-up, match-day seat at Chelsea, and a whopping £126 for the match-day tickets at Arsenal.

Tennis

Wimbledon Lawn Tennis Championships
The All England Club's Wimbledon Lawn Tennis Championships are famous for Centre Court, strawberries and cream, a gentle spot of rain, and a nostalgic old-school insistence on players wearing white. Thankfully, the rain has been banished on Centre Court by the nifty retractable roof, but whether you can get tickets for Centre Court all comes down to the luck of the draw—there's a ballot system for advance purchase (see website for more details). ⊠ *The All England Lawn Tennis Club, Church Rd.* ☎ *020/8971–2473 for general inquiries* ⊕ *www.wimbledon.com.*

ⓨ Nightlife

BARS

Aqua Shard

BARS/PUBS | This sophisticated bar on level 31 of the iconic Shard is worth a visit for the phenomenal views alone. The cocktail list is pretty special, too—big on fruit purees and unusual bitters. No reservations are taken in the bar, so be prepared to wait during busy periods. ⊠ *The Shard, 31 St. Thomas St., Level 31, London Bridge* ☎ *020/3011–1256* ⊕ *www.aquashard.co.uk* Ⓜ *London Bridge.*

Three Eight Four

BARS/PUBS | Epitomizing a new breed of Brixton bar, Three Eight Four is known for its innovative cocktails and tapas-style shared plates. The cocktail menu changes seasonally but always involves artisinal spirits and unusual mixing techniques—try the Nightshade, which comes with a pipette that you use to add the final ingredient (crème de cassis) yourself. The bare lightbulbs and stripped brick walls are a bit of a hipster bar cliché, but this place manages it with particular panache. ⊠ *384 Coldharbour La., Brixton* ☎ *020/3417–7309* ⊕ *www.threeeightfour.com* Ⓜ *Brixton.*

🎭 Performing Arts

★ **Battersea Arts Centre** (*BAC*)
ARTS CENTERS | Battersea Arts Centre has a reputation for producing innovative new work as well as hosting top alternative stand-up comics. Performances take place in quirky spaces all over this atmospheric former town hall. Check out Scratch events, low-tech theater where the audience provides feedback on works-in-progress. Entry for Scratch events is pay-what-you-can (minimum £3). The bar, which serves snacks and sharing plates, is open all day. ⊠ *176 Lavender Hill, Battersea* ☎ *020/7223–2223* ⊕ *www.bac.org.uk* ⊠ *Pay what you can (£3 suggested)–£30* Ⓜ *National Rail: Clapham Junction.*

BFI Southbank

FILM | With the best repertory programming in London, the four movie theaters here are effectively a national film center run by the British Film Institute. More than 1,000 titles are screened each year, with art-house, foreign, silent, overlooked, classic, noir, and short films favored over recent Hollywood blockbusters. The center also has a gallery, bookshop, and "mediatheque" where visitors can watch film and television from the National Archive for free (closed Monday). The Riverfront Bar and Kitchen offers dining with views while the Benugo BFI Bar and Kitchen is informal and buzzy. This is one of the venues for the BFI London Film Festival; throughout the year there are minifestivals, seminars, and guest speakers. ⊠ Belvedere Rd., South Bank ☎ 020/7928–3232 ⊕ www.bfi.org.uk ✑ From £10 Ⓜ Waterloo.

★ National Theatre

THEATER | FAMILY | When this complex designed by Sir Denys Lasdun opened in 1976, Londoners were slow to warm-up to the low-rise Brutalist block, with Prince Charles describing it as "a clever way of building a nuclear power station in the middle of London without anyone objecting." But whatever you think of the outside, the inside offers generally superb theatrical experiences at (relatively) friendly prices—several of which (like War Horse or One Man, Two Guvnors) have gone on to become long-running Broadway hits. Interspersed with the three theaters—the 1,150-seat Olivier, the 890-seat Lyttelton, and the 450-seat Dorfman—is a multilayered foyer with exhibitions, bars, restaurants, and free entertainment. Musicals, classics, and plays are performed by top-flight professionals, who you can sometimes catch giving foyer talks as well. Backstage, costume, and architecture tours are available daily at 9:45 am except Sunday. The Clore Learning Centre offers courses and events on different aspects of theater production, and you can watch staff at work on set building and scenery painting from the Sherling High-Level Walkway. Each weekend in August, the free outdoor River Stage Festival presents live music, dance, family workshops, and DJ sets in front of the theater. ⊠ Belvedere Rd., South Bank ☎ 020/7452–3000 ⊕ www.nationaltheatre.org.uk ✑ From £15, tours £13 Ⓜ Waterloo.

★ Southbank Centre

ART GALLERIES—ARTS | FAMILY | The general public has never really warmed to the Southbank Centre's hulking concrete buildings (beloved by architecture aficionados), products of the Brutalist style popular when the center was built in the 1950s and '60s—but all the same, the masses flock to the concerts, recitals, festivals, and exhibitions held here, Europe's largest arts center. The **Royal Festival Hall** is truly a People's Palace, with seats for 2,900 and a schedule that ranges from major symphony orchestras to pop stars. The smaller **Queen Elizabeth Hall** is more classically oriented. It contains the **Purcell Room,** which hosts lectures and chamber performances. For art, head to the **Hayward Gallery**, which hosts shows on top contemporary artists such as Antony Gormley and Cy Twombly. The center's riverside street level has a terrific assortment of restaurants and bars, though you'll need to head to the Cut, just south of here, for independent eateries. ⊠ Belvedere Rd., South Bank ☎ 020/3879–9555 ⊕ www.southbankcentre.co.uk ✑ Free–£120 Ⓜ Waterloo, Embankment.

Young Vic

THEATER | Just down the road from its elder sibling the Old Vic, this offshoot hosts big names performing alongside emerging talent, often in daring innovative productions of both new and classic plays that appeal to a more diverse audience than is traditionally found on the London scene. Good food is served all day at the bustling bar. ⊠ 66 The Cut, Waterloo, South Bank ☎ 020/7922–2922 ⊕ www.youngvic.org ✑ From £10 Ⓜ Southwark, Waterloo.

Kensington, Chelsea, Knightsbridge, and Notting Hill

The Royal Borough of Kensington & Chelsea (or K&C, as the locals call it) is where you'll find London at its richest, and not just in the moneyed sense. South Kensington offers a concentration of great museums near Cromwell Road, with historic Kensington Palace and Kensington Gardens nearby in Hyde Park. Once-raffish Chelsea, where the Pre-Raphaelites painted and Mick Jagger partied, is now a thoroughly respectable home for the discreetly wealthy, while flashier Knightsbridge has become a haven for international plutocrats, with shopping to match their tastes.

The center of London's West Indian community from the 1950s through the '70s, Notting Hill these days is the address of choice for the well-heeled, be they bankers, rock stars, media and advertising types, or rich hippies.

GETTING HERE

Several Tube stations are nearby: Sloane Square and High Street Kensington on the District and Circle lines; Knightsbridge and Hyde Park Corner on the Piccadilly Line; and South Kensington and Gloucester Road on the District, Circle, and Piccadilly lines. For Portobello Market and environs, the best Tube stops are Ladbroke Grove and Westbourne Park (Hammersmith and City Line); ask for directions when you emerge. The Notting Hill Gate stop on the District, Circle, and Central lines enables you to walk the length of Portobello Road while going slightly downhill.

◉ Sights

Harrods

STORE/MALL | With an encyclopedic assortment of luxury brands, this Knightsbridge institution, currently owned by the Qatar Investment Authority, has more than 300 departments and 25 eating and drinking options, all spread over 1 million square feet on a 4½-acre site. Now populated more by window-shopping tourists and superrich visitors from abroad than by the bling-averse natives, Harrods is best approached as the world's largest, most upscale and expensive mall. After a two year redesign of the food hall, you can now find a variety of dining options on-site, including sushi, Indian, pasta, and more; all have counter seating so you can watch the chefs at work. At the center is the Wine Bar, with over a hundred wines by the glass and food by Caviar House and Prunier. There's also a giant coffee roasting station, ceiling-high shelves of fresh bread at the Bakery, a vegetable butchery, and an expanded deli counter. In addition, the revamped Beauty Hall now offers cult brands, innovative "Magic Mirrors" that allow shoppers to instantly see a new make-up look via digital technology, beauty master classes, and over 46,000 different lipsticks, as well as 13 treatment rooms where you can try on make-up in private. ✉ 87–135 Brompton Rd., Knightsbridge ☎ 020/7730–1234 ⊕ www.harrods.com Ⓜ Knightsbridge.

★ Hyde Park

CITY PARK | FAMILY | Along with the smaller St. James's and Green parks to the east, the 350-acre Hyde Park started as Henry VIII's hunting grounds. Along its south side runs Rotten Row, once Henry's royal path to the hunt—the name is a corruption of *Route du Roi* (Route of the King). It's still used by the Household Cavalry, who live at the Hyde Park Barracks to the left. Hyde Park is wonderful for

Kensington, Chelsea, Knightsbridge, and Notting Hill

Sights ▼

1 Harrods **G5**
2 Hyde Park. **G3**
3 Kensington Gardens. **C3**
4 Kensington Palace **C3**
5 Natural History Museum **E5**
6 Portobello Market **A1**
7 Science Museum. **E5**
8 Victoria & Albert Museum **E5**

Restaurants ▼

1 Bar Boulud **G4**
2 Dinner by Heston Blumenthal **G4**
3 Elystan Street **F6**
4 The Harwood Arms. **A9**
5 Hereford Road **B1**
6 Mari Vanna **G4**
7 Six Portland Road. **A2**
8 Yashin Ocean House ... **D7**

Hotels ▼

1 Ampersand **E6**
2 Ashburn Hotel. **C6**
3 The Berkeley **H4**
4 The Draycott **G6**
5 easyHotel South Kensington. **B6**
6 Egerton House **F5**
7 London House Hotel. ... **B1**
8 Mandarin Oriental Hyde Park. **G4**
9 Number Sixteen. **E6**
10 The Pelham Hotel. **E6**
11 The Portobello Hotel ... **A1**
12 The Rockwell. **B6**

KEY

● Exploring Sights
● Restaurants
● Hotels

Inside the Natural History Museum, you'll find a fascinating array of dinosaur fossils.

strolling, cycling, or just relaxing by the Serpentine, the long body of water near its southern border. On the south side, by the Lido Café and Bar at the 1930s **Serpentine Lido**, is the site of the **Princess Diana Memorial Fountain.** On Sunday, close to Marble Arch, you'll find the uniquely British tribute to free speech, Speakers' Corner. ⊠ *Hyde Park* ☎ *030/0061–2114* ⊕ *www.royalparks.org.uk* ✉ *Free* Ⓜ *Hyde Park Corner, Knightsbridge, Lancaster Gate, Marble Arch.*

★ Kensington Gardens

GARDEN | FAMILY | Laid out in 1689 by William III, who commissioned Sir Christopher Wren to build Kensington Palace, the gardens are a formal counterpart to neighboring Hyde Park. Just to the north of the palace itself is the Dutch-style **Sunken Garden .** Nearby, the 1912 bronze statue *Peter Pan* commemorates the boy in J. M. Barrie's story who lived on an island in the Serpentine and who never grew up. Kids will enjoy the magical **Diana, Princess of Wales' Memorial Playground,** whose design was also inspired by Barrie's book. The **Elfin Oak** is a 900-year-old tree trunk that was carved with scores of tiny elves, fairies, and other fanciful creations in the 1920s. The **Italian Gardens,** an ornamental water garden commissioned by Prince Albert in 1860, comprise several ornamental ponds and fountains (there's also a nice café on-site), while the **Round Pond** attracts model-boat enthusiasts. ⊠ *Kensington* ☎ *030/0061–2000* ⊕ *www. royalparks.org.uk* ✉ *Free* Ⓜ *High St. Kensington, Lancaster Gate, Queensway, South Kensington.*

★ Kensington Palace

CASTLE/PALACE | FAMILY | Neither as imposing as Buckingham Palace nor as charming as Hampton Court, Kensington Palace is something of a Royal Family commune, with various close relatives of the queen occupying large apartments in the private part of the palace. Bought in 1689 by Queen Mary and King William III, it was converted into a palace by Sir Christopher Wren and Nicholas Hawksmoor, and royals have been in residence ever since. Princess Diana lived here with her sons after her divorce, and this is where Prince William now lives with his wife, Catherine, Duchess of Cambridge and their children. The State Apartments are open to the public, with both permanent and temporary exhibitions. Look for the King's Staircase, with its panoramic trompe-l'oeil painting, and the King's Gallery, with royal artworks surrounded by rich red damask walls, intricate gilding, and a beautiful painted ceiling. Outside, the grounds are almost as lovely as the palace itself. ⊠ *The Broad Walk, Kensington Gardens, Kensington* ☎ *0207/482–7799 for advance booking in U.K., 0203/166–6000* ⊕ *www.hrp. org.uk* ⊠ *£18* Ⓜ *Queensway, High St. Kensington.*

★ Natural History Museum

MUSEUM | FAMILY | The ornate terracotta facade of this enormous Victorian museum is embellished with relief panels depicting living creatures to the left of the entrance and extinct ones to the right (although some species have subsequently changed categories). Most are represented inside the museum, which contains more than 70 million different specimens. Only a small percentage is on public display, but you could still spend a day here and not come close to seeing everything. The skeleton of a giant blue whale dominates the vaulted, cathedral-like entrance hall, affording you perhaps the most irresistible photo op in the building. The **Darwin Centre** houses some of the millions of items the museum itself doesn't have room to display. If you want to see some of the other thousands of specimens on the shelves, you must book a behind-the-scenes **Spirit Collection** tour on the day (space is limited). ⊠ *Cromwell Rd., South Kensington* ☎ *0207/942–5000* ⊕ *www. nhm.ac.uk* ⊠ *Free (some fees for special exhibitions)* Ⓜ *South Kensington.*

Portobello Market

OUTDOOR/FLEA/GREEN MARKETS | Still considered the best all-around market in town by many fans, and certainly the most famous, Portobello Market stretches almost 2 miles, from fashionable Notting Hill to the lively cultural melting pot of North Kensington, changing character as it goes. The southern end, starting at Chepstow Villas and going to Elgin Crescent, is lined with shops and stalls, and, on Saturday, arcades selling antiques, silver, and bric-a-brac. The middle, from Elgin Crescent to Talbot, is devoted to fruit and vegetables, interspersed with excellent hot food stalls. On Friday and Saturday, the area between Talbot Road and the elevated highway (called the Westway) becomes more of a flea market, specializing in new household and mass-produced goods sold at a discount. North of the Westway up to Goldborne Road are more stalls selling even cheaper secondhand household goods and bric-a-brac. Scattered throughout but mostly concentrated under the Westway are clothing stalls selling vintage pieces and items from emerging designers, custom T-shirts, and supercool baby clothes, plus jewelry. New and established designers are also found in the boutiques of the Portobello Green Arcade.

Some say Portobello Road has become a tourist trap, but if you acknowledge that it's a circus and get into the spirit, it's a lot of fun. Perhaps you won't find many bargains, but this is such a fascinating part of town that just hanging out is a good enough excuse to come. There are some food and flower stalls throughout the week (try the Hummingbird Bakery for delicious cupcakes), but Saturday is when the market in full swing. Serious shoppers avoid the crowds and go on Friday morning. Bring cash—several vendors don't take credit cards—but also be sure to keep an eye on it. ⊠ *Portobello Rd., Notting Hill* ⊕ *www.portobelloroad. co.uk* ⊙ *Closed Sun.* Ⓜ *Notting Hill Gate.*

Choices, choices: there are plenty of prints—and much else—at the Portobello Road Market.

★ Science Museum

MUSEUM | **FAMILY** | With attractions ranging from entertaining yet educational exhibits like an interactive gallery where kids can perform their own hands-on scientific experiments to an exhibition on the fight against superbugs, the Science Museum brings the subject alive for visitors of all ages. One of the three great South Kensington museums, it stands next to the Natural History Museum in a more modern, plainer building. Highlights include the Launch Pad gallery, which demonstrates basic laws of physics; *Puffing Billy,* the oldest steam locomotive in the world; and the actual Apollo 10 capsule. The six floors are devoted to subjects as diverse as the history of flight, space exploration, jet flight simulators, the large Hadron collider, 3-D printing, and the history of robots over the last 400 years. The museum also contains a 450-seat IMAX theater and a motion simulator ride. ⊠ *Exhibition Rd., South Kensington* ☎ *0870/870–4868* ⊕ *www. sciencemuseum.org.uk* ⊠ *Free (charge for special exhibitions, IMAX, Wonderlab, and simulator rides)* Ⓜ *South Kensington.*

★ Victoria & Albert Museum

MUSEUM | **FAMILY** | Known to all as the V&A, this huge museum is devoted to the applied arts of all disciplines, all periods, and all nationalities. First opened as the South Kensington Museum in 1857, it was renamed in 1899 in honor of Queen Victoria's late husband and has since grown to become one of the country's best-loved cultural institutions. Many collections at the V&A are presented not by period but by category—textiles, sculpture, jewelry, and so on. Nowhere is the benefit of this more apparent than in the **Fashion Gallery,** known for its high-profile temporary exhibitions. There are galleries devoted to Britain, Japan, China, Korea, and the Islamic Middle East. More recently installed areas include the Ceramics Gallery and the Medieval and Renaissance galleries, which have the largest collection of works from the period outside of Italy. The **Europe Gallery** (Rooms 1–7) brings together more than 1,100 objects from 1600 to 1800. ⊠ *Cromwell Rd., South Kensington*

☎ *020/7942–2000* ⊕ *www.vam.ac.uk* ⊠ *Free (charge for some special exhibitions, from £5)* Ⓜ *South Kensington.*

Restaurants

Bar Boulud

$$ | **BRASSERIE** | New York–based French superchef Daniel Boulud combines French brasserie classics like escargot, salade nicoise, and poule au pot with American-style gourmet burgers at this sophisticated but casual restaurant located within the Mandarin Oriental. The excellent grazing menu has something for everyone, and the professional but informal waitstaff enhances the convivial vibe. **Known for:** excellent foie gras/beef/ short rib burgers; affordable set meals from noon until 6:30; superb take on French brasserie classics. ⑤ *Average main: £25* ⊠ *Mandarin Oriental Hyde Park, 66 Knightsbridge, Knightsbridge* ☎ *020/7201–3899 for reservations only* ⊕ *www.barboulud.com/london* Ⓜ *Knightsbridge.*

★ Dinner by Heston Blumenthal

$$$$ | **BRITISH** | Medieval English cuisine meets molecular gastronomy in this reassuringly luxurious, two Michelin star Blumenthal flagship within the Mandarin Oriental. Try the signature "Meat Fruit" appetizer (last popular in the 16th century), a ball of ultrasmooth chicken liver parfait encased in a citrus-flavored gel "peel" or the much-more-appetizing-than-it-sounds "Rice and Flesh", a 15th-century dish of yellow saffron rice with veal sweetbreads and wild smoked eel. **Known for:** handsome dining room with Hyde Park views; creative reinterpretations of historical dishes; pineapple Tipsy cake for dessert. ⑤ *Average main: £44* ⊠ *Mandarin Oriental Hyde Park, 66 Knightsbridge, Knightsbridge* ☎ *020/7201–3833* ⊕ *www.dinnerby-heston.com* Ⓜ *Knightsbridge.*

The Harwood Arms

$$$$ | **MODERN BRITISH** | Despite a Michelin star and a co-owner who's also the chef at one of Britain's (and indeed the world's) top restaurants, this is a relaxed neighborhood gastropub with an unusually fine kitchen. It specializes in British produce, wild food, and especially game, with dishes like crab royale with peas and lovage and game pie with Somerset cider jelly, all served via set menus only. **Known for:** Michelin-starred food in a gastropub setting; seasonal venison from the pub's own hunting estate; good value set menus. ⑤ *Average main: £38* ⊠ *27 Walham Grove, Chelsea* ☎ *020/7386– 1847* ⊕ *www.harwoodarms.com* ☾ *No lunch Mon.* Ⓜ *Fulham Broadway.*

Hereford Road

$ | **MODERN BRITISH** | **FAMILY** | A Bayswater favorite with the well-connected Notting Hill set, Hereford Road is renowned for its pared-down, pomp-free, and ingredient-driven seasonal British fare, with an emphasis on well-sourced regional British produce. Work your way through uncluttered combos like steamed mussels with cider and thyme, lemon sole with roast cauliflower and capers, or chilled English rice pudding with a dollop of strawberry jam. **Known for:** pared-back Modern British nose-to-tail dining; deceptively simple-sounding dishes like duck livers with green beans; famously affordable two- and three-course set lunches. ⑤ *Average main: £15* ⊠ *3 Hereford Rd., Bayswater* ☎ *020/7727–1144* ⊕ *www.herefordroad.org* ☾ *No lunch Mon.–Wed.* Ⓜ *Bayswater, Queensway.*

★ Elystan Street

$$$ | **MODERN BRITISH** | Chef Phil Howard is committed to seasonality, bringing together well-matched ingredients in this relaxed, loftlike space that leans toward the modernist and minimalist. The dishes are deeply flavored and accomplished, earning the restaurant a Michelin star (the vegetarian game is especially strong). **Known for:** Michelin-level cuisine

in a relaxed setting; roast grouse with celeriac and pear puree; convivial vibe enhanced by a smart wine list. ⑤ *Average main: £30* ✉ *43 Elystan St., Chelsea* ☎ *020/7628–5005* ⊕ *www.elystanstreet. com* Ⓜ *South Kensington.*

Mari Vanna

$$ | **RUSSIAN** | London's sizeable, well-heeled Russian community flocks to this maximalist evocation of a pre-Revolution *babushka*'s living room, overflowing with vintage chandeliers, porcelain figurines, tapestries, and nested Russian dolls. The menu leans toward traditional old-country comfort food like Siberian *pelmeni* (dumplings) filled with pork and beef, smoked salmon blinis, creamy beef Stroganoff with wild mushrooms, and, of course, borscht, finished off with a 12-layer honey cake. **Known for:** over-the-top nostalgic Russian décor; borscht, blinis, and beef Stroganoff; flavored vodka shot selection. ⑤ *Average main: £24* ✉ *The Wellington Court, 116 Knightsbridge, Knightsbridge* ☎ *020/7225–3122* ⊕ *www. marivanna.ru/london* Ⓜ *Knightsbridge.*

★ Six Portland Road

$$ | **FRENCH** | **FAMILY** | The ultimate neighborhood restaurant in west London's wealthy Holland Park section draws diners with its brilliant-but-understated French and Mediterranean classics, relaxed service, and interesting, largely French Caves de Pyrene–sourced wines. Treat yourself to sea trout with romesco and saffron or some superdelicate nettle and ricotta ravioli. **Known for:** intimate seating; unpretentious but pitch-perfect service; winning boutique wine list. ⑤ *Average main: £22* ✉ *6 Portland Rd., Notting Hill* ☎ *020/7229–3130* ⊕ *www. sixportlandroad.com* ⊘ *Closed Sun. No lunch Sat.* Ⓜ *Holland Park.*

Yashin Ocean House

$$$ | **JAPANESE** | Here at one of London's top Japanese restaurants, head chef and cofounder Yasuhiro Mineno creates fresh, colorful, and exquisite sushi, sashimi, salads, and carpaccios. Tofu-topped miso cappuccino comes in a Victorian cup and saucer, while *nigiri* might include signature flourishes such as truffle shavings on fatty tuna. **Known for:** exquisite sushi and sashimi with creative twists; 5- to 15-piece chef-decides omakase sets; head-to-tail seafood dishes. ⑤ *Average main: £30* ✉ *117–119 Old Brompton Rd., Kensington* ☎ *020/7373–3990* ⊕ *www. yashinocean.com* Ⓜ *High St. Kensington.*

Hotels

Ampersand

$$ | **HOTEL** | A sense of style emanates from every surface of this stylish hotel in the heart of Kensington, and the playful vintage vibe lends the property a refreshingly down-to-earth feel in a neighborhood that can feel stodgy. **Pros:** flawless design; great service; good restaurant. **Cons:** ground-floor rooms can be noisy; breakfast is not included in the price of a room; the area swarms with tourists visiting the museums on weekends. ⑤ *Rooms from: £234* ✉ *10 Harrington Rd., Kensington* ☎ *020/7589–5895* ⊕ *www.ampersandhotel.com* ⇱ *111 rooms* ⦿ *No meals* Ⓜ *Gloucester Rd.*

Ashburn Hotel

$$ | **HOTEL** | A short walk from Gloucester Road Tube station and within walking distance of Harrods and the Kensington museums, the Ashburn is one of the better "boutique" hotels in this part of town. **Pros:** friendly atmosphere; free Wi-Fi; different turndown gift every night. **Cons:** summer prices sometimes hike the cost; some rooms on the small side; on very busy road. ⑤ *Rooms from: £144* ✉ *111 Cromwell Rd., Kensington* ☎ *020/7244– 1999* ⊕ *www.ashburn-hotel.co.uk* ⇱ *38 rooms* ⦿ *Free breakfast* Ⓜ *Gloucester Rd.*

★ The Berkeley

$$$$ | **HOTEL** | **FAMILY** | Convenient for Knightsbridge shopping, the very elegant Berkeley is known for its excellent restaurants, splendid rooftop swimming pool and garden, and an excellent, if pricey, Bamford spa. **Pros:** lavish and elegant; attentive service; great drinking and dining options. **Cons:** you'll need your best designer clothes to fit in; even the cheapest rooms are expensive; while beautiful, the style is very traditional luxury. ⑤ *Rooms from: £450 ✉ Wilton Pl., Knightsbridge ☎ 020/7235–6000, 800/637–2869 in U.S. ⊕ www. the-berkeley.co.uk ➽ 190 rooms* ⑩ *Free breakfast* Ⓜ *Knightsbridge.*

★ The Draycott

$$$ | HOTEL | FAMILY | This elegant yet homey boutique hotel near Sloane Square is the stuff London dreams are made on—if your dream is to live like a pleasantly old-fashioned, impeccably mannered, effortlessly stylish Chelsea lady or gentleman. **Pros:** lovely traditional town house; attentive service; access to garden square. **Cons:** no restaurant or bar; single rooms are very small; elevator is tiny. ⑤ *Rooms from: £286 ✉ 26 Cadogan Gardens, Chelsea ☎ 020/7730–0236 ⊕ www.draycotthotel.com ➽ 35 rooms* ⑩ *Free breakfast* Ⓜ *Sloane Sq.*

easyHotel South Kensington

$ | HOTEL | London's original "pod hotel" has tiny rooms with a double bed, private shower room, and little else—each brightly decorated in the easyGroup's trademark orange and white (to match their budget airline easyJet). **Pros:** amazing rates; safe and decent-enough space; good location. **Cons:** not for the claustrophobic—rooms are truly tiny and most have no windows; six floors and no elevator; Wi-Fi is not included in the price of rooms. ⑤ *Rooms from: £48 ✉ 14 Lexham Gardens, Kensington ☎ 07951/440134 ⊕ www.easyhotel.com ➽ 34 rooms* ⑩ *No meals* Ⓜ *Gloucester Rd.*

★ Egerton House

$$$ | HOTEL | FAMILY | This welcoming boutique hotel is an oasis of understated country house chic in glitzy Knightsbridge, with guest rooms that don't stint on design touches, like bold, rich textiles. **Pros:** personalized, attentive service; luxurious but comfortable design; striking art.

Cons: some may find rooms over-decorated; the traditional elegance won't appeal to everyone; on the pricier side. ⑤ *Rooms from: £330 ✉ 17–19 Egerton Terr., Knightsbridge ☎ 020/7589–2412, 877/955–1515 in U.S. ⊕ www.redcarnationhotels.com ➽ 29 rooms* ⑩ *Free breakfast* Ⓜ *Knightsbridge, South Kensington.*

London House Hotel

$ | HOTEL | Set in a row of white Georgian town houses, this excellent budget option in hit-or-miss Bayswater is friendly, well run, and spotlessly clean. **Pros:** friendly and efficient; emphasis on value; good location. **Cons:** basement rooms lack sunlight; smallest rooms are tiny; the area isn't quite as vibrant as neighboring Notting Hill. ⑤ *Rooms from: £110 ✉ 81 Kensington Garden Sq., Bayswater ☎ 020/7243–1810 ⊕ www.londonhouse-hotels.com ➽ 103 rooms* ⑩ *No meals* Ⓜ *Queensway, Bayswater.*

★ Mandarin Oriental Hyde Park

$$$$ | HOTEL | Following an extensive postfire renovation, this ultraluxe hotel on the edge of Hyde Park welcomes you with one of the most exuberantly Edwardian facades in town, then fast-forwards you to high-trend modern London, thanks to striking and luxurious guest rooms filled with high-tech gadgets. **Pros:** several rooms have balconies or terraces overlooking Hyde Park; spacious rooms and bathrooms; excellent service. **Cons:** nothing comes cheap; rooms on lower floors on Knightsbridge side may have traffic noise; street outside often very busy. ⑤ *Rooms from: £720 ✉ 66 Knightsbridge, Knightsbridge ☎ 020/7235–2000 ⊕ www. mandarinoriental.com/london ➽ 181 rooms* ⑩ *Free breakfast* Ⓜ *Knightsbridge.*

★ Number Sixteen

$$$$ | HOTEL | Rooms at this lovely boutique hotel just around the corner from the Victoria & Albert Museum, look like they come from the pages of *Architectural Digest*, and the delightful garden is an added bonus. **Pros:** just the right level of helpful service; interiors are gorgeous; the afternoon tea is excellent. **Cons:** no restaurant; elevator doesn't go to third floor; intimacy of a small boutique hotel may not be for everyone. ⑤ *Rooms from: £336* ✉ *16 Sumner Pl., South Kensington* ☎ *020/7589–5232, 888/559–5508 in U.S.* ⊕ *www.firmdale.com* ⇋ *41 rooms* ⟨○⟩ *Free breakfast* Ⓜ *South Kensington.*

The Pelham Hotel

$$ | **HOTEL** | One of the first boutique hotels ever in London, this still-stylish choice is just a short stroll away from the Natural History, Science, and Victoria & Albert museums. **Pros:** great location for museum-hopping; elegant interior design; lovely staff. **Cons:** taller guests will find themselves cursing the top-floor rooms with sloping ceilings; some rooms are on the small side given the price; some suites are only accessible via the stairs. ⑤ *Rooms from: £200* ✉ *15 Cromwell Pl., South Kensington* ☎ *020/7589–8288, 888/757–5587 in U.S.* ⊕ *www.starhotelscollezione.com/en/our-hotels/the-pelham-london* ⇋ *52 rooms* ⟨○⟩ *Free breakfast* Ⓜ *South Kensington.*

The Portobello Hotel

$$ | **HOTEL** | One of London's quirkiest hotels, the little Portobello (formed from two adjoining Victorian houses) has attracted scores of celebrities to its small but stylish rooms over the years, and the decor reflects these hip credentials with joyous abandon. **Pros:** stylish and unique; pets are allowed; guests have use of nearby gym and pool. **Cons:** all but the priciest rooms are quite small; may be too eccentric for some; a continental breakfast is included in the price but cooked breakfasts are extra. ⑤ *Rooms from: £195* ✉ *22 Stanley Gardens, Notting Hill* ☎ *020/7727–2777* ⊕ *www.portobellohotel.com* ⇋ *21 rooms* ⟨○⟩ *Free breakfast* Ⓜ *Notting Hill Gate.*

The Rockwell

$ | **HOTEL** | Despite being on the notoriously traffic-clogged Cromwell Road, the Rockwell is one of the best boutique hotels in this part of London—and windows have triple-soundproofing. **Pros:** large bedrooms; good value for neighborhood; helpful staff. **Cons:** on busy road; no bathtubs; decor a bit tired in places. ⑤ *Rooms from: £108* ✉ *181 Cromwell Rd., South Kensington* ☎ *020/7244–2000* ⊕ *www.therockwell.com* ⇋ *40 rooms* ⟨○⟩ *Free breakfast* Ⓜ *Earl's Ct.*

▽ Nightlife

BARS

The Blue Bar at the Berkeley Hotel

BARS/PUBS | With its Lutyens blue walls, Edwardian plasterwork, white onyx bar, and black crocodile-print leather floor, this hotel bar oozes sultry sophistication. Immaculate service, an excellent seasonal cocktail list, and a glass extension make this an ideal spot for a romantic tête-à-tête, complete with a background soundtrack of lounge and deep house music. ✉ *The Berkeley, Wilton Pl., Knightsbridge* ☎ *020/7235–6000* ⊕ *www.the-berkeley.co.uk* Ⓜ *Knightsbridge, Hyde Park Corner.*

LIVE MUSIC

606 Club

MUSIC CLUBS | This Chelsea jazz club has been doing things speakeasy-style since long before it became a nightlife trend. Buzz the door near the far end of King's Road and you'll find a basement venue showcasing mainstream and contemporary jazz by well-known U.K.-based musicians. You must eat a meal in order to consume alcohol, so allow for an extra £30. Reservations are advisable. Lunchtime jazz takes place on select Sundays; call ahead. ✉ *90 Lots Rd., Chelsea* ☎ *020/7352–5953* ⊕ *www.606club.co.uk* 🎟 *From £10 music charge added to bill* Ⓜ *Fulham Broadway. Overground: Imperial Wharf.*

Royal Albert Hall is not only host to the acclaimed Proms performances, but it's also one of the city's most beautiful buildings.

🎭 Performing Arts

★ Royal Albert Hall

CONCERTS | Opened in 1871, this splendid iron-and-glass-domed auditorium hosts everything from pop and classical headliners to Cirque du Soleil, awards ceremonies, and sumo wrestling championships, but it is best known for the annual July–September BBC Promenade Concerts. Bargain-price standing-room (or promenading or sitting-on-the-floor) tickets for "the Proms" are sold on the night of the concert. The circular 5,272-seat auditorium has a terracotta exterior surmounted by a mosaic frieze depicting figures engaged in cultural pursuits. The hall is open most days for daytime guided tours and Tuesday through Sunday for afternoon tea. ✉ *Kensington Gore, Kensington* 🕾 *0207/589–8212* ⊕ *www.royalalberthall.com* ✍ *From £7; tours £14* Ⓜ *South Kensington.*

Royal Court Theatre

THEATER | For decades, the Royal Court was one of Britain's leading showcases for exciting new theatrical voices and premieres of ground-breaking works, and it still continues to produce important British and international dramas. For some productions, four 10-pence standing tickets go on sale one hour before each performance (but the view is severely restricted), and £12 tickets are available at 9 am Mondays for that night's performance. Monthly backstage and building tours are offered occasionally (check website for more information). ✉ *Sloane Sq., Chelsea* 🕾 *020/7565–5000* ⊕ *www.royalcourt-theatre.com* ✍ *From £12; tours £10* Ⓜ *Sloane Sq.*

🛍 Shopping

BOOKS

★ Books for Cooks

BOOKS/STATIONERY | It may seem odd to describe a bookshop as delicious-smelling, but on several days you can't but notice the aromas wafting out of the tiny café in the back of the shop—where the resident chef cooks a three-course set lunch for only £7, served from noon to 1 pm Tuesday through Friday (but be sure to get there early). The dishes are drawn from recipes in the 8,000 cookbooks on the shelves. Just about every world cuisine is represented, along with a complete lineup of works by celebrity chefs. Before you come to London, visit the shop's website to sign up for a specialized cooking workshop in the upstairs demonstration kitchen. ✉ *4 Blenheim Crescent, Notting Hill* ☎ *020/7221–1992* ⊕ *www.booksforcooks.com* Ⓜ *Notting Hill Gate, Ladbroke Grove.*

CLOTHING

Jigsaw

CLOTHING | The quality of fabrics and detailing belie the reasonable prices here, where clothes are classic yet trendy and elegant without being dull—and where cuts are kind to the womanly figure. The style is epitomized by the Duchess of Cambridge, who, as Kate Middleton before her marriage, was a buyer for the company. Although there are numerous branches across London, no two stores are the same. Preteens have their own line, Jigsaw Junior. ✉ *The Chapel, 6 Duke of York Sq., Chelsea* ☎ *020/730–4404* ⊕ *www.jigsaw-online.com* Ⓜ *Sloane Sq.*

Rigby & Peller

SPECIALTY STORES | Many of London's most affluent women find their luxury lingerie (plus swimwear) here because the quality is excellent and the service impeccably knowledgeable—and perhaps because it's the Queen's favored underwear supplier and has provided maternity wear to the Duchess of Cambridge.

Despite the upscale clientele, it's much friendlier than you might expect. Brands include Primadonna and Aubade as well as R&P's own line, and if the right fit eludes you, there's a made-to-measure service that starts at around £300. There are also branches in Mayfair, Chelsea, St. John's Wood, and the City. ✉ *2 Hans Rd., Knightsbridge* ☎ *020/7225–4760* ⊕ *www. rigbyandpeller.com* Ⓜ *Knightsbridge.*

DEPARTMENT STORES

Harvey Nichols

DEPARTMENT STORES | While visiting tourists flock to Harrods, local fashionistas shop at Harvey Nichols, aka "Harvey Nicks." The womenswear and accessories departments are outstanding, featuring top designers like Tom Ford, Loewe, Roland Mouret, Valentino, Tory Burch, and just about every fashionable name you can think of. The furniture and housewares are equally gorgeous (and pricey), although they become somewhat more affordable during the biannual sales in January and July. The Fifth Floor bar is the place to see and be seen, but if you're in search of food, the same floor also has an all-day Modern European café, a branch of Burger & Lobster, the carnivore-friendly Zelman Meats, or sushi-to-go from Yo! Sushi. To keep you looking as box-fresh as your purchases, the Beauty Lounge features a rotating menu of treatments from brands such as Elemis, La Mer, and Dermalogia, plus makeovers, LED facials, IV vitamin infusions, and blow-dry, nail, and brow bars. ✉ *109–125 Knightsbridge, Knightsbridge* ☎ *020/7235–5000* ⊕ *www. harveynichols.com* Ⓜ *Knightsbridge.*

JEWELRY

Butler & Wilson

JEWELRY/ACCESSORIES | Specialists in bold costume jewelry and affordable glamour, Butler & Wilson attracts fans including the Duchess of Cambridge. Semiprecious stones have been added to its foundation diamanté, colored rhinestone, and crystal collections. The British sense of humor is reflected in items like Champagne-bottle earrings or crystal studs in the shape of an eye. ✉ *189 Fulham Rd., South Kensington* ☎ *020/7352–3045* ⊕ *www.butlerandwilson.co.uk* ☽ *Closed Sun.* Ⓜ *South Kensington.*

MUSIC

Music & Video Exchange

MUSIC STORES | This store is a music collector's treasure trove, with a constantly changing stock refreshed by customers selling and exchanging as well as buying. The ground floor focuses on rock, pop, indie, and punk, both mainstream and obscure, in a variety of formats ranging from vinyl to CD, cassette, and even minidisk. Don't miss the classical music in the basement and the soul, jazz, house, techno, reggae, and more upstairs. Like movies? There's a wide variety of Blu-ray and DVD box sets, as well as bargain classic and cult films. Keep an eye out for rarities—including first pressings and one-offs—in all departments. Similar exchanges for comics (No. 32) and books (No. 30) are on nearby Pembridge Road (also a destination for vintage clothing for men [No. 34] and women [No. 20], plus more clothing, accessories, and retro homewares [No. 28]). Note: stock depends on what customers bring in to exchange, so you'll surely find many more DVDs with European (PAL) formatting than the North American–friendly NTSC format, but the store does get the latter occasionally. ✉ *38 Notting Hill Gate, Notting Hill* ☎ *020/7243–8573* ⊕ *www.mgeshops.com* Ⓜ *Notting Hill Gate.*

Regent's Park and Hampstead

Regent's Park, Primrose Hill, Belsize Park, and Hampstead are four of London's prettiest and most genteel neighborhoods. The city becomes noticeably calmer and greener as you head uphill from Marylebone Road through Regent's Park to the refreshing greenery of Primrose Hill and the handsome Georgian houses and Regency villas of Hampstead. To the west, the less bucolic but equally elegant St. John's Wood and Little Venice also provide a taste of moneyed London.

GETTING HERE

To get to Hampstead by Tube, take the Northern Line (the Edgware branch) to Hampstead or Golders Green Station, or take the London Overground to Hampstead Heath Station. The south side of Hampstead Heath can also be reached by the London Overground Gospel Oak Station. To get to Regent's Park, take the Bakerloo Line to Regent's Park Tube station or, for Primrose Hill, the Chalk Farm stop on the Northern Line. Little Venice is reachable by the Warwick Avenue stop on the Bakerloo Line, and St. John's Wood has its own stop on the Jubilee Line.

◉ Sights

★ Hampstead Heath

NATURE PRESERVE | **FAMILY** | For generations, Londoners have headed to Hampstead Heath to escape the dirt and noise of the city. A unique expanse of *rus in urbe* ("country in the city"), its 791 acres encompass a variety of wildlife as well as habitats: grassy meadows, woodland, scrub, wetlands, and some of Europe's most venerable oak forests. Be aware that, aside from the southern slope of Parliament Hill and Golders Hill Park, it is more like countryside than a park, with signs and facilities in short supply. Pick up a map at Kenwood House or at the "Enquiries" window of the Staff Yard near the tennis courts off Highgate Road, where you can also get details about the history of the Heath and the flora and fauna growing there. An excellent alfresco café near the Athletics Field serves Italian food.

Coming onto the Heath from the South End Green entrance, walk east past the children's **Playground** and **Paddling Pool,** turn left, and head to the top of **Parliament Hill.** At 321 feet above sea level,

Regent's Park and Hampstead

KEY
- **1** Sights
- **1** Hotels

Sights ▼
1 Hampstead Heath B2
2 Highgate Cemetery..... D1
3 Kenwood House C1
4 Regent's Park D7
5 ZSL London Zoo......... D6

Hotels ▼
1 Haverstock Hotel C4
2 York & Albany E6

it's one of the highest points in London. You'll find a stunning panorama over the city. On clear days you can see all the way to the South Downs, the hills beyond southern London.

If you keep heading east from the playground instead, you'll come to the **Lido,** an Olympic-size, outdoor, unheated swimming pool that gets packed on all-too-rare hot summer days. ⊠ *Hampstead* ☎ *020/7332–3322* ⊕ *www.cityoflondon. gov.uk/hampstead* ⊠ *Free* Ⓜ *Overground: Hampstead Heath for west of Heath or Gospel Oak for south and east of Heath and Lido. Northern Line: Golders Green, then Bus 210 or 268 to Whitestone Pond for north and west of Heath and Golders Hill Park.*

Highgate Cemetery

CEMETERY | Highgate is not the oldest cemetery in London, but it is probably the best known, both for its roster of famous "inhabitants" and the quality of its funerary architecture. After it was consecrated in 1839, Victorians came from miles around to appreciate the ornate headstones, the impressive tombs, and the view. Such was its popularity that 19 acres on the other side of the road were acquired in 1850, and this additional East Cemetery is the final resting place of numerous notables, including the most visited, Karl Marx (1818–83), as well as George Eliot and, a more recent internment, George Michael. At the summit is the **Circle of Lebanon,** a ring of vaults built around an ancient cypress tree, a legacy of the 17th-century gardens that formerly occupied the site. Leading from the circle is the **Egyptian Avenue,** a subterranean stone tunnel lined with catacombs, itself approached by a dramatic colonnade that screens the main cemetery from the road. Both sides are impressive, with a grand (locked) iron gate leading to a sweeping courtyard built for the approach of horses and carriages. By the 1970s the cemetery had become unkempt and neglected until a group of volunteers,

the Friends of Highgate Cemetery, undertook the huge upkeep. Tours are conducted by the Friends, who will show you the most interesting graves among the numerous statues and memorials once hidden by overgrowth. The West side can only be seen during a one-hour tour. Booking is essential for weekdays but not permitted for weekends; tours of the East side on Saturday are first-come, first-served. You're expected to dress respectfully, so skip the shorts and the baseball cap; children under eight are not admitted and neither are dogs, tripods, or video cameras. Note that unless you book online in advance, admission and tour fees are cash-only. ⊠ *Swains La., Highgate* ☎ *020/8340–1834* ⊕ *www. highgatecemetery.org* ⊠ *East Cemetery £4, tours £8; West Cemetery tours £12, includes admission to East Cemetery* Ⓜ *Archway, then Bus 210, 271, or 143 to Waterlow Park; Belsize Park, then Bus C11 to Brookfield Park.*

★ Kenwood House

HOUSE | This largely Palladian villa offers an escape to a gracious country house with a magnificent collection of Old Masters and beautiful grounds, all within a short Tube ride from central London. Originally built in 1616, Kenwood was expanded by Robert Adam starting in 1767 and later by George Saunders in 1795. Adam refaced most of the exterior and added the splendid library, which, with its vaulted ceiling and Corinthian columns, is the highlight of the house's interior. A major renovation restored four rooms to reflect Adam's intentions as closely as possible, incorporating the furniture he designed for them and his original color schemes. Kenwood is also home to the **Iveagh Bequest,** a world-class collection of some 60 paintings that includes masterworks like Rembrandt's *Self-Portrait with Two Circles* and Vermeer's *The Guitar Player,* along with major works by Reynolds, Van Dyck, Hals, Gainsborough, Turner, and more. The grounds, designed by Humphry Repton and bordered by Hampstead

Heath, are equally elegant and serene, with lawns sloping down to a little lake crossed by a trompe-l'oeil bridge. All in all, it's the perfect home for an 18th-century gentleman. In summer, the grounds host a series of popular and classical concerts, culminating in fireworks on the last night. The Brew House café, occupying part of the old coach house, has outdoor tables in the courtyard and a terraced garden. ⊠ *Hampstead La., Highgate* ☎ *0870/333–1181* ⊕ *www.english-heritage.org.uk/visit/places/kenwood* ⊠ *Free, house and estate tour £18* Ⓜ *Golders Green or Archway, then Bus 210. Overground: Gospel Oak.*

★ **Regent's Park**

CITY PARK | FAMILY | The formal cultivated Regent's Park, more country-house grounds than municipal amenity, began life in 1812, when John Nash was commissioned by the Prince Regent (later George IV) to create a master plan for the former royal hunting ground. Nash's original plan included a summer palace for the prince and 56 villas for friends, none of which were realized except for 8 villas (only 2 survive). However, the grand neoclassical terraced houses on the south, east, and west edges of the park were built by Nash and reflect the scope of his ambitions. Queen Mary's Gardens, which has some 30,000 roses and is a favorite spot for weddings, was created in the 1930s. Today the 395-acre park, with the largest outdoor sports area in central London, draws the athletically inclined from around the city.

At the center of the park is the **Queen Mary's Gardens,** a fragrant 17-acre circle containing more than 400 varieties of roses. Just to the east of the gardens is the **Regent's Park Open-Air Theatre** and the **Boating Lake,** which you can explore by renting a pedalo (paddleboat) or rowboat. Heading east from the rose gardens along Chester Road past the **Broad Walk** will bring you to Nash's iconic white-stucco **Cumberland Terrace,** with its central

Ionic columns surmounted by a triangular Wedgwood-blue pediment. At the north end of the Broad Walk you'll find the **London Zoo,** while to the northwest of the central circle is **The Hub** (*0300/061–2323*), a state-of-the-art community sports center that has changing rooms, exercise classes, and a café with 360-degree views of the surrounding sports fields, used for soccer, rugby, cricket, field hockey, and softball contests. There are also tennis courts toward the park's southeast (Baker Street) entrance, and the park is a favorite north–south route for cyclists. ⊠ *Chester Rd., Regent's Park* ☎ *0300/061–2300* ⊕ *www.royalparks.org.uk* ⊠ *Free* Ⓜ *Baker St., Regent's Park, Great Portland St.*

★ **ZSL London Zoo**

ZOO | FAMILY | With an emphasis on education, wildlife conservation, and the breeding of endangered species, London Zoo offers visitors the chance to see tigers, gorillas, meerkats, and more in something resembling a natural environment rather than a cage. Operated by the nonprofit Zoological Society of London, the zoo was begun with the royal animals collection, moved here from the Tower of London in 1828; the zoo itself did not open to the public until 1847. Big attractions include Land of the Lions, a walk-through re-creation of an Indian forest where you can see three resident Asiatic lions relaxing at close range; Gorilla Kingdom, which provides a similar re-created habitat (in this case an African rain forest) for its colony of six Western Lowland Gorillas; and the Attenborough Komodo Dragon House, renamed to honor the renowned naturalist. The zoo also offers the chance to get up close and personal with 15 ring-tailed lemurs. The huge B.U.G.S. pavilion (Biodiversity Underpinning Global Survival) is a self-sustaining, contained ecosystem for 140 less-cuddly species, including invertebrates such as spiders and millipedes, plus some reptiles and fish. Rainforest Life is an indoor tropical rain forest (complete

A Trip to Abbey Road

The black-and-white crosswalk (known as a "zebra crossing") near the Abbey Road Studios at No. 3, where the Beatles recorded their entire output from "Love Me Do" onward, is a place of pilgrimage for Beatles' fans from around the world, many of them teenagers born long after the band split up. They converge here to re-create the cover of the Beatles' 1969 *Abbey Road* album, posing on the crossing despite the onrushing traffic. ■TIP→ Be careful if you're going to attempt this; traffic on Abbey Road is busy. One of the best ways to explore landmarks in the Beatles' story is to take one of the excellent walking tours offered by **Original London Walks** (☎ 020/7624–3978 ⊕ www. walks.com). Try **The Beatles In-My-Life Walk** (Saturday and Tuesday at 11 am outside Marylebone Railway station) or **The Beatles Magical Mystery Tour** (Wednesday at 2 pm and Thursday except for December and January and Sunday at 11 am, at Underground Exit 1, Tottenham Court Road).

with humidity) inhabited by the likes of armadillos, monkeys, and sloths. A special nighttime section offers glimpses of nocturnal creatures like slow lorises and bats. The Animal Adventures Children's Zoo allows kids to closely observe coatis, as well as to interact with llamas, donkeys, small pigs, sheep, and goats. Two of the most popular attractions are Penguin Beach, especially at feeding time (1:30 and 4:30), and meerkat snack time (11:15), where you can see the sociable animals keeping watch over their own sandy territory.

If you're feeling flush, try to nab one of the six daily "Meet the Penguins" VIP tickets (1:45 pm) that offer a 20-minute guided close encounter with the locals (£54); there are similar VIP encounters with giraffes, meerkats, and various denizens of the rain forest. Other zoo highlights include Butterfly Paradise and Tiger Territory, an enclosure for four beautiful endangered Sumatran tigers (including two cubs born at the zoo). Adults-only Zoo Nights held Friday nights in June and July offer street food, alcoholic drinks, and entertainment. You can also experience the zoo after-hours by booking an overnight stay in one of the cozy cabins

near (not *in*) the lion enclosure. Check the website or the information board out front for free events, including creature close encounters and "ask the keeper" sessions. ⊠ *Outer Circle, Regent's Park* ☎ *0844/225–1826* ⊕ *www.zsl.org* ⊠ *From £27* Ⓜ *Camden Town, then Bus 274.*

🛏 Hotels

Haverstock Hotel

$$ | HOTEL | Just down the hill from Hampstead Village is this stylish boutique hotel located in a converted pub. **Pros:** cool, minimalist decor; convenient to Hampstead, Belsize Park, and Primrose Hill; free Wi-Fi and buffet breakfast. **Cons:** no elevator; rooms on the small side; some rooms can be noisy. $ *Rooms from: £135* ⊠ *154 Haverstock Hill, Hampstead* ☎ *020/7722–5097* ⊕ *www.haverstockhotel.com* ⇨ *22 rooms* ○ *Free breakfast* Ⓜ *Belsize Park.*

York & Albany

$$ | HOTEL | Located on the northern edge of Regent's Park opposite the zoo entrance, this town house hotel with stylish, individually decorated rooms is owned by noted chef Gordon Ramsay, who also operates the restaurant on

the ground floor. **Pros:** location close to Regent's Park and Camden town; excellent restaurant on-site; charming decor that is both traditional and modern. **Cons:** some traffic noise from outside road; hotel located at busy intersection; rooms not spacious for the price. $ *Rooms from: £210* ⊠ *127–129 Parkway* ☎ *207/387–5700* ⊕ *www.gordonramsay-restaurants.com/york-and-albany* 🛏 *9 rooms* 🍽 *No meals* Ⓜ *Camden Town.*

🎭 Performing Arts

Open Air Theatre

THEATER | FAMILY | Works by Shakespeare have been performed here every summer (from mid-May to mid-September) since 1932, with casts including luminaries such as Vivien Leigh, Dame Judi Dench, and Damien Lewis. Today the theater also mounts productions of classic plays, musicals, and shows for family audiences among its four annual productions. *A Midsummer Night's Dream* is the one to catch, if it's on—never has that enchanted Greek wood been better evoked, especially when enhanced by genuine birdsong and a rising moon. There's a covered restaurant for pretheater dining, an informal café, and, of course, a bar. You also can order picnic hampers in advance. The park can get chilly, so bring a blanket. Performances proceed rain or shine (umbrellas aren't allowed) with refunds only in case of a very heavy downpour. ⊠ *Inner Circle, Regent's Park* ☎ *0844/826–4242* ⊕ *www.openairtheatre.com* 🎟 *From £25* Ⓜ *Baker St., Regent's Park.*

Up and Down the Thames

Downstream—meaning seaward, or east—from central London, Greenwich will require a day to explore, especially if you have any interest in maritime history or technology. Upstream to the west are the royal palaces and grand houses that were built as country residences with easy access to London by river. Hampton Court Palace, with its famous maze, is the most notable.

GREENWICH

8 miles east of central London.

About 8 miles downstream (meaning seaward, to the east) from central London, Greenwich is a small borough that looms large across the world. Once the seat of British naval power, it is not only home to the Old Royal Observatory, which measures time for our entire planet, but also the Greenwich Meridian, which divides the world into two—you can stand astride it with one foot in either hemisphere.

The Docklands Light Railway (DLR) is a zippy way to get to Cutty Sark Station from Canary Wharf or Bank Tube station in The City. Or take the DLR to Island Gardens and walk the old Victorian Foot Tunnel under the river. (Sitting at the front of a train can be disconcerting, as you watch the controls in the fully automated driver's cab move about as if a ghost were at the helm.) The best way to arrive, however—time and weather permitting—is like a sea captain of old: by water (it takes an hour from central London).

Up and Down the Thames

Sights ▶
1 *Cutty Sark*...............**G1**
2 Hampton Court Palace....**A3**
3 Kew Gardens............**B1**
4 National Maritime
  Museum................**G1**
5 Richmond Park..........**B2**
6 Royal Observatory.......**G1**

Restaurants ▶
1 Chez Bruce.............**D2**

👁 Sights

★ Cutty Sark

HISTORIC SITE | FAMILY | This sleek, romantic clipper was built in 1869, one among a vast fleet of tall-masted wooden ships that plied the oceanic highways of the 19th century, trading in exotic commodities—in this case, tea. *Cutty Sark* (named after a racy witch in a Robert Burns poem) was the fastest in the fleet, sailing the London–China route in 1871 in only 107 days. The clipper has been preserved in dry dock as a museum ship since the 1950s, but was severely damaged in a devastating fire in 2007. Yet up from the ashes, as the song goes, grow the roses of success: after a major restoration project, the visitor facilities are now better than ever. Not only can you tour the ship in its entirety, but the glittering visitor center (which the ship now rests directly above) allows you to view the hull from below. There's plenty to see here, and the cramped quarters form a fantastic time capsule to walk around in—this boat was never too comfortable for the 28-strong crew (as you'll see). Don't forget to take in the amusing collection of figureheads. The ship also hosts comedy, cabaret, and theater shows. ✉ *King William Walk, Greenwich* ☎ *020/8858–4422* 🌐 *www.rmg.co.uk/cuttysark* 🎟 *From £15* Ⓜ *DLR: Cutty Sark.*

★ National Maritime Museum

MUSEUM | FAMILY | From the time of Henry VIII until the 1940s, Britain was the world's preeminent naval power, and the collections here trace half a millennia of that seafaring history. The story is as much about trade as it is warfare: *Atlantic: Slavery, Trade, Empire* gallery explores how trade in goods (and people) irrevocably changed the world, while *Traders: The East India Company and Asia* focuses on how the epoch-defining company shaped trade with Asia for 250 years. One gallery is devoted to Admiral Lord Nelson, Britain's most famous naval commander, and among the exhibits is the uniform he was wearing, complete with bloodstains, when he died

at the Battle of Trafalgar in 1805. ✉ *Romney Rd., Greenwich* ☎ *020/8312–6608* 🌐 *www.rmg.co.uk/national-maritime-museum* 🎟 *Free; tours £10; fee for special exhibitions* Ⓜ *DLR: Greenwich.*

★ Royal Observatory

MUSEUM | FAMILY | Greenwich is on the prime meridian at 0° longitude, and the ultimate standard for time around the world has been set here since 1884, when Britain was the world's maritime superpower.

The observatory is actually split into two sites, a short walk apart—one devoted to astronomy, the other to the study of time. The enchanting **Peter Harrison Planetarium** is London's only planetarium, its bronze-clad turret glinting in the sun. Shows on black holes and how to interpret the night sky are enthralling and enlightening. Even better for kids are the high-technology rooms of the **Astronomy Centre,** where space exploration is brought to life through cutting-edge interactive programs and fascinating exhibits—including the chance to touch a 4.5-billion-year-old meteorite.

Across the way is **Flamsteed House,** designed by Christopher Wren in 1675 for John Flamsteed, the first Astronomer Royal. A climb to the top of the house reveals a **28-inch telescope,** built in 1893 and now housed inside an onion-shape fiberglass dome. It doesn't compare with the range of modern optical telescopes, but it's still the largest in the United Kingdom. Regular wintertime viewing evenings reveal startlingly detailed views of the lunar surface. In the **Time Galleries,** linger over the superb workmanship of John Harrison (1693–1776), whose famous **Maritime Clocks** won him the Longitude Prize for solving the problem of accurate timekeeping at sea, which paved the way for modern navigation. ✉ *Romney Rd., Greenwich* ☎ *020/8858–4422* 🌐 *www.rmg.co.uk/royal-observatory* 🎟 *Royal Observatory £16, planetarium shows £10; combined ticket with Cutty Sark £27* Ⓜ *DLR: Greenwich.*

Among the botanical splendors of Kew Gardens is the Waterlily House.

RICHMOND

20 miles southwest of central London.

Named after the (long-vanished) palace Henry VII started here in 1500, Richmond is still a welcoming suburb with a small-town feel, marred only by choking levels of traffic. Duck away from the main streets to find many handsome Georgian and Victorian houses, antiques shops, a Victorian theater, a grand stately home—and, best of all, the largest of London's royal parks.

⊙ Sights

★ Hampton Court Palace

CASTLE/PALACE | FAMILY | The beloved seat of Henry VIII's court, sprawled elegantly beside the languid waters of the Thames, Hampton Court is steeped in more history than virtually any other royal building in England. Begun in 1515 by Cardinal Wolsey to curry favor with the young Henry, the Tudor palace actually conceals a larger 17th-century baroque building partly designed by Christopher Wren. George II moved the royal household closer to London in the early 18th century. Wander through the State Apartments before taking in the strikingly azure ceiling of the Chapel Royal. Well-handled reconstructions of Tudor life take place all year. Latter-day masters of the palace, the joint rulers William and Mary (reigned 1689–1702), were responsible for the beautiful King's and Queen's Apartments and the elaborate baroque of the Georgian Rooms. Don't miss the famous hedge maze and the Lower Orangery Garden, which shows off thousands of exotic species that William and Mary gathered from around the globe. ⊠ *Hampton Court Rd., East Molesey* ☎ *020/3166–6000* ⊕ *www.hrp. org.uk/hamptoncourtpalace* ⊠ *£24 palace, maze, and gardens; £5 maze only; £8 maze and gardens* Ⓜ *Richmond, then Bus R68. National Rail: Hampton Court, 35 mins from Waterloo (most trains require change at Surbiton).*

★ Richmond Park

CITY PARK | FAMILY | This enormous park was enclosed in 1637 for use as a royal hunting ground—like practically all other London parks. Unlike the others, however, Richmond Park still has wild red and fallow deer roaming its 2,500 acres (three times the size of New York's Central Park) of grassland and heath. Its ancient oaks are among the last remnants of the vast, wild forests that once encroached on London in medieval times. The Isabella Plantation (near the Ham Gate entrance) is an enchanting and colorful woodland garden, first laid out in 1831. There's a splendid protected view of St. Paul's Cathedral from King Henry VIII's Mound, the highest point in the park; find it, and you have a piece of magic in your sights. The park is also home to White Lodge, a 1727 hunting lodge that now houses the Royal Ballet School. ⊠ *Richmond* ☎ *030/0061–2200* ⊕ *www. royalparks.org.uk* 🎫 *Free* Ⓜ *Richmond, then Bus 371 or 65.*

🍴 Restaurants

Chez Bruce

$$$ | **MODERN FRENCH** | Top-notch French and Mediterranean cuisine, faultless service, and a winning wine list make this one of London's all-star favorite restaurants. At this cozy haunt over-looking Wandsworth Common, prepare for unfussy grown-up gastro wonders ranging from homemade charcuterie to lighter, simply grilled fish dishes. **Known for:** elegant neighborhood salon; luxe classics like lobster and scallop ravioli; impressive sommelier. Ⓢ *Average main: £27* ⊠ *2 Bellevue Rd., Wandsworth Common, Battersea* ☎ *020/8672–0114* ⊕ *www.chezbruce.co.uk* Ⓜ *Overland: Wandsworth Common.*

KEW

6 miles southwest of central London.

A leafy suburb, Kew offers little to see except for its two big attractions: the lovely Kew Palace and the Royal Botanic Gardens—anchored in the landscape for several miles around by a towering, mock-Chinese pagoda.

👁 Sights

★ Kew Gardens

GARDEN | FAMILY | Enter the Royal Botanic Gardens, as Kew Gardens are officially known, and you are enveloped by blazes of color, extraordinary blooms, hidden trails, and lovely old follies. Beautiful though it all is, Kew's charms are secondary to its true purpose as a major center for serious research: over 200 academics are consistently hard at work here on projects spanning 110 countries. First opened to the public in 1840, this 326-acre site has been supported by royalty and nurtured by landscapers, botanists, and architects since the 1720s. Today the gardens, now a UNESCO World Heritage Site, hold more than 30,000 species of plants from every corner of the globe. Although the plant houses make Kew worth visiting even in the depths of winter (there's also a seasonal garden), the flower beds are, of course, best enjoyed in the fullness of spring and summer.

Architect Sir William Chambers built a series of temples and follies, of which the crazy 10-story **Pagoda,** visible for miles around, is the star. The Princess of Wales Conservatory houses 10 climate zones, and the Xstrata Treetop Walkway takes you 59 feet up into the air. Two great 19th-century greenhouses—the **Palm House** and the **Temperate House**—are filled with exotic blooms, and many of the plants have been there since the final glass panel was fixed into place, including the largest greenhouse plant in the world, a Chilean wine palm planted in 1846 (and so big that you have to climb the spiral staircase to the roof to get a proper view of it). ⊠ *Kew Rd. at Lichfield Rd., for Victoria Gate entrance, Kew* ☎ *020/8332–5000* ⊕ *www.kew. org* 🎫 *£17, Explorer Land Train £5* Ⓜ *Kew Gardens. National Rail: Kew Gardens, Kew Bridge.*

Chapter 4

OXFORD AND THE THAMES VALLEY

Updated by
Toby Orton

👁 **Sights**
★★★★☆

🍴 **Restaurants**
★★★★☆

🛏 **Hotels**
★★★★☆

🛍 **Shopping**
★★★☆☆

🍸 **Nightlife**
★★★☆☆

WELCOME TO OXFORD AND THE THAMES VALLEY

TOP REASONS TO GO

★ **Oxford:** While scholars' noses are buried in their books, you get to sightsee among Oxford University's ancient stone buildings and memorable museums.

★ **Windsor Castle:** The mystique of eight successive royal houses of the British monarchy permeates Windsor and its famous castle, where a fraction of the current Queen's vast wealth is displayed.

★ **Blenheim Palace:** The only British historic home to be named a World Heritage Site has magnificent baroque architecture, stunning parkland, and remembrances of Winston Churchill.

★ **Boating on the Thames:** Life is slower on the river, and renting a boat or taking a cruise is an ideal way to see verdant riverside pastures and villages. Windsor, Marlow, Henley, and Oxford are good options.

An ideal place to begin any exploration of the Thames Valley is the town of Windsor, about an hour's drive west of central London. From there you can follow the river to Marlow and to Henley-on-Thames, site of the famous regatta, and then make a counterclockwise sweep west to the area around Henley-on-Thames. To the north is Oxford, with its pubs, colleges, and museums; it can make a good base for exploring some of the area's charming towns and notable stately homes. If you're extending your itinerary, west of the region but still nearby are the Cotswolds and Stratford-upon-Avon.

1 **Windsor.** A gorgeous town with one of England's most famous castles.

2 **Eton.** Home to England's most prestigious secondary school.

3 **Ascot.** A posh town famous for horse racing.

4 **Cliveden.** A stately mansion and one of the country's grandest hotels.

5 **Marlow.** A lovely Thames-side village.

6 **Henley-on-Thames.** A village famed for its rowing regatta.

7 **Oxford.** One of the world's oldest and greatest centers of learning.

8 **Woodstock.** Home to extraordinary Blenheim Palace, Winston Churchill's birthplace.

9 **Aylesbury.** A good base for exploring the area's grand manor houses.

10 **St. Albans.** A historical town that's close to the popular Harry Potter Studio Tour.

11 **Woburn Abbey.** A grand manor house.

12 **Althorp.** The alluring childhood home of the late Princess Diana.

Easy proximity to London has made the Thames Valley a favored hangout for the wealthy, just as it has been for centuries. The rich and powerful of centuries past built the lavish country estates and castles, including Windsor, that today form the area's most popular tourist attractions.

Many of these are easy day trips from London, as is Oxford and its famed university. Consider exploring this stretch of the River Thames by boat, either jumping aboard a cruiser or getting behind the oars. Windsor, Henley, and Marlow all make good starting points.

Once an aquatic highway connecting London to the rest of England and the world, the Thames was critical to the power of the city when the sun never set on the British Empire. By the 18th century, the Thames was one of the world's busiest water systems, declining in commercial importance only when the 20th century brought other means of transportation to the forefront. Traditionally, the area west of London is known as the Thames Valley, and the area to the east is called the Thames Gateway.

Anyone who wants to understand the mystique of the British monarchy should visit Windsor, home to the medieval and massive Windsor Castle. Farther upstream, the green quadrangles and graceful spires of Oxford are the hallmarks of one of the world's most famous universities. Within 10 miles of Oxford the storybook village of Woodstock and gracious Blenheim Palace, one of the grandest houses in England, are both well worth your time.

The railroads and motorways carrying traffic to and from London have turned much of this area into commuter territory, but you can still find timeless villages and miles of relaxing countryside. The stretches of the Thames near Marlow and Henley-on-Thames are lovely, with rowing clubs, piers, and sturdy waterside cottages and villas. It all conspires to make the Thames Valley a wonderful find, even for experienced travelers.

MAJOR REGIONS

Winsor, Marlow, and Nearby. Windsor Castle is one of the jewels of the area known as Royal Windsor, but a journey around this section of the Thames has other pleasures. The town of Eton holds the eponymous private school, Ascot has its famous racecourse, and Cliveden is a stately home turned into a grand hotel.

The stretch of the Thames Valley from Marlow to Henley-on-Thames is enchanting. Walking through its fields and along its waterways, it's easy to see how it inspired Kenneth Grahame's classic 1908 children's book, *The Wind in the Willows*. Whether by boat or on foot, you can discover some of the region's most delightful scenery. On each bank are fine wooded hills with spacious homes, greenhouses, flower gardens, and neat lawns that stretch to the water's edge. Grahame wrote his book in Pangbourne, and his illustrator, E. H. Shepard, used the great house at Mapledurham as the model for Toad Hall. It all still has the power to inspire.

Oxford. Wonderfully walkable, this university town has handsome, golden-stone buildings and museum after museum to explore. Take a punt on the local waterways for a break. Oxford's good bars, pubs, and restaurants keep you going late at night as well.

Oxfordshire. The River Thames takes on a new graciousness as it flows along the borders of Oxfordshire for 71 miles; with each league it increases in size and importance. Three tributaries swell the river as it passes through the landscape: the Windrush, the Evenlode, and the Cherwell. Tucked among the hills and dales are one of England's most impressive stately homes, an Edenic little town, and a former Rothschild estate. Closer to London in Hertfordshire is St. Albans, wtih its cathedral and Roman remains.

Planning

When to Go

High summer is lovely, but droves of visitors have the same effect on some travelers as bad weather. Consider visiting in late spring or early fall, when the weather isn't too bad, and the crowds have headed home. Book tickets and accommodations well in advance for Henley's Royal Regatta at the cusp of June and July and Ascot's Royal Meeting in mid-June. Visiting Eton and the Oxford colleges is much more restricted during term time (generally September to late March and late April to mid-July). Most stately homes are open March through September or October

only—call in advance. Avoid any driving in the London area during morning and afternoon rush hours.

FESTIVALS
Henley Festival
FESTIVALS | A floating stage and spectacular musical events, from classical to folk, draw a well-heeled crowd who dress to impress. The Henley Festival takes place during the week after the regatta in July. ✉ Henley ☎ 01491/843400 ⊕ www.henley-festival.co.uk.

★ Oxford Literary Festival
FESTIVALS | The festival takes place during the last week of March at Christ Church College, the Sheldonian, and other university venues. Leading authors come to give lectures and interviews, and there's plenty to entertain children. ✉ Christ Church College, St. Aldate's, Oxford ☎ 07444/318986 ⊕ www.oxfordliteraryfestival.org.

Windsor Festival
FESTIVALS | Concerts, poetry readings, and children's events highlight the Windsor Festival, held over the last two weeks in September, with events occasionally taking place in the castle. The festival also runs a smaller program in March, with a focus on classical music events. ☎ 01753/743585 ⊕ www.windsorfestival.com.

Planning Your Time

The major towns of the Thames Valley are easy to visit on a day trip from London. A train to Windsor, for example, takes about an hour, and you can fully explore the town and its environs in a day. Base yourself in Oxford for a couple of days, though, if you want to make a thorough exploration of the town and the surrounding countryside. To visit the great houses and the rural castles you need to either rent a car or join an organized tour. Blenheim Palace and Waddesdon Manor require at least half a day to do them justice, as do Stowe Landscape Gardens and Woburn Abbey.

Getting Here and Around

BUS

Oxford and the area's main towns are convenient by bus from London, as is Windsor (although trains are faster), but St. Albans is best reached by train.

You can travel between the major towns by local bus, but it's complicated and can require changing more than once. For information, contact Traveline. If you want to see more than one town in this area in a day, it's best to rent a car or join a tour.

CONTACTS Arriva. ⊕ *www.arrivabus. co.uk.* **First.** ☎ *01224/650100* ⊕ *www.first-group.com.* **Megabus.** ☎ *0900/160–0900 booking line, calls cost £0.60 per min* ⊕ *uk.megabus.com.* **Oxford Bus Company.** ☎ *01865/785400* ⊕ *www.oxfordbus. co.uk.* **Reading Buses.** ☎ *0118/959–4000* ⊕ *www.reading-buses.co.uk.* **Stagecoach Oxford Tube.** ☎ *01865/772250* ⊕ *www. oxfordtube.com.* **Traveline.** ☎ *0871/200–2233* ⊕ *www.traveline.info.*

CAR

Most towns in this area are within a one- or two-hour drive of central London—except during rush hour, of course. Although the roads are good, this wealthy section of the commuter belt has heavy traffic, even on the secondary roads. Parking in towns can be a problem, so take advantage of public parking lots near the outskirts of town centers.

TRAIN

Trains to Oxford (one hour) and the region depart from London's Paddington Station. Trains bound for Ascot (50 minutes) leave from Waterloo every 30 minutes. Trains to St. Albans (20 minutes) leave from St. Pancras Station. A number of lines, including Chiltern and First Great Western, serve the area; National Rail Enquiries has information.

CONTACTS National Rail Enquiries. ☎ *0845/748–4950* ⊕ *www.nationalrail. co.uk.*

Restaurants

Londoners weekend here, and where they go, stellar restaurants follow. Bray (near Windsor), Marlow, and Great Milton (near Oxford) claim some excellent tables; you need to book months ahead for these. Simple pub food, as well as classic French cuisine, can be enjoyed in waterside settings at many restaurants beside the Thames. Even in towns away from the river, well-heeled commuters and Oxford professors support top-flight establishments. Reservations are often not required but are strongly recommended, especially on weekends.

Hotels

From converted country houses to refurbished Elizabethan inns, the region's accommodations are rich in history and distinctive in appeal. Many hotels cultivate traditional gardens and retain a sense of the past with impressive collections of antiques. Book ahead, particularly in summer; you're competing for rooms with many Londoners in search of a getaway.

⇨ *Restaurant and hotel reviews have been shortened. For full information, visit Fodors.com. Restaurant prices are the average cost of a main course at dinner, or if dinner is not served, at lunch. Hotel prices are the lowest cost of a standard double room in high season, including 20% V.A.T.*

WHAT IT COSTS in Pounds			
$	$$	$$$	$$$$
RESTAURANTS			
under £16	£16–£23	£24–£30	over £30
HOTELS			
under £125	£125–£225	£226–£350	over £350

Visitor Information

CONTACTS Tourism Southeast.
☎ 02380/625400 ⊕ www.visitsouth-
eastengland.com. **Visit Thames.** ⊕ www.
visitthames.co.uk.

Windsor

21 miles west of London.

Only a small part of old Windsor—the
settlement that grew up around the
town's famous castle in the Middle
Ages—has survived. The town isn't what
it was in the time of Sir John Falstaff
and the *Merry Wives of Windsor,* when
it was famous for its convivial inns—in
1650, it had about 70 of them. Only a
handful remain today, with the others
replaced, it seems, by endless cafés.
Windsor can feel overrun by tourists in
summer, but even so, romantics appreciate cobbled Church Lane and noble
Queen Charlotte Street, opposite the
castle entrance.

GETTING HERE AND AROUND
Fast Green Line buses leave from the
Colonnades opposite London's Victoria
Coach Station every half hour for the
70-minute trip to Windsor. First Group
has frequent service from Heathrow
Airport's Terminal 5; the journey takes
less than an hour. First Group also runs
regional bus service to small towns and
villages near Windsor.

Trains travel from London Waterloo every
30 minutes, or you can catch a more frequent train from Paddington and change
at Slough. The trip takes less than an
hour from Waterloo and around 30 minutes from Paddington. If you're driving,
the M4 from London takes around an
hour. Park in one of the public lots near
the edge of the town center.

TOURS
Ascot Carriages
Year-round carriage rides depart from
the Savill Garden Visitor Centre, 4 miles
south of the castle (£60 for 30 minutes
or £120 per hour). You can combine a ride
with a vintage afternoon tea in the Savill
Garden Gallery Café (£9 per person) or a
picnic (the carriage stops for a long break
in a secluded spot—you bring the picnic).
✉ Savill Garden, Wick La., Englefield
Green ☎ 07811/543019 ⊕ www.ascotcar-
riages.co.uk.

City Sightseeing
Hop-on, hop-off tours of Windsor and Eton
are offered by City Sightseeing, though it's
easy to explore compact Windsor on foot.
☎ 01789/299123 ⊕ www.city-sightseeing.
com ⊠ From £12.

ESSENTIALS
BUS CONTACTS First Group. ☎ 0175/352–
4144 ⊕ www.firstgroup.com. **Green Line.**
☎ 0344/801–7261 ⊕ www.greenline.co.uk.

**VISITOR INFORMATION Royal Wind-
sor Information Centre.** ✉ Old Booking
Hall, Windsor Royal Station, Thames
St. ☎ 01753/743900, 01753/743907 for
accommodations ⊕ www.windsor.gov.uk.

◉ Sights

Savill Garden
GARDEN | The main horticultural delight of
Windsor Great Park, the exquisite Savill
Garden is about 4 miles from Windsor
Castle. The 35 acres of ornamental
gardens contain an impressive display
of 2,500 rosebushes and a tremendous
diversity of trees and shrubs. The Savill
Building, easily recognizable by its undulating roof in the shape of a leaf, holds
a visitor center, restaurant, and terrace
where you can dine overlooking the garden, as well as a large shopping area with
plenty of gifts, cards, and original artwork.
✉ Wick Rd., Egham ☎ 01753/860222
⊕ www.windsorgreatpark.co.uk ⊠ £12
Mar.–Oct., £6 Nov.–Feb.

Windsor, Marlow, and Nearby

★ Windsor Castle

CASTLE/PALACE | From William the Conqueror to Queen Victoria, the kings and queens of England added towers and wings to this brooding, imposing castle that is visible for miles. It's the largest inhabited castle in the world and the only royal residence in continuous use by the British Royal Family since the Middle Ages. Despite the multiplicity of hands involved in its design, the palace manages to have a unity of style and character. The most impressive view of Windsor Castle is from the A332 road, coming into town from the south. Admission includes an audio guide and, if you wish, a guided tour of the castle precincts. Entrance lines can be long in season, and you're likely to spend at least half a day here, so come early.

As you enter, **Henry VIII's gateway** leads uphill into the wide castle precincts, where you're free to wander. Across from the entrance is the exquisite **St. George's Chapel** (closed Sunday). Here lie 10 of the kings of England, including Henry VI, Charles I, and Henry VIII (Jane Seymour is the only one of his six wives buried here). One of the noblest buildings in England, the chapel was built in the Perpendicular style popular in the 15th and 16th centuries, with elegant stained-glass windows; a high, vaulted ceiling; and intricately carved choir stalls. The colorful heraldic banners of the Knights of the Garter—the oldest British Order of Chivalry, founded by Edward III in 1348—hang in the choir. The ceremony in which the knights are installed as members of the order has been held here with much pageantry for more than five centuries.

The elaborate **Albert Memorial Chapel** was created by Queen Victoria in memory of her husband.

The **North Terrace** provides especially good views across the Thames to Eton College, perhaps the most famous of Britain's exclusive public schools (confusingly, "public schools" in Britain are highly traditional, top-tier private schools). From the terrace, you enter the **State Apartments,** which are open to the public most days. On display to the left of the entrance to the State Apartments, **Queen Mary's Dolls' House** is a perfect miniature Georgian palace-within-a-palace, created in 1923. Electric lights glow, the doors all have tiny keys, and a miniature library holds Lilliputian-size books written especially for the young queen by famous authors of the 1920s. Five cars, including a Daimler and Rolls-Royce, stand at the ready. In the adjacent corridor are exquisite French couturier–designed costumes made for the two Jumeau dolls presented to the Princesses Elizabeth and Margaret by France in 1938.

Although a fire in 1992 gutted some of the State Apartments, hardly any works of art were lost. Phenomenal repair work brought to now life the **Grand Reception Room,** the **Green and Crimson Drawing Rooms,** and the **State and Octagonal Dining Rooms.** A green oak hammer-beam (a short horizontal beam that projects from the tops of walls for support) roof looms magnificently over the 600-year-old **St. George's Hall,** where the Queen gives state banquets. The State Apartments contain priceless furniture, including a magnificent Louis XVI bed and Gobelin tapestries; carvings by Grinling Gibbons; and paintings by Canaletto, Rubens, Van Dyck, Holbein, Dürer, and Bruegel. The tour's high points are the **Throne Room** and the **Waterloo Chamber,** where Sir Thomas Lawrence's portraits of Napoléon's victorious foes line the walls. You can also see arms and armor—look for Henry VIII's ample suit.

A visit October to March also includes the Semi-State rooms, the private apartments of George IV, resplendent with gilded ceilings.

To see the castle come magnificently alive, check out the Changing the Guard, which takes place daily at 11 am April to July and on alternate days at the same time August to March. Confirm the exact schedule before traveling to Windsor. Note that the State rooms (and sometimes the entire castle) are closed during official state occasions; dates of these closures are listed on the website, or you can call ahead to check. Oh, and if the Royal Standard flag is being flown, you'll know the Queen is in residence. ⊠ *Castle Hill* ☎ *0303/123–7304 for tickets* ⊕ *www. rct.uk/visit/windsor-castle* ⊠ *£23.50 for Precincts, State Apartments, Gallery, St. George's Chapel, and Queen Mary's Dolls' House; £12.90 when State Apartments are closed.*

★ Windsor Great Park

CITY PARK | The remains of an ancient royal hunting forest, this park stretches for some 5,000 acres south of Windsor Castle. Much of it is open to the public and can be explored by car or on foot. Its chief attractions are clustered around the southeastern section, known (or at least marketed) as the **Royal Landscape.** These include **Virginia Water,** a 2-mile-long lake that forms the park's main geographical focal point. More than anything, however, the Royal Landscape is defined by its two beautiful gardens. **Valley Gardens,** located on the north shore of Virginia Water, is particularly vibrant in April and May, when the dazzling multicolor azaleas are in full bloom. If you're feeling fit, the romantic **Long Walk** is one of England's most photographed footpaths—the 3-mile-long route, designed by Charles II, starts in the Great Park and leads all the way to Windsor Castle.

Boating on the Thames

Whether you're drifting lazily along in your own boat or taking a sight-seeing cruise past crucial points of English history, you'll see the River Thames from a new and delightful vantage point out on the water. It's hard to beat gliding peacefully on the river, water meadows on either side of you, and then tying up for a picnic or lunch at a riverside pub. You can just putter about in a rowboat for an hour or so, or hire a boat and organize your own itinerary for a few days. If this doesn't appeal, go on a romantic lunch cruise or take one of the many organized trips. There are 125 miles of navigable water to explore, quieter nearer the source of the Thames in the Cotswolds, perhaps most picturesque between Pangbourne and Marlow, and busiest nearer London. Wherever you go, your pace of life will slow right down: boats aren't allowed to travel above 5 mph.

Choosing a Boat

Most boats rented by the hour accommodate four people. Motorboats are noisy, but you can opt for electric canoes or launches that have the benefit of canopies. Punts (flat-bottom wooden boats) require a strong arm so you can maneuver the long wooden pole and push the boat along. Narrow boats carried freight on canals but are now well equipped for pleasure trips.

Renting Boats

The main hubs for boat rental are at Windsor, Henley-on-Thames, Oxford, and Lechlade. The costs are £15 an hour for a rowboat, £25 for an electric boat, £60 for half a day with a punt, and £175 a day for a motor cruiser. A short trip for four on a narrow boat from Oxfordshire Narrowboats ranges from around £160 to £1,000.

Hobbs of Henley ⊠ Station Rd., Henley on Thames ☎ 01491/572035 ⊕ www.hobbsofhenley.com.

Oxford River Cruises ⊠ Folly Bridge, Oxford ☎ 01865/987147, 0845/226–9396 ⊕ www.oxfordrivercruises.com.

Oxfordshire Narrowboats ⊠ Heyford Wharf, Station Rd., Lower Heyford ☎ 01869/340348 ⊕ www.oxfordshire-narrowboats.co.uk.

Hiring Boats

Hire a private boat with its own skipper to take you on a leisurely cruise. Compleat Angler in Marlow will take you on 1- or 2½-hour-long cruises down the river as far as Cliveden or even Windsor. The shortest trips available take about one hour.

Compleat Angler ⊠ Marlow Bridge, Bisham Rd., Marlow ☎ 0344/879–9210 ⊕ www.macdonaldhotels.co.uk/compleatangler.

Cruises

Windsor Castle, Runnymede, Henley (where you can stop for the River & Rowing Museum), and Mapledurham all lie on the banks of the Thames. Salter's Steamers runs short round-trips out of Windsor, Henley, Oxford, and Marlow, and French Brothers runs round-trips from Windsor.

French Brothers ⊠ The Promenade, Barry Ave. ☎ 01753/851900 ⊕ www.frenchbrothers.co.uk.

Salter's Steamers ⊠ Folly Bridge, Oxford ☎ 01865/243421 ⊕ www.salterssteamers.co.uk.

Divided from the Great Park by the busy A308 highway, the smaller **Windsor Home Park,** on the eastern side of Windsor Castle, is the private property of the Royal Family. It contains **Frogmore House,** a lavish royal residence. Completed in 1684, Frogmore was bought by George III as a gift for his wife, Queen Charlotte. The sprawling white mansion later became a beloved retreat of Queen Victoria. It was also formerly home to the Duke and Duchess of Sussex, otherwise known as Prince Harry and Meghan Markle, and can still only be visited by guided tour on a handful of days throughout August; see ⊕ www.rct.uk for more information. ⊠ *Entrances on A329, A332, B383, and Wick La.* ☎ *01753/860222* ⊕ *www.windsorgreatpark.co.uk* ⊡ *£12.50* ⊘ *Windsor Home Park closed Sept.–July and Mon. and weekends in Aug.*

🍴 Restaurants

Bel and the Dragon

$$ | MODERN BRITISH | Sit street side and watch as village life streams by, or cozy up in the oak-beamed bar of this historic inn dating from the 11th century. Rotisserie-cooked beef, pork, and chicken are specialties, and they do an exceptionally fine fish pie. **Known for:** excellent dishes right off the grill; perfect fish pie; hip and friendly staff. ⑤ *Average main: £18* ⊠ *Thames St.* ☎ *01753/866056* ⊕ *www. belandthedragon-windsor.co.uk.*

★ Fat Duck

$$$$ | MODERN BRITISH | One of the top restaurants in the country, and ranked by many food writers among the best in the world, this extraordinary place packs in fans of hypercreative, hyperexpensive cuisine, who enjoy it for the theater as much as for the food. Culinary alchemist Heston Blumenthal is famed for the so-called molecular gastronomy he creates in his laboratory-like kitchen, and his name has become synonymous with weird and funky taste combinations. **Known for:** creative and immersive dining experience; strict booking process and long waiting list for reservations; famed strange dishes like bacon-and-egg ice cream. ⑤ *Average main: £325* ⊠ *High St., Bray* ☎ *01628/580333* ⊕ *www.thefatduck.co.uk* ⊘ *Closed Sun. and Mon.*

Hinds Head

$$$$ | MODERN BRITISH | Fat Duck's esteemed chef Heston Blumenthal owns this Michelin-starred pub across the road, where he sells less extreme dishes at more reasonable prices. A brilliant modern take on traditional English cuisine, the menu may include roast chicken and smoked almonds, or stone bass with mussel and saffron broth. **Known for:** famed celebrity chef; historic ambience; big crowds so booking ahead is smart. ⑤ *Average main: £32* ⊠ *High St., Bray* ☎ *01628/626151* ⊕ *www.hindsheadbray. com* ⊘ *Closed Mon. No dinner Sun.*

★ Two Brewers

$$ | BRITISH | Locals congregate in a pair of low-ceiling rooms at this tiny 17th-century establishment by the gates of Windsor Great Park. Those under 18 aren't allowed inside the pub (although they can be served at a few outdoor tables), but adults will find a suitable collection of wine, espresso, and local beer, plus an excellent menu with dishes like roasted cod with butter sauce and samphire or steak frites with brandy and peppercorn. **Known for:** classic, adults-only British pub; traditional lunchtime roast on Sunday; historic setting. ⑤ *Average main: £16* ⊠ *34 Park St.* ☎ *01753/855426* ⊕ *www. twobrewerswindsor.co.uk.*

🛏 Hotels

Langton House

$ | B&B/INN | FAMILY | A former residence for representatives of the crown, this Victorian mansion on a quiet, leafy road is a 10-minute walk from Windsor Castle. **Pros:** soothing decor; family-friendly environment; friendly hosts. **Cons:** may hear some airplane noise; a little out of town;

At Eton College, students wear the school's traditional shirts, coats, and pinstripe pants.

cheaper rooms have shared bathrooms. $ *Rooms from: £102* ✉ *46 Alma Rd.* ☎ *01753/858299* ⊕ *www.langtonhouse. co.uk* ⇄ *5 rooms* ⍄ *Free breakfast.*

MGallery Windsor Castle Hotel

$$$ | **HOTEL** | You're treated to an exceptional view of Windsor Castle's Changing the Guard ceremony from this former coaching inn, parts of which date back to the 16th century. **Pros:** excellent location; wonderful afternoon tea; great view of the castle. **Cons:** older rooms are small; furniture is faux antique; a bit pricey. $ *Rooms from: £320* ✉ *18 High St.* ☎ *01753/851577* ⊕ *www.castlehotelwindsor.com* ⇄ *112 rooms* ⍄ *Free breakfast.*

Oakley Court

$$ | **HOTEL** | A romantic getaway on the Thames, this Victorian-era mansion stands on landscaped grounds 3 miles west of Windsor. **Pros:** stunning mansion; lots of pampering; friendly staff. **Cons:** bedrooms could do with an update; river views cost more; noisy parakeets on grounds. $ *Rooms from: £184* ✉ *Windsor Rd.* ☎ *01753/609988*

⊕ *www.theoakleycourthotel.co.uk* ⇄ *118 rooms* ⍄ *Free breakfast.*

★ Stoke Park

$$$$ | **HOTEL** | On a 350-acre estate, Stoke Park's neoclassical grandeur can make Windsor Castle, visible in the distance, seem almost humble in comparison. **Pros:** luxurious rooms; sweeping grounds; great spa. **Cons:** not for those lukewarm about golf; old-school atmosphere not for everyone; very pricey, even for what you get. $ *Rooms from: £350* ✉ *Park Rd., Stoke Poges* ☎ *01753/717171* ⊕ *www.stokepark.com* ⇄ *77 rooms* ⍄ *No meals.*

🎭 Performing Arts

The Old Court

ARTS CENTERS | **FAMILY** | Windsor's former fire station has a whole new lease on life as a contemporary arts venue, presenting films, theater, music, dance, and comedy, with plenty of events for kids. ✉ *The Old Court, St. Leonard's Rd.* ☎ *01753/911333* ⊕ *www.oldcourt.org.*

Theatre Royal

THEATER | FAMILY | Windsor's Theatre Royal, where productions have been staged since 1910, is one of Britain's leading provincial theaters. It puts on plays and musicals year-round, including a pantomime for five weeks around Christmas. ⊠ *Thames St.* ☎ *01753/853888* ⊕ *www.theatreroyalwindsor.co.uk.*

💼 Shopping

Windsor Royal Station

SHOPPING CENTERS/MALLS | Set within a handsome building that was once a Victorian-era train station, Windsor Royal Station is home to fashion outlets like Mint Velvet, Jigsaw, Whistles, and Vanilla. ⊠ *5 Goswell Hill* ☎ *01753/797070* ⊕ *www.windsorroyalstation.co.uk.*

🏃 Activities

John Logie Motorboats

BOATING | From April through October, John Logie Motorboats rents motorboats and rowboats, starting at £28 for a half hour (weather and river conditions permitting). ⊠ *Barry Ave.* ☎ *07774/983809* ⊕ *www.johnlogiemotorboats.com.*

Eton

23 miles west of London.

Some observers may find it symbolic that almost opposite Windsor Castle—which embodies the continuity of the royal tradition—stands Eton, a school that for centuries has educated many leaders of the country. With High Street, its single main street, leading from the river to the famous school, the old-fashioned town of Eton is much quieter than Windsor.

GETTING HERE AND AROUND

Eton is linked to Windsor by a footbridge across the Thames. Most visitors barely notice passing from one to the other.

👁 Sights

★ Eton College

COLLEGE | Signs warn drivers of "Boys Crossing" as you approach the splendid Tudor-style buildings of Eton College, the distinguished boarding school for boys ages 13–18 founded in 1440 by King Henry VI. It's all terrifically photogenic—during the college semester students still dress in pinstripe trousers, swallowtail coats, and stiff collars. Rivaling St. George's at Windsor in terms of size, the Gothic **Chapel** contains superb 15th-century grisaille wall paintings juxtaposed with modern stained glass by John Piper. Beyond the cloisters are the school's playing fields where, according to the Duke of Wellington, the Battle of Waterloo was really won, since so many of his officers had learned discipline and strategy during their school days. Boris Johnson is the most recent of the country's many prime ministers to have been educated here. The **Museum of Eton Life** has displays on the school's history and vignettes of school life. The school gives public tours on Friday afternoon from early April through August, bookable online. ⊠ *Brewhouse Yard* ☎ *01753/370100* ⊕ *www.etoncollege.com* 💳 *£10* ⊘ *Closed Sept.–early Apr.*

Runnymede

MEMORIAL | A giant step in the history of democracy was taken at Runnymede on the Thames outside Egham. Here King John, under his barons' compulsion, signed the Magna Carta in 1215, affirming in theory that individuals had the right to justice and liberty. There's not much to see, though you can stroll the woodlands. On the hillside, in a meadow given to the United States by Queen Elizabeth in 1965, stands a memorial to President John F. Kennedy. Nearby is another memorial, a classical temple in style, erected by the American Bar Association for the 750th anniversary of the signing. There is no visitor center at Runnymede, just informational plaques, a nice tearoom, and a parking lot (small charge). The site is on the south side of A308 (traffic is noisy); on the opposite bank of the Thames are the ruins of the 11th-century St. Mary's Priory and the 2,000-year-old Ankerwycke Yew. ⊠ *A308, Egham* ☎ *01784/432891* ⊕ *www.nationaltrust. org.uk/runnymede-and-ankerwycke* 🎫 *Free; parking £1.80 per hour.*

🍴 Restaurants

Gilbey's Eton

$$ | MODERN BRITISH | Just over the bridge from Windsor, this restaurant at the center of Eton's Antiques Row serves a changing menu of imaginative fare, from potted ham hock and rhubarb with sweet onion and mustard seed to crayfish and dill hot-smoked trout fish cakes. Well-priced wines, both French and from the restaurant's own English vineyard, are a specialty, as are the savories—meat, fish, and vegetarian pâtés. **Known for:** traditional English food; old-school charm; bargain fixed-price lunches. $ *Average main: £19* ⊠ *82–83 High St.* ☎ *01753/854921* ⊕ *www.gilbeygroup.com/restaurants/ gilbeys-eton.*

🛏 Hotels

Christopher Hotel

$$ | HOTEL | This former coaching inn on the village's main shopping street has spacious rooms in the handsome main building as well as in the courtyard mews. **Pros:** a nice mix of modern and historic; good restaurant; great location. **Cons:** steep stairs; courtyard rooms can be noisy; rooms could use a little sprucing up. $ *Rooms from: £160* ⊠ *110 High St.* ☎ *01753/852359* ⊕ *www.thechristopher.co.uk* 🛏 *34 rooms* ⏹ *Free breakfast.*

Ascot

8 miles southwest of Windsor, 28 miles southwest of London.

The posh town of Ascot (pronounced *as*-cut) has for centuries been famous for horse racing and for style. Queen Anne chose to have a racecourse here, and the first race meeting took place in 1711. The impressive show of millinery for which the Royal Meeting (or Royal Ascot, as it is also known) is famed was immortalized in *My Fair Lady,* in which a hat with osprey feathers and black-and-white silk roses transformed Eliza Doolittle into a grand lady. Betting on the races at England's most prestigious course is as important as dressing up; it's all part of the fun.

GETTING HERE AND AROUND
If you're driving, leave M4 at Junction 6 and take A332. Trains from London leave Waterloo Station every half hour, and the journey takes 50 minutes. The racecourse is a seven-minute walk from the train station.

👁 Sights

Ascot Racecourse

SPORTS—SIGHT | The races run regularly throughout the year, and Royal Ascot takes place annually in mid-June. ■ **TIP→ Tickets for Royal Ascot generally go on sale in November, so buy them well in advance.** Prices range from £26 for standing room on the heath to around £90 for seats in the stands. Car parking costs £40 in advance or £45 on the day. ⊠ *A329* ☎ *0844/346–3000* ⊕ *www.ascot. co.uk.*

🛏 Hotels

★ Coworth Park

$$$ | HOTEL | FAMILY | Much imaginative and thoughtful renovation has transformed this 18th-century mansion, set on 240 acres of parkland, into a playful and contemporary lodging. **Pros:**

Watching the horse races at Royal Ascot is a posh British tradition.

country-house atmosphere; attentive and friendly service; free activities for kids. **Cons:** not for traditionalists; eye-wateringly expensive; some bedrooms are small. ⑤ *Rooms from: £350* ✉ *Blacknest Rd.* ☎ *01344/876600* ⊕ *www.dorchestercollection.com/en/ascot/coworth-park* ⤴ *70 rooms* ⦿ *Free breakfast.*

Cliveden

8 miles northwest of Windsor, 16 miles north of Ascot, 26 miles west of London.

This grand stately home, designed by Charles Barry, the architect of the Houses of Parliament, and the setting of the notorious Profumo affair in the 1960s, has spectacular gardens and sweeping views to the Thames.

GETTING HERE AND AROUND

If you're driving, take the M4 to the A4, where brown signs lead you to the entrance off the A4094.

◉ Sights

Cliveden

HOUSE | FAMILY | Described by Queen Victoria as a "bijou of taste," Cliveden (pronounced *Cliv*-dn) is a magnificent country mansion that, for more than 300 years, has lived up to its Georgian heritage as a bastion of aesthetic delights. The house, set on 376 acres of gardens and parkland above the River Thames, was rebuilt in 1851; but it was the rich and powerful Astor family, who purchased it in 1893, that made Cliveden famous. In the 1920s and 1930s this was the meeting place for the influential salon known as the "Cliveden Set"—a group of strongly conservative thinkers who many accused of being Nazi sympathizers. Its doyenne was Nancy Astor, an American by birth, who became the first woman to sit in the British Parliament. The ground-floor rooms of the house are open, as is the Octagon Chapel, with its beautiful gilt-painted ceiling and wall panels. You can wander the lovely grounds, which include a water garden, miles of woodland and riverbank paths, a kids' play area, and a yew-tree maze. Book your timed ticket for the house beforehand or early on the day. Boat hire and trips are available daily in July and August. Note that opening times of the house can be unpredictable, even at the busiest times of the year; always call before setting out. ⊠ *Cliveden Rd., Taplow* ✛ *Near Maidenhead* ☎ *01628/605069* ⊕ *www.nationaltrust.org.uk/cliveden* ⊠ *Garden and woodland £16, house £2.*

🛏 Hotels

★ Cliveden House

$$$$ | **HOTEL** | If you've ever wondered what it would feel like to be an Edwardian grandee, then sweep up the drive to this stately home, one of Britain's grandest hotels. **Pros:** like stepping back in time; outstanding sense of luxury; beautiful grounds. **Cons:** airplanes fly overhead; two-night minimum on weekends; you'll need deep pockets. $ *Rooms from: £500* ⊠ *Cliveden Rd., Taplow* ☎ *01628/668561* ⊕ *www.clivedenhouse.co.uk* ⤳ *47 rooms* �‖ *Free breakfast.*

🏃 Activities

Cliveden Boathouse

BOATING | Here you can rent two vintage boats, rowing boats, and an electric canoe that ply the Thames. The 45-minute champagne sunset cruise is the most affordable at £70 per person. They sail most days April through October at 5 and 6 pm. ⊠ *Cliveden, Cliveden Rd., Taplow* ☎ *01628/668561.*

Marlow

7 miles west of Cliveden, 15 miles northwest of Windsor.

Just inside the Buckinghamshire border, Marlow and the surrounding area overflow with Thames-side prettiness. The unusual suspension bridge was built in the 1830s by William Tierney Clark, architect of the bridge in Hungary linking Buda and Pest. Marlow has a number of striking old buildings, particularly the privately owned Georgian houses along Peter and West streets. In 1817, the Romantic poet Percy Bysshe Shelley stayed with friends at 67 West Street and then bought **Albion House** on the same street. His second wife, Mary, completed her Gothic novel *Frankenstein* here. Ornate **Marlow Place,** on Station Road, dating from 1721, is reputedly the finest building in town.

Marlow hosts its own one-day regatta in mid-June. The town is a good base from which to join the **Thames Path** to Henley-on-Thames. On summer weekends tourism can often overwhelm the town.

GETTING HERE AND AROUND

Trains leave London from Paddington every half hour and involve a change at Maidenhead; the journey takes an hour. By car, leave M4 at Junction 8/9, following A404 and then A4155. From M40, join A404 at Junction 4.

👁 Sights

Swan-Upping

FESTIVAL | This traditional event, which dates back 800 years, takes place in Marlow during the third week of July. By bizarre ancient laws, the Queen owns every single one of the country's swans, so each year swan-markers in skiffs start from Sunbury-on-Thames, catching the new cygnets and marking their beaks to establish ownership. The Queen's Swan Marker, dressed in scarlet livery, presides over this colorful ceremony. ⊠ *Marlow* ☎ *01628/523030* ⊕ *www.royal.uk.*

Restaurants

Vanilla Pod

$$$$ | FRENCH | Discreet and intimate, this restaurant is a showcase for the French-inspired cuisine of chef Michael Macdonald, who, as the restaurant's name implies, holds vanilla in high esteem. The fixed-price menu borrows the flavor of a French bistro and shakes it up a bit, so you might have filet mignon with polenta or something more adventurous, such as fennel escabeche with mackerel and vanilla. **Known for:** French-inspired cooking; a flair for vanilla; great value set lunch. $ *Average main: £45* ⊠ *31 West St.* ☎ *01628/898101* ⊕ *www.thevanillapod.co.uk* ⊙ *Closed Sun. and Mon.*

🛏 Hotels

Macdonald Compleat Angler

$$ | HOTEL | Although fishing aficionados consider this luxurious, 17th century, Thames-side inn the ideal place to stay, the place is stylish enough to attract those with no interest in casting a line. **Pros:** gorgeous rooms; great views of the Thames; legendary fishing spot. **Cons:** river views cost more, except Rooms 9 and 10; need a car to get around; rooms could use some updating. $ *Rooms from: £180* ⊠ *Marlow Bridge, Bisham Rd.* ☎ *0844/879–9128, 01628/184444 international* ⊕ *www.macdonaldhotels. co.uk/our-hotels/south-england/marlow/ macdonald-compleat-angler* ⇆ *64 rooms* ⑩ *Free breakfast.*

Henley-on-Thames

7 miles southwest of Marlow, 8 miles north of Reading, 36 miles west of central London.

Henley's fame is based on one thing: rowing. The Henley Royal Regatta, held at the cusp of June and July on a long, straight stretch of the River Thames, has made the little riverside town famous throughout the world. Townspeople launched the Henley Regatta in 1839, initiating the Grand Challenge Cup, the most famous of its many trophies. The best amateur oarsmen from around the globe compete in crews of eight, four, or two, or as single scullers. For many spectators, the event is on par with Royal Ascot and Wimbledon.

The town is set in a broad valley between gentle hillsides. Henley's historic buildings, including half-timber Georgian cottages and inns (as well as one of Britain's oldest theaters, the Kenton), are all within a few minutes' walk. The river near Henley is alive with boats of every shape and size, from luxury cabin cruisers to tiny rowboats.

GETTING HERE AND AROUND

Frequent First Great Western trains depart for Henley from London Paddington; the journey time is around an hour. If you're driving from London or from the west, leave M4 at Junction 8/9 and follow A404(M) and then A4130 to Henley Bridge. From Marlow, Henley is a 7-mile drive southwest on A4155.

ESSENTIALS

VISITOR INFORMATION Henley Visitor Information Centre. ⊠ *Henley Town Hall, Market Pl., Henley* ☎ *01491/578034* ⊕ *www.henleytowncouncil.gov.uk/information-centre-including-tourism.aspx.*

The rowing competitions at the Henley Royal Regatta draw spectators all along the river.

Sights

River & Rowing Museum

MUSEUM | FAMILY | Focusing on the history and sport of rowing, this absorbing museum built on stilts includes exhibits devoted to actual vessels, from a Saxon log boat to an elegant Victorian steam launch to Olympic boats. One gallery tells the story of the Thames as it flows from its source to the ocean, while another explores the history of the town and its famed regatta. A charming *Wind in the Willows* walk-through exhibit evokes the settings of the famous children's book. ⊠ *Mill Meadows, Henley* ☎ *01491/415600* ⊕ *www.rrm.co.uk* ⊠ *£9.*

St. Mary's Church

RELIGIOUS SITE | With a 16th-century "checkerboard" tower, St. Mary's is a stone's throw from the bridge over the Thames. The adjacent, yellow-washed **Chantry House,** built in 1420, is one of England's few remaining merchant houses from the period. It's an unspoiled example of the rare timber-frame design, with upper floors jutting out. You can enjoy tea here on Sunday afternoon in summer. ⊠ *Hart St., Henley* ☎ *01491/577340* ⊕ *www.stmaryshenley.org.uk* ⊠ *Free.*

🍴 Restaurants

Crooked Billet

$$ | MODERN BRITISH | It's worth negotiating the maze of lanes leading to this cozy, 17th-century, country pub 6 miles west of Henley-on-Thames. Choices could include John Dory with anchovy beignet and duck leg and lardons cooked in red wine. **Known for:** old pub atmosphere; booking ahead is necessary; garden for open-air dining. ⑤ *Average main: £22* ⊠ *Newlands La., Stoke Row* ☎ *01491/681048* ⊕ *www.thecrookedbillet.co.uk.*

The Three Tuns

$$ | MODERN BRITISH | Walk past the cozy bar in this traditional 17th-century pub to eat in the snug dining room with the clutch of locals who come nightly for the traditional British comfort food. Plates such as beer-battered fish-and-chips or local butcher's sausages and mashed potatoes are easy crowd-pleasers. **Known for:** excellent traditional savory pies; lovely old pub atmosphere; delicious desserts. $ *Average main: £16* ⊠ *5 Market Pl., Henley on Thames* ☎ *01491/410138* ⊕ *www. threetunshenley.co.uk* ۩ *Closed Mon.*

 ## Hotels

Hotel du Vin

$$ | HOTEL | A sprawling brick brewery near the river has been transformed into a distinctive modern architectural showplace. **Pros:** very chic; lovely river views from upper floors; good for oenophiles. **Cons:** won't thrill traditionalists; a charge for parking; steps inside are tricky to navigate. $ *Rooms from: £160* ⊠ *New St., Henley* ☎ *01491/877579* ⊕ *www.hotelduvin.com* ➷ *43 rooms* ۩ *Free breakfast.*

The Row Barge

$ | B&B/INN | This historic, 15th-century pub certainly looks the part, with low-beamed ceilings and a fire crackling in the grate. **Pros:** historic inn with lots of character; friendly owners; good food. **Cons:** entrance to guest rooms through bar and up a staircase with very low ceiling; room No. 1 has no door to the bathroom; quirks of historic building not for everyone. $ *Rooms from: £95* ⊠ *West St.* ☎ *01491/572649* ➷ *4 rooms* ۩ *Free breakfast.*

 ## Activities

Henley Royal Regatta

CANOEING/ROWING/SKULLING | A series of rowing competitions attracting participants from many countries, the annual Henley Royal Regatta takes place over five days in late June and early July. Large tents are erected along both sides of a straight stretch of the river known as Henley Reach, and every surrounding field becomes a parking lot. There's plenty of space on the public towpath from which to watch the early stages of the races. ■**TIP→** If you want to attend, book a room months in advance. After all, 500,000 people turn out for the event. ⊠ *Henley* ☎ *01491/571900 for ticket line, 01491/572153 for inquiries* ⊕ *www.hrr.co.uk.*

Oxford

With arguably the most famous university in the world, Oxford has been a center of learning since 1167, with only the Sorbonne preceding it. It doesn't take more than a day or two to explore its winding medieval streets, photograph its ivy-covered stone buildings and ancient churches and libraries, and even take a punt down one of its placid waterways. The town center is compact and walkable, and at its heart is Oxford University. Alumni of this prestigious institution include 48 Nobel Prize winners, 26 British prime ministers (including Boris Johnson), and 28 foreign presidents (including Bill Clinton), along with poets, authors, and artists such as Percy Bysshe Shelley, Oscar Wilde, and W. H. Auden.

Oxford is 55 miles northwest of London, at the junction of the rivers Thames and Cherwell. The city is more interesting and more cosmopolitan than Cambridge, and although it's also bigger, its suburbs aren't remotely interesting to visitors. The charm is all at the center, where the old town curls around the grand stone buildings, good restaurants, and historic pubs. Victorian writer Matthew Arnold described Oxford's "dreaming spires," a phrase that has become famous. Students rush past you on the sidewalks on the way to their exams, clad with marvelous antiquarian style in their requisite mortar caps, flowing dark gowns, stiff collars, and crisp white bow ties. ■**TIP→** Watch your back when crossing roads, as bikes are everywhere.

GETTING HERE AND AROUND

Megabus, Oxford Bus Company, and Stagecoach Oxford Tube all have buses traveling from London 24 hours a day; the trip takes between one hour 40 minutes and two hours. In London, Megabus departs from Victoria Coach Station, while Oxford Bus Company and Stagecoach Oxford Tube have pickup points on Buckingham Palace Road, Victoria; Oxford Tube also picks up from the Marble Arch underground station. Oxford Bus Company runs round-trip shuttle service from Gatwick (£37) every hour and Heathrow (£30) every half hour. Most of the companies have multiple stops in Oxford, with Gloucester Green, the final stop, being the most convenient for travelers. You can easily traverse the town center on foot, but the Oxford Bus Company has a one-day ticket (£4.30) for unlimited travel in and around Oxford.

Trains to Oxford depart from London's Paddington Station for the one-hour trip. Oxford Station is at the western edge of the historic town center on Botley Road.

To drive, take the M40 northwest from London. It's an hour's drive, except during rush hour, when it can take twice as long. In-town parking is notoriously difficult, so use one of the five free park-and-ride lots and pay for the bus to the city. The Thornhill Park and Ride and the St. Clement's parking lot before the roundabout that leads to Magdalen Bridge are convenient for the M40.

TIMING

You can explore major sights in town in a day or so, but it takes longer than that to spend an hour in each of the key museums and absorb the scene at the colleges. Some colleges are open only in the afternoons during university terms. When the undergraduates are in residence, access is often restricted to the chapels, dining rooms, and libraries, too, and you're requested to refrain from picnicking in the quadrangles. All are closed certain days during exams, usually from mid-April to late June.

ESSENTIALS

BUS CONTACTS Megabus. ☎ *0871/266–3333 for inquiries, 0900/160–0900 booking line* ⊕ *www.megabus.com.* **Oxford Bus Company.** ☎ *01865/785400* ⊕ *www. oxfordbus.co.uk.* **Stagecoach Oxford Tube.** ☎ *01865/772250* ⊕ *www.oxfordtube. com.*

TOURS

City Sightseeing

ORIENTATION | This company runs hop-on, hop-off bus tours with 20 stops around Oxford. Your ticket, purchased from the driver, is good for 24 hours. ☎ *01865/790522* ⊕ *www.citysightseeingoxford.com* 🚌 *From £16.*

◉ Sights

Oxford University isn't one easily identifiable campus, but a sprawling mixture of 38 colleges scattered around the city center, each with its own distinctive identity and focus. Oxford students live and study at their own college, and also use the centralized resources of the overarching university. The individual colleges are deeply competitive. Most of the grounds and magnificent dining halls and chapels are open to visitors, though the opening times (displayed at the entrance gates) vary greatly.

The **city center** of Oxford is bordered by High Street, St. Giles, and Longwall Street. Most of Oxford University's most famous buildings are within this area. **Jericho,** the neighborhood where many students live, is west of St. Giles, just outside the city center. Its narrow streets are lined with lovely cottages. The area north of the center around Banbury and Marston Ferry roads is called **Summertown,** and the area east of the center, along St. Clement's Street, is known as **St. Clement's.**

Oxford's Ashmolean Museum is the oldest public museum in the United Kingdom.

★ Ashmolean Museum

MUSEUM | What might be Britain's greatest museum outside London is also the oldest public museum in the United Kingdom. "The Ash," as locals call it, displays its rich and varied collections from the Neolithic to the present day over five stunning floors. Innovative and spacious galleries explore connections between priceless Greek, Roman, and Indian artifacts, as well as Egyptian and Chinese objects, all of which are among the best in the country. In the superb art collection, don't miss drawings by Raphael, the shell-encrusted mantle of Powhatan (father of Pocahontas), the lantern belonging to Guy Fawkes, and the Alfred Jewel, set in gold, which dates from the reign of King Alfred the Great (ruled 871–899). ✉ *Beaumont St.* ☎ *01865/278000* ⊕ *www.ashmolean.org* ✉ *Free.*

The Bodleian Library and Radcliffe Camera

LIBRARY | A vast library, the domed Radcliffe Camera is Oxford's most spectacular building, built in 1737–49 by James Gibbs in Italian baroque style. It's usually surrounded by tourists with cameras trained at its golden-stone walls. The Camera contains part of the Bodleian Library's enormous collection, begun in 1602 and one of six "copyright libraries" in the United Kingdom. Like the Library of Congress in the United States, this means it must by law contain a copy of every book printed in Great Britain. In addition, the Bodleian is a vast repository for priceless historical documents—including a Gutenberg Bible and a Shakespeare First Folio. The collection continues to grow by more than 5,000 items a week. Tours reveal the magnificent Duke Humfrey's Library, which was the original chained library, completed in 1488 (the ancient tomes are dusted once a decade) as well as the spots used to create Hogwarts in the *Harry Potter* films. Arrive early to secure tickets for the three to six daily tours. The standard tours can be prebooked, as can the extended tours on Wednesday and Saturday; otherwise, tours are first-come, first-served. Audio tours don't require reservations. ✉ *Broad St.*

Oxford

KEY

1 Exploring Sights

1 Restaurants

1 Hotels

i Tourist information

Sights ▼

1 Ashmolean Museum ... **A3**

2 The Bodleian Library
and Radcliffe Camera ... **C4**

3 Carfax Tower **B4**

4 Christ Church **B5**

5 Christ Church
Picture Gallery **C4**

6 Dorchester Abbey **B5**

7 Magdalen College **E5**

8 Museum of the History
of Science **C3**

9 Oxford University
Museum of
Natural History **C1**

10 Pitt Rivers Museum **B1**

11 Sheldonian Theatre **C3**

12 St John's College **B2**

13 University Church of
St. Mary the Virgin **C4**

14 University of Oxford
Botanic Garden **E5**

15 White Horse Hill and
Uffington Castle **B5**

Restaurants ▼

1 Brasserie Blanc **A1**

2 Cote **A4**

3 CuttleFish **E5**

4 Gee's **A1**

5 Le Manoir aux
Quat'Saisons **E5**

Hotels ▼

1 Brown's Guest House ... **E5**

2 Coach and Horses **E5**

3 Le Manoir aux
Quat'Saisons **E5**

4 Malmaison Oxford **A5**

5 Newton House **B5**

6 Old Bank Hotel **C4**

7 Old Parsonage **A1**

☏ 01865/287400 ⊕ www.bodleian.ox.ac. uk ⊠ From £4 ⊘ Sometimes closed for events; call to confirm.

Carfax Tower

BUILDING | Passing through Carfax, the center of Oxford and where four roads meet, you can spot this tower. It's all that remains of **St. Martin's Church,** where Shakespeare stood as godfather for William Davenant, who himself became a playwright. Every 15 minutes, little mechanical "quarter boys" mark the passage of time on the tower front. Climb up the 99 steps of the dark stairwell for a good view of the town center. ⊠ Queen St. and Cornmarket ☏ 01865/792653 ⊠ £3.

Christ Church

COLLEGE | Built in 1546, the college of Christ Church is referred to by its members as "The House." This is the site of Oxford's largest quadrangle, Tom Quad, named after the huge bell (6¼ tons) that hangs in the Sir Christopher Wren–designed gate tower and rings 101 times at 9:05 every evening in honor of the original number of Christ Church scholars. The vaulted, 800-year-old chapel in one corner has been Oxford's cathedral since the time of Henry VIII. The college's medieval dining hall contains portraits of many famous alumni, including 13 of Britain's prime ministers, but you'll recognize it from its recurring role in the Harry Potter movies (although they didn't actually film here, the room was painstakingly re-created in a studio). ■TIP➔ **Plan carefully, as the dining hall is often closed between noon and 2 during term time.** Lewis Carroll, author of Alice in Wonderland, was a teacher of mathematics here for many years; a shop opposite the meadows on St. Aldate's sells Alice paraphernalia. ⊠ St. Aldate's ☏ 01865/276492 ⊕ www.chch.ox.ac.uk ⊠ £15 ⊘ Sometimes closed for events; check website to confirm.

Christ Church Picture Gallery

MUSEUM | This connoisseur's delight in Canterbury Quadrangle exhibits works by the Italian masters as well as Hals, Rubens, and Van Dyck. Drawings in the 2,000-strong collection are shown on a changing basis. ⊠ Oriel Sq. ☏ 01865/276172 ⊕ www.chch.ox.ac.uk/ gallery ⊠ £4 ⊘ Closed Tues. Oct.–June.

Dorchester Abbey

RELIGIOUS SITE | In addition to secluded cloisters and gardens, the abbey has a spacious church dating from 1170, with a rare lead baptismal font from the Norman period. There are two unique items from the 14th century: a sculptured stone Tree of Jesse window and a wall painting of the Crucifixion with an unusual cross design. The great tower was rebuilt in 1602, but incorporated the old 14th-century spiral staircase. The **Sanctuary** has unusual carved wooden niches, depicting figures representing the Seven Deadly Sins. In the **Lady Chapel,** you can see the so-called "Swaggering Knight" effigy, one of the best-preserved knight's effigies in England, which has faint traces of its original 13th-century coloring (extremely rare for statuary of this age). Be sure to check out the **People's Chapel** for its rare and beautiful fragments of 14th-century wall paintings. Dorchester Abbey is about 9 miles south of Oxford, on A4074. ⊠ Henley Rd., off A4074, Dorchester on Thames ☏ 01865/340007 ⊕ www. dorchester-abbey.org.uk ⊠ Free.

★ Magdalen College

COLLEGE | Founded in 1458, with a handsome main quadrangle and a supremely monastic air, Magdalen (pronounced maud-lin) is one of the most impressive of Oxford's colleges and attracts its most artistic students. Alumni include such diverse people as P. G. Wodehouse, Oscar Wilde, and John Betjeman. The school's large, square tower is a famous local landmark. ■TIP➔ **To enhance your visit, take a stroll around the Deer Park and along Addison's Walk; then have tea in the Old**

The grounds of Magdalen College are some of Oxford's most picturesque.

Kitchen, which overlooks the river. ⊠ *High St.* ☎ *01865/276000* ⊕ *www.magd.ox.ac. uk* ⊠ *£7* ⊙ *Closed mornings Oct.–June.*

Museum of the History of Science

MUSEUM | The Ashmolean, the world's oldest public museum, was originally housed in this 1683 building, which now holds scientific and mathematical instruments, from astrolabes to quadrants. Among the gems are a wonderful collection of 18th- and 19th-century models of the solar system and the chalkboard Einstein used in a lecture on the Theory of Relativity. There are guided tours on Thursday (2:30 and 3:15) and Saturday (12:30 and 1:15). ⊠ *Broad St.* ☎ *01865/277293* ⊕ *www.mhs.ox.ac. uk* ⊠ *Free (£5 suggested donation)* ⊙ *Closed Mon.*

Oxford University Museum of Natural History

MUSEUM | **FAMILY** | This highly decorative Victorian Gothic creation of cast iron and glass, more a cathedral than a museum, is worth a visit for its architecture alone. Among the eclectic collections of entomology, geology, mineralogy, and zoology are the towering skeleton of a *Tyrannosaurus rex* and casts of a dodo's foot and head. There's plenty for children to explore and touch. ⊠ *Parks Rd.* ☎ *01865/272950* ⊕ *www. oumnh.ox.ac.uk* ⊠ *Free.*

★ Pitt Rivers Museum

MUSEUM | **FAMILY** | More than half a million intriguing archaeological and anthropological items from around the globe, based on the collection bequeathed by Lieutenant-General Augustus Henry Lane Fox Pitt-Rivers in 1884, are crammed into a multitude of glass cases and drawers. In an eccentric touch that's surprisingly thought-provoking, labels are handwritten, and items are organized thematically rather than geographically—a novel way to gain perspective. Give yourself plenty of time to wander through the displays of shrunken heads, Hawaiian feather cloaks, and fearsome masks. ⊠ *S. Parks Rd.* ☎ *01865/270927* ⊕ *www.prm.ox.ac.uk* ⊠ *Free (donations welcome).*

Sheldonian Theatre

ARTS VENUE | This fabulously ornate theater is where Oxford's impressive graduation ceremonies are held, conducted almost entirely in Latin. Dating from 1663, it was the first building designed by Sir Christopher Wren when he served as professor of astronomy. The D-shaped auditorium has pillars, balconies, and an elaborately painted ceiling. The stone pillars outside are topped by 18 massive stone heads. Climb the stairs to the cupola for the best view of the city's "dreaming spires." Guided tours take place a few times per week; call in advance for details. ⊠ *Broad St.* ☎ *01865/277299* ⊕ *www.sheldon.ox.ac. uk* ⊠ *£3.80; tours £8.*

St. John's College

COLLEGE | One of Oxford's most attractive campuses, St. John's has seven quiet quadrangles surrounded by elaborately carved buildings. You enter the first through a low wooden door. This college dates to 1555, when Sir Thomas White, a merchant, founded it. His heart is buried in the chapel (it's a tradition for students to curse as they walk over it). The Canterbury Quad represented the first example of Italian Renaissance architecture in Oxford, and the Front Quad includes the buildings of the old St. Bernard's Monastery. ⊠ *St. Giles'* ☎ *01865/277300* ⊕ *www.sjc.ox.ac.uk* ⊠ *Free.*

University Church of St. Mary the Virgin

RELIGIOUS SITE | Seven hundred years' worth of funeral monuments crowd this galleried and spacious church, including the alter-step tombstone of Amy Robsart, the wife of Robert Dudley, who was Elizabeth I's favorite suitor. One pillar marks the site where Thomas Cranmer, author of the *Anglican Book of Common Prayer,* was brought to trial for heresy by Queen Mary I (Cranmer had been a key player in the Protestant reforms). He was later burned at the stake nearby on Broad Street. The top of the 14th-century tower has a panoramic view of the city's skyline—it's worth the 127 steps. The Vaults and Garden Café, part of the church accessible from Radcliffe Square, serves breakfasts and cream teas as well as good lunches. ⊠ *High St.* ☎ *01865/279111* ⊕ *www.universitychurch.ox.ac.uk* ⊠ *Church free, tower £5.*

University of Oxford Botanic Garden

GARDEN | Founded in 1621 as a healing garden, this is the oldest of its kind in the British Isles. Set on the river, the diverse garden displays 6,000 species ranging from lilies to citrus trees. There is a spacious walled garden, six luxuriant glass houses, including insectivorous and lily houses, and interesting medicinal, rock, and bog gardens to explore. Picnics are allowed, but you must bring your own food and drinks, as there's nowhere to buy them inside. ⊠ *Rose La.* ☎ *01865/286690* ⊕ *www. obga.ox.ac.uk* ⊠ *£5.45.*

White Horse Hill and Uffington Castle

NATURE SITE | Stretching up into the foothills of the Berkshire Downs between Swindon and Oxford is a wide fertile plain known as the Vale of the White Horse. Here, off B4507, cut into the turf of the hillside to expose the underlying chalk, is the 374-foot-long, 110-foot-high figure of a white horse (known as the the Uffington White Horse), an important prehistoric site. Some historians believed that the figure might have been carved to commemorate King Alfred's victory over the Danes in 871, whereas others date it to the Iron Age, around 750 BC. More current research suggests that it's at least 1,000 years older, created at the beginning of the second millennium BC. **Uffington Castle,** above the horse, is a prehistoric fort. English Heritage maintains these sites. To reach the Vale of the White Horse from Oxford (about 20 miles), follow A420, then B4508 to the village of Uffington. ⊠ *Dragon Hill Rd.* ☎ *01793/762209* ⊕ *www.nationaltrust. org.uk/white-horse-hill* ⊠ *Free.*

🍽 Restaurants

Brasserie Blanc

$$ | FRENCH | Raymond Blanc's sophisti-
cated brasserie in the Jericho neigh-
borhood is the more affordable chain
restaurant cousin of Le Manoir aux
Quat'Saisons in Great Milton. The
changing menu always lists a good
selection of steaks and innovative
adaptations of bourgeois French fare,
sometimes with Mediterranean or
Asian influences. **Known for:** French
classics like beef bourguignonne;
affordable prix-fixe lunch menu; good
wine selection. ⓢ *Average main: £17
⊠ 71–72 Walton St. ☎ 01865/510999
⊕ www.brasserieblanc.com.*

Cote

$ | FRENCH | This reliably good brasse-
rie serves decent French-influenced
cooking in a contemporary setting. Start
with an order of excellent calamari, fried
in bread crumbs with a subtle infusion
of garlic, before moving on to a main
of fish parmentier (pie with a potato
topping) or a classic steak in pepper-
corn sauce served with french fries.
Known for: reliably good French bistro
cooking; rich desserts; large crowds
so reservations are recommended.
ⓢ *Average main: £12 ⊠ 41–47 George
St. ☎ 01865/251992 ⊕ www.cote.co.uk/
restaurant/oxford.*

CuttleFish

$ | SEAFOOD | The clue's in the name
here—this popular local restaurant spe-
cializes in fresh, upscale seafood. Dishes
are prepared with a European touch and
frequently come with butter, cream, and
other sauces, such as sardines served
with lemon and parsley butter. **Known
for:** excellent seafood; nautical surround-
ings; good-value lunches. ⓢ *Average
main: £14 ⊠ 36–37 St. Clement's St.
☎ 01865/243003 ⊕ www.cuttlefishox-
ford.co.uk.*

Gee's

$$ | MODERN BRITISH | With its glass-and-
steel framework, this former florist's shop
just north of the town center makes a
charming conservatory dining room, full
of plants and twinkling with lights in the
evening. The menu concentrates on the
best of Oxfordshire produce and changes
daily, but you can expect to find the likes of
delicate seafood linguine, farm-fresh roasted vegetables, and wood-fired guinea fowl.
Known for: sophisticated British dishes with
local produce; chocolate nemesis and pistachio ice cream dessert; affordable lunch
and early dinner menus. ⓢ *Average main:
£18 ⊠ 61 Banbury Rd. ☎ 01865/553540
⊕ www.geesrestaurant.co.uk.*

★ Le Manoir aux Quat'Saisons

$$$$ | FRENCH | One of the original gastrono-
my-focused hotels, Le Manoir was opened
in 1984 by chef Raymond Blanc, whose
culinary talents have earned the hotel's restaurant two Michelin stars—now held for
an incredible 29 years and running. Decide
from among such innovative French
creations as spiced cauliflower velouté
with langoustines, beef fillet with braised
Jacob's ladder, or Dover sole with brown
butter and rosemary. **Known for:** one of the
top restaurants in the country; flawless
French-style fine dining; beautiful surroundings. ⓢ *Average main: £170 ⊠ Church Rd.,
Great Milton ☎ 01844/278881 ⊕ www.bel-
mond.com/hotels/europe/uk/oxfordshire/
belmond-le-manoir-aux-quat-saisons/.*

🛏 Hotels

Brown's Guest House

$ | B&B/INN | At the southern edge of cen-
tral Oxford, this redbrick Victorian house
is a good bet in a town that has precious
few affordable guesthouses. **Pros:** comfortable rooms; friendly owners; more
spacious than many B&Bs. **Cons:** a long
walk to the center; suburban location is
a bit dull; single rooms lack private bathroom. ⓢ *Rooms from: £90 ⊠ 281 Iffley
Rd. ☎ 07711/897168 ⊕ www.brownsox-
ford.com ⇆ 10 rooms ⓞ Free breakfast.*

Coach and Horses

$$ | **B&B/INN** | Everything is new in this airy and spacious lodging, but it doesn't mean the place lacks atmosphere or charm. **Pros:** lovely modern design; friendly hosts; central location. **Cons:** limited parking; gets booked up quickly; decor doesn't reflect the building's history. ⑤ *Rooms from: £140* ✉ *62 St. Clements St.* ☎ *01865/200017* ⊕ *www. oxfordcoachandhorses.co.uk* 🛏 *8 rooms* ⍾ *Free breakfast.*

★ Le Manoir aux Quat'Saisons

$$$$ | **HOTEL** | **FAMILY** | Standards are high at this 15th-century stone manor house, the ultimate place for a gourmet getaway, where master-chef Raymond Blanc's epicurean touch shows at every turn, including one of the country's finest kitchens. **Pros:** design is plush, but not stuffy; perfect for romance, but also accommodates kids; famous on-site cooking school and amazing food. **Cons:** every room is different, so if you have specific requirements, let them know when booking; all the food is tough on the waistline; price is even tougher on the wallet. ⑤ *Rooms from: £550* ✉ *Church Rd., Great Milton* ☎ *01844/278881* ⊕ *www.belmond.com/ hotels/europe/uk/oxfordshire/belmond-le-manoir-aux-quat-saisons* 🛏 *32 rooms* ⍾ *Free breakfast.*

Malmaison Oxford

$$$ | **HOTEL** | Housed in what was a 19th-century prison, this high-concept boutique hotel remains true to its unusual history by showing off the original metal doors and exposed-brick walls. **Pros:** modern luxury in a beautifully converted building; unique setting; great bar and restaurant. **Cons:** no matter how comfortable they make it, the prison ambience can still be weird; expensive parking; no elevator and lots of stairs. ⑤ *Rooms from: £230* ✉ *3 Oxford Castle* ☎ *01865/689944* ⊕ *www.malmaison. com/locations/oxford* 🛏 *95 rooms* ⍾ *Free breakfast.*

Newton House

$$ | **B&B/INN** | This handsome Victorian mansion, a five-minute walk from all of Oxford's action, is a sprawling, friendly place on three floors. **Pros:** great breakfasts; handy parking lot; excellent value for the location. **Cons:** on a main road; no elevator; some may be disappointed with the contemporary look. ⑤ *Rooms from: £127* ✉ *82 Abingdon Rd.* ☎ *01865/240561* ⊕ *www.newtonhouseoxford.co.uk* 🛏 *14 rooms* ⍾ *Free breakfast.*

Old Bank Hotel

$$ | **HOTEL** | From the impressive collection of modern artwork throughout the hotel to the sleek furnishings in the guest rooms, this stately converted bank building displays contemporary style in a city that favors the traditional. **Pros:** excellent location; interesting artwork at every turn; good restaurant. **Cons:** standard rooms can be small; breakfast costs extra; location a bit noisy. ⑤ *Rooms from: £220* ✉ *91–94 High St.* ☎ *01865/799599* ⊕ *www. oldbankhotel.co.uk* 🛏 *43 rooms* ⍾ *No meals.*

Old Parsonage

$$$ | **HOTEL** | A 17th-century gabled stone house in a small garden next to St. Giles Church, the Old Parsonage is a dignified retreat. **Pros:** beautiful vine-covered building; complimentary walking tours; free parking. **Cons:** pricey; some guest rooms are small; cool, contemporary look favored over period charm. ⑤ *Rooms from: £300* ✉ *1 Banbury Rd.* ☎ *01865/310210* ⊕ *www. oldparsonagehotel.co.uk* 🛏 *35 rooms* ⍾ *Free breakfast.*

▼ Nightlife

Head of the River

BARS/PUBS | Near Folly Bridge, the terrace at the Head of the River is the perfect place to watch life on the water. It gets very crowded on sunny afternoons, but there's a great, quintessentially Oxford atmosphere. The pub also offers 20 comfortable guest rooms if you want to stay and appreciate the views a little longer. ✉ *St. Aldate's* ☎ *01865/721600* ⊕ *www.headoftheriveroxford.co.uk.*

Kings Arms

BARS/PUBS | The capacious Kings Arms, popular with students and fairly quiet during the day, carries excellent local brews as well as inexpensive pub food. ✉ *40 Holywell St.* ☎ *01865/242369* ⊕ *www.kingsarmsoxford.co.uk.*

★ Raoul's

BARS/PUBS | This hip cocktail bar was named one of the 100 best cocktail bars in the world by the *Times* of London, and the bartenders can prove it with their encyclopedic knowledge of mixology and creative flair. The crowd is generally as bright and young as you'd expect. ✉ *32 Walton St.* ☎ *01865/553732* ⊕ *www.raoulsbar.com.*

Turf Tavern

BARS/PUBS | Off Holywell Street, the Turf Tavern has a higgledy-piggledy collection of little rooms and outdoor spaces where you can enjoy a quiet drink and inexpensive pub food. ✉ *Bath Pl.* ☎ *01865/243235* ⊕ *www.greenekingpubs.co.uk/pubs/oxfordshire/turf-tavern.*

White Horse

BARS/PUBS | This cozy pub, dating from at least 1823, serves real ales and traditional food all day. ✉ *52 Broad St.* ☎ *01865/204801* ⊕ *www.whitehorseoxford.co.uk.*

🎭 Performing Arts

Music at Oxford

CONCERTS | This acclaimed series of weekend classical concerts takes place October through June in such esteemed venues as Christ Church Cathedral and the Sheldonian Theatre. ☎ *01865/244806* for box office ⊕ *www.musicatoxford.com.*

New Theatre

THEATER | Oxford's main performance space, the New Theatre stages popular shows, comedy acts, and musicals. ✉ *George St.* ☎ *0844/871–3020* ⊕ *www.atgtickets.com/venues/new-theatre-oxford.*

Oxford Playhouse

THEATER | This theater presents classic and modern dramas as well as dance and music performances. ✉ *Beaumont St.* ☎ *01865/305305* ⊕ *www.oxfordplayhouse.com.*

🛍 Shopping

Alice's Shop

TOYS | This quaint little store is entirely devoted to *Alice in Wonderland* paraphernalia. ✉ *83 St. Aldate's* ☎ *01865/240338* ⊕ *www.aliceinwonderlandshop.com.*

Blackwell's

BOOKS/STATIONERY | Family owned and run since 1879, Blackwell's stocks an excellent selection of books. Inquire about the literary and historic walking tours that run from late April through October. ✉ *48–51 Broad St.* ☎ *01865/792792* ⊕ *blackwell.co.uk.*

★ Covered Market

OUTDOOR/FLEA/GREEN MARKETS | This is a fine place for a cheap sandwich and a leisurely browse; the smell of pastries and coffee follows you from cake shop to jeweler to cheesemonger. ✉ *High St.* ⊕ *www.oxford-coveredmarket.co.uk.*

Scriptum

GIFTS/SOUVENIRS | Cards, stationery, handmade paper, and leather-bound journals can be purchased here, alongside marvelously arcane stuff you didn't know you needed—like quills, sealing wax, and even Venetian masks. ✉ *3 Turl St.* ☎ *01865/200042* ⊕ *www.scriptum.co.uk.*

Fountains and formal Italian gardens set off the monumental baroque pile that is Blenheim Palace.

Shepherd & Woodward

CLOTHING | This traditional tailor specializes in university gowns, ties, and scarves. ✉ *109–113 High St.* ☎ *01865/249491* ⊕ *www.shepherdandwoodward.co.uk.*

Taylors Deli

FOOD/CANDY | If you're planning a picnic, Taylors Deli has everything you need. There are tasty cakes, pastries, and other snacks, as well as great tea and coffee. ✉ *31 St. Giles* ☎ *01865/558853* ⊕ *www. taylorsoxford.co.uk.*

University of Oxford Shop

GIFTS/SOUVENIRS | Run by the university, the University of Oxford Shop sells authorized clothing, ceramics, and tea towels, all emblazoned with university crests. ✉ *106 High St.* ☎ *01865/247414* ⊕ *www.oushop.com.*

☼ Activities

BIKING

Bainton Bikes

BICYCLING | Bicycles can be rented from Bainton Bikes, a family-owned company that's happy to deliver to your hotel. You can also hire a two-wheeler outside the train station in the summer. Prices start at around £10 per day. The shop also provides free support during your hire, including puncture repair. ✉ *78 Walton St.* ☎ *01865/311610* ⊕ *www.bainton-bikes.com.*

PUNTING

You may choose, like many an Oxford student, to spend a summer afternoon punting, while dangling your champagne bottle in the water to keep it cool. Punts—shallow-bottom boats that are poled slowly up the river—can be rented in several places, including at the foot of the Magdalen Bridge.

Cherwell Boathouse

LOCAL SPORTS | From mid-March through mid-October, Cherwell Boathouse rents boats and, if you call ahead, someone to punt it. Rentals cost £18 per hour weekdays (£20 on weekends) or £90 (£100 on weekends) per day and should be booked ahead. The facility, a mile north of the heart of Oxford, also includes a stylish restaurant. ⊠ *Bardwell Rd.* ☎ *01865/515978* ⊕ *www.cherwellboathouse.co.uk.*

Salter's Steamers

LOCAL SPORTS | At the St. Aldates Road end of Folly Bridge, Salter's Steamers rents out punts and skiffs (rowboats) for £20 per hour, £60 per half day, and £100 per day. Chauffeured punts are £60 per hour, booked in advance. Day cruises are also run from Christ Church meadows to nearby Abingdon. ⊠ *Folly Bridge* ☎ *01865/243421* ⊕ *www.salterssteamers.co.uk.*

SPECTATOR SPORTS
Eights Week

BOATING | At the end of May, during Oxford's Eights Week (also known as Summer Eights), men and women from the university's colleges compete to be "Head of the River." This is a particularly fun race to watch because the shape of the river provides an added element of excitement. It's too narrow for the eight-member teams to race side by side, so the boats set off one behind another. Each boat tries to catch and bump the one in front. ⊠ *Oxford* ⊕ *www.ourcs.co.uk.*

Woodstock

8 miles northwest of Oxford on A44.

Handsome 17th- and 18th-century houses line the trim streets of Woodstock, at the eastern edge of the Cotswolds. It's best known for nearby Blenheim Palace, and in summer tour buses clog the village's ancient streets. On a quiet fall or spring afternoon, however, Woodstock is a sublime experience: a mellowed 18th-century church and town hall mark the central square, and along its backstreets, you can find flower-bedecked houses and quiet lanes right out of a 19th-century etching.

GETTING HERE AND AROUND

The public bus service S3 runs (usually every half hour) between Oxford and Woodstock and costs £3.30 one way. It can drop you at the gates of Blenheim Palace.

◉ Sights

★ Blenheim Palace

CASTLE/PALACE | This magnificent palace has been called England's Versailles, and with good reason—it's still the only historic house in Britain to be named a World Heritage Site. Designed by Sir John Vanbrugh in the early 1700s in collaboration with Nicholas Hawksmoor, Blenheim was given by Queen Anne and the nation to General John Churchill, first duke of Marlborough, in gratitude for his military victories (including the Battle of Blenheim) against the French in 1704. The exterior is opulent and sumptuous, with huge columns, enormous pediments, and obelisks, all exemplars of English baroque. Inside, lavishness continues in extremes; you can join a free guided tour or simply walk through on your own. In most of the opulent rooms, family portraits look down at sumptuous furniture, elaborate carpets, fine Chinese porcelain, and immense pieces of silver. Exquisite tapestries in the three state rooms illustrate the first duke's victories. Book a tour of the current duke's private apartments for a more intimate view of ducal life. For some visitors, the most memorable room is the small, low-ceiling chamber where Winston Churchill (his father was the younger brother of the then-duke) was born in 1874; you can also see his paintings, his toy soldier collection, and a room devoted to his private letters (those he sent home from school in Marlborough as a young boy are both touching and tragic). He's buried in nearby Bladon.

Sir Winston wrote that the unique beauty of Blenheim lay in its perfect adaptation of English parkland to an Italian palace. Its 2,000 acres of grounds, the work of Capability Brown, 18th-century England's best-known landscape gardener, are arguably the best example of the "cunningly natural" park in the country. Looking across the park to Vanbrugh's semi-submerged Grand Bridge makes for an unforgettable vista. Blenheim's formal gardens include notable water terraces and an Italian garden with a mermaid fountain, all built in the 1920s.

The Pleasure Gardens, reached by a miniature train that stops outside the palace's main entrance, contain a butterfly house, a hedge maze, and a giant chess set. The herb-and-lavender garden is also delightful. Blenheim Palace stages a concert of Beethoven's *Battle Symphony* in mid-July, combined with a marvelous fireworks display. There are many other outdoor events throughout the summer, including jousting tournaments. Allow at least three hours for a full visit.

After taking in Blenheim Palace, stop by **Bladon,** 2 miles southeast of Woodstock on A4095 and 6 miles northwest of Oxford, to see the small, tree-lined churchyard that's the burial place of Sir Winston Churchill. His grave is all the more impressive for its simplicity. ⊠ *Off A4095, Woodstock* ☎ *01993/810530* ⊕ *www.blenheimpalace.com* ✉ *Palace, park, and gardens £28.50; park and gardens £18.50.*

🍴 Restaurants

★ Falkland Arms

$ | BRITISH | It's worth detouring a bit for this supremely appealing pub on the village green at Great Tew, about 8 miles northwest of Woodstock. The small restaurant offers a traditional but creative menu, which includes dishes like wild mushroom and garlic linguine or roast duck with herb roasted potatoes. **Known for:** cozy, traditional pub atmosphere; classic pub food done very well; pie of the day. ⑤ *Average main: £14* ✉ *19–21 The Green, Great Tew* ☎ *01608/683653* ⊕ *www.falklandarms.co.uk.*

🛏 Hotels

The Feathers

$$ | HOTEL | Antiques-bedecked guest rooms fill this stylish inn, which was cobbled together from five 17th-century houses in the heart of town. **Pros:** beautiful modern design; great food; good afternoon tea. **Cons:** two-night minimum stay on weekends in summer; narrow stairs for top rooms; no hotel parking. ⑤ *Rooms from: £165* ✉ *Market St., Woodstock* ☎ *01993/812291* ⊕ *www. feathers.co.uk* ↪ *21 rooms* ⦿l *Free breakfast.*

Macdonald Bear

$$ | HOTEL | Tudoresque wood paneling, beamed ceilings, wattle-and-daub walls, and blazing fireplaces help define this as an archetypal English coaching inn. **Pros:** plenty of character; historic (and some say haunted) house; lovely old English atmosphere. **Cons:** creaky old floors; old beams can get in the way; reputation for ghosts not for everyone. ⑤ *Rooms from: £190* ✉ *Park St., Woodstock* ☎ *0844/879–9143 local, 01993/811124 international* ⊕ *www.macdonaldhotels. co.uk/our-hotels/south-england/wood-stock/macdonald-bear-hotel* ↪ *54 rooms* ⦿l *Free breakfast.*

Aylesbury

22 miles east of Oxford, 46 miles north-west of London.

Aylesbury makes a good base for exploring the surrounding countryside, including stately homes and gardens. It's a pretty, historic place with a 13th-century church surrounded by small Tudor lanes and cottages. This market town has been associated with the Aylesbury duck since the 18th century, when flocks were walked 40 miles to the London markets. Kids appreciate a visit to the Roald Dahl's Children's Gallery, which is open all year.

GETTING HERE AND AROUND

From London, Chiltern Railways runs frequent trains from Marylebone Station (one hour). The town is easily accessible from Oxford by Arriva Bus 280, which runs every 30 minutes; travel time is 80 minutes. If you're driving from Oxford, take A40 and A418. From London, follow M1 and A41 and allow 90 minutes.

👁 Sights

★ Stowe Landscape Gardens

GARDEN | This exquisite example of a Georgian garden was created for the Temple family by the most famous gardeners of the 18th century. Capability Brown, Charles Bridgeman, and William Kent all worked on the land to create 980 acres of trees, valleys, and meadows. More than 40 striking monuments, follies, and temples dot the landscape of lakes, rivers, and pleasant vistas. This is a historically important place, but it's not for those who want primarily a flower garden. Allow at least half a day to explore the grounds. Stowe House, at the center, is now a fancy school with some magnificently restored rooms. It's open for tours most afternoons, but the actual schedule is notoriously changeable, so do call ahead or check ⊕ *www. stowe.co.uk* for more information. The gardens are about 3 miles northwest of

Thames Valley Hiking and Biking

The gentle hills, pretty towns, friendly pubs, and easily accessible lodgings of the Thames Valley make this prime territory to explore by bike. The Thames is almost completely free of car traffic along the Thames Path, a 184-mile national trail that traces the river from the London flood barrier to the river's source near Kemble, in the Cotswolds. The path follows towpaths from the outskirts of London, through Windsor, Oxford, and Lechlade.

Good public transportation in the region makes it possible to start and stop easily anywhere along this route. In summer, the walking is fine and no special gear is necessary, but in winter the path often floods—check ahead.

For the best information on the Thames paths, contact the National Trails Office or the Ramblers' Association, both good sources for advice and maps. The Chiltern Conservation Board promotes walking in the Chilterns peaks.

Biking is perhaps the best way to see the Chilterns. Routes include the 99-mile Thames Valley Cycle Route from London to Oxford and the 87-mile Ridgeway Path from Uffington that follows the Chilterns; the National Trails Office has information. The Thames Path also has plenty of biking opportunities.

Buckingham, which is 14 miles northwest of Aylesbury. You enter through the New Inn visitor center, where there are period parlor rooms to explore. ⊠ *New Inn Farm, off A422, Stowe* ☎ *01280/817156, 01280/818002 for tours* ⊕ *www.nationaltrust.org.uk/stowe-gardens* ⊠ *£14; house only £7.*

★ Waddesdon Manor

HOUSE | Many of the regal residences created by the Rothschild family throughout Europe are gone now, but this one is still a vision of the 19th century at its most sumptuous. G. H. Destailleur built the house in the 1880s for Baron Ferdinand de Rothschild in the style of a 16th-century French château, with perfectly balanced turrets and towers and walls of creamy stone. Although intended only for summer weekend house parties, it was lovingly furnished over 35 years with Savonnerie carpets; Sèvres porcelain; furniture made by Riesener for Marie Antoinette; and paintings by Guardi, Gainsborough, and Reynolds. The collection is brought into

the 21st century by an extraordinary broken porcelain chandelier, by artist Ingo Maurer, located in the Blue Dining Room. The gardens are equally extraordinary, with an aviary, colorful plants, and winding trails that provide panoramic views. In the restaurant you can dine on English or French fare and order excellent Rothschild wines. Admission is by timed ticket; arrive early or book in advance. The annual Christmas fairs and light festivals held here are well worth seeing; check the website in advance for details. ⊠ *Silk St., Waddesdon* ✛ *On A41 west of Aylesbury* ☎ *01296/820414* ⊕ *www. waddesdon.org.uk* ⊠ *House and gardens £21; gardens only £11.50* ⊘ *Closed Mon. and Tues.*

🛏 Hotels

The Five Arrows

$$ | B&B/INN | Fancifully patterned brick chimneys and purple gables decorate this elegant building next to the main entrance of Waddesdon Manor. **Pros:** historic building; lovely grounds; great suites. **Cons:** some rooms are small; on a busy main road; may get booked up for weddings. $ *Rooms from: £155* ✉ *High St., Waddesdon* ☎ *01296/651727* ⊕ *www.fivearrowshotel.co.uk* ⤳ *16 rooms* ❏ *Free breakfast.*

★ Hartwell House

$$ | **HOTEL** | Part Jacobean, part Georgian, this magnificent stately home provides formal luxury in an opulent country setting. **Pros:** truly elegant ambience; lovely garden views; surrounded by soothing parkland. **Cons:** very formal; not all rooms have direct access to park; expensive bar. $ *Rooms from: £210* ✉ *Oxford Rd.* ☎ *01296/747444* ⊕ *www.hartwell-house. com* ⤳ *48 rooms* ❏ *Free breakfast.*

St. Albans

25 miles east of Aylesbury, 20 miles northwest of London.

A lively town on the outskirts of London, St. Albans is known for its historic cathedral, and it also holds reminders of a long history. From AD 50 to 440, the town, then known as Verulamium, was one of the largest communities in Roman Britain. You can explore this past in the Verulamium Museum and splendid Roman sites around the area. For activities more focused on the present, every Wednesday and Saturday, the Market Place on St. Peter's Street bustles with traders from all over England selling everything from fish and farm produce to clothing. A 20-minute drive away from St. Albans is Warner Bros. Harry Potter Studio Tour, which has sets and props from the successful films.

GETTING HERE AND AROUND

About 20 miles northwest of London, St. Albans is off the M1 and M25 highways, about an hour's drive from the center of the capital. Thameslink has frequent trains from London's St. Pancras Station, arriving at St. Albans City Station in 30 minutes. The main train station is on Victoria Street, in the town center. A second station on the south side of town, St. Albans Abbey Station, serves smaller towns in the surrounding area. Trains on this line are operated by London Midland. Bus service is slow and not direct. Central St. Albans is small and walkable. There's a local bus service, but you're unlikely to need it. Taxis usually line up outside the train stations.

ESSENTIALS

TRAIN CONTACTS Southern Railway. ☎ *0345/1272920* ⊕ *www.southernrailway.com.*

VISITOR INFORMATION St. Albans Tourist and Information Centre. ✉ *Town Hall, Market Pl.* ☎ *01727/864511* ⊕ *www.enjoystalbans.com.*

◉ Sights

★ Hatfield House

HOUSE | Six miles east of St. Albans, this outstanding brick mansion surrounded by lovely formal gardens stands as a testament to the magnificence of Jacobean architecture. Robert Cecil, Earl of Salisbury, built Hatfield in 1611, and his descendants still live here. The interior, with its dark-wood paneling, lush tapestries, and Tudor and Jacobean portraits, reveals much about the era. The beautiful King James Drawing Room is a vision in ostentatious grandeur, with its gilded ceiling and portrait-covered walls. By contrast, the Chinese Bedroom is a charming example of the later 19th-century infatuation with Far Eastern design. The intricate Marble Hall, with its elaborate carved wooden panels, is one of the most impressive rooms in the house, although perhaps the building's finest single feature is the ornate Grand Staircase, with carved wooden figures on the banisters. The knot garden, near the Tudor Old Palace, where the first Queen Elizabeth spent much of her youth, is a

The grounds of Hatfield House have lovely woodland paths and masses of bluebell flowers.

highlight of the West Garden. Wednesday is the only day the East Garden, with topiaries, parterres, and rare plants, is open to the public. The Park has lovely woodland paths and masses of bluebells. There are various markets, theater performances, and shows throughout the season, including open-air film screenings and, occasionally, Elizabethan banquets. Check the website for the schedule. ⊠ *Great North Rd., Hatfield* 🕾 *01707/287010* ⊕ *www.hatfield-house. co.uk* ✉ *House, West Garden, and Park £19; West Garden and Park £11; East Garden Free.* ⊙ *Closed Oct.–Mar.*

Roman Theater

ARCHAEOLOGICAL SITE | Your imagination can take you back to AD 130 as you walk around the ruins of this 2,000-seat Roman Theater, one of the few in the country. Next to the theater are the scant ruins of a Roman town house, shops, and a shrine. ⊠ *Bluehouse Hill* 🕾 *01727/835035* ✉ *£3.*

Shaw's Corner

HOUSE | From 1906 to his death in 1950, the famed Irish playwright George Bernard Shaw lived in the small village of Ayot St. Lawrence, 9 miles northeast of St. Albans. Today, his small Edwardian home, Shaw's Corner, remains much as he left it. The most delightful curiosity is his little writing hut, which is in the garden and which can be turned to face the sun. ⊠ *Off Hill Farm La., Ayot St. Lawrence* 🕾 *01438/821968* ⊕ *www.national-trust.org.uk/shawscorner* ✉ *£9.20.*

St. Albans Cathedral

RELIGIOUS SITE | Medieval pilgrims came from far and wide to the hilltop St. Albans Cathedral to honor its patron saint, a Roman soldier turned Christian martyr. His red-canopied shrine beyond the choir has a rare loft from where guards kept watch over gifts that were left. Construction of the mainly Norman cathedral began in the early 11th century, but the nearly 300-foot-long nave dates from 1235; the pillars are decorated with

13th- and 14th-century paintings. The tower is even more historic and contains bricks from ancient Roman buildings. Join a free tour of the highlights daily at 1:05 pm, or come for the more extensive free tours at 11:30 and 2:30 on weekdays, 11:30 and 2 on Saturday, and 2:30 on Sunday. Tower tours take place on selected dates, mostly on Saturdays. Call or check the website for the schedule. ✉ *Holywell Hill* ☎ *01727/860780* ⊕ *www.stalbanscathedral.org* ⧠ *Free (donations welcome); tower tours £9.50.*

Verulamium Museum

MUSEUM | FAMILY | With exhibits on everything from food to burial practices, the Verulamium Museum, on the site of the ancient Roman city, explores life 2,000 years ago. The re-created Roman rooms contain colorful mosaics that are some of the finest in Britain. Every second weekend of the month, "Roman soldiers" invade the museum and demonstrate the skills of the Imperial Army. ✉ *St. Michael's St.* ☎ *01727/751810* ⊕ *www.stalbansmuseums.org.uk/visit/verulamium-museum* ⧠ *£6.*

Verulamium Park Hypocaust

CITY PARK | FAMILY | Adjacent to the Verulamium Museum, this park contains the usual—playground, wading pool, lake—and the unusual—Roman ruins that include part of the town hall and a hypocaust, or central-heating system. The hypocaust dates to AD 200 and included one of the first heated floors in Britain. Brick columns supported the floor, and hot air from a nearby fire was drawn underneath the floor to keep bathers warm. ✉ *St. Michael's St.* ☎ *01727/751810* ⊕ *www.stalbansmuseums.org.uk* ⧠ *Free.*

★ Warner Bros. Harry Potter Studio Tour

MUSEUM | FAMILY | Attention all Muggles: this spectacular attraction just outside Watford immerses you in the magical world of Harry Potter for hours. From the Great Hall of Hogwarts—faithfully re-created, down to the finest detail—to magical props beautifully displayed in the vast studio space, each section of this attraction showcases the real sets, props, and special effects used in the eight movies. Visitors enter the Great Hall, a fitting stage for costumes from each Hogwarts house. You can admire the intricacies of the huge Hogwarts Castle model, ride a broomstick, try butterbeer, explore the Forbidden Forest, and gaze through the shop windows of Diagon Alley. The Hogwarts Express section—at a faithfully reproduced Platform 9¾—allows you to walk through a carriage of the actual steam train and see what it's like to ride with Harry and the gang. Tickets, pegged to a 30-minute arrival time slot, must be prebooked online. The studio tour is a 20-minute drive from St. Albans. You can also get here by taking a 20-minute train ride from London's Euston Station to Watford Junction (then a 15-minute shuttle-bus ride; £3 round-trip, cash only). Via car from London, use M1 and M25—parking is free. ✉ *Studio Tour Dr., Leavesden Green* ☎ *0345/084–0900* ⊕ *www.wbstudiotour.co.uk* ⧠ *£47.*

🍽 Restaurants

Waffle House

$ | BELGIAN | Indoors or out, you can enjoy a great budget meal at the 16th-century Kingsbury Watermill, near the Verulamium Museum. The organic flour for the sweet-and-savory Belgian waffles comes from Redbournbury Watermill, north of the city. **Known for:** delicious waffles, sweet or savory; organic ingredients; lovely watermill setting. $ *Average main: £8* ✉ *Kingsbury Watermill, St. Michael's St.* ☎ *01727/853502* ⊕ *www.waffle-house.co.uk* ☉ *No dinner.*

Ye Olde Fighting Cocks

$ | BRITISH | Some claim this is England's oldest pub, but it should come as no surprise that the title is hotly contested. Still, this octagonal building certainly looks suitably aged and makes a cozy

At the Warner Bros. Harry Potter Studio Tour, you can visit Diagon Alley and Hogwarts.

stop for a pint and good home-cooked food. **Known for:** extremely old and atmospheric pub; good pub food; lots of summer crowds. ⑤ *Average main: £15* ✉ *16 Abbey Mill La.* ☎ *01727/869152* ⊕ *www.yeoldefightingcocks.co.uk* ⊙ *No dinner Sun.*

 Hotels

St. Michael's Manor
$$ | HOTEL | In the same family for three generations, this luxurious 16th-century manor house close to the center of St. Albans is set in 5 acres of sweeping grounds. **Pros:** spacious rooms; excellent food; beautiful grounds. **Cons:** a little too grand for some; afternoon tea could be better; popular for weddings. ⑤ *Rooms from: £155* ✉ *Fishpool St.* ☎ *01727/864444* ⊕ *www.stmichaelsmanor.com* ⇆ *30 rooms* ⑪ *Free breakfast.*

Woburn Abbey

30 miles west of St. Albans, 10 miles northeast of Aylesbury.

A stunning drive through the deer park at Woburn Abbey leads to a superb art collection within a Georgian mansion and roaming wildlife in a safari park.

GETTING HERE AND AROUND
Woburn Abbey is easily accessible for drivers from M1 at Junction 12 or 13; a car is needed to tour the safari park. The nearest train station, Flitwick, is a 15-minute taxi ride away. Frequent trains connect with St. Albans and London's St. Pancras Station in 50 minutes.

⊙ Sights

Woburn Abbey

HOUSE | FAMILY | Still the ancestral residence of the Duke of Bedford, Woburn Abbey houses countless Grand Tour treasures and Old Master paintings, including 20 stunning Canalettos that practically wallpaper the crimson dining salon, as well as excellent works by Gainsborough and Reynolds. The Palladian mansion contains a number of etchings by Queen Victoria, who left them behind after she stayed here. Outside, 10 species of deer roam grounds that include an antiques center and small restaurant. The adjacent **Woburn Safari Park** is a popular drive-through wildlife experience, home to big game from around the world. Be prepared for fearless monkeys who like to hitch a ride on your car without asking. There are plenty of play areas, a boating lake with swan boats, and walkabouts with small animals such as wallabies. Allow at least half a day for the safari park. If you buy a joint ticket with the house, you can use it on another day. Note that Woburn Abbey will be closed for renovations until spring 2021. ⊠ A4012, off A5, Woburn ☎ 01525/290333 abbey, 01525/290407 safari park ⊕ www.woburn.co.uk 🏷 House, gardens, and deer park £17; gardens and deer park only £8; safari park £21.

Althorp

5 miles west of Northampton, 27 miles northwest of Woburn Abbey.

Althorp, known as the childhood home and burial place of Princess Diana, has fine architecture and paintings, both Old Masters and new.

GETTING HERE AND AROUND

Signposted at Junction 16 of M1, Althorp is most easily reached by car. However, if you ask the driver, Stagecoach Bus 96 from Northampton's train station will drop you here (Monday through Saturday). Buses run every hour.

ESSENTIALS

BUS CONTACTS Stagecoach.
☎ 0871/200–2233 Traveline ⊕ www.stagecoachbus.com.

⊙ Sights

Althorp House

HOUSE | Deep in the heart of Northamptonshire sits the ancestral home of the Spencers, best known in recent years as the family home of Princess Diana. Here, on a tiny island in a lake known as the Round Oval, is Diana's final resting place. A lakeside temple is dedicated to her memory. The house has no permanent Diana exhibits on display, but it does have rooms filled with paintings by Van Dyck, Reynolds, and Rubens—all portraits of the Spencers going back 500 years—and an entry hall that architectural historian Nikolaus Pevsner called "the noblest Georgian room in the country." Two paintings by contemporary artist Mitch Griffiths stand out in complete contrast. A literary festival is held here in mid-June. On the west side of the estate park is Great Brington, the neighboring village where the church of St. Mary the Virgin holds the Spencer family crypt; it's best reached by the designated path from Althorp. The house is closed throughout the winter, but seasonal opening times vary so check the website in advance. ⊠ Rugby Rd., off A428, Northampton ☎ 01604/770107 ⊕ www.spencerofalthorp.com 🏷 £20 ⊙ Closed Oct.–June.

CANTERBURY AND THE SOUTHEAST

Updated by
Joseph Reaney

◉ Sights	🍴 Restaurants	🏨 Hotels	🛍 Shopping	🍸 Nightlife
★★★★☆	★★☆☆☆	★★☆☆☆	★★☆☆☆	★★★☆☆

WELCOME TO CANTERBURY AND THE SOUTHEAST

TOP REASONS TO GO

★ **Castles galore:** From Dover to Herstmonceux, these fortresses will dazzle with their architecture and fascinate with their histories.

★ **Brighton:** With its great bars and restaurants, top-notch nightlife, and sunbathing-friendly shoreline, this is the quintessential modern English seaside city.

★ **Canterbury Cathedral:** This enormous House of God, a masterpiece of medieval architecture, inspires awe with its soaring towers and flagstone corridors.

★ **Manors and Mansions:** West Kent is home to one of England's richest concentrations of historic homes, including the medieval moated Ightham Mote and the sprawling Jacobean-style Knole.

★ **Gardens:** Gardens of all kinds are an English specialty, and at Sissinghurst and Wisley, as well as in the gardens of Hever Castle and Chartwell, you can easily spend an entire afternoon wandering through acres of exotic flora.

The eastern part of the region takes in the cathedral town of Canterbury and the Kent coast, right down to the port city of Dover with its famous white cliffs. The next section heads inland to the pretty spa town of Royal Tunbridge Wells and the surrounding area of West Kent, where stately homes and castles dot the farmland. A third part encompasses the county of East Sussex, which includes the medieval hill town of Rye, the 1066 battlefield near Hastings, and the cool coastal city of Brighton. And the fourth section covers the western part of the region: coast-hugging West Sussex—including its county town of Chichester—and Surrey.

1 Canterbury. A UNESCO-listed medieval town dominated by a massive cathedral founded more than 1,000 years ago.

2 Deal. A quiet seaside town home to two famous coastal castles built during the reign of Henry VIII.

3 Dover. A busy port town, famed for its striking white cliffs.

4 Royal Tunbridge Wells. An ideal base for exploring nearby regal homes and gardens.

5 Hever. Home to Hever Castle—seat of Anne Boleyn's family—and close to Winston Churchill's residence Chartwell.

6 Tonbridge. A little market town within easy reach of renowned country houses like Knole and Ightham Mote.

7 Rochester. A historic cathedral city best known for its Norman castle and Georgian dockyard.

8 Rye. A pretty hill town popular with London day-trippers.

9 Hastings. A once-popular Victorian spa town, famed for the nearby 1066 battefield.

10 Lewes. A gem of a town with a crumbling medieval castle, a famous opera festival, and a penchant for bonfires.

11 Brighton. A funky and lively city that blends Victorian architecture with the best shopping and dining on the coast.

12 Arundel. A little hilltop town with an impressive castle, a neo-Gothic cathedral, and a medieval priory church.

13 Chichester. The charming capital of West Sussex, which once played an important role in ancient Rome.

14 Guildford. The largest town in Surrey, known for its historic merchants' houses and ruined Norman castle.

TEA TIME IN ENGLAND

Relaxing with tea and a scone with clotted cream and jam is a civilized pastime.

Tea is often called the national drink, and for good reason. Most people start their day with "a cuppa," have tea breaks in the afternoon, and a cup after dinner.

Yet despite its ubiquity, a patiently brewed cup of tea can also take on a rare sophistication when combined with a scone in a cream tea or, even better, as part of a fancier formal afternoon tea.

It's hard to imagine a time when tea wasn't part of English culture. But there was no tea in Europe until the 1600s, when it was first brought by Portuguese and Dutch traders. Charles II and his wife, Catherine of Braganza, were tea drinkers. When coffeehouses in London began serving the drink in the mid-17th century, it was seen as an expensive curiosity. By the early 18th century, tea was sold in coffeehouses all over the country, and consumed by all classes. The Duchess of Bedford is credited with popularizing formal afternoon tea in the early 1800s. Dinner in those days was often not served until after 8 pm, so a light meal in late afternoon was welcome. The tradition faded when more people began working in offices in the 20th century—though the love of tea remains.

WHICH TEA?

England's most popular tea is English Breakfast tea, a full-bodied blend of black teas. Second in line is Earl Grey: oil of bergamot orange creates an elegant perfume, but it's an acquired taste. Assam is one of the major teas blended into English Breakfast, and it tastes similar, if a bit more brisk. By contrast, Darjeeling is light and delicate; it's perfect for afternoons.

CREAM TEA

In popular tourist areas in Britain, signs everywhere advertise "cream tea." This is the national shorthand for "tea and scones." The "cream" part is delectable clotted cream—a cream so thick it has a texture like whipped butter. Some scones are fruity and have raisins or dried fruit; others are more like a cross between American biscuits and shortbread. Along with the cream, you'll usually be offered jam. It's customary to put both jam and cream on the scone, though there's no consensus on which should go first. In fact, it's a matter of some dispute, particularly between residents of southwestern counties Cornwall and Devon.

Cream teas are widely offered in areas favored by travelers, such as Stratford-upon-Avon, the Cotswolds, Devon, and Canterbury. In those regions, you'll see it advertised in pubs, restaurants, and dedicated tea shops. Cream tea is a casual afternoon affair: think of it as a coffee break, with tea. Your tea will likely be in a teabag rather than loose leaf. The cost is usually from £3 to £7.

AFTERNOON TEA

A pricey treat reserved for vacations and special occasions, afternoon tea (called "high tea" in America, but not in England, where that term referred to

Cucumber sandwiches at afternoon tea

a meal between 5 and 7 pm) is served in upscale hotels in London, as well as in Oxford, Cambridge, and Brighton, or anywhere popular with travelers. Along with tea—and you can choose from a variety of teas—you'll be served finger sandwiches (usually cucumber, egg, ham, and smoked salmon) and scones, as well as tiny cakes and pastries. These will usually be brought on tiered plate stands, with sweet options higher up and savory on the lower level. Tea will be brewed in a china pot and served with china cups and saucers; milk and lemon are accompaniments.

Afternoon tea is generally offered between 3 and 5:30 pm and can last for hours. It's generally quite formal, and most people dress up for the occasion. Expect to spend anything from £20 to £60.

TEA IN THE SOUTHEAST

Amberley Castle. If you're indulging in an English tradition, why not do it at a castle? Amberley Castle, now a very expensive hotel, does an excellent afternoon tea, with all the requisite cakes and finger sandwiches. Make reservations. ⊠ *Church St., Off B2139, Amberley* ☎ *01978/831992* ⊕ *www. amberleycastle.co.uk.*

Amberley Castle

Surrey, Kent, and Sussex form the breadbasket of England, where bucolic farmland stretches as far as the eye can see. Once a favorite destination of English nobility, this region is rich with history, visible in the great castles and stately homes that dot the countryside.

Its cities are similarly historic, especially ancient Canterbury, with its spectacular cathedral and medieval streets. Along the coast, funky seaside towns have a more relaxed attitude, especially artsy Brighton, where artists and musicians use the sea as inspiration for their work.

Although it's close to London (both Surrey and Kent reach all the way to London's suburbs) and is one of the most densely populated areas of Britain, the Southeast feels far away from the big city. In Kent, acres of orchards burst into a mass of pink-and-white blossoms in spring, while Dover's white cliffs and brooding castle have become symbols of coastal Britain. Historic mansions, such as Petworth House and Knole, are major draws for travelers, and lush gardens—such as Vita Sackville-West's Sissinghurst and the Royal Horticultural Society's Wisley—attract thousands to their vivid floral displays.

Because the English Channel is at its narrowest here, a great deal of British history has been forged in the Southeast. The Romans landed in this area and stayed to rule Britain for four centuries. So did the Saxons—*Sussex* means "the land of the South Saxons." The biggest invasion of them all took place here when William ("the Conqueror") of Normandy defeated the Saxons at a battle near Hastings in 1066, changing the island forever.

MAJOR REGIONS

Canterbury and the Kent Coast. The cathedral city of Canterbury is an ancient place that has attracted travelers since the 12th century. Its magnificent cathedral, the Mother Church of England, remains a powerful draw. Even in prehistoric times, this part of England was relatively well settled. Saxon settlers, Norman conquerors, and the folk who lived here in late-medieval times all left their mark. From Canterbury there's rewarding wandering to be done in the gentle Kentish countryside between the city and the busy port of Dover. Here the landscape ravishes the eye in spring with apple blossoms and in autumn with lush fields ready for harvest. In addition to orchards and market gardens, the county contains round oast houses. These buildings with tilted, pointed roofs were once used for drying hops; now many are expensive homes.

Tunbridge Wells and West Kent. England is world-renowned for its magnificent stately homes and castles, but many of them are scattered across the country, presenting a challenge for travelers. Within a 15-mile radius of Tunbridge Wells, however, in the area of hills and hidden dells known as the Weald, lies a wealth of architectural wonder in the historic homes, castles, and gardens found here: Penshurst Place, Hever Castle, Chartwell, Knole, Ightham Mote, Leeds Castle, and lovely Sissinghurst Castle Garden.

East Sussex. The area to the west of Canterbury, both along the coast and inland, is home to a host of history-rich sites, including the delightful medieval town of Rye, the famous 1066 battlefield at Battle (near Hastings), and the location of the long-standing Glyndebourne Opera House Festival near Lewes. One of the three steam railroads in the Southeast services part of the area: the Romney, Hythe, and Dymchurch Railway.

Brighton, West Sussex, and Surrey. The self-proclaimed belle of the coast, Brighton is upbeat, funky, and endlessly entertaining. To the west is Chichester, with its fascinating Roman foundations and its 900-year-old poem-in-stone cathedral. Outside town, the soft green downs of West Sussex and Surrey hold stately homes you can visit, including Arundel Castle and Petworth House, as well as the bustling and historic town of Guildford.

Planning

When to Go

It's best to visit in spring, summer, or early fall. Many privately owned castles and mansions are open only between April and September or October, though the parks surrounding the stately houses may be open all year. If crowds tend to spoil your fun, avoid August, Sunday, and national holidays, particularly in Canterbury and the seaside towns.

FESTIVALS
Arundel Festival
FESTIVALS | The popular Arundel Festival presents dramatic productions, classical and pop concerts, and a few more locally centered fun and games, such as a rubber duck race. Most events take place in and around the grounds of Arundel Castle for 10 days in late August. The full schedule is published on the website. ⊠ *Arundel* ☎ *01903/883690* ⊕ *www. arundelfestival.co.uk.*

Brighton Festival
FESTIVALS | The three-week-long Brighton Festival, one of England's biggest and liveliest arts festivals, takes place every May in venues around Brighton. The more than 600 events include drama, music, dance, and visual arts. ⊠ *Brighton* ☎ *01273/709709* ⊕ *www.brighton-festival.org.*

★ Brighton Fringe
FESTIVALS | One of the largest fringe festivals in the world—and second only to the Edinburgh Fringe in Scotland—this four-week-long arts extravaganza sees hundreds of stand-up, sketch comedy, music, dance, and circus acts descend on the city every May. ⊠ *Brighton* ☎ *01273/917272* ⊕ *www.brightonfringe.org.*

Broadstairs Dickens Festival
FESTIVALS | In 1937, Gladys Waterer, the then-resident of Dickens House in Broadstairs, put on a commemorative production of Charles Dickens's *David Copperfield* and had people about the town dress in Victorian clothing to publicize it. Since then, the town has hosted a Dickens Festival every June, incorporating everything from film screenings and walking tours to country fairs and dress-up mini-golf. ⊠ *Broadstairs* ☎ *01843/863701* ⊕ *www.broadstairsdickensfestival.co.uk.*

Canterbury Festival
FESTIVALS | Kent's biggest international arts festival fills the town with music, dance, theater, and other cultural events for two weeks every October. ⊠ *Canterbury* ☎ *01227/457568* ⊕ *www.canterburyfestival.co.uk.*

Rye Arts Festival

FESTIVALS | The town of Rye has long been a chosen residence for arty types, from Henry James and Anthony van Dyck to Paul McCartney and Spike Milligan. So it makes perfect sense that, for two weeks every September, the town hosts this art festival, filled with literary talks, film screenings, concerts, and theater performances. ⊠ *Rye* ☎ *01797/224442* ⊕ *www.ryeartsfestival.org.uk.*

Planning Your Time

With the exception of Brighton, you can easily see the highlights of each of the towns in less than a day. Brighton has more to offer, and you should allot at least two days to take it all in. Consider basing yourself in one town while exploring a region. For example, you could stay in Brighton and take in Lewes on a day trip. Base yourself in Rye for a couple of days while exploring Winchelsea, Battle, Hastings, and Herstmonceux Castle. Royal Tunbridge Wells is a great place to overnight if you plan on exploring the many stately homes and castles nearby.

Getting Here and Around

AIR

Although Heathrow isn't too far away, Gatwick Airport is the most convenient gateway for the Southeast. The rail station inside Gatwick has trains to Brighton and other major towns, and you can also take a taxi from Heathrow to Guildford for around £50.

BUS

National Express buses serve the region from London's Victoria Coach Station. Most of the larger towns can be reached this way; journey times vary from less than two hours (Canterbury) to more than three (Chichester). Megabus runs buses at budget prices from Victoria Coach Station to many of the same destinations as National Express and can be cheaper, although luggage limits are strict.

Bus service between towns can be useful but is often intermittent. Out in the country, don't expect buses more often than once every half hour or hour. Traveline is the best central place to call for bus information, and local tourist information centers can be a big help.

CONTACTS Megabus. ☎ *0900/160–0900* ⊕ *uk.megabus.com.* **National Express.** ☎ *0871/781–8181* ⊕ *www.nationalexpress.com.* **Traveline.** ☎ *0871/200–2233* ⊕ *www.traveline.info.*

CAR

While larger towns in the area can be easily reached by public transport (and having a car can be a bit of a nuisance), you will need your own wheels to visit most castles, grand country homes, and quiet villages. Major routes radiating outward from London to the Southeast are, from east to west, the A2/M2 via Canterbury (60 miles) to Dover (76 miles); the A21, passing by Royal Tunbridge Wells (42 miles) to Hastings (66 miles); the M23/A23 to Brighton (53 miles); and the A3 via Guildford (32 miles) to Chichester (72 miles).

TRAIN

Trains are the fastest and most efficient way to travel to major cities in the region, but they don't stop in many small towns. From London, Southeastern trains serve Sussex and Kent from Victoria and Charing Cross stations, and South Western Railway travels to Surrey from Waterloo Station. Getting to Brighton can take as little as one hour, Canterbury about 1½ hours, and Dover around two hours. A Network Railcard costing £30, valid throughout the Southeast for a year, entitles you and three companions to one-third off many off-peak rail fares.

CONTACTS National Rail Enquiries.
☎ 03457/484950 ⊕ www.nationalrail.
co.uk. **Network Railcard.** ☎ 0345/300–
0250 ⊕ www.network-railcard.co.uk.

Restaurants

If you're in a seaside town, look for that
great British staple, fish-and-chips. Perhaps "look" isn't the word—just follow
your nose. On the coast, locally caught
seafood is the specialty. Try local smoked
fish (haddock and mackerel) or the succulent local oysters. If you're inland, sample
fresh local lamb and beef. In cities such
as Canterbury, Brighton, and Tunbridge
Wells, there are numerous restaurants
and cafés, but out in the countryside the
best options are often pubs.

Hotels

All around the coast, resort towns
stretch along beaches, their hotels
standing cheek by jowl. Not all of the
smaller hotels and guesthouses remain
open year-round; many do business only
from mid-April to September or October.
Some hotels have all-inclusive rates for
a week's stay. Prices rise in July and
August, when the seaside resorts can
get solidly booked, especially Brighton.
On the flip side, hotels may drop rates by
up to 40% off-season. Places in Brighton
may not take a booking for a single night
in summer or on weekends.

*Restaurant and hotel reviews have been
shortened. For full information, visit
Fodors.com. Restaurant prices are per
person for a main course at dinner, or
if dinner is not served, at lunch. Hotel
prices are the lowest cost of a standard
double room in high season, including
20% V.A.T.*

WHAT IT COSTS in Pounds			
$	$$	$$$	$$$$
RESTAURANTS			
under £16	£16–£23	£24–£30	over £30
HOTELS			
under £125	£125–£225	£226–£350	over £350

Visitor Information

Tourist boards in the main towns can
help with information, and many will also
book local accommodations.

**CONTACTS Southeast England Tourist
Board.** ⊕ www.visitsoutheastengland.
com.

Canterbury

*60 miles southeast of London, 18 miles
northwest of Deal.*

Just mention Canterbury, and most
people are taken back to memories of
high-school English classes and Geoffrey
Chaucer's *Canterbury Tales*, about
medieval pilgrims making their way to
Canterbury Cathedral. Judging from the
tales, however, in those days Canterbury
was as much a party town as it was a
spiritual center.

The city has been the seat of the Primate
of All England, the archbishop of Canterbury, since Pope Gregory the Great
dispatched St. Augustine to convert
the pagan hordes of Britain in 597. The
height of Canterbury's popularity came
in the 12th century, when thousands of
pilgrims flocked here to see the shrine
of the murdered archbishop Thomas
Becket. This southeastern town became
one of the most visited in England, if not
Europe. Buildings that served as pilgrims'
inns (and that survived World War II
bombing of the city) still dominate the

streets of Canterbury's center, though it's tourists, not pilgrims, who flock to this city of about 40,000 people today.

Prices at city museums are higher than average, so if you plan to see more than one, ask at the tourist office if a combination ticket might be cheaper.

GETTING HERE AND AROUND

The fastest way to reach Canterbury from London is by train. Southeastern trains to Canterbury run every half hour in peak times from London's Charing Cross Station. The journey takes around 1½ hours. Canterbury has two centrally located train stations, Canterbury East and Canterbury West; both are about a 10-minute walk from the cathedral.

National Express and Megabus buses bound for Canterbury depart several times a day from London's Victoria Coach Station. Trips to Canterbury take around two hours and drop passengers at the bus station right in the center. If you're driving, take the A2/M2 to Canterbury from London (60 miles). Park in one of the signposted lots at the edge of the town center.

Canterbury has a small, walkable town center (there's also a good local bus service, but you're unlikely to need it). Most major tourist sites are on one street, though it changes name three times—from St. George's Street, to High Street, to St. Peter's Street.

TIMING

The town tends to get crowded around religious holidays—particularly Easter weekend—and on other national holiday weekends. If you'd rather avoid the tour buses, try visiting midweek.

ESSENTIALS

VISITOR INFORMATION Canterbury Visitor Information Centre. ⊠ *The Beaney House of Art & Knowledge, 18 High St.* ☎ *01227/862162* ⊕ *www.canterbury. co.uk.*

TOURS

Canterbury Guided Tours

Expert guides lead 90-minute walking tours at 11 am daily, with an additional tour at 2 pm on weekends from November to March and daily April through October. Tours start outside Christchurch Gate (the main cathedral gate) opposite the Buttermarket, and they cost £10. You can buy a ticket in advance online or during the tour. ⊠ *Christchurch Gate, The Precincts* ☎ *01227/459779* ⊕ *www. canterburyguidedtours.com* ⊠ *From £8.*

◉ Sights

The Beaney House of Art & Knowledge

MUSEUM | The medieval Poor Priests' Hospital is the site of this quirky local museum, where exhibits provide an overview of the city's history and architecture from Roman times to World War II. It covers everything and everyone associated with the town, including the mysterious death of the 16th-century writer Christopher Marlowe and the British children's book and TV characters Rupert the Bear and Bagpuss. One recent acquisition is a beautiful gold dragon pendant, made in Kent during the Anglo-Saxon era (410–1066). ⊠ *18 High St.* ☎ *01227/862162* ⊕ *www.canterburymuseums.co.uk/ beaney* ⊠ *Free.*

★ Canterbury Cathedral

RELIGIOUS SITE | The focal point of the city was the first of England's great Norman cathedrals. Nucleus of worldwide Anglicanism, the Cathedral Church of Christ Canterbury (its formal name) is a living textbook of medieval architecture. The building was begun in 1070, demolished, begun anew in 1096, and then systematically expanded over the next three centuries. When the original choir section burned to the ground in 1174, another replaced it, designed in the new Gothic style, with tall, pointed arches.

The cathedral was only a century old, and still relatively small, when Thomas

Impressive both inside and out, ancient Canterbury Cathedral dominates the town.

Becket, the archbishop of Canterbury, was murdered here in 1170. Becket, as head of the church, had been engaged in a political struggle with his old friend Henry II. Four knights supposedly over-heard Henry scream, "Will no one rid me of this turbulent priest?" (although there is no evidence that those were his actual words—the only contemporary record has him saying, "What miserable drones and traitors have I nourished and brought up in my household, who let their lord be treated with such shameful contempt by a low-born cleric?").

Thinking they were carrying out the king's wishes, the knights went immediately to Canterbury and hacked Becket to pieces in one of the side chapels. Henry, racked with guilt, went into deep mourning. Becket was canonized, and Canterbury's position as the center of English Christi-anity was assured.

For almost 400 years, Becket's tomb was one of the most extravagant shrines in Christendom, until it was destroyed by Henry VIII's troops during the Reformation. In **Trinity Chapel,** which held the shrine, you can still see a series of 13th-century stained-glass windows illustrating Becket's miracles. (The actual site of Becket's murder is down a flight of steps just to the left of the nave.) Nearby is the tomb of Edward, the Black Prince (1330–76), warrior son of Edward III and a national hero. In the corner of Trinity Chapel, a second flight of steps leads down to the enormous Norman **undercroft,** or vaulted cellar, built in the early 12th century. A row of squat pillars engraved with dancing beasts (mythical and otherwise) supports the roof.

To the north of the cathedral are the **cloisters** and a small compound of monastic buildings. The 12th-century octagonal water tower is still part of the cathedral's water supply. The Norman staircase in the northwest corner of the Green Court dates from 1167 and is a unique example of the architecture of the times. Another highlight is the almost Disney-like stained glass window "'Salva-tion" by Hungarian artist Ervin Bossányi.

Look out for a little padlock with a swastika, a reference to the atrocities that occured during World War II.

At the entrance to the cathedral, by Christchurch Gate, is a free-to-enter vistor center, which has more information on the history (and myth) of Canterbury Cathedral. ■TIP➜ **The cathedral is popular, so arrive early or late in the day to avoid the crowds.** ✉ *The Precincts* ☎ *01227/762862* ⊕ *www.canterbury-cathedral.org* 💷 *£12.50; free for services; £5 tour; £4 audio guide.*

Canterbury Roman Museum

MUSEUM | Below ground, at the level of the remnants of Roman Canterbury, this small but informative museum tells the story of the area's distant Roman past. Highlights of the collection include a hypocaust (the Roman version of central heating) and two colorful floor mosaics dating from around the year 270 that were unearthed in the aftermaths of the bombs that fell on Canterbury during World War II. Displays of excavated objects—some of which you can hold in the **Touch the Past** area—and computer-generated reconstructions of Roman buildings and the marketplace help recreate the past. ✉ *Butchery La.* ☎ *01227/785575* ⊕ *www.canterburymuseums.co.uk/romanmuseum* 💷 *£9.*

Christchurch Gate

RELIGIOUS SITE | This huge gate, built in 1517, leads into the cathedral close. As you pass through, look up at the sculpted heads of two young figures: Prince Arthur, elder brother of Henry VIII, and the young Catherine of Aragon, to whom Arthur was married in 1501 (when he was just 15). He died shortly afterwards, and Catherine married Henry. Jump forward 25 years, and Henry was king. But they had produced no male children, a fact Henry attributed to God's wrath for marrying his sister-in-law. The Pope refused to grant him a divorce, but Henry went ahead and did it anyway, creating an irrevocable breach with the Roman Catholic Church and altering the course of English history forever.

Outside the gate is the tiny Buttermarket, an old dairy market square with a sweet name and a dark past. Before the 16th century, it was called "the Bullstake," because animals were tied here and tortured (a popular activity of the time known as "baiting") before they were slaughtered. Today, it's surrounded by bars and restaurants and leads onto pretty Mercery Lane, with its medieval-style cottages and massive, overhanging timber roofs. ✉ *The Precincts, Off Sun St.* ⊕ *www.canterbury-cathedral.org.*

Eastbridge Hospital of St. Thomas

RELIGIOUS SITE | The 12th-century building (which would now be called a hostel) lodged pilgrims who came to pray at the tomb of Thomas Becket. It's a tiny place, fascinating in its simplicity. The refectory, the chapel, and the crypt are open to the public. ✉ *25 High St.* ☎ *01227/471668* ⊕ *www.eastbridgehospital.org.uk* 💷 *£3* ⊘ *Closed Sun. and Nov.–late Mar.*

Medieval City Walls

ARCHAEOLOGICAL SITE | For an essential Canterbury experience, follow the circuit of the 13th- and 14th-century walls, built on the line of the Roman walls. Roughly half survive; those to the east are intact, towering some 20 feet high and offering a sweeping view of the town. You can access these from a number of places, including Castle Street and Broad Street, but perhaps the most photo-worthy section is by Canterbury East Station Bridge. ✉ *Canterbury E. Station Bridge.*

Westgate Towers

LOCAL INTEREST | In medieval times, Canterbury had seven gatehouses guarding entry to the city, but today only this one survives. Still, with its twin castellated towers, it's one of England's finest. Currently under renovation but still open to the public, Westgate Towers contains a small museum with exhibits on the gate's history, including medieval armaments once used by the city guard and artifacts related to the city jail that was here from the 14th century. There are also some surprising links to the United States: one of the prisoners held here, Robert Cushman, was an organizer of the *Mayflower* voyage in 1620. Climb to the roof for a panoramic view of the city. The entrance is via a bar called The Pound Bar & Kitchen. Be aware that a trip to the top requires climbing five sets of narrow stairs. ⊠ *The Pound Bar & Kitchen, 1 Pound Ln.* ☎ *01227/458629* ⊕ *www.one-poundlane.co.uk/westgate-towers* 🎫 *£4 (£2 during renovation).*

🍴 Restaurants

City Fish Bar

$ | BRITISH | Long lines and lots of satisfied finger licking attest to the deserved popularity of this excellent fish-and-chip shop in the center of town, where all orders are takeout. Everything is freshly fried, the batter crisp, and the fish tasty; the fried mushrooms are also surprisingly good. **Known for:** fresh fish in crispy batter; chunky chips; good-quality fast food. ⑤ *Average main: £7* ⊠ *30 St. Margaret's St.* ☎ *01227/760873* ⊕ *www.facebook. com/cityfishbar.*

★ The Corner House

$$ | BRITISH | Set just outside the medieval city walls, this historic pub turned restaurant serves locally sourced British produce with creative culinary twists. Mains include confit pork belly with creamed kale and bacon and herb-crumbed cod loin with mash and cockles, but it's the "nibbles" (snacks) that are really inventive—try the sausage roll, served as three thick slices with homemade mushroom ketchup. **Known for:** building that dates back to 1574; to-die-for treacle bread; four guest rooms available on-site. ⑤ *Average main: £19* ⊠ *1 Dover St.* ☎ *01227/780793* ⊕ *www.cornerhous-erestaurants.co.uk.*

The Goods Shed

$$ | BRITISH | Next to Canterbury West Station, this farmers' market restaurant with wooden tables is well known for offering fresh, seasonal Kentish food—think monkfish with parsley dumplings and broccoli or guinea fowl with lentils and black pudding. Whatever is freshest that day appears on the menu, whether it's quail eggs, John Dory, or duck breast. **Known for:** fresh local produce; great seafood, including a catch of the day; cool historic design. ⑤ *Average main: £18* ⊠ *Station Rd. W* ☎ *01227/459153* ⊕ *www.thegoodsshed.co.uk* ⊗ *Closed Mon. No dinner Sun.*

The Old Buttermarket

$ | BRITISH | A colorful, friendly old pub near the cathedral, the Old Buttermarket is a great place to grab a hearty lunch and sample some traditional English fare with a modern inflection. You can sip a pint of fresh English ale from the ever-changing selection while sampling a wild boar and chorizo pie or perhaps a warming bowl of Applewood-smoked mac and cheese. **Known for:** great selection of ales; excellent savory pies; interesting history (there's been a pub in this spot for 500 years). ⑤ *Average main: £13* ⊠ *39 Burgate* ☎ *01227/462170* ⊕ *www. nicholsonspubs.co.uk/theoldbuttermar-ketcanterbury* ▭ *No credit cards.*

🛏 Hotels

ABode Canterbury

$ | HOTEL | This glossy boutique hotel inside the old city walls offers up-to-date style in traditional Canterbury, with good-size rooms—modern but not minimal—classed as Comfortable, Desirable, Enviable, and Most Enviable. **Pros:** central location; luxurious handmade beds; tasty afternoon tea. **Cons:** one of the pricier hotels in town; bar gets quite crowded; breakfast is extra. ⑤ *Rooms from: £110* ⊠ *30–33 High St.* ☎ *01227/766266* ⊕ *www.abodecanterbury.co.uk* 🔌 *72 rooms* 🍽 *No meals.*

Canterbury

KEY

- ① Exploring Sights
- ① Restaurants
- ① Hotels
- ⓘ Tourist information

Sights ▼

1. The Beaney House of
   Art & Knowledge **C3**
2. Canterbury Cathedral ...**C3**
3. Canterbury
   Roman Museum **C3**
4. Christchurch Gate **C3**
5. Eastbridge Hospital
   of St. Thomas............ **B3**
6. Medieval City Walls **C4**
7. Westgate Towers....... **B2**

Restaurants ▼

1. City Fish Bar **C3**
2. The Corner House **C4**
3. The Goods Shed **B2**
4. The Old Buttermarket ...**C3**

Hotels ▼

1. ABode Canterbury...... **B3**
2. Canterbury Cathedral
   Lodge.................... **D3**
3. Cathedral Gate...........**C3**
4. Ebury Hotel **E5**
5. House of Agnes......... **A2**

★ Canterbury Cathedral Lodge

$ | HOTEL | There is no more peaceful place to stay in Canterbury then at this small and modern hotel tucked away within the grounds of the famous cathedral. **Pros:** outstanding location; incredible cathedral views; free entry to the cathedral (worth £12.50). **Cons:** no lunch or dinner served in restaurant; double beds are small; gets booked up during conferences. $ *Rooms from: £120* ⊠ *The Precincts* ☎ *01227/865350* ⊕ *www.canterburycathedrallodge.org* ⇨ *35 rooms* ⦿ *Free breakfast.*

Cathedral Gate

$ | HOTEL | If you're looking for a hotel with history, you're in the right place: Cathedral Gate's ancient beamed ceilings, low doorways, and sloping floors reveal origins dating back to 1438 (that's 75 years earlier than Christchurch Gate next door). **Pros:** a real sense of history; convenient location right by cathedral; free tea and coffee served all day. **Cons:** cooked breakfast costs extra; patchy TV and Wi-Fi signal; some rooms share bathrooms. $ *Rooms from: £82* ⊠ *36 Burgate* ☎ *01227/464381* ⊕ *www.cathgate.co.uk* ⇨ *25 rooms* ⦿ *Free breakfast.*

Ebury Hotel

$$ | HOTEL | Family run, this hotel earns rave reviews for its laid-back attitude and comfortable accommodations inside two big Victorian buildings. **Pros:** cozy lounge; lovely indoor pool; three- and four-bedrooms good value for families. **Cons:** a bit of a walk to the town center; no elevator; pet-friendly ethos is great for dog lovers, not allergy sufferers. $ *Rooms from: £130* ⊠ *65–67 New Dover Rd.* ☎ *01227/768433* ⊕ *www.ebury-hotel.co.uk* ⇨ *15 rooms* ⦿ *Free breakfast.*

★ House of Agnes

$ | B&B/INN | This historic B&B, which dates back 600 years and was written about by Dickens, offers unique and stylish accommodations not far from Canterbury West Station. **Pros:** historic building; just enough modern touches;

honesty bar. **Cons:** rooms vary quite a bit in size; no elevator; quirky design not for everyone. $ *Rooms from: £95* ⊠ *71 St. Dunstans St.* ☎ *01227/472185* ⊕ *www.houseofagnes.co.uk* ⇨ *17 rooms* ⦿ *Free breakfast.*

ⓨ Nightlife

Canterbury is home to a popular university, and the town's many pubs and bars are busy and often crowded with college-age folks.

Alberry's Wine Bar

BARS/PUBS | With late-night jazz and hip-hop and a trendy crowd, Alberry's Wine Bar is one of Canterbury's coolest nightspots. At lunchtime they serve a fine burger, too. ⊠ *38 St. Margaret's St.* ☎ *01227/452378* ⊕ *www.alberrys.co.uk.*

Parrot

BARS/PUBS | Built in 1370 on Roman foundations, the Parrot is an atmospheric old pub known for its ever-changing selection of real ales. They also do good food; Sunday lunch here is particularly popular. ⊠ *1–9 Church La.* ☎ *01227/454170* ⊕ *www.parrotcanterbury.co.uk.*

Thomas Becket

BARS/PUBS | A traditional English pub, with bunches of hops hanging from the ceiling and a fire crackling in the hearth on a cold winter's day, the Thomas Becket is a convivial kind of place. There is food available, but most people just come for the ale and the atmosphere. ⊠ *21 Best La.* ☎ *01227/464384* ⊕ *www.facebook.com/thethomasbecketpubrestaurant.*

ⓣ Performing Arts

Gulbenkian Theatre

THEATER | Outside the town center, the Gulbenkian Theatre mounts all kinds of plays, particularly experimental plays, as well as dance performances, concerts, and comedy shows. It also screens films. ⊠ *University of Kent, Library Rd.*

☎ 01227/769075 ⊕ www.thegulbenkian.
co.uk.

The Marlowe Theatre

THEATER | This impressive modern performance space showcases Shakespeare productions, contemporary theater, music, dance, and comedy. It is also a venue for popular touring shows, including West End musicals. ✉ The Friars ☎ 01227/787787 ⊕ www.marlowetheatre.com.

🛍 Shopping

Canterbury's medieval streets are lined with shops, perfect for an afternoon of rummaging. The best are in the district just around the cathedral. The King's Mile, which stretches past the cathedral and down Palace Street and Northgate, is a good place to start.

★ Catching Lives Charity Bookshop

BOOKS/STATIONERY | One of Canterbury's most photographed buildings (and that's saying something), this wonderfully crooked half-timbered house dates back to the 17th century. Inside, volunteers sell a wide range of second-hand and collectable books, with all profits going to the local homeless charity Catching Lives. ✉ 28 Palace St. ☎ 07899/458961 ⊕ www.catchinglives.org/catching-lives-bookshop.

Crowthers of Canterbury

MUSIC STORES | Behind the delightfully old-style red shop front, Crowthers of Canterbury carries an extensive selection of musical instruments, gifts, and other souvenirs for music lovers. ✉ 1 Borough ☎ 01227/763965 ⊕ www.crowthersofcanterbury.co.uk.

925 Silver

JEWELRY/ACCESSORIES | This little shop has a great selection of handmade silver jewelry. ✉ 57 Palace St. ☎ 01227/785699 ⊕ www.925-silver.co.uk.

★ Revivals

CLOTHING | This amazing little vintage clothing store attracts customers from far and wide with its eclectic fashions—from waistcoats and ballgowns to shoes and jewelry—all at very reasonable prices. ✉ 42 St. Peter's St. ☎ 01227/768033 ⊕ www.facebook.com/revivalscanterbury.

Deal

18 miles southeast of Canterbury, 9 miles north of Dover.

The large seaside town of Deal, known for its castle, is famous in history books as the place where Caesar's legions landed in 55 BC, and it was from here that William Penn set sail in 1682 on his first journey to the American colony he founded, Pennsylvania.

GETTING HERE AND AROUND

Southeastern trains travel to Deal twice an hour from London's St. Pancras Station and once an hour from London's Charing Cross. The journey takes between 1½ and two hours. You can also get a National Express bus from London's Victoria Coach Station, but there's only one bus per day (late evening), and the trip takes around three hours. From Canterbury, drive east on the A258 to Sandwich, then south on the A258 into Deal. Direct bus number 12 (45 minutes) is the best public transport option from Canterbury; trains take longer, cost more, and require a change in Ashford.

ESSENTIALS

VISITOR INFORMATION **Deal Visitor Information Centre.** ✉ Town Hall, High St. ☎ 01304/369576 ⊕ www.deal.gov.uk.

👁 Sights

Deal Castle

CASTLE/PALACE | Erected in 1540 and intricately built to the shape of a Tudor rose, Deal Castle is the largest of the coastal

Canterbury and the Kent Coast

defenses constructed by Henry VIII. A moat surrounds its gloomy passages and austere walls. The castle museum has exhibits about prehistoric, Roman, and Saxon Britain. ✉ *Victoria Rd.* ☎ *0370/333–1181* ⊕ *www.english-heritage.org.uk/deal* ✉ *£7.60* ⊘ *Closed Mon. and Tues. in Mar. and weekdays Nov.–mid-Feb.*

Dickens House Museum
MUSEUM | This house was originally the home of Mary Pearson Strong, on whom Dickens based the character of Betsey Trotwood, David Copperfield's aunt. Dickens lived here from 1837 to 1839 while writing *The Pickwick Papers* and *Oliver Twist*. Some rooms have been decorated to look as they would have in Dickens's day, and there's a reconstruction of Miss Trotwood's room as described by Dickens. The house is in Broadstairs, 18 miles up the coast from Deal. ✉ *2 Victoria Parade, Broadstairs* ☎ *01843/861232* ⊕ *www.dickensmuseumbroadstairs. co.uk* ✉ *£3.75* ⊘ *Closed Dec.–Mar. and weekdays in Nov.*

Walmer Castle and Gardens
CASTLE/PALACE | Another of Henry VIII's coastal fortifications, this castle was converted in 1708 into a residence for the Lord Warden of the Cinque Ports, a ceremonial honor dating back to the early Middle Ages. Made up of four round towers around a circular keep, the castle has counted many famous figures among its lord wardens, including William Pitt the Younger (1759–1806), the Duke of Wellington (1769–1852), and Sir Winston Churchill (1874–1965). The small museum here homes in on Wellington (who lived here from 1829 until his death), telling the story of his victory at Waterloo through a rather random selection of

memorabilia, including an original pair of Wellington boots, which the duke is credited with inventing.

Visitors can enter the drawing and dining rooms of the castle (except when the lord warden is in residence) and explore the eight acres of award-winning gardens that surround the fortification. These include the Glen, a planted former chalk quarry that's now open for the first time in a century, and the sprawling lavender gardens, which come with gorgeous ocean views. The castle is about two miles south of Deal town center. ⊠ Off Kingsdown Rd. ☎ 0370/333–1181 ⊕ www.english-heritage.org.uk/walmer 🎫 £12.20 ⊙ Closed Mon. and Tues. in Mar. and weekdays Nov.–mid-Feb.

Dover

9 miles south of Deal, 78 miles east of London.

The busy passenger port of Dover has for centuries been Britain's gateway to Europe, famed for its pretty white cliffs. The town itself is, sadly, not a pretty place; the savage bombardments of World War II and the shortsightedness of postwar developers left the city center in something of a mess. Mostly Dover town is a place you go through to get to the ferry. However, there are a couple of notable exceptions, including the Roman-era legacy of a lighthouse adjoining a stout Anglo-Saxon church.

GETTING HERE AND AROUND

National Express buses depart from London's Victoria Coach Station for Dover about every 90 minutes. The journey takes between 2½ and 3 hours. Drivers from London take the M20, which makes a straight line southeast to Dover. The journey should take around two hours. Southeastern trains leave London's Charing Cross, Victoria, and St. Pancras stations about every 30 minutes for Dover Priory Station in Dover. Direct trains take

around two hours; a slightly quicker (but usually more expensive) service changes in Ashford.

To get to Dover from Deal, drive south on the A258. There are also regular direct trains (16 minutes) and buses (40 minutes).

For the best views of the cliffs, you need a car or taxi; it's a long way to walk from town.

ESSENTIALS

VISITOR INFORMATION Dover Visitor Information Centre. ⊠ Dover Museum, Market Sq. ☎ 01304/201066 ⊕ www.whitecliffscountry.org.uk.

◉ Sights

★ Dover Castle.

CASTLE/PALACE | **FAMILY** | Spectacular and with plenty to explore, Dover Castle, towering high above the ramparts of the white cliffs, is a mighty medieval castle that has served as an important strategic center over the centuries.

Most of the castle, including the keep, dates to Norman times. It was begun by Henry II in 1181 but incorporates additions from almost every succeeding century. The **Great Tower** re-creates how the opulent castle would have looked in Henry's time, complete with sound effects, interactive displays, and courtly characters in medieval costume.

History jumps forward the better part of a millennium (and becomes rather more sober in the telling) as you venture down into the labyrinthine **Secret Wartime Tunnels.** The castle played a surprisingly dramatic role in World War II, the full extent to which remained unknown for years afterward. These well-thought-out interactive galleries tell the complete story. The tunnels themselves, originally built during the Napoleonic Wars, were used as a top-secret intelligence-gathering base in the fight against Hitler. ⊠ Castle Hill Rd. ☎ 0370/333–1181 ⊕ www.

The majestic White Cliffs of Dover are a national icon.

english-heritage.org.uk/dover ✉ £20.90 ⊙ Closed weekdays Nov.–mid-Feb. and Mon. and Tues. mid-Feb.–Mar.

Roman Painted House

ARCHAEOLOGICAL SITE | Believed to have been a hotel, the remains of this nearly 2,000-year-old structure were excavated in the 1970s. It includes some Roman wall paintings (mostly dedicated to Bacchus, the god of revelry), along with the remnants of an ingenious heating system. ✉ 25 New St. ☎ 01304/203279 ⊕ karu.org.uk/roman_painted_house.html ✉ £4 ⊙ Closed Sun., Mon., Oct.–Mar., and Wed.–Fri. in May.

★ White Cliffs

NATURE SITE | Plunging hundreds of feet into the sea, Dover's startlingly white cliffs are a spectacular sight, and one of the most iconic symbols of England. The cliffs, which are composed mainly of chalk with slivers of flint, are eroding at a rather alarming rate: more than a foot (30 cm) a year on average. Because of this, you must be cautious when walking along the cliffs—experts recommend staying at least 20 feet from the edge. The cliffs stretch for around eight miles altogether, but the most popular section to visit is the one managed by the National Trust, about two miles east of town. The visitor center has five miles of walking trails heading farther east to the 19th-century South Foreland Lighthouse and St. Margaret's Bay, with spectacular views along the way. There are also some lovely coastal walks to the west of Dover with good views of the cliffs, inclduing Samphire Hoe, Folkestone East Cliff, and Warren Country Park. Signs will direct you from the roads to scenic spots. ✉ Visitor Centre, Upper Rd., Guston ⊕ www.nationaltrust.org.uk/the-white-cliffs-of-dover ✉ Free; parking £5.

🍴 Restaurants

The Allotment

$ | **BRITISH** | This charming, slightly quirky restaurant in the center of Dover doesn't look like much from the outside, but don't be fooled—delicious, creative Modern British meals are served within.

The menu is jam-packed with local and regional ingredients; try the pan-seared scallops to start, followed by Kentish venison steak or, even better, the bouillabaisse (a French seafood stew made with seasonal fish, shrimp, calamari, and clams in a garlic, white wine, and tomato sauce). **Known for:** house special fisherman's pie; lots of local produce; charming and quirky character. $ *Average main: £15* ✉ *9 High St.* ☎ *01304/214467* ⊕ *www.theallotmentrestaurant.com.*

La Scala

$ | SICILIAN | This cheerful Italian restaurant in the center of Dover is much favored by locals looking for an authentic, inexpensive Italian meal without feeling the need to sit up too straight. The menu is mostly Sicilian influenced; you might start with a simple caprese salad of fresh tomatoes with mozzarella and basil, before moving on to some homemade pasta with swordfish in a tomato and white wine sauce or a whole rump of lamb cooked with garlic and rosemary. **Known for:** delicious homemade pasta; authentic and informal Italian cooking; busy on weekends (so book early). $ *Average main: £13* ✉ *19 High St.* ☎ *01304/208044* ⊕ *lascaladover.business. site* ⊗ *Closed Sun.*

🛏 Hotels

White Cliffs Hotelwhite

$$ | B&B/INN | Situated near St. Margaret's Bay, four miles east of town along the famous White Cliffs of Dover, this colorful little hotel is attached to a friendly pub that serves good food. **Pros:** tons of character; beautiful cliff-top location; good food. **Cons:** a little way from central Dover; Wi-Fi comes and goes; quite pricey for what you get. $ *Rooms from: £180* ✉ *High St., St. Margaret's-at-Cliffe* ☎ *01304/852229* ⊕ *www.thewhitecliffs. com* ⇨ *17 rooms* �“❘ *Free breakfast.*

Royal Tunbridge Wells

54 miles west of Dover.

Nobody much bothers with the "Royal" anymore, but Tunbridge Wells is no less regal because of it. Because of its wealth and political conservatism, this historic bedroom community has been the subject of (somewhat envious) British humor for years. Its restaurants and lodgings make it a convenient base for exploring the many homes and gardens nearby.

The city owes its prosperity to the 17th- and 18th-century passion for spas and mineral baths. In 1606, a mineral-water spring was discovered here, drawing legions of royal visitors looking for eternal health. Tunbridge Wells reached its zenith in the mid-18th century, when Richard "Beau" Nash presided over its social life. The buildings at the lower end of High Street are mostly 18th century, but as the street climbs the hill north, changing its name to Mount Pleasant Road, structures become more modern.

GETTING HERE AND AROUND

Southeastern trains leave from London's Charing Cross Station every 15 to 20 minutes. The journey to Tunbridge Wells takes just under an hour. If you're traveling by car from London, head here on the A20/M25/A21; travel time is about an hour.

To get to Tunbridge Wells from Dover, drive west on the A20/M20, switching to the A228 heading south; the journey typically takes 1½ to two hours. You can also take an hourly train from Dover (1½ hours, with a change in Tonbridge).

Tunbridge Wells sprawls in all directions, but the historic center is compact. None of the sights is more than a 10-minute walk from the main train station. You can pick up a town map at the station.

Tunbridge Wells and West Kent

ESSENTIALS

VISITOR INFORMATION Tunbridge Wells Tourist Information Centre. ⊠ *The Corn Exchange, The Pantiles* ☎ *01892/515675* ⊕ *www.visittunbridgewells.com.*

◉ Sights

★ Church of King Charles the Martyr

RELIGIOUS SITE | This important parish church dates from 1678, when the area was little more than a mineral spring surrounded by fields; the modern town of Tunbridge Wells grew up around it. Dedicated to Charles I, who had been executed by Parliament in 1649—and whose son, Charles II, was restored 11 years later—the church's plain exterior belies its splendid interior, with a particularly beautiful plastered baroque ceiling. The entrance is on the corner of the A26 and the A267, across the road from the

Pantiles. ⊠ *Chapel Pl.* ☎ *01892/511745* ⊕ *www.kcmtw.org* 🖾 *Free; donations welcome* ⏱ *Closed Sun. except for services.*

Pantiles

PROMENADE | A good place to begin a visit to Tunbridge Wells is at the Pantiles, a famous promenade with colonnaded shops near the spring on one side of town. Its odd name derives from the Dutch "pan tiles" that originally paved the area. Now sandwiched between two busy main roads, the Pantiles remains an elegant, tranquil oasis, and the site of the actual well. ■ **TIP→ You can still drink the waters when a "dipper" (the traditional water dispenser) is in attendance, from Easter through September.** ⊠ *Royal Tunbridge Wells.*

🍴 Restaurants

★ Kitsu

$ | JAPANESE | This tiny, unassuming restaurant might seem like an unlikely venue for exceptional sushi, but it's the best for miles. Everything is fresh and delicious, from the fragrant miso soup to the light tempura to the sushi platters that are big enough to share. **Known for:** excellent sushi; good casual dining; BYOB and cash-only policies. $ *Average main: £13* ✉ *82a Victoria Rd.* ☎ *07425/900016* ⊕ *www.kitsu.co.uk* ▭ *No credit cards.*

★ Sankey's The Old Fishmarket

$$ | SEAFOOD | Serving the best of British seafood, as well as an extensive choice of champagne and sparkling wines, this intimate little restaurant has bar seating set around an open kitchen, so you can watch (and chat with) the chef preparing your food. But don't let the relaxed, friendly, and unstuffy atmosphere fool you; this is exceptional quality, fresh seafood cooked to perfection (or not cooked at all, in the case of the delicious oysters). **Known for:** intimate 20-seat setting; extensive oyster menu (including £1-an-oyster happy hour); historic old pavilion building. $ *Average main: £22* ✉ *The Pantiles, 19 The Upper* ☎ *01892/511422* ⊕ *www.sankeys.co.uk/ the-old-fishmarket* ⏱ *Closed Mon.*

★ Thackeray's

$$$$ | FRENCH | Once the home of Victorian novelist William Makepeace Thackeray, this mid-17th-century tile-hung house is now an elegant restaurant known for creative French cuisine, with à la carte dishes like monkfish "on the bone" with barbecued celeriac or saddle of venison with roast sweet potatoes. A starter, main (plus side), and dessert will set you back £60, so if you're feeling hungry, opt for one of the prix fixe menus instead: there's the five-course seasonal tasting menu (£59 per person, plus £30 for wine pairing) or the seven-course "Chef's Tasting Menu" (£78 per person, plus £95

for premium wine pairing). **Known for:** fine dining experience; extravagant wine list; very expensive prices. $ *Average main: £34* ✉ *85 London Rd.* ☎ *01892/511921* ⊕ *www.thackerays-restaurant.co.uk* ⏱ *Closed Mon. No dinner Sun.*

🛏 Hotels

Hotel du Vin

$$ | HOTEL | An elegant sandstone house dating from 1762 has been transformed into a chic boutique hotel with polished wood floors and luxurious furnishings. **Pros:** historic building; cute old-school elevator with mesh door; reliably good service. **Cons:** some rooms are small; bar can get crowded; big price hike in summer. $ *Rooms from: £170* ✉ *Crescent Rd.* ☎ *01892/320749* ⊕ *www.hotelduvin. com/locations/tunbridge-wells* ⇥ *34 rooms* ⦿ *Free breakfast.*

★ The Mount Edgcumbe

$$ | HOTEL | Perched on a hill overlooking the town below, this charming family-run boutique hotel has spacious, individually designed rooms that combine home comforts like Hypnos beds, walk-in showers, and roll-top baths, with quirky touches like bold print cushions, pineapple-shaped lamps, and antique chairs. **Pros:** excellent cellar restaurant; private parking available; delicious eggs royale at breakfast. **Cons:** an uphill walk from town; quirky touches not for everyone; no staffed reception. $ *Rooms from: £170* ✉ *Off A264* ☎ *01892/618854* ⊕ *www. themountedgcumbe.com* ⇥ *6 rooms* ⦿ *Free breakfast.*

One Warwick Park

$ | HOTEL | This stylish boutique hotel in the center of Tunbridge Wells used to be a brewery and then a schoolhouse; today it's a luxurious and intimate place to stay, with spacious, contemporary guest rooms and modern bathrooms. **Pros:** chic design including underground art gallery; great food; central setting near Pantiles. **Cons:** cheapest rooms are small;

no on-site parking; prices rise sharply for best rooms. $ *Rooms from: £115* ✉ *1 Warwick Park* ☎ *01892/520587* ⊕ *www. onewarwickpark.co.uk* ⇨ *39 rooms* ⍟ *Free breakfast.*

Spa Hotel

$$ | HOTEL | The country-house flavor of this 1766 Georgian mansion has been beautifully maintained by luxurious furnishings and preserved period details. **Pros:** lap-of-luxury feel; gorgeous countryside views; pony-riding lessons for kids. **Cons:** breakfast is extra; quite formal atmosphere; uphill walk from the town center. $ *Rooms from: £190* ✉ *Off Langton Rd.* ☎ *01892/520331* ⊕ *www. spahotel.co.uk* ⇨ *70 rooms* ⍟ *No meals.*

Hever

10 miles northwest of Royal Tunbridge Wells.

The pretty village of Hever is best known for its romantic, history-layered castle—a fairy-tale medieval fortification on the outside and a Tudor mansion within. However, it's also within easy reach of two other famous heritage properties: Chartwell, the beloved home of Winston Churchill and magnificent views across rolling Kentish hills; and Penshurst Place, an Elizabethan manor house with one of the oldest and grandest medieval halls in England.

GETTING HERE AND AROUND

Southern trains leave from London Bridge Station every hour. The journey to Hever takes around 40 minutes. If you're traveling by car from London, take the A2/M25/B2042; travel time is one to 1½ hours. If driving from Tunbridge Wells, take the A264 east then follow signs directing you north on the B2026 toward Hever. Bus 234 runs between Tunbridge Wells and Hever three times a day (there's no convenient train connection).

⊙ Sights

Chartwell

HOUSE | A grand Victorian mansion with a pond-dotted estate offering views over the surrounding countryside, Chartwell was the beloved private home of Sir Winston Churchill from 1924 until his death in 1965. Virtually everything has been kept as it was when he lived here, with his pictures, books, photos, and maps. There's even a half-smoked cigar that the World War II prime minister never finished. Churchill was an amateur artist, and his paintings show a softer side of the stiff-upper-lipped statesman; outdoor art trails show his work displayed at the points where he likely sat to paint them. Admission to the house is by timed ticket available only the day of your visit. To get here from Hever, head north on the B2027 and follow signs. ■**TIP**➔ **Be sure to explore the rose gardens and take a walk in the surrounding countryside.** ✉ *Mapleton Rd., Westerham* ☎ *01732/868381* ⊕ *www.nationaltrust.org.uk/chartwell* ▣ *£19; garden and studio only £11; parking £4* ⊙ *House closed Nov.–Feb.*

★ Hever Castle

CASTLE/PALACE | It's hard to imagine a more romantic castle than this: nestled within rolling hills, all turrets and battlements, the whole encircled by a water lily–bound moat filled with fabulous beasts (enormous Japanese koi carp). Here, at her childhood home, Anne Boleyn, second wife of Henry VIII and mother of Elizabeth I, was courted by Henry. He loved her dearly for a time, but had her beheaded in 1536 after she failed to give birth to a son. He then gifted Boleyn's home to his fourth wife, Anne of Cleves.

Famous though it was, the castle fell into disrepair in the 19th century. When American millionaire William Waldorf Astor acquired it in 1903, he needed additional space to house his staff. His novel solution was to build a replica Tudor village,

using only methods, materials, and even tools appropriate to the era. The result is more or less completely indistinguishable from the genuine Tudor parts.

Astor also created the stunning gardens, which today include an excellent yew maze, ponds, playgrounds, tea shops, gift shops, plant shops—you get the picture. There's a notable collection of Tudor portraits, and, in summer, activities are nonstop here, with jousting, falconry exhibitions, and country fairs, making this one of southern England's most rewarding castles to visit. In one of the Victorian wings, B&B rooms go for upwards of £145 per night for a basic room; there's also a four-bedroom holiday cottage available for £3,250 a week. ⊠ Off B2026, Hever ☎ 01732/865224 ⊕ www.hevercastle.co.uk ☙ £18/80; grounds only £15.55 ⊗ Closed Jan.–mid-Feb. and Mon. and Tues. in late Nov.–late Dec.

Penshurst Place

HOUSE | At the center of the adorable hamlet of Penshurst stands this fine medieval manor house, hidden behind tall trees and walls. Although it has a 14th-century hall, Penshurst is mainly Elizabethan and has been the family home of the Sidneys since 1552. The most famous Sidney is the Elizabethan poet Sir Philip, author of Arcadia. The **Baron's Hall,** topped with a chestnut roof, is the oldest and one of the grandest halls to survive from the early Middle Ages. Family portraits, furniture, tapestries, and armor help tell the story of the house, which was first inhabited in 1341 by Sir John de Pulteney, the very wealthy four-time London mayor. On the grounds are a toy museum, a gift shop, and the enchanting 11-acre walled Italian Garden, which displays tulips and daffodils in spring and roses in summer. Take time to study the village's late-15th-century half-timber structures adorned with soaring brick chimneys. To get here from Hever, take the B2027 east then follow signs to Penshurst. ⊠ Rogues

Hill, Penshurst ☎ 01892/870307 ⊕ www.penshurstplace.com ☙ £12.50; grounds only £10.50 ⊗ Closed Nov.–mid-Feb. and weekdays mid-Feb.–Mar.

🍴 Restaurants

The Spotted Dog

$ | BRITISH | One mile south of Penshurt, this historic pub first opened its doors in 1520 and in many ways hardly appears to have changed today. Its big inglenook fireplace and heavy beams give it character, the views from the hilltop are lovely, and the good food (a mixture of traditional pub grub and slightly more sophisticated fare) make it a pleasure to relax inside. **Known for:** mixture of casual and formal dining; atmospheric old pub; lovely beer garden in summer. ⑤ Average main: £13 ⊠ 6 Saint's Hill, Penshurst ☎ 01892/870253 ⊕ www.spotteddogpub.com.

Tonbridge

9 miles east of Hever.

This Kentish market town is a great base for exploring two magnificent Tudor properties. The first is Knole, perhaps the quintessential Tudor mansion, as famous for its literary connections and impressive collection of furniture and tapestries as it is for its elegant 15th- and 16th-century architecture. The second is Ightham Mote, a captivating, unreal-looking place that's almost unique among medieval manor houses in that it still has a moat (although that has nothing to do with the name).

GETTING HERE AND AROUND

Southeastern trains leave several times an hour from London Charing Cross to Tonbridge (40 minutes). Driving, via the A2/M25/A21, takes a little longer (one to 1½ hours). If driving from Hever, head east on the B2027 to reach Tonbridge. The town is five miles north of Tunbridge Wells; drive on the A26 or take one of the regular trains (10 minutes) or buses (25 minutes).

◉ Sights

All Saints Church

RELIGIOUS SITE | Situated two miles east of Tonbridge in the little village of Tudeley, this modest 13th-century church holds one of the glories of 20th-century church art. The building is awash with the luminous yellows and blues of 12 windows by Marc Chagall (1887–1985), commissioned as a tribute by the family of a young girl who drowned in a sailing accident in 1963. To get here, take the A26 from Tonbridge, then continue a mile or so east along B2017. ⊠ *Off B2017, Tudeley* ☎ *01892/833241* ⊕ *www.tudeley. org/allsaintstudeley.htm* ▨ *Free; £3 donation requested.*

★ Ightham Mote

HOUSE | This wonderful, higgledy-piggledy, timber-framed medieval manor house looks like something out of a fairy tale. Even its name is a bit of an enigma—"Ightham" is pronounced "Item" (we can't quite figure that out either) and "Mote" doesn't refer to the kind of moat you get in a castle, but an old English word for meeting place. Perhaps it's also fitting, then, that finding the place takes careful navigation down tiny, winding country lanes, and then even to reach the front door you must first cross a narrow stone bridge over the moat (yes, it has one of those, too). But it's all worth the effort to see a fanciful vision right out of the Middle Ages.

Built nearly 700 years ago, Ightham's magical exterior has hardly changed since the 14th century, but within you'll find that it encompasses styles of several periods, from Tudor to Victorian. The Great Hall, the Tudor chapel, and the drawing room are all highlights of the main property. Nearby is the smaller but equally pretty Laundry Hall, home to a second-hand bookshop and exhibition, as well as shaded woodland walks (awash with bluebells in spring), a pretty pond, and a natural play area for little ones.

Ightham Mote is six miles north of Tonbridge on the A227. ⊠ *Mote Rd., off A227, Sevenoaks* ☎ *01732/810378* ⊕ *www. nationaltrust.org.uk/ightham-mote* ▨ *£15.50 Mar.–Oct.; £5.40 Nov.–Feb.* ☉ *House closed Nov., Jan., and Feb.*

★ Knole

HOUSE | The pleasant but workaday town of Sevenoaks, seven miles northwest of Tonbridge, lies in London's commuter belt, a world away from the baronial air of its premier attraction: Knole, the grand, beloved estate of the Sackville family since the 16th century.

Begun in the 1400s and enlarged in 1603 by Thomas Sackville, Knole's sprawling complex of courtyards and outbuildings resembles a small town. In fact, with more that 300 rooms, 51 chimneys (count them!), and a total footprint covering five acres—the equivalent to almost four football fields—it's England's largest house. Factor in the supremely stroll-worthy (and free-roaming deer-filled) 1,000-acre park surrounding the property, and you'll need at least an afternoon to explore Knole thoroughly.

The house is noted for its wonderful tapestries, embroidered furnishings, and an extraordinary set of 17th-century silver furniture. Most of the salons are in the pre-baroque model, rather dark and armorial. The magnificently florid staircase was a novelty in its Elizabethan heyday. Vita Sackville-West grew up here and used it as the setting for her novel *The Edwardians,* a witty account of life among the gilded set.

Also on the property is the Conservation Studio, which showcases the work that the National Trust does at Knole and other local properties (you can also see the conservators in action), as well as the beautiful private garden, though this is only open on rare occasions.

In contrast to the property itself, the entrance is surprisingly low-key; look for the signposted track opposite St.

Nicholas Church. ⊠ *Knole La., off A225, Sevenoaks* ☎ *01732/462100* ⊕ *www. nationaltrust.org.uk/knole* ⬛ *£15.50; gatehouse tower £5; parking £5* ⊗ *House closed Nov.–early Mar.*

🍴 Restaurants

The Greyhound

$ | BRITISH | This cozy country pub, situated in the village of Charcott six miles west of Tonbridge, serves superior pub grub using fresh, local ingredients. The owners rear their own livestock, so you can be certain the lamb, beef, and pork on the menu is farm fresh. **Known for:** beautifully cooked Sunday roasts; wide choice of real ales; meat-heavy menu. ⑤ *Average main: £13* ⊠ *Off Camp Hill, Tonbridge* ☎ *01892/870275* ⊕ *www. thegreyhoundcharcott.co.uk* ⊗ *Closed Mon.*

Rochester

20 miles northeast of Tonbridge.

Positioned near the confluence of the Thames and the River Medway, this posh town has a history of Roman, Saxon, and Norman occupation, all of which have left architectural remains, including the vast castle at the town center. Novelist Charles Dickens called Rochester home for more than a decade, until his death in 1870, and would sometimes walk here all the way from London.

South of Rochester, in the corridor between Canterbury and Tunbridge Wells, lies a number of interesting historic sights, including Leeds Castle and Sissinghurst Castle Gardens.

GETTING HERE AND AROUND

From London, Rochester is a 45-minute drive via the M2/A2. Regular Southeastern trains from several London stations—including St. Pancras, Victoria, and Charing Cross—take a similar amount of time. To reach Rochester from Tonbridge, take

the A26 and A228 northeast. The journey takes about 45 minutes. Southeastern trains run regular services from Tonbridge to Strood (one hour), which is a 15-minute walk from Rochester town center.

ESSENTIALS

VISITOR INFORMATION Medway Visitor Information Centre. ⊠ *95 High St., The Precinct* ☎ *01634/338141* ⊕ *www.visit-medway.org.*

👁 Sights

Historic Dockyard

MARINA | FAMILY | The buildings and 47 retired ships at the 80-acre dockyard across the River Medway from Rochester constitute the country's most complete Georgian-to-early-Victorian dockyard. Fans of maritime history could easily spend a day at the exhibits and structures. The dockyard's origins go back to the time of Henry VIII; some 400 ships were built here over the centuries. Highlights include Maritime Treasures, a museum of naval artifacts including some fascinating 18th-century scale models; the Victorian Ropery, where costumed guides take you on a tour of an old rope factory, including its impressive quarter-mile-long "rope walk," where ropes are still made using old methods; and the Courtyard, part of the old Smithery (blacksmith), where special events are sometimes held, including pirate-themed fun days for kids in summer. There's also a guided tour of the submarine HMS *Ocelot*, the last warship to be built for the Royal Navy at Chatham. ■**TIP→ Book online in advance for good discounts on admission.** ⊠ *Main Gate Rd., Chatham* ☎ *01634/823800* ⊕ *thedockyard.co.uk* ⬛ *£22* ⊗ *Closed late Nov.–mid-Feb.*

★ Leeds Castle

CASTLE/PALACE | Every inch the grand medieval castle, Leeds is more like a storybook illustration of what an English castle should look like, from the fortress-like exterior to the breathtaking rooms within. Ramparts and battlements? Check. Moat? Check. Ancient stone walkways on which you just know a knight in shining armor might pass by at any second? Pretty much.

Leeds—not to be confused with the city in the north of England; the name comes from its mention as "Esledes" (meaning "hill" or "slope") in the Domesday Book of 1086—has all this and more. One of England's finest castles, it commands two small islands on a peaceful lake. Dating to the 9th century and rebuilt by the Normans in 1119, the castle became a favorite home of many medieval English queens. Henry VIII liked it so much he had it converted from a fortress into a grand palace.

The interior doesn't match the glories of the much-photographed exterior, although there are fine paintings and furniture, including many pieces from the 20th-century refurbishment by the castle's last private owner, Lady Baillie. The outside attractions are more impressive and include a surprisingly tricky maze (made from 2,400 yew trees), which leads to an atmospheric rock-carved grotto, as well as two adventure playgrounds, an aviary of native and exotic birds, and woodland gardens. There are also several dining options, including the informal but excellent Castle View Restaurant (try the haddock-and-chips).

Leeds Castle is 12 miles southeast of Rochester, off the M20 highway. ■ TIP→ **All tickets are valid for a year, in case you don't manage to see everything in one day.** ⊠ *Off A20, Maidstone* ☎ *01622/765400* ⊕ *www.leeds-castle. com* 🎫 *£27.*

Rochester Castle

CASTLE/PALACE | The impressive ruins of Rochester Castle comprise a superb example of Norman military architecture. The keep, built in the 1100s using the old Roman city wall as a foundation, is the tallest in England. In 1215, during King John's struggle against the barons who wanted him to sign the Magna Carta,

Rochester was subject to one of the most brutal seiges in English history. Thanks to the diarist Samuel Pepys (1633–1703) it's known that the ruins of Rochester Castle were already a popular tourist attraction in the 17th century. Today the structure has been shored up but left without floors, so that from the bottom you can see to the open roof and study the complex structure. At the shop you can pick up well-researched guides to the building. ⊠ *Castle Hill* ☎ *0370/333–1181* ⊕ *www. english-heritage.org.uk/rochester* 🎫 *£7.*

Rochester Cathedral

RELIGIOUS SITE | Augustine of Canterbury ordained the first English bishop in a small cathedral that stood on this site in the year 604. The current cathedral, England's second oldest, is a jumble of architectural styles. Much of the original Norman building from 1077 remains, including the striking west front, the highly carved portal, and the tympanum above the doorway. Some medieval art survives, including a 13th-century Wheel of Fortune on the choir walls; it's a reminder of how difficult medieval life was. Informative, full-length guided tours take place daily at 11:30 am (£4 per person), with 20-minute "spotlight" tours daily at 10:30 am and 1:15 pm (free). Check the website for special evening viewings (a small charge applies) and various events, including music and supper. ⊠ *Boley Hill* ☎ *01634/843366* ⊕ *www.rochestercathedral.org* 🎫 *Free (donations welcome).*

★ Sissinghurst Castle Garden

GARDEN | One of the most famous gardens in the world, unpretentiously beautiful and quintessentially English, Sissinghurst rests deep in the Kentish countryside. The gardens, with their many different themed "rooms," were laid out in the 1930s around the remains of part of a moated Tudor castle by writer Vita Sackville-West (one of the Sackvilles of Knole, her childhood home) and her husband, diplomat Harold Nicolson. The relationship was clearly loving but also complicated, as both had a string of extramarital same-sex affairs; Vita, famously, had a decade-long romance with Virginia Woolf.

Climb the tower for a wonderful overview of the gardens—as well as a peek inside Vita's study en route—then descend to see them up close. There's the stunning White Garden, filled with snow-color flowers and silver-gray foliage; the herb and cottage gardens, which showcase Sackville-West's encyclopedic knowledge of plants; and the Delos Garden, which brings a slice of the Mediterranean to the heart of Kent (as well as finally realizing a dream of Vita and Harold's following their visit to Greece in 1935). As well as the gardens, there are woodland and lake walks all around, making it easy to spend a half day or more here.

If you love it all so much you want to stay, you can—the National Trust rents the Priest's House on the property for a minimum stay of three nights; prices start at around £700 and rise to upwards of £1,600 in midsummer. See the National Trust website for details (but be warned, you'll need to book well ahead).

Sissinghurst Castle Garden is 22 miles south of Rochester on the A229, and 16 miles east of Tunbridge Wells on the A262. ⊠ *Off A262, Cranbrook* ☎ *01580/710700* ⊕ *www.nationaltrust.org.uk/sissinghurst-castle* ⊠ *£14.50; parking £4* ⊙ *Closed weekdays Nov.–mid-Mar.*

🍴 Restaurants

Don Vincenzo

$ | ITALIAN | This lively Italian trattoria in the center of Rochester specializes in delicious pizza and pasta, the best of which is the simple Napoletana, which is topped with mozarella, anchovies, capers, and tomato sauce. If that's just not enough to satisfy your appetite, try a hearty calzone stuffed with two types of Italian cheeses, spicy salami, and tomatoes. **Known for:** delicious pizza and pasta; filling calzones; cheap eats. ⑤ *Average main: £11* ⊠ *108*

High St. ☎ *01634/408373* ⊕ *www.donvincenzo.co.uk.*

🛏 Hotels

The Dog and Bear

$ | B&B/INN | This cozy, quaint country pub with guest rooms is located a few miles east of Leeds Castle, in the small village of Lenham. **Pros:** traditional village pub; convenient for Leeds Castle; family rooms available. **Cons:** basic amenities; rooms near bar can be noisy; food a mixed bag. ⑤ *Rooms from: £110* ⊠ *The Square, Lenham, Maidstone* ☎ *01622/858219* ⊕ *www.dogandbearlenham.co.uk* ⇨ *24 rooms* ❚⊙❚ *Free breakfast.*

★ Sissinghurst Castle Farmhouse

$$ | B&B/INN | This lovely, larger-than-you-expect farmhouse on the grounds of Sissinghurst Castle was originally built in 1885 and lovingly restored by the National Trust in 2009. **Pros:** beautiful location on the grounds of a historic home; delicious breakfast; barbecues on the lawn in summer. **Cons:** patchy TV signal in the rooms; need a car to get here; no restaurant for dinner. ⑤ *Rooms from: £160* ⊠ *Off A262, Sissinghurst* ☎ *01580/720992* ⊕ *www.sissinghurstcastlefarmhouse.com* ⇨ *9 rooms* ❚⊙❚ *Free breakfast.*

Rye

39 miles south of Rochester.

With cobbled streets and ancient timbered dwellings, Rye is an artist's dream. It was an important port town until the harbor silted up and the waters retreated more than 150 years ago; now the nearest harbor is two miles away. Virtually every building in the little town center is intriguingly historic. Rye is known for its many antiques stores and also for its sheer pleasantness. This place can be easily walked without a map, but if you need some direction, Campion Frames (71 The Mint) sells a fact-packed walking tour map for £2.

GETTING HERE AND AROUND

If you're driving to Rye from London, take the A2, followed by M2, M20, and A2070/A259. Trains from London's St. Pancras leave once an hour and take just over one hour, including a change in Ashford. Driving from Rochester is the same route as from London (though starting with the M2), while getting to Rye from Rochester by train means going via London.

 Sights

★ Bodiam Castle

CASTLE/PALACE | FAMILY | Immortalized in paintings, photographs, and films, Bodiam Castle (pronounced *Boe*-dee-um) rises out of the distance like a piece of medieval legend. From the outside it's one of Britain's most impressive castles, with turrets, battlements, a glassy moat (one of the very few still in use), and two-foot-thick walls. However, once you cross the drawbridge to the interior there's little to see but ruins, albeit on an impressive scale. Built in 1385 to withstand a threatened French invasion, it was partly demolished during the English Civil War of 1642–46 and has been uninhabited ever since. Still, you can climb the intact towers to take in sweeping countryside views, and kids love running around the keep. The castle, 12 miles northwest of Rye, schedules organized activities for kids during school holidays. ■**TIP**➜ **For a unique way to approach Bodiam Castle, take a 45-minute river cruise through the pretty Sussex countryside. Boats leave from the riverbank in Newenden; find more information and sailing times at www.bodiamboatingstation.co.uk.** ⊠ *Off Main Rd., Bodiam* ☎ *01580/830196* ⊕ *www.nationaltrust. org.uk/bodiamcastle* ☑ *£11.40.*

Chapel Down Winery

WINERY/DISTILLERY | After decades—centuries, even—as the butt of jokes, the English wine industry is at last being taken more seriously; in recent years, English wines have even been winning some prestigious international awards. Drop in at Chapel Down Winery, one of Britain's leading wine producers, to decide for yourself. You can visit the wine shop and explore the herb gardens for free, or pay for a (nearly) two-hour-long guided tour of the rest of the grounds—advanced booking is advisable in summer. The winery is eight miles north of Rye. ⊠ *Off B2082, Tenterden* ☎ *01580/766111* ⊕ *www. chapeldown.com* ☑ *Tours £20* ⊗ *No guided tours Dec.–mid-Feb.*

Church of St. Mary

RELIGIOUS SITE | At the top of the hill at the center of Rye, this classic English village church is more than 900 years old and encompasses a number of architectural styles. The turret clock dates to 1561 and still keeps excellent time. Its huge pendulum swings inside the church nave. ■**TIP**➜ **Climb the tower for amazing views of the surrounding area.** ⊠ *Church Sq.* ☎ *01797/222318* ⊕ *www.ryeparish-church.org.uk* ☑ *Free.*

Great Dixter House and Gardens

GARDEN | Combining a large timber-frame hall with a cottage garden on a grand scale, this place will get your green thumbs twitching. The house dates to 1464 (you can tour a few rooms) and was restored in 1910 by architect Edwin Lutyens, who also designed the garden. From these beginnings, the horticulturist and writer Christopher Lloyd (1921–2006), whose home this was, developed a series of creative, colorful "garden rooms" and a dazzling herbaceous Long Border. The house is nine miles northwest of Rye. ⊠ *Off A28, Northiam* ☎ *01797/252878* ⊕ *www.greatdixter. co.uk* ☑ *£13; gardens only £11* ⊗ *Closed Mon. and Nov.–Mar.*

Lamb House

HOUSE | Something about Lamb House, an early-18th-century dwelling, attracts writers. The novelist Henry James lived here from 1898 to 1916, while E. F. Benson, one-time mayor of Rye and author of the witty *Lucia* novels (written in the 1920s and 1930s), was a later resident. The ground-floor rooms contain some of James's furniture and personal belongings. ✉ *West St.* ☎ *01797/222909* ⊕ *www.nationaltrust.org.uk/lamb-house* ✉ *£7.90* ⏱ *Closed Nov.–Feb. and Wed. and Thurs. in Mar.–Oct.*

Mermaid Street
NEIGHBORHOOD | One of the town's original cobbled streets, and perhaps its most quintessential view, heads steeply from the top of the hill to the former harbor. Its name supposedly came from the night a drunken sailor swore he heard a mermaid call him down to the sea (back when Rye was still a seaside town). The houses here date from between the medieval and Georgian periods; a much-photographed pair have the delightfully fanciful names "The House with Two Front Doors" and "The House Opposite." △ **Be careful on your feet—the cobbles are very uneven.** ✉ *Rye.*

★ Winchelsea
TOWN | This small town, a few miles south of Rye, perches prettily atop its own small hill amid rolling farmland, and has a number of interesting attractions. There's the splendid (though damaged) church at its heart, built in the 14th century with stone from Normandy. The stained-glass windows are particularly captivating, with renowned Scottish artist Douglas Strachan (1875-1950) creating an almost three-dimensional effect with his bold illustrations.

Outside the church lies a grave with one of most quoted epitaphs in the English language. When English-Irish comedian Spike Milligan (of *The Goon Show* fame) was buried here in 2002, he requested to have the words "I told you I was ill" added to his gravestone. The diocese refused, but agreed to a compromise in which it was written in Irish instead. Take a walk around the graveyard and see if you can spot the headstone with the words: "Dúirt mé leat go raibh mé breoite".

Under the town's narrow streets are at least 56 medieval cellars, with some accessible by an interesting—if rather long—guided tour (£5) on various dates from April to October. A short walk from the town center is Winchelsea Beach, a pretty stretch of shingle coastline. ✉ *Winchelsea* ⊕ *www.winchelsea.com.*

Ypres Tower
BUILDING | Down the hill past Church Square, Ypres Tower (pronounced "Wipers" by locals) was originally built as part of the town's fortifications (now all but disappeared) in 1249; it later served as a prison. A row of defensive cannons is fixed to the rampart overlooking the (disappointingly industrial) edge of Rye and several miles of flatland beyond. When they were installed, however, the canons pointed directly out to sea. Inside the tower is the Rye Castle Museum, which has displays on the city's history, from medieval floor tiles to 15th-century suits of armor, as well an interesting exhibition on 1830s life as a female prisoner in the "women's tower."

A second (free to enter) outpost of the RCM on nearby East Street has even more exhibits, including examples of Rye pottery for which the town was famous and a fire engine that was built in 1745 and served the town for 120 years. ✉ *Gungarden* ☎ *01797/226728* ⊕ *www. ryemuseum.co.uk* ✉ *£4.*

🍴 Restaurants

★ Hayden's Coffee Shop
$ | BRITISH | This incredibly popular High Street café serves high quality and great value meals and snacks from mid-morning to late afternoon every day of the week. Come early for an excellent Full English breakfast or opt for a light lunch like homemade soup or Welsh rarebit (a fondue-like dish where a sauce of melted cheddar, ale, and mustard is poured over slices of toasted bread). **Known for:** lovely views of salt flats out the back; tasty

cream teas; long lines during weekend lunch. **$** *Average main: 9* ⌂ *108 High St.* ☎ *01797/224501* ⊕ *www.haydensinrye. co.uk/dining/* ⊙ *No dinner.*

★ Knoops Chocolate Bar

$ | **SOUTH AMERICAN** | Despite the fact it has no hot meals, no waiters, and no tables, Knoops has been one of Rye's most consistently popular "restaurants" for years. Step inside and it's easy to see why: this unassuming little shop serves perhaps the best hot chocolate in England. **Known for:** local Rye phenomenon; choosing your chocolate by cocoa percentage; tasty milkshakes and mochas. **$** *Average main: £4* ⌂ *East Cliff* ☎ *01797/225838* ⊕ *www. knoops.co.uk* ⊙ *No dinner.*

Simply Italian

$ | **ITALIAN** | In a quiet, edge-of-the-center location, this popular Italian eatery packs in the crowds on weekend nights with its inexpensive but classic pasta and pizza dishes. Try the rigatoni con salsiccia (with spicy sausage in a tomato and garlic sauce) or chicken breast topped with mozzarella and parma ham cooked in a tomato cream sauce. **Known for:** excellent pizza and pasta; cozy interiors; relaxed atmosphere. **$** *Average main: £9* ⌂ *12 Strand* ☎ *01797/226024* ⊕ *www.simply-italian.co.uk.*

★ Webbes at the Fish Café

$$ | **SEAFOOD** | One of Rye's most popular restaurants, where most of the seafood is freshly caught nearby, occupies a brick building that dates to 1907, but the interior has been redone in a sleek, modern style.

Sample the salt and Sichuan pepper squid with soy and sherry dressing or the pan-fried Rye Bay scallops with pancetta and chive vermouth sauce. **Known for:** top-quality and locally caught seafood; fast and friendly service; dinner reservations recommended. ⑤ *Average main: £17* ✉ *17 Tower St.* ☎ *01797/222210* ⊕ *www. webbesrestaurants.co.uk.*

Whitehouse

$ | **CAFÉ** | **FAMILY** | This chic, contemporary café serves delectable baked goods, all-day breakfasts, and tapas-style light bites. Come for the Turkish eggs, poached with yogurt and dill, or, if you're in the mood for something heartier, try the coconut red lentil dal with chili salsa. **Known for:** perfectly brewed coffee; healthful light bites; delicious cakes. ⑤ *Average main: £9* ✉ *24 High St.* ☎ *01797/224748* ⊕ *www.whitehouserye. co.uk* ⊗ *No dinner.*

Hotels

Jeake's House

$$ | **B&B/INN** | Antiques fill the cozy bedrooms of this rambling 1689 house, where the snug, painted-and-paneled parlor has a wood-burning stove for cold days. **Pros:** pleasant atmosphere; delicious breakfasts; lovely rooftop views from top-floor rooms. **Cons:** Mermaid Street is steep and cobbled; cheapest room has bathroom across the hall; some bedrooms are small. ⑤ *Rooms from: £125* ✉ *Mermaid St.* ☎ *01797/222828* ⊕ *www.jeakeshouse.com* ⊷ *11 rooms* ℗ *Free breakfast.*

★ The Mermaid Inn

$$ | **HOTEL** | Steeped in a history of smuggling—look for Rudyard Kipling's atmospheric poem *A Smuggler's Song* on the wall outside—the 600-year-old Mermaid is Rye's most historic inn; its sloping floors, oak beams, low ceilings, and huge open hearth look like a film set, but it's all totally authentic. **Pros:** dripping in atmosphere; good restaurant; one of England's oldest

inns. **Cons:** price is high for what's on offer; small bedrooms; allegedly haunted. ⑤ *Rooms from: £160* ✉ *Mermaid St.* ☎ *01797/223065* ⊕ *www.mermaidinn. com* ⊷ *31 rooms* ℗ *Free breakfast.*

★ Rye Windmill

$ | **HOTEL** | One of the Southeast's most unique B&Bs, this 450-year-old white-washed windmill overlooking the River Tillingham is home to 10 lovely bedrooms with large en suite bathrooms, including walk-in showers. **Pros:** unique and luxurious Windmill Suite; central location but feels rural; welcoming hosts. **Cons:** tap water not drinkable (refillable bottled water provided); no restaurant; two-night minimum in summer. ⑤ *Rooms from: £95* ✉ *Ferry Rd., Off B2089* ☎ *01797/224027* ⊕ *www.ryewindmill. co.uk* ⊷ *10 rooms* ℗ *Free breakfast.*

Nightlife

Globe Inn Marsh Rye

BARS/PUBS | On the outskirts of the city, this pretty clapboard gastro-pub has an intriguing setup: instead of a bar, the drinks are piled up on a table in the middle of the room and served from there. Along with a good selection of local ales and craft beers, there's also a choice of ciders straight from the barrel and an extensive menu of artisanal gins. The food—from stacked burgers to bonfire pizzas—is great, too. There's live music every Thursday evening starting at 7:30 pm. ✉ *10 Military Rd.* ☎ *01797/225220* ⊕ *www.ramblinns.com/the-globe-inn-rye.*

★ Rye Waterworks

BARS/PUBS | This cozy little micropub, set within a 17th-century pump house, offers eight (mostly local) beers on tap. The bar staff is friendly and chatty, and there's a real communal vibe to the place, with most drinkers sharing tables. If you get peckish, there's are tasty pub snacks available; try the pork pie with mustard and chutney. ■**TIP**➜ **If you like the pub furnishings, you can pick some up for yourself**

at the Waterworks Curios antiques shop next door. ⊠ *Tower St.* ☎ *01797/224110* ⊕ *www.ryewaterworks.co.uk.*

🛍 Shopping

Rye has great antiques shops, perfect for an afternoon of rummaging, with the biggest cluster at the foot of the hill near the tourist information center.

Britcher & Rivers

FOOD/CANDY | This traditional sweet shop is like something out of a bygone age. Choose from row upon row of tall jars packed with every imaginable type of candy, measured out into little paper bags. ⊠ *109 High St.* ☎ *01797/227152.*

★ Clive Sawyer Gallery (*Just Ten Gallery / Just One Gallery*)

ART GALLERIES | This little gallery shop showcases the eye-catching fine art photography of Clive Sawyer. The larger framed images are printed using the ChromaLuxe process, making them richly colorful and vibrant. ⊠ *103A High St.* ☎ *07738/715354* ⊕ *www.just-one.gallery.*

Glass Etc

CERAMICS/GLASSWARE | A glorious collection of quality antique glass can be found in this colorful, friendly shop near the train station. ⊠ *18–20 Rope Walk* ☎ *01797/226600* ⊕ *www.decanterman.com.*

Hastings

13 miles southwest of Rye.

In the 19th century, Hastings became one of England's most popular spa resorts. Tall Victorian row houses painted in lemony hues still cover the cliffs around the deep blue sea, and the views from the hilltops are extraordinary. The pretty Old Town, on the east side of the city, offers a glimpse into the city's 16th-century past. Hastings has been through difficult times in recent decades, and the town developed a reputation as a rough place. It's currently trying hard to reinvent itself—a clutch of trendy new boutique bed-and-breakfasts have opened, as well as an important new art gallery—but the town center can still be quite rowdy after dark. Expect a handsome but tattered town, with a mix of traditional English seaside amusements: miniature golf, shops selling junk, fish-and-chips stands, and a rocky beach that stretches for miles.

Of course, Hastings is also known for the famous battle that took place on October 14, 1066, when William of Normandy and his troops trounced King Harold's Anglo-Saxon army (although the battle itself actually took place six miles northwest of Hastings). Today, you can visit the battlefield and the abbey built in its honor, as well as the sweet little town around it (called, fittingly, Battle).

GETTING HERE AND AROUND

If you're driving to Hastings from London, take the A21. Trains travel to Hastings three or four times an hour from London's Victoria and St. Pancras stations. The journey takes between 1½ and two hours; some trains involve a change in Brighton or Ashford. The main station is within easy walking distance of most sights, though a second station—the more grandly titled St Leonards Warrior Square—may be more convenient if you're staying farther west. National Express buses travel from London Victoria Coach Station to Hastings once or twice a day in around 2½ hours.

From Rye, there are direct trains every hour to Hastings (20 minutes). It's a 30-minute drive along the A259.

ESSENTIALS

VISITOR INFORMATION Hastings Tourist Information Centre. ⊠ *Muriel Matters House, 2 Breeds Pl.* ☎ *01424/451111* ⊕ *www.visit1066country.com.*

Sussex Beach Huts

Rows of tiny, cheerfully painted, one-room wooden beach huts brighten the shoreline throughout Sussex (look for them in Hastings and Brighton) and elsewhere. The huts originated in the Victorian wheeled bathing machines that were rolled into the water so that women could swim modestly behind them. Eventually the wheels came off, and they and similar structures became favored for storage and as a windbreak. Most huts lack electricity or plumbing but are beloved for their sheer adorableness. Some are rented; others are owned, and prices can be surprisingly steep. In 2017, a beach hut in Dorset sold for £275,000, which is more than £40,000 above the average price of a house in Britain.

Sights

★ Battle Abbey

ARCHAEOLOGICAL SITE | Situated six miles northwest of Hastings, this great Benedictine abbey was erected by William the Conqueror on the site of the Battle of Hastings—one of the most decisive turning points in English history and the last time the country was successfully invaded. All of this meant little to Henry VIII, of course, who didn't spare the building from his violent dissolution of the monasteries. Today the abbey is just a ruin, but a very pretty one.

Start at the visitor center to get the full story through a series of films and interactive exhibits before taking a walk around the abbey site, including up to the first floor. A memorial stone marks the high altar, which in turn was supposedly laid on the spot where Harold II, the last Saxon king, was killed.

You can also follow a trail around the 1066 battlefield, lined with a series of intricately carved wooden sculptures of Norman and Saxon soldiers, or climb the gatehouse for an exhibiton on the site's post-invasion history as well as spectacular rooftop views of the town. For a potted history of Battle, head to nearby St. Mary's Church, where the three-meter-long Battle Tapestry artfully illustrates how the town developed around the abbey. ✉ High St., Battle ☎ 01424/775705 ⊕ www.english-heritage.org.uk/battle-abbey ☞ £12.30; parking £4 ⊙ Closed weekdays early Nov.–mid-Feb. and Mon. and Tues. mid-Feb.–Apr.

Hastings Castle

CASTLE/PALACE | **FAMILY** | Take a thrilling ride up the West Hill Cliff Railway from George Street precinct to the atmospheric ruins of the thousand-year-old fortress now known as Hastings Castle. It was built by William the Conqueror in 1066, before he had even won the Battle of Hastings and conquered England—that's confidence for you. Today all that remains of the country's first Norman castle are mere fragments of the fortifications, some ancient walls, and a number of gloomy dungeons. Nevertheless, you get an excellent view of the chalky cliffs, the rocky coast, and the town below. You can buy a joint ticket that covers admission to Smuggler's Adventure and the nearby Blue Reef aquarium for £19; you then have seven days to see the other attractions. ✉ West Hill, Off Castle Hill Rd. ☎ 01424/422964 ☞ £5.25 ⊙ Closed Nov.–Mar.

Hastings Contemporary

MUSEUM | A symbol of Hastings's slow but growing regeneration after decades of neglect, this spruced-up exhibition space in the Old Town has become one of the most talked-about contemporary art galleries outside London. Formerly known as the Jerwood Gallery, Hastings Contemporary's collection includes works by Walter Sickert, Stephen Lowry, and Augustus John, while temporary exhibitions change every couple of months. The glazed-tile building on the seafront was designed to reflect the row of distinctive old, blackened fishing sheds it sits alongside. ⊠ *Rock-a-Nore Rd.* ☎ *01424/728377* ⊕ *www.hastings-contemporary.org* ⊠ *£9* ⊗ *Closed Mon. except bank holidays.*

★ Herstmonceux Castle

CASTLE/PALACE | FAMILY | With a banner waving from one tower and a glassy moat crossed by what was once a drawbridge, this fairy-tale castle has everything except knights in shining armor. Situated 13 miles northwest of Hastings, the redbrick structure was originally built by Sir Roger Fiennes (ancestor of actor Ralph Fiennes) in 1444, although it was altered in the Elizabethan age and again early in the 20th century after it had largely fallen to ruin. Canadian Queen's University owns the castle, so only part of it is open for guided tours, usually once or twice a day except on Saturday; call in advance to schedule a tour in high season.

Highlights include the magnificent ballroom, a medieval room, and the stunning Elizabethan-era staircase. Explore the formal walled garden, lily-covered lakes, and miles of woodland—the perfect place for a picnic on a sunny afternoon. There's also a hands-on science center for kids.

When school isn't in session, the castle rents out its small, plain guest rooms from £40 per night. On the last weekend of August, the castle hosts a large **Medieval Festival,** complete with jousting, falconry shows, and around 100 craft stalls. ⊠ *Off Wartling Rd., Herstmonceux* ☎ *01323/833816* ⊕ *www.herstmonceux-castle.com* ⊠ *Castle, grounds, and science center £14.50; grounds only £7; castle tours £3* ⊗ *Closed Nov.–mid-Feb.*

Smuggler's Adventure

MUSEUM | FAMILY | The history of smuggling on the south coast is told through waxworks and other exhibits inside this labyrinth of caves underneath the West Hill, a 15-minute walk from Hastings Castle. You can buy a joint ticket with Hastings Castle and Blue Reef aquarium for £19. ⊠ *St. Clement Caves* ☎ *01424/422964* ⊕ *www.smugglersadventure.co.uk* ⊠ *£9* ⊗ *Closed mid-Nov.–mid-Feb.*

🍴 Restaurants

★ Blue Dolphin Fish Bar

$ | SEAFOOD | The crowds line up all day to make their way into this small fish-and-chip shop just off the seafront, down near the fish shacks. Although the decor is humble, reviewers consistently rank the battered fish and huge plates of double-cooked chips (chunky fries) as among the best in the country. **Known for:** popularity across Britain; beachside location; tasty traditional fish-and-chips. ⑤ *Average main: £7* ⊠ *61A High St.* ☎ *01424/547150.*

★ Sundial

$$$ | MODERN FRENCH | A 17th-century brick farmhouse with wood-beamed ceilings and lovely views of the South Downs is home to an excellent modern French restaurant. Situated near the castle in Herstmonceux, it features an imaginative three-course "Gourmet Menu" (£48 per person) that changes regularly but may include pan-fried wild turbot with truffle butter or beef fillet steak with a sauce of port and shallot. **Known for:** sophisticated Modern French cooking; lovely views; delicious pineapple tarte tatin dessert. ⑤ *Average main: £25* ⊠ *Gardner St., Herstmonceux* ☎ *01323/832217* ⊕ *www.sundialrestaurant.co.uk* ⊗ *Closed Mon. No dinner Sun.*

White's Seafood & Steak Bar

$$ | SEAFOOD | FAMILY | Great seafood in simple, unpretentious surroundings is the order of the day at this popular place in Hastings Old Town. Fresh-as-can-be seafood, huge platters of shellfish, creamy fish pies, and delicious plates of fish-and-chips are the epitome of unfussy local flavor. **Known for:** huge seafood platters; fresh catch of the day; hot-rock cooking at your table. $ Average main: £16 ✉ 44-45 George St. ☎ 01424/719846 ⊕ www.whitesbar.co.uk.

 ## Hotels

The Cloudesley

$ | B&B/INN | No TVs and a general Zen vibe at this boutique B&B in the quieter St. Leonard's district of Hastings make it a thoroughly relaxing place to stay. **Pros:** oasis of calm; great spa treatments; impeccable eco credentials. **Cons:** chill vibe won't be for everyone; two-night minimum at certain times; 20-minute walk into Hastings. $ Rooms from: £85 ✉ 7 Cloudesley Rd., St. Leonards-on-Sea ☎ 01424/722759 ⊕ www.thecloudesley. co.uk ⤸ 5 rooms ⊚ Free breakfast.

Hastings House

$$ | HOTEL | In Warrior Square at the edge of Hastings, this boutique guesthouse brings a funky, modern style to a grand Victorian building. **Pros:** spacious rooms; stylish and modern decor; near the sea. **Cons:** no restaurant; few services; area can be noisy at night. $ Rooms from: £125 ✉ 9 Warrior Sq., St. Leonards-on-Sea ☎ 01424/422709 ⊕ www.hastingshouse. co.uk ⤸ 9 rooms ⊚ Free breakfast.

★ Swan House

$ | B&B/INN | Originally a bakery, this extraordinary 15th-century building has been beautifully converted into an elegant and welcoming B&B, where the light and airy guest rooms are decorated in neutral modern tones and retain original features such as exposed wood beams. **Pros:** beautiful and historic building; welcoming

hosts; seriously delicious breakfasts. **Cons:** some bathrooms have shower only; two-night minimum on summer weekends; gets booked up. $ Rooms from: £120 ✉ 1 Hill St. ☎ 01424/430014 ⊕ www.swan-househastings.co.uk ⤸ 4 rooms ⊚ Free breakfast.

Zanzibar International Hotel

$$ | HOTEL | This spacious, light-filled hotel overlooking the sea has guest rooms designed as a playful yet restrained homage to exotic destinations. **Pros:** great facilities for a small hotel; lovely sea views; champagne is served with breakfast. **Cons:** a bit over-the-top for some tastes; pricey for Hastings; nonrefundable 50% deposit. $ Rooms from: £195 ✉ 9 Eversfield Pl., St. Leonards-on-Sea ☎ 01424/460109 ⊕ www.zanzibarhotel. co.uk ⤸ 8 rooms ⊚ Free breakfast.

Lewes

30 miles west of Hastings, 8 miles northeast of Brighton.

The town nearest to the celebrated Glyndebourne Opera House, Lewes is so rich in history that the Council for British Archaeology named it one of the 50 most important English towns. A walk is the best way to appreciate its steep streets and appealing jumble of building styles and materials—flint, stone, brick, tile—and the secret lanes (called "twittens") behind the castle, with their huge beeches. Here and there are smart antiques shops, good eateries, and secondhand-book dealers. Most of the buildings in the center date to the 18th and 19th centuries.

Something about this town has always attracted rebels. It was once the home of Thomas Paine (1737–1809), whose pamphlet *Common Sense* advocated that the American colonies break with Britain. It was also favored by Virginia Woolf and the Bloomsbury Group, early-20th-century countercultural artistic innovators.

Today Lewes's beauty and proximity to London mean that the counterculture crew can't really afford to live here anymore, but its rebel soul still peeks through, particularly on Guy Fawkes Night (November 5), the anniversary of Fawkes's foiled attempt to blow up the Houses of Parliament in 1605. Flaming tar barrels are rolled down High Street and into the River Ouse, while costumed processions fill the streets.

GETTING HERE AND AROUND

If you're driving to Lewes from London, take the M23 south. The journey takes around an hour and 45 minutes. Southern trains run direct to Lewes from Victoria Station about three times an hour (the journey takes an hour), but there's no good bus connection. To get to Lewes from Hastings, it's an hour drive west along the A259 and A27 or an hour by train (there are four Southern services an hour).

ESSENTIALS

VISITOR INFORMATION Lewes Information Centre. ⊠ *187 High St.* ☎ *01273/483448* ⊕ *www.visitlewes.co.uk.*

◉ Sights

Anne of Cleves House

HOUSE | FAMILY | This 16th-century structure, a fragile-looking, timber-frame building, holds a small collection of Sussex ironwork and other items of local interest, such as Sussex pottery. The house was part of Anne of Cleves's divorce settlement from Henry VIII, although she never lived in it. There are medieval dress-up clothes for kids. To get to the house, walk down steep, cobbled Keere Street, past lovely Grange Gardens, to Southover High Street. ⊠ *52 Southover High St.* ☎ *01273/474610* ⊕ *www.sussexpast.co.uk/anneofcleves* 🎟 *£6.50; combined ticket with Lewes Castle £13.40* ⊗ *Closed Nov.–mid-Feb.*

Beachy Head

NATURE SITE | Move over Dover: these are perhaps Britain's most spectacular white cliffs. Located 18 miles southeast of Lewes, off the A259 just before Eastbourne, this up-to-162-meter-high curtain of chalk has watched over the English Channel for nigh on 100 million years. Today, you can walk the windy path along the top of Beachy Head for lovely views of the cliffs, the sea, and the pretty red-and-white-striped lighthouse. For a longer clifftop walk, continue west along the Seven Sisters Cliffs; it's around 5½ miles (two hours) each way from the Beachy Head parking lot to the stony beach at Cuckmere Haven. ⊠ *Main Car Park, Beachy Head Rd.* ☎ *1323/410000* ⊕ *www.lewes-eastbourne.gov.uk.*

★ Charleston

HOUSE | Art and life mixed at Charleston, the farmhouse that Vanessa Bell—sister of Virginia Woolf—bought in 1916 and fancifully decorated, along with Duncan Grant (who lived here until 1978). The house, which is seven miles east of Lewes, soon became a refuge for the writers and artists of the Bloomsbury Group. On display are colorful ceramics and textiles of the Omega Workshop—in which Bell and Grant participated—and paintings by Picasso and Renoir, as well as by Bell and Grant themselves. Entry to the house is by guided tour; you can buy tickets when you arrive (first come, first served) or book in advance online. It's also possible to book private, themed tours that focus on different aspects of Charleston's heritage, such as its groundbreaking LGBTQ+ history or the influence French culture had on the Bloomsbury Group. ■TIP➔ **The house isn't suitable for those with mobility issues, although reduced-price ground-floor-only tickets are available.** ⊠ *Off A27, Firle* ☎ *01323/811626* ⊕ *www.charleston.org. uk* 🎟 *£14.50* ⊗ *Closed Mon. and Tues.*

Bonfire Night in Lewes

In 1605, a group of Catholic rebels attempted to blow up Parliament in the most famous failed coup in English history. Known as the Gunpowder Plot, it's still commemorated with fireworks every year on the Saturday closest to the anniversary on November 5 ("Remember, remember, the fifth of November; gunpowder, treason, and plot"). As befitting a 400-year-old custom, it's a night rich with tradition—nowhere more spectacularly than in Lewes. Thousands march through the town with flaming torches; many wear elaborate costumes and play instruments. By far the most arresting part of the night is the parade of giant, towering effigies, built with great craftsmanship. Many depict public figures and other bogeymen of the day in viciously satirical ways. Recent examples include Vladimir Putin standing amid the wreckage of an airplane, Donald Trump as a clown shooting himself in the foot,

and British prime minister Boris Johnson urinating on newspapers. Huge pyres are lit ("bonfires"), on which the effigies are burned. Think of it as the Macy's Thanksgiving Day Parade directed by David Lynch. The fireworks and merriment carry on well into the night. Admittedly, it may be too much for some people to stomach—there's nothing like the sight of burning crosses, anti-Catholic chants, and the torching of a papal effigy to make foreign visitors wonder just what they've stepped into. But, it's important to stress, it's all totally in the spirit of ancient tradition and bone-dry humor rather than actual anti-Catholic sentiment. It's a unique event with a carnival atmosphere and deep historic roots. Similar, though smaller, parades happen in Rye and Hastings, usually on different weeks. For more details see ⊕ www.lewesbonfirecelebrations.com or check the town websites.

Lewes Castle

CASTLE/PALACE | High above the valley of the River Ouse stand the majestic ruins of Lewes Castle, begun in 1100 by one of the country's Norman conquerors and completed 300 years later. The castle's barbican holds a small museum with archaeology collections, a changing temporary exhibition gallery, and a bookshop. There are panoramic views of the town and countryside. ⊠ 92 High St. ☎ 01273/486290 ⊕ www.sussexpast.co.uk/properties-to-discover/lewes-castle ⊠ £8.50; combined ticket with Anne of Cleves House £13.40 ☉ Closed Mon. in Jan.–Mar.

Long Man of Wilmington

PUBLIC ART | Ten miles southeast of Lewes on the A27, Wilmington has a famous landmark that people drive for miles to see. High on the downs to the south of the village (signposted off the A27), a 226-foot-tall white figure with a staff in each hand, known as the Long Man of Wilmington, is carved into the chalk. His age is a subject of great debate: some researchers think he might have been created as far back as Roman or even Neolithic times, but recent soil analysis places the figure closer to the 16th century. It's one of England's two most significant human hill figures, along with the Cerne

A mixture of architectural styles and good shops makes Lewes a wonderful town for a stroll.

Abbas Giant near Dorchester in Dorset. ⊠ *S. Downs Way, Wilmington* ⊕ *sussexpast.co.uk/properties-to-discover/the-long-man.*

Monk's House

HOUSE | Of particular interest to Bloomsbury Group fans, this property three miles south of Lewes was the home of novelist Virginia Woolf and her husband, Leonard Woolf, who bought it in 1919. Leonard lived here until his death in 1969. Rooms in the small cottage include Virginia's study and her bedroom. Artists Vanessa Bell (Virginia's sister) and Duncan Grant helped decorate the house. ⊠ *The St., Rodmell* ☎ *01273/474760* ⊕ *www.nationaltrust.org.uk/monks-house* 🎟 *£6.60* ⊙ *Closed Nov.–Mar., Mon., and Tues.*

🍴 Restaurants

Bill's

$ | **MODERN EUROPEAN** | **FAMILY** | What started in the early 2000s as a distinctly Lewes café-restaurant has since grown to become a full-blown chain, with more than 80 restaurants across the United Kingdom. This is where it all began, and the casual, mostly Modern European food remains as reliably good here as it is everywhere. **Known for:** lots of vegetarian and vegan options; great breakfasts; family atmosphere. ⑤ *Average main: £13* ⊠ *56 Cliffe High St.* ☎ *01273/476918* ⊕ *www.bills-website.co.uk.*

The Limetree Kitchen

$ | **BRITISH** | Elegant, imaginative menus and a commitment to locally sourced produce is at the heart of this popular restaurant in the center of Lewes. Menus are heavily influenced by what's in season, with just a few, well-chosen options available each day—examples might include tempura of Devonishire hake with tartare sauce or local rib-eye steak with parsley and shallot. **Known for:** excellent value main courses; seasonal menus; locally sourced produce. $ *Average main: £11* ⊠ *14 Station St.* ☎ *01273 /478636* ⊕ *www.limetreekitchen.co.uk* ⊘ *Closed Mon. and Tues.*

The Real Eating Company
$ | **CAFÉ** | This light-filled restaurant has big windows overlooking the bustling shopping street outside. The heavy wood tables are perfect for lingering over the home-style cooking. **Known for:** good breakfasts; great cakes; bustling street view. $ *Average main: £9* ⊠ *18 Cliffe High St.* ☎ *01273/402650* ⊕ *www.real-eating.co.uk* ⊘ *No dinner Sun.*

Robson's of Lewes
$ | **CAFÉ** | Good coffee, fresh produce, and delicious pastries make this coffee shop one of the best places in Lewes to drop by for an afternoon pick-me-up. A light-filled space with wood floors and simple tables creates a pleasant, casual spot to enjoy a cup of coffee with breakfast, a scone, or a light sandwich or salad lunch. **Known for:** great coffee; tasty light bites; good to-go options. $ *Average main: £6* ⊠ *22A High St.* ☎ *01273/480654* ⊕ *www.robsonsoflewes.co.uk* ⊘ *No dinner.*

 ## Hotels

Horsted Place
$$ | **B&B/INN** | On 1,100 acres, this luxurious Victorian manor house was built as a private home in 1850; it was owned by a friend of the current Queen until the 1980s, and she was a regular visitor. **Pros:** historic country manor; delicious food; lovely gardens. **Cons:** too formal for some; creaky floors bother light sleepers; the English manor lifestyle doesn't come cheap. $ *Rooms from: £200* ⊠ *Off A26, Little Horsted* ☎ *01825/750581* ⊕ *www.horstedplace.co.uk* ⇌ *20 rooms* ¶○¶ *Free breakfast.*

The Ram Inn
$$ | **B&B/INN** | Roaring fires, cozy rooms, and friendly locals give this 500-year-old inn its wonderful feeling of old-world authenticity. **Pros:** proper village pub atmosphere; excellent breakfast (try the croissants); well-designed rooms. **Cons:** you need a car to get here; rooms over the bar can be noisy; Wi-Fi is patchy. $ *Rooms from: £150* ⊠ *The St., West Firle* ☎ *01273/858222* ⊕ *www.raminn.co.uk* ⇌ *5 rooms* ¶○¶ *Free breakfast.*

The Shelleys
$$ | **B&B/INN** | The lounge and dining room in this 17th-century High Street building are on the grand scale, furnished with antiques that set the tone for the rest of the lovely building. **Pros:** historic atmosphere; fine French-influenced cuisine; location in the heart of Lewes. **Cons:** service a bit spotty; securing a restaurant table can be tough; could do with a facelift. $ *Rooms from: £220* ⊠ *136 High St.* ☎ *01273/472361* ⊕ *www.the-shelleys.co.uk* ⇌ *19 rooms* ¶○¶ *Breakfast.*

☿ Nightlife

Lewes has a relatively young population and a nightlife scene to match. There are also many lovely old pubs.

The Brewers Arms
BARS/PUBS | On High Street, this is a good pub with a friendly crowd. While the half-timbered building only dates from 1906, a pub has stood on this spot since the 16th century. ⊠ *91 High St.* ☎ *01273/475524* ⊕ *www.thebrewersarmslewes.com.*

King's Head
BARS/PUBS | A contemporary pub dating back to 1891, the King's Head has a good menu with locally sourced fish and meat dishes. There are also three quirky boutique rooms available. ⊠ *9 Southover High St.* ☎ *01273/474628* ⊕ *www.kingsheadlewes.co.uk.*

Brighton

NORTH LAINE

West Pier

English Channel

KEY

- Exploring Sights
- Restaurants
- Hotels

Tourist information

| 0 | 1,000 ft |
| 0 | 250 m |

Sights ▼

1 Brighton Beach **D5**

2 Brighton Museum and
   Art Gallery **D3**

3 Brighton Pier **D5**

4 i360 .... **A4**

5 The Lanes **C4**

6 Royal Pavilion **D3**

7 SEA LIFE Brighton **D4**

8 Standen **D1**

9 Volk's Electric
   Railway **E5**

Restaurants ▼

1 Gelato Gusto **D3**

2 Iydea **D2**

3 The Mock Turtle
   Tea Room **D4**

4 Riddle & Finns
   The Lanes **C3**

5 Terre à Terre **D4**

6 The Witchez **E4**

Hotels ▼

1 Brightonwave **E4**

2 Drakes **E4**

3 The Grand Brighton **B4**

4 Granville Hotel **A4**

5 Hotel du Vin **C4**

6 Nineteen Brighton **E4**

7 Oriental Brighton **A3**

🎭 Performing Arts

★ Glyndebourne Opera House

OPERA | Nestled beneath the Downs, three miles east of Lewes, this world-famous opera house combines first-class productions, a state-of-the-art auditorium, and a beautiful setting. Tickets are *very* expensive (the cheapest start at around £85, though for many productions it's twice that, rising to around £250), and you have to book months in advance. But it's worth every penny to aficionados, who traditionally wear evening dress and bring a hamper to picnic on the grounds. The main season runs from mid-May to the end of August. ■ TIP➔ **Save money by booking standing-room tickets (from £10), or look out for special nights when adults under 30 pay just £30.** ⊠ *New Rd., Ringmer* ☎ *01273/813321* ⊕ *www. glyndebourne.com.*

🛍 Shopping

Antiques shops offer temptation along the busy High Street. Lewes also has plenty of tiny boutiques and independent clothing stores vying for your pounds.

Cliffe Antiques Centre

ANTIQUES/COLLECTIBLES | This packed-to-the-rafters shop carries a fine mix of vintage English prints, estate jewelry, and art at reasonable prices. ⊠ *47 Cliffe High St.* ☎ *01273/473266* ⊕ *www.cliffeantiques.co.uk.*

The Fifteenth Century Bookshop

BOOKS/STATIONERY | A wide collection of rare and vintage books can be found at this ancient, timber-framed building in the center of Lewes. Antique children's books are a specialty. ⊠ *99–100 High St.* ☎ *01273/474160* ⊕ *www.oldenyoungbooks.co.uk.*

Louis Potts & Co.

CERAMICS/GLASSWARE | From frivolous knickkacks to full-on formal dining sets, Louis Potts specializes in stylish bone china and glassware. ⊠ *43 Cliffe High St.* ☎ *01273/472240* ⊕ *www.louispotts.com.*

Brighton

9 miles southwest of Lewes, 54 miles south of London.

For more than 200 years, Brighton has been England's most interesting seaside city, and today it's more vibrant, eccentric, and cosmopolitan than ever. A rich cultural mix—Regency architecture, specialty shops, sidewalk cafés, lively arts, and a flourishing gay scene—makes it unique and unpredictable.

In 1750, physician Richard Russell published a book recommending seawater treatment for glandular diseases. The fashionable world flocked to Brighton to take Dr. Russell's "cure," and sea bathing became a popular pastime. Few places in the south of England were better for it, since Brighton's broad beach of smooth pebbles stretches as far as the eye can see. It's been popular with sunbathers ever since.

The next windfall for the town was the arrival of the Prince of Wales (later George IV). "Prinny," as he was called, created the Royal Pavilion, a mock-Asian pleasure palace that attracted London society. This triggered a wave of villa building, and today the elegant terraces of Regency houses are among the town's greatest attractions. The coming of the railway set the seal on Brighton's popularity: the *Brighton Belle* brought Londoners to the coast in an hour.

Londoners still flock to Brighton. Add them to the many local university students, and you have a trendy, young, and laid-back city that does, occasionally, burst at its own seams. Property values have skyrocketed, but all visitors may notice is the good shopping and restaurants, attractive (if pebbly) beach, and wild nightlife. Brighton is also the place to go if you're looking for hotels with offbeat design and party nights.

GETTING HERE AND AROUND

Southeastern trains leave from London's Victoria and London Bridge stations several times per hour. The journey takes about an hour, and the trains stop at Gatwick Airport. Brighton-bound National Express buses depart from London's Victoria Coach Station every day on the hour and half hour. The direct buses take around 2½ hours. By car from London, head to Brighton on the M23/A23. The journey should take between 1½ and 2 hours, depending on traffic.

From Lewes, Southern train services leave every 10 minutes for Brighton (15 minutes). Otherwise, it's a simple drive down the A27 and A270 (20 to 30 minutes).

Brighton (and the adjacent Hove) sprawls in all directions, but the part of interest to travelers is fairly compact. All the major sights are within a 10-minute walk of the train station, where you can pick up a town map. City Sightseeing has a hop-on, hop-off tour bus that leaves Brighton Pier every 20 to 30 minutes. It operates April through October and costs £14.

TIMING

On summer weekends the town is packed with Londoners looking for a day by the sea. Oceanfront bars can be rowdy, especially on national holidays (like the last weekend of August) when concerts and events bring in crowds. But summer is also when Brighton looks its best, and revelers pack the shops, restaurants, and bars. At other times, it's much quieter. The Brighton Festival in May fills the town with music and other performances.

ESSENTIALS

VISITOR AND TOUR INFORMA-TION Brighton Visitor Information Point. ⊠ *The Brighton Centre, King's Rd.* ☎ *01273/290337* ⊕ *www.visitbrighton. com.* **City Sightseeing.** ☎ *01789/299123* ⊕ *www.city-sightseeing.com.*

◉ Sights

Brighton Beach

BEACH—SIGHT | Brighton's most iconic landmark is its famous beach, which sweeps smoothly from one end of town to the other. In summer, sunbathers, swimmers, and ice cream–sellers pack the shore; in winter, people stroll at the water's stormy edge, walking their dogs and searching for seashells. The water is bracingly cold, and the beach is covered in a thick blanket of large, smooth pebbles (615 billion of them, according to the tourism office). ■ **TIP→ Bring a pair of rubber swimming shoes if you're taking a dip—the stones are hard on bare feet.** **Amenities:** food and drink; lifeguards; toilets; parking (fee); water sports. **Best for:** partiers; sunset; swimming. ⊠ *Brighton.*

Brighton Museum and Art Gallery

MUSEUM | The grounds of the Royal Pavilion contain this museum, in a former stable block designed for the Prince Regent (1762–1830), son of George III. The museum has particularly interesting art nouveau and art deco collections. Look out for a tiny replica of Salvador Dalí's famous sofa in the shape of Mae West's lips. The Fashion & Style Gallery has clothes from the Regency period to the present day, and the Performance gallery has a collection of masks, puppets, and other theatrical curiosities. ⊠ *Royal Pavilion Gardens, Off Church St.* ☎ *0300/029–0900* ⊕ *brightonmuseums. org.uk/brighton* ⊠ *£6* ⊗ *Closed Mon. except holidays.*

Brighton Pier

MARINA | **FAMILY** | Opened in 1899, the pier is an amusement park set above the sea. In the early 20th century it had a music hall and entertainment; today it has roller coasters and other carnival rides, as well as game arcades, clairvoyants, candy stores, and greasy-food stalls. In summer it's packed with children by day and (on weekends) teenagers by night. There's no fee to enter the

The Brighton Pier makes for a lovely sunset backdrop.

pier, although the individual kiosks have their own charges. Alternatively, a wristband (£20 adults, £12 children) allows blanket entry, which can amount to a big savings if you're making the rounds of what's on offer. The skeletal shadow of a pier you can see off in the water is all that's left of the old West Pier. ⊠ *Off Madeira Dr.* ☎ *01273/609361* ⊕ *www. brightonpier.co.uk.*

★ i360

VIEWPOINT | FAMILY | Designed by the same people who made the London Eye, this seaside viewing platform ascends 531 feet into the air, allowing an incredible view of the coastline and the South Downs. On clear days you can see the Isle of Wight. The ride (or "flight" as sponsor British Airways insists on calling it) lasts about 25 minutes. Booking is advisable, especially in summer; it's also 10% cheaper if you reserve online. Check out the website for special packages that include dinner. i360 stays open in all weather, other than exceptionally strong winds. It's so peaceful inside the doughnut-shaped pods, you'd never guess the storm that raged over the £43 million structure, ahead of its eventual opening in 2016. Locals worried it would ruin the character of the promenade. After you take in the sweeping view, you've got the leisurely descent back to street level to decide if you agree with them. ⊠ *Lower King's Rd.* ☎ *0337/720360* ⊕ *www.britishairwaysi360.com* ⊠ *£13.50.*

The Lanes

NEIGHBORHOOD | This maze of tiny alleys and passageways was once the home of fishermen and their families. Closed to vehicular traffic, the area's narrow cobbled streets are filled with interesting restaurants, boutiques, and antiques shops. Fish and seafood restaurants line the heart of the Lanes, at Market Street and Market Square. ⊠ *Bordered by (clockwise) North St., Market St., Prince Albert St., and Ship St.*

George IV loved the sea at Brighton and built the flamboyant Royal Pavilion as a seaside escape.

★ Royal Pavilion

MUSEUM | The city's most remarkable building is this delightfully over-the-top domed and pinnacled fantasy. Built as a simple seaside villa in the fashionable classical style of 1787 by architect Henry Holland, the Pavilion was rebuilt between 1815 and 1822 by John Nash for the Prince Regent (later George IV). The result was an exotic, foppish Eastern design with opulent Chinese interiors. The two great set pieces are the **Music Room,** styled in the form of a Chinese pavilion, and the **Banqueting Room,** with its enormous flying-dragon "gasolier," or gaslight chandelier, a revolutionary invention in the early 19th century. The gardens, too, have been restored to Regency splendor, following John Nash's naturalistic design of 1826. For an elegant time-out, a tearoom serves snacks and light meals. ⊠ *Off Church St.* ☎ *0300/029–0900* ⊕ *brightonmuseums. org.uk/royalpavilion* ⊠ *£15.*

SEA LIFE Brighton

ZOO | FAMILY | Near Brighton Pier, this aquarium has thousands of sea-dwelling creatures—from sharks to seahorses to starfish—in more than 30 marine habitats. There's a glass-bottom-boat experience, a humid rain-forest adventure (featuring an eight-foot-long anaconda), and a extraordinary coral reef exhibition that shows how the ecosystem changes between day and night. Check online for the daily feeding schedules, all of which are accompanied by free talks (including sharks at 2 and turtles at 4). Book online at least a day in advance for big discounts on the ticket price. ⊠ *Marine Parade* ☎ *0371/226–6770* ⊕ *www.visit-sealife.com/brighton* ⊠ *£15.*

Standen

HOUSE | A well-preserved family country house dating from the 1890s and set in a beautiful hillside garden, Standen typifies the Arts and Crafts movement. Designed by the influential architect

Philip Webb (1831–1913), it contains a wealth of William Morris carpets, wallpapers, fabrics, and even original electric-light fittings. The house is 2 miles south of East Grinstead and 28 miles north of Brighton. ⊠ *West Hoathly Rd., East Grinstead* ✛ *28 miles north of Brighton* ☎ *01342/323029* ⊕ *www.nationaltrust.org.uk/standen* ☑ *£12* ⊙ *Closed Nov.–Jan. No tours on weekdays.*

Volk's Electric Railway

TRANSPORTATION SITE (AIRPORT/BUS/FERRY/TRAIN) | FAMILY | Built by Brighton inventor Magnus Volk in 1883, this was the first electric railway anywhere in the world—and it's recently been spruced-up in an extensive, £2 million restoration project. Between April and October, you can take the 1¼-mile, three-station trip along the beachfront Marine Parade. ⊠ *Marine Parade* ☎ *01273/292718* ⊕ *www.volksrailway.org.uk* ☑ *£3.80 single, £4.90 return* ⊙ *Closed Nov.–Easter.*

🍽 Restaurants

★ Gelato Gusto

$ | CAFÉ | FAMILY | No seaside town would be complete without an ice-cream store, and the delicious, homemade, artisanal gelato on sale here is a real treat. Everything is made fresh daily; try the cherry cheesecake flavor or maybe a scoop of the delicious chocolate and sea salt. **Known for:** delicious Italian ice cream; indulgent desserts; essential part of the Brighton seafront experience. ⑤ *Average main: £9* ⊠ *2 Gardner St.* ☎ *01273/673402* ⊕ *www.facebook.com/gelatogustobtn.*

Iydea

$ | VEGETARIAN | This popular restaurant and café is a must for visiting vegetarians, though even the most ardent carnivores are likely to leave satisfied. The food is laid out cafeteria style (or "canteen" style in British English), so you choose your meal based on choices of main dishes, sides, and toppings. **Known for:** top vegetarian restaurant; delicious, international cooking; popular veggie breakfast. ⑤ *Average main: £7* ⊠ *17 Kensington Gardens* ☎ *01273/667992* ⊕ *www.iydea.co.uk.*

The Mock Turtle Tea Room

$ | CAFÉ | Less than five minutes' walk from the Royal Pavilion, the Mock Turtle is a great old-fashioned, homey café. Alongside a decent selection of teas and coffees are four types of rarebit, soups, and scones as well as cakes and enormous doughnuts. **Known for:** popular stop for tea and coffee; excellent cakes; location close to Royal Pavilion. ⑤ *Average main: £7* ⊠ *4 Pool Valley* ☎ *01273/327380.*

★ Riddle & Finns The Lanes

$$ | SEAFOOD | White tiles, bare metal tables, and sparkling chandeliers set the tone as soon as you walk through the door of this casually elegant restaurant. The house specialty is oysters, fresh and sustainably sourced, served with or without a foaming tankard of black velvet (champagne and Guinness) on the side. **Known for:** romantic atmosphere; supremely fresh seafood; no reservations policy so be prepared to wait. ⑤ *Average main: £22* ⊠ *12B Meeting House La.* ☎ *01273/721667* ⊕ *www.riddleandfinns. co.uk.*

Terre à Terre

$$ | VEGETARIAN | This inspiring vegetarian restaurant is incredibly popular, so come early for a light lunch or later for a more sophisticated evening meal. Dishes have a pan-Asian influence, so you may have steamed rice buns stuffed with ginger pak choi or battered halloumi with the pleasingly tongue-twistery side of lemony Yemeni relish. **Known for:** Asian-influenced cooking; excellent vegetarian dishes; great wine list. ⑤ *Average main: £17* ⊠ *71 East St.* ☎ *01273/729051* ⊕ *www.terreaterre.co.uk.*

Brighton and the Regent

The term "Regency" comes from the last 10 years of the reign of George III (1811–20), who was ultimately deemed unfit to rule because of his mental illness. Real power was officially given to the Prince of Wales, also known as the Prince Regent, who became King George IV and ruled until his death in 1830.

Throughout his regency, George IV spent grand sums indulging his flamboyant tastes in architecture and interior decorating—while failing in affairs of state.

The distinctive architecture of the Royal Pavilion is a prime, if extreme, example of the Regency style, popularized by architect John Nash (1752–1835) in the early part of the 19th century. The style is characterized by a diversity of influences—French, Greek, Italian, Persian, Japanese, Chinese, Roman, Indian... you name it. Nash was George IV's favorite architect, beloved for his interest in Indian and Asian art and for his neoclassical designs, as evidenced in his other most famous work: Regent's Park and its terraces in London.

The Witchez

$ | EASTERN EUROPEAN | Owned by talented graphic designers and photo artists, the Witchez Photo Design Restaurant is certainly a unique concept: delicious German- and Polish-influenced comfort food served in the middle of a design studio (which means you can have your passport photo taken while you wait). Never mind the weirdness of the concept; this place is a whole lot of fun, and the food is good to boot—schnitzel, pierogi, German sausage, potato dumplings, and pizzas. **Known for:** truly unique concept; tasty German and Polish dishes; great atmosphere.
⑤ *Average main: £14* ⊠ *16 Marine Parade* ☎ *01273/673652* ⊕ *www.thewitchez. co.uk* ⊗ *Closed Sun. No lunch.*

🛏 Hotels

★ Brightonwave

$$ | B&B/INN | Chic and sleek, this hotel a little off the seafront (three minutes' walk from Brighton Pier) is all about relaxation. **Pros:** big and comfortable beds; beautiful design; lovely hosts. **Cons:** rooms on the small side; few extras; limited parking.
⑤ *Rooms from: £130* ⊠ *10 Madeira Pl.* ☎ *01273/676794* ⊕ *www.brightonwave. com* ⊃ *8 rooms* ⊚ *Free breakfast.*

★ Drakes

$$ | HOTEL | It's easy to miss the low-key sign for this elegant, modern hotel tucked away amid the frilly houses on Marine Parade, but it's worth the trouble of finding, because everything is cool, calm, and sleekly designed. **Pros:** attention to detail; well-designed bathrooms; excellent restaurant. **Cons:** two-night minimum on weekends; breakfast is extra; limited parking.
⑤ *Rooms from: £160* ⊠ *43–44 Marine Parade* ☎ *01273/696934* ⊕ *www.drake-sofbrighton.com* ⊃ *20 rooms* ⊚ *No meals.*

The Grand Brighton

$$ | HOTEL | The city's most famous hotel and a seafront landmark, the Grand Brighton is a huge, Victorian wedding cake of a building dating from 1864. **Pros:** as grand as its name; lovely sea views; luxurious spa. **Cons:** a bit impersonal; prices can rise sharply on weekends; cheaper rooms are small.
⑤ *Rooms from: £220* ⊠ *97–99 Kings Rd.* ☎ *01273/224300* ⊕ *www.grand-brighton.co.uk* ⊃ *201 rooms* ⊚ *Free breakfast.*

Granville Hotel

$$ | HOTEL | Three grand Victorian buildings facing the sea have been combined to create one great boutique hotel. **Pros:** creative design; friendly staff; rambunctious atmosphere. **Cons:** decor too quirky for some; sea-facing rooms can be noisy; not wheelchair accessible. $ *Rooms from: £125* ⊠ *124 King's Rd.* ☎ *01273/326302* ⊕ *www.granvillehotel. co.uk* ⥈ *24 rooms* ⦿ *Free breakfast.*

Hotel du Vin

$$ | HOTEL | In the Lanes area, this outpost of a snazzy boutique chain has chic, modern rooms. **Pros:** gorgeous rooms; comfortable beds; excellent restaurant. **Cons:** bar can get crowded; big price fluctuations in summer; often gets booked up. $ *Rooms from: £185* ⊠ *2 Ship St.* ☎ *01273/855221* ⊕ *www.hotelduvin.com* ⥈ *49 rooms* ⦿ *Free breakfast.*

Nineteen Brighton

$ | B&B/INN | A calm oasis in the heart of Brighton, this guesthouse is filled with contemporary art and designer accessories. **Pros:** innovative design; close to the beach; three nights for the price of two. **Cons:** not on the nicest street; two-night minimum on weekends; breakfast not included. $ *Rooms from: £95* ⊠ *19 Broad St.* ☎ *07426/043930* ⊕ *www.nineteenbrighton.com* ⥈ *7 rooms* ⦿ *No meals.*

Oriental Brighton

$$ | HOTEL | With a casual elegance that typifies Brighton, this Regency-era boutique hotel sits close to the seafront. **Pros:** close to the beach; chic and colorful rooms; tasty cooked breakfasts. **Cons:** lacking a restaurant; bar can get rowdy; no free parking. $ *Rooms from: £150* ⊠ *9 Oriental Pl.* ☎ *01273/205050* ⊕ *www. orientalbrighton.co.uk* ⥈ *9 rooms* ⦿ *Free breakfast.*

⏵ Nightlife

Brighton is a techno hub, largely because so many DJs have moved here from London. Clubs and bars present live music most nights, and on weekends the entire place can be a bit too raucous for some tastes. There's a large and enthusiastic gay scene.

Bohemia Brighton

MUSIC CLUBS | Though open throughout the day as an upscale café-bar, Bohemia Brighton really comes to life after dark. Its Champagne Late Lounge has great cocktails and live DJs every Saturday night, while regular jazz nights (usually Thursday starting at 9 pm) see the best local jazz acts take over the venue, which is laid out like a traditional jazz club with table service and a romantic, candlelit ambience. ⊠ *54-55 Meeting House La.* ☎ *01273/777770* ⊕ *www.bohemiabright-on.co.uk.*

Patterns

MUSIC CLUBS | One of Brighton's foremost venues, in an art deco building east of Brighton Pier, Patterns is the latest incarnation of a string of popular nightclubs that have occupied this spot. Expect to hear live acts during the week, including a regular local slot (this being Brighton, the quality is generally quite high) and techno and house on the weekend. ⊠ *10 Marine Parade* ☎ *01273/894777* ⊕ *www. patternsbrighton.com.*

The Plotting Parlour

BARS/PUBS | This ultrahip nightclub on Stein Street feels like a glamorous speakeasy. Cocktails are a specialty, and the bar staff certainly know what they're doing (try the fierce ginger and chili margarita). It's extremely popular with the cooler brand of local partygoer, and it's fabulously good fun to boot. ⊠ *6 Steine St.* ☎ *01273/621238* ⊕ *www.theplotting-parlour-brighton.co.uk.*

Proud Cabaret

CABARET | A mixture of vintage and avant-garde cabaret and burlesque is on offer at this stylish nightclub, which has a distinctly 1920s flavor. It's only open Friday and Saturday and can get very busy, so booking ahead is advisable. ⊠ 83 St. Georges Rd. ☎ 01273/605789 ⊕ proud-cabaret.com.

★ Performing Arts

Brighton Dome

ARTS CENTERS | West of the Royal Pavilion, the Brighton Dome was converted from the Prince Regent's stables in the 1930s. It includes a theater and a concert hall that stages classical and pop concerts, plays, stand-up comedy, and festive pantomimes (a traditional British children's play with songs and dance, usually featuring a mix of talented stage pros and low-rent TV stars). ⊠ Church St. ☎ 01273/709709 ⊕ www.brightondome.org.

Duke of York's Picture House

FILM | One of the oldest cinemas in the world, the elegant Duke of York's Picture House dates back to 1910 and shows an eclectic range of art-house movies and also hosts film-related discussions and events. It's a 10-minute walk north of the main train station. ⊠ Preston Rd. ☎ 0871/902–5747 ⊕ www.picturehouses.com.

Theatre Royal

THEATER | Close to the Royal Pavilion, the Theatre Royal has a gem of an auditorium that has been a favorite venue for shows on their way to, or fresh from, London's West End for more than 200 years. ⊠ New Rd. ☎ 0844/871–7650 ⊕ www.atgtickets.com/venues/theatre-royal-brighton.

⬤ Shopping

Brighton's best shopping can be found in two areas: the Lanes, a labyrinth of poky alleyways and passages full of boutique clothing, antiques, and jewelry and North Laine, a network of narrow streets full of fun, funky, and exotic little stores.

Dave's Comics

BOOKS/STATIONERY | This supercool independent comic book store is stocked with an enormous range of comic books. There's a sister store two doors down, specializing in graphic novels, toys, and other collectibles. ⊠ 5 Sydney St. ☎ 01273/691012 ⊕ www.davescomics.co.uk.

The Great Frog Paterson and Curiouser & Curiouser

JEWELRY/ACCESSORIES | A two-for-one of funky jewelry stores sharing the same premises, the Great Frog Paterson specializes in jewelry with a rock 'n' roll theme (the owners claim to be the creators of the original skull ring) while Curiouser & Curiouser is filled with unique handmade pieces (the shop made several pieces of jewelry for the Harry Potter movies). ⊠ 2 Sydney St. ☎ 01273/673120 ⊕ www.thegreatfrogpaterson.com.

Lavender Room

JEWELRY/ACCESSORIES | This relaxing boutique tempts with scented calendars, glittery handmade jewelry, and little things you just can't live without. ⊠ 16 Bond St. ☎ 01273/220380 ⊕ www.lavender-room.co.uk.

Pecksniff's Bespoke Perfumery

PERFUME/COSMETICS | This delightfully old-fashioned "British Fragrance and Cosmetic House" mixes and matches ingredients to suit your perfume wishes. ⊠ 45–46 Meeting House La. ☎ 01273/723292 ⊕ www.pecksniffs.com.

West Sussex
and Surrey

0   8 mi

0   8 km

Royal Pavilion Shop

GIFTS/SOUVENIRS | Next door to the Royal Pavilion, this little shop sells well-designed toys, trinkets, books, and cards, all with a loose Regency theme. There are also high-quality fabrics, wallpapers, and ceramics based on material in the pavilion itself. ⊠ *4–5 Pavilion Parade* ☎.

Arundel

21 miles west of Brighton.

The little hilltop town of Arundel is dominated by three oversized landmarks. First, a great—and greatly restored—castle, which has been home of the dukes of Norfolk for more than 700 years. Second, an imposing neo-Gothic Roman Catholic cathedral (the duke is Britain's leading Catholic peer). And third, a spectacular

medieval priory church. The town center, which spreads down the hill towards the river, is also full of interesting old buildings, the vast majority of which are either pubs, tea shops, or antiques dealers.

GETTING HERE AND AROUND

Arundel is located at the point where the A27 meets the A824, about a two-hour drive south of central London. Trains from London's Victoria Station leave every half hour and take 1½ hours. No direct buses run from London, and while it's possible to take a National Express bus to Worthing or Chichester and change to a local bus to Arundel, the journey is likely to take five hours or more.

From Brighton, there are regular Southern trains to Arundel (one to 1½ hours, changing in Barnham), or it's a 45-minute drive west along the A27.

ESSENTIALS
VISITOR INFORMATION Arundel Visitor Information Centre. ⊠ *Arundel Museum, River Rd.* ☎ *01903/885866* ⊕ *www. sussexbythesea.com.*

Sights

★ Arundel Castle
CASTLE/PALACE | FAMILY | You've probably already seen Arundel Castle without knowing it, at least on screen. Its striking resemblence to Windsor means that it's frequently used as a stand-in for its more famous cousin in movies and television.

Begun in the 11th century, this vast castle remains rich with the history of the Fitzalan and Howard families and holds paintings by Van Dyck, Gainsborough, and Reynolds. During the 18th century and in the Victorian era it was reconstructed in the fashionable Gothic style—although the keep, rising from its conical mound, is as old as the original castle (climb its 130 steps for great views of the River Arun), and the barbican and the Barons' Hall date from the 13th century. Among the treasures here are the rosary beads and prayer book used by Mary, Queen of Scots, in preparing for her execution.

The formal garden, a triumph of order and beauty, is also worth a visit. Special events happen year-round, including a week of jousting, usually in late July. (Ticket prices rise slightly during event weeks.) Although the castle's ceremonial entrance is at the top of High Street, you enter at the bottom, close to the parking lot. ⊠ *Off High St.* ☎ *01903/882173* ⊕ *www.arundelcastle.org* ☐ *£23; gardens only £13* ⊘ *Closed Mon. and Nov.–Mar.*

Arundel Cathedral
RELIGIOUS SITE | This far-too-big-for-a-small-town Catholic cathedral in the French-Gothic style was commissioned by Henry, Duke of Norfolk, to celebrate his coming of age. Designed by Joseph Hansom (of Hansom Cab horse-drawn carriage fame), it opened in 1873. Stroll around the gorgeous interior, renowned for its signature stained-glass rose window and beautiful 19th-century organ. Also look out for the roundels of Saxon saints high up on the walls of the aisles. ⊠ *London Rd.* ☎ *01903/882297* ⊕ *www. arundelcathedral.uk.*

★ St. Nicholas Church
RELIGIOUS SITE | Just across the road from Arundel Cathedral is another equally impressive—and equally oversized—religious building. This 14th-century parish church, built on the site of a far older priory, was almost certainly the work of Henry Yeveley and William Wynford, who also contributed to Canterbury and Winchester cathedrals. Interestingly, the church is today divided into two separate parts according to denomination: the main part, the nave, is Protestant, while the chancel is Catholic. The latter, seized during the Reformation, is where the dukes of Norfolk are buried. Wander around to see some of the decorative highlights, including the remarkable stone pulpit, the unusually large Royal Coat of Arms, and some surviving fragments of medieval wall paintings. ⊠ *Off London Rd.* ☎ *01903/882262* ⊕ *www. stnicholas-arundel.co.uk.*

Restaurants

★ The Town House
$$$ | BRITISH | This small but elegant restaurant in a beautifully converted Regency town house (look above you—the dining room ceiling is quite something) serves top-notch British and European cuisine. The fixed-price lunch and dinner menus change regularly but could include roast breast of local partridge with red-currant jelly or trout with a chive butter sauce. **Known for:** local meats and fish; seasonal menus; beautiful dining room. ⑤ *Average main: £30* ⊠ *65 High St.* ☎ *01903/883847* ⊕ *www.thetown-house.co.uk.*

Hotels

★ Amberley Castle

$$$ | HOTEL | Enter under the portcullis of this genuine medieval castle, where across the moat, present-day luxury dominates. **Pros:** sleep in a real castle; lovely gardens and grounds; good afternoon tea. **Cons:** you have to dress up for dinner; five miles outside Arundel; incredibly expensive. ⑤ *Rooms from: £295 ⊠ Church St., Off B2139, Amberley ☎ 01798/831992 ⊕ www.amberleycastle. co.uk ⇴ 19 rooms ⑩ Free breakfast.*

Bailiffscourt Hotel & Spa

$$$ | HOTEL | Situated a few miles south of Arundel, this charmingly out-of-the-way country escape offers lovely period features, expansive private gardens, and one of the region's finest spas. **Pros:** elegant tapestry-filled restaurant; lovely spa and tennis courts; a short walk to the beach. **Cons:** "medieval" decor in some rooms a little much; underwhelming afternoon tea; spa visit requires walking outside. ⑤ *Rooms from: £275 ⊠ Climping St. ☎ 01903/723511 ⊕ www. hshotels.co.uk/bailiffscourt ⇴ 39 rooms ⑩ Free breakfast.*

Norfolk Arms Hotel

$$ | HOTEL | The best accommodation option in the town center, this 18th-century coaching inn on the main street was, like Arundel's cathedral and castle, built by one of the dukes of Norfolk (during the Napoleonic Wars, it was used to house soldiers). **Pros:** charming old building; good pub food and craft beer; friendly and welcoming staff. **Cons:** older rooms on the small side; underpowered and slow-to-heat showers; no elevator. ⑤ *Rooms from: £130 ⊠ 22 High St. ☎ 01903/882101 ⊕ www.norfolkarmsarundel.com ⇴ 37 rooms ⑩ Free breakfast.*

Chichester

11 miles west of Arundel, 66 miles southwest of London.

The Romans founded Chichester, the capital city of West Sussex, on the low-lying plains between the wooded South Downs and the sea. The city walls and major streets follow the original Roman plan to this day. This cathedral town, a good base for exploring the area, is a well-respected theatrical hub, with a reputation for attracting good acting talent during its summer repertory season. North of town is Petworth House, one of the region's finest stately homes.

GETTING HERE AND AROUND

From London, take the A3 south and follow exit signs for Chichester. The journey takes around two hours, as much of it is on smaller highways. Southern trains run to Chichester at least twice-hourly from London Victoria Station, with a travel time of around 1½ hours. Buses leave from London's Victoria Coach Station a handful of times per day and take between 3½ and 4 hours with a change at Gatwick Airport.

From Arundel, it's a 25-minute drive west along the A27 to Chichester. There's also a regular 85A bus service (35 minutes), as well as trains via Barnham (25 minutes).

ESSENTIALS

VISITOR INFORMATION Chichester Tourist Information Centre. ⊠ *The Novium, Tower St. ☎ 01243/775888 ⊕ www.visitchichester.org.*

The outdoor cloisters of Chichester Cathedral are just as pretty as its interiors.

👁 Sights

★ Chichester Cathedral

RELIGIOUS SITE | Standing on Roman foundations, 900-year-old Chichester Cathedral has a glass panel that reveals Roman mosaics uncovered during restorations. Other treasures include the wonderful Saxon limestone reliefs of the raising of Lazarus and Christ arriving in Bethany, both in the choir area. Among the outstanding contemporary artworks are a stained-glass window by Marc Chagall and a colorful tapestry by John Piper. Keep an eye out, too, for the memorial to Gustav Holst: the composer's ashes were interred here as he wished to be close to his favorite Tudor musician, Thomas Weelkes.

Entrance to the cathedral is free—as are the guided tours that begin every day except Sunday at 11:15 and 2:30—though donations are very welcome, particularly as the roof is in the midst of an €8 million restoration. You can also prebook tours that concentrate on subjects including the English Civil War and the cathedral's art collection; call or go online for details. After visiting the cathedral's interior, be sure to walk around its pretty cloisters, where you'll also find a lovely café and shop. ✉ Off West St. ☎ 01243/782595 ⊕ www.chichestercathedral.org.uk 🎫 Free; £5 suggested donation.

Fishbourne Roman Palace

MUSEUM | In 1960, workers digging a water-main ditch uncovered a Roman wall; so began nine years of archaeological excavation of this site, the remains of the largest, grandest Roman villa in Britain. Intricate mosaics (including Cupid riding a dolphin) and painted walls lavishly decorate what is left of many of the 100 rooms of the palace, built in AD 1st century, possibly for local chieftain Tiberius Claudius Togidubnus. You can explore the sophisticated bathing and heating systems, along with the only example of a Roman garden in northern Europe. An extension has added many modern attributes, including a video reconstruction of how the palace might have looked. The site is 1½ miles west of Chichester, a 30-minute walk. ✉ *Roman Way, Fishbourne* ☎ *01243/785859* ⊕ *www.sussexpast.co.uk/fishbourne* ☎ *£10* ⊙ *Closed weekdays Dec.–mid-Feb.*

Novium Museum

MUSEUM | Set over three floors, this fascinating museum tells the story of Chichester and the surrounding area over the last 500,000 years. It's built around the remains of a Roman Bathhouse, so an entire floor is given over to life in Roman Chichester (or Noviomagus Reginorum, as it was known then). Explore further, and you'll delve both back and forward in time, with exhibits ranging from Bronze Age remains to 17th-century memorials. There are also excellent, regularly changing exhibitions on local history. ✉ *Tower St.* ☎ *01243/775888* ⊕ *www.thenovium. org* ⊙ *Closed Sun.*

★ Pallant House Gallery

MUSEUM | This small but important collection of mostly modern British art includes work by Henry Moore and Graham Sutherland. It's in a modern extension to Pallant House, a mansion built for a wealthy wine merchant in 1712 and considered one of the finest surviving examples of Chichcester's Georgian past. At that time, its state-of-the-art design showed the latest in complicated brickwork and superb wood carving. Appropriate antiques and porcelains furnish the faithfully restored rooms. Temporary and special exhibitions (usually around three at once) invariably find new and interesting angles to cover. ✉ *9 N. Pallant* ☎ *01243/774557* ⊕ *www.pallant.org. uk* ☎ *Ground-floor galleries free; rest of museum £12.50 (£6.50 Tues. and Thurs. evening)* ⊙ *Closed Mon.*

Petworth House and Park

HOUSE | One of the National Trust's greatest treasures, Petworth is the imposing 17th-century home of Lord and Lady Egremont and holds an outstanding collection of English paintings by Gainsborough, Reynolds, and Van Dyck. There are

also 19 oil paintings by J. M. W. Turner, the great proponent of romanticism who often visited Petworth and immortalized it in luminous drawings.

A 13th-century chapel is all that remains of the original manor house. The celebrated landscape architect Capability Brown (1716–83) added a 700-acre deer park; today, it has the largest herd of fallow deer in England. Other highlights include Greek and Roman sculpture and Grinling Gibbons wood carvings, such as those in the spectacular Carved Room. Six rooms in the servants' quarters, among them the old kitchen, are also open to the public.

You can reach Petworth off the A285/A283; the house is 14 miles northeast of Chichester. ✉ *A283, Petworth* ☎ *01798/343929* ⊕ *www.nationaltrust. org.uk/petworth* ☎ *£10.90; parking £4.*

Weald and Downland Open Air Museum

MUSEUM | FAMILY | On the outskirts of Singleton, a secluded village five miles north of Chichester, is this sanctuary for historical buildings dating from the 13th through 19th century. Among the 45 structures moved to 50 acres of pretty wooded meadows are a cluster of medieval houses, a working water mill, a Tudor market hall, and a Victorian schoolhouse. Look carefully, and you might recognize some of the structures from the hit Amazon/BBC TV show *Good Omens*. The buildings are brought to life with regular tours, talks, and demonstrations. ✉ *Town La., Off A286, Singleton* ☎ *01243/811363* ⊕ *www.wealddown.co.uk* ☎ *£14.*

🍽 Restaurants

Purchases

$$ | BRITISH | This excellent bistro is popular with locals for a special-occasion dinner and with the pre-theater crowd, who enjoy the fixed-price early-bird menus. The food strikes a nice balance between hearty, traditional fare and contemporary stylings. **Known for:** bargain pre-theater menus; traditional cooking

with a contemporary edge; tasty beef Wellington with spinach and tarragon sauce. $ *Average main: £23* ✉ *31 North St.* ☎ *01243/771444* ⊕ *www.purchases-restaurant.co.uk.*

🛏 Hotels

Chichester Harbour Hotel

$$ | HOTEL | This handsome 18th-century house, known for its flying (partially freestanding) staircase and colonnade, was once the residence of Admiral George Murray, one of Admiral Nelson's right-hand men. **Pros:** beautifully restored building; stylish design; great city center location. **Cons:** street-facing rooms can be noisy; prices are a little high; gets booked up during Glorious Goodwood horse racing season. $ *Rooms from: £160* ✉ *North St.* ☎ *01243/778000* ⊕ *www.har-bourhotels.co.uk/chichester* ↝ *37 rooms* ⏍ *Free breakfast.*

★ Nightingale Cottage

$$ | B&B/INN | Located in Boxgrove, a village just northeast of Chichester, this charming B&B offers space, comfort, and personalized service within a gorgeous, 17th-century thatched cottage. **Pros:** attractive 400-year-old property; spacious suites with armchairs and desks; location opposite a lovely ruined priory. **Cons:** limited space means it's often full; low ceilings can be a hazard; a little way out of town. $ *Rooms from: £125* ✉ *The St.* ☎ *01243/926389* ⊕ *www.nightingalecottagebedandbreak-fast.com* ↝ *2 suites* ⏍ *Free breakfast.*

🎭 Performing Arts

Chichester Festival Theatre

THEATER | The modernist, hexagonal Chichester Festival Theatre presents classics and modern plays from May through September and is a venue for touring companies the rest of the year. Built in 1962, it has an international reputation for innovative performances and attracts theatergoers from across the country. ✉ *Oaklands Park, Off A286* ☎ *01243/781312* ⊕ *www.cft.org.uk.*

Guildford

37 miles northeast of Chichester, 32 miles southwest of London.

Guildford, the largest town in Surrey and the county's capital, has a lovely historic center with charming original storefronts. Gabled merchants' houses line the steep, pleasantly provincial High Street, where the remains of a Norman castle are tucked away in a peaceful garden, and the iconic clock on the old guildhall dates from 1683. The area around the train station is rather seedy and crowded, but once you make your way to the center it's a much nicer town. Guildford is a good place to base yourself if you're planning to visit nearby attractions such as the Royal Horticultural Society gardens in Wisley or the ruins of Waverley Abbey.

GETTING HERE AND AROUND

From London, take the A3 south and then exit onto the A31, following signs for Guildford. The 28-mile journey takes about an hour in traffic. Southwest trains run to Guildford several times an hour from London's Waterloo Station; the trip takes between 30 minutes and 1¼ hours. If you're coming from Chichester, drive up the A3 to Guildford (one hour), or hop on one of the regular trains (1¼ hours, changing in Havant).

Guildford Station is extremely busy and surrounded by traffic, but fortunately the center is a five-minute walk; just follow the signs for High Street. National Express buses travel from London to Guildford every couple of hours; the trip takes an hour.

ESSENTIALS

VISITOR INFORMATION Guildford Tourist Information Centre. ✉ *155 High St.* ☎ *01483/444333* ⊕ *www.visitguildford.com.*

Sights

Guildford Castle

CASTLE/PALACE | Constructed shortly after the Norman invasion of England in 1066, the sturdy keep of Guildford Castle still stands watch over the city center, surrounded by beautiful and colorful gardens (look out for the statue of Alice Through the Looking Glass, in honor of local resident Lewis Carroll). Step inside the keep to learn more about its fascinating history, to see a model of the castle as it appeared circa 1300, and to enjoy stunning views of the gardens and the city from the rooftop terrace. Nearby, the castle's old gatehouse houses part of Guildford Museum, with exhibits on local history and archaeology, as well as memorabilia of Lewis Carroll. ⊠ *Castle St.* ☎ *01483/444751* ⊕ *www.guildford.gov. uk/castle* 💷 *£3.50; gardens free* ⊙ *Closed Nov.–Feb. and weekdays Mar.–Oct.*

Guildford Cathedral

RELIGIOUS SITE | On a hilltop across the River Wey, this is only the second Anglican cathedral to be built on a new site since the Reformation in the 1500s. It was consecrated in 1961, and the industrial-looking redbrick exterior is rather dauntingly severe, even brutal (so much so that it was even chosen as a key location for the 1976 horror movie *The Omen*). In contrast, the interior, with its stone and plaster, looks bright and cool.

Once inside, see if you can spot the brass stag on the floor, which marks the highest point of the hill. You'll also see some of the 1,468 "kneelers" which were individually designed for the cathedral with patterns appropriate to the time; look out for cushions dedicated to everything from Sputnik to the 1960 Olympics.

The cathedral has a lively program of events, including music recitals and art exhibitions, and is also used as a performance venue by the local Shakespeare society on certain dates in the summer. Call or check the website for details. ⊠ *Stag Hill* ☎ *01483/547860* ⊕ *www. guildford-cathedral.org* 💷 *Free.*

Polesden Lacey

HOUSE | This gorgeous, creamy-yellow Regency mansion, built in 1824, contains impressive collections of furniture, paintings, porcelain, and silver gathered in the early part of the 20th century. Edwardian society hostess Mrs. Ronald Greville was responsible for the lavish interiors, and the future King George VI stayed here for part of his honeymoon in 1923. On summer days you can wander its vast landscaped gardens or rent croquet equipment from the house and take advantage of its smooth lawns. The house is in Great Bookham, 10 miles east of Guildford. ⊠ *Off A246, Polesden Rd., Great Bookham* ☎ *01372/452048* ⊕ *www.nationaltrust.org.uk/polesden-lacey* 💷 *£13.60.*

★ RHS Garden Wisley

GARDEN | Wisley is the Royal Horticultural Society's innovative and inspirational 240-acre showpiece, beloved by horticulturalists across this garden-loving country. Both an ornamental and scientific center, it claims to have greater horticultural diversity than any other garden in the world. Highlights include the flower borders and displays in the central area, the rock garden and alpine meadow in spring, and the large and modern conservatories. There's also an impressive bookstore and a garden center that sells more than 10,000 types of plants. The garden is eight miles northeast of Guildford. ⊠ *Off A3, Woking* ☎ *01483/224234* ⊕ *www.rhs.org.uk/gardens/wisley* 💷 *£13.45.*

The Sculpture Park

PUBLIC ART | **FAMILY** | Set in a forested park 12 miles southwest of Guildford, this is a wild, fanciful place where giant steel spiders climb trees, bronze horses charge up hillsides, and metal girls and boys dance on lakes. You follow signposted paths across the parkland, spotting tiny sculptures up trees, in bushes, and walking through the legs of other more gigantic creations. You can also follow the footpath beside the little car park outside up to the **Devil's Jumps,** a ruggedly beautiful spot with views over the South Downs. The name derives from a piece of local folklore: one night the devil stole a cauldron from a witch who lived near Waverley Abbey. She gave chase on her broomstick, so with each leap the devil kicked up huge clods of earth, which in turn became hills—hence "jumps." ⊠ *Jumps Rd., Churt* ☎ *01428/605453* ⊕ *www.thesculpturepark.com* ⊠ *£10.*

★ Watts Gallery and Memorial Chapel

MUSEUM | An extraordinary small museum, the Watts Gallery was built in tiny Compton in 1904 by the late-19th-century artist George Frederic Watts (1817–1904) to display his work. His romantic, mystical paintings have been somewhat rediscovered in recent years, not least by Barack Obama, who counts Watts's 1886 painting *Hope* as one of his favorite works of art.

A marvellously higgeldy-piggeldy studio displays his sculptures, which are astonishing both for their size and the near-obsessive attention to detail. However, for all his skill and popularity, he has critics who contend that his artistic talent was eclipsed by that of his wife. Follow the signposted walk to the Watts Memorial Chapel, less than half a mile from the museum, and you may become one of them.

Mary Watts (1849–1938), virtually unknown as an artist both then and now, designed this tiny chapel, a masterpiece of art nouveau style, from the intricately carved redbrick exterior to the jaw-dropping painted interior. You could easily spend half an hour trying to decode all the symbolism and allegory woven meticulously into the gilded walls. The museum and chapel are three miles south of Guildford. ⊠ *Down La., Compton* ☎ *01483/810235* ⊕ *www.wattsgallery. uk* ⊠ *Museum £11.50; chapel free.*

Waverley Abbey

RELIGIOUS SITE | One of the oldest Cistercian abbeys in England, this was an important center of monastic power from 1128 until Henry VIII's dissolution of the monastries. What remains is a strikingly picturesque ruin surrounded by open countryside. Roofed sections of the undercroft and monks' dormitory survive, as does the refectory tunnel and a magnificent yew tree in the former churchyard, thought to be around 700 years old. A more unexpected historical footnote sits on the banks of the abbey stream: moss-covered tank traps, overlooked from across a field by a pillbox (sniper station). They were placed here during World War II after British generals role-played a Nazi invasion and decided this was the route they'd choose to attack London. Unused plans later found in Berlin showed they were precisely right. The abbey is off the B3001, 11 miles southwest of Guildford. ⊠ *Waverley La., Farnham* ☎ *0370/333–1181* ⊕ *www. english-heritage.org.uk/visit/places/ waverley-abbey* ⊠ *Free.*

🍴 Restaurants

The Mill

$ | BRITISH | A short hop down the road from Waverley Abbey and nine miles south of Guildford, this unusually handsome pub is in an old watermill, which is still working—you can see it in the lobby. The menu nicely balances British pub classics and more contemporary tastes; expect to find some excellent fish-and-chips alongside chicken breast with truffle mashed potatoes or a delicious plate of linguine with chili and basil. **Known for:** fresh and tasty pies; good gastro-pub fare; lovely beer garden. $ *Average main: £14* ⊠ *Farnham Rd.* ☎ *01252/703333* ⊕ *www. millelstead.co.uk.*

Hiking in the Southeast

For those who prefer to travel on their own two feet, the Southeast offers long sweeps of open terrain that make walking a pleasure. Ardent walkers can explore all or part of the popular **North Downs Way** (153 miles) and the **South Downs Way** (106 miles), following ancient paths along the tops of the downs—the undulating treeless uplands typical of the area. Both trails are now part of the **South Downs National Park** (⊕ www.south-downs.gov.uk), but each maintains its separate identity. Both are very popular with hikers (particularly on weekends).

Trails on the Downs

The North Downs Way starts outside Guildford, in the town of Farnham, alongside the A31. You can park at the train station, about ½ mile away. The path starts with absolutely no fanfare, on a traffic-choked bypass, but soon improves. It passes several scenic spots, including the White Cliffs of Dover, along the way and follows part of the old Pilgrim's Way to Canterbury that so fascinated Chaucer.

The South Downs Way starts in Winchester, at Water Lane, and ends on the promenade in the seaside town of Eastbourne. Along the way it crosses the chalk landscape of Sussex Downs, with parts of the route going through deep woodland. Charming little villages serve the walkers cool ale in inns that have been doing precisely that for centuries.

The 30-mile **Downs Link** joins the two routes. Along the Kent coast, the **Saxon Shore Way**, stretching 143 miles from Gravesend to Rye, passes four Roman forts.

Resources

Guides to these walks are available from the excellent website for **National Trails** (⊕ www.nationaltrail. co.uk). Tourist information offices throughout the region also have good information.

Rumwong

$ | **THAI** | Considered by locals to be one of the best Thai restaurants in the region, Rumwong has an incredibly long menu, with dozens of choices from all over Thailand. Tasty dishes include the *poh-taek*, a "seafarer's soup" made with lemongrass, lime leaves, and shellfish, and *kai pud krapraw*, a spicy stir-fry made with ground chicken, fresh chilies, and basil. **Known for:** one of region's best Thai restaurants; spicy stir-fries; delicious Thai curries. ⑤ *Average main: £10* ⊠ *18–20 London Rd.* ☎ *01483/536092* ⊕ *www. rumwong.co.uk* ▭ *No credit cards* ⊙ *Closed Mon.*

★ **Theion**

$$ | **GREEK** | This excellent Greek restaurant is set within a gorgeous space in the city center, with brick walls and high ceilings. The à la carte menu features delicious Mediterranean dishes including fried zucchini balls with fresh Greek yogurt, black pork casserole with roasted potatoes, and oven-baked sea bream stuffed with seasonal greens, while the lunchtime set menu offers excellent value (two courses for £12.95). **Known for:** delicious modern Greek cuisine; atmospheric dining room; extensive wine list. ⑤ *Average main: £16* ⊠ *Chapel St.* ☎ *01483/579786* ⊕ *www.theion.co.uk.*

🛏 Hotels

The Angel Hotel (*Angel Posting House*)
$ | HOTEL | Guildford was once famous for its coaching inns, and this handsome, 500-year-old hotel is the last to survive. **Pros:** historic building; central location; unique and quirky character. **Cons:** some rooms get very hot in summer; in need of some renovation; location can be noisy. ⑤ *Rooms from: £115 ✉ 91 High St. ☎ 01483/564555 ⊕ www.angelposting-house.com ⌷ 22 rooms ⦿ No meals.*

Guildford Harbour Hotel
$$ | HOTEL | Part of a small boutique chain, the Harbour Hotel is one of the more contemporary offerings in this part of Surrey, with its modern and well-designed rooms attracting mostly business travelers although the spa also brings in plenty of travelers who want a pampering getaway. **Pros:** efficient and modern design; centrally located; good spa and fitness center. **Cons:** lacks character; mostly business oriented; unromantic urban surroundings. ⑤ *Rooms from: £130 ✉ 3 Alexandra Terr. ☎ 01483/792300 ⊕ www.guildford-harbour-hotel.co.uk ⌷ 183 rooms ⦿ Breakfast.*

🎭 Performing Arts

Yvonne Arnaud Theatre
THEATER | This horseshoe-shape theater on an island in the River Wey frequently previews West End productions. The smaller Mill Studio showcases more intimate productions. ✉ *Off Millbrook ☎ 01483/440000 ⊕ www.yvonne-arnaud. co.uk.*

Chapter 6

STONEHENGE AND THE SOUTH

Updated by
Ellin Stein

👁 Sights   🍴 Restaurants   🛏 Hotels   🛍 Shopping   🍸 Nightlife

★★★★★   ★★★☆☆   ★★★★☆   ★★★☆☆   ★★☆☆☆

WELCOME TO STONEHENGE AND THE SOUTH

TOP REASONS TO GO

★ **Salisbury Cathedral:** Crowned with England's tallest church spire, this impressive cathedral offers spectacular views of the surrounding countryside from the roof and spire, accessible by daily tours.

★ **Stonehenge:** The power and mystery of this Neolithic stone circle on Salisbury Plain is still spellbinding.

★ **House and garden at Stourhead:** The cultivated English landscape at its finest, with an 18th-century Palladian stately home and beautiful gardens adorned with neoclassical temples.

★ **The New Forest:** Get away from it all in the South's most extensive woodland, crisscrossed by myriad trails ideal for horseback riding, hiking, and biking.

★ **Literary trails:** Jane Austen, Thomas Hardy, John Fowles, and Ian McEwan have made this area essential for book buffs, with a concentration of sights with literary associations in Chawton, Dorchester, Chesil Beach, and Lyme Regis.

The south of England's contrasting landscapes range from Salisbury Plain and the sheltered villages of coastal Hampshire and Dorset to the port cities of Southampton and Portsmouth and the woodlands of the New Forest. Culture-rich towns like Salisbury and Winchester are great places to spend the night. Salisbury puts you within easy reach of Stonehenge and the equally ancient stone circles at Avebury. The southern coast of Dorset has a couple of popular vacation resorts, Bournemouth and Weymouth, and historic sites like Corfe Castle. Lyme Regis is the gateway to the Jurassic Coast, a fossil-packed World Heritage Site.

1 Winchester. One of the region's most culturally and historically significant town.

2 Chawton. A genteel village once home to Jane Austen.

3 Portsmouth. A historically significant south-coast port town.

4 Southampton. Another major English port.

5 Isle of Wight. A charming island filled with

old-fashioned seaside resorts.

6 Salisbury. A great cathedral city often used as a home base for Stonehenge visits.

7 Stonehenge. One of the world's greatest and most enigmatic prehistoric monuments.

8 Avebury. A village home to the largest stone circles in the world.

9 Longleat House. A popular Elizabethan estate.

10 Stourhead. Wiltshire's most beautiful garden.

11 Lyndhurst. The hub of the rustic New Forest area.

12 Beaulieu. A classic English village.

13 Bournemouth. A coastal town with some of southern England's most pristine beaches.

14 Wimborne Minster. A small town with a famous church.

15 Corfe Castle. An atmospheric ruined castle.

16 Dorchester. The heart of Thomas Hardy country.

17 Cerne Abbas. A charming village with an interesting hill figure.

18 Sherborne. A market town with a beautiful abbey.

19 Weymouth. West Dorset's main coastal resort town.

20 Abbotsbury. A charming beachside village.

21 Lyme Regis. A seaside town on the Jurassic Coast.

With cathedrals, stately homes, stone circles, the South—consiting of the counties of Hampshire, Dorset, and Wiltshire—contains a variety of significant attractions, as well as several quieter pleasures. Two important cathedrals, Winchester and Salisbury (pronounced *sawls*-bree), are here, as are classic stately homes such as Longleat, Stourhead, and Wilton House, along with remarkable prehistoric sites like Avebury and Stonehenge.

And these are just the tourist-brochure highlights. Anyone spending time in the region should rent a bike or a car and set out to discover the back-road villages and larger market towns. Close to London, the green fields of Hampshire separate the cliffs and coves of the West Country from the sprawl of the suburbs. Even if you have a coastal destination in mind, slow down on your way there—there's plenty to see. Originally a Roman town, historic Winchester was made capital of the ancient kingdom of Wessex in the 9th century by Alfred the Great, a pioneer in establishing the rule of law and considered to be the first king of a united England. The city is dominated by its imposing cathedral; the final resting place of notables ranging from Saxon kings to the son of William the Conqueror to Jane Austen. It's a good base for visiting Austen's home village of Chawton, as well as other locations associated with several British literary greats such as Thomas Hardy.

North of Hampshire and the New Forest lies the somewhat harsher terrain of Salisbury Plain, part of it owned by the British army and used for training and weapons testing. Two monuments, millennia apart, dominate the plain. One is the 404-foot-tall stone spire of Salisbury Cathedral, the subject of one of John Constable's finest paintings. Not far away is the best-known prehistoric structure in Europe, the dramatic Stonehenge. The many theories about its construction and purpose only add to its otherworldly allure.

Other subregions have their own appeal, and many are of literary or historical interest. The Dorset countryside of grass-covered chalk hills known as the Dorset Downs—the wooded valleys, meandering rivers, and meadows immortalized in the novels of Thomas Hardy—is interspersed with unspoiled market towns and villages. Busy beach resorts such as Lyme Regis perch next to hidden coves on the fossil-rich

Jurassic Coast. Just off Hampshire is the Isle of Wight—Queen Victoria's favorite getaway—where colorful flags flutter from the many sailboats anchored at Cowes, home of the famous regatta.

The South has been quietly integral to England's history for well over 4,000 years, occupied successively by prehistoric people, the Celts, the Romans, the Saxons, the Normans, and the modern British. Though short on historic buildings due to wartime bombing, the port cities of Southampton and Portsmouth are rich in history itself. The *Mayflower* departed from the former, and the latter is home to the oldest dry dock in the world—Henry VIII's navy built its ships here. Portsmouth was also the departure point for Nelson to the Battle of Trafalgar, Allied forces to Normandy on D-Day, and British forces to the Falklands.

MAJOR REGIONS

Winchester, Portsmouth, and Southampton. From the cathedral city of Winchester, 70 miles southwest of London, you can meander southward to the coast, stopping at the bustling ports of Southampton and Portsmouth to explore their maritime heritage. From either port you can strike out for the restful shores of the Isle of Wight, vacation destination of Queen Victoria and thousands of modern-day Britons.

Isle of Wight. Osborne House, near Cowes, and Carisbrooke Castle, outside Newport, provide historic interest, while beach lovers and sailors head for the charming east-coast resorts of Ryde and Ventnor or the island's iconic Needles landmark on the western tip.

Salisbury, Stonehenge, and Salisbury Plain. Filled with sites of cultural and historical interest, this area includes the handsome city of Salisbury, renowned for its spectacular cathedral, and the iconic prehistoric stone circles at Stonehenge and Avebury. A trio of nearby

stately homes displays the ambitions and wealth of their original aristocratic inhabitants—Wilton House with its Inigo Jones–designed staterooms, Stourhead and its exquisite neoclassical gardens, and the Elizabethan splendor of Longleat. Your own transportation is essential to get to anything beyond Salisbury other than Stonehenge or Avebury.

New Forest, Dorset, and the South Coast. The New Forest, a woodland southwest of Southampton, was once a hunting preserve of William the Conqueror, so he could pursue his favorite sport close to the royal seat at Winchester. Thus protected from the worst of the deforestation that has befallen most of southern England's other forests, this relatively undeveloped, scenic national park has great possibilities for walking, riding, and biking. West of here stretches the largely unspoiled county of Dorset, which encompasses the beaches, coves, rolling hills, and lush fields that were the setting for most of Thomas Hardy's books, including *Far from the Madding Crowd*, and other classic Victorian-era novels. "I am convinced that it is better for a writer to know a little bit of the world remarkably well than to know a great part of the world remarkably little," Hardy wrote, and the bit he chose to know was the towns, villages, and countryside of this rural area, not least the county capital, Dorchester, an ancient agricultural center. North of here is the picturesque market town of Sherborne, with its impressive abbey. Other places of historic interest, such as Maiden Castle and the Cerne Abbas giant, are close to the bustling seaside resorts of Bournemouth and Weymouth. You may find Lyme Regis (associated with 20th-century novelist John Fowles) and the villages along the route closer to your ideal of coastal England. Fossil enthusiasts should head for the Jurassic Coast.

Planning

When to Go

In summer, the coastal resorts of Bournemouth and Weymouth are crowded; it may be difficult to find the accommodations you want. The Isle of Wight gets its fair share of summer visitors, too, especially during the weeklong Cowes Regatta in late July or early August. Because ferries fill up to capacity, you may have to wait for the next one. The New Forest is most alluring in spring and early summer (for the foaling season) and fall (for the colorful foliage), whereas summer can be busy with walkers and campers. In all seasons, take waterproof boots for the mud and puddles. Major attractions such as Stonehenge and Longleat House attract plenty of people at all times; bypass such sights on weekends, public holidays, or school vacations. Don't plan to visit the cathedrals of Salisbury and Winchester on a Sunday, when your visit will be restricted, or during services, when it won't be appreciated by worshippers.

FESTIVALS
Salisbury International Arts Festival
FESTIVALS | Held from late May through early June, the festival has outstanding classical recitals, plays, author talks, international cinema, dance, comedy, and family events. ⊠ *87 Crane St., Salisbury* ☎ *01722/332241* ⊕ *www.wiltshirecreative.co.uk.*

Planning Your Time

The South has no obvious hub, though many people base themselves in one or both of the cathedral cities of Winchester and Salisbury and make excursions to nearby destinations. The coastal cities of Portsmouth and Southampton have their charms, but neither of these large urban centers is particularly attractive as an overnight stop. Busy Bournemouth, whose major sight is a Victorian-era museum, has quieter areas that are more conducive to relaxation. To escape the bustle, the New Forest, southwest of Southampton, has space and semi-wilderness. It's easy to take a morning or afternoon break to enjoy the available activities, whether on foot, bike, or horseback. The Isle of Wight needs more time and is worth exploring at leisure over at least a couple of days.

Getting Here and Around

BUS
National Express buses at London's Victoria Coach Station on Buckingham Palace Road depart every 60–90 minutes for Bournemouth (2¾ hours), Southampton (2½ hours), and Portsmouth (2¼ hours), and every two hours for Winchester (2 hours). There are three buses daily to Salisbury (about 3 hours). Bluestar operates a comprehensive service in the Southampton and Winchester areas, as well as buses to the New Forest. Stagecoach South operates services in Portsmouth and around Hampshire. Salisbury Reds serves Salisbury; More travels to Bournemouth and Poole; First Bus serves Portsmouth, Southampton, and Dorset locations such as Weymouth and Dorchester; and Southern Vectis covers the Isle of Wight. More, Bluestar, Salisbury Reds, and Southern Vectis sell one-day (and two-day, five-day, and 15-day from Southern Vectis) passes as well as seven-, 30-, and 90-day passes for all routes. Ask about the Megarider tickets sold by Stagecoach South. Contact Traveline for all information on routes and tickets.

CONTACTS **Bluestar.** ☎ *01202/338421* ⊕ *www.bluestarbus.co.uk.* **First Bus.** ☎ *0345/646–0707* ⊕ *www.firstgroup.com.* **More.** ☎ *01202/338420* ⊕ *www.morebus.co.uk.* **National Express.** ☎ *0871/781–8181* ⊕ *www.nationalexpress.com.* **Salisbury Reds.**

🖷 01202/338420 ⊕ www.salisburyreds.
co.uk. **Southern Vectis.** 🖷 0330/053–9182
⊕ www.islandbuses.info. **Stagecoach
South.** 🖷 0345/121–0190 ⊕ www.stage-
coachbus.com. **Traveline.** 🖷 0871/200–
2233 ⊕ www.traveline.info.

CAR

On the whole, the region is easily
negotiable using public transportation.
But for rural spots, especially the grand
country estates, a car is useful. The
well-developed road network includes
M3 to Winchester (70 miles from
London) and Southampton (77 miles);
A3 to Portsmouth (77 miles); and M27
along the coast, from the New Forest
and Southampton to Portsmouth. For
Salisbury, take M3 to A303, then A30.
A35 connects Bournemouth to Dorchester and Lyme Regis, and A350 runs north
to Dorset's inland destinations.

TRAIN

South Western Railway serves the South
from London's Waterloo Station. Travel
times average 1 hour to Winchester,
1½ hours to Southampton, 2 hours to
Bournemouth, and 2¾ hours to Weymouth. The trip to Salisbury takes 1½
hours and that to Portsmouth about 1¾
hours. A yearlong Network Railcard, valid
throughout the South and Southeast,
entitles you and up to three accompanying adults to one-third off most train fares
and up to four accompanying children
ages 5–15 to a 60% discount off each
child fare. It costs £30. Weekend First
tickets, available on weekends and public
holidays, let you upgrade to first class
from £5–£25, depending on the train
operator.

CONTACTS National Rail Enquiries.
🖷 0845/748–4950 ⊕ www.nation-
alrail.co.uk. **South Western Railway.**
🖷 0345/600–0650 ⊕ www.southwest-
trains.co.uk.

Restaurants

In summer, and especially on summer
weekends, visitors can overrun the restaurants in small villages, so either book
a table in advance or prepare to wait. The
more popular or upscale the restaurant,
the more critical a reservation is. For local
specialties, try fresh-grilled river trout or
sea bass poached in brine, or dine like a
king on New Forest's renowned venison.
Hampshire is noted for its pig and sheep
farming, and you might zero in on pork and
lamb dishes on local restaurant menus.
The region places a strong emphasis on
seasonal produce, so venison, for example,
is best between September and February.

Hotels

Modern hotel chains are well represented,
and in rural areas you can choose between
elegant country-house hotels, traditional coaching inns (updated to different
degrees), and modest guesthouses. Some
seaside hotels don't accept one-night bookings in summer. If you plan to visit Cowes
on the Isle of Wight during Cowes Week,
the annual yachting jamboree in late July or
early August, book well in advance.

*Restaurant and hotel reviews have been
shortened. For full information, visit Fodors.
com. Restaurant prices are the average
cost of a main course at dinner, or if dinner
is not served, at lunch. Hotel prices are the
lowest cost of a standard double room in
high season, including 20% V.A.T.*

WHAT IT COSTS in Pounds			
$	$$	$$$	$$$$
RESTAURANTS			
under £16	£16–£23	£24–£30	over £30
HOTELS			
under £125	£125–£225	£226–£350	over £350

6

Stonehenge and the South **PLANNING**

Tours

British Guild of Tourist Guides
This organization maintains a directory of qualified Blue Badge guides who can meet you anywhere in the region for private tours. Tours are tailored to your particular interests or needs and generally start around £290 per full day, £180 per half day. ☎ 020/7403–1115 ⊕ www.britainsbestguides.org.

Visitor Information

CONTACTS Tourism South East.
☎ 023/8062–5400 ⊕ www.tourismsouth-east.com. **Visit South West .** ☎ 0203/117–0664 ⊕ www.swtourismalliance.org.uk.

Winchester

70 miles southwest of London, 12 miles northeast of Southampton.

Winchester is among the most historic of English cities, and as you walk the graceful streets and wander the many public gardens, a sense of the past envelops you. Although it's now merely the county seat of Hampshire, for more than four centuries Winchester served first as the capital of the ancient kingdom of Wessex and then of England. The first king of England, Egbert, was crowned here in AD 827, and the court of his successor Alfred the Great was based here until Alfred's death in 899. After the Norman Conquest in 1066, William I ("the Conqueror") had himself crowned in London, but took the precaution of repeating the ceremony in Winchester. William also commissioned the local monastery to produce the Domesday Book, a land survey begun in 1085. The city remained the center of ecclesiastical, commercial, and political power until the 13th century, when that power shifted to London. Despite its deep roots in the past, Winchester is also a thriving market town living firmly in the present, with numerous shops and restaurants on High Street.

GETTING HERE AND AROUND
On a main train line and on the M3 motorway, Winchester is easily accessible from London. The train station is a short walk from the sights; the bus station is in the center, opposite the tourist office. The one-way streets are notoriously confusing, so find a parking lot as soon as possible. The city center is very walkable, and most of the High Street is closed to vehicular traffic. A walk down High Street and Broadway brings you to St. Giles Hill, which has a panoramic view of the city.

TIMING
The city is busier than usual during the farmers' market, the largest in the country, held on the second and last Sunday of each month.

TOURS
Winchester Tourist Guides
A 90-minute "City Highlights" walking tour (which takes in central Winchester) departs from the tourist information center Monday through Saturday (weekdays at 2 pm and Saturday at 11 am and 2 pm) from mid-November to mid-December. The "Discover Upper Winchester" tour adds the cathedral and the Great Hall and leaves at 11 am Monday through Saturday in January through mid-November and Sunday at 11:30 am from May through September. The "Discover Lower Winchester" tour, which includes the city center, Jane Austen's House, and Winchester College, leaves at 2 pm Monday through Saturday January through mid-November and at 2 pm on Sunday from May through September. ☎ 01962/840500 ⊕ www.winchestertour-istguides.com ⌘ From £5.

ESSENTIALS
VISITOR INFORMATION Winchester Tourist Information Centre. ⊠ Winchester Guildhall, High St. ☎ 01962/840500 ⊕ www.visitwinchester.co.uk.

Sights

City Mill

FACTORY | Set over the River Itchen at the east end of the High Street, this rare surviving example of an 18th-century urban water mill, complete with small island garden, is probably the oldest working water mill in Britain, with timbers dating back to the 11th century. The medieval corn mill on the site was rebuilt in 1744 and remained in use until the early 20th century. Restored by the National Trust in 2004, it still operates as a working mill on weekends, and you can purchase stone-ground flour produced here in the gift shop. ⊠ *Bridge St.* ☎ *01962/870057* ⊕ *www.nationaltrust.org.uk* ⊠ *£5.85.*

City Museum

MUSEUM | **FAMILY** | This museum reflects Winchester's history, from the Iron Age to the present. One gallery covers the 1,000 years of the Anglo-Saxon and Medieval eras (guided tours at 10:30 am and noon), which includes displays of pottery, jewelry, and coins from the former and agricultural tools from the latter. Other collections feature two of Jane Austen's purses and a detailed scale model of the city in Victorian times. It's an imaginative, well-presented collection that appeals to children and adults alike. The hands-on activities include a history detective quiz and costumes for kids of every time period starting with the Romans. On the top floor are some well-restored Roman mosaics. Pick up an audio guide at the entrance (£2) to get the most out of the museum. ⊠ *The Square, next to cathedral* ☎ *01962/863064* ⊕ *www.hampshirecul-turaltrust.org.uk/winchester-city-museum* ⊠ *Free (suggested donation £3).*

★ The Great Hall

HISTORIC SITE | A short walk west of the cathedral, this outstanding example of early English Gothic architecture, and one of Britain's finest surviving 13th-century halls, is all that remains of the city's original Norman castle built by William the Conqueror (later razed by Oliver Cromwell). It's also the site of numerous historically significant events: the English Parliament is thought to have had one of its first meetings here in 1246, Sir Walter Raleigh was tried for conspiracy against King James I in 1603, and Dame Alice Lisle was sentenced to death by the brutal Judge Jeffreys for sheltering fugitives after Monmouth's Rebellion in 1685. Hanging on the west wall is the hall's greatest artifact, a huge oak table, which, legend has it, was King Arthur's original Round Table. In fact, it was probably created around 1290 at the beginning of the reign of Edward I for a tournament. It is not clear when the green and white stripes that divide the table into 24 places, each with the name of a knight of the mythical Round Table, were added, but it is certain that the Tudor Rose in the center surmounted by a portrait of King Arthur was commissioned by Henry VIII. Take time to wander through the garden—a re-creation of a medieval shady retreat, named for two queens: Eleanor of Provence and Eleanor of Castile. ⊠ *Castle Ave.* ☎ *01962/846476* ⊕ *www.hants.gov.uk/greathall* ⊠ *£3* ⚲ *May be closed for events—check website.*

Gurkha Museum

MUSEUM | This unique museum tells the story of the British Army's Gurkha brigade, whose Nepalese soldiers have fought alongside the British since the early 19th century in virtually every deployment, through tableaux, dioramas, uniforms, weapons, artifacts, and interactive touch-screen displays. A program of lectures includes a curry lunch (£35). ⊠ *Peninsula Barracks, Romsey Rd.* ☎ *01962/842832* ⊕ *www.thegurkhamu-seum.co.uk* ⊠ *£3* ⊙ *Closed Sun.*

★ Highclere Castle

CASTLE/PALACE | Set in 1,000 acres of parkland designed by Capability Brown, this is the historic home of the actual earls of Carnarvon—as opposed to the imaginary earls of Grantham that are portrayed

The historic city of Winchester, with its graceful cathedral, is well worth exploring.

living within it in the television drama *Downton Abbey*. Victorian Gothic rather than actual Gothic, this huge country house was designed by Sir Charles Barry, architect of the similar Houses of Parliament. Commissioned by the third earl in 1838 to transform a simpler Georgian mansion, Barry used golden Bath stone to create this fantasy castle bristling with turrets. Like its fictional counterpart, it served as a hospital during World War I. Highlights of the State Rooms include Van Dyke's equestrian portrait of Charles I in the Dining Room and the imposing library (Lord Grantham's retreat). There's also an exhibit of Egyptian antiquities collected by the fifth earl, known for his pivotal role in the 1920s excavation of ancient Egyptian tombs, notably Tutankhamun's. Find pleasant views of the house and countryside by walking the gardens and grounds. From January through Easter, the estate is only open for guided tours of the house, exhibition, grounds, and garden at a pricey £120; tickets are either for morning tours (10 am–1 pm) or afternoon (1 pm–4 pm).

Two lodges on the estate are available for two-night stays on limited dates from February through December. The house is 25 miles north of Winchester and 5 miles south of Newbury. There's train service from London and Winchester to Newbury, and taxis can take you the 5 miles to Highclere. ✉ *Highclere Castle, Highclere Park, Newbury* ✛ *Off A34* ☎ *01635/253204* ⊕ *www.highclerecastle.co.uk* ✉ *£24 castle, exhibition, and gardens; £17 castle or exhibition plus gardens; £7 gardens only* ☉ *Closed June.*

King's Gate

HISTORIC SITE | One of two surviving gateways in the city's original ancient walls, this structure to the south of the Close is thought to have been built in the 12th century as a remodeling of a Roman gate on the site. The tiny 13th-century church of St. Swithun-upon-Kingsgate, a rare surviving example of a "gateway church" (built into the walls of medieval cities), is on the upper floor. Nearby, 8 College Street is the house where Jane Austen died on July 18, 1817, three days after writing a comic poem about the legend of St. Swithun's Day (copies are usually available in the cathedral). ⊠ *St. Swithun St.*

Watercress Line
SCENIC DRIVE | FAMILY | This 10-mile-long scenic railroad line named for the area's watercress beds is reserved for steam locomotives and takes in both the highest station in southern England and several locomotive restoration workshops. It starts at Alresford (8 miles northeast of Winchester by A31 and B3046), where you'll find some antiques shops and Georgian houses, and runs to Alton. ⊠ *The Railway Station, Station Rd., New Alresford* ☎ *01962/733810* ⊕ *www.watercressline.co.uk* ⊠ *£16* ⊗ *Closed Jan. and Nov., Mon. in June and Sept., Fri. in May and Sept., and other select dates; check website for timetables.*

Westgate Museum
MUSEUM | FAMILY | This atmospheric museum atop the last of the city's fortified medieval gateways was a debtor's prison for 150 years and now holds a motley assortment of items relating to Tudor and Stuart times. There's a stunning painted ceiling from 1554 and walls inscribed with 16th- through 18th-century graffiti by former prisoners. Child-size replicas of authentic 16th-century armor that can be tried on, as well as the opportunity to make brass rubbings, make it popular with kids. You can take in a view of Winchester from the roof. ⊠ *High St.* ☎ *01962/869864* ⊕ *www.winchester.gov.uk* ⊠ *Free* ⊗ *Closed weekdays.*

★ Winchester Cathedral
RELIGIOUS SITE | The imposing Norman exterior of the city's greatest monument, begun in 1079 and consecrated in 1093, makes the Gothic lightness within even more breathtaking. It's one of the largest cathedrals in Europe, and throughout it you will find outstanding examples of every major architectural style from the 11th to 16th century: the transepts and crypt are 11th-century Romanesque; the great nave, the longest in Europe,

is 14th- and 15th-century Perpendicular Gothic; and the presbytery (behind the choir, holding the high altar) is 14th-century Decorated Gothic. Other notable features include the richly carved 14th-century choir stalls, the ornate 15th-century stone screen behind the high altar, and the largest surviving spread of 13th-century floor tiles in England. Little of the original stained glass has survived, except in the large window over the entrance. When Cromwell's troops ransacked the cathedral in the 17th century, locals hid away bits of stained glass they found on the ground so that it could later be replaced. Free tours are run year-round. The Library's Winchester Bible, one of the finest remaining 12th-century illuminated manuscripts, is on display in an exhibition space in the South Transept. The patron saint of the cathedral is St. Swithun (died AD 862), an Anglo-Saxon bishop who is also buried here. He had requested an outdoor burial plot, but his body was transferred to the newly restored church in 971, accompanied by, legend has it, 40 days of rain. Since then, folklore says that rain on St. Swithun's Day (July 15) means 40 more days of wet weather.

Among the other well-known people buried here are William the Conqueror's son, William II ("Rufus"), mysteriously murdered in the New Forest in 1100, and Jane Austen, whose grave lies in the north aisle of the nave. The tombstone makes no mention of Austen's literary status, though a brass plaque in the wall, dating from 80 years after her death, celebrates her achievements, and modern panels provide an overview of her life and work. You can also explore the tower—with far-reaching views in fair weather—and other recesses of the building on a tour. Special services or ceremonies may mean the cathedral, the crypt, and the Treasury are closed to visits, so call ahead. Outside the cathedral, explore the Close, the area to the south of the cathedral with neat lawns, the Deanery, Dome Alley, and Cheyney Court. ⊠ *The Close,*

Cathedral Precincts ☎ 01962/857200 ⊕ www.winchester-cathedral.org.uk ⌨ Cathedral £9.50; tower tour £7.50.

Winchester College

COLLEGE | This prestigious "public" (meaning private) school—Britain's oldest in continuous operation, with several buildings still in use after six centuries—was founded in 1382 by Bishop William of Wykeham, whose alabaster tomb sits in a chapel dedicated to him in Winchester Cathedral. The wooden ceiling of the school's own 14th-century chapel is notable for its delicate fan vaulting. The boys wearing monk-style cassocks are "scholars"—students holding academic scholarships. Tours are sometimes canceled due to college events, so call ahead. ✉ College St. ☎ 01962/621209 ⊕ www. winchestercollege.org/guided-tours ⌨ £8 ☞ Admission by guided tour only.

🍴 Restaurants

The Black Rat

$$$$ | MODERN BRITISH | This former pub retains relatively reasonable prices despite being Winchester's only Michelin-starred restaurant. The Black Rat specializes in hearty Modern British dishes that use locally sourced, seasonal ingredients, several from the restaurant's own kitchen garden. **Known for:** imaginative flavor combinations; four huts for outdoor dining; extensive wine list. ⑤ Average main: £45 ✉ 88 Chesil St. ☎ 01962/844465 ⊕ www. theblackrat.co.uk.

Cathedral Refectory

$ | BRITISH | With a vaulted glass roof on steel supports, this self-service cafeteria across from the cathedral combines contemporary style with locally sourced, freshly prepared dishes to create a refreshing stop for lunch or afternoon tea. Food is served daily until 4:30 or 5, and there are tables outside for fair-weather eating. **Known for:** locally sourced ingredients; homemade cakes; walled garden for picnics. ⑤ Average main: £10 ✉ 1 The

Close ☎ 01962/857258 ⊕ www.winchester-cathedral.org.uk ☾ No dinner.

Chesil Rectory

$$ | MODERN BRITISH | The timbered and gabled building may be venerable—it dates back to the mid-15th century—but the cuisine is Modern British, using locally sourced ingredients. The small but well-executed menu is particularly strong on game dishes, like pressed duck with golden raisins, a Sauternes gel, and brioche or vegetarian options like a King Oyster mushroom with miso butter, puffed black rice, and a confit egg yolk. **Known for:** historic, romantic ambience; fresh takes on British classics like the roast beef traditional Sunday lunch; good-value set-price lunches. ⑤ Average main: £20 ✉ 1 Chesil St. ☎ 01962/851555 ⊕ www.chesilrectory.co.uk.

Forte Kitchen

$ | CAFÉ | This unfussy but elegant café-restaurant serving breakfast, lunch, and afternoon tea offers freshly made soups, sandwiches, hot dishes, and cakes made with locally sourced ingredients. Favorites include beer-battered cod loin, fried mushrooms on sourdough toast with creamed spinach and a poached egg, and a confit duck Scotch egg with red cabbage ketchup. **Known for:** excellent breakfasts; fast, friendly service; no reservations so waits are possible. ⑤ Average main: £12 ✉ 78 Parchment St. ☎ 01962/856840 ⊕ www. fortekitchen.co.uk ☾ No dinner.

Green's Bar and Kitchen

$ | BRITISH | Reasonably priced comfort food is served cafeteria-style at this established, family-run favorite, including dishes like a meat pie of the day, jerk chicken wrap, and vegan cassoulet. Serving breakfast (including a great full English) and lunch, the place transforms into a busy cocktail bar in the evening. **Known for:** home-cooked comfort food; outdoor seating in good weather; great cocktails. ⑤ Average main: £11 ✉ 4 Jewry St. ☎ 01962/869630.

★ Rick Stein, Winchester

$$$ | SEAFOOD | Renowned as Britain's finest seafood chef, Rick Stein chose Winchester for his first venture away from the Cornish coast. The menu is largely focused on fish and crustaceans, but carnivores and vegetarians are catered to as well. **Known for:** simply but confidently prepared classics like turbot hollandaise; exotic choices like spicy Indonesian curry with prawn and squid; good-value set menus for lunch and early evening dinner. $ *Average main: £27* ⊠ *7 High St.* ☎ *01962/353535* ⊕ *www.rickstein.com.*

Hotels

★ Lainston House

$$$ | HOTEL | The 63 acres surrounding this elegant 17th-century country house retain many original features, including the walls of the kitchen garden (still in use), the apple trees in the former orchard, and a mile-long avenue of linden trees, the longest in Europe. **Pros:** beautiful setting; period detail in guest and public rooms; excellent bar and restaurant. **Cons:** lower-priced modern rooms small; noise from functions can bleed into some rooms; restaurant service can be erratic. $ *Rooms from: £230* ⊠ *Woodman La., off B3049, Sparsholt* ☎ *01962/776088* ⊕ *www.exclusive.co.uk/lainston-house* ⤴ *50 rooms* ¹⊚¹ *No meals.*

Old Vine

$$ | B&B/INN | Ideally located opposite the cathedral, this 18th-century inn, now a gastro-pub with rooms, has received a smart, modern makeover without losing any of its character. **Pros:** comfortable, stylish rooms; delicious food; attentive service. **Cons:** rooms over bar may be noisy on weekends; soundproofing between rooms could be better; some rooms on the dark side. $ *Rooms from: £155* ⊠ *8 Great Minster St.* ☎ *01962/854616* ⊕ *www.oldvinewinchester.com* ⤴ *6 rooms* ¹⊚¹ *Free breakfast.*

Wykeham Arms

$$ | B&B/INN | A watering hole since 1755, this pub with rooms near the cathedral and the college wears its Britishness proudly, with photos of national heroes like Nelson and Churchill, military artifacts, and an assortment of pewter mugs hanging from the ceiling. **Pros:** quirky charm; lively bar; central location. **Cons:** rooms above bar can be noisy; not for those looking for luxury; housekeeping erratic. $ *Rooms from: £149* ⊠ *75 Kingsgate St.* ☎ *01962/853834* ⊕ *wykehamarmswinchester.co.uk* ⤴ *14 rooms* ¹⊚¹ *Free breakfast* ⌕ *No children under 14.*

🛍 Shopping

Kingsgate Books and Prints

ART GALLERIES | Located under the medieval Kingsgate Arch, this atmospheric shop is filled with drawings, prints, and engravings (many by local artists); rare antique county maps; and secondhand books. ⊠ *1 Kingsgate St.* ☎ *01962/864710* ⊕ *www.kingsgatebooksandprints.co.uk.*

P&G Wells

BOOKS/STATIONERY | The oldest bookshop in the country (in business for more than 250 years), P&G Wells has numerous books by and about Jane Austen, who had an account here and, in 1817, died almost next door. It also has the region's largest selection of children's books. ⊠ *11 College St.* ☎ *01962/852016* ⊕ *bookwells.co.uk.*

Chawton

16 miles northeast of Winchester.

In Chawton you can visit the home of Jane Austen (1775–1817), who lived the last eight years of her life in the village, moving to Winchester only during her final illness. The site has always drawn literary pilgrims, but with the ongoing release of successful films based on her novels, the town's popularity among visitors has grown enormously.

GETTING HERE AND AROUND

Hourly Stagecoach Bus 64 service connects Winchester and Alresford with Chawton. It's a 10-minute walk from the bus stop to Jane Austen's House. By car, take A31. Alternatively, take a 40-minute stroll along the footpath from Alton.

◉ Sights

★ Chawton House Library

LIBRARY | Located in an Elizabethan country house on a 275-acre estate (part of the South Downs National Park), this library specializes in works by English women writers from 1600 to 1830, including authors such as Mary Shelley, Mary Wollstonecraft, and Frances Burney. It also houses the Knight Collection, the private library of the family who owned the house for over 400 years. Jane Austen's brother, Edward, eventually inherited the property and added the walled kitchen garden, shrubberies, and parkland. You can see the dining room table where Austen joined her family for meals and the library collection that contains a manuscript written in her own hand. ✉ Chawton ☎ 01420/541010 ⊕ www.chawtonhouse.org ✉ Library and gardens £10; gardens only £6; gardens free Jan.–mid-Feb. ⊙ House closed Jan., Feb., and some Sat. in June and July (check website).

★ Jane Austen's House Museum

HOUSE | This unassuming redbrick house is where Jane Austen spent the last eight years of her life, writing Emma, Persuasion, and Mansfield Park, and revising Sense and Sensibility, Northanger Abbey, and Pride and Prejudice. Now a museum, the house retains a modest but genteel atmosphere suitable for the home of a clergyman's widow and her unmarried daughters. The drawing room contains a piano similar to the one Jane would play every morning before retiring to a small writing table in the family dining parlor—leaving her sister, Cassandra, to do the household chores ("I find composition

impossible with my head full of joints of mutton and doses of rhubarb," Jane wrote). In the early 19th century, the road near the house was a bustling thoroughfare, and although Jane was famous for working through interruptions, she retained one protection against the outside world—the famous creaking door, its hinges deliberately unoiled to better warn her when someone was entering her workspace. ■TIP→ The museum is often closed for special events, so call ahead. ✉ Winchester Rd., signed off A31/A32 roundabout ☎ 01420/83262 ⊕ www.jane-austens-house-museum.org.uk ✉ £9 ⊙ Closed Jan.

Open-Air Markets 🛍

Among the best markets in the area is the Winchester Farmers' Market held in Winchester's Cathedral Close on the second and last Sunday (and some Saturdays) of each month. The largest in the United Kingdom with some 95 stalls, it specializes in local produce. Also worth a look are Salisbury's traditional Charter Market (Tuesday and Saturday), Southampton's Bargate Market for artisanal foods and local produce (Friday), and Dorchester's large produce and flea market (Wednesday) and flea market (Sunday).

🛏 Hotels

Four Seasons Hotel Hampshire

$$$$ | HOTEL | FAMILY | Although deep in the peaceful British countryside, this country-house hotel on a 500-acre estate is only a half hour from Heathrow. **Pros:** peaceful location; great spa; plenty of activities. **Cons:** pricey; pool dominated by children at some times; inconsistent dining service.

In Search of Jane Austen 👁

Jane Austen country—verdant countryside interspersed with relatively unspoiled villages—still bears traces of the decorous early-19th-century life she described with wry wit in novels such as *Emma, Persuasion, Sense and Sensibility*, and *Pride and Prejudice*. Serious Janeites will want to retrace her life in Bath, Chawton, Winchester, and Lyme Regis.

Bath

Bath provided the elegant backdrop for the society Austen observed with such razor sharpness. Austen lived in Bath between 1801 and 1806, and although she wrote relatively little during this time, it provided the setting for *Northanger Abbey* and *Persuasion*. The Jane Austen Centre in Bath explores her relationship to the city.

Chawton

About 83 miles southeast of Bath is the heart of Jane Austen country, where you'll find the tiny Hampshire village of Chawton. Here you will find the

tastefully understated house, a former bailiff's cottage on her brother's estate, where Austen worked on three of her novels. It's now a museum that sensitively evokes her life there.

Winchester

Driving southwest from Chawton, take the A31 for about 15 miles to Winchester, where you can visit Austen's austere grave within the cathedral and view an exhibit about her life. Then see the commemorative plaque on No. 8 College Street, where Addison's disease ended her life on July 18, 1817.

Lyme Regis

Lyme Regis, 110 miles southwest of Winchester, is the 18th-century seaside resort on the Devon border where Austen spent the summers of 1804 and 1805. It's home to the Cobb, the stone jetty that juts into Lyme Bay, where poor Louisa Musgrove jumps off the steps known as Granny's Teeth—a turning point in *Persuasion*.

$ *Rooms from: £450* ⊠ *Dogmersfield Park, Chalky La., Hook* ☎ *01252/853000* ⊕ *www.fourseasons.com/hampshire* ⤴ *133 rooms* ⑩ *No meals.*

★ **Heckfield Place**

$$$$ | HOTEL | Because this property reflects the owner's precise vision and attention to detail, a stay here is like a stay at a friend's home, if your friend has an exquisitely tasteful but comfortable, eco-friendly Georgian house on a 400-acre estate an hour from London. **Pros:** understatedly luxurious decor; imaginative menus using ingredients from property; dedicated eco-friendly ethos. **Cons:** ubiquitous "relaxing" music in public rooms may not be for everyone; some rooms don't have phone reception; complicated

AV system. $ *Rooms from: £500* ⊠ *Heckfield Place, Hook* ☎ *0118/932–6868* ⊕ *www.heckfieldplace.com* ⤴ *44 rooms, 1 cottage* ⑩ *Free breakfast.*

Portsmouth

24 miles south of Chawton, 77 miles southwest of London.

In addition to a historic harbor and revitalized waterfront, Portsmouth has the energy of a working port. At Gunwharf Quays is the soaring Spinnaker Tower, as well as shops, restaurants, bars, and a contemporary art gallery. The main attractions for many visitors are the HMS *Victory,* the well-preserved flagship from which Nelson won the Battle of Trafalgar, on view at the Portsmouth Historic Dockyard; the extraordinary record of seafaring history at the National Museum of the Royal Navy; and the D-Day Museum (Operation Overlord embarked from Portsmouth). For others, Portsmouth is primarily of interest for the ferries that set off from here to the Isle of Wight and more distant destinations.

GETTING HERE AND AROUND
The M27 motorway from Southampton and the A3 from London take you to Portsmouth. There are also frequent buses and trains that drop you off at the Hard, the main transport terminus. It's only a few steps from the Historic Dockyard and Gunwharf Quays. Regular passenger ferries cross Portsmouth Harbour from the Hard for Gosport's Royal Navy Submarine Museum. Attractions in the nearby town of Southsea are best reached by car or by buses departing from the Hard.

ESSENTIALS
VISITOR INFORMATION Portsmouth Visitor Information Centre. ⊠ *Portsmouth Museum, Museum Rd.* ☎ *023/9282–6722* ⊕ *www.visitportsmouth.co.uk.*

◉ Sights

The D-Day Story
MUSEUM | FAMILY | Here three galleries tell the absorbing story of the planning and preparation for the invasion of Europe during WWII and the actual landings on D-Day—June 6, 1944—through an eclectic range of exhibits including maps, uniforms, and even actual landing craft, as well as filmed testimonies from those who were there. The museum's centerpiece is the Overlord Embroidery ("Overlord" was the invasion's code name), a 272-foot-long embroidered cloth with 34 panels illustrating the history of the operation, from the Battle of Britain in 1940 to victory in Normandy in 1944. ⊠ *Clarence Esplanade* ☎ *023/9288–2555* ⊕ *www.theddaystory.com* 🎟 *£10.*

Explosion! The Museum of Naval Firepower
MILITARY SITE | FAMILY | This museum located in a Georgian building used by the Royal Navy to store weapons and ammunition since 1771 explores the history of warfare at sea with interactive touch-screen exhibits on naval armaments, from cannonballs to mines, missiles, torpedoes, and even a decommissioned nuclear bomb. Reached by water bus from the Historic Dockyard, the museum also tells the story of the local people who manufactured the weapons. ⊠ *Priddy's Hard, Gosport* ☎ *023/9250–5600* ⊕ *www.explosion.org.uk* 🎟 *£18* ⊘ *Closed weekdays Nov.–Mar.*

★ The Mary Rose
MUSEUM | FAMILY | An on-site museum houses the *Mary Rose,* the former flagship of Henry VIII's navy and the world's only 16th-century warship on display. Built in this same dockyard more than 500 years ago, the ship sank in the harbor in 1545 and remained there until raised in 1982. In an accompanying exhibition, you can see artifacts retrieved from the seabed ranging from the ship's large guns to personal possessions like surgeon's tools, tankards, bowls, combs, and games. ⊠ *Main Rd.* ☎ *023/9281–2931* ⊕ *www.maryrose.org* 🎟 *£18 (£14.40 online), includes admission to the Portsmouth Historic Dockyard.*

Millennium Promenade
PROMENADE | Starting at the Spur Redoubt (supposedly the point from which Nelson set sail for Trafalgar) near Clarence Pier in Southsea, the Millennium Promenade follows the waterfront through Old Portsmouth and Gunwharf Quays, ending up at the Hard near the Historic Dockyard. The 4-mile self-guided walk, marked by a rope pattern on the sidewalk, passes a variety of fortifications built in the 13th

Winchester, Portsmouth, Southampton, and the Isle of Wight

century, the early 20th century, and everything in between. ⊠ *Spur Redoubt, Long Curtain Rd.* ☎ *023/9282–6722* ⊕ *www.visitportsmouth.co.uk.*

Portchester Castle

ARCHAEOLOGICAL SITE | With a commanding position over the harbor, this medieval castle is surrounded by what is believed to be the most complete set of Roman walls in northern Europe, a Roman "Saxon Shore" fort dating back to the 3rd century. On its completion in the mid-12th century, the castle was appropriated by Henry II and remained a royal residence until the 17th century. From the keep's central tower you can take in sweeping views of the harbor and coastline. ⊠ *Church Rd., Portchester* ⊹ *Off A27 near Fareham* ☎ *02392/378291* ⊕ *www.english-heritage.org.uk* ⊠ *£7.20* ⊗ *Closed weekdays Nov.–Mar.*

★ Portsmouth Historic Dockyard

HISTORIC SITE | **FAMILY** | The city's most impressive attraction includes an unrivaled collection of historic ships, including the HMS *Warrior* (1860), Britain's first iron-clad battleship and perhaps the Royal Navy's best-known warship. It served as the flagship of Vice-Admiral Lord Nelson, Britain's most celebrated naval hero at the Battle of Trafalgar (1805) and is still the ceremonial flagship of Britain's First Sea Lord. You can inspect the cramped gun decks, visit the cabin where Nelson met his officers, and stand on the spot where he was mortally wounded by a French sniper. There's also an interactive gallery that explores the ship's history and audio guides to take along your visit.

The **National Museum of the Royal Navy** has extensive exhibits about Nelson and the Battle of Trafalgar, a fine collection of painted figureheads, and galleries of paintings and mementos recalling naval history from King Alfred to the present. **Action Stations,** an interactive attraction, gives insight into life in the modern Royal Navy and tests your sea legs with tasks such as piloting boats through gales. **Boathouse 4** explores the role of smaller wooden boats in the Navy's history and challenges the adventurous to a "Mast and Rigging" experience. You should allow one or two days to tour all the attractions in the Historic Dockyard. The entrance fee includes a boat ride around the harbor, and the all-attractions ticket is valid for one year. ⊠ *Victory Gate, HM Naval Base* ☎ *023/9283–9766* ⊕ *www. historicdockyard.co.uk* ✉ *£18 for one attraction; £27 for any two attractions; £36 for any three attractions; Full Navy Ticket £39 (includes HMS Warrior, HMS Victory, Horrible Histories Pirates, Action Stations, National Museum of the Royal Navy, HMS M.33, Harbour Tours, Waterbus, Boathouse 4, Dockyard Apprentice, Royal Navy Submarine Museum, and Explosion Museum).*

Royal Navy Submarine Museum

MILITARY SITE | FAMILY | Here you can learn about submarine history and the rigors of life below the waves with the help of family-friendly interactive games. The highlight is a tour of the only surviving World War II submarines in the United Kingdom, the HMS *Alliance* and the midget-class HMS *X24*, from the cramped living quarters to the engine rooms. Also on the large site is the first Royal Navy sub, *Holland 1*, built in 1901, and a *Biber*, a German WWII midget submarine. From Portsmouth Harbour, take the ferry to Gosport and walk along Millennium Promenade past the huge sundial clock. From April to October, an hourly free water bus runs from the Historic Dockyard. ⊠ *Haslar Jetty Rd., Gosport* ☎ *023/9251–0354*

⊕ *www.submarine-museum.co.uk* ✉ *£18* ⊙ *Closed Nov.–Mar., Mon., and Tues. except bank holidays.*

Spinnaker Tower

VIEWPOINT | The focal point of the lively Gunwharf Quays development of shops and bars, the Spinnaker Tower is a striking addition to Portsmouth's skyline. The slender structure evokes a mast with a billowing sail, and rises to a height of 558 feet. An elevator whisks you to three viewing platforms 330 feet high for thrilling all-around views of the harbor and up to 23 miles beyond. ⊠ *Gunwharf Quays* ☎ *023/9285–7520* ⊕ *www.spinnakertower.co.uk* ✉ *£11.50; £43 with Portsmouth Historic Dockyard all-attraction ticket; £34.90 with PHD two-attraction ticket; £26.55 with Mary Rose Museum ticket.*

🍴 Restaurants

Abarbistro

$$ | MODERN BRITISH | A relaxed, modern bistro midway between Old Portsmouth and Gunwharf Quays, this place is ideal for a snack, meal, or glass of wine from the thoughtfully chosen wine list. The changing Modern British menu specializes in seafood dishes like seared scallops with butternut squash puree or beer-battered fish-and-chips, mostly sourced from Portsmouth's fish market directly opposite. **Known for:** super fresh seafood; friendly service; extensive wine list. ⑤ *Average main: £16* ⊠ *58 White Hart Rd.* ☎ *023/9281–1585* ⊕ *www.abarbistro. co.uk* ⊟ *No credit cards.*

Restaurant 27

$$$$ | FRENCH FUSION | Owned by chef Kevin Bingham (who lives upstairs) and his family, this 35-seat global French restaurant serving set-price tasting menus for the whole table only is very much a personal vision, with Bingham's sophisticated, technically assured take on French classics (expect gels, foams, "soil," and smears) winning rave reviews. The four set-menus (one at £49 and one at £59,

You can tour Admiral Nelson's famous flagship, the HMS *Victory*, at Portsmouth's Historic Dockyard.

plus vegetarian versions of each) change daily according to what fresh ingredients are available, but dishes might include duck with apple and sage, a starter of whipped goat cheese with pumpkin and pistachio, or Devon crab spaetzle at Sunday lunch. **Known for:** excellent distinctive dishes; extensive wine list; set-price tasting menus. ⑤ *Average main: £55* ⊠ *27a South Parade, Southsea* ☎ *023/9287–6272* ⊕ *www.restaurant27.com* ⊘ *Closed Mon. and Tues. No dinner Sun.*

🛏 Hotels

Fortitude Cottage

$ | B&B/INN | With sleek modern bedrooms, this friendly B&B provides top-class waterside accommodation in two buildings in the center of Old Portsmouth, within walking distance of the Historic Dockyard via the Millennium Promenade just across the street. **Pros:** central but quiet location; helpful, friendly owners; great view from penthouse suite. **Cons:** a good amount of stairs; not

all rooms have great views; some rooms on small side. ⑤ *Rooms from: £99* ⊠ *51 Broad St.* ☎ *023/9282–3748* �よ *6 rooms* ⦿I *Free breakfast.*

🏃 Activities

Queen Elizabeth Country Park

PARK—SPORTS-OUTDOORS | FAMILY | Designated an Area of Outstanding Natural Beauty, this park has more than 2,000 acres of woodland and rolling hills, including 20 miles of scenic trails for hikers, cyclists, and horse riders. You can climb to the top of 888-foot-tall Butser Hill to take in a panoramic view of the coast. Part of the South Downs National Park, it lies 15 miles north of Portsmouth and 4 miles south of the Georgian market town of Petersfield. A visitor center has a theater, café, and shop. ⊠ *Gravel Hill, Horndean* ✛ *Park has its own signed sliproads off the A3* ☎ *023/9259–5040* ⊕ *www.hants.gov.uk/thingstodo/countryparks/qecp* ⧄ *Free.*

Southampton

17 miles northwest of Portsmouth, 24 miles southeast of Salisbury, 77 miles southwest of London.

Southampton is England's leading passenger port. It is rich in historic embarkations, from Henry V's fleet bound for France and the battle of Agincourt to the *Mayflower*, the ill-fated *Titanic*, and the maiden voyages of the great ocean liners of the 20th century such as the *Queen Mary* and the *Queen Elizabeth*. Parts of the town center can seem mundane, having been hastily rebuilt after World War II bombing, but bits of the city's history emerge from between modern buildings. The Old Town retains its medieval feel, and some remnants of the old castellated town walls remain. Other attractions include a decent art gallery, extensive parks, and a couple of good museums. The Southampton Boat Show, a 10-day event in mid-September, draws huge crowds.

GETTING HERE AND AROUND

Located on the M3 motorway from London and Winchester, and on the M27 from Portsmouth, Southampton is also easily accessed by bus or train from these cities. The bus and train stations are a few minutes' walk from the tourist office, and the main sights can be reached by foot.

◉ Sights

Broadlands

HOUSE | This 60-room Palladian mansion located on 5,000 acres near the town of Romsey was the home of 19th-century British Prime Minister Lord Palmerston and later of Earl Mountbatten of Burma (1900–79), uncle of Prince Philip (who spent his honeymoon here with the Queen) and mentor to Prince Charles. As the last viceroy of India, Mountbatten was in charge of that country's transition to independence before being killed by the IRA. One of the grandest houses in Hampshire, Broadlands dates back to the 18th century and holds a large collection of antiques, Greek and Roman marbles, and Old Master paintings, including three Van Dycks. Landscape designer Capability Brown laid out the grounds, which include wide lawns sweeping down to the banks of the River Test. The only way to see the house is through a one-hour guided tour (cash-only). ⊠ *Broadlands Park, Romsey* ✚ *Off A3090 Romsey Bypass* ☎ *01794/505058* ⊕ *www.broadlandsestates.co.uk* ⊠ *£10* ⊗ *Closed Jan.–early Apr.*

God's House Tower

BUILDING | Incorporated in the medieval town walls are a number of buildings, including this late-13th-century gatehouse, which was expanded at the start of the 100 Years' War in the early 14th century to incorporate a two-story gallery and three-story tower. It subsequently became a gunpowder factory, the town jail, and an archeology museum. After extensive restoration, the gallery space is now used for art installations, while a "Stories Behind the Stones" multimedia installation in the tower tells the story of the building itself. Don't miss the far-reaching views over the city from the roof. ⊠ *Town Quay Rd.* ☎ *07733/092291* ⊕ *www.godshousetower.org.uk* ⊠ *£5* ⊗ *Closed Mon.*

Mayflower Park and the Pilgrim Fathers' Memorial

MEMORIAL | This memorial was built to commemorate the departure of the 102 passengers who, on August 15, 1620, left for North America on the *Mayflower* from the city. A plaque also honors the 2 million U.S. troops who embarked from Southampton for occupied Europe during World War II. ⊠ *Town Quay, Western Esplanade.*

SeaCity Museum

MUSEUM | This museum tells the story of the city's residents—from the earliest settlers through the Romans and Saxons to the present —via artifacts from maritime, local history, archaeology, and archive collections as well as through audiovisual installations. Ships, including the great clippers, feature prominently, especially in the main exhibition, which is devoted to the impact on the city of the sinking of the *Titanic,*which departed from here in 1912. An interactive model of the ill-fated ship and a wealth of footage and photos provide insight into the lives of the crew, many of whom were recruited locally. ✉ *Civic Centre, Havelock Rd.* ☎ *023/8083–4536* ⊕ *www.seacitymuseum.co.uk* 🎫 *£8.50.*

🍴 Restaurants

Oxford Brasserie

$$ | ECLECTIC | This airy modern brasserie on a restaurant-heavy street close to the docks is known for its melt-in-your-mouth meat dishes but also offers vegetarian options. The cosmopolitan menu draws on French, Modern British, and Italian influences. **Known for:** excellent meat-focused menu; good traditional roast Sunday lunches; nice vegetarian options. 💲 *Average main: £16* ✉ *33–34 Oxford St.* ☎ *023/8063–5043* ⊕ *www.theoxfordbrasserie.co.uk.*

🛏 Hotels

The Pig In The Wall

$$ | B&B/INN | On a quiet street across from Mayflower Park, this snug hotel in two converted town houses is set into the city's medieval walls and has a funky but chic aesthetic in guest rooms and public areas. **Pros:** stylish rooms; lovely common areas; limited but good menu. **Cons:** breakfast not included; very steep stairs to top-floor room; wood floors mean some overhead noise. 💲 *Rooms from: £170* ✉ *8 Western Esplanade* ☎ *0845/077–9494* ⊕ *www.thepighotel.com/in-the-wall* 🛏 *12 rooms* 🍴 *No meals.*

★ Southampton Harbour Hotel and Spa

$$ | HOTEL | Staying at this snazzy five-star hotel directly on the marina is like staying on a cruise ship (or perhaps a super-yacht) without ever leaving land, a design theme reinforced by tiered balconies and floor-to-ceiling windows. **Pros:** luxurious, comfortable rooms; terraces with views over the harbor; excellent spa and restaurant. **Cons:** expensive rates for the area; check-in process can be long at busy times; rooms under bar area can be noisy. 💲 *Rooms from: £225* ✉ *5 Maritime Walk, Ocean Village* ☎ *238/110–3456* ⊕ *www.harbourhotels.co.uk/southampton* 🛏 *119 rooms* 🍴 *Free breakfast.*

🎭 Performing Arts

Mayflower

THEATER | This is one of the larger theaters outside London. The Royal Shakespeare Company and Matthew Bourne's *Swan Lake* are among the productions that have attracted packed houses. ✉ *22-26 Commercial Rd.* ☎ *023/8071–1811* ⊕ *www.mayflower.org.uk.*

Nuffield Theatre

THEATER | Located on the Southampton University campus, the Nuffield hosts national touring companies and leading stand-up comedians, as well as productions by its own repertory company. ✉ *University Rd.* ☎ *023/8067–1771* ⊕ *www.nstheatres.co.uk.*

Isle of Wight

Drawn by the island's slightly old-fashioned and unspoiled feel, throngs of visitors flock to the 23-mile-long Isle of Wight (pronounced white) in summer. It became a fashionable holiday destination during the reign of Queen Victoria, who spent her own vacations and last days here at her favorite residence, Osborne House. The island attracted the cream of Victorian society, including Darwin, Thackeray, and Tennyson, with the latter living here until tourist harassment drove him away. Perhaps understandably, islanders have a love-hate relationship with the crowds of tourists who disembark from the ferries and hydrofoils that connect the island with Southampton, Portsmouth, Southsea, and Lymington. The attractions include its seaside resorts—Ryde, Bembridge, Ventnor, and Freshwater (stay away from rather tacky Sandown and Shanklin)—and its green interior landscape, narrow lanes, curving bays, sandy beaches, and walking paths. Although the revitalizing ocean air is, to quote Tennyson, "worth sixpence a pint," the island offers more than sailing and the sea. There are splendid scenic roads to explore in Brading Down, Ashley Down, Mersely Down, and along Military Road, as well as historic holiday getaways to visit, notably Osborne House itself.

GETTING HERE AND AROUND

Wightlink operates a car ferry between the mainland and the Isle of Wight. The crossing takes about 40 minutes from Lymington to Yarmouth and 45 minutes from Portsmouth to Fishbourne. The company also operates a catamaran service between Portsmouth and Ryde (22 minutes). Red Funnel runs a car ferry (one hour) between Southampton and East Cowes and a hydrofoil service (25 minutes) to West Cowes. Hovertravel runs a hovercraft shuttle between Southsea (Portsmouth) and Ryde (15 minutes). The island is covered by a good network of roads, and you can rely on a regular local bus service. Southern Vectis, the local bus company, operates hop-on, hop-off open-top tours. The Needles Breezer goes to Dimbola Lodge, the Needles, and Alum Bay between mid-March and early November, while the Downs Breezer, which goes to Sandown and Brading, runs from late May through August. You can board and disembark at different points for £10, and the fare includes unlimited access to all Southern Vectis services for 24 hours.

TIMING

Summer traffic slows things down considerably. Try to avoid Cowes Week in late July or early August, the Garlic Festival in mid-August, and the two major rock festivals that take place in mid-June and mid-September.

ESSENTIALS

FERRY INFORMATION Hovertravel.
☎ *01983/717717* ⊕ *www.hovertravel. co.uk.* **Red Funnel.** ☎ *02380/019912* ⊕ *www.redfunnel.co.uk.* **Wightlink.** ☎ *0333/999–7333* ⊕ *www.wightlink. co.uk.*

VISITOR INFORMATION Isle of Wight Tourism. ✉ *The Guildhall, High St.* ☎ *01983/521555* ⊕ *www.visitisleofwight. co.uk.*

Cowes

7 miles northwest of Ryde.

If you embark from Southampton, your ferry crosses the Solent channel and docks at Cowes, near Queen Victoria's Osborne House. Cowes is a magic name in the sailing world because of the internationally known Cowes Week yachting festival (⊕ *www.aamcowesweek.co.uk*), held each July or August. At the north end of the high street, on the Parade, a tablet commemorates the two ships that sailed from here in 1633 carrying the English settlers who founded what later became Maryland.

GETTING HERE AND AROUND

A car ferry and a hydrofoil shuttle passengers from Southampton. Southern Vectis runs numerous buses connecting Cowes with other destinations on the island.

◉ Sights

Carisbrooke Castle

CASTLE/PALACE | Built more than a thousand years ago, this Norman castle was remodeled extensively during the Middle Ages and surrounded by a mile of artillery fortifications in 1600 to defend against the threat of the Spanish Armada. During the English Civil War, Carisbrooke served as a prison for Royalists, most notably King Charles I, who tried (unsuccessfully) to escape through a still-visible tiny window in the north curtain wall. (The small museum has memorabilia relating to the imprisoned king.) The castle was restored during Victoria's reign and served as the residence of her daughter, Princess Beatrice, memorialized in a namesake Edwardian-style garden here. There are excellent views from the top of the Norman keep and battlements. Children love meeting the donkeys who still pull the wheel that draws water from the castle well. The castle is about a mile southwest of the Isle of Wight's capital, Newport. From Cowes, take Bus 1 or 5 (1 from West Cowes, near Holmwood Hotel; 5 from East Cowes, near Osborne House) to Newport, from where it's a 30-minute walk or a short ride on Bus 6, 7, 12, or 38 to The Mall in Carisbrooke, ¼ mile away. ⊠ *Castle Hill, Newport* ⊹ *Off B3401* ☎ *01983/522107* ⊕ *www.english-heritage.org.uk* ⌾ *£10.50* ⊗ *Closed weekdays Nov.–mid-Feb. and Mon. and Tues. late Feb.–Mar.*

★ Osborne House

HOUSE | This palazzo-style Italianate house, much of it designed by Prince Albert in collaboration with Thomas Cubitt, was the royal family's private retreat and Queen Victoria's favorite residence. The house reveals Albert's interest in engineering through clever innovations like an early form of central heating, as well as Victoria's determination to give her children a normal but disciplined upbringing. After Albert's death in 1861, the queen retreated to Osborne to mourn her loss in relative seclusion, and the antiques-filled rooms have scarcely been altered since she died here in 1901. The house and extensive grounds (also designed by Albert)—which can be quite crowded during July and August—were used as a location for the 2019 television series *Victoria.* During the summer, a minibus takes you to what used to be Victoria's private beach, now open to the public, where you can see her personal bathing machine. Another minibus goes to the Swiss Cottage, a replica Alpine chalet built as a playhouse for Victoria and Albert's nine children; there are also two playgrounds for young children on-site. ◼ TIP➔ **Book ahead for guided tours of the house and gardens.** Buses 4 (from Ryde) and 5 (from Cowes and Newport) stop outside. ⊠ *York Ave.* ⊹ *Off A3021* ☎ *01983/200022* ⊕ *www.english-heritage.org.uk* ⌾ *£18.50 house and grounds, Apr.–Oct.; £13 house (ground floor only) and grounds Nov.–Mar.* ⊗ *Closed weekdays Nov.–mid-Feb. and Mon. and Tues. mid-Feb.–Mar.; Swiss Cottage closed Nov.–Mar.*

▭ Hotels

Best Western New Holmwood Hotel

$$ | HOTEL | The rooms may be unremarkable and basic, but the staff is friendly, and the views are special from the hotel's unrivaled location above the western end of the Esplanade—ideal for watching yachts in the Solent. **Pros:** good sea views; friendly staff; within walking distance of passenger ferry. **Cons:** tired decor; rooms without views are dark; food service can be slow. ⑤ *Rooms from: £140* ⊠ *65 Queens Rd., Egypt Pt.* ☎ *01983/292508* ⊕ *www.newholmwoodhotel.co.uk* ⇱ *26 rooms* ⦿⦶ *Free breakfast.*

No. 1 and No. 2 Sovereign's Gate

$$$ | RENTAL | English Heritage has created two lovely cottages out of what was the ceremonial entrance to the Osborne estate (it's still the entrance the Royal Family uses when they visit the property). **Pros:** unusual location; out-of-hours access to Osborne House grounds; lots of privacy. **Cons:** limited booking options (three-, four-, or seven-night stays only); no staff services; pricey. ⑤ *Rooms from: £230* ⌧ *Royal Entrance, York Ave.* ☎ *0370/333–1187* ⊕ *www.english-heritage.org.uk* ⌔ *2 lodges* ⏀ *No meals.*

Ryde

7 miles southeast of Cowes.

The town of Ryde has long been one of the Isle of Wight's most popular summer resorts with several family attractions. After the construction of Ryde Pier in 1814, elegant town houses sprang up along the seafront and on the slopes behind, commanding fine views of the harbor. In addition to its long, sandy beach, Ryde has a large lake (you can rent rowboats and pedal boats) and playgrounds.

GETTING HERE AND AROUND

From Portsmouth, catamaran service takes about 22 minutes. If you're driving from Cowes, take the A3021 to the A3054.

🍴 Restaurants

Seaview Hotel Restaurant and Bar

$$$ | MODERN BRITISH | A strong maritime flavor defines this outstanding restaurant, the only Michelin Bib Gourmand on the island, located in the heart of a harbor village just outside Ryde. Much of the fresh produce is from the Seaview's own farm. **Known for:** fresh seafood with local ingredients; charming nautical theme; good value prix-fixe menus. ⑤ *Average main: £28* ⌧ *Seaview Hotel,*

The High St., Seaview ☎ *01983/612711* ⊕ *www.seaviewhotel.co.uk* ⊗ *No dinner Sun. in Nov.–Mar.*

🛏 Hotels

Lakeside Park Hotel & Spa

$$ | HOTEL | Halfway between Cowes and Ryde in the tiny town of Wootton Bridge, this waterfront hotel on a 20-acre tidal lake is perfectly located for exploring the northern part of the island. **Pros:** scenic location; pretty views; comfortable rooms. **Cons:** restaurant quality uneven; somewhat characterless; spa maintenance could be better. ⑤ *Rooms from: £200* ⌧ *High St., Wootton Bridge* ☎ *01983/882266* ⊕ *www.lakesideparkhotel.com* ⌔ *47 rooms* ⏀ *Free breakfast.*

Brading

3 miles south of Ryde on A3055.

The Anglo-Norman St. Mary's Church in Brading dates back to 1180. It contains the tombs of the Oglanders, a local family whose Norman ancestor is thought to have fought under William the Conqueror at the Battle of Hastings in 1066. You can still see the old lockup, dating from 1750, complete with stocks and whipping post at the Hall.

GETTING HERE AND AROUND

To get here from Ryde, take the Island Line trains or local bus services.

CONTACTS Island Line. ☎ *01983/812591* ⊕ *www.southwesternrailway.com.*

👁 Sights

Brading Roman Villa

BUILDING | Housed within a striking wooden-walled, glass-roofed building one mile south of Brading are the remains of this substantial 3rd-century Roman villa, with original walls, splendid mosaic floors, and a well-preserved heating system. The mosaics, depicting peacocks (symbolizing eternal life), gods, gladiators, sea beasts, and reclining nymphs, are a rare example of this type of floor preserved in situ in a domestic building. A dedicated space hosts related temporary exhibitions, and there's also a café on-site. ✉ *Morton Old Rd.* ✛ *Off A3055* ☎ *01983/406223* ⊕ *www.bradingroman-villa.org.uk* ✉ *£9.50.*

Ventnor

11 miles south of Ryde.

The south-coast resorts are the sunniest and most sheltered on the Isle of Wight. Handsome Ventnor rises from such a steep slope that the ground floors of some of its houses are level with the roofs of those across the road.

GETTING HERE AND AROUND

Local bus service connects Ventnor with the rest of the island.

 ## Sights

★ **Ventnor Botanic Garden**

GARDEN | Laid out over 22 acres, these gardens contain more than 3,500 species of trees, plants, and shrubs. Thanks to a unique microclimate, subtropical flora from the Mediterranean, Antipodes, and South Africa flourish outdoors. The impressive greenhouse includes banana trees and a waterfall; a visitor center, with a gift shop that sells plants and seeds, puts the gardens into context. Admission includes a guided tour. You can also stay overnight on the grounds, either in a three-bedroom cottage, in one of two wooden cabins, or in a teepee (July and August only). All include admission and after-hours access to the gardens. ✉ *Undercliff Dr.* ☎ *01983/855397* ⊕ *www.botanic.co.uk* ✉ *£9.50.*

Alum Bay and the Needles

19 miles northwest of Ventnor, 18 miles southwest of Cowes.

At the western tip of the Isle of Wight is the island's most famous natural landmark, the **Needles,** a long line of jagged chalk stacks jutting out of the sea like giant teeth, with a lighthouse at the end. It's part of the Needles Pleasure Park, which has mostly child-oriented attractions. Adjacent is **Alum Bay,** accessed from the Needles by chairlift. Here you can catch a good view of the "colored sand" in the cliff strata or take a boat to view the lighthouse. **Yarmouth,** a charming fishing village, is a 10-minute drive from Alum Bay.

GETTING HERE AND AROUND

Wightlink car and passenger ferries from Lymington dock at nearby Yarmouth. The spectacular A3055 runs along the south-west coast from Ventnor to Freshwater, the nearest town. From there you can follow the coast road to Alum Bay. Local bus services connect Freshwater with the rest of the island.

Sights

Alum Bay Glass

LOCAL INTEREST | **FAMILY** | In addition to being famous for sailing and its connections to Queen Victoria, the Isle of Wight is also renowned for its glassmaking. Local craftspeople have given live demonstrations of glassblowing here since 1972. The perfume bottles, vases, bowls, doorknobs, ornaments, and other items they create are available for sale in the showroom. ✉ *Alum Bay New Rd., Totland Bay, Alum Bay* ☎ *0871/720–0022* ⊕ *www.alumbayglass.co.uk.*

Dimbola

HOUSE | This was the home of Julia Margaret Cameron (1815–79), the eminent Victorian portrait photographer and friend of Lord Tennyson. A gallery includes more than 60 examples of her work, including striking images of Carlyle, Tennyson, and Browning. In addition, there's much here that will appeal to fans of decorative textiles and wall coverings. There's also a room devoted to the various Isle of Wight rock festivals, most famously the five-day event in 1970 that featured the Who, the Doors, Joni Mitchell, and Jimi Hendrix. On the ground floor is a shop and a good Alice in Wonderland–themed tearoom for snacks, hot lunches, and a traditional cream tea. ⊠ *Terrace La., Freshwater Bay* ⚓ *Off Gate La.* ☎ *01983/756814* ⊕ *www. dimbola.co.uk* ⧉ *£5.45* ⊙ *Closed mid-Dec.–Feb. and Mon. in Mar.*

Salisbury

24 miles northwest of Southampton, 44 miles southeast of Bristol, 79 miles southwest of London.

The silhouette of Salisbury Cathedral's majestic spire signals your approach to this historic city long before you arrive. Although the cathedral is the principal focus of interest here, and its Cathedral Close is one of the country's most atmospheric spots (especially on a foggy night), Salisbury has much more to see, not least its largely unspoiled—and relatively traffic-free—old center. Here are stone shops and houses that over the centuries grew up in the shadow of the great church. You're never far from any of the five rivers that meet here or from the bucolic water meadows that stretch out to the west of the cathedral and provide the best views of it. Salisbury didn't become important until the early 13th century, when the seat of the diocese was transferred here from Old Sarum, the original settlement 2 miles to the north, of which only ruins remain. In the 19th century, novelist Anthony Trollope based his tales of ecclesiastical life, notably *Barchester Towers*, on life here, although his fictional city of Barchester is really an amalgam of Salisbury and Winchester. The local tourist office organizes walks—of differing lengths for varying stamina—to guide you to the must-sees. And speaking of must-sees, prehistoric Stonehenge is less than 10 miles away and easily visited from the city.

GETTING HERE AND AROUND

Salisbury is on main bus and train routes from London and Southampton; regular buses also connect Salisbury with Winchester. The bus station is centrally located on Endless Street. Trains stop west of the center. After negotiating a ring-road system, drivers will want to park as soon as possible. The largest of the central parking lots is by Salisbury Playhouse. The city center is compact, so you won't need to use local buses for most sights. For Wilton House, take Bus Red 3 or Red 8 from Salisbury town center.

TIMING

Market Place hosts the Charter Market every Tuesday and Saturday and farmers' markets on the first and third Wednesday of the month (a farmers' market is also incorporated into the Charter Market). It's also the venue for other fairs and festivals, notably the one-day Food & Drink Festival in mid-September and the four-day Charter Fair in October. The city gets busy during the arts festival in May and June, when accommodations may be scarce.

TOURS

Salisbury City Guides

Blue Badge guides lead 90-minute city tours from the tourist information center at 11 every morning from April through October and on weekends the rest of the year. Tickets are £7. ☎ *07873/212941* ⊕ *www.salisburycityguides.co.uk.*

Stonehenge Tour

Hop-on, hop-off open-top buses leave once or twice an hour all year from the train station and the bus station, and the route includes Old Sarum and Salisbury Cathedral as well as Stonehenge. Tickets for a tour of all three attractions are £38; an Old Sarum and Stonehenge tour is £31.50; and bus only without a tour is £16. ☎ 01202/338420 ⊕ www.thestonehengetour.info.

ESSENTIALS

VISITOR INFORMATION Salisbury Information Centre. ✉ Fish Row, off Market Pl. ☎ 01722/342860 ⊕ www.visitwiltshire.co.uk/explore/salisbury.

 Sights

Cathedral Close

HISTORIC SITE | Eighty acres of rolling lawns and splendid period architecture provide one of Britain's finest settings for a cathedral. The Close, the largest in the country, contains three museums: historic Mompesson House, the Salisbury Museum, and the Rifles Museum devoted to the county's infantry regiments. ✉ The Close ⊹ Bounded by West Walk, North Walk, and Exeter St. ⊕ www.salisburycathedral.org.uk.

High Street Gate

BUILDING | One of four castellated gateways originally built between 1327 and 1342 using stones taken from the original settlement at Old Sarum, this is the north passage through the wall that surrounds the Cathedral Close. The mullioned windows over the archway mark the site of a small lock-up jail to which anyone who committed offences within the Close was taken. ✉ Salisbury.

Long Bridge

LOCAL INTEREST | For a classic view of Salisbury, head to Long Bridge and Town Path. From the main street, walk west to Mill Road, which leads you across the Queen Elizabeth Gardens. Cross the bridge and continue on Town Path

through the water meadows, from which you can see the vista that inspired John Constable's 1831 Salisbury Cathedral from the Meadows, one of Britain's most iconic paintings, now on view in London's Tate Britain. ✉ Salisbury.

Market Place

MARKET | The Charter Market, one of southern England's most popular markets, fills this square on Tuesday and Saturday. Permission to hold an annual fair here was granted in 1221, and that right is still exercised for three days every October, when the Charter Fair takes place. A narrow side street links Poultry Cross to Market Place. ✉ Salisbury.

Mompesson House

HOUSE | A perfect example of Queen Anne architecture, this family home, built in 1701, sits on the north side of Cathedral Close. It's notable for magnificent plasterwork, an exceptionally carved oak staircase, fine period furniture, and a superb collection of 18th-century drinking glasses. Tea and refreshments are served in a walled garden. ✉ The Close ☎ 01722/335569 ⊕ www.nationaltrust.org.uk ≥ £7.30 ⊙ Closed early–mid-Nov., Jan.–early Mar., and Mon. and Tues. in late Nov.–Dec.

Old Mill

LOCAL INTEREST | This 15th-century building with some 13th-century features became England's first paper mill in the early 16th century and is now a hotel and atmospheric pub. It makes a pleasant destination for a 20-minute walk along Town Path southwest of the town center. ✉ Town Path, West Harnham ⊕ oldmillhotelsalisbury.co.uk.

Old Sarum

ARCHAEOLOGICAL SITE | Massive earthwork ramparts on a bare sweep of Wiltshire countryside are all that remain of this impressive Iron Age hill fort, which was successively taken over by Romans, Saxons, and Normans (you can still see the ruins of a castle built by William the

Salisbury Cathedral has a towering spire—the tallest in England—that you can tour.

Conqueror in 1070 within the earth-works). The site was still fortified in Tudor times, though the population had mostly decamped in the 13th century to New Sarum, or Salisbury. Clamber over the huge banks to take in the far-reaching views to Salisbury Cathedral. ⊠ *Castle Rd.* ⊹ *Off A345* ☎ *01722/335398* ⊕ *www. english-heritage.org.uk* ⊡ *£5.40.*

Poultry Cross

LOCAL INTEREST | One of Salisbury's best-known landmarks, the hexagonal Poultry Cross is the last remaining of the four original medieval market crosses that gave shelter to market traders (other crosses indicated the dairy, wool, and livestock markets). A cross on the site was first mentioned in 1307, though the current structure dates from the late 15th century. The canopy and flying buttresses were added in 1852. ⊠ *Silver St.*

St. Thomas and St. Edmund Church

RELIGIOUS SITE | Dating back to 1229, this church contains a rare medieval "Doom painting" of Judgment Day that is considered to be one of the best preserved and most complete of the few such works left in Britain. Created around 1470 and covering the chancel arch, the scenes of heaven and hell served to instill the fear of damnation into the congregation. ■**TIP→ It's best seen on a spring or summer evening when the light through the west window illuminates the details.** ⊠ *St. Thomas's Sq., Beckets* ☎ *01722/322537* ⊕ *www.stthomassalisbury.co.uk* ⊡ *Free.*

★ Salisbury Cathedral

RELIGIOUS SITE | Salisbury is dominated by the towering cathedral, a soaring hymn in stone. It is unique among cathedrals in that it was conceived and built as a whole in the amazingly short span of 38 years (1220–58). The spire, added in 1320, is the tallest in England and a miraculous feat of medieval engineering—even though the point, 404 feet above the ground, is 2½ feet off vertical. The excellent model of the cathedral in the north nave aisle, directly in front of you as you enter, shows the building about 20 years into construction, and makes clear the ambition of Salisbury's medieval builders. For all their sophistication, the height and immense weight of the great spire have always posed structural problems. In the late 17th century, Sir Christopher Wren was summoned from London to strengthen the spire, and in the mid-19th century Sir George Gilbert Scott, the leading Victorian Gothicist who designed the Houses of Parliament, undertook a major program of restoration. He also initiated a clearing out of the interior and removed some less-than-sympathetic 18th-century alterations, returning a more authentically Gothic feel. Despite this, the interior seems spartan and a little gloomy, but check out the remarkable lancet windows and sculpted tombs of crusaders and other medieval notables. Next to the cathedral model in the north aisle is a medieval clock—probably the oldest working mechanism in Europe, if not the world—made in 1386.

The **cloisters** are the largest in England, and the octagonal **Chapter House** contains a marvelous 13th-century frieze showing scenes from the Old Testament. Here you can also see one of the four original copies of the **Magna Carta,** the charter of rights the English barons forced King John to accept in 1215; it was sent here for safekeeping in the 13th century.

■ TIP→ Join a free one-hour tour of the cathedral, leaving two or more times a day. For a peaceful break, the café in the cloister serves freshly baked cakes and pastries, plus hot lunches. ⊠ *Cathedral Close* ☎ *01722/555120* ⊕ *www.salisburycathedral.org.uk* ⊠ *Cathedral and Chapter House free, suggested donation £7.50; tower tour £13.50.*

The Salisbury Museum

MUSEUM | Opposite the cathedral's west front, this excellent museum is in the King's House, parts of which date to the 15th century (James I stayed here in 1610 and 1613). The history of the area from prehistoric times through the Norman Conquest is explored in the Wessex gallery, which houses some of Britain's most important archaeological finds and where Stonehenge-related exhibits provide helpful background information for a visit to the famous megaliths. Also on view are collections of local costumes dating back 250 years, outstanding British ceramics, and Turner watercolors, all dwarfed by the 12-foot Salisbury Giant, a 13-century pageant figure, and his companion hobbyhorse, Hob Nob. A cozy café is in one of the oldest sections of the building. ⊠ *The King's House, 65 The Close* ☎ *01722/332151* ⊕ *www. salisburymuseum.org.uk* ⊠ *£8 (tickets good for 1 year).*

★ Wilton House

CASTLE/PALACE | This is considered to be one of the loveliest stately homes in England and, along with its grounds, a fine example of the English Palladian style. The seat of the earls of Pembroke since Tudor times, the south wing of the current building was rebuilt in the early 17th century by Isaac de Caus, with input from Inigo Jones, Ben Jonson's stage designer and the architect of London's Banqueting House. It was completed by James Webb, again with input from Jones, Webb's uncle-by-marriage, after the recently finished south wing was ravaged by fire in 1647. Most noteworthy are the seven state rooms in the south wing, among them the Single Cube Room (built as a perfect 30-foot cube) and, one of the most extravagantly beautiful rooms in the history of interior decoration, the aptly named Double Cube Room. The name refers to its proportions (60 feet long by 30 feet wide and 30 feet high), evidence of Jones's classically inspired belief that beauty in architecture derives from harmony and balance. The room's headliner is the spectacular Van Dyck portrait of the Pembroke family. Elsewhere at Wilton House, the art collection includes several other Old Master paintings, including works by Rembrandt and members of the

With its art and gilded furniture, the Double Cube Room at Wilton House may well be one of England's most beautiful interiors.

Brueghel family. Another exhibition is devoted to Cecil Beaton's photo portraits of 20th-century notables and the current Lord Pembroke's collection of classic cars. Also of note are the 22 acres of lovely grounds, which have sweeping lawns dotted with towering oaks; the gardens; and the Palladian bridge crossing the small River Nadder, designed by the 9th earl after the Rialto Bridge in Venice. Some public rooms may be closed on some open days—check website for more information. ⊠ Off A36, Wilton ✛ The town of Wilton is 3 miles west of Salisbury. Buses Red 3 and Red 8 from Salisbury depart every 10 to 15 mins and stop outside Wilton House. ☎ 01722/746728 ⊕ www. wiltonhouse.co.uk ✉ £15.50; grounds only £6.50 ⊙ Closed early Sept.–early May, Fri., and Sat.

🍴 Restaurants

★ Allium

$$ | MODERN BRITISH | This family-run, centrally located restaurant has been winning rave reviews for both the taste and presentation of its creative Modern British dishes. Produce is largely fresh and local while meats and poultry are free-range and sustainably farmed. **Known for:** high quality, creative dishes; pork belly confit with curry-spiced scallops; reasonable prices. ⑤ Average main: £20 ⊠ 6–7 Ox Row ☎ 01722/326057 ⊕ alliumsalisbury.restaurant ⊙ Closed Sun. and Mon.

★ Anokaa

$$ | INDIAN | For a refreshingly modern take on Indian cuisine, try this bustling restaurant a few minutes from the center. Classic recipes are taken as starting points for the artistically presented dishes, which include tandoori-seared rack of lamb, cinnamon-glazed duck

breast stuffed with garlicky spinach, and a seasonal (and local) vegetable curry. **Known for:** creative, well-executed Indian dishes; excellent service; buffet lunch. $ *Average main: £16* ⊠ *60 Fisherton St.* ☎ *01722/414142* ⊕ *www.anokaa.com.*

Boston Tea Party

$ | **CAFÉ** | **FAMILY** | Specializing in quick, nourishing meals, this relaxed café in a 14th-century building serves hot and cold breakfasts, lunches, and afternoon snacks. Choices include cheeseburgers served with bacon jam, a veggie version with portobello mushroom, pulled-pork buns, or a huge vegan super salad with mango and avocado. **Known for:** child-friendly atmosphere and dishes; freshly roasted coffee and homemade cakes; casual dining in impressive historic setting. $ *Average main: £9* ⊠ *Old George Inn, 13 High St.* ☎ *01722/330731* ⊕ *www. bostonteaparty.co.uk* ⊗ *No dinner.*

Howard's House

$$$$ | **MODERN BRITISH** | If you're after complete tranquility, head for this early-17th-century house surrounded by two acres of grounds in the Nadder Valley. The excellent restaurant has fixed-price menus specializing in contemporary English cooking using local and seasonal ingredients, such as a butter-baked fillet of wild brill or roast loin of Wiltshire venison. **Known for:** excellent five-course tasting menu; relaxed and romantic atmosphere; terrace dining in the summer. $ *Average main: £42* ⊠ *Teffont Evias, Teffont Evias* ⊹ *Off B3089* ☎ *01722/716392* ⊕ *www. howardshousehotel.co.uk.*

🛏 Hotels

Cricket Field House

$ | **B&B/INN** | Located halfway between Wilton and Salisbury, this comfortable ex-gamekeeper's cottage overlooks a cricket ground and has a large, peaceful garden of its own. **Pros:** efficient, helpful management; well-maintained rooms; good breakfasts. **Cons:** 20-minute walk

from town; on a busy road; no restaurant on-site. $ *Rooms from: £110* ⊠ *Wilton Rd.* ☎ *01722/322595* ⊕ *www. cricketfieldhouse.co.uk* ⇆ *18 rooms* ⏹ *Free breakfast.*

Mercure Salisbury White Hart Hotel

$ | **HOTEL** | Behind the pillared portico and imposing 17th-century classical facade of this city center hotel (part of the Mercure chain) are modern bedrooms (of various sizes) with a muted cream-and-brown color scheme. **Pros:** central location; cozy public areas; friendly service. **Cons:** some rooms are small; impersonal, corporate feel; tired decor in rooms. $ *Rooms from: £120* ⊠ *1 St. John St.* ☎ *01722/312801* ⊕ *www.mercure.com* ⇆ *68 rooms* ⏹ *Free breakfast.*

Wyndham Park Lodge

$ | **B&B/INN** | This simple Victorian house in a quiet part of town (off Castle Street) provides an excellent place to rest and a delicious breakfast, as well as a garden. **Pros:** efficient and hospitable owners; good breakfast; handy parking. **Cons:** spotty Wi-Fi; furnishings a bit dated; books up quickly. $ *Rooms from: £85* ⊠ *51 Wyndham Rd.* ☎ *01722/416517* ⊕ *www.wyndhamparklodge.co.uk* ⇆ *4 rooms* ⏹ *Free breakfast.*

🎭 Performing Arts

Salisbury Playhouse

THEATER | The playhouse presents high-caliber drama all year and is the main venue for the Salisbury Arts Festival. ⊠ *Malthouse La.* ☎ *01722/320333* ⊕ *www.salisburyplayhouse.com.*

🛍 Shopping

Most of the shops are found around Market Place, the venue for twice-weekly markets and the annual Charter Fair, and along the High Street, where chain stores predominate.

Dauwalders of Salisbury

GIFTS/SOUVENIRS | This shop specializes in coins, medals, and die-cast models, but primarily stamps. It's a good source for quirky gift ideas. ⊠ *42 Fisherton St.* ☎ *01722/412100.*

Activities

Hayball Cyclesport

BICYCLING | Bike rentals here start at £20 for 8 hours, £30 for 24 hours, or £150 for a week. ⊠ *26–30 Winchester St.* ☎ *01722/411378* ⊕ *www.hayballcyclesport.co.uk* ☉ *Closed Sun.*

Stonehenge

8 miles north of Salisbury, 20 miles south of Avebury.

Almost five millennia after their construction, these stone circles on the Salisbury Plain continue to pose fascinating questions. How were the giant stones, some weighing as much as 45 tons, brought here, possibly from as far away as Wales? What was the site used for? Why were the stones aligned with the midsummer sunrise and the midwinter sunset? But Stonehenge is more than just the megaliths; the surrounding landscape is dotted with ancient earthworks, remains of Neolithic settlements, and processional pathways, creating a complex of ceremonial structures that testifies to the sophisticated belief system of these early Britons.

GETTING HERE AND AROUND

Stonehenge Tour buses leave from Salisbury's train and bus stations every half hour from 9:30 to 2:30, and then hourly from 3 to 5, from early June to August; hourly from 10 to 4 from April to early June and September through October; and 10 to 2 in November through March. Tickets cost £16 or £31.50 (includes Stonehenge and a visit to Old Sarum). Other options are a taxi or a custom tour. Drivers can find the monument near the junction of A303 with A344.

⊙ Sights

★ Stonehenge

ARCHAEOLOGICAL SITE | FAMILY | Mysterious and ancient, Stonehenge has baffled archaeologists, not to mention the general public, for centuries. One of England's most visited monuments (attracting over a million visitors a year) and a UNESCO World Heritage Site, the circle of giant stones standing starkly against the wide sweep of Salisbury Plain still has the capacity to fascinate and move those who view it. Unattractive visitor facilities have been removed to better establish the stones in their original context of grass fields, other nearby monuments, and their original processional approach, the Avenue. Although general visitors can no longer enter the stone circle itself (except by special arrangement; call for further information), you can roam free over the surrounding landscape with its Neolithic earthworks, some of which predate the stones. To best experience the awe and mystery of Stonehenge, visit the circle in the early morning or in the evening, when the crowds have dispersed.

Stonehenge was begun as early as 3000 BC with the construction of a circular earthwork enclosure. The nearby Cursus, long rectangular earthwork banks, were also created around this time. The stone circle itself was completed in stages, beginning around 2500 BC with the inner circle of bluestones, and continued to be changed and in use until around 1600 BC. The early inner circle was later surrounded by an outer circle of 30 sarsen stones, huge sandstone blocks weighing up to 25 tons, which are believed to have originated from the Marlborough Downs. Within these two circles was a horseshoe-shape group of sarsen trilithons (two large vertical stones supporting a third stone laid horizontally across it) and within that another horseshoe-shape grouping of bluestones. The sarsens used in the trilithons averaged 45 tons. Many of the huge stones were brought here

Salisbury, Stonehenge, and Salisbury Plain

from great distances before the invention of the wheel, and it's not certain what ancient form of transportation was used to move them. Every time a reconstruction of the journey has been attempted, it has failed. The labor involved in quarrying, transporting, and carving these stones is astonishing, all the more so when you realize that it was accomplished about the same time as the construction of Egypt's major pyramids.

Stonehenge (the name derives from the Saxon term for "hanging stones") has been excavated several times over the centuries, but the primary reason for its erection remains unknown. It's fairly certain that it was a religious site, and that worship here involved the cycles of the sun; the alignment of the stones on the axis of the midsummer sunrise and midwinter sunset makes this clear. Viewed from the center of the stone circle, the sun rises adjacent to the Heel Stone at midsummer and sets between the stones of the tallest trilithon at midwinter. The Druids certainly had nothing to do with the construction: the monument had already been in existence for nearly 2,000 years by the time they appeared. Some historians have maintained that Stonehenge was a kind of Neolithic computer, with a sophisticated astronomical purpose—an observatory of sorts—though evidence from excavations in the early 20th century shows that it had once been used as a burial ground. Another possibility is that this Neolithic village was home to those who performed the religious rites at Stonehenge, where people gathered from far and wide to feast and worship.

Without direct access to the stones, it is not possible to closely examine their prehistoric carvings, some of which show axes and daggers, so bring a pair of binoculars to help make out the details on the monoliths. To fully engage your imagination, or to get that magical photo, it's worth exploring all aspects of the site, both near and far. An informative visitor center is located 1½ miles away (access to the stone circle is via a frequent shuttle), with parking, audio guide rental, a café, loads of branded merchandise, and an exhibition of prehistoric objects found at the site. There's also a dramatic display using time-lapse photography that puts you (virtually) in the center of the circle as the seasons change. Next to the visitor center are some re-created Neolithic huts that show how the people who built and used Stonehenge might have lived. Visits are by timed admission slots only. ✉ Amesbury ✚ Junction of A360 and Airman's Corner ☎ 0370/333–1181 ⊕ www.english-heritage.org.uk ✉ £21.10 (walk-up); £19 (advance).

Avebury

24 miles north of Stonehenge, 34 miles north of Salisbury, 25 miles northeast of Longleat, 27 miles east of Bath.

The village of Avebury was built much later than its famous stone circles; it has an informative museum with an outstanding collection of Bronze Age artifacts from the area around here and Stonehenge. You can also explore a cluster of other prehistoric sites nearby.

GETTING HERE AND AROUND
From Salisbury, follow A345 north to Upavon and take the A342 to Devizes; then continue 7 miles northeast on the A361. You can also take the hourly Stagecoach bus No. 49 from Swindon to Avebury (30 minutes).

◉ Sights

Alexander Keiller Museum
MUSEUM | FAMILY | The Avebury Stone Circles are put into context by this collection of Neolithic and Bronze Age artifacts from the site, one of the most important prehistoric archaeological collections in Britain. The museum contains charts, photos, models, and home movies taken by its namesake, archaeologist Alexander Keiller. It has been suggested that Keiller, responsible for the excavation of Avebury in the 1930s, may have adapted the site's layout to highlight presentation more than authenticity. The exhibits are divided between the 17th-century **Stables Gallery,** which displays finds from Keiller's excavations, the child-friendly **Barn Gallery**, where you find interactive exhibits about the history of Avebury, and an activity area where kids can dress up in Bronze Age clothes. You can also visit the **Manor House**, where Keiller lived, and its surrounding gardens. The Tudor-era building received several subsequent (Queen Anne, Regency, and art deco) additions, and the rooms have been filled with acquired or commissioned period-appropriate furniture to illustrate how previous occupants lived. ✉ High St. ✚ Off A4361 ☎ 01672/539250 ⊕ www.nationaltrust. org.uk ✉ Museum £4.40; manor house and gardens £9 ⊗ Manor House and gardens closed Jan.–mid-Feb.

★ Avebury Stone Circles
ARCHAEOLOGICAL SITE | Surrounding part of Avebury village, the Avebury Stone Circles, the largest in the world, are one of England's most evocative prehistoric monuments—not as famous as Stonehenge, but all the more powerful for their lack of commercial exploitation. The stones were erected around 2600 BC, about the same time as the better-known monument. As with Stonehenge, the purpose of this stone circle has never been ascertained, although it most likely was used for similar ritual purposes. Unlike Stonehenge, however, there are

no certain astronomical alignments at Avebury, at least none that have survived. The main site consists of a wide, circular ditch and bank, about 1,400 feet across and more than half a mile around. Entrances break the perimeter at roughly the four points of the compass, and inside stand the remains of three stone circles. The largest one originally had 98 stones, although only 27 remain. Many stones on the site were destroyed centuries ago, especially in the 14th century when they were buried for unclear reasons, possibly religious fanaticism. Others were later pillaged in the 18th century to build the thatched cottages you see flanking the fields. You can walk around the circles, a World Heritage Site, at any time; early morning and early evening are recommended. As with Stonehenge, the summer solstice tends to draw the crowds. ⊠ *Avebury* ✛ *1 mile north of A4* ☎ *01672/539–250* ⊕ *www. english-heritage.org.uk* ✉ *Free.*

Cherhill Down

LOCAL INTEREST | Four miles west of Avebury, Cherhill Down is a prominent hill carved with a vivid white horse and topped with a towering obelisk. The horse is one of a number of hillside etchings in Wiltshire, all but two of which date back no further than the late 18th century. This one was put there in 1780 to indicate the highest point of the downs between London and Bath. The views from the top are well worth the half-hour climb. The best view of the horse is from A4, on the approach from Calne. ⊠ *Avebury* ✛ *A4 south of Cherhill village, near Calne* ☎ *01672/539167* ⊕ *www.nationaltrust.org.uk.*

Silbury Hill

LOCAL INTEREST | Rising 130 feet and comparable in height and volume to the roughly contemporary pyramids in Egypt, this largest man-made mound in Europe dates from about 2400 BC. Though there have been periodic excavations of the mound

since the 17th century, its original purpose remains unknown. The viewing area, less than 1 mile east of Avebury, is open only during daylight hours, but there's no direct access to the mound itself ⊠ *Avebury* ✛ *A4, 1 mile west of West Kennett* ⊕ *www.english-heritage.org.uk.*

West Kennet Avenue

ARCHAEOLOGICAL SITE | Lined with what remains of the original 100 standing stones, spaced 80 feet apart, this 1½-mile path was once a prehistoric processional way leading to the stone circles at Avebury. Only the half mile nearest the main monument survives intact. The lost stones are marked with concrete obelisks. ⊠ *Avebury* ✛ *Off B4003, south of Avebury* ☎ *01672/539250* ⊕ *www. english-heritage.org.uk* ✉ *Free.*

★ West Kennet Long Barrow

ARCHAEOLOGICAL SITE | One of the largest Neolithic chambered tombs in Britain, West Kennet Long Barrow was built around 3400 BC. You can explore all around the site and also enter the tomb, which was used for more than 1,000 years before the main passage was blocked and the entrance closed, around 2000 BC. More than 300 feet long, it has an elevated position with a great view of Silbury Hill and the surrounding countryside. It's about 1 mile east of Avebury. ⊠ *Avebury* ✛ *¾ mile southwest of West Kennett, along footpath off A4* ☎ *01672/539250* ⊕ *www.english-heritage.org.uk* ✉ *Free.*

🍴 Restaurants

Waggon and Horses

$ | **BRITISH** | A 17th-century thatched-roof building with foundations made from sarsen stones, this traditional inn and pub (Dickens mentions the building in the *Pickwick Papers)*is a two-minute drive from the Avebury stone circles. With a beer garden that has views of Silbury Hill, it's something of a tourist

Continued on page 315

MYSTERIOUS
STONEHENGE

A circle of giant stones sitting on the wide sweep of Salisbury Plain, Stonehenge is one of the most famous prehistoric sites in England. It still has the capacity to fascinate and move those who view it, but Stonehenge can also be perplexing. The site seems to pose more questions than it answers about its 5,000-year-long history, and its meaning and purpose are continually reevaluated and debated. With some context, you can experience Stonehenge as it once was: deeply mystical and awe-inspiring.

The ineffable mystery of Stonehenge—the name derives from the Anglo-Saxon term for "hanging stones"—remains despite the presence of a busy road nearby and close to a million visitors a year. Since the opening of a visitor center 1½ miles from the site, the experience of seeing Stonehenge has been hugely improved. But timing your visit and taking advantage of what the site offers—including a good audio guide—are important.

It also helps to sort through the theories, and to look at the landscape. Stonehenge was created in, broadly speaking, three stages: the earliest stage around 3000 BC, the stone settings around 2500 BC, and the rearrangement of the stones around 2300 BC. It was built on Salisbury Plain, an area devoid of trees since the last ice age—but it does not stand in isolation. The Stonehenge part of the UNESCO World Heritage Site of Stonehenge and Avebury (a nearby stone circle) covers almost 6,500 acres containing more than 350 burial mounds and prehistoric monuments. Archaeologists continue to rewrite the site's history as they uncover more evidence about Stonehenge and the surrounding ancient structures.

—by Ellin Stein

Opposite: Theories about the sun and its alignment with Stonehenge continue to invite debate. Above: An aerial view provides perspective on the great stone circle.

VIEWING STONEHENGE TODAY

Heel Stone ④

The Avenue ③

Principal Entrance

⑥ **Slaughter Stone**

Circular Bank and Ditch

Station Stone

Circle of Bluestones

Horseshoe of Sarsen Trilithons

Circle of Sarsen Stones with lintels

⑤ **Altar Stone**

Horseshoe of Bluestones

North Barrow ①

Station Stone

LAYOUT OF THE CIRCLE

Stonehenge today has an **outer circle of sarsen stones**, sandstone blocks from nearby Marlborough Downs. It is the only stone circle in the world with lintels. The huge stones are around 13 feet high, 7 feet wide, and weigh about 25 tons each. This sarsen circle surrounds a smaller **circle of bluestones**, a dolerite stone that appears blue when wet. Bluestones were possibly the first stones at the site, brought from the Preseli Hills in West Wales 150 miles away.

Sarsen stones form the **trilithons**, the tall (over 20 feet) pairs of upright stones with lintels across the top, in the center of the circle, part of an **inner horseshoe of sarsen stones and bluestones**. The sandstone **Altar Stone** is also in the center. The horseshoe's open end and central upright stones face midsummer sunrise and midwinter sunset.

The word "henge" refers to another feature of the site: a henge is a **circular earthwork bank with an internal ditch** surrounding flattened ground. Stonehenge is unusual in that the ditch is outside the earthwork bank.

OVER THE CENTURIES

Circular ditch with interior bank constructed	2850 BC Construction of nearby Avebury stone circles begins	2500 BC Large sarsen stones brought to Stonehenge; first bluestones brought from Wales

| 3000 BC | 2800 BC | 2500 BC | 2400 |

Heel Stone

South Barrow

Secondary Entrance

Aubrey Holes
❷

❶ North Barrow. The outer ditch and bank intersect with the largely unexcavated North Barrow, thought to have been used for burials. The barrow may predate Stonehenge.

❷ Aubrey Holes. These 56 pits inside the outer bank, now with concrete markers, are named after John Aubrey, the antiquarian who identified them in 1666. Evidence suggests they may once have contained bluestone or timber uprights and were later used for cremated remains.

❸ The Avenue. The Avenue's parallel ditches and banks stretch over 2.8 km (1.7 miles) to the bank of the River Avon. It was discovered in 2009, but little remains. Periglacial stripes, a natural geographic feature, run parallel to the banks of the Avenue and align in place with the solstice axis.

❹ Heel Stone. This sarsen block stands at the entrance to the Avenue, on the edge of the current site. At midsummer solstice, the sun rises over the Heel Stone.

❺ Altar Stone. Now recumbent, the great sandstone Altar Stone stood nearly 6 feet tall at the center of Stonehenge. Unlike the sarsen stones, it probably came from Milford Haven in

Wales. Despite the name, its purpose remains unknown. Today the stone is the centerpiece for rituals around the summer and winter solstice.

❻ Slaughter Stone. This stone, originally upright, now lies within the northeast entrance, and may have formed part of a portal. It is stained a rusty red by rainwater acting on the iron in the stone, rather than by the blood of human sacrifice, as 18th-century legend says.

Trilithon standing stones

HOW MANY STONES?

Many of the site's original stones have been lost over the years to builders of roads and houses and souvenir hunters, and some have fallen down. However, out of the original 30 large sarsen uprights, 17 remain, with 3 of the 5 trilithons still standing. Forty-three bluestones are left from the original 80 or so, and other major stones remain at the site.

MOVING THE STONES

The first 80 bluestones were brought by sea and river over 150 miles from Wales around 2500 BC. People probably used rafts to transport the bluestones over water. The heavier sarsen stones were dragged about 25 miles over land from the Marlborough Downs, and tipped into pits dug in the chalk plain. It is possible that people used wooden rollers for transporting the stones.

LEGENDS, MYTHS, and CURRENT THEORIES

LEGENDARY STONEHENGE

Because of its prominence, Stonehenge has become steeped in myths assigning it any number of religious, mystical, and spiritual functions: it was built by the legendary Arthurian wizard Merlin, by the devil, giants, even aliens. The rebel queen Boudicca, who fought against the Romans, was said to have been buried at Stonehenge after the Romans fought the Druids, giving rise to the myth that the Druids built the stone circle to mark her tomb. One thing is certain: the Druids had nothing to do with the construction of Stonehenge, which had already stood for 2,000 years when they appeared.

WHO BUILT STONEHENGE?

The Neolithic and Bronze Age people who built Stonehenge, beginning around the time that the great pyramids in Egypt were built, had only hand tools for shaping the stones and their own manpower for moving them. No other stone circle contains such carefully shaped and meticulously placed stones. Some stones also show carvings of daggers and axes.

The first Neolithic people at what is now the World Heritage Site were semi-nomadic farmers who buried their dead in large, east-west facing barrows. Later, between 2500 and 2200 BC, the "Beaker People" started to use the site. Their name comes from their tradition of burying their dead with pottery (seen in displays at the Salisbury and South Wiltshire Museum), and they may have been sun worshipers. The final group was the Wessex people, around 1600 BC, who probably made the carvings in the stones and finalized Stonehenge's structure.

NEW THEORIES

Recent excavations have put forward two major new theories about its purpose. Evidence from the Stonehenge Riverside Project, a major ongoing archaeological study running since 2003, indicates that it was a domain of the dead: both a burial ground and a memorial. Numerous burials have been found all over the site and the surrounding area. Stonehenge is joined to Durrington Walls, the world's largest known henge and a nearby ancient settlement, by the River Avon and the Avenue. The journey along

Above: Many stones have fallen, but Stonehenge is still a powerful sight.

the river to Stonehenge may have been a ritual passage from life to death.

Another theory is that Stonehenge was a place of healing, accounting for the number of burials with physical injury and disease found in the tombs here as well as the unusual number of people who were not native to the area. That the bluestones were brought from so far away suggests that they were thought to harbor great powers.

STONEHENGE AND THE SUN

Stonehenge's design offers an intriguing clue as to its purpose, although there are no definitive answers. The horseshoe of trilithons and other stone settings align on the solstitial (midsummer sunrise and midwinter sunset) axis. This has led to much speculation and a variety of ideas. The centuries-old theory persists that Stonehenge was an astronomical observatory, a calendar, or a sun temple. It is fairly certain that it was a religious site, and worship here may have involved cycles of the sun.

On Summer Solstice (June 21), thousands gather to watch the sun rise over the Heel Stone. But the discovery of a neighboring stone to the Heel Stone questions even this, suggesting it may not itself have been a marker of sunrise, but part of a "solar corridor" that framed the sunrise.

Ongoing archaeological research, not to mention speculation, continues to revise the story of Stonehenge.

EXPLORING NEARBY SITES

NEAR STONEHENGE

Hundreds of Neolithic monuments and barrows dot the landscape around Stonehenge. Excavations at **Durrington Walls**, a couple of miles northeast of Stonehenge off A345, have unearthed a substantial settlement dating from around 2500 BC, probably occupied by Stonehenge's builders. Although there is little left of most Neolithic sites today, concrete posts mark nearby **Woodhenge** (also off A345), which dates from around 2300 BC. Its long axis is aligned to the midsummer sunrise and the midwinter sunset. Admission and parking are free at both these sites.

AVEBURY AND ENVIRONS

Twenty-four miles to the north lie Avebury and the **Avebury Stone Circles**, the largest stone circles in the world (dating to around 2850 BC). You can walk freely among the stones— a major attraction for those who prefer the site to Stonehenge.
Silbury Hill, the last of the great monuments, and **West Kennet Long Barrow**, a tomb, are close by.

Above, Silbury Hill

MAKING THE MOST OF YOUR VISIT

Avebury, Wiltshire

WHEN TO VISIT

Come early before the crowds arrive, or in the evening when the light is low and skies darkening. Summer weekends and school holidays can be especially crowded. Stonehenge is packed at Summer Solstice, when visitors stay all night to watch the sun rise.

English Heritage, which manages the site, can arrange access to the inner circle (not a guided tour) outside of regular hours. This requires application and a fee well in advance, as Stone Circle Access visits are popular.

The visitor center is located a mile-and-a-half from the stones. Frequent shuttles take you to the circles, a 10-minute trip. You can also walk.

TIPS AND WHAT TO BRING

Since the stones are roped off, bring binoculars to see the Broze Age carvings on them. Spend a few hours: walk all around the site to get that perfect photo and to observe the changing light on the plain. The free audio guide is essential, and the shop sells plenty of books.

MAKING A DAY OF IT

The Salisbury and South Wiltshire Museum in Salisbury has models and burial reconstructions that help put Stonehenge into perspective. The smaller Alexander Keiller Museum in Avebury has finds from the area.

It's an easy drive between nearby prehistoric sites. Stonehenge is set in 1,500 acres of National Trust land with excellent walks. The 36.5 mile Great Stone Way is a walking route that links Avebury with Stonehenge and runs to Old Sarum, near Salisbury.

GETTING HERE

By car, Stonehenge is 2 miles west of Amesbury off A36. The **Stonehenge Tour Bus** departs from Salisbury rail and bus stations frequently; buses leave every half hour or hour. Other options are a taxi or an organized tour. **Salisbury and Stonehenge Guided Tours** operates small-group tours from Salisbury and London.

hub in high season, but lunches and dinners are still excellent. **Known for:** cozy atmosphere with open fire; homemade food using locally sourced ingredients; crowds in high season. ⑤ *Average main: £15 ✉ Beckhampton ✛ A4, 300 feet east of junction with A361 ☎ 01672/539418 ⊕ www.waggonandhorsesbeckhampton. co.uk.*

Hotels

The Lodge
$$ | B&B/INN | With their eclectic design, rare prints, and antique furnishings, the two spacious guest rooms of this charming B&B are full of character. **Pros:** unique location and views; comfortable rooms; vegetarian breakfasts. **Cons:** can book up; expensive; early 10 am checkout. ⑤ *Rooms from: £195 ✉ Rawlings Park ✛ Off A4361 ☎ 01672/539023 ⊕ www. averburylodge.co.uk ⥽ 2 rooms ⁑ Free breakfast.*

Longleat House

31 miles southwest of Avebury, 6 miles north of Stourhead, 19 miles south of Bath, 27 miles northwest of Salisbury.

With its popular safari park and a richly decorated High Elizabethan house to explore, Longleat can provide a day of diversions.

GETTING HERE AND AROUND
Longleat House is off A36 between Bath and Salisbury. The nearest train station is Warminster, about 5 miles away. Your best option is to take a taxi from there.

◉ Sights

★ Longleat House
CASTLE/PALACE | FAMILY | The family seat of the Marquesses of Bath, Longleat House is one of southern England's most famous stately homes, and possibly the most ambitiously, even eccentrically,

commercialized, as evidenced by the presence of a drive-through safari park (open since 1966) with giraffes, zebras, gorillas, monkeys, rhinos, and lions. The house, considered to be one of the finest remaining examples of High Elizabethan, was largely completed in 1580 for more than £8,000, an astronomical sum at the time. It contains outstanding tapestries, paintings, porcelain, furniture, and one of the largest private collections of books in England (more than 40,000 volumes housed in seven libraries). Notable period features include Victorian kitchens, an Elizabethan minstrels' gallery, painted ceilings, and a great hall with massive wooden beams. You can wander at will or take one of the specialized guided tours (such as the "Rooftop" tour or the "Scandalous History" tour). In addition to 900 acres of parkland designed by Capability Brown, plus formal and pleasure gardens and the safari park, the property has a miniature railway, a petting zoo, an extensive (and fairly fiendish) hedge maze, and an "adventure castle," all of which make it extremely popular, particularly in summer and during school vacations. A first-come, first-served safari bus service is available (£5) for those arriving without their own transport. ✉ *Warminster ✛ Off A362 ☎ 01985/844400 ⊕ www.longleat. co.uk ⊠ £34.90, £29.70 online ⊙ Closed Jan.–mid-Feb., Mon.–Thurs. in Mar., and Mon.–Wed. in Nov.*

Hotels

Bishopstrow Hotel and Spa
$$ | HOTEL | This ivy-covered Regency manor house set on 27 acres has been converted into a relaxed country-house hotel that combines well-chosen antiques with modern amenities. **Pros:** country-house ambience; impressive suites; friendly staff. **Cons:** drink prices high; dinner service can be understaffed and slow; maintenance needs more attention. ⑤ *Rooms from: £150 ✉ Boreham Rd., Warminster ☎ 01985/212312*

The gardens of Stourhead are perhaps the most beautiful in all of England.

⊕ *www.bishopstrow.co.uk* ⇥ *32 rooms* ⦿ *Free breakfast.*

Stourhead

9 miles southwest of Longleat, 15 miles northeast of Sherborne, 30 miles west of Salisbury.

England has many memorable gardens, but Stourhead is one of the most glorious. Its centerpiece is a magnificent artificial lake surrounded by neoclassical temples, atmospheric grottos, and rare trees. The Palladian stately home is also worth a look.

GETTING HERE AND AROUND

By car, you can reach Stourhead via B3092. It's signposted off the main road. From London, board a train to Gillingham and take a five-minute cab ride to Stourton.

⊙ Sights

★ Stourhead

GARDEN | Close to the village of Stourton lies one of Wiltshire's most breathtaking sights—Stourhead, a Palladian mansion whose gardens are the most celebrated example of the English 18th-century taste for "natural" landscaping. Both house and grounds have few parallels for beauty anywhere in Europe. Stourhead was built between 1721 and 1725 by wealthy banker Henry Hoare, popularly known as "Good Henry" (he died the same year as the mansion's completion), with his descendants adding the portico and wings (a fire gutted the building in 1902 shortly after a restoration, but it was able to be largely reconstructed unaltered). Henry's grandson added a wing for the elegant Regency library and a picture gallery built to house his collections of paintings and books. There are also significant collections of Chippendale furniture and Chinese and French porcelain collected by the early Hoares on their Grand Tours. Still, Stourhead's greatest masterpiece is its gardens, designed by Henry Hoare II. Influenced by the neoclassical dream landscapes of 17th century painters Claude Lorrain and Nicolas Poussin, Henry "the Magnificent" used hills, water (notably the central lake), and a remarkable collection of trees and shrubs—interspersed with classically inspired temples, grottoes, follies, and bridges—to create the effect of a three-dimensional oil painting. Discover the changing vistas on a walk around the artificial lake (1½ miles; walk counterclockwise for the best views). ■TIP→ **The best times to visit are early summer when the massive banks of rhododendrons are in full bloom or mid-October for autumn color, but the gardens are beautiful at any time of year.** You can get a fine view of the surrounding area from King Alfred's Tower, a 1772 folly (a structure built for picturesque effect). ⊠ *Stourton* ✛ *Off B3092, near Mere* ☎ *01747/841152* ⊕ *www.nationaltrust.org.uk* ✉ *House and gardens £20.40; King Alfred's Tower £5* ⊗ *House closed mid-Dec.–mid-Mar. and mid–late Nov.; King Alfred's Tower closed late Oct.–mid-Mar. and weekdays mid-Mar.–late Oct.*

🛏 Hotels

The Spread Eagle Inn
$$ | **B&B/INN** | You can't stay at Stourhead, but you can stay at this popular inn built at the beginning of the 19th century just inside the main entrance. **Pros:** period character; lovely rooms; free access to Stourhead. **Cons:** needs some modernization; food can be disappointing; handheld shower attachments as opposed to real showers. ⑤ *Rooms from: £125* ⊠ *Church Lawn, near Warminster, Stourton* ☎ *01747/840587* ⊕ *www.spreadeagleinn. com* ⤿ *5 rooms* ⑨❘ *Free breakfast.*

Lyndhurst

26 miles southeast of Stonehenge, 18 miles southeast of Salisbury, 9 miles west of Southampton.

Lyndhurst is famous as the capital of the New Forest. Although some popular spots can get crowded in summer, there are ample parking lots, picnic areas, and campgrounds. Miles of trails crisscross the region.

GETTING HERE AND AROUND
From Salisbury, follow A36, B3079, and continue along A337 another 4 miles or so. To explore the New Forest, take A35 out of Lyndhurst (the road continues southwest to Bournemouth) or A337 south. The New Forest Tour is a hop-on, hop-off open-top bus. Regular bus services are operated by Bluestar and Wilts & Dorset. Many parts of the New Forest are readily accessible by train from London via the centrally located Brockenhurst Station.

TOURS
New Forest Tour
The bus runs three circular routes with hourly departures through the New Forest daily between July and mid-September; all-day hop on-hop off tickets, beginning at £17, are purchased onboard. ☎ *01202/338420* ⊕ *www.thenewforest-tour.info.*

👁 Sights

★ New Forest
NATIONAL/STATE PARK | **FAMILY** | This national park, still largely owned by the Crown, consists of 150 square miles of woodland, heaths, grassland, bogs, and the remains of coppices and timber plantations established in the 17th to 19th century. Residents have had grazing rights since the 12th century, and you can still encounter free-roaming cattle, and, most famously, the hardy New Forest ponies. An extensive network of trails makes it a

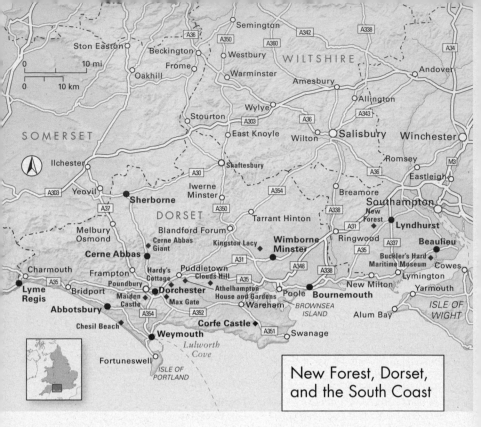

New Forest, Dorset, and the South Coast

wonderful place for biking, walking, and horseback riding. ⊠ *Lyndhurst* ⊕ *www. thenewforest.co.uk* 🚉 *Free.*

New Forest Heritage Centre

INFO CENTER | FAMILY | This visitor complex with a gallery, museum, and reference library devoted to the New Forest contains displays and activities related to the area's geology, history, wildlife, and culture. The museum is packed with quizzes and other interactive elements that keep children engaged. There's also a café. ⊠ *Main Car Park, Avenue Rd.* ☎ *023/8028–3444* ⊕ *www.newforestheritage.org.uk* 🚉 *Free.*

St. Michael and All Angels

RELIGIOUS SITE | Lyndhurst's High Street is dominated by this imposing redbrick, Victorian Gothic church, notable for its stained-glass windows designed by Pre-Raphaelites William Morris and Edward Burne-Jones, as well as a large fresco of the Parable of the Wise and Foolish Virgins by Frederick Leighton. Fans of Lewis Carroll's *Alice in Wonderland* should note that Alice Hargreaves (née Liddell), the inspiration for the fictional Alice, is buried in the churchyard. ⊠ *High St.* ☎ *023/8028–3175* ⊕ *www. newforestparishes.com.*

🍽 Restaurants

★ The Pig

$$ | MODERN BRITISH | Funkier sister of glamorous Lime Wood, this New Forest "restaurant with rooms" puts the emphasis on localism and seasonality and is a local favorite. Lunch and dinner are served in a large Victorian greenhouse overlooking lawns, and the frequently changing menu may include dishes like pork belly with oyster mushrooms

Fossil Hunting on the Jurassic Coast 👁

Besides the dramatic beauty of its jagged cliffs and hidden coves, the lure of the Jurassic Coast for visitors is fossils and fossil hunting. The varied and dramatic coastline is a World Heritage Site encompassing 200 million years of geological history, and constant erosion makes finding fossils a distinct possibility.

A 65-million-year geological journey through time forming an almost complete record of the Mesozoic era, the Jurassic Coast stretches for 95 miles between the younger, Cretaceous chalk stacks known as "Old Harry Rocks" at Studland Bay in Dorset in the east to the older, striking red Triassic cliffs at Exmouth (Devon) in the west. The earliest Jurassic cliffs of West Dorset formed in a tropical sea that flooded a vast desert. After the sea level dropped 140 million years ago, forest, swampland, and dinosaurs thrived, before the rising sea flooded the area once again. Fossils are continually uncovered, and both amateurs and professionals have made many important finds here.

When to Go

If you're intent on collecting fossils, consider visiting in winter, when storms and rough seas encourage cliff erosion that sweeps fossils onto the beaches below. Search at low tide if you want the very best chance of making discoveries. Winter is less crowded, too. In summer the seas are calmer and the weather is more reliable. Although summer has more visitor traffic, the days are longer and buses more frequent—a plus if you're exploring the coastal path.

What to Look For

Fossil hunters should stick to the area around Charmouth (the beach below Stonebarrow Hill, east of Charmouth, is especially fruitful) and Lyme Regis. The rock here is rich in fossils of the creatures that lived in the Jurassic oceans and especially prone to rapid erosion. You're free to pick and chip at the rocks; no permit is needed.

Seeing the Coast

The South West Coast Path National Trail, more than 600 miles long, passes through the area and is a great way to get closer to the Jurassic Coast. The Jurassic Coaster X53 bus travels along the Jurassic Coast from Poole to Weymouth and Exeter, and allows you to walk a section of the path and return by bus.

You can join a pro: information on guided walks is available from local tourist offices and the Lyme Regis Museum. Operators run boat trips from gateway towns, an easy way to appreciate the coastline. See the boards at harbors, or ask at information centers. A mile east of Lyme Regis, the **Charmouth Heritage Coast Centre** (☎ 01297/560772 ⊕ www. charmouth.org, £8 walks) organizes two-hour walks, kids' events, and has a permanent exhibit. Late March through November, **Harry May** (☎ 07974/753287 ⊕ www.mackerelfishinglymeregis.com, £10) operates mackerel fishing and sightseeing boat trips on the Marie F and the Sunbeam from the Cobb in Lyme Regis.

and a basil-and-sunflower-seed salsa verde or poached silver mullet with fennel, Dorset olives, and samphire. **Known for:** nearly all ingredients come from their own garden or other sources within 25 miles; porcine dishes, as the name suggests; foraging expeditions with the staff. ⑤ *Average main: £20* ✉ *Beaulieu Rd., Brockenhurst* ☎ *01590/622354* ⊕ *www. thepighotel.com.*

Verveine

$$$$ | SEAFOOD | This small but acclaimed seafood restaurant attached to a fishmongers' specializes in innovative fish cuisine using the freshest ingredients. Options change daily, but might include dishes like roast Devon hake, hispi cabbage, ventrenche ham (French pancetta), and burnt apple puree or grilled megrim fillet with artichokes and wild garlic. **Known for:** creative seafood dishes using the freshest ingredients; excellent wine list; multicourse tasting menus. ⑤ *Average main: £44* ✉ *98 High St.* ☎ *01540/642176* ⊕ *www.verveine. co.uk* ☉ *Closed Sun. and Mon.*

🛏 Hotels

Chewton Glen Hotel and Spa

$$$$ | HOTEL | This grand early-19th-century country-house hotel and spa on extensive manicured grounds ranks among Britain's most acclaimed—and most expensive— lodgings. **Pros:** classic English luxury; top-notch leisure facilities; high staff-to-guest ratio. **Cons:** expensive rates; somewhat lacking in atmosphere; service not always up to five-star expectations. ⑤ *Rooms from: £370* ✉ *Christchurch Rd., New Milton* ☎ *01425/275341, 800/344–5087 in U.S.* ⊕ *www.chewtonglen.com* ⇗ *70 rooms* ⏺ *No meals.*

★ Lime Wood

$$$$ | HOTEL | If you're looking for a discreet, luxurious hideaway in a woodland setting with uninterrupted views and an excellent spa, this hugely relaxing country-house hotel is hard to beat. **Pros:** great location; stylish yet comfortable design; friendly staff. **Cons:** hard to reach without a car; breakfast not included; pricey. ⑤ *Rooms from: £395* ✉ *Beaulieu Rd.* ☎ *023/8028–7177* ⊕ *www.limewood-hotel.co.uk* ⇗ *29 rooms* ⏺ *No meals.*

Spot in the Woods

$ | B&B/INN | A Victorian house with a chalet-style addition in the back, this comfortable, boutique bed-and-breakfast on the edge of the New Forest has individually designed, rustic chic rooms with homey hand-knitted blankets in orange, taupe, or blue. **Pros:** relaxed atmosphere; in-house deli serving locally sourced food; spacious rooms. **Cons:** no evening meals; a little remote; café can be noisy when busy. ⑤ *Rooms from: £115* ✉ *174 Woodlands Rd., Woodlands, Netley Marsh* ☎ *023/8029–3784* ⊕ *www. spotinthewoods.co.uk* ⇗ *11 rooms* ⏺ *No meals.*

🏃 Activities

Largely unspoiled and undeveloped, yet accessible even to those not normally given to long walks or bike rides, the New Forest provides numerous opportunities to explore the outdoors. Bike rental and horseback riding are widely available. Numerous trails lead through thickly wooded country, across open heaths, and through the occasional bog. With very few hills, it's fairly easy terrain, and it's rich with wildlife. You're almost guaranteed to see wild ponies, deer, and, occasionally, free-roaming cattle and pigs.

BIKING

Cycle Experience

BICYCLING | Bike rentals from £18.50 per day allow you to explore a range of trails weaving through the New Forest, one of Britain's best terrains for off-road biking. ✉ *2 Brookley Rd., Brockenhurst* ☎ *01590/624808* ⊕ *www.cyclex.co.uk.*

HORSEBACK RIDING
Brockenhurst Riding Stables
HORSEBACK RIDING | FAMILY | The stable offers rides on forest trails for all levels. Hour-long treks are £38, and two-hour outings are £76. ✉ *Warren Farm, Balmer Lawn Rd., Brockenhurst* ☎ *01590/624747* ⊕ *www.brockenhurstridingstables.co.uk.*

WALKING
New Forest
HIKING/WALKING | The area is crisscrossed with short, easy trails, as well as longer hikes. For an easy walk (about 4 miles), start from Lyndhurst and head directly south for Brockenhurst, a commuter village. The path goes through woods, pastureland, and heath—and you'll see plenty of New Forest ponies. ✉ *Lyndhurst.*

Beaulieu

7 miles southeast of Lyndhurst.

The unspoiled village of Beaulieu (pronounced *byoo*-lee) has three major attractions in one at Beaulieu Abbey and is near the museum village of Buckler's Hard.

GETTING HERE AND AROUND
Beaulieu is best reached by car on B3056 from Lyndhurst or B3054 from Lymington. It's signposted off A326 from Southampton. Bus 112 has a limited service (three times daily on Tuesday and Thursday) between Beaulieu and Lymington and Hythe, and runs daily. During the summer, the New Forest Tour bus extends to Beaulieu.

 Sights

Beaulieu
TOWN | FAMILY | With a ruined 13th-century abbey, a stately home, and an automobile museum, Beaulieu appeals to several different interests. **Beaulieu Abbey** was founded in 1204 by Cistercian monks on land given to them by King John (the name means "beautiful place" in French). You can still see the ruins of the cloister and the herb garden, as well as two remaining buildings, one containing an exhibition re-creating daily life in the monastery. **Palace House and Gardens** incorporates the abbey's original 14th-century gatehouse and has been the home of the Montagu family since they purchased it in 1538, after the dissolution of the monasteries, when the abbey was badly damaged. You can explore the drawing rooms, dining halls, fine family portraits, and the beautiful grounds. The father of the present Lord Montagu established the **National Motor Museum,** which traces the history of British motoring. The collection contains more than 280 classic cars and motorcycles, from late-19th-century vehicles to futuristic F1 racing cars, rally cars, and luxury cars, plus famous film cars like the flying Ford Anglia from *Harry Potter and the Chamber of Secrets.* Other museum attractions include interactive experiences, audiovisual displays, a World of *Top Gear* attraction devoted to the popular British TV show (complete with test track), and rides in vehicles ranging from a monorail to a 1912 London bus. ✉ *Beaulieu* ✛ *Off B3056* ☎ *01590/612345* ⊕ *www.beaulieu.co.uk* ✉ *Abbey, Palace House, World of Top Gear, and Motor Museum £24.75 (£19.50 in advance).*

Buckler's Hard Maritime Museum
MUSEUM VILLAGE | FAMILY | This restored 18th-century shipbuilding village, two miles south of Beaulieu, is home to a re-created Shipwright's Cottage along with a Shipwright School in a replica 18th-century timber workshop, where courses are given in traditional shipbuilding techniques. There's also a fascinating **Maritime Museum,** which traces the village's role in British history, including the building of Nelson's warships (the New Forest lost many of its trees from the 16th to 18th centuries, when it served as the principal source of timber for British Navy ships). From Easter

through September, you can cruise down the privately owned Beaulieu River. The **Master Builder's House Hotel** has a bar and restaurant. ⊠ *Off B3056* ☎ *01590/616203* ⊕ *www.bucklershard.co.uk* ✉ *£7.50 (£6.90 advance); river cruise £5.50 (£5 advance).*

Bournemouth

26 miles southwest of Southampton, 26 miles south of Salisbury, 24 miles east of Dorchester.

Bournemouth has seven miles of beaches, and the waters are said to be some of southern England's most pristine. The resort was founded in 1810 by Lewis Tregonwell, an ex-army officer. He settled near what is now the Square and planted the first pine trees in the distinctive steep little valleys—or chines—cutting through the cliffs to the Bournemouth sands. The scent of fir trees was said to benefit consumption (tuberculosis) sufferers, and the town grew steadily.

Today the city has expanded to swallow up neighboring settlements, making it a somewhat amorphous sprawl on first view. Its stodgier, more traditional side is kept in check by the presence of a lively student population—partly made up of foreign-language students from abroad. Gardens laid out with trees and lawns link the Square and the beach. This is an excellent spot to relax and listen to music wafting from the Pine Walk bandstand. Regular musical programs take place at the Pavilion.

GETTING HERE AND AROUND

From the New Forest, take A35 or A31/A338 southwest to Bournemouth. The center of town is best explored on foot, but to reach East Cliff or Boscombe you need to drive or hop aboard the frequent local buses. Fast trains from London take about two hours.

ESSENTIALS

VISITOR INFORMATION Bournemouth Tourist Information Centre. ⊠ *Pier Approach* ☎ *01202/451781* ⊕ *www.bournemouth. co.uk.*

◉ Sights

Bournemouth Beach

BEACH—SIGHT | FAMILY | With seven miles of clean sandy beaches tucked beneath its cliffs, Bournemouth is said to enjoy some of the country's warmest sea temperatures. You can descend to the seafront either by taking the zigzag paths through the public gardens near Bournemouth Pier (where there's a family-friendly amusement arcade) or by taking the three outdoor elevators from the cliffs. If you're not tempted to swim, you can stroll along the nearby promenade. Windsurfing, sailing, and other water sports are also big here. **Amenities**: food and drink; lifeguards; parking (from £1.50 an hour, varies seasonally); water sports. **Best for:** walking. ⊠ *Westover Rd.* ☎ *01212/451734.*

Russell-Cotes Art Gallery and Museum

MUSEUM | Perched on East Cliff, this lavish late-Victorian villa overflows with sculpture, paintings, and artifacts, including cases of butterflies and an exquisite suit of Japanese armor—just a few of the treasures collected from around the world by Russell-Cotes, a widely traveled Victorian couple. The house, a combination of Italian Renaissance and Scottish Baronial, with added Moorish-, Japanese-, and French-themed rooms, was designed to showcase the collection. There's also a small landscaped garden and café. The museum hosts temporary exhibitions as well, such as ones devoted to the legacy of the Pre-Raphaelites or to the role of fans in Victorian society. ⊠ *East Cliff* ☎ *01202/451800* ⊕ *www. russellcotes.com* ✉ *£7.50* ⊙ *Closed Mon. except bank holidays.*

St. Peter's Church
RELIGIOUS SITE | This parish church is easily recognizable by its 200-foot-high tower and spire. Lewis Tregonwell, founder and developer of Bournemouth, is buried in the churchyard. Here, too, is the elaborate tombstone of Mary Shelley, author of *Frankenstein* and wife of the great Romantic poet Percy Bysshe Shelley, whose heart is buried with her. ⊠ *Hinton Rd.* ☎ *01202/290986* ⊕ *www.stpeters-bournemouth.org.uk.*

Restaurants

WestBeach
$$ | SEAFOOD | Superbly positioned on the marine promenade, close to Bournemouth Pier, this fish restaurant serves the best seafood in town, whether grilled, baked, or in fish pies and stews. The menu usually lists haddock, wild locally caught sea bass, plaice, and shellfish (local oysters, crab, mussels, clams, lobster). **Known for:** fresh fish and shellfish; sea views from right on beach; minimalist decor. ⑤ *Average main: £22* ⊠ *Pier Approach* ☎ *01202/587785* ⊕ *west-beach.co.uk.*

🛏 Hotels

The Urban Beach
$ | HOTEL | A short walk from the seafront and a 10-minute drive from Bournemouth's center, this funky boutique hotel provides the contemporary style and energy so needed by the town. **Pros:** well-designed decor; friendly staff; power showers. **Cons:** location not central; food quality variable; parking difficult. ⑤ *Rooms from: £116* ⊠ *23 Argyll Rd., Boscombe* ☎ *01202/301509* ⊕ *www. urbanbeach.co.uk* ⇝ *12 rooms* ⑩ *Free breakfast.*

Wimborne Minster

7 miles northwest of Bournemouth.

The impressive minster of this quiet market town makes it seem like a miniature cathedral city. The town is exceptionally quiet on Sunday.

GETTING HERE AND AROUND
To reach Wimborne Minster from central Bournemouth, take any main road heading west, following signs for A341 or A349, or take advantage of the regular bus service.

ESSENTIALS
VISITOR INFORMATION Wimborne Minster Tourist Information Centre. ⊠ *29 High St.* ☎ *01202/886116* ⊕ *www.visit-dorset. com/visitor-information.*

◉ Sights

Kingston Lacy
HOUSE | Sir Charles Barry, co-architect of the Houses of Parliament in London, created this grand 19th-century country house built to resemble an 18th-century Venetian palazzo. It contains notable paintings by Titian, Rubens, Van Dyck, Brueghel, and Velásquez as well as a fabulous Spanish Room lined with gilded leather and topped by an ornate Venetian ceiling. There's also a fine collection of Egyptian artifacts, the largest private collection in the country. Formal gardens (including a Japanese garden with a teahouse) and extensive parkland with walking paths surround the house. Admission is by a timed guided tour ticket only. ⊠ *Blandford Rd.* ⬦ *Off B3082, 1½ miles northwest of Wimborne Minster* ☎ *01202/883402* ⊕ *www.nationaltrust. org.uk* 🎫 *£17.20; £11.80 gardens only, Mar.–Oct. 4–6 pm* ⊗ *Top floor closed Nov.–Mar.*

Priest's House Museum & Garden

HOUSE | With an emphasis on local archaeological finds (largely Roman and Iron Age), costume, and history, this museum in an Elizabethan town house charts the development of the East Dorset area. You can see how residents might have lived in the house through rooms furnished in the styles of several periods, including a 17th-century hall and working Victorian kitchen. In the garden are displays of agricultural and horticultural tools plus a tearoom. ⊠ 23–27 High St. ☎ 01202/882533 ⊕ www.priest-house. co.uk ☜ £5.75 ⊗ Closed Sun.

Wimborne Minster

LIBRARY | Although there has been a church here since the 8th century, the current building, with its crenellated and pinnacled twin towers, was built between 1120 and 1180. The nave reflects these Norman origins in its zigzag molding interspersed with carved heads. Several Gothic components were added later, as were fine Victorian geometric tiles and stained-glass windows. Don't miss the late-17th-century chained library (where books are chained to shelves), one of the first public libraries in Britain and still the country's second-largest chained library. Its collection includes a 14th-century manuscript and a 1522 book with a title page designed by Hans Holbein. Also look out for the pre-Copernican astronomical clock, which dates to before the 15th century. It's on the inside wall of the west tower. ⊠ High St. ☎ 01202/884753 ⊕ www.wimborneminster.org.uk ⊗ Library closed Nov.–Easter except 1st Sat. of month.

🛏 Hotels

★ Museum Inn

$$ | B&B/INN | It's worth seeking out this characterful inn, located 10 miles north of Wimborne Minster, in an Area of Outstanding Natural Beauty. **Pros:** pretty village location; great food; comfortable beds. **Cons:** car required; service

can be slow; portions can be small for some. ⑤ Rooms from: £135 ⊠ High St. ✛ Off A354, near Blandford Forum ☎ 01725/516261 ⊕ www.museuminn. co.uk ☜ 8 rooms ❍ Free breakfast.

Corfe Castle

25 miles south of Wimborne Minster, 15 miles south of Poole, 5 miles southeast of Wareham.

The village of Corfe Castle is best known for the ancient, ruined castle that overlooks it.

ESSENTIALS
VISITOR INFORMATION Discover Purbeck Information Centre. ⊠ Wareham Library, South St. ☎ 01929/552740 ⊕ www. visit-dorset.com.

◉ Sights

Clouds Hill

HOUSE | This brick-and-tile cottage served as the retreat of T. E. Lawrence, better known as Lawrence of Arabia, before he was killed in a motorcycle accident on the road from Bovington in 1935. The house remains very much as he left it, with photos and memorabilia from his time in the Middle East. It's particularly atmospheric on a gloomy day, as there's no electric light. Clouds Hill is 8 miles northwest of Corfe. ⊠ King George V Rd. ☎ 01929/405616 ⊕ www.nationaltrust. org.uk/cloudshill ☜ £7.70 ⊗ Closed Nov.–Feb.

Corfe Castle

ARCHAEOLOGICAL SITE | One of the most dramatic ruins in Britain, Corfe Castle overlooks the picturesque gray limestone village of the same name. The present ruins are of the castle built in 1086, when the great central keep was erected by William the Conqueror to guard the principal route through the surrounding Purbeck Hills. The outer walls and towers were added in the 1270s. Cromwell's

The ruins of Corfe Castle, destroyed during the 17th-century English Civil War, are evocative after a snowfall.

soldiers blew up the castle in 1646 during the Civil War, after a long siege during which its Royalist chatelaine, Lady Bankes, led its defense. ⊠ *Off A351* ☎ *01929/481294* ⊕ *www.nationaltrust. org.uk* ✉ *£12 Apr.–Oct. weekends and bank holidays; £11 all other times.*

Swanage Railway

SCENIC DRIVE | **FAMILY** | Train enthusiasts love this largely volunteer-run railroad that makes 25-minute, 6-mile scenic trips, with steam (and some diesel) locomotives pulling vintage train carriages across the Isle of Purbeck—actually a peninsula. Trips begin from Norden in the center and go to the seaside town of Swanage via Corfe Castle. Small, pretty stations with flower baskets, painted signs, and water bowls for dogs add to the excursion's charm. Trains leave approximately every 80 to 120 minutes in low season, and every 40 minutes in high season. ⊠ *Station House, Springfield Rd.,* *Swanage* ☎ *01929/425800* ⊕ *www.swanagerailway.co.uk* ✉ *£3–£15* ⊙ *Closed Jan., Nov., Feb. except school midterm holiday, Sun.–Fri. in Mar., and weekdays in Dec. except school Christmas holiday.*

🍴 Restaurants

Duke of Wellington

$ | **BRITISH** | This family-run traditional pub that dates back to the 16th century has flagstones, bare stone walls, an inglenook fireplace, an open fire in winter, and a beer garden in the summer. The homemade food leans towards the traditional, with superior versions of old favorites like fish pie. **Known for:** highly regarded beer and ale selection; fresh fish specials; organic and locally sourced Sunday roast lunch. ⑤ *Average main: £14* ⊠ *63 East St.* ☎ *01929/480208* ⊕ *www. dukewareham.co.uk.*

🛏 Hotels

Castle Inn

$$ | B&B/INN | This small inn has a thatched roof, flagstone bar, and other 16th-century features while bedrooms are individually furnished and make the most of the original beams, exposed brickwork, and stone fireplaces. **Pros:** close to Lulworth Cove; great for dog lovers; charming decor. **Cons:** food can be disappointing; rooms over the bar are noisy; some rooms stuffy. ⑤ *Rooms from: £155* ✉ *Main Rd., West Lulworth* ✛ *10 miles west of Corfe Castle* ☎ *01929/400311* ⊕ *www.castleinn-lulworth.co.uk* 🛏 *11 rooms* ⑩ *Free breakfast.*

★ The Pig on the Beach

$$$ | HOTEL | The latest outpost of the Hampshire luxury minichain is in a Victorian Gothic former private residence in an unspoiled village on the scenic, peaceful Studland Peninsula. **Pros:** beautiful location; comfortable bedrooms and welcoming public rooms; excellent restaurant. **Cons:** on the pricey side; breakfast not included; ubiquitous piped music not for everyone. ⑤ *Rooms from: £230* ✉ *Manor House, Manor Rd., Swanage* ☎ *01929/450288* ⊕ *www.thepighotel.com/on-the-beach* 🛏 *23 rooms, 2 cottages, 1 hut* ⑩ *No meals.*

Dorchester

21 miles west of Corfe, 30 miles west of Bournemouth, 43 miles southwest of Salisbury.

The traditional market town of Dorchester was immortalized as Casterbridge by Thomas Hardy in his 19th-century novel *The Mayor of Casterbridge.* In fact, the whole area around here, including a number of villages tucked away in the rolling hills of Dorset, has become known as "Hardy country" because of its connection with the author. Hardy was born in a cottage in the hamlet of Higher Bockhampton, about 3 miles northeast of the town, and his bronze statue looks westward from a bank on Colliton Walk. Two important historical sites, as well as the author's birthplace and a former residence, are a short drive from Dorchester.

Dorchester has many reminders of its Roman heritage. A stroll along Bowling Alley Walk, West Walk, and Colliton Walk follows the approximate line of the original Roman town walls, part of a city plan laid out around AD 70. On the north side of Colliton Park is an excavated Roman villa with a marvelously preserved mosaic floor. While the high street in the center of town can be busy with vehicular traffic, the tourist office has walking itineraries that cover the main points of interest along quieter routes and help you appreciate the character of Dorchester today.

GETTING HERE AND AROUND

Dorchester can be reached from Corfe Castle via A351 and A352. From Salisbury take A354. Park wherever you can (pay parking lots are scattered around the center) and explore the town on foot.

ESSENTIALS

VISITOR INFORMATION Dorchester Tourist Information Centre. ✉ *Dorchester Library and Learning Centre, Charles St.* ☎ *01305/267992* ⊕ *www.visit-dorset.com.*

👁 Sights

Athelhampton House and Gardens

HOUSE | Largely unchanged since it was built in 1485, this outstandingly well-preserved example of domestic Tudor architecture (with 16th- and 20th-century additions) turns up as "Athelhall" in some of Thomas Hardy's writings (Hardy was a frequent visitor and his father, a stonemason, worked on roof repairs here). Don't miss the Great Hall, still with its original linenfold paneling, heraldic stained glass, and vaulted timber

Hardy's Dorset

Among this region's proudest claims is its connection with one of England's most celebrated novelists, Thomas Hardy (1840–1928). Today, it is still possible to get a sense of the landscapes and streetscapes that inspired the writer. If you read some of Hardy's novels before coming to Dorset—evoked as Hardy's partly factual, partly fictional county of Wessex—some places may be immediately recognizable from his descriptions, lending his books a greater resonance. The tranquil countryside surrounding Dorchester is lovingly described in *Far from the Madding Crowd*, while Casterbridge, in *The Mayor of Casterbridge*, stands in for Dorchester itself. Salisbury makes an appearance as "Melchester" in *Jude the Obscure*, and any reader will recognize the village of Shaftesbury, with its steep Gold Hill, a street lined with cottages, as the book's "Shaston." A pilgrimage to Hardy's Wessex should begin at the author's birthplace in Higher Bockhampton, three miles east of Dorchester, and, although his body is in Westminster Abbey in London, his heart is buried in the churchyard in the village of Stinsford, a mile east of Dorchester.

roof. The paneled Library contains more than 3,000 books. Outside, 20 acres of grounds include eight formal walled gardens created in the 19th century and 12 yew pyramids, each 30 feet high. ⊠ *Dorchester ✦ A35, 5 miles east of Dorchester* ☎ *01305/848363* ⊕ *www. athelhampton.com* ⊠ *House and garden £14.50; garden only £10* ⊗ *Closed Sat. year-round and weekdays Nov.–mid-Feb.*

Dinosaur Museum

MUSEUM | FAMILY | This family-oriented museum engages children with fossils, skeletons, life-size dinosaur reconstructions, multimedia displays, and interactive exhibits. ⊠ *Icen Way ✦ Off High East St.* ☎ *01305/269880* ⊕ *www. thedinosaurmuseum.com* ⊠ *£8.99* ⊗ *Closed mid-late Dec.*

Hardy's Cottage

HOUSE | Thomas Hardy's grandfather built this small thatch-and-cob cottage, where the writer was born in 1840, and little has changed since the family left. Here Hardy grew up and wrote many of his early works, including *Far from the Madding Crowd*, at a desk you can still see. Access is by foot only, via a walk through woodland or down a country lane from the parking lot. There's a visitor center with information about the surrounding landscape and trails that let you follow in Hardy's footsteps. ⊠ *Brockhampton La., Higher Bockhampton ✦ ½ mile south of Blandford Rd.* ☎ *01305/262366* ⊕ *www. nationaltrust.org.uk* ⊠ *£7.90* ⊗ *Closed Nov.–mid-Feb. and Mon.–Wed.*

Maiden Castle

ARCHAEOLOGICAL SITE | Although called a castle, this is actually one of the most important pre-Roman archaeological sites in England and the largest, most complex Iron Age hill fort in Europe, made of stone and earth with ramparts that enclose about 45 acres. England's Neolithic inhabitants built the fort some 4,000 years ago, and many centuries later it was a Celtic stronghold. In AD 43 invading Romans, under the general (later emperor) Vespasian, stormed the fort. Finds from the site are on display in the Dorset County Museum in Dorchester. To experience an uncanny silence and sense of mystery, climb Maiden Castle early in the day. Leave your car in the lot at the end of Maiden Castle Way, a 1½-mile lane. ⊠ *Winterborne Monkton ✦ Off A354, 2 miles southwest of Dorchester* ☎ *0370/333–1181* ⊕ *www. english-heritage.org.uk.*

Maumbury Rings

ARCHAEOLOGICAL SITE | This large Neolithic henge, 278 feet in diameter, is the oldest monument in Dorchester and has survived by adapting. In the 1st century AD it became a Roman amphitheater, one of the largest in Britain, and the site of gladiatorial contests and executions. In the Middle Ages it was used for jousting tournaments, while during the English Civil War it was converted into an artillery fort. After the Restoration, it once again became a place of public execution, notoriously that of 80 rebels ordered by the infamous Judge Jeffreys. Vividly evoked in Hardy's *Mayor of Casterbridge*, it's now used for public events such as the Dorset Arts Festival. ⊠ *Maumbury Rd.* ✢ *Off Weymouth Ave.* ⊕ *www.maumburyrings.co.uk.*

Max Gate

HOUSE | Thomas Hardy lived in Max Gate from 1885 until his death in 1928. An architect by profession, Hardy designed the handsome Victorian house himself, and visitors can now see the study where he wrote *Tess of the d'Urbervilles, The Mayor of Casterbridge,* and *Jude the Obscure.* The dining room, the drawing room, and the garden are open to the public. ⊠ *Off Syward Rd.* ✢ *1 mile east of Dorchester* ☎ *01305/262538* ⊕ *www. nationaltrust.org.uk* ⊠ *£7.40* ⊙ *Closed Nov.–mid-Feb. and Mon.–Wed.*

Poundbury

TOWN | Owned by the Duchy of Cornwall and under the aegis of the Prince of Wales, this development in a traditional architectural vernacular style showcases Prince Charles's vision of urban planning, environmental sustainability, and community living. Zoning is strict, with an emphasis on conservation and energy efficiency; private houses coexist with shops, offices, small-scale factories, and leisure facilities. Dorchester's Farmers' Market is held in the Queen Mother's Square the first Saturday of the month. Poundbury, a mile west of Dorchester on the B3150, has attracted the ire of modernist architects, but any properties for sale are quickly snapped up. ⊠ *Poundbury* ⊕ *duchyofcornwall.org/poundbury.html.*

🍴 Restaurants

Yalbury Cottage

$$$$ | **MODERN FRENCH** | Oak-beamed ceilings, exposed stone walls, and inglenook fireplaces add to the charm of this restaurant in a 300-year-old cottage aross the road from where Thomas Hardy went to school. It specializes in set menus featuring superior modern French cooking using locally sourced produce, with dishes like Portland crab fritter with Lyme Bay scallop, beef brisket with Dorset black garlic, and Cornish brill in phyllo pastry. **Known for:** French cuisine with an English twist; good-value fixed-price two- or three-course dinner menus; booking up quickly so making reservations is a good idea. ⑤ *Average main: £43* ⊠ *Bockhampton La., Lower Bockhampton* ☎ *01305/262382* ⊕ *www. yalburycottage.com* ⊙ *No dinner Sun. No lunch Tues.–Sat.*

🛏 Hotels

The Casterbridge

$$ | **B&B/INN** | Small but full of character, this family-owned inn in a Georgian building dating from 1790 is elegantly decorated with period antiques. **Pros:** central location; hospitable owners; good breakfasts. **Cons:** traffic noise in front rooms; water pressure could be better; Wi-Fi not in all bedrooms. ⑤ *Rooms from: £140* ⊠ *49 High East St.* ☎ *01305/264043* ⊕ *www.thecasterbridge.co.uk* ⇌ *11 rooms* ⊙ *Free breakfast.*

Shopping

Wednesday Market

OUTDOOR/FLEA/GREEN MARKETS | This large traditional market sells bric-a-brac and antiques inside and organic local produce and Dorset delicacies such as Blue Vinny cheese (which some connoisseurs prefer to Blue Stilton) outside. ⊠ *Cattle Market, off Weymouth Ave.* ⊕ *www.wimborne-market.co.uk/dorchester-market.*

Activities

Thomas Hardy Society

HIKING/WALKING | From April through October, the Thomas Hardy Society organizes guided walks to sites that inspired locations in Hardy's novels. Readings and discussions accompany the walks, which range from a couple of hours to most of a day. ⊠ *Dorset County Museum, 19 North Sq.* ☎ *01305/251501* ⊕ *www.hardysociety.org.*

Cerne Abbas

6 miles north of Dorchester.

The village of Cerne Abbas, worth a short exploration on foot, has some Tudor houses on the road beside the church. Nearby you can also see the original village stocks.

GETTING HERE AND AROUND

Cerne Abbas is best reached by car from Dorchester to the south or Sherborne to the north via A352.

Sights

Cerne Abbas Giant

LOCAL INTEREST | This colossal and unblushingly priapic figure, 180 feet long, dominates a hillside overlooking the village of Cerne Abbas. The giant carries a huge club and may have originated as a pre-Roman tribal fertility symbol. Alternatively, historians have tended to believe he is a representation of Hercules dating back to the 2nd century AD, but more recent research suggests he may be a 17th-century gibe at Oliver Cromwell. The figure's outlines are formed by 1-foot-wide trenches cut into the ground to reveal the chalk beneath. The best place to view the figure is from the A352 itself, where you can park in one of the numerous nearby turnouts. ⊠ *Cerne Abbas* ✢ *Off A352, 8 miles north of Dorchester* ☎ *01297/489481* ⊕ *www.nationaltrust.org.uk.*

Cerne Abbey

RELIGIOUS SITE | Little remains of this 10th-century Benedictine abbey. However, the grounds of the South Gate House (a private residence constructed in the 16th and 18th centuries using materials from the abbey, including its original Saxon doorway) has some later remnants. The Abbot's Porch, built in 1509, was once the entrance to the abbot's quarters and is notable for its double oriel window with carvings of small animals; the 15th-century guesthouse is one of the few surviving monastic hospices in the United Kingdom. At the other end of the village is the monastery's original Tithe Barn. You are welcome to look around the grounds at the owner's discretion for a small donation. There is also a cottage available for short-term vacation rentals on the grounds. ⊠ *A352* ☒ *Suggested donation £1.*

Sherborne

20 miles north of Dorchester, 15 miles west of Shaftesbury, 40 miles west of Wilton, 43 miles west of Salisbury.

Originally the capital of Wessex (the actual Saxon kingdom, not Hardy's retro conceit), this unspoiled market town is populated with medieval buildings built using the local honey-colored stone. The focal point of the winding streets is Sherborne Abbey, where King Alfred's older brothers are buried. Also worth visiting are the ruins of Sherborne Castle, a Tudor mansion originally built by Sir Walter Raleigh, and its Capability Brown–designed gardens.

GETTING HERE AND AROUND

Hourly trains from Salisbury take 45 minutes to reach Sherborne. The station is at the bottom of Digby Road, near the abbey. Drivers should take A30, passing through Shaftesbury.

ESSENTIALS

VISITOR INFORMATION Sherborne Tourist Information Centre. ⊠ *3 Tilton Ct., Digby Rd.* ☎ *01935/815341* ⊕ *www.visit-dorset. com.*

Sights

Shaftesbury

TOWN | This small market town, the model for "Shaston" in Thomas Hardy's *Jude the Obscure*, sits on a ridge overlooking Blackmore Vale—you can catch a sweeping view of the surrounding countryside from the top of Gold Hill, a steep street lined with cottages so picturesque it was used in an iconic TV commercial to evoke the quintessential British village of yore. Shaftesbury is 20 miles west of Salisbury and 15 miles east of Sherborne. ⊠ *Sherborne* ✛ *Intersection of A30 and A350* ⊕ *www.shaftesburytourism.co.uk.*

Sherborne Abbey

RELIGIOUS SITE | As much as the golden hamstone exterior, majestic tower, and fine flying buttresses impress, the glory of Sherborne Abbey is the delicate 15th-century fan vaulting that extends the length of the soaring nave and choir. Some features from the original 8th-century cathedral, like a Saxon doorway in the northwest corner, still remain. If you're lucky, you might hear "Great Tom," one of the heaviest bells in the world, pealing out from the bell tower. Guided tours are run from April through September on Tuesday (10:30) and Friday (2:30), or by prior arrangement. ⊠ *3 Abbey Close* ☎ *01935/812452* ⊕ *www.sherborneabbey.com.*

★ Sherborne Castle

CASTLE/PALACE | After building this castle in 1594, Sir Walter Raleigh made it his home for 10 years before it passed into the custodianship of the Digby family. The castle's interiors cover a variety of periods, including Tudor, Jacobean, and Georgian. The Victorian Gothic rooms are notable for their splendid plaster ceiling moldings. After admiring the extensive collections of Meissen and Asian porcelain, stroll around the lake and 45 acres of landscaped grounds (a designated English Heritage Grade I site), the work of Capability Brown. The house is less than a mile southeast of town. ⊠ *New Rd.* ☎ *01935/812072* ⊕ *www.sherborne-castle.com* ◹ *Castle and gardens £13.50; gardens only £9* ⊗ *Closed Nov.–early Apr. and Mon. and Fri. except bank holidays.*

🛏 Hotels

The Alders

$ | **B&B/INN** | This homey B&B, a secluded stone house set in an old walled garden opposite a 13th-century church, is in a quiet, unspoiled village 3 miles north of Sherborne. **Pros:** peaceful setting; hospitable owners; excellent breakfasts. **Cons:** a bit remote; unlit walk to dinner; small towels. ⑤ *Rooms from: £85* ⊠ *Off B3145, Sandford Orcas* ☎ *01963/220666* ⊕ *www.thealdersbb.com* ◹ *3 rooms* ☕ *Free breakfast.*

Weymouth

8 miles south of Dorchester, 28 miles south of Sherbourne.

West Dorset's main coastal resort, Weymouth, is known for its sandy and pebble beaches and its royal connections. King George III began seawater bathing here for his health in 1789, setting a trend among the wealthy and fashionable of the day. The legacy of this popularity is Weymouth's many fine buildings, including the Georgian row houses lining the Esplanade. Striking historical details command attention: a wall on Maiden Street holds a cannonball that was embedded in it during the English Civil War, while a nearby column commemorates the embarkation of U.S. forces from Weymouth on D-Day.

Weymouth and its lively harbor provide the full bucket-and-spade seaside experience: donkey rides, sand castles, and plenty of fish-and-chips. Weymouth and Portland hosted the 2012 Olympic sailing events.

GETTING HERE AND AROUND

You can reach Weymouth on frequent local buses and trains from Dorchester or on less frequent services from Bournemouth. The bus and train stations are close to each other near King's Statue, on the Esplanade. If you're driving, take A354 from Dorchester and park on or near the Esplanade—an easy walk from the center—or in a lot near the harbor.

◉ Sights

★ Chesil Beach

BEACH—SIGHT | The unique geological curiosity known as Chesil Beach (official slogan: "18 miles and 180 billion pebbles") is in fact not a beach but a tombolo, a thin strip of sand and shingle that joins two bits of land together. Part of the Jurassic Coast World Heritage Site, Chesil, 18 miles long, is remarkable for its pebbles that decrease in size from east to west. It's also known as the setting for Ian McEwan's novel and its 2018 film adaptation, *On Chesil Beach*. You can access the eastern section leading to the Isle of Portland (a peninsula) and the western section beyond Abbotsbury year-round. However, access to the central section is restricted, with its environmentally sensitive eastern side facing the

shallow saltwater Fleet Lagoon entirely off-limits and its western side closed April to August to protect nesting birds. The entire beach is better suited to walking and fossil hunting than sunbathing and swimming since powerful undertows make the water dangerous (plus it's cold). There are walking and cycle trails along the rugged coastline. **Amenities:** parking (at five access points, £6–£8 per day); toilets (at five access points). **Best for:** walking; windsurfing. ⊠ *Portland Beach Rd., Portland* ☎ *03108/807000* ⊕ *www.jurassiccoast.org.*

🍴 Restaurants

Pascal's Brasserie

$ | BISTRO | Tucked away from the busy harbor, this French-owned local favorite serves classic Gallic dishes such as onion soup, eggs Benedict, and croque monsieur, plus pastas and salads. If you're looking for an afternoon pit stop, try the substantial, and very English, cream tea selection and other superlative baked goods. **Known for:** delicious homemade cakes and scones; gluten-free options; excellent breakfasts. ⑤ *Average main: £9* ⊠ *8 Cove St.* ☎ *01305/777500* 🚫 *No credit cards* ☾ *No dinner.*

The Ship Inn

$ | BRITISH | Whether you're in the mood for a hearty steak-and-ale pie or crayfish spaghetti with lobster sauce, this welcoming pub-restaurant with great views over the harbor specializes in a well-executed, modern approach to classic British pub fare. Service is attentive and friendly, and there's an excellent selection of beers and ales. **Known for:** outdoor seating overlooking harbor; several vegetarian and even vegan options; Sunday roast lunch. ⑤ *Average main: £14* ⊠ *Custom House Quay* ☎ *01305/773879* ⊕ *www.shipweymouth.co.uk.*

Sunrise is lovely at the Cobb, the harbor wall built by Edward I in Lyme Regis.

Abbotsbury

10 miles northwest of Weymouth.

Pretty Abbotsbury is at the western end of Chesil Beach and has a swannery. In other parts of the village, you can also visit a children's farm, housed in an impressive medieval barn, and subtropical gardens.

GETTING HERE AND AROUND

By car, take B3157 from Weymouth or the steep and very minor road passing through Martinstown off A35 from Dorchester; the latter route has marvelous views of the coast.

ESSENTIALS

VISITOR INFORMATION Abbotsbury Tourism. ⊠ *West Yard Barn, West St.* ☏ *01305/871130* ⊕ *www.abbotsbury. co.uk.*

◉ Sights

Abbotsbury Swannery

NATURE PRESERVE | FAMILY | Just outside Abbotsbury is this lagoon, a famous swan breeding ground and the only managed colony of nesting mute swans in the world. Originally tended by Benedictine monks as a source of meat in winter, the swans have remained for centuries, drawn by the lagoon's soft, moist eelgrass—a favorite food—and fresh water. They now build nests in reeds provided by the swannery. Cygnets hatch between mid-May and late June. You can try hand-feeding the birds at noon and 4 pm daily. There's also a giant maze, the largest willow maze in the county. ⊠ *New Barn Rd.* ☏ *01305/871858* ⊕ *www.abbots-bury-tourism.co.uk/swannery* ⛱ *£12.75; £19.50 includes subtropical gardens and children's farm* ⊗ *Closed Nov.–mid-Mar.*

Hardy Monument

MEMORIAL | On the hills above Abbotsbury stands this monument dedicated to Sir Thomas Masterman Hardy, Lord Nelson's flag captain at Trafalgar, to whom Nelson's dying words, "Kiss me, Hardy," were addressed. The monument lacks charm, but in clear weather you can scan the whole coastline between the Isle of Wight and Start Point in Devon. ⊠ *Black Down, Portesham* ☎ *01297/489481* ⊕ *www. nationaltrust.org.uk* 🖃 *£2* ⊙ *Closed Oct.– Mar. and Mon. and Tues. in Apr.–Sept.*

🍴 Restaurants

The Seaside Boarding House
$$ | MODERN BRITISH | Perched on a bluff overlooking sandy Burton Beach, this airy restaurant in a hamlet at the western end of Chesil Beach specializes in freshly caught seafood and locally raised meat and produce. The small but focused menu includes dishes like turbot with leeks in mussel broth, whole lemon sole with spinach, and grilled Cornish sardines on toast. **Known for:** fresh seafood; excellent cocktails; great views from terrace. ⑤ *Average main: £20* ⊠ *Cliff Rd.* ☎ *01308/897205* ⊕ *www.theseasideboardinghouse.com.*

Lyme Regis

19 miles west of Abbotsbury.

"A very strange stranger it must be, who does not see the charms of the immediate environs of Lyme, to make him wish to know it better," wrote Jane Austen in *Persuasion.* Judging from the summer crowds, many people agree with her. The scenic seaside town of Lyme Regis and the so-called Jurassic Coast are highlights of southwest Dorset. The crumbling Channel-facing cliffs in this area are especially fossil rich.

GETTING HERE AND AROUND
Lyme Regis is off the A35, extending west from Bournemouth and Dorchester. Drivers should park as soon as possible—there are lots at the top of town—and explore the town on foot. First buses run here from Dorchester and Axminster,

6 miles northwest; the latter town is on the main rail route from London Waterloo and Salisbury, as is Exeter, from which you can take the X53 bus.

ESSENTIALS
VISITOR INFORMATION Lyme Regis Tourist Information Centre. ⊠ *Guildhall Cottage, Church St.* ☎ *01297/442138* ⊕ *www. visit-dorset.com.*

👁 Sights

The Cobb
MARINA | Lyme Regis is famous for its curving stone harbor breakwater, the Cobb, built by King Edward I in the 13th century to improve the harbor. The Duke of Monmouth landed here in 1685 during his ill-fated attempt to overthrow his uncle, James II, and the Cobb figured prominently in the movie of John Fowles's novel *The French Lieutenant's Woman,* as well as in the 1995 film version of Jane Austen's *Persuasion.* There's a sweeping coastal view to Chesil Beach to the east. ⊠ *Lyme Regis* ⊕ *www. lymeregis.org/the-cobb.aspx.*

Dinosaurland Fossil Museum
MUSEUM | FAMILY | Located in a former church, this compact private museum run by a paleontologist has an excellent collection of local fossils with more than 12,000 specimens dating back 200 million years. It also provides information on regional geology, how fossils develop, and guided fossil-hunting walks. There are more fossils for sale in the shop on the ground floor along with minerals. ⊠ *Coombe St.* ☎ *01297/443541* ⊕ *www.dinosaurland. co.uk* 🖃 *£5* ⊙ *Closed mid-Oct.–mid-Feb.*

Lyme Regis Marine Aquarium
ZOO | FAMILY | This small but child-friendly aquarium has the usual up-close look at maritime creatures, from spider crabs to fish found in nearby Lyme Bay. Children love hand-feeding the gray mullets and getting up-close to starfish, lobsters, and crabs. ⊠ *The Cobb Lower Walkway* ☎ *01297/444230* ⊕ *www.*

lymeregismarineaquarium.co.uk ⌦ £6
⊘ Closed weekdays Nov.–Feb.

Lyme Regis Museum

MUSEUM | A gabled and turreted Edwardian building on the site of fossilist Mary Anning's former home, this lively museum is devoted to the town's maritime and domestic history, geology, local artists, writers (John Fowles was an honorary curator for a decade), and, of course, fossils. The museum also leads fossil-hunting and local history walks throughout the year. ⊠ Bridge St. ☎ 01297/443370 ⊕ www.lymeregismuseum.co.uk ⌦ £4.95 ⊘ Closed Mon. and Tues. in Nov.–late Mar.

🍴 Restaurants

The Bell Cliff Restaurant and Tea Rooms

$ | BRITISH | This cozy, child-and-dog-friendly restaurant in a 17th-century building at the bottom of Lyme Regis's main street makes a great spot for a light lunch or a cream tea with views over the bay. Apart from hot drinks and sandwiches (including fresh crab), you can order more substantial dishes like sausages and mashed potatoes, mac-and-cheese, or mussels with bacon and cider. **Known for:** large portions; vegan full English breakfast; noisy and cramped ambience. ⑤ Average main: £11 ⊠ 5–6 Broad St. ☎ 01297/442459 ⊘ No dinner Nov.–Mar.

★ Hix Oyster & Fish House

$$ | SEAFOOD | This coastal outpost of one of London's trendiest restaurants combines stunning views overlooking the Cobb with the celebrity-chef's trademark high standards and originality. Simply cooked and beautifully presented seafood rules here, including fillet of pollock with wild garlic, grilled fish on the bone, and, of course, local oysters. **Known for:** expertly prepared and locally sourced seafood; great views of the coast; extensive dessert menus. ⑤ Average main: £19 ⊠ Cobb Rd. ☎ 01297/446910 ⊕ www.hixoysterandfishhouse.co.uk ⊘ No lunch Mon. and Tues. No dinner Sun.

🛏 Hotels

Alexandra

$$$ | HOTEL | Magnificently sited above the Cobb, this family-owned boutique hotel combines contemporary design with the genteel charm of yesteryear. **Pros:** helpful staff; deck overlooking the Cobb and bay; central location. **Cons:** cheaper rooms have no sea views; food can be uneven; restricted parking. ⑤ Rooms from: £229 ⊠ Pound St. ☎ 01297/442010 ⊕ www.hotelalexandra.co.uk ⊘ Closed Jan. ⌔ 25 rooms ⑩ Free breakfast.

Coombe House

$ | B&B/INN | Tucked away in a stone house one minute from the seafront on one of the oldest lanes in Lyme, this uncluttered, stylish B&B has genial hosts and airy, modern guest rooms decorated in maritime blue and white. **Pros:** friendly owners; pleasant rooms; central location. **Cons:** books up fast; simple amenities; relaxed atmosphere not for everyone. ⑤ Rooms from: £72 ⊠ 41 Coombe St. ☎ 01297/443849 ⊕ www.coombe-house.co.uk ⌔ 3 rooms ⑩ Free breakfast.

🏃 Activities

Dorset Coast Path

HIKING/WALKING | This 95-mile path—a section of the 630-mile-long South West Coast Path National Trail—runs east from Lyme Regis to Old Harry Rocks near Studland, bypassing Weymouth and taking in the quiet bays, shingle beaches, and low chalk cliffs of the coast. Some highlights are Golden Cap, the highest point on the South Coast; the Swannery at Abbotsbury; Chesil Beach; Durdle Door; and Lulworth Cove (between Weymouth and Corfe Castle). Villages and isolated pubs dot the route, as do many rural B&Bs. ⊠ Lyme Regis ☎ 01752/896237 ⊕ www.southwest-coastpath.org.uk.

Chapter 7

CORNWALL AND
THE WEST COUNTRY

7

Updated by
Robert Andrews

👁 Sights   🍴 Restaurants   🛏 Hotels   🛍 Shopping   🍸 Nightlife

★★★★☆   ★★★★☆   ★★★☆☆   ★★☆☆☆   ★★☆☆☆

WELCOME TO CORNWALL AND THE WEST COUNTRY

TOP REASONS TO GO

★ **Coastal walks:** For high, dramatic cliff scenery, choose the Exmoor coast around Lynmouth or the coast around Tintagel. The South West Coast Path is 630 miles long.

★ **Riding or hiking on Dartmoor:** Escape to southern England's greatest wilderness—a treeless expanse dotted with rocky outcrops. There are many organized walks and pony-trekking operations.

★ **Tate St. Ives Gallery:** There's nowhere better to absorb the local arts scene than this offshoot of London's Tate Museum in the pretty seaside town of St. Ives. A rooftop café claims views over Porthmeor Beach.

★ **A visit to Eden:** It's worth the journey west for Cornwall's Eden Project alone—a wonderland of plant life in a former clay pit. Two gigantic geodesic "biomes" are filled with flora.

★ **Wells Cathedral:** A perfect example of medieval craftsmanship, the building is a stunning spectacle.

1 Bristol.

2 Wells.

3 Glastonbury.

4 Dunster.

5 Exmoor National Park.

6 Porlock.

7 Lynton and Lynmouth.

8 Clovelly.

9 Cornwall.

10 Plymouth.

11 Dartmoor National Park.

12 Tavistock and around.

13 Lydford.

14 Okehampton.

15 Chagford.

16 Exeter.

17 Topsham.

18 Beer.

19 Torquay.

20 Totnes.

21 Dartmouth.

Clevedon
Bristol
Weston
Super Mare
M5

Bristol Channel

Lynmouth 7
Lynton
6 Porlock
4
Dunster
A39
Wells
2
Glastonbury
3
A37

Exmoor
National Park
5
Bridgwater

Barnstaple
Taunton
SOMERSET
A303

Barnstaple
Bay
8
Clovelly
A361

DEVON
A377
M5

Honiton
DORSET

A39
A386
A30
Exeter
16
Topsham
18
A35

Boscastle
Okehampton
17
Beer

Tintagel
Launceston
13
14
15

Port Isaac
A30
Lydford
Chagford
Exmouth

CORNWALL
Tavistock
12
Dartmoor
National Park
A380
19

Bodmin
A388
11
A38
Torquay
Torbay

A390
A38
20
Paignton

St. Austell
Fowey
10
Plymouth
Totnes
21
Brixham
Dartmouth

St Austell
Bay
A379

English Channel

England's West Country is a land of granite promontories, windswept moors, hideaway hamlets, and—above all—the sea. Leafy, narrow country roads lead through miles of buttercup meadows and cider-apple orchards to heathery heights and mellow villages. With their secluded beaches and dreamy backwaters, Somerset, Devon, and Cornwall can be some of England's most relaxing regions to visit.

The counties of the West Country each have their own distinct flavor, and each comes with a regionalism that borders on patriotism. Somerset is noted for its rolling green countryside; Devon's wild and dramatic moors—bare, boggy, upland heath dominated by heathers and gorse—contrast with the restfulness of its many sandy beaches and coves; and Cornwall has managed to retain a touch of its old insularity, despite the annual invasion of thousands of people lured by the Atlantic waves or the ripples of the English Channel.

The historic port of Bristol is where you come across the first unmistakable burrs of the western brogue. Its Georgian architecture and a dramatic gorge create a backdrop to what has become one of Britain's most dynamic cities. To the south lie the cathedral city of Wells and Glastonbury, with its ruined abbey and Arthurian associations. Abutting the north coast is heather-covered Exmoor National Park.

There's more wild moorland in Devon, where Dartmoor is famed for its ponies roaming amid an assortment of strange tors (rocky outcroppings eroded into weird shapes). Devon's coastal towns are as interesting for their cultural and historical appeal—many were smuggler havens—as for their scenic beauty. Parts of south Devon resemble some balmy Mediterranean shore—hence its sobriquet, the English Riviera.

Cornwall, England's westernmost county, has always regarded itself as separate from the rest of Britain, and the Arthurian legends really took root here, not least at Tintagel Castle, the legendary birthplace of Arthur. The south coast is filled with sandy beaches, delightful coves, and popular resorts.

MAJOR REGIONS
Bristol, Wells, and North Devon. On the eastern side of this region is the vibrant city of Bristol. From here you might head south to the pretty cathedral city of Wells and continue on via Glastonbury, which

just might be the Avalon of Arthurian legend. Proceed west along the Somerset coast into Devon, skirting the moorlands of Exmoor and tracing the northern shore via Clovelly.

Cornwall. You're never more than 20 miles from the sea in this western outpost of Britain, and the maritime flavor imbues such port towns as Padstow and Falmouth. A string of good beaches and resort towns such as St. Ives pull in the summer crowds.

Plymouth and Dartmoor. Just over the border from Cornwall is Plymouth, an unprepossessing city but one with a historic old core and splendid harbor that recall a rich maritime heritage. North of Plymouth, you can explore the vast, boggy reaches of hilly Dartmoor, the setting for the Sherlock Holmes classic *The Hound of the Baskervilles*. This national park is a great place to hike or go horseback riding away from the crowds.

Exeter and South Devon. The ancient city of Exeter, Devon's county seat, has preserved some of its historical character despite wartime bombing. From Exeter you can explore southeast to the estuary village of Topsham. Sheltered by the high mass of Dartmoor to the west, the coastal resort area of Torbay, known as the English Riviera, enjoys a mild, warm climate that allows for subtropical vegetation, including palm trees. Between the two, on the banks of the River Dart, is the pretty market town of Totnes, while the well-to-do yachting center of Dartmouth lies south of Torbay at the river's estuary.

Planning

When to Go

In July and August, traffic chokes the roads leading into the West Country. Somehow the region squeezes in all the "grockles," or tourists, and the chances of finding

a remote oasis of peace and quiet are severely curtailed. The beaches and resort towns are either bubbling with zest or unbearably tacky, depending on your point of view. In summer, your best option is to find a secluded hotel and make brief excursions from there. Avoid traveling on Saturday, when weekly rentals start and finish, and the roads are jammed. Most properties that don't accept business year-round open for Easter and close in late September or October. Those that remain open have reduced hours. Winter has its own appeal: the Atlantic waves crash dramatically against the coast, and the austere Cornish cliffs are at their most spectacular.

The most notable festivals are Padstow's Obby Oss, a traditional celebration of the arrival of summer that takes place around May 1; the Cornish-themed Golowan Festival in Penzance in late June; and the St. Ives September Festival of music and art in mid-September. In addition, many West Country maritime towns host regattas over summer weekends. The best times to visit Devon are late summer and early fall, during the end-of-summer festivals, especially popular in the coastal towns of east Devon.

FESTIVALS
Exeter Festival of South West Food and Drink

FESTIVALS | FAMILY | This festival, which showcases local producers, chefs, and their gastronomic specialties, takes place in Northernhay Gardens over three days in early May. There are talks, demonstrations, kids' cookery classes, and live music in the evenings. ⊠ *Exeter* ⊕ *www. exeterfoodanddrinkfestival.co.uk.*

Glastonbury Festival

FESTIVALS | Held in Pilton (a few miles from the town of Glastonbury), the Glastonbury Festival is England's biggest and perhaps best annual rock festival. For five days over the last weekend in June, it hosts hundreds of bands—established and up-and-coming—on three main stages and myriad smaller venues. Tickets are steeply priced—around £270—and sell out months in advance; they include entertainment, a camping area, and service facilities. ✉ Pilton ⊕ www.glastonburyfestivals.co.uk.

Planning Your Time

The elongated shape of Britain's southwestern peninsula means that you may well spend more time traveling than seeing the sights. The key is to base yourself in one or two places and make day trips to the surrounding region. The cities of Bristol, Exeter, and Plymouth make handy bases from which to explore the region, but they can also swallow up a lot of time, at the expense of smaller, less demanding places. The same is true of the resorts of Torquay, Newquay, and Falmouth, which can get very busy. Choose instead towns and villages such as Wells, Lynmouth, Port Isaac, St. Mawes, and Fowey to soak up local atmosphere. If you stick to just a few towns in Somerset and Devon (Bristol, Wells, and Exeter) you could get a taste of the area in four or five days. If you intend to cover Cornwall, at the end of the peninsula, you'll need at least a week. Allow time for aimless rambling—the best way to explore the moors and the coast—and leave enough free time for doing nothing at all.

Getting Here and Around

AIR

Bristol International Airport, a few miles southwest of the city, has frequent flights from London, as well as from Dublin, Amsterdam, and other international cities. Exeter International Airport, 5 miles east of the city, and Cornwall Airport Newquay, 5 miles northeast of town, both have daily flights to London.

AIRPORT INFORMATION Bristol International Airport. ✉ A38, Lulsgate Bottom ☎ 0371/334–4444 ⊕ www.bristolairport.co.uk. **Cornwall Airport Newquay.** ✉ Off A3059, St. Mawgan ☎ 01637/860600 ⊕ www.cornwallairportnewquay.com. **Exeter International Airport.** ✉ A30, Clyst Honiton ☎ 01392/367433 ⊕ www.exeter-airport.co.uk.

BUS

National Express buses leave London's Victoria Coach Station for Bristol (2½ hours), Exeter (4–5 hours), Plymouth (5–6 hours), and Penzance (8–10 hours). Megabus offers cheap service to Bristol, Exeter, Plymouth, Newquay, Bodmin, and Falmouth (book online to avoid premium-line costs). There's also a good network of regional bus services. First buses serve Somerset, Devon, and Cornwall, and Stagecoach South West covers mainly south Devon and the north Devon coast. Dartline Coaches has a small network in Devon, and Plymouth Citybus operate around Plymouth and north and east Cornwall. First and Stagecoach South West offer money-saving one- or seven-day passes good for unlimited bus travel. Traveline can help you plan your trip.

CONTACTS Dartline Coaches. ☎ 01392/872900 ⊕ www.dartline-coaches.co.uk. **First.** ☎ 0345/602–0121 ⊕ www.firstgroup.com. **Megabus.** ☎ 0900/160–0900 for booking, 0141/352–4444 for general inquiries ⊕ uk.megabus.com. **National Express.** ☎ 0871/781–8181 ⊕ www.nationalexpress.com. **Plymouth Citybus.** ☎ 01752/662271 ⊕ www.plymouthbus.co.uk. **Stagecoach South West.** ☎ 01392/427711 ⊕ www.stagecoachbus.com. **Traveline.** ☎ 0871/200–2233 ⊕ www.travelinesw.com.

CAR

Unless you confine yourself to a few towns—for example, Exeter, Penzance, and Plymouth—you'll be at a huge disadvantage without your own transportation. The region has a few main arteries, but you should take minor roads whenever possible, if only to see the real West Country at a leisurely pace.

The fastest route from London to the West Country is via the M4 and M5 motorways. Allow at least two hours to drive to Bristol, three to Exeter. The main roads heading west are the A30 (burrowing through the center of Devon and Cornwall all the way to the tip of Cornwall), the A39 (near the northern shore), and the A38 (near the southern shore, south of Dartmoor and taking in Plymouth).

TRAIN

Rail travelers can make use of a fast service connecting Exeter, Plymouth, and Penzance. Great Western Railway and South Western Railway serve the region from London's Paddington and Waterloo stations. Average travel time to Exeter is 2½ hours, to Plymouth 3¼ hours, and to Penzance about 5½ hours. Once you've arrived, however, you'll find trains to be of limited use in the West Country, as only a few branch lines leave the main line between Exeter and Penzance.

Freedom of the South West tickets provide three days of unlimited travel throughout the West Country in any seven-day period or eight days in any 15-day period. Localized Ranger passes cover Devon or Cornwall.

CONTACTS National Rail Enquiries. ☎ 0345/748–4950 ⊕ www.nationalrail. co.uk.

Restaurants

The last several years have seen a food renaissance in England's West Country. In the top restaurants the accent is firmly on local and seasonal products. Seafood, from Atlantic pollock to Helford River oysters, is the number one choice along the coasts, and it's available in places from haute restaurants to harborside fish shacks. Celebrity chefs have marked their pitch all over the region, including Michael Caines outside Exeter, Mitch Tonks in Dartmouth, Nathan Outlaw in Port Isaac, and Rick Stein and Paul Ainsworth in Padstow. Better-known establishments are often completely booked on Friday or Saturday, so reserve well in advance.

Hotels

Accommodations include national hotel chains, represented in all of the region's principal centers, as well as ancient inns and ubiquitous bed-and-breakfast places. Availability can be limited on the coasts during August and during the weekend everywhere, so book well ahead. Many farmhouses also rent out rooms—offering tranquil rural surroundings—but these lodgings are often difficult to reach without a car. If you have a car, though, renting a house or cottage with a kitchen may be ideal. It's worth finding out about the weekend and winter deals that many hotels offer.

Restaurant and hotel reviews have been shortened. For full information, visit Fodors. com. Restaurant prices are the average cost of a main course at dinner, or if dinner is not served, at lunch. Hotel prices are the lowest cost of a standard double room in high season, including 20% V.A.T.

WHAT IT COSTS in Pounds			
$	$$	$$$	$$$$
RESTAURANTS			
under £16	£16–£23	£24–£30	over £30
HOTELS			
under £125	£125–£225	£226–£350	over £350

Visitor Information

CONTACTS Visit Cornwall. ✉ 30 Boscawen St., Truro ☎ 01872/261735 ⊕ www. visitcornwall.com Ⓜ. **Visit Devon.** ⊕ www.visitdevon.co.uk. **Visit Somerset.** ☎ 01749/835416 ⊕ www.visitsomerset. co.uk.

Bristol

120 miles west of London, 46 miles south of Birmingham, 45 miles east of Cardiff, 13 miles northwest of Bath.

The West Country's biggest city (population 430,000), Bristol has, in recent years, become one of the country's most vibrant centers, with a thriving cultural scene encompassing some of the best contemporary art, theater, and music. Buzzing bars, cafés, and restaurants, and a largely youthful population make it an attractive place to spend time.

Now that the city's industries no longer rely on the docks, the historic harbor along the River Avon has been given over to recreation. Arts and entertainment complexes, museums, and galleries fill the quayside. The pubs and clubs here draw the under-25 set and make the area fairly boisterous (and best avoided) on Friday and Saturday nights.

Bristol also trails a great deal of history in its wake. It can be called the "birthplace of America" with some confidence, for John Cabot and his son Sebastian sailed from the old city docks in 1497 to touch down on the North American mainland, which he claimed for the English crown. The city had been a major center since medieval times, but in the 17th and 18th centuries it became the foremost port for trade with North America, and it played a leading role in the Caribbean slave trade. Bristol was the home of William Penn, developer of Pennsylvania, and a haven for John Wesley, whose Methodist movement played an important role in colonial Georgia.

GETTING HERE AND AROUND

Bristol has good connections by bus and train to most cities in the country. From London, calculate about 2½ hours by bus or 1¾ hours by train. From Cardiff it's about 50 minutes by bus or train. By train, make sure you get tickets for Bristol Temple Meads Station (not Bristol Parkway), which is a short bus, taxi, or river-bus ride from the center. The bus station is more central, near the Broadmead shopping center. Most sights can be visited on foot, though a bus or a taxi is necessary to reach the Clifton neighborhood.

ESSENTIALS

VISITOR INFORMATION Bristol Tourist Information Centre. ⊠ *E Shed, Canon's Rd.* ☎ *0117/929–9205* ⊕ *www.visitbristol. co.uk.*

◉ Sights

Berkeley Castle

CASTLE/PALACE | In the sleepy village of Berkeley (pronounced *bark*-ley), this castle is perfectly preserved, down to its medieval turrets, and full of family treasures. It witnessed the murder of King Edward II in 1327—the cell in which it occurred can still be seen. Edward was betrayed by his French consort, Queen Isabella, and her paramour, the Earl of Mortimer. Roger De Berkeley, a Norman knight, began work on the castle in 1153, and it has remained in the family ever since. Magnificent furniture, tapestries, and pictures fill the state apartments, but even the ancient buttery and kitchen are interesting. Guided tours and entry to the Butterfly House (May–September) are included in the ticket price. The castle is 20 miles north of Bristol, accessed from M5. ⊠ *Off A38, Berkeley* ☎ *01453/810303* ⊕ *www. berkeley-castle.com* 🎟 *£14* 🕙 *Closed Thurs.–Sat. and Nov.–late Mar.*

Bristol Zoo Gardens

ZOO | FAMILY | Alongside the leafy expanse of Clifton Down is one of the country's most famous zoos, with more than 400 animal species living in 12 acres of gardens. The Seal and Penguin coasts, with underwater viewing, are rival attractions for Gorilla Island, Bug World, and Twilight World. Take Bus 8 from Temple Meads Station or the city center. ■TIP➔ **Online tickets bought at least a day in advance are cheaper than tickets bought at the gate. In**

Bristol, Wells, and North Devon

Map labels: WALES, Newport, Berkeley Castle, Bridgend, Cardiff, Clevedon, Bristol, A470, A48, M4, Barry, Penarth, Tyntesfield, A38, A37, Weston Super Mare, Churchill, Stanton Drew Circles, M5, Chew Magna, Bristol Channel, East Brent, Cheddar, Farrington Gurney, Highbridge, Wookey Hole Caves, Wells, Ilfracombe, Lynton, Lynmouth, Porlock, Minehead, Dunster, Nether Stowey, Glastonbury, A361, Porlock Weir, A39, Woolacombe, Exmoor National Park, A509, Bridgwater, A39, Knowle, A399, Barnstaple, A396, North Petherton, Barnstaple Bay, SOMERSET, A37, Taunton, A303, Clovelly, Umberleigh, A361, A3065, South Petherton, A39, Yeovil, Great Torrington, Colleton Mills, Buckland Saint Mary, A386, A377, Tiverton, Waterloo Cross, A303, A37, DEVON, M5, DORSET, Hele Bridge, Copplestone, Honiton, Fairmile, Kilmington, Okehampton, A30, A3052, Lyme Regis, A35, Launceston, A30, Exeter, Topsham, Dartmoor National Park, A38, Exmouth, A388, A380, 0   10 mi, 0   10 km

addition, travelers to the zoo by bus or cycle can download a voucher from the website and present it with their bus ticket or bike helmet at the gate for a **33% discounted entry.** ✉ *Clifton Down* ☎ *0117/428–5300* ⊕ *www.bristolzoo.org.uk* ✈ *£13.40– £17.85, depending on day.*

Church of St. Mary Redcliffe

RELIGIOUS SITE | Built by Bristol merchants who wanted a place in which to pray for the safe (and profitable) voyages of their ships, the rib-vaulted, 14th-century church was called "the fairest in England" by Queen Elizabeth I. High up on the nave wall hang the arms and armor of Sir William Penn, father of the founder of Pennsylvania. The church is a five-minute walk from Temple Meads train station toward the docks. ✉ *Redcliffe Way* ☎ *0117/231–0060* ⊕ *www. stmaryredcliffe.co.uk* ✈ *Free.*

Clifton Suspension Bridge

BRIDGE/TUNNEL | FAMILY | A monument to Victorian engineering, this 702-foot-long bridge spans the Avon Gorge. Work began on Isambard Kingdom Brunel's design in 1831, but the bridge wasn't completed until 1864. Free hour-long guided tours usually take place on weekends at 3 between Easter and October or 2 from November to Easter, departing from the tollbooth at the Clifton end of the bridge. At the far end of the bridge, the **Clifton Suspension Bridge Visitor Centre** has an engaging exhibition on the bridge and its construction, including a range of videos and hands-on experiences. Near the bridge lies **Clifton Village,** studded with boutiques, antiques shops, and smart crafts shops in its lanes and squares. Bus No. 8 from Bristol Temple Meads Station and the city center

stops in Clifton Village. ✉ *Bridge Rd., Leigh Woods* ☎ *0117/974–4664* ⊕ *www. cliftonbridge.org.uk* ⬛ *Free.*

★ M Shed

MUSEUM | FAMILY | In a refurbished transit shed on the harborside, this museum is dedicated to the city's history. The collection comprises three main galleries—Bristol People, Bristol Places, and Bristol Life—that focus on everything from the slave trade to scientific inventions to recent cultural innovations associated with the city. Check out the artifacts, photos, and sound and video recordings of and by Bristolians, all jazzed up with the latest interactive technology. Don't forget to take in the magnificent harbor views from the top-floor terrace. ✉ *Princes Wharf, Wapping Rd.* ☎ *0117/352–6600* ⊕ *www. mshed.org* ⬛ *Free* ✆ *Closed Mon., except bank holidays and school vacations.*

New Room

RELIGIOUS SITE | John Wesley and Charles Wesley were among the Dissenters from the Church of England who found a home in Bristol, and in 1739 they built the New Room, a meeting place that became the first Methodist chapel. Its simplicity contrasts with the style of Anglican churches and with the modern shopping center hemming it in. Upstairs you can visit the Preachers' Rooms, now containing a small museum. Charles Wesley's house, situated nearby, is also visitable (⊕ *www. charleswesleyhouse.org.uk*). ✉ *36 The Horsefair* ☎ *0117/926–4740* ⊕ *www. newroombristol.org.uk* ⬛ *Chapel free, museum £7* ✆ *Closed Sun.*

★ SS *Great Britain*

MILITARY SITE | FAMILY | On view in the harbor is the first iron ship to cross the Atlantic. Built by the great English engineer Isambard Kingdom Brunel in 1843, it remained in service until 1970, first as a transatlantic liner and ultimately as a coal storage hulk. Everything from the bakery to the officers' quarters comes complete with sounds and smells of the time, and there are even shadowy glimpses of rats in the galley. You can try on typical garments of the time, descend into the ship's dry dock for a view of the hull and propeller, and climb the ship's rigging (daily between Easter and October and during school vacations, or weekends at other times; £10, or free for under-18s). Your entry ticket also admits you to engrossing exhibits on the ship's history and to Being Brunel, a separate museum dedicated to the life of Isambard Brunel. A short walk east along the harborside from here will bring you to a replica of the *Matthew*, the tiny craft that carried John Cabot to North America in 1497, moored here when it is not sailing on the high seas. ■**TIP➔ Tickets are valid for one year. Buy online for a 5% discount.** ✉ *Great Western Dockyard, Gas Ferry Rd.* ☎ *0117/926–0680* ⊕ *www.ssgreatbritain. org* ⬛ *£17.*

★ Tyntesfield

HOUSE | This extravagant, 35-bedroom Victorian–Gothic Revival mansion has been magnificently restored to reveal a showcase of the decorative arts where every ornate detail compels attention. Besides magnificent woodwork, stained glass, tiles, and original furniture and fabrics, the house contains the modern conveniences of the 1860s, such as a heated billiards table; the servants' quarters are equally absorbing. There's a restaurant and family play area, too. You can see the house, garden, and chapel at your own pace, or join a free garden tour. ■**TIP➔ Arrive early in the day to avoid the crowds competing for timed tickets—Monday and Tuesday are the quietest days.** Tyntesfield is 7 miles southwest of Bristol; the daily bus service X6 is the most convenient public transport from the city (present your ticket for a 20% discount in the café and shop). The house is a 15-minute walk from the bus stop. ✉ *B3128, Wraxall* ☎ *01275/461900* ⊕ *www.nationaltrust.org.uk* ⬛ *£17.40; gardens only £10.75.*

Stanton Drew Circles

ARCHAEOLOGICAL SITE | Three rings, two avenues of standing stones, and a burial chamber make up the Stanton Drew Circles, one of the largest and most mysterious monuments in Britain, dating from 3000 to 2000 BC. It's far less well known than Stonehenge and other circles, however. The size of the circles suggests that the site was once as important as Stonehenge for its ceremonial functions, although little of great visual impact remains. English Heritage supervises the stones, which stand on private land. Access is given at any reasonable time, and a donation of £1 is requested. ■TIP→ **You have to walk through a farmyard to reach the field where the site lies, so wear sturdy shoes.** To get here from Bristol, head south on the A37 and turn right after about 5 miles onto the B3130, marked Stanton Drew. The circles are just east of the village, where more of the stones may be seen in the garden of the Druid's Arms pub. ⊠ *Off B3130, Stanton Drew* ☎ *0370/333–1181* ⊕ *www.english-heritage.org.uk.*

★ We The Curious

MUSEUM | **FAMILY** | One of the country's top family-friendly science centers, this multimedia attraction provides a "hands-on, minds-on" exploration of science and technology in more than 300 interactive exhibits and displays. "All About Us" is dedicated to the inner workings of the human body. Another section allows you to create your own animations. A 3D planetarium in a gleaming stainless-steel sphere takes you on a 30-minute voyage through the galaxy. There are up to 10 shows a day, bookable when you buy your ticket (£2.50–3.50). A popular exhibit lets kids test their skills at creating animations. Allow at least three hours to see it all. ■TIP→ **Buy tickets online for a 5% discount.** ⊠ *Anchor Rd., Harbourside* ☎ *0117/915–1000* ⊕ *www.wethecurious. org* ⊠ *£14.50.*

🍴 Restaurants

Boston Tea Party

$ | **BRITISH** | Despite the name, this laid-back and vaguely eccentric place is quintessentially English and ideal for a relaxed lunch away from the nearby rigors of the Park Street shopping scene. Generous salads, soups, and burgers are available, as are all-day breakfasts and brunches. **Known for:** wholesome snacks and delicious cakes; secluded garden perfect for lounging; ethical food policy. ⑤ *Average main: £8* ⊠ *75 Park St.* ☎ *0117/334–3008* ⊕ *www. bostonteaparty.co.uk.*

Box-E

$$ | **MODERN BRITISH** | The finest of a slew of restaurants and cafés clustered in Bristol's trendy, newly developed Wapping Wharf harborside district, this compact venue might be squeezed into a shipping container, but punches way above what its diminutive dimensions might suggest. The daily changing menu is also on the small side, but every dish is startlingly original, and each is a winner. **Known for:** cutting-edge menus; unique (and very small) setting; hipster clientele. ⑤ *Average main: £16* ⊠ *Unit 10, Cargo 1, Gas Ferry Steps, Wapping Wharf* ⊕ *www. boxebristol.com* ⊘ *Closed Sun. and Mon. No lunch Tues.*

Goram & Vincent

$$ | **MODERN BRITISH** | For glorious views of Bristol's most iconic sight, this restaurant with floor-to-ceiling windows overlooking the Avon Gorge and Clifton Suspension Bridge can't be beat. Sited inside the Avon Gorge Hotel and part of the Hotel du Vin group, it is named after the two legendary giants whose competition for the hand of the beautiful Avona led to the carving of the gorge. **Known for:** spectacular views; steaks and smoked meats; lavish Sunday lunch. ⑤ *Average main: £18* ⊠ *Sion Hill, Clifton* ☎ *0117/403–0210* ⊕ *www.hotelduvin.com.*

Eating Well in the West Country

From cider to cream teas, many specialties tempt your palate in the West Country. Lamb, venison, and, in Devon and Cornwall, seafood, are favored in restaurants, which have risen to heights of gastronomic excellence, notably through the influence of Rick Stein's seafood-based culinary empire in Padstow, in Cornwall. Seafood is celebrated at fishy frolics that include the Newlyn Fish Festival (late August) and Falmouth's Oyster Festival (early or mid-October).

What to Eat

Cheddar. Somerset is the home of Britain's most famous cheese—the ubiquitous cheddar, originally from the Mendip Hills village of the same name. Make certain that you sample a real farmhouse cheddar, made in the traditional barrel shape known as a truckle.

Cream teas. Devon's caloric cream teas consist of a pot of tea, homemade scones, and lots of strawberry jam and thickened clotted cream (a regional specialty, which is sometimes called Devonshire cream).

Pasties. Cornwall's specialty is the pasty, a pastry shell filled with chopped meat, onions, and potatoes. The pasty was devised as a handy way for miners to carry their dinner to work; today's versions are generally pale imitations of the original, though you can still find delicious home-cooked pasties if you're willing to search a little.

Seafood. In many towns in Devon and Cornwall, the day's catch is unloaded from the harbor and transported directly to eateries. The catch varies by season, but lobster is available year-round, as is crab, stuffed into sandwiches at quayside stalls and in pubs.

What to Drink

Perry. This is similar to cider but made from pears.

Scrumpy. For liquid refreshment, try scrumpy, a homemade dry cider that's refreshing but carries a surprising kick.

Wine and mead. English wine, similar to German wine, is made in all three counties (you may see it on local menus), and in Devon and Cornwall you can find a variant of age-old mead made from local honey.

Old India

$ | **INDIAN** | Bristol's former stock exchange has found a new role as an atmospheric Indian eatery. It's the perfect setting for classic and innovative Indian dishes such as *nilgiri korma* (chicken or lamb in a creamy almond sauce with rose petals) and *machi mazadaar* (salmon with mustard seeds and tamarind water). **Known for:** evocative, historic surroundings; tasty Indian cuisine; wide-ranging menu. ⑤ *Average main: £12* ⊠ *34 St.* *Nicholas St.* ☎ *0117/922–1136* ⊕ *www. oldindia.co.uk* ⊘ *Closed Sun. No lunch.*

★ Riverstation

$$ | **MODERN BRITISH** | Occupying a former police station, this modern, clean-lined restaurant affords serene views over the passing swans and boats. Upstairs, the more formal restaurant serves delicately cooked dishes like pigeon breast with date puree and smoked bacon in a madeira jus, and trout with new potatoes, baby leek, and samphires, while the irresistible desserts include coconut and blood

orange mousse, and caramel and apple cheesecake with honey ice cream. **Known for:** warm, friendly environment; soothing river views; good fixed-price menus. ⑤ *Average main: £18* ✉ *The Grove, Harbourside* ☎ *0117/914–4434* ⊕ *www. riverstation.co.uk* ⊗ *No dinner Sun.*

Source Food Hall & Café

$ | **MODERN BRITISH** | In the heart of the old city, this trendy eatery benefits from its location in the St. Nicholas Market by offering a range of fresh seasonal produce, either to eat in or take out from the deli, meat, and fish counters. The wholesome lunch menu might feature Italian cold meats, spiced aubergine with almond couscous and mint yogurt, or Bavette steak with fries. **Known for:** quality local ingredients; great breakfast and coffee; microbrewery beers and ciders. ⑤ *Average main: £11* ✉ *St. Nicholas Market, 1–3 Exchange Ave.* ☎ *0117/927–2998* ⊕ *www.sourcefood.co.uk* ⊗ *Closed Sun. No dinner.*

Watershed

$ | **BRITISH** | The excellent café-restaurant upstairs at Watershed overlooks part of the harborside. Sandwiches and hot snacks are served all day, along with coffees and cakes. **Known for:** artsy environment; harborside views; coffees, beers, and tasty snacks. ⑤ *Average main: £9* ✉ *1 Canon's Rd., Harbourside* ☎ *0117/927–5101* ⊕ *www.watershed.co.uk.*

🛏 Hotels

Bristol Marriott Royal Hotel

$$ | **HOTEL** | With a superb location next to the city's medieval cathedral, this is the more palatial of Bristol's two links in this large chain. **Pros:** good leisure facilities; very central location; helpful staff. **Cons:** not much personality; pricey parking; street noise in some rooms. ⑤ *Rooms from: £127* ✉ *College Green* ☎ *0117/925–5100* ⊕ *www.marriott.co.uk* ⤴ *241 rooms* ⑪ *No meals.*

★ Hotel du Vin

$$ | **HOTEL** | This hip chain has brought high-tech flair to six former sugar-refining warehouses, built in 1728 when the River Frome ran outside the front door. **Pros:** tastefully restored old building; great bathrooms; excellent bar and bistro. **Cons:** traffic-dominated location; dim lighting in rooms; limited parking. ⑤ *Rooms from: £129* ✉ *The Sugar House, Narrow Lewins Mead* ☎ *0117/403–2979* ⊕ *www.hotelduvin.com* ⤴ *40 rooms* ⑪ *No meals.*

★ 9 Prince's Buildings

$$ | **B&B/INN** | With Clifton Suspension Bridge at the end of the street and the Avon Gorge directly below, this elegant Georgian B&B offers classic views of Bristol from its windows. **Pros:** beautiful house in a historic neighborhood; friendly hosts; views of gorge. **Cons:** no elevator; credit cards not accepted; limited capacity. ⑤ *Rooms from: £125* ✉ *9 Prince's Buildings, Clifton* ☎ *0117/973–4615* ⊕ *www.9princesbuildings.co.uk* ⊟ *No credit cards* ⤴ *4 rooms* ⑪ *Free breakfast.*

★ Thornbury Castle

$$ | **HOTEL** | An impressive lodging, Thornbury has everything a genuine 16th-century Tudor castle needs: huge fireplaces, moody paintings, mullioned windows, and a large garden. **Pros:** grand medieval surroundings; sumptuous rooms; doting service. **Cons:** many steps to climb; some rooms and bathrooms are relatively small; unexciting location. ⑤ *Rooms from: £199* ✉ *Castle St., off A38, Thornbury* ☎ *01454/281182* ⊕ *www.thornburycastle.co.uk* ⤴ *28 rooms* ⑪ *Free breakfast.*

Victoria Square Hotel

$ | **HOTEL** | In two mellow Victorian buildings overlooking one of Clifton's leafiest squares, this somewhat functional hotel makes a useful base for exploring this part of Bristol. **Pros:** reasonable rates; pleasant location in Clifton; friendly staff. **Cons:** numerous steps and no elevator; some rooms are small and shabby; limited parking costs extra. ⑤ *Rooms from: £89* ✉ *Victoria*

Sq., Clifton ☎ *0117/973–9058* ⊕ *www. victoriasquarehotel.co.uk* ⤴ *41 rooms* ⦿ *Free breakfast.*

✪ Performing Arts

Arnolfini

ARTS CENTERS | In a converted warehouse on the harbor, the Arnolfini is one of the country's most prestigious contemporary-art venues, known for uncovering innovative yet accessible art. There are galleries, a cinema, a bookshop, and a lively café-bar. ✉ *16 Narrow Quay* ☎ *0117/917–2300* ⊕ *www.arnolfini.org.uk.*

St. George's

CONCERTS | A church built in the 18th century, St. George's now serves as one of the country's leading venues for classical, jazz, and world music, with near-perfect acoustics. Stop by for lunchtime concerts. ✉ *Great George St., off Park St.* ☎ *0845/402–4001* ⊕ *www.stgeorgesbristol.co.uk.*

Watershed

ART GALLERIES—ARTS | A contemporary arts center by the harbor, the Watershed also has a movie theater that screens excellent international films. ✉ *1 Canon's Rd., Harbourside* ☎ *0117/927–5100* ⊕ *www.watershed.co.uk.*

Wells

22 miles south of Bristol, 132 miles west of London.

England's smallest cathedral city, with a population of 10,000, lies at the foot of the Mendip Hills. Although set in what feels like a quiet country town, the great cathedral is a masterpiece of Gothic architecture—the first to be built in the Early English style. The city's name refers to the underground streams that bubble up into St. Andrew's Well within the grounds of the Bishop's Palace. Spring water has run through High Street since the 15th century. Seventeenth-century buildings surround the ancient marketplace, which hosts market days on Wednesday and Saturday.

GETTING HERE AND AROUND

Regular First buses from Bristol take one hour to reach Wells; the bus station is a few minutes south of the cathedral. Drivers should take A37, and park outside the compact and eminently walkable center.

ESSENTIALS

VISITOR INFORMATION Wells Visitor Information Service. ✉ *Wells Museum, 8 Cathedral Green* ☎ *01749/671770* ⊕ *www.wellssomerset.com.*

⊙ Sights

Bishop's Palace

CASTLE/PALACE | The Bishop's Eye gate leading from Market Place takes you to the magnificent, moat-ringed Bishop's Palace, which retains parts of the original 13th-century residence. The peaceful grounds command the most attention, including the gatehouse, the ramparts, and the impressive remains of a late-13th-century great hall that fell into ruin after the lead in its roof was sold in the 16th century. Most rooms of the palace are closed to the public, but you can see the undercroft, the private chapel, and the sumptuously decorated Long Gallery. In summer, ticket-holders can join a free tour of the palace and chapel at 11 am and 2 pm, and of the grounds at noon and 3 pm; in winter there are tours of the palace and gardens at noon. ✉ *Market Pl.* ☎ *01749/988111* ⊕ *www. bishopspalace.org.uk* 🎫 *£9.10.*

Vicar's Close

HISTORIC SITE | To the north of the cathedral, the cobbled Vicar's Close, one of Europe's oldest streets, has terraces of handsome 14th-century houses with strange, tall chimneys. A tiny medieval chapel here is still in use. ✉ *Wells.*

Harmonious and stately, Wells Cathedral has a monumental west front decorated with medieval statues of kings and saints.

Wells Cathedral

RELIGIOUS SITE | The great west towers of the Cathedral Church of St. Andrew, the oldest surviving English Gothic church, can be seen for miles. Dating from the 12th century, Wells Cathedral (as it's more commonly known) derives its beauty from the perfect harmony of all of its parts, the glowing colors of its original stained-glass windows, and its peaceful setting among stately trees and majestic lawns. To appreciate the elaborate west-front facade, approach the building from the cathedral green, accessible from Market Place through a great medieval gate called "penniless porch" (named after the beggars who once waited here to collect alms from worshippers). The cathedral's west front is twice as wide as it is high, and some 300 statues of kings and saints adorn it. Inside, vast inverted arches—known as scissor arches—were added in 1338 to stop the central tower from sinking to one side.

The cathedral has a rare and beautiful medieval clock, the second-oldest working clock in the world, consisting of the seated figure of a man called Jack Blandifer, who strikes a bell on the quarter hour while mounted knights circle in a joust. Near the clock is the entrance to the Chapter House—a small wooden door opening onto a great sweep of stairs worn down on one side by the tread of pilgrims over the centuries. Free guided tours lasting approximately one hour begin at the back of the cathedral; the website also has details of "High Parts" tours (taking in the galleries and roof spaces) and chained library tours, which need booking and are charged, as well as free tours exploring the cathedral's stained glass, stone carvings, and embroidery (usually on Wednesday and Saturday mornings in summer). A cloister restaurant serves snacks and teas. ⊠ *Cathedral Green* ☎ *01749/674483* ⊕ *www.wellscathedral.org.uk* ✉ *£6 suggested donation.*

Wookey Hole Caves

CAVE | FAMILY | These limestone caves in the Mendip Hills, 2 miles northwest of Wells, may have been the home of Iron Age people. Here, according to ancient legend, the Witch of Wookey turned to stone. You can tour the caves, dip your fingers in an underground river (artful lighting keeps things lively), and visit a museum, a penny arcade full of Victorian amusement machines, a mirror maze, fairy gardens, and a working paper mill that once supplied banknotes for the Confederate States of America. ⊠ *Off High St., Wookey Hole* ☎ *01749/672243* ⊕ *www.wookey.co.uk* ⊠ *£19.95* ⊙ *Closed weekdays Dec.–mid-Feb., except school vacations.*

🍴 Restaurants

The Fountain Inn

$ | MODERN BRITISH | Slightly off the tourist track but only a few minutes from the cathedral, this classic gastro-pub offers a winning combination of traditional decor lightened with tasteful modern touches and great, locally sourced food. The eclectic menu includes such standout dishes as Madras chicken curry, confit of duck, and beer-battered haddock. **Known for:** warm, intimate atmosphere; extensive menu with some good English classics; great range of beers, including local ales. ⑤ *Average main: £15* ⊠ *1 St. Thomas St.* ☎ *01749/672317* ⊕ *www.fountaininn.co.uk* ⊙ *No lunch Mon. No dinner Sun.*

Goodfellows

$$ | MODERN EUROPEAN | This little café-resaurant near the cathedral adds a continental touch to sedate Wells. By day exquisite cakes and pastries, chocolate concoctions, and excellent coffee are available, as well as soups, sandwiches, and light meals. **Known for:** Mediterranean style and menus; fresh seafood; tasty patisserie and desserts. ⑤ *Average main: £19* ⊠ *5 Sadler St.* ☎ *01749/673866* ⊕ *www.goodfellowswells.co.uk* ⊙ *No dinner Sun.–Tues.*

🛏 Hotels

Ancient Gate House

$ | B&B/INN | This venerable hostelry makes a convenient and atmospheric base for exploring the area. **Pros:** historic character; cathedral views; good restaurant. **Cons:** steps to climb; cramped rooms; some street noise in front rooms. ⑤ *Rooms from: £120* ⊠ *20 Sadler St.* ☎ *01749/672029* ⊕ *www.ancientgate-house.com* ⊅ *9 rooms* ⦿ *Free breakfast.*

Swan Hotel

$ | HOTEL | A former coaching inn built in the 15th century, the Swan has an ideal spot facing the cathedral. **Pros:** friendly and helpful service; some great views; good restaurant. **Cons:** dated in places; occasional noise issues; parking lot tricky to navigate. ⑤ *Rooms from: £103* ⊠ *11 Sadler St.* ☎ *01749/836300* ⊕ *www.swan-hotelwells.co.uk* ⊅ *55 rooms* ⦿ *Free breakfast.*

Glastonbury

5 miles southwest of Wells, 27 miles south of Bristol, 27 miles southwest of Bath.

A town steeped in history, myth, and legend, Glastonbury lies in the lea of Glastonbury Tor, a grassy hill rising 520 feet above the drained marshes known as the Somerset Levels. The Tor is supposedly the site of crossing ley lines (hypothetical alignments of significant places), and, in legend, Glastonbury is identified with Avalon, the paradise into which King Arthur was reborn after his death.

Partly because of these associations but also because of its world-class rock-music festival, the town has acquired renown as a New Age center, mixing crystal gazers with druids, yogis, and hippies, variously in search of Arthur, Merlin, Jesus—and even Elvis. ■TIP➔ **Between April and September, a shuttle bus runs every half hour between all of Glastonbury's major sights. Tickets are £3.50 and are valid all day.**

GETTING HERE AND AROUND

Frequent buses link Glastonbury to Wells and Bristol, pulling in close to the abbey. Drivers should take the A39. You can walk to all the sights or take the shuttle bus, though you'll need a stock of energy for ascending the Tor.

ESSENTIALS

VISITOR INFORMATION Glastonbury Tourist Information Centre. ⊠ *St. Dunstan's House, 1 Magdalene St.* ☎ *01458/832954* ⊕ *www.glastonburytic.co.uk.*

Sights

Glastonbury Abbey

RELIGIOUS SITE | The ruins of this great abbey, in the center of town, are on the site where, according to legend, Joseph of Arimathea built a church in the 1st century. A monastery had certainly been erected here by the 9th century, and the site drew many pilgrims. The ruins are those of the abbey completed in 1524 and destroyed in 1539, during Henry VIII's dissolution of the monasteries. A sign south of the Lady Chapel marks the sites where Arthur and Guinevere were supposedly buried. Between April and October, guides in period costumes are on hand to point out some of the abbey's most interesting features. The visitor center has a scale model of the abbey as well as carvings and decorations salvaged from the ruins. ■**TIP→ Tickets bought online are cheaper.** ⊠ *Magdalene St.* ☎ *01458/832267* ⊕ *www.glastonbury-abbey.com* ⊠ *£8.60.*

Glastonbury Tor

MOUNTAIN—SIGHT | It's a stiff climb up the conical Glastonbury Tor, but your reward is the fabulous view across the Vale of Avalon. At the top stands a ruined tower, all that remains of **St. Michael's Church,** which collapsed after a landslide in 1271. Take the Glastonbury Tor bus to the base

of the hill. Nearby at the foot of the Tor is **Chalice Well,** the legendary burial place of the Grail. ⊠ *Glastonbury.*

★ Somerset Rural Life Museum

MUSEUM | FAMILY | Occupying a Victorian farmhouse and a 14th-century abbey tithe barn, this museum tells the story of life in Somerset throughout the ages. Exhibits in the six galleries illustrate farming practices and daily life in the 19th century using sound recordings and projections as well as an array of tools and domestic objects. The barn, more than 90 feet in length, once stored the one-tenth portion of the town's produce that was owed to the church and now holds exhibitions. Soups and crusty sandwiches are available at the Grain Store Café, which has tables in the yard. The grounds also contain an apple cider orchard. For a good walk, take the scenic footpath from the museum that leads up to the Tor, a half mile east. ⊠ *Chilkwell St.* ☎ *01458/831197* ⊕ *www. swheritage.org.uk/rural-life-museum* ⊠ *£7.50* ⊘ *Closed Mon. year-round and Sun. Nov.–Easter.*

Restaurants

Who'd a Thought It

$ | BRITISH | As an antidote to the natural-food cafés of Glastonbury's High Street, try this traditional backstreet inn for some more down-to-earth fare that doesn't compromise on quality. Bar classics such as beer-battered fish-and-chips and Somerset sausages appear alongside chicken curry, vegan dishes, and sizzling steaks. **Known for:** fast and friendly service; quirky interior crammed with memorabilia; traditional dishes served alongside local beers and ciders. $ *Average main: £15* ⊠ *17 Northload St.* ☎ *01458/834460* ⊕ *www.whodathought-tit.co.uk.*

Hotels

Magdalene House

$ | B&B/INN | Formerly a convent, this Georgian B&B sits directly opposite the Abbey grounds, with views over the walls. **Pros:** adjacent to Abbey; convenient for anyone with mobility issues; elegant ambience. **Cons:** slightly overdecorated; no credit card payments unless online via PayPal; no single-night stays on weekends between March and November. ⓢ *Rooms from: £97* ✉ *Magdalene St.* ☎ *01458/830202* ⊕ *www.magdalenehouseglastonbury.com* ▤ *No credit cards* ⤳ *3 rooms* ⦿⚬ *Free breakfast* ☞ *No children under 7 allowed.*

★ Melrose House

$ | B&B/INN | Superbly situated at the base of Glastonbury Tor, this elegant B&B on the edge of town is surrounded by lush gardens with far-reaching views over the Vale of Avalon. **Pros:** tranquil setting; easy access to Glastonbury Tor; superb breakfasts. **Cons:** not very central; one-night stays not always possible; does not accept credit cards. ⓢ *Rooms from: £90* ✉ *Coursing Batch* ☎ *01458/834706* ⊕ *www.melrose-bandb.co.uk* ⤳ *3 rooms* ⦿⚬ *Free breakfast* ▤ *No credit cards.*

Dunster

35 miles west of Glastonbury, 43 miles north of Exeter.

Lying between the Somerset coast and the edge of Exmoor National Park, Dunster is a picture-book village with a broad main street. The eight-sided yarn market building on High Street dates from 1589.

GETTING HERE AND AROUND

To reach Dunster by car, follow the A39. By bus, there are frequent departures from nearby Minehead and Taunton. Dunster Castle is a brief walk from the village center. In the village is the Exmoor National Park Visitor Centre, which can give you plenty of information about local activities.

ESSENTIALS

VISITOR INFORMATION Exmoor National Park Visitor Centre. ✉ *Dunster Steep* ☎ *01643/821835* ⊕ *www.exmoor-nationalpark.gov.uk.*

⊙ Sights

★ Dunster Castle

CASTLE/PALACE | A 13th-century fortress remodeled in 1868, Dunster Castle dominates the village from its site on a hill. Parkland and unusual gardens with subtropical plants surround the building, which has fine plaster ceilings, stacks of family portraits (including one by Joshua Reynolds), 17th-century Dutch leather hangings, and a magnificent 17th-century oak staircase. The climb to the castle from the parking lot is steep. In winter, visits are by guided tour only, on a first-come-first-served basis and at a reduced price ✉ *Off A39* ☎ *01643/821314* ⊕ *www.nationaltrust.org.uk* 🎟 *£12.90.*

Tale of the Grail ⊙

According to tradition, Glastonbury was where Joseph of Arimathea brought the Holy Grail, the chalice used by Jesus at the Last Supper. Centuries later, the Grail was said to be the objective of the quests of King Arthur and the Knights of the Round Table. When monks claimed to have found the bones of Arthur and Guinevere at Glastonbury in 1191, the popular association of the town with the mythical Avalon was sealed. Arthur and Guinevere's presumed remains were lost to history after Glastonbury Abbey was plundered for its riches in 1539.

7

Cornwall and the West Country **DUNSTER**

🏨 Hotels

Luttrell Arms

$ | B&B/INN | In style and atmosphere, this classic inn harmonizes perfectly with Dunster village and castle; it was used as a guesthouse by the abbots of Cleeve in the 14th century. **Pros:** central location; historic trappings; good dining options. **Cons:** some standard rooms are small and viewless; no parking; heavy presence of dogs in the bar not great for allergy sufferers. ⑤ *Rooms from: £102* ✉ *High St.* ☎ *01643/821555* ⊕ *www.luttrellarms. co.uk* ⇨ *29 rooms* ⚟ *Free breakfast.*

Exmoor National Park

16 miles southwest of Dunster.

When you're headed to Exmoor National Park, stop by a visitor information center at Dulverton, Dunster, or Lynmouth for information and maps. Guided walks, many of which have themes (archaeology, for example), are mostly free to join, although some are subject to a small charge. If you're walking on your own, check the weather, take water and a map, and tell someone where you're going.

GETTING HERE AND AROUND

A car is usually necessary for getting around Exmoor. Bus 10, operated by Atwest and Ridlers, connects Minehead with Porlock and Porlock Weir twice daily on weekdays, and bus 300, a summer service run by Quantock Heritage on weekdays only, traces the coast between Minehead and Lynmouth. Bus 198, operated by Atwest, runs from Minehead to Dunster and inland to Dulverton (Monday to Saturday).

ESSENTIALS

BUS CONTACTS Atwest. ☎ *01643/709701* ⊕ *www.atwest.org.uk.* **Quantock Heritage.** ☎ *01984/624906* ⊕ *www.quantockheritage.com.* **Ridlers.** ☎ *01398/323398* ⊕ *www.ridlers.co.uk.*

VISITOR INFORMATION Dulverton National Park Centre. ✉ *7–9 Fore St., Dulverton* ☎ *01398/323841* ⊕ *www.exmoor-nationalpark.gov.uk.* **Lynmouth National Park Centre.** ✉ *The Pavilion, The Esplanade, Lynmouth* ☎ *01598/752509* ⊕ *www.exmoor-nationalpark.gov.uk.*

👁 Sights

Exmoor National Park

NATIONAL/STATE PARK | Less wild and forbidding than Dartmoor to its south, 267-square-mile Exmoor National Park is no less majestic for its bare heath and lofty views. The park extends right up to the coast and straddles the county border between Somerset and Devon. Some walks offer spectacular views over the Bristol Channel. Taking one of the more than 700 miles of paths and bridle ways through the bracken and heather (at its best in fall), you might glimpse the ponies and red deer for which the region is noted. Be careful: the proximity of the coast means that mists and squalls can descend with alarming suddenness. ✉ *Exmoor National Park Authority, Exmoor House, Dulverton* ☎ *01398/323665* ⊕ *www.exmoor-nationalpark.gov.uk.*

Porlock

6 miles west of Dunster, 45 miles north of Exeter.

Buried at the bottom of a valley, with the slopes of Exmoor all about, the small, unspoiled town of Porlock lies near "Doone Country," the setting for R. D. Blackmore's swashbuckling saga *Lorna Doone.* Porlock had already achieved a place in literary history by the late 1790s, when Samuel Taylor Coleridge declared it was a "man from Porlock" who interrupted his opium trance while the poet was composing "Kubla Khan."

GETTING HERE AND AROUND
Porlock is best reached via the A39 coastal route. Atwest and Ridlers operate buses between Porlock and Minehead. The village can be easily explored by foot.

ESSENTIALS
BUS CONTACTS Atwest. ☎ *01643/709701* ⊕ *www.atwest.org.uk.* **Ridlers.** ☎ *01398/323398* ⊕ *www.ridlers.co.uk.*

VISITOR INFORMATION Porlock Visitor Centre. ⊠ *The Old School, West End* ☎ *01643/863150* ⊕ *www.porlock.co.uk.*

 Sights

Porlock Hill
SCENIC DRIVE | As you're heading west from Porlock to Lynton, the coast road A39 mounts Porlock Hill, an incline so steep that signs encourage drivers to "keep going." The views across Exmoor and north to the Bristol Channel and Wales are worth it. Less steep but quieter and equally scenic routes, up the hill on toll roads, can be accessed from Porlock and Porlock Weir. ⊠ *Porlock.*

Porlock Weir
TOWN | Two miles west of Porlock, this tiny harbor is the starting point for an undemanding 2-mile walk along the coast through chestnut and walnut trees to **Culbone Church,** reputedly the smallest and most isolated church in England. Saxon in origin, it has a small Victorian spire and is lighted by candles, making it hard to find a more enchanting spot. ⊠ *Porlock.*

Restaurants

⭐ **Locanda on the Weir**
$$$ | **MODERN ITALIAN** | Set in a sea-facing Georgian building on one of the West Country's most enchanting stretches of coast, this restaurant with rooms run by an Anglo-Italian husband-and-wife team offers modern revisitations of classic Italian dishes executed with consummate artistry and originality. Expect to find such antipasti as home-cured salmon with horseradish cream, candied lemon and pickled beetroot, or a simple platter of cold meats and cheeses, which you might follow with gnocchi al Gorgonzola, made with Gorgonzola and Somerset Blue cheeses, Alba truffle-infused oil and thirty-months-aged Parmesan, or *baccalà alla livornese* (lightly salted cod with olives and capers). **Known for:** high-quality Italian cuisine using local ingredients; graceful surrroundings and serene sea views; enthusiastic, friendly service. ⑤ *Average main: £25* ⊠ *Porlock Weir* ☎ *01643/863300* ⊕ *www.locandaontheweir.co.uk* ⓧ *No lunch.*

Lynton and Lynmouth

13 miles west of Porlock, 60 miles northwest of Exeter.

A steep hill separates this pretty pair of Devonshire villages, which are linked by a Victorian cliff railway you can still ride. Lynmouth, a fishing village at the bottom of the hill, crouches below 1,000-foot-high cliffs at the mouths of the East and West Lyn rivers; Lynton is higher up. The poet Percy Bysshe Shelley visited Lynmouth in 1812, in the company of his 16-year-old bride, Harriet Westbrook. During their nine-week sojourn, the poet found time to write his polemical *Queen Mab.* The grand landscape of Exmoor lies all about, with walks to local beauty spots: Watersmeet, Hollerday Hill, or the Valley of Rocks, where rare feral goats graze.

GETTING HERE AND AROUND
These towns are best reached via the A39. Lynton is a stop on Quantock Heritage Bus 300, which runs Monday through Saturday from Minehead. It's a steep and winding ascent to Lynton from Lynmouth; take the cliff railway to travel between them.

ESSENTIALS

VISITOR INFORMATION Lynton and Lymouth Tourist Information Centre. ⊠ *26 Lee Rd., Lynton* ☎ *01598/752225* ⊕ *www.visitlyntonandlynmouth.com.*

👁 Sights

Coleridge Way

TRAIL | The 51-mile Coleridge Way runs between Nether Stowey (site of Coleridge's home) and Lynmouth, passing through the northern fringes of the Quantock Hills, the isolated villages of the Brendon Hills, and along the Exmoor coast. ⊠ *Lynmouth* ⊕ *www.visit-exmoor. co.uk/coleridge-way.*

Lynton and Lynmouth Cliff Railway

TRANSPORTATION SITE (AIRPORT/BUS/FERRY/TRAIN) | Water and a cable system power the 862-foot cliff railway that connects these two towns. As it ascends a rocky cliff, you are treated to fine views over the harbor. Inaugurated in 1890, it was the gift of publisher George Newnes, who also donated Lynton's imposing town hall, near the top station on Lee Road. ⊠ *The Esplanade, Lynmouth* ☎ *01598/753908* ⊕ *www.cliffrailwaylynton.co.uk* 🎫 *£4 round-trip* ⏱ *Closed early Nov.–early Feb.*

🍴 Restaurants

Rising Sun

$$ | **MODERN BRITISH** | A 14th-century inn and a row of thatched cottages make up this pub-restaurant with great views over the Bristol Channel. The kitchen specializes in local cuisine with European influences, so expect dishes like roast quail with black garlic gnocchi. **Known for:** traditional pub decor and ambience; good range of local ales; delicious seafood like lobster risotto and bouillabaisse. ⑤ *Average main: £21* ⊠ *Riverside Rd., Lynmouth* ☎ *01598/753223* ⊕ *www. risingsunlynmouth.co.uk.*

🛏 Hotels

Highcliffe House

$$ | **B&B/INN** | As the name suggests, this luxury Victorian B&B in Lynton occupies a lofty position with spectacular vistas over the Bristol Channel. **Pros:** romantic ambience; inspiring views; generous and wide-ranging breakfasts. **Cons:** design not for everyone; unsightly parking lot directly below; relatively high room rates. ⑤ *Rooms from: £150* ⊠ *Sinai Hill, Lynton* ☎ *01598/752235* ⊕ *www.highcliffehouse. co.uk* 🛏 *6 rooms* 🍴 *Free breakfast* ☞ *No guests under 18 allowed.*

🏃 Activities

BEACHES

West of Lynton, the Atlantic-facing beaches of Saunton Sands, Croyde Bay, and Woolacombe Bay are much beloved by surfers, with plenty of outlets renting equipment and offering lessons. Croyde Bay and Woolacombe Bay are more family-friendly.

Woolacombe Bay

BEACHES | One of the most famous beaches in the country, North Devon's Woolacombe is popular with surfers for its waves and with families for its soft sand and tidal pools that are great for kids to explore. This broad and extensive stretch of sand has all you could need for a dreamy day by the sea. At its northern end you'll find cafés, loungers, surfing equipment to rent, lifeguards, ice cream—you name it. If you're not looking for crowds and kids, you may want to head to the southernmost section of the beach, around Putsborough. The beach is 17 miles west of Lynton: to get here, take A361 and follow signs. **Amenities:** food and drink; lifeguards; parking (fee); toilets; water sports. **Best for:** surfing; swimming. ⊠ *Woolacombe.*

BOATING
Exmoor Coast Boat Cruises
BOATING | Cruise around the dramatic Devon coast on a boat trip departing from Lynmouth Harbour. The round-trip journey to Lee Bay costs £10 and takes 45 minutes. The 90-minute excursion to Heddon's Mouth (£20) lets you experience the clamorous birdlife on the cliffs. The trips are weather and tide dependant, so always call ahead, or check in at the Glen Lyn Gorge attraction in Lynmouth. ⊠ *Lynmouth.Harbour, Watersmeet Rd., Lynmouth* ☎ *01598/753207* ⊕ *www.theglenlyngorge.co.uk.*

Clovelly

40 miles southwest of Lynton, 60 miles northwest of Exeter.

Lovely Clovelly always seems to have the sun shining on its flower-lined cottages and stepped and cobbled streets. Alas, its beauty is well-known, and day-trippers can overrun the village in summer. Perched precariously among cliffs, a steep, cobbled road—tumbling down at such an angle that it's closed to cars—leads to the toylike harbor with its 14th-century quay. Allow about two hours (more if you stop for a drink or a meal) to take in the village. Hobby Drive, a 3-mile cliff-top carriageway laid out in 1829 through thick woods, gives scintillating views over the village and coast.

GETTING HERE AND AROUND
To get to Clovelly by bus, take Stagecoach service 319 from Barnstaple or Bideford. If you're driving, take the A39 and park at the Clovelly Visitor Centre for £7.75. The center of town is steep and cobbled. The climb from the harbor to the parking lot can be exhausting, but from Easter through October a reasonably priced shuttle service brings you back.

Donkeys at Work ⊙

Donkey stables, donkey rides for kids, and abundant donkey souvenirs in Clovelly recall the days when these animals played an essential role in town life, carrying food, packages, and more up and down the village streets. Even in the 1990s, donkeys helped carry bags from the hotels. Today sleds do the work, but the animals' labor is remembered.

⊙ Sights

Clovelly Visitor Centre
INFO CENTER | Here you'll see a 25-minute film that puts Clovelly into context. In the village you can visit a 1930s-style fisherman's cottage and an exhibition about Victorian writer Charles Kingsley, who lived here as a child. The admission fee includes parking, and you can book walking tours of the village at the Visitor Centre (£5). To avoid the worst crowds, arrive early or late in the day. ⊠ *Off A39* ☎ *01237/431781* ⊕ *www.clovelly.co.uk* 🎫 *£7.95.*

🛏 Hotels

Red Lion Hotel
$$ | **HOTEL** | You can soak up the tranquility of Clovelly after the day-trippers have gone at the 18th-century Red Lion, located right on the harbor in this coastal village. **Pros:** superb location; clean and comfortable; friendly staff. **Cons:** some rooms and bathrooms are small; bar lacks character; steep walk to get anywhere. 💲 *Rooms from: £170* ⊠ *The Quay* ☎ *01237/431237* ⊕ *www.clovelly.co.uk* 🔄 *17 rooms* 🍴 *Free breakfast.*

Clovelly may have it all: cobbled streets, quaint houses, and the endless blue sea.

Cornwall

Cornwall stretches west into the sea, with plenty of magnificent coastline to explore, along with tranquil towns and some bustling resorts. One way to discover it all is to travel southwest from Boscastle and the cliff-top ruins of Tintagel Castle, the legendary birthplace of Arthur, along the north Cornish coast to Land's End. This predominantly cliff-lined coast, interspersed with broad expanses of sand, has many tempting places to stop, including Padstow (for a seafood feast), Newquay (a surfing and tourist center), or St. Ives (a delightful artists' colony).

From Land's End, the westernmost tip of Britain, known for its savage land- and seascapes and panoramic views, return to the popular seaside resort of Penzance, the harbor town of Falmouth, and the river port of Fowey. The Channel coast is less rugged than the northern coast, with more sheltered beaches. Leave time to visit the excellent Eden Project, with its surrealistic-looking conservatories in an abandoned clay pit, and to explore the boggy, heath-covered expanse of Bodmin Moor.

Boscastle

15 miles north of Bodmin, 30 miles south of Clovelly.

In tranquil Boscastle, some of the stone-and-slate cottages at the foot of the steep valley date from the 1300s. A good place to relax and walk, the town is centered on a little harbor and set snugly within towering cliffs. Nearby, 2 miles up the Valency valley, is St. Juliot's, the "Endelstow" referred to in Thomas Hardy's *A Pair of Blue Eyes*—the young author was involved with the restoration of this church while he was working as an architect.

Port Isaac
Bay

Padstow Bay

DEVON

Wainhouse
Corner
Boscastle
Tintagel
Hallworthy
Launceston

CORNWALL

Port Isaac
Padstow
Wadebridge
Dozmary
Pool
Bodmin
Dobwalls
Newquay
Lanhydrock
Carkeel
Quintrell Downs
Trevarren
Eden
Project
Trerule Foot
Summercourt
St. Austell
Fowey
Plymouth
Perranporth
Charlestown
St Austell Bay
Blackwater
Lost Gardens
of Heligan
Redruth
Truro
St Ives Bay
Trelissick
Camborne
St. Just in Roseland
Geevor
Tin Mine
Whitecross
St. Mawes
Penzance
Falmouth
Newlyn
St. Michael's
Mount
Helston
St Keveme
Mousehole
Porthcurno
Land's
End
Lizard
Peninsula
Kynance
Cove
Lizard
Isles of Scilly

0   10 mi
0   10 km

GETTING HERE AND AROUND

Drivers can reach Boscastle along A39 and B3263. There are regular First Kernow buses from Wadebridge, which is reachable on Plymouth Citybus services from Bodmin Parkway, the nearest rail connection. The village is easily explored on foot.

VISITOR INFORMATION Boscastle Visitor

Centre. ⊠ The Harbour ☎ 01840/250010 ⊕ www.visitboscastleandtintagel.com.

🛏 Hotels

★ The Old Rectory

$ | B&B/INN | While restoring St. Juliot's Church, Thomas Hardy stayed in the building that now holds this delightful B&B; the stone house, set on 3 acres of lush grounds about 1½ miles from Boscastle, has been in the same family for

five generations. **Pros:** secluded setting; romantic ambience; environmentally friendly. **Cons:** a little hard to find; two-night minimum stay usually required; no kids under 12. ⑤ Rooms from: £100 ⊠ Off B3263, St. Juliot ☎ 01840/250225 ⊕ www.stjuliot.com ➵ 4 rooms ⓘ Free breakfast ⌇ No children under 12 allowed.

Tintagel

3 miles southwest of Boscastle.

The romance of Arthurian legend thrives around Tintagel's ruined castle on the coast. Ever since the somewhat unreliable 12th-century chronicler Geoffrey of Monmouth identified Tintagel as the home of Arthur, son of Uther Pendragon and Ygrayne, devotees of the legend

The coast near Tintagel Castle has lovely views.

cycle have revered the site. In the 19th century Alfred, Lord Tennyson described Tintagel's Arthurian connection in *The Idylls of the King*. Today the village has its share of tourist junk—including Excaliburgers—but the headland around Tintagel is still splendidly scenic.

GETTING HERE AND AROUND

To drive to Tintagel, take the A39 to the B3263. Numerous parking lots are found in the village center. There's a bus stop near the tourist office for First Kernow buses from Wadebridge, which has connections from Bodmin Parkway, the nearest train station. Between April and October, a shuttle service brings mobility impaired passengers to the castle.

VISITOR INFORMATION Tintagel Visitor Centre. ⊠ *Bossiney Rd.* ☏ *01840/779084* ⊕ *www.tintagelparishcouncil.gov.uk.*

◉ Sights

Old Post Office

HOUSE | This gorgeous, 14th-century, stone manor house with yard-thick walls, smoke-blackened beams, and an undulating slate-tile roof has been furnished with items from the 17th and 18th centuries. The walls are hung with "samplers"— embroidered poems and prayers usually produced by young girls. One room originally served as a post office and has been restored to its Victorian appearance. ⊠ *Fore St.* ☏ *01840/770024* ⊕ *www. nationaltrust.org.uk* ✉ *£5* ⊙ *Closed Nov.–mid-Mar.*

★ Tintagel Castle

CASTLE/PALACE | Although all that remains of the ruined cliff-top Tintagel Castle, legendary birthplace of King Arthur, is the outline of its walls, moats, and towers, it requires only a bit of imagination to conjure up a picture of Sir Lancelot and Sir Galahad riding out in search of the

All About King Arthur

Legends about King Arthur have resonated through the centuries, enthusiastically taken up by writers and poets, from 7th-century Welsh and Breton troubadours to Alfred, Lord Tennyson and Mark Twain in the 19th century, and T. H. White in the 20th century.

Who Was Arthur?

The historical Arthur was probably a Christian Celtic chieftain battling against the Saxons in the 6th century, although most of the tales surrounding him have a much later setting, thanks to the vivid but somewhat fanciful chronicles of his exploits by medieval scholars.

The virtuous warrior-hero of popular myth has always been treated with generous helpings of nostalgia for a golden age. For Sir Thomas Malory (circa 1408–71), author of *Le Morte d'Arthur*, the finest medieval prose collection of Arthurian romance, Arthur represented a lost era of chivalry and noble romance before the loosening of the traditional bonds of feudal society and the gradual collapse of the medieval social order.

Finding King Arthur

Places associated with Arthur and his consort, Guinevere, the wizard Merlin, the knights of the Round Table, and the related legends of Tristan and Isolde (or Iseult) can be found all over Europe, but the West Country claims the closest association. Arthur was said to have had his court of Camelot at Cadbury Castle (17 miles south of Wells) and to have been buried at Glastonbury.

Cornwall holds the greatest concentration of Arthurian links, notably his supposed birthplace, Tintagel, and the site of his last battle, on Bodmin Moor. However tenuous the links—and, barring the odd, somewhat ambiguous inscription, there's nothing in the way of hard evidence of Arthur's existence—the Cornish have taken the Once and Future King to their hearts, and his spirit is said to reside in the now-rare bird, the Cornish chough.

Holy Grail over the narrow causeway above the seething breakers. Archaeological evidence, however, suggests that the castle dates from much later—about 1150, when it was the stronghold of the earls of Cornwall. Long before that, Romans may have occupied the site. The earliest identified remains here are of Celtic (AD 5th century) origin, and these may have some connection with the legendary Arthur. Legends aside, nothing can detract from the castle ruins, dramatically set off by the wild, windswept Cornish coast, on an island joined to the mainland by a narrow isthmus. Paths lead down to the pebble beach and a cavern known as **Merlin's Cave.** Exploring Tintagel Castle involves some arduous climbing on steep steps, but even on a summer's day, when people swarm over the battlements and a westerly Atlantic wind sweeps through Tintagel, you can feel the proximity of the distant past. ✉ *Castle Rd., ½ mile west of the village* ☎ *01840/770328* ⊕ *www.english-heritage.org.uk* 🎟 *£13* ⊘ *Closed Mon. and Tues. in Nov.; closed Mon.–Thurs. in Dec.–mid-Feb. (except week after Christmas).*

Port Isaac

6 miles southwest of Tintagel.

A mixture of granite, slate, and white-washed cottages tumbles precipitously down the cliff to the tiny harbor at Port Isaac, still dedicated to the crab-and-lobster trade. Low tide reveals a pebbly beach and rock pools. Even with the daytime crowds attracted by the various TV dramas filmed here, it makes for a peaceful and secluded stay. For an extra slice of authentic Cornwall life, you can hear the local Fisherman's Friends choir sing shanties at the harborside on Friday nights in summer.

GETTING HERE AND AROUND

If you're driving, Port Isaac is reached via the A39, then the B3314. Park at the lot at the top of the village rather than attempting to drive into the center. By bus, take Plymouth Citybus service 11A from the train station at Bodmin Parkway, changing to First Kernow 96 at Wadebridge. Bus 96 does not run on Sunday.

🍴 Restaurants

Outlaw's Fish Kitchen

$ | SEAFOOD | One of the country's foremost chefs, Nathan Outlaw, has established a base in Port Isaac, where he has two top-notch seafood restaurants. The Fish Kitchen, right on the quay, is the more casual of the two, occupying a 15th-century fisherman's cottage with just eight tables. **Known for:** fresh local seafood; cozy but cramped ambience; friendly, informative staff. ⑤ *Average main: £14* ⊠ *1 Middle St.* ☎ *01208/881183* ⊕ *www.nathan-outlaw. com* ⊗ *Closed Sun., Mon., and late Dec.–early Feb.*

🛏 Hotels

The Old School Hotel and Restaurant

$ | HOTEL | Perched on the cliffs above Port Isaac's minuscule harbor, this idiosyncratic lodging was a Victorian schoolhouse until the 1980s, and it nostalgically retains many of the features of its previous role. **Pros:** lots of character; welcoming staff; picture-postcard views. **Cons:** minimum two-night stay in summer; some rooms are tiny; village can get overwhelmed by tourists by day. ⑤ *Rooms from: £120* ⊠ *Fore St.* ☎ *01208/880721* ⊕ *www.theoldschoolhotel.co.uk* ⊅ *12 rooms* ⊙I *Free breakfast.*

Padstow

10 miles southwest of Port Isaac.

A small fishing port at the mouth of the River Camel, Padstow attracts attention and visitors as a center of culinary excellence, largely because of the presence here since 1975 of pioneering seafood chef Rick Stein. Stein's empire includes two restaurants, a café, a fish-and-chips joint, a delicatessen, a patisserie, and a cooking school where classes fill up months in advance.

Even if seafood isn't your favorite fare, Padstow is worth visiting. The cries of seagulls fill its lively harbor, a string of fine beaches lies within a short ride—including some choice strands highly prized by surfers—and two scenic walking routes await: the Saints Way across the peninsula to Fowey and the Camel Trail, a footpath and cycling path that follows the river as far as Bodmin Moor. If you can avoid peak visiting times—summer weekends—so much the better.

GETTING HERE AND AROUND

Regular buses connect Padstow with Bodmin, the main transportation hub hereabouts, and on the main Plymouth–Penzance train line. To get here from Port Isaac, change buses at Wadebridge. Alternatively, take the bus to Rock and the passenger ferry across the river. There are numerous direct buses on the Newquay–Padstow route. Drivers should take A39/A389 and park in the waterside parking lot before reaching the harbor.

FERRY CONTACTS Padstow Rock Ferry. ☎ *01841/532239 Harbour Office, 0777/308–1574 Ferry Office* ⊕ *www. padstow-harbour.co.uk.*

VISITOR INFORMATION Padstow Tourist Information Centre. ✉ *The Mariner's Clock Building, South Quay* ☎ *01841/533449* ⊕ *www.padstowlive.com* Ⓜ *.*

🍴 Restaurants

★ Paul Ainsworth at no6

$$$$ | **MODERN BRITISH** | Paul Ainsworth is gradually expanding his culinary presence in Padstow to rival that of Rick Stein, and for many foodies, Ainsworth offers the better experience. His innovative creations can best be sampled at this intimate bistro that was his original foothold in the town, where diners seated in a series of small, stylish rooms feast on ingeniously concocted dishes that make the most of local and seasonal produce. **Known for:** exciting, creative cuisine like black truffle with morels and chicken tournedos Rossini; affordable set-price lunches; vivacious atmosphere. $ *Average main: £85* ✉ *6 Middle St.* ☎ *01841/532093* ⊕ *www.paul-ainsworth.co.uk* ☉ *Closed Sun., Mon., and mid-Jan.–early Feb.*

St. Petroc's Bistro

$$ | **MODERN BRITISH** | Part of chef Rick Stein's empire, this bistro with contemporary art adorning its walls has a secluded feel. The menu is strong on seafood but also offers succulent steaks and tasty vegetarian choices, featuring dishes like chicken fricassée, char-grilled monkfish tail, and ravioli of caramelized onion and fennel seeds with porcini mushrooms. **Known for:** unpretentious fine dining; smart but lively ambience; walled garden for eating outside. $ *Average main: £19* ✉ *4 New St.* ☎ *01841/532700* ⊕ *www. rickstein.com.*

★ The Seafood Restaurant

$$$ | **SEAFOOD** | Just across from where the lobster boats and trawlers unload their catches, Rick Stein's flagship restaurant has built its reputation on the freshest fish and the highest culinary artistry. The exclusively fish and shellfish menu includes everything from grilled Padstow lobster with herbs to stir-fried Singapore chili crab. **Known for:** top-quality, eclectic seafood dishes creatively prepared; famous regional chef; attentive service. $ *Average main: £30* ✉ *Riverside* ☎ *01841/532700* ⊕ *www.rickstein.com.*

🛏 Hotels

St. Edmund's House

$$$$ | **B&B/INN** | The most luxurious Rick Stein lodgings in town are distinguished by their sophisticated and minimalist style. **Pros:** stylish and spacious bedrooms; top-notch service; central but secluded. **Cons:** short walk to breakfast; extravagant prices; some noise issues. $ *Rooms from: £320* ✉ *St. Edmund's La.* ☎ *01841/532700* ⊕ *www.rickstein.com* ⇨ *6 rooms* ⎮⊙⎮ *Free breakfast.*

🏃 Activities

BIKING
Padstow Cycle Hire

BICYCLING | Bikes of all shapes and sizes can be rented at Padstow Cycle Hire, near the start of the Camel Trail. ✉ *South Quay* ☎ *01841/533533* ⊕ *www.padstow-cyclehire.com.*

SURFING
Harlyn Surf School
SURFING | This school can arrange two-hour to three-day surfing courses at its base in Harlyn Bay, 3 miles west of Padstow. ✉ *Harlyn Bay Beach* ☎ *07757/779008* ⊕ *www.harlynsurf-school.co.uk.*

WALKING
Saints Way
HIKING/WALKING | This 30-mile inland path takes you between Padstow and the Camel Estuary on Cornwall's north coast to Fowey on the south coast. It follows a Bronze Age trading route, later used by Celtic pilgrims to cross the peninsula. Several relics of such times can be seen along the way. ✉ *Padstow.*

Newquay

14 miles southwest of Padstow, 30 miles southwest of Tintagel.

The biggest, most developed resort on the north Cornwall coast is a fairly large town established in 1439. It was once the center of the trade in pilchards (a small herringlike fish), and on the headland you can still see a white hut where a lookout known as a "huer" watched for pilchard schools and directed the boats to the fishing grounds. Newquay has become Britain's surfing capital, and, in summer, young California-dreamin' devotees often pack the wide, cliff-backed beaches.

GETTING HERE AND AROUND
A branch line links Newquay with the main Plymouth–Penzance train line at Par, and there are regular buses from Padstow, Bodmin, and St. Austell. Train and bus stations are both in the center of town. Newquay has good road connections with the rest of the peninsula via the A30 and A39 and is linked to the rest of the country by its airport. The best beaches are a long walk or a short bus ride from the center.

Surfers Welcome 👁

The four-story Tate St. Ives, at the base of a cliff fronted by Porthmeor Beach, may be the only art museum with special storage space for visitors' surfboards.

VISITOR INFORMATION **Newquay Tourist Information Centre.** ✉ *Marcus Hill* ☎ *01637/838516* ⊕ *www.visitnewquay. org.*

🛏 Hotels

★ The Scarlet
$$$$ | HOTEL | The pampering begins the moment you enter this adults-only beachside hotel when you are greeted with a drink by the enthusiastic and highly professional staff, followed by a tour of the facilties. **Pros:** impeccable service; inspiring sea views; excellent dining. **Cons:** staff can be over-zealous; no children; some rooms only accessible by stairs. ⑤ *Rooms from: £340* ✉ *Tredragon Rd.* ☎ *01637/861800* ⊕ *www.scarlethotel.co.uk* ⤢ *37 rooms* ⏲ *Free breakfast.*

🏃 Activities

Surfing is Newquay's raison d'être for many of the enthusiasts who flock here throughout the year. Great Western and Tolcarne beaches are most suitable for beginners, while Fistral Beach is better for those with more experience. There are dozens of surf schools around town, many offering accommodation packages, and rental outlets are also ubiquitous.

BEACHES
Fistral Bay
BEACHES | This favorite of serious surfers is a long stretch of flat, soft sand, renowned for its powerful tides and

strong currents. Surf shops rent equipment and offer lessons on the beach, or you can just check out the scene. Lifeguards watch the water in summer, and there are cafés and shops selling beach supplies. The beach is at the western edge of Newquay. **Amenities:** food and drink; lifeguards; parking (fee); toilets; water sports. **Best for:** partiers; surfing; swimming. ⊠ *Off Headland Rd.*

SURFING
Extreme Academy

SURFING | One of the West Country's water-sports specialists, Extreme Academy based at Watergate Bay offers courses in wave skiing, kite surfing, kite buggying, paddle surfing, and just plain old surfing. It also has equipment for hire. ⊠ *Trevarrian Hill, Watergate Bay* ☎ *01637/860840* ⊕ *www.extremeacademy.co.uk.*

St. Ives

25 miles southwest of Newquay, 10 miles north of Penzance.

James McNeill Whistler came here to paint his landscapes, Barbara Hepworth to fashion her modernist sculptures, and Virginia Woolf to write her novels. Today sand, sun, and superb art continue to attract thousands of vacationers to the fishing village of St. Ives, named after Saint Ia, a 5th-century female Irish missionary said to have arrived on a floating leaf. Many come to St. Ives for the sheltered beaches; the best are Porthmeor, on the northern side of town, and, facing east, Porthminster—the choice for those seeking more space to spread out.

GETTING HERE AND AROUND
St. Ives has good bus and train connections with Bristol, Exeter, and Penzance. Train journeys usually involve a change at St. Erth (the brief St. Erth–St. Ives stretch is one of the West Country's most scenic train routes). The adjacent bus and train stations are within a few minutes' walk of the center. Drivers should avoid the center—parking lots are well marked in the higher parts of town.

VISITOR INFORMATION Visit St. Ives Information Centre. ⊠ *St. Ives Library, Gabriel St.* ☎ *01736/796297* ⊕ *www.stives-cornwall.co.uk* Ⓜ .

◉ Sights

Barbara Hepworth Museum and Sculpture Garden

GARDEN | The studio and garden of Dame Barbara Hepworth (1903–75), who pioneered abstract sculpture in England, are now a museum and sculpture garden, managed by Tate St. Ives. The artist lived here for 26 years. ⊠ *Trewyn Studio, Barnoon Hill* ☎ *01736/796226* ⊕ *www.tate. org.uk* ✍ *£7, £13 combined ticket with Tate St. Ives* ⊘ *Closed Mon. Nov.–Mar.*

Geevor Tin Mine

MINE | **FAMILY** | The winding B3306 coastal road southwest from St. Ives passes through some of Cornwall's starkest yet most beautiful countryside. Barren hills crisscrossed by low stone walls drop abruptly to granite cliffs and wide bays. Evidence of the ancient tin-mining industry is everywhere. Now a fascinating mining heritage center, the early-20th-century Geevor Tin Mine employed 400 men, but in 1985 the collapse of the world tin market wiped Cornwall from the mining map. Wear sturdy footwear for the surface and underground tours. A museum, shop, and café are at the site. ⊠ *B3306, Pendeen* ☎ *01736/788662* ⊕ *www.geevor.com* ✍ *£16.10* ⊘ *Closed Sat.*

St. Ives Society of Artists Gallery

MUSEUM | Local artists display selections of their current work for sale at this gallery in the former Mariners' Church. The Crypt Gallery in the basement is used for private exhibitions. ⊠ *Norway Sq.* ☎ *01736/795582* ⊕ *www.stisa.co.uk* ⊘ *Closed Sun. Nov.–Mar.*

★ Tate St. Ives

MUSEUM | The most spectacular branch of the renowned London gallery displays the work of artists who lived and worked in St. Ives, mostly from 1925 to 1975. The collection occupies a modernist building—a fantasia of seaside art deco–period architecture with panoramic views of the rippling ocean. Works of other international artists who influenced the St. Ives school—Picasso, Braque, and Mondrian among them—are exhibited alongside the local figures, and there are frequent exhibitions of contemporary art connected to West Cornwall. A four-story extension has significantly increased the exhibition space, and the rooftop café provides excellent food and views. ⊠ *Porthmeor Beach* ☎ *01736/796226* ⊕ *www.tate.org.uk* 🎫 *£9.50, £13 combined ticket with Barbara Hepworth Museum and Sculpture Garden* ⊗ *Closed Mon. Nov.–Mar.*

🍴 Restaurants

Blas Burgerworks

$ | **BURGER** | **FAMILY** | This tiny backstreet burger joint has been drawing enthusiastic crowds and critical plaudits since it first joined the St. Ives dining scene. Its popularity has as much to do with its rough-and-ready feel—with diners sharing the large, reconditioned tables in a spirit of cheerful solidarity—as with its delicious burgers made of pure Cornish beef or vegan and vegetarian ingredients, with such toppings as portobello mushrooms and spinach. ⑤ *Average main: £13* ⊠ *The Warren* ☎ *01736/797272* ⊕ *www. blasburgerworks.co.uk* ⊗ *Closed Nov.–Mar. No lunch during school terms.*

★ Gurnard's Head

$$ | **MODERN BRITISH** | This pub with bright, homey furnishings and a relaxed ambience looks past green fields to the ocean beyond. The frequently changing menu features fresh, inventively prepared meat and seafood dishes; look for spiced lamb parcel with harissa hummus, cucumber, and mint or red gurnard with tomato, anchovy, olive, and samphire—and leave room for some stupendous desserts. **Known for:** unusual dishes alongside old English favorites; remote coastal location; good set-price deals. ⑤ *Average main: £19* ⊠ *B3306, near Zennor, Treen* ☎ *01736/796928* ⊕ *www. gurnardshead.co.uk.*

Porthminster Café

$$ | **SEAFOOD** | Unbeatable for its location alone—on the broad, golden sands of Porthminster Beach—this sleek, modern eatery prepares imaginative breakfasts, lunches, teas, and evening meals that you can savor while you take in the marvelous vista across the bay. The accent is on Mediterranean and Asian seafood dishes, and typical choices include tuna sashimi, fried whole sea-bass with tempura prawns and a sweet and sour chili sauce, and seafood curry. **Known for:** beachside location; consistently high quality of food; famous seafood curry. ⑤ *Average main: £22* ⊠ *Porthminster Beach* ☎ *01736/795352* ⊕ *www.porthminstercafe.co.uk.*

Sloop Inn

$ | **BRITISH** | One of Cornwall's oldest pubs, the 1312 Sloop Inn serves simple lunches as well as evening meals in wood-beam rooms that display the work of local artists. There's also a separate restaurant upstairs. **Known for:** lively harborside atmosphere; traditional pub kitchen; Cornish beers. ⑤ *Average main: £12* ⊠ *The Wharf* ☎ *01736/796584* ⊕ *www.sloop-inn.co.uk.*

🛏 Hotels

★ Cornerways

$$ | **B&B/INN** | Everything in St. Ives seems squeezed into the tiniest of spaces, and this cottage B&B in the quiet Downalong quarter is no exception. **Pros:** friendly owners; tasteful decor; excellent breakfast choices. **Cons:** rooms are mostly small; narrow stairways to climb; very limited parking. ⑤ *Rooms from: £140* ⊠ *1*

Bethesda Pl. ☎ 01736/796706 ⊕ www.
cornerwaysstives.co.uk ▭ No credit
cards ⊷ 6 rooms ⦿ Free breakfast.

Primrose House

$$ | **HOTEL** | Blending the elegance of an
Edwardian villa with clean-lined mod-
ern style, this friendly hotel close to
Porthminster Beach has the best of both
worlds. **Pros:** close to beach and train
and bus stations; friendly atmosphere;
attention to detail. **Cons:** some rooms are
small and lack views; steep and narrow
car access; stairs to climb for some
rooms. ⑂ Rooms from: £170 ✉ Porth-
minster Beach ☎ 01736/794939 ⊕ www.
primroseonline.co.uk ⊗ Closed weekdays
in Jan. ⊷ 11 rooms ⦿ Free breakfast.

Land's End

*17 miles southwest of St. Ives, 9 miles
southwest of Penzance.*

The coastal road, B3306, ends at the
western tip of Britain at what is, quite
literally, Land's End.

GETTING HERE AND AROUND

Frequent buses serve Land's End from
Penzance (around one hour). There is no
direct service from St. Ives in winter, but,
in summer, an open-top double-decker
tracks the coast between St. Ives and
Penzance, taking in Land's End en route.

◎ Sights

Land's End

VIEWPOINT | The sea crashes against the
rocks at Land's End and lashes ships
battling their way around the point.
■**TIP**➔ **Approach from one of the coastal
footpaths for the best panoramic view.**
Over the years, sightseers have caused
some erosion of the paths, but new ones
are constantly being built, and Cornish
"hedges" (granite walls covered with
turf) have been planted to prevent ero-
sion. The scenic grandeur of Land's End
remains undiminished. The Land's End

Hotel here is undistinguished, though the
restaurant has good views. ✉ Sennen.

☺ Beaches

Porthcurno Beach

BEACHES | A protected, blue bay in South
Cornwall, Porthcurno has a crescent moon
of white sand (from crushed shells) at the
foot of imposing dark, blocklike granite
cliffs. The extraordinary Minack Theatre—
carved from solid rock—is on one side,
and there are pubs and cafés nearby.
A steep slope can make swimming a
challenge at times, but one area near
a stream is good for families. The town
and beach are signed off B3315, and the
coastal path is nearby. **Amenities:** food and
drink; lifeguards; parking (fee); toilets. **Best
for:** swimming; walking. ✉ 3 miles east of
Land's End, Porthcurno.

Sennen Cove

BEACHES | Located in the aptly named
Whitesand Bay, Sennen Cove is a gor-
geous expanse of creamy soft sand on
the western tip of Cornwall. When the tide
is coming in, the waves attract legions of
surfers. When the tide's out, kids paddle
in the tidal pools, and the sand stretches
as far as you can see. Cafés are nearby,
and surfing equipment is for rent on the
beach. Sennen is off A30 less than 2
miles north of Land's End, and can be
reached on foot on the South West Coast
Path. **Amenities:** food and drink; lifeguards;
parking (fee); toilets; water sports. **Best for:**
sunset; surfing; swimming; walking. ✉ Off
A30, Whitesand Bay.

Mousehole

*7 miles east of Land's End, 3 miles south
of Penzance.*

Between Land's End and Penzance,
Mousehole (pronounced *mow*-zel, the
first syllable rhyming with "cow") merits
a stop—and plenty of people do stop—to
see this archetypal Cornish fishing village
of tiny stone cottages. It was the home

of Dolly Pentreath, supposedly the last person to speak solely in Cornish, who died in 1777.

GETTING HERE AND AROUND
Frequent buses take 20 minutes to travel from Penzance to Mousehole. From Land's End, change buses at Newlyn. Drivers should take the B3315 coastal route and park in one of the seaside lots before entering the village.

🍴 Restaurants

2 Fore Street
$$ | MODERN BRITISH | Within view of Mousehole's tiny harbor, you can dine on some of the area's freshest seafood in this popular bistro. The seasonal, Mediterranean-inspired menu takes in everything from crab soup with saffron rouille (a sauce with breadcrumbs and garlic) and Parmesan toast to grilled lemon sole fillets with asparagus, smoked bacon sourdough crumb and hollandaise sauce. **Known for:** panoramic eating in a bright setting; fresh and locally sourced dishes; enclosed back garden. $ *Average main: £18 ✉ 2 Fore St. ☎ 01736/731164 ⊕ www.2forestreet.co.uk ⊘ Closed Jan. and early Feb.*

🛏 Hotels

★ Old Coastguard
$$ | HOTEL | The best views in Mousehole can be enjoyed from the bedrooms of this lodging; some rooms have balconies or terraces, all have modern bathrooms, and all come with Cornish tea and proper coffee with fresh milk. **Pros:** panoramic views; spacious garden; excellent bar-restaurant. **Cons:** unprepossessing exterior; could do with a scrub-up in places; no elevator to reach top rooms. $ *Rooms from: £150 ✉ The Parade ☎ 01736/731222 ⊕ www.oldcoast-guardhotel.co.uk ⇆ 14 rooms ⦿ Free breakfast.*

Detour: En Route 👁

About 2 miles north of Mousehole on B3315, **Newlyn** has long been Cornwall's most important fishing port. The annual Fish Festival takes over the town at the end of August. Newlyn became the magnet for artists at the end of the 19th century, and a few of the fishermen's cottages that first attracted them remain. Today the village has a good gallery of contemporary art.

Penzance

3 miles north of Mousehole, 1½ miles north of Newlyn, 10 miles south of St. Ives.

Superb views over Mount's Bay are one lure of this popular, unpretentious seaside resort. Even though it does get very crowded in summer, Penzance makes a good base for exploring the area. The town's isolated position has always made it vulnerable to attacks from the sea. During the 16th century, Spanish raiders destroyed most of the original town, and the majority of old buildings date from as late as the 18th century. The main street is Market Jew Street, a folk mistranslation of the Cornish expression Marghas Yow, which means "Thursday Market." Where Market Jew Street meets Causeway Head is Market House, an impressive, domed granite building constructed in 1837, with a statue of locally born chemist Humphry Davy in front.

In contrast to artsy St. Ives, Penzance is a no-nonsense working town. Though lacking the traffic-free lanes and quaint cottages of St. Ives, Penzance preserves pockets of handsome Georgian architecture.

GETTING HERE AND AROUND

The main train line from Plymouth terminates at Penzance, which is also served by National Express buses. Bus and train stations are next to each other at the east end of town. A car is an encumbrance here, so use one of the parking lots near the tourist office or the bus and train stations.

VISITOR INFORMATION Penzance Welcome Centre. ⊠ *Station Approach* ☎ *01736/335530* ⊕ *www.lovepenzance. co.uk.*

Sights

Chapel Street

NEIGHBORHOOD | One of the prettiest thoroughfares in Penzance, Chapel Street winds down from Market House to the harbor. Its predominantly Georgian and Regency houses suddenly give way to the extraordinary **Egyptian House,** whose facade recalls the Middle East. Built around 1830 as a geological museum, today it houses vacation apartments. Across Chapel Street is the 17th-century **Union Hotel,** where, in 1805, the death of Lord Nelson and the victory of Trafalgar were first announced. Near the Union Hotel on Chapel Street is the **Turk's Head,** an inn said to date from the 13th century. ⊠ *Penzance.*

Isles of Scilly

ISLAND | FAMILY | Fondly regarded in folklore as the lost land of Lyonesse, this compact group of more than 100 islands 30 miles southwest of Land's End is equally famed for the warm summer climate and ferocious winter storms. In fair weather you can find peace, flowers—wild, cultivated, and subtropical—swarms of seabirds, and unspoiled beaches galore. There's a 2¾-hour ferry service from Penzance, a plane service from Land's End airport and other mainland airports, and a helicopter service from Penzance. Planes and ferries both arrive at the largest of the five inhabited islands, St. Mary's, while up to 17 helicopter flights daily connect Penzance with St. Mary's and Tresco. St. Mary's has the bulk of the lodgings, though the most palatial retreats are on the islands of Tresco and St. Martin's. ⊠ *Penzance* ⊕ *www.visitislesofscilly.com.*

Penlee House Gallery and Museum

MUSEUM | A small collection in this gracious Victorian villa in Penlee Park focuses on paintings by members of the so-called Newlyn School from about 1880 to 1930. These works evoke the life of the inhabitants of Penzance and Newlyn, mostly fisherfolk. The museum also covers 5,000 years of West Cornwall history through archaeology, decorative arts, costume, and photography exhibits. ⊠ *Morrab Rd.* ☎ *01736/363625* ⊕ *www. penleehouse.org.uk* 🗓 *£5* ⊙ *Closed Sun.*

St. Michael's Mount

ISLAND | FAMILY | Rising out of Mount's Bay just off the coast, this spectacular granite-and-slate island is one of Cornwall's greatest natural attractions. The 14th-century castle perched at the highest point—200 feet above the sea—was built on the site of a Benedictine chapel founded by Edward the Confessor. In its time, the island has served as a church (Brittany's island abbey of Mont St. Michel was an inspiration), a fortress, and a private residence. The castle rooms you can tour include the Chevy Chase Room—a name probably associated with the Cheviot Hills or the French word *chevaux* (horses), after the hunting frieze that decorates the walls of this former monks' refectory. Family portraits include works by Reynolds and Gainsborough. Don't miss the wonderful views from the castle battlements. Around the base of the rock are buildings from medieval to Victorian times, but they appear harmonious. Fascinating gardens surround the Mount, and many kinds of plants flourish in its microclimate.

The stunning ocean setting of the open-air Minack Theatre near Penzance may distract you from the onstage drama.

To get to the island, walk the cobbled causeway from the village of Marazion or, when the tide is in, take the £2 ferry during summer or the £3 amphicraft in winter. There are pubs and restaurants in the village, but the island also has a café and restaurant. ■ **TIP→ Wear stout shoes for your visit, which requires a steep climb.** Visits may be canceled in severe weather. ✉ *A394, Marazion* ✛ *3 miles east of Penzance* ☎ *01736/710265* ⊕ *www. stmichaelsmount.co.uk* ✆ *£17.50; castle only £11.50; garden only £8.50* ☾ *Closed Sat., Nov.–mid-Feb., and Thurs.–Sun. in late Feb.–mid-Mar.*

🍴 Restaurants

Admiral Benbow

$ | **BRITISH** | One of the town's most famous inns, the 17th-century Admiral Benbow was once a smugglers' pub— look for the figure of a smuggler on the roof. In the family-friendly dining room, decorated to resemble a ship's galley, you can enjoy seafood or a steak-and-ale pie. **Known for:** great historic character; cozy and relaxed atmosphere; classic pub cuisine. ⑤ *Average main: £12* ✉ *46 Chapel St.* ☎ *01736/363448* ⊕ *www. thebenbow.com.*

Harris's

$$ | **MODERN BRITISH** | Seafood is the main event in the two small, pink-toned rooms of this restaurant off Market Jew Street. The menu showcases whatever the boats bring, though crab Florentine, grilled on a bed of spinach with a cheese sauce, is usually available. **Known for:** refined and elegant dining; fresh, expertly prepared seafood; great meat dishes like Cornish lamb and guinea fowl. ⑤ *Average main: £22* ✉ *46 New St.* ☎ *01736/364408* ⊕ *www.harrissres-taurant.co.uk* ☾ *Closed Sun., Mon., and 3 wks Nov. and Feb. No lunch.*

Hotels

★ Artist Residence
$$ | B&B/INN | A classic Georgian building has been converted with flair and wit to create a contemporary guesthouse with a strong artistic bent. **Pros:** idiosyncratic style; central location; excellent restaurant. **Cons:** noise intrusion in some rooms; no parking; no elevator. ⑤ *Rooms from: £140* ✉ *20 Chapel St.* ☎ *01736/365664* ⊕ *www.artistresidence. co.uk* ⟿ *25 rooms* ⦿| *Free breakfast.*

Camilla House
$ | B&B/INN | This flower-bedecked Georgian house close to the harbor has smartly decorated guest rooms with sea views from those at the front—top-floor rooms have all-round views but low ceilings. **Pros:** friendly and helpful management; immaculate decor; quiet location near seafront. **Cons:** some rooms are small; lengthy walk from bus and train stations; stairs to climb for uppermost rooms. ⑤ *Rooms from: £100* ✉ *12 Regent Terr.* ☎ *01736/363771* ⊕ *www.camillahouse.co.uk* ۞ *Closed Nov.–Mar.* ⟿ *8 rooms* ⦿| *Free breakfast.*

The Godolphin
$$ | HOTEL | Situated in the village of Marazion and very close to St. Michael's Mount, this dapper Georgian restaurant and hotel—whose large windows drink in the view of the turreted castle, the foreshore, and the ever-changing waters of Mount's Bay—has been given a modern makeover, with a bright and spacious feel that extends to the guest rooms. **Pros:** unrivaled views; relaxing bar and restaurant; friendly and attentive staff. **Cons:** not all rooms are sea-facing; some bathrooms are dated; housekeeping a bit slapdash. ⑤ *Rooms from: £190* ✉ *West End, Marazion* ☎ *01736/888510* ⊕ *www.thegodolphin. com* ⟿ *10 rooms* ⦿| *Free breakfast.*

Union Hotel
$ | HOTEL | Strong on historical atmosphere, this central lodging is housed the town's assembly rooms, where news of Admiral Nelson's victory at Trafalgar and of the death of Nelson himself were first announced from the minstrels' gallery in 1805. **Pros:** historic character; central location; good value. **Cons:** needs refurbishment; sparse staff; no elevator. ⑤ *Rooms from: £93* ✉ *Chapel St.* ☎ *01736/362319* ⊕ *www.unionhotel. co.uk* ⟿ *28 rooms* ⦿| *Free breakfast* Ⓜ.

🎭 Performing Arts

Minack Theatre
THEATER | The open-air Minack Theatre perches high above a beach 3 miles southeast of Land's End and about 6 miles southwest of Penzance. The slope of the cliff forms a natural amphitheater, with bench seats on the terraces and the sea as a magnificent backdrop. Different companies present everything from classic dramas to modern comedies, as well as operas and concerts, on afternoons and evenings between late March and late September. An exhibition center tells the story of the theater's creation. Note that this center is closed afternoons when matinee performances are scheduled. ✉ *Off B3315, Porthcurno* ☎ *01736/810181* ⊕ *www.minack.com* ▣ *Exhibition center £6, performances £12–£17.*

🏃 Activities

Many ships have foundered on Cornwall's rocky coastline, resulting in an estimated 3,600 shipwrecks. The area around Land's End has some of the best diving in Europe, in part because the convergence of the Atlantic and the Gulf Stream here results in impressive visibility and unusual subtropical marine life.

Cornish Diving Centre
DIVING/SNORKELING | This small company offers year-round dive excursions in the waters around West Cornwall. ✉ *Bar Rd., Falmouth* ☎ *01326/311265, 07885/771282* ⊕ *www.cornishdiving.co.uk.*

Lizard Peninsula

23 miles southeast of Penzance.

The southernmost point on mainland Britain, this peninsula is a government-designated Area of Outstanding Natural Beauty, named so for the rocky, dramatic coast rather than the flat and boring interior. The huge, eerily rotating dish antennae of the Goonhilly Satellite Earth Station are visible from the road as it crosses Goonhilly Downs, the backbone of the peninsula. There's no coast road, unlike Land's End, but the coastal path offers marvelous opportunities to explore on foot—and is often the only way to reach the best beaches. With no large town (Helston at the northern end is the biggest but isn't a tourist center), it's far less busy than the Land's End peninsula.

GETTING HERE AND AROUND
If you're driving, take A394 to reach Helston, gateway town to the Lizard Peninsula. From Helston, A3083 heads straight down to Lizard Point. Helston is the main public transport hub, but bus service to the villages is infrequent.

⊙ Sights

Kynance Cove
BEACH—SIGHT | A path close to the tip of the peninsula plunges down 200-foot cliffs to this tiny cove dotted with a handful of pint-size islands. The sands here are reachable only during the 2½ hours before and after low tide. The peninsula's cliffs are made of greenish serpentine rock, interspersed with granite; souvenirs of the area are carved out of the stone. ⊠ *Lizard.*

Falmouth

8 miles northeast of Lizard Peninsula.

The bustle of this resort town's fishing harbor, yachting center, and commercial port only adds to its charm. In the 18th century, Falmouth was the main mail-boat port for North America, and in Flushing, a village across the inlet, you can see the slate-covered houses built by prosperous mail-boat captains. A ferry service now links the two towns. On Custom House Quay, off Arwenack Street, is the King's Pipe, an oven in which seized contraband was burned.

GETTING HERE AND AROUND
Falmouth can be reached from Truro on a branch rail line or by frequent bus service, and is also served by local and National Express buses from other towns. Running parallel to the seafront, the long, partly pedestrianized main drag links the town's main sights. Visitors to Pendennis Castle traveling by train should use Falmouth Docks Station, from which it's a short walk. Alternatively, drive or take a local bus to the castle to save legwork.

VISITOR INFORMATION Fal River Visitor Information Centre. ⊠ *Prince of Wales Pier, 11 Market Strand* ☎ *01326/741194* ⊕ *www.falmouth.co.uk.*

⊙ Sights

National Maritime Museum Cornwall
MUSEUM | FAMILY | The granite-and-oak-clad structure by the harbor is an excellent place to come to grips with Cornish maritime heritage, weather lore, and navigational science. You can view approximately 30 of the collection of 140 or so boats, examine the tools associated with Cornish boatbuilders, and gaze down from the lighthouselike lookout, which is equipped with maps, telescopes, and binoculars. In the glass-fronted Tidal Zone below sea level, you come face-to-face with the sea itself. Between May and September, hour-long boat tours of the harbor and nearby coast depart from the museum three times daily. ■TIP→ **Buy museum tickets online for a 10% discount.** ⊠ *Discovery Quay* ☎ *01326/313388* ⊕ *www.nmmc.co.uk* ☜ *£14.50.*

★ Pendennis Castle

CASTLE/PALACE | FAMILY | At the end of its own peninsula stands this formidable castle, built by Henry VIII in the 1540s and improved by his daughter Elizabeth I. You can explore the defenses developed over the centuries. In the Royal Artillery Barracks, the Pendennis Unlocked exhibit explores the castle's history and its connection to Cornwall and England. The castle has sweeping views over the English Channel and across to St. Mawes Castle, designed as a companion fortress to guard the roads. There are free tours of the Half Moon Battery and regular performances, historical reenactments, and shows for kids. ⊠ *Pendennis Head* ☎ *01326/316594* ⊕ *www.english-heritage.org.uk* ⊴ *£10.90* ☉ *Closed Mon. and Tues. in late Feb.–late Mar. and weekdays in Nov.–mid-Feb.*

🍴 Restaurants

Gylly Beach

$$ | MODERN BRITISH | For views and location, this beachside eatery with a crisp, modern interior and deck seating can't be beat. By day, it's a breezy café offering burgers, salads, and sandwiches, while the evening menu presents a judicious balance of meat, seafood, and vegetarian dishes, from smoked fish trio to beef sirloin. **Known for:** amazing views; family-friendly setting; live music on Sunday night. ⑤ *Average main: £17* ⊠ *Gyllyngvase Beach, Cliff Rd.* ☎ *01326/312884* ⊕ *www.gyllybeach.com* ☉ *No dinner Mon. and Tues. Nov.–Easter.*

Pandora Inn

$ | BRITISH | This thatched pub on a creek 4 miles north of Falmouth is a great retreat, with both a patio and a moored pontoon for summer dining. The menu highlight is fresh seafood—try the fish pie in a shallot and pastis cream sauce. **Known for:** serene riverside setting; great local ales; lovely outside dining. ⑤ *Average main: £14* ⊠ *Restronguet Creek, Mylor Bridge* ☎ *01326/372678* ⊕ *www. pandorainn.com.*

Rick Stein's Fish

$$ | SEAFOOD | Celebrity-chef Rick Stein has expanded his seafood empire to Falmouth, where this spruced-up takeaway and restaurant opposite the National Maritime Museum makes a welcome addition to the local dining scene. The hake, plaice, and haddock are grilled, fried to a golden hue, or charcoal roasted and served with salad. **Known for:** celebrity-chef status; down-to-earth ambience; perfect seafood including classic fish-and-chips. ⑤ *Average main: £16* ⊠ *Discovery Quay* ☎ *01841/532700* ⊕ *www.rickstein.com* ☉ *No dinner Sun. and Mon. Oct.–Easter.*

🛏 Hotels

St. Michaels Resort

$$ | HOTEL | A cool, contemporary ambience pervades this seaside hotel overlooking Falmouth Bay and fronted by a lush, subtropical garden. **Pros:** excellent facilities; good restaurants; attentive and amiable staff. **Cons:** spa facilities can be busy; cheapest rooms are small and viewless; some rooms are noisy. ⑤ *Rooms from: £191* ⊠ *Gyllyngvase Beach* ☎ *01326/312707* ⊕ *www.stmichaelshotel.co.uk* ➪ *61 rooms* �‖ *Free breakfast.*

Trelissick

6 miles northeast of Falmouth.

Trelissick is known for the colorful Trelissick Garden, owned by the National Trust.

GETTING HERE AND AROUND

Between Easter and October, the most rewarding way to arrive at Trelissick is by ferry from Falmouth or St. Mawes. There are also frequent year-round buses from these towns. By car, it's on B3289, between A39 and A3078.

⊙ Sights

King Harry Ferry
TRANSPORTATION SITE (AIRPORT/BUS/FERRY/TRAIN) | A chain-drawn car ferry, the *King Harry* runs to the scenically splendid Roseland Peninsula each day three times an hour. From its decks you can see up and down the Fal, a deep, narrow river with steep, wooded banks. The river's great depth provides mooring for old ships waiting to be sold; these mammoth shapes often lend a surreal touch to the riverscape. On very rare occasions, you may even spot deer swimming across. ⊠ *B3289, Truro* ☎ *01872/862312* ⊕ *www.falriver.co.uk* ☒ *£6.*

Trelissick
GARDEN | Cornwall's mild climate has endowed it with some of the country's most spectacular gardens, among which is Trelissick Garden on the banks of the River Fal. Famous for its camellias, hydrangeas, magnolias, and rhododendrons, the terraced garden is set within 375 acres of wooded parkland, offering wonderful panoramic views and making this a paradise for walkers. There are also tranquil views from the porticoed Trelissick House and exhibitions of contemporary Cornish art in the gallery. ⊠ *B3289, Feock* ☎ *01872/862090* ⊕ *www.nationaltrust.org.uk* ☒ *£12.80.*

St. Mawes

6 miles south of Trelissick, 16 miles east of Falmouth.

At the tip of the Roseland Peninsula is the quiet, unspoiled village of St. Mawes, where subtropical plants thrive. The peninsula itself is a lovely backwater with old churches, a lighthouse, and good coast walking. One or two sailing and boating options are available in summer, but most companies operate from Falmouth.

Rent a Cottage 🛏

You can experience rural peace in a rented cottage in the West Country, but book early for summer.

Classic Cottages ☎ *01326/555555* ⊕ *www.classic.co.uk.*

Cornish Cottage Holidays ☎ *01244/617652* ⊕ *www.cornishcottageholidays.co.uk.*

Cornish Traditional Cottages ☎ *01208/895354* ⊕ *www.corncott.com.*

Helpful Holidays ☎ *01647/433593* ⊕ *www.helpfulholidays.co.uk.*

GETTING HERE AND AROUND
By road, St. Mawes lies at the end of A3078. You could drive from Falmouth, but it's easier to hop on a ferry crossing the estuary. Shuttling passengers between the ports in Falmouth and St. Mawes, the St. Mawes Ferry passes by two atmospheric castles along the way. It runs all year from Falmouth's Prince of Wales Pier and, between April and October, the Custom House Quay.

FERRY CONTACTS St. Mawes Ferry.
☎ *01326/741194* ⊕ *www.falriver.co.uk.*

⊙ Sights

St. Just in Roseland
TOWN | North of St. Mawes on the A3078 is St. Just in Roseland, one of the most beautiful spots in the West Country. The tiny hamlet has a 13th-century church set within a subtropical garden, often abloom with magnolias and rhododendrons, as well as a holy well and a graveyard on the banks of a secluded creek. ⊠ *Roseland.*

St. Mawes Castle
CASTLE/PALACE | Outside the village, the well-preserved Tudor-era St. Mawes Castle has a cloverleaf shape that makes it seemingly impregnable, yet during

the Civil War its Royalist commander surrendered without firing a shot. (In contrast, Pendennis Castle in Falmouth held out at this time for 23 weeks before submitting to a siege.) Outdoor theater productions occasionally take place here in summer. ✉ *Castle Dr.* ☎ *01326/270526* ⊕ *www.english-heritage.org.uk* ✉ *£6.84* ⊘ *Closed weekdays Nov.–mid-Feb. and Mon. and Tues. late Feb.–late Mar.*

Hotels

★ Hotel Tresanton

$$$ | HOTEL | It's the Cornish Riviera, Italian style: this former yachtsman's club, owned by hotelier Olga Polizzi, makes for a luxuriously relaxed stay. **Pros:** relaxed but professional service; terrific views; stylishly luxurious setting. **Cons:** some steps to climb; occasional noise intrusion in rooms; remote parking. ⑤ *Rooms from: £295* ✉ *Lower Castle Rd.* ☎ *01326/270055* ⊕ *www.tresanton.com* ⇨ *30 rooms* |○| *Free breakfast.*

Lugger Hotel

$$ | HOTEL | It's worth the winding drive on some of Cornwall's narrowest roads to get to this waterfront hideaway in a tiny fishing village. **Pros:** unforgettable seaside setting; attention to detail; quality cuisine. **Cons:** location is remote; some rooms are cramped with limited views; could pose issues for those with mobility problems. ⑤ *Rooms from: £166* ✉ *Portloe* ☎ *01872/501322* ⊕ *www.luggerhotel.co.uk* ⇨ *24 rooms* |○| *Free breakfast.*

Truro

8 miles northwest of St. Mawes, 8 miles northeast of Falmouth.

The county seat and Cornwall's only real city, Truro is a good option mostly for food and shopping and for cathedral and museum buffs. For an overview of the Georgian houses, take a stroll down steep, broad Lemon Street. The elegant 18th-century facades are of pale stone—unusual for Cornwall, where granite predominates. Like Lemon Street, Walsingham Place is a typical Georgian street, a curving, flower-lined pedestrian oasis. The city nestles in a crook of the River Truro.

GETTING HERE AND AROUND

Truro is on the main rail line between Penzance and Plymouth and is served by local and National Express buses. The compact center can be easily walked from the bus and train stations.

VISITOR INFORMATION Truro Tourist Information Centre. ✉ *30 Boscawen St.* ☎ *01872/274555* ⊕ *www.visittruro.org.uk.*

⊙ Sights

Cathedral Church of St. Mary

RELIGIOUS SITE | Although built between 1880 and 1910, this cathedral evokes a medieval church, with an exterior in Early English Gothic style. The interior is filled with relics from the 16th-century parish church that stood on this site, part of which has been incorporated into a side chapel. Lunchtime organ recitals take place on most Fridays between March and October. An open, cobbled area called High Cross lies in front of the west porch, and the city's main shopping streets fan out from here. ✉ *High Cross* ☎ *01872/276782* ⊕ *www.trurocathedral.org.uk* ✉ *Free, donations requested* ⊘ *Closed for visits during services.*

Royal Cornwall Museum

MUSEUM | FAMILY | In a Georgian building, this museum displays some fine examples of Cornwall-inspired art, a sampling of Cornish archaeology, an absorbing hodgepodge of local history, and an extensive collection of minerals. There's also a shop and a small café. ✉ *River St.* ☎ *01872/272205* ⊕ *www.royalcornwallmuseum.org.uk* ✉ *£5.50* ⊘ *Closed Mon. except bank holidays and school vacations.*

⊞ Hotels

The Alverton

$$ | HOTEL | Formerly a convent, this atmospheric lodging still holds a chapel that was designed by J. L. **Pros:** spacious rooms; friendly and helpful staff; secluded garden setting. **Cons:** decor could do with an upgrade; no elevator; slightly corporate feel. ⑤ *Rooms from: £135* ✉ *Tregolls Rd.* ☎ *01872/276633* ⊕ *www. thealverton.co.uk* ↗ *51 rooms* ◎| *Free breakfast.*

Fowey

25 miles northeast of St. Mawes.

Nestled in the mouth of a wooded estuary, Fowey (pronounced Foy) is still very much a working china-clay port as well as a focal point for the sailing fraternity. Increasingly, it's also a favored home of the rich and famous. Good and varied dining and lodging options abound, and these are most in demand during Regatta Week in mid- to late August and the annual Fowey Festival of Words and Music in mid-May. The Bodinnick and Polruan ferries take cars as well as foot passengers across the river for the coast road on to Looe.

A few miles west of Fowey are a pair of very different gardens: the Eden Project, a futuristic display of plants from around the world, and the Lost Gardens of Heligan, a revitalized reminder of the Victorian age.

GETTING HERE AND AROUND

Fowey isn't on any train line, but the town is served by frequent buses from St. Austell. Don't attempt to drive into the steep and narrow-lane town center, which is ideal for strolling around. Parking lots are signposted on the approach roads.

VISITOR INFORMATION Fowey Tourist Information. ⊕ *www.fowey.co.uk.*

⊙ Sights

Charlestown

TOWN | Seven miles west of Fowey, Charlestown has a Georgian harbor so well preserved that it often appears in period film and television productions (antique-looking square-riggers are usually moored here). This port was built by a local merchant in 1791 to export the huge reserves of china clay from nearby St. Austell. It was also one of the ports from which 19th-century emigrants left for North America. ✉ *Fowey.*

★ Eden Project

GARDEN | FAMILY | Spectacularly set in a former china-clay pit, this garden presents the world's major plant systems in microcosm. The crater contains more than 70,000 plants—many of them rare or endangered species—from three climate zones. Plants from the temperate zone are outdoors, and those from other zones are housed in hexagonally paneled geodesic domes. In the Mediterranean Biome, olive and citrus groves mix with cacti and other plants indigenous to warmer climates. The Rainforest Biome steams with heat, resounds to the gushing of a waterfall, and blooms with exotic flora; the elevated Canopy Walkway enables you to experience a monkey's-eye view of all of it. The emphasis is on conservation and ecology, but is free of any editorializing. A free shuttle helps the footsore, and well-informed guides provide information. An entertaining exhibition in the visitor center gives you the lowdown on the project, and the Core, an education center, provides amusement and instruction for children—if you can drag them away from the zipwire and giant swing. ■**TIP→ Buy tickets online at least a day before your visit for a discounted entry.** There are open-air concerts in summer and an ice-skating rink in winter. The Eden Project is 3 miles northeast of Charleston and 5 miles northwest of Fowey. There's frequent bus service from Fowey to St. Austell and from St. Austell train station to Eden. ✉ *Bodelva Rd., off A30, A390, and A391, St. Austell* ☎ *01726/811911* ⊕ *www.edenproject.com* ✉ *£28.50; £24.50 if arriving by bike, on foot, or on public transport; £39.50 combined ticket with Lost Gardens of Heligan (available online in advance only)* ⊙ *Usually closed Mon. and Tues. Jan.–mid-Feb.*

Lost Gardens of Heligan

GARDEN | These sprawling grounds have something for all garden lovers, as well as an intriguing history. Begun by the Tremayne family in the late 18th century, they were rediscovered and spruced up in the early 1990s by former rock music producer Tim Smit (the force behind the Eden Project). In Victorian times the gardens displayed plants from around the British Empire. The Jungle area contains surviving plants from this era, including a lone Monterey pine, as well as giant redwood, clumps of bamboo, and a wobbly rope bridge crossing the subtropical valley. The Italian Garden and walled Flower Gardens are delightful, but don't overlook the fruit and vegetable gardens or Flora's Green, bordered by a ravine. It's easy to spend half a day here. Guided tours can be arranged for groups. ■ **TIP→ Travel via St. Austell to avoid confusing country lanes, then follow signs to Mevagissey.** ✉ *B3273, Pentewan* ☎ *01726/845100* ⊕ *www.heligan.com* ✉ *£15, £39.50 combined ticket with Eden Project (when bought online at least one day before visit).*

🍴 Restaurants

Sam's

$ | **AMERICAN** | **FAMILY** | This small and buzzing bistro has a rock-and-roll flavor, thanks to the walls adorned with posters of music icons. Diners squeeze onto benches and into booths to savor dishes made with local seafood, including a majestic bouillabaisse, or just a simple "Samburger". **Known for:** convivial atmosphere; best burgers in Cornwall; long waits for a table. ⑤ *Average main: £13* ✉ *20 Fore St.* ☎ *01726/832273* ⊕ *www.samscornwall.co.uk.*

🛏 Hotels

Fowey Hall

$$ | **HOTEL** | **FAMILY** | A showy Victorian edifice, all turrets and elaborate plasterwork, this hotel with 5 acres of gardens, a spa, and a pool was the original inspiration for Toad Hall in *The Wind in the Willows*. **Pros:** grand manorial setting; family-friendly rates; spacious rooms with good views. **Cons:** no elevator; not ideal for anyone seeking an adult ambience; steep walk from town center. ⑤ *Rooms from: £159* ✉ *Hanson Dr.* ☎ *01726/833866* ⊕ *www.foweyhallhotel.co.uk* ☞ *36 rooms* ⑩ *Free breakfast.*

St. Michaels Resort

$$ | **HOTEL** | A cool, contemporary ambience pervades this seaside hotel overlooking Falmouth Bay and fronted by a lush, subtropical garden. **Pros:** excellent facilities; good restaurants; attentive and amiable staff. **Cons:** spa facilities can be busy; cheapest rooms are small and viewless; some rooms are noisy. ⑤ *Rooms from: £191* ✉ *Gyllyngvase Beach, Falmouth* ☎ *01326/312707* ⊕ *www.stmichaelshotel.co.uk* ☞ *61 rooms* ⑩ *Free breakfast.*

🏃 Activities

Fowey River Hire

CANOEING/ROWING/SKULLING | **FAMILY** | Between April and September, Fowey River Hire runs daily kayak trips up the tranquil River Fowey, the best way to observe the area's abundant wildlife. Kayaks, paddleboards, and motorboats are also available to rent. ✉ *Albert Quay* ☎ *01726/833627 office, 07515/353936 cell* ⊕ *www.foweyriverhire.co.uk.*

Upstairs, downstairs: at Lanhydrock you can tour both the elegant picture gallery and the vast kitchens, pantries, and sculleries.

Bodmin

12 miles north of Fowey.

Bodmin was the only Cornish town recorded in the 11th-century Domesday Book, William the Conqueror's census. During World War I, the Domesday Book and the crown jewels were sent to Bodmin Prison for safekeeping. From the Gilbert Memorial on Beacon Hill you can see both of Cornwall's coasts. Lanhydrock, a stately home, is also near Bodmin.

GETTING HERE AND AROUND

At the junction of A38 and A30, Bodmin is a major transport hub for north Cornwall. Trains stop at Bodmin Parkway, 3 miles southeast of the center. A car is your best bet for touring Bodmin Moor and visiting Lanhydrock.

VISITOR INFORMATION Bodmin Visitor Information Centre. ⊠ *The Shire Hall, Mount Folly Sq.* ☎ *01208/76616* ⊕ *www. bodminlive.com.*

◉ Sights

Dozmary Pool

POOL | For a taste of Arthurian legend, follow A30 northeast out of Bodmin across the boggy, heather-clad granite plateau of Bodmin Moor. After about 10 miles, turn right at Bolventor to get to Dozmary Pool. A lake rather than a pool, it was here that King Arthur's legendary magic sword, Excalibur, was supposedly returned to the Lady of the Lake after Arthur's final battle. ⊠ *Bodmin.*

★ Lanhydrock

HOUSE | One of Cornwall's greatest country piles, Lanhydrock gives a look into the lives of the upper classes in the 19th century. The former home of the powerful, wealthy Robartes family was originally constructed in the 17th century but was totally rebuilt after a fire in 1881. Its granite exterior remains true to the house's original form, however, and the long picture gallery in the north wing, with its barrel-vaulted plaster ceiling depicting 24 biblical scenes, survived the devastation. A small museum shows photographs and letters relating to the family. The house's endless pantries, sculleries, dairies, nurseries, and linen cupboards bear witness to the immense amount of work involved in maintaining this lifestyle. About 900 acres of wooded parkland border the River Fowey, and in spring the gardens present an exquisite ensemble of magnolias, azaleas, and rhododendrons. Allow two hours to see the house and more time to stroll the grounds. The house is 3 miles southeast of Bodmin. ⊠ *Off A30, A38, and B3268* ☎ *01208/265950* ⊕ *www.nationaltrust. org.uk* ☜ *£16.45; Nov.–Dec. £9.05* ⊗ *House closed Nov., Jan., and Feb., gardens closed Nov.–mid-Feb., estate remains open daily.*

Launceston

25 miles northwest of Plymouth.

Cornwall's ancient capital, Launceston, on the eastern side of Bodmin Moor, retains parts of its medieval walls, including the South Gate.

VISITOR INFORMATION Launceston Tourist Information Centre. ⊠ *White Hart Arcade, Broad St.* ☎ *01566/772321* ⊕ *www. visitlaunceston.co.uk.*

⊙ Sights

Launceston Castle

CASTLE/PALACE | For a superb view of the surrounding countryside, climb to the hilltop ruins of this 13th-century castle. George Fox, founder of the Quakers, was imprisoned here in 1656. ⊠ *Castle Lodge* ☎ *01566/772365* ⊕ *www.english-herit-age.org.uk* ☜ *£5.85* ⊗ *Closed Nov.–Mar.*

Plymouth

48 miles southwest of Exeter, 124 miles southwest of Bristol, 240 miles southwest of London.

Devon's largest city has long been linked with England's commercial and maritime history. The Pilgrims sailed from here to the New World on the *Mayflower* in 1620. Although much of the city center was destroyed by air raids in World War II and has been rebuilt in an uninspiring style, there are worthwhile sights. A harbor tour is also a good way to see the city.

GETTING HERE AND AROUND

Frequent trains arrive from Bodmin, Penzance, and Exeter. From London Paddington, trains take three to four hours; Megabus and National Express buses from London's Victoria Coach Station take five or six hours. The train station is 1 mile north of the seafront, connected by frequent buses. Long-distance buses stop at the centrally located bus station off Royal Parade. Drivers can leave their cars in one of the numerous parking lots, including a couple right by the harbor. The seafront and central city areas are best explored on foot.

ESSENTIALS

VISITOR INFORMATION Plymouth Tourism Information Centre. ⊠ *Mayflower Museum, 3–5 The Barbican* ☎ *01752/306330* ⊕ *www.visitplymouth.co.uk.*

⊙ Sights

The Barbican

NEIGHBORHOOD | East of the Royal Citadel is the Barbican, the oldest surviving section of Plymouth. Here Tudor houses and warehouses rise from a maze of narrow streets leading down to the fishing harbor and marina. Many of these buildings have become antiques shops, art shops, and cafés. It's well worth a stroll for the atmosphere. ⊠ *Plymouth.*

The Box

MUSEUM | FAMILY | Consisting of a museum, gallery, and archive, The Box opened in 2020 as Plymouth's state-of-the-art exhibition space dedicated to all cultural and historical aspects of the city. Upon entering, visitors pass below 14 giant wooden ship's figureheads dating from the 1800s, a theme explored further in the 100 Journeys gallery, focusing on the city's long relationship with the sea and the various voyages that began from Plymouth, and the Port of Plymouth gallery. More than 3,000 natural history specimens are displayed in the Mammoth gallery, while the Photo Album gallery and Media Lab provide visual images from the past. Lastly, the Salon holds an excellent art collection that highlights artists associated with the West Country such as Sir Joshua Reynolds, Stanhope Forbes, Barbara Hepworth, and, more recently, Robert Lenkiewicz. Numerous interactive touchscreens will engage all ages, and there are regular temporary exhibitions. ⊠ *Tavistock Pl.* ☎ *01752/304774* ⊕ *www. theboxplymouth.com* ⊘ *Closed Mon.*

Elizabethan House

MUSEUM | In the heart of the Barbican section, this former sea captain's home offers a fascinating insight into how well-to-do Plymothians lived during the city's golden age. The three floors of the timber-frame house are filled with 16th- and 17th-century furnishings, and there's a reconstructed kitchen and a spiral staircase built around a ship's mast. The museum will remain closed until renovation work is complete in 2021. ⊠ *32 New St.* ☎ *01752/304774* ⊕ *www.plymhearts. org* ⊛ *£2.80.*

Hoe

VIEWPOINT | From the Hoe, a wide, grassy esplanade with crisscrossing walkways high above the city, you can take in a magnificent view of the inlets, bays, and harbors that make up Plymouth Sound. ⊠ *Plymouth.*

Mayflower Museum

MUSEUM | FAMILY | On three floors, this interactive exhibition narrates the story of Plymouth, from its beginnings as a fishing and trading port to the modern industrial city it is today. Along the way, you'll take in the stories of various expeditions that embarked from here to the New World, including the *Mayflower* itself. The city's tourist office is also in this building. ⊠ *3–5 The Barbican* ☎ *01752/306330* ⊕ *www.visitplymouth.co.uk* ⊛ *£3.50* ⊘ *Closed Sun. Nov.–Mar.*

Mayflower Steps

MEMORIAL | By the harbor you can visit the Mayflower Steps, marking where the Pilgrims embarked in 1620. The actual steps no longer exist, but a granite block, the **Mayflower Stone,** marks the approximate spot, and there is a commemorative portico with Doric columns of Portland stone. Local historians believe that the true site is roughly where a Victorian pub, the Admiral MacBride, now stands. The Pilgrims had originally sailed from Southampton but had to stop in Plymouth because of damage from a storm. ⊠ *The Barbican.*

National Marine Aquarium

ZOO | FAMILY | This excellent aquarium—the U.K.'s largest—on the harbor presents aqueous environments, from a freshwater stream to the Great Barrier Reef and the Blue Planet Biozone. Not to be missed is the chance to walk beneath sharks in the Atlantic Ocean tank, alongside clown fish, octopuses, and humphead wrasses in the Biozone. Feeding times are fun for the kids, and Waves Café, with its harbor views, makes a good spot for a rest and refreshment. ■**TIP→ Tickets are valid for one year. Buy online for a set day at least three days in advance for a 10% discount.** ⊠ *Rope Walk, Coxside* ☎ *0844/893–7938* ⊕ *www.national-aquarium.co.uk* ⊛ *£17.95.*

Plymouth Boat Trips

TOUR—SIGHT | Harbor cruises leave from the Mayflower Steps and Cremyll Quay all year, while longer scenic trips on the rivers Tamar and Yealm operate between

Plymouth, Exeter, and South Devon

April and October. Check the website for daily times. ✉ *Mayflower Steps, 2–5 Commercial Wharf* ☎ *01752/253153* 🌐 *www.plymouthboattrips.co.uk.*

Plymouth Gin Distillery

WINERY/DISTILLERY | At the Black Friars Distillery, Plymouth's most famous export, gin, has been distilled since 1793. You can purchase bottles of sloe gin, damson liqueur, fruit cup, or the fiery "Navy Strength" gin that traditionally was issued to the Royal Navy. Learn the full story on walking tours around the distillery, ending with a sampling in the wood-paneled Refectory Bar. The building originally housed a friary and was where the Pilgrims spent their last night on English soil in 1620. ✉ *Black Friars Distillery, 60 Southside St.* ☎ *01752/665292* 🌐 *www. plymouthgin.com* ☞ *Tours £12.50–£55.*

Saltram

HOUSE | An exquisite 18th-century home with many of its original furnishings, Saltram was built around the remains of a late-Tudor mansion. Its jewel is one of Britain's grandest neoclassical rooms—a vast, double-cube salon designed by Robert Adam and hung with paintings by Sir Joshua Reynolds, first president of the Royal Academy of Arts, who was born nearby in 1723. Fine plasterwork adorns many rooms, and three have original Chinese wallpaper. The outstanding garden includes rare trees and shrubs, and there's a restaurant and a cafeteria. Saltram is 3½ miles east of Plymouth city center. ✉ *South of A38, Plympton* ☎ *01752/333500* 🌐 *www.nationaltrust. org.uk* ☞ *£12.80* ⏱ *House may close for a few weeks in Jan. and Nov.*

Pony trekking in Dartmoor National Park lets you get off the beaten path.

Smeaton's Tower

MEMORIAL | This lighthouse, transferred here at the end of the 19th century from its original site 14 miles out to sea, provides a sweeping vista over Plymouth Sound and the city as far as Dartmoor. Brace yourself for the 93 steps to the top. ⊠ *Hoe Rd.* ☎ *01752/304774* ⊕ *www. plymhearts.org* ⊠ *£5.*

🍴 Restaurants

The Barbican Kitchen

$$ | **MODERN BRITISH** | Housed within the historic Black Friars Distillery in the heart of the Barbican, this restaurant owned by a distinguished local culinary duo is a cheerful spot for a quick lunch or a more leisurely evening meal. The menu might include slow-cooked pork belly with tiger prawns and caramelized cauliflower or smoked haddock risotto. **Known for:** buzzy atmosphere; cool distillery location (with plenty of house-made gin on the menu); good selection of steaks. ⑤ *Average main: £16* ⊠ *Plymouth Gin Distillery, 60 Southside St.* ☎ *01752/604448* ⊕ *www. barbicankitchen.com* ⊘ *Closed Sun.*

Quay 33

$$ | **MODERN BRITISH** | Fresh seafood landed at the nearby quays, such as sea bass and hake, features high on the menu at this Barbican eatery, but you will also find pastas, risottos, steaks, and slow-cooked duck-leg confit. Exmouth mussels or grilled scallops make an ideal light lunch, while desserts include crème brûlée and homemade cheesecake. **Known for:** first-class service; creative and delicious food; tasty desserts. ⑤ *Average main: £16* ⊠ *33 Southside St.* ☎ *01752/229345* ⊕ *www.quay33.co.uk* ⊘ *Closed Sun.*

🛏 Hotels

Boringdon Hall Hotel

$$ | **HOTEL** | One of the foremost manor houses in the West Country during Tudor times, this battlemented pile oozes historic character. **Pros:** country house splendor; quality restaurant; luxury spa facilities. **Cons:** cheaper rooms are very ordinary; no elevator; remote from Plymouth's center. $ *Rooms from: £146* ✉ *Colebrook* ☎ *01752/546196* ⊕ *www. boringdonhall.co.uk* ⌁ *42 rooms* ❍❙ *Free breakfast.*

Crowne Plaza

$$ | HOTEL | Grandly located in a tall block overlooking Plymouth Hoe, this modern chain hotel has a businesslike tone but doesn't skimp on comforts. **Pros:** excellent location for sights; large rooms; lofty views. **Cons:** impersonal feel; some bathrooms are small; tight parking. $ *Rooms from: £182* ✉ *Armada Way* ☎ *01752/639988, 0800/890410* ⊕ *www.ihg.com* ⌁ *211 rooms* ❍❙ *Free breakfast.*

Rooms by Bistrot Pierre

$ | B&B/INN | Looking onto a placid sward of lawn in the newly fashionable Royal William Yard district of Plymouth—formerly the navy's victualling quarter—this classic Georgian building once housed naval officers and now offers well-appointed guest accommodations with a touch of class. **Pros:** classic Georgian rooms; interesting dockyard environment; easy parking. **Cons:** not close to the main tourist sites; little in the way of service or staff presence; breakfast is sparse. $ *Rooms from: £100* ✉ *Residence One, 7 Royal William Yard* ☎ *01752/262318* ⊕ *www. bistrotpierre.co.uk* ⌁ *14 rooms* ❍❙ *Free breakfast.*

⚡ Performing Arts

Theatre Royal

THEATER | Plymouth's Theatre Royal presents ballet, musicals, and plays by some of Britain's best companies. ✉ *Royal Parade* ☎ *01752/267222* ⊕ *www. theatreroyal.com.*

Dartmoor National Park

10 miles north of Plymouth, 13 miles west of Exeter.

Devon presents no greater contrast to the country's quaint and picturesque image than the bleak, deserted expanses of Dartmoor. Southern England's greatest natural wilderness is largely a treeless landscape of sometimes alarming emptiness, though it also harbors surprises in the form of hidden lakes, abandoned quarries, and the dramatically wind-sculpted tors, or craggy peaks, that puncture the horizon in every direction. Sudden mists and above-average rainfall levels add to the simultaneously inhospitable and alluring scene.

GETTING HERE AND AROUND

Public transport services are extremely sparse on Dartmoor, making a car indispensable for anywhere off the beaten track. The peripheral towns of Okehampton and Tavistock are well served by bus from Exeter and Plymouth, and Chagford also has direct connections to Exeter, but central Princetown has only sporadic links with the outside world.

ESSENTIALS

VISITOR INFORMATION National Park Visitor Centre. ✉ *Tavistock Rd., Princetown* ☎ *01822/890414* ⊕ *www.dartmoor.gov. uk.*

⊙ Sights

Dartmoor National Park

NATIONAL/STATE PARK | Even on a summer's day, the brooding hills of this sprawling wilderness appear a likely haunt for such monsters as the hound of the Baskervilles, and it seems entirely fitting that Sir Arthur Conan Doyle set his Sherlock Holmes thriller in this landscape. Sometimes the wet, peaty wasteland of Dartmoor National Park vanishes in rain and mist, although in clear weather you can see north to Exmoor, south over the English Channel, and west far into Cornwall. Much of Dartmoor consists of open heath and moorland, unspoiled by roads—wonderful walking and horseback-riding territory but an easy place to lose your bearings. Dartmoor's earliest inhabitants left behind stone monuments and burial mounds that help you envision prehistoric man roaming these pastures. Ponies, sheep, and birds are the main animals to be seen.

Several villages scattered along the borders of this 368-square-mile reserve—one-third of which is owned by Prince Charles—make useful bases for hiking excursions. Accommodations include simple inns and some elegant havens. **Okehampton** is a main gateway, and **Chagford** is a good base for exploring north Dartmoor. Other scenic spots include **Buckland-in-the-Moor,** a hamlet with thatch-roof cottages; **Widecombe-in-the-Moor,** whose church is known as the Cathedral of the Moor; and **Grimspound,** the Bronze Age site featured in Conan Doyle's most famous tale. Transmoor Link buses connect many of Dartmoor's towns and villages. The **National Park Visitor Centre** in Princetown is a good place to start your trip, as are centers in Postbridge and Haytor. You can also pick up information in Ivybridge, Ashburton, Okehampton, Moretonhampstead, Bovey Tracey, Tavistock, and Buckfastleigh. ⊠ *National Park Visitor Centre, Tavistock Rd., Princetown* ☎ *01822/890414* ⊕ *www.dartmoor.gov.uk.*

🏃 Activities

Hiking is extremely popular in Dartmoor National Park. The areas around Widgery Cross, Becky Falls, and the Bovey Valley, as well as the short but dramatic walk along Lydford Gorge, have wide appeal, as do the many valleys around the southern edge of the moors. Guided hikes, typically costing £3 to £8, are available through the park's visitor information centers. Reservations are usually not

necessary. Longer hikes in the bleak, less-populated regions—for example, the tors south of Okehampton—are appropriate only for most experienced walkers. Dartmoor is a great area for horseback riding; many towns have stables for guided rides.

Tavistock and Around

13 miles north of Plymouth.

On the River Tavy, the ancient town of Tavistock historically owed its importance to its Benedictine abbey (dissolved by Henry VIII in the 16th century) and to its status as a stannary town, where tin was weighed, stamped, and assessed. Today the town of 11,000 preserves a prosperous, predominantly Victorian appearance, especially at the bustling indoor Pannier Market off central Bedford Square. Tavistock makes a useful base for exploring a scattering of nearby sights—Buckland Abbey, Cotehele House, and Morwellham Quay—and for touring Dartmoor's western reaches.

GETTING HERE AND AROUND

Tavistock, on A386 and A390, is easily accessed via the frequent buses from Plymouth, which take about an hour. You'll need your own transportation to visit the attractions scattered around it, however.

👁 Sights

Buckland Abbey

HOUSE | A 13th-century Cistercian monastery, Buckland Abbey became the home of Sir Francis Drake in 1581. Today it's filled with mementos of Drake and the Spanish Armada, but the highlight is a beautifully expressive self-portrait by Rembrandt, displayed in its own gallery. Part of a bequest, the painting was only identified, painstakingly restored, and revealed to the public in 2014. The house, which has a restaurant, is 6 miles south of Tavistock; to get here, take A386 south to Crapstone and then head west. ⊠ *Off A386, Yelverton* ☎ *01822/853607* ⊕ *www. nationaltrust.org.uk* ⌁ *£12.80; £8.40 for garden and estate in Jan.* ⊘ *House closed Jan.*

Cotehele House and Quay

HOUSE | About 4 miles west of Buckland Abbey and 9 miles southwest of Tavistock, Cotehele House and Quay was formerly a busy port on the River Tamar, but it is now usually visited for the well-preserved, atmospheric late-medieval manor, home of the Edgcumbe family for centuries. The house has original furniture, tapestries, embroideries, and armor, and you can also visit the impressive gardens, a quay museum, and a restored mill (usually in operation on Sunday and Thursday—call for other days). A limited number of visitors are allowed per day, so arrive early and be prepared to wait during busy periods. Choose a bright day, because the rooms have no electric light. Shops, crafts studios, a gallery, and a restaurant provide other diversions. ■TIP→ **Take advantage of the shuttle bus that runs every half hour between the house, quay, and mill.** ⊠ *Off A390, St. Dominick* ☎ *01579/351346* ⊕ *www.nationaltrust.org.uk* ⌁ *£12.80, £8.80 Jan.–early Mar.* ⊘ *Restricted access and mill closed Nov.–Dec.*

Morwellham Quay

MUSEUM VILLAGE | FAMILY | In the 19th century, Morwellham (pronounced More-*wel*-ham) was England's main copper-exporting port, and it has been carefully restored as a working museum, with quay workers and coachmen in costume. Visitors can board a special train that goes along the River Tamar and into the George and Charlotte Copper Mine. Fairs and other special events take place throughout the year. The site lies 2 miles east of Cotehele House and 5 miles southwest of Tavistock. ⊠ *Off B3257, Tavistock* ☎ *01822/832766* ⊕ *www. morwellham-quay.co.uk* ⌁ *£11.95, mine train £4.80.*

Stay on a Farm 🛏

One way to experience the authentic rural life in Somerset, Devon, and Cornwall is to stay on a farm. **Cartwheel Holidays** (⊕ *www.cartwheel-holidays.co.uk*) has details about working farms that supply accommodations—including bed-and-breakfasts, cottage rentals, and campsites—throughout the region. Other reference points are **Devon Farms** (⊕ *www.devonfarms.co.uk*), for farms in Devon, and **Cornish Farm Holidays** (⊕ *www.cornishfarmholidays.co.uk*), for Cornwall.

🍴 Restaurants

★ The Horn of Plenty

$$$$ | MODERN BRITISH | The restaurant within this Georgian house has magnificent views across the wooded, rhododendron-filled Tamar Valley and a sophisticated menu featuring traditional British cuisine with French and Asian elements. A typical starter and main course might be seared scallops with cauliflower, cumin, and mango followed by Creedy Carver duck with baby leeks and Jerusalem artichokes, while desserts include warm rum baba with marinated pineapple, banana, and coconut. **Known for:** extravagant and exceptional fine dining; stunning views; affordable potluck set-menu on Monday night. ⑤ *Average main: £52.50* ⊠ *A390, Gulworthy* ☎ *01822/832528* ⊕ *www.thehornofplenty.co.uk.*

🛏 Hotels

Bedford Hotel

$$ | HOTEL | This grand, castellated hotel in the center of town harks back to its Victorian heyday, with lounge areas furnished with comfy armchairs, warmed by open fires, and dotted with old artifacts and local photos. **Pros:** traditional style; staff

are welcoming and friendly; good food. **Cons:** some noise in street-facing rooms; old-fashioned and frayed in places; no elevator. $ *Rooms from: £140* ✉ *1 Plymouth Rd., Tavistock* ☎ *01822/613221* ⊕ *www.bedford-hotel.co.uk* ⤳ *31 rooms* ♢ *Free breakfast.*

★ Hotel Endsleigh

$$$ | HOTEL | Under the auspices of hotelier Olga Polizzi, the Endsleigh has risen to be one of the country's best-loved hotels, nestled in a fold of the Tamar Valley with the river itself rolling serenely by at the bottom of the garden. **Pros:** elegant without being pompous; discreet but ever-present staff; beautiful rural setting. **Cons:** few leisure facilities; a bit rickety in places; remote location. $ *Rooms from: £295* ✉ *Milton Abbot* ☎ *01822/870000* ⊕ *www.hotelendsleigh.com* ⤳ *19 rooms* ♢ *Free breakfast.*

Lydford

7 miles north of Tavistock, 24 miles north of Plymouth.

The sequestered hamlet of Lydford packs a lot into a small area: there's the dramatic scenery of the gorge just outside the village, the remains of a medieval castle, and some attractive options for eating and sleeping. The Granite Way cycle and walking track, much of it running along a disused railway route, connects Lydford with Okehampton.

GETTING HERE AND AROUND

The gorge is easily accessed on Stagecoach South West buses from Plymouth to Tavistock, then Dartline Coaches to Lydford, and on Dartline Coaches from Okehampton (connected to Exeter). By car, take A386 between Tavistock and Okehampton.

◉ Sights

★ Lydford Gorge

NATURE SITE | The River Lyd carved a spectacular 1½-mile-long chasm through the rock at Lydford Gorge, outside the pretty village of Lydford, midway between Okehampton and Tavistock. Two paths follow the gorge past gurgling whirlpools and waterfalls with evocative names such as the Devil's Cauldron and the White Lady Waterfall. ■ **TIP→ Sturdy footwear is recommended.** Although the walk can be quite challenging, the paths can still get congested during busy periods. Two tearooms are open early March through October. In winter, access is restricted to the waterfall and the top of the gorge. ✉ *Off A386, Lydford* ☎ *01822/820320* ⊕ *www.nationaltrust.org.uk* ⬛ *£10.50; £5 in winter.*

⑪ Restaurants

Dartmoor Inn

$$ | MODERN BRITISH | Locals and visitors alike make a beeline for this gastro-pub in a 16th-century building with a number of small dining spaces done in spare, contemporary country style. The elegantly presented dishes may include dry-aged moorland sirloin in a peppercorn sauce, beer-battered hake, or venison with celeriac, cavolo nero, and quince. **Known for:** cozy ambience; fresh, locally sourced food; affordable lunch menu. $ *Average main: £18* ✉ *Moorside, on A386, Lydford* ☎ *01822/820221* ⊕ *www.dartmoorinn. com.*

▦ Hotels

Castle Inn

$ | B&B/INN | In the heart of Lydford village, this 16th-century inn sits next to Lydford Castle. **Pros:** antique character; tasty pub food; peaceful rural setting. **Cons:** shabby in places; some small rooms; occasionally sloping floors and low ceilings. $ *Rooms from:*

A walk in Lydford Gorge takes you through lush forest.

£75 ✉ School Rd., off A386, Lydford
☎ 01822/820242 ⊕ www.castleinnlyd-
ford.com ⇌ 9 rooms ⫶◉⫶ Free breakfast.

★ Lewtrenchard Manor

$$ | HOTEL | Paneled rooms, stone fireplac-
es, leaded-glass windows, and hand-
some gardens outfit this spacious 1620
manor house on the northwestern edge
of Dartmoor. **Pros:** beautiful Jacobean
setting; conscientious service; outstand-
ing food. **Cons:** rooms in outbuildings
have less atmosphere; restaurant service
sometimes slow; not very child-friend-
ly. ⑤ Rooms from: £180 ✉ Off A30,
Lewdown ☎ 01566/464077 ⊕ www.
lewtrenchard.co.uk ⇌ 14 rooms ⫶◉⫶ Free
breakfast.

Activities

Cholwell Riding Stables

HORSEBACK RIDING | One- and two-hour
horseback rides through some of Dart-
moor's wilder tracts are available with
Cholwell Riding Stables. Riders of all

abilities are escorted, and equipment is
provided. The stables are about 2 miles
southeast of Lydford. ✉ Off A386, Mary
Tavy ☎ 01822/810526 ⊕ www.cholwell-
ridingstables.co.uk.

Okehampton

*8 miles northeast of Lydford Gorge, 28
miles north of Plymouth, 23 miles west
of Exeter.*

This town at the confluence of the rivers
East and West Okement is a good base
for exploring north Dartmoor. It has a fas-
cinating museum dedicated to the moor,
as well as a helpful tourist office.

GETTING HERE AND AROUND

There's good bus service to Okehampton
from Plymouth, Tavistock, and Exeter,
and on summer Sundays (May–Sept.) you
can travel by train from Exeter. If you're
driving, the town is on A30 and A386;
parking is easy in the center of town.

👁 Sights

Museum of Dartmoor Life

MUSEUM | FAMILY | The three floors of this informative museum contain historical artifacts, domestic knickknacks, traditional agricultural and mining tools, and fascinating insights into the lives of ordinary folk living on the moor. The museum also provides tourist information for Dartmoor and the Okehampton area. ✉ Museum Courtyard, 3 West St. ☎ 01837/52295 ⊕ www.dartmoorlife.org.uk ✍ £5 ⊘ Closed Dec.– late Mar. and Sun. late Mar.–late May and mid-Sept.–Nov.

Okehampton Castle

CASTLE/PALACE | On the riverbank a mile southwest of the town center, the jagged ruins of this Norman castle occupy a verdant site with a picnic area and woodland walks. ✉ Castle Lodge, Off B3260 ☎ 01837/52844 ⊕ www.english-heritage.org.uk ✍ £5.85 ⊘ Closed Nov.–Mar.

Hotels

White Hart Hotel

$ | B&B/INN | This venerable 17th-century coaching inn has counted the eminent statesman William Pitt the Elder among its guests, and, since his visit, it has retained much of its antique style. **Pros:** reasonable rates; historical character; helpful and accommodating staff. **Cons:** no elevator; unexciting restaurant menu; parking available only for guests with disabilities. ⑤ Rooms from: £79 ✉ Fore St. ☎ 01837/658533 ⊕ www.jdwetherspoon.com ⤶ 23 rooms ⑪ No meals.

🏃 Activities

Easter Hall Park

HORSEBACK RIDING | Eight miles north of Okehampton, Easter Hall Park arranges horseback rides throughout the year. Following an initial capability assessment, excursions can last anywhere from 30 minutes to a half day. ✉ Off A386 ☎ 01837/810350 ⊕ www.easterhallpark.co.uk.

Chagford

9 miles southeast of Okehampton, 30 miles northeast of Plymouth.

Once a tin-weighing station, Chagford was an area of fierce fighting between the Roundheads and the Cavaliers during the English Civil War. Although officially a "town" since 1305, Chagford is more of a village, with taverns grouped around a seasoned old church and a curious "pepper-pot" market house on the site of the old Stannary Court. With a handful of cafés and shops to browse around, it makes a convenient base from which to explore north Dartmoor.

GETTING HERE AND AROUND

Infrequent local buses connect Chagford with Okehampton and Exeter (except on Sunday, when there's no service). The village is off A382; a car or bicycle is the best way to see its far-flung sights.

👁 Sights

Castle Drogo

CASTLE/PALACE | Northeast of Chagford, this castle looks like a stout medieval fortress, complete with battlements, but construction actually took place between 1910 and 1930. Designed by noted architect Sir Edwin Lutyens for Julius Drewe, a wealthy grocer, the castle is only half finished (funds ran out). Inside, medieval grandeur is combined with early-20th-century comforts, and there are awesome views over Dartmoor's Teign Valley. The grounds are well worth a prolonged wander, with paths leading down to the river at Fingle Bridge. Turn off the A30 Exeter–Okehampton road at Whiddon Down to reach the castle. ✉ Off A30 and A382, Drewsteignton ☎ 01647/433306 ⊕ www.nationaltrust.org.uk ✍ £12.80 ⊘ Castle closed Nov. and late Dec.–Feb.

Devon Guild of Craftsmen

MUSEUM | One of the Southwest's most important contemporary arts and crafts centers, the Devon Guild is in a converted 19th-century coach house in the village of Bovey Tracey, 10 miles southeast of Chagford and 14 miles southwest of Exeter. The center has excellent exhibitions of local, national, and international crafts, as well as a shop and café. ⊠ *Riverside Mill, Fore St., Bovey Tracey* ☎ *01626/832223* ⊕ *www.crafts.org.uk* ➲ *Free.*

🍴 Restaurants

★ Gidleigh Park

$$$$ | MODERN BRITISH | One of England's foremost country-house hotels, Gidleigh Park occupies an enclave of landscaped gardens and streams, reached via a lengthy, winding country lane and private drive at the edge of Dartmoor. The extremely pricey contemporary restaurant, directed by chef Chris Ede, has been showered with culinary awards. **Known for:** top-notch dining experience; prix-fixe menus with multicourse options; excellent wine menu. [$] *Average main: £125* ⊠ *Gidleigh Park* ☎ *01647/432367* ⊕ *www.gidleigh.co.uk.*

The Old Cottage Tea Shop

$ | BRITISH | This is the real deal, perfect for a light lunch or, even better, a cream tea served on bone china. Warm scones come in baskets, with black currant and other homemade jams and plenty of clotted cream. **Known for:** perfect English cream tea; charming ambience; homemade cakes and desserts. [$] *Average main: £5* ⊠ *20 Fore St., Bovey Tracey* ☎ *01626/833430* ⊕ *www.theoldcottage-teashop.co.uk* ⊟ *No credit cards.*

🛏 Hotels

★ Bovey Castle

$$ | HOTEL | FAMILY | With the grandeur of a country estate and the amenities of a modern hotel, Bovey Castle, built in 1906 for Viscount Hambledon, has it all. **Pros:** baronial splendor; range of activities; good for families. **Cons:** spa facilities not always up to expectations; overpriced drinks and extras; remote location. [$] *Rooms from: £184* ⊠ *Off B3212, North Bovey* ☎ *01647/445000* ⊕ *www.bovey-castle.com* ➲ *82 rooms* 🍴 *No meals.*

Three Crowns

$ | B&B/INN | Facing the churchyard in the heart of Chagford village, this venerable inn retains its authentic, gnarled character; behind the granite facade, it has a smart restaurant, grandly located within a glass atrium, among its modern facilities. **Pros:** traditional flavor; modern atrium restaurant; friendly and attentive staff. **Cons:** some rooms are pokey with uneven floors; possible noise intrusion from churchbells at the front, fans at the back; parking spaces not available for all room categories. [$] *Rooms from: £115* ⊠ *High St.* ☎ *01647/433444* ⊕ *www. threecrowns-chagford.co.uk* ➲ *21 rooms* 🍴 *Free breakfast.*

Exeter

18 miles east of Chagford, 48 miles northeast of Plymouth, 85 miles southwest of Bristol, 205 miles southwest of London.

Exeter has been the capital of the region since the Romans established a fortress here 2,000 years ago, and evidence of the Roman occupation remains in the city walls. Although it was heavily bombed in 1942, Exeter retains much of its medieval character, as well as examples of the gracious architecture of the 18th and 19th centuries. It's convenient to both Torquay and Dartmoor.

GETTING HERE AND AROUND

Once- or twice-hourly train service from London Paddington takes about 2¼ hours; the less frequent service from London Waterloo via Salisbury takes just under 3½ hours. From London's Victoria Coach Station, National Express buses leave every two hours, and Megabus has four daily departures, all taking between 4½ and 5¼ hours. With its own airport, Exeter is a major transportation hub for Devon. Trains from Bristol, Salisbury, and Plymouth stop at Exeter St. David's and connect to the center by frequent buses. Some trains also stop at the more useful Exeter Central. The bus station is off Paris Street near the tourist office. Cars are unnecessary in town, so park yours as soon as possible—all the sights are within an easy walk.

TOURS
Red Coat Guided Tours
Free 90-minute walking tours of Exeter by Red Coat Guided Tours take place daily all year, focusing on different aspects of the city. See the website for details, or contact the tourist office. You can also pick up a leaflet on self-guided walks from here. ⊠ *Exeter* ☎ *01392/265203* ⊕ *www.exeter.gov.uk/guidedtours.*

ESSENTIALS
VISITOR INFORMATION Exeter Visitor Information and Tickets. ⊠ *Dix's Field* ☎ *01392/665700* ⊕ *www.visitexeter.com.*

 ## ◉ Sights

★ Cathedral of St. Peter
RELIGIOUS SITE | At the heart of Exeter, the great Gothic cathedral was begun in 1275 and completed almost a century later. Its twin towers are even older survivors of an earlier Norman cathedral. Rising from a forest of ribbed columns, the nave's 300-foot stretch of unbroken Gothic vaulting is the longest in the world. Myriad statues, tombs, and memorial plaques adorn the interior. In the minstrels' gallery, high up on the left of the nave, stands a group of carved figures singing and playing musical instruments, including bagpipes. Guided tours of the interior (up to four a day Monday through Saturday), roof, chapel, garden, and precinct are available, as are audio tours. Outside in Cathedral Close, don't miss Mol's Coffee House at No. 1 (now a gift shop), whose half-timber facade bearing the coat of arms of Elizabeth I is redolent of bygone times, and the 400-year-old door to No. 10, the bishop of Crediton's house, is ornately carved with angels' and lions' heads. ⊠ *Cathedral Close* ☎ *01392/285983* ⊕ *www.exeter-cathedral.org.uk* ☎ *£7.50, cathedral tours free, audio tours £2.50, other tours £14 (including admission).*

Custom House
GOVERNMENT BUILDING | Exeter's historic waterfront on the River Exe was the center of the city's medieval wool industry, and the Custom House, built in 1680, attests to the city's prosperity. The city's earliest surviving brick building is now flanked by Victorian warehouses and houses a visitor center where you can view documents on the city's maritime history and an audiovisual display. ⊠ *The Quay* ☎ *01392/271611* ⊕ *www.exeter.gov.uk* ☎ *Free* ⏱ *Closed Mon.–Wed. in Nov.–Mar.*

Guildhall
GOVERNMENT BUILDING | On the city's main shopping street, this is said to be the oldest municipal building in the country still in use. The current hall, with its Renaissance portico, dates from 1330, although a guildhall has occupied this site since at least 1160. The walls are adorned with imposing portraits of royal figures and noteworthy locals, and its timber-braced roof, one of the earliest in England, dates from about 1460. ⊠ *High St.* ☎ *01392/665500* ⊕ *www.exeter.gov. uk* ☎ *Free* ⏱ *Closed Sun. and during municipal functions.*

Powderham Castle
CASTLE/PALACE | FAMILY | Seat of the earls of Devon, this notable stately home 8 miles south of Exeter is famed for its staircase hall, a soaring fantasia of white stuccowork on a turquoise background, constructed in 1739–69. Other sumptuous rooms, adorned with family portraits by Sir Godfrey Kneller and Sir Joshua Reynolds, were used in the

Merchant-Ivory film *Remains of the Day.*
The Belvedere Tower built in the 1770s
offers inspiring views over the Exe Estuary, and a second tower, built in 1400
by Sir Philip Courtenay (ancestor of the
current owners), stands in the deer park.
"Safari" rides (a tractor pulling a trailer)
to see the 600-odd fallow deer depart
at 1:45 (not Tuesday, Friday, or in bad
weather), and October sees daily "Deer
Rut Safaris." There are also falconry displays in summer. The restaurant serves
light lunches, and there's a children's play
area, a pets' corner, a farm shop, and a
plant center. ■ TIP➜ **Check the website for
online discounts. Tickets are valid for seven
days.** ✉ *A379, Kenton* ☎ *01626/890243*
⊕ *www.powderham.co.uk* 🎟 *£12.95,
deer park £3.50* ⊗ *Closed Sat. and late
Oct.–late Mar. Occasionally closed for
functions: check website.*

Rougemont Gardens

GARDEN | These gardens behind the Royal
Albert Memorial Museum were laid out
at the end of the 18th century. The land
was once part of the defensive ditch
of Rougemont Castle, built in 1068 by
decree of William the Conqueror. The
adjoining Northernhay Gardens contain
the original Norman gatehouse and the
remains of the Roman city wall, the latter
forming part of the ancient castle's outer
wall. ✉ *Off Queen St.*

★ Royal Albert Memorial Museum

MUSEUM | **FAMILY** | This family-friendly
museum is housed in a recently refurbished Victorian building. The centerpiece
is the extensive Making History gallery,
a giddy mix of objects imaginatively
illustrating the city's history and covering
everything from Roman pottery to memorabilia from World War II. The geology
section is thrillingly enhanced by the latest video technology, and there are also
excellent ethnography and archaeological
collections, natural-history displays, and
works by West Country artists. ✉ *Queen
St.* ☎ *01392/265858* ⊕ *www.rammuse-
um.org.uk* 🎟 *Free* ⊗ *Closed Mon.*

Underground Passages

ARCHAEOLOGICAL SITE | **FAMILY** | Exeter's
Underground Passages, which once
served as conduits for fresh water, are
the only medieval vaulted passages open
to the public in Britain. They date to the
mid-14th century, although some were
enlarged by the Victorians. An exhibition
and video precede the 25-minute guided
tour. Many of the passages are narrow
and low: be prepared to stoop. The tours
often sell out during school vacations, so
come early. Children under five are not
permitted in the tunnels. ✉ *2 Paris St.*
☎ *01392/665887* ⊕ *www.exeter.gov.uk*
🎟 *£7* ⊗ *Closed Mon. Oct.–May.*

🍴 Restaurants

Ask Italian

$ | **ITALIAN** | This outpost of an Italian
chain has secured an enviable site in a
part-medieval, part-Georgian building
opposite the cathedral. With three dining
areas, it has windows with superb views
across the Close, as well as a courtyard
that is perfect for warm days. **Known for:**
relaxed lunches; tasty pizza and pastas;
views of the cathedral. ⑤ *Average main:
£14* ✉ *5 Cathedral Close* ☎ *01392/920202*
⊕ *www.askitalian.co.uk.*

Herbie's

$ | **VEGETARIAN** | A mellow stop, this
friendly vegetarian and vegan bistro with
wood floors and simple tables is ideal
for unwinding over leisurely conversation. You can snack on pita bread
with hummus and salad, or tackle the
Mediterranean platter, Moroccan tagine,
warm vegetable salad made with feta
cheese and pine nuts, or a stir fry with
brown rice. **Known for:** tasty and inventive
vegetarian and vegan food; laid-back
atmosphere; organic wine and beers.
⑤ *Average main: £12* ✉ *15 North St.*
☎ *01392/258473* ⊕ *www.herbiesrestau-
rant.co.uk* ⊗ *Closed Sun. No dinner Mon.*

Lympstone Manor

$$$$ | **MODERN BRITISH** | Exeter-born master chef Michael Caines has breathed new life into this elegant Georgian mansion overlooking the Exe estuary 5 miles south of Exeter, where he has installed three separate dining rooms to showcase his highly original recipes. The wow-factor starts the moment you arrive, with unforgettable estuary views forming a fitting prelude to the gastronomic feast to follow. **Known for:** fabulous location; stylishly presented and eclectic gourmet cuisine; frequently changing fixed-price menus and multicourse tasting menus. $ *Average main: £140* ⊠ *Courtlands La., Exmouth* ☎ *01395/202040* ⊕ *www. lympstonemanor.co.uk.*

The Prospect

$ | **BRITISH** | At this pub you can contemplate the quayside comings and goings over a pint of real ale and a hot or cold meal. The nautical theme comes through in pictures and the ship's wheel hanging from the ceiling. **Known for:** classic British pub grub; fun nautical decor; quayside location. $ *Average main: £10* ⊠ *The Quay* ☎ *01392/273152* ⊕ *www. heavitreebrewery.co.uk.*

Ship Inn

$ | **BRITISH** | Here you can lift a tankard of stout in the very rooms where Sir Francis Drake and Sir Walter Raleigh enjoyed their ale. The pub dishes out casual bar fare, from sandwiches to grills and steak and ale pie, either in the bar or in the beamed and paneled upstairs restaurant. **Known for:** famous former patrons; traditional English pub fare; lively and welcoming environment. $ *Average main: £9* ⊠ *1–3 St. Martin's La.* ☎ *01392/272040* ⊕ *www.greeneking-pubs.co.uk.*

Tea on the Green

$ | **BRITISH** | **FAMILY** | Near the cathedral, this child-friendly tearoom is ideal for lunch, coffee, or snacks when you're seeing the sights. You can also sample one of Devon's famous cream teas, served with jam, scones, and clotted cream, or show up earlier for eggs Benedict or a cooked English breakfast. **Known for:** friendly and polite service; great range of gluten-free options; ethically produced and locally sourced food. $ *Average main: £12* ⊠ *2 Cathedral Close* ☎ *01392/276913* ⊕ *www. teaonthegreen.com* ⊘ *No dinner.*

🛏 Hotels

★ Hotel du Vin

$ | **HOTEL** | This former hospital has been reimagined as a modish hotel with a zippy, happening vibe and add-ons that include a heated indoor-outdoor pool, a fitness room, and spa treatments. **Pros:** contemporary style; great food; nice wellness facilities. **Cons:** rooms on the small side; tiny gym and pool; limited parking. $ *Rooms from: £115* ⊠ *Magdalen St.* ☎ *0330/016–0391* ⊕ *www. hotelduvin.com* ⇆ *59 rooms* ⦿ *Free breakfast.*

The Pig-at Combe

$$ | **HOTEL** | Rolling parkland surrounds this stately Elizabethan manor house, which is 16 miles east of Exeter and has been converted into a hipster retreat run with energy and enthusiasm. **Pros:** beautiful rural surroundings; relaxed ambience; attentive but informal staff. **Cons:** rather remote; defiantly untraditional; crowded tables in restaurant. $ *Rooms from: £199* ⊠ *Off A30, Gittisham* ☎ *01404/540400* ⊕ *www.thepighotel.com* ⇆ *30 rooms* ⦿ *No meals.*

★ Raffles

$ | **B&B/INN** | A 10-minute walk from the center, this quirky B&B in a quiet neighborhood makes an ideal base for a night or two in town. **Pros:** peaceful location; plenty of character; great breakfasts. **Cons:** single room is small; parking costs £5; no elevator. $ *Rooms from: £95* ⊠ *11 Blackall Rd.* ☎ *01392/270200* ⊕ *www.raffles-exeter.co.uk* ⇆ *6 rooms* ⦿ *Free breakfast.*

Southernhay House

$$ | **HOTEL** | Located close to the cathedral on the elegant Southernhay, this graceful Georgian hotel with a secluded garden was originally built for a merchant of the East India Company in 1815, hence the paintings commemorating the Battle of Waterloo (fought in the same year) and the names of the spacious and elegantly furnished guest rooms—Silk, Cotton, Ivory, Spice, and Opium, etc.—that recall some of the merchandise that made the company's fortune. **Pros:** central location; charming building; discreet service. **Cons:** few rooms and often booked up; no elevator; no private parking. Ⓢ *Rooms from: £135* ⊠ *36 Southernhay East* ☎ *01392/439000* ⊕ *www.southernhay-house.com* ⤳ *11 rooms* ⦿ *No meals.*

White Hart

$ | **HOTEL** | Guests have been welcomed to this inn since the 15th century, and it is said that Oliver Cromwell stabled his horses here. **Pros:** close to center; historic building; on-site parking. **Cons:** can be noisy; drab and dated in parts; below average food in restaurant. Ⓢ *Rooms from: £70* ⊠ *66 South St.* ☎ *01392/279897* ⊕ *www.marstonsinns. co.uk/inns/white-hart-hotel-exeter* ⤳ *55 rooms* ⦿ *Free breakfast.*

🎟 Performing Arts

Northcott Theatre

THEATER | A range of innovative and traditional productions are staged at this central venue, including plays, comedy, musical revues, and dance performances. ⊠ *Stocker Rd.* ☎ *01392/726363* ⊕ *www.exeternorthcott.co.uk.*

🛍 Shopping

Some of Exeter's most interesting shops are along Gandy Street, off the main High Street drag, with several good food and clothes outlets. Exeter was the silver-assay office for the West Country, and the earliest example of Exeter silver (now a museum piece) dates from 1218; Victorian pieces are still sold. The Exeter assay mark is three castles.

Exeter Quay Antiques

ANTIQUES/COLLECTIBLES | Twenty dealers display their diverse wares in Exeter's former fish market, including everything from silverware and ceramics to "royalty thimbles." It also includes a quayside café. ⊠ *The Quay* ☎ *01392/493501* ⊕ *www.exeterquayantiques.co.uk.*

🏃 Activities

Saddles and Paddles

BICYCLING | Renting out bikes, kayaks, canoes, and paddle boards, this shop is handily placed for a 7-mile trip along the scenic Exeter Canal Trail, which follows the River Exe and the Exeter Ship Canal. ⊠ *4 Kings Wharf* ☎ *01392/424241* ⊕ *www.sadpad.com.*

Topsham

4 miles southeast of Exeter on B3182.

This small town, full of narrow streets and hidden courtyards, was once a bustling river port, and it remains rich in 18th-century houses and inns.

GETTING HERE AND AROUND
Frequent bus service connects Topsham with Exeter; the village is also a stop for twice-hourly trains running between Exmouth and Exeter. Topsham is best negotiated on foot.

👁 Sights

A la Ronde

HOUSE | The 16-sided, nearly circular A la Ronde was built in 1798 by two cousins inspired by the Church of San Vitale in Ravenna, Italy. Among the 18th- and 19th-century curiosities here is an elaborate display of feathers and shells. The house is 5 miles south of Topsham. ⊠ *Summer La.* ☎ *01395/265514* ⊕ *www.*

nationaltrust.org.uk ✉ *£10.50* ⊗ *Closed Jan. and weekdays early Nov.–late Dec.*

Topsham Museum

MUSEUM | Occupying a 17th-century Dutch-style merchant's house beside the river, this museum has period-furnished rooms and displays on local and maritime history. One room has memorabilia belonging to the late actress Vivien Leigh, who spent much time in the region. ✉ *25 The Strand* ☎ *01392/873244* ⊕ *www.topshammuseum.org.uk* ✉ *Free* ⊗ *Closed Nov.–Mar. and Tues.*

Beer

22 miles east of Topsham, 26 miles east of Exeter, 33 miles south of Taunton.

Beer, just outside Seaton, was once a favorite smugglers' haunt, and the fishing village has remained fairly unchanged. It was the source of the white stone used for numerous Devon churches, Exeter Cathedral, and, farther afield, Winchester Cathedral, Westminster Abbey, and the Tower of London.

◉ Sights

Beer Quarry Caves

CAVE | FAMILY | Worked from Roman times until 1900, this impressive underground network of caves make for an interesting tour. A small exhibition includes tools and examples of carved stone. ✉ *Quarry La.* ☎ *01297/680282* ⊕ *www.beerquarrycaves. co.uk* ✉ *£9* ⊗ *Closed Nov.–late Mar.*

Torquay

26 miles south of Topsham, 23 miles south of Exeter.

The most important resort area in South Devon, Torquay envisions itself as the center of the "English Riviera." Since 1968 the towns of Paignton and Torquay (pronounced tor- *kee*) have been amalgamated under the common moniker of Torbay. Torquay is the supposed site of the hotel in the popular British television comedy *Fawlty Towers* and was the home of mystery writer Agatha Christie. Fans should check out the exhibit devoted to Christie at the town museum and visit Greenway, her holiday home on the River Dart. Torquay's tourist office has leaflets outlining an Agatha Christie Trail that takes in all the Christie-related places in town.

The town has shed some of its old-fashioned image in recent years with modern hotels, luxury villas, and apartments that climb the hillsides above the harbor. Still, Torquay is more like Brighton's maiden aunt in terms of energy and fizz, though a pubs-and-clubs culture makes an appearance on Friday and Saturday nights. Palm trees and other semitropical plants (a benefit of being near the warming Gulf Stream) flourish in the seafront gardens; the sea is a clear and intense blue.

GETTING HERE AND AROUND

Buses arrive near Torquay's harbor and the tourist office. The train station is close to Torre Abbey, but other points in town are best reached on local buses or by taxi. Drivers should take A38 and A380 from Exeter.

ESSENTIALS

VISITOR INFORMATION English Riviera Visitor Information Centre. ✉ *5 Vaughan Parade* ☎ *01803/211211* ⊕ *www.eng-lishriviera.co.uk.*

◉ Sights

Cockington

TOWN | Just a mile outside the heart of Torbay by bus or car lies this chocolate-box village with thatched cottages, a 14th-century forge, and the square-tower Church of St. George and St. Mary. Repair to the Old Mill for a café lunch, or head to the Drum Inn, designed by Sir Edwin Lutyens to be an archetypal pub. On the village outskirts lies Cockington Court—a grand estate with crafts studios, shops, and an eatery. Cockington has, however, more than a touch of the faux: cottages that don't sell anything put up signs to this effect. ⊠ *Torquay*.

★ Torre Abbey

MUSEUM | FAMILY | For lovers of fine things, Torquay's chief attraction is Torre Abbey, surrounded by parkland but close to the seafront. The abbey itself, founded in 1196, was razed in 1539, though you can still see traces of the old construction. The mansion that now occupies the site was the home of the Cary family for nearly 300 years, and it was later converted into a museum and art gallery. Artistic riches lie within the main building: marine paintings, Victorian sculptures, Pre-Raphaelite window designs, and drawings by William Blake. There are plenty of family-friendly activities, including brass-rubbing. ⊠ *King's Dr.* ☎ *01803/293593* ⊕ *www.torre-abbey.org. uk* ☜ *£8* ☯ *Closed Mon.*

♨ Restaurants

The Elephant

$$$ | MODERN BRITISH | Set back from Torquay's harbor, this elegant eatery offers sophisticated but relaxed dining, with views over Torbay from its Georgian windows. The innovative menus offer such starters as chili crab ravioli and Tokyo turnip broth with a bantam egg and seaweed, and, among the mains, rump of lamb with celeriac risotto and cod with Jerusalem artichoke and curry sauce. **Known for:** first-class service; delectable dishes; fixed-price tasting menu in upstairs dining room. ⑤ *Average main: £24* ⊠ *3-4 Beacon Terr.* ☎ *01803/200044* ⊕ *www.elephantrestaurant.co.uk* ☯ *Closed Sun., Mon., and 2 wks early Jan.*

★ Number 7 Fish Bistro

$$ | SEAFOOD | Seafood fans can indulge their passion at this unpretentious, convivial spot near the harbor; wood floors and an array of maritime knickknacks

Fawlty Towers

John Cleese was inspired to write the TV series *Fawlty Towers* after he and the Monty Python team stayed at a hotel in Torquay while filming the series *Monty Python's Flying Circus* in the early 1970s. The "wonderfully rude" owner became the model for Basil Fawlty, the exasperated, accident-prone manager in the series. The owner died in 1981, but his hotel, the Gleneagles, is still going strong—though happily nothing like the chaotic Fawlty Towers.

set the mood. Fresh, locally caught fish is brought to your table for inspection before being simply but imaginatively prepared. **Known for:** freshest seafood in Torquay; wine bar upstairs; lively atmosphere. ⑤ *Average main: £19* ⊠ *7 Beacon Terr.* ☎ *01803/295055* ⊕ *www.no7-fish. com* ☯ *Closed Sun. Oct.–June, Mon. Nov.–May. No lunch Sun.–Tues. Closed 3 wks Feb. and 1st wk Nov.*

▣ Hotels

Cary Arms & Spa

$$$ | B&B/INN | Squeezed into a narrow space at the bottom of a steep lane just outside Torquay, this secluded coastal spot lies just feet from the rocky shore and the waters of Babbacombe Bay, where dolphins and seals are occasional visitors. **Pros:** splendid seaside location; quality toiletries and thoughtful complimentary extras; excellent bar and restaurant. **Cons:** very steep approach road; spa facilities are comparatively modest; five-star prices not always justified. ⑤ *Rooms from: £233* ⊠ *Babbacombe Beach* ☎ *01803/327110* ⊕ *www.caryarms.co.uk* ☞ *22 rooms* ❑ *Free breakfast.*

The Imperial Torquay

$$ | **HOTEL** | This enormous pile perched above the sea exudes slightly faded Victorian splendor. **Pros:** grand setting; great views; good advance booking rates. **Cons:** lackluster food; back rooms face parking lot; dated in parts. ⑤ *Rooms from: £140* ✉ *Park Hill Rd.* ☎ *01803/294301* ⊕ *www. theimperialtorquay.co.uk* ⇆ *152 rooms* ⑩ *Free breakfast.*

🏃 Activities

Torbay's beaches, a mixture of sand and coarse gravel, have won awards for their water quality and facilities, and can get crowded in summer. Apart from the central Torre Abbey Sands, they're mainly to the north of town, often separated by the crumbly red cliffs characteristic of the area. To sun and swim, head for Anstey's Cove, a favorite spot for scuba divers, with more beaches farther along at neighboring Babbacombe.

Totnes

8 miles west of Torquay, 28 miles southwest of Exeter.

This busy market town on the banks of the River Dart preserves plenty of its medieval past, and, on summer Tuesdays, vendors dress in period costume for the Elizabethan Market. Market days are Friday and Saturday, when the town's status as a center of alternative medicine and culture becomes especially clear, and on the third Sunday of the month, when there's a local produce market on Civic Square. The historic buildings include a guildhall and St. Mary's Church.

GETTING HERE AND AROUND

Totnes is on a regular fast bus route between Plymouth and Torbay and is a stop for main-line trains between Plymouth and Exeter. Buses pull into the center, and the train station is a few minutes' walk north of the center. Drivers should take A38 and A385 from Plymouth or A385 from Torbay.

ESSENTIALS
VISITOR INFORMATION Visit Totnes.
☎ *01803/411183 Telephone service available Apr.–Oct.* ⊕ *www.visittotnes.co.uk.*

👁 Sights

Brixham

TOWN | At the southern point of Tor Bay, Brixham has kept much of its original charm, partly because it still has an active fishing harbor. Much of the catch goes straight to restaurants as far away as London. Sample fish-and-chips on the quayside, where there's a (surprisingly petite) full-scale reproduction of the vessel on which Sir Francis Drake circumnavigated the world. The village is 10 miles southeast of Totnes by A385 and A3022. ✉ *Brixham.*

South Devon Railway

TRANSPORTATION SITE (AIRPORT/BUS/ FERRY/TRAIN) | **FAMILY** | Steam trains of this railway run through 7 miles of the wooded Dart Valley between Totnes and Buckfastleigh, on the edge of Dartmoor. Call about special trips around Christmas. ■**TIP→ Keep your train tickets to receive discounts at local English Heritage sites.** ✉ *Dart Bridge Rd., Buckfastleigh* ☎ *01364/644370* ⊕ *www.southdevonrailway.co.uk* 🎫 *£16 round-trip* ⊙ *Closed Nov., part of Dec., Jan., most of Feb., and early Mar.*

Totnes Castle

CASTLE/PALACE | You can climb up the hill in town to the ruins of this castle—a fine Norman motte and bailey design—for a wonderful view of Totnes and the River Dart. ✉ *Castle St.* ☎ *01803/864406* ⊕ *www.english-heritage.org.uk* 🎫 *£5.85* ⊙ *Closed weekdays Nov.–Mar.*

Hotels

★ Royal Seven Stars Hotel
$ | HOTEL | Conveniently located at the bottom of the main street, this centuries-old coaching inn has counted Daniel Defoe and Edward VII among its former guests. **Pros:** central location; friendly staff; spotless rooms. **Cons:** standard accommodations and bathrooms are small; rooms over bars can be noisy; busy public areas. ⑤ *Rooms from: £120* ✉ *The Plains* ☎ *01803/862125* ⊕ *www.royalsevenstars. co.uk* ↪ *21 rooms* ⑩ *Free breakfast.*

Performing Arts

Dartington Hall
ARTS CENTERS | One of the foremost arts centers of the West Country, Dartington Hall lies 2 miles northwest of Totnes. There are concerts, film screenings, and exhibitions. The gardens, free year-round, are the setting for outdoor performances of Shakespeare in summer. There's a café, and you can stay overnight in rooms in the hall. ✉ *Off A384 and A385, Dartington* ☎ *01803/847070* ⊕ *www.dartington. org/whats-on.*

Shopping

Shops at Dartington
SHOPPING CENTERS/MALLS | Near Dartington Hall, 15 stores and four cafés and restaurants in and around an old cider press make up the Shops at Dartington. Open daily, it's a good place to find handmade Dartington crystal glassware, kitchenware, crafts, books, and toys. The Food Shop sells local food and drink, including fudge, ice cream, and cider, and Bayards Kitchen has an excellent selection of organic, vegetarian, vegan, gluten-free, and meat dishes. ✉ *Shinners Bridge, Dartington* ☎ *01803/847500* ⊕ *www.dartington.org/shops.*

Dartmouth

13 miles southeast of Totnes, 35 miles east of Plymouth, 35 miles south of Exeter, 5 miles southwest of Brixham.

An important port in the Middle Ages, Dartmouth is today a favorite haunt of yacht owners. Traces of its past include the old houses in Bayard's Cove at the bottom of Lower Street, where the *Mayflower* made a stop in 1620, the 16th-century covered Butterwalk, and the two castles guarding the entrance to the River Dart. The Royal Naval College, built in 1905, dominates the heights above the town. A few miles south of Dartmouth on Start Bay there are a number of pretty beaches including Blackpool Sands, popular with families.

GETTING HERE AND AROUND
Frequent buses connect Dartmouth with Plymouth and Totnes. Drivers coming from the west should follow A381 and A3122. Approaching from the Torbay area via A3022 and A379, you can save mileage by using the passenger and car ferries crossing the Dart. Travelers on foot can take advantage of a vintage steam train service operating between Paignton and Kingswear, where there are ferry connections with Dartmouth. River ferries also link Dartmouth with Totnes.

ESSENTIALS
VISITOR INFORMATION Dartmouth Visitor Centre. ✉ *The Engine House, Mayors Ave.* ☎ *01803/834224* ⊕ *www.discoverdartmouth.com.*

Sights

Dartmouth Steam Railway
TRANSPORTATION SITE (AIRPORT/BUS/FERRY/ TRAIN) | FAMILY | These lovingly restored trains chug along on tracks beside the River Dart between Paignton and Kingswear (across the river from Dartmouth). You can combine a train ride with a river excursion between Dartmouth and Totnes and a bus

between Totnes and Paignton or Torquay on a Round Robin ticket (£28.75 or £29.50). ✉ *5 Lower St.* ☎ *01803/555872* ⊕ *www.dartmouthrailriver.co.uk* 💲 *£18.90* ⊘ *Closed Jan.–mid-Feb.*

Greenway

HOUSE | A rewarding way to experience the River Dart is to join a cruise from Dartmouth's quay to visit Greenway, the 16th-century riverside home of the Gilbert family (Sir Humphrey Gilbert claimed Newfoundland on behalf of Elizabeth I), more famous today for its association with the crime writer Agatha Christie. Mrs. Mallowan (Christie's married name) made it her holiday home beginning in 1938, and the house displays collections of archaeological finds, china, and silver. The gorgeous gardens are thickly planted with magnolias, camellias, and rare shrubs and are richly endowed with panoramic views. Beware, however, that the grounds are steeply laid out, and those arriving by boat face a daunting uphill climb. Allow three hours to see everything; in busy periods, timed tickets for the house are given on arrival. Parking spaces here are restricted and must be booked in advance. Alternatively, ask at the tourist office about walking and cycling routes to reach the house, as well as about the bus service from Greenway Halt (a stop on the Dartmouth Steam Railway). A round-trip ticket between Dartmouth and Greenway costs £9.50 on the Greenway Ferry (⊕ *www.greenwayferry.co.uk*). ✉ *Greenway Rd., Galmpton* ☎ *01803/842382* ⊕ *www.nationaltrust.org.uk* 💲 *£12.80* ⊘ *Closed Jan.–early Feb., and weekdays early Nov.–late Dec.*

Restaurants

The Seahorse

$$$ | **SEAFOOD** | In a prime riverside location, this seafood restaurant epitomizes the region's ongoing food revolution. The knowledgeable staff guides diners through the Italian-inspired menu, which primarily depends on the day's catch: look for scallops with garlic and white port,

zuppa di pescatore (seafood soup), or Dover sole or gurnard grilled over charcoal with rosemary. **Known for:** relaxed and convivial atmosphere; good set-price menus; charming and attentive staff. ⑤ *Average main: £30* ✉ *5 S. Embankment* ☎ *01803/835147* ⊕ *www.seahorserestaurant.co.uk* ⊘ *Closed Sun. and Mon.*

🛏 Hotels

★ Royal Castle Hotel

$ | **HOTEL** | Part of Dartmouth's historic waterfront (and consequently a hub of activity), this hotel has truly earned the name "Royal"—several monarchs have slept here. **Pros:** historical resonance; superb central location; professional staff. **Cons:** some cheaper rooms are nondescript; many steps, no elevator; noise intrusion in some rooms. ⑤ *Rooms from: £115* ✉ *11 The Quay* ☎ *01803/833033* ⊕ *www.royalcastle.co.uk* ⇗ *24 rooms* ⑩ *No meals.*

🏃 Activities

Blackpool Sands

BEACHES | Located on Start Bay, this privately managed beach sits at the edge of an extraordinary natural setting of meadows and forest. It's favored for its clear water and long, wide stretch of shingle. Popular with families, the beach is big enough that you can always find a quiet stretch. Take A379 south of Dartmouth and look for signs. **Amenities:** food and drink; lifeguards; parking (fee); showers, toilets; water sports. **Best for:** swimming. ✉ *3 miles south of Dartmouth* ☎ *01803/771800.*

Chapter 8

BATH AND THE COTSWOLDS

Updated by
Sophie Ibbotson

👁 Sights	🍴 Restaurants	🛏 Hotels	🏷 Shopping	🍸 Nightlife
★★☆☆☆	★★★★☆	★★★★☆	★★★★☆	★★☆☆☆

WELCOME TO BATH AND THE COTSWOLDS

TOP REASONS TO GO

★ **Bath's architecture:** Bath is perhaps the most perfectly preserved and harmonious English city. Close up, the elegance and finesse of the Georgian buildings is a perpetual delight.

★ **Hidcote Manor Garden:** In a region rich with imaginative garden displays, Hidcote lays good claim to eminence. Exotic shrubs from around the world and the famous "garden rooms" are the highlights of this Arts and Crafts masterpiece.

★ **Perfect villages:** With their stone cottages, Cotswold villages tend to be improbably picturesque; the hamlets of Upper and Lower Slaughter are among the most charming.

★ **Roman baths:** Take a break from Bath's Georgian elegance and return to its Roman days on a tour around this ancient bath complex.

★ **Gloucester Cathedral:** The Great East Window, Whispering Gallery, and cloisters are especially noteworthy in this ancient monument, one of the country's finest cathedrals.

1 **Bath.**

2 **Castle Combe.**

3 **Lacock.**

4 **Cheltenham.**

5 **Winchcombe.**

6 **Broadway.**

7 **Chipping Camden.**

8 **Moreton-in-Marsh.**

9 **Stow-on-the-Wold.**

10 **Bourton-on-the-Water.**

11 **Lower Slaughter and Upper Slaughter.**

12 **Northleach.**

13 **Burford.**

14 **Bibury.**

15 **Cirencester.**

16 **Malmesbury.**

17 **Painswick.**

18 **Tetbury.**

The rolling uplands of the Cotswolds represent all the beauty and charm rural England has to offer, as immortalized in countless books, paintings, and films.

In eloquently named settlements from Bourton-on-the-Water to Stow-on-the-Wold, you can taste the glories of the old English village—its stone slate roofs, low-ceiling rooms, and gardens; the atmosphere is as thick as honey, and equally as sweet. On the edge of the Cotswolds is Bath, among the most alluring small cities in Europe.

The blissfully unspoiled Cotswolds, deservedly popular with visitors and convenient to London, occupy much of the county of Gloucestershire, in west-central England. They also take in slices of neighboring Oxfordshire, Worcestershire, Wiltshire, and Somerset. Together these make up a sweep of land stretching from close to Stratford-upon-Avon and Shakespeare Country in the north almost as far as the Bristol Channel in the south. On the edge of the area, two historic towns have been absorbed, rather than compromised. Bath, offering up "18th-century England in all its urban glory," to use a phrase by writer Nigel Nicolson, is one. The other is Regency-era Cheltenham, which, like Bath, is a spa town with elegant architecture.

Bath rightly boasts of being the best-planned town in England. Although the Romans founded the city when they discovered there the only true hot springs in England, its popularity during the 17th and 18th centuries luckily coincided with one of Britain's most creative architectural eras. Today people come to walk in the footsteps of Jane Austen, visit Bath Abbey and the excavated Roman baths, shop in an elegant setting, or have a modern spa experience at the stunning Thermae spa.

North of Bath are the Cotswolds—an area that more than one writer has called the very soul of England. This idyllic region, which from medieval times grew prosperous on the wool trade, remains a vision of rural England. Here are time-defying churches, sleepy hamlets, sequestered ancient farmsteads, and such fabled abodes as Sudeley Castle. The Cotswolds can hardly claim to be undiscovered, but the area's poetic appeal has survived the tour buses and gift shops.

MAJOR REGIONS
Bath and nearby. On the eastern edge of the county of Somerset, the city of Bath has strong links with the Cotswolds stretching north, the source of the wool that for centuries underpinned its economy. The stone mansions and cottages of that region are recalled in Bath's Georgian architecture and in the mellow stone that it shares with two of the villages across the Wiltshire border, Lacock and Castle Combe.

The Cotswolds. A gently undulating area of limestone uplands, the Cotswolds are among England's best-preserved rural districts, and the quiet but lovely grays and ambers of the stone buildings here are truly unsurpassed. Much has been written about the area's age-mellowed towns, but the architecture of the villages actually differs little from that of villages elsewhere in England. Their distinction lies in their surroundings: the valleys are lush and rolling, and cozy hamlets appear covered in foliage from church tower to garden gate. Beyond the town limits, you can explore, on foot or by car, the "high wild hills and rough uneven ways" that Shakespeare wrote about.

Over the centuries, quarries of honey-color stone have yielded building blocks for many Cotswold houses and churches and have transformed little towns into realms of gold. Make Chipping Campden, Moreton-in-Marsh, or Stow-on-the-Wold your headquarters and wander for a few days. Then ask yourself what the area is all about. Its secret seems shared by two things—sheep and stone. These were once the great sheep-rearing areas of England, and during the peak of prosperity in the Middle Ages, Cotswold wool was in demand the world over. This made the local merchants rich, but many gave back to the Cotswolds by restoring old churches (the famous "wool churches" of the region) or building rows of limestone almshouses now seasoned to a glorious golden-gray. These days the wool merchants have gone but the wealth remains—the region includes some of the most exclusive real estate in the country.

One possible route is to begin with Cheltenham—the largest town in the area and a gateway to the Cotswolds, but slightly outside the boundaries and more of a small city in atmosphere—then move on to the beauty spots in and around Winchcombe. Next are Sudeley Castle, Stanway House, and Snowshill Manor, among the most impressive houses of the region; the oversold village of Broadway; Chipping Campden, the Cotswold cognoscenti's favorite; and Hidcote Manor, one of the most spectacular gardens in England. Then circle back south, down through Moreton-in-Marsh, Stow-on-the-Wold, Upper Slaughter, Lower Slaughter, and Bourton-on-the-Water, and end with Bibury and Tetbury. This is definitely a region where it pays to go off the beaten track to take a look at that village among the trees.

Planning

When to Go

This area contains some of England's most popular destinations, and it's best to avoid weekends in the busier areas of the Cotswolds. During the week, even in summer, you may hardly see a soul in the more remote spots. Bath is particularly congested in summer, when students flock to its language schools. On the other hand, Cheltenham is a relatively workaday place that can absorb many tour buses comfortably.

Book your room well ahead if you visit during the two weeks in May and June, when the Bath Festival hits town, or if you visit Cheltenham during the National Hunt Festival (horse racing) in mid-March. Note that the private properties of Hidcote Manor, Snowshill Manor, and Sudeley Castle close in winter; Hidcote Manor Garden is at its best in spring and fall.

FESTIVALS
Bath Comedy Festival
FESTIVALS | Running for 10 days, April's Bath Comedy Festival features comedy events at venues throughout the city. ⊠ *Bath Box Office, Abbey Chambers, Abbey Courtyard, Bath* ☎ *01225/463362* ⊕ *www.bathcomedy.com.*

★ Bath Festival
FESTIVALS | Held over 17 days in May, the Bath Festival is a multi-arts celebration of literature and music in and around the city. Events include classical, jazz, and world-music concerts, dance performances, literary talks, and exhibitions, many in the Assembly Rooms and Bath Abbey. ⊠ *Bath Box Office, 2 Terrace Walk, Bath* ☎ *01225/463362* ⊕ *www.bathfestivals. org.uk.*

Cheltenham Jazz Festival

MUSIC FESTIVALS | Held over a week in late April and early May, the Cheltenham Jazz Festival presents noted musicians from around the world. ☒ *Cheltenham* ☏ *01242/850270 box office* ⊕ *www. cheltenhamfestivals.com.*

Jane Austen Festival

FESTIVALS | Celebrating the great writer with films, plays, walks, and talks over nine days in mid-September, the Jane Austen Festival is a feast for Janeites. ☒ *Bath* ☏ *01225/443000* ⊕ *www. janeaustenfestivalbath.co.uk.*

★ Literature Festival

ARTS FESTIVALS | The 10-day Literature Festival in October brings world-renowned authors, actors, and critics to Cheltenham for hundreds of readings, lectures, and other events. ☒ *Cheltenham* ☏ *01242/850270 box office* ⊕ *www. cheltenhamfestivals.com.*

Music Festival

MUSIC FESTIVALS | Cheltenham's famous Music Festival, held over 10 days in early July, highlights new compositions, often conducted by the composers themselves, plus a wide variety of choral and instrumental classical pieces. ☒ *Cheltenham* ☏ *01242/850270 box office* ⊕ *www. cheltenhamfestivals.com.*

Science Festival

FESTIVALS | For five days in early June, the Science Festival attracts leading scientists and writers to Cheltenham. ☒ *Cheltenham* ☏ *01242/850270 tickets* ⊕ *www.cheltenhamfestivals.com.*

Planning Your Time

Bath and Cheltenham are the most compelling larger towns in the region, and the obvious centers for an exploration of the Cotswolds. Cheltenham is closer to the heart of the Cotswolds and is far less touristy, but it has less immediate appeal. Bath is 29 miles from Cirencester in the southern Cotswolds and 45 miles from Stow-on-the-Wold in the north. It's also worth finding accommodations in the smaller Cotswold settlements, though overnight stops in this well-heeled area can be costly. Good choices include Cirencester, Stow-on-the-Wold, and Broadway.

You can get a taste of Bath and the Cotswolds in three hurried days; a weeklong visit gives you plenty of time for the slow wandering this small region deserves. Near Bath, it's an easy drive to Lacock and Castle Combe, two stately villages on the southern edge of the Cotswolds, and Winchcombe makes a good entry into the area from Cheltenham. At the heart of the Cotswolds, Stow-on-the-Wold, Bourton-on-the-Water, and Broadway should on no account be missed. Within a short distance of these, Chipping Campden and Moreton-in-Marsh are less showy, with a more relaxed feel. Northleach is fairly low-key but boasts a fine example of a Cotswold wool church, while Bibury and Upper and Lower Slaughter are tiny settlements that can easily be appreciated on a brief passage. On the southern fringes of the area, Burford, Tetbury, and Cirencester have antiques and tea shops galore while avoiding the worst of the crowds.

Getting Oriented

The major points of interest in this part of west-central England—Bath, the Cotswolds, and Cheltenham—are one way to organize your explorations. Bath, in the southwestern corner of this area, is a good place to start; it can also be visited on a day trip out from London. The Cotswolds, about two hours northwest of London by car, cover some of southern England's most beautiful terrain. To the west of the Cotswolds lies the city of Cheltenham, an elegant former spa town.

Getting Here and Around

AIR

This area is about two hours from London; Bristol and Birmingham have the closest regional airports.

BUS

National Express buses head to the region from London's Victoria Coach Station. Megabus, a budget bus company best booked online, also serves Cheltenham and Bath from London. It takes about three hours to get to both Cheltenham and to Bath via bus. Bus service between some towns can be extremely limited. The First company covers the area around Bath. Stagecoach, Johnson's Coaches, Cotswold Green, Swanbrook, Marchants, and Pulham's Coaches operate in the Cotswolds region. Traveline has comprehensive information about all public transportation.

CONTACTS Cotswold Green.
☎ 01453/835153 ⊕ www.bustimes. org/operators/cotswold-green. **First.** ☎ 0871/2002233 ⊕ www.firstgroup. com. **Johnson's Coaches.** ☎ 01564/797000 ⊕ www.johnsonscoaches.co.uk. **Marchants.** ☎ 01242/257714 ⊕ www. marchants-coaches.com. **Megabus.** ☎ 0141/352–4444 for general inquiries, 0900/160–0900 for bookings ⊕ www.megabus.com. **National Express.** ☎ 0871/781–8181 ⊕ www. nationalexpress.com. **Pulham's Coaches.** ☎ 01451/820369 ⊕ www.pulhamscoaches.com. **Stagecoach.** ☎ 0871/200–2233 ⊕ www.stagecoachbus.com. **Swanbrook.** ☎ 01452/712386 ⊕ www.swanbrook. co.uk. **Traveline.** ☎ 0871/200–2233 ⊕ www.traveline.info.

CAR

A car is the best way to make a thorough tour of the area, given the limitations of public transportation. M4 is the main route west from London to Bath and southern Gloucestershire; expect about a two-hour drive. From Exit 18, take A46 south to Bath. From Exit 20, take M5 north to Cheltenham; from Exit 15, take A419 to A429 north to the Cotswolds. From London you can also take M40 and A40 to the Cotswolds, where a network of minor roads links the villages.

TRAIN

First Great Western trains serve the region from London's Paddington Station; First Great Western and CrossCountry trains connect Cheltenham and Birmingham. Travel time from Paddington to Bath is about 90 minutes. Most trains to Cheltenham (two hours and 20 minutes) involve a change at Swindon or Bristol Parkway. Train service within the Cotswold area is extremely limited, with Kemble (near Cirencester) and Moreton-in-Marsh being the most useful stops, both serviced by regular trains from London Paddington. A three-day or seven-day Heart of England Rover pass is valid for unlimited travel within the region. National Rail Enquiries can help with schedules and other information.

CONTACTS National Rail Enquiries. ☎ 03457/484950 ⊕ www.nationalrail. co.uk.

Restaurants

Good restaurants dot the region, thanks to a steady flow of fine chefs seeking to cater to wealthy locals and waves of demanding visitors. The country's food revolution is in full evidence here. Restaurants have never had a problem with a fresh food supply: excellent regional produce; salmon from the rivers Severn and Wye; local lamb and pork; venison from the Forest of Dean; and pheasant, partridge, quail, and grouse in season. Also look for Gloucestershire Old Spot pork, bacon (try a delicious Old Spot bacon sandwich), and sausage on area menus.

Hotels

The hotels of this region are among Britain's most highly rated—from bed-and-breakfasts in village homes and farmhouses to luxurious country-house hotels. Many hotels present themselves as deeply traditional rural retreats, but some have opted for a sleeker, fresher style, with boldly contemporary or minimalist furnishings. Spas are becoming increasingly popular at these hotels. Book ahead whenever possible, and brace yourself for some high prices. B&Bs are a cheaper alternative to the fancier hotels, and most places offer two- and three-day packages. Note that the majority of lodgings in Bath and many in the Cotswolds require a two-night minimum stay on weekends and holidays; rates are often higher on weekends. Accommodation in Cheltenham and the Cotswolds is especially hard to find during the week of Cheltenham's National Hunt Festival in March.

There are numerous possibilities for renting a cottage in and around Bath and the Cotswolds, and accommodations are usually available by the week. Check out Manor Cottages or Cotswolds Hideaways for a range of self-catering options.

CONTACTS Cotswolds Hideaways. ☎ *01386/702654* ⊕ *www.cotswoldshideaways.co.uk.* **Manor Cottages.** ☎ *01993/223410* ⊕ *www.manorcottages. co.uk.*

Restaurant and hotel reviews have been shortened. For full information, visit Fodors.com. Restaurant prices are the average cost of a main course at dinner or, if dinner is not served, at lunch. Hotel prices are the lowest cost of a standard double room in high season, including 20% V.A.T.

WHAT IT COSTS in Pounds

	$	$$	$$$	$$$$
RESTAURANTS				
	under £16	£16–£23	£24–£30	over £30
HOTELS				
	under £125	£125–£225	£226–£350	over £350

Visitor Information

The South West Tourism website has information about the entire region. The Cotswolds site is a government one that has a useful section on tourism. The major towns have Tourist Information Centres that provide advice and help with accommodations.

CONTACTS The Cotswolds. ⊕ *www. cotswolds.com.* **South West Tourism.** ⊕ *www.visitsouthwest.co.uk.*

Bath

13 miles southeast of Bristol, 115 miles west of London.

In Bath, a UNESCO World Heritage Site, you're surrounded by magnificent 18th-century architecture, a lasting reminder of a vanished world often described by the likes of Jane Austen. In the 19th century, the city lost its fashionable luster and slid into a refined gentility that still remains. Bath is no museum, though: it's lively, with good dining and shopping; excellent art galleries and museums; the remarkable excavated Roman baths; and theater, music, and other performances all year. Many people rush through Bath in a day, but there's enough to do to merit an overnight stay—or more. In summer, the sheer volume of sightseers may hamper your progress.

The Romans put Bath on the map in the 1st century when they built a temple here, in honor of the goddess Minerva, and a sophisticated network of baths to make full use of the mineral springs that gush from the earth at a constant temperature of 116°F (46.5°C). ■TIP→ **Don't miss the remains of the baths, one of the city's glories.** Visits by Queen Anne in 1702 and 1703 brought attention to the town, and soon 18th-century "people of quality" took it to heart. Assembly rooms, theaters, and pleasure gardens were built to entertain the rich and titled when they weren't busy attending the parties of Beau Nash (the city's master of ceremonies and chief social organizer, who helped increase Bath's popularity) and having their portraits painted by Gainsborough.

GETTING HERE AND AROUND

Frequent trains from Paddington and National Express buses from Victoria connect Bath with London. The bus and train stations are close to each other south of the center. By car from London, take M4 to Exit 18, from which A46 leads 10 miles south to Bath.

Drivers should note that parking is extremely limited within the city, and any car illegally parked will be ticketed. Fees for towed cars can be hundreds of pounds. Public lots in the historic area fill up early, but the park-and-ride lots on the outskirts provide inexpensive shuttle service into the center, which is pleasant to stroll around.

TIMING

Schedule a visit to Bath during the week, as weekends see an influx of visitors. The city gets similarly crowded during its various festivals, though the added conviviality and cultural activity during these events are big draws in themselves.

TOURS

City Sightseeing

Fifty-minute guided tours of Bath are run by City Sightseeing on open-top buses year-round, leaving two to four times an hour from High Street, near the abbey. They allow for hopping on and off at 17 different stops. Tickets, valid for 24 hours, give discounts on entry to some of Bath's top attractions. ☎ 01225/444102 ⊕ www.city-sightseeing.com ✉ From £16.50.

Mad Max Tours

During spring and summer, Mad Max Tours runs full- or half-day tours through the Cotswolds departing outside the Abbey Hotel near Bath Abbey and going through some of the main Cotswold highlights. Depending on the chosen itinerary, this can include Stonehenge, Castle Combe, and many of the area's prettiest villages. Advance booking is essential and the ticket may not include the price of entry to certain sites. ☎ 07990/505970 ⊕ www.madmaxtours. co.uk ✉ From £35.

Mayor of Bath's Honorary Guides

Free two-hour walking tours of Bath are offered year-round by the Mayor of Bath's Honorary Guides. Individuals can just show up outside the Roman Baths. Tours are Sunday through Friday at 10:30 am and 2 pm, Saturday at 10:30 am, and there's an additional tour at 7 pm Tuesday and Thursday from May to August. Note that unlike many other free tours, these guides don't accept tips. ☎ 01225/477411 ⊕ www.bathguides.org.uk.

ESSENTIALS

VISITOR INFORMATION Bath Tourist Information Centre. ✉ Bridgwater House, 2 Terrace Walk ☎ 01225/614420 ⊕ www. visitbath.co.uk.

⊙ Sights

American Museum in Britain

MUSEUM | A 19th-century Greek Revival mansion in a majestic setting on a hill 2½ miles southeast of the city holds the only museum of American decorative arts outside the United States. Rooms are furnished in historical

Sights ▼

1	American Museum in Britain	J6
2	Bath Abbey	F5
3	Bath Skyline Walk	J6
4	Circus	D3
5	Fashion Museum and Assembly Rooms	D3
6	Herschel Museum of Astronomy	C5
7	Holburne Museum	H3
8	Jane Austen Centre	D4
9	Museum of Bath Architecture	E3
10	Museum of Bath at Work	D2
11	Museum of East Asian Art	D3
12	Number 1 Royal Crescent	C3
13	Prior Park Landscape Garden	H9
14	Pulteney Bridge	F5
15	Queen Square	D4
16	Roman Baths and the Pump Room	E6
17	Royal Victoria Park	B3
18	Thermae Bath Spa	E6

Restaurants ▼

1	Bathwick Boatman	I1
2	The Bertinet Bakery	E5
3	Boston Tea Party	D5
4	Chez Dominique	F5
5	The Circus Restaurant	D3
6	The Grand Eastern	E5
7	The Herd Steak Restaurant	F5
8	Menu Gordon Jones	C9
9	The Pig Near Bath	A6
10	Pump Room	E6
11	The Roman Baths Kitchen	E5
12	Rustico	C3
13	Sally Lunn's	F6

Hotels ▼

1	The Albany	B4
2	Cranleigh	A4
3	Dukes Hotel	H4
4	The Gainsborough Bath Spa	E6
5	Halcyon Apartments	D4
6	Harington's Hotel	E5
7	Marlborough House	A4
8	Paradise House	D8
9	Queensberry Hotel	D3
10	The Royal Crescent	C2
11	Three Abbey Green	F6

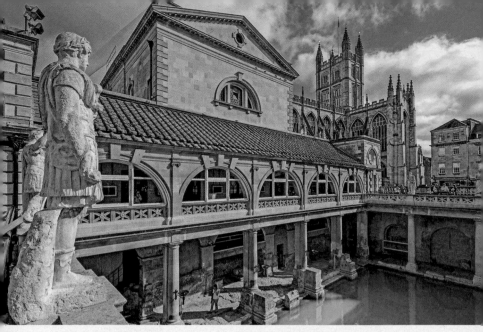

The remains of the Roman baths evoke the days when the Romans gathered here to socialize and bathe.

styles, such as the 17th-century Conkey's Tavern, the beautifully elegant Greek Revival room, and the lavish, richly red New Orleans bedroom from the 1860s. Other galleries explore historical themes (the settlement of the West, the Civil War) or contain a large collection of quilts, as well as porcelain and Shaker objects; a separate building is devoted to folk art, including a fine collection of decoy wildfowl. The parkland includes a reproduction of George Washington's garden at Mount Vernon, and the New American Garden Project features many plants native to the United States. Take a bus headed to the University of Bath and get off at the Avenue, where signs point to the museum, half a mile away. The City Sightseeing bus also drops off here. ⊠ *Claverton Manor, Off A36* ☎ *01225/460503* ⊕ *www.americanmuseum.org* ⊠ *£14; Gardens only £9* ⊘ *Closed Mon. (except bank holidays) and Nov.–mid-Mar.*

Bath Abbey

RELIGIOUS SITE | Dominating Bath's center, this 15th-century edifice of golden, glowing stone has a splendid west front, with carved figures of angels ascending ladders on either side. Notice, too, the miter, olive tree, and crown motif, a play on the name of the building's founder, Bishop Oliver King. More than 50 stained-glass windows fill about 80% of the building's wall space, giving the interior an impression of lightness. The abbey was built in the Perpendicular (English late-Gothic) style on the site of a Saxon abbey, and the nave and side aisles contain superb fan-vaulted ceilings. Look for the 21st-century expressively carved angels on the choir screens. The building's heating comes from the adjacent Roman baths. There are four services on Sunday, including choral evensong at 3 pm. **Tower tours** (45 minutes; on the hour every hour daily except Sunday) allow close-up views of the massive bells and panoramic cityscapes from the roof; the 212 dizzying steps demand a level of fitness. ⊠ *Abbey Churchyard*

☎ *01225/422462* ⊕ *www.bathabbey.org* ✉ *Abbey £4 suggested donation, tower tours £6* ⊙ *No tower tours Sun.*

Bath Skyline Walk

TRAIL | An excellent way to appreciate the beauty and uniqueness of Bath is through the Bath Skyline Walk. One of England's most popular walks, it is 6 miles of greenery that encircles the city and includes woodlands, valleys, meadows, and trails with captivating views of the city's architecture. Grab a picnic and some strong shoes and head out on the waymarked path. The starting point is on Bathwick Hill near the entrance to the National Trust Bathwick Fields; you can download a free walking guide from the National Trust website. ■ TIP➔ **If you don't have the time (or energy) for the full walk, take the 3-mile "Walk to the View" waymarked from Bath Abbey.** ✉ *Bathwick Hill* ☎ *01225/833977* ⊕ *www.nationaltrust. org.uk/bath-skyline/trails/bath-skyline-walk* ✉ *Free.*

Circus

PLAZA | John Wood designed the masterful Circus, a circle of curving, perfectly proportioned Georgian houses interrupted just three times for intersecting streets. Wood died shortly after work began; his son, the younger John Wood, completed the project. Notice the carved acorns atop the houses: Wood nurtured the myth that Prince Bladud founded Bath, ostensibly with the help of an errant pig rooting for acorns (this is one of a number of variations of Bladud's story). A garden with large plane trees fills the center of the Circus. The painter Thomas Gainsborough (1727–88) lived at No. 17 from 1760 to 1774. ✉ *Intersection of Bennett, Brock, and Gay Sts.*

★ Fashion Museum and Assembly Rooms

MUSEUM | In its role as the **Assembly Rooms,** this neoclassical building was one of the leading centers for social life in 18th-century Bath. Jane Austen came here often, and it's in the Ballroom that Catherine Morland has her first,

disappointing encounter with Bath's beau monde in *Northanger Abbey;* the Octagon Room is the setting for an important encounter between Anne Elliot and Captain Wentworth in *Persuasion.* Built by John Wood the Younger in 1771, the building was badly damaged by wartime bombing in 1942 but was faithfully restored. Its stunning chandeliers are the 18th-century originals. Throughout the year, classical concerts are given here, just as they were in bygone days. The Assembly Rooms are also known today for the entertaining **Fashion Museum,** displaying apparel from Jacobean times up to the present. You can see examples of what would have been worn in the heydays here, as well as glamorous frocks from the 20th century—a dress of the year is an annual addition. Besides admiring the changing exhibits, you can have fun trying on corsets and crinolines. An audio guide and daily guided tours at noon and 3:30 are included in the admission. ✉ *Bennett St.* ☎ *01225/477789* ⊕ *www.fashionmuseum.co.uk* ✉ *Assembly Rooms free; Fashion Museum £9.50; £26 combined ticket includes Roman Baths and the Victoria Art Gallery.*

Herschel Museum of Astronomy

MUSEUM | In the garden of this modest Bath town house, which he shared with his sister Caroline (an astronomer in her own right), William Herschel (1738–1822) identified the planet Uranus. He used a handmade telescope of his own devising, and this small museum, devoted to his studies and discoveries, shows his telescopes, the workshop abutting the kitchen where he cast his speculum metal mirrors, as well as orreries, caricatures, and musical instruments of his time (Herschel was the organist at Bath's Octagon Chapel). ✉ *19 New King St.* ☎ *01225/446865* ⊕ *www. herschelmuseum.org.uk* ✉ *£6.90; joint ticket with Number 1 Royal Crescent, Musuem of Bath Architecture, and Beckford's Tower £16.*

★ Holburne Museum

MUSEUM | One of Bath's gems, this elegant 18th-century building and its modern extension house a superb collection of 17th- and 18th-century decorative arts, ceramics, and silverware. Highlights include paintings by Gainsborough (*The Byam Family*, on indefinite loan) and George Stubbs (*Reverend Carter Thelwall and Family*), and a hilarious collection of caricatures of the Georgian city's fashionable elite. In its original incarnation as the Sydney Hotel, the house was one of the pivots of Bath's high society, which came to perambulate the pleasure gardens (Sydney Gardens) that still lie behind it. One visitor was Jane Austen, whose main Bath residence was No. 4 Sydney Place, a brief stroll from the museum. There's also an excellent café and tea garden on-site. ✉ *Great Pulteney St.* ☎ *01225/388569* ⊕ *www.holburne.org* 💷 *£12.50.*

Jane Austen Centre

MUSEUM | The one place in Bath that gives Austen any space provides a briefly diverting exhibition about the influence of Bath on her writings; *Northanger Abbey* and *Persuasion* are both set primarily in the city. The center is brought to life by characters in costume, and displays and a short film give a pictorial overview of life in Bath around 1800. Immerse yourself further by dressing up in costume; assistants are on hand to take your photo. The cozy Georgian house, a few doors up from where the writer lived in 1805 (one of several addresses she had in Bath), also includes the Austen-themed Regency Tea Rooms, open to the public. ✉ *40 Gay St.* ☎ *01225/443000* ⊕ *www. janeausten.co.uk* 💷 *£12.*

Museum of Bath Architecture

MUSEUM | This absorbing museum in the Georgian Gothic–style Countess of Huntingdon's Chapel is an essential stop on any exploration of Bath, particularly for fans of Georgian architecture. It illustrates the evolution of the city, with examples

Jane Austen in Bath 👁

Though born and brought up in Hampshire, Jane Austen had close connections with Bath and lived here from 1801 to 1806. She wasn't overly fond of the place, peppering her letters with caustic comments about it. Austen wrote her sister, Cassandra, that she left "with what happy feelings of escape." However, she is thought to have fallen in love here, and she received her only known offer of marriage while in Bath. Bath's eight-day Jane Austen Festival celebrates the writer in late September.

of everything from window design and wrought-iron railings to marbling and other interior decoration, while an informative film puts what you see into context. ✉ *The Paragon* ☎ *01225/333895* ⊕ *www.museumofbatharchitecture.org.uk* 💷 *£6.90; joint ticket with Number 1 Royal Crescent, Herschel Museum of Astronomy, and Beckford's Tower £16* 🕐 *Closed Dec. and Jan.*

Museum of Bath at Work

MUSEUM | The core of this industrial-history collection, which gives a novel perspective on the city, is an engineering works and fizzy drinks factory. This building once belonged to Bath entrepreneur Jonathan Bowler, who started his many businesses in 1872. The collection includes the original clanking machinery and offers glimpses into Bath's stone industry and cabinetmaking. Look out for the Bath in Particular exhibition, an illuminating collection chosen by locals. ✉ *Julian Rd.* ☎ *01225/318348* ⊕ *www. bath-at-work.org.uk* 💷 *£8 including audio guide* 🕐 *Closed Dec. and weekdays Nov. and Jan.–Mar.*

Museum of East Asian Art

MUSEUM | Intimate galleries on three floors display ancient and modern pieces, mostly from China but with other exhibits from Japan, Korea, and Southeast Asia. Highlights are the Chinese jade figures, especially the animals, both mythical and real, Buddhist objects, and Japanese lacquerware and prints. Don't miss the charming *netsuke* (toggles) and *inro* (seal cases) on the staircase to the lower ground floor. ⊠ *12 Bennett St.* ☎ *01225/464640* ⊕ *www.meaa.org.uk* ⊠ *£5* ⊘ *Closed Mon.*

★ Number 1 Royal Crescent

BUILDING | The majestic arc of the Royal Crescent, much used as a film location, is the crowning glory of Palladian architecture in Bath. The work of John Wood the Younger, these 30 houses fronted by 114 columns were laid out between 1767 and 1774. The first house to be built, on the corner of Brock Street and the Royal Crescent, was Number 1 Royal Crescent. The museum now crystallizes a view of the English class system in the 18th century—the status, wealth, and elegance of the upstairs in contrast with the extensive servants' quarters and kitchen downstairs. You can witness the predilections of the first resident, Henry Sandford, in the cabinet of curiosities and the electrical machine, as well as a Georgian love of display in the sumptuous dessert table arrangement in the dining room. Several varieties of historic mousetraps make their appearance downstairs. Everything is presented with elegant attention to authenticity and detail. ⊠ *Royal Crescent* ☎ *01225/428126* ⊕ *no1royalcrescent.org. uk* ⊠ *£10.90; joint ticket with Museum of Bath Architecture, Herschel Museum, and Beckford's Tower £16* ⊘ *Closed Jan.*

Prior Park Landscape Garden

GARDEN | A vision to warm Jane Austen's heart, Bath's grandest house lies a mile or so southeast of the center, with splendid views over the Georgian townscape. Built around 1738 by John Wood the Elder, the Palladian mansion was the home of quarry owner and philanthropist Ralph Allen (1693–1764), whose guests included such luminaries as poet Alexander Pope and novelists Henry Fielding and Samuel Richardson. Today it's a school, and the interior is not open to the public, but you may wander through the beautiful grounds, designed by Capability Brown and embellished with a Palladian bridge and lake. A leisurely circuit of the park should take around an hour. ■TIP➔ **The parking here is reserved for people with disabilities, so take a taxi or bus from the center. The City Sightseeing bus also calls here.** ⊠ *Ralph Allen Dr.* ☎ *01225/833977* ⊕ *www. nationaltrust.org.uk* ⊠ *£8.40* ⊘ *Closed weekdays Nov.–Jan.*

Pulteney Bridge

BRIDGE/TUNNEL | Florence's Ponte Vecchio inspired this 18th-century span, one of the most famous landmarks in the city and the only work of Robert Adam in Bath. It's unique in Great Britain because shops line both sides of the bridge. ⊠ *Between Bridge St. and Argyle St.*

Queen Square

PLAZA | Palatial houses and the Francis Hotel surround the garden in the center of this square designed by the older John Wood. An obelisk financed by Beau Nash celebrates the 1738 visit of Frederick, Prince of Wales. ⊠ *South end of Gay St.*

★ Roman Baths and the Pump Room

MUSEUM | The hot springs have drawn people here since prehistoric times, so it's quite appropriate to begin an exploration of Bath at this excellent museum on the site of the ancient city's primary "watering hole." Roman patricians would gather to immerse themselves, drink the mineral waters, and socialize. With the departure of the Romans, the baths fell into disuse. When bathing again became fashionable at the end of the 18th century, this magnificent Georgian building was erected.

Almost the entire Roman bath complex was excavated in the 19th century, and the museum displays relics that include a memorable mustachioed, Celtic-influenced Gorgon's head, fragments of colorful curses invoked by the Romans against their neighbors, and information about Roman bathing practices. The **Great Bath** is now roofless, and the statuary and pillars belong to the 19th century, but much remains from the original complex (the Roman characters strutting around, however, are 21st century) and the steaming, somewhat murky waters are undeniably evocative. Tours take place hourly for no additional charge, and you can visit after 6:30 pm in July and August to experience the baths lighted by torches. Wear sensible shoes as the ancient stones are uneven and can be slippery. The ongoing Archway project will see new educational spaces and more of the Roman site being opened up to the public starting in 2021.

Adjacent to the Roman bath complex is the famed **Pump Room,** built in 1792–96, a rendezvous for members of 18th- and 19th-century Bath society. Here Catherine Morland and Mrs. Allen "paraded up and down for an hour, looking at everybody and speaking to no one," to quote from Jane Austen's *Northanger Abbey.* Today you can take in the elegant space—or you can simply, for a small fee, taste the fairly vile mineral water. Charles Dickens described it as tasting like warm flatirons. ✉ *Abbey Churchyard* ☎ *01225/477785* ⊕ *www.romanbaths.co.uk* ✉ *£18.50; £26 combined ticket includes the Fashion Museum and Assembly Rooms and the Victoria Art Gallery.*

Royal Victoria Park
CITY PARK | FAMILY | Originally designed as an arboretum, this tidy expanse of lawns and shady walks just west of the Royal Crescent provides the perfect setting for pleasant strolls and leisurely picnics. The park has a pond, a **Botanic Garden,** and an adventure playground with plenty for kids. The Great Dell Aerial Walkway has also been restored at the northern end of the park. Hot-air balloon launches and open-air shows at festival time enliven the atmosphere. ✉ *Upper Bristol Rd.* ⊕ *www.bathnes. gov.uk/services/sport-leisure-and-parks/ parks-green-spaces/find-park/royal-victoria-park* ✉ *Free.*

Thermae Bath Spa
HOT SPRINGS | One of the few places in Britain where you can bathe in natural hot-spring water, and in an open-air rooftop location as well, this striking complex designed by Nicholas Grimshaw consists of a Bath-stone building surrounded by a glass curtain wall. The only difficulty is in deciding where to spend more time—in the sleekly luxurious, light-filled Minerva Bath, with its curves and gentle currents, or in the smaller, open-air rooftop pool for the unique sensation of bathing with views of Bath's operatic skyline (twilight is particularly atmospheric here). Two 18th-century thermal baths, the Cross Bath and the Hot Bath, are back in use, too (the latter for treatments only). End your session in the crisp third-floor café and restaurant. ■TIP→ **It's essential to book spa treatments ahead of time.** Towels, robes, and slippers are available for rent. Note that changing rooms are co-ed. Weekdays are the quietest time to visit. You must be 16 to bathe here and 18 to book a spa treatment. A separate, free **Visitor Centre** (April through October, Monday through Saturday 10–5, Sunday 11–4) opposite the entrance gives an overview of the project and provides audio guides (£2) for a brief tour of the exterior. ✉ *Hot Bath St.* ☎ *01225/331234* ⊕ *www.thermaebathspa.com* ✉ *£37 for 2 hrs (£42 on weekends) and £10 for each additional hr.*

Bath's Georgian Architecture

Bath wouldn't be Bath without its distinctive 18th-century Georgian architecture, much of which was conceived by John Wood the Elder (1704–54), an antiquarian and architect. Wood saw Bath as a city destined for almost mythic greatness. Arriving in Bath in 1727, he sought a suitable architectural style, and found it in the Palladian style, made popular in Britain by Inigo Jones.

Elements of Style

Derived from the Italian architect Andrea Palladio (1508–80), who in turn was inspired by ancient Roman architecture, Palladianism accentuated symmetry and proportion. The plain facades of buildings, dignified with columns, pilasters, and pediments over doors and windows, often contrasted with rich interiors. The Building of Bath Collection has more information.

Buildings to See

Wood created a harmonious city, building graceful terraces (row houses), crescents (curving rows of houses), and villas of the same golden local limestone used by the Romans. Influenced by nearby ancient stone circles as well as round Roman temples, Wood broke from convention in his design for Bath's Circus, a circle of houses broken only three times for intersecting streets.

After the death of Wood the Elder, John Wood the Younger (1728–82) carried out his father's plans for the Royal Crescent, a regal crescent of 30 houses. Today you can stop in at Number 1 Royal Crescent for a look at one of these homes—it's like eavesdropping on the 18th century. He also built the Assembly Rooms, which are open to the public.

8

Bath and the Cotswolds BATH

🍽 Restaurants

Bathwick Boatman

$ | MODERN BRITISH | Just five minutes from the Holburne Museum, this former rowing club house serves quality food in a picturesque setting. The global menu ranges from tandoori marinated salmon to tagliatelle. **Known for:** riverside setting; quality food with a global influence; warm atmosphere. $ *Average main: £15* ✉ *Forester Rd.* ☎ *01225/428844* ⊕ *www. bathwickboatman.com* ☾ *Closed Mon.*

The Bertinet Bakery

$ | BAKERY | This popular artisanal bakery serves tasty breads, pastries, and savory light meals to eat in or take out. All the breads are hand-baked daily under the leadership of local baker Richard Bertinet. **Known for:**

mouthwatering almond croissants; bread-making classes at bakery school; freshly baked artisanal bread. $ *Average main: £5* ✉ *1 New Bond St Place* ☎ *01225/313296* ⊕ *www.bertinetbakery.com.*

Boston Tea Party

$ | MODERN BRITISH | Sit in this bustling café and watch the comings and goings of the Bath square outside and take your pick from the all-day menu. Impressive choices include everything from croque monsieurs to Cuban sandwiches. **Known for:** all-day menu of sandwiches, teas, and coffee; friendly staff; lively atmosphere. $ *Average main: £9* ✉ *19 Kingsmead Sq.* ☎ *01225/727677* ⊕ *www. bostonteaparty.co.uk.*

Chez Dominique

$$ | FRENCH | The enticing prix-fixe menu attracts diners to this award-winning French restaurant, which is renowned for its signature dishes from sea bass to duck breast. The Sunday roast is very popular but should be booked ahead. **Known for:** good-value prix-fixe menu; private dining room with a view of Pulteney Weir; fabulous Sunday roast lunch. $ *Average main: £19* ✉ *15 Argyle St.* ☎ *01225/463482* ⊕ *www. chezdominique.co.uk.*

The Circus Restaurant

$$ | MODERN BRITISH | This sophicticated and popular restaurant on the corner of the Circus has an enticing seasonal menu that covers everything from morning coffee to late-night dinners. The husband-and-wife team prioritize locally sourced ingredients, and wines come from old-world small growers. **Known for:** local ingredients; family-run ethos; classic English cuisine. $ *Average main: £16* ✉ *34 Brock St.* ☎ *01225/466020* ⊕ *www.thecircusrestaurant.co.uk* ⊘ *Closed Sun.*

The Grand Eastern

$ | INDIAN | Delicious Indian dishes are the main draw, but the three magnificent glass domes of the large Georgian interior and the arresting South Asian murals mean that a meal here becomes an event. Specialties of the house include *mughlai* chicken (flavored with egg, ginger, and garlic and fried in a sauce of yogurt, coconut, and poppy seeds) and salmon *bhaja* (panfried with Bengali spices and served with diced potatoes). **Known for:** classic Indian and Bengali cuisine; elaborate setting; long menu with lots of options. $ *Average main: £13* ✉ *8a Quiet St.* ☎ *01225/422323* ⊕ *grandeastern.co.uk.*

The Herd Steak Restaurant

$$$ | BRITISH | In this popular Argyle Street eatery with stripped-back white walls, it's all about the steak. The mouthwatering meats all come from Aberdeen Angus and Hereford Cross cows on local area farms. **Known for:** the best steaks in the region; friendly staff; locally sourced meat and seasonal ingredients. $ *Average main: £25* ✉ *12 Argyle St.* ☎ *01225/316583* ⊕ *www. theherdrestaurant.co.uk.*

Menu Gordon Jones

$$$$ | MODERN BRITISH | Step away from the center of town to sample the ingenious cuisine that Michelin-trained chef Gordon Jones conjures up in his open kitchen. There is no set menu, but each course is carefully explained before it's served; there might be smoked eel with maple syrup and purple potatoes, a crisp haggis, roasted turbot with giant raisins and caper dressing, and blackberry sorbet with marinated cucumber. **Known for:** imaginative cuisine served with style; tasting menus that change every single day (so it's always a surprise); reservations required far in advance. $ *Average main: £65* ✉ *2 Wellsway* ☎ *01225/480871* ⊕ *www.menugordonjones.co.uk* ⊘ *Closed Mon.*

★ The Pig Near Bath

$$ | MODERN BRITISH | The Bath outpost of the growing Pig empire is a funky but chic "restaurant with rooms" in a converted country house in the Mendip Hills. It's all about the local and seasonal here (everything comes from within a 25-mile radius): kale, arugula, and other leaves and veggies are sourced from the Pig's kitchen garden; apples, pears, and apricots come from its orchard; and pork, chicken, quail, and venison are provided by animals raised on the property. **Known for:** salmon, bacon, and pancetta smoked on-site; relaxed atmosphere in a quaint deer park setting; alfresco dining in summer. $ *Average main: £18* ✉ *Hunstrete House, Pensford* ☎ *01761/49049* ⊕ *www.thepighotel.com.*

Pump Room

$$ | BRITISH | The 18th-century Pump Room, with views over the Roman baths, serves morning coffee, lunches, and afternoon tea, to music by a pianist or string trio who play every day. The stately setting is the selling point rather than the food, but do sample the West Country cheese board and the homemade cakes and pastries. **Known for:** gorgeous setting from a bygone era; classic afternoon tea, coffee, and cakes; long waits during the day and reservations required for dinner. $ Average main: £16 ⊠ Abbey Churchyard ☎ 01225/444477 ⊕ www.thepumproombath.co.uk ⊘ No dinner Sept.–Jan. and Mar.–June.

The Roman Baths Kitchen

$ | BRITISH | This bustling brasserie is located in a town house in the center of Bath and serves traditional British and European dishes. Locally sourced ingredients are used to create tasty menu options like wild mushroom risotto and confit duck leg. **Known for:** classic English dishes served with sophistication; terrace dining; ideal lunch stop. $ Average main: £13 ⊠ Abbey Churchyard ☎ 01225/477877 ⊕ www.romanbathkitchen.co.uk.

Rustico

$ | ITALIAN | Serving old-fashioned Italian country fare along with a dash of dolce vita, this delightful restaurant has a cozy, intimate atmosphere. The welcoming staff gladly serves you homemade pastas like grandma used to make, quantities of seafood casserole, handsome steaks, and pork in sage and white wine sauce, for instance. **Known for:** traditional Italian home-cooking; the area's best tiramisu; cozy outdoor seating. $ Average main: £15 ⊠ 2 Margaret's Buildings ☎ 01225/310064 ⊕ www.rusticobistroitaliano.co.uk ⊘ Closed Mon.

Sally Lunn's

$ | BRITISH | Small and slightly twee, this tourist magnet near Bath Abbey occupies the oldest house in Bath, dating from 1482. It's famous for the Sally Lunn bun, a semisweet bread served here since 1680. **Known for:** famed Sally Lunn buns with sweet and savory toppings; lots of tourists; tiny but interesting on-site museum. $ Average main: £12 ⊠ 4 N. Parade Passage ☎ 01225/461634 ⊕ www.sallylunns.co.uk.

🛏 Hotels

The Albany

$ | B&B/INN | Homey and friendly, this Edwardian house close to the Royal Crescent has simply furnished rooms decorated with neutral shades of beige and cream. **Pros:** spotless rooms; convenient location; excellent breakfasts. **Cons:** some rooms are very small; limited parking; on a main road so can get noisy. $ Rooms from: £85 ⊠ 24 Crescent Gardens ☎ 01225/313339 ⊕ www.albanybath.co.uk ➥ 6 rooms ❖ Free breakfast.

Cranleigh

$ | B&B/INN | On a quiet hilltop above the city center, this Victorian guesthouse has wonderful views of the Avon Valley. **Pros:** quiet rooms; many choices at breakfast; free parking. **Cons:** far from center; along a busy road; steps to climb. $ Rooms from: £115 ⊠ 159 Newbridge Hill ☎ 01225/310197 ⊕ cranleighbath.com ➥ 9 rooms ❖ Free breakfast.

Dukes Hotel

$ | HOTEL | True Georgian grandeur is evident in the refurbished rooms of this Palladian-style mansion–turned–elegant small hotel, which comes with one of the best addresses in Bath. **Pros:** excellent central location; historic building; friendly and helpful service. **Cons:** some rooms are small; limited parking; no elevator. $ Rooms from: £120 ⊠ 53–54 Great Pulteney St., entrance on Edward St. ☎ 01225/787960 ⊕ www.dukesbath.co.uk ➥ 17 rooms ❖ Free breakfast.

★ The Gainsborough Bath Spa

$$$ | HOTEL | As the only hotel in the United Kingdom with access to Bath's natural thermal waters, thanks to its location in a custom-designed Spa Village, the Gainsborough has a unique appeal. **Pros:** spectacular Georgian setting in a central location; exclusive spa facilities; flawless service. **Cons:** only showers in some rooms; a little pricey; spa not always accessible without booking a treatment. $ *Rooms from: £250* ⊠ *Beau St.* ☎ *01225/358888* ⊕ *www.thegainsboroughbathspa.co.uk* ⇆ *98 rooms* ¡○¡ *Free breakfast.*

Halcyon Apartments

$$ | HOTEL | For those who like more privacy and to fend for themselves, these spacious, chic, contemporary apartments are perfect. **Pros:** central location; good for those who are independent; parking available. **Cons:** not for those who like to be waited on; advance notice of check-in needed; plenty of stairs. $ *Rooms from: £129* ⊠ *15a George St.* ☎ *01225/585100* ⊕ *www.thehalcyon.com* ⇆ *7 apartments* ¡○¡ *No meals:*

Harington's Hotel

$$ | HOTEL | It's rare to find a compact hotel in the cobblestone heart of Bath, and this informal three-story lodging converted from a group of Georgian town houses fits the bill nicely. **Pros:** good breakfasts; helpful staff; central location. **Cons:** occasional street noise from revelers; steps to climb; many small rooms. $ *Rooms from: £126* ⊠ *8-10 Queen St.* ☎ *01225/461728* ⊕ *www.haringtonshotel. co.uk* ⇆ *13 rooms* ¡○¡ *Free breakfast.*

Marlborough House

$$ | B&B/INN | A warm, informal welcome greets all who stay at this Victorian establishment not too far from the Royal Crescent, where each room charms with period furniture, fresh flowers, and antique beds. **Pros:** obliging and helpful hosts; immaculate rooms; parking available. **Cons:** walk to the center is along a busy road; minimum two-night stay on weekends; gets booked up quickly at peak times. $ *Rooms from: £145* ⊠ *1 Marlborough La.* ☎ *01225/318175* ⊕ *www.marlborough-house.net* ⇆ *6 rooms* ¡○¡ *Free breakfast.*

Paradise House

$$ | B&B/INN | Don't be put off by the 10-minute uphill walk from the center of Bath—you'll be rewarded by a wonderful view of the city from the lovely garden and upper stories of this Georgian guesthouse. **Pros:** great attention to detail; spectacular views from some rooms; parking is available. **Cons:** uphill walk from the city center; books up far in advance; some low ceilings and doors. $ *Rooms from: £150* ⊠ *88 Holloway* ☎ *01225/317723* ⊕ *www.paradise-house. co.uk* ⇆ *12 rooms* ¡○¡ *Free breakfast.*

Queensberry Hotel

$ | HOTEL | Intimate and elegant, this boutique hotel on a residential street near the Circus occupies three 1772 town houses built by John Wood the Younger for the Marquis of Queensberry; it's a perfect marriage of chic sophistication, homey comforts, and attentive service. **Pros:** efficient service; tranquil ambience; valet parking. **Cons:** occasional street noise; no tea/coffee-making facilities in rooms; slight uphill walk from the city center. $ *Rooms from: £110* ⊠ *7 Russel St.* ☎ *01225/447928* ⊕ *www. thequeensberry.co.uk* ⇆ *29 rooms* ¡○¡ *Free breakfast.*

The Royal Crescent

$$$$ | HOTEL | You can't get a more prestigious address in Bath than the Royal Crescent, and this hotel, discreetly plumb center, overlooks parkland and the town. **Pros:** historic building; total comfort; great location. **Cons:** most bedrooms are very modern in feel; some rooms have no views; some bathrooms are small. $ *Rooms from: £360* ⊠ *16 Royal Crescent* ☎ *01225/823333* ⊕ *www.royalcrescent.co.uk* ⇆ *45 rooms* ¡○¡ *Free breakfast.*

Three Abbey Green

$$ | B&B/INN | Just steps from Bath Abbey, a gorgeous square dominated by a majestic plane tree is home to this welcoming B&B. **Pros:** superb location; airy rooms; delicious breakfasts. **Cons:** some noise from pub-goers; only suites have bathtubs; no parking. $ *Rooms from: £130* ⊠ *3 Abbey Green* ☎ *01225/428558* ⊕ *www.threeabbeygreen.com* ⊑ *10 rooms* ⭘ *Free breakfast.*

Nightlife

The Bell

BARS/PUBS | Owned by a co-op and a favorite among locals, the Bell has live music—jazz, blues, and folk—on Monday, Wednesday, and Sunday, as well as a selection of real ales, good food, computer access, and even self-service laundry. ⊠ *103 Walcot St.* ☎ *01225/460426* ⊕ *www.thebellinnbath.co.uk.*

Circo

WINE BARS—NIGHTLIFE | This buzzing circular bar whips up a sassy cocktail or glass of champagne in this popular venue. There are movie nights on Wednesday, Cuban Thursdays, and even a gin high tea. Circo also serves tapas-style food. ⊠ *16 George St.* ☎ *01225/465905* ⊕ *www.circobar.co.uk.*

Raven

BARS/PUBS | Pub aficionados will relish the friendly, unspoiled ambience of the Raven, a great spot for a pie and a pint. There are regular arts, science, and storytelling nights upstairs. ⊠ *6-7 Queen St.* ☎ *01225/425045* ⊕ *www.theravenofbath.co.uk.*

Performing Arts

Theatre Royal

THEATER | A gemlike Regency playhouse from 1805, the Theatre Royal has a year-round program that often includes pre- or post-London tours. You must reserve the best seats well in advance, but you can line up for same-day standby seats or standing room. ■**TIP→ Take care with your seat location—sight lines can be poor.** ⊠ *Box Office, Saw Close* ☎ *01225/448844* ⊕ *www.theatreroyal.org.uk.*

🛍 Shopping

Bath has excellent small, family-run, and specialty shops; many close Sunday. Check out the shopping district centers on Stall and Union streets, the SouthGate shopping center near the train station (modern stores), Milsom Street (traditional stores), and Walcot Street (arts and crafts). Leading off these main streets are alleyways and passages lined with galleries and antiques shops.

Bartlett Street Antiques Centre

ANTIQUES/COLLECTIBLES | This place has more than 60 showcases and stands selling every kind of antique imaginable, including silver, porcelain, and jewelry. ⊠ *Bartlett St.* ⊕ *www.bartlettstreetantiquescentre.com.*

Bath Christmas Market

CRAFTS | For 18 days in late November and early December, the outdoor Bath Christmas Market sells gift items and regional specialties—from handcrafted toys to candles, cards, and edible delights—in over 200 chalet-style stalls concentrated in the area just south of the Abbey. ⊠ *York St.* ☎ *0844/8475256* ⊕ *www.bathchristmasmarket.co.uk.*

Bath Sweet Shop

FOOD/CANDY | The city's oldest candy store, Bath Sweet Shop boasts of stocking some 350 different varieties, including traditional licorice torpedoes, pear drops, and aniseed balls. Sugar-free treats are available. ⊠ *8 N. Parade Passage* ☎ *01225/428040.*

Beaux Arts Bath

CERAMICS/GLASSWARE | This gallery, close by the Abbey, carries the work of prominent artists, potters, sculptors, painters, and printmakers. ⊠ *12–13 York St.* ☎ *01225/464850* ⊕ *www.beauxartsbath.co.uk.*

The charm of tiny Castle Combe, with its one main street of stone cottages, far exceeds its size.

Guildhall Market

OUTDOOR/FLEA/GREEN MARKETS | The covered Guildhall Market, open Monday through Saturday 9–5, is the place for everything from jewelry and gifts to delicatessen food, secondhand books, bags, and batteries. There's a café, too. ✉ *Entrances on High St. and Grand Parade* ⊕ *www.bathguildhallmarket. co.uk.*

Activities

Bath Boating Station

BOATING | To explore the River Avon by rented skiff, punt, or canoe, head for the Bath Boating Station, behind the Holburne Museum. It's open April to September. ✉ *Forester Rd.* ☎ *01225/312900* ⊕ *www.bathboating.co.uk.*

Castle Combe

12 miles northeast of Bath, 5 miles northwest of Chippenham.

This Wiltshire village lived a sleepy existence until 1962, when it was voted the "prettiest village" in England—without any of its inhabitants knowing that it had even been a contender. The village's magic is that it's so delightfully toylike, you can see almost the whole town at one glance from any one position. Castle Combe consists of little more than a brook, a pack bridge, a street (which is called the Street) of simple stone cottages, a market cross from the 13th century, and the Perpendicular-style church of St. Andrew. The grandest house in the village (on its outskirts) is the Upper Manor House, which was built in the 15th century by Sir John Fastolf and is now the Manor House Hotel. If you're coming by car, use the village parking lot at the top of the hill and walk down.

GETTING HERE AND AROUND

Regular buses and trains go to Chippenham, where you can pick up a bus for Castle Combe, but it's easier to drive or join a tour.

 Hotels

Lucknam Park Hotel & Spa

$$$ | HOTEL | Driving up Lucknam Park's mile-long avenue of lime and beech trees towards the 18th-century Palladian mansion, you may feel like you've bagged an invitation to stay with Jane Austen's demanding dragon, Lady Catherine de Burgh. **Pros:** attentive service; country estate setting; well-equipped spa. **Cons:** pricey; some rooms on the small side; a little off the beaten track. ⑤ *Rooms from: £275* ✉ *Colerne, Chippenham* ☎ *01225/742777* ⊕ *www.lucknampark. co.uk* ⇆ *42 rooms* ⦿❙ *Free breakfast.*

★ Manor House Hotel

$$$ | HOTEL | Secluded in a 23-acre park on the edge of the village, this partly 14th-century manor house has guest rooms—some in mews cottages—that brim with antique character. **Pros:** romantic getaway; rich historical setting; good golf course. **Cons:** some rooms not in main house; not for those who dislike sound of constant running water; might be too stuffy for some. ⑤ *Rooms from: £240* ✉ *Castle Combe* ☎ *01249/782206* ⊕ *www.exclusive.co.uk/the-manor-house* ⇆ *48 rooms* ⦿❙ *Free breakfast.*

Lacock

8 miles southeast of Castle Combe, 12 miles east of Bath.

Owned by the National Trust, this lovely Wiltshire village is the victim of its own charm, its unspoiled gabled and stone-tile cottages drawing tour buses aplenty. Off-season, however, Lacock slips back into its profound slumber, the mellow stone and brick buildings little changed in 500 years and well worth a wander. Besides Lacock Abbey, there's the handsome church of St. Cyriac (built with money earned in the wool trade), a 14th-century tithe barn, and, in the village, a few antiques shops and a scattering of pubs that serve bar meals in atmospheric surroundings.

GETTING HERE AND AROUND

All buses from Bath to Lacock involve a change and take 60 to 110 minutes, so it's best to drive or join a tour.

Sights

Lacock Abbey

HOUSE | Well-preserved Lacock Abbey reflects the fate of many religious establishments in England—a spiritual center became a home. The abbey, at the town's center, was founded in the 13th century and closed down during the dissolution of the monasteries in 1539, when its new owner, Sir William Sharington, demolished the church and converted the cloisters, sacristy, chapter house, and monastic quarters into a private dwelling. The house passed to the Talbot family, the most notable descendant of whom was William Henry Fox Talbot (1800–77), who developed the world's first photographic negative. You can see the oriel window, the subject of this photograph in the upper rooms of the abbey, along with a rare 16th-century purpose-built strong room in the octagonal tower. Look for the sugar lump on the goat's nose in the Great Hall. The last descendant, Matilda Talbot, donated the property as well as Lacock itself to the National Trust in the 1940s. The abbey's grounds and Victorian woodland are also worth a wander. Harry Potter fans, take note: Lacock Abbey was used for some scenes at Hogwarts School in the film *Harry Potter and the Sorcerer's Stone.*

The **Fox Talbot Museum,** in a 16th-century barn at the gates of Lacock Abbey, commemorates the work of Fox Talbot as well as other pioneers and contemporary artists in this field. ⊠ *High St.* ☎ *01249/730459* ⊕ *www.nationaltrust. org.uk* ⊠ *£15.20; excluding Abbey rooms £11.60.*

🍽 Restaurants

Sign of the Angel

$ | **BRITISH** | A 15th-century inn just five minutes from Lacock Abbey, Sign of the Angel serves traditional food in a cozy and intimate setting. Some dishes, such as the roast loin of beef with Yorkshire pudding or the seasonal pie of the day are as traditional as the decor, but modern touches— orange butter sauce, for instance—adds an extra dimension. **Known for:** historical and antique features; classic cream teas; traditional British pub fare. ⑤ *Average main: £15* ⊠ *6 Church St.* ☎ *01249/730230* ⊕ *www. signoftheangel.co.uk.*

Cheltenham

50 miles north of Bath, 13 miles east of Gloucester, 99 miles west of London.

Although Cheltenham has acquired a reputation as snooty—the population (around 110,000) is generally well-heeled and conservative—it's also cosmopolitan. The town has excellent restaurants and bars, fashionable stores, and a thriving cultural life. Its primary claim to renown, however, is its architecture, rivaling Bath's in its Georgian elegance, with wide, tree-lined streets, crescents, and terraces with row houses, balconies, and iron railings.

The Cotswolds

Like Bath, Cheltenham owes part of its fame to mineral springs. By 1740 the first spa was built, and after a visit from George III and Queen Charlotte in 1788, the town dedicated itself to idleness and enjoyment. "A polka, parson-worshipping place"—in the words of resident Lord Tennyson—Cheltenham gained its reputation for snobbishness when stiff-collared Raj majordomos returned from India to find that the springs—the only purely natural alkaline waters in England—were the most effective cure for their "tropical ailments."

Great Regency architectural set pieces—Lansdown Crescent, Pittville Spa, and the Lower Assembly Rooms, among them—were built solely to adorn the town. The Rotunda building (1826) at the top of Montpellier Walk—now a bank—contains the spa's original "pump room," in which the mineral waters were on tap. More than 30 statues adorn the storefronts of Montpellier Walk. Wander past Imperial Square, with its ironwork balconies, past the ornate Neptune's Fountain, and along the Promenade. In spring and summer, lush flower gardens enhance the town's buildings, attracting many visitors.

GETTING HERE AND AROUND
Trains from London Paddington and buses from London Victoria head to Cheltenham. The train station is west of the center, and the bus station is centrally located off Royal Well Road. Drivers should leave their vehicles in one of the numerous parking lots. The town center is easily negotiable on foot.

TOURS

Walking Tours of Regency Cheltenham

Leaving from the Wilson Museum & Tourist Information Centre at the main art gallery, Cheltenham's tourist office arranges walking tours of the town at 11 on Saturday from April until mid-October and on Sunday in July and August. ⊠ *Cheltenham Art Gallery and Museum, Clarence St.* ☎ *01242/387492* ⊕ *www. visitcheltenham.com* ✉ *From £6.*

 ## ◉ Sights

★ Gloucester Cathedral

RELIGIOUS SITE | In the center of Gloucester, magnificent Gloucester Cathedral, with its soaring, elegant exterior, was originally a Norman abbey church, consecrated in 1100. Reflecting different periods, the cathedral mirrors perfectly the slow growth of ecclesiastical taste and the development of the Perpendicular style. The interior has largely been spared the sterilizing attentions of modern architects and is almost completely Norman, with the massive pillars of the nave left untouched since their completion. The fan-vaulted roof of the 14th-century cloisters is the finest in Europe, and the cloisters enclose a peaceful garden (used in the filming of *Harry Potter and the Sorcerer's Stone*). ■TIP→ **Don't miss the Whispering Gallery, which has a permanent exhibition devoted to the splendid, 14th-century stained glass of the Great East Window.** Tours of the tower (269 steps up) are available, as are guided tours. Gloucester is 13 miles southwest of Cheltenham and reachable from there on frequent buses and trains. ⊠ *12 College Green* ☎ *01452/528095* ⊕ *www.gloucestercathedral.org.uk* ✉ *£5 requested donation, photography permit £3, tower tours £5* ۞ *Whispering Gallery closed during services.*

Pittville Pump Room

BUILDING | The grandest of the remaining spa buildings, the pump room is set amid parkland, a 20-minute walk from the town center. The classic Regency structure, built in the late 1820s, now serves mainly as a concert hall and a theatrical venue but still offers its musty mineral waters to the strong of stomach. It's wise to check before visiting as there's often a function taking place. ⊠ *E. Approach Dr.* ☎ *0844/576–2210* ⊕ *www. cheltenhamtownhall.org.uk* ✉ *Free* ۞ *Closed Mon. and Tues.*

★ The Wilson, Cheltenham Art Gallery and Museum

MUSEUM | From the 1880s onward, Cheltenham was at the forefront of the Arts and Crafts movement, and this is still demonstrated by the fine displays of William Morris textiles, furniture by Charles Voysey, and wood and metal pieces by Ernest Gimson at this museum and art gallery. Decorative arts, such as Chinese ceramics, are also well represented, and British artists, including Stanley Spencer, Vanessa Bell, and Jake and Dinos Chapman, make their mark. The Summerfield Galleries demonstrate life through the ages in easily digestible chunks. Exhibits on Cheltenham's history complete the picture; one is devoted to Edward Wilson, who traveled with Robert Scott to the Antarctic on Scott's ill-fated 1912 expedition. ⊠ *Clarence St.* ☎ *01242/237431* ⊕ *www. cheltenhammuseum.org.uk* ✉ *Suggested donation £4* ۞ *Galleries closed Mon.*

① Restaurants

Brasserie Blanc

$$ | MODERN FRENCH | Housed in the former ballroom of Queen's Hotel, this offshoot of renowned chef Raymond Blanc's Manoir aux Quat' Saisons in Great Milton offers French provincial cooking in contemporary surroundings that harmonize well with the expansive Regency windows. Though part of a chain of restaurants, it has an impressive menu that features a range of dishes from typical French cuisine to British favorites with a Gallic twist. **Known for:** French provincial cooking; good value set menus; stylish surroundings.

A tour of Gloucester Cathedral provides a visual lesson in architectural styles from Norman through Perpendicular Gothic.

⑤ *Average main: £16* ⊠ *The Promenade* ☎ *01242/266800* ⊕ *www.brasserie-blanc.com.*

The Coffee Dispensary

$ | **BRITISH** | Located in a former pharmacy, the Coffee Dispensary is a small independent café that sources its beans from single estates, aiming to bring the best flavors to the people of Cheltenham. It also serves cakes and savory snacks. **Known for:** the best coffee in Cheltenham; friendly vibe; sourcing from single-estate coffee producers. ⑤ *Average main: £3* ⊠ *18 Regent St.* ☎ *01242/260597* ⊕ *www.the-coffee-dispensary.co.uk.*

The Daffodil

$$ | **MODERN BRITISH** | Housed in a former art deco cinema, the Daffodil is themed along 1920s lines with a touch of glamour and an enticing menu. The menu features dishes like twice-baked Double Gloucester soufflé, calves' liver with mustard mash, and curry spiced chicken breast. **Known for:** 1920s decor and style; great cocktail menu; live jazz on Monday nights and Saturday afternoons.

⑤ *Average main: £19* ⊠ *18–20 Suffolk Parade* ☎ *01242/700055* ⊕ *www.thedaffodil.com* ⊗ *Closed Mon. and Tues.*

The Ivy Montpellier Brasserie

$$ | **BRITISH** | Set in an opulent Regency building with a statement bar, the Ivy Brasserie serves first-class food with British and European specialties. In its heyday, the Rotunda building was a bathing pool with spa water on tap, and its domed roof and seating area have been exquisitely restored to house the smart restaurant. **Known for:** gorgeous Regency building and dramatic bar; fun cocktails like salted caramel espresso martinis; weekend brunch menu. ⑤ *Average main: £17* ⊠ *Rotunda Terrace, Montpellier Walk* ☎ *01242/894200* ⊕ *www.theivycheltenhambrasserie.com.*

Purslane

$$ | **MODERN BRITISH** | Lured by the fresh ingredients and cool, unfussy surroundings, diners come here to enjoy the freshest of Cornish fish, Salcombe Bay crab, and Forest of Dean ham accompanied by unusual but delicious vegetables

Great Walks in the Cotswolds

The gentle Cotswolds countryside, designated an Area of Outstanding Natural Beauty, is threaded with more than 3,000 miles of pleasant walking routes that enable you to appreciate these upland tracts at their best. It's easy to plan an afternoon walk or a multiday exploration.

Waymarked routes crisscross the area, and none of them are too challenging. No specialized equipment is required; it's healthy, and it's free. Walks come in all lengths, but unless you decide to tackle one of the more ambitious regional trails, it may be easiest to pick a circular route. Just look for the "Public Footpath" and "Public Bridleway" signs, which indicate a right-of-way even when this passes through private property. Before you know it, you'll be opening gates and crossing stiles on the trails along with everyone else.

Choose Your Walking Route

The most celebrated route travers-ing the area is the **Cotswold Way** (⊕ *www.nationaltrail.co.uk*), a 102-mile national trail that traces the escarp-ment marking the western edge of the Cotswolds, stretching north to south between Chipping Campden and Bath and taking in Broadway, Winchcombe, and Painswick, among many other villages. The trail has incomparable views across the Severn Vale to the Malvern Hills and takes you through varied scenery: limestone grasslands crossed by drystone walls, beech woodlands, and stone-built villages

with ancient churches. You can select a route rather than walk the entire trail, which might take 7–10 days.

The **Heart of England Way** (⊕ *www. heartofenglandway.org*) runs a linear route from Bourton-on-the-Water north to Lower Slaughter, Bourton-on-the-Hill, and Chipping Campden, and continues north into the West Midlands. It's 104 miles in all, and the Cotswold section takes in hills and deep wooded valleys.

The **Warden's Way** and the **Windrush Way** both run between Winchcombe and Bourton-on-the-Water, 14-mile rambles that link the Cotswold Way (at Winchcombe) with the Oxfordshire Way (at Bourton-on-the-Water). The Warden's Way takes you through Upper and Lower Slaughter; the Windrush Way follows the meander-ing River Windrush and touches on Sudeley Castle, but without entering any village en route.

Part of the Cotswold Way can be incor-porated into an easy circular route between **Chipping Campden and Broadway**, along mostly level ground but including the elevated viewpoints of Dover's Hill and Broadway Tower. The circular route adds up to around 12 miles.

One of the most scenic Cotswolds walks explores the **Coln Valley**, a 6-mile circular route beginning and ending at Bibury. The path follows the banks of the lovely River Coln for part of the way, through meadows and woodland.

like borage, wild garlic, and sea cabbage. The accent is on fish, but you will also find hay-baked Cotswold lamb, vegetarian dishes, and plenty of local cheeses. **Known for:** focus on fresh seafood; unusual vegetables prepared creatively; menu of local cheeses. $ *Average main: £18 ⊠ 16 Rodney Rd.* ☎ *01242/321639* ⊕ *www.purslane-restaurant.co.uk* ⊘ *Closed Sun. and Mon.*

Well Walk Tea Room

$ | **CAFÉ** | Squeeze past all the antiques and knickknacks in this pretty bow-fronted shop and tearoom for a soup, pasta, or sandwich lunch, or treat yourself to an afternoon tea with crumpets and cakes. Along with traditional English Breakfast and Earl Grey, you can sample nettle and sweet fennel, jasmine, green, and white tea. **Known for:** family-run tearoom; quaint atmosphere; homemade lemonade in summer. $ *Average main: £3 ⊠ 5–6 Well Walk* ☎ *01242/574546* ⊕ *www.wellwalktearoom.co.uk* ⊘ *Closed Sun. and Mon. No dinner.*

Hotels

The Bradley

$ | **B&B/INN** | The thoughtful and hospitable owners take great pride in this town house, near the town center, that has been in the same family for more than 100 years. **Pros:** good value; attentive hosts; well-designed rooms. **Cons:** lots of stairs to top rooms; no private parking; some bathrooms are very small. $ *Rooms from: £115 ⊠ 19 Bayshill Rd.* ☎ *01242/519077* ⊕ *www.thebradleyhotel. co.uk* ↝ *10 rooms* ⦿| *Free breakfast* ↝ *No children under 11 are allowed.*

Cowley Manor

$$ | **HOTEL** | This Georgian mansion on 55 acres brings country-house style into the 21st century with a mellow atmosphere and modern fabrics and furnishings. **Pros:** beautiful grounds; excellent spa facilities; relaxed vibe. **Cons:** slightly corporate feel; spa is set away from the main house;

no elevator to second floor. $ *Rooms from: £205 ⊠ Off A435, Cowley* ☎ *01242/870900* ⊕ *www.cowleymanor. com* ↝ *30 rooms* ⦿| *Free breakfast.*

Malmaison Cheltenham

$ | **HOTEL** | Just around the corner from the calming Montpelier Gardens, the Malmaison's classic white building blends with the local architecture. **Pros:** quiet, beautiful rooms; short walk to Montpellier and the Suffolks; very relaxed atmosphere. **Cons:** limited parking; restaurant is sometimes closed for private functions; gets booked quickly at peak times. $ *Rooms from: £110 ⊠ Bayshill Rd.* ☎ *01242/370655* ⊕ *www.malmaison.com/locations/cheltenham* ↝ *60 rooms* ⦿| *Free breakfast.*

🎭 Performing Arts

Everyman Theatre

THEATER | The late-Victorian Everyman Theatre is an intimate venue for opera, dance, concerts, and plays. ■**TIP→ You can often catch pre– or post–West End productions here, at a fraction of big-city prices.** ⊠ *Regent St.* ☎ *01242/572573* ⊕ *www.everymantheatre.org.uk.*

Festivals Box Office

FESTIVALS | For information on the town's ambitious lineup of festivals, contact the Festivals Box Office via phone from Tuesday to Friday. ⊠ *109-111 Bath Rd.* ☎ *01242/850270 box office* ⊕ *www. cheltenhamfestivals.com.*

🛍 Shopping

This is serious shopping territory. A stroll along Montpellier Walk and then along the flower-bedecked Promenade brings you to high-end specialty stores and boutiques. A bubble-blowing Wishing Fish Clock, designed by Kit Williams, dominates the Regent Arcade, a modern shopping area behind the Promenade. A farmers' market enlivens the Promenade on the second and last Friday of the month.

Cavendish House

DEPARTMENT STORES | The town's oldest department store, now run by House of Fraser, stocks designer fashions. ✉ *32–48 The Promenade* ☏ *01242/521300* ⊕ *www.houseoffraser. co.uk/cheltenham-hof-store-2013.*

Martin & Co

JEWELRY/ACCESSORIES | This shop carries a good stock of classic and modern jewelry. ✉ *19 The Promenade* ☏ *01242/522821* ⊕ *www.martin-and-co.com.*

Q and C Militaria

SPECIALTY STORES | A treasure trove for military buffs, Q and C Militaria offers badges and medals, breastplates, helmets, coats of arms, and books. It's run by ex-soldiers. ✉ *22 Suffolk Rd.* ☏ *01242/519815* ⊕ *www.qcmilitaria.com.*

⚡ Activities

Cheltenham Racecourse

HORSE RACING/SHOW | Important steeplechase races take place at Cheltenham Racecourse, north of the town center. The Gold Cup awards crown the last day of the National Hunt Festival in mid-March. ✉ *Cheltenham Racecourse, Evesham Rd.* ☏ *0344/5793003 tickets, 01242/513014 general inquiries* ⊕ *www. thejockeyclub.co.uk/cheltenham.*

Winchcombe

7 miles northeast of Cheltenham.

The sleepy, unspoiled village of Winchcombe (population 4,500), once the capital of the Anglo-Saxon kingdom of Mercia, has some attractive half-timber and stone houses, as well as a clutch of appealing old inns serving food. A good place to escape the crowds, it's near Sudeley Castle and is also on several walking routes: the Cotswold Way; the Warden's Way and Windrush Way, both linking Winchcombe with Bourton-on-the-Water; and the Winchcombe Way, a 42-mile figure-eight trail around the northern Cotswolds. A three-day walking festival (⊕ *www.winchcombe-welcomeswalkers.com*) takes place here in mid-May.

GETTING HERE AND AROUND

Hourly Marchants buses take 20 minutes to get to Winchcombe from Cheltenham (no Sunday service). By car, take B4632, leading over the steep and panoramic Cleeve Hill.

ESSENTIALS

VISITOR INFORMATION **Winchcombe Tourist Information Centre.** ✉ *Town Hall, High St.* ☏ *01242/602925* ⊕ *www.winchcombe.co.uk.*

⊙ Sights

Belas Knap Long Barrow

ARCHAEOLOGICAL SITE | A bracing 2-mile walk south of Winchcombe on the Cotswold Way, one of Britain's national walking trails, leads to the hilltop site of Belas Knap, a Neolithic long barrow, or submerged burial chamber, above Humblebee Wood. ■TIP→ **The site isn't much to see, but you hike through one of the most enchanting natural domains in England, with views stretching over to Sudeley Castle.** ✉ *Winchcombe* ☏ *0370/333–1181* ⊕ *www.english-heritage.org.uk/visit/ places/belas-knap-long-barrow.*

Gloucestershire and Warwickshire Railway

TRANSPORTATION SITE (AIRPORT/BUS/FERRY/TRAIN) | FAMILY | Less than a mile north of Winchcombe at Greet, this steam-hauled train, run by a team of volunteers, chugs its way along the foot of the Cotswolds connecting Winchcombe with Toddington, Cheltenham Racecourse, and the northern hub at Broadway. ✉ *Winchcombe Station, Greet Rd.* ☏ *01242/621405* ⊕ *www.gwsr.com* 🎫 *£13 round-trip to Cheltenham, all-day rover ticket £20* ⊗ *Closed Nov., Jan., Feb.; Mon. and Fri. year-round; and weekdays Mar. and Dec.*

As enchanting as the house, the gardens at Sudeley Castle provide a perfect spot for summer meanderings.

St. Peter's Church

RELIGIOUS SITE | Almost 40 outlandish gargoyles adorn this mid-15th-century Perpendicular-style building, a typical Cotswold wool church full of light. The interior displays an embroidered altar frontal said to have been worked by Catherine of Aragon, first wife of King Henry VIII. Look for the Winchcombe Imp, an unusual figure for a rood screen, now at the back of the church. ✉ *Gloucester St.* ☎ *01242/602067* ⊕ *www.winchcombeparish.org.uk.*

★ Sudeley Castle

CASTLE/PALACE | One of the grand showpieces of the Cotswolds, Sudeley Castle was the home and burial place of Catherine Parr (1512–48), Henry VIII's sixth and last wife, who outlived him by one year. Here Catherine undertook, in her later years, the education of the ill-fated Lady Jane Grey and the future queen, Princess Elizabeth. Sudeley, for good reason, has been called a woman's castle. The term "castle" is misleading, though, for it looks more like a Tudor-era palace, with a peaceful air that belies its turbulent history. In

the 17th century Charles I took refuge here, causing Oliver Cromwell's army to besiege the castle. It remained in ruins until the Dent-Brocklehurst family stepped in with a 19th-century renovation.

The 14 acres of gardens, which include the roses of the Queen's Garden (best seen in June) and a Tudor knot garden, are the setting for Tudor fun days in summer. Inside the castle, visitors see the West Wing, with the Long Room where exhibitions illustrate the castle's history, and the East Wing which contains the private apartments of Lord and Lady Ashcombe, where you can see paintings by Van Dyck, Rubens, Turner, and Reynolds. Art tours can also be booked in advance. Rare and exotically colored birds strut in the pheasantry. The 11 cottages and apartments on the grounds are booked for a minimum of three-night stays. The castle is a mile southeast of Winchcombe. ✉ *Off B4632* ☎ *01242/604244, 01242/609481 cottages* ⊕ *www.sudeleycastle.co.uk* 🎫 *£17.25* ⊗ *Closed mid-Dec.–mid-Feb.*

🍴 Restaurants

Wesley House

$$ | MODERN BRITISH | Wooden beams and stone walls distinguish this 15th-century half-timber building, where the elegant dining room and sunny conservatory make a fine backdrop for superior Modern British dishes. You can eat and drink less formally in the adjoining snug or bar and grill, where sharing platters of cheeses, cured meats, or fish lets you sample a bit of everything. **Known for:** affordable prix-fixe lunch and evening menus; historic building; sophisticated seasonal dishes. $ *Average main: £16* ✉ *High St.* ☎ *01242/602366* ⊕ *www.wesleyhouse. co.uk* ⊘ *Closed Mon. No dinner Sun.*

Broadway

8 miles north of Winchcombe, 17 miles northeast of Cheltenham.

The Cotswold town to end all Cotswold towns, Broadway has become a favorite of day-trippers. William Morris first discovered the delights of this village, and J. M. Barrie, Vaughan Williams, and Edward Elgar soon followed. Today you may want to avoid Broadway in summer, when it's clogged with cars and buses. Named for its handsome, wide main street (well worth a stroll), the village includes numerous antiques shops, tea parlors, and boutiques. Step into Broadway's back-roads and alleys and you can discover any number of honey-color houses and colorful gardens.

GETTING HERE AND AROUND

Broadway can be reached by car via A44; park in one of the lots signposted from the main street. Johnson's Coaches connects the town with Stratford-upon-Avon, Chipping Campden, and Moreton-in-Marsh; Marchants connects Broadway with Winchcombe and Cheltenham. No buses run on Sunday. You'll need a car to reach Broadway Tower, Stanway House, and Snowshill Manor.

ESSENTIALS

VISITOR INFORMATION Broadway Tourist Information Centre. ✉ *Russell Sq.* ☎ *01386/852937* ⊕ *www. broadway-cotswolds.co.uk/ tourist-information-centre.*

👁 Sights

Broadway Tower Country Park

NATIONAL/STATE PARK | Among the attractions of this park on the outskirts of town is its crenelated tower, an 18th-century "folly" built by the sixth earl of Coventry and later used by William Morris as a retreat. The panoramic view from the top takes in three counties and looks over peaceful countryside and wandering deer. There are plenty of nature trails and good spots for picnics, as well as a café. Wall panels on the three floors inside describe the tower's connection with the local Arts and Crafts movement and World War II. Note that the spiral staircase is narrow and steep. A nuclear bunker is open on weekends during the summer. ✉ *Middle Hill, off A44* ☎ *01386/852390* ⊕ *www. broadwaytower.co.uk* 🎫 *Park free, tower £5, bunker £4.50.*

★ Snowshill Manor

HOUSE | FAMILY | Three miles south of Broadway and 13 miles northeast of Cheltenham, Snowshill is one of the most unspoiled of all Cotswold villages. Snuggled beneath Oat Hill, with little room for expansion, the hamlet is centered on an old burial ground, the 19th-century St. Barnabas Church, and Snowshill Manor, a splendid 17th-century house that brims with the collections of Charles Paget Wade, gathered between 1919 and 1956. Over the door of the house is Wade's family motto, *Nequid pereat* ("Let nothing perish"). The rooms are bursting with Tibetan scrolls, spinners' tools, ship models, Persian lamps, and bric-a-brac; the Green Room displays 26 suits of Japanese samurai armor. Outside, an imaginative terraced garden provides an exquisite frame for the house. ■TIP➡ **Admission is by timed tickets issued on a first-come, first-served basis, so arrive early in peak season.** ⊠ *Off A44, Snowshill* ☎ *01386/852410* ⊕ *www. nationaltrust.org.uk/snowshill-man-or-and-garden* 🎟 *£12.80; garden only £7.60* ⊗ *Closed Nov.–mid-Mar.*

Stanway House & Fountain

HOUSE | This perfect Cotswold manor of glowing limestone, Stanway House dates from the Jacobean era. Its triple-gabled gatehouse is a Cotswold landmark, and towering windows dominate the house's Great Hall. They illuminate a 22-foot-long shuffleboard table from 1620 and an 18th-century bouncing exercise machine. The other well-worn rooms are adorned with family portraits, tattered tapestries, vintage armchairs, and, at times, Lord or Lady Neidpath themselves, the current owners. The partly restored baroque water garden has a modern fountain that shoots up 300 feet. The tallest in Britain, it shoots at 2:45 and 4. To get to Stanway, about 5 miles south of Broadway, take B4632 south from town, turning left at B4077. ■TIP➡ **Admission to the house and fountain is cash-only.** ⊠ *Off B4077, Stanway* ☎ *01386/584469* ⊕ *www. stanwayfountain.co.uk* 🎟 *House and fountain £11; fountain only £7* ⊗ *Closed Sept.–May, Fri.–Mon., and Wed.*

🍴 Restaurants

Broadway Deli

$ | **BRITISH** | A bustling small café, Broadway Deli serves breakfasts, coffee, and light lunches. You can browse local cheeses, honey, fresh fruit, and vegetables amid a constant stream of locals and visitors alike. **Known for:** friendly store with a community spirit; local specialties; great coffee. ⑤ *Average main: £7* ⊠ *St. Patricks, 29 High St.* ☎ *01386/853040* ⊕ *www.broadwaydeli.co.uk* ⊗ *Closed Sun. and Mon.*

Russell's

$$$ | **MODERN BRITISH** | With a courtyard at the back and a patio at the front, this chic "restaurant with rooms" is perfect for a light lunch at midday or a full meal in the evening. Menus concentrate on Modern British dishes and change seasonally. **Known for:** good-value fixed-price menu; fresh local produce; stylish setting. ⑤ *Average main: £25* ⊠ *20 High St.* ☎ *01386/853555* ⊕ *www.russellsofbroadway.co.uk* ⊗ *No dinner Sun.*

The Swan

$ | **MODERN BRITISH** | **FAMILY** | In the center of Broadway, this pub-restaurant makes a handy stop for a snack, lunch, drink, or something more substantial. Among the hot dishes you're likely to find slow-cooked corned salt-beef hash or sticky crispy duck salad; tapots (small British tapas-style dishes) and tasting platters are a popular alternative. **Known for:** hearty pub food; cask ales; Sunday lunch menu. ⑤ *Average main: £15* ⊠ *2 The Green* ☎ *01386/852278* ⊕ *www.theswanbroadway.co.uk.*

🛏 Hotels

Dormy House Hotel

$$$ | **HOTEL** | Luxury rules at this converted 17th-century farmhouse overlooking the Vale of Evesham, two miles north of Broadway. **Pros:** unstuffy service; good food; great views. **Cons:** steep prices; isolated; can get very busy. ⑤ *Rooms from: £270* ⊠ *Willersey Hill* ☎ *01386/852711* ⊕ *www.dormyhouse.co.uk* 🍴 *40 rooms* ⦿❘ *Free breakfast.*

★ Lygon Arms

$$$ | **HOTEL** | Occupying a sprawling 600 year-old coaching inn on High Street, the Lygon Arms is a charming warren, filled with cozy nooks for afternoon tea, a separate wine bar, a vaulted dining hall serving locally-sourced menus, and plush luxury at every turn. **Pros:** excellent food; beautiful, historical setting with all modern amenities; great staff and service.

Continued on page 440

GLORIOUS ENGLISH GARDENS

by Kate Hughes

The English have been masters of the garden for centuries; gardening is in the blood. No one, from the owner of vast acres in the country to a town dweller with a modest window box, is able to resist this pull. Since the 18th century they have also been inveterate garden visitors, with people from around the world following in their wake. Here's how to make the most of your garden visit, from the variety of styles you'll see to the best bets for all tastes around England.

Magnificent vista of the Palladian bridge and lake at Stourhead gardens.

For many people the quintessential English garden conjures up swaths of close-clipped lawns (the landscape garden), beds of roses, or colorful flowers (the herbaceous border) lining a path to a cottage door framed with honeysuckle.

This is not the whole story, however. Cathedrals and colleges yield up their sequestered cloister gardens; grand houses their patterned beds of flowers by the thousand; manor houses their amusing topiary shapes, orchards, and wildflower meadows; sweeping landscaped parks their classical temples and serpentine lakes; a Cornish ravine its jungle tumbling down to the sea. And this is not to mention the magnificent glasshouses and biomes of the botanical gardens housing spectacular plant treasures. Around the country, gardens large and small invite exploration.

GARDEN STYLES THROUGH THE AGES

In the gardens you'll be visiting, one theme remains constant no matter the style: the combination of usefulness and beauty. Gardens were larders as well as ornaments; plants were grown and birds and animals kept both for decoration and for eating. Behind each great garden was wealth, and gardens became as great a status symbol as the houses they surrounded. Growing the best pineapple, building the most elaborate terraces, flooding a valley to make a lake were all signs that you had made it in the world.

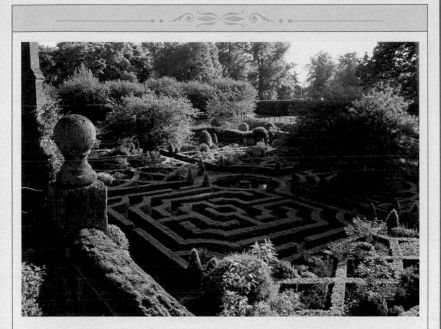

SYMBOLS AND PATTERNS: TUDOR GARDENS

Since Tudor times the rose has been the emblem of England, and it still is the most loved English flower. Musk roses entwine the arbors in the garden created to impress Queen Elizabeth I on her visit to Kenilworth Castle in 1575, now magnificently restored. Here the formal arrangement of trellises, obelisks, fountain, statues, and aviary set in gravel paths and overlooked by a viewing platform exemplify gardens of the time. Also here is the first uniquely English garden feature—the knot garden. Low evergreen hedges, most famously planted with box, were interlaced in geometric patterns, the spaces filled with flowers and herbs. Good examples of knot gardens can be found at Hampton Court Palace and Hatfield House.

WEALTH AND POWER: THE 17TH-CENTURY FORMAL GARDEN

Landed gentry with time on their hands took gardening to their hearts. After the ravages of the Civil War (1642–49) and the Great Fire of London (1666) they felt the lure of the rural idyll, and country houses with small estates proliferated. The garden rectangle in front of the house was divided into smaller rectangles—the forerunner of garden "rooms" as at Sissinghurst and Hidcote Manor—and filled with formal walkways, fishponds, and fountains. Topiary gardens (Levens Hall and Packwood House) became popular, and an increase in foreign travel led to the introduction of a greater variety of bulbs and flowers. In 1621 the first botanic garden was set up in Oxford.

Opposite page clockwise from top left: Stowe Landscape Gardens; Chatsworth; Hidcote Manor Garden
Above: Hampton Court Palace (formal Privy Garden) Knot garden at Hatfield House

GEOMETRY TO LANDSCAPE: THE 18TH CENTURY

Gradually the formal approach gave way. One product of the fashionable Grand Tour, when aristocratic young bloods were exposed to new landscapes and ideas, was William Kent (1685–1748), the "father of modern gardening." His innovative genius was his English take on the Italian garden, converting the natural landscape into a pleasure ground for the rich, dotting it with statues, obelisks, and classical temples and ornamenting it with trees and serpentine lakes (Rousham and Stowe).

Kent was eclipsed by Lancelot "Capability" Brown (1715–83), who created 100 gardens between 1750 and 1780 (Stowe, Stourhead, Petworth, Kew Gardens). He brought the landscape right to the front door and created lakes and parkland that also provided timber, cover for game, and grazing for sheep and deer.

SHOW AND TECHNOLOGY: THE VICTORIAN PERIOD

This was an age of new technology, variety, and the return of flowers. Wealthy industrialists could afford to move out of town and create rose gardens, ferneries, and rockeries, and display showier flowers such as chrysanthemums, dahlias, and rhododendrons. The invention of the lawn mower in 1830 made the English obsession with close-clipped lawns accessible to all. Bedding schemes and patterns reappeared in the new public parks of the 1830s and 1840s. One spectacular scheme is the parterre (ornamental flower garden with paths) at Waddesdon Manor, planted with lavish displays each spring and summer. Joseph Paxton (1803–1865) head gardener at Chatworth, created the first greenhouse, which started a fashion for conservatories and the growing of exotic fruit such as figs and peaches.

The parterre at Waddesdon Manor

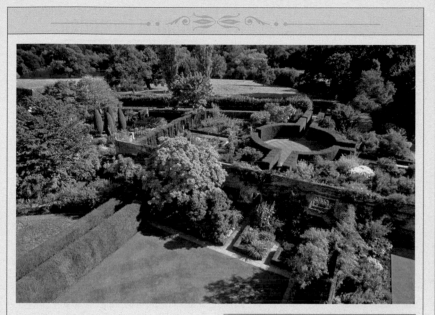

ARTS AND CRAFTS: INTO THE 20TH CENTURY

The Arts and Crafts movement drew inspiration from medieval romance and nature and preferred the informal cottage garden look, seen particularly in the Cotswolds (Hidcote Manor, Kiftsgate, Rodmarton Manor). Female gardeners came to the fore. Gertrude Jekyll (pronounced Jee-kill; 1843–1932), often working with the architect Edwin Lutyens (1869–1944), set the fashion for using drifts of single color, and Vita Sackville West (1892–1962) created the enduringly romantic Sissinghurst.

ANYTHING GOES: MODERN TIMES

The reaction to the drab years of the Second World War was to create garden cities and increasingly versatile gardens using all modern materials available. The bold approach and strong colors of Christopher Lloyd (1921–2006) at Great Dixter has remained influential. Environmental awareness has led to more educational gardens, such as the spectacular Eden Project in Cornwall.

Overview of part of Sissinghurst (top); house and garden at Great Dixter (bottom)

Cons: a tad pricy; rooms vary in size; old building with lots of stairs and uneven floors. ⑤ *Rooms from: £245* ✉ *High St.* ☎ *01386/852255* ⊕ *www.lygonarmshotel.co.uk* ↝ *82 rooms* ⦿ *Free breakfast.*

Mill Hay House

$$ | B&B/INN | If the rose garden, trout-filled pond, and sheep on the hill at this 18th-century Queen Anne house aren't appealing enough, then the stone-flagged floors, leather sofas, and grandfather clocks should satisfy. **Pros:** delightful owners; beautifully landscaped gardens; gourmet breakfasts. **Cons:** books up quickly; two-night minimum stay for most of the year; entrance can be hard to find. ⑤ *Rooms from: £195* ✉ *Snowshill Rd.* ☎ *01386/852498* ⊕ *www.millhay.co.uk* ↝ *3 rooms* ⦿ *Free breakfast* ↝ *No young children allowed.*

Old Station House

$ | B&B/INN | With its acre of lawns and gardens, this former stationmaster's home, now a bed-and-breakfast, makes a peaceful refuge from the tourist traffic of Broadway, a 10-minute walk away. **Pros:** thoughtful and welcoming hosts; peaceful location; Wi-Fi available. **Cons:** outside the village; lacks old-world ambience; not good for young families. ⑤ *Rooms from: £120* ✉ *Station Rd.* ☎ *01386/852659* ⊕ *www.broadwaybedandbreakfast.com* ↝ *4 rooms* ⦿ *Free breakfast* ↝ *No children under 12.*

The Olive Branch

$$ | B&B/INN | Right on the main drag, this 16th-century cottage has authentic period charm and is strewn with antique knickknacks like a brass wind-up gramophone. **Pros:** cottage character; central location; hospitable hosts. **Cons:** small bathrooms; narrow stairs; low ceilings. ⑤ *Rooms from: £130* ✉ *78 High St.* ☎ *01386/853440* ⊕ *www.theolivebranch-broadway.com* ↝ *8 rooms* ⦿ *Free breakfast.*

Chipping Campden

4 miles east of Broadway, 18 miles north-east of Cheltenham.

Undoubtedly one of the most beautiful towns in the area, Chipping Campden, with its population of about 2,500, is the Cotswolds in a microcosm. It has St. James, the region's most impressive church; frozen-in-time streets; a silk mill that was once the center of the Guild of Handicraft; and pleasant, untouristy shops. One of the area's most seductive settings unfolds before you as you travel on B4081 through sublime English countryside and happen upon the town, tucked in a slight valley. North of town is lovely Hidcote Manor Garden. ∎**TIP→ Chipping Campden can easily be reached on foot along a level section of the Cotswold Way from Broadway Tower, outside Broadway; the walk takes about 75 minutes.**

GETTING HERE AND AROUND

By car, Chipping Campden can be reached on minor roads from A44 or A429. There's a small car park in the center and spaces on the outskirts of the village. By bus, take Johnson's Coaches from Stratford-upon-Avon, Broadway, and Moreton-in-Marsh, or Pulham's Coaches from Bourton-on-the-Water and Cheltenham, changing at Moreton-in-Marsh (no Sunday service).

ESSENTIALS

VISITOR INFORMATION Chipping Campden Tourism Information Centre. ✉ *The Old Police Station, High St.* ☎ *01386/841206* ⊕ *www.chippingcampdenonline.org.*

⦿ Sights

Court Barn Museum

MUSEUM | Near the church of St. James, this museum occupies an old agricultural building that has been smartly renovated to showcase the area's prominence in the fields of craft and design. You can admire examples of silverware, ceramics, printing, woodcarving, jewelry, and cutlery, as well as changing exhibitions. Opposite the barn is an important row of almshouses dating from the reign of King James I. ⊠ *Church St.* ☎ *01386/841951* ⊕ *www.courtbarn.org.uk* ⊠ *£5* ⊗ *Closed Mon. except bank holidays.*

Guild of Handicraft

HISTORIC SITE | In 1902, the Guild of Handicraft took over this former silk mill. Arts and Crafts evangelist Charles Robert Ashbee (1863–1942) brought 150 acolytes from London, including 50 guildsmen, to revive and practice such skills as cabinetmaking and bookbinding. The operation folded in 1920, but the refurbished building now houses the intriguing and very full workshop of a silversmith and has a café and gallery on the ground floor. ⊠ *The Old Silk Mill, Sheep St.* ☎ *01386/840345* ⊕ *www. thegalleryattheguild.co.uk* ⊠ *Free* ⊗ *Workshop closed Sun.*

★ Hidcote Manor Garden

GARDEN | Laid out around a Cotswold manor house, Hidcote Manor Garden is arguably the most interesting and attractive large garden in Britain. Crowds are large at the height of the season, but it's worthwhile anytime. A horticulturist from the United States, Major Lawrence Johnston, created the garden in 1907 in the Arts and Crafts style. Johnston was an imaginative gardener and avid traveler who brought back specimens from all over the world. The formal part of the garden is arranged in "rooms" separated by hedges and often with fine topiary work and walls. Besides the variety of plants, what's impressive are the different effects created, from calm open spaces to areas packed with flowers. ■TIP→ **Look for one of Johnston's earliest schemes, the red borders of dahlias, poppies, fuchsias, lobelias, and roses; the tall hornbeam hedges; and the Bathing Pool garden, where the pool is so wide there's scarcely space to walk.** The White

Garden was probably the forerunner of the popular white gardens at Sissinghurst and Glyndebourne. If you have time, explore the tiny village of Hidcote Bartrim with its thatched stone houses; it borders the garden and fills a storybook dell. The garden is 4 miles northeast of Chipping Campden. ⊠ *Hidcote Bartrim* ☎ *01386/438333* ⊕ *www.nationaltrust. org.uk/hidcote* ⊠ *£14.20* ⊗ *Closed late Dec.–mid-Feb. and weekdays Nov.–mid-Dec.*

Kiftsgate Court Gardens

GARDEN | While not as spectacular as Hidcote Manor Garden, this intimate, privately-owned garden, just a five-minute stroll away, still captivates. It's skipped by the majority of visitors to Hidcote, so you won't be jostled by the crowds. The interconnecting flower beds present harmonious arrays of color, and the contemporary formal water garden adds an elegant contrast. Don't miss the prized Kiftsgate rose, supposed to be the largest in England, flowering gloriously in mid-July. ⊠ *Off B4081, Mickleton* ☎ *01386/438777* ⊕ *www.kiftsgate.co.uk* ⊠ *£9* ⊗ *Closed Oct.–Mar., Thurs. and Fri. year-round, and Sat. and Tues. Apr. and Sept.*

Market Hall

BUILDING | The broad High Street, lined with stone houses and shops, follows a captivating curve. In the center, on Market Street, is the Market Hall, a gabled Jacobean structure built by Sir Baptiste Hycks in 1627 "for the sale of local produce." ⊠ *Market St.*

St. James

RELIGIOUS SITE | The soaring pinnacled tower of St. James, a prime example of a Cotswold wool church (it was rebuilt in the 15th century with money from wool merchants), announces Chipping Campden from a distance; it's worth stepping inside to see the lofty, light-filled nave. The church recalls the old saying, which became popular because of the vast numbers of houses of worship in the Cotswolds, "As sure as

God's in Gloucestershire." ⊠ *Church St.*
☎ *01386/841927* ⊕ *www.stjameschurch-*
campden.co.uk 🎫 *£3 donation suggested.*

🍴 Restaurants

★ Churchill Arms

$$ | MODERN BRITISH | FAMILY | With chef
Neil Deverell-Smith at the helm, this
is the epitome of cozy Cotswolds fine
dining. In the small country pub just outside Chipping Campden, plain wooden
tables and benches, a flagstone floor,
light-colored walls, and a roaring fire
provide the backdrop for excellent food.
Known for: British classics reimagined;
family-run atmosphere; a focus on local
produce and gin. [$] *Average main: £16*
⊠ *Paxford, Off B4479* ☎ *01386/593159*
⊕ *www.churchillarms.co.*

Eight Bells

$ | BRITISH | Close to St. James Church,
this traditional tavern has low beams, a
flagstone floor, and a small courtyard. The
long menu includes daily specials, local
ales, and enticing dishes like confit duck
and deep-fried fish-and-chips. **Known
for:** historic pub with lots of character;
affordable ciabatta sandwich lunches; local beers. [$] *Average main: £14*
⊠ *Church St.* ☎ *01386/840371* ⊕ *www.*
eightbellsinn.co.uk.

Huxleys

$$ | CAFÉ | At this beamed and buzzing lit-
tle café, locals drop in to discuss horses
and dogs over a glass of wine, families
gather around the big round table for
lunch, and tired shoppers sink into arm-
chairs for a reviving coffee. The Italian-in-
spired menu is filled with light dishes
like antipasti, bruschetta, soups, baked
potatoes, and salads. **Known for:** Italian
light bites; superb coffee and cakes; terrace for outdoor dining. [$] *Average main:*
£16 ⊠ *High St.* ☎ *01386/849077* ⊕ *www.*
huxleys.org ⊘ *No dinner Sun.–Wed.*

🛏 Hotels

Badgers Hall

$$ | B&B/INN | Expect a friendly welcome
at this antique B&B above a tearoom
just across from the Market Hall,
where the spacious, spotless rooms
have beamed ceilings and exposed
stonework. **Pros:** atmospheric building;
attentive hosts; delicious breakfasts.
Cons: low ceilings; entrance is through
tea shop; two-night minimum stay
required. [$] *Rooms from: £155* ⊠ *High*
St. ☎ *01386/840839* ⊕ *www.badger-*
shall.com 🛏 *4 rooms* ⦿ *Free breakfast*
☞ *No kids under 10.*

Charingworth Manor

$ | HOTEL | Views of the countryside
are limitless from this 14th-century
manor-house hotel where mullioned
windows and oak beams enhance the
sitting room. **Pros:** helpful and friendly
staff; great breakfasts; lots of amenities.
Cons: some low beams in bedrooms;
a lot of birds on property; decor a bit
dated. [$] *Rooms from: £120* ⊠ *Off B4035*
☎ *01386/593555, 08446/593555* ⊕ *www.*
classiclodges.co.uk/charingworth-manor
🛏 *26 rooms* ⦿ *Free breakfast.*

Cotswold House Hotel and Spa

$$ | HOTEL | This luxury hotel in the heart
of Chipping Campden injects contemporary design into a stately 18th-century
manor house, and from the swirling
staircase in the entrance to the individually designed guest rooms studded with
contemporary art, it's a winning formula.
Pros: plenty of pampering; pleasant
garden; personalized service. **Cons:**
some bathrooms are small; additional
charge to use spa; no swimming pool.
[$] *Rooms from: £150* ⊠ *The Square*
☎ *01386/840330* ⊕ *www.bespokeho-*
tels.com/cotswoldhouse 🛏 *28 rooms*
⦿ *Free breakfast.*

Arts and Crafts in the Cotswolds

The Arts and Crafts movement flourished throughout Britain in the late 19th and early 20th centuries, but the Cotswolds are most closely associated with it. The godfather of the movement was designer William Morris (1834–96), whose home for the last 25 years of his life, Kelmscott Manor in Gloucestershire, became the headquarters of the school. A lecture by Morris, "The Beauty of Life," delivered in Birmingham in 1880, included the injunction that became the guiding principle of the movement: "Have nothing in your houses which you do not know to be useful or believe to be beautiful."

Driven by the belief that the spirit of medieval arts and crafts was being degraded and destroyed by the mass production and aggressive capitalism of the Victorian era, and aided by a dedicated core of artisans, Morris revolutionized the art of house design and decoration. His work with textiles was particularly influential.

Where to See It

Many of Morris's followers were influenced by the Cotswold countryside, such as the designer and architect Charles Robert Ashbee, who transferred his Guild of Handicraft from London to Chipping Campden in 1902. The village holds the small Court Barn Museum dedicated to local craftwork, including a permanent exhibition of pieces by the original group and those who followed in their wake.

Their work can also be seen at the Wilson, Cheltenham Art Gallery and Museum, and, in its original context, at Rodmarton Manor outside Tetbury—which Ashbee declared the finest application of the movement's ideals. (Farther afield, Blackwell in the Lake District is a notable Arts and Crafts house.)

To see the Arts and Crafts ethic applied to horticulture, visit Hidcote Manor Garden, near Chipping Campden.

Noel Arms Hotel

$$ | HOTEL | Dating to the 14th century, Chipping Campden's oldest inn was built to accommodate foreign wool traders, and even though it's been enlarged, the building retains its exposed beams and stonework. **Pros:** traditional character; friendly staff; excellent curries at restaurant. **Cons:** rooms can be noisy and overheated; annex overlooks car park; some rooms are small. $ *Rooms from: £125* ✉ *High St.* ☎ *0844/8159833* ⊕ *www. bespokehotels.com/noelarmshotel* 28 *rooms* ❍❘ *Free breakfast.*

🛍 Shopping

Hart

JEWELRY/ACCESSORIES | Descendants of an original member of the Guild of Handicraft specialize in fashioning lovely items from silver at this shop. ✉ *Guild of Handicraft, Sheep St.* ☎ *01386/841100* ⊕ *www.hartsilversmiths.co.uk.*

Stuart House Antiques

ANTIQUES/COLLECTIBLES | Three bay windows filled with silverware and copperware, porcelain, Doulton figurines, and Staffordshire figures show you only a fraction of what's available here over two floors overflowing with antiques. ✉ *High St.* ☎ *01386/840995* ⊕ *www.antiques-at-las.com/stuarthouseantiques.*

Moreton-in-Marsh

5 miles south of Chipping Campden, 18 miles northeast of Cheltenham, 5 miles north of Stow-on-the-Wold.

In Moreton-in-Marsh, the houses have been built not around a central square but along a street wide enough to accommodate a market. The village has fine views across the hills. One local landmark, St. David's Church, has a tower of honey-gold ashlar. This town of about 3,500 also possesses one of the last remaining curfew towers, dated 1633. Curfew dates to the time of the Norman Conquest, when a bell was rung to "cover-fire" for the night against any invaders.

GETTING HERE AND AROUND

Moreton-in-Marsh is on the A429 north of Cirencester. Park along the main street or in the lot on Station Road. The town has a train station with frequent connections to London Paddington. There are good bus services except on Sundays. Pulham's Coaches connect with Cirencester, Cheltenham, Stow-on-the-Wold, and Bourton-on-the-Water; Johnson's Coaches with Stratford-upon-Avon, Chipping Campden, and Broadway. For Sezincote, a car is necessary.

ESSENTIALS

VISITOR INFORMATION Moreton-in-Marsh Visitor Information Centre. ⊠ *Moreton Area Centre, High St., Moreton in Marsh* ☎ *01608/650881* ⊕ *www.cotswolds.com.*

◉ Sights

Rollright Stones

ARCHAEOLOGICAL SITE | A reminder of the ancient civilizations of Britain can be seen about 8 miles east of Moreton, where three stone groups occupy a high position on the wolds. The site lacks the grandeur of Stonehenge and Avebury, but has a peace and beauty of its own and is almost as important. Legend gives the stones, dating from before 1500 BC, the names of the King's Men, the King Stone, and the Whispering Knights. ⊠ *Off A3400, Moreton in Marsh* ⊕ *www.english-heritage.org.uk* ☞ *£2 donation requested.*

Sezincote

GARDEN | It comes as somewhat of a surprise to see the blue onion domes and miniature minarets of Sezincote, a mellow stone house and garden tucked into a valley near Moreton-in-Marsh. Created in the early 19th century, Sezincote (pronounced *see*-zincot) was the vision of Sir Charles Cockerell, who made a fortune in the East India Company. He employed his architect brother, Samuel Pepys Cockerell, to "Indianize" the residence with Hindu and Muslim motifs. Note the peacock-tail arches surrounding the windows of the first floor. The exotic garden, Hindu temple folly, and Indian-style bridge were favorites of the future George IV, who was inspired to create that Xanadu of Brighton, the Royal Pavilion. If you come in spring, glorious aconites and snowdrops greet you. Children under 10 are allowed inside only at the owners' discretion. ⊠ *Off A44, Moreton in Marsh* ☎ *01386/700444* ⊕ *www. sezincote.co.uk* ☞ *House and grounds £10; grounds only £5* ☽ *House closed Oct.–Apr. and Sat.–Wed.*

Tuesday Market

MARKET | Supposed to be the largest street market in the Cotswolds, the Tuesday Market takes over the center of the main street between 8 am and 3:30 pm, with a mix of household goods, fruits and vegetables, and some arts-and-crafts and jewelry stalls. It's no newcomer to the market scene either: it was chartered in 1227. ⊠ *High St., Moreton in Marsh.*

🍴 Restaurants

Horse and Groom

$ | **MODERN BRITISH** | Located between Broadway and Moreton-in-Marsh, this laid-back Cotswold pub has its dishes of the day (all made with local seasonal ingredients) written on the chalkboard inside. Options might include Dexter sirloin steak with watercress, shallot, and horseradish butter or a beetroot-and-thyme risotto. **Known for:** busy crowds; beautiful garden for dining outside; good menu for kids. $ *Average main: £14* ✉ *Bourton-on-the-Hill, Moreton in Marsh* ☎ *01386/700413* ⊕ *www.horseandgroom.info.*

🛏 Hotels

Manor House Hotel

$$ | **HOTEL** | Secret passageways and a priest hole testify to the age of this 16th-century building, where the mullioned windows, original stonework, and log fires in winter are tastefully balanced by smart, contemporary furnishings in the public areas. **Pros:** accommodating staff; historical ambience; set back from the main road. **Cons:** smallish rooms; lots of stairs; some noise intrusion. $ *Rooms from: £160* ✉ *High St., Moreton in Marsh* ☎ *01608/650501* ⊕ *www.cotswold-inns-hotels.co.uk/the-manor-house-hotel* ⤴ *35 rooms* ⦿ *Free breakfast.*

Stow-on-the-Wold

5 miles south of Moreton-in-Marsh, 15 miles east of Cheltenham.

At an elevation of 800 feet, Stow is the highest town in the Cotswolds—"Stow-on-the-Wold, where the wind blows cold" is the age-old saying. Built around a wide square, Stow's imposing golden stone houses have been discreetly converted into high-quality antiques stores, shops, and tea parlors. The Square, as it's known, has a fascinating history. In the 18th century, Daniel Defoe wrote that more than 20,000 sheep could be sold here on a busy day. Such was the press of livestock that sheep runs, known as "tures," were used to control the sheep, and these narrow streets still run off the main square. Today pubs and antiques shops fill the area.

Also here are St. Edward's Church and the Kings Arms Old Posting House, its wide entrance still seeming to wait for the stagecoaches that used to stop here on their way to Cheltenham.

GETTING HERE AND AROUND

Stow-on-the-Wold is well connected by road (A429, A424, and A436) and bus (from Moreton-in-Marsh, Bourton-on-the-Water, Northleach, Cirencester, and Cheltenham). There are parking lots off Sheep Street and Fosseway (A429). Chastleton House is reachable only by car.

👁 Sights

Chastleton House

HOUSE | One of the most complete Jacobean properties in Britain opts for a beguilingly lived-in appearance, taking advantage of almost 400 years' worth of furniture and trappings accumulated by many generations of the single family that owned it until 1991. The house was built between 1605 and 1612 for William Jones, a wealthy wool merchant, and has an appealing authenticity: bric-a-brac is strewn around, wood and pewter are unpolished, upholstery is uncleaned. The top floor is a glorious, barrel-vaulted long gallery, and throughout the house you can see exquisite plasterwork, paneling, and tapestries. The gardens include rotund topiaries and the first croquet lawn (the rules of croquet were codified here in 1865). During busy periods, admission is by timed ticket on a first-come, first-served basis. Note that there is no tearoom or shop here, but the church next door sells tea and snacks when the house is open. Chastleton is 6 miles northeast of Stow, signposted off A436 between Stow and A44. ✉ *Off*

A436, Stow on the Wold ☎ 01608/674355
⊕ www.nationaltrust.org.uk/chastle-
ton-house ⊠ £10.50; garden only £5
⊙ Closed Nov.–Feb., Mon., and Tues.

🍴 Restaurants

★ Feathered Nest Inn

$$$$ | BRITISH | A ten-minute drive from
Stow-on-the-Wold, this popular gastro-pub is as cozy and comforting as the
name would suggest. The food here is
exceptional, and the products so local
that the staff can usually point to the
farm the meat was sourced from, con-
tributing to a generous prix-fixe menu, or,
for those who brought their appetites, a
superb tasting menu. **Known for:** locally
sourced produce; high-end presentation;
lovely valley views. $ Average main: £45
⊠ Nether Westcote ☎ 01993/833030
⊕ www.thefeatherednestinn.co.uk.

🛏 Hotels

Number Nine

$ | B&B/INN | Beyond the traditional
Cotswold stone exterior of this former
coaching inn—now a bed-and-breakfast—are unfussy, spacious bedrooms
done in soothing white and pale colors.
Pros: helpful and amiable hosts; close to
pubs and restaurants; delicious breakfasts. **Cons:** two bathrooms have tubs,
not showers; low ceilings; steps to climb.
$ Rooms from: £75 ⊠ 9 Park St., Stow
on the Wold ☎ 01451/870333 ➪ 3 rooms
🍴 Free breakfast.

Stow Lodge

$$ | HOTEL | A former rectory, this stately,
family-run hotel couldn't be better placed,
separated from Stow's main square by a
tidy garden. **Pros:** central location; hospita-
ble service; good breakfasts. **Cons:** chiming
church clock can be disturbing; steep steps
to top-floor rooms; minimum stay on week-
ends. $ Rooms from: £150 ⊠ The Square,
Stow on the Wold ☎ 01451/830485
⊕ www.stowlodge.co.uk ➪ 20 rooms
🍴 Free breakfast ☞ No children under 5.

🛍 Shopping

Stow-on-the-Wold is the leading center
for antiques stores in the Cotswolds,
with dealers centered on the Square,
Sheep Street, and Church Street.

Baggott Church St. Limited

ANTIQUES/COLLECTIBLES | This shop displays
fine old furniture, portraits and landscape
paintings, silver, and toys, with their
price tags tied on with ribbon. ⊠ Church
St., Stow on the Wold ☎ 01451/830370
⊕ www.baggottantiques.com.

Durham House Antiques

ANTIQUES/COLLECTIBLES | Showcases of
jewelry, silver items, and ceramics, along
with antiquarian books and period furniture,
are on display over two floors. ⊠ 48 Sheep
St., Stow on the Wold ☎ 01451/870404
⊕ www.durhamhouseantiques.co.uk.

Tudor House

ANTIQUES/COLLECTIBLES | Three floors
of showcases contain the finds of 20
antiques dealers presenting anything
from tiny mother-of-pearl pieces and
beaded bags to wooden dressers full of
plates and jugs. ⊠ 40 Sheep St., Stow on
the Wold ☎ 01451/830021.

Bourton-on-the-Water

4 miles southwest of Stow-on-the-Wold,
12 miles northeast of Cheltenham.

Off A429 on the eastern edge of the
Cotswolds, Bourton-on-the-Water is
deservedly famous as a classic Cotswold
village. Like many others, it became
wealthy in the Middle Ages because
of wool. The little River Windrush runs
through Bourton, crossed by low stone
bridges; it's as pretty as it sounds. This
village makes a good touring base and has
a collection of quirky small museums, but
in summer it can be overcrowded. A stroll
through Bourton takes you past stone
cottages, many converted to small stores
and fish-and-chips and tea shops.

Antiques and Markets in the Cotswolds

The Cotswolds contain one of the largest concentrations of art and antiques dealers outside London. The famous antiques shops here are, it's sometimes whispered, "temporary storerooms" for the great families of the region, filled with tole-ware, treen, faience firedogs, toby jugs, and silhouettes, plus country furniture, and ravishing 17th- to 19th-century furniture.

The center of antiquing is Stow-on-the-Wold, in terms of volume of dealers. Other towns that have a number of antiques shops are Broadway, Burford, Cirencester, Tetbury, and Moreton-in-Marsh. The Cotswolds have few of those "anything in this tray for £10" shops, however. The **Cotswold Antique Dealers' Association** (☎ 07831/850544, ⊕ www. cotswolds-antiques-art.com) represents 50 or so dealers in the area.

As across England, many towns in the region have market days, when you can purchase local produce (including special treats ranging from Cotswold cheeses to fruit juices), crafts, and items such as clothes, books, and toys. Moreton-in-Marsh has a market on Tuesday, while Cirencester is busy on Monday and Friday. Attending a farmers' market or a general market is a great way to mingle with the locals and perhaps find a special treasure or a tasty treat.

GETTING HERE AND AROUND

Bourton-on-the-Water is served by Pulham's Coaches from Stow-on-the-Wold, Moreton-in-Marsh, Cirencester, and Cheltenham. By car, take A40 and A436 from Cheltenham. You may find parking in the center, but if not, use the lot outside the village.

ESSENTIALS

VISITOR INFORMATION Bourton-on-the-Water Visitor Information Centre. ⊠ Victoria St. ☎ 01451/820211 ⊕ www.bourtoninfo. com.

Sights

Bourton Model Railway

MUSEUM | FAMILY | Kids get a kick out of the more than 40 model trains running through 500 square feet of detailed layouts depicting everything from industrial areas to a county fair. There are plenty of trains and toys to buy in the shop. ⊠ Box Bush, High St. ☎ 01451/820686 ⊕ www.bourtonmodelrailway.co.uk ☎ £3 ⊘ Closed Jan. and weekdays Sept.–May.

Cotswold Motoring Museum and Toy Collection

MUSEUM | FAMILY | Housed in an old mill and marked by a topiary vintage Mini car, this museum has seven rooms crammed to the rafters with more than 30 shiny vintage and classic cars, delightful caravans from the 1920s and 1960s, ancient motorbikes and bicycles, road signs from past times, and a shepherd's hut on wheels. If this and the assortment of motoring memorabilia is not enough, there are also children's toys, pedal cars, models, and board games. ⊠ The Old Mill, Sherborne St. ☎ 01451/821255 ⊕ www.cotswoldmotoringmuseum.co.uk ☎ £6.50 ⊘ Closed mid-Dec.–mid-Feb.

Model Village

MUSEUM | FAMILY | Built in 1937, this knee-high model of Bourton-on-the-Water took five years to complete. As you walk down its tiny lanes, you'll see how little has changed over the past decades. The small exhibition at Miniature World shows miniature scenes and rooms; some you can make come to life. Particularly entertaining is the model village within the model village, which, much like an infinity mirror, is perpetuated to an increasingly smaller scale. ⊠ *Old New Inn, High St.* ☎ *01451/820467* ⊕ *www.themodelvillage.com* ⌕ *£4.25.*

🍴 Restaurants

The Plough Inn

$ | BRITISH | A few minutes' drive from Bourton in a quiet hamlet, the Plough occupies an old, restored 17th-century inn. Flagstones, original beams, a fireplace, a quiet bar area, and simple, classic pub fare done well make this an ideal retreat from the Bourton crowds in high season. **Known for:** farm-to-table menu; warm atmosphere; dog-friendly policies. ⑤ *Average main: £15* ⊠ *Chapel Ln., Cold Aston* ☎ *01451/822602* ⊕ *www. coldastonplough.com.*

Rose Tree

$ | BRITISH | Plain wooden tables and understated decor are the setting for the wholesome British dishes served in this traditional restaurant beautifully sited on the banks of the Windrush with a large outdoor area. Sip a cocktail on the riverside terrace while you wait for your order. **Known for:** beautiful riverside setting; classic ploughman's lunches; locally sourced food. ⑤ *Average main: £15* ⊠ *Victoria St.* ☎ *01451/820635* ⊕ *www. therosetreeinbourton.co.uk* ⊗ *Closed Mon. No dinner Sun.*

🛏 Hotels

Chester House Hotel

$ | HOTEL | Just steps from the River Windrush, this traditional stone building has been tastefully adapted with contemporary fittings and style. **Pros:** friendly staff; stylish rooms; ideal location for exploring the area. **Cons:** busy on weekends; coachhouse rooms overlook car park; limited parking. ⑤ *Rooms from: £120* ⊠ *Victoria St.* ☎ *01451/820286* ⊕ *www.chesterhousehotel.com* ⌕ *22 rooms* ⧀ *Free breakfast.*

🛍 Shopping

Cotswold Perfumery

PERFUME/COSMETICS | This popular, family-owned shop carries many perfumes that are manufactured on the premises by hand, and also stocks perfume bottles, diffusers, and essential oils, as well as jewelry. Classes are also available on-site for those who want to learn to mix their own perfume. ⊠ *Victoria St.* ☎ *01451/820698* ⊕ *www.cotswold-perfumery.co.uk* ⌕ *Factory tour £5.*

Lower Slaughter and Upper Slaughter

2 miles north of Bourton-on-the-Water, 15 miles east of Cheltenham.

To see the quieter, more typical Cotswold villages, seek out the evocatively named Lower Slaughter and Upper Slaughter (the names have nothing to do with mass murder, but come from the Saxon word *sloh,* which means "a marshy place"). Lower Slaughter is one of the "water villages," with Slaughter Brook running down the center road of the town. Little stone footbridges cross the brook, and the town's resident gaggle of geese can often be seen paddling through the sparkling water. Nearby, Lower and Upper Swell are two other quiet towns to explore.

GETTING HERE AND AROUND

The Slaughters are best explored by car.

👁 Sights

Warden's Way

TRAIL | Connecting the two Slaughters is the Warden's Way, a mile-long pathway that begins in Upper Slaughter at the town-center parking lot and passes stone houses, green meadows, ancient trees, and a 19th-century corn mill with a waterwheel and brick chimney. The

Blue skies, stone buildings, a peaceful brook: villages such as Upper Slaughter demonstrate the enduring appeal of the Cotswolds.

Warden's Way continues south to Bourton-on-the-Water; the full walk from Winchcombe to Bourton is 14 miles. You can pick up maps from local tourist offices. ✉ *Lower Slaughter.*

Hotels

Lords of the Manor Hotel

$$ | **HOTEL** | You'll find refinement and a warm welcome in this rambling 17th-century manor house with Victorian additions, tucked away in a quintessential Cotswold village. **Pros:** heavenly setting; understated elegance; outstanding food. **Cons:** some rooms on the small side; limited Wi-Fi; packages book up quickly. $ *Rooms from: £192* ✉ *Off A429, Upper Slaughter* ☎ *01451/820243* ⊕ *www.lordsofthemanor.com* 🛏 *26 rooms* ❑ *Free breakfast.*

Northleach

7 miles southwest of Lower and Upper Slaughter, 14 miles southeast of Cheltenham.

Just off the Fosse Way (and bypassed by the busy A40), little Northleach—population around 2,000—has remained one of the least spoiled of Cotswold towns. Trim cottages, many with traditional stone-tile roofs, line the streets that converge on the spacious central square. By the 13th century Northleach had acquired substantial wealth thanks to the wool trade. The wool of the local Cotswold Lion sheep (so called because of their thick, manelike fleece) was praised above all others by weavers in Flanders, to whom it was exported.

GETTING HERE AND AROUND

Pulham's Coaches links Northleach with Bourton-on-the-Water and Cheltenham. It's an out-of-the-way village—signposted from A40 and A429—where you should be able to park near the central square and walk to the sights.

 Sights

St. Peter and St. Paul

RELIGIOUS SITE | Besides its soaring pillars and clerestory windows, this 15th-century light-filled church, known as the cathedral of the Cotswolds, contains notable memorial brasses, monuments to the merchants who endowed the church. Each merchant has a wool sack and sheep at his feet. ✉ Mill End ☎ 01451/861132 ⊕ www.northleach.org ⛁ Free.

 Restaurants

Wheatsheaf Inn

$$ | MODERN BRITISH | This popular pub dating from the 17th century specializes in Modern British cuisine with choices ranging from local venison to fresh fish. The courtyard garden is a delight in summer. **Known for:** twice-baked cheddar soufflé; dessert menu; great breakfasts. ⑤ Average main: £16 ✉ West End ☎ 01451/860244 ⊕ www.cotswoldswheatsheaf.com.

🛏 Hotels

Yew Tree Cottage

$ | B&B/INN | For a peaceful stay in a traditional Cotswold cottage, you can't beat this guesthouse. **Pros:** full of character; charming hostess; tasty meals. **Cons:** a bit remote; dogs in the house; no showers (just baths). ⑤ Rooms from: £100 ✉ Off A429, Turkdean ☎ 01451/860222 ⊕ www.bestcotswold.com ⤿ 2 rooms ⑩ Free breakfast.

Burford

9 miles east of Northleach, 18 miles north of Swindon, 18 miles west of Oxford.

Burford's broad main street leads steeply down to a narrow bridge across the River Windrush. The village served as a stagecoach stop for centuries and has many historic inns; it's now a popular stop for tour buses and seekers of antiques.

GETTING HERE AND AROUND

Burford can be easily reached by bus from Oxford and Northleach. Once here, it's easy to stroll around. Drivers should park as soon as possible; there are possibilities on and off High Street.

ESSENTIALS

VISITOR INFORMATION Burford Visitor Information Centre. ✉ 33A High St. ☎ 01993/823558 ⊕ www.oxfordshirecotswolds.org.

👁 Sights

Bampton

TOWN | Fans of the television drama *Downton Abbey* probably already know that the interior shots of the series are filmed at Highclere Castle in southern Winchester, but they might be interested to learn that most of the exterior shots are concentrated on the Oxfordshire village of Bampton, on the eastern edge of the Cotswolds. Visitors can walk the sleepy streets of mellow stone, see the library in Church View which doubled as the Downton Cottage Hospital, and visit the church of St. Mary, the setting of both Mary and Edith's weddings. Lady Sybil and Branson planned their elopement in the Swan Inn at the nearby village of Swinbook, 2 miles east of Burford. Bampton is 6 miles southeast of Burford and 18 miles southwest of Oxford, from where there is a regular bus. Drivers should take the road signed Brize Norton off the A40. ⊕ www.bamptonoxon-parishcouncil.gov.uk.

St. John the Baptist

RELIGIOUS SITE | Hidden away at the end of a lane at the bottom of High Street is the splendid parish church of St. John the Baptist, its interior a warren of arches, chapels, and shrines. The church was remodeled in the 15th century from Norman beginnings. Among the monuments is one dedicated to Henry VIII's barber, Edmund Harman, that depicts four Amazonian Indians; it's said to be the first depiction of native people from the Americas in Britain. Also look for the elaborate Tanfield monument and the grave of Christopher Kempster, master mason to Christopher Wren during the rebuilding of St. Paul's Cathedral in London. ⊠ *Church Green* ☎ *01993/823788* ⊕ *www.burford-church.org* ✉ *Suggested donation £2.*

Restaurants

The Angel at Burford

$ | **MODERN BRITISH** | At this informal eatery in a 16th-century coaching inn, the farmhouse-style tables are filled with traditional dishes with locally sourced ingredients. The secluded garden is the perfect place to enjoy lunchtime baguettes or sandwiches in nice weather. **Known for:** fantastic steaks and other meats; relaxed and informal atmosphere; beautiful garden. ⑤ *Average main: £15* ⊠ *14 Witney St.* ☎ *01993/822714* ⊕ *www.theangelatburford.co.uk.*

Hotels

Burford House

$$ | **HOTEL** | Family photographs, old books, and toys scattered throughout this 17th-century building make it feel more like home than a hotel. **Pros:** friendly, unobtrusive service; comfortable public rooms; very homey decor. **Cons:** rooms at front subject to traffic noise; parking difficult at peak times; not for those averse to teddy bears. ⑤ *Rooms from: £125* ⊠ *99 High St.* ☎ *01993/823151* ⊕ *www.burford-house.co.uk* ✉ *6 rooms* ⦿ *Free breakfast.*

The Lamb Inn

$$ | **HOTEL** | Step through the door of this ancient coaching inn and be greeted by huge flagstones, gateleg tables, armchairs, and a roaring fire, then wind your way along the tartan carpet through creaking passages and stairways to the immaculate and cozy bedrooms. **Pros:** idyllic location; attentive service; historical building. **Cons:** some rooms are small; some street parking; very pet-friendly, so not for non-dog lovers. ⑤ *Rooms from: £205* ⊠ *Sheep St.* ☎ *01993/823155* ⊕ *www.cotswold-inns-hotels.co.uk/the-lamb-inn* ✉ *17 rooms* ⦿ *Free breakfast.*

Bibury

10 miles southwest of Burford, 6 miles northeast of Cirencester, 15 miles north of Swindon.

The tiny town of Bibury, with a population of less than 1,000, sits idyllically beside the little River Coln on B4425. It was famed Arts and Crafts designer William Morris's choice for Britain's most beautiful village. Fine old cottages, a river meadow, and the church of St. Mary's are some of the delights here.

GETTING HERE AND AROUND

There are a few buses to Bibury operated on weekdays only by Pulham's Coaches from Cirencester which continue on to Bourton-on-the-Water. You'll need a car to reach Chedworth Roman Villa.

⦿ Sights

Arlington Row

NEIGHBORHOOD | The town has a famously pretty and much-photographed group of 17th-century weavers' cottages made of stone. ⊠ *Bibury.*

Chedworth Roman Villa

ARCHAEOLOGICAL SITE | **FAMILY** | The remains of a mile of walls are what's left of one of the largest Roman villas in England, beautifully set in a wooded valley on the eastern fringe of the Cotswolds. Thirty-two rooms, including two complete bath suites, have been identified, and covered walkways take you over the colorful mosaics, some of the most complete in England. Audio guides are available, and there's a small museum. Look out for the rare large snails, fattened on milk and herbs during Roman times, in the grounds; they come out on warm, wet days. There's a café here, but it's also an ideal place for a picnic. ■ TIP→ **Look carefully for the signs for the villa: from Bibury, go across A429 to Yanworth and Chedworth. The villa is also signposted from A40. Roads are narrow.** The site is 6 miles northwest of Bibury and 10 miles southeast of Cheltenham. ⊠ Off A429, Yanworth ☎ 01242/890256 ⊕ www.nationaltrust.org.uk/ched-worth-roman-villa ➔ £11.50 ⊗ Closed mid-Nov.–mid-Feb.

 ## Hotels

Swan Hotel
$$ | HOTEL | Few inns can boast of a more idyllic setting than this mid-17th-century coaching inn, originally a row of cottages on the banks of the gently flowing River Coln. **Pros:** idyllic spot; helpful staff; tasty local food. **Cons:** busy with day-trippers, and wedding parties on weekends; most standard rooms lack views; not enough electrical plugs in rooms. ⑤ Rooms from: £180 ⊠ B4425 ☎ 01285/740695 ⊕ www.cotswold-inns-hotels.co.uk/the-swan-hotel ➔ 22 rooms ⊗ Free breakfast.

Cirencester

6 miles southwest of Bibury, 9 miles south of Chedworth, 14 miles southeast of Cheltenham.

A hub of the Cotswolds since Roman times, when it was called Corinium, Cirencester (pronounced *siren*-sester) was second only to London in importance. Today this old market town is the area's largest, with a population of 19,000. It sits at the intersection of two major Roman roads, the Fosse Way and Ermin Street (now A429 and A417). In the Middle Ages, Cirencester grew rich on wool, which funded its 15th-century parish church. It preserves many mellow stone buildings dating mainly from the 17th and 18th centuries and bow-fronted shops that still have one foot in the past.

GETTING HERE AND AROUND
Cirencester has hourly bus service from Cheltenham and less frequent service from Moreton-in-Marsh, Tetbury, and Kemble (for rail links). By road, the town can be accessed on A417, A419, and A429. Its compact center is easily walkable.

ESSENTIALS
VISITOR INFORMATION Cirencester Visitor Information Centre. ⊠ Corinium Museum, Park St. ☎ 01285/654180 ⊕ www.cirencester.co.uk/visitorinformationcentre.

Sights

★ Corinium Museum
MUSEUM | FAMILY | Not much of the Roman town remains visible, but the museum displays an outstanding collection of Roman artifacts, including jewelry and coins, as well as mosaic pavements and full-scale reconstructions of local Roman interiors. Spacious and light-filled galleries that explore the town's history in Roman and Anglo-Saxon times and in the 18th century include plenty of hands-on exhibits for kids. ⊠ Park St. ☎ 01285/655611 ⊕ www.coriniummuseum.org ➔ £5.80.

St. John the Baptist
RELIGIOUS SITE | At the top of Market Place is this magnificent Gothic parish church, known as the cathedral of the "woolgothic" style. Its gleaming, elaborate, three-tier, three-bay south porch is the largest in England and once served as the town hall. The chantry chapels and many coats of arms

bear witness to the importance of the wool merchants as benefactors of the church. A rare example of a delicate 15th-century wineglass pulpit sits in the nave. ⊠ *Market Pl.* ☎ *01285/659317* ⊕ *www.cirenparish. co.uk* ⊋ *£3 donation suggested.*

🍴 Restaurants

The Fleece

$$ | BRITISH | This 17th-century inn retains its historic past while serving fabulous modern food, real ales, and gin cocktails. Choose from a wide range of dishes including venison, steak, and seafood, or the varied selections on the daily specials board. **Known for:** lots of locals; real ales on tap; cool history with plenty of famous guests. $ *Average main: £17* ⊠ *Market Pl.* ☎ *01285/ 658507* ⊕ *www.thefleece-cirencester.co.uk.*

Jesse's Bistro

$$ | MODERN BRITISH | Tucked away in a little courtyard, Jesse's is an intimate yet roomy bistro where you can treat yourself to a chilled sherry, local Gatcombe lamb, or fish straight up from Cornwall. The charcoal is glowing in the oven as you sit at your mosaic-topped table and watch the chefs at work. **Known for:** quality ingredients from local providers; tables that book up in advance; great British cheese boards. $ *Average main: £18* ⊠ *The Stableyard, 14 Black Jack St.* ☎ *01285/641497* ⊕ *www.jessesbistro. co.uk* ⊗ *Closed Mon. No dinner Sun.*

Made by Bob

$$ | MODERN BRITISH | There's energy and buzz at this plate-glass-and-chrome eatery, situated right by the Cornhall, which serves breakfasts, coffees, lunches, and afternoon teas with a smile. Choose from coffee and pastry, afternoon tea with cakes, or a soup and focaccia lunch. **Known for:** locally sourced food on menus that change with the seasons; monthly supper clubs; excellent brunch. $ *Average main: £16* ⊠ *Unit 6 The Cornhall, 26 Market Pl.*

☎ *01285/641818* ⊕ *www.mbbbrasserie. co.uk* ⊗ *No dinner Sun. and Mon.*

🛏️ Hotels

Barnsley House

$$$ | HOTEL | A honey-and-cream Georgian mansion, the former home of garden designer Rosemary Verey, has been discreetly modernized and converted into a luxurious retreat without sacrificing its essential charm. **Pros:** romantic setting; great attention to detail; beautiful gardens. **Cons:** some rooms at the top of three flights of stairs; no kids under 14; farm next door not for everyone. $ *Rooms from: £350* ⊠ *Off the B4425, Barnsley* ☎ *01285/740000* ⊕ *www. barnsleyhouse.com* ⊋ *18 rooms* ⊗ *Free breakfast.*

The Barrel Store

$ | B&B/INN | For a no-frills stay in the Cotswolds, the Barrel Store offers comfortable rooms with self-catering facilities in a refurbished building that was once a store for the town brewery. **Pros:** affordable; stylish and comfortable rooms; close to local restaurants and attractions. **Cons:** communal ethos not for everyone; no electric plugs in the bedrooms; some rooms have shared bathroom facilities. $ *Rooms from: £55* ⊠ *Brewery Court* ☎ *01285/657181* ⊕ *www.thebarrelstore. co.uk* ⊋ *14 rooms* ⊗ *No meals.*

Ivy House

$ | B&B/INN | Delicious breakfasts, hospitable owners, and reasonable rates enhance a stay at this stone Victorian house, close to the center of town. **Pros:** homemade granola at breakfast; child-friendly atmosphere; easy 10-minute walk to town center. **Cons:** on a main road; rooms can be the small side; some ground-floor rooms can be viewed by passing pedestrians. $ *Rooms from: £100* ⊠ *2 Victoria Rd.* ☎ *01285/656626* ⊕ *www.ivyhousecotswolds.com* ⊋ *4 rooms* ⊗ *Free breakfast.*

🛍 Shopping

Corn Hall

ANTIQUES/COLLECTIBLES | This is the venue for a home, garden, and fashion market Monday through Thursday; an antiques market on Friday; and a crafts market on Saturday. ⊠ *Market Pl.* ⊕ *www.cornhall-cirencester.com.*

Makers and Designers Emporium

JEWELRY/ACCESSORIES | Better known as m.a.d.e., this shop is a cornucopia of unusual designer items, including stationery, textiles, housewares, toys, and jewelry. ⊠ *9 Silver St.* ☎ *01285/658225* ⊕ *www.made-gallery.com.*

Market Place

OUTDOOR/FLEA/GREEN MARKETS | Every Monday and Friday, Cirencester's central Market Place is packed with stalls selling a motley assortment of goods, mainly household items but some local produce and crafts, too. A farmers' market takes place here every second and fourth Saturday of the month. ⊠ *Cirencester* ⊕ *www.cirencester.gov.uk/markets.*

🏃 Activities

Cotswold Water Park

WATER SPORTS | FAMILY | You can indulge in water sports such as waterskiing and windsurfing at the Cotswold Water Park, 4 miles south of Cirencester. This group of 150 lakes covers 40 square miles and has multiple entrances. There's swimming March through October, and plenty to do for walkers, cyclists, and kayakers as well. You pay individual charges for the activities, and you can rent equipment on-site. ⊠ *B4696, South Cerney* ☎ *01793/752413* ⊕ *www.waterpark.org* 🎫 *Free.*

Malmesbury

15 miles south of Cirencester, 24 miles northwest of Bath.

Malmesbury is the oldest continually inhabited town in England and its ancient walls and abbey are still a delight to explore. The town started off as an Iron Age hillfort in a defensive position between the River Avon tributaries, and saw action during the English Civil War (1642–51). Later on, it thrived on the wool trade and today is known as the gateway to the Cotswolds. At the center of the rural community, the ornate 500-year-old market cross stands in front of Malmesbury Abbey, a landmark that can be seen for miles. ■TIP➔ **Malmesbury is renowned for its historic bridges and riverside walk. Buy a guide and map (£1) from the tourist office in the town hall to enjoy a scenic walk around town.**

GETTING HERE AND AROUND

There are regular buses from Bath, Chippenham, and Cirencester.

👁 Sights

Athelstan Museum

MUSEUM | Located within the town hall, the Athelstan Museum contains a general history of the town of Malmesbury, as well as details on the Abbey and King Athelstan. The museum also has exhibits about the lace-making industry, the town's wool trade, and locally made clocks and bikes. Local-born philosopher Thomas Hobbes gets special attention, too. ⊠ *Town Hall, Cross Hayes* ☎ *01666/829258* ⊕ *www.athelstanmuseum.org.uk* 🎫 *Free.*

★ Malmesbury Abbey

RELIGIOUS SITE | Although now a fraction of its original size, Malmesbury Abbey is still the defining feature of the entire town. There has been an abbey on this site since 1180; the current abbey is the third. During the dissolution of the monasteries, the abbey was used as a wool store and many parts were destroyed. But during the 16th century, the magnificent building became the parish church of Malmesbury, which it has remained since. The breathtaking Norman porch and its ornate carved figures depict the story of Creation through the death of Christ; it is considered one of the best examples of such in Europe. In the northern section of the building is King Athelstan's tomb; Athelstan was crowned king of Wessex in 925 and united England by 927. Malmesbury Abbey is also famed for its stained-glass windows; the Luce window is by Burne-Jones. ⊠ *Gloucester St.* ☎ *01666/826666* ⊕ *www.malmesbury-abbey.com* ⊠ *Free (donations appreciated).*

Hotels

Old Bell Hotel
$ | **HOTEL** | Just a few steps from Malmesbury Abbey, the Old Bell Hotel dates from 1220 and is reputedly the oldest hotel in England. **Pros:** central location; good restaurant on-site; lots of history. **Cons:** on one of the main roads so can be noisy; some bathrooms are small; parking can be cramped during busy times. ⑤ *Rooms from: £125* ⊠ *Abbey Row* ☎ *01666/822344* ⊕ *www.oldbellhotel. co.uk* ⇌ *41 rooms* ⦿ *Free breakfast.*

Painswick

16 miles northwest of Cirencester, 8 miles southwest of Cheltenham, 5 miles south of Gloucester.

An old Cotswold wool town of around 2,000 inhabitants, Painswick has become a chocolate-box picture of quaintness, attracting day-trippers and tour buses. But come during the week and you can discover the place in relative tranquility. The huddled gray-stone houses and inns date from as early as the 14th century and include a notable group from the Georgian era. It's worth a stroll through the churchyard of St. Mary's, renowned for its table tombs and monuments and its 100 yew trees planted in 1792. The Cotswold Way passes near the center of the village, making it easy to take a pleasant walk in the countryside.

GETTING HERE AND AROUND
Painswick is on A46 between Stroud and Cheltenham. Stagecoach runs hourly bus connections with Stroud (15 minutes) and Cheltenham (35 minutes), with reduced service on Sunday.

ESSENTIALS
VISITOR INFORMATION Painswick Visitor Information Centre. ⊠ *Grave Diggers Hut, St. Mary's Church* ☎ *01452/812278* ⊕ *www.painswicktouristinfo.co.uk.*

👁 Sights

Painswick Rococo Garden
GARDEN | Half a mile north of town, this delightful garden is a rare survivor from the exuberant rococo period of English garden design (1720–60). After 50 years in its original form, the 6-acre garden became overgrown. Fortunately, the rediscovery of a 1748 painting of the garden by local artist Thomas Robins sparked a full-scale restoration in the 1980s. Now you can view the original structures—such as the pretty Gothic Eagle House and curved Exedra—take in the asymmetrical vistas, and try the modern maze, which, unusually, has three centers you can discover. It's also famous for the snowdrops that bloom in January and February. There's a restaurant and a shop, too. ⊠ *B4073* ☎ *01452/813204* ⊕ *www.rococogarden. org.uk* ⊠ *£10* ⊙ *Closed Oct.–mid-Jan.*

🍴 Restaurants

Falcon Inn
$$ | **BRITISH** | With views of the church of St. Mary's, this historic pub dating from 1554 offers a reassuring traditional and charming milieu for food and refreshment. Light meals are available at lunchtime, teas in the afternoon, and

for the evening meal you might start with deep-fried calamari and whitebait with caper sauce, then try the rump of lamb with minted mashed potato for your main course. **Known for:** traditional British food; beautiful views; plenty of history. $ *Average main: £17* ⊠ *New St.* ☎ *01452/814222* ⊕ *www.falconpainswick.co.uk.*

Hotels

Cardynham House

$ | **HOTEL** | In the heart of the village, this 15th- to 16th-century former wool merchant's house, which retains its beamed ceilings, Jacobean staircase, and Elizabethan fireplace, has four-poster beds in almost all of its rooms. **Pros:** romantic and quirky; great food in restaurant; tasty breakfasts. **Cons:** some low ceilings; mainly small bathrooms; no Wi-Fi in rooms. $ *Rooms from: £110* ⊠ *The Cross, Tibbiwell La.* ☎ *01452/814006 guesthouse, 01452/810030 restaurant* ⊕ *www.cardynham.co.uk* ⇨ *9 rooms* ⊚ *Free breakfast.*

Tetbury

12 miles south of Painswick, 8 miles southwest of Cirencester.

With about 5,300 inhabitants, Tetbury claims royal connections. Indeed, the soaring spire of the church that presides over this Elizabethan market town is within sight of Highgrove House, the Prince of Wales's abode. The house isn't open to the public, but you can book well in advance for a tour of the gardens. Tetbury is known as one of the area's antiques centers.

GETTING HERE AND AROUND

Tetbury is connected to Cirencester by buses operated by Cotswold Green. There is no Sunday service. It's easy to stroll around the compact town.

ESSENTIALS

VISITOR INFORMATION Tetbury Tourist Information Centre. ⊠ *33 Church St.* ☎ *01666/503552* ⊕ *www.visittetbury.co.uk.*

◉ Sights

Chavenage

HOUSE | Tall gate piers and spreading trees frame the family-owned Chavenage, a gray Cotswold-stone Elizabethan manor house. The tour includes a room with fine tapestries, where Cromwell lodged during the Civil War, and a main hall with minstrels' gallery and spy holes. The house is 2 miles northwest of Tetbury. It has recently been used as a filming location for the popular television show *Poldark.* ⊠ *Between B4104 and A4135* ☎ *01666/502329* ⊕ *www. chavenage.com* ⊡ *£10* ⊗ *Closed Oct.–Apr., Mon.–Wed., and Sat.*

★ Highgrove House

GARDEN | Highgrove House is the much-loved country home of Prince Charles and Camilla, Duchess of Cornwall. Here the prince has been making the 37-acre estate his personal showcase for traditional and organic growing methods and conservation of native plants and animals since 1980. Joining a tour of 26 people, you can appreciate the amazing industry on the part of the royal gardeners who have created the orchards, kitchen garden, and woodland garden almost from nothing. Look for the stumpery, the immaculate and quirky topiaries, and the national collection of hostas. You can sample the estate's produce in the restaurant and shop or from its retail outlet in Tetbury. Tickets go on sale in February and sell out quickly, though extra dates are released through the year via a mailing list. Be sure to book well ahead. Allow three to four hours for a visit to the garden, which is 1½ miles southwest of Tetbury. Those under 12 aren't permitted. ⊠ *Highgrove House, Off A433, Doughton* ☎ *0300/1237310 tours* ⊕ *www.highgrovegardens.com* ⊡ *£27.50, prebooked only* ⊗ *Closed late Oct.–early Apr.*

With its majestic trees, Westonbirt National Arboretum is the perfect place to take in fall's splendor.

Market House

BUILDING | In the center of Tetbury, look for the eye-catching Market House, dating from 1655. Constructed of white-painted stone, it's built up on rows of Tuscan pillars. Various markets are held here during the week. ⊠ *Market Sq.* ⊕ *www.thefeoffeesoftetbury.co.uk/ the-market-house.*

Rodmarton Manor

HOUSE | One of the last English country houses constructed using traditional methods and materials, Rodmarton Manor (built 1909–29) is furnished with specially commissioned pieces in the Arts and Crafts style. Ernest Barnsley, a follower of William Morris, worked on the house and gardens. The notable gardens—wild, winter, sunken, and white—are divided into "rooms" bounded by hedges of holly, beech, and yew. The manor is 5 miles northeast of Tetbury. Admission is cash-only. ⊠ *Off A433, Rodmarton* ☎ *01285/841442* ⊕ *www. rodmarton-manor.co.uk* ✉ *£10; garden only £7.50* ⊙ *Closed Oct.–Mar., Sun.–Tues., Thurs., and Fri.*

St. Mary the Virgin

RELIGIOUS SITE | This church, a fine example of 18th-century neo-Gothic style, has a galleried interior with pews and fine slender pillars. The entrance porch has a striking contemporary mural of the Annunciation. The churchyard is a wildflower haven with around 300 species of native wildflowers including snowdrops, cyclamen, bluebells, and more. Donations are welcome. ⊠ *Church St.* ☎ *01666/500088* ⊕ *www.tetburychurch.btck.co.uk* ✉ *Free.*

Westonbirt National Arboretum

GARDEN | FAMILY | Spread over 600 acres and with 17 miles of paths, this arboretum contains one of the most extensive collections of trees and shrubs in Europe. A lovely place to spend an hour or two, it's 3 miles southwest of Tetbury and 10 miles north of Bath. The best times to come for color are in late spring, when the rhododendrons, azaleas, and magnolias are blooming, and in fall, when the maples come into their own. Open-air concerts take place in summer, and there are exhibitions throughout the year. A gift shop, café, and restaurant are on the grounds. ✉ Off A433 ☎ 0300/0674890 ⊕ www. forestryengland.uk/westonbirt-the-national-arboretum 🎫 £11 Mar.–Nov.; £7 Dec.–Feb.

🍴 Restaurants

The Royal Oak

$ | **MODERN BRITISH** | This mellow-stone gabled pub, located in the snug village of Leighterton just five miles west of Tetbury, likes to satisfy the crowds that assemble here with the best local fare in the area. Draw up a stool at the bar or take a seat at one of the many wooden tables to try the squid, chorizo, and tomato stew or cauliflower, squash, and chickpea tagine. **Known for:** traditional English country pub; huge desserts; walled garden for summer dining. $ Average main: £14 ✉ 1 The Street, Leighterton ☎ 0166/890250 ⊕ www.royaloakleighterton.co.uk ⊗ No dinner Sun.

The Snooty Fox

$ | **BRITISH** | Just steps from Market House and in the heart of village life, the Snooty Fox is a bustling inn and restaurant that makes the most of quality ingredients from local Cotswolds producers. Real ales and local ciders are served at the bar, and teas, coffees, and hot and cold meals are available all day. **Known for:** the heart of the local community; locally sourced ingredients; cozy ambience. $ Average main: £13 ✉ Market Pl. ☎ 01666/502436 ⊕ www. snooty-fox.co.uk.

🛏 Hotels

★ Calcot Manor

$$$ | **HOTEL** | **FAMILY** | In an ideal world everyone would sojourn in this oasis of opulence at least once; however, the luxury never gets in the way of the overall air of relaxation, a tribute to the warmth and efficiency of the staff. **Pros:** delightful rural setting; excellent spa facilities; children love it. **Cons:** all but 12 rooms are separate from main building; some traffic noise; steep prices. $ Rooms from: £310 ✉ A4135 ☎ 01666/890391 ⊕ www.calcot. co ⇆ 35 rooms ⊙ Free breakfast.

King's Arms

$ | **B&B/INN** | **FAMILY** | A short drive from Tetbury in a small hamlet, the King's Arms is a paragon of modern rustic chic, with cozy rooms furnished with sheepskin rugs and big, soft beds. **Pros:** excellent food; vintage charm; comfortable rooms and public spaces. **Cons:** decor can be a little dark; out of the way location; bathrooms a little outdated. $ Rooms from: £110 ✉ The Street, Didmarton ☎ 01454/238245 ⊕ www.kingsarmsdidmarton.co.uk ⇆ 6 rooms ⊙ No meals.

🛍 Shopping

Highgrove Shop

GIFTS/SOUVENIRS | This pleasant, though pricey, shop sells organic products and gifts inspired by Prince Charles's gardens. ✉ 10 Long St. ☎ 01666/505666 ⊕ www. highgrovegardens.com/collections.

House of Cheese

FOOD/CANDY | Farm-produced cheeses, all wonderfully fresh and flavorsome, are on offer at the House of Cheese. Pâtés, preserves, and olive-wood cheese boards are other goodies at this tiny shop. ✉ 13 Church St. ☎ 01666/502865 ⊕ www. houseofcheese.co.uk.

Chapter 9

STRATFORD-UPON-AVON AND THE HEART OF ENGLAND

Updated by
Sally Coffey

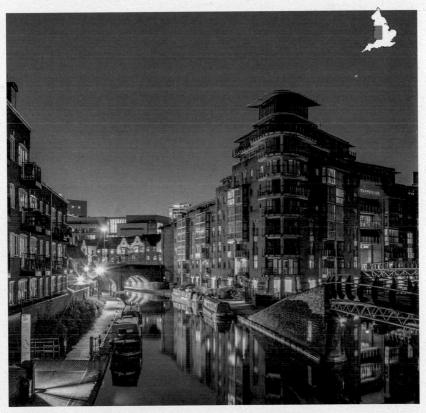

👁 **Sights**
★★★★★

🍽 **Restaurants**
★★★★☆

🛏 **Hotels**
★★★☆☆

🛍 **Shopping**
★★★☆☆

🍸 **Nightlife**
★★☆☆☆

WELCOME TO STRATFORD-UPON-AVON AND THE HEART OF ENGLAND

TOP REASONS TO GO

★ **Shakespeare in Stratford:** To see a play by Shakespeare in the town where he was born—and perhaps after you've visited his birthplace or other sights—is a magical experience.

★ **The city of Birmingham:** The revamped city center shows off its superb art collections and cultural facilities, international cuisine, and renowned Jewellery Quarter.

★ **Half-timber architecture:** Black-and-white half-timber houses are a mark of pride throughout the region; there are concentrations of buildings from medieval times to the Jacobean era in Chester, Shrewsbury, Ludlow, and Stratford-upon-Avon.

★ **Ironbridge Gorge:** Recall the beginnings of England's Industrial Revolution at this fine complex of industrial-heritage museums.

★ **Castles of Warwickshire:** Explore the sprawling medieval Warwick Castle, or take in the Elizabethan romance of nearby Kenilworth Castle.

Stratford-upon-Avon is northwest of London in the Midlands county of Warwickshire, known as Shakespeare Country. Tiny villages surround it; to the north are two magnificent castles, Warwick and Kenilworth. A little farther northwest is the region's main city, Birmingham. To the southwest, along the Malvern Hills, lie the peaceful spa town of Great Malvern and the prosperous agricultural city of Hereford. The western part of the region, bordering Wales, is hugged by the River Severn. The town of Shrewsbury is here, close to Ironbridge, home to the first major cast-iron bridge in the world. To the south of Ironbridge lies Ludlow, an architectural and culinary hotspot; at the northwestern edge of the region is the ancient city of Chester.

1 Stratford-upon-Avon. Shakespeare's famous hometown.

2 Henley-in-Arden. A sleepy village with stately homes.

3 Warwick. Home to a historic castle.

4 Kenilworth Castle. Warwickshire's most romantic ruined castle.

5 Birmingham. The cultural hub of the region.

6 Great Malvern. A genteel suburb and a good base for the Malvern Hills.

7 Ledbury. A bucolic town filled with charming half-timber buildings.

8 Ross-on-Wye. A small market town trapped in time.

9 Hereford. A famous cathedral city.

10 Shrewsbury. An important medieval town.

11 Ironbridge Gorge. A World Heritage Site considered the cradle of the Industrial Revolution.

12 Ludlow. An old market town with an impressive food scene.

13 Chester. The thriving historical center of Cheshire.

GREAT INDIAN FOOD IN ENGLAND

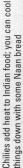

Chilies add heat to Indian food; you can cool things down with some Naan bread

"Going for an Indian" or "going for a curry"—the two are synonymous—is part of English life. On even the smallest town's main street you'll usually find an Indian restaurant or takeout place, from inexpensive to high-end establishments.

British trade with India and its subsequent rule over the country for two centuries before 1947 has ensured an enduring national appetite for spices. Immigration from India, Pakistan, and Bangladesh in the mid-20th century led to a concentration of restaurants in Birmingham, Manchester, and London. Today, you can also find South Indian, Nepalese, and Sri Lankan establishments. The exotic mix of herbs and spices gives Indian food its distinctive appeal. Typically, ginger, garlic, cilantro (coriander on English menus), cumin, cardamom, fenugreek, and cayenne enhance fresh vegetables and meat (chicken or lamb), fish, or cheese (paneer). Fresh cilantro is a common garnish. But it's the addition of chili that makes things hot; feel free to ask advice on how spicy to expect a dish when ordering.

ON THE SIDE

Starters include lime pickle, mango chutney, and *raita* (diced cucumber in mint yogurt), all scooped up with *pappadams* (crispy, fried tortilla-like disks made from chickpeas). For the main course, there's plain or pilau Basmati rice, naan bread from the tandoor (barrel-shape clay oven), or chapatis (flat bread). Side dishes include onion or eggplant *bhajis* (spiced fritters) and *sag aloo* (potato with spinach).

Curry is a general term for dishes with a hot, spicy sauce. The strength of each dish is given in italics after the description.

BALTI

Literally meaning "bucket," a *balti* dish is a popular Birmingham invention dating from the 1970s. Different combinations of meat, spices, and vegetables are stir-fried and served at the table in a small wok with handles. *Mild to Medium.*

BIRYANI

Made with stir-fried chicken, lamb, or prawns (shrimp), plus almonds and golden raisins, this rice-based dish has a dry texture. It is usually served with a vegetable curry. *Medium.*

CHICKEN TIKKA MASALA

A British-Bangladeshi invention, boneless chunks of chicken breast are marinated in yogurt and garam masala (dry-roasted spices), threaded on a skewer, and cooked in a tandoor. The accompanying creamy, tomato-based sauce is either orange-red from turmeric and paprika or deep red from food coloring. *Mild.*

DOPIAZA

The name means two or double onions, so expect lots of onions, mixed with green bell peppers. The sauce

Rogan josh, a spicy choice

is reduced, producing concentrated flavors. *Medium hot.*

JALFREZI

This dish is derived from British rule in India, when the Indian cook would heat up leftover cold roast meat and potatoes. Fresh meat is cooked with green bell peppers, onions, and plenty of green chilies in a little sauce. *Hot.*

KORMA

Mild and sweet, this curry is very popular and is considered by many to be Britain's favorite curry. Chicken or lamb is braised in a cream- or yogurt-based sauce to which almonds and coconut are added. *Mild.*

ROGAN JOSH

A staple dish, rogan josh is quite highly spiced. Its deep-red color originally came from dried red Kashmiri chilies, but now red bell peppers and tomatoes are used. *Medium hot.*

TANDOORI CHICKEN

Chicken pieces are marinated in a yogurt and spice paste and then cooked in a tandoor. The red color comes from cayenne pepper, chili powder, or food coloring. It's served dry with slices of lemon or lime, naan, and salad. *Mild.*

Chicken tikka masala, a favorite

The lyricism of England's geographical heartland is found in the remote, half-timber market towns of Herefordshire, Worcestershire, and Shropshire, as well as in the bucolic villages of Warwickshire. It melts away around the edges of Birmingham— England's second-largest city. Although often maligned by Britons as a grubby post-industrial metropolis, it is, nonetheless, forging a new identity for itself as a cultural hub.

However, it's the countryside around here that most invokes the England of our imaginations—nowhere more so than Stratford-upon-Avon, birthplace of perhaps the nation's most famous son, William Shakespeare. You get new insight into the great playwright when you visit the stretch of country where he was born and raised. The sculpted, rolling farmland of Warwickshire may look nothing like the forested countryside of the 16th century, but plenty of sturdy Tudor buildings that Shakespeare knew survive to this day (including his birthplace). There's beauty in this—but also the possibility of tourist overkill. Stratford itself, with its Shakespeare sites and the theaters of the Royal Shakespeare Company, sometimes can feel like "Shakespeare World." And while Shakespeare himself would recognize plenty of the ancient, timber-framed buildings that line the main shopping streets, the same cannot be said of the bland, cookie-cutter chain stores that occupy most of these buildings today.

Still, there's much more to see—magnificent castles, pastoral churches, and gentle countryside—in this famously lovely part of England. Stop in at Charlecote Park, a grand Elizabethan manor house, and moated Baddesley Clinton, a superb example of late-medieval domestic architecture. The huge fortresses of Warwick Castle and Kenilworth Castle also provide glimpses into the past.

To the west, some of England's prettiest countryside lies along the 160-mile border with Wales in the counties of Herefordshire, Worcestershire, and Shropshire. The Welsh borders are remote and tranquil, dotted with small villages and market towns full of 13th- and 14th-century, black-and-white, half-timber buildings—the legacy of a forested countryside. The Victorians were responsible for the more recent fashion of painting these structures black and white. The more elaborately decorated half-timber buildings in market towns such as Shrewsbury and Chester are monuments to wealth, dating mostly from the early 17th century. More half-timbered structures are found in Ludlow, now a culinary center nestled in the lee of its majestic ruined castle.

In the 18th century, in a wooded stretch of the Severn Gorge in Shropshire, the coke blast furnace was invented, and the first iron bridge was erected (1779), heralding the birth of the Industrial Revolution. You can get a sense of this history at the museums at Ironbridge Gorge.

The ramifications of that technological leap are what led to the rapid growth of Birmingham, the capital of the Midlands. Its industrial center, which suffered decades of decline in the 20th century, inspired culture as diverse as the heavy metal sound of Black Sabbath and the dark realm of Mordor in J. R. R. Tolkien's *The Lord of the Rings*, while the modern success of the television series *Peaky Blinders* has encouraged a whole new generation of visitors. Today, an imaginative makeover and active, varied cultural life are draws for anyone interested in the rebirth of modern urban Britain.

MAJOR REGIONS

Stratford-upon-Avon. The birthplace of Shakespeare, the bustling historic town of Stratford-upon-Avon is liberally dotted with 16th-century buildings the playwright would recognize.

Around Shakespeare Country. This section of Warwickshire is marked by gentle hills, green fields; slow-moving rivers; quiet villages; and time-burnished halls, churches, and castles (Warwick and Kenilworth are the best examples and well worth visiting). Historic houses such as moated Baddesley Clinton and Packwood House are another reason to explore. All the sights are close enough to Stratford-upon-Avon that you can easily use the town as a base if you wish.

Birmingham. Britain's second-largest city, once known as "the city of 1,001 trades," now makes the most of its industrial past through some outstanding museums and the biggest canal network outside Venice. There's also buzzing nightlife and an excellent restaurant scene.

Great Malvern and Hereford. In the arc of towns to the west of Birmingham and around the banks of the River Wye to the south, history and tradition rub up against deepest rural England. Great Malvern and the cathedral town of Hereford are great bases from which to soak up the bucolic flavor of the Malvern Hills and Elgar country or to view the spectacular swing of the Wye at the wonderfully named Symonds Yat.

Shrewsbury and Chester. Rural Shropshire, one of the least populated English counties, is far removed from most people's preconceptions of the industrial Midlands. Within its spread are towns long famed for their beauty, such as Ludlow. Two important urban centers, Shrewsbury and Chester, are both renowned for their medieval heritage and their wealth of half-timber buildings. The six-mile stretch of the Ironbridge Gorge, however, gives you the chance to experience the cradle of the Industrial Revolution with none of the reeking smoke that gave this region west of Birmingham its name— the Black Country—during the mid-19th century. Now taken over by the Ironbridge Gorge Museum Trust, the bridge, the first of its kind to be built of iron, opened in 1781 and today is the centerpiece of this vast museum complex.

Planning

When to Go

The Shakespeare sights get very crowded on weekends and school vacations; Warwick Castle usually brims with visitors, so arrive early in the day. Throughout the region, some country properties fill up quickly on weekends. Most rural sights have limited opening hours in winter and some stately homes have limited hours even in summer, which is when the countryside is at its most appealing. Each year, Shakespeare's birthday is celebrated with a two-day event held on the weekend closest to the Bard's birthday (April 23) in Stratford-upon-Avon. The Ludlow Fringe Festival takes place from late June to early July, while the Autumn in Malvern Festival takes place each October.

FESTIVALS
Autumn in Malvern Festival

FESTIVALS | The Autumn in Malvern Festival takes place each October at a variety of venues in and around the Malvern Hills. Classical music is the mainstay of the festival (local hero Elgar is featured heavily) with plenty of literary events as well. Full listings are released each July. ⊠ *Great Malvern* ☎ *01684/892277* ⊕ *www.malvernfestival.co.uk.*

Ludlow Food Festival

FESTIVAL | Held on the grounds of the Norman Ludlow Castle, this annual celebration of local produce is held over three days each September and features more than 180 food and drink suppliers. Many offer free tastings. ⊠ *Castle Square, Ludlow* ☎ *01584/873957* ⊕ *www.ludlowfoodfestival.co.uk* 🎫 *£9.*

Mop Fair

FESTIVALS | Dating from medieval times, the Mop Fair takes place on or around October 12, traditionally the time when laborers and apprentices from the surrounding area came to seek work. They carried implements of their trades so that prospective employers could identify them. The fair still attracts entertainers and fairground amusements. ⊠ *Town Center, Stratford-upon-Avon* ⊕ *www.stratford.gov.uk/markets/stratford-upon-avon-mop-fair.cfm.*

★ **Shakespeare Birthday Celebrations**

CULTURAL FESTIVALS | These festivities have taken place on and around the weekend closest to April 23, the Bard's birthday, since 1824. Over several days, the streets are filled with performers, impromptu concerts, and pageantry, and special events are held at various venues. The celebrations culminate with a spectacular procession. ⊠ *Stratford-upon-Avon* ☎ *01789/269332* ⊕ *www.shakespearescelebrations.com.*

Planning Your Time

Stratford-upon-Avon is ideal for day visits from London or as a base for exploring nearby, but even ardent Shakespeare lovers probably won't need more than a day or two here. Warwick can be explored in an hour or two, but allow half a day to tackle the many lines at busy Warwick Castle. A drive through the area's country lanes is a pleasant way to spend a day; a stop at any stately home will take a few hours. You're also near the northern Cotswolds if you want to explore the countryside further.

The museums and major sights of Birmingham can take a couple of days, and it's a good city for modern, budget hotels. However, the smaller towns and cities of Hereford, Shrewsbury, and Chester have more obvious charms. If you want to walk the hills, Great Malvern or Ledbury are good gateways for the Malvern Hills. In the north of the region, Ironbridge Gorge and Chester demand a full day each. Ludlow and Shrewsbury take less time. Once you've gone as far north as this, you could consider going on to Liverpool or hopping across the border into north Wales.

Getting Here and Around

AIR

The region is served by Birmingham International Airport, six miles east of the city center. It has connections to all of Britain's major cities and limited service to the United States.

CONTACTS Birmingham International Airport. ✉ A45, off M42, Birmingham ☎ 0871/222–0072 ⊕ www.birminghamairport.co.uk.

BUS

The cheapest way to travel is by bus, and National Express serves the region from London's Victoria Coach Station. You can reach Birmingham in less than three hours; Hereford and Shrewsbury take between four and five hours. National Express also operates services from London's Heathrow (2¾ hours) and Gatwick (4 hours) airports to Birmingham.

Stagecoach Midlands serves local routes throughout the Stratford and Birmingham areas. Megabus, a budget service booked online, runs buses from Victoria Station in London to Birmingham (3½ hours). A number of different companies run local services between Birmingham, Hereford, Ludlow, and other parts of the Midlands. Traveline is an excellent resource for planning local travel.

CONTACTS Megabus. ☎ 0141/352–4444 for inquiries, 0900/160–0900 for bookings ⊕ uk.megabus.com. **National Express.** ☎ 0871/781–8181 ⊕ www.nationalexpress.com. **Stagecoach.** ⊕ www.stagecoachbus.com. **Traveline.** ☎ 0114/221–1282 ⊕ www.traveline.info.

CAR

To reach Stratford (100 miles), Birmingham (120 miles), Shrewsbury (160 miles), Ludlow (150 miles), and Chester (200 miles) from London, take the M40. For the farther areas, keep on it until it becomes the M42, then take the M6. From London, the M4 and then the A417 and A40 take you to Hereford in just under three hours. Driving can be difficult in the region's western reaches—especially in the hills and valleys west of Hereford, where steep, twisting roads often narrow down into mere trackways.

Around Stratford, one pleasure of this rural area is driving the smaller "B" roads, which lead deep into the countryside. Local bus services don't do Warwickshire justice—renting a car or taking a tour bus are the two best options, although trains serve the major towns.

TRAIN

Stratford has good train connections and can be seen as a day trip from London if your time is limited (a matinee is your best bet if you want to squeeze in a play). Chiltern Railways trains leave from London Marylebone Station and take two hours direct or 2½–3 hours with transfers. They also go to Warwick. West Midlands and Avanti West Coast both run direct trains to Birmingham (about 40 miles from Stratford). From London, Avanti West Coast and West Midlands trains leave from Euston (it's 1½–2 hours to Birmingham), while Chiltern Railways trains leave from Marylebone. Trains from Euston tend to be quicker (around 1½ hours). Travel times from Paddington to Hereford and Ludlow are about 3 hours (most change at Newport); Euston to Shrewsbury, with a change at Crewe or Birmingham, is 2½ hours; and to Chester, direct or with a change at Crewe, takes two hours.

CONTACTS Chiltern Railways. ☎ 03456/005165 ⊕ www.chilternrailways.co.uk. **Trainline.** ⊕ www.thetrainline.com. **West Midlands Rail.** ☎ 0344/811–0133 ⊕ www.westmidlandsrailway.co.uk.

Restaurants

Stratford has many reasonably priced bistros and unpretentious eateries offering a broad choice of international fare; Warwick and Kenilworth both have good restaurant options. Birmingham has an exciting food scene but is probably most famous for its Indian and Pakistani "curry houses." You'll find good choices both in the city center and out of town. The city also hosts the United Kingdom's biggest food festival, Foodies Festival, at Cannon Hills Park every June. Across the rest of the Midlands, casual spots dominate, although Ludlow has some exceptionally good restaurants.

Hotels

Stratford and Warwick have accommodations to suit every price range. Because Stratford is so popular with theatergoers, you need to book well ahead. Most hotels offer discounted two- and three-day packages. Near Stratford, a number of top-notch country hotels guarantee discreet but attentive service—at fancy prices. Birmingham's hotels, geared to the convention crowd and often booked well in advance, can be bland and impersonal, but a few more sophisticated options are popping up; look for midweek discounts. In the countryside, many ancient inns and venerable Regency-style houses have been converted into hotels.

Restaurant and hotel reviews have been shortened. For full information, visit Fodors.com. Restaurant prices are the average cost of a main course at dinner, or, if dinner is not served, at lunch. Hotel prices are the lowest cost of a standard double room in high season, including 20% V.A.T.

WHAT IT COSTS in Pounds

	$	$$	$$$	$$$$
RESTAURANTS				
	under £16	£16–£23	£24–£30	over £30
HOTELS				
	under £125	£125–£225	£226–£350	over £350

Visitor Information

Traveline can field all general transportation inquiries. Shakespeare's England offers the Explorer Pass, available for one, two, or three days (£39, £50, and £60 respectively), which allows entry to 18 attractions, including the five Shakespeare family homes, plus Kenilworth and Warwick castles. Local tourist offices can recommend day or half-day tours of the region and will have the names of registered Blue Badge guides—a mark of prestige among tour companies.

CONTACTS Shakespeare's England. 🕾 *01789/260677* ⊕ *www.shakespeares-england.co.uk.* **Traveline.** 🕾 *0871/200–2233 general information, 0114/221–1282 customer support* ⊕ *www.traveline.info.*

Stratford-upon-Avon

Even under the weight of busloads of visitors, Stratford, on the banks of the slow-flowing River Avon, has somehow hung on to much of its ancient character and, on a good day, can still feel like a traditional English market town. It doesn't take long to figure out who's the center of attention here. Born in a half-timber, early-16th-century building in the center of Stratford on April 23, 1564, William Shakespeare died on April 23, 1616, his 52nd birthday, in a more imposing house at New Place, also in the center of

With its thatched roof, half-timbering, and countryside setting, Anne Hathaway's Cottage is a vision from the past.

Stratford. Although he spent much of his life in London, the world still associates him with his hometown, so much so that the town's river is sometimes referred to as "Shakespeare's Avon."

Here, in the years between his birth and 1587, he played as a young lad, attended grammar school, and married Anne Hathaway; and here he returned as a prosperous man. You can see Shakespeare's whole life here: his birthplace on Henley Street; his burial place in Holy Trinity Church; the home of his wife, Anne Hathaway's Cottage; the home of his mother, Mary Arden's Farm, at Wilmcote; New Place; and Hall's Croft, the home of Shakespeare's daughter, Susanna; her husband, Dr. John Hall; and their daughter, Elizabeth.

By the 16th century, Stratford was a prosperous market town with thriving guilds and industries. Half-timber houses from this era have been preserved, and they're set off by later architecture, such as the elegant Georgian storefronts on Bridge Street, with their 18th-century porticoes and arched doorways.

Most sights cluster around Henley Street (off the roundabout as you come in on the A3400 Birmingham road), the High Street, and Waterside, which skirts the public gardens through which the River Avon flows. Bridge Street and the parallel Sheep Street are Stratford's main thoroughfares and where you will find mostly banks, shops, and restaurants. Bridgefoot, between the canal and the river, is next to Clopton Bridge, built in the 15th century by Sir Hugh Clopton, once lord mayor of London and one of Stratford's richest and most philanthropic residents.

GETTING HERE AND AROUND

Stratford lies about 100 miles northwest of London; take the M40 to Junction 15. The town is 35 miles southeast of Birmingham by the A38, M6, M42, and M40 (Junction 16).

Chiltern Railways serves the area from London's Marylebone Station, with trains taking an average of two hours; some are direct, but most have one change. West Midlands Railway operates direct routes from Birmingham's Snow Hill Station (journey time under an hour). Stratford has two stations, Stratford-upon-Avon Parkway, northwest of the center at Bishopston, and Stratford-upon-Avon at the edge of the town center on Alcester Road, from where it is a short walk into town.

PLANNING YOUR TIME

If you have only a day here, arrive early and confine your visit to two or three Shakespeare Birthplace Trust properties, a few other town sights, a pub lunch, and a walk along the river, capped off with a stroll to Anne Hathaway's Cottage (25 minutes on foot). If you don't like crowds, avoid visiting on weekends and during school vacations, and take in the main Shakespeare shrines in the early morning to see them at their least frenetic. One high point of Stratford's calendar is the Shakespeare's Birthday Celebrations, usually on the weekend nearest to April 23.

TOURS

★ City Sightseeing

GUIDED TOURS | Running from early April to early November, these double-decker tour buses offer two options: a hop-on, hop-off bus tour that allows you to create your own itinerary around 11 landmarks in and around the town or a ticket that includes entry to each of the five Shakespeare family homes. ☎ *01789/299123* ⊕ *www.city-sightseeing.com/en/100/ stratford-upon-avon* ⊠ *From £15.*

★ Shakespeare Birthplace Trust

The main places of Shakespearean interest (Anne Hathaway's Cottage, Hall's Croft, Mary Arden's Farm, Shakespeare's New Place, and Shakespeare's Birthplace) are run by the Shakespeare Birthplace Trust, an independent charity that aims to preserve and promote the properties. By far the most economical way to visit the properties is to get a Full Story ticket (£23), which gives unlimited

access to all five houses for a year. ☎ *01789/204016* ⊕ *www.shakespeare. org.uk.*

Stratford Town Walk

WALKING TOURS | This walking tour runs every day of the year, even on Christmas Day, at 11 am, with an extra tour on Saturday at 2 pm. There's no need to book in advance; you can just show up. The tours, which take around two hours, will take you on a journey through the town, unravelling Shakespeare's story as you go. The meeting point is by the yellow sign outside the Royal Shakespeare Company, opposite the junction with Sheep Street. ☎ *01789/292478* ⊕ *www. stratfordtownwalk.co.uk* ⊠ *From £6.*

ESSENTIALS

VISITOR INFORMATION Stratford-upon-Avon Tourist Information Centre. ⊠ *Bridgefoot* ☎ *01789/264293* ⊕ *www.visitstratfordu- ponavon.co.uk.*

⊙ Sights

★ Anne Hathaway's Cottage

BUILDING | The most picturesque of the Shakespeare Birthplace Trust properties, this thatched cottage on the western outskirts of Stratford is the family home of the woman Shakespeare married in 1582. The "cottage," actually a substantial Tudor farmhouse with latticed windows, is astonishingly beautiful. Inside, it is surprisingly cozy with lots of period furniture, including the loveseat on which Shakespeare reputedly conducted his courtship and a rare carved Elizabethan bed. The cottage garden is planted in lush Edwardian style with herbs and flowers. Wildflowers are grown in the adjacent orchard (a nod to what was grown in the garden in the Hathaways' time), and the neighboring arboretum has trees, shrubs, and roses mentioned in Shakespeare's works. ■TIP→ **The best way to get here is on foot, especially in late spring when the apple trees are in blossom.** The signed path runs from Evesham

Place (an extension of Grove Road) opposite Chestnut Walk. Pick up a leaflet with a map from the tourist office; the walk takes 25–30 minutes. ✉ *Cottage La.* 🕾 *01789/338532* ⊕ *www.shakespeare. org.uk* ✑ *£13; Full Story ticket (includes entry to Hall's Croft, Mary Arden's Farm, Shakespeare's New Place, and Shakespeare's Birthplace) £23.*

Bancroft Gardens

GARDEN | Between the Royal Shakespeare Theatre and Clopton Bridge lie these well-tended expanses of lawns and flower beds. The swans gliding gracefully along the river are permanent residents, coexisting with the pleasure craft on the river and the nearby canal. The centerpiece of the gardens is the Gower Memorial statue, designed in 1888 by Lord Gower and adorned with bronze figures of Hamlet, Lady Macbeth, Falstaff, and Prince Hal—symbols of philosophy, tragedy, comedy, and history, respectively. ✉ *Off Waterside.*

Charlecote Park

HISTORIC SITE | A celebrated house in the village of Hampton Lucy just outside Stratford, Charlecote Park is a Prodigy house, built in 1558 by Sir Thomas Lucy to impress Queen Elizabeth I (the house is even shaped like the letter "E" in her honor). Shakespeare knew the house—he was supposedly even caught poaching deer here. Overlooking the River Avon, the redbrick manor is striking and sprawling. It was renovated in neo-Elizabethan style by the Lucy family, represented here by numerous portraits, during the mid-19th century. A carved ebony bed is one of many spectacular pieces of furniture. The Tudor gatehouse is unchanged since Shakespeare's day, and a collection of carriages, a Victorian kitchen, and a small brewery occupy the outbuildings. Indulge in a game of croquet near the quirky, thatched, Victorian-era summer hut, or explore the deer park landscaped by Capability Brown. Interesting themed tours and walks

take place in summer—call in advance to find out what's on offer. The house is five miles northeast of Stratford; by car it is reached via the B4086 or it costs around £15 in a taxi from Stratford-upon-Avon. ✉ *Wellesbourne, Warwick* 🕾 *01789/470277* ⊕ *www.nationaltrust. org.uk* ✑ *£14.80; winter admission to grounds and outbuildings £11* ⊙ *House closed Nov.–mid-Feb.*

Compton Verney

HOUSE | A neoclassical country mansion remodeled in the 1760s by Scottish architect Robert Adam has been repurposed by the Peter Moores Foundation as an art museum with more than 800 works. The house is set on 120 acres of spectacular rolling parkland landscaped by Capability Brown. Intriguingly varied works of art are beautifully displayed in restored rooms: British folk art and portraits, textiles, Chinese pottery and bronzes, southern Italian art from 1600 to 1800, and German art from 1450 to 1600 are the main focus. Tours take place Tuesday through Sunday and bank holidays at noon. It's 10 miles east of Stratford; by car, take the B4086. ✉ *Off B4086, Kineton* 🕾 *01926/645500* ⊕ *www. comptonverney.org.uk* ✑ *£10.25; £14.90 for museum plus special exhibitions* ⊙ *Closed Dec.–Mar. except certain weekends in Feb.*

Guild Chapel

RELIGIOUS SITE | This historic chapel is the noble centerpiece of Stratford's Guild buildings, including the Guildhall, the Grammar School, and the almshouses—all well known to Shakespeare. It also houses some of the finest surviving medieval wall paintings in Europe. The ancient structure was rebuilt in the late Perpendicular style in the 5th century. The paintings were covered with limewash during the Reformation on orders given to Shakespeare's father, who was mayor at the time. Some of the most impressive paintings, rediscovered hundreds of years later, have now been

Stratford-upon-Avon

Sights ▼

1 Anne Hathaway's Cottage........ A3
2 Bancroft Gardens................... F5
3 Charlecote Park..................... J4
4 Compton Verney J6
5 Guild Chapel....................... D5
6 Hall's Croft D7
7 Holy Trinity Church D9
8 MAD Museum D3
9 Mary Arden's Farm A3
10 Royal Shakespeare Theatre....... F5
11 Shakespeare Distillery............ A3
12 Shakespeare's Birthplace D2
13 Shakespeare's New Place D5
14 Shakespeare's Schoolroom
   and Guildhall D5
15 Stratford-upon-Avon
   Butterfly Farm.................... H6
16 Tudor World E4

Restaurants ▼

1 The Black Swan/
  The Dirty Duck E6
2 Hobsons Patisseries E3
3 Hussain's D5
4 Lambs of Sheep Street............ E4
5 Le Bistrot Pierre................... I5
6 Opposition E4
7 Sorrento D4
8 33 The Scullery.................... B3
9 The Townhouse D5
10 The Vintner E4

Hotels ▼

1 Arden Hotel......................... F5
2 Arden House B5
3 The Bell Alderminster............. H9
4 Crowne Plaza
  Stratford-upon-Avon H3
5 Ettington Park Hotel H9
6 Hallmark Hotel
  The Welcombe.................... G1
7 Hotel Indigo
  Stratford-upon-Avon C5
8 Macdonald Alveston Manor J5
9 Mercure Stratford-Upon-Avon
  Shakespeare Hotel D5
10 The Stratford,
   DoubleTree by Hilton............. A2
11 Victoria Spa Lodge C1
12 White Swan C3

KEY

1 Exploring Sights
1 Restaurants
1 Hotels

Bancroft
Gardens

Avon River

0 — 500 ft
0 — 100 m

restored and can be viewed, including an ornate painting known as *The Doom* above the chancel arch. Restoration on other paintings continues. ⊠ *Chapel La.* ☎ *01789/207111* ⊕ *www.guildchapel.org. uk* ✉ *Free, donations welcome.*

Hall's Croft

HISTORIC SITE | One of the finest surviving Jacobean (early-17th-century) town houses in England, this impressive residence (one of the best preserved of the Shakespeare family homes) has a delightful walled garden and was once the home of Shakespeare's eldest daughter, Susanna, and her husband, Dr. John Hall. John Hall was a wealthy physician who, by prescribing an herbal cure for scurvy, was well ahead of his time. One room is furnished as a medical dispensary of the period, and throughout the building are fine examples of heavy oak Jacobean furniture, including a child's high chair and some 17th-century portraits. The café serves light lunches and afternoon teas. ⊠ *Old Town* ☎ *01789/338533* ⊕ *www. shakespeare.org.uk* ✉ *£9; Full Story ticket (includes Anne Hathaway's Cottage and Gardens, Shakespeare's Birthplace, Shakespeare's New Place, and Mary Arden's Farm) £23.*

★ Holy Trinity Church

RELIGIOUS SITE | This 13th-century church on the banks of the River Avon is the final resting place of William Shakespeare. He was buried here not because he was a famed poet but because he was a lay rector of Stratford, owning a portion of the township tithes. On the north wall of the sanctuary, over the altar steps, is the famous marble bust created by Gerard Jansen in 1623 and thought to be a true likeness of Shakespeare. The bust offers a more human, even humorous, perspective when viewed from the side. Also in the chancel are the graves of Shakespeare's wife, Anne; his daughter, Susanna; his son-in-law, John Hall; and his granddaughter's first husband, Thomas Nash. Also here is the christening font in which Shakespeare was baptized. ⊠ *Old Town* ☎ *01789/266316* ⊕ *www. stratford-upon-avon.org* ✉ *£4 donation requested.*

MAD Museum

MUSEUM | **FAMILY** | Push buttons and pedals to your heart's content to make the exhibits in the Mechanical Art & Design Museum come alive. Witty, beautiful, and intricate automata and examples of kinetic art will clank, whir, and rattle away. Marbles and Ping-Pong balls thread and bounce through looping runs, a typewriter plays tunes on glasses and bottles, and two trains chuff around high up on the walls. Kids will love constructing their own marble run, and grown-ups will marvel at the Kitchenator display. There's also a shop full of weird and wonderful things to buy. Tickets last all day so you can come and go as you please. ⊠ *4–5 Henley St.* ☎ *01789/269356* ⊕ *themad-museum.co.uk* ✉ *£7.80.*

★ Mary Arden's Farm

HOUSE | **FAMILY** | This charming working farm was the childhood home of Shakespeare's mother, Mary Arden, and offers great insight into the farming methods employed in Tudor England. The rural heritage attraction, just three miles outside Stratford, is great for kids, who can try their hand at basket weaving and gardening, listen as the farmers explain their work in the fields, watch the cooks prepare food in the Tudor farmhouse kitchen, or play in the amazing timber-framed adventure playground. There are also daily falconry and archery displays and opportunities to meet the farm animals, as well as a good café. ⊠ *Station Rd., Wilmcote* ☎ *01789/338535* ⊕ *www.shakespeare.org.uk* ✉ *Adult £15.50; Full Story ticket (includes Anne Hathaway's Cottage and Gardens, Hall's Croft, Shakespeare's New Place, and Shakespeare's Birthplace) £23* ⊗ *Closed Nov.–mid-Mar.*

Kayaking along the River Avon (a popular excursion) will bring you past the Royal Shakespeare Theatre.

★ Royal Shakespeare Theatre

ARTS VENUE | FAMILY | Overlooking Bancroft Gardens and with views along the River Avon, the Stratford home of the world-renowned Royal Shakespeare Company is undoubtedly one of the best places in the world to watch a Shakespearean play. The company has existed since 1879 and today boasts three Stratford venues: the Royal Shakespeare Theatre, the Swan Theatre (on the site of the original Shakespeare Memorial Theatre), and The Other Place. There's a great rooftop restaurant at the Royal Shakespeare Theatre, plus a popular Behind the Scenes tour. You can also ascend to the theater's tower, for a panoramic view of Stratford. ⊠ *Waterside* ☎ *01789/331111* ⊕ *www.rsc.org.uk* ✉ *Behind the Scenes tour £9; tower £3.*

★ Shakespeare's Birthplace

MUSEUM | A half-timber house typical of its time, the playwright's birthplace is a much-visited shrine that has been altered and restored since Shakespeare lived here. Passing through the modern visitor center, you are immersed in the world of Shakespeare through a state-of-the-art exhibition that includes evocative audio and visuals from contemporary stagings of his plays. The house itself is across the garden from the visitor center. Colorful wall decorations and furnishings reflect comfortable, middle-class Elizabethan domestic life. You can view his father's workshop and you can see the very room where Shakespeare was born. Mark Twain and Charles Dickens were both pilgrims here, and you can see the signatures of Thomas Carlyle and Walter Scott scratched into the windowpanes. In the garden, actors present excerpts from his plays. There's also a café and bookshop on the grounds. ⊠ *Henley St.* ☎ *01789/204016* ⊕ *www.shakespeare. org.uk* ✉ *£18; Full Story ticket (includes Anne Hathaway's Cottage and Gardens, Hall's Croft, Shakespeare's New Place, and Mary Arden's Farm) £23.*

Stratford-upon-Avon has plenty of pubs and restaurants when you need a break from the Shakespeare trail.

Shakespeare Distillery

WINERY/DISTILLERY | Gin is really having a moment in England right now, and this distillery is embracing the trend while combining traditional Tudor ingredients with modern handcrafting techniques. Tours (1¼ hours) give a concise overview of how gin is made and also include a complimentary gin and tonic, plus a guided tasting of three spirits. ✉ *Drayton Manor Dr.* ☎ *01789/336559* ⊕ *www. shakespearedistillery.com* ✉ *£15* ⊘ *Closed Mon. and Tues.*

★ Shakespeare's New Place

HOUSE | This is the spot where Shakespeare lived for the last 19 years of his life and where he wrote many of his plays, including *The Tempest*. Though the actual 15th-century building he inhabited was torn down in the 18th century, the site was imaginatively reinterpreted in 2016 as an outdoor space where the footprint of the original house can be traced. Each of his 38 plays is represented by a pennant in the Golden Garden, and his sonnets are engraved into the stone paving. Highlights include a mulberry tree that some believe was given to Shakespeare by King James I and a restored Elizabethan knot garden. A permanent exhibition inside the neighboring Nash's House tells the story of the New House and Shakespeare's family life within it; there's also a roof terrace, which provides views of the gardens. Nash's House was once home to Thomas Nash, the husband of Shakespeare's granddaughter, Elizabeth Hall. ✉ *22 Chapel St.* ☎ *01789/338536* ⊕ *www.shakespeare. org.uk* ✉ *£13; Full Story ticket (includes Anne Hathaway's Cottage and Gardens, Shakespeare's Birthplace, Hall's Croft, and Mary Arden's Farm) £23.*

Shakespeare's Schoolroom and Guildhall

HISTORIC SITE | Dating from the early 15th century, the Guildhall is where a young Shakespeare went to school and where he was allegedly first introduced to the world of theater. Once the administrative center of the town, it now serves as a heritage center where visitors can see newly discovered medieval wall paintings, including two of the oldest surviving Tudor roses in England, plus take part in a lesson in the very room where Shakespeare was once taught. In the 16th century, the Guildhall was where the city council once sat, including John Shakespeare, Shakespeare's father, who was town mayor in the 1560s. Around this time it also became home to the King's New School, and shortly afterwards William Shakespeare attended as a pupil. On the first floor is the Guildhall proper, where traveling acting companies performed to obtain their licenses. Many historians believe that it was after seeing the troupe known as the Earl of Leicester's Men in 1587 that Shakespeare got the acting bug and set off for London. Today the building is still home to a school, and lessons take place on weekday mornings during term time before the attraction opens at 11 am. ⊠ *Church St.* ☎ *01789/203170* ⊕ *www. shakespearesschoolroom.org* 🖃 *£8.50.*

Stratford-upon-Avon Butterfly Farm
NATURE PRESERVE | FAMILY | The United Kingdom's largest exotic butterfly collection is housed in a tropical greenhouse, a two-minute walk past the Bridgefoot footbridge (spiders, caterpillars, and insects from all over the world also make their home here). Kids can watch as butterflies emerge from pupae, search for caterpillars among the plants, or take a look at a toxic black widow spider. The ant colony is another highlight. There is also a fantastic shop, plus places to picnic in the lovely garden. ⊠ *Swan's Nest La.* ☎ *01789/299288* ⊕ *www.butterfly-farm.co.uk* 🖃 *£7.25.*

Tudor World
MUSEUM | FAMILY | Tread carefully over the cobbles, and enter Tudor World on Sheep Street to find a dimly lit and quirky maze of displays that explore, with the help of Tudor mannequins, aspects of the 16th century, including the plague years, early medicine, witch trials, bearbaiting, punishment, and alleged ghosts. Kids

will enjoy peering round the curtains and opening the boxes of smells. At night, ghost tours by lantern light (suitable only for adults and older children) explore the house's paranormal history in spooky detail. ⊠ *The Shrieves House Barn, 40 Sheep St.* ☎ *01789/298070* ⊕ *www. tudorworld.com* 🖃 *£6; ghost tours £7.50.*

🍴 Restaurants

The Black Swan/The Dirty Duck
$ | BRITISH | The only pub in Britain to be licensed under two names (the more informal one came courtesy of American GIs who were stationed here during World War II), this is one of Stratford's most celebrated and consistently rated pubs, attracting actors since the 18th-century days of thespian David Garrick. Along with your pint of bitter, you can choose from the extensive pub-grub menu of fish-and-chips, steaks, burgers, and grills; there are also good-value light bites. **Known for:** classic English pub atmosphere; reservations-only for dinner; veranda overlooking the river. ⑤ *Average main: £10* ⊠ *Waterside* ☎ *01789/297312* ⊕ *www.greeneking-pubs.co.uk.*

★ Hobsons Patisseries
$ | BRITISH | Visitors and locals alike head for the half-timber Hobsons Patisseries to indulge in the famous savory pies or scrumptious afternoon teas. Just a couple of minutes walk from Shakespeare's Birthplace, it's an almost obligatory lunch stop. **Known for:** delicious cakes and pies; cheap eats; low-key afternoon tea. ⑤ *Average main: £7* ⊠ *1 Henley St.* ☎ *01789/293330* ⊕ *www.hobsonspatis-series.com.*

Hussain's
$ | INDIAN | The luxuriant marigolds in the window might draw you in, but locals will tell you it's the Indian dishes that are the real appeal here. The extensive menu lists plenty of balti and rogan josh choices; for a little less heat, try the tandoori chicken with mild spices, cream, ground

almonds, and mixed fruits, or increase the heat a bit with *jhinga bhuna* (king-size prawns in a spicy tomato sauce with onions, green peppers, and coriander). **Known for:** range of tandoori specialties; local curry-house atmosphere; prompt, friendly service. $ *Average main: £12* ⊠ *6A Chapel St.* ☎ *01789/267506* ⊕ *www.hussains-restaurant.com* ⊘ *No lunch Mon.–Wed.*

★ Lambs of Sheep Street
$$ | BRITISH | Sit downstairs to appreciate the hardwood floors and oak beams of this local epicurean favorite; upstairs, the look is a bit more contemporary. The updates of tried-and-true dishes include herb-crusted rack of English lamb and panfried calf's liver with creamed potato, wilted spinach, pancetta, and crisp shallot. **Known for:** good-value set meals; one of the oldest buildings in Stratford; modern twists on British classics. $ *Average main: £19* ⊠ *12 Sheep St.* ☎ *01789/292554* ⊕ *www.lambsrestaurant.co.uk* ⊘ *No lunch Mon. and Sun.*

Le Bistrot Pierre
$$ | FRENCH | There's always a satisfied hum in the air at this large, modern, and bustling bistro, part of a small chain, that's close to the river. It's French and the menu makes that known; olives from Provence, sausage from the Beaujolais region, pâtés, mussels in a Roquefort sauce, beef bourguignon, and rustic French cheeses all appear. **Known for:** regional French cuisine; riverside dining; good menu for kids. $ *Average main: £18* ⊠ *Swan's Nest La., Bridgefoot* ☎ *01789/264804* ⊕ *www.bistrotpierre.co.uk.*

Opposition
$$ | MODERN BRITISH | Hearty, warming meals are offered at this informal, family-style restaurant in a 16th-century building on the main dining street near the theaters. The English and international dishes—chicken roasted with banana in lime butter and served with curry sauce and basmati rice, for instance—win praise from the locals. **Known for:** historical ambience; plenty of vegetarian and healthy options; summertime crowds. $ *Average main: £20* ⊠ *13 Sheep St.* ☎ *01789/269980* ⊕ *www.theoppo.co.uk* ⊘ *Closed Sun.*

Sorrento
$$ | ITALIAN | Family run, this Italian restaurant takes a respectable, old-fashioned approach to service. The menu of traditional favorites is cooked from family recipes and includes main dishes such as veal sirloin grilled with rosemary and garlic butter and black linguine with crab-claw meat and scallops. **Known for:** alfresco dining in summer; family restaurant for over 30 years; old-fashioned table service. $ *Average main: £17* ⊠ *8 Ely St.* ☎ *01789/297999* ⊕ *www.sorrentorestaurant.co.uk* ⊘ *Closed Sun. and Mon.*

★ 33 The Scullery
$$ | BRITISH | This small restaurant has attracted quite a following thanks to its fresh, seasonal ingredients. This is British cooking at its best and includes good options for seafood, game, and vegetarian dishes. **Known for:** buzzy atmosphere; seasonal ingredients; high-quality British dishes. $ *Average main: £18* ⊠ *33a Greenhill St.* ☎ *01789/205–700* ⊕ *www.33scy.co.uk* ⊘ *Closed Mon.*

★ The Townhouse
$$ | MODERN BRITISH | Theatergoers tucking into an early supper to the strains of the piano in the bar, grandmothers enjoying afternoon tea, and couples lingering over candlelit suppers can all happily be found at this restaurant with rooms, which is part of the Brakspear Brewery. Chefs source the best ingredients locally where possible and serve up dishes such as oven-roasted duck breast and whole grilled plaice. **Known for:** good-value pretheater menus; chic decor; Sunday roast with all the trimmings. $ *Average main: £16* ⊠ *16 Church St.* ☎ *01789/262222* ⊕ *www.stratfordtownhouse.co.uk.*

The Vintner

$$ | **BISTRO** | The imaginative, bistro-inspired menu varies each day at this café and wine bar set in a 15th-century building. Tempting British and European-style dishes include confit leg of duck bigarade with dauphinoise potatoes and seared beef fillet Stroganoff. **Known for:** inventive pretheater menu; historic setting; excellent wine list. $ Average main: £18 ⊠ 4 and 5 Sheep St. ☎ 01789/297259 ⊕ www.the-vintner.co.uk.

 Hotels

★ Arden Hotel

$$ | **HOTEL** | Bedrooms are spacious and discreet with splashes of green, violet, and dark crimson in this redbrick boutique hotel across the road from the Royal Shakespeare Theatre. **Pros:** convenient for theatergoers; crisp and modern style; gorgeous guest areas. **Cons:** gets booked up quickly; may be too noisy for some; can be popular with business travelers. $ Rooms from: £200 ⊠ Waterside ☎ 01789/298682 ⊕ www.theardenhotelstratford.com ⊷ 45 rooms ⦷ Free breakfast.

★ Arden House

$$ | **B&B/INN** | This luxury guesthouse, sister property to the nearby Arden Hotel, offers a first-class stay, with a help-yourself pantry, books to borrow, afternoon tea, and a daily gin o'clock. **Pros:** welcoming atmosphere; free afternoon tea and gin; amazing breakfast selection. **Cons:** hosts can seem overeager to please; no tea- and coffee-making facilities in rooms; you may feel obliged to chat with other guests. $ Rooms from: £169 ⊠ 58–59 Rother St. ☎ 01789/298682 ⊕ www.theardenhotelstratford.com ⊷ 10 rooms ⦷ Some meals.

The Bell Alderminster

$$ | **B&B/INN** | Just a few miles south of Stratford, this pub with rooms oozes imagination and individuality. **Pros:** rural setting, close to the Cotswolds; excellent food; homemade biscuits and fresh milk in the rooms. **Cons:** on a loud main road; bar can get busy; a bit inconvenient for the Shakespeare attractions. $ Rooms from: £125 ⊠ Shipston Rd., Alderminster ☎ 01789/335671 ⊕ www.brunningandprice.co.uk/bell ⊷ 8 rooms ⦷ Free breakfast.

Crowne Plaza Stratford-upon-Avon

$ | **HOTEL** | **FAMILY** | This spick-and-span, good-value hotel's selling points are its excellent location near the center of the historic district and views across the river. **Pros:** good location; nice leisure facilities, including pool; free accommodation and dinners for kids. **Cons:** not much old England charm; big and impersonal; a bit overrun with conferences. $ Rooms from: £75 ⊠ Bridgefoot ☎ 0371/423–4876 reservations, 01789/279988 inquiries ⊕ www.crowneplaza.com ⊷ 259 rooms ⦷ Free breakfast.

★ Ettington Park Hotel

$ | **HOTEL** | This Victorian Gothic mansion, featuring arched windows and romantic turrets, is approached along a private avenue and is a soothing retreat for theatergoers who want to escape Stratford's crowds. **Pros:** gorgeous building; spacious rooms; relaxing lounge. **Cons:** a bit too formal for some; well outside Stratford; a lot of wedding guests on weekends. $ Rooms from: £105 ⊠ Off A3400, Alderminster ☎ 0845/072–7454 reservations, 01789/451401 inquiries ⊕ www.handpickedhotels.co.uk/hotels/ettington-park-hotel ⊷ 48 rooms ⦷ Free breakfast.

Hallmark Hotel The Welcombe

$ | **HOTEL** | With its mullioned bay windows, gables, and tall chimneys, this hotel in an 1886 neo-Jacobean-style building evokes the luxury of bygone days. **Pros:** great for golfers; lovely spa facilities; stunning grounds. **Cons:** dining too formal for some; need a car to get here; can feel a bit too impersonal. $ Rooms from: £121 ⊠ Warwick Rd. ☎ 0330/028–3422 ⊕ www.

hallmarkhotels.co.uk/hotels/hallmark-ho-tel-the-welcombe-stratford-upon-avon/ ➠ 85 rooms ⦿l Free breakfast.

★ Hotel Indigo Stratford-upon-Avon

$ | HOTEL | This hotel in a black-and-white timber-frame building in the center of town has a great location just opposite Shakespeare's New Place and a gor-geous, stripped-back feel that works well within the confines of a historic building. **Pros:** great location; excellent restaurant; plenty of character that combines old and new. **Cons:** part of a chain; neighborhood can be a little busy; some rooms on the small side. $ Rooms from: £95 ✉ Chapel St. ☎ 0330/102–7244 ⊕ stratford.hotelin-digo.com ➠ 93 rooms ⦿l Free breakfast.

Macdonald Alveston Manor

$ | HOTEL | This redbrick Elizabethan manor house across the River Avon has plenty of historic features, as well as a modern spa with a long list of treatments. **Pros:** a nice mix of the modern and historic; award-winning restaurant; interesting theatrical history. **Cons:** a lack of charm; no elevator and lots of stairs; fee for parking. $ Rooms from: £113 ✉ Clopton Bridge ☎ 0344/879–9138, 01789/205478 for international calls ⊕ www.macdonald-hotels.co.uk/our-hotels/alveston ➠ 113 rooms ⦿l Free breakfast.

Mercure Stratford-Upon-Avon Shakespeare Hotel

$ | HOTEL | Built in the 1400s, this Elizabe-than town house in the heart of Stratford is a vision right out of The Merry Wives of Windsor, with its nine gables and long, stunning, black-and-white, half-timber facade. **Pros:** historic building; relaxing lounge; great food. **Cons:** some very small bedrooms; parking fee; a bit dated in places. $ Rooms from: £105 ✉ Chapel St. ☎ 01789/294997 ⊕ www.mercure.com ➠ 78 rooms ⦿l No meals.

The Stratford, DoubleTree by Hilton

$$ | HOTEL | Although this modern hotel may lack the period charm of older hotels, its up-to-date facilities, spacious rooms, and ample grounds make it a good option if Tudor beamed ceilings aren't a must. **Pros:** friendly staff; handy location near train station; lots of modern conveniences. **Cons:** largely used as a conference hotel; rooms lack personality; fee for parking. $ Rooms from: £163 ✉ Arden St. ☎ 01789/271000 ⊕ www.qhotels.co.uk/our-locations/the-stratford ➠ 102 rooms ⦿l Free breakfast.

Victoria Spa Lodge

$$ | B&B/INN | This B&B lies 1½ miles outside town and backs on to the Stratford-upon-Avon Canal; the grand building dates from 1837 and is brimming with character. **Pros:** beautiful building; charming common spaces; free parking. **Cons:** away from the town center; too old-fashioned for some; quite small rooms. $ Rooms from: £129 ✉ Bish-opton La. ☎ 01789/267985 ➠ 6 rooms ⦿l Free breakfast.

★ White Swan

$ | HOTEL | None of the character of this black-and-white timbered hotel, in one of Stratford's most historic buildings, has been lost in its swanky but sympathetic update. **Pros:** great sense of history; large bathrooms; friendly service. **Cons:** fee for parking, which is not on-site; food not impressive; Shakespeare motif can feel a bit overdone. $ Rooms from: £107 ✉ Rother St. ☎ 01789/297022 ⊕ www.white-swan-stratford.co.uk ➠ 41 rooms ⦿l Free breakfast.

🎭 Performing Arts

★ Royal Shakespeare Company

THEATER | One of the finest reperto-ry troupes in the world and long the backbone of England's theatrical life, the Royal Shakespeare Company (RSC) per-forms plays year-round in Stratford and at venues across Britain. The stunning Royal Shakespeare Theatre, home of the RSC, has a thrust stage based on the original Globe Theater in London. The Swan Theatre, part of the theater complex and also built in the style of Shakespeare's Globe, stages plays by Shakespeare and his contemporaries such as Christopher Marlowe and Ben Jonson. Contemporary works are staged at The Other Place nearby. Prices start from £5 for rehearsals and previews. ■ TIP➔ **Seats book up fast, but day-of-performance and returned tickets are sometimes available.** ✉ *Waterside* ☎ *01789/403493* ⊕ *www.rsc.org.uk* ✐ *General tickets from £16.*

🛍 Shopping

Chain stores and shops sell tourist junk, but this is also a good place to shop for high-quality (and high-price) silver, jewelry, and china. Check out the regular open markets on Rother Street—the Friday one is particularly good for bargains—and don't miss Upmarket held on Waterside every Sunday (and bank holidays) from Easter to Christmas. It's a great place to browse for unusual gifts and souvenirs.

Antiques Centre
ANTIQUES/COLLECTIBLES | This building set in a Tudor courtyard contains around 50 stalls displaying jewelry, silver, linens, porcelain, and memorabilia. There's also a lovely tearoom next door. ✉ *59–60 Ely St.* ☎ *01789/204180.*

B&W Thornton
CERAMICS/GLASSWARE | Above Shakespeare's Birthplace, B&W Thornton stocks Moorcroft pottery and glass along with Shakespearean figurines. ✉ *23 Henley St.* ☎ *01789/269405* ⊕ *www. bwthornton.co.uk.*

★ Chaucer Head Bookshop
BOOKS/STATIONERY | This is the best of Stratford's many secondhand bookshops and a great place to pick up books on British history and travel. ✉ *21 Chapel St.* ☎ *01789/204330* ⊕ *www.chaucer-head.com.*

★ Shakespeare Bookshop
BOOKS/STATIONERY | Run by the Shakespeare Birthplace, the Shakespeare Bookshop carries Elizabethan plays, Shakespeare studies, children's books, and general paraphernalia. ✉ *Shakespeare's Birthplace, Henley St.* ☎ *01789/292176* ⊕ *www.shakespeare. org.uk/shop/bookshop.*

🏃 Activities

★ Avon Boating
BOATING | From April to October, Avon Boating rents out rowboats, punts, and canoes by the hour (£7). You can also hire a motorboat (£35 per hour), and river cruises (£7) are available onboard one of the quaint Edwardian passenger vessels. There are also gin cruises (£22.50) offered in conjunction with Shakespeare Distillery. ✉ *Swan's Nest Boathouse, Swan's Nest La.* ☎ *01789/267073* ⊕ *www.avon-boating.co.uk.*

Bancroft Cruisers
BOATING | A family-run business, Bancroft Cruises runs regular 45-minute guided excursions (£7) along the Avon with lots of Shakespeare trivia thrown in. When booking, ask about the afternoon tea package. ✉ *Crowne Plaza, Bridgefoot* ☎ *01789/269669* ⊕ *www.bancroftcruisers.co.uk.*

Henley-in-Arden

8 miles northwest of Stratford.

A brief drive out of Stratford will take you under the Stratford-upon-Avon Canal aqueduct to pretty Henley-in-Arden, whose wide main street is an architectural pageant of many periods. This area was once the Forest of Arden, where Shakespeare set one of his greatest comedies, *As You Like It*. Among the buildings to look for are the former Guild

Hall, dating from the 15th century, and the White Swan pub, built in the early 1600s. Near Henley-in-Arden are two stately homes worth a stop, Packwood House and Baddesley Clinton.

GETTING HERE AND AROUND
The town is on the A3400. West Midlands trains for Henley-in-Arden depart every hour from Stratford; the journey takes about 15 minutes. Train service from Birmingham Moor Street takes about 35 minutes, and trains leave every hour. The town heritage center is open from April through October.

ESSENTIALS
VISITOR INFORMATION Henley-in-Arden Heritage Centre. ⊠ *Joseph Hardy House, 150 High St., Henley in Arden* ☎ *01564/795919* ⊕ *www.heritagehenley. org.uk.*

◉ Sights

★ Baddesley Clinton
HOUSE | The eminent architectural historian Sir Nikolaus Pevsner described this as "the perfect late medieval manor house," and it's hard to argue with that assessment. The Tudor mansion, with its elegant Queen Anne brick bridge reaching over the moat, is like something out of a period drama. Set off a winding back-road, this grand manor dating from the 15th century retains its great fireplaces, 17th-century paneling, and three priest holes (secret chambers for Roman Catholic priests, who were hidden by sympathizers when Catholicism was banned in the 16th and 17th centuries). Admission to the house is by timed ticket. Baddesley Clinton is two miles east of Packwood House and 15 miles north of Stratford-upon-Avon. ⊠ *Rising La., Knowle, Henley in Arden* ⊕ *Off A4141 near Chadwick End* ☎ *01564/783294* ⊕ *www.nationaltrust.org.uk/baddesley-clinton* ⚐ *£12.60.*

Packwood House
HOUSE | Garden enthusiasts are drawn to Packwood's re-created 17th-century gardens, highlighted by an ambitious topiary Tudor garden in which yew trees represent Jesus's Sermon on the Mount. With tall chimneys, the house combines redbrick and half-timbering. Exquisite collections of 16th-century furniture and tapestries in the interior's 20th-century version of Tudor architecture make this one of the area's finest historic houses open to the public. It's five miles north of Henley-in-Arden and 12 miles north of Stratford-upon-Avon. ⊠ *Packwood La., Lapworth, Henley in Arden* ⊕ *Off B4439, 2 miles east of Hockley Heath* ☎ *01564/782024* ⊕ *www.nationaltrust. org.uk/packwood-house* ⚐ *£12.60; £8.40 in winter.*

Warwick

8 miles east of Henley-in-Arden, 4 miles south of Kenilworth, 9 miles northeast of Stratford-upon-Avon.

Most famous for Warwick Castle—that vision out of the feudal ages—the town of Warwick (pronounced *war*-ick) is an interesting architectural mix of Georgian redbrick and Elizabethan half-timbered buildings.

GETTING HERE AND AROUND
Frequent trains to Warwick leave London's Marylebone Station; travel time is about 90 minutes. The journey between Stratford-upon-Avon and Warwick takes around 40 minutes by train or bus. Stagecoach Bus X18 is more frequent, running every half hour.

ESSENTIALS
VISITOR INFORMATION Warwick Tourist Information Centre. ⊠ *Court House, Jury St.* ☎ *01926/492212* ⊕ *www.visitwarwick.co.uk.*

👁 Sights

Collegiate Church of St. Mary

RELIGIOUS SITE | Crowded with gilded, carved, and painted tombs, the Beauchamp Chantry within this church is considered one of the finest medieval chapels in England. Despite the wealth of late-medieval and Tudor chivalry, the chapel was built in the 15th century in honor of the somewhat-less-than-chivalrous Richard de Beauchamp, who consigned Joan of Arc to burn at the stake. Alongside his impressive effigy in gilded bronze lie the fine tombs of Robert Dudley, Earl of Leicester, adviser and favorite of Queen Elizabeth I, and Dudley's brother, Ambrose. The church's chancel, distinguished by its flying ribs, houses the alabaster table tomb of Thomas Beauchamp, one of the first knights of the Order of the Garter, and his wife.

In the Norman crypt, look for the rare ducking stool (a chair in which people were tied for public punishment). You can also climb St. Mary's Tower for views of Warwick Castle, just a five-minute walk away. ✉ Old Sq. ☎ 01926/403940 🌐 www.stmaryswarwick.org.uk 💷 £2 donation suggested; tower £3.

★ Lord Leycester Hospital

BUILDING | Unattractive postwar development has spoiled much of Warwick's town center, but look for the 14th-century half-timber Lord Leycester Hospital at the Norman gate, which is a genuine hidden gem. The Lord Leycester has effectively been a retirement home for soldiers since Robert Dudley, the Earl of Leicester, dedicated it to that purpose in 1571. Within the complex, there is a 12th-century chapel, an impressive beamed hall, and a fine courtyard with a wattle-and-daub balcony and 500-year-old gardens. You can book a tour with one of the guides dressed in Elizabethan robes and afterwards have cream tea in the very friendly Brethren's Kitchen, where food has been served for centuries. ✉ *60 High St.* ☎ *01926/491422* ⊕ *www.lordleycester.com* ✑ *£8.50; gardens only £2* ⊘ *Closed Mon. except bank holidays.*

St. John's House Museum

HOUSE | FAMILY | Kids as well as adults appreciate the well-thought-out St. John's House Museum, with its period costumes and scenes of domestic life, as well as a Victorian schoolroom and kitchen. Beautiful gardens where you can picnic surround the Jacobean building near the castle. ✉ *St. Johns* ☎ *01926/412069* ⊕ *heritage.warwickshire.gov.uk/museum-service/st-johns-house-museum-planning-your-visit* ✑ *Free* ⊘ *Closed Mon.*

★ Warwick Castle

CASTLE/PALACE | FAMILY | The vast bulk of this medieval castle rests on a cliff overlooking the Avon River and is considered "the fairest monument of ancient and chivalrous splendor which yet remains uninjured by time," to use the words of Sir Walter Scott. Today, the company that runs the Madame Tussauds wax museums owns the castle, and it has become more theme park than authentic heritage site, but it is still a lot of fun. Warwick's two soaring towers, bristling with battlements, can be seen for miles: the 147-foot-high Caesar's Tower, built in 1356, and the 128-foot-high Guy's Tower, built in 1380. Warwick Castle's monumental walls enclose an impressive armory of medieval weapons, as well as state rooms with historic furnishings and paintings. Other exhibits explore the castle's history through the ages, display the sights and sounds of a great medieval household as it prepares for an important battle, and tell the story of a princess's fairy-tale wedding. Be prepared both to play your part and be spooked in the gruesome dungeon experience (50 minutes and not recommended for under-10s) as you travel through scenes of torture, poisonings, and death sentences. Elsewhere, a working trebuchet (a kind of catapult), falconry displays, and rat-throwing (stuffed, not live) games add to the atmosphere. Below the castle, strutting peacocks patrol the 64 acres of grounds elegantly landscaped by Capability Brown in the 18th century. ■**TIP➜ Arrive early to beat the crowds. If you book online, you save 30% on ticket prices.** Lavish medieval banquets take place throughout the year, and plenty of food stalls serve lunch. For the ultimate castle experience, you can "glamp" (glamorously camp) in a medieval tent, stay in a wooden lodge in the Knight's Village, or spend the night in your own luxury suite in the 14th-century Caesar's Tower. ✉ *Castle La. off Mill St.* ☎ *0371/265–2000* ⊕ *www.warwick-castle.com* ✑ *Castle £20, £13 in advance; castle and dungeon £18 (in advance only).*

🍴 Restaurants

The Art Kitchen

$$ | THAI | Thai chefs enjoy fine-tuning the recipes at this chic and contemporary restaurant. The green and red curries are favorites, especially the chicken or lamb Masaman curry. **Known for:** modern Thai cuisine; interesting artwork; dependable set menus. ⑤ *Average main: £16* ✉ *7 Swan St.* ☎ *01926/494303* ⊕ *www.theartkitchen.com.*

★ Rose & Crown

$$ | MODERN BRITISH | Plain wood floorboards, comfy sofas, sturdy wooden tables, and solidly good food and drink set the tone at this contemporary gastro-pub with rooms on the town's main square. It's popular with locals, and the owners take pride in offering seasonal

Now in impressive ruins, mighty Kenilworth Castle once hosted Queen Elizabeth I. Today it has gardens, exhibitions, and a great setting.

food that mixes British and international influences with only the best ingredients. **Known for:** seasonal produce; great pub; warm atmosphere. ⑤ *Average main: £16* ✉ *30 Market Pl.* ☎ *01926/411117* ⊕ *www. roseandcrownwarwick.co.uk.*

🛏 Hotels

★ Mallory Court Country House Hotel and Spa

$$ | HOTEL | This elegant country-house hotel four miles southeast of Warwick makes for a quiet, luxurious getaway; it has 43 rooms but still manages to make you feel like you're visiting friends (albeit very wealthy ones). **Pros:** good for pampering; excellent restaurant; real English country-house experience. **Cons:** outside town; lots of weekend weddings; some traffic noise. ⑤ *Rooms from: £220* ✉ *Harbury La., Bishops Tachbrook* ☎ *01926/330214* ⊕ *www.mallory.co.uk* ⤵ *43 rooms* ❚❘ *Free breakfast.*

Kenilworth Castle

5 miles north of Warwick.

The sprawling, graceful red ruins of Kenilworth Castle loom over the green fields of Warwickshire, surrounded by the low grassy impression of what was once a lake.

GETTING HERE AND AROUND

The local Stagecoach company offers bus services to and from Stratford and Warwick on the X17 and X18 routes. The castle is 1½ miles from the town center.

ESSENTIALS

VISITOR INFORMATION Kenilworth Library and Information Centre. ✉ *Kenilworth Library, 11 Smalley Pl., Kenilworth* ☎ *0300/555–8171* ⊕ *www.warwickshire. gov.uk/kenilworthlibrary.*

👁 Sights

★ Kenilworth Castle & Elizabethan Garden

CASTLE/PALACE | The romantic ruins of Kenilworth give some sense of the turbulent times the castle has witnessed in its 900-year history. In 1326, King Edward II was imprisoned here and forced to renounce the throne before he was transferred to Berkeley Castle in Gloucestershire and allegedly murdered with a red-hot poker. Here the ambitious Robert Dudley, Earl of Leicester, one of Elizabeth I's favorites, entertained the queen four times, most notably in 1575 with 19 days of revelry. It was for this extended visit that Dudley created the elaborate Elizabethan garden in which to woo the queen; the garden has since been restored to its original splendor with arbors, an aviary, and an 18-foot-high Carrara marble fountain. The top of the keep has commanding views of the countryside, one good indication of why this was such a formidable fortress from 1120 until it was dismantled by Oliver Cromwell after the English Civil War in the mid-17th century. Still intact are its keep, with 20-foot-thick walls; its great hall built by John of Gaunt in the 14th century; and its curtain walls, the low outer walls forming the castle's first line of defense. You can climb the stairs to the viewing platforms for the vista that Queen Elizabeth would have had when she stayed and visit the restored gatehouse where an excellent exhibition explores her relationship with Dudley. The fine gift shop sells excellent replicas of tapestries and swords. ⊠ *Castle Green, off A452, Kenilworth* ☎ *01926/852078* ⊕ *www.english-heritage.org.uk* 🎫 *£11.80* ⊗ *Closed weekdays Jan.–mid-Feb.*

🍴 Restaurants

Clarendon Arms

$ | BRITISH | FAMILY | A location close to Kenilworth Castle and some good hand-pulled ales helps make this pub a nice spot for lunch. You can order home-cooked food, including steaks and grills from the bar or the ever-classic fish-and-chips. **Known for:** classic pub grub; good kids' menu; closed kitchen from 3 to 5:30 pm on weekdays. 💲 *Average main: £11* ⊠ *44 Castle Hill, Kenilworth* ☎ *01926/852017* ⊕ *www.clarendonarms-pub.co.uk.*

Birmingham

25 miles north of Stratford-upon-Avon and 115 miles northwest of London.

Though it doesn't have the reputation of being one of the United Kingdom's most visually appealing cities—thanks to the decline of heavy industry, bombing during World War II, and some drab civic architecture in the decades afterwards—21st-century Birmingham is a vibrant and diverse metropolis in the midst of a major cultural rebirth, and it's a lot more attractive than you might think.

The city first flourished in the boom years of the 19th-century's Industrial Revolution, allowing its inventive citizens to accumulate enormous wealth that was evident in the city streets: at one time, the city had some of the finest Victorian buildings in the country. It still has some of the most ravishingly beautiful Pre-Raphaelite paintings, on view in the Birmingham Museum and Art Gallery.

Today, art galleries, museums, ballet, theater, and a symphony orchestra all thrive here. Creative redevelopment and public art are also making areas more attractive for the city's 1.2 million residents. The redeveloped Bullring shopping center, part of which has a striking, curving facade of 15,000 aluminum disks, has won widespread critical acclaim.

The city has a distinctive, almost sing-song local accent—known as "Brummie"—that's often the butt of unfair jokes in the United Kingdom. A favorite local rebuttal is to point out that Shakespeare, born and raised just 25 miles away, would have had a Brummie accent.

GETTING HERE AND AROUND

The X1 and X12 buses connect Birmingham International Airport to the city center 24 hours a day, and you can get into the city center in just over 30 minutes by train; a taxi will cost you around £30. Try to avoid the city's convoluted road network. Drivers are often surprised that Birmingham's inner ring road twists through the city center.

New Street train station is right in the center of the city, home to the Grand Central shopping center and close to the Bullring shopping center. Trams stop directly outside the train station at the Grand Central stop.

Most of the central sights, which are well signposted, form a tight-knit group. The easiest way to get around the city is on foot, though you'll need a bus for the Barber Institute and Cadbury World, and it's a short Metro (tram) ride to the Jewellery Quarter, which also has its own train station (though this, too, can be walked to in around 20 minutes). A Daytripper ticket covering bus, Metro, and most trains costs £6.90. The tourist information center, the best place to pick up a map, is close to the public bus and rail stations. It has details on heritage walks.

PLANNING YOUR TIME

A couple of days gives you time to linger in the Jewellery Quarter and browse the excellent art galleries and museums. Much of Birmingham is now pedestrian-friendly, the downtown shopping area transformed into arcades and buses-only streets. You can also explore restored canals and canal towpaths.

ESSENTIALS

VISITOR INFORMATION Visit Birmingham.
⊕ *www.visitbirmingham.com.*

◉ Sights

Avoncroft Museum of Historic Buildings

MUSEUM VILLAGE | You can see old architecture typical of Worcestershire at this 19-acre open-air museum, which is situated 15 miles outside the city center and which has rescued more than 30 structures from destruction. Alongside half-timber buildings are Victorian chimneys, a collection of phone booths, a three-seater "earth closet" (lavatory), a 1946 prefabricated house, and a working windmill. ■**TIP→ During the week, school groups usually arrive at the museum in the morning, making afternoons a less crowded time to visit. Wear good walking shoes.**
⊠ *Stokeheath, Bromsgrove* ✣ *2 miles south of Bromsgrove* ☎ *01527/831363* ⊕ *www.avoncroft.org.uk* ✉ *£11* ⊘ *Closed Mon. in Sept.–Dec. and Mar.–June. Closed weekdays in Jan. and Feb.*

★ Barber Institute of Fine Arts

MUSEUM | Part of the University of Birmingham, this museum has a small but astounding collection of European paintings, prints, drawings, and sculpture, including works by Botticelli, Van Dyck, Gainsborough, Turner, Manet, Monet, Degas, van Gogh, and Magritte. The museum also has a lively program of temporary exhibitions and a weekly lunchtime concert at 1 pm on Friday, as well as occasional evening concerts. The museum is three miles from the city center; to get here, take a train from New Street Station to University Station, which is a 10-minute walk from the gallery, or jump on a No. 61 or 63 bus, operated by National Express West Midlands. ⊠ *University of Birmingham, Off Edgbaston Park Rd., near East Gate, Edgbaston* ☎ *0121/414–7333* ⊕ *www.barber.org.uk* ✉ *Free.*

Birmingham

Sights ▼

1 Avoncroft Museum of Historic Buildings **F9**
2 Barber Institute of Fine Arts **F9**
3 Birmingham Back to Backs **G9**
4 Birmingham Cathedral **F5**
5 Birmingham Museum and Art Gallery **E6**
6 Black Country Living Museum ... **A4**
7 Cadbury World **F9**
8 Coffin Works **D5**
9 Ikon Gallery **B7**
10 Jewellery Quarter **C3**
11 Lichfield Cathedral **I2**
12 Museum of the Jewellery Quarter **B1**
13 National Sea Life Centre **B7**
14 Pen Room **B4**
15 Thinktank Birmingham Science Museum **J5**

Restaurants ▼

1 Itihaas **D5**
2 Opus **E5**
3 Purnell's **E5**
4 Pushkar **B8**
5 Shabab's **F9**
6 Siamais **B7**
7 Simpsons **A9**

Hotels ▼

1 The Bloc Hotel **C3**
2 Eaton Hotel **A9**
3 Hampton Manor **J2**
4 Hilton Garden Inn **J2**
5 Hotel du Vin & Bistro **F5**
6 Macdonald Burlington Hotel **F7**
7 Malmaison **E7**
8 New Hall Hotel & Spa **I2**
9 Staying Cool at Rotunda **G7**

KEY

0 ——— 500 ft
0 ——— 100 m

1 *Exploring Sights*
1 *Restaurants*
1 *Hotels*

Cruising Birmingham's Canals 👁

With eight canals and 100 miles of waterways, Birmingham can genuinely lay claim to having more canals in its center than Venice. The city is at the heart of a system of waterways built during the Industrial Revolution to connect inland factories to rivers and seaports—by 1840, the canals extended more than 4,000 miles throughout the British Isles. These canals, which carried nine million tons of cargo a year in the late 19th century and helped make the city an industrial power-house, have undergone an extensive cleanup and renovation and are now a tourist attraction.

A walk along the Birmingham Canal Main Line near the Gas Street Basin will bring you to modern shops, restaurants, and more developments such as Brindleyplace in one direction and the Mailbox in the other, and you can see the city from an attractive new perspective. Churchills at the Mailbox (⊕ *www.mailboxlife.com/ brand/churchills*) offers canal-side views, an indoor fire pit, and a choice of over 300 wines to sip as you watch canal life go by. One of the best ways to enjoy the canal network is by bike. Cycle Chain hires out bikes from £3 per hour and can also provide free maps. Alternatively, you can take a narrowboat cruise along the historic canal network with Bosworth Cruises (⊕ *www.sherbornewharf.co.uk*).

★ Birmingham Back to Backs

MUSEUM | Of the 20,000 courtyards of back-to-back houses (houses that quite literally back onto each other) built in the 19th century for the city's expanding working-class population, this is the only survivor. Three houses tell the stories of families (a clock-maker, locksmith, and glass-eye maker were among the residents) who lived in these charming properties, which were rescued from decay by the National Trust and opened as a heritage site. Each of the properties is decorated for a different period in the courtyard's history, from the outdoor privies to the long johns hanging over the bedstead. Admission is by guided tour only, which must be booked in advance. Allow at least one hour for the tour and be prepared for steep stairs; ground-floor tours are available for those with limited mobility. ⊠ *55–63 Hurst St., City Centre* ☎ *0121/666–7671* ⊕ *www.nationaltrust. co.uk* 🖾 *£8.65* ⊗ *Closed Mon. and Jan.*

Birmingham Cathedral

RELIGIOUS SITE | The early-18th-century Cathedral Church of St. Philip, a few blocks from Victoria Square, contains some lovely plasterwork in its elegant, gilded Georgian interior. The stained-glass windows behind the altar, designed by the Pre-Raphaelite Edward Burne-Jones (1833–98) and executed by the firm of William Morris & Company, glow with sensuous hues. There are regular free guided tours (most Monday at 12:30 pm and Wednesday at 11:30 am) where you can find out about how this church became a cathedral. ⊠ *Colmore Row, City Centre* ☎ *0121/262–1840* ⊕ *www. birminghamcathedral.com*.

★ Birmingham Museum and Art Gallery

MUSEUM | Vast and impressive, this museum holds a magnificent collection of Victorian art and is known internation-ally for its works by the Pre-Raphaelites. All the big names are here—among them Rubens, Renoir, Constable, and Francis Bacon—reflecting the enormous wealth of 19th-century Birmingham and the aesthetic taste of its industrialists. Galleries of metalwork, silver, and ceramics reveal some of the city's history, and works from the Renaissance, the Arts and Crafts movement, and the present day are also well represented. One gallery displays part of the incredible **Staffordshire Hoard,** the greatest collection of Anglo-Saxon treasure ever discovered. The 3,500-strong haul was unearthed in a field 16 miles north of Birmingham; among the hundreds of items on permanent display here include helmets, gold, jewelry, and metalwork. The Edwardian Tearoom is a good place to have lunch, and there is a great play area for kids just outside. ⊠ *Chamberlain Sq., City Centre* ☎ *0121/348–8000* ⊕ *www.birmingham-museums.org.uk* ✉ *Free, some charges for exhibitions.*

★ Black Country Living Museum
MUSEUM VILLAGE | FAMILY | This 26-acre museum on social history gives insight into what life was like centuries ago for the men and women who worked in the coal-producing region known as the Black Country (a term that arose from the resulting air pollution), and it's a little like walking onto a film set. The town of Dudley, 10 miles northwest of Birmingham, was where coal was first used for smelting iron way back in the 17th century. The replicated village is made up of buildings from around the region, including a chain maker's workshop; a trap-works (where animal snares were fashioned); his-and-hers hardware stores (pots and pans for women, tools and sacks for men); a druggist; and a general store where costumed women describe life in a poor industrial community in the 19th century. You can also sit on a hard bench and watch Charlie Chaplin films in the 1920s cinema, peer into the depths of a mine, or ride on a barge to experience canal travel of yesteryear. For sustenance, there is a café, a 1930s-era fried-fish shop, and the Bottle & Glass Inn for ales and drinks. ■**TIP→ To avoid the numerous school parties, visit on the**

weekend or during school vacations. The museum, three miles from the M5, is best reached by car. Leave M5 at Junction 2 by the A4123, and then take A4037 at Tipton. Trains from Birmingham New Street to Tipton Station take 17 minutes; buses from the train station run past the museum, which is one mile away. ⊠ *Tipton Rd., Dudley* ☎ *0121/557–9643* ⊕ *www.bclm.co.uk* ✉ *£19.95* ☉ *Closed 1st 2 wks Jan. and Mon. and Tues. early Nov.–mid-Mar.*

Cadbury World
MUSEUM | FAMILY | The village of Bournville (five miles south of Birmingham city center) contains this museum devoted to—what else?—chocolate. In 1879, the Quaker Cadbury brothers moved the family business from the city to this "factory in a garden." The museum traces the history of the cocoa bean and the Cadbury dynasty. The 4D Chocolate Adventure Zone and the accompanying play areas may seem like overkill, but Cadbury World is extremely popular with kids. You can watch (and smell) chocolates being made by hand, enjoy free samples, and then stock up from the cut-price shop. The restaurant has specialty chocolate cakes as well as lunches. Opening times change almost daily, and reservations are essential; call or go online to check times and book tickets. ⊠ *Linden Rd., Off A38, Bournville* ☎ *0121/393–6004* ⊕ *www.cadburyworld.co.uk* ✉ *£18* ☉ *Closed early–mid-Jan. and select days in Dec.*

★ Coffin Works
MUSEUM | On paper this museum might not be the obvious choice for a fun afternoon on your vacation, but it's actually a very lovely time capsule of an interesting and important part of Birmingham's industrial history. It was on this very site that Alfred and Edwin Newman (the Newman Brothers, who were previously accomplished brass fitters) first started making coffins in the late Victorian era. The company quickly established themselves as the area's best coffin-makers

and were soon making coffins for the likes of Queen Mary, King George V, and Winston Churchill. Though the company fell into decline starting in the 1960s, eventually closing in the 1990s, guided tours now let you clock in as workers once did before taking you behind the scenes in the manager's office (where you can listen to spooky audio of one of the most prominent figures in the company's history), onto the factory floor, and even into the shroud room. Tours occur every hour on the hour between 11 am and 3 pm, Wednesday through Sunday. ⊠ *13-15 Fleet St.* ☎ *0121/233–4790* ⊕ *www.coffinworks.org* ✉ *Tours £7.50* ☾ *Closed Mon. and Tues.*

★ Ikon Gallery

MUSEUM | Converted from a Victorian Gothic–style school, this gallery is among the city's top venues for contemporary art from Britain and abroad and rightly so. The bright, white interior is divided into two main galleries, which host rolling exhibitions. There's also a third space called The Tower, which hosts more site-specific shows. The bookshop is great, and there's a very nice café on the ground floor of the building. Ikon exemplifies how Birmingham is embracing its past while moving very much into the future. ⊠ *1 Oozells Sq., Brindleyplace, City Centre* ☎ *0121/248–0708* ⊕ *www. ikon-gallery.co.uk* ✉ *Free* ☾ *Closed Mon., except bank holidays.*

★ Jewellery Quarter

NEIGHBORHOOD | For more than two centuries, jewelers have worked in the district of Hockley, northwest of the city center. Today, hundreds of manufacturing jewelers continue the tradition in the Jewellery Quarter, producing more than a third of the jewelry made in Britain. It's a fun area to explore, with many of the jewelers working out of pretty redbrick houses. In the Museum of the Jewellery Quarter, you can tour a former workshop and see how unique pieces are made. ■ **TIP→ A free booklet from the tourist office gives you** the lowdown on shopping in the area. The city's Assay Office hallmarks 12 million items each year with the anchor symbol, denoting Birmingham origin. The ornate green and gilded Chamberlain Clock, at the intersection of Vyse Street, Warstone Lane, and Frederick Street, marks the center of the district. The quarter is two stops on the Metro from Birmingham New Street, and although it is a lot calmer than the city center, it has a hip café and restaurant scene. ⊠ *Hockley* ⊕ *www. jewelleryquarter.net* ☾ *Some shops closed on Sun.*

Lichfield Cathedral

RELIGIOUS SITE | It's worth a detour 15 miles northeast of Birmingham to explore the only medieval English cathedral with three spires. The sandstone building, beautifully sited by a tree-fringed pool, dates mainly from the 12th and 13th centuries, and the Lady Chapel glows with some 16th-century stained glass from the Cistercian abbey of Herkenrode, near Liège, in Belgium. Half-timber houses surround the peaceful grounds, and the town itself has Georgian buildings as well as the birthplace (now a museum) of lexicographer Dr. Samuel Johnson. Free tours run Monday through Saturday at 11 am and 2 pm. Visitors can also pay to tour the recently restored historic library (£18), accessed up 35 spiral steps, which includes many early books, including 15th-century manuscripts of Chaucer's *Canterbury Tales.* Frequent trains from Birmingham New Street take 45 minutes. ⊠ *19A The Close, Lichfield* ☎ *01543/306100* ⊕ *www.lichfield-cathedral.org* ✉ *Free; donations encouraged.*

★ Museum of the Jewellery Quarter

MUSEUM | This museum is built around the workshops of Smith & Pepper, a firm that operated in the Jewellery Quarter for more than 80 years. Little changed here from when the firm was founded in 1899 to when it finally closed its doors in 1981. A factory tour (about an hour) and exhibits explain the history of the neighborhood and the jeweler's craft, and you can watch demonstrations of jewelry being made in the traditional way. The Earth's Riches gallery displays intriguing jewelry made from an assortment of natural materials, the on-site shop sells beautiful pieces by local jewelers, and a lovely café also displays photography of the city. ⊠ 75–80 Vyse St., Hockley, Jewellery Quarter ☎ 0121/348–8263 ⊕ www.birminghammuseums.org.uk/jewellery 🎫 Tours £7; exhibits free but donations welcome ⊗ Closed Sun. and Mon. (except bank holidays).

National Sea Life Centre

ZOO | FAMILY | Almost as far from the sea as you can get in Britain (which isn't very far), this imaginatively landscaped aquarium allows a glimpse into Davey Jones's locker. An underwater tunnel lets you view sharks and stingrays up close, or you can book a feeding experience with the sharks or the green sea turtle. The resident Gentoo penguins that greet you on arrival are a crowd-pleaser. Children gravitate to the touch pools and other interactive activities. Buy your tickets online for discounts of up to 35%. ⊠ The Water's Edge, Brindleyplace, City Centre ☎ 0871/423–2110 ⊕ www.visitsealife.com/birmingham 🎫 From £13.95 online.

Pen Room

MUSEUM | During the 19th century, Birmingham was the hub of the world pen trade with 129 factories employing nearly 8,000 people. This museum celebrates the heritage of this lost city trade and tells the stories of past workers in poignant detail. Located within a former pen factory, the exhibits illustrate the industry's heyday through a decorative array of nibs, quills, fountain pens, inks, and all the paraphernalia of the pre-ballpoint era. You can try your hand at calligraphy, make your own nib, and listen to recollections of previous employees for insight about the working conditions of yesteryear. ⊠ Unit 3, the Argent Centre, 60 Frederick

Eat Balti in Brum 🍴

Birmingham is home to the *balti*, a popular cuisine created in the mid-1970s by the Pakistani community. The food is cooked and brought to the table in a woklike dish and eaten with naan, not rice. Curry and other spices season the meat and vegetables. There are more than 30 restaurants in the "Balti Triangle" of the Moseley and Sparkbrook districts.

St., Jewellery Quarter ☎ 0121/236–9834 ⊕ www.penmuseum.org.uk 🎫 £6 ⊗ Closed Mon.

Thinktank Birmingham Science Museum

MUSEUM | FAMILY | This interactive museum in the state-of-the-art Millennium Point Center allows kids to explore science and the history of Birmingham over four floors of galleries. Mini-Brum, an interactive gallery for under-eights, is hugely popular, while older kids will love exploring deep space in the planetarium (an extra £2.50 on the admission price). When the weather is nice, head outdoors to the play area and the Science Garden. The museum is a 10-minute walk from Moor Street railway station or a 15-minute walk from Birmingham New Street. ⊠ Millennium Point, Curzon St., Digbeth ☎ 0121/348–8000 ⊕ www.birminghammuseums.org.uk/thinktank 🎫 £13 ⊗ Science Garden closed early Jan.–mid-Feb.

🍴 Restaurants

Itihaas

$$ | INDIAN | Birmingham has some of the country's finest Indian restaurants, and this is one of the best in the city. The cooking concentrates on north Indian dishes like *koila murgh* (chicken marinated in yogurt and seared over charcoal)

and *hara bara gosht* (a casserole of lamb cooked with garlic, chili, and spinach). **Known for:** delicious Indian food; colonial-style decor; tasty tandoori starters. $ *Average main: £18* ⊠ *18 Fleet St., City Centre* ☎ *0121/212–3383* ⊕ *www.itihaas.co.uk* ⊗ *No lunch weekends.*

★ Opus

$$$ | **MODERN BRITISH** | This stylish, modern restaurant specializes in local, seasonal British flavors. Expect Aberdeen beef with duck-fat chips or perhaps some grilled sole with rich, brown shrimp butter. **Known for:** free-range meat and fresh fish; fabulous tasting menu with wine pairings; chef's table that puts you front and center in kitchen. $ *Average main: £25* ⊠ *54 Cornwall St., City Centre* ☎ *0121/200–2323* ⊕ *www.opusrestaurant.co.uk* ⊗ *Closed Sun.*

★ Purnell's

$$$$ | **MODERN BRITISH** | Business moguls and sophisticated foodies alike can be found sampling an aperitif in a comfy armchair before moving to the sleek, slate-floor dining room at this establishment run by a Michelin-starred chef. Located in a Victorian terracotta and redbrick building, this is where chef Glyn Purnell creates his adventurous modern British fare. **Known for:** innovative take on British cooking, including some impressive tasting menus; tables booked up two months in advance; affordable lunchtime prices. $ *Average main: £45* ⊠ *55 Cornwall St., City Centre* ☎ *0121/212–9799* ⊕ *www.purnellsrestaurant.com* ⊗ *Closed Sun. and Mon.*

★ Pushkar

$ | **INDIAN** | A vogueish dining room is the perfect setting for the inventive Punjabi cuisine at this popular curry palace and cocktail bar on bustling Broad Street. White linen tablecloths and accents of gold and amber create a plush dining setting, and the food doesn't disappoint either. **Known for:** good cocktail menu; independent curry restaurant in a sea of chains; late-night dinner service. $ *Average main: £15* ⊠ *245 Broad St., City Centre* ☎ *0121/643–7978* ⊕ *www.pushkardining.com* ⊗ *No lunch weekends.*

Shabab's

$ | **INDIAN** | This stalwart of the Birmingham curry scene is something of a local institution, serving up impressive balti since 1987. Tradition dictates that proper balti must be eaten from the same dish it is cooked in, and Shabab's long history guarantees a lot of flavor in its dishes. **Known for:** traditional lamb balti; BYOB policy; spices galore. $ *Average main: £7* ⊠ *163-165 Ladypool Rd.* ☎ *0121/440–2893* ⊕ *www.shababs.co.uk.*

Siamais

$ | **THAI** | In the trendy Brindleyplace neighborhood by the canal, this Thai restaurant makes itself stand out from your typical southeastern Asian restaurants by pairing each course with its very own cocktail. Still, classic Thai dishes such as green and red curry abound in an atmosphere that is more Gothic than Old Siam. **Known for:** some of the best cocktails in the city; traditional Thai food; fashionable location. $ *Average main: £15* ⊠ *6 Brindleyplace, 7 Oozells St., City Centre* ☎ *0121/643–3993* ⊕ *www.siamais.co.uk.*

★ Simpsons

$$$$ | **FRENCH** | This bright and modern restaurant with rooms housed in a gleaming Georgian villa is known for its French-influenced cuisine with resolutely British ingredients. The assured and welcoming service makes it easy to savor specialties such as Aberdeenshire beef bavette and cheek or quail with elderberries and parsley, which have secured its Michelin star since 2000. **Known for:** impressive tasting menus; adventurous kids' options; beautiful Georgian decor. $ *Average main: £35* ⊠ *20 Highfield Rd., Edgbaston* ☎ *0121/454–3434* ⊕ *www.simpsonsrestaurant.co.uk* ⊗ *Closed Mon.*

Hotels

★ The Bloc Hotel

$ | HOTEL | This budget hotel in the Jewellery Quarter has pod-style bedrooms, plus a selection of mini-apartments for those who want to use their hotel as little more than somewhere to sleep between exploring. **Pros:** comfortable rooms; unbeatable prices; well designed. **Cons:** few home comforts; breakfast costs extra; no storage space. ⑤ *Rooms from: £79* ✉ *77 Caroline St., City Centre* ☎ *0121/212–1223* ⊕ *www.blochotels.com* ⇨ *105 rooms* ⦿ *No meals.*

Eaton Hotel

$ | HOTEL | With an elegant, gleaming white facade, this mansion in leafy Edgbaston provides a peaceful, cozy stay two miles from the bustle of Birmingham's center. **Pros:** complimentary parking; great breakfasts; boutique-hotel ambience. **Cons:** not in city center; rooms aren't the most inspiring; on a loud main road. ⑤ *Rooms from: £98* ✉ *279 Hagley Rd., Edgbaston* ☎ *0121/454–3311* ⊕ *eaton-hotel.business.site* ⇨ *55 rooms* ⦿ *Free breakfast.*

★ Hampton Manor

$$ | HOTEL | Just a five-minute walk from the village of Hampton-in-Arden, this hotel (and its restaurant's accompanying Michelin star) is proof that Birmingham lodging isn't all about business travel. **Pros:** amazing restaurant; free parking; country-retreat feel. **Cons:** a bit out of town; popular with weddings; pricey for the area. ⑤ *Rooms from: £180* ✉ *Shadowbrook La., Hampton-in-Arden* ☎ *01675/446080* ⊕ *www.hamptonmanor. com* ⇨ *15 rooms.*

Hilton Garden Inn

$ | HOTEL | An excellent central location near the waterside nightlife scene is just one perk to staying at this smoothly run hotel. **Pros:** nice location; stylish bar and restaurant; frequent special offers. **Cons:** mostly for business travelers; breakfast not always included; not a lot of character. ⑤ *Rooms from: £80* ✉ *Brindleyplace, 1 Brunswick Sq., City Centre* ☎ *0121/643–1003* ⊕ *www.hilton.com* ⇨ *238 rooms* ⦿ *No meals.*

Hotel du Vin & Bistro

$ | HOTEL | A Victorian hospital in the city center got a makeover from this superhip chain, but it retains such original details as the ironwork double stairway and marble columns. **Pros:** chic and comfortable; central location; nice spa on-site. **Cons:** expensive valet parking; a little tired in places; popular for business meetings. ⑤ *Rooms from: £99* ✉ *25 Church St., City Centre* ☎ *0121/794–3005* ⊕ *www. hotelduvin.com/locations/birmingham* ⇨ *66 rooms* ⦿ *No meals.*

Macdonald Burlington Hotel

$ | HOTEL | Housed in one of the city's grand Victorian buildings, this traditional hotel is a surprisingly good value option in the center of Birmingham. **Pros:** close to New Street Station and shops; affordable weekend rates; nice bar and restaurant. **Cons:** attracts a mainly business clientele; no personality; streets around it can get rowdy. ⑤ *Rooms from: £110* ✉ *Burlington Arcade, 126 New St., City Centre* ☎ *0344/879–9019* ⊕ *www. macdonaldhotels.co.uk* ⇨ *112 rooms* ⦿ *No meals.*

Malmaison

$ | HOTEL | Retail therapy is on your doorstep at this chic hotel in the Mailbox shopping center, where large windows make the guest rooms light and airy by day, and there's subtle lighting by night. **Pros:** handy for shopping and dining; vibrant rooms; great spa. **Cons:** drab views; expensive parking (cheaper alternatives are close by); breakfast not included. ⑤ *Rooms from: £98* ✉ *1 Wharfside St., City Centre* ☎ *0121/794–3004* ⊕ *www.malmaison.com/locations/birmingham* ⇨ *193 rooms* ⦿ *No meals.*

★ New Hall Hotel & Spa

$ | HOTEL | A tree-lined drive leads through 26 acres of gardens and open fields to this moated, 12th-century manor house, where public rooms reflect the hotel's long history with touches such as 16th-century oak paneling and Flemish glass, 18th-century chandeliers, and a 17th-century stone fireplace. **Pros:** historic building; beautiful grounds; excellent spa. **Cons:** a little difficult to locate; far from city center; might be a bit staid for some. $ *Rooms from: £98* ✉ *Walmley Rd., Sutton Coldfield* ☎ *0121/378–2442* ⊕ *www.handpickedhotels.co.uk/newhall* ⊷ *60 rooms* ⦿ *Free breakfast.*

★ Staying Cool at the Rotunda

$ | RENTAL | The top five floors of the Rotunda, an iconic, cylindrical office building from 1965, now contain spacious studio, one-, and two-bedroom apartments, designed to the hilt in sleek mid-century style. **Pros:** well-stocked kitchens; dreamy beds; awesome views. **Cons:** no designated parking; not much old English charm; no actual restaurant on-site. $ *Rooms from: £105* ✉ *Rotunda, 150 New St., City Centre* ☎ *0121/285–1250* ⊕ *www.stayingcool.com/locations/birmingham* ⊷ *35 apartments* ⦿ *No meals.*

▼ Nightlife

The city's thriving nightlife scene is concentrated around Broad Street and Hurst Street, as well as the Brindleyplace and Mailbox areas.

Asha's

BARS/PUBS | This colorful bar and restaurant has superb fresh fruit cocktails and Asian cuisine. ✉ *12–22 Newhall St., City Centre* ☎ *0121/200–2767* ⊕ *www.ashas-birmingham.co.uk* ☾ *No lunch weekends.*

Digbeth Dining Club

GATHERING PLACES | If you want to know where locals come to hang, this is it. Held every Thursday through Sunday, it's a collection of street-food stalls—largely from homegrown cooks—and bars, all with a buzzy, fun atmosphere. There's a heady mix of music, too, and you should buy a ticket (£1) in advance to avoid missing out. From time to time it also decamps to other Midlands locations. ✉ *Lower Trinity St.* ⊕ *www.digbethdiningclub.com.*

★ The Fighting Cocks

BARS/PUBS | This handsome, trendy pub in the southern suburb of Moseley is full of polished wood tables, colorful cushions, and stained-glass windows. The beer selection is huge, and the high-class pub food is delicious. This place gets rammed to the rafters for the traditional "roasts"—beef, pork, lamb, chicken, or nut—on Sunday at lunchtime. ✉ *1 St. Mary's Row, Moseley* ☎ *0121/449–0811* ⊕ *www.thefightingcocksmoseley.co.uk.*

★ Jam House

BARS/PUBS | This is the place to come for live music in the city. The excellent drinking, dining, and dancing venue has live jazz, soul, or funk nightly. ✉ *3–5 St. Paul's Sq., Jewellery Quarter* ☎ *0121/200–3030* ⊕ *www.thejamhouse.com/birmingham.*

Old Joint Stock

BARS/PUBS | The spacious and high-domed Old Joint Stock serves good ales and pies in an old bank. There's a theater attached, with a steady stream of good plays and comedy gigs. ✉ *4 Temple Row West, off Colmore Row, City Centre* ☎ *0121/200–1892 pub, 0121/200–0946 theater* ⊕ *www.oldjointstocktheatre.co.uk.*

🎬 Performing Arts

Birmingham's performing arts companies are well regarded throughout the country. Catch a performance if you can.

BALLET

★ Birmingham Royal Ballet

DANCE | The second company of the Royal Ballet, the touring Birmingham Royal Ballet is based at the Hippodrome Theatre, which also plays host to visiting companies such as the Welsh National Opera. ⊠ *Hurst St., Southside, City Centre* ☎ *0844/338–5000 Birmingham Hippodrome* ⊕ *www.brb.org.uk.*

CONCERTS

Resorts World Arena

CONCERTS | Formerly known as the Genting Arena, this huge stadium within the massive National Exhibition Centre (universally known as "the N.E.C.") is located close to the airport. Tickets for all events here should be bought through the Ticket Factory. ⊠ *National Exhibition Centre, Off M42* ☎ *0844/338–8000* ⊕ *www.theticketfactory.com.*

Symphony Hall

CONCERTS | This is the home of the distinguished City of Birmingham Symphony Orchestra and a venue for jazz, pop, and classical concerts. With its shoebox-shape, 6,000-pipe organ, and impeccable acoustics, the Symphony Hall is easily one of the finest concert halls in England. ⊠ *8 Centenery Sq., City Centre* ☎ *0121/780–3333* ⊕ *www.thsh.co.uk.*

★ Town Hall Birmingham

CONCERTS | The splendidly neoclassical Town Hall Birmingham holds a wide range of events, including organ recitals, opera, and contemporary music concerts. Monthly tours teach about the history of this magnificent building, where both Mendelssohn and Charles Dickens debuted new works. ⊠ *Victoria Sq., City Centre* ☎ *0121/780–3333* ⊕ *www.thsh. co.uk* 🎫 *Tours £8.50.*

FILM

★ Electric Cinema

FILM | This movie theater, a genuine survivor from the art deco age, is now the U.K.'s oldest working movie theater. Sofas and waiter service enhance the decadent viewing experience. ⊠ *47–49 Station St., City Centre* ☎ *0121/643–7879* ⊕ *www.theelectric.co.uk* 🎫 *From £11.50.*

THEATER

★ Birmingham Repertory Theatre

THEATER | Set within an ultramodern building next to the staggering contemporary design of Birmingham's library, the revered Birmingham Repertory Theatre is one of England's oldest (founded in 1913) and most esteemed theater companies. It's equally at home performing modern or classical works. ⊠ *Centenary Sq., Broad St., City Centre* ☎ *0121/236–4455 box office, 0121/245–2000 general information* ⊕ *www.birmingham-rep.co.uk.*

Alexandra Theatre

THEATER | First opened in 1901, the Alexandra Theatre, or "the Alex" as it is more affectionately known, welcomes touring companies on their way to or from London's West End. ⊠ *Suffolk Queensway, City Centre* ☎ *0844/871–3011* ⊕ *www.atgtickets.com/venues/the-alexandra-theatre-birmingham.*

🛍 Shopping

ARTWORK

St. Paul's Gallery

ART GALLERIES | An entertaining and quirky treasure trove, St. Paul's Gallery specializes in hand-signed fine-art prints of album covers, past and present. ⊠ *94–108 Norwood St., Jewellery Quarter* ☎ *0121/236–5800* ⊕ *www.stpaulsgallery.com.*

JEWELRY

★ Crescent Silver

JEWELRY/ACCESSORIES | In the heart of the Jewellery Quarter, this shop sells a range of interesting silver jewelry and gifts. It currently stocks its wares at sales outlets at Highgrove (Prince Charles's private home) and royal palaces. ✉ *83–85 Spencer St., Jewellery Quarter* ☎ *0121/236-9006* ⊕ *www.crescentsilver.co.uk.*

SHOPPING CENTERS

★ Bullring & Grand Central

SHOPPING CENTERS/MALLS | This huge dual complex consists of the Bullring, built on the site of a medieval marketplace, and Grand Central, based in Birmingham New Street Station; together they offer over 200 stores to browse. Don't miss the stunningly curved architecture of Selfridge's and its awesome food hall. ✉ *Between New St. and High St., City Centre* ☎ *0121/632-1526 Bullring, 0121/654-1000 Grand Central* ⊕ *www.bullring.co.uk.*

★ Great Western Arcade

SHOPPING CENTERS/MALLS | This Victorian shopping mall near Snow Hill Station is a nice respite from the city's chain stores. Built with a similar design to Gallerio Vittoria Emmanuele in Milan, it's a more elegant place to shop than most. Peruse the charming boutiques and specialist shops, and you may end up going back with a couture hat, some Scottish whiskey, or even a cigar or two. ✉ *Colmore Row* ☎ *0121/236-5417* ⊕ *www.greatwesternarcade.co.uk.*

The Mailbox

SHOPPING CENTERS/MALLS | Once a Royal Mail sorting office, the Mailbox is now filled with trendy shops and designer outlets such as Harvey Nichols and Savile Row tailor Gieves & Hawkes, as well as some fine restaurants. ✉ *7 Commercial St., City Centre* ☎ *0121/632-1000* ⊕ *www.mailboxlife.com.*

Activities

CRICKET

Edgbaston Stadium

CRICKET | To watch first-class cricket at one of the country's most hallowed venues, head to Edgbaston Stadium. Tickets for test matches sell out months ahead, but those at the county level are not so sought after. ✉ *The County Ground, Edgbaston* ☎ *0121/369-1994* ⊕ *www.edgbaston.com.*

Great Malvern

35 miles southwest of Birmingham, 20 miles northeast of Hereford.

Great Malvern feels a bit like a seaside resort, though instead of the ocean your eyes plunge into an expanse of green meadows rolling away into the Vale of Evesham. This attractive Victorian spa town's architecture has changed little since the mid-1800s. It's a good base for walks in the surrounding Malvern Hills. These hills, with their long, low, purple profiles rising from the surrounding plain, inspired much of the music of Sir Edward Elgar (1857–1934), who composed "Pomp and Circumstance" and the "Enigma Variations." They also inspired his remark that "there is music in the air, music all around us."

GETTING HERE AND AROUND

Great Malvern is off the A449 road; getting here from Hereford will take 40 minutes or so by car. West Midlands trains take a half hour. Birmingham is an hour away by car and rail.

ESSENTIALS

VISITOR INFORMATION Malvern Tourist Information Centre. ✉ *The Lyttelton Well Courtyard, 6 Church St.* ☎ *01684/892289* ⊕ *www.visitthemalverns.org.*

◉ Sights

★ The Firs, Elgar's Birthplace

BUILDING | The composer Sir Edward Elgar was born in the village of Lower Broadheath, eight miles north of Great Malvern, in this tiny brick cottage. Set in a peaceful garden, the museum contains personal memorabilia, including photographs, musical scores, and letters. Be sure to take a seat next to the statue of the musician as he admires the Malvern Hills that so inspired him. ✉ *Crown East*

La., Lower Broadheath ☎ 01905/333330 ⊕ www.nationaltrust.org.uk/the-firs ☒ £8 ⏱ Closed Tues.–Thurs. in Nov. and Dec.

Great Malvern Priory

RELIGIOUS SITE | A solidly built, early-Norman, Benedictine abbey restored in the mid-19th century, the priory dominates the steep streets downtown. The fine glass spans from the 15th century—including a magnificent east window and the vibrantly blue Magnificat window in the north transept—to the beautifully evocative Millennium Windows, installed in 1999. There's also a splendid set of misericords (the elaborately carved undersides of choir seats). ☒ Church St. ☎ 01684/561020 ⊕ www.greatmalvern-priory.org.uk ☒ Free ⏱ Closed Sun.

Royal Three Counties Show

FESTIVAL | For three days in mid-June, this agricultural show presents rare animal breeds, equestrian events, competitions for the best cows, pigs, and sheep, and plenty of food. Other events, from collectors' fairs to dog shows, take place at the showground year-round; check the website for listings. ☒ Three Counties Showground ☎ 01684/584900 ⊕ www.royalthreecounties.co.uk ☒ £21.

★ Worcester Cathedral

RELIGIOUS SITE | There are few more quintessentially English sights than that of Worcester Cathedral, its towers overlooking the green expanse of the county cricket ground and its majestic image reflected in the swift-flowing waters of the River Severn. A cathedral has stood

Worcester Cathedral has a blissfully English setting near the River Severn.

on this site since 680, and much of what remains dates from the 13th and 14th centuries. Notable exceptions are the Norman crypt (built in the 1080s), the largest in England, and the ambulatory, a cloister built around the east end. The most important tomb in the cathedral is that of King John (1167–1216), one of the country's least-admired monarchs, who alienated his barons and subjects through bad administration and heavy taxation, and, in 1215, was forced to sign that great charter of liberty, the Magna Carta. ■TIP➜ **Don't miss the beautiful decoration in the vaulted chantry chapel of Prince Arthur, Henry VIII's elder brother, whose body was brought to Worcester after his death at Ludlow in 1502.** The medieval library (accessible by prebooked tour only) holds around 300 medieval manuscripts, dating from the 10th century onwards. Worcester is eight miles north of Great Malvern. ⊠ *8 College Yard, at High St., Worcester* ☎ *01905/732900* ⊕ *www.worcestercathedral.co.uk* ⊠ *Free; cathedral tours £6; library tours £6.*

🍴 Restaurants

★ L'amuse Bouche

$$ | MODERN FRENCH | One of Malvern's best restaurants, L'amuse Bouche specializes in French cuisine with a contemporary English edge. Start with the scallops with samphire and pancetta dust before sampling the seared Malvern Hills lamb's liver or the apple-cider-braised pork belly. **Known for:** one of the best restaurants in the region; garden views from the elegant dining room; French-inspired cuisine with English ingredients. ⑤ *Average main: £20* ⊠ *Cotford Hotel, 51 Graham Rd.* ☎ *01684/572427* ⊕ *www.cotfordhotel.co.uk/lamuse-bouche-restaurant* ⊘ *No lunch Mon.–Sat.*

🛏 Hotels

Cottage in the Wood

$ | HOTEL | Amid shady grounds, this family-run hotel sits high up the side of the Malvern Hills, with splendid views of the landscape. **Pros:** tremendous views; great food; choice between heritage

Eating Well in the Heart of England 🍴

"The Malvern water," said John Wall in 1756, "is famous for containing nothing at all." The famously pure water is still bottled in the town and exported worldwide; it's said that the Queen never travels without it.

Outside Birmingham, this area is rich farming country where the orchards produce succulent fruit, especially apples and plums. Hereford cider is popular because it tastes much sweeter than the cider brewed farther south in Devon.

The meat and milk products, which come from the local red-and-white Hereford breed of cattle, are second to none. Cheshire cheese, one of the country's oldest cheeses, is noted for its rich, crumbly texture; blue-veined Shropshire cheese is more unusual and worth trying. Ludlow produces a formidable assortment of local meat products and is noted for its sausages.

or modern rooms. **Cons:** three separate buildings; steep and narrow approach; cheaper rooms don't have the best views. $ *Rooms from: £119* ✉ *Holywell Rd.* ☎ *01684/588860* ⊕ *www.cottage-inthewood.co.uk* ⇨ *30 rooms* ⦿l *Free Breakfast.*

★ Sidney House

$ | **B&B/INN** | In addition to having stunning views, this dignified yet quirky early-19th-century bed-and-breakfast sits near the town center. **Pros:** great views; easy access to Malvern Hills; personable host. **Cons:** on a busy road; some of the rooms are quite small; no formal bar or restaurant. $ *Rooms from: £70* ✉ *40 Worcester Rd.* ☎ *01684/574994* ⊕ *www.sidneyhouse.co.uk* ⇨ *6 rooms* ⦿l *Free breakfast.*

🎭 Performing Arts

Malvern has links with Sir Edward Elgar as well as with George Bernard Shaw, who premiered many of his plays here.

Ledbury

10 miles southwest of Great Malvern on A449.

Among the 16th-century black-and-white half-timber buildings in the center of Ledbury, take special note of the Feathers Hotel and the Talbot Inn. They're considered to be among the finest timber-frame buildings of their age left in England. The cobbled Church Lane, almost hidden behind the 17th-century market house, is crowded with other medieval half-timber buildings and leads to St. Michael's and All Angels Church.

GETTING HERE AND AROUND

If you're driving, Ledbury is 25 minutes from Hereford via the A438 and 15 minutes from Great Malvern via the A449. There are local buses from both Hereford and Great Malvern, which have rail links with the rest of the country.

ESSENTIALS

VISITOR INFORMATION Ledbury Tourist Information Centre. ✉ *Ice Bytes Café, 38 The Homend* ☎ *0844/567–8650* ⊕ *www.visitherefordshire.co.uk.*

◉ Sights

Eastnor Castle

CASTLE/PALACE | FAMILY | Completed in 1820, Eastnor Castle, a turreted Norman-revival extravaganza on the eastern outskirts of Ledbury, includes some magnificent neo-Gothic salons designed by 19th-century architect Augustus Pugin. The Hervey-Bathurst family has restored other grand rooms, full of tapestries, gilt-framed paintings, Regency chandeliers, old armchairs, and enormous sofas, making Eastnor a must-see for lovers of English interior decoration. In the Little Library, look out for the rare game of Life Pool, originally played on the billiards table. Within the grounds, there is a knight's maze and adventure playground to keep kids amused. Opening days vary throughout the season; check the website in advance before you visit. There is also a campsite and two cottages within the castle's deer park, if you'd like to stay the night. ⊠ *Off the A438* ☎ *01531/633160* ⊕ *www. eastnorcastle.com* ✉ *House and grounds £12.50 online; grounds only £8.50 online* ⊙ *Closed Oct.–Easter.*

★ Hellens Manor

HOUSE | Just outside the village of Much Marcle, four miles southwest of Ledbury, lies the beautiful 17th-century manor of Hellens, kept like a time capsule in virtually unspoiled condition. The gloom and dust are part of the experience of visiting; candles illuminate the interior, and there's no central heating. Part of the house dates from the 13th century and contains fine Old Master paintings. Take a walk in the gardens and, if you have time, also check out the 13th-century village church. Entry is by guided tour only, which takes place at 1, 2, and 3 pm on Wednesday, Sunday, and bank holiday Mondays from Easter through early October. There is also a rather charming tearoom on-site. ⊠ *Much Marcle* ⊹ *Just off the A449 between Ledbury and Ross-on-Wye road* ☎ *01531/660504* ⊕ *www.*

hellensmanor.com ✉ *£9.50* ⊙ *Closed early-Oct.–Easter and Mon., Tues., and Thurs.–Sat. except bank holidays.*

Ledbury Heritage Centre

MUSEUM | In the old grammar school, this museum traces the history of the building, town, railroad, and canal, mostly through local postcards. It also has displays on two literary celebrities linked to the area, John Masefield and Elizabeth Barrett Browning. ⊠ *Church La.* ☎ *1531/636147* ✉ *Free* ⊙ *Closed Oct.–Easter.*

⊟ Hotels

★ Feathers Hotel

$ | HOTEL | You can't miss the striking black-and-white facade of this centrally located Tudor hotel, which dates from the 16th century. **Pros:** rooms retain period feel; great restaurant; afternoon tea available. **Cons:** some rooms on the small side; steps to climb; may be a bit creaky for some. ⑤ *Rooms from: £96* ⊠ *25 High St.* ☎ *01531/635266* ⊕ *www.feathersledbury.co.uk* ⤵ *22 rooms* ⊙❘ *Free breakfast.*

Ross-on-Wye

10 miles southwest of Ledbury.

Perched high above the River Wye in the Malvern Hills, Ross-on-Wye seems oblivious to modern-day intrusions and remains at heart a small market town. Its steep streets come alive on Thursday and Saturday—market days—but they're always a happy hunting ground for antiques. Nearby towns have sights from a castle to a scenic overlook on the river.

GETTING HERE AND AROUND

The A449 connects Ross-on-Wye with Great Malvern and Ledbury, and the M50 leads directly to Ross from Junction 8 of the M5.

Sights

Goodrich Castle

CASTLE/PALACE | Looming dramatically over the River Wye at Kerne Bridge, from the south, the castle looks like a fortress from the Rhineland amid the green fields; you quickly see its grimmer face from the battlements on its north side. Dating from the late 12th century, the red sandstone castle is surrounded by a deep moat carved out of solid rock, from which its walls appear to soar upward. Built to repel Welsh raiders, it was destroyed in the 17th century during the Civil War, and it's where you can view the only surviving Civil War mortar. ⊠ *Castle La., Goodrich* ☎ *01600/890538* ⊕ *www.english-heritage.org.uk/visit/ places/goodrich-castle* 🎫 *£8.40* ⊗ *Closed weekdays Nov.–mid-Feb.*

Symonds Yat and King Arthur's Cave

VIEWPOINT | Six miles south of Ross-on-Wye, outside the village of Symonds Yat (a local dialect word for "gate"), the 473-foot-high Yat Rock commands superb views of the River Wye as it winds through a narrow gorge in a great five-mile loop. It's best approached from the south on B4432, and from there, it's a short walk. A small, hand-pulled ferry takes passengers across the river from the Saracens Head pub (£1.20). About a mile northeast of Symonds Yat is **King Arthur's Cave**, although any link to the legendary monarch is, well, just a legend. Several important Paleolithic finds have been made in the cave, including flint tools and the bones of a woolly mammoth and a saber-toothed cat. Today, it is home to a colony of bats. To find the cave, take the exit marked Symonds Yat West from the A40. Park at the rest area just before Downard Park campsite, and follow the path a short way into the woods. ⊠ *Symonds Yat, Ross on Wye.*

Activities

Symonds Yat Canoe Hire

BOATING | FAMILY | This well-regarded company rents canoes and kayaks by the day or half day. It's a popular way to experience the River Wye. Prices start at £20 for a two-person canoe or kayak, and you'll need to pay cash on arrival. ⊠ *Leisure Park, Symonds Yat* ☎ *01600/891069* ⊕ *www.canoehire.com.*

Hereford

13 miles northwest of Ross-on-Wye, 52 miles southwest of Birmingham, 53 miles northeast of Cardiff.

Before 1066, Hereford was the capital of the Anglo-Saxon kingdom of Mercia and, earlier still, the site of Roman, Celtic, and Iron Age settlements. Today, people come primarily to see the massive Norman cathedral but quickly discover the charms of this busy country town. Hereford is the center of a wealthy agricultural area known for its cider, fruit, and cattle—the white-faced Hereford breed of cow has spread across the world.

GETTING HERE AND AROUND

The bus and train stations are about a ½ mile northeast of the center. A train from Birmingham will take around 1½ hours. Traveling by car, take the M50 off Junction 8 of the M5, then the A417 and A438 to Hereford. Stagecoach West buses cover the local area, and the city is compact enough to explore on foot.

ESSENTIALS

VISITOR INFORMATION Visit Herefordshire & The Wye Valley. ⊕ *www.visithereford-shire.co.uk.*

👁 Sights

All Saints Church

RELIGIOUS SITE | On the west side of High Town, this 13th-century church contains superb canopied choir stalls and misericords, as well as unusual renovations in the south chapel, dating from the reign of Queen Anne (1702–14). It also has an excellent coffee shop and restaurant. ✉ *Bewell St.* ☎ *01432/370414* ⊕ *www. achurchnearyou.com/church/10548* ✆ *Free.*

Black and White House Museum

HOUSE | The half-timber Old House, crisscrossed with black beams and whitewashed walls, is a fine example of domestic Jacobean architecture. Built in 1621, the house started out as a private home, before spending years as a butcher's shop and then a bank, but has been preserved as a museum since 1929. It's kept in the style it would have been in the early 17th century. Across the three floors you can explore a kitchen, dining hall, parlor, and bedrooms complete with four-poster beds. Look for the rare wall paintings and the unusual dog's door between the nursery and master bedroom. ✉ *High Town* ☎ *01432/260694* ⊕ *www.herefordshire.gov.uk/info/200172/ history_lives_here/648/hereford_museums_and_art_gallery* ✆ *£3* ☉ *Closed Mon. except bank holidays.*

Cider Museum

MUSEUM | A farm's cider house (the alcoholic, European kind) and a cooper's workshop have been re-created at the Cider Museum, where you can tour ancient cellars with huge oak vats. Cider brandy is made here, and the museum sells its own brand, along with other cider items. ✉ *Pomona Pl., at Whitecross Rd.* ☎ *01432/354207* ⊕ *www.cidermuseum.co.uk* ✆ *£5.50* ☉ *Closed Sun.*

★ Hereford Cathedral

RELIGIOUS SITE | Built of local red sandstone, Hereford Cathedral is a treasure trove of historical artifacts, including Mappa Mundi, the largest medieval map in the world; the largest chained library to survive with its locks and chains intact; and many fine 11th-century Norman carvings. The cathedral retains a large central tower, and most of the interior is 19th century. Nevertheless, there are some exquisite contemporary stained-glass windows in the Audley Chapel and a 12th-century chair that is one of the oldest pieces of furniture in the country and was reputedly used by King Stephen (1092–1154). The Mappa Mundi is undoubtedly the biggest draw here. Drawn in about 1300, it's a fascinating glimpse of how the medieval mind viewed the world: Jerusalem is shown dead center, the Garden of Eden at the edge, Europe and Africa are the wrong way round—and, of course, there are no Americas. In addition to land masses, the map details 500 individual drawings, including cities, Biblical stories, mythical creatures, and images of how people in different corners of the globe were thought to look—the last two frequently overlapping in wildly imaginative fashion. The map is held inside the chained library, containing some 1,500 books, among them an 8th-century copy of the Four Gospels. Chained libraries, in which books were attached to cupboards to discourage theft, are extremely rare: they date from medieval times, when books were as precious as gold. The cathedral also holds a copy of the 1217 revision of the Magna Carta; it's not on permanent display, but it's sometimes brought out for temporary exhibits. Tours of the cathedral (without the library) and the tower run on set days throughout the year. Garden tours run in summer. ✉ *Cathedral Close* ☎ *01432/374200* ⊕ *www.herefordcathedral.org* ✆ *Mappa Mundi and chained library exhibition £6; all tours £5* ☉ *Mappa Mundi and chained library closed Sun.*

On the grounds of Attingham Park, you'll find parkland home to deer and flowers.

Restaurants

Café at All Saints

$ | **BRITISH** | A good spot for lunch, this coffee bar and restaurant occupies the western end and gallery of All Saints Church in the heart of Hereford. The imaginative dishes are cooked fresh each day, with Herefordshire wild venison and mushroom casserole frequently appearing on the menu. **Known for:** inventive lunchtime menu; delicious coffee; half-priced menu from 3 to 4 pm. ⑤ *Average main: £10* ⊠ *High St.* ☎ *01432/370415* ⊕ *www.billskitchen.uk/hereford.html* ⊙ *Closed Sun. No dinner.*

🛏 Hotels

★ Castle House

$$ | **HOTEL** | These conjoined Georgian villas next to the moat (all that remains of Hereford Castle) offer luxurious lodgings, a warm welcome, and good food. **Pros:** close to cathedral; quiet setting; castle suites are steeped in history. **Cons:** can get busy with weddings; on the expensive side; some rooms are away form the main house. ⑤ *Rooms from: £155* ⊠ *Castle St.* ☎ *01432/356321* ⊕ *www.castlehse.co.uk* ⊅ *24 rooms* ⦿❘ *Free breakfast.*

Sink Green Farm Bed and Breakfast

$ | **HOTEL** | Peace and seclusion await three miles southeast of Hereford at this informal working farm, which dates back to the 16th century, as do magnificent views of the Wye Valley—and a hot tub from which to enjoy them. **Pros:** friendly and casual; lovely garden; hot tub on-site. **Cons:** car needed to get around; you may feel obliged to make friends; decor a tad old-fashioned. ⑤ *Rooms from: £80* ⊠ *B4399, Rotherwas* ☎ *01432/870223* ⊕ *www.sinkgreenfarm.co.uk* ⊅ *3 rooms* ⦿❘ *Free breakfast.*

Shrewsbury

55 miles north of Hereford, 46 miles south of Chester, 48 miles northwest of Birmingham.

One of England's most important medieval towns, Shrewsbury (pronounced *shrose*-bury), the county seat of Shropshire, lies within a great horseshoe loop of the Severn. It has numerous 16th-century half-timber buildings—many built by well-to-do wool merchants—plus elegant ones from later periods. Today the town retains a romantic air—there are many bridal shops along with churches—and it can be a lovely experience to stroll the Shrewsbury "shuts." These narrow alleys overhung with timbered gables lead off the central market square, which was designed to be closed off at night to protect local residents. You can also relax in Quarry Park on the river.

A good starting point for exploring the city is the small square between Fish Street and Butcher Row. These streets are little changed since medieval times, when some of them took their names from the principal trades carried on there, but Peacock Alley, Gullet Passage, and Grope Lane clearly got their names from somewhere else.

GETTING HERE AND AROUND

The train station is at the neck of the river that loops the center, a little farther out than the bus station on Raven Meadows. A direct train service runs here from Hereford (50 minutes) and Birmingham (one hour). If you're coming from London by car, take the M40 and M42 north, then the M6 and M54, which becomes the A5 to Shrewsbury; the trip is 150 miles. The streets are full of twists, but the town is small enough not to get lost. Walking tours of Shrewsbury depart from the tourist office daily in summer and Saturday only from November to May (£7.50).

ESSENTIALS

VISITOR INFORMATION Shrewsbury Visitor Information Centre. ☒ *The Music Hall, The Square* ☎ *01743/258888* ⊕ *www.originalshrewsbury.co.uk/see-do/visitor-information.*

Sights

★ Attingham Park

HOUSE | Built in 1785 by George Steuart (architect of the church of St. Chad in Shrewsbury) for the first Lord Berwick, this elegant stone mansion has a three-story portico, with a pediment carried on four tall columns. The building overlooks a sweep of parkland, part of which is home to around 300 deer. Inside the house are painted ceilings and delicate plasterwork, a fine picture gallery designed by John Nash (1752–1835), and 19th-century Neapolitan furniture. Attingham Park is four miles southeast of Shrewsbury. ☒ *B4380, off A5, Atcham* ☎ *01743/708123* ⊕ *www.nationaltrust. org.uk/attingham-park* ☒ *£13.45.*

Ireland's Mansion

HISTORIC SITE | The cluster of restored half-timber buildings that link Fish Street with Market Square is known as Bear Steps. This mansion, built in 1575 with elaborate Jacobean timbering and richly decorated with quatrefoils, is the most notable. It's not open to the public, but it's worth a look. ☒ *Fish St. and Market Sq.*

★ St. Chad's Church

RELIGIOUS SITE | On a hilltop west of the town center, this church designed by George Steuart, the architect of Attingham Park, is one of England's most distinctive ecclesiastical buildings. Completed in 1792, the round Georgian church is surmounted by a tower that is in turn square, octagonal, and circular,

as well as topped by a dome. When built, it provoked riots among townsfolk averse to its radical style. The interior has a fine Venetian east window and a brass Arts and Crafts pulpit. ☒ *St. Chad's Terr.* ☎ *01743/365478* ⊕ *www.stchadschurchshrewsbury.com* ☒ *Free.*

Shrewsbury Abbey

HISTORIC SITE | Now unbecomingly surrounded by busy roads, the abbey was founded in 1083 and later became a powerful Benedictine monastery. The abbey church has survived many ups and downs and retains a 14th-century west window above a Norman doorway. A more recent addition is a memorial to World War I poet Wilfred Owen. To reach the abbey from the center, cross the river by the English Bridge. ☒ *Abbey Foregate* ☎ *01743/232723* ⊕ *www.shrewsburyabbey.com* ☒ *Free; donations of £2 encouraged.*

Shrewsbury Castle

CASTLE/PALACE | Guarding the northern approaches to the town, the sandstone castle rises over the River Severn at the bottom of Pride Hill. Originally Norman, it was dismantled during the Civil War and later rebuilt by Thomas Telford, the Scottish engineer who designed many notable buildings and bridges in the early 19th century. Military history buffs will enjoy the **Shropshire Regimental Museum** based in the castle, although there's enough history about the area and its people thrown in to satisfy even the casually interested. ■**TIP→ The numerous benches in the gardens are good for a quiet sit-down.** ☒ *Castle Court* ☎ *01743/358516* ⊕ *www. shrewsburymuseum.org.uk/visit-shrewsbury/shrewsbury-castle* ☒ *£4; grounds free* ⊘ *Closed mid-Dec.–mid-Feb., Thurs., and Sun. in mid-Sept.–mid-Dec.*

Shrewsbury Museum and Art Gallery

MUSEUM | Located in the the town's former Music Hall, this museum chronicles the history of the area, from prehistoric times to the present day. One gallery tells the story of Roman occupation; some genuine finds include a unique silver

The sprawling Ironbridge Gorge Museum interprets the country's industrial history and includes a re-created Victorian town.

mirror from nearby Wroxeter. Another gallery focuses on the boom years of the 19th century, including a display on the life of Shrewsbury's most famous son, Charles Darwin. Special exhibitions change regularly. ✉ *The Music Hall, The Square* ☎ *01743/258885* ⊕ *www.shrewsburymuseum.org.uk* 🖃 *£4.50* ⏰ *Closed Mon. except bank holidays.*

Wrekin
NATURE SITE | If you head south of Shrewsbury on B4380 for around five miles, you can see, rising on the left, the Wrekin, a strange, wooded, conical, extinct volcano that is 1,335 feet high and which may have been the inspiration behind Middle Earth in the *Lord of the Rings* series of books; J. R. R. Tolkien lived nearby. The walk to the summit, which has panoramic views, is about five miles. A few miles farther on, you enter the wooded gorge of the River Severn. ✉ *Atcham.*

🍽 Restaurants

★ Draper's Hall
$$$ | **MODERN BRITISH** | The dark-wood paneling, antique furniture, and intimate lighting of this 16th-century hall make this a distinctive dining spot for modern British cuisine. You might try the loin of Rhug Estate pheasant breast or loin of halibut. **Known for:** Modern British food; chic decor; wild game dishes. ⑤ *Average main: £24* ✉ *10 St. Mary's Pl.* ☎ *01743/344679* ⊕ *www.drapers-hall.co.uk.*

The Walrus
$$$$ | **CONTEMPORARY** | Run by chef couple Ben and Carla, half the excitement here lies in the ever-changing menu, which is genuinely committed to using local and seasonal produce. All the vegetables come from the restaurant's walled garden in nearby Ford, and the resulting dishes are impressive. **Known for:** local produce; low-key fine dining; friendly service. ⑤ *Average main: £35* ✉ *5 Roushill* ☎ *01743/240005* ⊕ *www.the-walrus.co.uk* ⏰ *Closed Sun.–Tues.*

Hotels

Albright Hussey Manor

$ | HOTEL | Lovely gardens surround this moated Tudor manor house, originally the home of the Hussey family, which dates back to 1524; black-and-white half-timbering combines with a later redbrick-and-stone extension. **Pros:** beautiful period setting; fine food; lovely grounds. **Cons:** location a bit out of town; could do with a face-lift; newer rooms less attractive. $ *Rooms from: £78* ⊠ *Broad Oak* ☎ *01939/290571* ⊕ *www.albrighthussey. co.uk* ⇨ *26 rooms* ❍ *No meals.*

★ Lion & Pheasant

$$ | B&B/INN | This elegant townhouse in the popular Wyle Cop area of Shrewsbury has an excellent restaurant, unique and blissful rooms, and lots of character. **Pros:** reputable restaurant; original features; luxury linens. **Cons:** some may find the decor too vanilla; can be on the busy side; no elevator. $ *Rooms from: £130* ⊠ *49-50 Wyle Cop* ☎ *01743/770345* ⊕ *www.lionandpheasant.co.uk* ⇨ *22 rooms* ❍ *No meals.*

Performing Arts

Theatre Severn

ARTS CENTERS | This theater covers all the lively arts: classical and popular music, dance, and drama. ⊠ *Frankwell Quay* ☎ *01743/281281* ⊕ *www.theatresevern. co.uk.*

Shopping

★ Parade

SHOPPING CENTERS/MALLS | Behind St. Mary's church, this shopping center is in a neoclassical building from 1830 that once held the Royal Infirmary. One of the most appealing malls in England, it has over 20 attractive boutiques, a coffee shop, and a river terrace. ⊠ *St. Mary's Pl.* ☎ *01743/343178* ⊕ *www. paradeshops.co.uk.*

Ironbridge Gorge

4 miles east of Much Wenlock, 15 miles east of Shrewsbury, 28 miles northwest of Birmingham.

The River Severn and its tree-cloaked banks make an attractive backdrop to this cluster of villages; within a mile of the graceful span of the world's first substantial iron bridge are fascinating museums exploring the area's industrial past and the reasons why it's been described as the "cradle of the Industrial Revolution."

GETTING HERE AND AROUND

To drive here from Shrewsbury, take the A5 east, A442 south, and then the A4169 west before following the brown signs for Ironbridge. On weekends and bank holidays from Easter to late October, the Gorge Connect Bus shuttles passengers between Ironbridge's museums every 30 minutes; it's just £2 for museum passport holders and £2.50 for anyone else.

ESSENTIALS

VISITOR INFORMATION Ironbridge Visitor Information Centre. ⊠ *The Museum of the Gorge, The Wharfage, Telford* ☎ *01952/433424* ⊕ *www.ironbridge.org.uk.*

Sights

★ Ironbridge Gorge Museum

MUSEUM | FAMILY | The 10 sites that make up the Ironbridge Gorge Museum—a World Heritage Site spread over 6 square miles—preserve the area's fascinating industrial history in spectacular fashion. The best starting point is the **Museum of the Gorge,** which has a good selection of literature and an audiovisual show on the history of the area. In nearby Coalbrookdale, the **Museum of Iron** explains the production of iron and steel. You can see the blast furnace built by Abraham Darby, who developed the original coke process in 1709. The adjacent **Enginuity** exhibition is a hands-on, feet-on interactive exploration of engineering that's good for kids. From here, drive the few miles along the river until the arches of the **Iron Bridge** come into view. Designed by T. F. Pritchard, smelted by Darby, and erected between 1777 and 1779, this graceful arch spanning the River Severn can best be seen—and photographed—from the towpath, a riverside walk edged with wildflowers and shrubs. The tollhouse on the far side houses an exhibition on the bridge's history and restoration.

A mile farther along the river is the **Jackfield Tile Museum,** a repository of decorative tiles from the 19th and 20th centuries. Another half mile brings you to the **Coalport China Museum.** Exhibits show some of the factory's most beautiful wares, and craftspeople give demonstrations; visit the restrooms for the unique communal washbasins. A short walk from Coalport is the **Tar Tunnel**, part of a 1787 tar mine; note the black bitumen still seeping through the walls. Nearby is Ironbridge's star attraction: **Blists Hill Victorian Town,** where you can see old mines, furnaces, and a wrought-iron works. The main draw is the re-creation of the "town" itself, with its doctor's office, bakery, grocer, candle maker, sawmill, printing shop, and candy store. At the entrance you can change some money for specially minted pennies and make purchases from the shops. Shopkeepers, the bank manager, and the doctor's wife are on hand to give you advice. If you don't fancy the refreshments at the Fried Fish Dealers, you could drop into the **New Inn** pub (in Blists Hill) for a traditional ale or ginger beer and join one of the singalongs around the piano that take place a couple of times every afternoon; or, for something more formal, try the **Club Room** restaurant next door. Allow at least a full day to appreciate all the major sights and perhaps to take a stroll around the famous Iron Bridge or hunt for Coalport china in the stores clustered near it. On weekends and national holidays from April through October, a shuttle bus takes you between sites. ✉ *B4380, Telford* ☎ *01952/433424* ⊕ *www.ironbridge.org.uk* ✉ *Passport ticket (all attractions, valid 1 year) £25.15. Individual sites: Blists Hill £18.50; Enginuity, Coalport China Museum, Jackfield Tile Museum, and Museum of Iron £9.50 each; Museum of the Gorge £4.50.*

Restaurants

Restaurant Severn

$$$ | MODERN BRITISH | At this discreet restaurant set back from the main road in the center of Ironbridge, the concept is simple: locally sourced produce and modern techniques are combined to serve up a twist of British classics and European favorites. Start with a Scotch egg with brown sauce and pancetta before moving on to pork belly stuffed with black pudding, kale, and spiced red cabbage. **Known for:** British classics with a modern slant; personal service; fabulous wines. ⑤ *Average main: £29* ✉ *33 High St., Ironbridge* ☎ *01952/432233* ⊕ *www.restaurantsevern.co.uk* ⊗ *Closed Mon. and Tues.*

🛏 Hotels

Hundred House Hotel

$$ | HOTEL | The low beams, stained glass, wood paneling, and patchwork cushions that greet you as you enter this Georgian inn set the tone for the whimsical guest rooms, fancifully named after herbs and flowers (the latter, of course, being the most colorful). **Pros:** full of fanciful touches and quirky nooks and corners; good food; welcoming country inn. **Cons:** not for those who favor the plain and simple; a little out of town; a bit on the pricey side. ⑤ *Rooms from: £198* ✉ *Bridgnorth Rd. (A442), Norton* ☎ *01952/580240* ⊕ *www.hundredhouse.co.uk* ⤴ *8 rooms* ⑩ *Free breakfast.*

★ Library House

$ | **B&B/INN** | Built in 1740 and at one time the village's library, this small guesthouse sits on the hillside near the Ironbridge museums and just a few steps from the bridge. **Pros:** welcoming hosts; good location; elegant bedrooms. **Cons:** no restaurant; books up quickly; might be too personable for some. ⑤ *Rooms from: £100* ✉ *11 Severn Bank, Telford* ☎ *01952/432299* ⊕ *www.libraryhouse. com* ⤳ *3 rooms* ⑩ *Free breakfast.*

Ludlow

25 miles south of Ironbridge Gorge, 27 miles south of Shrewsbury, 24 miles north of Hereford.

Medieval, Georgian, and Victorian build ings jostle for attention in pretty Ludlow, which has a finer display of black-and-white half-timber buildings than even Shrewsbury. Dominating the center is the Church of St. Laurence, its extravagant size a testimony to the town's prosperous medieval wool trade. Cross the River Teme and climb Whitcliffe Common for a spectacular view of the church and the Norman castle.

Several outstanding restaurants have given the town of just 11,000 a reputation as a culinary hot spot. Ludlow is a proponent of the Slow Food movement, which focuses on food traditions and responsible production with the aim of protecting forgotten foods, such as the Shropshire prune, from being lost forever.

GETTING HERE AND AROUND

From London Paddington, the journey time by train is 3½ hours (changing at Newport in southern Wales), from Shrewsbury 30 minutes, and from Birmingham just under two hours with a change in Shrewsbury. From the train station, it's less than a 10-minute walk to the city center. Driving

from London, take the M40, M42, and A448 to Kidderminster, then the A456 and A4117 to Ludlow. The town has good parking and is easily walkable.

ESSENTIALS

VISITOR INFORMATION Ludlow Visitor Information Centre. ✉ *Ludlow Assembly Rooms, 1 Mill St.* ☎ *01584/875053* ⊕ *www.ludlow.org.uk.*

◉ Sights

★ Ludlow Castle

CASTLE/PALACE | **FAMILY** | The "very perfection of decay," according to author Daniel Defoe, the ruins of this red sandstone castle date from 1085. No wonder the massive structure dwarfs the town: it served as a vital stronghold for centuries and was the seat of the Marcher Lords who ruled "the Marches," the local name for the border region. The two sons of Edward IV—the little princes of the Tower of London—spent time here before being dispatched to London and before their death in 1483. Follow the terraced walk around the castle for a lovely view of the countryside. ✉ *Castle Sq.* ☎ *01584/873355* ⊕ *www.ludlowcastle.com* 🎟 *£7* ⊙ *Closed weekdays early Jan.–early Feb.*

Stokesay Castle

HOUSE | This 13th-century fortified manor house built by a wealthy merchant is among the finest of its kind in England. Inside the main hall, the wooden cruck roof and timber staircase (a rare survival) demonstrate state-of-the-art building methods of the day. Outside, the cottage-style garden creates a bewitching backdrop for the magnificent Jacobean timber-frame gatehouse. The castle is seven miles northwest of Ludlow. ✉ *Craven Arms* ☎ *01588/672544* ⊕ *www. english-heritage.org.uk/visit/places/stokesay-castle* 🎟 *£8.60* ⊙ *Closed weekdays Nov.–late Feb.*

Restaurants

The Cliffe at Dinham

$$ | BRITISH | Although there are lovely rooms in this 1850s redbrick inn near Ludlow Castle, the main draw is the food. The dining room serves up good quality local dishes, but what really makes the modern British menu standout are its special evenings, such as Fish Night, in which fresh oysters and langoustines are cooked to perfection. **Known for:** classic British cuisine; nice cocktail menu and wine list; castle views. $ *Average main: £18* ✉ *Dinham* ☎ *01584/872063* ⊕ *www.thecliffeatdinham.co.uk.*

Hotels

The Feathers

$$ | HOTEL | Even if you're not staying here, take time to admire the extravagant half-timber facade of this hotel, built in the early 17th century and described by many as one of the most beautiful inns in the world. **Pros:** ornate plasterwork; unpretentious feel; some four-poster beds. **Cons:** most guest rooms lack traditional feel; can be very tourist heavy; it's an old building and sometimes this shows. $ *Rooms from: £129* ✉ *21 Bullring* ☎ *01584/875261* ⊕ *www.feathersatludlow.co.uk* ➵ *42 rooms* ❚◎❙ *Free breakfast.*

★ Fishmore Hall

$$ | HOTEL | Saved from dereliction in the late 2000s, Fishmore Hall has been beautifully converted from a crumbling old mansion into a relaxing, contemporary lodge. **Pros:** lovely location; well-designed rooms; serene, luxurious spa. **Cons:** restaurant is pricey; a little out of town; outdoor hot tub is not to everyone's liking. $ *Rooms from: £145* ✉ *Fishmore Rd.* ☎ *01584/875148* ⊕ *www.fishmorehall.co.uk* ➵ *15 rooms* ❚◎❙ *Free breakfast.*

★ Timberstone

$ | B&B/INN | FAMILY | The Read family has turned a rambling stone cottage in the Clee Hills into a welcoming haven with rooms furnished in neutral tones in a soothing, contemporary style. **Pros:** relaxing and hospitable; geared to families; great food. **Cons:** far from the center of Ludlow; rustic living may not appeal to everyone; dinner menu is limited. $ *Rooms from: £120* ✉ *B4363, Cleestanton* ☎ *01584/823519* ⊕ *www.timberstoneludlow.co.uk* ➵ *5 rooms* ❚◎❙ *Free breakfast.*

Chester

75 miles north of Ludlow, 46 miles north of Shrewsbury.

Cheshire's thriving center is Chester, a city similar in some ways to Shrewsbury, though it has many more black-and-white half-timber buildings (some built in Georgian and Victorian times), and its medieval walls still stand. History seems more tangible in Chester than in many other ancient cities, as modern buildings haven't been allowed to intrude on the center. A negative result of this perfection is that Chester has become a favorite tour bus destination, with gift shops, noise, and crowds aplenty.

Chester has been a prominent city since the late 1st century, when the Roman Empire expanded north to the banks of the River Dee. The original Roman town plan is still evident: the principal streets, Eastgate, Northgate, Watergate, and Bridge Street, lead out from the Cross—the site of the central area of the Roman fortress—to the four city gates. The partly excavated remains of what is thought to have been the country's largest Roman amphitheater lie to the south of Chester's medieval castle.

Lined with handsome brick, stone, and half-timber buildings, Chester's compact center is perfect for shopping and strolling.

GETTING HERE AND AROUND

There's a free shuttle bus to the center if you arrive by train, and buses pull up at Vicar's Lane in the center (Monday to Saturday). Chester is 180 miles from London and about two hours by train; some trains change at Crewe. If you're driving and here for a day only, use the city's Park and Ride lots, as central parking lots fill quickly, especially in summer.

Guided walks leave the town hall daily at 10:30 am with an additional tour at 2 pm from Easter to October (£8). In summer, the 10:30 am tour ends with a proclamation from the Town Crier, who is dressed in traditional attire.

ESSENTIALS

VISITOR AND TOUR INFORMATION Chester Tourist Information Centre. ⊠ *Town Hall, Northgate St.* ☎ *01244/405340* ⊕ *www. visitcheshire.com/chester.* **City Sightseeing.** ☎ *01244/347452* ⊕ *www.city-sight-seeing.com/en/89/chester.*

⊙ Sights

ChesterBoat

TOUR—SIGHT | This company runs excursions on the River Dee every 30 minutes daily from 11–5 in late March through November and hourly from 11–4 on weekends in November and December. Special themed cruises include retro disco nights; see the website for listings. ⊠ *Boating Station, Souters La.* ☎ *01244/325394* ⊕ *www.chesterboat. co.uk* ✉ *£7 in advance, £7.50 quayside* ⊙ *Closed weekdays Jan.–mid-Feb.*

★ Chester Cathedral

RELIGIOUS SITE | Tradition has it that, in Roman, times a church of some sort stood on the site of what is now Chester Cathedral, but records date construction to around AD 900. The earliest work traceable today, mainly in the north transept, is that of the 11th-century Benedictine abbey. After Henry VIII dissolved the monasteries in the 16th century, the abbey church became the cathedral church of the new diocese of

Historic Chester Cathedral was built around 900 AD.

Chester. The misericords in the choir stalls reveal carved figures of people and animals, both real and mythical, and above is a gilded and colorful vaulted ceiling. Cathedral at Height tours (£8) take you to parts of the building usually off-limits to visitors, including the roof—from which you can see two countries (England and Wales) and five separate counties. ⊠ *St. Werburgh St., off Market Sq.* ☎ *01244/500959* ⊕ *www.chesterca-thedral.com* ⊙ *No tours Sun.*

Chester Rows

BUILDING | Chester's unique Rows, which originated in the 12th and 13th centuries, are essentially double rows of stores, one at street level and the other on the second floor with galleries overlooking the street. The Rows line the junction of the four streets in the old town. They have medieval crypts below them, and some reveal Roman foundations ⊠ *Chester* ⊕ *www.visitchester.com/things-to-do/chester-rows-p22731.*

Chester Zoo

ZOO | FAMILY | Well-landscaped grounds and natural enclosures make the 80-acre zoo one of Britain's most popular and also one of its largest. Highlights include the Realm of the Red Ape, the jaguar enclosure, and the Dragons in Danger habitat. Baby animals are often on display. Eleven miles of paths wind through the zoo, and you can use the water-bus boats or the overhead train to tour the grounds. Fun 10-minute animal talks, aimed at kids, take place at various locations around the zoo throughout the day; little ones will especially love the Madagascar PLAY zone. ⊠ *A41* ☎ *01244/380280* ⊕ *www.chesterzoo.org* ⊠ *From £20.*

City Walls

BUILDING | Accessible from several points, the city walls provide splendid views of Chester and its surroundings. The whole circuit is two miles, but if your time is short, climb the steps at Newgate and walk along toward Eastgate to see the great ornamental **Eastgate Clock,** erected to commemorate Queen Victoria's Diamond Jubilee in 1897. Lots of small shops near this part of the walls sell old books, old postcards, antiques, and jewelry. Where the **Bridge of Sighs** (named after the enclosed bridge in Venice that it closely resembles) crosses the canal, descend to street level and walk up Northgate Street into Market Square. ✉ *Chester.*

Grosvenor Museum

MUSEUM | **FAMILY** | Start a visit to this museum with a look at the Roman Stones Gallery, which displays Roman-era tombstones previously used to repair city walls (keep an eye out for the wounded barbarian). Afterwards you can skip a few centuries to explore the period house for a tour from 1680 to the 1920s. ✉ *27 Grosvenor St.* 🕾 *01244/972197* ⊕ *www.grosvenormuseum.westcheshiremuseums.co.uk* 🎫 *Free.*

Restaurants

Albion Inn

$ | **BRITISH** | You feel as if you're stepping back in time at this Victorian pub; the posters, advertisements, flags, and curios tell you the idiosyncratic landlord keeps it as it would have been during World War I. The candlelit restaurant forms one of the three snug rooms and, unsurprisingly, serves up traditional fare such as lamb's liver, corned beef hash, and gammon (thick-sliced ham) with pease pudding. **Known for:** old-fashioned British food; historic, old-school ambience; local hangout. ⑤ *Average main: £10* ✉ *Park St.* 🕾 *01244/340345* ⊕ *www.albioninnchester.co.uk* 🕙 *No dinner Sun.*

Chez Jules

$$ | **BISTRO** | Once a fire station, this bustling bistro is now unashamedly French and rustic, with red-and-white-check tablecloths and a menu chalked up on the blackboard. Start perhaps with some *moules marinières* (mussels cooked in a white-wine-and-onion sauce) or French onion soup, followed by grilled sea bass or a classic rib-eye steak with Café du Paris butter. **Known for:** rural French cooking; dishes that change daily; good value set menus. ⑤ *Average main: £18* ✉ *71 Northgate St.* 🕾 *01244/400014* ⊕ *www.chezjules.com.*

Simon Radley at the Chester Grosvenor

$$$$ | **FRENCH** | Named for its noted chef, this Michelin-starred restaurant has a sophisticated panache and prices to match. Expect the seasonal but not the usual: the Two Hens features black-leg chicken alongside lobster, while the wild halibut comes with shaved octopus and seaweed dumplings. **Known for:** unexpected flavor combinations; smart dress code and no children under 12; reservations needed for weekend. ⑤ *Average main: £45* ✉ *Chester Grosvenor Hotel, Eastgate St.* 🕾 *01244/324024* ⊕ *www.chestergrosvenor.com/simon-radley-restaurant* 🕙 *Closed Sun. and Mon.* 🎩 *Jacket required.*

🛏 Hotels

Abode Chester

$ | **HOTEL** | Perched at a busy traffic intersection on the edge of Chester's old town, this gleaming, modern hotel from the trendy Abode chain may not occupy the city's most romantic spot, but it's well run and comfortable. **Pros:** spacious guest rooms; good food; great bar. **Cons:** lacks historic charm of older hotels; parking lot is hard to find; a bit of a stroll into town. ⑤ *Rooms from: £94* ✉ *Grosvenor Rd.* 🕾 *01244/347000* ⊕ *www.abodehotels.co.uk/chester* 🛏 *85 rooms* 🍴 *No meals.*

★ Chester Grosvenor Hotel

$$ | **HOTEL** | Handmade Italian furniture and swaths of French silk fill this deluxe downtown hotel in a Tudor-style building, which was established in 1865. **Pros:** pampered luxury; superb food; excellent service and facilities. **Cons:** no private

parking; spa is small; extra for cooked breakfast. $ Rooms from: £162 ⊠ East-gate ☎ 01244/324024 ⊕ www.chester-grosvenor.com ⤳ 80 rooms ⦿| Free breakfast.

Grove Villa

$ | B&B/INN | This family-run B&B—in a charming Victorian building with antique furnishings on the banks of the River Dee—has just three guest rooms to choose from, two of which overlook the river. **Pros:** beautiful river location; breakfast around a communal table; friendly and welcoming hosts. **Cons:** no credit cards; no Internet connection; 15 minutes to town center. $ Rooms from: £90 ⊠ 18 The Groves ☎ 01244/349713 ⊕ www.grovevillachester.co.uk ▭ No credit cards ⤳ 3 rooms ⦿| Free breakfast.

🛍 Shopping

Chester Market

SHOPPING CENTERS/MALLS | This indoor market, near the Town Hall, has more than 50 stalls, including Chester's only fishmonger. It's a great place to try local food delicacies. It's open Monday through Saturday from 8 am until 5 pm (except for bank holidays). ⊠ 6 Princess St. ⊕ www.chester.market.

Chapter 10

MANCHESTER, LIVERPOOL, AND THE PEAK DISTRICT

Updated by
Rhonda Carrier

⊙ **Sights** ★★★★☆ 🍴 **Restaurants** ★★★★☆ 🛏 **Hotels** ★★★★☆ 🛍 **Shopping** ★★★★☆ 🍸 **Nightlife** ★★★★☆

WELCOME TO MANCHESTER, LIVERPOOL, AND THE PEAK DISTRICT

TOP REASONS TO GO

★ **Manchester theater and nightlife:** The city's theater scene keeps getting more exciting, while bustling café-bars and pubs, together with ornate Victorian-era beer houses, mean there are plenty of ways to continue your night out in style.

★ **Liverpool culture, old and new:** This once-run-down merchant city, already a must-see for fans of the Fab Four, has reinvented itself as a cultural hub with plenty of dining, lodging, and nightlife hot spots.

★ **Outdoor activities in the Peak District:** Even a short hike in Edale or High Peak reveals the craggy, austere beauty for which the area is famous, but cycling, caving, and other sports make the Peaks a veritable natural playground.

★ **Grand country houses:** The stately Chatsworth House and the Tudor manor Haddon Hall will enchant fans of both *Downton Abbey* and quintessentially English architecture alike.

Manchester lies at the heart of a tangle of motorways in the northwest of England, about a half hour across the Pennines from Yorkshire. It's 70 miles from the southern edge of the Lake District. The city spreads west toward the coast and the mouth of the River Mersey and Liverpool. To see any great natural beauty, you must head east to the Peak District, a national park less than an hour's drive southeast of Manchester. It's also where you'll find two of the grandest and best-preserved historic homes in all of Britain: Chatsworth and Haddon Hall.

1 Manchester. England's second city and the main setting of the Industrial Revolution.

2 Liverpool. A waterfront city famous for its maritime history and as the birthplace of the Beatles.

3 Buxton. A good base for the Peak District, Britain's first national park.

4 Bakewell. The commercial hub of the Peak District.

5 Matlock. A former spa town now known for its beautiful setting.

6 Castleton. Famed for its Peak District geology.

7 Edale. A popular hiking center.

8 Stoke-on-Trent. The center of Britain's ceramics industry.

THE BEATLES IN LIVERPOOL

The Beatles' music and style—and their haircuts—rocked the 1960s.

This distinctive northern English city was the birthplace of the Beatles, who changed rock music forever using recording techniques unheard of at the time.

The Fab Four became counterculture icons who defined the look and sound of the 1960s, but despite their international success, they remained true sons of Liverpool. The city remains a site of pilgrimage for fans more than half a century after the Beatles' early gigs here. Liverpool may no longer be the rough, postwar city the Beatles grew up in, but it makes the most of its connections to Paul McCartney, John Lennon, George Harrison, and Ringo Starr. John and Paul's childhood homes, Mendips and 20 Forthlin Road, are in south Liverpool; both are National Trust sites. You can take in a show at Mathew Street's (re-created) Cavern Club, where the band played in its early days, or tour Penny Lane, Strawberry Fields, and other mop-top nostalgia spots. Located on two sites at Albert Dock and Pier Head, the Beatles Story museum provides a state-of-the-art overview of the group's career.

THEIR WORDS

"I knew the words to 25 rock songs, so I got into the group. 'Long Tall Sally' and 'Tutti Frutti,' that got me in. That was my audition." —Paul McCartney

"Paul wasn't quite strong enough, I didn't have enough girl appeal, George was too quiet, and Ringo was the drummer. But we thought everyone would be able to dig at least one of us, and that's how it turned out." —John Lennon

FOLLOW IN THE FOOTSTEPS

SEE THE MAIN SIGHTS

The three key shrines of Beatle-dom in Liverpool are John and Paul's childhood homes in south Liverpool and the legendary Cavern Club on Mathew Street downtown, where the Beatles were discovered by their future manager Brian Epstein in 1961. A combined ticket for both Beatle homes includes a bus between the city center and the two sites.

CHECK OUT THE BEATLES STORY

At two venues at the Albert Dock and Pier Head, entertaining scenes re-create stages in the Fab Four's lives—from early gigs in Germany and the Cavern Club to each member's solo career—with 3D computer animations, band artifacts, and more.

CHOOSE THE RIGHT TOUR

The two-hour Magical Mystery Tour (⊕ *www.cavern-club.org*) departing from the Albert Dock (Anchor Courtyard) is a great way to zoom around Penny Lane, Strawberry Field, and other landmarks it would otherwise be difficult to find. Liverpool Beatles Tours (⊕ *www.beatlestours.co.uk*) can cram in every Beatles haunt on three-, four- or five-hour or full-day tours. Other options are private guides or personalized tours.

GO TO BEATLEWEEK

The annual **International Beatleweek** (www.internationalbeatleweek.com) is usually held the last week in August. Attend John and Yoko fancy-dress parties; listen to Beatles tribute bands; and check out record fairs, exhibitions, and conventions.

(top, right) Mendips, John's childhood home and now a National Trust site; (below) The rebuilt Cavern Club.

TAKING STOCK

When these four local rapscallions appeared on the Liverpool pop circuit in the early 1960s, they were just another group of lads struggling to get gigs on the city's "Merseybeat" scene. What followed was extraordinary: Beatlemania swept over fans around the world, including the United States, which the group first visited in 1964. Before their 1969 breakup, the Beatles achieved phenomenal commercial and creative success, bringing bohemianism to the masses and embodying a generation's ideals of social liberation and peace. They reinvented pop music, bridging styles and genres as diverse as Celtic folk, psychedelia, and Indian raga; starring in epoch-making movies such as *A Hard Day's Night* and *Help!*; and causing such hysteria they couldn't even hear their own guitars on stage. Though adulation followed them everywhere, the Beatles remained obstinate "Scousers," showing a grounded charm and irreverent humor characteristic of their native city.

For those looking for picture-postcard England, the northwest region of the country might not top many sightseeing lists, but it has plenty to offer. Manchester, Britain's third-largest city by size and second by cultural significance, bustles with redevelopment, and Liverpool is undergoing similar revitalization.

Yes, the 200 years of smokestack industry that abated only in the 1980s have taken a toll on the landscape, but the region does have some lovely scenery inland in Derbyshire (pronounced *Dar-be-sha*)—notably the spectacular Peak District, a national park at the southern end of the Pennine range.

Manchester and Liverpool, the economic engines that propelled Britain in the 18th and 19th centuries, have sloughed off their mid-20th-century decline and celebrate their rich industrial and maritime heritage through some excellent museums—either in converted Victorian edifices, strikingly modern buildings, or, in the case of the Manchester Art Gallery and Whitworth Art Gallery, a stunning combination of the two.

The cities, each with a population of about 500,000, have reestablished themselves as centers of sporting and musical excellence, as well as hot spots for culture and nightlife. Since 1962, the Manchester United, Manchester City, Everton, and Liverpool football (soccer) clubs have between them won everything worth winning in Britain and Europe. The Beatles launched the Mersey sound of the '60s; contemporary Manchester groups and acts from the Smiths to Bugzy Malone still punch above their weight on both sides of the Atlantic. On the classical side of music, Manchester is the home of Britain's oldest leading orchestra, the Hallé (founded in 1857)—just one legacy of 19th-century industrialists' investments in culture.

As you head inland to the Peak District, nature comes to the forefront in the form of crags that rear violently out of the plains. The Pennines, a line of hills that begins in the Peak District and runs as far north as Scotland, are sometimes called the "backbone of England." In this landscape of rocky outcrops and undulating meadowland you'll see nothing for miles but sheep, drystone walls (built without mortar), and farms, interrupted—spectacularly—by 19th-century villages and stately homes. In and around this area are Victorian-era spas such as Buxton, pretty towns such as Bakewell, and magnificent houses such as Chatsworth and Haddon Hall. The delight of the Peak District is being able to ramble for days in rugged countryside but still enjoy the pleasures of civilization.

MAJOR REGIONS

Manchester. This vibrant city mixes a compelling industrial heritage with cutting-edge urban design and thriving music and club scenes. Great museums and art galleries justify its blossoming status as the United Kingdom's second city of culture.

Liverpool. The imposing waterfront, the pair of cathedrals, and the grand architecture make it clear that this city—now undergoing a postindustrial rebirth—is more than just the Beatles. Even so, the many museums don't leave out the city's place in rock-and-roll history.

The Peak District. Heading southeast, away from the urban congestion of Manchester and Liverpool, it's not far to the southernmost contortions of the Pennine Hills. Here, about an hour southeast of Manchester, sheltered in a great natural bowl, is the spa town of Buxton: at an elevation of more than 1,000 feet, it's the second-highest town in England. Buxton makes a convenient base for exploring the 540 square miles of the Peak District, Britain's oldest—and, its fans say, most beautiful—national park. About 38,000 people live in the towns throughout the park.

"Peak" is perhaps misleading; despite being a hilly area, it contains only gentle rises that don't reach much higher than 2,000 feet. Yet a trip around destinations such as Bakewell, Matlock, Castleton, and Edale, as well as around the grand estates of Chatsworth House and Haddon Hall, involves negotiating fairly perilous country roads, each of which repays the effort with enchanting views.

Outdoor activities are popular in the Peaks, particularly caving (or "potholing"), walking, and hiking. Bring all-weather clothing and waterproof shoes.

Planning

When to Go

Manchester has a reputation as one of the wettest cities in Britain, and visiting in summer won't guarantee dry weather. Nevertheless, the damp or cold shouldn't spoil a visit because of the many indoor sights and cultural activities here and in Liverpool. Summer is the optimal time to see the Peak District, especially because traditional festivities take place in many villages. The only time to see the great houses of Derbyshire's Wye Valley is from spring through fall.

Planning Your Time

It's possible to see the main sights of Manchester or Liverpool in two days, but you'd have to take the museums at a real gallop. In Manchester, the Museum of Science and Industry and the Imperial War Museum North could easily absorb a day by themselves, as could the Albert Dock and waterfront area of Liverpool, where the Beatles Story's main venue, the Tate Liverpool, and the Merseyside Maritime and International Slavery museums, as well as the neighboring Museum of Liverpool, all vie for your attention. In Liverpool, an additional half day is needed to see the homes of John Lennon and Paul McCartney. The excellent nightlife of each city demands at least an overnight stay at each. You can explore the Peak District on a day trip from Manchester in a pinch, but allow longer to visit the stately homes or to hike.

FESTIVALS
Buxton Festival
FESTIVALS | This renowned event, held for two weeks during mid-July each year, includes opera, drama, and concerts. ⊠ *The Square, Buxton* ☎ *01298/72190 box office* ⊕ *www.buxtonfestival.co.uk.*

★ Manchester International Festival

FESTIVALS | This biennial multi-arts festival has played a major role in Manchester's cultural development since it launched in 2007. With international artists such as Björk and Marina Abramović making appearances, it often premieres events that go on to tour nationally or globally. Events take place in some of the city's most popular performing arts spaces, as well as obscure locations such as disused buildings. ⊠ *Manchester* ⊕ *www. mif.co.uk.*

Getting Here and Around

AIR

Both Manchester and Liverpool are well served by their international airports. Manchester, the third-largest airport in the country (and the busiest outside London), has the greater number of flights, including some from the United States. East Midlands Airport southwest of Derby also provides an alternative international air route into the region.

AIRPORTS **East Midlands Airport.** ⊠ *Castle Donington* ☎ *0808/169–7032* ⊕ *www. eastmidlandsairport.com.* **Liverpool John Lennon Airport.** ⊠ *Hale Rd., Liverpool* ☎ *0871/521–8484* ⊕ *www. liverpoolairport.com.* **Manchester Airport.** ☎ *0808/169–7030* ⊕ *www.manchesterairport.co.uk.*

BUS

National Express buses serve the region from London's Victoria Coach Station. Average travel time to Manchester or Liverpool is five hours. To reach Matlock, Bakewell, and Buxton, you can take a bus from London to Derby and change to the TransPeak bus service, though you might find it more convenient to travel first to Manchester.

CONTACTS **National Express.** ☎ *0871/781– 8181* ⊕ *www.nationalexpress.com.* **TransPeak.** ☎ *0844/351–1120* ⊕ *www. highpeakbuses.com.*

CAR

If you're traveling by road, expect heavy traffic out of London on weekends. Travel time to Manchester or Liverpool from London via the M6 is 3 to 3½ hours. Although a car may not be an asset in touring the centers of Manchester and Liverpool, it's helpful in getting around the Peak District. Bus service is quite good, but a car allows the most flexibility.

Roads within the region are generally very good, but the deeper you get into the countryside, the more likely you are to encounter narrow, one-lane farm roads once you turn off the main routes. In summer, Peak District traffic is very heavy; watch out for speeding motorbikes, especially on the A6. In winter, know the weather forecast, as moorland roads can quickly become impassable.

In Manchester and Liverpool, try to sightsee on foot to avoid parking issues. In the Peak District, park in signposted parking lots whenever possible.

TRAIN

Virgin Trains serves the region from London's Euston Station. Direct services to Manchester and Liverpool take between 2 and 2½ hours. There are trains between Manchester's Piccadilly Station and Liverpool's Lime Street roughly four times an hour during the day; the trip takes 50 minutes. (Trains also go less frequently from Manchester's Victoria and Oxford Road stations.) Get schedules and other information through National Rail Enquiries.

To reach Buxton in the Peak District from London, take the train to Manchester that stops at Stockport and change there; to Buxton it's another 45-minute ride. The local service—one train an hour (more at peak times)—from Manchester Piccadilly to Buxton takes just under one hour.

CONTACTS **National Rail Enquiries.** ☎ *03457/484950* ⊕ *www.nationalrail. co.uk.*

TRANSPORTATION DISCOUNTS AND DEALS

A Greater Manchester Wayfarer ticket (£14.40; £28.80 for groups of up to two adults and two children) covers a day's travel on all forms of transport in Manchester and parts of Lancashire, Cheshire, Staffordshire, Derbyshire, and the Peak District. See ⊕ www.tfgm.com or call ☎ 0161/244–1000 for information.

Restaurants

Dining options in Manchester and Liverpool vary from smart cafés offering Modern British, Continental, or global fare to world-class international restaurants for all budgets. Manchester has one of Britain's biggest Chinatowns, as well as its "Curry Mile" of 40 odd Bangladeshi, Pakistani, and Indian restaurants a mile south of the city center (although delicious modern Indian restaurants certainly exist in the city center, too).

One local dish that has survived is Bakewell pudding (never called "tart" in these areas, as its imitations are elsewhere in England). Served with custard or cream, the pudding—a pastry covered with jam and a thin layer of almond-flavor filling—can't be missed if visiting Bakewell.

Hotels

Because the larger city-center hotels in Manchester and Liverpool rely on business travelers during the week, they may markedly reduce their rates on weekends. Smaller hotels and guesthouses abound, often in nearby suburbs, many just a short bus ride from downtown. The Manchester and Liverpool visitor information centers operate room-booking services. Also worth investigating are serviced apartments, which are becoming more popular in the cities. The Peak District has inns, bed-and-breakfasts, and hotels, as well as a network of youth hostels and campsites. Local tourist offices have details; reserve well in advance for Easter and summer.

Restaurant and hotel reviews have been shortened. For full information, visit Fodors.com. Restaurant prices are the average cost of a main course at dinner, or if dinner is not served, at lunch. Hotel prices are the lowest cost of a standard double room in high season, including 20% V.A.T.

WHAT IT COSTS in Pounds			
$	$$	$$$	$$$$
RESTAURANTS			
under £16	£16–£23	£24–£30	over £30
HOTELS			
under £125	£125–£225	£226–£350	over £350

Manchester

Central Manchester is alive with the vibe of cutting-edge popular music and a swank, often fancy café, cocktail bar, and restaurant culture that keeps evolving at a dizzying speed. The city's once-grim industrial landscape, redeveloped since the late 1980s, includes tidied-up canals, cotton mills transformed into loft apartments, and stylish contemporary architecture that has pushed the skyline ever higher. Beetham Tower, the 12th-tallest building in Britain (the second tallest outside London since the addition of the Deansgate Square South Tower to the Manchester cityscape), stands proud and prominent. Since 2020, over £300 million of investment has unleashed another cultural boom that includes or will include several major city projects, including the expansion of several museums and music venues, the reopening of the Contact Theatre and the Manchester Jewish Museum, the launch of the OMA/Rem Koolhas-designed Factory cultural space (which will serve as the permanent home to the Manchester International Festival), and the opening of the RHS Garden Bridgewater. Manchester's imposing Town Hall is closed until 2024, but you can still admire its 280-foot-tall clock tower from the outside.

The now-defunct Haçienda Club marketed the 1980s rock band New Order to the world, and Manchester became the clubbing capital of England. Other Manchester-based bands like Joy Division, the Smiths, Stone Roses, Happy Mondays, and Oasis also rose to the top of the charts throughout the '70s, '80s, and '90s. The extraordinary success of the Manchester United and Manchester City football clubs has kept the eyes of sports fans around the world fixed firmly on Manchester.

GETTING HERE AND AROUND

Manchester Airport has many international flights, so you might not even have to travel through London. There are frequent trains from the airport to Piccadilly Railway Station (15–20 minutes), Metrolink trams to the city center (50 minutes), and buses to Piccadilly Gardens Bus Station (70-80 minutes). A taxi from the airport to Manchester city center costs around £30. For details about public transportation in Manchester, see ⊕ www.tfgm. com or call ☎ 0161/244–1000.

Driving to Manchester from London (3 to 3½ hours), take the M1 north to the M6, then the M62 east, which becomes the M602 as it enters Greater Manchester.

Trains from London's Euston Station drop passengers at the centrally located Piccadilly railway station. The journey takes just over two hours. Manchester Central (Chorlton Street) Coach Station, a five-minute walk west of Piccadilly railway station, is the main bus station for regional and long-distance buses.

Most local buses leave from Piccadilly Gardens bus station, the hub of the urban bus network. Metroshuttle

operates three free circular routes around the city center; frequency and times vary by route.

The ever-expanding Metrolink electric tram service runs through the city center and out to the suburbs and the airport. The Eccles extension has a stop for the Lowry (Harbour City) and the Altrincham line a stop for Manchester United Stadium (Old Trafford). Buy a ticket from the platform machine before you board.

SystemOne Travelcards are priced according to the times of day, number of days, and modes of transport you want to include (for example: unlimited buses, trams, and trains after 9:30 am cost £10); buy from the bus driver or a train- or tram-stop ticket machine.

TOURS

City Centre Cruises

Take a three-hour round-trip cruise (prices starting from £18) on a barge to the Manchester Ship Canal; some include a traditional Sunday lunch or afternoon tea. Another includes entry to the Manchester United football stadium tour. Times vary; call or go online for departure schedule. ☎ 0161/902–0222 ⊕ www. citycentrecruises.com ✉ From £25.

Manchester Guided Tours

Group tours run by this tourism board–recommended firm include daily Discover Manchester walks. Prices start at £10. ☎ 07505/685942 ⊕ www.manchester-guidedtours.com.

GETTING ORIENTED

Manchester is compact enough that you can easily walk across the city center in 40 minutes. Deansgate and Princess Street, the main thoroughfares, run roughly north–south and west–east; the lofty terracotta Victorian **Town Hall** sits in the middle, close to the fine **Manchester Art Gallery**. Dominating the skyline at the southern end of Deansgate is Manchester's second-highest building, Beetham Tower, which houses a Hilton Hotel and marks the beginning of the

Castlefield Urban Heritage Park, with the Museum of Science and Industry and the canal system. The Whitworth Art Gallery is a bus ride from downtown; otherwise, all other central sights are within easy walking distance of the Town Hall. Take a Metrolink tram 2 miles south for the Salford Quays dockland area, with the Lowry and the Imperial War Museum North; you can spend half a day or more in this area. ■TIP→ Keep in mind that the museums mentioned above are excellent and free.

ESSENTIALS

TRANSPORTATION CONTACTS Metrolink. ☎ 0161/205–2000 ⊕ www.tfgm. com. Transport for Greater Manchester. ☎ 0161/244–1000 ⊕ www.tfgm.com.

VISITOR INFORMATION Manchester Visitor Information Centre. ⊠ Manchester Central Library, St Peter's Sq., City Centre ☎ ⊕ www.visitmanchester.com.

👁 Sights

Castlefield Urban Heritage Park
ARCHAEOLOGICAL SITE | FAMILY | Site of an early Roman fort, the district of Castlefield was later the center of the city's industrial boom, which resulted in the building of Britain's first modern canal in 1764 and the world's first railway station in 1830. It has been beautifully restored into an urban park with canal-side walks, landscaped open spaces, and refurbished warehouses. The 7-acre site contains the reconstructed gate to the Roman fort of Mamucium, the buildings of the Museum of Science and Industry, and several bars and restaurants, many with outdoor terraces. You can easily spend a day here. ⊠ Liverpool Rd., Castlefield.

★ Central Library
LIBRARY | This 1930s structure was once the biggest municipal library in the world, and today its circular exterior, topped by a line of Doric columns and a massive Corinthian portico facing St. Peter's Square, is a major focus for Manchester's most prestigious civic

quarter. Notable sights within the library are the British Film Institute Mediatheque, a free-to-view collection of 2,000 films and TV programs relating to the United Kingdom and its people; the Media Lounge with creative software and gaming stations; the Music Library with a DJ-mixing desk and instrument collection that is free to use; and the Children's Library, as well as free Wi-Fi, displays on local history, and a convenient café. ⊠ St. Peter's Sq., City Centre ☎ 0161/234–1983 ⊕ www.manchester. gov.uk/centrallibrary ⊙ Closed Sun.

Chetham's Library
BUILDING | The oldest public library in the English-speaking world (founded in 1653), as well as the meeting place of Marx and Engels when the former visited Manchester, is now an accredited museum. Among its collection of over 100,000 printed works—including some 16th- and 17th-century books and journals—are the economics books that Marx read here. ■TIP→ Tours are available at 11 am and 2:30 pm weekdays via advance booking. ⊠ Long Millgate, City Centre ☎ 0161/834–7961 ⊕ library. chethams.com ⊠ Tours £6.50 ⊙ Closed weekends.

★ IWM North
MUSEUM | FAMILY | The thought-provoking exhibits in this striking, aluminum-clad building, which architect Daniel Libeskind described as representing three shards of an exploded globe, present the reasons for war and show its effects on society. Hourly Big Picture audiovisual shows envelop you in the sights and sounds of conflicts while a time line from 1914 to the present examines objects and personal stories from veterans showing how war changes lives. Excellent special exhibitions cover everything from life in Britain during the Blitz to artistic responses to conflict. The museum is on the banks of the Manchester Ship Canal in The Quays, across the footbridge from the Lowry. It's a five-minute

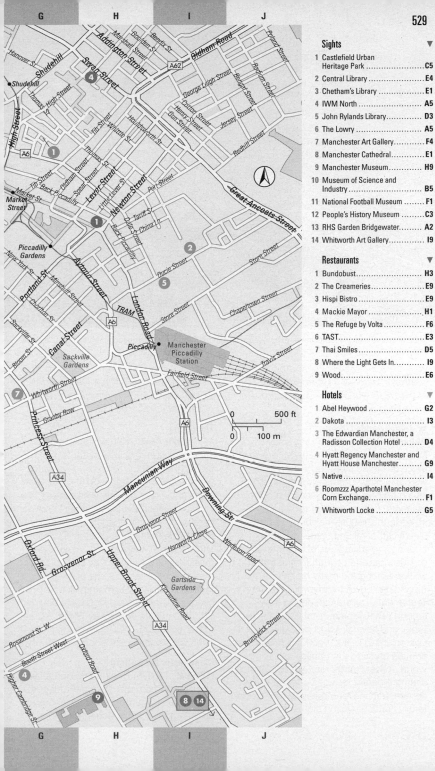

Sights ▼

1 Castlefield Urban Heritage Park **C5**
2 Central Library **E4**
3 Chetham's Library **E1**
4 IWM North **A5**
5 John Rylands Library.............. **D3**
6 The Lowry **A5**
7 Manchester Art Gallery............ **F4**
8 Manchester Cathedral............. **E1**
9 Manchester Museum............. **H9**
10 Museum of Science and Industry **B5**
11 National Football Museum **F1**
12 People's History Museum **C3**
13 RHS Garden Bridgewater......... **A2**
14 Whitworth Art Gallery.............. **I9**

Restaurants ▼

1 Bundobust.......................... **H3**
2 The Creameries.................... **E9**
3 Hispi Bistro **E9**
4 Mackie Mayor **H1**
5 The Refuge by Volta **F6**
6 TAST................................ **E3**
7 Thai Smiles **D5**
8 Where the Light Gets In........... **I9**
9 Wood................................ **E6**

Hotels ▼

1 Abel Heywood **G2**
2 Dakota **I3**
3 The Edwardian Manchester, a Radisson Collection Hotel **D4**
4 Hyatt Regency Manchester and Hyatt House Manchester......... **G9**
5 Native **I4**
6 Roomzzz Aparthotel Manchester Corn Exchange..................... **F1**
7 Whitworth Locke **G5**

Manchester was an industrial powerhouse; learn all about this history at the engaging Museum of Science and Industry.

walk from the MediaCityUK stop of the Metrolink tram. ⊠ *Trafford Wharf Rd.* ☎ *0161/836–4000* ⊕ *www.iwm.org.uk/ visits/iwm-north.*

★ John Rylands Library

LIBRARY | Owned by the University of Manchester, this Gothic Revival masterpiece designed by Alfred Waterhouse was built by Enriqueta Augustina Rylands as a memorial to her husband, a cotton magnate. Constructed of red sandstone in the 1890s, the library resembles a cathedral and contains some outstanding collections of illuminated manuscripts and beautifully illustrated books. Among the many highlights are the oldest known fragment of the New Testament in existence, dating from around AD 100; an original Gutenberg Bible; and several works by William Caxton (c.1417–92), who introduced the printing press to the English-speaking world. A lively temporary exhibition and events program includes printing press demonstrations, photography tours, and family crafts based on elements of the building's decor or other related objects. ⊠ *150 Deansgate, Millennium Quarter* ☎ *0161/306–0555* ⊕ *www.library.manchester.ac.uk* ⌨ *Free.*

The Lowry

ARTS VENUE | **FAMILY** | Clad in perforated steel and glass, this arts center is one of the highlights of the Salford Quays waterways. L. S. Lowry (1887–1976) was a local artist, and one of the few who painted the industrial landscape; galleries here showcase his work alongside that of contemporary artists. The theater has three spaces showcasing everything from West End musicals and new works by up-and-coming theater companies to some of the U.K.'s most popular stand-up comedians. The nearest Metrolink tram stop is Harbour City, a 10-minute walk away. ⊠ *Pier 8, Salford* ☎ *0343/235–8888* ⊕ *www.thelowry. com* ⌨ *Galleries free, performances vary.*

Manchester Art Gallery

MUSEUM | **FAMILY** | Behind an impressive classical portico, this splendid museum and its sparkling modern atrium houses an outstanding collection of paintings by the Pre-Raphaelites and their circle, notably Ford Madox Brown's masterpiece *Work* and Holman Hunt's *The Hireling Shepherd* . British artwork from the 18th and the 20th centuries is also well represented. The second-floor Craft and Design Gallery shows off the best of the decorative arts in ceramics, glass, metalwork, and furniture. The Clore Art Studio is a creative space for families. ⊠ *Mosley St., City Centre* ☎ *0161/235–8888* ⊕ *www.manchesterartgallery.org* ⛇ *Free.*

Manchester Cathedral
RELIGIOUS SITE | The city's sandstone cathedral, set beside the River Irwell and originally a medieval parish church dating in part from the 15th century, is unusually broad for its length and has the widest medieval nave in Britain. Inside, angels with gilded instruments look down from the roof of the nave, and misericords (the undersides of choristers' seats) in the early-16th-century choir stalls reveal intriguing carvings. The octagonal chapter house dates from 1485. ■**TIP**➜ **On weekends and school holidays kids get free Explorer activity packs.** ⊠ *Victoria St., City Centre* ☎ *0161/833–2220* ⊕ *www. manchestercathedral.org* ⛇ *Free.*

★ Manchester Museum
MUSEUM | FAMILY | Run by the University of Manchester and located in a superb Gothic Revival building with modern add-ons, this museum is currently undergoing a £13½ million transformation that will culminate in a new South Asia gallery, a Chinese culture gallery, and the world's first center for age-friendly culture. Embracing anthropology, natural history, and archaeology, it features one of the U.K.'s largest ancient Egyptian collections as part of the extensive Ancient Worlds galleries, a beautiful Living Worlds gallery designed to raise questions about our attitude towards nature, and a vivarium complete with live frogs and other amphibians and reptiles. A lively events program for all ages helps lure in repeat visitors. ⊠ *Oxford Rd., University Quarter* ☎ *0161/275–2648* ⊕ *www.museum. manchester.ac.uk.*

★ Museum of Science and Industry
HISTORIC SITE | FAMILY | The venue's historic buildings, one of which is the world's oldest passenger rail station (1830), hold marvelous collections relating to the city's industrial past and present, although conservation, restoration, and expansion over the next few years will mean certain areas are off-limits or obscured by scaffolding. You can walk through a reconstructed Victorian sewer, be blasted by the heat and noise of working steam engines, see cotton looms whirring in action, and watch a planetarium show. The Air and Space Gallery fills a graceful cast-iron-and-glass building, constructed as a market hall in 1877. ■**TIP**➜ **Allow at least half a day to get the most out of all the sites, temporary exhibitions, talks, and events.** ⊠ *Castlefield Urban Heritage Park, Liverpool Rd., main entrance on Lower Byrom St., Castlefield* ☎ *0161/832–2244* ⊕ *www.scienceandindustrymuseum.org.uk* ⛇ *Free, charges vary for special exhibits.*

National Football Museum
MUSEUM | FAMILY | This striking, glass-skinned triangle of a building includes a galaxy of footballing (soccer) memorabilia, from historic trophies, souvenirs, and shirts (many of them match-worn and signed by legends of the sport) to such near-sacred items as the ball from the 1966 World Cup—the last time England won the sport's ultimate prize. There's also lots of interactive fun to be had, like in the penalty shoot-out area, the Performance section that looks at how football affects the body, and the under-5s discovery zone. ⊠ *Urbis Bldg., Cathedral Gardens, City Centre* ☎ *0161/605–8200* ⊕ *www.nationalfootballmuseum.com* ⛇ *£10.*

Manchester's History: Cottonopolis

Manchester's spectacular rise from a small town to the world's cotton capital—with the nickname Cottonopolis—in only 100 years began with the first steam-powered cotton mill, built in 1783. Dredging made the rivers Irwell and Mersey navigable to ship coal to the factories. The world's first passenger railway opened in 1830, and construction of the Manchester Ship Canal in 1894 provided the infrastructure for Manchester to dominate the industrial world.

A few people acquired great wealth, but factory hands worked under appalling conditions. Working-class discontent came to a head in 1819 in the Peterloo Massacre, when soldiers killed 15 workers at a protest meeting. The conditions under which factory hands worked were later recorded by Friedrich Engels (co-author with Karl Marx of the *Communist Manifesto*), who managed a cotton mill in the city. More formal political opposition to the government emerged in the shape of the Chartist movement (which campaigned for universal suffrage) and the Anti–Corn Law League (which opposed trade tariffs), forerunners of the British trade unions. From Victorian times until the 1960s, daily life for the average Mancunian was so oppressive that it bred the desire to escape, although most stayed put and endured the harsh conditions.

People's History Museum

MUSEUM | Not everyone in 19th-century Manchester owned a cotton mill or made a fortune on the trading floor. This museum recounts powerfully the struggles of working people in the city and in the United Kingdom as a whole since the Industrial Revolution. Displays include the story of the 1819 Peterloo Massacre—when the army attacked a crowd of civil rights protesters in Manchester's St. Peter's Square, killing 15 and almost sparking revolution—together with an unrivaled collection of trade-union banners, tools, toys, utensils, and photographs, all illustrating the working lives and pastimes of the city's people. ⊠ *Left Bank, City Centre* ☎ *0161/838–9190* ⊕ *www.phm.org.uk* ⊠ *Free.*

★ RHS Garden Bridgewater

GARDEN | FAMILY | This 154-acre garden has transformed the heritage grounds of Worsley New Hall into a delightful green space for both locals and visitors. There's a kitchen garden, a stream-side Chinese garden, community growing spaces, a learning garden, and a play area. ⊠ *Worsley New Hall, Off Leigh Rd., Salford* ✛ *About a 15-min drive west of city center* ☎ *020/7821–3187* ⊕ *www. rhs.org.uk/gardens.*

★ Whitworth Art Gallery

MUSEUM | FAMILY | This University of Manchester–owned art museum is beautifully—and uniquely—integrated into the surrounding parkland through its art garden, sculpture terrace, orchard garden, and landscape gallery. Some of the free events and activities take you into the park itself, including children's outdoor art clubs. The renowned collections inside the gallery embrace British watercolors, Old Master drawings, postimpressionist works, wallpapers, and an outstanding textile gallery befitting a city built on textile manufacturing. There's also a learning studio for families and a "café in the trees" overlooking the art garden, with a seasonal British menu. ⊠ *University of Manchester, Oxford Rd., University Quarter* ☎ *0161/275–7450* ⊕ *www.whitworth. manchester.ac.uk* ⊠ *Free.*

🍴 Restaurants

Britain's culinary renaissance over the last three decades is nowhere more apparent than in Manchester, where new and ever-more exciting restaurants are continually opening and adding to the scene of long-established classics. Curry Mile south of the city center has long been popular for its dishes from the Indian subcontinent, but its dominance is being increasingly challenged by the arrival of contemporary Indian eateries. There's also been a street-food boom, with venues like Stretford Food Hall and Hatch (a cluster of old sea containers with pop-up restaurants, bars, and shops inside). Manchester's vegetarian and vegan scene is also one of the country's most vibrant while artisan cafés and bakeries abound, too.

Bundobost

$ | INDIAN | Tasty Gujurat-inspired vegetarian street food lures the budget-conscious to this colorful and vivacious canteen-style restaurant tucked away in a basement on Piccadilly Gardens. Order from the bar, and watch chefs get busy in a semi-open kitchen on Indian dishes both classic and modern. **Known for:** sociable Indian sharing dishes; local and global craft beers; inventive cocktails. ⑤ *Average main: £6* ✉ *61 Piccadilly, City Centre* ☎ *0161/359–6757* ⊕ *www. bundobust.com.*

The Creameries

$$$$ | MODERN BRITISH | An exciting venture by seasoned local chef Mary-Ellen McTague (who cooked under Heston Blumenthal at the legendary Fat Duck for many years), this airy suburban dining room in a former bakery offers great-value three-course lunch and five-course supper menus. This is contemporary comfort food at its finest; you can sample the likes of home-smoked mackerel, goat cheese beignets, and treacle tart. **Known for:** ethically sourced produce including wild meats; zero-waste policy; on-site

wine bar and shop offering low-intervention wines. ⑤ *Average main: £35* ✉ *406 Wilbraham Rd., Chorlton, South Manchester* ☎ *0161/312–8328* ⊕ *www. thecreameries.co.uk.*

★ Hispi Bistro

$$ | MODERN EUROPEAN | Part of a small group of famously crowd-funded (yup, people liked the owner-chef so much they raised money so he could open a place in their 'hood) restaurants found across northwest England, this neighborhood bistro offers ambitious dining at remarkably fair prices. In pared-back surroundings, expect the likes of torched mackerel, cured cod loin, and crottin cheese baked in truffle honey, plus wonderful accompaniments including hard-to-find vegetables. **Known for:** great-value early dinners; exceptional kids' menu; Sunday lunch. ⑤ *Average main: £20* ✉ *1C School La., Didsbury* ☎ *0161/445–3996* ⊕ *www.hispi.net.*

Mackie Mayor

$ | INTERNATIONAL | Located in a 19th-century market building, this food court brings together several casual dining experiences under one stunningly restored roof. Choose from sourdough pizza, rotisserie chicken, fish-and-chips, rare cuts of beef, Thai street food, and tortillas, tacos, and nachos, all ordered from the counters and delivered to long shared tables. **Known for:** convivial atmosphere; local artisanal produce; fabulous breakfasts and brunches. ⑤ *Average main: £7* ✉ *1 Eagle St., Northern Quarter* ⊕ *www.mackiemayor.co.uk* ⊗ *Closed Mon. No dinner Sun.*

★ The Refuge by Volta

$ | INTERNATIONAL | This glamorous spot serves eclectic global food amidst the original features of a stunning Victorian Gothic building that's been given new life as the Principal Hotel. Expect dishes from Spanish salt cod croquettes and Asian-inspired ceviche to Middle Eastern *mutabal* (an eggplant dish similar to baba ghanoush) and lamb shawarma. **Known**

for: Sunday lunches; local ingredients; buzzy atmosphere. $ *Average main: £9* ✉ *The Principal Hotel, Oxford St., City Centre* ☎ *0161/233–5151* ⊕ *www. refugemcr.co.uk.*

★ TAST

$$$ | CATALAN | Financed by one-time Barcelona soccer legend and Manchester City FC manager Pep Guardiola, this Catalonian restaurant pulls no punches when it comes to contemporary cooking, with dishes courtesy of two Michelin-star chef Paco Pérez. The unifying overall concept is "tastets": small tastes of food with greater complexity than tapas. **Known for:** groundbreaking cuisine; quirky, theatrical presentation; special occasion dining. $ *Average main: £30* ✉ *20-22 King St., City Centre* ☎ *0161/806–0547* ⊕ *www.tastcatala.com* ⊘ *Closed Mon.*

Thai Smiles

$ | THAI | This no-frills but charming venue serves authentic Thai street food to a largely non-Western crowd from a small, noodle-centric menu. There's a couple of tables outdoors for warmer days, and you're free to bring in your own alcohol. **Known for:** authentic dishes; excellent value for money; sporadic closing hours. $ *Average main: £7* ✉ *Deansgate Mews, City Centre* ☎ *07702 /741759* ⊘ *Closed Mon. No dinner Wed.*

★ Where the Light Gets In

$$$$ | MODERN BRITISH | Much-loved by food critics, this groundbreaking "New Northern" restaurant in a former coffee warehouse offers a no-choice tasting menu (£90) that depends on "the day's catch, harvest, and slaughter." Regular ingredients include Macclesfield trout, cured Middle White pork, and salt-baked beets in delicious combinations; much of the produce comes from the restaurant's own farm. **Known for:** immense creativity; excellent wine flights; hip atmosphere. $ *Average main: £90* ✉ *7 Rostron Brow* ✛ *7 miles southeast of central Manchester in Stockport* ☎ *0161/477–5744* ⊕ *www.wtlgi.co* ⊘ *Closed Sun.–Tues. No lunch Wed.–Fri.*

Wood

$$$ | MODERN BRITISH | The first opening by former *Masterchef* winner Simon Wood, this scene-setting restaurant in the pedestrianized First Street arts and leisure complex serves up high-end, creative British dishes from an open kitchen. Think adventurous ingredients such as red deer, Douglas fir, and crapaudine beetroot combined with modern takes on traditional dishes like neeps and tatties (Scottish mash). **Known for:** meat-heavy menu; multicourse "mystery tour" tasting menus; wonderful staff. $ *Average main: £30* ✉ *Jack Rosenthal St., City Centre* ☎ *0161/236–5211* ⊕ *www. woodrestaurantgroup.com/manchester* ⊘ *Closed Mon.*

🛏 Hotels

Abel Heywood

$ | HOTEL | Ideal for those who want a true Mancunian feel to their accommodation, this well-priced boutique hotel and bar in the funky Northern Quarter was named for a local mayor, radical, and publisher. **Pros:** in-room visitor guide to the Northern Quarter and Manchester; historic ambience and local charm; great location for nightlife. **Cons:** rooms are small; some rooms have noise from the kitchen; tempermamental/noisy air-conditioning. $ *Rooms from: £85* ✉ *38 Turner St., Northern Quarter* ☎ *0161/819–1441* ⊕ *www.abelheywood. co.uk* ⇨ *15 rooms* ⦿ *No meals.*

Dakota

$ | HOTEL | This boutique hotel has brought some glamorous decadence to the Manchester hotel scene, with its low-lit vibe, bold palette of mainly pale and chocolate browns, and sumptuous fabrics mixing well with the champagne bar and cigar garden. **Pros:** just a five-minute walk from Piccadilly Station; outdoor terraces in some rooms; great cocktails. **Cons:** room service is not 24 hours; building a bit severe; not all rooms have robes. $ *Rooms from: £120* ✉ *29 Ducie St.,*

City Centre ☎ 0161/674–9180 ⊕ www.
dakotahotels.co.uk/manchester 🛏 137
rooms ⊙| No meals.

★ The Edwardian Manchester, a Radisson Collection Hotel

$$ | HOTEL | In the heart of the city, this elegant option invites you to unwind with its atmospheric spa (complete with a urban subterranean swimming pool, sauna, steam rooms and cutting-edge gym), luxurious afternoon teas, and memorable dining including contemporary Japanese and Mexican small plates in Peter Street Kitchen. **Pros:** great central location; highly attentive staff; some suites with private verandas. **Cons:** spa can get very busy; some rooms small by city standards; bars sometimes fully booked for private events. ⓢ *Rooms from: £144* ⊠ *Free Trade Hall, Peter St., City Centre* ☎ 0161/835–9929 ⊕ www.radissonhotels.com/en-us/hotels/radisson-collection-edwardian-manchester 🛏 263 rooms ⊙| Free breakfast.

Hyatt Regency Manchester and Hyatt House Manchester

$$ | HOTEL | This sleek upscale hotel and its sister apart-hotel (the U.K.'s very first Hyatt House property) are located within the same modern building and are ideal for those who like to be away from the fray of the city center with all its nightlife noise. It's also very handy for visiting the University of Manchester campus, Manchester Museum, and The Whitworth. **Pros:** floor-to-ceiling windows with city or university green views; nice amenities including gym; 24-hour H Market for snacks and groceries. **Cons:** a walk away from the city's best restaurants and bar areas; strange layout (Hyatt House reception on 18th floor); hotel may feel corporate to some. ⓢ *Rooms from: £135* ⊠ *55 Booth St. West, University Quarter* ☎ 0161/359–5550 ⊕ www.hyatthousemanchester.com 🛏 328 rooms ⊙| Free breakfast.

★ Native

$ | RENTAL | A charming reincarnation of a one-time cotton warehouse, Native retains its impressive original brick barrelled ceilings, exposed beams, and wrought-iron girders (now painted a hip powder-blue). **Pros:** unique historic building with gorgeous wooden floors; sociable community hub on-site; just steps from Piccadilly Station. **Cons:** early check-out time if not booked direct; some rooms a bit dark; can suffer from outside noise. ⓢ *Rooms from: £95* ⊠ *Ducie Street Warehouse, Ducie St., City Centre* ☎ 0161/503–9551 ⊕ www.nativeplaces.com 🛏 166 rooms ⊙| No meals.

Roomzzz Aparthotel Manchester Corn Exchange

$$ | RENTAL | The architecture and the original features of the iconic Manchester Corn Exchange—which also has served as a shopping mall and is now largely a dining hub—are the stars at this apartment hotel. **Pros:** free grab-and-go breakfasts and 24-hour coffee; on-site gym; round-the-clock essentials shop. **Cons:** specific rooms can be requested but not booked; not all rooms have bathtubs; water pressure not reliably powerful. ⓢ *Rooms from: £130* ⊠ *Corn Exchange, Exchange Sq., City Centre* ☎ 0203/504–5555 ⊕ www.roomzzz.com 🛏 114 apartments ⊙| Free breakfast.

Whitworth Locke

$ | RENTAL | Just off the Gay Village a 10-minute walk from Piccadilly Station, this imposing 19th-century cotton mill now holds suites and studios that combine hip contemporary decor with nods to the building's Victorian quirks and eccentricities plus the practicality of full kitchens. **Pros:** on-site restaurant hosting pop-up global dining experiences; sociable hub with cocktail masterclasses and movie nights; washer-dryers and dishwashers by request. **Cons:** area can be noisy at night; windows are small; unique interior design may not be to everyone's

Manchester's pubs and café-bars, whether Victorian or modern, are well worth a stop.

taste. $ Rooms from: £70 ⊠ 74 Princess St., City Centre ☎ 0330/320–0690 ⊕ www.lockeliving.com/whitworth-locke ⇥ 160 rooms ⍵ No meals.

Nightlife

Manchester vies with London as Britain's capital of youth culture, but it has vibrant nightlife and entertainment options for all ages. Spending time at a bar, pub, or club is an essential part of any trip. For event listings, check out the free *Manchester Evening News,* widely available throughout the city or as a website or app. Other helpful websites include ⊕ *www. manchesterconfidential.co.uk*, ⊕ *www. manchesterwire.co.uk*, and ⊕ *creativetourist.com*.

The neighborhood of Gay Village lines up stylish bars and cafés along the Rochdale Canal; Canal Street is its heart. There are several gay bars, but most attract a mixed crowd.

BARS

Cloud 23

BARS/PUBS | This dressy champagne and cocktail bar in the city's tallest building has stunning 360-degree views. Some of its inventive concoctions make a playful nod to local culture. You can also get afternoon tea or dine from a small menu of tacos, flatbreads, and desserts. ⊠ *Hilton Manchester Deansgate, Beetham Tower, 303 Deansgate, City Centre* ☎ *0161/870–1670* ⊕ *www. cloud23bar.com*.

Folk

BARS/PUBS | Bars and restaurants come and go on trendy, ever-evolving Burton Road, but this bar and café has stood the test of time thanks to its heated terrace (complete with palm trees), eclectic tunes by live DJs, chic interiors, and good food. ⊠ *169 Burton Rd., West Didsbury* ☎ *0161/445–2912* ⊕ *www. folkcafebar.co.uk*.

Kosmonaut

BARS/PUBS | With stripped-down decor of exposed brick walls, old tiles, and leather benches, this bar exudes a hipster vibe. There's a Ping-Pong table and changing art exhibitions, as well as a wine list and beer selection, although it's the inventive cocktails that draw the crowds. ⊠ *10 Tariff St., Northern Quarter* ☎ *07496/977443* ⊕ *www.kosmonaut.co.*

The Liars Club

BARS/PUBS | This self-described "tiki dive bar" serves up generously sized cocktails in its kitschy Polynesian beach–style bar. Order a Zombie if you like your drinks set on fire. They also serve a hundred types of rum. ⊠ *19A Back Bridge St., City Centre* ☎ *0161/834–5111* ⊕ *www.theliarsclub.co.uk.*

The Molly House

BARS/PUBS | This lively Gay Village bar has an outstanding selection of beers from around the world, in addition to good wine and cocktail lists. The tapas nibbles are delicious and surprisingly inexpensive. ⊠ *26 Richmond St., City Centre* ☎ *0161/237–9329* ⊕ *www.themollyhouse.com.*

PUBS

The Angel

BARS/PUBS | You won't find any televisions in this atmospheric real ale pub that serves beers from small independent breweries. British comfort food (sometimes with a modern twist like Lancashire cheese croquettes) is also offered in both the bar and its cozy restaurant, which comes with a log fire and grand piano. ⊠ *6 Angel St., Northern Quarter* ☎ *0161/833–4786.*

The Briton's Protection

BARS/PUBS | You can sample more than 230 whiskies and bourbons at this gorgeous pub with stained-glass windows, cozy back rooms, a spacious beer garden, and a mural of the Peterloo Massacre. ⊠ *50 Great Bridgewater St.* ☎ *0161/236–5895.*

Dukes 92

BARS/PUBS | Once a stable block for horses working the canals, this is a great spot for a pub lunch or drink, especially in the summer, thanks to its waterside terrace, balcony, and outdoor kitchen. ⊠ *18 Castle St., Castlefield* ☎ *0161/839–8642* ⊕ *www.dukes92.com.*

The Marble Arch Inn

BREWPUBS/BEER GARDENS | This handsome, unspoiled Victorian pub specializes in craft beers brewed by local firm Manchester Marble and offers a dedicated cheese menu. ⊠ *73 Rochdale Rd., Northern Quarter* ☎ *0161/832–5914* ⊕ *www.marblebeers.com/marble-arch.*

The Oast House

BARS/PUBS | This unique pub is surrounded by a large terrace and occupies a 16th-century oasthouse (where brewers roasted hops) that was brought here, brick by brick, from Kent. The emphasis here is on craft beers and ales, accompanied by food like hanging kebabs and grilled meats. ⊠ *The Avenue Courtyard, Crown Sq.* ☎ *0161/829–3830* ⊕ *www.theoasthouse.uk.com.*

Peveril of the Peak

BARS/PUBS | This iconic throwback Victorian pub with a green-tile exterior draws a crush of locals to its tiny rooms. ⊠ *127 Great Bridgewater St., St Peters Square* ☎ *0161/236–6364.*

DANCE CLUBS

Aatma

DANCE CLUBS | Formerly Kraak, this multipurpose, fairly intimate, stripped-back space hosts club nights from northern soul to electro, live music, poetry, and more. ⊠ *11 Stevenson Sq., Northern Quarter* ⊕ *www.aatmavenue.co.uk.*

★ Depot at Mayfield

GATHERING PLACES | This vast cultural venue in the historic former Mayfield railway station showcases the city's industrial past alongside a lively roster of arts, music, industry, culture, and community events. Its atmospheric spaces include the old concourse and the roof-top, open-air platform. ✉ *Baring St., City Centre* ☎ *0161 /806–0161* ⊕ *www.depotmayfield.com.*

★ Factory 251

DANCE CLUBS | This club and occasional live music venue brings the old offices of the legendary Factory Records to life with sounds ranging from drum 'n' bass to indie. ✉ *118 Princess St., City Centre* ☎ *0161/637–2570* ⊕ *www.factorymanchester.com.*

42's

DANCE CLUBS | Off Deansgate, this venue plays retro, indie, singalong anthems, and classic rock, with Manchester's proud musical heritage at the fore. ✉ *2 Bootle St., City Centre* ☎ *0161/831–7108* ⊕ *www.42s.co.uk.*

Gorilla

MUSIC CLUBS | Nestled under old railway arches, Gorilla is a live-music venue and gin parlor with an intimate vibe. ✉ *54–56 Whitworth St., University Quarter* ☎ *0161/826–2998* ⊕ *www.thisisgorilla.com.*

Hidden

DANCE CLUBS | This former industrial building near the iconic Strangeways prison hosts house, disco, and techno nights. ✉ *16–18 Mary St.* ⊕ *www.hidden.club.*

LIVE MUSIC

★ Albert Hall

MUSIC CLUBS | One of the city's most exciting venues, this former Wesleyan chapel was abandoned and forgotten about for over four decades; it's now a superb indie music hall and clubbing venue retaining many of the site's original features, including an organ and stained-glass windows. ✉ *27 Peter St., City Centre* ☎ *0161/817–3490* ⊕ *www.alberthallmanchester.com.*

Band on the Wall

MUSIC CLUBS | This famous venue, set to expand to include a movie-screening space, has a reputation for hosting both established and pioneering acts. ✉ *25 Swan St., Northern Quarter* ☎ *0161/834–1786* ⊕ *bandonthewall.org.*

★ The Deaf Institute

MUSIC CLUBS | Good acoustics characterize the intimate domed music hall of this landmark building (a onetime institute for those with hearing and speech impairments) that regularly hosts cutting-edge indie acts. There are also club nights, open mics, and quiz nights. ✉ *135 Grosvenor St., University Quarter* ☎ *0161/276–9350* ⊕ *www.thedeafinstitute.co.uk.*

Manchester Arena

MUSIC CLUBS | Europe's largest indoor arena by capacity hosts shows by major rock and pop stars, as well as large-scale sporting events. ✉ *21 Hunts Bank* ☎ *0845/337–0717 box office* ⊕ *www.manchester-arena.com.*

Night & Day Café

MUSIC CLUBS | This was a major player in Manchester's musical history: many bands who played here eventually went on to huge success, including Elbow. Now this venue and café-bar covers all genres, from indie and folk to jazz and electronica. ✉ *26 Oldham St., Northern Quarter* ☎ *0161/236–1822* ⊕ *www.nightnday.org.*

O2 Apollo Manchester

MUSIC CLUBS | Housed in an art deco venue, the 3,500-seat venue (known by locals as just "the Apollo") showcases live rock and comedy acts before a mixed-age crowd. ✉ *Stockport Rd., Ardwick Green* ☎ *08444/777677* ⊕ *www.academymusicgroup.com.*

🎭 Performing Arts

Bridgewater Hall

CONCERTS | This dramatically modern venue—which sits on 280 springs to reduce external noise—is home to Manchester's renowned Hallé Orchestra, as well as the BBC Symphony Orchestra and the Manchester Camerata. It also hosts rock and pop concerts. ✉ *Lower Mosley St., St Peters Square* ☏ *0161/907–9000* ⊕ *www.bridgewater-hall.co.uk.*

★ HOME

ARTS CENTERS | This cutting-edge contemporary arts venue houses a main 450-seat theater, a studio theater space, a gallery, five cinema screens, and digital production and broadcast facilities, as well as a bar, a café, and a bookshop. ✉ *2 Tony Wilson Pl., University Quarter* ☏ *0161/200–1500* ⊕ *homemcr.org.*

The Kings Arms

MUSIC | Live music, plays, and comedy feature on the bill of this intimate, bohemian space above a traditional pub. ✉ *11 Bloom St., Salford* ☏ *0161/832–3605* ⊕ *www.kingsarmssalford.com.*

Opera House

CONCERTS | This elegant venue hosts West End musicals as well as opera and classical ballet performances. ✉ *3 Quay St., City Centre* ☏ *0844/871–3018* ⊕ *www.atgtickets.com/venues/manchester.*

Palace Theatre

ARTS CENTERS | One of the city's largest theaters presents mainly touring musicals and tribute acts. ✉ *97 Oxford St., City Centre* ☏ *0844/871–3019* ⊕ *www.atgtickets.com/venues/palace-theatre-manchester.*

★ Royal Exchange Theatre

THEATER | Housed in the city's one-time cotton exchange, this innovative venue for classic and contemporary works includes a glass-and-metal structure cradling a theater-in-the-round, plus a studio space. ✉ *St. Ann's Sq., City Centre* ☏ *0161/833–9833* ⊕ *www.royalexchange.co.uk.*

Royal Northern College of Music

ARTS CENTERS | The College hosts classical and contemporary music concerts—everything from opera to jazz. ✉ *124 Oxford Rd., University Quarter* ☏ *0161/907–5200* ⊕ *www.rncm.ac.uk.*

🛍 Shopping

The city is nothing if not fashion-conscious; take your pick from glitzy department stores, huge retail outlets, designer shops, and idiosyncratic boutiques. Famous names are centered on Exchange Square (including branches of big-name department stores Harvey Nichols and Selfridges), Deansgate, and King Street, and designer boutiques are colonizing nearby Spinningfields; the Northern Quarter provides edgier style for young trendsetters as well as a wide variety of vinyl record and music shops. Outside the city, the vast Trafford Centre mall houses a multitude of stores, entertainment options, and eateries under one roof.

Afflecks

CLOTHING | With a collection that ranges from top hats to punk skinny jeans and skate wear, this emporium has been purveying indie fashion and lifestyle paraphernalia to its many fans for decades. ✉ *52 Church St., Northern Quarter* ☏ *0161/839–0718* ⊕ *www.afflecks.com.*

Barton Arcade

SHOPPING CENTERS/MALLS | This charming Victorian arcade houses various specialty stores selling fashion and shoes, as well as bars and restaurants. ✉ *51–63 Deansgate, City Centre* ⊕ *www.barton-arcade.co.uk.*

★ Manchester Craft and Design Centre

CRAFTS | This vibrant, airy space in a onetime Victorian fish-market building houses two floors of studios for resident artists and craft makers selling to the public. Crafts workshops are hosted, too, and there's a wonderful café. ✉ *17 Oak St., Northern Quarter* ☏ *0161/832–4274* ⊕ *www.craftanddesign.com.*

⚡ Activities

FOOTBALL

Football (soccer in the United States) is *the* reigning passion in Manchester. Locals tend to be torn between Manchester City and Manchester United, the two local clubs. Matches for both are usually sold out months in advance; stadium tours can be a good alternative if you can't snag match tickets.

Manchester City Etihad Stadium

SOCCER | This is the place to see Manchester City in action and also to inspect club memorabilia, visit the changing rooms, and explore the pitch. There are also daily tours, including on match days. ✉ *Etihad Campus, Rowsley St., Sportcity* ☎ *0161/444–1894* ⊕ *www.mancity.com* 🎫 *£25.*

Old Trafford

SOCCER | Matches at Manchester United's home stadium attract fans of one of the biggest names in soccer from near and far. The museum and tour take you behind the scenes into the changing rooms and players' lounge, as well as down the tunnel. ✉ *Sir Matt Busby Way, Trafford Park* ☎ *0161/868–8000* ⊕ *www.manutd.com* 🎫 *£25.*

Liverpool

A city lined with one of the most famous waterfronts in England, celebrated around the world as the birthplace of the Beatles, and still the place to catch that "Ferry 'Cross the Mersey," Liverpool reversed a downturn in its fortunes with late 1980s developments, such as the impressively refurbished Albert Dock area. In 2004, UNESCO named six historic areas in the city center together as one World Heritage Site, in recognition of the city's maritime and mercantile achievements during the height of Britain's global influence. The city's heritage, together with famous attractions and a legacy of cultural vibrancy that includes an ever-growing events program, draws an increasing number of visitors each year—in turn impacting its growing hotel and dining scenes.

The 1960s produced Liverpool's most famous export: the Beatles. The group was one of hundreds influenced by the rock and roll they heard from visiting American GIs and merchant seamen in the late 1950s and one of many that played local venues such as the Cavern Club (demolished but rebuilt nearby). All four Beatles were born in Liverpool, but the group's success dates from the time they left for London. Nevertheless, the city has milked the group's Liverpool connections for all they're worth, with a multitude of local attractions such as Paul McCartney's and John Lennon's childhood homes.

GETTING HERE AND AROUND

Liverpool John Lennon Airport, about 5 miles southeast of the city, receives mostly domestic and European flights. The Arriva 500 bus service runs to the city center up to every 30 minutes; other buses to the center are the 80 and 80A. A taxi to the center of Liverpool costs around £30.

Long-distance National Express buses, including a service from London, use the Liverpool One bus station, as do some local buses. Other local bus terminals are Sir Thomas Street and Queen Square. Train service on Virgin Trains from London's Euston Station takes 2½ hours.

If you're walking (easier than driving), you'll find the downtown sights well signposted. Take care when crossing the busy inner ring road separating the Albert Dock from the rest of the city.

TOURS
Liverpool Beatles Tours
These personalized tours of Beatles-related sites are tailored to what you want to see. They last from three hours to an entire day (or more), and there's the option to focus on your favorite Beatle. ⊠ *25 Victoria St., City Centre* ☎ *07939/069553* ⊕ *www. beatlestours.co.uk.*

Magical Mystery Tours
This ever-popular tour departs daily from the Albert Dock's Anchor Courtyard. The bus—decked out in full psychedelic colors—takes you around all the Beatles-related high points, including Penny Lane and Strawberry Fields, in two hours. The ticket price includes entry to the Cavern Club on the evening of your tour day. The firm also offers private tours. ⊠ *City Centre* ☎ *0151/703–9100* ⊕ *www. cavernclub.org/the-magical-mystery-tour* ☎ *£18.95.*

Mersey Guides
PERSONAL GUIDES | This is your point of contact for dozens of different tours of the city, bringing together professional local guides with in-depth knowledge on topics as diverse as Manchester's maritime or wartime histories. ⊕ *www. showmeliverpool.com.*

GETTING ORIENTED
Liverpool has a fairly compact center, and you can see most of the city highlights on foot. The skyline helps with orientation: the Radio City tower on **Queen Square** marks the center of the city. The Liver Birds, on top of the **Royal Liver Building,** signal the waterfront and River Mersey. North of the Radio City tower lie Lime Street Station and William Brown Street, a showcase boulevard of municipal buildings, including the outstanding **Walker Art Gallery** and **World Museum Liverpool.** The city's other museums, including the dazzling Museum of Liverpool and the two-venue **Beatles Story,** are concentrated westward on the waterfront in the **Albert Dock** and **Pier Head** area, a 20-minute walk or five-minute bus

ride away. **Hope Street,** to the east of the center, connects the city's two cathedrals, both easily recognizable on the skyline. On nearby Berry Street the red, green, and gold **Chinese Arch,** the largest multiple-span arch outside China, marks the small Chinatown area. ■**TIP→ Allow extra time to tour the childhood homes of Paul McCartney and John Lennon, as they lie outside the city center.**

ESSENTIALS
BUS CONTACTS Merseytravel. ☎ *0151/330–1000* ⊕ *www.merseytravel. gov.uk.*

VISITOR INFORMATION Visit Liverpool. ⊠ *William Brown St. Liverpool, City Centre*

Sights

Albert Dock
MARINA | To understand the city's prosperous maritime past, head for these 7 acres of restored waterfront warehouses built in 1846. Named after Queen Victoria's consort, Prince Albert, the dock provided storage for silk, tea, and tobacco from the Far East until it was closed in 1972. Today the fine colonnaded brick buildings contain the **Merseyside Maritime Museum,** the **International Slavery Museum, Tate Liverpool,** and the main venue of the **Beatles Story.** When weather allows, you can sit at an outdoor café overlooking the dock; there are also bars, restaurants, and even hotels on the site. For a bird's-eye view of the Albert Dock area, take the rotating Liverpool Wheel—a 60-meter-tall version of the London Eye. ■**TIP→ Much of the pedestrian area of the Albert Dock and waterfront area is cobblestone, so wear comfortable shoes.** ⊠ *Off Strand St. (A5036), Waterfront* ☎ ⊕ *www.albertdock.com.*

★ Another Place
PUBLIC ART | A hundred naked, life-size, cast-iron figures by sculptor Antony Gormley stand proudly on the 2 miles of foreshore at Crosby Beach, weathered

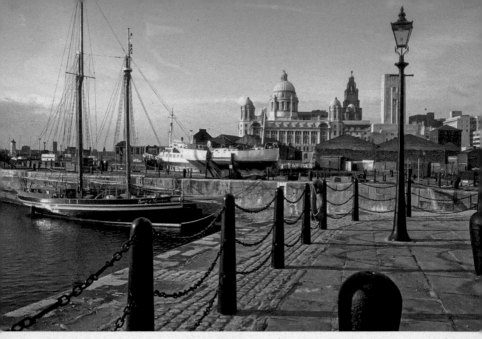

Once a major shipping center and now transformed with museums, restaurants, and shops, the Albert Dock has views of the green dome of the Royal Liver Building.

by sand and sea. Unlike most other statues, you are permitted to interact with these and even clothe them if you wish. Check tide times before you go, and be aware that it's not safe to walk out to the farthest figures. The site is 6 miles north of downtown Liverpool; to get here, take the Merseyrail train to Blundellsands or Crosby from Liverpool Central or Moorfields Stations. A taxi will cost around £30. ⊠ *Mariners Rd., Crosby Beach* ☎ *0845/140–0845 for tide times* ⊕ *www.visitliverpool.com* ⊠ *Free.*

★ The Beatles' Childhood Homes

HOUSE | A must-see for Beatles pilgrims, this tour takes you to Mendips, the 1930s middle-class, semidetached house that was the home of John Lennon from 1946 to 1963, and 20 Forthlin Road, Paul McCartney's childhood home. After his parents separated, John joined his aunt Mimi at Mendips; she gave him his first guitar but banished him to the porch, saying, "The guitar's all very well, John, but you'll never make a living out of it." Meanwhile, Forthlin Road is a modest

1950s council house where a number of the Beatles' songs were written. The tour leaves from Jury's Inn hotel next to Albert Dock (mornings) or Speke Hall (afternoons). ■**TIP**➔ **Advanced bookings are essential—places are strictly limited to 15.** ⊠ *City Centre* ☎ *0344/249–1985* ⊕ *www.nationaltrust.org.uk/beatles-child-hood-homes* ⊠ *From £27.50* ⊗ *Closed Dec.–Feb.*

★ Beatles Story

MUSEUM | Entertaining scenes at this popular attraction in the Albert Dock complex re-create stages in the Beatles' story (and their later careers as solo artists). You'll find everything from the enthusiastic early days in Germany and the Cavern Club to the White Room, where "Imagine" seems to emanate from softly billowing curtains. A second location at the Mersey Ferries Terminal at Pier Head is included in the admission price; here you can see changing exhibitions. On-site shops sell every conceivable kind of souvenir a Fab Four fan could wish for. ⊠ *Britannia*

Vaults, Albert Dock ☎ 0151/709–1963 ⊕ www.beatlesstory.com 🖾 £17.

British Music Experience

MUSEUM | FAMILY | Located in the former first-class lounge of the historic Cunard Building, this venue traces the story of British music through a colorful array of costumes, instruments, and other memorabilia. Regular events include celebrations of particular musical icons, and there are school-holiday activities for kids. ☒ Cunard Building, Pier Head, Waterfront ☎ 00151/519–0915 ⊕ www. britishmusicexperience.com 🖾 £14 ⊘ Closed Mon. and Tues. mid-Nov.–Mar.

Casbah Coffee Club

MUSEUM | A coffee shop owned by original drummer Pete Best's mother, this is where The Beatles played some of their earliest gigs. Decorated by the band themselves, it's now a museum offering an authentic taste of those exciting early days. Entry is by guided tour only. ☒ 8 Hayman's Green, West Derby ✛ Take bus No. 11 or 12 from Queen's Sq. to West Derby; it's 3½ miles from the city center. ☎ 0787/201–7473 ⊕ www.petebest.com/ casbah-coffee-club 🖾 From £15.

★ International Slavery Museum

MUSEUM | In the same building as the Merseyside Maritime Museum, this museum's four dynamic galleries recount the history of transatlantic slavery and trace its significance in contemporary society. "Life in West Africa" reproduces a Nigerian Igbo compound; life aboard slave ships bound for the Americas is revealed in the "Enslavement and the Middle Passage" section; and "Legacy" examines the effect of the African diaspora on contemporary society. ☒ Albert Dock, Hartley Quay, Waterfront ☎ 0151/478–4499 ⊕ www.liverpoolmuse- ums.org.uk 🖾 Free.

Liverpool Cathedral

RELIGIOUS SITE | The world's fifth-largest Anglican cathedral, this Gothic-style edi- fice was begun in 1903 by architect Giles Gilbert Scott and finally finished in 1978. The tower is a popular climb; two eleva- tors and 108 steps take you to panoramic views (from April to October, twilight ascents are available). There's also a gallery of ecclesiastical embroidery. ☒ St. James' Mount, City Centre ☎ 0151/709– 6271 ⊕ www.liverpoolcathedral.org.uk 🖾 Free; £5.50 combined ticket for tower, audio tour, and embroidery gallery.

Mersey Ferries

TRANSPORTATION SITE (AIRPORT/BUS/FERRY/ TRAIN) | Hop on a ferry across the River Mersey to Birkenhead and Seacombe, for fine views of the city—a jour- ney celebrated in "Ferry 'Cross the Mersey," Gerry and the Pacemakers' 1964 hit song. These cruises last 50 minutes, but you can hop off to explore the U-Boat Story (a docked German World War II museum with interactive displays) on the other side of the water. It was from Pier Head that 9 million British, Irish, and other European emigrants set sail between 1830 and 1930 for new lives in North America, Australia, and Africa. ☒ Pier Head Ferry Terminal, Off A5036, Waterfront ☎ 0151/330–1003 ⊕ www.merseyfer- ries.co.uk 🖾 £11 round-trip including U-Boat Story ticket.

★ Merseyside Maritime Museum

MUSEUM | This wonderful museum captures the triumphs and tragedies of Liverpool's seafaring history over five floors. Besides exhibits of maritime paintings, models, ceramics, and ships in bottles, it brings to life the ill-fated stories of the Titanic and Lusitania; the Battle of the Atlantic; and the city's role during World War II. Seized, the gallery for the Border Force National Museum, explores the heroes and villains of the world of smuggling, together with the story of mass emigration from the port in the 19th century, while the Life on Board gallery looks at everyone from merchant sailors to leisure cruise-liner passengers. ☒ Albert Dock, Hartley Quay, Waterfront

Liverpool

Sights ▼

1 Albert Dock........................ **D7**
2 Another Place..................... **B1**
3 The Beatles'
   Childhood Homes................... **I9**
4 Beatles Story...................... **C7**
5 British Music Experience.......... **C4**
6 Casbah Coffee Club **J2**
7 International Slavery Museum....**C6**
8 Liverpool Cathedral................ **I8**
9 Mersey Ferries.................... **B5**
10 Merseyside Maritime Museum ...**C6**
11 Metropolitan Cathedral of
    Christ the King **J4**
12 Museum of Liverpool............. **C5**
13 RIBA North **C5**
14 Royal Liver Building **B4**
15 St. George's Hall **G3**
16 Speke Hall, Garden & Estate **I9**
17 Sudley House **I9**
18 Tate Liverpool **C6**
19 Walker Art Gallery................ **G2**
20 Western Approaches Museum ...**C3**
21 World Museum Liverpool......... **G2**

Restaurants ▼

1 Bakchich.......................... **G5**
2 Lunya............................. **F5**
3 Maray **H6**
4 Mowgli **H5**
5 Oktopus **I6**
6 Panoramic 34..................... **B2**
7 Salt House Bacaro **D4**
8 Wreckfish......................... **G6**

Hotels ▼

1 Aloft Liverpool.................... **D3**
2 Aparthotel Adagio
   Liverpool City Centre **G4**
3 Hope Street Hotel................. **J6**
4 The Resident **G5**
5 2 Blackburne Terrace **J7**
6 Z Liverpool....................... **D3**

Liverpool's History: Shipping Center 👁

Liverpool, on the east bank of the Mersey River estuary, at the point where it merges with the Irish Sea, developed from the 17th century through the slave trade. It became Britain's leading port for ferrying Africans to North America and for handling sugar, tobacco, rum, and cotton, which began to dominate the local economy after the abolition of the slave trade in 1807.

Because of its proximity to Ireland, the city was also the first port of call for those fleeing famine, poverty, and persecution in that country. Similarly, Liverpool was often the last British port of call for thousands of mostly Jewish refugees fleeing Eastern Europe.

Many of the best-known liner companies were based in Liverpool, including Cunard and White Star, whose most famous vessel, the *Titanic*, was registered in Liverpool. The city was dealt an economic blow in 1894 with the opening of the Manchester Ship Canal, which allowed traders to bypass Liverpool and head to Manchester, 35 miles east. Britain's entry into the European Common Market saw more trade move from the west coast to the east, and the postwar growth of air travel diverted passengers from the sea. But as a sign of the city's revival, oceangoing liners returned to the city in 2008 after the building of a new cruise liner terminal at the Pier Head.

☎ *0151/478–4499* ⊕ *www.liverpoolmuseums.org.uk* ✉ *Free.*

Metropolitan Cathedral of Christ the King
RELIGIOUS SITE | Consecrated in 1967, this Roman Catholic cathedral is a modernistic, funnel-like structure of concrete, stone, and mosaic, topped with a glass lantern. Long, narrow, blue-glass windows separate chapels, each with modern works of art. An earlier design by classically inspired architect Edwin Lutyens was abandoned when World War II began (the current design is by Frederick Gibberd), but you can still take a look at Lutyen's vast brick-and-granite crypt and barrel-vaulted ceilings. ✉ *Mount Pleasant, City Centre* ☎ *0151/709–9222* ⊕ *www.liverpoolmetrocathedral.org.uk* ✉ *Free; crypt and treasury £3* ⊙ *Crypt and treasury closed Sun.*

Museum of Liverpool
MUSEUM | **FAMILY** | Clad in Jura stone and shaped like a ship, with a spectacular spiral staircase running from the atrium to each floor, this ambitious museum tells the story of the city from its earliest settlement in the Neolithic Age. Highlights include an extraordinary 3D map with different perspectives of the city as you move around it, an engrossing film about soccer culture, and an interactive time line peeling away layers of Liverpool's history. There's a children's gallery and family museum trails, too. ✉ *Pier Head, Waterfront* ☎ *0151/478–4545* ⊕ *www.liverpoolmuseums.org.uk* ✉ *Free.*

RIBA North
MUSEUM | Located within a cutting-edge waterside building, this architecture center hosts changing exhibitions, talks, hands-on workshops, and city tours. There's a café and a shop, too. ✉ *21 Mann Island, Waterfront* ☎ *0151/703–0107* ⊕ *www.architecture.com/contact-and-visit/riba-north* ✉ *Free* ⊙ *Closed Sun. and Mon.*

Royal Liver Building
BUILDING | The 322-foot-tall Royal Liver (pronounced *lie-ver*) Building with its twin

towers is topped by two 18-foot-high copper birds representing the mythical Liver Birds, the town symbol; local legend has it that if they fly away, Liverpool will cease to exist. For decades Liverpudlians looked to the Royal Liver Society for assistance—it was originally a burial club to which families paid contributions to ensure a decent send-off. ■TIP→ **The building, now offices, can best be seen from one of the Mersey ferries.** ☒ *Water St., Waterfront.*

St. George's Hall

BUILDING | Built between 1839 and 1847, St. George's Hall is among the world's finest examples of Greek Revivalist architecture. When Queen Victoria visited Liverpool in 1851, she declared it "worthy of ancient Athens." Tours—led by '"footmen"' in Georgian costume—tell the story of the building, which today hosts music festivals, concerts, and fairs. ☒ *Lime St., City Centre* ☎ *0151/233–3020* ⊕ *www.liverpoolcityhalls.co.uk/st-georges-hall* ☒ *Tours £20* ☉ *Closed Sun.*

Speke Hall, Garden & Estate

HOUSE | This black-and-white mansion 6 miles from downtown Liverpool is one of the best examples of half-timbering in Britain. Built around a cobbled courtyard, the great hall dates to 1490; an elaborate western bay with a vast chimneypiece was added in 1560. The house, owned by the National Trust, was heavily restored in the 19th century, though a Tudor priest hole and Jacobean plasterwork remain intact. The Victorian landscaped gardens enjoy views over the Mersey toward North Wales. ■TIP→ **Speke Hall is beside the airport, and Arriva buses between the airport and the center drop you a pleasant 10-minute walk away; ask the driver to let you off at the nearest stop.** ☒ *The Walk, Speke* ☎ *0151/427–7231* ⊕ *www.nationaltrust.org.uk/speke-hall-garden-and-estate* ☒ *£15.40; gardens only £10.80* ☉ *Hall closed Nov.–early Feb.*

Sudley House

HOUSE | This handsome 19th-century mansion contains the extraordinary art collection amassed by shipping magnate George Holt (1825–96), including paintings by J. M. W. Turner, Thomas Gainsborough, Dante Gabriel Rossetti, and Joshua Reynolds. The interior is an immaculately maintained example of high Victorian domestic style. Permanent displays include historic children's toys and women's fashion from the 18th century to the present day. Sudley House is about 5 miles southeast of the city center; if you're not driving, take a train to Mossley Hill and then it's an 11-minute walk. ☒ *Mossley Hill Rd., Aigburth* ✛ *Drive south down the A5036 along the river, take Bus 61 to Elmswood Rd., 80 or 80A to Rose La., or 82 to Aigburth Rd.* ☎ *0151/478–4016* ⊕ *www.liverpoolmuseums.org.uk* ☒ *Free.*

★ Tate Liverpool

MUSEUM | FAMILY | This offshoot of the London-based art galleries of the same name occupies a handsome conversion of Albert Dock warehouses by the late James Stirling, one of Britain's leading 20th-century architects. There is no permanent collection; challenging exhibitions of modern and contemporary art change every couple of months. There are children's activities, an excellent gift shop, and a dockside café-restaurant. ☒ *Albert Dock, Waterfront* ☎ *0151/702–7400* ⊕ *www.tate.org.uk* ☒ *Free; charges for certain special exhibitions vary.*

★ Walker Art Gallery

MUSEUM | FAMILY | With a superb display of British art and some outstanding Italian and Flemish works, this is one of the best British art collections outside London. Don't miss the unrivaled collection of paintings by 18th-century Liverpudlian equestrian artist George Stubbs or works by J. M. W. Turner, Claude Monet, Frederic Lord Leighton, and the Pre-Raphaelites. Modern artists are included, too; on display is one of David Hockney's typically Californian pool scenes. Other excellent exhibits showcase classical Greek and Roman sculptures as well as china, silver, and furniture that once adorned the mansions of Liverpool's industrial barons. There are temporary exhibitions, including those focusing on photography, and a dedicated children's art space. The café holds center stage in the airy museum lobby. ⊠ *William Brown St., City Centre* ☎ *0151/478–4199* ⊕ *www.liverpoolmuseums.org.uk* ⊠ *Free; charge for temporary exhibitions.*

Western Approaches Museum

MUSEUM | Winston Churchill said that the threat of a U-boat attack from the Atlantic was his greatest fear during World War II. At this evocative war museum you can explore the warren of rooms under the city streets that served the top-secret "Western Approaches Command HQ" from 1941 to 1945. The lofty Operations Room, full of the state-of-the-art technology of the time, is especially interesting. ⊠ *1–3 Rumford St., Exchange Flags, City Centre* ☎ *0151/227–2008* ⊕ *www.liverpoolwarmuseum.co.uk* ⊠ *£13.50.*

World Museum Liverpool

MUSEUM | **FAMILY** | Travel from the prehistoric to the space age through the stunning displays in these state-of-the-art galleries. Ethnology, the natural and physical sciences, and archaeology all get their due over five floors. Highlights include a collection of Egyptian mummies and a beautiful assemblage of Japanese arms and armory in the World Cultures Gallery. There's plenty to keep kids amused, like fish and other sea creatures in the Aquarium, monster bugs in the Bug House, and life-size casts of prehistoric monsters in the Dinosaurs and Natural World Gallery, plus a planetarium and a busy program of events and activities. ⊠ *William Brown St., City*

Centre ☎ *0151/478–4393* ⊕ *www.liverpoolmuseums.org.uk* ⊠ *Free.*

🍴 Restaurants

★ Bakchich

$ | **LEBANESE** | **FAMILY** | Those who like good food at great prices head to Bakchich, a Lebanese street-food joint featuring a large communal table with smaller tables dotted around it for convivial or more intimate dining. On offer are delicious hot and cold meze, *meshawi* charcoal grills (chicken, lamb, and seafood), wraps, salads, and a small but tasty kids' menu. **Known for:** Middle Eastern breakfasts; fresh juices and mocktails; huge portions. $ *Average main: £8* ⊠ *54 Bold St., City Centre* ☎ *0151/707–1255* ⊕ *www.bakchich.co.uk.*

★ Lunya

$ | **CATALAN** | **FAMILY** | An 18th-century warehouse on the edge of the Liverpool One shopping district houses this impressive Catalan fusion restaurant and deli, where you can feast on classic and creative tapas dishes. An extensive breakfast menu makes this a great place to start your day, while the children's menu tempts those with junior foodies. **Known for:** wine, cheese, and sherry tastings along with other events; Catalan breakfasts and brunches; deli platters to share. $ *Average main: £9* ⊠ *55 Hanover St., City Centre* ☎ *0151/706–9770* ⊕ *www.lunya.co.uk.*

Maray

$ | **INTERNATIONAL** | Tapping into Liverpool's love affair with the sharing experience, this tiny bistro serves eclectic and inventive dishes with global inspirations, ranging from the Middle East and the southern United States to Scandinavia. The place—all bare bricks, upcycled furniture, and edgy artwork—takes its name from the Marais district of Paris, though it's actually inspired more by the falafel joints of the French capital's less scenic Bastille district. **Known for:** falafel (homemade daily); member of the Sustainable Restaurant Association; luscious after-dinner cocktails. ⑤ *Average main: £7* ✉ *91 Bold St., City Centre* ☎ *0151/709–5820* ⊕ *www.maray.co.uk.*

★ Mowgli

$ | **INDIAN** | **FAMILY** | Indian street food is the draw at this fun and colorful spot that has lights upcycled from old birdcages and a bar created from former railway sleepers. Many of the vibrant dishes, such as the hugely popular yogurt chat bombs (crispy, filled bread puffs), are served in tiffin boxes (traditional Indian lunch containers) to charming effect. **Known for:** innovative cocktails; enthusiastic, informative staff; handmade ice-cream cones. ⑤ *Average main: £7* ✉ *69 Bold St., City Centre* ☎ *0151/708–9356* ⊕ *www.mowglistreetfood.com.*

Oktopus

$ | **MODERN EUROPEAN** | This noisy, social space has an open kitchen that serves exciting Modern European sharing plates amidst a hip but cozy thrift-store decor in a brick-lined courtyard. The sourdough bread brought in from the bakery next door is not to be missed, nor are the artisanal British cheeses. **Known for:** very fair prices; local beers; superb snacks. ⑤ *Average main: £10* ✉ *24 Hardman St., Hardman Yard, City Centre* ☎ *0151/709–8799* ⊗ *No dinner Sun. No lunch Mon.–Thurs.*

Panoramic 34

$$$$ | **MODERN EUROPEAN** | For some, the waterfront and city views through the floor-to-ceiling windows of this 34th-floor restaurant might outdo the food, but there's no denying the ambition and love that's gone into the Modern European set menus. You can also just come here to soak up that vista over afternoon tea or a cocktail. **Known for:** best views in town; fantastic seven-course tasting menu; dressed-up atmosphere. ⑤ *Average main:*

£34 ✉ *West Tower, Brook St., 34th fl., Waterfront* ☎ *0151/236–5534* ⊕ *www. panoramic34.com* ⊗ *Closed Mon.*

★ Salt House Bacaro

$ | **ITALIAN** | This stylish place—a lively take on the workingmen's canteens of backstreet Venice, known as *bacaros*—offers highly creative small plates and charcuterie. Options include croquettes, fried mixed fish, and *pizzette* (mini-pizzas). **Known for:** cicchetti (sharing plates); casual eating at the bar—great for solo diners; fabulous cocktails, some with Italian bitters. ⑤ *Average main: £8* ✉ *47 Castle St., City Centre* ☎ *0151/665–0047* ⊕ *www.salthousebacaro.com.*

★ Wreckfish

$$ | **MODERN BRITISH** | Part of the same crowd-funded group as Manchester's Hispi Bistro and KALA Bistro, this hip spot serves up seriously good modern global cuisine from an open kitchen in a once derelict building in the Ropewalks district. As with its sister restaurants, think excellent local ingredients—duck's heart or featherblade of beef—taken to the next level through the use of ingredients such as orange blossom vinegar, 'nduja butter, and truffles. **Known for:** great value lunch and early dinner menu; fantastic service; choice of communal and private tables. ⑤ *Average main: £20* ✉ *Slater St., City Centre* ☎ *0151/707– 1960* ⊕ *www.wreckfish.co.*

🛏 Hotels

Aloft Liverpool

$ | **HOTEL** | It's a lot about the architecture and the original features at this hotel in the landmark Victorian Royal Insurance Building, with green-marble wall tiles, sleek dark-wood paneling, and a grand staircase winding up to a domed rotunda. **Pros:** central location near the Cavern Club; good snack bar; hip Bliss Spa toiletries. **Cons:** noise from bar can transfer to rooms; some rooms have odd layout due to historic building; some rooms are in basement. $ *Rooms from: £83* ✉ *No. 1 North John St., City Centre* ☎ *0151/294–3970* ⊕ *www.marriott.com/ hotels/travel/lplal-aloft-liverpool* ⤢ *116 rooms* |O| *No meals.*

Aparthotel Adagio Liverpool City Centre

$ | RENTAL | FAMILY | A particular boon for families visiting Liverpool, this place comes with the freedom and flexibility of an apartment with the services and facilities of a hotel: private kitchens but also access to a bar, gym, laundry, and virtual concierge. **Pros:** family welcome packs with baby/toddler equipment; great location for sightseeing; five-minute walk from the train stations. **Cons:** optional breakfast but no lunch or dinner; close to noisy bars (request the top floor); some rooms very compact. $ *Rooms from: £72* ✉ *1 Fairclough St., City Centre* ☎ *0151/318–0580* ⊕ *www.adagio-city. com* ⤢ *125 rooms* |O| *No meals.*

Hope Street Hotel

$ | HOTEL | In Liverpool's Georgian Quarter, this chic but relaxed hotel happily blends old (an 1890s building inspired by Venetian palazzos) and new (a contemporary steel-and-glass facade fitted over part of the frontage) with rooms with minimalist, Scandinavian-esque decor. **Pros:** lovely spa; frequent upgrades; very good deals in off-season. **Cons:** reception can be very busy; food in restaurant not as impressive as the rooms; rooms can be noisy due to wooden floors. $ *Rooms from: £92* ✉ *40 Hope St., City Centre* ☎ *0151/709–3000* ⊕ *www.hopestreethotel.co.uk* ⤢ *89 rooms* |O| *No meals.*

★ The Resident

$ | HOTEL | FAMILY | This hip hotel brand focuses on the guest experience and growing its visitors' connections with the city by offering hosted evening drinks (with a wine list curated by renowned oenologist Joe Flatiron) where guests can socialize while getting insider tips on what to see and do during their stay.

Pros: focus on local artisan produce; room-service drinks and snacks; immersive city experience. **Cons:** no restaurant; small doubles may be too cozy for some; soundproofing not 100%. $ *Rooms from: £59* ✉ *29 Seel St., City Centre* ☎ *0151/705–2626* ⊕ *www.residenthotels. com/the-resident-liverpool* ⤢ *106 rooms* |O| *No meals* ▭ *No credit cards.*

★ 2 Blackburne Terrace

$$ | B&B/INN | On a cobbled lane in Liverpool's charming Georgian Quarter, this boutique town house B&B is an intimate haven within a hectic city. **Pros:** complimentary in-room treats such as bath oils and artisan gin; personal coffee machines; free parking. **Cons:** no restaurant; hilltop setting not great for those with mobility issues; one of the city's pricer options. $ *Rooms from: £207* ✉ *2 Blackburne Terr., City Centre* ☎ *0151/708–5474* ⊕ *2blackburneterrace. com* ⤢ *4 rooms* |O| *Free breakfast.*

Z Liverpool

$ | HOTEL | Modern urban style on a budget and a supercentral location make the Z a superb option; rooms are all clean and simple, with bespoke beds, crisp linen, and flat-screen TVs. **Pros:** free wine and cheese in the evening; thoughtful design features; great views from some rooms. **Cons:** street noise in some rooms; not all rooms have windows; glassed-in shower rooms and toilets don't feel private enough for some guests. $ *Rooms from: £35* ✉ *2 N. John St., City Centre* ☎ *0151/ 556–1770* ⊕ *www.thezhotels. com* ⤢ *92 rooms* |O| *Free breakfast.*

▼ Nightlife

Alma de Cuba

BARS/PUBS | A church transformed into a luxurious bar, Alma de Cuba has a huge mirrored altar and hundreds of dripping candles. They also serve a popular Sunday brunch with a live gospel choir. ✉ *St. Peter's Church, Seel St., City*

Centre ☎ 0151/305–3744 ⊕ www.alma-de-cuba.com.

Arts Club

MUSIC CLUBS | Music, art, science events, and casual dining are all in the mix at this long-standing venue reinvented as a creative space and bar. ✉ 90 Seel St., City Centre ☎ 0151/559–3773 ⊕ academymusicgroup.com.

Berry and Rye

BARS/PUBS | Hidden away behind an unassuming and umarked facade, Berry and Rye is a Prohibition-era speakeasy that brings together expertly mixed cocktails and cakes in a stylish candlelit space. ✉ 48 Berry St., City Centre.

Camp and Furnace

MUSIC CLUBS | This huge bar, live music venue, and restaurant complex in a former Edwardian foundry and blade-making factory retains a suitably industrial vibe. ✉ 67 Greenland St., City Centre ☎ 0151/708–2890 ⊕ www.campandfurnace.com.

Cavern Club

MUSIC CLUBS | While not the original venue—that was demolished years ago—this is still a popular music spot, drawing in rock-and-roll fans with its live acts including Beatles tribute bands. ✉ 10 Mathew St., City Centre ☎ 0151/236–9091 ⊕ www.cavernclub.com.

Heebie Jeebies

MUSIC CLUBS | A roster of local indie bands and talented DJs makes this two-story club with a courtyard a top option for the young alternative crowd. ✉ 80–82 Seel St., City Centre ☎ 0151/709–3678.

Invisible Wind Factory

MUSIC CLUBS | This quirky entertainment complex in a former warehouse just north of the city center bills itself as a cultural theme park of the future. Expect live music and makers' workshops, as well as on-site artists' studios and a

garden. ✉ 3 Regent Rd. ☎ 0151/236–3160 ⊕ www.thekazimier.co.uk.

Kazimier Garden

MUSIC CLUBS | This eccentric outdoor venue with heaters hosts live music accompanied by food from its barbecue. ✉ 4–5 Wolstenholme Sq., City Centre ☎ 0151/236–3160 ⊕ www.thekazimier.co.uk.

★ LEAF on Bold Street

CAFES—NIGHTLIFE | Tea shop meets bar and live music venue (with club nights) at this bohemian spot in a former art deco cinema. ✉ 65–67 Bold St., City Centre ☎ 0151/707–7747 ⊕ www.thisisleaf.co.uk.

The Shipping Forecast

MUSIC CLUBS | Big-name acts mean this intimate venue often gets packed to the rafters, but that only adds to the clubby vibe. There are also club nights that range from hip-hop to indie, vintage fairs, plus a menu of well-executed American comfort food classics. ✉ 15 Slater St., City Centre ☎ 0151/709–6901 ⊕ www.theshippingforecastliverpool.com.

⚅ Performing Arts

FILM
FACT Centre

ART GALLERIES—ARTS | The Foundation for Art and Creative Technology offers up a unique mix of exhibitions, films, and participant-led art projects, plus a café. ✉ 88 Wood St., City Centre ☎ 0151/707–4444 ⊕ www.fact.co.uk.

PERFORMING ARTS VENUES
★ Bluecoat

ART GALLERIES—ARTS | The city center's oldest building is now a creative hub encompassing contemporary visual arts, live art, literature, music, and dance, along with a café and bistro. ✉ School La., City Centre ☎ 0151/702–5324 ⊕ www.thebluecoat.org.uk.

Liverpool Empire

ARTS CENTERS | This theater presents musicals, live music acts, and occasionally dance and opera. ✉ *Lime St., City Centre* ☎ *0844/871–3017* ⊕ *www.atgtickets. com/venues/liverpool-empire.*

Philharmonic Hall

CONCERTS | This large art deco concert hall and sometime cinema plays host to concerts by the resident Royal Liverpool Philharmonic Orchestra, as well as contemporary rock, pop, folk, roots, jazz, and blues performances. ✉ *Hope St., City Centre* ☎ *0151/709–3789* ⊕ *www. liverpoolphil.com.*

THEATER

Everyman Theatre

THEATER | This vibrant theater in a prize-winning contemporary building focuses on British playwrights and experimental productions from around the world, as well as hosting a playwrights' workspace. There's also a café and a basement bistro. A nearby sister theater, the Playhouse, stages slightly more mainstream productions. ✉ *5–11 Hope St., City Centre* ☎ *0151/709–4776 box office (both theaters)* ⊕ *www.everymanplayhouse.com.*

Royal Court Theatre

THEATER | This restored art deco venue currently undergoing long-term restoration is one of the city's most appealing sites for stand-up comedy, theater, and more. Visitors can also take a heritage tour of the building. ✉ *1 Roe St., City Centre* ☎ *0151/709–4321* ⊕ *www.royalcourtliverpool.co.uk.*

🛍 Shopping

The Beatles Shop

GIFTS/SOUVENIRS | All the mop-top knick-knacks of your dreams are available at this hugely popular, official Beatles souvenir shop. ✉ *31 Mathew St., City Centre* ☎ *0151/236–8066* ⊕ *www.thebeatlesonline.co.uk.*

★ Liverpool One

SHOPPING CENTERS/MALLS | The city's largest shopping complex comprises four districts (Peter's Lane, South John Street, Paradise Street, and Hanover Street) totaling more than 160 stores, from small independent shops to international chains, plus restaurants and leisure amenities. ✉ *Paradise St., City Centre* ☎ *0151/232–3100* ⊕ *www.liverpool-one. com.*

Metquarter

SHOPPING CENTERS/MALLS | This luxury shopping district is the place for upscale boutiques, designer names, and cutting-edge fashions. ✉ *35 Whitechapel, City Centre* ☎ *0151/224–2390* ⊕ *www. metquarter.com.*

🏃 Activities

FOOTBALL

Football matches are played on weekends and, increasingly, some weekdays. Tickets for Liverpool sell out months in advance; you should have more luck with Everton.

Anfield Stadium

SOCCER | If you can't get tickets to a match at the stadium of Liverpool FC, one of England's top teams, take a trip into the dressing rooms and down the tunnel of Anfield Football Stadium as part of a tour. You can also visit the interactive museum, on the tour or separately. ✉ *Anfield Rd., Anfield* ☎ *0151/260–2500* ⊕ *www.liverpoolfc.com* 🎫 *£20 tour.*

Goodison Park

SOCCER | Home to Everton, one of Liverpool's two great football teams, this 40,000-capacity stadium now also hosts tours. ✉ *Goodison Rd.* ☎ *0151/556–1878* ⊕ *www.evertonfc.com* 🎫 *£15 tours.*

The Peak District

HORSE RACING
Aintree Racecourse
HORSE RACING/SHOW | Britain's most famous horse race, the Grand National Steeplechase, has been run here almost every year since 1839. The race is held in March or April; book well ahead to attend (the event is also televised). Admission starts at around £27, depending on the race day and your level of access. ✉ Ormskirk Rd., Aintree ☎ 0844/579–3001 ⊕ aintree.thejockeyclub.co.uk.

Buxton

25 miles southeast of Manchester.

Just outside the Peak District National Park yet almost entirely surrounded by it, Buxton makes a good base for park excursions but it has its own attractions as well. The town's spa days left a notable legacy of 18th- and 19th-century buildings, parks, and open spaces that give the place an air of faded grandeur. The Romans arrived in AD 79 and named Buxton Aquae Arnemetiae, loosely translated as "Waters of the Goddess of the Grove." The mineral springs, which emerge from 3,500 to 5,000 feet belowground at a constant 82°F, were believed to cure assorted ailments. In the 18th century, the town became established as a popular spa, a minor rival to Bath. You can still drink water, which is also sold throughout Britain, from the ancient St. Ann's Well. The architecturally revered semicircular 18th-century Crescent Building houses heritage displays in the Pump Room where the 7th Duke of Devonshire used to "take the waters," and several major thermal hotel and spa openings are planned, putting Buxton back in contention for the title of England's leading spa town.

GETTING HERE AND AROUND

Some National Express bus services to and from London stop at Buxton, departing from Manchester's Central Coach Station. There are also Skyline buses between Buxton and Manchester Airport and buses between Buxton and Chatsworth House. If you're driving to Buxton from Manchester, take the A6 southeast to Buxton. The journey takes one hour, as does the hourly train from Manchester.

ESSENTIALS

VISITOR INFORMATION Buxton Visitor Centre & Crescent Heritage Experience.
✉ The Pump House, The Crescent ☎ 01298/214577 ⊕ www.visitpeakdistrict. com.

Sights

Buxton Museum and Art Gallery

MUSEUM | The highlight of this venue is its "Wonders of the Peak" gallery with displays on Derbyshire's geology, archaeology, history, and art. It's a good place to see Blue John, a colorful, semiprecious mineral found only in the Peak District (the name comes from *bleu jaune*—literally "blue yellow"—a term supposedly coined by visiting French mine workers). ✉ Terrace Rd. ☎ 01629/533540 ⊕ www. derbyshire.gov.uk/leisure/buxton-museum ⊠ Free ⊗ Closed Mon.

Buxton Opera House

ARTS VENUE | Built in 1903, this lovely Edwardian edifice is one of England's best examples of Frank Matcham theater design, with its marble columns, carved cherubs, and gold leaf. A varied performance program includes classical music, opera, dance, drama, and comedy, and it's also host to the Buxton Festival. ✉ Water St. ☎ 01298/72190 ⊕ www. buxtonoperahouse.org.uk.

Devonshire Royal Hospital

BUILDING | This impressive 18th-century building was designed by John Carr as a stable with room for 110 horses. In 1859, the circular area for exercising horses was covered with a massive 156-footwide slate-color dome—bigger than that of St. Paul's Cathedral in London—and incorporated into a hospital. The University of Derby has taken over the building, and visitors can access it for free when school is in session. ✉ 1 Devonshire Rd.

Pavilion Gardens

GARDEN | These 23 acres are home to a miniature train, a boating lake, a play area, and the 1870s Pavilion building. With its ornate iron-and-glass roof, the latter was originally a concert hall and ballroom, but it's now the setting for an arts center, three cafés, an ice-cream parlor, a market hall, and a gift boutique. ✉ St. John's Rd. ☎ 01298/23114 ⊕ www. paviliongardens.co.uk.

★ Poole's Cavern and Buxton Country Park

ARCHAEOLOGICAL SITE | FAMILY | The Peak District's extraordinary geology can be seen up close in this large limestone cave far beneath the 100 acres of Buxton Country Park. Inhabited in prehistoric times, the cave contains, in addition to the standard stalactites and stalagmites, the source of the River Wye, which flows through Buxton. The Country Park paths take you up to Grin Low, home to the Victorian fortified hill marker Solomon's Tower, the remains of several Bronze Age burial chambers, and views of Mam Tor and Kinder Scout. There's also a fun Go Ape! treetop adventure course on site. Admission to the cave includes a guided tour lasting nearly an hour. ✉ Green La. ☎ 01298/26978 ⊕ www.poolescavern. co.uk ⊠ £11.

🍽 Restaurants

Columbine

$$$ | MODERN BRITISH | In a town blessed with good cafés but few noteworthy restaurants, this option run by a husband-and-wife team has a somewhat old-fashioned feel but stands out for its fine use of local ingredients, including High Peak lamb and beef, in the inventive cuisine. The cozy venue, with upstairs and downstairs cellar seating, is especially good for pre- and post-theater meals. **Known for:** produce from small local producers; advance booking needed outside festival and Christmas seasons; proximity to opera house. ⑤ *Average main: £24 ✉ 7 Hall Bank ☎ 01298/78752 ⊕ www.columbinerestaurant.co.uk ⊗ Closed Tues. No lunch Sun. and late Dec.–mid-Jan.*

🛏 Hotels

Old Hall

$ | B&B/INN | FAMILY | In a refurbished 16th-century building claiming to be England's oldest hotel and rumored to have once accommodated Mary, Queen of Scots, this hotel overlooks the ornate Buxton Opera House. **Pros:** family-friendly, with picnics to take to the Pavilion Gardens; good food in the restaurant; historic ambience. **Cons:** no private parking; rooms may be a bit chintzy for some; bathrooms are uninspiring. ⑤ *Rooms from: £69 ✉ The Square ☎ 01298/22841 ⊕ www.oldhallhotelbuxton.co.uk ⇌ 35 rooms ⍩ Free breakfast.*

Roseleigh Guesthouse

$ | B&B/INN | This prize-winning B&B overlooking Pavilion Gardens has comfortable, classic rooms that chime well with the Victorian atmosphere. **Pros:** adventurous hosts who can advise on local activities; some rooms with lake views; private parking. **Cons:** no family rooms; one room has private but not en suite bathroom; some of the quirkier decorative elements might not be to everyone's taste. ⑤ *Rooms from: £78 ✉ 19 Broad Walk ☎ 01298/24904 ⊕ www.roseleighhotel.co.uk ⊗ Closed Dec.–mid-Jan. ⇌ 13 rooms ⍩ Free breakfast.*

🎭 Performing Arts

Buxton Festival

FESTIVALS | This renowned event, held for two weeks during mid-July each year, includes opera, drama, and concerts. ✉ *The Square ☎ 01298/72190 box office ⊕ www.buxtonfestival.co.uk.*

🛍 Shopping

Buxton has a wide variety of stores, especially around Spring Gardens, the main shopping street.

Cavendish Arcade

SHOPPING CENTERS/MALLS | The independent stores in this beautifully tiled building on the site of the old thermal baths sell handmade chocolates, fashion, housewares, pottery, and gifts. ✉ *The Crescent ⊕ www.cavendisharcade.co.uk.*

🍽 Bakewell Pudding

Bakewell is the source of Bakewell pudding, said to have been created inadvertently, when, sometime in the 19th century, a cook at the town's Rutland Arms Hotel (which is still in business) dropped some rich cake mixture over jam tarts and baked it. Every local bakery and tearoom claims an original recipe, so it's easy to spend a gustatory afternoon tasting rival puddings.

Chatsworth House is one of England's great country houses.

Bakewell

12 miles southeast of Buxton.

In Bakewell, a medieval bridge crosses the winding River Wye in five graceful arches. A 9th-century Saxon cross that stands outside the parish church reveals the town's great age. Narrow streets and houses built out of the local gray-brown stone also make the town extremely appealing. Ceaseless traffic can take the shine off—though there's respite down on the quiet riverside paths.

This market town is the commercial hub of the Peak District, for locals and visitors. The crowds are really substantial on market day (Monday), attended by area farmers. For a self-guided hour-long stroll, pick up a map at the tourist office, where the town trail begins.

GETTING HERE AND AROUND

TransPeak buses between Derby and Buxton via Matlock also stop at Bakewell. By car, Bakewell is a 1½-hour drive southeast on the A6 from Manchester.

ESSENTIALS

VISITOR INFORMATION Bakewell Visitor Centre. ⊠ *Old Market Hall, Bridge St.* ☎ *01629/813227* ⊕ *www.peakdistrict. gov.uk.*

Sights

Caudwell's Mill

BUILDING | This unique roller flour mill still runs most days, and visitors can experience the result in the on-site shop in the form of cookies, flours, and yeast. Among the displays are hands-on models and mechanical features. ⊠ *Rowsley* ☎ *01629/734374* ⊕ *www.caudwellsmill. co.uk* ⊠ *Free.*

★ Chatsworth House

HOUSE | FAMILY | One of England's greatest country houses, the "Palace of the Peak" is the ancestral home of the dukes of Devonshire and stands in vast parkland grazed by deer and sheep. Originally an Elizabethan house, it was altered over several generations starting in 1686 and now has a hodgepodge look, though the Palladian facade remains untouched. It's surrounded by woods, elaborate gardens, greenhouses, rock gardens, and a beautiful water cascade—all designed by Capability Brown in the 18th century and, in the 19th, Joseph Paxton, an engineer as well as a brilliant gardener. ■**TIP→ Plan on at least a half day to explore the grounds; avoid Sunday if you can as it gets very crowded.** Inside are intricate carvings, superb furniture, Van Dyck portraits, Sir Joshua Reynolds's *Georgiana, Duchess of Devonshire and Her Baby,* John Singer Sargent's enormous *Acheson Sisters,* and fabulous rooms, including the Sculpture Gallery, the library, and the Painted Hall. On the estate, you'll also find a working farm with milking demonstrations, an adventure playground, cafés, restaurants, a tea shop, and a farm shop; you can even stay in several cottages scattered throughout the grounds. ⊠ *Off B6012 ✛ 4 miles northeast of Bakewell* ☎ *01246/565300* ⊕ *www.chatsworth.org* ✆ *House, gardens, farm, and adventure playground £24; house and gardens £22; gardens only £13; farmyard and adventure playground £7; parking £4 (free with online tickets)* ⊘ *Closed 2nd wk of Jan.–late Mar.*

Eyam Plague Village

HISTORIC SITE | After a local tailor died of the plague in this tiny, idyllic, gray-stone village in 1665, locals isolated themselves from the outside world rather than risk the spread of Black Death (the area had hitherto been spared). They succeeded in containing the disease, but at huge cost; by the time it had run its course, most of the residents were dead. Their heroism is commemorated in florid memorials in the village churchyard. The small **Eyam Museum** puts everything into context, while **Eyam Hall and Craft Centre,** run by the National Trust, hosts history walks on the topic. ⊠ *Hawkhill Rd., Eyam ✛ 6 miles north of Bakewell off A623* ☎ *01433/631371 museum* ⊕ *www.eyam-museum.org.uk* ✆ *Museum £3* ⊘ *Museum closed Mon. and Nov.–late Mar.*

★ Haddon Hall

HOUSE | One of England's finest stately homes, and perhaps the most authentically Tudor of all the great houses, Haddon Hall bristles with intricate period detail. Built between 1180 and 1565, the house passed into the ownership of the dukes of Rutland and remained largely untouched until the early 20th century, when the ninth duke undertook a superlative restoration that revealed a series of early decorative 15th-century frescoes in the chapel. The finest of the intricate plasterwork and wooden paneling is best seen in the superb Long Gallery on the first floor. A popular filming location, Haddon's starring roles include *The Princess Bride* (1985), *Pride and Prejudice* (2005), and *The Other Boleyn Girl* (2008). ⊠ *A6* ☎ *01629/812855* ⊕ *www.haddonhall. co.uk* ✆ *£18.50, parking £3* ⊘ *Closed Nov. and late Dec.–early Apr.*

★ Peak District National Park

NATIONAL/STATE PARK | The United Kingdom's first-ever national park (inaugurated in 1951, paving the way for a further nine parks), the Peak District provides a wild green space for the estimated 20 million people who live within an hour's journey of it, including the inhabitants of Manchester and Stoke-on-Trent, as well as to the millions people who visit each year. Located mostly in northern Derbyshire but including parts of Greater Manchester, Staffordshire, Cheshire, and Yorkshire, the national park is generally divided into the Dark Peak (gritstone moorlands) and the White Peak (limestone), but it has a remarkable diversity of landscapes that make it popular with hikers, cyclists, climbers, and cavers. It's also much-loved for the spa towns, country houses, and heritage sites that are found within the park itself. Visitor centers with information on outdoor activities in the region can be found in Bakewell, Castleton, Derwent, and Edale. Public transport is patchy; it's best explored by car. ☏ 1629/816200 ⊕ www.peakdistrict.gov.uk.

🍴 Restaurants

The Old Original Bakewell Pudding Shop

$ | **BRITISH** | Given the plethora of local rivals, it takes a bold establishment to claim its Bakewell puddings as "original," but those served here are among the best. The "pudding" in question is actually a dense, sugary pie with a jam and almond filling and a puff pastry crust, eaten cold or hot with custard or cream. **Known for:** breakfast sandwiches; afternoon teas ("All Things Bakewell" includes both pudding and tart); on-site deli counter. ⑤ Average main: £12 ⊠ The Square ☏ 01629/812193 ⊕ www.bakewellpuddingshop.co.uk ⊗ No dinner.

Hotels

Bagshaw Hall

$ | **HOTEL** | This characterful 17th-century property offers upscale suites with kitchenettes or full kitchens as well as luxury touches including bathrobes and slippers. **Pros:** a short stroll from the center of Bakewell; self-catering facilities; attractive grounds. **Cons:** no restaurant (breakfast can be brought to rooms); no reception (need to call on arrival); early checkout (10 am). ⑤ Rooms from: £80 ⊠ Bagshaw Hill ☏ 01629/810333 ⊕ www.bagshawhall.com ➔ 12 rooms ❌ No meals.

★ The Cavendish at Baslow

$$ | **B&B/INN** | In a pretty village on the Chatsworth Estate just a 20-minute walk from Chatsworth House itself, this intimate hotel oozes history as well as a quintessentially English country-house style that stems partly from the use of original furniture and artwork from Chatsworth. **Pros:** direct access to wonderful walking routes; great views from the terrace; excellent afternoon teas. **Cons:** restaurant service can be a little slow; standard rooms are unexciting; lounge is small for the size of hotel. ⑤ Rooms from: £130 ⊠ Church Ln., Baslow ☏ 01246/582311 ⊕ www.cavendishbaslow.co.uk ➔ 28 rooms ❌ No meals.

Matlock

8 miles southeast of Bakewell, 5 miles south of Haddon Hall.

In the heart of the Derbyshire Dales just outside Peak District National Park, Matlock and its near neighbor Matlock Bath are former spa towns compressed into a narrow gorge on the River Derwent. The area's beautiful scenery led Daniel Defoe to nickname this area "Little Switzerland." Some surviving Regency buildings in Matlock testify to its former importance, although it's less impressive an ensemble than that presented by Buxton.

Matlock Bath Illuminations, a flotilla of lighted and decorated boats, shimmers after dark on weekends in September and October along the still waters of the Derwent; on Saturday there are also firework displays.

GETTING HERE AND AROUND

There are TransPeak buses to Matlock from Buxton, via Bakewell. The town is about a one-hour, 40-minute drive southeast on the A6 from Manchester.

ESSENTIALS
VISITOR INFORMATION Matlock Visitor
Information Point. ⊠ *Matlock Station, Off A6* ☎ *01335/343666* ⊕ *www.visitpeakdistrict.com.*

Sights

★ Crich Tramway Village
MUSEUM VILLAGE | FAMILY | A 15-minute drive outside Matlock, this period village includes the **National Tramway Museum of Antique Vehicles** and a tram restoration workshop with a public viewing gallery. On the vintage streets, you can board old trams that take you to the surrounding countryside and back. Spend your pennies in the old-fashioned sweets shop or ice cream parlor before exploring the woodland walk and play areas. ⊠ *Crich Village* ☎ *01773/854321* ⊕ *www.tramway.co.uk* ⊠ *£18* ⊙ *Closed Nov.–mid-Mar.*

Hardwick Hall
HOUSE | Few houses in England evoke the late Elizabethan era as vividly as Hardwick Hall, a beautiful stone mansion and walled gardens 10 miles east of Matlock. The vast state apartments well befit their original chatelaine, Bess of Hardwick, who, by marrying a succession of four rich husbands, was second only to Queen Elizabeth in her wealth when work on this house began. Unique patchwork hangings, probably made from clerical copes and altar frontals taken from monasteries and abbeys, grace the entrance hall, and superb 16th- and 17th-century tapestries cover the walls of the main staircase and first-floor High Great Chamber. Access is signposted from Junction 29 of the M1 motorway. ⊠ *Doe Lea, Chesterfield* ☎ *01246/850430* ⊕ *www.nationaltrust.org.uk/hardwick-hall* ⊠ *£16.50; gardens only £7.50; parking £5* ⊙ *House closed Mon., Tues., and Jan.–mid-Feb.*

Heights of Abraham
CAVE | FAMILY | A cable-car ride across the River Derwent takes you to this country park on the crags above the small village of Matlock Bath. The ticket includes access to the woodland walks and nature trails of the 60-acre park, guided tours of two caverns and a former lead mine where workers toiled by candlelight, and entry to a local fossils exhibition. There are also two adventure playgrounds and a restaurant. ⊠ *A6, Matlock Bath* ☎ *01629/582365* ⊕ *www.heightsofabraham.com* ⊠ *£19 cable car, park, exhibition, and caverns* ⊙ *Closed Nov.–mid-Feb., and weekdays in Mar.*

🍴 Restaurants

★ Stones
$$$ | MODERN BRITISH | This charming restaurant with its riverside terrace serves top-notch Modern British food. The tasting menus (with or without a paired wine flight) take regional flavors and infuse them with contemporary flair. **Known for:** dedicated vegetarian menus; alfresco dining; emphasis on seasonality. ⑤ *Average main: £25* ⊠ *1C Dale Rd.* ☎ *01629/56061* ⊕ *www.stones-restaurant.co.uk* ⊙ *No lunch Tues. Closed Sun. and Mon.*

🛏️ Hotels

Sheriff Lodge
$ | B&B/INN | Huge beds and luxury bedding demonstrate the hosts' commitment to guest comfort at this intimate dog-friendly B&B in a former gentleman's residence; there's also a lovely garden with views across the valley towards Riber Castle. **Pros:** 7-foot-long beds; homemade cake on arrival; complimentary essentials boxes in rooms. **Cons:** a resident dog precludes those with allergies; steep walk from town center; not all rooms have baths. ⑤ *Rooms from: £96* ⊠ *The Dimple, Dimple Rd.*

☎ 01629/760760 ⊕ www.sherifflodge.
co.uk ⌁ 5 rooms ⦿ Free breakfast.

🏃 Activities

High Peak Trail

HIKING/WALKING | One of the major walking, cycling, and horse-riding trails in the Peak District, High Peak Trail runs for 17 miles from Cromford (just south of Matlock Bath) to Dowlow, following the route of an old railroad. ⊠ Matlock ⊕ www.peakdistrict.gov.uk.

Castleton

24 miles northwest of Matlock, 10 miles northwest of Chatsworth, 9 miles northeast of Buxton.

The area around Castleton, in the Hope Valley, contains the most famous manifestations of the geology of the Peak District. A number of caves and mines are open to the public, including some former lead mines and Blue John mines (amethystine spar; the unusual name is a corruption of the French *bleu-jaune*, meaning "blue yellow"). The limestone caverns attract many people, which means that pretty Castleton is marred by a certain commercialization. Summer brings the crowds, many of which poke around in the numerous shops displaying Blue John jewelry and wares.

GETTING HERE AND AROUND

Hope Rail Station, 1½ miles from the center of Castleton, is served by rail on the Manchester Piccadilly–Sheffield line every one to two hours. The journey takes 50 minutes. By car, Castleton is a one-hour drive southeast on the A6 from Manchester.

ESSENTIALS

VISITOR INFORMATION **Castleton Visitor Centre.** ⊠ Buxton Rd. ☎ 01629/816572 ⊕ www.peakdistrict.gov.uk.

👁 Sights

Peak Cavern

CAVE | FAMILY | Caves riddle the entire town and the surrounding area, and in this massive example, rope making has been done on a great ropewalk for more than 400 years. You can still see the remains of the 17th-century rope-makers' village. Some trivia to keep kids amused: the cavern was traditionally called the "Devil's Arse" due to the flatulent noise that water makes when draining out of the caves. Events held here include ghost tours and Christmas carols. ⊠ Off Goosehill ☎ 01433/620285 ⊕ www.peakcavern.co.uk ⚏ £11.75 Peak Cavern; £20 joint ticket with Speedwell Caverns.

Peveril Castle

CASTLE/PALACE | In 1176, Henry II added the square tower to this Norman castle, whose ruins occupy a dramatic crag above the town. The castle has superb views—from here you can still clearly see a curving section of the medieval defensive earthworks in the town center below. Peveril Castle is protected on its west side by a 230-foot-deep gorge formed by a collapsed cave; unsurprisingly, it was considered to be the best-defended castle in England in its day, and was never captured or besieged. However, its relative lack of strategic importance meant that the castle wasn't well maintained, and, in 1609, it was finally abandoned altogether. Park in the town center, from which it's a steep climb up. ⊠ Market Pl. ☎ 01433/620613 ⊕ www.english-heritage.org.uk ⚏ £6.20 ⊙ Closed weekdays Nov.–Mar.

★ Speedwell Cavern

CAVE | FAMILY | This is the area's most exciting cavern by far, with 105 slippery steps leading down to old lead-mine tunnels blasted out by 19th-century miners. Here you transfer to a small boat for the claustrophobic ¼-mile trip through an illuminated access tunnel to the cavern itself. At this point you're 600 feet

underground, with views farther down to the so-called Bottomless Pit, a cavern entirely filled with water. An on-site shop sells items made of Blue John, a mineral found nowhere else in the world. ⊠ *Winnats Pass* ✛ *1 mile west of Castleton* ☎ *01433/623018* ⊕ *www.speedwellcavern.co.uk* ✇ *£12.50; £20 combination ticket with Peak Cavern.*

Winnats Pass

SCENIC DRIVE | Heading northwest to Edale, the most spectacular driving route is over Winnats Pass, through a narrow, boulder-strewn valley. The name means "wind gate," due to the wind-tunnel effect of the peaks on each side. Beyond are the tops of Mam Tor (where there's a lookout point) and the hamlet of Barber Booth, after which you run into Edale. ⊠ *Castleton.*

🛏 Hotels

Innkeepers' Lodge (Castle Hotel)

$ | **B&B/INN** | Right by Peveril Castle, this former coaching inn—also known as The Castle and reputed to be haunted—has rooms that blend modern convenience and slick bathrooms with original features such as old wooden beams and exposed stone walls. **Pros:** charming atmosphere, with real fire places in bar; good value; delicious Sunday roast. **Cons:** sloping floors; building is a bit warrenlike; parking gets full quickly. ⑤ *Rooms from: £89* ⊠ *Castle St.* ☎ *01433/620578* ⊕ *www. innkeeperslodge.com* ✇ *15 rooms* ⧖ *Free breakfast.*

★ Losehill Hotel and Spa

$$ | **HOTEL** | Originally an Edwardian ramblers' hostel, this country hotel remains a great place from which to hike in the magnificent surrounding countryside, including to Castleton itself. **Pros:** away-from-it-all setting; expansive grounds; excellent restaurant. **Cons:** sound-proofing poor between certain rooms; some rooms very small; Wi-Fi is intermittent. ⑤ *Rooms from: £140* ⊠ *Edale Rd., Hope* ☎ *01433/621219* ⊕ *www.losehillhouse. co.uk* ✇ *23 rooms* ⧖ *Free breakfast.*

Edale

5 miles northwest of Castleton.

At Edale, an extremely popular hiking center, you're truly in the Peak District wilds. This sleepy, straggling village, in the shadow of Mam Tor and Lose Hill and the moorlands of the high plateau known as Kinder Scout (2,088 feet), lies among some of the most breathtaking scenery in Derbyshire. England has little wilder scenery than Kinder Scout, with its ragged edges of grit stone and its interminable leagues of heather and peat.

GETTING HERE AND AROUND

Edale Rail Station has services every one or two hours from Manchester (35 minutes) on the Sheffield line. By car, Edale is a one-hour drive southeast on the A6 from Manchester.

ESSENTIALS

VISITOR INFORMATION The Moorland Centre. ⊠ *Fieldhead* ☎ *01433/670207* ⊕ *www.peakdistrict.gov.uk.*

👁 Sights

Pennine Way

HIKING/WALKING | The 250-mile-long Pennine Way starts in the village of Edale, 4 miles northeast of Castleton, and crosses Kinder Scout, a moorland plateau and nature reserve. If you plan to attempt this, seek local advice first, because bad weather can make the walk treacherous. However, several much shorter routes into the Edale Valley, such as the 8-mile route west to Hayfield, give you a taste. ⊠ *Edale* ⊕ *www.nationaltrail.co.uk.*

🍴 Restaurants

Old Nag's Head

$ | **BRITISH** | This pub at the top of the village has marked the official start of the Pennine Way since 1965, but the building itself dates back as far as 1577. Call in at the Hiker's Bar, sit by the fire, and tuck into hearty traditional meals. **Known for:** classic pub dining; homey atmosphere; a real wood fireplace. ⑤ *Average main: £10* ✉ *Grinsbrook Booth* ☎ *01433/670291* 🌐 *www.dorbiere.co.uk.*

★ Penny Pot Cafe

$ | **CAFÉ** | Nestled away in the trees beside Edale Station, this charming little spot has outdoor seating and cozy interiors warmed by a log-burner in the chillier months. Walker-, cyclist- and dog-friendly, it serves everything from delicious panini and fresh soups to homemade cakes and scones amid images of local spots accompanied by poems. **Known for:** warm, personal welcome; live music; nice starting/finishing point for wonderful walks. ⑤ *Average main: £5* ✉ *Station Approach* ☎ *01433/670688* 🌐 *www. facebook.com/pennypotcafe.*

Stoke-on-Trent

55 miles southeast of Liverpool.

Just west of the Peak District, the area known as the Potteries is still the center of Britain's ceramics industry, though production is increasingly being transferred overseas. There are, in fact, six towns, now administered as "the city of Stoke-on-Trent." Famous names such as Wedgwood, Royal Doulton, Spode, and Coalport carry on, though they've been taken over by other companies.

The most famous manufacturer, Josiah Wedgwood, established his pottery works at Etruria, near Burslem, in 1759. More recent innovators include the very collectible Clarice Cliff, who strove to brighten plain whiteware in the 1920s with her colorful geometric and floral designs. Also bold and colorful were the classic art deco pieces of Susie Cooper. Museums portray the history of this area, and there's still plenty of shopping, with good prices for seconds.

GETTING HERE AND AROUND
Stoke-on-Trent is on the main rail route between London (90 minutes) and Manchester (an hour). If you're driving, it's just off Junctions 15 and 16 on the M6 motorway. National Express coaches between Manchester and Birmingham, and between London and Colne or Southport, call here. Traveline West Midlands (🌐 *www.travelinemidlands.co.uk*) has information on local bus services.

ESSENTIALS
VISITOR INFORMATION Tourist Information Centre. ✉ *The Potteries Museum & Art Gallery, Bethesda St.* ☎ *01782/236000* 🌐 *www.visitstoke.co.uk.*

👁 Sights

Emma Bridgewater

FACTORY | This highly successful local firm is known across Britain for its whimsical pottery designs. The hour-long factory tour (advance booking required) shows how Emma Bridgewater herself adapted 200-year-old techniques, and you can book a session in the decorating studio to try your hand at designs of your own. There's also a gift shop, a cute café, and a walled country-style garden in the summer. ✉ *Lichfield St., Hanley*

☎ 01782/201328 ⊕ www.emmabridge-water.co.uk ✉ Free ⊙ No tours Fri. afternoon or weekends.

Gladstone Pottery Museum

FACTORY | The country's only remaining old-style Victorian pottery factory's traditional bottle kilns are surrounded by original workshops where you can watch demonstrations of the old skills of throwing, casting, and decorating or even try your hand at throwing a pot. ⊠ Uttoxeter Rd., Longton ☎ 01782/237777 ⊕ www.stokemuseums.org.uk ✉ £7.75 ⊙ Closed Mon.

The Potteries Museum & Art Gallery

MUSEUM | This modern museum and gallery displays a 5,000-piece ceramic collection of international repute and is recognized worldwide for its unique Staffordshire pottery, as well as for a number of items from the Staffordshire Hoard, the largest collection of Anglo-Saxon gold and metalworks ever found. Other highlights are an original World War II Spitfire plane and works by Picasso, Degas, and Dürer. You'll also find the area's tourism information headquarters here. ⊠ Bethesda St. ☎ 01782/232323 ⊕ www.stokemuseums.org.uk ✉ Free.

World of Wedgwood

FACTORY | FAMILY | This slick modern attraction on the Wedgewood Estate's 240-acre garden factory site offers a factory tour, a V&A Collection of ceramics, works of art, manuscripts, and photographs, creative studios hosting activities and events, woodland walks, and a children's play area. There's also a restaurant, a tearoom, as well as the obligatory pottery and gift store. ⊠ Wedgewood Dr., Off A5035, Barlaston ☎ 01782/204141 ⊕ www.worldofwedgwood.com ✉ Factory tour £10, V&A Collection free.

🛏 Hotels

Upper House Hotel

$ | HOTEL | This handsome mansion located among gardens and woodlands was built in 1845 for Francis Wedgwood, heir to the family property firm. **Pros:** good food on-site; lovely views; peaceful surroundings. **Cons:** popular with weddings; bar sometimes unattended; limited breakfast hours including weekends. ⑤ Rooms from: £105 ⊠ The Green, Barlaston ☎ 01782/373790 ⊕ www.theupperhouse.com ⟿ 24 rooms ⦿ Free breakfast.

Chapter 11

THE LAKE DISTRICT

Updated by
Sophie Ibbotson

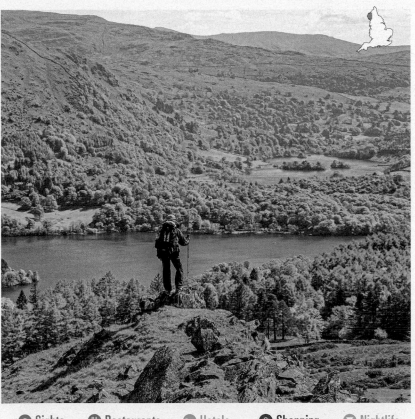

👁 **Sights**
★★★☆☆

🍴 **Restaurants**
★★★☆☆

🛏 **Hotels**
★★★☆☆

🛍 **Shopping**
★★☆☆☆

🍸 **Nightlife**
★☆☆☆☆

WELCOME TO THE LAKE DISTRICT

TOP REASONS TO GO

★ **Hiking:** Whether it's a demanding trek or a gentle stroll, walking is the way to see the Lake District at its best.

★ **Boating:** There's nowhere better for renting a small boat or taking a cruise. The Coniston Boating Centre and Derwent Water Marina near Keswick are possible places to start.

★ **Literary landscapes:** The Lake District has a rich literary history, in the children's books of Beatrix Potter, in the writings of John Ruskin, and in the poems of William Wordsworth. Stop at any of the writers' homes to enrich your experience.

★ **Pints and pubs:** A pint of real ale in one of the region's inns, such as the Drunken Duck near Hawkshead, may never taste as good as after a day of walking.

★ **Sunrise at Castlerigg:** The stone circle at Castlerigg, in a hollow ringed by peaks, is a reminder of the region's ancient history.

The Lake District is in northwest England, some 70 miles north of the industrial belt that stretches from Liverpool to Manchester and south of Scotland. The major gateway from the south is Kendal, and from the north, Penrith. Both are on the M6 motorway. Main-line trains stop at Oxenholme, near Kendal, with a branch linking Oxenholme to Kendal and Windermere. Windermere, in the south, is the most obvious starting point and has museums, cafés, and gift shops. But the farther (and higher) you can get from the southern towns, the more you'll appreciate the area's spectacular landscapes. Lake District National Park breaks into two reasonably distinct sections: the gentler, rolling south and the craggier, wilder north.

1 Kendal. The southern gateway to the Lake District.

2 Windermere and Bowness-on-Windermere. The region's largest body of water.

3 Ambleside. A quintessential Lakeland town.

4 Rydal. Once home to poet William Wordsworth.

5 Grasmere. A romantic village with literary connections.

6 Elterwater and the Langdales. Beautiful upland country great for hikers.

7 Coniston. A small lake resort and boating center.

8 Hawkshead. A market town in the Vale of Esthwaite.

9 Cartmel. The southern Lakeland area's most attractive village.

10 Penrith. A bustling market town and capital of old Cumbria.

11 Ullswater. The region's second largest lake.

12 Keswick. A good base to explore the less crowded northern lakes.

13 Borrowdale. Challenging, spectacular walking country.

14 Cockermouth. A charming village that was the birthplace of William Wordsworth.

15 Bassenthwaite Lake. The only "official" lake in the Lake District.

"Let nature be your teacher." Wordsworth's ideal comes true in this popular national park of jagged mountains, waterfalls, wooded valleys, and stone-built villages. No mountains in Britain give a greater impression of majesty; deeper and bluer lakes can be found, but none that fit so readily into the surrounding scene. Outdoors enthusiasts flock to this region for boating or hiking, while literary types visit the homes of Beatrix Potter, William Wordsworth, and other classic writers.

In 1951, the Lake District National Park was created here from parts of the old counties of Cumberland, Westmorland, and Lancashire. The Lake District is a contour map come to life, covering an area of approximately 885 square miles and holding 16 major lakes and countless smaller stretches of water. The scenery is key to all the park's best activities: you can cross it by car in about an hour, but this is an area meant to be walked or boated or climbed. The mountains aren't high by international standards—Scafell Pike, England's highest peak, is only 3,210 feet above sea level—but they can be tricky to climb. In spring, many summits remain snowcapped long after the weather below has turned mild.

The poets Wordsworth and Coleridge, and other English writers, found the Lake District an inspiring setting for their work, and visitors have followed ever since, to walk, go boating, or just relax and take in the views. Seeing the homes and other sights associated with these writers can occupy part of a trip.

This area can be one of Britain's most appealing reservoirs of calm, though, in summer, the lakeside towns can lose their charm when cars and tour buses clog the narrow streets. Similarly, the walks and hiking trails that crisscross the region seem less inviting when you share them with a crowd. Despite the challenges of popularity, the Lake District has managed tourism and the landscape in a manner that retains the character of the villages and the natural environment. Explore beyond Windermere and Keswick to discover little farming communities eking out a living despite the occasionally harsh conditions.

Today, too, a new generation of hotel and restaurant owners is making more creative use of the local foods and other assets of the Lakeland fells, and chic modern or foodie-oriented establishments are springing up next to traditional tearooms and chintz-filled inns.

Off-season visits can be a real treat. All those inns and bed-and-breakfasts that turn away crowds in summer are eager for business the rest of the year (and their rates drop accordingly). It's not an easy task to find a succession of sunny days in the Lake District—some malicious statisticians allot to it about 250 rainy days a year—but when the sun breaks through and brightens the surfaces of the lakes, it's an away-from-it-all place to remember.

MAJOR REGIONS

The Southern Lakes. The southern lakes and valleys contain the park's most popular destinations and, thus, those most overcrowded in summer. Among the many attractions here are the small resort towns clustered around Windermere, England's largest lake, and the area's hideaway valleys, rugged walking centers, and monuments rich in literary associations. This is the easiest part of the Lake District to reach, with Kendal, the largest town, just a short distance from the M6 motorway. An obvious route from Kendal takes in Windermere, the area's natural touring center, before moving north through Ambleside and Rydal Water to Grasmere. Some of the loveliest Lakeland scenery is to be found by then turning south, through Elterwater, Hawkshead, and Coniston.

Penrith and the North Lakes. The scenery of the northern lakes is considerably more dramatic—some would say bleaker—than much of the landscape to the south, a change that becomes apparent on your way north from Kendal to Penrith. A 30-mile drive on the A6 takes you through the wild and desolate Shap Fells, which rise to a height of 1,304 feet. This is one

of the most notorious moorland crossings in the country: even in summer it's a lonely place to be, and in winter, snow on the road can be dangerous. From Penrith the road leads to Ullswater, possibly the grandest of all the lakes; then there's a winding route west past Keswick, south through the marvelous Borrowdale Valley, and on to Cockermouth. Outside the main towns such as Keswick it can be easier to escape the summer crowds in the northern lakes.

Planning

When to Go

The Lake District is one of the rainiest areas in Britain, but June, July, and August hold the best hope of fine weather, and summer is the time for all the major festivals. You will, however, be sharing the lakes with thousands of other people. If you travel at this time, turn up early at popular museums and attractions, and expect to work to find parking. April and May, as well as September and October, are good alternatives. Later and earlier in the year there'll be even more space and freedom, but many attractions close, and from December to March, snow and ice can sometimes block high passes and may preclude serious hill walking without heavy-duty equipment.

Planning Your Time

You could spend months tramping the hills, valleys, and fells of the Lake District, or, in three days you could drive through the major towns and villages. The key is not to do too much in too short a time. If you're traveling by public transportation, many places will be off-limits. As a base, Windermere has the best transport links, but it can be crowded, and it has less character than some of the smaller towns like Ambleside and Keswick, which also have plenty of sleeping and eating options. For a more intimate version of village life, try Coniston, Hawkshead, or Grasmere. Keep in mind that the northern and western lakes have the most dramatic scenery and offer the best opportunity to escape the summertime hordes.

The Lake District may be compact, but it's not a place to hurry. Allow plenty of time for walking: paths can be steep and rocky, and, in any case, you'll want to stop frequently to look at the great views. A good day's walking with a picnic can be done from nearly anywhere. Driving brings its own speed inhibitors, from sheep on the roads to slow tractors.

You're likely to be based down near lake level, but try to experience the hills, too. If you're short of time, a drive over one of the high passes such as Honister will give you a glimpse of the enormity of the landscape.

Getting Here and Around

AIR
Manchester Airport has its own rail station with direct service to Carlisle, Windermere, and Barrow-in-Furness. Manchester is 70 miles from the southern part of the Lake District.

CONTACT Manchester Airport. ✉ *M56, Near Junctions 5 and 6* ☎ *0808/169–7030* ⊕ *www.manchesterairport.co.uk.*

BOAT
Whether you rent a boat or take a ride on a modern launch or vintage vessel, getting out on the water is a fun (and often useful) way to see the Lake District. Windermere, Coniston Water, and Derwentwater all have boat rental facilities.

BUS
National Express serves the region from London's Victoria Coach Station and from Manchester's Chorlton Street Station. Average travel time to Kendal is just over 7 hours from London; to Windermere,

7½ hours; and to Keswick, 8¼ hours. From Manchester there's one bus a day to Windermere via Ambleside, Grasmere, and Keswick. There's direct bus service to the Lake District from Carlisle, Lancaster, and York.

Stagecoach in Cumbria provides local service between Lakeland towns and through the valleys and high passes. Bus service between main tourist centers is fairly frequent on weekdays, but much reduced on weekends and bank holidays. Don't count on reaching the more remote parts of the area by bus. Off-the-beaten-track touring requires a car or strong legs. A one-week Cumbria Megarider ticket (£28), available on the bus, is valid on all routes. Dayrider tickets (£6–£8) are valid for a day; the price varies depending on how far you wish to travel. Contact Traveline for up-to-date timetables.

CONTACTS National Express. ☎ *0871/781–8181* ⊕ *www.nationalexpress.com.* **Stagecoach.** ☎ *01539/722217* ⊕ *www.stagecoachbus.com.* **Traveline.** ☎ *0871/200–2233* ⊕ *www.traveline.info.*

CAR
A car is almost essential in the Lake District; bus service is limited and trains can get you to the edge of the national park but no farther. You can rent cars in Penrith and Kendal. Roads within the region are generally good, although minor routes and mountain passes can be steep and narrow. Warning signs are often posted if snow or ice has made a road impassable; check local weather forecasts in winter before heading out. In July and August and during the long public holiday weekends, expect heavy traffic. The Lake District has plenty of parking lots; use them to avoid blocking narrow lanes. Most parking lots require payment; it's smart to keep some change on hand.

To reach the Lake District by car from London, take M1 north to M6, getting off either at Junction 36 and joining A590/

A591 west (around the Kendal bypass to Windermere) or at Junction 40, joining A66 direct to Keswick and the northern lakes region. Travel time to Kendal is about four to five hours, to Keswick five to six hours. Expect heavy traffic out of London on weekends.

TRAIN

There are direct trains from Manchester and Manchester airport to Windermere. For schedule information, call National Rail Enquiries. Two train companies serve the region from London's Euston Station: take an Avanti West Coast or Northern Rail train bound for Carlisle, Edinburgh, or Glasgow and change at Oxenholme for the branch line service to Kendal and Windermere. Average travel time from London to Windermere (including the change) is 3¼ hours. If you're heading for Keswick, you can either take the train to Windermere and continue from there by Stagecoach bus (Bus 554/555/556; 70 minutes) or stay on the main London–Carlisle train to Penrith Station (4 hours), from which Stagecoach buses (Bus X5) also run to Keswick (45 minutes). Direct trains from Manchester depart for Windermere five times daily (travel time 2 hours). First North Western runs a local service from Windermere and Barrow-in-Furness to Manchester Airport. National Rail can handle all questions about trains.

Train connections are good around the edges of the Lake District, but you must take the bus or drive to reach the central Lakeland region. Trains are sometimes reduced, or nonexistent, on Sunday.

CONTACTS Avanti West Coast.
☎ 0344/556–1394 ⊕ www.avantiwest-coast.co.uk. **National Rail Enquiries.** ☎ 03457/484950 ⊕ www.nationalrail.co.uk. **Northern Rail.** ☎ 0800/200–6060 ⊕ www.northernrailway.co.uk.

The Lake District National Park

The Lake District National Park head office (and main visitor center) is at Brockhole, north of Windermere. Helpful regional national-park information centers sell books and maps, book accommodations, and provide walking advice.

CONTACTS Bowness Bay Information Centre. ⊠ Glebe Rd., Bowness-on-Windermere ☎ 0845/901–0845 ⊕ www.lakedistrict.gov.uk. **Keswick Information Centre.** ⊠ Moot Hall, 12-14 Main St., Keswick ☎ 0845/901–0845 ⊕ www.keswick.org. **Lake District Visitor Centre.** ⊠ Brockhole, Ambleside Rd., Windermere ☎ 015394/46601 ⊕ www.brockhole.co.uk. **Ullswater Information Centre.** ⊠ Beckside Car Park, off Greenside Rd., Glenridding ☎ 0845/901–0845 ⊕ www.lakedistrict.gov.uk.

Tours

Cumbria Tourist Guides

This organization of Blue Badge–accredited guides, who are all experts on the area, offers a large range of customized tours, from low-impact country ambles to brewery crawls. From £175 for a half day. ☎ 01228/562096 ⊕ www.cumbriatourist-guides.org.

English Lakeland Ramblers

Arrange single-base and inn-to-inn guided tours of the Lake District from the United States through this organization. Prices start at US$3,850 per person for seven days. ☎ 800/724–8801 ⊕ www.ramblers.com.

Lake District Walker

ADVENTURE TOURS | This outfitter offers guided day hikes for different abilities. ⊠ Cockermouth ☎ 01900/826291 landline, 07805/592–9132 cell ⊕ www.thelakedistrictwalker.co.uk ⊠ From £25.

Mountain Goat

EXCURSIONS | Half- and full-day tours, some of which really get off the beaten track, depart from Windermere, Ambleside, and Keswick, and offer pick-ups from as far as Manchester, Chester, Liverpool, Glasgow, and Edinburgh. ⊠ *Victoria St., Windermere* ☎ *015394/45161* ⊕ *www.mountain-goat.com* ⊠ *From £26.*

★ **Swim the Lakes**

ADVENTURE TOURS | With more than 80 lakes, meres, and tarns, Cumbria is a great place for open-water swimming. Swim the Lakes has specialized swimming wet suits and a wealth of knowledge and enthusiasm about the best places to swim. Guided trips range from a couple of hours to weekends with accommodation and food included. As a way to see the lakes, the view and the experience from the water is hard to beat. ⊠ *2 Compston Rd., Ambleside* ☎ *015394/33826* ⊕ *www. swimthelakes.co.uk* ⊠ *From £30 for guided short wild swims.*

Restaurants

Lakeland restaurants increasingly reflect a growing British awareness of good food. Local sourcing and international influences are common, and even old Cumberland favorites are being creatively reinvented. Pub dining in the Lake District can be excellent—the hearty fare often makes use of local ingredients such as Herdwick lamb, and real ales are a good accompaniment. If you're going walking, ask your hotel or B&B about making you a packed lunch. Some local delicatessens also offer this service.

Hotels

Your choices include everything from small country inns to grand lakeside hotels. Many hotels offer the option of paying a higher price that includes dinner as well as breakfast. The regional mainstay is the bed-and-breakfast, from the house

on Main Street to an isolated farmhouse. Most country hotels and B&Bs gladly cater to hikers and can provide on-the-spot information. Wherever you stay, book well in advance for summer visits, especially those in late July and August. In winter, many accommodations close for a month or two. On weekends and in summer it may be hard to get a reservation for a single night. Internet access is improving, and an increasing number of hotels and cafés offer Wi-Fi.

Restaurant and hotel reviews have been shortened. For full information, visit Fodors.com. Restaurant prices are the average cost of a main course at dinner, or if dinner is not served, at lunch. Hotel prices are the lowest cost of a standard double room in high season, including 20% V.A.T.

WHAT IT COSTS in Pounds

	$	$$	$$$	$$$$
RESTAURANTS				
	under £16	£16–£23	£24–£30	over £30
HOTELS				
	under £125	£125–£225	£226–£350	over £350

Visitor Information

CONTACTS **Cumbria Tourism.** ⊠ *Windermere Rd., Staveley* ☎ *01539/822222* ⊕ *www.golakes.co.uk.*

Kendal

70 miles north of Manchester.

The southern gateway to the Lake District is the "Auld Gray Town" of Kendal, outside the national park and less touristy than the towns to the northwest. You may want to stay closer to the action, but the town has some worthwhile sights. Nearby hills frame Kendal's gray stone

The Lake
District

houses and provide some delightful walks; you can also explore the ruins of Kendal Castle. ■ **TIP→ Pack a slab of Kendal mint cake, the local peppermint candy that British walkers and climbers swear by. It's for sale around the region.**

The town's motto, "Wool Is My Bread," refers to its importance as a textile center in northern England before the Industrial Revolution. It was known for manufacturing woolen cloth, especially Kendal Green, which archers favored. Away from the main road are quiet courtyards and winding medieval streets known as "ginnels." Wool merchants used these for easy access to the River Kent.

GETTING HERE AND AROUND

Kendal is just off the M6, about 70 miles north of Manchester. It has train service via a branch line from Oxenholme and National Express bus service from

London as well. It's the largest town in the area but is still plenty small enough to walk around.

ESSENTIALS

VISITOR INFORMATION Kendal Tourist Information Centre. ✉ *Fantastic Kendal, 26–28 Finkle St.* ☎ *01539/725139* ⊕ *www. exploresouthlakeland.co.uk.*

◉ Sights

Kendal Museum

MUSEUM | Focusing on natural history and archaeology, this grand, old-fashioned museum details splendidly the flora and fauna of the Lake District. The museum is at the northern end of town, close to the train station. ✉ *Station Rd.* ☎ *01539/815597* ⊕ *www.kendalmuseum. org.uk* ✦ *£5* ⊗ *Closed Sun.–Wed.*

The design of the famous, fanciful topiary garden at Levens Hall dates back to the 17th century.

Levens Hall

GARDEN | FAMILY | An Elizabethan house and the home of the Bagot family since 1590, Levens Hall is famous for its topiary garden, probably the most distinctive in the world. Laid out in 1694, the garden retains its original design, and the yew and beech hedges, cut into complex shapes that resemble enormous chess pieces, rise among a profusion of flowers. The house contains a stunning medieval hall with oak paneling, ornate plasterwork, Jacobean furniture, and Cordova goat-leather wallpaper. You can easily spend a couple of hours here admiring the place or getting lost in the living willow labyrinth. There's a play area for children. Levens Hall is 4 miles south of Kendal. ⊠ *Off A590, Levens* ☎ *01539/560321* ⊕ *www.levenshall.co.uk* ⊠ *£14.50; gardens only £10.50* ⊙ *Closed early Oct.–mid-Apr. and Fri.–Sat.*

Sizergh Castle

CASTLE/PALACE | One of the Lake District's finest fortified houses, Sizergh Castle has a 58-foot-tall tower that dates from 1340, more than 1,600 acres of grounds, and the national fern collection. Expanded in Elizabethan times, the castle includes outstanding oak-paneled interiors with intricately carved chimneypieces and oak furniture. The estate has ancient woodland, and there are good walks here. Sizergh is 3½ miles south of Kendal. ⊠ *Off A591, Sizergh* ☎ *015395/60951* ⊕ *www. nationaltrust.org.uk/sizergh* ⊠ *£11.50; gardens only £7.50* ⊙ *Castle closed Nov.– mid-Mar. and Mon.*

🍴 Restaurants

The Famous 1657 Chocolate House

$ | BRITISH | Chocolate rules at this old spot serving 16 chocolate drinks. You can choose among 300 kinds of chocolates in the shop, too. **Known for:** period costumed staff; traditional English desserts; all things chocolate. ⑤ *Average main: £5* ⊠ *54 Branthwaite Brow* ☎ *01539/740702* ⊕ *www.chocolatehouse1657.co.uk* ⊙ *Closed Sun. No dinner.*

Classic English Desserts

The English love to round off lunch or dinner with something sweet. British food is experiencing an ongoing revival that has cooks bringing back favorites such as fool, trifle, spotted dick, and sticky toffee pudding and making the most of seasonal fruits and traditional spices.

Winter is the perfect time for steamed puddings, made with currants, dried fruits, and spices such as cinnamon, nutmeg, cloves, and ginger, or for hot fruit crumbles with custard. The warmer months bring an avalanche of fresh berries, and with them light, creamy desserts such as syllabub and fool come into their own. For many, the classic desserts such as sticky toffee pudding and spotted dick capture memories of growing up in the 20th century. Today, dessert bars are becoming a trend in cities including London.

Hot Steamed Puddings

These puddings are cooked slowly over boiling water. Sticky toffee pudding is a dark sponge cake made with finely chopped dates or prunes, and covered in a thick toffee sauce. The oddly named spotted dick is traditionally made with suet and steamed in a hot cloth, "spotted" with currants and other dried fruits, and served with custard. Another classic, Christmas pudding, dates from medieval times. Also known as plum pudding, it contains brandy, currants, and dried fruit, and is strong-flavored. Before the pudding steams for many hours, each family member stirs the mixture and makes a wish.

Fruit Crumbles

Crumbles, similar to American crisps, were invented during wartime rationing when butter, flour, and sugar were too scarce to make pastry for pie. Tart Bramley apples native to England work well with cinnamon and cloves. Don't pass up rhubarb crumble, especially around February when the delicate bright pink variety of rhubarb from Yorkshire makes its brief appearance.

Trifle, Fool, and Syllabub

Dating from Tudor times, fool is simply a sharp fruit, usually gooseberry, swirled with whipped cream and a little sugar. Trifle evolved from fool and begins with a layer of sponge cake (soaked in port, sherry, or Madeira wine) and Jell-O or jam, topped with custard and whipped cream. Light but flavorful, syllabub is made from wine or brandy infused overnight with lemon and sugar and whipped with cream.

Eton Mess

Invented at the famous Eton College, after, it's said, a Labrador dog accidentally sat on a picnic basket, Eton Mess is still served at the annual prize-giving ceremony. This unfussy summer dessert consists of strawberries mixed with whipped cream and crushed meringue.

Summer Pudding

Fresh summer berries, bread, and a little sugar are all that should go into a summer pudding. Left for several hours so that the sweet and sharp flavors develop, the pudding turns out a deep red color and is often served with a touch of cream.

The Moon Highgate

$$ | **MODERN BRITISH** | Small but sleek, this restaurant with an open fire and artfully battered floorboards has won a good local reputation for high-quality dishes. The vegetarian selections are always worthwhile, and the sometimes adventurous Modern British cooking shows Mediterranean flourishes. **Known for:** imaginative British menu; seasonal ingredients; fixed-price early dinners. ⑤ *Average main: £17* ⊠ *129 Highgate* ☎ *01539/729254* ⊕ *www.themoonhighgate.com* ⊘ *Closed Sun. and Mon.*

🛏 Hotels

Kendal Hostel

$ | **HOTEL** | Right on Kendal's main street, this upscale hostel is located in an attractive building with plenty of character. **Pros:** central location; friendly staff; self-catering facilities. **Cons:** shared bathrooms; can get noisy with large groups; no free parking. ⑤ *Rooms from: £40* ⊠ *118-120 Highgate* ☎ *01539/724066* ⊕ *www.kendalhostel.com* ⇋ *14 rooms* ⑩ *No meals.*

Performing Arts

★ Brewery Arts Centre

ARTS CENTERS | A contemporary complex in a converted brewery, the Brewery Arts Centre includes a gallery, theater, cinemas, and workshop spaces. The Vats Bar, an on-site freehouse, serves up a tasty selection of pizzas and hearty mains, as well as a variety of craft beers and wine. In November, the Mountain Film Festival presents productions aimed at climbers and walkers. ⊠ *122A Highgate* ☎ *01539/725133* ⊕ *www.breweryarts.co.uk* ⊠ *Free* ☞ *Kitchen closed Sun.–Mon.*

🛍 Shopping

Kendal has a pleasant mix of chains, factory outlet stores, specialty shops, and traditional markets. The most interesting stores are tucked away in the quiet lanes and courtyards around Market Place, Finkle Street, and Stramongate. There's been a market in Kendal since 1189, and outdoor market stalls still line the center of town along Stramongate and Market Place every Wednesday and Saturday.

Windermere and Bowness-on-Windermere

10 miles northwest of Kendal.

For a natural touring base for the southern half of the Lake District, you don't need to look much farther than Windermere, though it does get crowded in summer. The resort became popular in the Victorian era when the arrival of the railway made the remote and rugged area accessible. Wordsworth and Ruskin opposed the railway, fearing an influx of tourists would ruin the tranquil place. Sure enough, the railway terminus in 1847 brought with it Victorian day-trippers, and the original hamlet of Birthwaite was subsumed by the new town of Windermere, named after the lake.

Windermere has continued to flourish, despite being a mile or so from the water. The development now spreads to envelop the slate-gray lakeside village of Bowness-on-Windermere. Bowness is the more attractive of the two, but they're so close that it doesn't matter where you stay.

GETTING HERE AND AROUND

Windermere is easily reached by car, less than a half hour off the M6. There's also a train station at the eastern edge of town; change at Oxenholme for the branch line to Kendal and Windermere.

Bus 599, leaving every 20 minutes in summer (hourly the rest of the year) from outside the Windermere train station, links the town with Bowness.

The Windermere Ferry, which carries cars and pedestrians, crosses from Ferry Nab on the Bowness side of the lake to reach Far Sawrey and the road to Hawkshead. With year-round ferry service between Ambleside, Bowness, Brockhole, and Lakeside, Windermere Lake Cruises is a pleasant way to experience the lake.

ESSENTIALS

CONTACTS Windermere Ferry.
☎ *01228/227653* ⊕ *www.cumbria.gov. uk/roads-transport/highways-pavements/ windermereferry.asp.* **Windermere Lake Cruises.** ☎ *015394/43360* ⊕ *www.winder- mere-lakecruises.co.uk.*

 ## Sights

★ Blackwell

HOUSE | From 1898 to 1900, architect Mackay Hugh Baillie Scott (1865–1945) designed Blackwell, a quintessential Arts and Crafts house with carved paneling, delicate plasterwork, and a startling sense of light and space. Originally a retreat for a Manchester brewery owner, the house is a refined mix of modern style and the local vernacular. Lime-washed walls and sloping slate roofs make it fit elegantly into the landscape above Windermere, and the artful integration of decorative features into stained glass, stonework, friezes, and wrought iron gives the house a sleekly contemporary feel. Accessibility is wonderful here: nothing is roped off, and you can even play the piano. There's some Baillie Scott furniture, too, and an exhibition space upstairs. Peruse the shop, and try

the honey-roast ham in the excellent tea-room. The grounds are also worth a visit; they often host contemporary sculpture installations. ⊠ *Off the B5360, Winder- mere* ☎ *01539/446139* ⊕ *www.blackwell. org.uk* ✉ *£9.*

Brockhole

GARDEN | FAMILY | A lakeside 19th-century mansion with 30 acres of terraced gardens sloping down to the water, Brockhole serves as the park's official visitor center and has some exhilarating activities. Among them are "treetop trek"—a rope bridge and zipline route high up through oak trees—and the U.K.'s only "treetop nets," allowing everyone over the age of three to climb and bounce around safely among the twigs and leaves more than 25 feet up, supported by elastic ropes. There's also a 30-foot climbing wall. The gardens, designed in the Arts and Crafts style by Thomas Mawson, are at their best in spring, when daffodils punctuate the lawns and azaleas burst into bloom. There's an adventure playground, pony rides, minigolf, and rowboats for rent. The bookstore carries hiking guides and maps, and you can picnic here or eat at the café-restaurant. Bus 555/559 goes to the visitor center from Windermere, and boats from Waterhead stop at a pier. Windermere Lake Cruises has seasonal ferry service to Brockhole from Water-head in Ambleside. ⊠ *Ambleside Rd., Windermere* ☎ *015394/46601* ⊕ *www. brockhole.co.uk* ✉ *Free; treetop trek £22; treetop nets from £13.*

Hawkshead Brewery

WINERY/DISTILLERY | It may not have the Lake District's most picturesque setting—in Staveley, between Windermere and Kendal—but for beer lovers, there are few better places than this brewery, which brews and serves more than a dozen award-winning beers, including some by guest brewers. Sample the wares and "beer tapas" (sweet corn and coriander fritters with apricot chutney, chickpea, and red lentil dal) at the large bar, where there's often live music in the evenings. Brewery tours happen daily at 1 pm and include two half pints of Hawkshead beer. ⊠ *Mill Yard, Staveley* ☎ *01539/822644* ⊕ *www.hawkshead-brewery.co.uk* ⊠ *Free; tours £10 including 1 pint (or 2 halves) during the tour.*

★ Lakes Aquarium

ZOO | FAMILY | On the quayside at the southern end of Windermere, this excellent aquarium has wildlife and waterside exhibits. One highlight is an underwater tunnel walk along a re-created lake bed, complete with diving ducks and Asian short-clawed otters. Piranhas, rays, and tropical frogs also have their fans, and there are some unexpected treats such as marmosets. A friendly, knowledgeable staff is eager to talk about the animals. ■**TIP→ Animal handling takes place daily at 1 pm in the rain-forest areas.** Tickets are cheapest if booked in advance online. ⊠ *C5062, Newby Bridge* ☎ *01539/430153* ⊕ *www.lakesaquarium.co.uk* ⊠ *£7.50.*

Lakeside & Haverthwaite Railway Company

TRANSPORTATION SITE (AIRPORT/BUS/FERRY/ TRAIN) | FAMILY | Vintage steam trains chug along on the 18-minute, 4-mile branch line between Lakeside and Haverthwaite, giving you a great view of the lake's southern tip. You can add on a lake cruise for another perspective on the region's natural beauty. Departures from Lakeside coincide with ferry arrivals from Bowness and Ambleside. See the website for timetables. ⊠ *Haverthwaite Railway Station, A590, Haverthwaite* ☎ *01539/531594* ⊕ *www.lakesiderailway.co.uk* ⊠ *£7.10 round-trip; £12 unlimited 1-day travel.*

Orrest Head

VIEWPOINT | To escape the traffic and have a view of Windermere, set out on foot and follow the signs to the left of the Windermere Hotel to Orrest Head. The shady, uphill path winds through Elleray Wood, and after a 20-minute hike you arrive at a rocky little summit (784 feet)

with a panoramic view that encompasses the Yorkshire fells, Morecambe Bay, and the beautiful Troutbeck Valley. ⊠ *Windermere.*

Windermere

BODY OF WATER | No sights in Windermere or Bowness compete with that of Windermere itself. At 11 miles long, 1½ miles wide, and 220 feet deep, the lake is England's largest and stretches from Newby Bridge almost to Ambleside, filling a rocky gorge between thickly wooded hills. The cold waters are superb for fishing, especially for Windermere char, a rare lake trout. In summer, steamers and pleasure craft travel the lake, and a trip across the island-studded waters, particularly the round-trip from Bowness to Ambleside or down to Lakeside, is wonderful. Although the lake's marinas and piers have some charm, you can bypass the busier stretches of shoreline (in summer they can be packed solid) by walking beyond the boathouses. Here, from among the pine trees, are fine views across the lake. Windermere Lake Cruises offers a variety of excursions. ⊠ *Windermere* ⊕ *www.windermere-lake-cruises.co.uk.*

Windermere Jetty

MARINA | Right beside the lake, the center houses the world's finest collection of Victorian and Edwardian steam- and motor-powered yachts and launches. Displays about Windermere's nautical history include the famous names of motorboat racing on the lake. The *Dolly*, built around 1850, is one of the two oldest mechanically powered boats in the world. Among the many other vessels on view are Beatrix Potter's rowing boat and a dinghy that belonged to Arthur Ransome. ■**TIP→ For £14, you can take a boat ride on Windermere in an antique vessel—if the weather is good.** ⊠ *Rayrigg Rd., Bowness-on-Windermere* ☎ *01539/445565* ⊕ *windermerejetty.org* ⊠ *£9* ☉ *Closed mid-Jan. for maintenance.*

Walk through an underwater tunnel and learn about the Lake District's fish, frogs, and otters at the Lakes Aquarium near Windermere.

World of Beatrix Potter

MUSEUM | **FAMILY** | A touristy attraction aimed at kids interprets the author's 23 tales with three-dimensional scenes of Peter Rabbit and more. Skip it if you can, and visit Potter's former home at Hill Top and the Beatrix Potter Gallery in Hawkshead. ⊠ *The Old Laundry, Crag Brow, Bowness-on-Windermere* ☎ *01539/488444* ⊕ *www.hop-skip-jump. com* 🍴 *£8.20*.

🍴 Restaurants

Angel Inn

$ | **BRITISH** | Up the steep slope from the water's edge in Bowness, this spacious, stylish pub serves good home-cooked fare as well as a fine collection of beers that includes its own Hawkshead brew. Specials, chalked on a board, may include dishes such as roasted cod with bok choy or goat cheese and fig tart. **Known for:** draft beers and ciders; landscaped gardens; local, seasonal food. ⑤ *Average main: £14*

⊠ *Helm Rd., Bowness-on-Windermere* ☎ *01539/444080* ⊕ *www.angelbowness. com*.

Masons Arms

$ | **BRITISH** | **FAMILY** | With fabulous views over the rolling countryside of the Winster Valley to the east of Windermere, the Masons Arms is a slate-floored traditional old inn serving local ales and good pub food. Old mirrors and tankards decorate the walls, and there's a speciality gin list as well as a menu showcasing the best local ingredients. **Known for:** locally farmed meats; homemade desserts; popular children's menu. ⑤ *Average main: £15* ⊠ *Strawberry Bank, Windermere* ☎ *01539/568486* ⊕ *www.mason-sarmsstrawberrybank.co.uk*.

Queen's Head Hotel

$ | **BRITISH** | This unpretentious 17th-century inn in the pretty little village of Troutbeck is in a superb location. The Queen's Head is owned by Robinsons Brewery, and though its menu is not particularly imaginative, it does serve good, wholesome pub grub throughout the day, as well as Robinsons' cask ales. **Known for:** historic building; plenty of cask ales; weekly fish-and-chips night. $ *Average main: £15* ✉ *Town Head, off A592, Troutbeck* ☎ *01539/432404* ⊕ *www.queensheadtroutbeck.co.uk.*

🛏 Hotels

★ Gilpin Hotel and Lake House

$$$ | **HOTEL** | Hidden among 22 acres of grounds with meandering paths leading to sleek, spacious lodges, this rambling country house provides the ultimate pampering. **Pros:** plenty of pampering; notable food; a policy of no weddings or conferences. **Cons:** a little out of the way; expensive rates; might be too posh for some. $ *Rooms from: £295* ✉ *Crook Rd., Bowness-on-Windermere* ✛ *2 miles east of Windermere* ☎ *01539/488818* ⊕ *thegilpin.co.uk* ⤳ *20 rooms, 5 lodges* ⦿ *All-inclusive* ⌇ *No children under 7.*

Ivy Bank

$ | **B&B/INN** | One of Windermere's smartest bed-and-breakfasts, spotless Ivy Bank is in a quiet, leafy part of town. **Pros:** bike storage; good walks nearby; family room. **Cons:** most rooms have showers, but no tubs; rooms are quite small; not on the lakeside of Windermere. $ *Rooms from: £85* ✉ *Holly Rd., Windermere* ☎ *01539/442601* ⊕ *www.ivy-bank.co.uk* ⤳ *5 rooms* ⦿ *Free breakfast.*

★ Miller Howe

$$$ | **HOTEL** | A lovely location, lake views, and superb service help set this luxurious Edwardian country-house hotel apart. **Pros:** more than 5 acres of grounds; great lake views; staff that take care of the little extras. **Cons:** sometimes closes for a couple of weeks in winter; not in the center of Windermere; on a noisy main road. $ *Rooms from: £230* ✉ *Rayrigg Rd., Bowness-on-Windermere* ☎ *015394/42536* ⊕ *www.millerhowe.com* ⤳ *14 rooms* ⦿ *Some meals.*

★ 1 Park Road

$ | **B&B/INN** | On a quiet corner, this upscale boutique B&B has spacious guest rooms with carefully chosen fabrics and wallpaper, comfortable mattresses, and contemporary touches. **Pros:** welcoming and stylish; hosts will pick guests up from the station; good food, wine, and beer. **Cons:** a 15-minute walk to the lake; limited car parking; not handicap accessible. $ *Rooms from: £90* ✉ *1 Park Rd., Windermere* ☎ *01539/442107* ⊕ *1parkroad.co.uk* ⤳ *6 rooms* ⦿ *Free breakfast.*

★ Punch Bowl Inn

$$ | **HOTEL** | An outstanding inn and restaurant, the Punch Bowl is a stylish but down-to-earth retreat in the peaceful Lyth Valley, between Windermere and Kendal. **Pros:** contemporary design; relaxed atmosphere; excellent food. **Cons:** remote location; limited parking; often booked for weddings in summer. $ *Rooms from: £150* ✉ *Totter Bank, Off A5074, Crosthwaite* ☎ *01539/568237* ⊕ *www.the-punchbowl.co.uk* ⤳ *9 rooms* ⦿ *Free breakfast.*

Rum Doodle

$ | **B&B/INN** | Named after a classic climbing novel, Rum Doodle is an immaculately and imaginatively designed B&B. **Pros:** wonderfully stylish with lots of fun quirks; friendly welcome; sumptuous breakfast. **Cons:** some distance from both Bowness and Windermere centers; two-night minimum stay in high season; not suitable for young children. $ *Rooms from: £119* ✉ *Sunny Bank Rd., Windermere* ☎ *01539/445967* ⊕ *www.rumdoodlewindermere.com* ⤳ *9 rooms* ⦿ *Free breakfast.*

🛍 Shopping

The best selection of shops is at the Bowness end of Windermere, on Lake Road, and around Queen's Square: clothing stores, crafts shops, and souvenir stores of all kinds.

★ More? The Artisan Bakery

FOOD/CANDY | Between Kendal and Windermere, this bakery is the place to stop for mouthwatering, award-winning bread, cakes, and sandwiches, including an unforgettable bright green matcha tea blondie. It also brews fine coffee. Proximity to the neighboring Hawkshead Brewery makes for a couple of hours of true indulgence. ⊠ *Mill Yard, Staveley* ☎ *01539/822297* ⊕ *www.moreartisan. co.uk.*

Peter Hall & Son

CRAFTS | This woodcraft workshop, between Kendal and Windermere, sells bespoke furniture and finely honed boxes and bowls, among other items. ⊠ *Danes Rd., Staveley* ☎ *01539/821633* ⊕ *www. peter-hall.co.uk.*

Activities

BIKING

Country Lanes Cycle Hire

BICYCLING | This shop rents a variety of bikes from £26 per day. Helmets and a number of other useful accessories are included in the price. ⊠ *Windermere Railway Station, off A591, Windermere* ☎ *01539/444544* ⊕ *www.countrylaneslakedistrict.co.uk.*

Ambleside

7 miles northwest of Windermere.

Unlike Kendal and Windermere, Ambleside seems almost part of the hills and fells. Its buildings, mainly of local stone and many built in the traditional style that forgoes the use of mortar in the outer walls, blend perfectly into their setting. The small town sits at the northern end of Windermere along A591, making it a popular center for Lake District excursions. It has recently seen a sharp rise in quality restaurants, and the numerous outdoor shops are handy for walkers. Ambleside does, however, suffer from overcrowding in high season. Wednesday, when the local market takes place, is particularly busy.

GETTING HERE AND AROUND

An easy drive along A591 from Windermere, Ambleside can also be reached by ferry.

ESSENTIALS

VISITOR INFORMATION Ambleside Tourist Information Centre. ⊠ *In the Post Office, Central Bldgs., 8-9 Market Pl.* ☎ *01539/432582 Post Office/Tourist Information, 0844/225–0544 Ambleside Online* ⊕ *www.visitcumbria.com/amb/ ambleside, www.amblesideonline.co.uk.*

Sights

Armitt Museum

MUSEUM | Ambleside's fine local museum is a scholarly place, focusing on influential German artist Kurt Schwitters and Beatrix Potter. Schwitters lived out his final years in Ambleside, and the museum now has a room filled with his art. The museum also shows the less well-known aspects of Beatrix Potter, revealing her work as an important scientific and intellectual figure. Exhibits shed light on her as a naturalist, mycologist, sheep breeder, and conservationist. A large collection of her natural-history watercolors and a huge number of photographic portraits can be viewed by appointment in the excellent library upstairs. ⊠ *Rydal Rd.* ☎ *01539/431212* ⊕ *www.armitt.com* 🎟 *£5.*

Bridge House

BUILDING | This tiny 17th-century stone building, once an apple store, perches on an arched stone bridge spanning Stone Beck. It may have been built here to avoid land tax. This much-photographed building, which is cared for by the National Trust, holds a shop and an information center. ⊠ *Rydal Rd.* ☎ *015394/32617* ⊕ *www.nationaltrust.org.uk/ambleside/ features/bridge-house—a-17th-century-survivor* 🎟 *Free.*

🍴 Restaurants

★ Fellinis

$ | **VEGETARIAN** | Billing itself as "Vege-terranean" to reflect its Mediterranean culinary influences, Fellinis is one of Cumbria's finest foodie destinations and a particular treat for vegetarians. Upstairs is a plush studio cinema screening art-house releases, while downstairs the restaurant rustles up sumptuous concoctions for a sophisticated crowd. **Known for:** unpretentious fine dining; vegetarian and vegan dishes; romantic dinner-and-a-movie ambience. ⑤ *Average main: £14* ✉ *Church St.* ☎ *01539/432487* ⊕ *www.fellinisambleside.com* ⊙ *No lunch.*

Lake Road Kitchen

$$$$ | **MODERN BRITISH** | Cuttlefish shells piled in the window and a Nordic-style wood-paneled interior give a clue as to the culinary style of Lake Road Kitchen, quite possibly the most awarded restaurant in Ambleside. About 80% of everything green on the menu is foraged; the remainder comes from the highest-quality, mainly local suppliers. **Known for:** homegrown and foraged produce; mouthwatering set menu with wine pairings; small space so reservations necessary. ⑤ *Average main: £65* ✉ *Lake Rd.* ☎ *01539/422012* ⊕ *www.lakeroadkitchen.co.uk* ⊙ *Closed Mon. and Tues. No lunch.*

Matthew's Bistro

$$ | **BRITISH** | **FAMILY** | Matthew Colley is a charismatic chef who opened his own restaurant in 2001 to serve "retro classic" dishes to hungry Lake District walkers. He's passionate about local, artisanal produce and makes almost everything from scratch, including his own Cumbrian sausages. **Known for:** family-friendly atmosphere; good value set menu; special (and tasty) dessert of the day. ⑤ *Average main: £22* ✉ *Compston Rd.* ☎ *01539/431234* ⊙ *No lunch.*

★ Old Stamp House

$$$ | **BRITISH** | The quality of locally sourced and foraged food has been raised to a new level by this startlingly good restaurant, which, together with the Lake Road Kitchen, has given Ambleside unexpected status on the British gastro map. Chef Ryan Blackburn has created a menu anchored to Cumbrian traditions but at the same time mouthwateringly creative and contemporary. **Known for:** creative seasonal menu; celebrity chef; excellent wine list. ⑤ *Average main: £26* ✉ *Church St.* ☎ *01539/432775* ⊕ *www.oldstamphouse.com* ⊙ *Closed Sun. and Mon. No lunch Tues.*

Rattle Ghyll

$ | **VEGETARIAN** | Hidden away up a winding lane past the old mill waterwheel, homey Rattle Ghyll is a deservedly popular little café serving great homemade cakes, soups, sandwiches, and salads. The tasting plate of cakes is an especially good option. **Known for:** homemade soups; tasting plates of cakes; outdoor seating. ⑤ *Average main: £7* ✉ *2 Bridge St.* ☎ *07975/912990* ⊕ *www.rattleghyll.com* ⊙ *Closed Mon. and Tues. No dinner.*

🛏 Hotels

Nanny Brow

$$ | **B&B/INN** | Outside Ambleside toward the Langdales, this smart guesthouse feels more like a hotel, with a huge lounge, named rooms, antique furniture, and award-winning breakfasts. **Pros:** great setting and views; easy access to the Fells; historic building. **Cons:** no evening meals; remote location; need a car to get here. ⑤ *Rooms from: £160* ✉ *Clappersgate* ✛ *Off the A593 between Clappersgate and Skelwith Bridge* ☎ *01539/433232* ⊕ *www.nannybrow.co.uk* ⊋ *14 rooms* ⑩ *Free breakfast.*

Rooms at the Apple Pie

$ | B&B/INN | Converted from what were once the offices of Beatrix Potter's solicitor husband, this Ambleside café has branched out into accommodations, with eight simple but stylishly furnished rooms decorated with photos of delights from the café next door. **Pros:** scrumptious breakfasts; central location; stylish rooms. **Cons:** not staffed 24 hours a day; breakfast is extra; limited parking. $ Rooms from: £56 ⊠ Rydal Rd., Keswick ☎ 01539/433679 ⊕ www.applepieambleside.co.uk ⤴ 8 rooms ¹⊙¹ No meals.

★ Rothay Manor

$$ | HOTELHOTEL | One of the original luxury hotels of the Lakes, Rothay Manor was recently purchased from previous owners, a family who owned it for most of a century and gave it a loving facelift. **Pros:** spectacular, experimental cuisine; spacious rooms; quiet location. **Cons:** can feel a little intimidating; on the more expensive end; not all bathrooms have tubs. $ Rooms from: £220 ⊠ Off the A593 ☎ 01539/433605 ⊕ www.rothaymanor.co.uk ⤴ 18 rooms ¹⊙¹ Free breakfast.

The Samling

$$$ | HOTEL | On its own sculpture-dotted 67 acres not far from Ambleside and Windermere, this place oozes exclusivity from the moment you enter the long, winding drive. **Pros:** set on gorgeous private estate; superb restaurant; celebrity guest list. **Cons:** exclusivity doesn't come cheap; steep climb up from the lake; outside Ambleside. $ Rooms from: £330 ⊠ Ambleside Rd. ☎ 015394/431922 ⊕ www.thesamlinghotel.co.uk ⤴ 12 rooms ¹⊙¹ Free breakfast.

3 Cambridge Villas

$ | B&B/INN | It's hard to find a more welcoming spot than this lofty Victorian house right in the center of town, thanks to hosts who know a thing or two about local walks. **Pros:** especially good value for single travelers; warm family welcome; central location. **Cons:** some rooms are a little cramped; can occasionally be noisy; street parking only. $ Rooms from: £98 ⊠ 3 Church St. ☎ 01539/432307 ⊕ www.3cambridgevillas.co.uk ⤴ 7 rooms ¹⊙¹ Free breakfast.

Waterhead

$$ | HOTEL | If you want hotel benefits, Waterhead is a good bet; near the water's edge, with good views, it's comfortable and spotless, with excellent service and amenities that include underfloor heating, espresso machines, and even the occasional trouser press. **Pros:** welcoming and professional; a stone's throw from Lake Windermere; great views. **Cons:** style is a little dated; a walk from Ambleside's best pubs and restaurants; standard rooms quite small. $ Rooms from: £135 ⊠ Lake Rd. ☎ 015394/32566 ⊕ www.englishlakes.co.uk/waterhead ⤴ 41 rooms ¹⊙¹ Free breakfast.

🏃 Activities

The fine walks in the vicinity include routes north to Rydal Mount or southeast over Wansfell to Troutbeck. Each walk will take up to a half day, there and back. Ferries from Bowness-on-Windermere dock at Ambleside's harbor, called Waterhead. ■**TIP**→ **To escape the crowds, rent a rowboat at the harbor for an hour or two.**

Rydal

1 mile northwest of Ambleside.

The village of Rydal, on the small glacial lake called Rydal Water, is rich with Wordsworthian associations.

👁 Sights

Dora's Field

NATURE PRESERVE | One famous beauty spot linked with Wordsworth is Dora's Field, below Rydal Mount next to the church of **St. Mary's** (where you can still see the poet's pew). In spring, the field is awash in yellow daffodils, planted by William Wordsworth and his wife in memory of their beloved daughter Dora, who died in 1847. ⊠ *A591* ⊕ *www. nationaltrust.org.uk/ambleside/features/ daffodils-at-doras-field-*.

Rydal Mount

HOUSE | If there's one poet associated with the Lake District, it is Wordsworth, who made his home at Rydal Mount from 1813 until his death. Wordsworth and his family moved to these grand surroundings when he was nearing the height of his career, and his descendants still live here, surrounded by his furniture, his books, his barometer, and portraits. You can see the study in which he worked, Dorothy's bedroom, and the 4½-acre garden, laid out by the poet himself, that gave him so much pleasure. ■ TIP→ **Wordsworth's favorite footpath can be found on the hill past White Moss Common and the River Rothay.** Spend an hour or two walking the paths and you may understand why the great poet composed most of his verse in the open air. A tearoom in the former saddlery provides cakes and drinks; in winter, it moves into the dining room. ⊠ *Off A591* ☎ *01539/433002* ⊕ *www.rydalmount. co.uk* ⊠ *£7.50; garden only £5* ⊘ *Closed Jan.; closed Mon. and Tues. in Nov.–Mar.*

Grasmere

3 miles north of Rydal, 4 miles northwest of Ambleside.

Lovely Grasmere, on a tiny, wood-fringed lake, is made up of crooked lanes in which Westmorland slate–built cottages hold shops and galleries. The village is a focal point for literary and landscape associations because this area was the adopted heartland of the Romantic poets, notably Wordsworth and Coleridge. The Vale of Grasmere has changed over the years, but many features Wordsworth wrote about are still visible. Wordsworth lived on the town's outskirts for almost 50 years and described the area as "the loveliest spot that man hath ever known."

GETTING HERE AND AROUND

On the main A591 between Ambleside and Keswick, Grasmere is easily reached by car.

ESSENTIALS

VISITOR INFORMATION Grasmere Tourist Information Centre. ⊠ *Church Stile* ☎ *01539/435665* ⊕ *www.nationaltrust. org.uk/allan-bank-and-grasmere.*

◉ Sights

★ Allan Bank

HOUSE | FAMILY | Rope swings on the grounds, picnics in atmospheric old rooms, free tea and coffee, and huge blackboards you can write on: Allan Bank is unlike most other historic houses cared for by the National Trust. On a hill above the lake near Grasmere village, this grand house was once home to poet William Wordsworth as well as to Canon Rawnsley, the founder of the National Trust. Seriously damaged by fire in 2011, it has been partially restored but also left deliberately undecorated. It offers a much less formal experience than other stops on the Wordsworth trail. There are frequent activities for both children and adults: arts and crafts but also music and astronomy. Red squirrels can be seen on the 30-minute woodland walk through the beautiful grounds. ⊠ *Off A591* ☎ *01539/435143* ⊕ *www.nationaltrust. org.uk/allan-bank-and-grasmere* ⊠ *£7.90* ⊘ *Closed Jan.–mid-Feb.*

Dove Cottage and Wordsworth Museum

HOUSE | William Wordsworth lived in Dove Cottage from 1799 to 1808, a prolific and happy time for the poet. During this time he wrote some of his most famous works, including "Ode: Intimations of Immortality" and *The Prelude*. Built in the early 17th century as an inn, this tiny,

Poetry, Prose, and the Lakes 👁

The Lake District's beauty has whetted the creativity of many a famous poet and artist over the centuries. Here's a quick rundown of some of the writers inspired by the area's vistas.

William Wordsworth (1770–1850), one of the first English Romantics, redefined poetry by replacing the mannered style of his predecessors with a more conversational style. Many of his greatest works, such as *The Prelude*, draw directly from his experiences in the Lake District, where he spent much of his life. Wordsworth and his work had an enormous effect on Coleridge, Keats, Shelley, Byron, and countless other writers. Explore his homes in Cockermouth, Rydal, and Grasmere, among other sites.

John Ruskin (1819–1900), writer, art critic, and early conservationist, was an impassioned champion of new ways of seeing. He defended contemporary artists such as William Turner and the Pre-Raphaelites. His five-volume masterwork, *Modern Painters*, changed the role of the art critic from that of approver or naysayer to that of interpreter. Stop by Coniston to see his home and the Ruskin Museum.

Thomas De Quincey (1785–1859) wrote essays whose impressionistic style influenced many 19th-century writers, including Poe and Baudelaire. His most famous work, *Confessions of an English Opium-Eater* (1822), is an imaginative memoir of his young life, which indeed included opium addiction. He settled in Grasmere in 1809.

Beatrix Potter (1866–1943) never had a formal education; instead, she spent her childhood studying nature. Her love of the outdoors, and Lakeland scenery in particular, influenced her delightfully illustrated children's books, including *The Tale of Peter Rabbit* and *The Tale of Jemima Puddle-Duck*. Potter also became a noted conservationist who donated land to the National Trust. Today you can visit Hill Top, the writer-artist's home in Hawkshead.

dim, and, in some places, dank house is beautifully preserved, with an oak-paneled hall and floors of Westmorland slate. It first opened to the public in 1891 and remains as it was when Wordsworth lived here with his sister, Dorothy, and wife, Mary. Bedrooms and living areas contain much of Wordsworth's furniture and many personal belongings. Coleridge was a frequent visitor, as was Thomas De Quincey, best known for his 1822 autobiographical masterpiece *Confessions of an English Opium-Eater*. De Quincey moved in after the Wordsworths left. You visit the house on a timed guided tour, and the ticket includes admission to the spacious, modern **Wordsworth Museum,** which documents the poet's life and the literary contributions of Wordsworth and the Lake Poets. The museum includes space for major art exhibitions. The **Jerwood Centre,** open to researchers by appointment, houses 50,000 letters, first editions, and manuscripts. Afternoon tea is served at a café next to the parking lot. ✉ *A591, south of Grasmere* ☎ *01539/435544* ⊕ *www.wordsworth. org.uk* 🎫 *£8.95* ⊘ *Closed Jan.*

St. Oswald's

RELIGIOUS SITE | William Wordsworth, his wife Mary, his sister Dorothy, and four of his children are buried in the churchyard of this historical church with a curious split interior on the River Rothay. The poet planted eight of the yew trees here, including the one under which he was interred. As you leave the churchyard, stop at the Gingerbread Shop, in a tiny cottage, for a special local treat. ⊠ *Stock La.* ⊕ *www.stoswaldsgrasmere.uk.*

Restaurants

Heidi's

$ | **CAFÉ** | This bustling, cozy little café and deli is lined with jars of locally made jams and chutneys. Bang in the center of Grasmere, it's great for coffee and a homemade pastry or flapjack (bars made with syrup, butter, and oats). **Known for:** locally made products; delicious coffee; cozy breakfast spot. $ *Average main: £10* ⊠ *Red Lion Sq.* ☎ *01539/435248* ⊕ *www. heidisgrasmerelodge.co.uk.*

★ The Jumble Room

$$ | **BRITISH** | A small stone building dating to the 18th century, Grasmere's first shop is now a friendly, fashionable, and colorful restaurant, with children's books, bold animal paintings, and hanging lamps. The food is an eclectic mix of international and traditional British; think porcini mushroom arancini, beetroot and pumpkin ravioli, or Lebanese chicken with clementine and fennel. **Known for:** freshly baked bread; lively atmosphere; imaginative menu. $ *Average main: £16* ⊠ *Langdale Rd.* ☎ *01539/435188* ⊕ *www.thejumbleroom.co.uk* ⊗ *No lunch, closed Mon. and Tues.*

Tweedies Bar & Lodge

$$ | **MODERN BRITISH** | One of the region's best gastro-pubs, Tweedies attracts many locals as well as visitors. Delicious updated British classics include beer-battered Fleetwood haddock, braised ox cheek with lardons, and an 8-ounce burger with roasted shallots. **Known for:** live music; classic British menu including great burgers; awesome local ales. $ *Average main: £16* ⊠ *Langdale Rd.* ☎ *01539/435300* ⊕ *www.tweediesgrasmere.com.*

🛏 Hotels

Banerigg House

$ | **B&B/INN** | A cozy family home less than a mile south of the village, Banerigg House has unfussy, well-appointed rooms, most with lake views. **Pros:** welcoming hosts; good value for single rooms; canoes available. **Cons:** a little out of town; the house has an awkward turn onto the busy road; rooms are quite dated. $ *Rooms from: £99* ⊠ *Lake Rd.* ☎ *01539/435204* ⊕ *www.banerigg.co.uk* ⇥ *6 rooms* ⏐○⏐ *Free breakfast.*

★ Heidi's Grasmere Lodge

$ | **B&B/INN** | Small but sumptuous, this lodging has a distinctly feminine sensibility, with floral wallpaper, curly steel lamps, and painted woodwork. **Pros:** chic bathrooms with whirlpool tubs; warm welcome; some rooms have mountain views. **Cons:** no children allowed; so pristine you may worry about your muddy boots; rooms vary in size. $ *Rooms from: £99* ⊠ *Red Lion Sq.* ☎ *01539/435248* ⊕ *www.heidisgrasmerelodge.co.uk* ⇥ *6 rooms* ⏐○⏐ *Free breakfast.*

Moss Grove Organic

$ | **B&B/INN** | A Victorian building in the heart of Grasmere, the chic and spacious Moss Grove Organic puts an emphasis on its environmental credentials. **Pros:** roaring fire in the evenings; homemade marmalade at breakfast; modern design with a conscience. **Cons:** tight parking; not the place for a big fry-up breakfast; service can be slow. $ *Rooms from: £124* ⊠ *Red Lion Sq.* ☎ *01539/435251* ⊕ *www.mossgrove.com* ⇥ *11 rooms* ⏐○⏐ *Free breakfast.*

Raise View

$$ | B&B/INN | Out of the center of Grasmere toward Dunmail Raise (hence the name), Raise View has some of Grasmere's more stylish rooms and a reputation for hospitality. **Pros:** high-quality, homey accommodation; gorgeous views; generous breakfast. **Cons:** on the edge of town; books up quickly; limited parking. ⑤ *Rooms from: £126* ✉ *White Bridge* ☎ *01539/435215* ⊕ *www.raiseview.uk* ⇨ *5 rooms* ⑩ *Free breakfast.*

⊖ Shopping

★ Grasmere Gingerbread Shop

FOOD/CANDY | The smells wafting across the churchyard draw many people to the Grasmere Gingerbread Shop. Since 1854, Sarah Nelson's gingerbread has been sold from this cramped 17th-century cottage, which was once the village school. The delicious treats, still made from a secret recipe, are sold by costumed ladies and packed into attractive tins for the journey home or to eat right away. ✉ *Church Cottage* ☎ *01539/435428* ⊕ *www.grasmeregingerbread.co.uk.*

⊛ Activities

Loughrigg Terrace

HIKING/WALKING | The most panoramic views of lake and village are from the south of Grasmere, from the bare slopes of Loughrigg Terrace, reached along a well-signposted track on the western side of the lake or through the woods from parking lots on the A591 between Grasmere and Rydal Water. It's less than an hour's walk from the village, though your stroll can be extended by continuing around Rydal Water, passing Rydal Mount, detouring onto White Moss Common before returning to Dove Cottage and Grasmere, a 4-mile (three-hour) walk in total. ✉ *Grasmere.*

Elterwater and the Langdales

2½ miles south of Grasmere, 4 miles west of Ambleside.

The delightful village of Elterwater, at the eastern end of the Great Langdale Valley on B5343, is a good stop for hikers. It's barely more than a cluster of houses around a village green, but from here you can choose from a selection of excellent circular walks. Great Langdale winds up past hills known as the Langdale Pikes towards Great End and England's highest hill, Scafell Pike. To the south, Little Langdale is another of Cumbria's most beautiful valleys with walks aplenty. At its head, the high passes of Wrynose and Hardknott lead west across wild fells to Eskdale and one of the most beautiful and remote lakes, Wast Water. Beyond that, at Ravenglass, the national park reaches all the way to the Cumbrian coast. Between the two Langdales are plenty more great walking opportunities over fells and past far-flung beauty spots such as Blea Tarn.

⑪ Restaurants

Britannia Inn

$ | BRITISH | At this 500-year-old pub, restaurant, and inn in the heart of superb walking country, antiques, comfortable chairs, and prints and oil paintings furnish the cozy, beamed public rooms. The hearty traditional British food—from grilled haggis with homemade plum jam to pan-seared sea bass and wild-mushroom stroganoff—is popular with locals, as are the many whiskies and ales, including a specially brewed Britannia Gold beer. **Known for:** specialty beers; traditional oak-beamed interior; annual beer festival in November. ⑤ *Average main: £14* ✉ *B5343* ☎ *01539/437210* ⊕ *www.thebritanniainn.com.*

Continued on page 594

HIKING IN THE LAKE DISTRICT

From easy strolls around lakes to mountain climbs, the Lake District has some of England's best hiking. The landscape is generally accessible but also spectacular, with crashing streams cascading from towering mountains into the rivers and lakes that define the region. The scenery that inspired Wordsworth and Ruskin, among many others, is best experienced on an exhilarating walk.

With its highest mountain topping out at just 3,209 feet, the Lake District has peaks that are sometimes sniffed at by hardcore hikers, but they provide a stunning and not always benevolent setting. In winter the peaks are often ice- and snow-bound, and even routes at lower levels can occasionally be impassable.

There is plenty of variety to suit all abilities and enthusiasms, and almost everywhere you go in the national park you'll come across wooden footpath signs pointing the way over stiles and across fields. Paths are usually well maintained and, especially in summer, the most popular trails can be busy with booted walking hordes. Many people don't venture far from their cars, however, and peace and solitude are usually only a hillside or two away.

Many lakes and tarns (small mountain lakes) have paths that skirt their edges, though to see the best of the region you should head upward into the fells (mountains) and valleys, where the landscape becomes increasingly grand. Some of the best routes combine a boat ride with a walk up a fellside. When your walk is over, be sure to reward yourself with a pint at the pub.

Above: View of Troutbeck Park, a farm near Troutbeck that writer Beatrix Potter left to the National Trust

CHOOSE YOUR BEST DAY HIKE

Trails are abundant in the Lake District: you can walk just about anywhere, but a little planning will be rewarded. It's worthwhile to buy a good Ordnance Survey map, too. The routes included here, from 90 minutes to 5 hours, all show the national park at its best, from the southern lakes to the wilder, bleaker northern lakes. A couple of the trails are fairly popular, well-trodden routes; others take you off the most beaten paths. Several include a boat trip for extra enjoyment—just don't miss the last boat home.

Newlands Valley from Catbells

CATBELLS

Medium; 3.6 miles walking, plus boat ride to and from Keswick; 1 hour, 30 minutes walking
Starting point: Hawes End

This classic, popular Lakes route climbs the long, fairly gently sloping hill of Catbells, above Derwentwater. You'll need to catch the ferry from Keswick to the beginning of the route at Hawes End.

From the ferry landing stage, climb straight uphill before heading right (south) along the spine of the hill to the summit. From Catbells, the views over Derwenwater and beyond to the high fells of Skiddaw and Blencathra are breathtaking. Take the lower path, nearer the lake, on the return in order to make this a circular route. The route can be shortened by catching a

Borrowdale

On Pillar mountain, western Lake District

boat back from High Brandelhow or Low Brandelhow (other landing stages) instead of Hawes End.

STONETHWAITE UP LANGSTRATH BECK

Easy; 6 miles; 2 hours, 30 minutes
Starting point: Stonethwaite

In the high valleys in the middle of the Lake District, rivers become streams and wind through a wonderfully wild, largely treeless landscape away from the lakes themselves. Running south from Derwentwater, Borrowdale is one of the most beautiful valleys around, but for even more spectacular walking country continue to the hamlet of Stonethwaite, from where the road becomes a track and then a path as it leads up beside the beck, the valley opening out into moorland. At the bottom of the valley, the climb is a fairly gentle one. About 3 miles upstream,

cross a bridge and return on the other side of the stream. The Langstrath Inn makes a good food and drink spot at the end of the walk.

TROUTBECK TO THORNTHWAITE CRAG

Difficult; 9.8 miles; 4–5 hours
Starting point: Troutbeck

Windermere is more known for its boating, but you can find great mountain routes. Starting in the village of Troutbeck, 3 miles north of Windermere, this walk drops down into the valley, following the stream of Hagg Gill and climbing around a hill known as the Troutbeck Tongue. The trail then rises onto the ridge of Thornthwaite Crag, from where there are vertiginous views. Parts of this upper section are steep. For the return to Troutbeck, head west into the valley of the Trout Beck (stream) itself. Back in the village of Troutbeck, the Queen's Head Hotel is a great pub for food and drink.

Red deer

Looking away from Martindale, toward Ullswater.

KENTMERE TO LONG SLEDDALE

Medium; 4.5 miles; 2 hours, 30 minutes
Starting point: Kentmere

Easily accessible from popular centers in the south of the region such as Windermere or Kendal, Kentmere and Long Sleddale are nevertheless in a part of the national park that many visitors bypass in their haste to get to the lakes—and that's a shame. These two valleys are beautiful examples of rural Cumbria, and the easy climb from one to another has some great views.

For a circular route, head south along the road from the village of Kentmere before heading left up the hill and across high moorland and down into the grand valley of Long Sleddale. The trail is a pleasant loop.

LAKELAND LINGO

If someone tells you to walk along the "beck" to the "force" and then climb the "fell" to the "tarn," you've just been told to hike along the stream or river (beck) to the waterfall (force) before climbing the hill or mountain (fell) to reach a small mountain lake (tarn).

You should also keep in mind that town or place names in the Lake District can be the same as the name of the lake on which the town stands. For example, Windermere is both the town and the lake itself—a "mere" is a lake in Old English.

HOWTOWN TO MARTINDALE

Medium; 7.6 miles plus optional boat ride from Pooley Bridge; 3 hours, 30 minutes plus 25-minute boat ride
Starting point: Howtown

To get to Howtown, you can drive the long, narrow road down the eastern side of Ullswater; but to arrive at this spot in style, catch an antique Ullswater Steamer from Pooley Bridge at the lake's northern end.

Martindale is a magically hidden valley, enclosed on all sides by large fells. Climbing the steep switchback road up the bare hillside of Hallin Fell to the pass from the hamlet of Howtown, there is nothing to suggest the beautifully pastoral landscape beyond. Sheep graze at lower levels; higher up the steep sides of the valley are wild and rocky.

To turn this into a circular route, turn left at the top of the valley and return along the ridge of Beda Fell. In Howtown, the eponymous hotel serves food and drink and will make you a take-out lunch.

AROUND GRASMERE

Easy; 3.4 miles (can easily be extended to go around Rydal Water); 1 hour, 30 minutes
Starting point: Grasmere village

Rich with literary and artistic traditions, Grasmere is a bijou little lake easily walked around in an afternoon.

Starting in the village, where there is parking, head counter-clockwise around the lake, skirting the lower edge of Loughrigg Terrace. At the southeastern end of the lake, follow the stream through woods that link Grasmere to Rydal Water. If you want something a little longer, the walk can be extended around Rydal before you cross the A591 and return to Grasmere across White Moss Common.

In Grasmere, Tweedies Bar is a good place for a post-stroll pint.

Snow in the Lake District

View of the Langdale Fells

OLD MAN OF CONISTON

Difficult; 4.6 miles; 2 hours, 30 minutes to 3 hours
Starting point: Coniston village

Of all the area's classic peaks, the Old Man of Coniston is one of the most accessible. Though it's a fairly steep route that can be difficult in winter, the paths are well-trodden and well-maintained and it doesn't require any climbing to reach the summit, 2,634 feet up. From the top on a clear day, there are extraordinary views down to Coniston Water and around and beyond the Furness Fells.

Set off from the center of the village of Coniston, where the Black Bull Inn offers good hearty food and some excellent ales. Multiple paths to the summit make it easy to turn the walk into a circular route.

PREPARING FOR YOUR HIKE

CHOOSING A HIKE

A glance at a map of the Lake District National Park reveals a lacework mesh of footpaths; stop your car at random on a country road and there will probably be a path somewhere nearby. In the Lake District meticulous planning is not necessarily required in order to go for a walk: possibilities for short strolls abound.

The walks suggested offer good options; for other choices and for maps, stop in any town visitor information office or at the Lake District National Park Visitor Centre at Brockhole. There are trails from this visitor center. You can also join a guided hike. *(For more information on these offices, see the towns in this chapter and the Lake District Planner.)*

WHAT TO WEAR

Check the weather, but expect the unexpected. Good clothing, and clothing for rain, is essential: even at the height of summer, wet weather can roll in from the west and spoil a sunny day. Higher up, too, temperatures are noticeably colder than at lake level, and it's usually much breezier. Generally a good pair of walking boots will suffice, and for lakeside walks you'd probably get by with flat-soled shoes. For the highest routes, snow and ice in winter can linger until spring and a set of slip-on spikes can be useful. The national park is overflowing with shops selling walking clothes, maps, and equipment.

WHAT TO BRING

Carry plenty of water and lightweight, high-energy food—or whatever you want for a picnic. Kendal mint cake is a favorite snack. Don't forget sunscreen and insect repellent. Bring a map: Ordnance Survey maps, available in area bookstores and visitor centers, are the best.

Sticklebarn

$ | **BRITISH** | The National Trust owns other pubs, but Sticklebarn is the first one it has run. With its own water supply and hydroelectric power, the pub's aim is sustainability; the kitchen uses as much produce as possible from the immediate area and makes its own gin and vodka. **Known for:** real ales on tap; family friendly; wood-fired pizzas and other standard pub fare. ⑤ *Average main: £13* ✉ *Great Langdale* ☎ *01539/437356* ⊕ *www.nationaltrust. org.uk/sticklebarn-and-the-langdales.*

🛏 Hotels

Old Dungeon Ghyll Hotel

$ | **HOTEL** | There's no more comforting stop after a day outdoors than the Hiker's Bar of this 300-year-old hotel at the head of the Great Langdale Valley. **Pros:** ideally situated for walking; wonderfully isolated; spectacular views all around. **Cons:** no-nonsense approach not to everyone's taste; busy in summer; remote location. ⑤ *Rooms from: £116* ✉ *Off B5343, Great Langdale* ☎ *01539/437272* ⊕ *www.odg.co.uk* ⇱ *12 rooms* ⦿ *Some meals.*

🏃 Activities

There are access points to Langdale Fell from several spots along B5343, the main road; look for information boards at local parking places. You can also stroll up the river valley or embark on more energetic hikes to Stickle Tarn or to one of the summits of the Langdale Pikes. Beyond the Old Dungeon Ghyll Hotel, the Great Langdale Valley splits in two around a hill known as the Band—a path up its spine has particularly good views back down over the valley and can be continued to the summit of Scafell Pike.

Coniston

5 miles south of Elterwater.

This small lake resort and boating center attracts climbers to the steep peak of the **Old Man of Coniston** (2,635 feet), which towers above the slate-roof houses. It also has sites related to John Ruskin. Quieter than Windermere, Coniston is a good introduction to the pastoral and watery charms of the area, though the small town itself can get crowded in summer.

GETTING HERE AND AROUND

The Coniston Launch connects Coniston Pier with Ruskin's home at Brantwood and some other stops around the lake, offering hourly service (£11.25 for a daylong, hop-on, hop-off ticket; £18.25 including entry to Brantwood) on its wooden Ruskin and Ransome launches.

ESSENTIALS

VISITOR INFORMATION Coniston Launch. ☎ *01768/775753* ⊕ *www.conistonlaunch. co.uk.* **Coniston Tourist Information Centre.** ✉ *Ruskin Ave.* ☎ *01539/441533.*

👁 Sights

★ Brantwood

HOUSE | On the eastern shore of Coniston Water, Brantwood was the cherished home of John Ruskin (1819–1900), the noted Victorian artist, writer, critic, and social reformer, after 1872. The rambling 18th-century house (with Victorian alterations) is on a 250-acre estate that stretches high above the lake. Here, alongside mementos such as his mahogany desk, are Ruskin's own paintings, drawings, and books. On display is art that this great connoisseur collected, and in cerebral corners such as the Ideas Room visitors are encouraged to think about meaning and change. Ruskin's Rocks explores his fascinations with stones and music with a brilliant bit of modern technology. A video on Ruskin's life shows the lasting influence of his thoughts, and the Severn Studio has rotating art exhibitions. Ruskin himself laid out the extensive grounds. Take time to explore the gardens and woodland walks, which include some multilayered features: Ziggy Zaggy, for example, originally a garden built by Ruskin to reflect Dante's Purgatorial Mount, is now an allegory of the seven deadly sins. Brantwood hosts a series of classical concerts on some Saturdays, as well as talks, guided walks, and study days. ✉ Off B5285 ☎ 01539/441396 ⊕ www. brantwood.org.uk ✍ £8.70; gardens only £6.20 ⊙ Closed Mon. and Tues. in Nov.–mid-Mar.

Coniston Boating Centre
TRANSPORTATION SITE (AIRPORT/BUS/FERRY/ TRAIN) | The National Trust's restored Victorian steam yacht and the slightly more utilitarian Coniston Launch both leave from the town's spruced-up waterside satellite, a 15-minute stroll from the center. There's a parking lot, a smart café, and various boat- and bike-hire options, too. Originally launched in 1859 and restored in the 1970s, the Steam Yacht (⊕ www.nationaltrust.org.uk/gondola) runs between Coniston Pier, Brantwood, and Park-a-Moor at the south end of Coniston Water daily from late March through October (half-lake cruise £11; 10% discount for National Trust members). The Coniston Launch (⊕ www. conistonlaunch.co.uk) runs similar routes and is marginally cheaper, though also a little less romantic. Both will get you across the lake to Brantwood, and a stop at Monk Coniston jetty, at the lake's northern tip, connects to the footpaths through the Monk Coniston Estate and the beauty spot of Tarn Hows. ✉ Coniston Pier ☎ 01539/441366 ⊕ www.conistonboatingcentre.co.uk.

Coniston Water
BODY OF WATER | The lake came to prominence in the 1930s when Arthur Ransome made it the setting for *Swallows and Amazons,* one of a series of novels about a group of children and their adventures. The lake is about 5 miles long, a tempting stretch that drew Donald Campbell here in 1959 to set a water-speed record of 260 mph. He was killed when trying to beat it in 1967. His body and the wreckage of *Bluebird K7* were retrieved from the lake in 2001. Campbell is buried in St. Andrew's church in Coniston, and a stone memorial on the village green commemorates him. ✉ Coniston.

Monk Coniston Estate
BODY OF WATER | Two miles north of Coniston on the A593, just past Beatrix Potter's beautifully situated Yew Tree Farm, is a small National Trust parking lot from where paths lead up through oak woods beside the tumbling stream of Tom Gill to Tarn Hows, a celebrated Lake District beauty spot, albeit a man-made one, created when the gill was dammed in the mid-19th century. The paths are steep in places, but two waterfalls make it well worth the effort. ✉ Coniston.

Ruskin Museum
MUSEUM | This repository of fascinating and thought-provoking manuscripts, personal items, and watercolors by John Ruskin illuminates his thinking and influence. There is also a focus on speedboat racer Donald Campbell; his *Bluebird K7,* dragged up from Coniston Water, will eventually rest here once it has been painstakingly put back together. Good local-interest exhibits include copper mining, geology, lace, and more. Upstairs, the Dawson Gallery occasionally hosts high-profile artists. ✉ Yewdale Rd. ☎ 01539/441164 ⊕ www.ruskinmuseum.com ✍ £6.50 ⊙ Closed Mon. in mid-Nov.–mid-Mar.

🍴 Restaurants

Black Bull Inn

$ | **BRITISH** | Attached to the Coniston Brewing Company, whose ales are on tap here, the Black Bull is an old-fashioned pub in the heart of the village. It can feel a little dated, but it's a good pick for simple, hearty food such as fried whitebait, homemade leek-and-potato soup, and a tasty steak-and-ale pie. **Known for:** locally sourced ingredients; large range of real ales; old-fashioned decor. $ *Average main: £13* ☒ *Coppermines Rd.* ☎ *01539/441335* ⊕ *www.blackbullconiston.co.uk.*

🛏 Hotels

★ Bank Ground Farm

$$ | **HOTEL** | Used by Arthur Ransome as the setting for *Swallows and Amazons,* 15th-century Bank Ground is beautifully situated on the eastern shore of Coniston Water, opposite the village of Coniston on the western shore. **Pros:** stunning lake views; homey atmosphere; traditional welcome. **Cons:** a fair walk from the village; some rooms are cramped; low ceilings in the cottage. $ *Rooms from: £150* ☒ *Off B5285* ☎ *01539/441264* ⊕ *www.bankground.com* ⊙ *Guesthouse closed Nov.–Easter* ↵ *6 rooms, 4 cottages* ⦿ *Free breakfast.*

Lakeland House

$ | **B&B/INN** | In the middle of Coniston, Lakeland House has smart, modern rooms with bold wallpaper, beamed ceilings, and slate-floored bathrooms. **Pros:** café downstairs; good value; open fire for cozy evenings. **Cons:** not as homey as a traditional B&B; on a main road; attic rooms have low ceilings. $ *Rooms from: £80* ☒ *Tilberthwaite Ave., Keswick* ☎ *01539/441303* ⊕ *www.lakelandhouse.co.uk* ↵ *12 rooms* ⦿ *Free breakfast.*

🛍 Shopping

Heritage Meats

FOOD/CANDY | Once owned by Beatrix Potter, Yew Tree Farm is nestled in some especially attractive hills. The owners have a conservation-based approach to farming and sell great free-range meat. If you're staying nearby in a self-catering cottage, ring ahead to arrange to pick up some Herdwick chops or wild Lakeland game. ☒ *A593* ☎ *01539/441433* ⊕ *www.heritagemeats.co.uk.*

🏃 Activities

HIKING

Steep tracks lead up from the village to the **Old Man of Coniston.** The trail starts near the Sun Hotel on Brow Hill and goes past an old copper mine to the peak, which you can reach in about two hours. It's one of the Lake District's most satisfying hikes—not too arduous, but high enough to feel a sense of accomplishment and get fantastic views (west to the sea, south to Morecambe Bay, and east to Windermere). Experienced hikers include the peak in a seven-hour circular walk from the village, also taking in the heights and ridges of Swirl How and Wetherlam.

Hawkshead

3 miles east of Coniston.

In the Vale of Esthwaite, this small market town is a pleasing hodgepodge of tiny squares, cobbled lanes, and whitewashed houses. There's a good deal more history here than in most local villages, however. The Hawkshead Courthouse, just outside town, was built by the monks of Furness Abbey in the 15th century. Hawkshead later derived much wealth from the wool trade, which flourished here in the 17th and 18th centuries.

Children's writer Beatrix Potter used details from her house at Hill Top, near Hawkshead, in the illustrations for her stories.

As a thriving market center, Hawkshead could afford to maintain the **Hawkshead Grammar School,** at which William Wordsworth was a pupil from 1779 to 1787; he carved his name on a desk inside, now on display. In the village, Ann Tyson's House claims the honor of having provided the young William with lodgings. The twin draws of Wordsworth and Beatrix Potter—apart from her home, Hill Top, there's a Potter gallery—conspire to make Hawkshead crowded year-round.

GETTING HERE AND AROUND

Hawkshead is east of Coniston on B5285 and south of Ambleside via B5286. An alternative route is to cross Windermere via the car ferry from Ferry Nab, south of Bowness. Local buses link the village to others nearby.

ESSENTIALS

VISITOR INFORMATION Hawkshead Tourist Information Centre. ⊠ *Main St.* ☎ *01539/436946* ⊕ *www.hawksheadtouristinfo.org.uk.*

◉ Sights

★ Beatrix Potter Gallery

MUSEUM | FAMILY | In the 17th-century solicitor's offices formerly used by Potter's husband, the Beatrix Potter Gallery displays a selection of the artist-writer's original illustrations, watercolors, and drawings. There's also information about her interest in conservation and her early support of the National Trust. The house looks almost as it would have in her day, though with touch screens in wooden frames and a children's play area upstairs. Admission is by timed ticket when the place gets busy. ⊠ *Main St.* ☎ *01539/436355* ⊕ *www.nationaltrust.org.uk/beatrix-potter-gallery-and-hawkshead* ⊠ *£8* ⊗ *Closed Jan.–mid Feb.*

★ Hill Top

HOUSE | Children's author and illustrator Beatrix Potter (1866–1943), most famous for her *Peter Rabbit* stories, called this place home. The house looks much the same as when Potter bequeathed it to the National Trust, and fans will

What's Real About Real Ale?

The English can be passionate about their drink, as the growing interest in real ale shows. It differs from other beers by the use of natural ingredients and the fact that it's matured by fermentation in the barrel from which the ale is served. The process doesn't use carbon dioxide, so pure taste wins out over fizz.

The **Directory of U.K. Real Ale Breweries** (⊕ *www.quaffale.org.uk*) lists 35 operating real-ale breweries in Cumbria, of which the Coniston Brewing Company, Barngates Brewery (at the Drunken Duck Inn), and Hawkshead (in Staveley, between Kendal and Windermere) are three of the best. Most real ales are caramel in color and hoppy, malty, and slightly bitter to taste. A pint of ale is the usual quantity to be consumed, though a half is acceptable; you can also find it in bottles.

Most pubs in the Lake District offer some sort of local brew—the better ones take enormous pride in their careful tending of the beer, from barrel to glass. Interested in the subject, or just in the taste? Check out the website of the **Campaign for Real Ale** (⊕ *www.camra.org.uk*).

recognize details such as the porch and garden gate, old kitchen range, Victorian dollhouse, and four-poster bed, which were depicted in the book illustrations. ■ **TIP→ Admission to this often-crowded spot is by timed ticket; book in advance and avoid summer weekends and school vacations.** Hill Top lies 2 miles south of Hawkshead by car or foot, though you can also approach via the car ferry from Bowness-on-Windermere. ⊠ *Off B5285, Near Sawrey* ☎ *01539/436269* ⊕ *www.nationaltrust. org.uk/hill-top* 🎫 *£12.60* ☉ *Closed mid-Feb. and weekdays in Nov.–Dec.*

🍴 Restaurants

★ Tower Bank Arms

$ | BRITISH | With a porch that appears in a Beatrix Potter story and a location just a rabbit's hop from the author's home, you might expect this pub to be something of a tourist trap, but luckily it's anything but. The meals are tasty and copious, making use of local ingredients. **Known for:** literary influences; standard pub fare; some of the area's best ales. $ *Average main: £12* ⊠ *Off B5285, Near Sawrey* ☎ *01539/436334* ⊕ *www.towerbankarms. co.uk* ☉ *Closed Mon. in winter.*

🛏 Hotels

★ Drunken Duck Inn

$$ | HOTEL | After four centuries, this friendly old coaching inn remains an outstanding place for both food and lodging. **Pros:** superchic rural style; excellent dining and drinking; exceptionally friendly staff. **Cons:** chic interior at odds with the rustic setting; can feel isolated; standard rooms are small. $ *Rooms from: £125* ⊠ *Off B5286, Ambleside* ☎ *01539/436347* ⊕ *www.drunkenduck-inn.co.uk* 🛏 *16 rooms* ⊙ *Free breakfast.*

Randy Pike

$$ | B&B/INN | Built in the 19th century as the shooting lodge for Wray Castle, Randy Pike is filled with stylish, imaginative, and playful touches. **Pros:** plenty of space; good food; big garden. **Cons:** a little out of the way; pricey rates; two-night minimum on weekends. $ *Rooms from: £200* ⊠ *Off B5286, between Outgate and Clappersgate* ☎ *01539/436088* ⊕ *www.randypike. co.uk* 🛏 *3 rooms* ⊙ *Free breakfast.*

★ Yewfield Vegetarian Guesthouse

$ | B&B/INN | With the laid-back friendliness of a B&B and the sophisticated style of a country house, Yewfield is a very good value—especially if you can score one of the rooms at the front of the house with a great view across the valley. **Pros:** good location to begin walks; pretty garden; apartments are great for weeklong stays. **Cons:** not good for families with young kids; remote; closed in winter. ⓢ *Rooms from: £110* ✉ *Hawkshead Hill* ☎ *01539/436765* ⊕ *www.yewfield.co.uk* ⊘ *Closed Dec. and Jan.* ⤢ *19 rooms, 2 apartments* ⦿ *Free breakfast.*

Activities

Grizedale Forest Park

BICYCLING | Stretching southwest from Hawkshead and blanketing the hills between Coniston and Windermere, Grizedale Forest Park has a thick mix of oak, pine, and larch woods crisscrossed with biking and walking paths. Forty permanent outdoor sculptures are scattered beside the trails and more are planned. The **visitor center** has information, maps, a café, and an adventure playground. ✉ *Off B5286* ☎ *0300/067–4495* ⊕ *www.forestryengland.uk/grizedale.*

Grizedale Mountain Bikes

BICYCLING | If you have the urge to explore the trails of the national park, Grizedale Mountain Bikes rents all the right equipment, with bicycles from £35 per day. They also have a workshop staffed by mechanics if you need to service or repair your own bike. ✉ *Grizedale Forest Park Visitor Centre, off B5286* ☎ *01229/860335* ⊕ *www.grizedalemountainbikes.co.uk.*

Cartmel

17 miles south of Hawkshead.

The village of Cartmel is the southern Lakeland area's most attractive, set in a gentler Cumbrian landscape of hills and fields beyond the trees of Grizedale and the southern tip of Windermere. It comes alive when more than 20,000 people descend on Cartmel Racecourse for steeplechasing on holiday weekends in May and August. Dominating the town is the ancient priory, now the village church. Market Square has pubs, bookshops, and the village shop, rightly famed for its delicious sticky toffee pudding. Helped by the L'Enclume restaurant, the town has a large and growing foodie reputation and some excellent gourmet shops, including a great cheese shop.

Sights

Cartmel Priory

ARCHAEOLOGICAL SITE | Founded in 1190, the huge Cartmel Priory survived the dissolution of the monasteries in the 16th century because it was also the village church. Four monks and 10 villagers were hanged, however. The 25 wooden misericords are from 1440 and include a carved depiction of the Green Man, with a face made of leaves. Guided tours take place on Wednesday from April through October at 11 am and 2 pm (£5). ✉ *Priest La.* ☎ *01539/536261* ⊕ *www.cartmelpriory.org.uk* ⊠ *Free; tours £5.*

Holker Hall

HOUSE | The red sandstone towers of Holker Hall rise above elegant English gardens. The Cavendish family still lives in the house, which has a fine cantilevered staircase and a library with more than 3,000 books. Much of the house was rebuilt in Elizabethan style after an 1871 fire. Topiaries, a labyrinth, and an enormous lime tree are the highlights of the 25 acres of gardens. The three-day Holker Festival in early June celebrates the gardens and local culture and food. ⊠ *Off A5278, Cark* ⊹ *2 miles west of Cartmel* ☎ *01539/558328* ⊕ *www.holker. co.uk* ✍ *House and gardens £13; gardens only £9* ⊘ *Closed Mon. and Tues. and Nov.–mid-Mar.*

🍴 Restaurants

★ L'Enclume

$$$$ | MODERN BRITISH | The village of Cartmel has earned a place on England's culinary map with this ambitious restaurant with rooms. Chef Simon Rogan's innovative food incorporates long-forgotten herbs and cutting-edge techinques. **Known for:** fresh seasonal ingredients; carefully chosen wine pairings; decadent tasting menus. ⑤ *Average main: £159* ⊠ *Cavendish St.* ☎ *01539/536362* ⊕ *www.lenclume. co.uk* ⊘ *Closed Mon.*

🛍 Shopping

Cartmel Cheeses

FOOD/CANDY | A huge range of delicious cheeses, mostly British, can be purchased in this welcoming, pungent little shop. Free tastings are often available, and you can also find their stall at the Saturday market in Keswick. ⊠ *1 Unsworth Yard* ☎ *01539/534307* ⊕ *www.cartmelcheeses.co.uk.*

Cartmel Village Shop

FOOD/CANDY | This fabulous delicatessen, famous for its deliciously rich sticky toffee pudding, is also a great place to purchase picnic provisions. ⊠ *The Square* ☎ *01539/536280* ⊕ *www.cartmelvillageshop.co.uk.*

Penrith

30 miles north of Kendal.

The red-sandstone town of Penrith was the capital of old Cumbria, part of the Scottish kingdom of Strathclyde in the 9th and 10th centuries. It was rather neglected after the Normans arrived, and the Scots sacked it on several occasions. Penrith has been a thriving market town for centuries; the market still takes place on Tuesday, and it continues to be known for good shopping.

The tourist information center, in the Penrith Museum, has information about the historic town trail, which takes you through narrow byways to the plague stone on King Street, where food was left for the stricken, to St. Andrew's churchyard and its 1,000-year-old "hog back" tombstones (stones carved as stylized "houses of the dead"), and finally to the ruins of Penrith Castle.

GETTING HERE AND AROUND

Penrith is just off the M6, 30 miles north of Kendal and 100 miles north of Manchester. Both the M6 and the alternative A6 cross the Pennines spectacularly at Shap Fells. From Windermere you can reach Penrith by going over the Kirkstone Pass to Ullswater. There are some direct trains from Euston Station in London to Penrith; sometimes it's necessary to change.

ESSENTIALS

VISITOR INFORMATION Penrith Tourist Information Centre. ⊠ *Penrith Museum, Middlegate* ☎ *01768/867466* ⊕ *www. visiteden.co.uk.*

⊙ Sights

Dalemain

HOUSE | Home of the Hasell family since 1679, Dalemain began with a 12th-century peel tower, built to protect the occupants from raiding Scots, and is now a delightful hodgepodge of architectural styles. An imposing Georgian facade of local pink sandstone encompasses a medieval hall and extensions from the 16th through the 18th century. Inside are a magnificent oak staircase, furniture dating from the mid-17th century, a Chinese drawing room, a 16th-century room with intricate plasterwork, and many fine paintings, including masterpieces by Van Dyck. The gardens are worth a look, too, and deer roam the estate. At the end of winter, the house hosts the World Marmalade Awards and Festival. Dalemain is 3 miles southwest of Penrith. ✉ A592 ☎ 017684/86450 ⊕ www.dalemain.com ✉ £12.50; gardens only £9.50 ⊗ Closed Dec.–Jan. and Fri. and Sat. rest of year; Mansion closed Dec.–Mar.

★ Little Salkeld Watermill

FACTORY | This fully functioning stone-ground flour mill is well worth a visit for its delicious baked goods and for a tour of the fascinating workings of the mill itself. There's been a mill here since the 13th century, and the current structure was built in 1760. Tours are officially self-guided (take an information sheet), but the miller will probably take a break to show you around. Just up the road is the Bronze Age stone circle of Long Meg and her Daughters. According to folklore, the 51 stones (27 of which are still upright) were a coven of witches turned to stone by a Scottish wizard. ✉ Off A66, 6 miles northeast of Penrith, Little Salkeld ☎ 01768/881523 ⊕ www.organicmill.co.uk ✉ £2 ⊗ Closed Tues., Wed., and Jan.

Lowther Castle

CASTLE/PALACE | **FAMILY** | On 130 acres of parkland and gardens, the 1806 Lowther Castle fell into disrepair during the second half of the 20th century. Once used as a chicken farm, this fairy-tale structure is currently being carefully restored. Its romantic ruined turrets can be seen from all over the grounds, which are carpeted with wildflowers, dotted with living willow sculptures, and filled with tree swings and other play areas for the kids. The gallery has ornate Italian plaster decoration, and the café is a fine spot for afternoon tea and cake. Walks in the grounds are glorious on a sunny day. ✉ Off A6, Lowther ☎ 01931/712192 ⊕ www.lowthercastle.org ✉ £11.

Penrith Castle

ARCHAEOLOGICAL SITE | The evocative remains of this 15th-century redbrick castle stand high above a steep, now-dry moat. Home of the maligned Richard, Duke of Gloucester (later Richard III), who was responsible for keeping peace along the border, it was one of England's first lines of defense against the Scots. By the Civil War, the castle was in ruins, and the townsfolk used some of the fallen stones to build their houses. The ruins stand in a park, across from the town's train station. ✉ Off Castlegate ☎ 0870/333–1181 ⊕ www.english-heritage.org.uk ✉ Free.

Penrith Museum

MUSEUM | In a 16th-century building that served as a school from 1670 to the 1970s, this museum contains Stone Age axe heads, interesting fossils and minerals, and an informative film about Cumbria's Neolithic history. The Penrith Tourist Information Centre is here, too. ✉ Middlegate ☎ 01768/865105 ⊕ www.eden.gov.uk/museum ✉ Free ⊗ Closed Sun.

Rheged

ARTS VENUE | FAMILY | Named for the Celtic kingdom of Cumbria, Rheged is a modern, grass-covered visitor center with activities for kids and some interesting free exhibits about the history, culture, and other aspects of the Lake District. A gallery hosts rotating art and photography exhibits, and a massive theater shows 3-D and large-format movies. Shops showcase Cumbrian food, drink, and crafts, and three different cafés offer drinks and light meals. Rheged is 2 miles southwest of Penrith and 1 mile west of Junction 40 on the M6. ⊠ *A66* ☎ *01768/868000* ⊕ *www.rheged.com* ⊠ *Free.*

🍴 Restaurants

Four and Twenty

$$ | MODERN BRITISH | High ceilings, shabby-chic chairs, and old-fashioned filament bulbs in jars set the scene for this handsome conversion of what was once a bank: the restaurant's name references the financially themed nursery rhyme. A warm salad of pancetta and Cumbrian chorizo, slow-cooked beef brisket, and twice-baked Cumberland farmhouse cheddar cheese soufflé are just three of the pleasures on the menu. **Known for:** cocktails and whiskies; beautifully presented food; busy nights should be booked in advance. $ *Average main: £19* ⊠ *42 King St.* ☎ *01768/210231* ⊕ *www.fourandtwentypenrith.co.uk.*

★ George and Dragon

$$ | BRITISH | This pub and restaurant makes good use of local produce for tasty traditional dishes, including goat cheese mousse with caramelized fig, home-cured salmon gravlax, and roasted shallot, leek, and chestnut tarte tatin. Sausages come from the Eden Valley, brown trout from the River Lowther, and many of the greens are grown in the restaurant's gardens at Askham Hall. **Known for:** courtyard and garden for summer dining; beautifully restored Georgian interior; fresh produce grown in kitchen garden. $ *Average main: £18* ⊠ *A6, south of Penrith, Clifton* ☎ *01768/865381* ⊕ *www.georgeanddragonclifton.co.uk.*

🛏 Hotels

★ Askham Hall

$$ | B&B/INN | Ancient hub of the Lowther Estate, beautiful Askham Hall's spectacular gardens and fairy-tale rooms are now open to guests. **Pros:** royally stylish; beautiful gardens and surrounding countryside; excellent restaurant. **Cons:** not in the heart of the Lake District; can be busy in high season; full payment required 1 month before stay. $ *Rooms from: £170* ⊠ *Off A6, Askham* ☎ *01931/712350* ⊕ *www.askhamhall. co.uk* ⊠ *18 rooms* ⊠ *Free breakfast.*

Brooklands

$ | B&B/INN | The welcome is friendly, the breakfast is hearty (salmon fish cakes with poached eggs and a full English breakfast are among the options), and the rooms have patterned wallpaper and heavy, luxurious fabrics at this Victorian terraced house. **Pros:** well-looked-after B&B; tasty breakfasts; fancy toiletries. **Cons:** a drive from the spectacular Lakeland scenery; some rooms are very small; bathrooms have showers but no tubs. $ *Rooms from: £90* ⊠ *2 Portland Pl.* ☎ *01768/863395* ⊕ *www.brooklands-guesthouse.com* ⊠ *7 rooms* ⊠ *Free breakfast.*

The George Hotel

$$ | HOTEL | Right on Penrith's lively market square is this attractive redbrick hotel, which dates back more than 300 years. **Pros:** historic building; modern rooms; central location. **Cons:** restaurant underwhelming; parking limited; can be noisy. $ *Rooms from: £155* ⊠ *Devonshire St.* ☎ *01768/862696* ⊕ *www.lakedistricthotels.net/georgehotel* ⊠ *35 rooms* ⊠ *Free breakfast.*

Even in winter, expert climbers will attempt an ascent of Helvellyn along the perilously narrow Striding Edge.

🛍 Shopping

Penrith is a diverting place to shop, with its narrow streets and arcades chockablock with family-run specialty shops. Major shopping areas include Devonshire Arcade, with its brand-name stores; the pedestrian-only Angel Lane and Little Dockray; and Angel Square.

Brunswick Yard

ANTIQUES/COLLECTIBLES | Clocks, hip flasks, doors, tools, kettles, toys, furniture, and all sorts of old treasure can be found in this wonderful antiques shop and salvage yard just up the hill from the town center. ⊠ *Brunswick Rd.* ☎ *07887/867741* ⊕ *www.brunswickyard.com* ⊗ *Closed Sun. and Mon.*

The Hedgehog Bookshop

BOOKS/STATIONERY | This welcoming little bookshop, hidden on a quiet pedestrian street, has a well-chosen selection of children's books on the ground floor and adult books upstairs, as well as a lovely selection of stationery. ⊠ *19 Little Dockray* ☎ *01768/863003* ⊕ *www.thehedgehogbookshop.co.uk* ⊗ *Closed Sun.*

★ **James & John Graham of Penrith Ltd.**

FOOD/CANDY | Artisanal cheese and the best of Cumbria's local produce, including the town's famously good toffee, are available at this mouthwateringly good bakery and deli. The hot steak pie is perhaps the best you'll ever taste. ⊠ *Market Sq.* ☎ *01768/862281* ⊕ *www.jjgraham. co.uk.*

Penrith Farmers' Market

OUTDOOR/FLEA/GREEN MARKETS | The stalls of the outdoor market line Dockray, Corn Market, and Market Square fon the third Tuesday of the month from 9:30 to 2:30 between March and December. They sell fine local produce and original crafts, and many of the award-winning farmers are happy to talk about what they've grown and raised. ⊠ *Penrith* ☎ *01768/212150 Eden District Council (Markets)* ⊕ *www. visiteden.co.uk.*

Ullswater

6 miles southwest of Penrith.

Hemmed in by towering hills, Ullswater, the region's second-largest lake, is one of the least developed, drawing people for its calm waters and good access to the mountain slopes of Helvellyn. The A592 winds along the lake's pastoral western shore, through the adjacent hamlets of Glenridding and Patterdale at the southern end. Lakeside strolls, great views, tea shops, and rowboat rentals provide the full Lakeland experience.

ESSENTIALS

VISITOR INFORMATION Ullswater Tourist Information Centre. ⊠ *Beckside Car Park, off A592, Glenridding* ☎ *017684/82414* ⊕ *www.lakedistrict.gov.uk.*

⊙ Sights

Aira Force

BODY OF WATER | A spectacular 65-foot waterfall pounds under a stone bridge and through a wooded ravine to feed into Ullswater. From the parking lot it's a 10-minute walk to the falls, with more-serious walks on Gowbarrow Fell and to the village of Dockray beyond. A new 1¼-mile footpath allows visitors to leave their cars at Glencoyne Bay, to the south, and walk through a deer park. ■TIP➔ **Bring sturdy shoes, especially in wet or icy weather, when the paths can be treacherous.** Just above Aira Force in the woods of Gowbarrow Park is the spot where, in 1802, William Wordsworth's sister, Dorothy, observed daffodils that, as she wrote, "tossed and reeled and danced and seemed as if they verily laughed with the wind that blew upon them." Two years later, Wordsworth transformed his sister's words into the famous poem "I Wandered Lonely as a Cloud." Two centuries later, national park wardens patrol Gowbarrow Park in season to prevent tourists from picking the few remaining daffodils. ⊠ *A592, near A5091* ⊕ *www. nationaltrust.org.uk/aira-force-and-ullswater* 🅿 *Parking £5 for 2 hrs.*

Helvellyn

MOUNTAIN—SIGHT | West of Ullswater's southern end, the brooding presence of Helvellyn (3,118 feet), one of the Lake District's most formidable mountains and England's third highest, recalls the region's fundamental character. It's an arduous climb to the top, especially via the challenging ridge known as Striding Edge, and the ascent shouldn't be attempted in poor weather or by inexperienced hikers. Signposted paths to the peak run from the road between Glenridding and Patterdale and pass by **Red Tarn,** which is the highest small mountain lake in the region at 2,356 feet. ⊠ *Glenridding.*

★ Ullswater Steamers

TRANSPORTATION SITE (AIRPORT/BUS/FERRY/ TRAIN) | These antique vessels, including a 19th-century steamer that is said to be the oldest working passenger ship in the world, run the length of Ullswater between Glenridding in the south and Pooley Bridge in the north, via Howtown on the eastern shore. It's a pleasant tour, especially if you combine it with a lakeside walk. One-way trips start at £6.50, or you can sail the entire day for £16.80 with the Cruise All Piers Pass. ⊠ *Pier House, off A592, Glenridding* ☎ *017684/82229* ⊕ *www.ullswater-steamers.co.uk.*

🛏 Hotels

Another Place, the Lake

$$ | HOTEL | Dark carved wood, antique tiles, and a stunning location overlooking Ullswater give the Lake plenty of country-house style, and the hotel also manages to be more relaxed than some of its competition. **Pros:** great lake location; quiet; excellent restaurant. **Cons:** isolated from other amenities; closed for part of January; grounds only partially

Festivals and Folk Sports

With everything from rushbearing to Westmorland wrestling to traditional music, the Lake District hosts some of Britain's most unusual country festivals, as well as some excellent but more typical ones.

Major Events

Major festivals include the Keswick Film Festival (February), Words by the Water (a literary festival in Keswick, March), Keswick Jazz Festival (May), Cockermouth and Keswick carnivals (June), Ambleside and Grasmere rushbearing (August), and the Lake District Summer Music (regionwide, in August)—but there are many others. Horse racing comes to Cartmel over May and August holiday weekends.

Special Activities

Rushbearing dates back to medieval times, when rushes covered church floors. Today, processions of flower-bedecked children and adults bring rushes to churches in a number of villages. Folk sports, often the highlights at local festivals, include Cumberland and Westmorland wrestling, in which the opponents must maintain a grip around each other's body. Fell running, a sort of cross-country run where the route goes roughly straight up and down a mountain, is also popular.

A calendar of events is available at tourist information centers or on the Cumbria Tourism website, ⊕ *www. golakes.co.uk.*

handicap accessible. $ *Rooms from: £210* ✉ *Watermillock* ☎ *017684/86442* ⊕ *www.another.place* ➘ *19 rooms* ⊗ *Free breakfast.*

Howtown Hotel

$$ | HOTEL | Near the end of the road on the isolated eastern side of Ullswater, this gloriously quiet family-run hotel is low-key and low-tech. **Pros:** exceptionally quiet; spectacular location; dinner included in price. **Cons:** not for those who must be plugged in; a bit remote; books up fast. $ *Rooms from: £200* ✉ *Howtown Rd., Howtown* ☎ *01768/486514* ⊕ *www. howtown-hotel.co.uk* ➡ *No credit cards* ⊘ *Closed mid-Nov.–late Mar.* ➘ *12 rooms, 4 cottages* ⊗ *Free breakfast.*

Inn on the Lake

$$$ | HOTEL | With some of the best lake views in the Lake District, Inn on the Lake is a large Victorian property right on the edge of Ullswater, with only its own terrace and lawns separating it from the water. **Pros:** right on the lakeshore;

beautiful scenery; plenty of parking. **Cons:** very busy in summer; can be noisy if there's a wedding; decor in the rooms is a bit fussy. $ *Rooms from: £250* ✉ *Ullswater, Glenridding* ☎ *0800/840–1245 reservations, 017684/82444 reception* ⊕ *www.lakedistricthotels.net/innon-thelake* ➘ *47 rooms* ⊗ *Free breakfast.*

Keswick

14 miles west of Ullswater.

The great mountains of Skiddaw and Blencathra brood over the gray slate houses of Keswick (pronounced *kezz*-ick), on the scenic shores of Derwentwater. The town is a natural base for exploring the rounded, heather-clad Skiddaw range to the north, while the hidden valleys of Borrowdale and Buttermere (the latter reached by stunning Honister Pass) take you into the rugged heart of the Lake District. Nearby, five beautiful lakes are set among the three highest mountain ranges in England. The tourist information center here has regional information and is the place to get fishing permits for Derwentwater.

Keswick's narrow, cobbled streets have a grittier charm compared to the refined Victorian elegance of Grasmere or Ambleside. However, it's the best spot in the Lake District to purchase mountaineering gear and outdoor clothing. There are also many hotels, guesthouses, restaurants, and pubs.

GETTING HERE AND AROUND

Keswick is easily reached along A66 from Penrith, though you can get there more scenically via Grasmere in the south. Buses run from the train station in Penrith to Keswick. The town center is pedestrianized.

■ TIP→ Traffic can be horrendous in summer, so consider leaving your car in Keswick. The open-top Borrowdale bus service between Keswick and Seatoller (to the south) runs frequently, and the Honister Rambler minibus is perfect for walkers aiming for the high fells of the central lakes; it makes stops from Keswick to Buttermere. The Keswick Launch service on Derwentwater links to many walks as well as the Borrowdale bus service.

ESSENTIALS

VISITOR INFORMATION Keswick Information Centre. ⊠ *Moot Hall, Market Sq.* ☎ *0845/9010845* ⊕ *www.lakedistrict. gov.uk.*

⊙ Sights

★ Castlerigg Stone Circle

ARCHAEOLOGICAL SITE | A Neolithic monument about 100 feet in diameter, this stone circle was built around 3,000 years ago on a hill overlooking St. John's Vale. The brooding northern peaks of Skiddaw and Blencathra loom to the north, and there are views of Helvellyn to the south. The 38 stones aren't large, but the site

makes them particularly impressive. Wordsworth described them as "a dismal cirque of Druid stones upon a forlorn moor." The site, always open to visitors, is 4 miles east of Keswick. There's usually space for cars to park beside the road that leads along the northern edge of the site: head up Eleventrees off Penrith Road at the eastern edge of Keswick. ⊠ *Off A66* ⊕ *www.english-heritage.org. uk* ☜ *Free.*

Derwent Pencil Museum

MUSEUM | FAMILY | Legend has it that shepherds found graphite on Seathwaite Fell after a storm uprooted trees in the 16th century. The Derwent company still makes pencils here, and the museum contains the world's longest colored pencil (it takes 28 men to lift it), a pencil produced for World War II spies that contains a rolled-up map, and displays about graphite mining. There's a café and plenty of opportunities for kids to draw, so it's a good, family-friendly option on a rainy day. ⊠ *Southey Works, Carding Mill La.* ☎ *01768/773626* ⊕ *www.pencilmuseum. co.uk* ☜ *£4.95.*

Derwentwater

BODY OF WATER | To understand why Derwentwater is considered one of England's finest lakes, take a short walk from Keswick's town center to the lakeshore and past the jetty, and follow the **Friar's Crag** path, about a 15-minute level walk from the center. This pine-tree-fringed peninsula is a favorite vantage point, with its view of the lake, the ring of mountains, and many tiny islands. Ahead, crags line the **Jaws of Borrowdale** and overhang a mountain ravine—a scene that looks as if it emerged from a Romantic painting. ⊠ *Keswick.*

Keswick Launch Company

TOUR—SIGHT | For the best lake views, take a wooden-launch cruise around Derwentwater. Between late March and November, circular cruises set off every half hour in alternate directions from a dock; there's a more limited (roughly

The setting of the Castlerigg Stone Circle, ringed by stunning mountains, makes this Neolithic monument deeply memorable.

hourly) winter timetable. You can also rent a rowboat here in summer. Buy a hop-on, hop-off Around the Lake ticket (£10.50) and take advantage of the seven landing stages around the lake that provide access to hiking trails, such as the two-hour climb up and down Cat Bells, a celebrated lookout point on the western shore of Derwentwater. ■TIP→ **Buy slightly discounted tickets at the Moot Hall information office in the center of town.** ✉ *Lake Rd.* ☎ *017687/72263* ⊕ *www. keswick-launch.co.uk* 🎫 *From £2.35* ⊘ *Closed mid-Dec.–early Feb.*

Moot Hall

INFO CENTER | The handsome 19th-century Moot Hall, with its one-handed clock, has served as both the town hall and the local prison. Now it houses the main **tourist information center** for the region. It's also the place to get fishing permits for Derwentwater and Bassenthwaite. ✉ *Market Pl.* ☎ *017687/72645* ⊕ *www. lakedistrict.gov.uk.*

🍴 Restaurants

★ Fellpack

$ | BRITISH | Created by four friends who have returned home to the Lakes, the menu at Fellpack is designed as a celebration of Cumbria's ingredients and traditional recipes, albeit with a quirky twist. Fellpack has a gallery of incredible landscape images shot by photographer James Appleton, as well as a collection of fell running jerseys from clubs across the United Kingdom. **Known for:** food served in handmade dishes; delicious, hearty cuisine; awesome landscape photography. ⑤ *Average main: £15* ✉ *Lake Rd.* ☎ *01768/771177* ⊕ *www.fellpack. co.uk* ⊘ *No lunch.*

Morrels

$$ | MODERN BRITISH | One of the town's better eateries, Morrels has local art and wooden floors that give a sophisticated edge to the bar and dining area. Modern British fare is the specialty at this mellow place, with dishes like poached pear with feta and walnut salad or roast

halibut with cherry tomatoes and orzo. **Known for:** pretheater dinners; traditional Sunday roast; no children under 5 policy. $ *Average main: £17* ✉ *34 Lake Rd.* ☎ *017687/72666* ⊕ *www.morrels.co.uk/ restaurant* ✹ *Closed Mon. No lunch.*

Square Orange Café Bar

$ | CAFÉ | Young locals and windblown walkers gather in Keswick's liveliest café for excellent coffee or tea, fruit-flavored cordials, and some serious hot chocolate. The music is laid-back; the staff is undeniably cool; the walls are hung with paintings and photos; and there are homemade pizzas, tapas, and pints of local beer for long rainy days or cold winter nights. **Known for:** decadent chocolate orange cake; ethically sourced tea and coffee; live music on Wednesday evening. $ *Average main: £10* ✉ *20 St. John's St.* ☎ *017687/73888* ⊕ *www. thesquareorange.co.uk.*

Hotels

Ferndene

$ | B&B/INN | FAMILY | Exceptionally friendly, this spotless B&B a 10-minute walk from the lake is carefully tended by its kindly owners, who offer plenty of advice on walking and local sights when you want it. **Pros:** family-focused; good value; bicycle storage. **Cons:** lacks style of more expensive lodgings; road busy in summer; limited parking. $ *Rooms from: £90* ✉ *6 St. John's Terr.* ☎ *017687/74612* ⊕ *www.ferndene-keswick.co.uk* ⤙ *6 rooms* ⊙ *Free breakfast.*

Highfield Hotel

$ | HOTEL | Slightly austere on the outside but charming within, this Victorian hotel overlooks the lawns of Hope Park and has accommodations with great character, including rooms in the turret and the former chapel. **Pros:** good service; tasty food; great views. **Cons:** some downstairs bedrooms are small; not in the town center; a few bathrooms need updating. $ *Rooms from: £110* ✉ *The*

Heads ☎ *017687/72508* ⊕ *www.high-fieldkeswick.co.uk* ✹ *Closed Jan.* ⤙ *18 rooms* ⊙ *Free breakfast.*

★ Howe Keld

$ | B&B/INN | In a town that overflows with B&Bs, this comfortable town house stands out because of its contemporary flair and pampering touches. **Pros:** famously filling breakfasts; good ecological practices; one room accessible for people with disabilities. **Cons:** a short distance from the heart of town; backs onto a busy road; some rooms have low ceilings. $ *Rooms from: £120* ✉ *5–7 The Heads* ☎ *017687/72417* ⊕ *www. howekeld.co.uk* ✹ *Closed Jan.* ⤙ *14 rooms* ⊙ *Free breakfast.*

🎭 Performing Arts

Keswick Film Club

FILM | With an excellent festival in February and a program of international and classic films, the Keswick Film Club lights up the beautiful, 100-year-old, redbrick Alhambra Cinema on St. John's Street and the Theatre by the Lake. ✉ *The Alhambra Cinema, St. John's St.* ☎ *017687/72195* ⊕ *www.keswickalhambra.co.uk* 🎟 *£7.50.*

Keswick Jazz Festival

CONCERTS | Held each May, the popular Keswick Jazz Festival consists of four days of music. Reservations are accepted from November. ✉ *Keswick* ☎ *0845/8621460 box office* ⊕ *www. keswickjazzandbluesfestival.co.uk.*

Theatre by the Lake

ARTS CENTERS | In one of Cumbria's most vibrant cultural settings, the company at the Theatre by the Lake presents classic and contemporary productions year-round. The Keswick Music Society season runs from September through January, and the Words by the Water literary festival takes place here in March. ✉ *Lake Rd.* ☎ *017687/74411* ⊕ *www. theatrebythelake.com.*

🛍 Shopping

Keswick has a good choice of book-stores, crafts shops, and wool-clothing stores tucked away in its cobbled streets, as well as excellent outdoor shops. Keswick's market is held Saturday.

George Fisher

SPORTING GOODS | The area's largest and best outdoor equipment store, George Fisher sells sportswear, travel books, and maps. The staff is faultlessly friendly, helpful, and well informed. Daily weather information is posted in the window, and there's a children's play den. ✉ *2 Borrowdale Rd.* ☎ *017687/72178* ⊕ *www. georgefisher.co.uk.*

Needle Sports

SPORTING GOODS | This company stocks all the best equipment for mountaineering and for rock and ice climbing. They also provide information about local climbing and fell running clubs. ✉ *56 Main St.* ☎ *01768/772227* ⊕ *www.needlesports.com.*

Thomasons

FOOD/CANDY | A butcher and delicatessen, Thomasons sells some very good meat pies—just the thing for putting in your pocket before you climb a Lakeland fell. The homemade sausages are fantastic if you're planning a barbecue. ✉ *8–10 Station St.* ☎ *017687/80169* ⊘ *Closed Sun.*

🏃 Activities

BIKING

Keswick Bikes

BICYCLING | This company rents bikes (from £30 per day) and provides information on all the nearby trails. Guided tours can be arranged with advance notice. ✉ *133 Main St.* ☎ *017687/73355* ⊕ *www. keswickbikes.co.uk.*

WATER SPORTS

Derwent Water Marina

WATER SPORTS | Rental boats in all shapes and sizes and instruction in canoeing, sailing, and windsurfing can be had at Derwent Water Marina. Other

---

Detour: Enroute 👁

The most scenic route from Keswick, B5289 south, runs along the eastern edge of Derwentwater, past turnoffs to natural attractions such as Ashness Bridge, the idyllic tarn of Watendlath, the Lodore Falls (best after a good rain), and the precariously balanced Bowder Stone. Farther south is the tiny village of **Grange**, a walking center at the head of Borrowdale, where there's a riverside café.

---

water-related activities include ghyll scrambling—the fine art of walking up or down a steep Lakeland stream. A two-day sailing or windsurfing course costs £230 (⊕ *www.getonthelake. co.uk/tuition-courses*). ✉ *Portinscale* ☎ *017687/72912* ⊕ *www.derwentwater-marina.co.uk.*

Borrowdale

7 miles south of Keswick.

South of Keswick and its lake lies the valley of Borrowdale, whose varied landscape of green valley floor and surrounding crags has long been considered one of the region's most magnificent treasures. **Rosthwaite,** a tranquil farming village, and **Seatoller,** the southernmost settlement, are the two main centers (both are accessible by bus from Keswick), though they're little more than clusters of aged buildings surrounded by glorious countryside.

GETTING HERE AND AROUND

The valley is south of Keswick on B5289. The Borrowdale bus service between Keswick and Seatoller runs frequently.

◉ Sights

★ Borrowdale Fells

MOUNTAIN—SIGHT | These steep fells rise up dramatically behind Seatoller. Get out and walk whenever inspiration strikes. Trails are well signposted, or you can pick up maps and any gear in Keswick. ⊠ *Seatoller*.

Honister Pass and Buttermere

BODY OF WATER | Beyond Seatoller, B5289 turns westward through Honister Pass (1,176 feet) and Buttermere Fell. Boulders line the road, which is one of the most dramatic in the region. The road sweeps down from the pass to the village of Buttermere, sandwiched between its namesake lake and Crummock Water at the foot of high, craggy fells. Beyond the pass, at the edge of Buttermere village, Syke Farm sells fantastic local ice cream, with flavors including marmalade and brown bread. Both Buttermere and Crummock Water have excellent walking options, away from many of the crowds farther east. Newlands Pass is an equally spectacular route back to Keswick via the pastoral Newlands Valley. ⊠ *Seatoller*.

Scafell Pike

MOUNTAIN—SIGHT | England's highest mountain at 3,210 feet, Scafell (pronounced *scar*-fell) Pike is visible from Seatoller. One route up the mountain, for experienced walkers, is from the hamlet of Seathwaite, a mile south of Seatoller. ⊠ *Seatoller*.

🛏 Hotels

★ Hazel Bank Country House

$$ | B&B/INN | Though this stately, carefully restored home retains original elements from its days as a grand Victorian country pile, its welcoming owners have invested in handsome local furniture and stripped away some of the chintz, opening up inspiring views across the pristine lawns to the valley and the central Lakeland peaks beyond. **Pros:** serene location; immaculate gardens; attentive staff. **Cons:** not near many amenities; car required to get here; deposit required for bookings. ⑤ *Rooms from: £160* ⊠ *Off B5289, Rosthwaite* ☎ *017687/77248* ⊕ *www.hazelbankhotel.co.uk* ⟿ *7 rooms* ⦿❘ *Free breakfast.*

Langstrath Country Inn

$$ | HOTEL | FAMILY | In the tranquil hamlet of Stonethwaite, the welcoming Langstrath was originally built as a miner's cottage in the 16th century but has expanded into a spacious inn with chunky wooden tables and logs burning on a slate open fire. **Pros:** great walks right out the door; excellent food and drink selection; wonderfully peaceful. **Cons:** few other places to eat or shop nearby; some rooms are quite small; lounge decor is dated. ⑤ *Rooms from: £125* ⊠ *Off B5289, Seatoller* ☎ *017687/77239* ⊕ *www.thelangstrath.co.uk* ⊗ *Closed Dec.–mid-Feb.* ⟿ *8 rooms* ⦿❘ *Free breakfast.*

Cockermouth

15 miles northwest of Borrowdale, 14 miles northwest of Seatoller.

This small but bustling town, at the confluence of the rivers Derwent and Cocker, has colorful buildings, history, and narrow streets that are a delight to wander. The ruined 13th-century castle is open only on special occasions. Over a weekend in September, the town holds the Taste Cumbria Food Festival.

GETTING HERE AND AROUND

The most straightforward access to the town is along the busy A66 from Penrith. For a more scenic, roundabout route, head over the Whinlatter or Honister passes from Keswick.

ESSENTIALS

VISITOR INFORMATION Cockermouth Tourist Information Centre. ⊠ *Cockermouth Library and Tourist Information, 80 Main St.* ☎ *01900/822634* ⊕ *www.cockermouth.org.uk.*

One of the Lake District's literary landmarks, Wordsworth House near Cockermouth was where poet William Wordsworth was born.

👁 Sights

★ Castlegate House Gallery

MUSEUM | One of the region's best galleries, Castlegate displays and sells outstanding contemporary works, many by Cumbrian artists. There's a wonderful permanent collection, and changing exhibitions focus on paintings, sculpture, glass, ceramics, and jewelry. ✉ *Castlegate* ☎ *01900/822149* ⊕ *www.castlegate-house.co.uk* ⊗ *Closed Tues. and Sun.*

★ Wordsworth House

HOUSE | Cockermouth was the birthplace of William Wordsworth and his sister, Dorothy, whose childhood home was this 18th-century town house, carefully kept as it would have been in their day. There is no sense of dusty preservation here, though, and nothing is roped off; the house achieves a rare sense of natural authenticity, with clutter and period cooking in the kitchen and herbs and vegetables growing outside in the beautiful traditional Georgian garden. A café makes good use of the homegrown produce. Enthusiastic staffers are both knowledgable and approachable, and the busy calendar of activities adds to the sense of a house still very much alive. ✉ *Main St.* ☎ *01900/824805* ⊕ *www. nationaltrust.org.uk/wordsworth-house* 💷 *£8.80* ⊗ *Closed mid-Dec.–mid-Feb.; Fri. in mid-Feb.–Oct.; Sun.–Tues. in mid-Nov.–mid-Dec.*

🍴 Restaurants

Bitter End

$ | BRITISH | Flocked floral wallpaper, old lamps, an open fire, and a handsome wooden floor set the tone at this appealing pub. Homey and intimate, the pub serves big, tasty portions of traditional British food such as scampi tails, chicken-and-leek pie, and gammon with egg and pineapple. **Known for:** popular Sunday roasts; hearty British favorites; eight real ales on tap. 💲 *Average main: £12* ✉ *15 Kirkgate* ☎ *01900/828993* ⊕ *www.bitter-end.co.uk* ⊗ *No lunch Mon.*

Quince & Medlar

$$ | VEGETARIAN | Sophisticated and imaginative vegetarian cuisine, served by candlelight, is the specialty at this refined, wood-paneled Georgian town house. You'll probably be offered a drink in the sitting room before being called to your table; you choose from at least six main courses, such as baked pumpkin and cheese gnocchi, gingered quinoa roast, or watercress and red pepper soufflé. **Known for:** imaginative vegetarian menu; Cumbrian art on the walls; local dairy, eggs, and fresh produce. $ *Average main: £16* ✉ *13 Castlegate* ☎ *01900/823579* ⊕ *www.quinceandmedlar.co.uk* ⊘ *Closed Sun. and Mon. No lunch.*

🛏 Hotels

★ Six Castlegate

$ | B&B/INN | After a day of exploring, relax in style at this elegant B&B in a Georgian town house with spacious rooms immaculately decorated in pale, natural tones; all have good views, generous showers, and comfortable beds. **Pros:** modern facilities and antique style blend nicely; near galleries and attractions; exceptional value. **Cons:** road noise in some rooms; no check-in before 5 pm; standard doubles are small. $ *Rooms from: £90* ✉ *6 Castlegate* ☎ *01900/826786* ⊕ *www.sixcastlegate.co.uk* ⇥ *6 rooms* ⏺ *Free breakfast.*

Bassenthwaite Lake

5 miles east of Cockermouth, 3 miles north of Keswick.

Bassenthwaite is the only body of water officially called a lake in the Lake District; the others are known as "meres" or "waters." Bird-watchers know this less-frequented lake well because of the many migratory species found here, including ospreys (check out ⊕ *www.ospreywatch.co.uk*). The shoreline habitat is the best preserved in the national park—in part because most of it is privately owned and also because motorboats are not allowed. Posh accommodations and good restaurants dot the area, and popular walks include the climb up Skiddaw (3,054 feet), which, on a clear day, has panoramic views of the Lake District, the Pennines, Scotland, and the Isle of Man from its summit.

👁 Sights

Lakes Distillery

WINERY/DISTILLERY | England's largest whiskey distillery, converted from a Victorian model farm, serves as a great visitor attraction. Hour-long tours get you up close to the process and include a history of illicit distilling in the area and a thrilling aerial film that follows the River Derwent from source to sea. Visits include a tasting of either gin or whiskey; the home-produced whiskey has a slightly smoky flavor with hints of spice, and the gin is distilled with wild juniper picked in the fells of the Lake District. The popular bistro, in the old milking parlor, offers high-quality dishes such as a distiller's lunch—a take on the traditional ploughman's—and slow-cooked pork with caramelized apples and mash. Desserts are especially good, and seating spills out into the courtyard in good weather. ✉ *Setmurthy, Nr Bassenthwaite Lake* ☎ *017687/88850* ⊕ *www.lakesdistillery.com* 🍴 *£12.50.*

🛏 Hotels

★ The Pheasant

$$ | B&B/INN | Halfway between Cockermouth and Keswick at the northern end of Bassenthwaite Lake, this traditional 18th-century coaching inn exudes English coziness without the usual Lakeland fussiness. **Pros:** atmosphere of a well-loved local inn; fantastic bar; great food. **Cons:** a little out of the way; busy in summer; avoid if you don't like dogs. $ *Rooms from: £129* ✉ *Off A66* ☎ *017687/76234* ⇥ *15 rooms* ⏺ *Free breakfast.*

CAMBRIDGE AND EAST ANGLIA

12

Updated by
Toby Orton

◉ Sights	🍴 Restaurants	🛏 Hotels	🛍 Shopping	🍸 Nightlife
★★★☆☆	★★★☆☆	★★★☆☆	★★★☆☆	★★★☆☆

WELCOME TO CAMBRIDGE AND EAST ANGLIA

TOP REASONS TO GO

★ **Cambridge:** A walk through the colleges is grand, but the best views of the university's buildings and immaculate lawns (and some famous bridges) are from a punt on the river.

★ **Constable country:** In the area where Constable grew up, you can walk or row downstream from Dedham straight into the setting of one of the English landscape painter's masterpieces at Flatford Mill.

★ **Lincoln's old center:** The ancient center of the city has a vast, soaring cathedral, a proper rampart-ringed castle, and winding medieval streets.

★ **Wild North Sea coast:** North Norfolk has enormous sandy beaches (great for walking) and opportunities to see seals and birds, especially on the salt marshes around Blakeney.

★ **Lavenham:** This old town is the most comely of the tight-knit cluster of places that prospered from the medieval wool trade, with architecture including timber-frame houses gnarled into crookedness by age.

East Anglia, in southeastern England, can be divided into distinct areas for sightseeing. The central area surrounds the ancient university city of Cambridge and includes Ely, with its magnificent cathedral rising out of the flatlands, and the towns of inland Suffolk. The Suffolk Heritage Coast is home to historic small towns and villages; while the northeast, with the region's capital, Norwich, encompasses the waterways of the Broads and the beaches and salt marshes of the North Norfolk coast. Farther north, in Lincolnshire, the historic town of Stamford sits just south of the city of Lincoln, famous for its tall, fluted cathedral towers.

1 Cambridge. Home to one of the world's most famous universities.

2 Ely. A village with a lofty cathedral that dominates the surrounding flatlands.

3 Sudbury. A silk-weaving town with a rich historical flavor.

4 Long Melford. A charming wool town.

5 Lavenham. A perfectly preserved Tudor village.

6 Bury St. Edmonds. One of East Anglia's prettiest towns.

7 Dedham. An idyllic village in the heart of Constable Country.

8 Woodbridge. An atmospheric seaside town.

9 Aldeburgh. A quiet seaside resort.

10 Norwich. Home to a famous cathedral and castle.

11 Blakeney. A quiet coastal resort.

12 Wells-next-the-Sea. A good base to explore the area's stately homes, including royal Sandringham.

13 Stamford. Home to Burghley House, an impressive Elizabethan mansion.

14 Lincoln. A city on the western fringes of East Anglia and home to a majestic Norman cathedral.

EAST ANGLIA'S SEAFOOD BOUNTY

Fish-and-chips taste perfect during a day by the sea in East Anglia.

Perhaps unsurprisingly in an island nation, the harvest of the rivers and the sea forms an essential part of the British culinary tradition. Few regions are so closely associated with a love of good seafood as East Anglia.

The coastlines of Essex, Suffolk, and Norfolk overflow with towns that specialize in one type of seaborne bounty or another. Shrimp, crab, and oysters are still caught using centuries-old methods; and lobsters, crabs, and mussels from Norfolk are sent to the top restaurants in London. Changing tastes tell a kind of social history of their own: oysters, now an expensive luxury, were once considered peasant food; and a new generation of chefs, eager to reconnect with forgotten ingredients and methods, is rediscovering old-fashioned flavors such as eel and samphire. Then there's that most famous of British seafood dishes—humble fish-and-chips. Some of the best in the country can be found in Suffolk towns such as Aldeburgh, where savvy fish-and-chip shop owners have installed webcams so customers can check how far the line stretches down the street.

SEA SALT

Evidence suggests that sea salt has been harvested in East Anglia for 2,000 years. It's popular today—but only one regional company still produces sea salt in the local style. Based in and named after the harbor town of Maldon in Essex, Maldon Crystal Salt Company uses a distinctive method that yields thin, flaky crystals with a delicate piquancy. Praised by chefs, Maldon salt is widely available at English supermarkets.

CHOOSING YOUR FISH-AND-CHIPS

The key word is simplicity: very fresh fish, deep-fried in batter, served immediately. Chips (slices of fried potato) must be thick cut and slightly soft, not crisp like fries, and sprinkled with salt and vinegar. The kind you get in fish-and-chips shops is almost always better than pub offerings. Cod, plaice, and haddock are the most popular choices, but the concern about cod overfishing means that you may see pollock, coley, or skate as alternatives.

Potted shrimp, a tasty appetizer

CROMER CRAB

Known for its juicy flesh and higher-than-average white meat content, the best East Anglian crab comes from the area around Cromer in Norfolk. It's often served in salads, pasta dishes, and savory crab cakes.

EEL

A staple of the East Anglian diet for centuries but long out of favor, the humble eel is making a comeback at fashionable restaurants. Eels are usually served smoked (on their own, or in soups or salads) or jellied in a flavored stock with the consistency of aspic.

MUSSELS

This type of small clam is particularly associated with the towns of Brancaster and Stiffkey. Cheap and

Cromer crab dressed with lemon mayonnaise

versatile, mussels can be served on their own. with other seafood, or in soups and stews.

OYSTERS

The Essex coast has been producing oysters since Roman times. A luxury item, oysters are usually served raw with few accompaniments—as a main course by the dozen or as a starter by the half dozen.

SAMPHIRE

A green sea vegetable that grows wild on shores and marshland, samphire is abundant in East Anglia, where it's an accompaniment to local seafood. Crisp and slightly salty, it's often described as "tasting like the sea."

SHERINGHAM LOBSTER

This well-regarded lobster is usually served with melted butter or with fries as a kind of upper-class cousin of fish-and-chips. Lobster bisque—a rich, creamy soup—is also popular.

YARMOUTH BLOATERS

A form of cured herring produced in Great Yarmouth, near Norwich, these fat, slightly salted fish aren't gutted before being smoked. This gives them a particularly strong, almost gamey flavor.

One of those beautiful English inconsistencies, East Anglia has no spectacular mountains or rivers to disturb the quiet, storied land of rural delights. Occupying an area of southeastern England that pushes out into the North Sea, its counties of Essex, Norfolk, Suffolk, Lincolnshire, and Cambridgeshire feel cut off from the pulse of the country.

Among its highlights is Cambridge, a lovely and ancient university city. East Anglia also has four of the country's greatest stately homes: Holkham Hall, Blickling Hall, Houghton Hall, and Sandringham—where the Queen spends Christmas.

In times past, East Anglia was one of the most important centers of power in northern Europe. Towns like Lincoln were major Roman settlements, and the medieval wool trade brought huge prosperity to the higgledy-piggledy streets of tiny Lavenham. Thanks to its relative lack of thoroughfares and canals, however, East Anglia was mercifully untouched by the Industrial Revolution. The area is rich in idyllic, quintessentially English villages: sleepy, sylvan settlements in the midst of otherwise deserted lowlands. Even the towns feel small and manageable; the biggest city, Norwich, has a population of just 130,000. Cambridge, with its ancient university, is the area's most famous draw, along with incomparable cathedrals, at Ely and Lincoln particularly, and one of the finest Gothic buildings in Europe, King's College Chapel.

And yet, despite all of these treasures, the real joy of visiting East Anglia is making your own discoveries. Spend a couple of days exploring the hidden byways of the fens or just taking in the subtle beauties of the many England-like-it-looks-in-the-movies villages. If you find yourself driving down a small country lane and an old church or mysterious, ivy-covered ruin peeks out from behind the trees, give in to your curiosity and look inside. Such places are East Anglia's best-kept secrets.

MAJOR REGIONS

Cambridge. The home of the ancient university is East Anglia's liveliest town. The city center is perfect for ambling around the colleges, museums, and King's College Chapel, one of England's greatest monuments.

Ely and Central Suffolk. This central area of towns and villages within easy reach of Cambridge is testament to the amazing changeability of the English landscape. The town of Ely is set in an eerie, flat, and apparently endless marsh, or fenland. (A medieval term, "the fens," is still used informally to describe the surrounding region.) Only a few miles south and east into Suffolk, however, all this changes to pastoral landscapes of gently undulating hills and clusters of villages including pretty Sudbury and Lavenham.

The Suffolk Coast. The 40-mile Suffolk Heritage Coast, which wanders northward from Felixstowe up to Kessingland, is one of the most unspoiled shorelines in the country. The lower part of the coast is the most impressive; however, some of the loveliest towns and villages, such as Dedham and the older part of Flatford, are inland. The best way to experience the countryside around here is to be willing to get lost along its tiny, ancient back roads. Try to avoid the coastal area between Lowestoft and Great Yarmouth; it has little to offer but run-down beach resorts.

Norwich and North Norfolk. Norwich, unofficial capital of East Anglia, is dominated by the 15th-century spire of its impressive cathedral. Norfolk's continuing isolation from the rest of the country, and its unspoiled landscape and architecture—largely bypassed by the Industrial Revolution—have proved to be a draw. Many of the flint-knapped (decorated with broken flint) houses in North Norfolk's newly trendy villages are now weekend or holiday homes. Windmills, churches, and waterways are the area's chief defining characteristics. A few miles inland from the Norfolk coast you reach the Broads, a national park made up of a network of shallow, reed-bordered lakes, many linked by wide rivers. Boating and fishing are great lures; rent a boat for a day or a week and the waterside pubs, churches, villages, and nature reserves are all within easy reach.

Stamford and Lincoln. The fens of northern Cambridgeshire pass imperceptibly into the three divisions of Lincolnshire: Holland, Kesteven, and Lindsey. Holland borders the Isle of Ely and the Soke of Peterborough. This marshland spreads far and wide south of the Wash. The chief attractions are two towns: Stamford, to the southwest, and Lincoln, with its magnificent cathedral.

Planning

When to Go

Summer and late spring are the best times to visit East Anglia. Late fall and winter can be cold, windy, and rainy, though this is England's driest region and crisp, frosty days here are beautiful. To escape crowds, avoid the popular Norfolk Broads in late July and August. You can't visit most of the Cambridge colleges during exam period (late May to mid-June), and the competition for hotel rooms heats up during graduation week (late June). The Aldeburgh Festival of Music and the Arts, one of the biggest events on the British classical music calendar, takes place in June.

Planning Your Time

Cambridge is the region's most interesting city, and ideally you should allow two days to absorb its various sights. (In a pinch, you could do it as a day trip from London but only with an early start and a good pair of walking shoes.) You could easily use the city as a base for exploring Ely, Bury St. Edmunds, Lavenham, Long Melford, and Sudbury, although accommodations are available in these towns as well. The Suffolk Coast has enticing overnight stops in such small towns as Dedham and Aldeburgh. In the northern part of the region, Norwich makes a good place to stop for the night and has enough sights to keep you interested for a day. If you're here to see the coast, you'll do better staying in villages such as Blakeney or Wells. Allow several hours to see the large Blickling Hall, near Norwich, and Burghley House, outside Stamford. Lincoln, notable for its cathedral, and Stamford are west and north of Norfolk if you want to work them into an itinerary.

Getting Here and Around

AIR

Norwich International Airport serves a limited number of domestic and international destinations, though not the United States. London Stansted Airport, 30 miles south of Cambridge, is used mainly for European flights. The vast majority of travelers to the region arrive by train, car, or bus.

AIRPORTS London Stansted Airport. ⊠ Bassingbourn Rd., Bishop's Stortford ☎ 0808/169–7031 ⊕ www.stanstedairport.com. **Norwich International Airport.** ⊠ Amsterdam Way, off A140, Norwich ☎ 01603/411923 ⊕ www.norwichairport.co.uk.

BUS

National Express buses serve the region from London's Victoria Coach Station. Average travel times are 3 hours to Cambridge and Norwich, 2½ hours to Bury St. Edmunds, and 4½ hours to Lincoln.

Long-distance buses are useful for reaching the region and traveling between its major centers, but for smaller hops, local buses are best. First and Stagecoach buses cover the Cambridge, Lincolnshire, and Norwich areas. Information about local Norfolk service and county service is available from the Norfolk Bus Information Centre. Traveline can answer public transportation questions.

A FirstDay ticket, which covers a day of unlimited bus travel around Norwich and the Norfolk coast, costs £14, while a FirstWeek pass, good for seven days, costs £26. These tickets cover all buses except the Park and Ride shuttles that link parking lots with the town center. There are also various local passes that cost from around £4 to £10 daily, £10 to £21 weekly. You can buy any of these tickets from the driver.

CONTACTS Norfolk Bus Information Centre. ☎ 0845/300–6116. **Stagecoach.** ☎ 01223/433250 ⊕ www.stagecoachbus.com/about/east. **Traveline.** ☎ 0871/200–2233, 84268 text "Traveline" from mobile phone for link to bus finder ⊕ www.traveline.info.

CAR

If you're driving from London, Cambridge (54 miles) is off M11. At Exit 9, M11 connects with A11 to Norwich (114 miles); A14 off A11 goes to Bury St. Edmunds. A12 from London goes through east Suffolk via Ipswich. For Lincoln (131 miles), take A1 via Huntingdon, Peterborough, and Grantham to A46 at Newark-on-Trent. A more scenic alternative is to leave A1 at Grantham and take A607 to Lincoln.

East Anglia has few fast main roads besides those mentioned here. Once off the A roads, traveling within the region often means taking country lanes that have many twists and turns. Going even just a few miles can take much longer than you think.

TRAIN

The entire region is well served by trains from London's Liverpool Street and King's Cross stations. The quality and convenience of these services varies enormously, however. Cambridge trains leave from King's Cross and Liverpool Street, take about 45 minutes to an hour, and cost about £26. On the other hand, getting to Lincoln from King's Cross entails at least one transfer, takes two to three hours, and costs between about £35 and £95, depending on when you travel. ■TIP➔ **Tickets for trains between London and Lincoln can be a fraction of the price if you buy online in advance.** A good way to save money on local trains in East Anglia is to buy an Anglia Plus Ranger Pass. It costs £24.70 for one day or £49.40 for three days and allows unlimited rail travel in Norfolk, Suffolk, and part of Cambridgeshire. You can add up to four kids for an extra £4 each.

CONTACTS Abellio Greater Anglia.
☎ *0345/600–7245* ⊕ *www.great-eranglia.co.uk.* **East Midlands Trains.**
☎ *03457/125678* ⊕ *www.eastmid-landsrailway.co.uk.* **Great Northern Rail.**
☎ *0345/026–4700* ⊕ *www.greatnorth-ernrail.com.* **National Rail Enquiries.**
☎ *03457/484950* ⊕ *www.nationalrail.co.uk.*

Restaurants

In summer, the coast gets so packed with people that reservations are essential at restaurants. Getting something to eat at other than regular mealtime hours isn't always possible in small towns; head to cafés if you want a midmorning or after-lunch snack. Look for area specialties, such as crab, lobster, duckling, Norfolk black turkey, hare, and partridge, on menus around the region. In Norwich there's no escaping the hot, bright-yellow Colman's mustard, which is perfect smeared gingerly on some sausage and mash.

Hotels

The region is full of centuries-old, half-timber inns with rooms full of roaring fires and cozy bars. Bed-and-breakfasts are a good option in pricey Cambridge. It's always busy in Cambridge and along the coast in summer, so reserve well in advance.

Restaurant and hotel reviews have been shortened. For full information, visit Fodors.com. Restaurant prices are the average cost of a main course at dinner, or if dinner is not served, at lunch. Hotel prices are the lowest cost of a standard double room in high season, including 20% V.A.T.

WHAT IT COSTS in Pounds			
$	$$	$$$	$$$$
RESTAURANTS			
under £16	£16–£23	£24–£30	over £30
HOTELS			
under £125	£125–£225	£226–£350	over £350

Visitor Information

Broads Authority. ⊠ *Yare House, 62 Thorpe Rd., Norwich* ☎ *01603/610734* ⊕ *www.broads-authority.gov.uk.* **East of England Tourism.** ⊠ *Dettingen House, Dettingen Way, Bury St. Edmunds* ☎ *0333/320–4202* ⊕ *www.visiteastofengland.com.*

Cambridge

With the spires of its university buildings framed by towering trees and expansive meadows, and its medieval streets and passages enhanced by gardens and riverbanks, the city of Cambridge is among the loveliest in England. The city predates the Roman occupation of Britain, but there's confusion over exactly how and when the university was founded. The most widely accepted story is that it was established in 1209 by a pair of scholars from Oxford, who left their university in protest over the wrongful execution of a colleague for murder.

Keep in mind there's no recognizable campus: the scattered colleges *are* the university. The town reveals itself only slowly, filled with tiny gardens, ancient courtyards, imposing classic buildings, alleyways that lead past medieval churches, and wisteria-hung facades. Perhaps the best views are from the Backs, the green parkland that extends along the River Cam behind several colleges. This

12

Cambridge and East Anglia CAMBRIDGE

sweeping openness, a result of the larger size of the colleges and lack of industrialization in the city center, is what distinguishes Cambridge from Oxford.

This university town may be beautiful, but it's no museum. Well-preserved medieval buildings sit cheek by jowl with the latest in modern architecture (for example, the William Gates Building, which houses Cambridge University's computer laboratory) in this growing city dominated culturally and architecturally by its famous university (students make up around one-fifth of the city's 109,000 inhabitants), and beautified by parks, gardens, and the quietly flowing River Cam.

The exquisite King's College choir defines the traditional English Christmas, when the *Festival of Nine Lessons and Carols* is broadcast live on Christmas Eve. On top of all its tradition and history, Cambridge remains a lively city and an extraordinary center of learning and research where innovation and discovery still happen behind its ancient walls.

GETTING HERE AND AROUND

Good bus (three hours) and train (one hour) services connect London and Cambridge. The long-distance bus terminal is on Drummer Street, very close to Emmanuel and Christ's colleges. Several local buses connect the station with central Cambridge, including the frequent Citi 7 and 8 services, although any bus listing City Centre or Emmanuel Street among its stops will do. The journey takes just under 10 minutes. If you're driving, don't attempt to venture very far into the center—parking is scarce and pricey. The center is amenable to explorations on foot, or you could join the throng by renting a bicycle.

Stagecoach sells Dayrider (£4.50) tickets for all-day bus travel within Cambridge, and Megarider tickets (£15) for seven days of travel within the city. You can extend these to cover the whole county of Cambridgeshire (£7 and £25, respectively), or even an extension to a week as far as Oxford (£42.40). Buy any of them from the driver.

TIMING

In summer and over the Easter and Christmas holidays Cambridge is devoid of students, its heart and soul. To see the city in full swing, visit between October and June. In summer there are arts and music festivals, notably the Strawberry Fair and the Arts Festival (both June) and the Folk Festival (late July to early August). The May Bumps, intercollegiate boat races, are, confusingly, held the first week of June. This is also the month when students celebrate the end of exam season, so expect to encounter some boisterous nightlife.

TOURS

City Sightseeing

BUS TOURS | This company operates open-top bus tours of Cambridge, including the Backs, colleges, and Botanic Gardens. Tours can be joined at marked bus stops in the city. Ask the tourist office about additional tours. ⊠ *Silver, Street East* ☎ *01789/299123* ⊕ *www.city-sightseeing.com* ✉ *From £19.91.*

Visit Cambridge

WALKING TOURS | Walking tours are led by official Blue or Green Badge guides. The 1½- or 2-hour tours leave from the tourist information center at Peas Hill. Hours vary according to the tour, with the earliest leaving at 11 am and the latest at 2 pm. ⊠ *The Guildhall, Peas Hill* ☎ *01223/791501* ⊕ *www.visitcambridge. org/official-tours* ✉ *From £8.*

ESSENTIALS

VISITOR INFORMATION Cambridge Visitor Information Centre. ⊠ *The Guildhall, Peas Hill* ☎ *01223/791500* ⊕ *www.visitcambridge.org.*

Audley End, a 17th-century house, serves as an idyllic backdrop for a cricket match.

👁 Sights

Exploring the city means, in large part, exploring the university. Each of the 25 oldest colleges is built around a series of courts, or quadrangles, framing manicured, velvety lawns. Because students and fellows (faculty) live and work in these courts, access is sometimes restricted, and you're asked not to picnic in the quadrangles at any time.

Visitors aren't normally allowed into college buildings other than chapels, dining halls, and some libraries; some colleges charge admission for certain buildings. Public visiting hours vary from college to college, depending on the time of year, and it's best to call or to check with the city tourist office. Colleges close to visitors during the main exam time, late May to mid-June. Term time (when classes are in session) means roughly October to December, January to March, and April to June; summer term, or vacation, runs from July to September. ■ TIP→ Bring a pair of binoculars, as some college

buildings have highly intricate details, such as the spectacular ceiling at King's College Chapel. When the colleges are open, the best way to gain access is to join a walking tour led by an official Blue Badge guide—many areas are off-limits unless you do. The 90-minute and two-hour tours (£8 to £18) leave up to four times daily from the city tourist office. The other traditional view of the colleges is gained from a punt—the boats propelled by pole on the River Cam.

Audley End House and Gardens

HOUSE | FAMILY | A famous example of early-17th-century architecture, Audley End was once owned by Charles II, who bought it as a convenient place to break his journey on the way to the Newmarket races. Although the palatial building was remodeled in the 18th and 19th centuries, the Jacobean style is still on display in the magnificent Great Hall. You can walk in the park, landscaped by Capability Brown in the 18th century, and the fine Victorian gardens. Exhibitions focus on the lives of domestic servants in

Sights ▼

1 Audley End
  House and Gardens **G9**
2 Cambridge University
  Botanic Gardens.................... **F9**
3 Christ's College..................... **E5**
4 Emmanuel College.................. **E6**
5 Fitzwilliam Museum **D7**
6 Great St. Mary's.................... **D5**
7 Imperial War Museum
  Duxford **G9**
8 Kettle's Yard **C3**
9 King's College **C6**
10 King's College Chapel **C5**
11 Museum of Archaeology
  and Anthropology................ **D6**
12 Polar Museum **F7**
13 Queens' College **C6**
14 Trinity College **C5**
15 Whipple Museum of the
  History of Science................ **D6**

Restaurants ▼

1 Loch Fyne.......................... **D7**
2 Midsummer House **F3**
3 The Oak............................ **F7**
4 Pickerel Inn........................ **C4**
5 Restaurant 22 .... **E2**
6 River Bar
  Steakhouse & Grill................ **D4**
7 Three Horseshoes................. **A2**

Hotels ▼

1 Duke House **F5**
2 5 Chapel St **H1**
3 Regent Hotel **E7**
4 University Arms.................... **E6**
5 The Varsity......................... **D4**

KEY

① Exploring Sights
① Restaurants
① Hotels

the late 19th century. A recent renovation opened up the Nursery Suite, bedecked in the style of the 1830s, and the Coal Gallery, which once provided hot water for the family upstairs (though not the servants). The Service Wing lets you look "below stairs" at the kitchen, scullery (where fish were descaled and chickens plucked), and game larder (where pheasants, partridges, and rabbits were hung), while the Stable Yard gives kids the chance to see old saddles and tack and don Victorian riding costumes. The house is in Saffron Waldon, 14 miles south of Cambridge. ⊠ *Audley End Road, Off London Rd., Saffron Walden* ☎ *01799/522842* ⊕ *www.english-heritage.org.uk/visit/ places/audley-end-house-and-gardens* 🖾 *£18.50 Apr.–Oct., £13 Nov.–Mar.* ⊙ *House closed Nov.–Mar.*

Cambridge University Botanic Gardens

GARDEN | **FAMILY** | Opened in 1846, these 40 acres contain rare specimens like the jade vine, greenhouses filled with orchids and other tropical beauties, and a rock garden with delicate plants from all over the world. The gardens are a five-minute walk from the Fitzwilliam Museum. ⊠ *Cory Lodge, Bateman St.* ☎ *01223/336265* ⊕ *www.botanic.cam. ac.uk* 🖾 *£6.*

Christ's College

COLLEGE | To see the way a college has grown over the centuries you could not do better than a visit here. The main gateway bears the enormous coat of arms of its patroness, Lady Margaret Beaufort, mother of Henry VII, who established the institution in 1505. It leads into a fine courtyard, with the chapel framed by an ancient magnolia. In the dining hall hang portraits of John Milton and Charles Darwin, two of the college's most famous students. Next, walk past a fellows' building credited to Inigo Jones, who transformed English architecture in the early 17th century, to the spacious garden (once a favorite haunt of Milton's), and finally to a modern ziggurat-like confection from the 1960s. ⊠ *St. Andrew's St.* ☎ *01223/334900* ⊕ *www. christs.cam.ac.uk* 🖾 *Free* ⊙ *Gardens closed weekends. Closed during exam periods.*

Emmanuel College

COLLEGE | The master hand of architect Sir Christopher Wren (1632–1723) is evident throughout much of Cambridge, particularly at Emmanuel, built on the site of a Dominican friary, where he designed the chapel and colonnade. A stained-glass window in the chapel has a likeness of John Harvard, founder of Harvard University, who studied here. The college, founded in 1584, was an early center of Puritan learning; a number of the Pilgrims were Emmanuel alumni, and they remembered their alma mater in naming Cambridge, Massachusetts. ⊠ *St. Andrew's St.* ☎ *01223/334200* ⊕ *www.emma.cam.ac.uk* 🖾 *Free* ⊙ *Closed during exam periods.*

★ Fitzwilliam Museum

MUSEUM | In a classical-revival building renowned for its grand Corinthian portico, "The Fitz," founded by the 7th Viscount Fitzwilliam of Merrion in 1816, has one of Britain's most outstanding collections of art and antiquities. Highlights include two large Titians, an extensive collection of French impressionist paintings, and many works by Matisse and Picasso. The opulent interior displays these treasures to marvelous effect, from Egyptian pieces like inch-high figurines and painted coffins to sculptures from the Chinese Han dynasty of the 3rd century BC. Other collections of note here include a fine collection of flower paintings, an assortment of medieval illuminated manuscripts, and a fascinating room full of armor and muskets. ⊠ *Trumpington St.* ☎ *01223/332900* ⊕ *www.fitzmuseum.cam.ac.uk* 🖾 *Free* ⊙ *Closed Mon. except bank holidays.*

A must-see at Cambridge is King's College Chapel, a masterpiece of Perpendicular Gothic style.

Great St. Mary's

RELIGIOUS SITE | Known as the "university church," Great St. Mary's has its origins in the 11th century, although the current building dates from 1478. The main reason to visit is to climb the 113-foot tower, which has a superb view over the colleges and marketplace (though it may be closed in bad weather). Also here is the Michaelhouse Centre, a small café, gallery, and performing arts venue with frequent free lunchtime concerts. Tours must be booked in advance. ⊠ *Market Hill, King's Parade* ☎ *01223/747273* ⊕ *www.gsm.cam.ac.uk* ✉ *Free; tower £5; guided tours £10.*

Imperial War Museum Duxford

MUSEUM | Europe's leading aviation museum houses a remarkable collection of 180 aircrafts from Europe and the United States. The former airfield is effectively a complex of several museums under one banner. The **Land Warfare Hall** features tanks and other military vehicles. The striking **American Air Museum** honors the 30,000 Americans killed in action flying from Britain during World War II. It contains the largest display of American fighter planes outside the United States. **AirSpace** holds a vast array of military and civil aircraft in a 3-acre hangar. Directly underneath is the **Airborne Assault Museum,** which chronicles the history of airborne forces, such as the British Parachute Regiment, which played a pivotal role in the Normandy Landings. One of the most popular exhibits is a Spitfire plane that was shot down over Calais during World War II and recovered in 1986. After a massive restoration project, the plane was restored to full airworthiness in 2014. There are also hangars where you can see restoration work taking place on other WWII planes and exhibitions on maritime warfare and the Battle of Britain. See the planes in action with the historic air shows that are held on a handful of dates every summer; check the website for details. ⊠ *A505, Duxford* ☎ *01223/835000* ⊕ *www.iwm. org.uk/visits/iwm-duxford* ✉ *£17.10.*

★ Kettle's Yard

MUSEUM | Originally a private house owned by a former curator of London's Tate galleries, Kettle's Yard contains a fine collection of 20th-century art, sculpture, furniture, and decorative arts, including works by Henry Moore, Barbara Hepworth, and Alfred Wallis. The museum reopened in 2018 after a two-year renovation project. A separate gallery shows changing exhibitions of modern art and crafts, and weekly concerts and lectures attract an eclectic mix of enthusiasts. Ring the bell for admission. ⊠ Castle St. ☏ 01223/748100 ⊕ www. kettlesyard.co.uk ✉ Free ⊘ Closed Mon. except bank holidays.

King's College

COLLEGE | Founded in 1441 by Henry VI, King's College has a magnificent late-15th-century chapel that is its most famous landmark. Other notable architecture includes the neo-Gothic Porters' Lodge, facing King's Parade, which was a comparatively recent addition in the 1830s, and the classical Gibbs building. ■TIP➔ Head down to the river, from where the panorama of college and chapel is one of the university's most photographed views. Past students of King's College include the novelist E. M. Forster, the economist John Maynard Keynes, and the World War I poet Rupert Brooke. ⊠ King's Parade ☏ 01223/331100 ⊕ www.kings. cam.ac.uk ✉ £9, includes chapel.

★ King's College Chapel

RELIGIOUS SITE | Based on Sainte-Chapelle, the 13th-century royal chapel in Paris, this house of worship is perhaps the most glorious flowering of Perpendicular Gothic in Britain. Henry VI, the king after whom the college is named, oversaw the work. From the outside, the most prominent features are the massive flying buttresses and the fingerlike spires that line the length of the building. Inside, the most obvious impression is of great space—the chapel was once described as "the noblest barn in Europe"—and of light flooding in from its huge windows.

The brilliantly colored bosses (carved panels at the intersections of the roof ribs) are particularly intense, although hard to see without binoculars. An exhibition in the chantries, or side chapels, explains more about the chapel's construction. Behind the altar is The Adoration of the Magi, an enormous painting by Peter Paul Rubens. ■TIP➔ The chapel, unlike the rest of King's College, stays open during exam periods. Every Christmas Eve, a festival of carols is sung by the chapel's famous choir. It's broadcast on national television and considered a quintessential part of the traditional English Christmas. To compete for the small number of tickets available, join the line at the college's main entrance in the early hours—doors open at 7 am. ⊠ King's Parade ☏ 01223/331212 ⊕ www.kings. cam.ac.uk ✉ £9, includes college and grounds ⊘ Sometimes closed for events; check ahead to confirm.

★ Museum of Archaeology and Anthropology

MUSEUM | Cambridge University maintains some fine museums in its research halls on Downing Street—the wonder is that they're not better known to visitors. At the recently renovated Museum of

Archaeology and Anthropology, highlights include an array of objects brought back from Captain Cook's pioneering voyages to the Pacific; Roman and medieval-era British artifacts; and the oldest human-made tools ever discovered, from the African expeditions of British archaeologist Louis Leakey (1903–72). ⊠ *Downing St.* ☎ *01223/333516* ⊕ *maa.cam.ac.uk* ⊠ *Free* ⊙ *Closed Mon.*

★ Polar Museum

MUSEUM | Beautifully designed, this museum at Cambridge University's Scott Polar Research Institute chronicles the history of polar exploration. There's a particular emphasis on the British expeditions of the 20th century, including the ill-fated attempt by Robert Falcon Scott to be the first to reach the South Pole in 1912. Norwegian explorer Roald Amundsen reached the pole first; Scott and his men perished on the return journey, but their story became legendary. There are also collections devoted to the science of modern polar exploration; the indigenous people of northern Canada, Greenland, and Alaska; and frequently changing art installations. ⊠ *Scott Polar Research Institute, Lensfield Rd.* ☎ *01223/336540* ⊕ *www.spri.cam.ac.uk/museum* ⊠ *Free* ⊙ *Closed Mon. except bank holidays.*

Queens' College

COLLEGE | One of the most eye-catching colleges, with a secluded "cloister court" look, Queens' is named after Margaret, wife of Henry VI, and Elizabeth, wife of Edward IV. Founded in 1448 and completed in the 1540s, the college is tucked away on Queens' Lane, next to the wide lawns that lead down from King's College to the Backs. The college's most famed piece of architecture is the wooden lattice Mathematical Bridge, first built in 1749. The original version is said to have been built without any fastenings, though the current bridge (reconstructed in 1902) is securely bolted. ⊠ *Queens' La.* ☎ *01223/335500* ⊕ *www.quns.cam.ac.uk* ⊠ *£3.50* ⊙ *Closed weekends Jan. and*

Feb. and during exam periods, certain wks Apr.–July; call to confirm.

Trinity College

COLLEGE | Founded in 1546 by Henry VIII, Trinity replaced a 14th-century educational foundation and is the largest college in either Cambridge or Oxford, with nearly 1,000 undergraduates. In the 17th-century great court, with its massive gatehouse, is **Great Tom,** a giant clock that strikes each hour with high and low notes. The college's true masterpiece is Sir Christopher Wren's **library,** colonnaded and seemingly constructed with as much light as stone. Among the things you can see here is A. A. Milne's handwritten manuscript of *The House at Pooh Corner.* Trinity alumni include Sir Isaac Newton, William Thackeray, Lord Byron, Lord Tennyson, and 31 Nobel Prize winners. ⊠ *St. John's St.* ☎ *01223/338400* ⊕ *www.trin.cam.ac.uk* ⊠ *£3* ⊙ *College and chapel closed exam period and event days; Wren library closed Sun.*

Whipple Museum of the History of Science

MUSEUM | This rather delightful, dusty old cupboard of a museum contains all manner of scientific artifacts, instruments, and doodads from the medieval period to the early 20th century. Most fun is the section on astronomy, including a beautiful 18th-century grand orrery—an elaborate three-dimensional model of the solar system, minus the planets that had yet to be discovered at the time. ⊠ *Free School La.* ☎ *01223/330906* ⊕ *www. hps.cam.ac.uk/whipple* ⊠ *Free* ⊙ *Closed weekends and bank holidays.*

🍴 Restaurants

Loch Fyne

$$ | SEAFOOD | Part of a Scottish chain that harvests its own oysters, this airy, casual place across from the Fitzwilliam Museum is deservedly popular. The seafood is fresh and well prepared, served in a traditional setting with a modern ambience. **Known for:** Bradan Rost smoked salmon;

Scottish oysters; great Scotch whiskey menu. $ *Average main: £17* ✉ *37 Trumpington St.* ☎ *01223/362433* ⊕ *www. lochfyneseafoodandgrill.co.uk.*

★ **Midsummer House**

$$$$ | FRENCH | Beside the River Cam on the edge of Midsummer Common, this gray-brick 19th-century villa holds a two–Michelin star restaurant set in a comfortable conservatory. Fixed-price menus for lunch and dinner (with five to eight courses) present innovative French and Mediterranean-influenced dishes that often include apples from the trees in the garden. **Known for:** great river views; beautiful historic setting; special-occasion dining. $ *Average main: £135* ✉ *Midsummer Common* ☎ *01223/369299* ⊕ *www.midsummerhouse.co.uk* ☉ *Closed Sun.–Tues.*

The Oak

$$ | BRITISH | This charming, intimate restaurant is a local favorite. It's near an uncompromisingly busy intersection, but the friendliness of the staff and classic bistro food more than make up for it. **Known for:** bistro-style menus; excellent steaks; delicious, regional seafood. $ *Average main: £20* ✉ *6 Lensfield Rd.* ☎ *01223/323361* ⊕ *www.theoakbistro. co.uk* ☉ *Closed Sun.*

Pickerel Inn

$ | BRITISH | This 600-year-old inn is home to one of the city's oldest pubs, making it a good stop for an afternoon pint of real ale and bowl of doorstop-sized potato wedges. Watch for the low beams. **Known for:** traditional pub atmosphere; excellent steak pie; classsic English pints. $ *Average main: £10* ✉ *30 Magdalene St.* ☎ *01223/355068* ⊕ *www. greeneking-pubs.co.uk/pubs/cambridgeshire/pickerel-inn* ▭ *No credit cards.*

Restaurant 22

$$$$ | BRITISH | Pretty stained-glass windows separate this sophisticated little restaurant from bustling Chesterton Road. The setting, in a terrace of houses, is low-key, but the food is creative and eye-catching. **Known for:** low-key setting; creative approach to classics; delicious desserts. $ *Average main: £50* ✉ *22 Chesterton Rd.* ☎ *01223/351880* ⊕ *www. restaurant22.co.uk* ☉ *Closed Sun. and Mon. No lunch.*

River Bar Steakhouse & Grill

$$ | MODERN BRITISH | Across the river from Magdalene College, this popular waterfront bar and grill serves delicious steak, burgers, and pies, plus specialties such as lobster mac and cheese or salmon steak with molasses and spices. There's an extensive cocktail menu as well. **Known for:** classic British mains; rooftop terrace dining; huge cocktail menu. $ *Average main: £23* ✉ *Quayside, 3 Thompsons La., off Bridge St.* ☎ *01223/307030* ⊕ *www.riverbarsteakhouse.com.*

Three Horseshoes

$$ | MEDITERRANEAN | This early-19th-century pub and restaurant in a thatched cottage has an elegant dining space in the conservatory and more casual tables in the airy bar. Sourcing of ingredients is taken seriously here—the menu lists not only the suppliers, but specific reasons for choosing them—and this is all put to good use in Modern British dishes with hints of the Mediterranean. **Known for:** local ingredients; seafood board; excellent wine. $ *Average main: £19* ✉ *High St., Madingley* ☎ *01954/210221* ⊕ *www. threehorseshoesmadingley.co.uk.*

🛏 Hotels

There aren't many hotels downtown. For more (and cheaper) options, consider one of the numerous guesthouses on the arterial roads and in the suburbs. These average around £40 to £90 per person per night and can be booked through the tourist information center.

★ Duke House

$$ | B&B/INN | This beautifully converted town house (home of the Duke of Gloucester when he was a student) is forever cropping up in British newspaper articles about the best B&Bs in the country. **Pros:** beautiful house; great location; suites are quite spacious. **Cons:** books up fast; two-night minimum on weekends; cheaper rooms are small. ⑤ *Rooms from: £150 ⊠ 1 Victoria St. ☎ 01223/314773 ⊕ www.dukehousecambridge.co.uk ⌇ 5 rooms ⧉ Free breakfast.*

5 Chapel Street

$ | B&B/INN | This sweet Georgian town house and B&B in the northeastern corner of the city is a beautiful 20-minute walk along the river from central Cambridge. **Pros:** quiet location; wonderful host; excellent breakfast. **Cons:** some rooms are small; suburban location; 20-minute walk to the center. ⑤ *Rooms from: £110 ⊠ 5 Chapel St., Chesterton ☎ 01223/514856 ⊕ www.5chapelstreet. com ⌇ 3 rooms ⧉ Free breakfast.*

Regent Hotel

$$ | HOTEL | A rare small hotel in central Cambridge, this handsome Georgian town house has wooden sash windows that look out over a tree-lined park called Parker's Piece. **Pros:** good view from top rooms; close to bars and restaurants; cozy atmosphere. **Cons:** no parking; a tad scruffy; no breakfast. ⑤ *Rooms from: £140 ⊠ 41 Regent St. ☎ 01223/351470 ⊕ www.regenthotel. co.uk ⌇ 22 rooms ⧉ No meals.*

University Arms

$$ | HOTEL | Decorated with a chic, contemporary flair that contributes to its rich historical status as Cambridge's oldest hotel, the University Arms is a welcome luxurious option on the city's hotel scene. **Pros:** beautiful historic building; charming, contemporary interior design; lively bar and dining room. **Cons:** prices are high in peak season;

parking is limited; busy location on one of the city's main thoroughfares. ⑤ *Rooms from: £170 ⊠ Regent St. ☎ 01223/606066 ⊕ www.universityarms. com ⌇ 192 rooms ⧉ No meals.*

★ The Varsity

$$$ | HOTEL | This stylish boutique hotel with an adjoining spa has wide windows that flood the place with light. **Pros:** beautiful location; gorgeous views; stylish design. **Cons:** not such great views in the less expensive rooms; prices are a bit high (particularly on weekdays); not much choice at breakfast. ⑤ *Rooms from: £250 ⊠ Thompson's La., off Bridge St. ☎ 01223/306030 ⊕ www.thevarsityhotel. co.uk ⌇ 44 rooms ⧉ No meals.*

▼ Nightlife

The city's pubs provide the mainstay of Cambridge's nightlife and shouldn't be missed.

The Eagle

BARS/PUBS | This 16th-century coaching inn with a cobbled courtyard has lost none of its old-time character. It also played a walk-on part in scientific history when, on February 28, 1953, a pair of excited Cambridge scientists announced to a roomful of rather surprised lunchtime patrons that they'd just discovered the secret of life: DNA. (Unfortunately they forgot to mention their third colleague, Rosalind Franklin, who has been largely erased from the history of their discovery). A plaque outside commemorates the event. ⊠ *8 Benet St. ☎ 01223/505020 ⊕ www.greeneking-pubs.co.uk/pubs/cambridgeshire/eagle.*

Fort St. George

BARS/PUBS | Overlooking the university boathouses, this lovely old pub gets honors for its riverside views. ⊠ *Midsummer Common ☎ 01223/354327 ⊕ www.greeneking-pubs.co.uk/pubs/ cambridgeshire/fort-st-george.*

Free Press
BARS/PUBS | A favorite of student rowers, this small pub has an excellent selection of traditional ales. ⊠ *7 Prospect Row* ☎ *01223/368337* ⊕ *www.freepresscambridge.com.*

🎭 Performing Arts

CONCERTS
Cambridge supports its own symphony orchestra, and regular musical events are held in many colleges, especially those with large chapels.

★ Cambridge Folk Festival
FESTIVALS | Spread over four days in late July or early August at Cherry Hinton Hall, the Cambridge Folk Festival attracts major international folk singers and groups. ⊠ *Cambridge* ☎ *01223/357851* ⊕ *www.cambridgelive.org.uk/folk-festival.*

Corn Exchange
CONCERTS | The beautifully restored Corn Exchange presents classical and rock concerts, stand-up comedy, musicals, opera, and ballet. ⊠ *Wheeler St.* ☎ *01223/357851* ⊕ *www.cambridgelive.org.uk/cornex.*

King's College Chapel
CONCERTS | During regular terms, King's College Chapel has evensong services Monday through Saturday at 5:30 and Sunday at 10:30 and 3:30. ■TIP➜ **Your best chance of seeing the full choir is Thursday to Sunday.** ⊠ *King's Parade* ☎ *01223/331212* ⊕ *www.kings.cam.ac.uk.*

THEATER
ADC Theatre
THEATER | Home of the famous *Cambridge Footlights Revue*, the ADC Theatre hosts mainly student and fringe theater productions. ⊠ *Park St.* ☎ *01223/300085* ⊕ *www.adctheatre.com.*

Arts Theatre
THEATER | The city's main repertory theater, built in 1936 by John Maynard Keynes (one of the most influential economists of the 20th century and a Cambridge University alumnus), still supports a full program of plays and concerts. It also has three lively bars and serves food. ⊠ *6 St. Edward's Passage* ☎ *01223/503333* ⊕ *www.cambridgeartstheatre.com.*

🛍 Shopping

Head to the specialty shops in the center of town, especially in and around Rose Crescent and King's Parade. Bookshops, including antiquarian stores, are Cambridge's pride and joy.

BOOKS
Cambridge University Press Bookshop
BOOKS/STATIONERY | In business since at least 1581, the Cambridge University Press runs this store on Trinity Street. ⊠ *1 Trinity St.* ☎ *01223/333333* ⊕ *www.cambridge.org/about-us/visit-bookshop.*

David's
BOOKS/STATIONERY | Near the Arts Theatre, G. David (known locally as just David's) sells antiquarian books. ⊠ *16 St. Edward's Passage* ☎ *01223/354619.*

Haunted Bookshop
BOOKS/STATIONERY | This shop carries a great selection of old, illustrated books and British classics. And (the clue's in the name) apparently it has a ghost, too. ⊠ *9 St. Edward's Passage* ☎ *01223/312913* ⊕ *www.sarahkeybooks.co.uk.*

Heffers
BOOKS/STATIONERY | Filled with rare and imported books, Heffers' boasts a particularly fine arts section. ⊠ *20 Trinity St.* ☎ *01223/463200* ⊕ *heffersbookshop.business.site.*

CLOTHING
Ryder & Amies
CLOTHING | Need a straw boater? This shop is the official outlet for Cambridge University products, from hoodies to ties to cuff links. ⊠ *22 King's Parade* ☎ *01223/350371* ⊕ *www.ryderamies.co.uk.*

Punting on the Cam

To punt is to maneuver a flat-bottom, wooden, gondolalike boat—in this case, through the shallow River Cam along the verdant Backs behind the colleges of Cambridge. One benefit of this popular activity is that you get a better view of the ivy-covered walls from the water. Mastery of the sport lies in your ability to control a 15-foot pole, used to propel the punt. With a bottle of wine, some food, and a few friends, you may find yourself saying things such as, "It doesn't get any better than this." One piece of advice: if your pole gets stuck, let go. You can use the smaller paddle to go back and retrieve it. Hang on to a stuck punt for too long and you'll probably fall in with it.

The lazier-at-heart may prefer chauffeured punting, with food supplied. Students from Cambridge often do the work, and you get a fairly informative spiel on the colleges. For a romantic evening trip, there are illuminated punts.

One university punting society once published a useful "Bluffer's Guide to Punting" featuring detailed instructions and tips on how to master the art. It has been archived online at ⊕ *duramecho.com/Misc/HowToPunt.html.*

MARKETS
All Saints Garden Art & Craft Market
CRAFTS | This market displays the wares of local artists outdoors on Saturday. It's also open Fridays in July and August and some weekends in December (weather permitting). ⊠ *Trinity St.* ⊕ *www.visitcambridge.org/shopping/all-saints-garden-art-and-craft-market.*

 Activities

BIKING
City Cycle Hire
BICYCLING | This shop charges supercheap rates of £8 per half day, £15 per day, and £25 for a week. All bikes are mountain or hybrid bikes. Reservations are essential in July and August. ⊠ *61 Newnham Rd.* ☎ *01223/365629* ⊕ *www.citycyclehire.com.*

PUNTING
You can rent punts at several places, notably at Silver Street Bridge–Mill Lane, at Magdalene Bridge, and from outside the Rat and Parrot pub on Thompson's Lane on Jesus Green. Hourly rental costs around £16 to £25. Chauffeured punting, usually by a Cambridge student, is also popular. It costs upwards of £15 to £20 per person.

★ Scudamore's Punting Co.
BOATING | This company rents chauffeured and self-drive punts. Daily, 45-minute tours start at around £20 per person (less if booked online). Scudamore's also runs various special tours—for afternoon tea or Halloween, for example. Private tours and punting lessons are also available. High-stakes romantics can even arrange a "Proposal Tour," which includes champagne and roses if your beloved says yes. ⊠ *Granta Place, Mill La.* ☎ *01223/359750* ⊕ *www.scudamores.com.*

Ely

16 miles north of Cambridge.

Known for its magnificent cathedral, Ely is the "capital" of the fens, the center of what used to be a separate county called the Isle of Ely (literally "island of eels"). Until the land was drained in the 17th century, Ely was surrounded by treacherous marshland, which inhabitants crossed wearing stilts. Today Wicken

Fen, a nature reserve 9 miles southeast of town (off A1123), preserves the sole remaining example of fenland in an undrained state.

Enveloped by fields of wheat, sugar beets, and carrots, Ely is a small, dense town that somewhat fails to live up to the high expectations created by its big attraction, its magnificent cathedral. The shopping area and market square lie to the north and lead down to the riverside, and the medieval buildings of the cathedral grounds and the King's School (which trains cathedral choristers) spread out to the south and west. Ely's most famous resident was Oliver Cromwell, whose house is now a museum.

GETTING HERE AND AROUND

The 9 and 12 buses leave twice an hour from the Drummer Street bus station in Cambridge. The journey to Ely takes around an hour. To drive there from Cambridge, simply take the A10 road going north out of the city. Ely is quite small, so find somewhere to park and walk to the center. Trains from Cambridge to Ely leave three times an hour and take 15 minutes.

ESSENTIALS

VISITOR INFORMATION Visit Ely. ⊠ *Oliver Cromwell's House, 29 St. Mary's St.* ☏ *01353/662062* ⊕ *www.visitely.org.uk.*

◉ Sights

★ Ely Cathedral

RELIGIOUS SITE | Known affectionately as the Ship of the Fens, Ely Cathedral can be seen for miles, towering above the flat landscape on one of the few ridges in the fens. In 1083, the Normans began work on the cathedral, which stands on the site of a Benedictine monastery founded by the Anglo-Saxon princess Etheldreda in 673. In the center of the cathedral you see a marvel of medieval construction—the unique octagonal

Lantern Tower, a sort of stained-glass skylight of colossal proportions, built to replace the central tower that collapsed in 1322. The cathedral's **West Tower** is even taller; the view from the top (if you can manage the 288 steps) is spectacular. Tours of both towers run daily. The cathedral is also notable for its 248-foot-long **nave,** with its simple Norman arches and Victorian painted ceiling. Much of the decorative carving of the 14th-century **Lady Chapel** was defaced during the Reformation (mostly by knocking off the heads of the statuary), but enough traces remain to show its original beauty.

The cathedral also houses the wonderful **Stained Glass Museum** (⊕ *www.stainedglassmuseum.com*). Exhibits trace the history of stained glass from medieval to modern times, including some stunning contemporary pieces. Ely Cathedral is a popular filming location; it doubled for Westminster Abbey in *The King's Speech* (2010) and *The Crown* (2015).

▪ **TIP** → There are guided tours of the cathedral from Monday to Saturday (and Sunday in summer). Generally they start at 10:45, noon, and 2, with extra tours in the summer, but times vary so it's a good idea to call ahead. ⊠ *The Gallery* ☏ *01353/667735* ⊕ *www.elycathedral.org* 🎟 *£8–£19.*

Oliver Cromwell's House

HOUSE | This half-timber medieval building stands in the shadows of Ely Cathedral. During the 10 years he lived here, Cromwell (1599–1658) was leading the rebellious Roundheads in their eventually victorious struggle against King Charles I in the English Civil War. A hero to some, a tyrant to others, he remains a controversial figure today. The house contains an exhibition about its former occupant, who was Britain's Lord Protector from 1653 to 1658. It's also the site of Ely's tourist information center. ⊠ *29 St. Mary's St.* ☏ *01353/662062* ⊕ *www. olivercromwellshouse.co.uk* 🎟 *£5.20.*

🍴 Restaurants

★ Old Fire Engine House

$$ | **BRITISH** | Scrubbed pine tables fill the main dining room of this converted fire station near Ely Cathedral; another room, used when there's a crowd, has an open fireplace and a polished wood floor, and also serves as an art gallery. The menu could include fenland recipes like sea bass with shrimp and dill sauce, as well as more familiar English fare, such as steak and kidney pie. **Known for:** seasonal produce; regularly changing menus; afternoon tea. $ *Average main: £18* ⊠ *25 St. Mary's St.* ☎ *01353/662582* ⊕ *www.theoldfireenginehouse.co.uk* ⊙ *No dinner Sun.*

🛏 Hotels

Cathedral House

$ | **B&B/INN** | This Georgian house, full of interesting period details such as an oriel window and a handsome staircase, makes a pleasant overnight stop in Ely. The bedrooms are small but cozy, with antique furniture; bathrooms are also small. **Pros:** heaps of character; steps from the cathedral; handy parking. **Cons:** on a busy road; two-night minimum on weekends; late check-in and early check-out times. $ *Rooms from: £90* ⊠ *17 St. Mary's St.* ☎ *01353/662124* ⊕ *www.cathedralhouse.co.uk* ➪ *2 rooms* ⫶◎⫶ *Free breakfast.*

Sudbury

32 miles southeast of Ely, 16 miles south of Bury St. Edmunds.

An early silk-weaving industry (still in existence, on a smaller scale) as well as the wool trade brought prosperity to Sudbury, which has three fine Perpendicular Gothic churches and some half-timber houses.

Draining East Anglia 👁

Large areas of East Anglia were originally barely inhabited, swampy marshes. Drainage of the wetlands by the creation of waterways was carried out most energetically in the 17th and 18th centuries. The process was far from smooth. Locals, whose fishing rights were threatened, sometimes destroyed the work. Also, as the marshland dried out, it shrank and sank, requiring pumps to stop renewed flooding. Hundreds of windmills were used to pump water away; some of them can still be seen today.

Thomas Gainsborough, one of the greatest English portrait and landscape painters, was born here in 1727; a statue of him holding his palette stands on Market Hill. In Charles Dickens's first novel, *The Pickwick Papers,* Sudbury was the model for the fictional Eatanswill, where Mr. Pickwick stands for Parliament.

GETTING HERE AND AROUND
From Cambridge, driving to Sudbury requires a circuitous route that takes about an hour. The A14 is slightly quicker, but the A3107 is more picturesque. There are no easy bus or train connections from Cambridge or Ely.

ESSENTIALS
VISITOR INFORMATION Sudbury Tourist Information Centre. ⊠ *The Library, Market Hill* ☎ *01787/881320* ⊕ *www.sudburytowncouncil.co.uk/tourist-information-centre-1.*

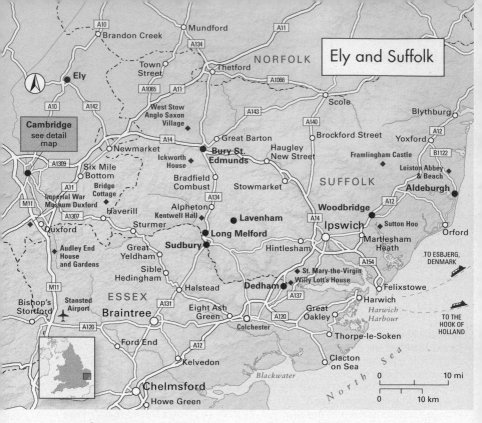

Long Melford

2 miles north of Sudbury, 14 miles south of Bury St. Edmunds.

It's easy to see how this village got its name, especially if you walk the full length of its 2-mile-long main street, which gradually broadens to include green squares and trees and finally opens into a large triangular green on the hill. Long Melford grew rich on its wool trade in the 15th century, and the town's buildings are an appealing mix, mostly Tudor half-timber or Georgian. Many house antiques shops. Away from the main road, Long Melford returns to its resolutely late-medieval roots.

GETTING HERE AND AROUND

Long Melford is just off the main A134. If you're driving from Sudbury, take the smaller B1064; it's much quicker than it looks on the map. There are several bus connections with Sudbury, Bury St. Edmunds, and Ipswich.

⊙ Sights

Holy Trinity Church

RELIGIOUS SITE | This largely 15th-century church, founded by the rich clothiers of Long Melford, stands on a hill at the north end of the village. Close up, the delicate flint flush-work (shaped flints set into a pattern) and huge Perpendicular Gothic windows that take up most of the church's walls have great impact, especially because the nave is 150 feet long. The Clopton Chapel, with an ornate (and incredibly rare) painted medieval ceiling, predates the rest of the church by 150 years. The beautiful Lady Chapel has an unusual cloister; the stone on the wall in the corner is an ancient multiplication table, used when the chapel served as a school in the 17th and 18th centuries. ■TIP➜ Tours can be arranged in advance; email alisonewbankis@gmail.com for more details and to make reservations. ⊠ Main St. ☎ 01787/310845 ⊕ www.longmelford-church.com ⊠ Free.

Kentwell Hall

HOUSE | FAMILY | A wide moat surrounds this redbrick Tudor manor house with tall chimneys and domed turrets. Built between 1520 and 1550, it was heavily restored inside after a fire in the early 19th century. On some weekends, costumed "servants" and "farmworkers" perform reenactments of Tudor life or life during World War II. There are also evening events, such as open-air theater performances. Check the website for notice of the spring lambing days. The house and farm are a half mile north of Long Melford Green. ■TIP➜ Always call ahead, as this place has notoriously variable opening times and sometimes contradictory listings. Family tickets (£28) are good value but can only be purchased online. ⊠ Off A134 ☎ 01787/310207 ⊕ www.kentwell.co.uk ⊠ £12; gardens and farm only £9 ⊗ Closed Oct.–Mar.

Melford Hall

HOUSE | Distinguished from the outside by its turrets and topiaries, Melford Hall is an Elizabethan house with its original banqueting room, a fair number of 18th-century additions, and pleasant gardens. Much of the porcelain and other fine pieces here come from the *Santisima Trinidad*, a ship loaded with gifts from the emperor of China and bound for Spain that was captured in the 18th century. Children's writer Beatrix Potter, related to the owners, visited often; there's a small collection of Potter memorabilia. ⊠ Off A134 ☎ 01787/379228 ⊕ www.nationaltrust.org.uk/melfordhall ⊠ £9.50 ⊗ Closed Nov.–Mar.

🛏 Hotels

The Bull

$ | HOTEL | This half-timber Elizabethan building reveals its long history with stone-flagged floors, bowed and twisted oak beams, and heavy antique furniture. **Pros:** historic atmosphere; comfortable bedrooms; friendly staff. **Cons:** minimum stay on summer weekends; popular with wedding parties; small bathrooms. ⑤ *Rooms from: £110* ⊠ *Hall St.* ☎ *01787/378494* ⊕ *www.greenekinginns.co.uk/hotels/bull-hotel-sudbury* ⤳ *25 rooms* ℠ *Some meals.*

Lavenham

4 miles northeast of Long Melford, 10 miles southeast of Bury St. Edmunds.

Virtually unchanged since the height of its wealth in the 15th and 16th centuries, Lavenham is one of the most perfectly preserved examples of a Tudor village in England. The weavers' and wool merchants' houses occupy not just one show street but most of the town. The houses are timber-frame in black oak, the main posts looking as if they could last another 400 years, although their walls are often no longer entirely perpendicular to the ground. The town has many examples of so-called "Suffolk pink" buildings—actually a catch-all term for brightly painted colors, including rose, yellow, and apricot; many of these house small galleries selling paintings and crafts.

GETTING HERE AND AROUND

Lavenham is on the A1141 and B1071. Take the latter if possible, as it's a prettier drive. There are hourly buses from Sudbury and Bury St. Edmunds and slightly less frequent buses from Ipswich.

ESSENTIALS

VISITOR INFORMATION Lavenham Tourist Information Centre. ⊠ *Lady St.* ☎ *01787/247983* ⊕ *www.lovelavenham.co.uk.*

Colorful and ancient, the timbered houses in pretty towns such as Lavenham recall the days when these buildings housed weavers and wool merchants.

Sights

Church of St. Peter and St. Paul

RELIGIOUS SITE | Set apart from the village on a hill, this grand 15th-century church was built between 1480 and 1520 by cloth merchant Thomas Spring. The height of its tower (141 feet) was meant to surpass those of the neighboring churches—and perhaps to impress rival towns. The rest of the church is perfectly proportioned, with intricately carved wood. ⌧ *Church St.* ☎ *01787/247244* ⊕ *www.lavenhamchurch. onesuffolk.net* ⌧ *Free.*

Lavenham Guildhall

BUILDING | Also known as the Guildhall of Corpus Christi, this higgledy-piggledy timber-framed building dating from 1529 dominates Market Place, an almost flawlessly preserved medieval square. Upstairs is a rather dull exhibition on local agriculture and the wool trade, although looking around the building itself is worth the admission charge. ⌧ *Market Pl.* ☎ *01787/247646* ⊕ *www.nationaltrust. org.uk/lavenham-guildhall* ⌧ *£8* ⊘ *Closed weekdays in Jan. and Feb., and Tues.– Thurs. in early Nov.–late Dec.*

Little Hall

BUILDING | This timber-frame wool merchant's house (brightly painted on the outside, in the local custom) contains a display showing the building's progress from its creation in the 14th century to its subsequent "modernization" in the 17th century. It also has a beautiful garden at the back. ⌧ *Market Pl.* ☎ *01787/247019* ⊕ *www.littlehall.org.uk* ⌧ *£4.50* ⊘ *Closed Nov.–Mar.*

Restaurants

★ Great House

$$$ | **FRENCH** | This excellent "restaurant with rooms" on the medieval Market Square takes deeply traditional flavors of the British countryside and updates them with a slight French twist in dishes like grilled salmon with spinach fondue or lamb with onion and thyme pie. Served in an elegant, whitewashed dining room, the three-course, fixed-price menus use a reassuring amount of local and regional ingredients. **Known for:** elegant, refined menus; local ingredients; a French touch. $ *Average main: £25* ✉ *Market Pl.* ☎ *01787/247431* ⊕ *www.greathouse. co.uk* ⊗ *Closed Mon. and Jan. No dinner Sun. No lunch Tues.*

★ Memsaab

$ | INDIAN | In a town ready to burst with cream teas, it's a bit of a surprise to find an Indian restaurant, let alone such an exceptional one. Among the classics one would expect from a curry house—from mild kormas to spicy *madrases* and *jalfrezies* (traditional curries made with chili and tomato)—are some finely executed specialties, including Nizami chicken (a fiery dish prepared with yogurt and fresh ginger) and king prawn *bhuna* (with ginger, garlic, and spring onion). **Known for:** top-notch Indian food; diverse choices; lively atmosphere. $ *Average main: £11* ✉ *2 Church St.* ☎ *01787/249431* ⊕ *www. memsaaboflavenham.co.uk.*

Munnings Tea Room

$ | CAFÉ | Probably one of the most photographed buildings in Lavenham, the wonderfully jumbled exterior of this adorable tearoom draws you in as surely as the promise of a delicious scone or slice of cake. Delightfully old-fashioned and quirky, this is what the British call a "proper tearoom," where tea is served in real china and diet-busting treats keep you going until dinner. **Known for:** famous building exterior; delicious cakes; quirky decor. $ *Average main: £14* ✉ *The Crooked House, 7 High St.* ☎ *0782/482–5623* ⊕ *www.munningstearoom.co.uk.*

⊟ Hotels

Lavenham Priory

$$$$ | RENTAL | You can immerse yourself in Lavenham's Tudor heritage at this sprawling house, one of the most widely photographed in the village. **Pros:** historic building; charming rooms; lovely garden. **Cons:** minimum two-night stay; no amenities; traffic noise in side rooms. $ *Rooms from: £365* ✉ *Water St.* ☎ *01787/247404* ⊕ *www.lavenhampriory. co.uk* ⇆ *2 rooms* ⦿ *No meals* ⌁ *2-night minimum.*

Swan Hotel

$$$ | HOTEL | This half-timber 14th-century lodging has rambling public rooms, roaring fireplaces, and corridors so low that cushions are strategically placed on beams. **Pros:** lovely old building; atmospheric rooms; beautiful spa. **Cons:** creaky floors; lots of steps to climb; popular wedding venue. $ *Rooms from: £235* ✉ *High St.* ☎ *01787/247477* ⊕ *www. theswanatlavenham.co.uk* ⇆ *49 rooms* ⦿ *Some meals.*

Bury St. Edmunds

10 miles north of Lavenham, 28 miles east of Cambridge.

The Georgian streetscape helps make the town one of the area's prettiest, and the nearby Greene King Westgate Brewery adds the smell of sweet hops to the air. The town hall dates from 1774.

Bury St. Edmunds owes its name, and indeed its existence, to Edmund, the last king of East Anglia and medieval patron saint of England, who was hacked to death by marauding Danes in 869. He was subsequently canonized, and his shrine attracted pilgrims, settlement, and commerce. In the 11th century the erection of a great Norman abbey (now only ruins) confirmed the town's importance as a religious center. The tourist office has a leaflet about the ruins and can arrange a guided tour.

GETTING HERE AND AROUND

The 11 bus from Cambridge's Drummer Street bus station takes about an hour to reach Bury St. Edmunds. By car, the town is a short drive from either Lavenham or Cambridge. Trains from Cambridge to Bury St. Edmunds leave once or twice an hour and take about 40 minutes.

ESSENTIALS
VISITOR INFORMATION Visit Bury St. **Edmunds.** ⊠ *Charter Sq.* ☎ *01284/764667* ⊕ *www.visit-burystedmunds.co.uk.*

 Sights

Angel Hill
NEIGHBORHOOD | A walk here is a journey through the history of Bury St. Edmunds. Along one side, the Abbey Gate, Norman Gate Tower, and St. Mary's Church make up a continuous display of medieval architecture. Elegant Georgian houses line Angel Hill on the side opposite St. Mary's Church; these include the Athenaeum, an 18th-century social and cultural meeting place that has a fine Adam-style ballroom. ⊠ *Angel Hill.*

Angel Hotel
HOTEL—SIGHT | This splendid, ivy-clad hotel was the location for Sam Weller's meeting with Job Trotter in Dickens's *The Pickwick Papers.* Dickens himself stayed here while he was giving readings at the nearby Athenaeum Hall. Now it's a great place to stop for lunch or afternoon tea. ⊠ *3 Angel Hill* ☎ *01284/714000* ⊕ *www. theangel.co.uk.*

Bury St. Edmunds Abbey
GARDEN | These scattered ruins are all that remain of the Abbey of Bury St. Edmunds, which fell during Henry VIII's dissolution of the monasteries. The Benedictine abbey's enormous scale is still evident in the surviving Norman Gate Tower on Angel Hill (incongruously, but quite appealingly, overlooked by a row of Georgian houses). Besides this, only the fortified Abbot's Bridge over the River Lark and a few ruins are left standing. There are explanatory plaques amid the ruins, which are now the site of the Abbey Botanical Gardens, with roses, elegant hedges, and rare trees, including a Chinese tree of heaven planted in the 1830s. There's also an aviary, a putting green, and a children's play area. ⊠ *Angel Hill* ☎ *01284/757490* ⊕ *www.english-heritage.org.uk* 🎟 *Free.*

Ickworth House
HOUSE | The creation of the eccentric Frederick Hervey, fourth earl of Bristol and bishop of Derry, this unusual 18th-century home was owned by the Hervey family until the 1960s. Inspired by his travels, Hervey wanted an Italianate palace and gardens. The two wings are arranged around a striking central rotunda. The east wing now contains a hotel, while the west has paintings by Hogarth, Titian, and Gainsborough. Behind the house, the rose gardens and vineyards spread out to join a vast, 1,800-acre wood. A stroll over the hills gives the best views of the house, which is 7 miles southwest of Bury St. Edmunds. Current renovation work means access to the house is limited (gardens are open as normal), so check with the venue before arrival. ⊠ *Off A143, Horringer* ☎ *01284/735270* ⊕ *www.nationaltrust. org.uk/ickworth* 🎟 *£15.22; gardens and park only £9.43.*

Moyse's Hall Museum
HOUSE | This 12th-century building, probably the oldest extant building in East Anglia, is a rare surviving example of a Norman house. The rooms hold exhibitions on Suffolk throughout the ages. One macabre display relates to the Red Barn Murder, a grisly local case that gained notoriety in a 19th-century play. ⊠ *Cornhill* ☎ *01284/706183* ⊕ *www.moy-seshall.org* 🎟 *£5; £12 combined ticket with West Stow Anglo Saxon Village.*

St. Edmundsbury Cathedral
RELIGIOUS SITE | Although the main body of this cathedral dates from the 15th century, its brilliant ceiling and gleaming stained-glass windows are the result of 19th-century restoration by architect Sir Gilbert Scott. Be sure to look near the altar to see the memorial to an event in 1214 when the barons of England took an oath here to force King John to grant the Magna Carta. There was a war, he lost, and the rest, as they say, is history. The cathedral's

original Abbey Gate was destroyed in a riot, and it was rebuilt in the 14th century with defense in mind—you can see the arrow slits. From Easter to September, guided tours are available Monday to Saturday at 11:30. There's also a small but popular café. ✉ *Angel Hill* ☎ *01284/748720* ⊕ *stedscathedral. org* ✉ *Free, suggested donation £3; tours £5* ⊗ *No guided public tours Oct.–Apr.*

St. Mary's Church

RELIGIOUS SITE | Built in the 15th century, St. Mary's has a blue-and-gold embossed "wagon" (barrel-shape) roof over the choir. Mary Tudor, Henry VIII's sister and queen of France, is buried here. ✉ *Angel Hill, at Honey Hill* ☎ *01284/754680* ⊕ *www.wearechurch. net* ✉ *Free.*

Theatre Royal

BUILDING | Built in 1819, the Theatre Royal is an outstanding example of Regency design. Guided tours can be booked at the box office. ✉ *6 Westgate St.* ☎ *01284/769505* ⊕ *www.theatreroyal.org* ✉ *Free; tours £7.50.*

West Stow Anglo Saxon Village

MUSEUM VILLAGE | **FAMILY** | This family-friendly museum past the outskirts of Bury St. Edmunds has indoor galleries displaying finds from the Anglo-Saxon period (410–1066) and a reconstruction of a village from that period with thatched-roof houses. Costumed performers give demonstrations of traditional crafts. There's also a small farm that's home to rare breeds of pigs and chickens. It's best to call ahead in winter as the hours can vary. ✉ *Icklingham Rd., West Stow* ☎ *01284/728718* ⊕ *www.weststow.org* ✉ *£6; £12 combined ticket with Moyse's Hall Museum.*

🍴 Restaurants

★ Maison Bleue

$$$ | **FRENCH** | This stylish French restaurant, with the same owners as the Great House in nearby Lavenham, specializes in locally caught seafood. Typical choices include king scallops with squid ink and duck breast with braised chicory, in addition to meatier options like Suffolk beef fillet with parsnip and walnut puree. **Known for:** elegant French cooking; special-occasion dining; great seafood. ⑤ *Average main: £26* ✉ *31 Churchgate St.* ☎ *01284/760623* ⊕ *www.maison-bleue.co.uk* ⊗ *Closed Sun. and Mon.*

Really Rather Good

$ | **BRITISH** | A prime location looking out over the town square adds an extra incentive to dine in this charming, independent café and coffeehouse. Sandwiches, artisan cofffee, cakes, and pancakes are the order here, and you can't go wrong with a classic cream tea, which is, ahem, really rather good. **Known for:** delicious cream teas; great location; warm service. ⑤ *Average main: £8* ✉ *31A Abbeygate St.* ☎ *01284/756181* ⊗ *No dinner.*

🛏 Hotels

Ickworth Hotel

$$ | **HOTEL** | **FAMILY** | You can live like nobility in the east wing of the Italianate Ickworth House, set on 1,800 acres. **Pros:** gorgeous grounds; relaxed atmosphere; family-friendly vibe. **Cons:** price can double at certain times in summer; two-night minimum on weekends; "family-friendly" can feel more like "overrun with kids". ⑤ *Rooms from: £129* ✉ *Off A143, 5 miles southwest of Bury St. Edmunds, Horringer* ☎ *01284/735350* ⊕ *www.ickworthhotel.co.uk* ⇌ *43 rooms* ⑪ *Free breakfast.*

The Old Cannon Brewery

$ | **B&B/INN** | This delightful old inn near the Bury St. Edmunds train station has a handful of bedrooms in its converted Victorian brewhouse. **Pros:** full of character; good food and beer; friendly hosts. **Cons:** pub is noisy until closing time; bathrooms are a little basic; few extras. ⑤ *Rooms from: £120* ✉ *86 Cannon St.* ☎ *01284/768769* ⊕ *www.oldcannonbrewery.co.uk* ⌁ *7 rooms* ⑩ *Free breakfast.*

 Nightlife

The Nutshell

BARS/PUBS | While you're in Bury St. Edmunds, pop in for a pint of the local Greene King ale at the Nutshell, which claims to be Britain's smallest pub—measuring just 16 feet by 7½ feet. ✉ *17 The Traverse* ☎ *01284/764867* ⊕ *www.thenutshellpub.co.uk.*

Dedham

62 miles southeast of Cambridge, 15 miles southeast of Bury St. Edmunds.

Dedham is the heart of Constable country. Here, gentle hills and the cornfields of Dedham Vale, set under the district's delicate, pale skies, inspired John Constable (1776–1837) to paint some of his most celebrated canvases. He went to school in Dedham, a picture-book village that did well from the wool trade in the 15th and 16th centuries and has retained a prosperous air ever since. The 15th-century church looms large over handsomely sturdy, pastel-color houses.

Nearby towns have several other sites of interest to Constable fans. About 2 miles from Dedham is Flatford, where you can see Flatford Mill, one of the two water mills owned by Constable's father. Northeast of Dedham, off A12, the Constable trail continues in East Bergholt, where Constable was born in 1776. Although the town is mostly modern, the older part has some atmospheric buildings like the church of St. Mary-the-Virgin.

GETTING HERE AND AROUND
From the main A12 road, Dedham is easily reached by car via B1029. Public transportation is extremely limited; there's no nearby train station.

👁 **Sights**

Bridge Cottage

HOUSE | On the north bank of the Stour, this 16th-century home in East Bergholt has a shop, an exhibition about Constable's life, and a pleasant tearoom overlooking the river. You can also rent rowboats here. ✉ *Off B1070, East Bergholt* ☎ *01206/298260* ⊕ *www.nationaltrust.org.uk/flatford* 💰 *Free* ⊗ *Closed mid-Dec.–late Dec. and weekdays Jan., Feb., and Nov.–mid-Dec.*

Colchester

TOWN | Nobody knows for sure whether Colchester is, as it claims, the oldest town in Britain. What's certain, however, is that it was a major stronghold during the Roman occupation. History buffs enjoy the impressive Roman amphitheater, where parts of the walls and floor are visible. Sections of the original Roman walls are also still standing. Colchester Castle was built on the foundations of the huge Roman Temple of Claudius. Colchester is off the A12, 9 miles southwest of Dedham.

★ St. Mary-the-Virgin

RELIGIOUS SITE | One of the most remarkable churches in the region, St. Mary-the-Virgin was started just before the Reformation. The doors underneath the ruined archways outside (remnants of a much older church) contain a series of mysterious symbols—actually a coded message left by Catholic sympathizers of the time. The striking interior contains a mini-museum of treasures, including an ancient wall painting of the Virgin Mary in one of the rear chapels, a 14th-century chest, and an extraordinary series of florid memorial stones on the nave wall opposite the main entrance. A unique feature of the church is that its bells are rung from a cage in the graveyard; this was erected as a temporary measure, pending the construction of a tower in 1531 that was never completed. ⊠ *Flatford Rd., East Bergholt* ☎ *01206/392646* 🖘 *Free.*

Willy Lott's House

HOUSE | A five-minute stroll down the path from Bridge Cottage brings you to this 16th-century structure that is instantly recognizable from Constable's painting *The Hay Wain* (1821). Although the house is not usually open to the public, the road is a public thoroughfare, so you can just walk right on up to see the famous—and completely unchanged— view for yourself. Just stand across from the two trees on the far bank, with the mill on your right, and look upstream. On the outside wall of the mill is a handy reproduction of the painting to help you compose your own photo. ⊠ *Flatford Rd., off B1070, East Bergholt.*

🍴 Restaurants

★ Le Talbooth

$$$ | BRITISH | This sophisticated restaurant serving excellent British-French fare is set in a Tudor house beside the idyllic River Stour. Outside, there are lighted terraces where food and drinks are served on warm evenings and jazz and steel bands play on Sunday evening in summer; inside, original beams, leaded-glass windows, and a brick fireplace add to the sense of history. **Known for:** superb British-French cooking; excellent service; summer barbecues. $ *Average main: £28* ⊠ *Gun Hill* ☎ *01206/323150* ⊕ *www.milsomhotels.com/letalbooth* ⊘ *No dinner Sun. mid-Sept.–early June.*

Marlborough Head

$ | BRITISH | This friendly, 300-year-old pub across from Constable's school in Dedham serves traditional English pub food. Dishes such as bangers and mash (sausages and mashed potatoes) and roast chicken share the menu with fish-and-chips and burgers. **Known for:** traditional pub food; proper village "local" feel; good old-school comfort eating. $ *Average main: £11* ⊠ *Mill La.* ☎ *01206/323250* ⊘ *No dinner Sun.*

🛏 Hotels

★ Maison Talbooth

$$$ | HOTEL | Constable painted the rich meadowlands in which this luxurious Victorian country-house hotel is set. **Pros:** good food; lovely views over Dedham Vale; some private hot tubs. **Cons:** restaurant books up fast; prices are high; need a car to get here. $ *Rooms from: £300* ⊠ *Stratford Rd.* ☎ *01206/322367* ⊕ *www. milsomhotels.com/maison-talbooth* 🖙 *12 rooms* ⏐⊙⏐ *Free breakfast.*

Milsoms Hotel

$$ | HOTEL | This Victorian-era hotel combines an old-fashioned feel with a modern style. **Pros:** comfortable rooms; stylish surroundings; delicious food. **Cons:** breakfast is a little pricey; a little way outside town; really need a car to get here. $ *Rooms from: £145* ⊠ *Stratford Rd.* ☎ *01206/322795* ⊕ *www.milsomhotels.com/milsoms* 🖙 *15 rooms* ⏐⊙⏐ *Free Breakfast.*

🏃 Activities

Boathouse Restaurant

BOATING | FAMILY | From Dedham, on the banks of the River Stour, you can rent a rowboat from the Boathouse Restaurant. They're available daily, April through October (depending on weather). The cost is £16 per hour, although you can rent for 30 minutes for £8 if you only want a brief sojourn in the water. ⊠ *Mill La.* ☎ *01206/323153* ⊕ *www.dedham-boathouse.com.*

Woodbridge

18 miles northeast of Dedham.

One of the first good ports of call on the Suffolk Heritage Coast, Woodbridge is a town whose upper reaches center on a fine old market square, site of the 16th-century Shire Hall. Woodbridge is at its best around its old quayside, where boatbuilding has been carried out since the 16th century. The most prominent building is a white-clapboard mill, which dates from the 18th century and is powered by the tides.

GETTING HERE AND AROUND

Woodbridge is on A12. There are a few local buses, but they mostly serve commuters. By train, Woodbridge is 1½ hours from London and just under 2 hours from Cambridge (with connections).

ESSENTIALS

VISITOR INFORMATION Woodbridge Tourist Information Centre. ⊠ *Station Building, Station Rd.* ☎ *01394/383789* ⊕ *choosewoodbridge.co.uk/listings/tourist-information-centre.*

◉ Sights

Framlingham Castle

CASTLE/PALACE | From the outside, this moated castle looks much as it would have in the 12th century. Upon entering, however, you'll notice that the keep is missing, although it still has 13 towers along the curtain wall. Most of the chimneys along the same wall are fake; they were Tudor additions meant to give the impression to passersby that this was a great mansion. Framlingham gradually fell into disrepair in the mid-1500s but not before it played its part in a pivotal moment in English history. After the death of Edward VI (Henry VIII's 15 year-old son), a succession crisis ensued, as, for the first time in English history, the only heirs to the throne were women. This sparked a battle between Mary (Edward's Catholic older sister) and Jane Grey, her teenage cousin, who was declared Queen by Protestant lords hoping to stage a coup. Mary, who was hopelessly outnumbered, fortified herself at Framlingham. Within just nine days she had rallied the great lords and ordinary folk alike to her cause, won the war, and taken back the crown. Today Framlingham is a peaceful place, except in summer, when it's an occasional venue for open-air concerts. ⊠ *B1116, Framlingham* ☎ *01728/724922* ⊕ *www.english-heritage.org.uk/framlingham* ☑ *£11.30* ⊘ *Closed weekdays Nov.–Mar.*

★ Sutton Hoo

INFO CENTER | The visitor center at Sutton Hoo tells the story of one of Britain's most significant Anglo-Saxon archaeological sites. In 1938, a local archaeologist excavated a series of earth mounds and discovered a 7th-century burial ship, probably that of King Raedwald of East Anglia. A complete replica of the 90-foot-long ship stands in the visitor center, which has artifacts and displays about Anglo-Saxon society. Nothing can quite make up for the fact that the best finds have been moved to the British Museum in London, but it is, nonetheless, all quite fascinating. Trails around the 245-acre site explore the area along the River Deben. ⊠ *Off B1083* ☎ *01394/389700* ⊕ *www.nationaltrust.org.uk/suttonhoo* ☑ *£15.*

🍽 Restaurants

★ Butley Orford Oysterage

$ | SEAFOOD | What started as a little café that sold oysters and cups of tea is now a bustling restaurant, with a nationwide reputation. It has no pretenses of grandeur but serves some of the best smoked fish you're likely to taste anywhere. **Known for:** legendary fish pie; traditional, local flavors; great, simple seafood. ⑤ *Average main: £13* ⊠ *Market Hill, Orford* ☎ *01394/450277* ⊕ *www.pinneysoforford.co.uk* ⊘ *No dinner Sun.–Tues. in Apr.–July, Sept., and Oct. No dinner Sun.–Thurs. in Nov.–Mar.*

Hotels

★ Crown and Castle

$$ | B&B/INN | Artsy, laid-back, and genuinely friendly, this little gem occupies an 18th-century building in the village of Orford, 10 miles east of Woodbridge. **Pros:** warm service; relaxed atmosphere; good restaurant. **Cons:** need a car to get around; not great for families; not close to major sights. $ *Rooms from: £160* ⊠ *Market Hill, Orford* ☎ *01394/450205* ⊕ *www.crownandcastle.co.uk* ⌂ *21 rooms* ⧖*I Free breakfast.*

Seckford Hall

$$ | HOTEL | The sense of history at this delightfully old-school hotel comes from more than just the magnificent Tudor architecture; several pieces of furniture are castoffs from Buckingham Palace, and one of the beds was supposedly slept in by Elizabeth I. Rooms are large and comfortable, with modern bathrooms (some have whirlpool tubs). **Pros:** antique charm; lovely setting; great atmosphere. **Cons:** no elevator; antique beds are creaky; minimum stay on weekends. $ *Rooms from: £150* ⊠ *Off A12* ☎ *01394/385678* ⊕ *www.seckford.co.uk* ⌂ *32 rooms* ⧖*I Free breakfast.*

Aldeburgh

15 miles northeast of Woodbridge.

Aldeburgh (pronounced *orl*-bruh) is a quiet seaside resort, except in June, when the town fills with people attending the noted Aldeburgh Festival. Its beach is backed by a promenade lined with candy-color dwellings. The 20th-century composer Benjamin Britten lived here for some time. He was interested in the story of Aldeburgh's native son, poet George Crabbe (1754–1832), and turned his life story into *Peter Grimes,* a celebrated opera that perfectly captures the atmosphere of the Suffolk Coast.

GETTING HERE AND AROUND

You have little choice but to drive to Aldeburgh; turn off A12 near Farnham and follow signs. There's no train station and no bus service.

ESSENTIALS

VISITOR INFORMATION Aldeburgh Tourist Information Centre. ⊠ *51 High St.* ☎ *01728/454884* ⊕ *www.thesuffolk-coast.co.uk/things-to-do/attractions/aldeburgh–visitor-information.*

Sights

★ Aldeburgh Beach Lookout

ARTS VENUE | This tiny, disused lookout tower is in the middle of the main beachfront in Aldeburgh and has been converted into a bijou space for contemporary art and performances. Artists take up weekly residences here, welcoming the public each Saturday to observe what they've created during the week. This isn't just a space for local talent, however; some big names in the British arts world have taken part in recent years, including the poet Michael Horovitz and painter Eileen Cooper, the first female head of the Royal Academy. They also sometimes show art films projected on the side of the building—an arresting sight against a backdrop of dark seas lapping on the nighttime shore. ⊠ *31 Crag Path* ☎ *01728/452754* ⊕ *www.aldeburgh-beachlookout.com* ⧖ *Free* ⊙ *Closed Sun.–Fri. Sometimes closed in winter.*

Leiston Abbey & Beach

BEACH—SIGHT | This Augustinian abbey, founded in 1186, was one of the most important religious orders in the area until it fell victim to Henry VIII's troops during the dissolution of the monasteries. It has a highly unusual feature—a 17th-century church built *inside* (and partially out of) the abbey ruins, effectively making it a church-within-a-church. Just opposite the row of little cottages leading up to the abbey, you'll see a small sign for a walking path to **Leiston Beach**.

The beach sculpture known as the Aldeburgh Scallop was created in honor of local composer Benjamin Britten.

The track starts rather unpromisingly by crossing a pig farm, but persevere, because the ¼-mile trail across fields, woods, and cliffs is the only way to access this beautiful sandy beach, one of the area's best-kept secrets. The water here is good for swimming, and the seclusion can be heavenly. There are no facilities whatsoever, but plenty of locals make the trek on a sunny day. Look out for the scattered remains of a few brick houses on your way down. These are all that's left of a village that was completely destroyed by coastal erosion in the 1960s. Leiston Abbey is 5½ miles north of Aldeburgh. ⊠ *B1122, Theberton* ☎ *01728/831354* ⊕ *www.english-heritage.org.uk* ▭ *Free.*

Moot Hall and Aldeburgh Museum

BUILDING | Moot Hall was the place where local elders met to debate and make decisions about the locality. Built of flint and timber, the 16th-century building once stood in the center of a thriving town; the fact that it's now just a few steps from the beach is testament to the erosive powers of the North Sea. Today, it contains the Aldeburgh Museum, a low-key collection that includes finds from an Anglo-Saxon ship burial. ⊠ *Moot Hall, Market Cross Pl.* ☎ *01728/454666* ⊕ *www.aldeburghmuseum.org.uk* ▭ *£3* ⊙ *Closed Nov.–Feb. and weekdays in Mar.*

🍴 Restaurants

★ Aldeburgh Fish and Chip Shop

$ | **BRITISH** | A frequent (and deserving) entry on "best fish-and-chips in Britain" lists, Aldeburgh's most celebrated eatery always has a long line of eager customers come frying time. The fish is fresh and local, the batter melts in your mouth, and the chips (from locally grown potatoes) are satisfyingly chunky. **Known for:** one of the most famous fish-and-chips shops in Britain; BYO wine or beer if you sit upstairs; long lines. ⑤ *Average main: £6* ⊠ *226 High St.* ☎ *01728/452250* ⊕ *www.aldeburghfishandchips.co.uk* ⊙ *Closed Mon. No dinner Sun., Tues., and Wed.*

The Lighthouse

$ | MODERN BRITISH | Excellent value, this low-key brasserie with tightly packed wooden tables relies exclusively on local produce for its Modern British dishes, all imaginatively prepared. The menu focuses on seafood, including oysters and Cromer crabs. **Known for:** fantastic fresh seafood; Grand Marnier fudge cake for dessert; great wine and beer selection. $ *Average main: £14* ⊠ *77 High St.* ☎ *01728/453377* ⊕ *www.lighthouserestaurant.co.uk.*

Hotels

Brudenell

$$ | HOTEL | With its good food, modest but comfortable rooms, and sweeping views of the sea, Brudenell is the very definition of an English seaside hotel. **Pros:** laid-back atmosphere; the beach is literally a stone's throw away; pleasant and quiet bedrooms. **Cons:** rooms are small for the price; car park is tiny; beach bar gets full early. $ *Rooms from: £160* ⊠ *The Parade* ☎ *01728/452071* ⊕ *www.brudenellhotel.co.uk* ➔ *44 rooms* ⧉ *Free breakfast.*

Performing Arts

★ Aldeburgh Festival

FESTIVALS | East Anglia's most important arts festival, and one of the best known in Britain, is the Aldeburgh Festival. It's held for two weeks in June in the small village of Snape, 5 miles west of Aldeburgh. Founded by Benjamin Britten, the festival concentrates on music but includes exhibitions, poetry readings, and lectures. A handful of events are aimed specifically at children. ⊠ *Snape* ☎ *01728/687100 for inquiries, 01728/687110 for box office* ⊕ *www.snapemaltings.co.uk/season/aldeburgh-festival.*

Witches in East Anglia 👁

Aldeburgh wasn't always the peaceful village it is today. In 1646, seven suspected witches were arrested and imprisoned at Moot Hall. They confessed after being tortured, and their public hanging in the town square was overseen by Matthew Hopkins, England's feared "Witchfinder General." From 1645 to 1647, he and his cronies killed around 300 women and children by torture, hanging, or burning. His methods were widely imitated, particularly during the 1692 witch trials in Salem, Massachusetts.

★ Snape Maltings

ARTS CENTERS | It's worth a stop to take in the peaceful River Alde location of this cultural center. It includes nine art galleries and crafts shops in distinctive large brick buildings once used to malt barley, plus a café and tearoom. There's a farmers' market on the first Saturday of the month, a major food festival in September, and a Benjamin Britten festival in October. Leisurely 45-minute river cruises (£7.50) leave from the quayside in spring and summer. From the Maltings, you can stroll out along an elevated trail through some reed marshes for beautiful views—just watch for uneven ground. ⊠ *Off B1069, Snape* ☎ *01728/688303* ⊕ *www.snapemaltings.co.uk.*

Norwich

63 miles northeast of Cambridge.

It used to be said that Norwich had a pub for each day of the year and a church in which to repent every Sunday. Although this is no longer true, real ales and steeples (including that of its grand cathedral) are still much in evidence in this pleasant city of 130,000. The University of East Anglia brings a cosmopolitan touch, including a lively arts scene and a love of literature evident by the city's many independent bookstores. It's a good base from which to explore the Norfolk Broads and the coast.

Established by the Saxons because of its prime trading position on the rivers Yare and Wensum, the town sits in the triangle between the two waterways. The inner beltway follows the line of the old city wall, much of which is still visible. It's worth walking or driving around after dark to see the floodlit buildings. By the time of the Norman Conquest, Norwich was one of the largest settlements in England, although much was destroyed by the Normans to create a new town. You can see the old flint buildings as you walk down the medieval streets and alleyways. Despite some industrial sites and many modern shopping centers, the town remains engaging.

GETTING HERE AND AROUND

Two Norwich-bound trains per hour leave from London's Liverpool Street station; the journey takes two hours. Buses to Norwich leave London's Victoria Coach Station every couple of hours; the trip takes three hours. The bus and train stations are a 10- to 15-minute walk from the city center. If you're driving, leave your car in any of the numerous lots scattered around the center.

TOURS

Broads Tours

TOUR—SIGHT | Based in Wroxham, 7 miles northeast of Norwich, Broads Tours has day cruises around the Broads rivers and canals, as well as cruiser boat rentals for a few days or a few weeks. ⊠ *Norfolk Broads Direct, The Bridge, Wroxham* ☎ *01603/782207* ⊕ *www.broadstours.co.uk.*

City Sightseeing

Forty-five-minute open-top bus tours of Norwich leave hourly (starting at 10:30) from Castle Meadow, April through September. Prices start at £14. ⊠ *Castle Meadow* ✛ *Castle Meadow West Side* ☎ *01263/587005* ⊕ *www.city-sightseeing.com.*

ESSENTIALS

VISITOR INFORMATION Visit Norwich. ⊠ *The Forum, Millennium Plain* ☎ *01603/213999* ⊕ *www.visitnorwich.co.uk.*

◉ Sights

★ Blickling Estate

HOUSE | Behind the wrought-iron entrance gate to Blickling Estate, two mighty yew hedges form a magnificent frame for this perfectly symmetrical Jacobean masterpiece. The redbrick mansion, 15 miles north of Norwich, has towers and chimneys, baroque Dutch gables, and, in the center, a three-story timber clock tower. The grounds include a formal flower garden and parkland with woods that conceal a temple, an orangery, and a pyramid. Blickling belonged to a succession of historic figures, including Sir John Fastolf, the model for Shakespeare's Falstaff; Anne Boleyn's family; and finally, Lord Lothian, ambassador to United States at the outbreak of the World War II. The Long Gallery (127 feet) has an intricate plasterwork ceiling with Jacobean emblems. ⊠ *B1354, Blickling*

☎ 01263/738030 ⊕ www.nationaltrust.
org.uk/blickling-estate 🎫 £15.50.

Norwich Castle

CASTLE/PALACE | FAMILY | The decorated stone facade of this castle, now a museum on the hill in the center of the city, makes it look like a children's-book illustration. Dating from 1130, the castle is Norman, but a stone keep replaced the original wooden bailey (wall). The thick walls and other defenses attest to its military function. Galleries contain a somewhat eclectic mix of artifacts and interactive displays, covering everything from ancient Egypt to Norman Norfolk and even the history of teapots. One gallery is devoted to the Norwich School of painters who, like John Constable, focused on the everyday landscape and seascape. ■TIP➔ Admission is £2 the last hour before closing and between noon and 1 on weekdays during school terms. ✉ Castle Meadow ☎ 01603/493625 ⊕ www. museums.norfolk.gov.uk/norwich-castle 🎫 £9.90; special exhibitions £6.

★ Norwich Cathedral

RELIGIOUS SITE | The grandest example of Norman architecture in Norwich has a towering 315-foot spire and the second-largest monastic cloisters in Britain (only Salisbury's are bigger). The cathedral was begun in 1096 by Herbert de Losinga, who had come from Normandy in 1091 to be its first bishop; his splendid tomb is by the high altar. The remarkable length of the nave is immediately impressive; the similarly striking height of the vaulted ceiling makes it a strain to study the delightful colored bosses, which illustrate Bible stories with great vigor and detail (binoculars are handy). The grave of Norfolk born nurse Edith Cavell, a British World War I heroine shot by the Germans in 1915, is at the eastern end. There's also a medieval-style herb garden, a Japanese garden, a restaurant, and a coffee shop. Guided tours are run Monday to Saturday at 10, 11, noon, 1, 2,

> ## Experiencing 👁 Norfolk's Broads
>
> Breathtakingly lovely, the Broads are a network of rivers and canals that stretch for about 150 miles across East Anglia, mostly in North Norfolk. It's a unique landscape of glassy waters, reed-covered marshlands, and impossibly photogenic windmills. At sunset, the whole area turns the color of honey. The Broads can be seen fleetingly from your car window, but it's nothing compared to floating through them on a boat. You can also see much of the Broads by bike.

and 3. The Cathedral Close is one of the most idyllic places in Norwich. Keep an eye out for peregrine falcons; they nest in the spire. Past the mixture of medieval and Georgian houses, a path leads down to the ancient water gate, Pulls Ferry. ✉ 62 The Close ☎ 01603/218300 ⊕ www. cathedral.org.uk 🎫 Free.

Plantation Garden

GARDEN | Abandoned and overgrown for more than 40 years after World War II, these beautiful Victorian gardens have been painstakingly returned to their former glory by a team of volunteers. Originally planted in 1856, the 2-acre site, dotted with fanciful Gothic follies, includes original features like an Italianate terrace and a huge rockery. It's a particularly tranquil spot when the spring and summer flowers are in full bloom—bring a picnic if the weather's good, or have a bite in the café. The entrance is somewhat hard to find; look for the little gate next to the Beeches Hotel. There's no car park, but you can use the lot at the nearby Black Horse Pub. ✉ 4 Earlham Rd. ☎ ⊕ www.plantationgarden.co.uk 🎫 £2.

★ Sainsbury Centre for the Visual Arts

COLLEGE | Designed by Norman Foster, this hangarlike building on the campus of the University of East Anglia holds the collection of the Sainsbury family (British supermarket billionaires). It includes a remarkable quantity of 20th-century works, including pieces by Picasso, Degas, Giacometti, Bacon, and Modigliani. Rotating exhibitions include big-name photography and art shows. If this museum were in London, it would be wall-to-wall crowded, every day. Buses 22, 25A, and X25 run from downtown Norwich. ⊠ *University of East Anglia, Earlham Rd.* ☎ *01603/593199* ⊕ *www.sainsburycentre.ac.uk* ⊠ *Free; special exhibitions from £9* ⊗ *Closed Mon.*

Restaurants

Adam and Eve

$ | BRITISH | Reputedly one of Norwich's oldest pubs, and one of the oldest in the country as a whole, this place dates back to at least 1249. From noon until 7, the kitchen serves such hearty pub staples as fresh, hot pies. **Known for:** extremely old pub; good comfort food; bit of a Norwich institution. ⑤ *Average main: £8* ⊠ *17 Bishopsgate* ☎ *01603/667423.*

Britons Arms

$ | BRITISH | A converted pub, this cozy, thatched café and restaurant has famously good homemade cakes as well as pies and tarts. The building, which dates from 1347, has low ceilings, a garden that's open in summer, and a crackling fire in winter. **Known for:** another impossibly old pub; cozy atmosphere; amazing cakes. ⑤ *Average main: £8* ⊠ *9 Elm Hill* ☎ *01603/623367* ⊕ *www.britonsarms.co.uk* ⊟ *No credit cards* ⊗ *Closed Sun. No dinner.*

Waffle House

$ | BELGIAN | FAMILY | This is the perfect antidote to all those meat-heavy English breakfasts—waffles, waffles, and more waffles on an imaginative menu.

Breakfast choices include toppings like bacon and bananas, while later in the day you can order them with anything from hummus and avocado to free-range sausage. **Known for:** duh, waffles; imaginative menu; savory or sweet options. ⑤ *Average main: £7* ⊠ *39 St. Giles St.* ☎ *01603/612790* ⊕ *www.wafflehousenorwich.co.uk.*

🛏 Hotels

The Maid's Head Hotel

$ | HOTEL | A charming and eccentric lodging in the middle of Norwich, the Maid's Head claims to be the oldest hotel in England. **Pros:** historic and full of character; modern comforts where they count; good restaurant. **Cons:** low ceilings; restaurant is pricey; breakfast not included in lower rates. ⑤ *Rooms from: £110* ⊠ *20 Tombland* ☎ *01603/209955* ⊕ *www.maidsheadhotel.co.uk* ⇦ *84 rooms* ⦿ *Free breakfast.*

🎭 Performing Arts

Maddermarket Theatre

THEATER | Patterned on the layout of Elizabethan theaters, the Maddermarket has been the base of amateur and community theater in Norwich since 1911. ⊠ *St. John's Alley* ☎ *01603/620917* ⊕ *www.maddermarket.co.uk.*

Norwich Arts Centre

ARTS CENTERS | This eclectic venue hosts a busy program of live music, dance, and comedy. ⊠ *St. Benedict's St.* ☎ *01603/660352* ⊕ *www.norwichartscentre.co.uk.*

Norwich Playhouse

THEATER | This professional repertory group performs everything from Shakespeare to world premieres of new plays. ⊠ *42–58 St. George's St.* ☎ *01603/598598* ⊕ *www.norwichtheatre.org.*

Walking Paths in East Anglia 👁

East Anglia is a walker's dream, especially if a relatively flat trail appeals to you. The regional website ⊕ www.visiteastofengland.com has further details about these paths.

The long-distance footpath known as the **Peddars Way** follows the line of a pre-Roman road, running from near Thetford through heathland, pine forests, and arable fields, and on through rolling chalk lands to the Norfolk coast near Hunstanton.

The **Norfolk Coastal Path** then continues eastward along the coast, joining at Cromer with the delightfully varied **Weaver's Way**, which passes through medieval weaving villages and deeply rural parts of the Norfolk Broads on its 56-mile route from Cromer to Great Yarmouth. Anyone interested in birds should carry binoculars and a field guide, as both of these routes have abundant avian life—both local and migratory.

Theatre Royal
THEATER | Norwich's biggest and best-known theater, the Theatre Royal hosts touring companies staging musicals, ballet, opera, and plays. ⊠ *Theatre St.* 🕾 *01603/630000* ⊕ *www.norwichtheatre.org.*

🛍 Shopping

The medieval lanes of Norwich, around Elm Hill and Tombland, contain the best antiques, book, and crafts stores.

★ Book Hive
BOOKS/STATIONERY | Considered by many to be among the best bookstores in England, the Book Hive has a rounded glass facade that gives you a hint of the treasures within. The three-story independent shop specializes in fiction, poetry, art and design, cooking, and children's books. Drop by, and you might stumble onto a book reading, cooking class, or other event. ⊠ *53 London St.* 🕾 *01603/219268* ⊕ *www.thebookhive.co.uk.*

Norwich Market
OUTDOOR/FLEA/GREEN MARKETS | Open Monday to Saturday, the city's main outdoor market has been the heart of the city's commerce for 900 years. Two hundred vendors sell everything from jewelry to clothing and food. ⊠ *Market Pl.* 🕾 *01603/213537* ⊕ *www.norwich.gov.uk.*

🏃 Activities

Broadland Cycle Hire
SPORTS—SIGHT | Located 8 miles northeast of Norwich, Broadland Cycle Hire charges £18 per day for rental (with discounts for couples and families). The company can recommend several good bike routes around the Broads rivers and canals. ⊠ *Horning Rd., Hoveton* 🕾 *07887/480331* ⊕ *www.norfolkbroadscycling.co.uk.*

Blakeney

28 miles northwest of Norwich.

The Norfolk coast begins to feel wild and remote near Blakeney, 14 miles west of Cromer. Driving the coast road from Cromer, you pass marshes, sandbanks, and coves, as well as villages. Blakeney is one of the most appealing, with harbors for small fishing boats and yachts. Once a bustling port town exporting corn and salt, it enjoys a quiet existence today, and a reputation for wildlife viewing at Blakeney Point.

The Wash

Old Hunstanton
Heacham

Brancaster Wells-next-the-Sea Blakeney National Nature Reserve

Burnham Market Holkham Hall Letheringsett Blakeney Cromer
Crossdale Street

Docking Holt Thursford A148
B1355

Lincoln

Sandringham House Houghton Hall Fakenham Blickling Estate

Sutton Crosses King's Lynn Hilington Harpley Saxthorpe Aylsham Smallburgh

Wisbech

Weasenham Saint Peter

NORFOLK Newton Saint Faith

Setchey Little Fransham

Swaffham Norwich THE BROADS

Ring's End

Stamford

Wereham Whitington Thurton Tasburgh

Fordham

Brandon Creek Mundford Larling

CAMBRIDGESHIRE Town Street Thetford South Lopham Needham

Ely Scole

Ingham SUFFOLK Brockford Street

Great Barton Haugley New Street

Bury St. Edmunds

0 8 mi
0 8 km

Norwich, North Norfolk, and Lincoln

GETTING HERE AND AROUND

A48 passes through the center of Blakeney. There are few bus connections, though the 46 and CH3 Coasthopper connect the town with Wells-next-the-Sea.

Sights

Blakeney National Nature Reserve

NATURE PRESERVE | The 1,000 acres of grassy dunes at Blakeney Point are home to nesting terns and about 500 common and gray seals. The 3½-mile walk here from Cley Beach is beautiful, but a boat trip from Blakeney or Morston Quay is fun and educational. An information center and a tearoom at Morston Quay are open according to tides and weather. ☒ Morston Quay, Quay Rd., Morston ☎ 01263/740241 ⊕ www.nationaltrust. org.uk/blakeney ☝ Free ⊘ Closed dusk–dawn.

Restaurants

White Horse at Blakeney

$$ | MODERN BRITISH | Traditional British food with an imaginative twist is the draw at this former coaching inn. The hearty, house special fish pie is excellent, or you may opt for a plate of fresh local mussels. **Known for:** seaside ambience; good seafood; cozy bar. $ Average main: £17 ☒ 4 High St. ☎ 01263/740574 ⊕ www.whitehorseblakeney.com.

Hotels

★ Byfords

$$ | HOTEL | In a market town 5 miles, southeast of Blakeney, Byfords epitomizes the increasing trendiness of North Norfolk. **Pros:** plush rooms; amiable staff; relaxed atmosphere. **Cons:** minimum stay on weekends; top-floor rooms have low ceilings; rooms can get hot in summer. ⑤ *Rooms from: £185* ⊠ *1–3 Shirehall Plain, Holt* ☎ *01263/711400* ⊕ *www.byfords.org. uk* ⊅ *16 rooms* ⦿ *Free breakfast.*

🏃 Activities

Bishop's Boats

TOUR—SPORTS | This company runs one- or two-hour seal-watching trips daily between March and early November for £13 per person. ⊠ *The Quay, at the end of High St.* ☎ *0800/074–0753 toll-free, 01263/740753* ⊕ *www.bishopsboats.co.uk.*

Temples Seal Watching Trips

TOUR—SPORTS | Temples Seal Watching Trips organizes two-hour boat trips out to Blakeney Point, where you can watch seals in their natural environment. Certain sailings drop you off at the Point for an hour before taking you back. Tours cost £13; there are usually two or three daily departures in high season. The ticket office is in Morston, 1½ miles west of Blakeney. ⊠ *Anchor Inn, 22 The Street, Morston* ☎ *01263/740791* ⊕ *www.seal-trips.co.uk.*

Wells-next-the-Sea

10 miles west of Blakeney, 34 miles northwest of Norwich.

A quiet base from which to explore other nearby towns, the harbor town of Wells-next-the-Sea and the nearby coastline remain untouched, with many excellent places for bird-watching and walking on the sandy beaches of Holkham Bay, near Holkham Hall. Today the town is a mile from the sea, but in Tudor times, when it was closer to the ocean, it served as one of the main ports of East Anglia. The remains of a medieval priory point to the town's past as a major pilgrimage destination in the Middle Ages. Along the nearby beach, a narrow-gauge steam train makes the short journey to Walsingham between Easter and October.

Queen Boudicca

After King Prasutagus died around AD 60, his wife, Boudicca, became queen of the Iceni Kingdom, which covered roughly the same area as modern-day Norfolk. Alas, the Romans annexed Iceni, flogged Boudicca, and raped her daughters. In revenge, she led an uprising, destroying first Roman Colchester, then London and St. Albans. Although she was later defeated, the warrior queen, with her flowing red hair and her chariot, has become something of a national symbol of Britain.

GETTING HERE AND AROUND
Wells-next-the-Sea is on the main A149 coastal road but can also be reached via B1105 from Fakenham. The nearest train station is about 16 miles away in Sheringham. There are regular buses from Sheringham, Fakenham, and Norwich.

ESSENTIALS
VISITOR INFORMATION Wells-next-the-Sea Tourist Information Centre. ⊠ *Staithe St.* ☎ *01328/710885* ⊕ *www.wellsguide. com.*

⊙ Sights

★ Holkham Hall

HOUSE | One of the most splendid mansions in Britain, Holkham Hall is the seat of the Coke family, the earls of Leicester. In the late 18th century, Thomas Coke went on a grand tour of the Continent, returning with art treasures and determined to build a house according to the new Italian ideas. Centered by a grand staircase and modeled after the Baths of Diocletian, the 60-foot-tall Marble Hall (mostly alabaster, in fact), may well be the most spectacular room in Britain. Beyond are salons filled with works from Coke's collection of masterpieces, including paintings by Gainsborough, Van Dyck, Rubens, and Raphael. Surrounding the house is a park landscaped by Capability Brown in 1762. A major upgrade of the visitor facilities was completed a couple of years ago, adding a new museum and a large coffee shop and restaurant in what used to be the stable blocks. The grounds are huge and populated by herds of deer, curious enough not to run away unless you get too close—in fact, there are so many that you'd be hard-pressed to walk through without spotting several. ■TIP➔ A good way to see the grounds is a half-hour-long lake cruise. The original walled kitchen gardens have been restored and once again provide produce for the estate. The gardens include an adventure playground for children. ⊠ Off A149 ☎ 01328/713111 for tickets, 01328/710227 for estate office ⊕ www.holkham.co.uk ⊠ Hall, museum, and gardens £17; gardens only £3.50; park free; parking £3 ☉ No vehicle access to park Nov.–Mar. Hall closed Nov.–Mar. and Tues., Wed., Fri., and Sat. in Apr.–Oct.

★ Houghton Hall

HOUSE | Built in the 1720s by the first British prime minister, Sir Robert Walpole, this extraordinary Palladian pile has been carefully restored by its current owner, the seventh marquess of Cholmondeley (pronounced "Chumley"). The double-height Stone Hall and the sumptuous private quarters reveal designer William Kent's preference for gilt, stucco, plush fabrics, and elaborate carvings. Don't leave the grounds without viewing the beautiful medieval simplicity of St. Martin's Church. Candlelight tours, light shows, and other special events are sometimes held on weekends; check the website for the schedule. Houghton Hall is 14 miles southwest of Wells-next-the-Sea. ⊠ Off A148, King's Lynn ☎ 01485/528569 ⊕ www.houghton-hall.com ⊠ £15–£18; park and grounds only £12 ☉ Closed Oct.–Mar. and Mon. (except bank holidays), Tues., and Fri.

★ Sandringham House

HOUSE | Not far from the old-fashioned seaside resort of Hunstanton, Sandringham House is where the Royal Family traditionally spends Christmas. The redbrick Victorian mansion was clearly designed for enormous country-house parties, with a ballroom, billiard room, and bowling alley, as well as a shooting lodge on the grounds. The house and gardens close when the Queen is in residence, but the woodlands, nature trails, and museum of royal memorabilia in the old stables remain open, as does the church, which is medieval but in heavy Victorian disguise. Tours give you access to most rooms, but steer clear of those occupied by current royals. The house is 20 miles southwest of Wells-next-the-Sea. ⊠ Off B1440, Sandringham ☎ 01485/545400 ⊕ www.sandringhamestate.co.uk ⊠ House, gardens, and museum £17.50; gardens and museum only £12.50 ☉ Closed mid-Oct.–early Apr.

🛏 Hotels

The Crown Hotel

$$ | HOTEL | Overlooking a tiny park in the middle of Wells-next-the-Sea, this cozy little hotel and restaurant is owned by New Zealand–born TV chef Chris Coubrough. **Pros:** cozy atmosphere; great restaurant; wonderful beds. **Cons:** some rooms on the small side; some bathrooms are Lilliputian; historic nature of the building makes parts inaccessible for those with mobility problems. ⑤ Rooms from: £160 ⊠ The Buttlands ☎ 01328/710209 ⊕ www.crownhotelnorfolk.co.uk ⇥ 12 rooms ❈ Free breakfast.

Victoria at Holkham

$$ | **HOTEL** | **FAMILY** | A colorful, whimsical hideaway, this hotel on the Holkham Hall estate is more laid-back and family-friendly than the austere Victorian exterior suggests, and inside, the shabby-chic design contrasts with a hip and sophisticated vibe. **Pros:** original character; excellent location; outstanding food. **Cons:** minimum stay on weekends; extremely busy in summer; no elevator. $ *Rooms from: £210* ⊠ *Park Rd., Holkham* ☎ *01328/711008* ⊕ *www.holkham.co.uk/victoria* ⌁ *20 rooms* ⦿ *Free breakfast.*

Activities

On Yer Bike Cycle Hire

BICYCLING | For £20 per day (plus a small delivery charge), On Yer Bike Cycle Hire will deliver bikes to your local lodging—and collect them, too. Reservations are required (but no credit cards accepted). ⊠ *Nutwood Farm, The Laurels, Wighton* ☎ *07584/308120, 07584/308120 cell phone* ⊕ *www.norfolkcyclehire.co.uk.*

Stamford

48 miles northwest of Cambridge.

Serene, honey-hued Stamford, on a hillside overlooking the River Welland, has a well-preserved center, in part because in 1967 it was designated England's first conservation area. This unspoiled town, which grew rich from the medieval wool and cloth trades, has a delightful, harmonious mixture of Georgian and medieval architecture.

GETTING HERE AND AROUND

Stamford is on the A43 and A1. Trains from London (King's Cross and St. Pancras stations) depart about every 30 minutes and those from Lincoln about every hour (all with connections). The journey from London takes between one and two hours, or between two and three from Lincoln due to connections.

ESSENTIALS

VISITOR INFORMATION Stamford Tourist Information Centre. ⊠ *Stamford Arts Centre, 27 St. Mary's St.* ☎ *01780/755611* ⊕ *www.stamfordartscentre.com/about-us/tourist-information.*

👁 Sights

★ Burghley House

HOUSE | **FAMILY** | Considered one of the grandest houses of the Elizabethan age, this architectural masterpiece is celebrated for its rooftops bristling with pepper-pot chimneys and slate-roof towers. It was built between 1565 and 1587 to the design of William Cecil, when he was Elizabeth I's high treasurer, and his descendants still occupy the house. The interior was remodeled in the late 17th century with treasures from Europe. On view are 18 sumptuous rooms, with carvings by Grinling Gibbons and ceiling paintings by Antonio Verrio (including the Heaven Room and the Hell Staircase—just as dramatic as they sound), as well as innumerable paintings and priceless porcelain. You can tour on your own or join the 80-minute guided tour daily at 10:30 am and 3 pm (£10). Capability Brown landscaped the grounds in the 18th century; herds of deer roam free, and open-air concerts are staged in summer. Brown also added the Gothic-revival orangery, where today you can take tea or lunch. More contemporary additions come in the form of the aptly named Garden of Surprise and the adjacent Sculpture Garden, filled with imaginative creations, water jets, and a mirrored maze. Burghley is a mile southeast of Stamford. ⊠ *Off A1* ☎ *01780/752451* ⊕ *www.burghley.co.uk* ⌁ *House and gardens £20; gardens only £13.50* ⊘ *Closed Nov.–mid-Mar., Fri. in mid-Mar.–Oct., and wk of the international Burghley Horse Trials (late Aug. or early Sept.).*

In the Heaven Room at Burghley House, 17th-century painter Antonio Verrio shows the classical gods and goddesses of Mount Olympus hard at play. Their frolicking looks almost three-dimensional. In the center of this opulence is a massive 18th-century silver wine cooler, an item the gods (and more earthly lords) might have found useful.

Lincoln

53 miles north of Stamford, 93 miles northwest of Cambridge, 97 miles northwest of Norwich.

Celts, Romans, and Danes all had important settlements here, but it was the Normans who gave Lincoln its medieval stature after William the Conqueror founded Lincoln Castle as a stronghold in 1068. Four years later, William appointed Bishop Remigius to run the huge diocese stretching from the Humber to the Thames, resulting in the construction of Lincoln Cathedral, the third-largest in England after York Minster and St. Paul's. Since medieval times, Lincoln's status has declined. However, its somewhat remote location (there are no major motorways or railways nearby) has helped preserve its traditional character.

The cathedral is on the aptly named Steep Hill; to its south, narrow medieval streets cling to the hillside. Jews House, on the Strait, dating from the early 12th century, is one of several well-preserved domestic buildings in this area. The name is almost as old as the house itself—it refers to a former resident, Belaset of Wallingford, a Jewish woman who was murdered by a mob in 1290, the same year the Jews were expelled from England (they remained in exile for nearly 400 years). The River Witham flows unobtrusively under the incongruously named High Bridge, a low, vaulted Norman bridge topped by timber-frame houses from the 16th century. West from here, you can rent boats, or, in summer, go on a river cruise.

GETTING HERE AND AROUND

There are direct buses (four to five hours) from London, but most rail journeys (two to three hours) involve changing trains. The bus and train stations are south of the center, and it's a steep walk uphill to the cathedral and castle. Drivers will find parking lots around the bus and train stations and in the center at the Lawn and Westgate.

ESSENTIALS

VISITOR INFORMATION Lincoln Tourist Information Centre. ⊠ *9 Castle Hill* ☎ *01522/545458* ⊕ *www.visitlincoln.com.*

◉ Sights

★ Lincoln Castle

CASTLE/PALACE | FAMILY | Facing the cathedral across Exchequer Gate, this castle was built by William the Conqueror in 1068, incorporating the remains of Roman walls. The castle was used as a debtor's prison from 1787 to 1878. In the chapel you can see cagelike stalls where convicts heard sermons; they were designed this way so inmates couldn't tell who their fellow prisoners were, thus supposedly preserving a modicum of dignity. The castle's star exhibit is an original copy of **Magna Carta**, signed by King John in 1215. This is one of only four surviving copies of the original document, and one of few ever to have left the country—it was secretly moved to Fort Knox for safekeeping during World War II. A major renovation in 2015 opened up the wall walk for the first time, allowing visitors to make a complete circuit of the battlements (totaling more than ¼ mile). In addition, a 3D cinema shows a high-tech film about the history of Magna Carta. ⊠ *Castle Hill* ☎ *01522/554559* ⊕ *www.lincolncastle.com* ⊠ *All attractions £14; Medieval Wall Walk £8; joint ticket with Lincoln Cathedral £18.*

★ Lincoln Cathedral

RELIGIOUS SITE | Lincoln's crowning glory (properly known as the Cathedral of St. Mary, although nobody calls it that), this was, for centuries, the tallest building in Europe. The Norman Bishop Remigius began work in 1072. The Romanesque church he built was irremediably damaged, first by fire, then by earthquake. Today, its most striking feature is the west front's strikingly tall towers, best

Both the castle and cathedral in Lincoln are two of the city's most magnificient sites.

viewed from the 14th-century Exchequer Gate in front of the cathedral or from the castle battlements beyond. Inside, a breathtaking impression of space and unity belies the many centuries of building and rebuilding. The stained-glass window at the north end of the transept (known as the Dean's Eye) dates from the 13th century. ■ TIP→ Look for the Lincoln Imp on the pillar nearest St. Hugh's shrine; according to legend, an angel turned this creature to stone.

Through a door on the north side is the chapterhouse, a 10-sided building with one of the oldest vaulted ceilings in the world. It sometimes housed the medieval Parliament of England during the reigns of Edward I and Edward II. The cathedral library, designed by Christopher Wren (1632–1723), was built onto the north side of the cloisters after the original library collapsed. Guided tours of the ground floor are included in the price. You can also book tours of the roof and tower, but these must be arranged in advance with the visitor services team. For

safety reasons, children under 14 are not allowed on those tours. ✉ Minster Yard ☎ 01522/561600 ⊕ www.lincolncathedral. com ✉ Nave free; rest of cathedral £8; joint ticket with Lincoln Castle £18.

Medieval Bishop's Palace

HOUSE | On the south side of Minster Yard, this building has exhibits about the former administrative center of the diocese, plus a garden and working vineyard. Renovation work currently restricts access, but you can prebook hard hat guided tours in advance. ✉ Minster Yard ☎ 01522/527 468 ⊕ www.english-heritage.org.uk/visit/places/lincoln-medieval-bishops-palace ✉ £5.90 ⊙ Closed weekdays in Nov.–Mar., and Mon. and Tues. in Apr.–Oct.

Minster Yard

NEIGHBORHOOD | Surrounding the cathedral on three sides, Minster Yard contains buildings of different periods, including graceful Georgian architecture. A statue of Alfred, Lord Tennyson, who was born in Lincolnshire, stands on the green near the chapter house. ✉ Minster Yard.

🍽 Restaurants

Brown's Pie Shop
$ | **BRITISH** | More than you might imagine from the modest name, Brown's Pie Shop serves the best of old-school British food. Enjoy succulent beef, great desserts, and some very good, freshly made savory pies. **Known for:** old-school pies; cheap and cheerful eats; hearty meals. $ *Average main: £10* ✉ *33 Steep Hill* ☎ *01522/527330* ⊕ *www.brownspieshop.co.uk.*

★ Jews House
$$ | **MODERN BRITISH** | This intimate restaurant is one of Lincoln's oldest buildings, a rare survivor of 12th-century Norman domestic architecture and worth a visit even if the cosmopolitan menu weren't so outstanding. Typical main dishes include duck breast with carrot and turmeric puree or wild turbot with caviar hollandaise. **Known for:** extremely historic building; long-standing favorite with locals; great, contemporary cooking. $ *Average main: £26* ✉ *15 The Strait* ☎ *01522/524851* ⊕ *www.jewshouserestaurant.co.uk* ☿ *Closed Sun.–Tues.*

Pimento
$ | **VEGETARIAN** | Having made the arduous walk up the aptly named Steep Hill, you'll be pleased to find the excellent Pimento waiting for you. A highly regarded vegan and vegetarian restaurant, you can expect to find a mix of classic English tearoom fare, from filled jacket potatoes and scones with jam to salads and sandwiches (all vegetarian or vegan, of course). **Known for:** all vegetarian and vegan menu; classic English dishes; focus on fresh produce. $ *Average main: £7* ✉ *27 Steep Hill* ☎ *01522/533225* ⊕ *www.pimentosteephill.com.*

Wig and Mitre
$ | **BRITISH** | This pub-café-restaurant serves everything from breakfast to full evening meals in its old-fashioned dining room. The produce comes from the local markets; expect dishes such as rib eye with triple-cooked chips (thick-cut fries) or sea bass and crab risotto. **Known for:** market produce; handsome, traditional pub interior; good wine list. $ *Average main: £15* ✉ *30–32 Steep Hill* ☎ *01522/535190* ⊕ *www.wigandmitre.com.*

🛏 Hotels

★ Cathedral View Guest House
$ | **B&B/INN** | This B&B in the medieval quarter is just a three-minute walk from Lincoln Cathedral and almost as old; those exposed beam roofs you're sleeping under date from the 12th century. **Pros:** historic building in a great location; good breakfast; private parking lot. **Cons:** some rooms are tiny; some street noise; early checkout. $ *Rooms from: £88* ✉ *6 Eastgate* ☎ *01522/537469* ⊕ *www.cathedralviewlincoln.co.uk* ⤶ *10 rooms* 🍽 *Free breakfast.*

🎭 Performing Arts

New Theatre Royal
THEATER | A fine Victorian auditorium, the New Theatre Royal previews plays and musicals before their London runs and also hosts touring productions and comedy. ✉ *Clasketgate* ☎ *01522/519999* ⊕ *www.newtheatreroyallincoln.co.uk.*

🛍 Shopping

The best stores are on Bailgate, Steep Hill, and the medieval streets leading directly down from the cathedral and castle.

Cheese Society

FOOD/CANDY | Just off Steep Hill, this shop has a great selection of English and French cheeses, including the delicious local Lincoln Blue. There's also an adjacent café. ✉ *1 St. Martin's La.* ☎ *01522/511003* ⊕ *www.thecheesesociety.co.uk.*

Harding House Gallery

ART GALLERIES | Steep Hill has good bookstores, antiques shops, and art galleries, including the delightful Harding House Gallery, a cooperative of contemporary visual artists. ✉ *Steep Hill* ☎ *01522/523537* ⊕ *www.hardinghousegallery.co.uk.*

Chapter 13

YORKSHIRE

Updated by
Ellin Stein

⊙ Sights   🍴 Restaurants   🛏 Hotels   🛍 Shopping   🍸 Nightlife

★★★☆☆   ★★★☆☆   ★★★☆☆   ★★☆☆☆   ★★☆☆☆

WELCOME TO YORKSHIRE

TOP REASONS TO GO

★ **York Minster:** The largest Gothic cathedral in Northern Europe helps make York one of the country's most visited cities. An interactive exhibit in the undercroft explores the site's history from Roman times onward.

★ **North York Moors:** The wide-open spaces of this national park let walkers find glorious solitude amid the heather-covered hills that glow crimson and purple in late summer and early fall.

★ **Rievaulx Abbey:** The ruins of this great Cistercian abbey can be approached by a tiny lane that provides a view of its soaring arches dramatically appearing out of the trees.

★ **Coastal towns:** Seafront Whitby inspired Bram Stoker to set some of *Dracula* there. Robin Hood's Bay, a village set in a ravine, has an outstanding beach.

★ **Haworth:** Looking as if it were carved from stone, this picture-perfect hillside town where the Brontë sisters lived is a lovely place to learn about them.

Yorkshire is the largest of England's historic counties. At its heart is the ancient city of York, with its Gothic cathedral and medieval city walls. To the west is the bustling city of Leeds, while a few miles away are the unspoiled hills that form what the tourist office calls Brontë Country—Haworth, where the Brontë family lived, and the valleys and villages of the Yorkshire Dales. North of York is North York Moors National Park. Isolated stone villages, moorland walks, and Rievaulx Abbey are within easy reach.

Along the east coast of Yorkshire, beaches and a fascinating history await you in the resort town of Scarborough, the former whaling port of Whitby, and Robin Hood's Bay.

1 York. Yorkshire's major city with its famous Gothic cathedral.

2 Harrogate. An elegant Georgian and Victorian spa town.

3 Knaresborough. A historic market town in the beautiful Nidd Gorge.

4 Ripon. Quite possibly England's second oldest city.

5 Castle Howard. A baroque masterpiece near York.

6 Leeds. A former industrial powerhouse reinvented as a shopping and entertainment hub.

7 Saltaire. A planned village that's also a UNESCO World Heritage Site.

8 Haworth. The heart of Brontë country.

9 Bolton Abbey. A pretty town in the Yorkshire Dales.

10 Skipton. A true market town.

11 Hawes. A center of English cheese-making.

12 Richmond. A charming market town.

13 Danby. A good base for Moors National Park.

14 Hutton-le-Hole. A picturesque village in the heart of moorland.

15 Helmsley. Home to the atmospheric ruins of Rievaulx Abbey.

16 Hull. The gateway to England's north.

17 Scarborough. The largest resort town on the Yorkshire coast.

18 Robin Hood's Bay. A tiny fishing villge with rugged, steep cliffs pounded by the North Sea.

19 Whitby. A Gothic fishing port and busy tourist hub.

GREAT ENGLISH CHEESES

Strong-flavored Blue Stilton is a classic.

England's lush pastures yield more than 700 types of cheese, which the English eat at any time except breakfast. Smooth and creamy, nutty and tasty, or blue and smelly, cheese turns up in sandwiches and soups, on toast, as a topping, and on cheese boards at the end of a meal.

Cheeses come in three strengths: mild, medium, and mature. Young cheese is mild and crumbly; as it ages, the flavor gets sharper and the texture firmer. Protected Designation of Origin (PDO) applies to 15 cheeses that are produced in a designated area. An increasing number of small artisan makers produce distinctive and organic cheeses as well as those made from the milk of goats (Quickes) or sheep (Blacksticks); they aren't afraid to experiment. Cornish Yarg is covered with nettles, Stinking Bishop is washed in perry (an alcoholic drink made from pears), and White Stilton is often stuffed with fruit. Some pubs offer local cheese as part of a "ploughman's lunch," served with crusty bread, relish, and pickled onion.

ON THE SIDE

For **ploughman's lunches**, look for fruit chutneys made from raisins, apples, onions, vinegar, and sugar. Branston pickle is a crunchy, spicy-sweet mix of chopped vegetables. Small pickled onions and gherkins are common. Piccalilli consists of cauliflower florets pickled in a thick yellow spicy sauce. **Cheese boards** have three or four cheeses, grapes, apples, pears, biscuits, and crackers.

BLUE STILTON

This has been the king of English cheeses since the 18th century. With a strong taste and scent, it's now the cheese traditionally served at Christmas, often with port. Distinguished by blue veins and a crusty exterior, the whole cheeses are wheel-shape and become softer and creamier as they age. As a condition of its PDO status, it must be made in Nottinghamshire, Derbyshire, or Leicestershire.

CHEDDAR

Originally matured only in caves at Cheddar in Somerset, this is the best known of all English cheeses. Ranging from mild to extra-mature (nuttier), it's firm in texture. If you're looking for the best, aim for West Country Farmhouse Cheddar, which has PDO status when it's made traditionally in Devon, Cornwall, Somerset, and Dorset.

CHESHIRE

The oldest named English cheese has appeared on the menu since Roman times. Usually white in color, it has a crumbly texture and salty tang, and it's sometimes colored with annatto, a derivative of the achiote tree that gives a yellow hue to orange color.

Lancashire cheese

DOUBLE AND SINGLE GLOUCESTER

Both varieties have a smooth, dense texture and creamy flavor. Double is more common, and its buttery color is due to annatto. Single Gloucester has PDO status; this requires the cheese to be made in Gloucestershire, to be wheel-shaped, and to be natural in color.

LANCASHIRE

This cheese comes in three strengths according to age: creamy, crumbly, and tasty. The creamy, young cheese is ideal for cheese on toast (Welsh rarebit); the crumbly goes well with fruitcake or an apple and is also good in a salad.

SHROPSHIRE BLUE

Contrary to expectation, this cheese has never been made in Shropshire. Now produced exclusively in the East Midlands, it's a soft, mellow, orange-color cheese with blue veins, created by injecting the *penicillium* mold.

WENSLEYDALE

Made all over the country, the cheese is traditionally produced at Hawes in Wensleydale in Yorkshire. It has a white, crumbly texture and a salty taste; it's best eaten when young and fresh. Wensleydale is often served with fruitcake, fresh apples, or hot apple dishes.

You can buy pieces of cheese both small and large around England.

A hauntingly beautiful region, Yorkshire is known for its wide-open spaces and dramatic landscapes. The hills of the North York Moors and the Yorkshire Dales glow pink and purple with heather in summer, turning to black in winter.

Rugged fishing villages like Robin Hood's Bay cling to the edges of cliffs in one of England's most unspoiled areas. Period architecture abounds in York, with its narrow medieval streets, or in historic spa towns like Harrogate, while ancient cathedrals, abbeys, and castles provide majestic backdrops to day-to-day life in the area.

Some of the region's biggest attractions are the result of human endeavor: York's towering Gothic cathedral, created by unknown master craftsmen; Castle Howard, Vanbrugh and Hawksmoor's baroque masterpiece near York; and the dramatic Fountains Abbey near Ripon, the largest monastic ruins in England.

The Yorkshire landscape, however, is just as compelling. The most rugged terrain is the North York Moors, a large windswept moorland (crossed by cultivated valleys), where flocks of Scottish Blackface or Swaledale sheep graze freely. The landscape that inspired the Brontë sisters (whose former home in the small hilltop village of Haworth is now a museum) is found in the West Yorkshire Pennines, with their moors and rocky crags punctuated by gray-stone villages. Farther to the north are the lush, green uplands and valleys known as the Yorkshire Dales, where the high rainfall produces swift rivers and sparkling streams. These are wonderfully peaceful places, except in summer, when hundreds of hikers (or "ramblers," as they're known in England) appear over the hills, injecting life into the local economy. ⚠ **In recent years, severe winter storms have caused major flooding in the Yorkshire Dales and surrounding areas, leading to the closure of roads and sites. Be sure to check the weather before you travel.**

The area isn't all green fields and perfect villages—there's also a gritty, urban aspect to the region. In West Yorkshire, once down-at-heels Leeds has remade itself with trendy restaurants and cafés, along with a buzzing music industry and nightlife scene.

MAJOR REGIONS

York. Still enclosed within its medieval city walls, this beautifully preserved city makes the perfect introduction to Yorkshire. Its towering Minster and narrow streets are alive with history.

Around York. West and north of York a number of sights make easy, appealing day trips from the city: the spa town of Harrogate, atmospheric Knaresborough, the ruins of Fountain Abbey, the market town of Ripon, and nearby Newby Hall. If you're heading northwest from York to Harrogate, you might take the less direct B1224 across Marston Moor, where, in 1644, Oliver Cromwell won a decisive victory over the Royalists during the English Civil War. A few miles beyond, at Wetherby, you can cut northwest along the A661 to Harrogate. Also nearby toward the northeast is Castle Howard, a magnificent stately home.

Leeds and Brontë Country. Rocky and bleak, this windswept stretch of country provides an appropriate setting for the dark, dramatic narratives penned by the Brontë sisters in Haworth. The busy city of Leeds provides a good starting point for a tour of West Yorkshire. From here you can strike out for the traditional wool towns, such as Saltaire, a UNESCO-protected gem, and the Magna museum at Rotherham, which draws long lines for its surprisingly interesting exploration of steel production. But the main thrust of many visits to West Yorkshire is to the west of Leeds, where the stark hills north of the Calder Valley and south of the River Aire form the landscape immortalized in the equally unsparing novels of the Brontë sisters. The gray-stone village of Haworth might have faded into obscurity were it not for the enduring fame of the literary sisters. Every summer, thousands toil up the steep main street to visit their former home. To truly appreciate the setting that inspired their books, though, you need to go farther afield to the ruined farm of Top Withens, which, in popular mythology, if not in fact, was the model for *Wuthering Heights*.

The Yorkshire Dales. Waterfalls, ancient woodlands, rugged uplands, and exceptionally scenic valleys make for splendid views. To the west of the North York Moors, this landscape has been shaped by limestone: lush green valleys (known as dales, the Viking word for valley) lie between white limestone scars (cliffs), while broad uplands are punctuated with dark fells (crags). The limestone cliffs, filled with caves, invite exploration.

As well as dramatic landscapes like the spectacular cliffs and gorges at Malham Cove and Gordale Scar, the area has some breathtaking waterfalls. Ruined priories, narrow roads, drystone walls made without mortar, and babbling rivers make for a quintessentially English landscape, full of paths and trails to explore.

The North York Moors. The North York Moors are a dramatic swath of high moorland starting 25 miles north of the city of York and stretching east to the coast and west to the Cleveland Hills. Only a few pockets remain of the dense forest that once covered the area. The transformation began during the Middle Ages, when the monks of Rievaulx and Whitby abbeys began raising huge flocks of sheep. Over the course of centuries, the sheep have kept the moors deforested, which ensures that the pink heather on which they feed spreads lushly across the hills. A series of isolated, medieval "standing stones" that once served as signposts on the paths between the abbeys are still handy for hikers.

For more than four decades, the area has been a national park, ensuring the protection of the bleak moors and grassy valleys that shelter brownstone villages and hamlets. Minor roads and tracks crisscross the hills, but there's no single, obvious route through the region. You can approach from York; another approach is from the coast at Whitby, along the Esk Valley to Danby, which is also accessible on the Esk Valley branch-train line running between Middlesbrough and Whitby. From Danby, minor roads run south over the high moors reaching Hutton-le-Hole, beyond which main roads lead to such interesting market towns as Helmsley, on the moors' edge. Completing the route in this direction leaves you with an easy side trip to Castle Howard before returning to York.

The North Yorkshire Coast. The coastline of the North York Moors paints a dramatic view of spectacular white cliffs covered in pink heather plummeting down to the dark sea hundreds of feet below. The red roofs of Robin Hood's Bay, the sharply curved bay at Whitby, and the gold-and-white buildings of Scarborough capture the imagination at first sight. Most coastal towns still support an active fishing industry, and every harbor offers fishing and leisure trips throughout summer. Beaches at Scarborough and Whitby have patrolled areas: swim between the red-and-yellow flags, and don't swim when a red flag is flying. All the North Sea beaches are ideal for fossil hunting and seashell collecting.

Planning

When to Go

To see the heather at its most vibrant, visit in summer (but despite the season, be prepared for some chilly days). It's also the best time to see the coast, as colorful regattas and arts festivals are underway. York Minster makes a splendidly atmospheric focal point for the prestigious York Early Music Festival in early July. Spring and fall bring their own rewards: far fewer crowds and crisp, clear days, although there's an increased risk of rain and fog. The harsh winter is tricky: while the moors and dales are beautiful covered in snow, and the coast sparkles on a clear, bright day, storms and blizzards can set in quickly, making the moorland roads impassable and villages at risk of being cut off entirely. In recent years, major flooding from rain storms has been increasing throughout Yorkshire. In winter, stick to York and the main towns.

FESTIVALS

Early Music Festival

CONCERTS | Devoted to compositions written before the 18th century, the Early Music Festival is held each July in York. There's also a Christmas program in early December. ⊠ St. Margaret's Church, Walmgate, York ☎ 01904/658338 ⊕ www.ncem.co.uk.

Harrogate Festival

ARTS FESTIVALS | The town of Harrogate plays host to music and writing festivals with top artists in July and comedy and literature festivals in October, as well as musical recital and lecture programs throughout the year. ⊠ 32 Cheltenham Parade, Harrogate ☎ 01423/562303 ⊕ www.harrogateinternationalfestivals.com.

Viking Festival

FESTIVALS | FAMILY | Held every February in York, this weeklong commemoration of the conquest of England by the Great Viking Army in 866 (only the British would hold a festival celebrating a losing battle) has more than 60 events, including a longship regatta and workshops for kids ranging from Viking-era crafts to fighting skills like archery and swordplay, as well as historical lectures, a banquet, and a beard competition. It ends with the Jorvik Viking Centre combat reenactment, where the invading Norsemen confront the Anglo-Saxon defenders. ⊠ Jorvik Viking Centre, Coppergate, York ☎ 01904/615505 ⊕ www.jorvikvikingfestival.co.uk.

Planning Your Time

Yorkshire is a vast region and difficult to explore in a short amount of time. If you're in a hurry, you could see the highlights of York or Leeds as a day trip from London; the fastest trains take just two hours. But it's an awful lot to pack into one day, and you're bound to leave out places you'll probably regret missing. Proper exploration—especially of the countryside—requires time and effort. In a few days you could explore York and some highlights such as Castle Howard and Studley Royal Park. You need the better part of a week to take in the small towns, abandoned abbeys, and inspiring moors and coast. It's well worth it: this is the path less traveled. The York Pass (⊕ www.yorkpass.com), good for one, two, or three days, can save you money on more than 30 attractions, but check it against your itinerary.

Getting Here and Around

AIR

Leeds Bradford Airport, 11 miles northwest of Leeds, has frequent flights from other cities in England and Europe. Look for cheap fares on British Airways, Jet2, or Ryanair. Another good choice for this region is Manchester Airport, about 40 miles southwest of Leeds. This larger airport is well served by domestic and international carriers.

AIRPORTS Leeds Bradford International Airport. ⊠ *Whitehouse Lane, Yeadon, Leeds* ⊹ *Off A658* ☎ *0871/288–2288* ⊕ *www. leedsbradfordairport.co.uk.* **Manchester Airport.** ⊠ *M56, near Junctions 5 and 6, Manchester* ☎ *0808/169–7030* ⊕ *www. manchesterairport.co.uk.*

BUS

National Express and Megabus have numerous daily departures from London's Victoria Coach Station to major cities in Yorkshire. Average travel times are five hours to Leeds, six hours to York, and nine hours to Scarborough. Once you're in the region, local bus companies take over the routes. There are Metro buses from Leeds and Bradford into the more remote parts of the Yorkshire Dales. Other companies are Harrogate Bus Company for services to Ripon, Harrogate, and Leeds; the Keighley Bus Company to Haworth; Coastliner for Castle Howard, Scarborough, Whitby, and Malton; the express Cityzap bus between Leeds and York; Arriva for Whitby, Scarborough, and Middlesbrough; and the volunteer-run DalesBus for Hawes and other destinations, mainly on Sunday and holiday Mondays May–September. In York the main local bus operator is Transdev. Traveline has route information.

CONTACTS Arriva. ☎ *0344/800–4411 customer service* ⊕ *www.arrivabus. co.uk.* **Coastliner.** ☎ *01653/692556* ⊕ *www.transdevbus.co.uk/coastliner.* **DalesBus.** ☎ *0871/200–2233* ⊕ *www.*

dalesbus.org. **The Harrogate Bus Company.** ☎ *01423/566061* ⊕ *www.transdevbus. co.uk/harrogate.* **Keighley Bus Company.** ☎ *01535/603284* ⊕ *www.transdevbus. co.uk/keighley.* **Megabus.** ☎ *0141/352– 4444* ⊕ *uk.megabus.com.* **Metro.** ☎ *0113/245–7676* ⊕ *www.wymetro. com.* **National Express.** ☎ *0871/781–8181* ⊕ *www.nationalexpress.com.* **York & Country.** ☎ *01653/692556* ⊕ *www. transdevbus.co.uk/york.* **Traveline.** ☎ *0871/200–2233* ⊕ *www.traveline.info.*

CAR

If you're driving, the M1 is the principal route north from London. This major highway gets you to Leeds in about four hours. For York (215 miles) and the Scarborough areas, stay on M1 to Leeds (197 miles), and then take A64. For the Yorkshire Dales, take M1 to Leeds, then A65 north and west to Skipton. For the North York Moors, take the A64 and then the A169 north from York to Pickering, then continue north on the A169 to Whitby or west on the A170 to Helmsley. The trans-Pennine motorway, the M62 between Liverpool and Hull, crosses the bottom of this region. North of Leeds, the A1 is the major north–south road, although narrow stretches, roadworks, and heavy traffic make this route slow going at times.

Some of the steep, narrow roads in the countryside off the main routes are difficult drives and can be perilous (or closed altogether) in winter. Main roads often closed by snowdrifts are the moorland A169 and the coast-and-moor A171. If you plan to drive in the dales or moors in winter, check the weather forecast in advance.

TRAIN

London North Eastern Railway (LNER) trains travel to York and Leeds from London's King's Cross Station. Grand Central trains head to York, Bradford, and Thirsk. Average travel times from King's Cross are 3¼ hours to York and 3 hours to Leeds. Northern Rail trains operate throughout the region. Contact National Rail for train times, and to find out if any discounted Rover tickets are available for your journey.

CONTACTS Grand Central Trains.
☎ 0345/603–4852 ⊕ www.grandcentral-rail.com. **London North Eastern Railway.** ☎ 03457/225333 ⊕ www.lner.co.uk. **National Rail Enquiries.** ☎ 0345/748–4950 ⊕ www.nationalrail.co.uk. **Northern Rail.** ☎ 0800/200–6060 ⊕ www.northernrail-way.co.uk.

Restaurants

Yorkshire is known for hearty food, though bacon-based breakfasts and lunches of pork pies do tend to get old fairly quickly. Increasingly, the larger towns and cities, particularly Leeds, have developed a foodie scene of sorts. Indian restaurants (often called curry houses) can be very good in northern cities. Out in the countryside, pubs are your best bet for dining. Many serve excellent home-cooked food and locally reared meat (especially lamb) and vegetables. Roast beef dinners generally come with Yorkshire pudding, the tasty, puffy, oven-baked dish made from egg batter, similar to a popover in the United States. It's generally served with lots of gravy. Be sure to sample local cheeses, especially Wensleydale, which has a delicate flavor and honey aftertaste.

Hotels

Traditional hotels are limited primarily to major towns and cities; those in the country tend to be guesthouses, inns, bed-and-breakfasts, or pubs with rooms, plus the occasional luxurious country-house hotel. Many of the better guesthouses are at the edge of town, but some proprietors will pick you up at the main station if you're relying on public transportation—verify before booking. Rooms fill quickly at seaside resorts in

July and August, and some places in the moors and dales close in winter. Always call ahead to make sure a hotel is open and has space available.

Restaurant and hotel reviews have been shortened. For full information, visit Fodors.com. Restaurant prices are the average cost of a main course at dinner or, if dinner is not served, at lunch. Hotel prices are the lowest cost of a standard double room in high season, including 20% V.A.T.

WHAT IT COSTS in Pounds

	$	$$	$$$	$$$$
RESTAURANTS				
	under £16	£16–£23	£24–£30	over £30
HOTELS				
	under £125	£125–£225	£226–£350	over £350

Visitor Information

CONTACT Welcome to Yorkshire. ☎ 0113/322–3500 ⊕ www.yorkshire.com.

York

For many people, the first stop in Yorkshire is the historic cathedral city of York. Much of the city's medieval and 18th-century architecture has survived, making it a delight to explore. It's one of the most popular short-stay destinations in Britain and only three hours by train from London's King's Cross Station.

York was the military capital of Roman Britain, when it was known as Eboracum, and traces of Roman garrison buildings survive throughout the city. After the Empire's collapse in the 5th century, the Saxons built Eoforwic on the ruins of a fort, but were soon defeated by Vikings, who called the city Jorvik and used it as a base from which to subjugate the countryside. When the Normans arrived in the 11th century, they emulated the Vikings by using the city as a military base. They also established the foundations of York Minster, the largest Gothic cathedral in northern Europe. The timber-framed buildings on the medieval street known as the Shambles suggest what the city looked like in Tudor times.

GETTING HERE AND AROUND

If you're driving, take the M1 north from London. Stay on it to Leeds, and then take the A64 northeast for 25 miles to York. The journey should take around 4 to 5 hours. Megabus coaches leave from Victoria Coach Station 7 times a day (6–7½ hours) and National Express buses depart from London's Victoria Coach Station approximately 11 times a day (5½–8 hours). Grand Central and London North East Line trains run from London's King's Cross Station every 6–30 minutes during the week (2 hours). York Station, just outside the city walls, has a line of taxis out front to take you to your hotel. If you don't have bags, the walk to town takes 8 minutes.

York's city center is mostly closed to traffic and very walkable. The old center is a compact, dense web of narrow streets and tiny medieval alleys called "snickelways." These provide shortcuts across the city center, but they're not on maps, so you never quite know where you'll end up, which in York is often a pleasant surprise.

TOURS

Association of Voluntary Guides to the City of York
Established more than 60 years ago, this organization arranges short walking tours around the city, taking in two medieval gateways, a walk along the ancient walls, and a visit to a medieval church, in addition to well-known sights. The tours are free, but tips are appreciated. Tours happen three times a day in June through August and two times a day the rest of the year. ⊠ 1 Museum St. ☎ 01904/550098 ⊕ www. avgyork.co.uk ⊠ Free.

City Sightseeing
TOUR—SIGHT | This tour company runs frequent hop-on, hop-off bus tours of York that stop at the Castle Museum, the Merchants Adventurers' Hall, Clifford's Tower, the Jorvik Viking Centre, and the Museum Gardens, among other attractions. Tickets are valid for three months. ☎ 01904/634296 ⊕ www.city-sightseeing.com ⊠ From £19.51.

Ghost Hunt of York
TOUR—SIGHT | FAMILY | This tour for "boils and ghouls" takes a slightly tongue-in-cheek approach to the haunted locations, employing props, illusion, jokes, and audience participation. The tours start at 7:30 pm nightly in the Shambles. ⊠ York ⊹ Bottom of The Shambles, opposite The Golden Fleece ☎ 01904/608700 ⊕ www. ghosthunt.co.uk ⊠ £7.50.

Ghost Keeper
TOUR—SIGHT | FAMILY | Take a "bloodcurdling" tour down narrow passageways and dark streets on Friday through Sunday nights in November, December, and February through June and nightly from July through Halloween. The 75-minute tours start at 7:30 pm from St. Mary's Graveyard, next to the Jorvik Viking Centre. ⊠ York ⊹ St. Mary's Churchyard, near Jorvik Viking Centre ☎ 07947/325239 ⊕ www.ghostkeeper.co.uk ⊠ £10.

Ghost Trail of York
TOUR—SIGHT | FAMILY | Still going strong after 21 years, the Ghost Trail of York has guides well versed in local lore, combining traditional spooky tales, Victorian tragedies, and more recent reports of modern ghostly phenomena. The 70-minute tours start at 7:30 pm at the west doors of the Minster. ⊠ York ⊹ By west doors of the Minster ☎ 01904/633276 ⊕ www.ghosttrail.co.uk ⊠ £4.

Original Ghost Walk of York
TOUR—SIGHT | FAMILY | Claiming to be the world's first Ghost Walk, the Original Ghost Walk of York presents the city's ghost tales as a combination of "history and mystery,"

with an emphasis on accuracy and authenticity. The tours depart at 8 pm from in front of the King's Arms Pub near Ouse Bridge. ⊠ *Kings St.* ✛ *In front of King's Arms Pub* ☎ *01759/373090* ⊕ *www.theoriginalghost-walkofyork.co.uk* ☜ *£5.*

TIMING
In July and August, tourists choke the narrow streets and form long lines at the Minster. April, May, June, and September are less crowded, but the weather can be unpredictable. April is also the time to see the embankments beneath the city walls rippling with pale gold daffodils.

ESSENTIALS
VISITOR INFORMATION Visit York. ⊠ *1 Museum St.* ☎ *01904/555670* ⊕ *www. visityork.org.*

 Sights

Castle Museum
MUSEUM | FAMILY | In an 18th-century building whose elegance belies its former role as a debtors' prison, this quirky museum includes a replica York street that re-creates the Victorian shopping experience, notable domestic interiors, more than 100 historic patchwork quilts, a toy gallery, and Christmas cards sent during World War I. You can also visit the cell where Dick Turpin, the 18th-century highwayman and folk hero, spent the night before his execution. ⊠ *Eye of York* ☎ *01904/687687* ⊕ *www.yorkcastlemuseum.org.uk* ☜ *£10.90.*

City of York Walls
HISTORIC SITE | Almost 3 miles of original medieval town walls remain around York, more than any other city in England. In the 9th century, invading Vikings buried the original Roman defensive walls, built some 1,900 years ago, under earthen ramparts topped with wooden stakes. These in turn were replaced by the current stone walls in the 13th and 14th centuries. In the mid-19th century, the walls, which had fallen into disrepair, were restored and maintained for public access, and you can now walk along a narrow paved path at the top and enjoy outstanding views (the whole circuit takes about two hours). In spring, the remains of the Viking embankment at the base are alive with daffodils. The walls are crossed periodically by York's distinctive "bars," or fortified gates: the portcullis on Monk's Bar on Goodramgate is still in working order, and Walmgate Bar in the east is the only gate in England with an intact barbican, although one scarred by the cannonballs fired during the Civil War. Bootham Bar in Exhibition Square was the defensive bastion for the north road, and Micklegate Bar, in the city's southwest corner, was traditionally the monarch's entrance. To access the path and lookout towers, find a staircase at one of the many breaks in the walls. ⊠ *York* ☎ *01904/551550* ⊕ *www.yorkwalls.org. uk.*

Clifford's Tower
BUILDING | This rather battered-looking keep at the top of a steep mound is all that remains of the old York castle, one of the greatest fortresses of medieval England. Sitting on a grassy mound, this squat stone tower dates from the mid-13th century. The Norman tower that preceded it, built in 1068 by William the Conqueror, was destroyed in 1190 when more than 150 Jews locked themselves inside to protect themselves from a violent mob. Trapped with no food or water, they committed mass suicide by setting their own prison aflame. From the top of the tower you have good views of the city. Plans are currently underway to reveal parts of the structure that have been hidden for decades and to create a new viewing platform, but the Tower will still be open to visitors during the renovation. ⊠ *Tower St.* ☎ *0370/333–1181* ⊕ *www. english-heritage.org.uk* ☜ *£5.70.*

Sights ▼

1 Castle Museum **C5**
2 City of York Walls **E2**
3 Clifford's Tower **C4**
4 DIG **E4**
5 Fairfax House **C4**
6 Jorvik Viking Centre **C4**
7 Merchant
   Adventurers' Hall **D4**
8 National
   Railway Museum **A1**
9 The Shambles **D3**
10 Stonegate............... **D2**
11 Treasurer's House **E2**
12 York Dungeon **C4**
13 York Minster............ **D2**
14 Yorkshire
   Air Museum **E4**
15 Yorkshire Museum....... **E4**

Restaurants ▼

1 Betty's Cafe
   Tea Rooms................ **C2**
2 The Blue Darbakan..... **D5**
3 Café Concerto........... **D2**
4 Melton's................. **A5**

Hotels ▼

1 Dairy Guest House...... **A5**
2 The Grand Hotel
   and Spa **B2**
3 Grange Hotel **D1**
4 Gray's Court Hotel **E2**
5 Hotel du Vin **A3**
6 Middlethorpe
   Hall & Spa **C5**
7 Mount Royale Hotel **A3**

DIG

ARCHAEOLOGICAL SITE | FAMILY | This reproduction of an archaeological dig in and beneath an old church is a great way to inspire an interest in history and archaeology in young people. A venture by the people behind the Jorvik Viking Centre, DIG is supervised by knowledgeable experts. Kids dig in the dirt to "find" Roman or Viking artifacts, and everyone heads to the lab afterwards to learn what previous archaeological finds discovered on the site have revealed about former inhabitants. ✉ *St. Saviour's Church, St. Saviourgate* ☎ *01904/615505* ⊕ *digyork. com* ✉ *£7; joint admission with Jorvik Viking Centre £15.50.*

Fairfax House

HOUSE | This museum of decorative arts, inside an elegant, beautifully decorated Georgian town house, contains crystal chandeliers, silk damask wallpaper, and one of the country's finest collections of 18th-century furniture. Entrance on Monday is restricted to guided tours at 11 and 2. ✉ *Castlegate* ☎ *01904/655543* ⊕ *www.fairfaxhouse.co.uk* ✉ *£7.50* ⊘ *Closed Jan.–Mar.*

Jorvik Viking Centre

ARCHAEOLOGICAL SITE | FAMILY | This kid-focused exhibition re-creates, based on extensive research, a 10th-century Viking village, with everything from the blind storyteller to the slaughter yard awash in offal. The olfactory element is especially popular with children (even the open sewer), as is the Disneyesque "travel through time" machine that propels you above straw huts and mannequins wearing Viking dress. Commentary is provided in six languages. Kids get a lot out of it, but adults are unlikely to learn anything new. A small collection of Viking-era artifacts is on display at the end of the ride. ✉ *Coppergate* ☎ *01904/615505* ⊕ *www. jorvikvikingcentre.co.uk* ✉ *£12.50; joint admission with DIG £15.50.*

Merchant Adventurers' Hall

HOUSE | Built between 1357 and 1361 by a wealthy medieval guild, this is the largest half-timbered hall in York. It has fine collections of silver and furniture, along with paintings that provide insight into the history of the Hall and its founders. The building itself is much of the attraction. A riverfront garden lies behind it. ✉ *Fossgate* ☎ *01904/654818* ⊕ *www. merchantshallyork.org* ✉ *£3.*

★ National Railway Museum

MUSEUM | FAMILY | A must for train lovers, Britain's biggest railway museum houses part of the national collection of rail vehicles. Don't miss such gleaming giants of the steam era as the *Mallard*, holder of the world speed record for a steam engine (126 mph), and a replica of the prototype steam engine, the *Rocket*. Passenger cars used by Queen Victoria are on display, as is the only Japanese bullet train to be seen outside Japan, along with railway-related art, posters, and memorabilia. You can climb aboard some of the trains and occasionally take a short trip on one. There's also a little tourist train that makes the short journey to York Minster (£3). ✉ *Leeman Rd.* ☎ *03330/161010* ⊕ *www. railwaymuseum.org.uk.*

The Shambles, a narrow medieval street in York, once held butchers' shops, but now has stores that serve the city's many shoppers and visitors.

The Shambles

NEIGHBORHOOD | York's best-preserved medieval street has shops and residences in half-timbered buildings with overhangs so massive you could almost reach across the narrow gap from one second-floor window to another. Once a hub of butchers (meat hooks are still fastened outside some of the doors), today it's mostly filled with independent shops and remains highly atmospheric. ⊠ *York ⊹ Off The Stonebow* ⊕ *www. insideyork.co.uk.*

Stonegate

NEIGHBORHOOD | This narrow, pedestrian-only street lined with Tudor and 18th-century storefronts retains considerable charm. First paved during Roman times (the original Roman road lies six feet below), it's been a central thoroughfare for almost 2,000 years. Today it's lined with interesting independent shops including upscale boutiques, jewelers, and quirky one-offs. A passage just off Stonegate, at 52A, leads to the remains of a 12th-century Norman stone house

attached to a more recent structure. You can still see the old Norman wall and window. ■**TIP→ Look out for the little red "printer's devil" at No. 33, a medieval symbol of a printer's premises. And above the doorway of No. 35 at the intersection of Stonegate and High Petergate, Minerva reclines on a stack of books, indicating they were once sold within.** ⊠ *Stonegate between Petergate and Davygate.*

Treasurer's House

HOUSE | Surprises await inside this large townhouse built during the 16th and 17th centuries. With an eye for texture, decoration, and pattern, industrialist Frank Green—who lived here from 1897 to 1930—re-created 13 period rooms, including a medieval great hall, as a showcase for his collection of antique furniture, ceramics, art, and textiles. Delft tiles decorate the former kitchen (now a shop), and the dining room retains its original 16th-century paneling and 18th-century plasterwork. Stumpwork from the 17th century is the highlight of the textiles in the Tapestry Room. There's an actual Roman road in the cellar, plus a display about Roman York and one resident's account of seeing a ghostly Roman legion in the 1950s. Access to the house is by guided tour only. ✉ *Minster Yard* ☎ *01904/624247* ⊕ *www.nationaltrust.org.uk* ✉ *House £8.90; Garden free* ۞ *Closed mid-Dec.–Mar.*

York Dungeon

AMUSEMENT PARK/WATER PARK | FAMILY |
This history-themed attraction takes a tongue-in-cheek approach to exploring the more violent and gory aspects of York's history. Lurid lighting, lots of fake blood, and costumed actors enliven episodes from the careers of infamous residents like highwayman Dick Turpin, revolutionary Guy Fawkes, Viking king Eric Bloodaxe, the Lost Roman Legion, and more, all to a soundtrack of wailing, screaming, and agonized moaning. As you might imagine, it's popular with kids, though not suitable for those under 9. ✉ *12 Clifford St.* ☎ *01904/632599* ⊕ *www.thedungeons.com/york* ✉ *£16.95; £13.95 online.*

★ York Minster

BUILDING | The city's focal point, this vast cathedral is the largest Gothic building north of the Alps and attracts almost as many visitors as London's Westminster Abbey. Inside, the effect created by its soaring pillars and lofty vaulted ceilings is almost overpowering. Binoculars may be helpful for viewing the loftiest of the 128 dazzling stained-glass windows. While mere numbers can't convey the scale of the building, the central towers are 200 feet high while the Minster itself is 519 feet long, 249 feet across its transepts, and 90 feet from floor to roof. Among the especially notable contributions to the building's uplifting splendor is the ornamentation of the 14th-century nave: the east window, one of the greatest pieces of medieval glazing in the world; the north transept's Five Sisters windows, five tall lancets of gray-tinged 13th-century glass; the enormous choir screen depicting stylized images of every king of England from William the Conqueror to Henry VI; and the masterful tracery of the Rose Window, with elements commemorating the 1486 marriage of Henry VII and Elizabeth of York, a union which ended the Wars of the Roses and started the Tudor dynasty. Don't miss the exquisite 13th-century **Chapter House,** with its superb medieval ribbed wooden roof and fine traceried stained-glass windows; the **Treasury;** the **Crypt;** and the interactive Revealing York Minster exhibition in the **undercroft,** where you can see the remains of a Roman barracks, the Minster's Norman foundations, stained glass, and the 10th-century Horn of Ulf carved from an elephant tusk and donated by a Viking nobleman. After exploring the cathedral at ground level, climb the 275 winding steps to the roof of the great **Central Tower,** which offers both close-up glimpses of the cathedral's detailed carvings and panoramic views of the city. Allow 45 minutes for the Tower tour, which is by timed admission only. Don't miss the newly restored great east window, Britain's largest expanse of medieval stained glass with its 311 stained-glass panels dating back to the 15th century. ■**TIP**➔ **To experience the cathedral at its most atmospheric, attend one of the evensong services with organ and choir.** ✉ *Minster Yard* ☎ *01904/557200* ⊕ *www.yorkminster.org* ✉ *Minster £11.50, Minster and Tower £16.50.*

Yorkshire Air Museum

MILITARY SITE | FAMILY | Located on 22 acres of parkland, this is the country's largest World War II airfield that's open to the public. The independent museum showcases more than 60 historic vehicles and aircraft, many of which are still in working condition and are certain to delight aviation enthusiasts. Planes range from early-20th-century biplanes and gliders, such as the Eastchurch Kitten (the only surviving one in the world), to Spitfires, other World War II–era planes, and contemporary fighter jets. There are also exhibits devoted to military vehicles, aircraft weaponry, and Royal Air Force uniforms. The museum is home to a memorial and gardens commemorating British and Allied service members who lost their lives in conflict. ⊠ *Halifax Way, Elvington* ☎ *01904/608595* ⊕ *www. yorkshireairmuseum.org* ✉ *£12.*

Yorkshire Museum

MUSEUM | The ecological and archaeo-logical history of the county is the focus of this museum in an early-19th-cen-tury Greek Revival–style building with massive Doric columns. Themed galleries focus mostly on Roman, Anglian, Viking, and medieval periods, with nearly 1 mil-lion objects, including the 15th-century Middleham Jewel, a pendant gleaming with a large sapphire; a Paleolithic hand axe; and an extremely rare copper-plate helmet, a 1,200-year-old Viking artifact. Another exhibition documents Yorkshire during the Jurassic period. ⊠ *St. Mary's Lodge, Museum Gardens* ☎ *01904/687687* ⊕ *www.yorkshiremu-seum.org.uk* ✉ *Museum £7.27; gardens and observatory free.*

🍴 Restaurants

Betty's Cafe Tea Rooms

$ | CAFÉ | Betty's has been a York insti-tution since 1936. The decor—inspired by the art deco ocean liner the *Queen Mary*—the dessert trollies, and the solic-itous white-aproned staff all contribute to an impression of stepping back in time to a more genteel era. **Known for:** charming afternoon tea; cool World War II history; pastries and old-fashioned sweets. ⑤ *Average main: £12* ⊠ *6–8 Helen's Sq., off Stonegate* ☎ *01904/659142* ⊕ *www. bettys.co.uk* ☽ *Closed Sun.*

The Blue Barbakan

$ | EASTERN EUROPEAN | This cozy independ-ent restaurant receives rave reviews for its hearty Eastern European fare. You'll find largely Polish dishes, including favorites

like pierogi, bigos (a hunter's stew made with cabbage, wild mushroom, and sau-sage), pancetta-wrapped rabbit leg, and schnitzel, as well as vegetarian options. **Known for:** excellent Polish-inspired dishes; big crowds; good value. ⑤ *Average main: 15* ⊠ *34 Fossgate* ☎ *01904/672474* ⊕ *www.bluebarbakan.co.uk.*

Café Concerto

$$ | BRITISH | Wallpaper made from sheet music reiterates the musical theme at this relaxed, intimate bistro in sight of York Minster. The kitchen serves simple, house-made café classics with an empha-sis on local ingredients. **Known for:** hearty portions; vegan and gluten-free options; friendly atmosphere. ⑤ *Average main: £16* ⊠ *21 High Petergate* ☎ *01904/610478* ⊕ *www.cafeconcerto.biz.*

Melton's

$$$$ | MODERN BRITISH | This family-run res-taurant in what was once a Victorian shop uses locally sourced Yorkshire produce to create a seasonal, highly imaginative take on Modern British cuisine. Selections include slow-cooked duck egg with Jeru-salem artichoke and oyster mushrooms; venison with celeriac and damson plums; and cod in smoked cream, apples, dates, and raisins. **Known for:** informal atmos-phere despite Michelin star; friendly, involved owners; lots of extras like amuse-bouches and palate cleansers. ⑤ *Average main: £38* ⊠ *7 Scarcroft Rd.* ☎ *01904/634341* ⊕ *www.meltonsrestau-rant.co.uk* ☽ *Closed Sun., Mon., and 3 wks at Christmas. No lunch Tues.*

🛏 Hotels

Dairy Guest House

$$ | B&B/INN | This former dairy in a Victorian town house near the city walls retains atmospheric original features like stained or etched glass, period fireplac-es, and ornate plaster cornices. **Pros:** nice period details; comfortable rooms; good breakfast. **Cons:** small bathrooms;

Continued on page 683

DID YOU KNOW?

York Minster is the largest Gothic cathedral in Britain. The towers of its west front rise 174 feet, and its nave is an imposing 138 feet wide and 276 feet long. The west front includes the window known as the Heart of York-shire because of the shape of the tracery near its top.

YORK MINSTER
GOTHIC GRANDEUR

You can see this vast cathedral from 10 miles away, the tall Gothic towers rising over the flat horizon. The focal point of York, it encompasses centuries of the city's history, and its treasures include 128 dazzling medieval glass windows. The Minster today is a tranquil place, but over the centuries it has survived structural threats and political upheaval.

The present York Minster is the fourth attempt to build a church on this site. The first, a Saxon minster from the 7th century, was built of wood. In the 8th century it was rebuilt in stone. Norman invaders badly damaged the first stone church in 1069 as they conquered the recalcitrant north. They later rebuilt it in their own style, and you can see Norman elements—foundations, masonry, columns—in the undercroft. Marauding Vikings, however, damaged that building. Much of the limestone building you see is the result of the vision of one 13th-century archbishop, Walter de Gray. He wanted to build one of the world's greatest cathedrals, on the scale of Canterbury, with vaulted ceilings soaring hundreds of feet high. York Minster was finally completed in 1472. De Gray stayed with his beloved building beyond the end. He died in 1255, and his effigy lies atop his tomb inside the south transept near the main entrance.

(top left) York Minster interior, (top right) A stone gargoyle, (bottom right) Chapter House ceiling

MINSTER ORIENTATION AND HIGHLIGHTS

The Minster is designed in cruciform, meaning in the shape of a cross. As you walk through the main doors, you're entering the south transept, one of the arms of the cross. These transepts were built in Archbishop de Gray's time in the 13th century. Ahead of you, the grand, soaring, light-filled nave stretches out to your left and right, with massive stained-glass windows at both ends. Across the nave is the northern transept—the other arm of the cross—and off of it a corridor leads to the octagonal Chapter House. The nave's ceiling is supported by flying buttresses on the exterior of the building. In the 13th and 14th centuries, this architectural feature was so experimental that the builders could not be certain the structure would not simply collapse.

Nave

❶ Nave. The 14th-century builders of the nave used painted wood for the nave's soaring ceilings out of practicality: they feared stone would be too heavy. A fire in 1840 destroyed the roof, but the vaulting and bosses are exact replicas. Giant stained-glass windows glow from each end: the Heart of Yorkshire to the west, and opposite it the great East Window.

❷ Great West Window. The heart-shaped tracery in the window that dominates the west end of the nave dates to 1338, and is remarkable both for its shape and its intricate design.

❸ Rose Window. This extraordinary stained-glass window in the south transept has 13th-century stonework, but it has early 16th-century glass in which white and red Tudor roses show the union of the houses of York and Lancaster. It was nearly lost when lightning struck the building in 1984, causing a fire.

❹ The Five Sisters. At the end of the north transept, these five tall, blade-shaped windows from around 1260 are rare pieces of medieval glass art made of more than 100,000 pieces of glass. Each blade is more than five feet wide and towers 52 feet high. All were painted

The Rose Window

on gray-tinged glass using a technique known as grisaille.

❺ Chapter House. With a beautifully painted and gilded ceiling (restored in 1845), the octagonal 13th-century Chapter House is a marvel, lined with exquisite stained glass and decorated with fanciful animals and gargoyles with human faces that could be caricatures of early monks.

❻ Choir Screen. Stretching along one section of the nave, an elegantly carved 15th-century stone panel, known as the choir screen, contains almost life-size sculptures of 15 kings of England from William the Conqueror to Henry VI.

Choir Screen

1069 Normans destroy Saxon structure

1220 Walter de Gray begins church

1472 The Minster is consecrated

1829 Arson attack damages choir

1967 Tower is structurally threatened

1200   1400   1600   1800   2000

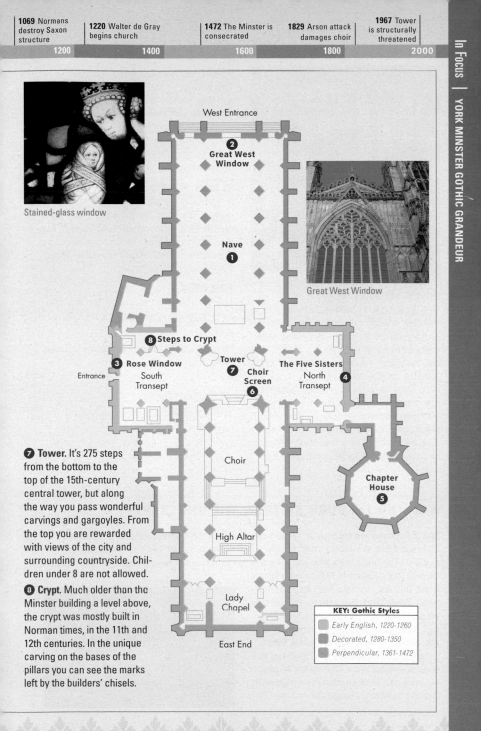

Stained-glass window

West Entrance

2 Great West Window

Nave **1**

Great West Window

8 Steps to Crypt

3 Rose Window
South Transept

Entrance

Tower **7**

Choir Screen **6**

The Five Sisters
North Transept **4**

Choir

Chapter House **5**

High Altar

Lady Chapel

East End

KEY: Gothic Styles

Early English, 1220-1260
Decorated, 1280-1350
Perpendicular, 1361-1472

7 Tower. It's 275 steps from the bottom to the top of the 15th-century central tower, but along the way you pass wonderful carvings and gargoyles. From the top you are rewarded with views of the city and surrounding countryside. Children under 8 are not allowed.

8 Crypt. Much older than the Minster building a level above, the crypt was mostly built in Norman times, in the 11th and 12th centuries. In the unique carving on the bases of the pillars you can see the marks left by the builders' chisels.

MAKING THE MOST OF YOUR VISIT

Five Sisters

WHEN TO VISIT

The best time to visit is early or late in the day. The church is busiest between 11 am and 2 pm. If you can avoid weekends or holidays, do, as the church can be crowded. You may encounter choir practice in the early evening. Look for occasional evening concerts; attending Evensong service can also be lovely. The building sometimes closes for church events and meetings, and it is closed to visitors (except those attending services) on most major religious holidays.

WHAT TO WEAR AND BRING

The church is enormous, so wear comfortable shoes. Bring binoculars to see the glass and higher carvings. The stone walls keep it cool inside year-round. There are no restrictions on attire. You may want to bring a bottle of water; there's no tea shop.

PLANNING YOUR TIME

A thorough visit, including the crypt, undercroft, and central tower, can take two hours, and could take longer for those who read all the displays or study the stained glass. The Orb exhibit shows some glass at eye level.

FOR FREE

The church is always free for worshippers or those who wish to pray.

TOURS

Free tours may be available without reservations.

WALKING THROUGH HISTORY: THE UNDERCROFT

One of the must-see sections of York Minster isn't in the Gothic building at all, but underneath it. The undercroft was excavated in the late 1960s and early 1970s after a survey found that the central tower was near collapse. While working frantically to shore up the foundations, builders uncovered extensive remains of previous structures on this site. Now the ruins and remnants they uncovered form the basis for the Revealing York Minster exhibit in the Undercroft Museum. You walk past Norman pillars and stonework, Viking gravestones, Saxon carvings and coffins, and the remains of a Roman basilica. The displays put all that you are seeing into the context of the region's history.

York Minster crypt

two-night minimum stay; few amenities. $ *Rooms from: £160* ✉ *3 Scarcroft Rd.* ☎ *01904/639367* ⊕ *www.dairyguesthouse.co.uk* ⤳ *6 rooms* ❤ *Free breakfast.*

The Grand Hotel and Spa

$$ | **HOTEL** | This handsome, comfortable hotel near the train station—not surprising, considering it was formerly the headquarters of the regional railroad—was built in 1906 and retains many original features, such as solid mahogany doors, beautiful tilework on the stairwells, and art nouveau ironwork. **Pros:** beautiful building; spacious rooms; good location. **Cons:** continental breakfast is average; occasional lapses in service; some unexpected charges. $ *Rooms from: £162* ✉ *Station Rise* ☎ *01904/380038* ⊕ *www.thegrandyork. co.uk* ⤳ *207 rooms* ❤ *Free breakfast.*

Grange Hotel

$ | **HOTEL** | Built in the early 19th century as the home for two wealthy members of the York clergy, this luxurious boutique hotel decorated with racing memorabilia goes in for traditional country house style, with tastefully decorated bedrooms boasting lovely period textiles, mantelpieces, and four-poster beds. **Pros:** nice ambience; some on-site parking; helpful staff. **Cons:** some rooms small; restaurant food uneven; no elevator. $ *Rooms from: £116* ✉ *1 Clifton* ☎ *01904/644744* ⊕ *www.grangehotel. co.uk* ⤳ *41 rooms* ❤ *Free breakfast.*

Gray's Court Hotel

$$ | **HOTEL** | Close to York Minster yet with its own half-acre garden, Gray's Court is an oasis of countryhouse peacefulness in the city center and the oldest inhabited house in York. **Pros:** peaceful but central location; lovely period decor; access to City Walls. **Cons:** expensive parking; breakfast service slow; decor not for everyone. $ *Rooms from: £170*

✉ *Chapter House St.* ☎ *01904/612613* ⊕ *www.grayscourtyork.com* ⤳ *11 rooms* ❤ *Free breakfast.*

Hotel du Vin

$$ | **HOTEL** | A converted 19th-century orphanage, the York outpost of this boutique hotel mini-chain has preserved the exposed brick walls and arched doorways of the original building. **Pros:** makes great use of the space; good-sized rooms; comfortable beds. **Cons:** some rooms can be damp; low bathroom lighting; on outskirts of city. $ *Rooms from: £129* ✉ *89 The Mount* ☎ *0844/748–9268* ⊕ *www.hotelduvin. com* ⤳ *44 rooms* ❤ *Free breakfast.*

Middlethorpe Hall & Spa

$$$ | **HOTEL** | Aimed at visitors who prize period details like oak-paneled walls, four-poster beds, carved wood bannisters, and window seats, and whose idea of luxury is a bowl of fresh daffodils, this splendidly restored Queen Anne building with mid-18th-century additions feels less like a country-house hotel than an actual country house. **Pros:** period luxury; gorgeous grounds; attentive staff. **Cons:** poor water pressure; outside city center; might be too formal for some. $ *Rooms from: £229* ✉ *Bishopthorpe Rd.* ☎ *01904/641241* ⊕ *www.middlethorpe.com* ⤳ *29 rooms* ❤ *Free breakfast.*

Mount Royale Hotel

$$ | **HOTEL** | This hotel has the feel of a relaxing country house despite being close to the city center in an upscale residential neighborhood. **Pros:** large rooms; lovely pool and garden; good service. **Cons:** well outside the town center; some rooms dated; property shows its age in places. $ *Rooms from: £135* ✉ *117–119 The Mount* ☎ *01904/628856* ⊕ *www.mountroyale.co.uk* ⤳ *24 rooms* ❤ *Free breakfast.*

Haunted York

Given its lengthy history, dark streets, and atmospheric buildings, it's no surprise that York feels as if it could be haunted. Indeed, a body called the Ghost Research Foundation International has determined that, with 500 recorded cases of ghostly encounters, York is the most haunted city in England and one of the most haunted in the world.

Not everybody believes in earth-bound spirits, but that hasn't stopped the local tourism industry from assuming many do. Should you choose to explore the town's spookier side, try Ghost Keeper, Ghost Hunt, Ghost Trail of York, or the Original Ghost Tour of York.

Nightlife

The Black Swan

BARS/PUBS | Located in a half-timbered 15th-century building complete with wood paneling, flagstone floors, and mullioned windows, this pub (there's been one here since the 16th century) serves home-cooked bar food and hosts folk and acoustic music nights. There are three rooms upstairs if you wish to spend the night. ⊠ *Peasholme Green* ☎ *01904/679131* ⊕ *www.blackswanyork. com.*

Old White Swan

BARS/PUBS | Spreading across five half-timbered 16th-century buildings on busy Goodramgate, the Old White Swan is known for its good pub lunches and its ghosts—it claims to have more than the equally venerable Black Swan. ⊠ *80 Goodramgate* ☎ *01904/540911* ⊕ *www. nicholsonspubs.co.uk.*

Snickleway Inn

BARS/PUBS | With its wood paneling and open brick fireplaces, the allegedly haunted Snickleway Inn provides a real sense of stepping back into the 15th century (when it was built). Its colorful past includes being used by Royalists during the English Civil War to store ammunition and explosives. ⊠ *47 Goodramgate* ☎ *01904/656138.*

Performing Arts

York Theatre Royal

ARTS CENTERS | Based in a lovely 18th-century building, the York Theatre Royal hosts theater, dance, music, and comedy performances, as well as readings, lectures, and children's entertainment. ⊠ *St. Leonard's Pl.* ☎ *01904/623568* ⊕ *www. yorktheatreroyal.co.uk.*

Shopping

Stonegate is the city's main shopping street. Winding down from the Minster toward the river, it's lined with a mix of unique shops and boutiques. The Shambles is another prime shopping area, with an eclectic mix of shops geared toward locals and tourists, while Petergate, which has mostly chain stores, is best for practical shopping.

The Antiques Centre York

ANTIQUES/COLLECTIBLES | With five showrooms spread over three floors of a Georgian town house, this antiques mecca sells furniture, jewelry, ceramics, coins, vintage fashion, and collectibles—Roman, Georgian, Victorian, Edwardian, and art deco—from more than 120 dealers, who display their wares in "cabinets." ⊠ *41 Stonegate* ☎ *01904/635888* ⊕ *www.theantiquescentreyork.co.uk.*

The town of Harrogate was the prime spa destination in Yorkshire in Victorian England.

Minster Gate Bookshop

BOOKS/STATIONERY | This bookshop in a Georgian town house has been in the trade since 1580 and sells secondhand and antiquarian books as well as new children's books, illustrated editions, old maps, and prints, largely of Yorkshire in general and York in particular. ✉ *8 Minster Gate* ☎ *01904/621812* ⊕ *www.minster-gatebooks.co.uk.*

Harrogate

21 miles west of York, 11 miles south of Ripon, 16 miles north of Leeds.

During the Regency and early Victorian periods, it became fashionable for the aristocratic and wealthy to "take the waters" at British spa towns, combining the alleged health benefits with socializing. In Yorkshire, the most elegant spa destination was Harrogate, and today its mainly Victorian buildings, parks, and spas still provide a relaxing getaway.

GETTING HERE AND AROUND

Trains from York leave every hour or so, and the journey takes about 40 minutes. There's at least one direct train daily from London. National Express buses leave from York every 30 minutes most days; the journey takes about 35 minutes. By car, Harrogate is off A59 and well marked. It's a walkable town, so you can park in one of its central lots and explore on foot.

Within and around Harrogate, the Harrogate & District bus company provides area services, and taxis are plentiful.

ESSENTIALS

VISITOR INFORMATION Harrogate Tourist Information Centre. ✉ *Royal Baths, Crescent Rd.* ☎ *01423/537300* ⊕ *www.visitharrogate.co.uk.*

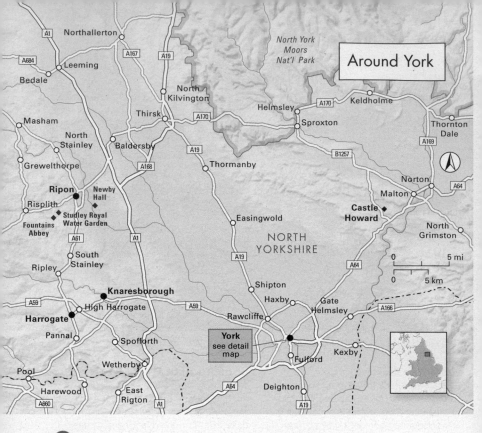

Sights

Royal Pump Room Museum

LOCAL INTEREST | Built in 1842 over the original sulfur well that made Harrogate a destination, the Pump Room housed in this octagonal structure sold 1,500 glasses of water to spa goers each morning in its heyday (so no, designer water is not a modern phenomenon). The pungent odor of Europe's strongest sulfuric well is still very much present. The museum has displays of bygone spa treatment paraphernalia alongside a somewhat eccentric collection of 19th-century clothes, fine china, and bicycles. ⊠ Crown Pl. ☎ 01423/556188 ⊕ www.harrogate.gov.uk ☞ £3.50.

The Stray

CITY PARK | These 200 acres of grassy parkland wrapped around Harrogate's Old Town become a riot of color in spring. Many of the mineral springs that made the town famous bubble below. ⊠ Harrogate ☎ 01423/841097 ⊕ www.harrogate.gov.uk.

Turkish Baths Harrogate

HOT SPRINGS | Dating from 1897, these Moorish-inspired, fully restored Turkish baths look virtually the same as they would have to the many Victorians who visited them. After changing into your bathing suit, relax on luxurious lounge chairs in the stunning mosaic-tile warming room. Move on to the increasingly hot sauna rooms, and then soak up eucalyptus mist in the steam room before braving the icy plunge pool. You can also book a massage or facial. Open hours are divided into single-sex and mixed sessions, so book in advance. ✉ *Royal Baths, Parliament St.* ☎ *01423/556746* ⊕ *www.turkishbathsharrogate.co.uk* ✆ *£19–£32 per session; 45-minute guided tour £3.80.*

Valley Gardens

CITY PARK | FAMILY | Southwest of the town center, these 17 acres of formal gardens include a children's boating lake, tennis courts, skate park, adventure playground, paddling pool, and a little café. ✉ *Valley Dr.* ✛ *Junction with Cornwall Rd. and Royal Parade* ☎ *01423/500600* ⊕ *www.harrogate.gov.uk.*

🍴 Restaurants

★ Bettys Cafe Tea Rooms

$ | CAFÉ | This celebrated Yorkshire tearoom began life in Harrogate in 1919, when a Swiss restaurateur brought his Alpine pastries and chocolates to England. The welcoming interior has changed little since it first opened, and the extensive array of teas not at all. **Known for:** classic English afternoon tea; traditional cakes, pastries, and sandwiches; nightly live piano music. 💲 *Average main: £14* ✉ *1 Parliament St.* ☎ *01423/814070* ⊕ *www.bettys.co.uk.*

The Ilkley Cow

$$ | STEAKHOUSE | This family-friendly Yorkshire take on an American steak house is bright and modern, with an emphasis on locally sourced food, particularly slow-roasted rotisserie meats and traditional steaks. Specialties include beer-braised brisket, baby back barbecue ribs, grilled steak from local herds, and, of course, burgers. **Known for:** big portions of steaks and other meats; family-friendly atmosphere; decent vegetarian options. 💲 *Average main: £16* ✉ *1–2 New Brook St., Ilkley* ☎ *01943/602030* ⊕ *www.theilkleycow.co.uk* ⊗ *Closed Mon.*

★ The Yorke Arms

$$$ | MODERN BRITISH | The peaceful rural location of this restaurant with rooms in the scenic Nidderdale Valley belies the sophistication of its distinctive cooking: it has been consistently rated as one of the top five dining spots not only in Yorkshire, but in the United Kingdom. It won its Michelin star with an emphasis on seasonal ingredients, creative combinations of flavors, and elegant presentations. **Known for:** daily changing menu of high-quality Modern British dishes; fabulous dessert selection; historic building in a peaceful setting. 💲 *Average main: £30* ✉ *Ramsgill-in-Nidderdale, Pateley Bridge* ☎ *01423/755243* ⊕ *www.theyorkearms.co.uk* ⊗ *Closed Sun.–Tues.*

🛏 Hotels

Hotel du Vin

$$ | HOTEL | This boutique hotel may sprawl through eight Georgian houses, but the public rooms, with their stripped-wood floors and clubby leather sofas, combine a contemporary, relaxed atmosphere with period charm. **Pros:** knowledgeable spa therapists; wonderful wine list; good breakfasts. **Cons:** some rooms tired; toilet maintenance could be better; bistro food uneven. 💲 *Rooms from: £134* ✉ *Prospect Pl.* ☎ *01423/608121* ⊕ *www.hotelduvin.com* ⇌ *52 rooms* 🍽 *No meals.*

Knaresborough

3 miles northeast of Harrogate, 17 miles west of York.

At the bottom of a precipitously deep, rocky gorge along the River Nidd, the little town of Knaresborough could hardly be more photogenic. It's best seen from a train, crossing the high Victorian viaduct above the gorge. In summer, you can rent a boat and row down the slow-moving river or stroll through the

You can paddle on the River Nidd in the pretty town of Knaresborough.

town's square, the site of a market since the early 14th century. Climb stone staircases through medieval streets winding their way up a hill to the ruins of the castle where Richard II was briefly imprisoned in 1399.

GETTING HERE AND AROUND

Northern Rail trains leave from Leeds every 10–30 minutes (a 45-minute trip) and from York every 40–60 minutes or so (a 30-minute trip). Local buses travel here from nearby towns, but they're less frequent. By car, the village is on A59 and is well signposted.

The village sits on a precipitous hill. The town is easily walkable, although it helps to be in good shape. There are clearly marked public parking areas.

 ## Sights

Mother Shipton's Cave

CAVE | Tucked away in beautiful woodland across the river from the center of town is the birthplace (according to local lore) of the titular 16th-century prophetess who supposedly foretold events such as the defeat of the Spanish Armada. Next to the cave is the mineral-rich Petrifying Well, England's oldest entrance-charging tourist attraction (it's been taking in tickets since 1630), famously able to petrify soft objects in three to five months. ✉ *Prophesy Lodge, Harrogate Rd., High Bridge* ☎ *01423/864600* ⊕ *www.mothershipton.co.uk* 🎫 *£9; £10 during school holidays and events; parking £2* ⊗ *Closed Nov.–Feb. and weekdays in Mar.*

Ripon

12 miles north of Knaresborough, 24 miles northwest of York.

Said to be England's second-oldest city and still one of its smallest, Ripon has been the site of a market since the 10th century, and probably before. A basilica was built here in the 7th century, and its chapel remains within the existing building, which is a mostly 12th-century minster. The church was designated a cathedral in the mid-19th century, making Ripon technically a city, despite a population of only about 16,000. Don't miss the Hornblower announcing he's on duty by blowing his horn at 9 pm every evening in the town square, an unbroken tradition that goes back 900 years. Market day, Thursday, is probably the best day to stop by.

GETTING HERE AND AROUND

Ripon is just off A1 via the A61, 12 miles north of Harrogate. There's no train service to Ripon, but local buses run from Harrogate several times a day.

◉ Sights

Newby Hall

GARDEN | FAMILY | Built in the 1690s by Sir Christopher Wren with 18th-century additions and interiors by Robert Adam, this country house, still home to the original family, is one of Britain's finest examples of 18th-century interior decoration. Of particular note is the ornamental plasterwork, Chippendale furniture, the domed Sculpture Hall devoted to Roman statuary, and the Tapestry Hall, which boasts priceless Gobelin tapestries. The 25 acres of gardens are justifiably famous; a double herbaceous border running down to the river separates garden "rooms," each flowering during a different season. A miniature railroad, playground, dollhouse and teddy bear exhibitions, and pedal boats amuse kids. Entry to the house is restricted to guided tours, which run April to September and can't be booked in advance. ⊠ *Skelton-on-Ure ✛ Off A1, 6 miles from Ripon exit* ☎ *01423/322583* ⊕ *www.newbyhall. com* ☜ *£21; gardens only £14.50* ☉ *Closed Oct.–Mar. and Mon. Apr.–June and Sept.*

Ripon Cathedral

BUILDING | The site's original 7th-century church was destroyed by the Vikings, though its Saxon crypt (AD 672), the oldest structure in any English cathedral, remains. The Romanesque transepts of the current cathedral date from the 12th century, while the west front (circa 1220) is an outstanding example of Early English Gothic. The nave was rebuilt in 1500 in a Perpendicular Gothic style. Note the recently restored, finely carved choir stalls—one carving, of a rabbit going down a rabbit hole, is said to have inspired Lewis Carroll, whose father was a canon here. ⊠ *Liberty Court House, Minster Rd.* ☎ *01765/603462* ⊕ *www. riponcathedral.org.uk.*

★ Studley Royal Water Garden & Fountains Abbey

ARCHAEOLOGICAL SITE | You can easily spend a day at this UNESCO World Heritage Site, an 822-acre complex made up of an 18th-century water garden and deer park; a Jacobean mansion; and, on the banks of the River Skell, Fountains Abbey, the largest monastic ruins in Britain. The landscape's neoclassical vision of an ordered universe—with spectacular terraces, classical temples, and a grotto—blends with the majestic Gothic abbey founded in 1132 and completed in the early 1500s. It housed Cistercian monks, known as "White Monks" after the color of their robes, who devoted their lives to silence, prayer, and work. Of the surviving buildings, the lay brothers' echoing refectory and dormitory are the most complete. Fountains Mill, built by the monks in the 12th century to grind grain for the monastery and one of the oldest buildings on the estate, was in operation until 1927. Fountains Hall is an elegant Elizabethan mansion partially built with stones taken from the abbey. The water garden and Fountains Abbey are 9 miles northwest of Knaresborough, 4 miles southwest of Ripon. ⊠ *Ripon* ✛ *Off A1, B6265 exit to Pateley Bridge* ☎ *01765/608888* ⊕ *www.nationaltrust. org.uk/fountainsabbey* ⊠ *£16.80.*

🍴 Restaurants

The Black Swan at Oldstead

$$$$ | **MODERN BRITISH** | With a Michelin-starred chef whose family farm is right down the road, this former drover's inn has a high reputation among foodies that belies its secluded location in a small Yorkshire village. Menus are based on what is available from the nearby garden or can be foraged locally; even cocktails include fruits and herbs made into alcohol with wood sorrel replacing lemons and limes. **Known for:** inventive high-quality cooking using local ingredients; multicourse tasting menus with no à la carte options; limited wine selection. ⑤ *Average main: £110* ⊠ *Oldstead* ✛ *At the southeast end of Oldstead on the junction towards Byland Abbey* ☎ *01347/868387* ⊕ *www.blackswanoldstead.co.uk* ⊗ *No lunch Sun.–Fri.*

🛏 Hotels

Grantley Hall

$$$ | **HOTEL** | Part Palladian country house hotel, part lively resort, and part luxury wellness retreat, Grantley Hall is set on 30 acres of parkland, combining grandeur with glitz. **Pros:** lovely house and grounds, including a fabulous pool; good food; big, well-decorated rooms. **Cons:** pricey; some housekeeping issues; loud music in bar not to everyone's taste. ⑤ *Rooms from: £325* ⊠ *Ripon* ☎ *01765/620070* ⊕ *www. grantleyhall.co.uk* ⇄ *47 rooms.*

★ Swinton Park

$$ | **HOTEL** | If you've ever wanted to experience the *Downton Abbey* lifestyle, head for this luxury hotel situated in a Victorian Gothic castle complete with battlements, a tower, and a turret. **Pros:** superior spa; spacious bedrooms; beautiful setting

with plenty of extras. **Cons:** restaurant kitchen can be disorganized; not big on heating; main house a bit old-fashioned. ⑤ *Rooms from: £205* ⊠ *Swinton Park, Swinton Rd., Masham* ☎ *01765/680966* ⊕ *www.swintonestate.com* ⇄ *32 rooms* ⏹ *Free breakfast.*

Castle Howard

15 miles northeast of York.

The baroque grandeur of Castle Howard is without equal in northern England. The grounds, enhanced by groves of trees, a twinkling lake, and a perfect lawn, add to the splendor.

GETTING HERE AND AROUND

There's daily scheduled bus service between Malton and Castle Howard, which is well outside any town and several miles off any public road. The nearest train stop is Malton, and you can take a taxi from there. By car, follow signs off A64 from York.

👁 Sights

★ Castle Howard

CASTLE/PALACE | Standing in the Howardian Hills to the west of Malton, Castle Howard is an outstanding example of English baroque architecture, with a distinctive roofline punctuated by a magnificent central dome. It served as Brideshead, the home of the fictional Flyte family in *Brideshead Revisited,* Evelyn Waugh's tale of aristocratic woe, in both its 1981 TV and 2008 film adaptations. The house was the first commission for playwright-turned-architect Sir John Vanbrugh, who, assisted by Nicholas Hawksmoor, designed it for the third Earl of Carlisle, a member of the Howard family. The central structure was started in 1701 and took 25 years to complete (with a Palladian wing added subsequently), but the end result was a stately home of audacious grandeur.

At Castle Howard, a baroque masterpiece, the splendor of the grounds matches the opulence of the sprawling house.

A spectacular central hallway with soaring columns supports a hand-painted ceiling that dwarfs all visitors, and there's no shortage of splendor elsewhere: vast family portraits, intricate marble fireplaces, immense tapestries, Victorian silver on polished tables, and a great many marble busts. Outside, the neoclassical landscape of carefully arranged woods, lakes, and lawns led 18th-century bon vivant Horace Walpole to comment that a pheasant at Castle Howard lived better than a duke elsewhere. Hidden throughout the 1,000 acres of formal and woodland gardens are temples, statues, fountains, and a grand mausoleum—even a fanciful children's playground. There's also a restaurant, two cafés, and three shops. Hourly tours of the grounds, included in the admission price, fill you in on more background and history. ✉ *Castle Howard, Malton* ✢ *A64 past York, then B1257* ☎ *01653/648333* ⊕ *www.castlehoward.co.uk* ✉ *House and gardens £19.95; gardens only £9.95 in winer, £12.95 in high season* ☉ *House closed Nov.–late Mar.*

Leeds

25 miles southwest of York, 43 miles northeast of Manchester.

Once an industrial powerhouse, Leeds has reinvented itself as a vibrant dining, drinking, and shopping destination with numerous trendy restaurants, sleek bars, and cafés, whose outdoor tables defy the northern weather. A large student population, supporting the city's good music shops and funky boutiques, keeps the town young and hip.

The 20th century was not kind to Leeds: World War II air raids destroyed the city's most distinguished landmarks, and, in the 1960s, urban planners replaced much of what was left with undistinguished modern buildings and inner-city highways. The city is currently restoring its surviving Victorian buildings and converting riverfront factories and warehouses into pricey loft apartments and office buildings.

GETTING HERE AND AROUND

Leeds Bradford Airport, 8 miles north-west of the city, is the main gateway to this part of the country. National Express and Megabus have frequent buses here from London's Victoria Coach Station. The journey takes about 4½ hours. East Coast trains depart from London's King's Cross Station to Leeds Station about every 30 minutes during the week. The trip takes about 2¼ hours. Leeds Station is in the middle of central Leeds and usually has a line of taxis waiting out front.

A city of nearly 750,000 people, Leeds has an efficient local bus service. Most visitors never use it as most sights are in the easily walkable downtown.

ESSENTIALS

VISITOR INFORMATION Leeds Visitor Centre. ⊠ *The Headrow* ☎ *0113/378–6977* ⊕ *www.visitleeds.co.uk.*

Sights

The Calls

NEIGHBORHOOD | East of Granary Wharf, the Calls, now the heart of Leeds's gay nightlife, has old riverfront warehouses converted into snazzy bars and restaurants that enliven the cobbled streets. The best have pleasant terraces overlooking the river. ⊠ *Leeds.*

Granary Wharf

NEIGHBORHOOD | Once at the heart of Leeds's decaying industrial zone, this regenerated development in the Canal Basin along the River Aire is now a trendy hub of chic bars and pleasant cafés. Granary Wharf is reached via the Dark Arches, brick railway tunnels now full of shops, where the River Aire flows under City Station. ⊠ *Dark Neville St.* ⊕ *www.granarywharfleeds.uk.*

★ Harewood House

CASTLE/PALACE | The home of the Earl of Harewood, a cousin of the Queen, Harewood House (pronounced *har*-wood) is a spectacular 1759 neoclassical mansion designed by York architect John Carr and the period's leading interior designer, Robert Adam (the money, sad to say, came from sugar plantations and the slave trade). Highlights include important paintings by Gainsborough and Reynolds, fine ceramics, and a ravishingly beautiful collection of Chippendale furniture (Chippendale was born in nearby Otley), notably the magnificent State Bed. The Old Kitchen and Below Stairs exhibition illustrates life from the servants' point of view. Capability Brown designed the handsome grounds, and Charles Barry added a lovely Italian garden with fountains in the 1840s. Children will love the bird garden with over 40 rare and endangered species and the adventure playground. The house is seven miles north of Leeds; you can take Harrogate and District Bus 36. ⊠ *Harewood* ✛ *Junction of A61 and A659 (on Leeds-Harrogate road)* ☎ *0113/218–1010* ⊕ *www.harewood.org* ⊠ *£15 (£13.50 online)* ☉ *Closed Nov.–late Mar.*

★ Hepworth Wakefield

MUSEUM | The largest purpose-built gallery in the United Kingdom (outside London) focuses on 20th-century British art, notably sculptors Henry Moore and Barbara Hepworth, with important works by both. The unique design of slightly skewed concrete building blocks by architect David Chipperfield is combined with the powerful permanent collection and rolling exhibitions devoted to contemporary artists in the Calder gallery. It's in the down-to-earth West Yorkshire town of Wakefield, 12 miles south of Leeds off M1. ⊠ *Gallery Walk, Wakefield* ☎ *01924/247360* ⊕ *www.hepworth-wakefield.org* ⊠ *Free.*

Leeds Art Gallery

MUSEUM | Next door to the Victorian Town Hall, Yorkshire's most impressive art museum has a strong core collection of works by Courbet, Sisley, Constable, Crome, multiple 20th-century British masters, and the internationally

Leeds, Brontë Country, and the Yorkshire Dales

acclaimed Yorkshire sculptor Henry Moore, who studied at the Leeds School of Art. The graceful statue on the steps outside the gallery is Moore's *Reclining Woman*. More works by Moore are at the adjacent **Henry Moore Institute,** which also has regular exhibitions of modern sculpture. The **Craft Centre and Design Gallery,** also in the museum, exhibits and sells fine contemporary crafts. ⊠ *The Headrow* ☎ *0113/378 5350* ⊕ *www.museumsand galleries.leeds.gov.uk* ⊘ *Closed Mon.*

Magna Science Adventure Centre

MUSEUM | FAMILY | A 45-minute drive south from Leeds to Rotherham brings Yorkshire's industrial past into focus at Magna, a widely respected science museum housed in a former steelworks. Smoke, flames, and sparking electricity bring one of the original six arc furnaces roaring to life in a sound-and-light show.

Four pavilions engagingly illustrate the use of fire, earth, air, and water in the production of steel. ⊠ *Sheffield Rd., Templeborough, Rotherham* ✛ *Junction 33 or 35 off M1* ☎ *01709/720002* ⊕ *www.visit-magna.co.uk* ⊠ *£12.95 (£11.95 online).*

Royal Armouries

MUSEUM | FAMILY | Occupying a redeveloped 13-acre dockland site 15 minutes from the city center, this National Museum of Arms and Armour now houses a collection that originally began in the reign of Elizabeth I, when selected objects were displayed at the Tower of London, making it the United Kingdom's oldest museum. Four collections (the 100 Years War, the Battle of Waterloo, Arms of the First World War, and Arms from the Tower) and five themed galleries (War, Tournament, Self-Defense, Hunting, and Oriental) trace the history of weaponry through some 8,500 objects. The state-of-the-art building is stunningly designed: see a full-sized elephant in armor, models of warriors on horseback, and floor-to-ceiling tents, as well as spirited interactive displays and live jousting demonstrations. Shoot a crossbow (extra charge), direct operations on a battlefield, or experience an Elizabethan joust (around Easter and the end of August). ⊠ *Clarence Dock, Armouries Dr.* ✛ *M621 to Junction 4* ☎ *0113/220–1999* ⊕ *www. royalarmouries.org.*

Temple Newsam

HOUSE | FAMILY | A grand country estate in the middle of a city, this huge Elizabethan and Jacobean building— the family home and birthplace of Lord Darnley (1545–67), the notorious husband of Mary, Queen of Scots— contains one of Britain's most important collections of fine and decorative arts, including furniture, paintings, and ceramics. Surrounding the house are 1,500 acres of parkland, lakes, gardens, miles of woodland walks, as well as a working rare breeds farm, where kids can enjoy a petting zoo. The park and gardens were created by noted 18th-century landscape designer, Capability Brown. Temple Newsam is 4 miles east of Leeds on A63; Bus 10 runs directly from Leeds Central Bus station from Easter to mid-September. ⊠ *Temple Newsam Rd., off Selby Rd.* ☎ *0113/336–7461* ⊕ *www.leeds.gov.uk/ museumsandgalleries* ⊠ *House £7.25; farm £4.10; joint ticket £10.30* ☉ *Closed Mon.*

★ Yorkshire Sculpture Park

GARDEN | This outdoor gallery near Wakefield is part of a former 18th-century estate encompassing more than 500 acres of fields, lakes, exotic trees, and rolling hills. The park, garden, and Underground Gallery—three galleries cut into a hillside—are filled with a carefully curated collection that includes works by Henry Moore and Barbara Hepworth, as well as modern sculptors like Antony Gormley, Anthony Caro, and David Nash. A visitor center offers a restaurant, a gallery for temporary exhibitions, and information about the ecology and history of the estate. You can get here easily from Leeds by train or car. ⊠ *West Bretton, Wakefield* ☎ *01924/832631* ⊕ *www.ysp.co.uk* ⊠ *Museum free, parking £3.50 per hr.*

🍴 Restaurants

Mill Kitchen

$ | CAFÉ | Located in a converted Victorian textile mill on the outskirts of town that now serves as a live-and-work complex for artists, this café and deli has been winning fans with all-day healthy breakfast dishes as well as freshly made sandwiches, soups, and heartier dishes like slow-roast pork belly with applesauce that use seasonal, locally sourced produce. When you've finished eating, check out the exhibitions in the complex's 3,500-square-foot art gallery. **Known for:** lots of vegan and vegetarian options; reasonable prices; family-friendly atmosphere. ⑤ *Average main: £8* ⊠ *1 The Old Combing, Sunnybank Mills, 83–85 Town St., Farsley* ☎ *0113/257–1417* ⊕ *www. millkitchen.co.uk* ☉ *No dinner.*

New Conservatory

$ | MODERN BRITISH | This book-lined, below-ground gastropub serves fresh sandwiches, homemade burgers, and hot dishes like a steak-and-ale stewpot or smoked haddock risotto along with several vegetarian and gluten-free options. There's an open-mic night on Thursday and a DJ on Friday. **Known for:** convivial atmosphere; excellent desserts; curated beer selection. ⑤ *Average main: £14* ⊠ *The Albions, Albion Pl., off Briggate* ☎ *0113/246–1853* ⊕ *www.thenewconservatory.co.uk.*

Trinity Kitchen

$ | **FAST FOOD** | This shopping center takes five of the best street-food traders and pop-up restaurants from around the country and installs them on its first floor under the name Trinity Kitchen. Vendors change every two months, and recent lineups have included Spuds & Bros poutine specialists, El Cubano Cuban steak sandwiches, and Hong Bao Asian street food. **Known for:** hip food truck vibe; wide variety of choices; high-quality, distinctive food. ⑤ *Average main: £8* ✉ *Trinity Leeds, 27 Albion St.* ☎ *0113/394–2415* ⊕ *www.trinityleeds.com* ⊟ *No credit cards.*

Whitelocks Ale House

$ | **BRITISH** | Claiming to date to 1715, this narrow, atmospheric bar in a quiet alley off bustling Briggate retains 19th- and 20th-century features, like beveled mirrors, copper-topped tables, art nouveau stained glass, and mosaic tiles. It serves superior pub food with an emphasis on the local and seasonal, like a warm butternut squash salad or homemade beef in ale pie. **Known for:** generous portions of classic pub food; lots of locals; beers from nearby microbreweries. ⑤ *Average main: £12* ✉ *6–8 Turks Head Yard, off Briggate* ☎ *0113/245–3950* ⊕ *www.whitelocksleeds.com.*

🛏 Hotels

Dakota Deluxe Leeds

$$ | **HOTEL** | This sleek boutique hotel from the founder of the Malmaison group puts the emphasis on contemporary minimalist comfort, with soundproofed, media-and-amenity-stuffed rooms in subdued purples and taupes. **Pros:** very helpful service; central location; good attention to detail. **Cons:** rooms on the small side; boring views; parking tricky and expensive. ⑤ *Rooms from: £154* ✉ *8 Russell St.* ☎ *0133/322–6261* ⊕ *leeds.dakotahotels.co.uk* ⤳ *88 rooms.*

Malmaison

$ | **HOTEL** | Once the headquarters of the local tram company, this Edwardian building has been reinvented as a funky hotel and Leeds outpost of the boutique mini-chain. **Pros:** friendly service; good food; comfortable beds. **Cons:** some rooms on small side; front rooms may get street noise on weekends; quirky decor may not be for everyone. ⑤ *Rooms from: £108* ✉ *1 Swinegate* ☎ *0844/693–0654* ⊕ *www.malmaison.com* ⤳ *100 rooms* ⦿ *Free breakfast.*

★ Quebecs

$$ | **HOTEL** | This independently owned boutique hotel, a favorite with visiting celebrities, is full of elegant Victorian touches, especially the sweeping oak-paneled staircase illuminated by tall stained-glass windows. **Pros:** lovely building; stylish rooms; friendly service. **Cons:** limited parking; some rooms have drab outlooks; traditional style not for everyone. ⑤ *Rooms from: £139* ✉ *9 Quebec St.* ☎ *0113/244–8989* ⊕ *www.quebecshotel.co.uk* ⤳ *51 rooms* ⦿ *Free breakfast.*

▼ Nightlife

Mojo

MUSIC CLUBS | This cocktail and rum bar proudly flies the flag for rock 'n' roll, with the old-school vinyl and dive style to match. ✉ *18 Merrion St.* ☎ *07815/457814* ⊕ *www.mojobar.co.uk.*

Roxy Ball Room

BARS/PUBS | This sceney bar in the Trinity Square shopping mall has an extensive menu of craft beers and classic cocktails, but the main attractions are the games: Ping-Pong, pool, a 9-hole mini-golf course, shuffleboard, and even beer pong. Slots can be booked in advance (from £4.50 per half hour), but a couple of Ping-Pong tables are open for walk-ins. ✉ *Trinity Sq., 1st fl., Boar La.* ☎ *0113/467–2200* ⊕ *www.roxyballroom.co.uk.*

The Ship

BARS/PUBS | A tavern for 300 years, this cozy, historic pub has a friendly atmosphere, fine ales, and homemade pub grub. ✉ 71A Briggate ☎ 0113/246–8031 ⊕ www.theshipleeds.co.uk.

🎭 Performing Arts

Leeds Grand Theatre

CONCERTS | This lavish Victorian Gothic auditorium dating back to 1878 hosts touring musicals, ballet, and dramas, in addition to performances by the leading regional opera company, Opera North, which is based here. ✉ 46 New Briggate ☎ 0844/848–2700 ⊕ www.leeds-grandtheatre.com.

Leeds International Concert Season

CONCERTS | The Victorian Town Hall hosts an international concert season (October through May) that attracts top national and international orchestras. Jazz, world music, rock, and brass bands also play free shows at outdoor bandstands in city parks. ✉ The Headrow ☎ 0113/376–0318 ⊕ www.leedsconcertseason.co.uk.

Leeds Playhouse

THEATER | In the heart of Leeds's cultural quarter, this ultramodern theater's adaptable space makes it eminently suitable for staging both new works and classics. ✉ Playhouse Sq., Quarry Hill ☎ 0113/213–7700 ⊕ www.leedsplayhouse.org.uk.

🛍 Shopping

Kirkgate Market

OUTDOOR/FLEA/GREEN MARKETS | The city has some excellent markets, notably Kirkgate Market, an Edwardian beauty that's one of the largest indoor markets in Europe. ✉ 34 George St. ☎ 0113/378–1950 ⊕ www.leeds.gov.uk/leedsmarkets.

Leeds Corn Exchange

SHOPPING CENTERS/MALLS | Housed in a grand mid-19th-century former mercantile exchange, this glass-roofed, oval shopping mall has independent boutiques, laid-back restaurants, and specialty stores across three levels. ✉ Call La. ☎ 0113/234–0363 ⊕ www.leedscorn-exchange.co.uk.

Victoria Quarter

SHOPPING CENTERS/MALLS | Notable for the soaring glass-covered arches of its beautiful turn-of-the-century shopping arcades, the spiffy Victoria Quarter combines 19th-century design and 21st-century style. ✉ 10 Queen Victoria St., Briggate ☎ 0113/245–5333 ⊕ www.victorialeeds.co.uk.

Saltaire

12 miles east of Leeds, 8 miles east of Haworth.

This planned community, built by a philanthropic Victorian industrialist in the wool trade to house his workers, perfectly preserves the architecture—both residential and industrial—of the period.

GETTING HERE AND AROUND

Saltaire has regular bus and train services from the nearby town of Bradford. Drivers should take A650 from Bradford and follow the signs.

ESSENTIALS

VISITOR INFORMATION Saltaire Visitor Information Centre. ✉ Victoria Hall, Victoria Rd., Shipley ☎ 01274/433678 ⊕ www.saltairevillage.info.

👁 Sights

Hockney 1853 Gallery

MUSEUM | Housed in a historic mill building that dates back to 1853, this gallery is devoted to a remarkable exhibition of over 300 works by Bradford-born artist David Hockney. The gallery also sells art materials and art books, plus there's a shopping complex and two restaurants in the building. ✉ Salt's Mill, Victoria Rd., Shipley ☎ 01274/531163 ⊕ www.saltsmill.org.uk.

National Science and Media Museum

MUSEUM | FAMILY | Bradford, 10 miles west of Leeds, is known for this renowned museum that looks at the science and culture of audiovisual technologies. It's a huge and highly entertaining place, with seven galleries displaying the world's first photographic negative, the latest digital imaging, and everything in between. There are also three cinemas, including an IMAX theater, that show recent releases. ⊠ *Little Horton La., Bradford* ☎ *01274/202–030* ⊕ *www.scienceandmediamuseum.org.uk.*

Saltaire

FACTORY | A UNESCO World Heritage Site, Saltaire was built as a model village in the mid-19th century by textile magnate Sir Titus Salt, who, aspiring to create the ideal industrial community, decided to relocate his factories from the dark mills of Bradford to the countryside. The Italianate village (the main building resembles a palazzo) is remarkably well preserved, with its former mills and houses now turned into shops, restaurants, and galleries, as well as private homes. The largest factory in the world when it was built in 1853, today it contains an art gallery, along with crafts and furniture shops. ⊠ *Saltaire Rd., Shipley* ☎ *01274/433678* ⊕ *www.saltairevillage.info.*

Haworth: Heart of Brontë Country

8 miles west of Saltaire.

Whatever Haworth might have been in the past, today it's Brontë country. This old stone-built textile village on the edge of the Yorkshire Moors long ago gave up its own personality and allowed itself to be taken over by the literary sisters, their powerful novels, and legions of fans. In 1820, when Anne, Emily, and Charlotte were very young, their father relocated them and their other three siblings away from their old home in Bradford to Haworth. The sisters—Emily (author of *Wuthering Heights,* 1847), Charlotte (*Jane Eyre,* 1847), and Anne (*The Tenant of Wildfell Hall,* 1848) were all influenced by the stark, dramatic landscape.

These days, it seems that every building they ever glanced at has been turned into a memorial, shop, or museum. The Haworth Visitor Center has good information about accommodations, maps, books on the Brontës, and inexpensive leaflets to help you find your way to such outlying *Wuthering Heights* sites as Ponden Hall (Thrushcross Grange) and Ponden Kirk (Penistone Crag).

GETTING HERE AND AROUND

To reach Haworth by bus or train, buy a Metro Day Rover for bus and rail (£8.40), take the Metro train from Leeds train station to Keighley, and walk to the bus stop, where you change to a Keighley & District bus to Haworth. On weekends and bank holidays you can opt to take the old-school steam-engined Keighley and Worth Valley Railway to continue on to Haworth.

By car, Haworth is an easy 25-mile drive on A629 from Leeds; it's well signposted, and there's plenty of cheap parking in town.

ESSENTIALS

VISITOR INFORMATION Haworth Visitor Information Centre. ⊠ *2–4 West La., Haworth* ☎ *01535/642329* ⊕ *www.visitbradford.com.*

◉ Sights

★ Brontë Parsonage Museum

HOUSE | The most evocative of Haworth's Brontë sights is this somber Georgian (1778) house, the sisters' family home, where you can see original furniture (some bought by Charlotte after the success of *Jane Eyre*), portraits, and books. The Brontës moved here when the Reverend Patrick Brontë was appointed vicar of the local church, but tragedy soon struck—his wife, Maria, and their

The streets and houses of Haworth look much as they did when the Brontë sisters lived and wrote their famous novels in this village near the moors.

two eldest children died within five years. The museum explores the family's tragic story, bringing it to life with a strong collection of enchanting mementos of the four children. These include tiny books they made when they were still very young; Charlotte's wedding bonnet; and the sisters' spidery, youthful graffiti on the nursery wall. Branwell, the Brontës' only brother, painted several of the portraits on display. ⊠ *Church St., Haworth* ☎ *01535/642323* ⊕ *www.bronte.org.uk* 🎫 *£9.50* ⊘ *Closed Jan.*

Brontë Waterfall

BODY OF WATER | If you have the time, pack a lunch and walk for 2¾ miles or so from Haworth along a field path, lane, and moorland track to the lovely, isolated waterfall that has, inevitably, been renamed in honor of the sisters. It was one of their favorite haunts, which they wrote about in poems and letters. ⊠ *Haworth* ✢ *From Haworth Church on Main St., follow signs* ⊕ *www.bronteadventures.co.uk/moors/bronte-waterfall.*

Keighley and Worth Valley Railway

TOUR—SIGHT | **FAMILY** | Haworth is one stop along the route of this scenic 5-mile heritage railway between Keighley and Oxenhope through the picturesque Worth Valley, as seen in numerous film and television shows including *Peaky Blinders.* Many of the trains are pulled by handsome steam engines. Frequent themed special events add to the fun. ⊠ *Haworth Station, Station Rd., Haworth* ☎ *01535/645214* ⊕ *www.kwvr.co.uk* 🎫 *£13 round-trip, £18 Day Rover ticket* ⊘ *Closed Jan.; weekdays Feb.–early Apr., late Apr.–mid-May, and Nov.–Dec.; Mon., Tues., Thurs., and Fri. mid-May–late May and mid-Sept.–late Oct.; and Mon. and Tues. mid-June–mid-July.*

Main Street

NEIGHBORHOOD | Haworth's steep, cobbled high street has changed little in outward appearance since the early 19th century, but it now acts as a funnel for crowds heading for points of interest: the **Black Bull** pub, where the reprobate Branwell Brontë drank himself into an early grave (his stool is kept in mint condition); the former **post office** (now a bookshop) from which Charlotte, Emily, and Anne sent their manuscripts to their London publishers; and the **church,** with its atmospheric graveyard (Charlotte and Emily are buried in the family vault inside the church; Anne is buried in Scarborough). ⊠ *Haworth.*

Top Withens
LOCAL INTEREST | The foreboding ruin of a mansion perched on a bleak hilltop three miles from Haworth, Top Withens is often assumed to be the inspiration for the fictional Wuthering Heights. Brontë scholars say it probably isn't; even in its heyday, the house never fit the book's description of Heathcliff's domain. Still, it's an inspirational walk across the moors. There and back from Haworth is a 3½-hour walk along a well-marked footpath that goes past the Brontë waterfall. If you've read *Wuthering Heights,* you don't need to be reminded to wear sturdy shoes and protective clothing. ⊠ *Haworth* ⊕ *www. haworth-village.org.uk.*

🍴 Restaurants

Haworth Old Hall
$ | **BRITISH** | This 16th-century building with two magnificent stone fireplaces is now a welcoming gastro-pub, and the friendly and efficient service gets high marks. The menu is hearty British food, with mains like pan-fried chicken breast in a creamy mushroom and brandy sauce as well as modern lighter options like jackfruit croquettes or a winter vegetable pot pie, plus sandwiches and burgers. **Known for:** good beer selection; filling portions of classic British dishes; atmospheric setting. $ *Average main: £13* ⊠ *Sun St., Haworth* ☎ *01535/642709* ⊕ *www.hawortholdhall.co.uk.*

The Hawthorn
$$ | **MODERN BRITISH** | This gastro-pub's weekly changing menu emphasizes fresh, seasonal ingredients, with meats sourced from local small farms' rare and native breeds (much of it cooked over a charcoal grill) and fish delivered from nearby Hartlepool, plus a good selection of gluten-free and vegetarian options. The downstairs bar evokes a snug Georgian tavern with its wood-paneling and open fire, while upstairs is an elegant Georgian dining room that features several antique clocks made by John Barraclough, clockmaker to the Brontës, who lived in this building. **Known for:** excellent grilled meats; cozy ambience; friendly service. $ *Average main: £20* ⊠ *103–109 Main St., Haworth* ☎ *01535/644477* ⊕ *www. thehawthornhaworth.co.uk* ⊘ *Closed Mon. and Tues.*

🛏 Hotels

The Apothecary Guest House
$ | **B&B/INN** | Built in 1640, this family-run B&B is located at the top of the cobbled main street, opposite the Brontë church. **Pros:** scenic views; town center location; helpful hosts. **Cons:** rooms at front may have noise from pub; limited time to order breakfast; decor may be too basic for some. $ *Rooms from: £60* ⊠ *86 Main St., Haworth* ☎ *01535/643642* ⊕ *www. theapothecaryguesthouse.co.uk* ⇌ *7 rooms* ⦿ *Free breakfast.*

Ashmount Country House
$$ | **B&B/INN** | A short walk from the Parsonage, this charming stone building was once home to the Brontë sisters' physician, Amos Ingham. **Pros:** lovely period building; ideal location; great views. **Cons:** some bedrooms small; cleaning standards uneven; afternoon tea could be better. $ *Rooms from: £139* ⊠ *Mytholmes La., Haworth* ☎ *01535/645726* ⊕ *www.ashmounthaworth.co.uk* ⇌ *12 rooms* ⦿ *Free breakfast.*

The imposing ruins of Bolton Priory provide a scenic backdrop for a walk along the River Wharfe.

Bolton Abbey

12 miles north of Haworth, 24 miles northwest of Leeds.

A leafy, picturesque village amid the rolling hills of the Yorkshire Dales, Bolton Abbey is a famously attractive town with a stone church and an evocative ruined priory. It is on a huge estate owned by the Duke of Devonshire, who still technically owns much of the area—a lingering reminder of the country's feudal past.

GETTING HERE AND AROUND

Bolton Abbey, off the A59 between Skipton and Harrogate, is best reached by car.

◉ Sights

Bolton Abbey

ARCHAEOLOGICAL SITE | Some of the loveliest Wharfedale scenery comes into view near Bolton Priory, the ruins of a 12th-century Augustinian priory that sit on a grassy embankment over a great curve of the River Wharfe. The view inspired J. M. W. Turner to create a number of watercolors of the priory ruins and nearby sites. Close to Bolton Priory and surrounded by romantic woodland scenery, the River Wharfe plunges between a narrow chasm in the rocks (called the Strid) before reaching **Barden Tower,** a ruined medieval hunting lodge that can be visited just as easily as Bolton Priory. Both are part of the 30,000-acre Bolton Abbey estate owned by the dukes of Devonshire. The priory is just a short walk or drive from the village of Bolton Abbey. You can also visit the priory church.

Guides are available weekdays from March to October. ✉ *Bolton Abbey, Skipton* ✛ *B6160 off A59* ☎ *01756/718000* ⊕ *www.boltonabbey.com* 🅿 *Parking £10.*

Embsay and Bolton Abbey Steam Railway
SCENIC DRIVE | FAMILY | You can take a scenic ride on this preserved heritage railway from the station in Bolton Abbey. Steam trains run every Sunday and daily in summer, but hours vary greatly, so it's best to call ahead. ✉ *Bolton Abbey Station, off A59* ☎ *01756/710614, 01756/795189 recorded timetable* ⊕ *www.embsaybol-tonabbeyrailway.org.uk* 🅿 *£12 round-trip.*

 Hotels

Devonshire Arms Country House Hotel & Spa
$$$ | HOTEL | Originally a 17th-century coaching inn, this luxurious country-house hotel near the River Wharfe is an easy walk from Bolton Abbey. **Pros:** one of the region's best hotels; real country-house atmosphere; great restaurant. **Cons:** you pay for all that charm; some new wing rooms small; older rooms a bit dated. ⑤ *Rooms from: £249* ✉ *Bolton Abbey, Skipton* ✛ *B6160 off A59* ☎ *01756/718100* ⊕ *www.thede-vonshirearms.co.uk* ↪ *40 rooms* ⑪ *Free breakfast.*

Skipton

6 miles west of Bolton Abbey, 12 miles north of Haworth, 22 miles west of Harrogate.

Skipton in Airedale, capital of the limestone district of Craven, is a country market town with as many farmers as visitors milling in the streets. There are markets Monday, Wednesday, Friday, and Saturday, with a farmers' market on Sunday. Shops selling local produce are the main retail experience.

Skipton is off A59 and A65 at the southern edge of the Yorkshire Dales National Park. From Leeds, First Leeds buses run regularly to Skipton. Little Red Bus buses depart once a day on Saturday from Harrogate. There are regular trains from Leeds; the journey takes about 40 minutes.

ESSENTIALS
VISITOR INFORMATION Skipton Tourist Information Centre. ✉ *Town Hall, High St.* ☎ *01756/792809* ⊕ *www.cravendc.gov. uk/tourism.*

 Sights

Grassington National Park Centre
INFO CENTER | This visitor center 10 miles north of Skipton has guidebooks, maps, and bus schedules to help you enjoy a day in Yorkshire Dales National Park. Grassington is deep in the dales on the tiny B6265, also known as the Grassington Road; buses travel here from nearby towns. A small stone village, it makes a good base for exploring Upper Wharfedale. The Dales Way footpath passes through the village, where there are stores, pubs, and cafés. In summer, it becomes overwhelmed by day-trippers and hikers, but you can escape them on the many local walks. ✉ *Hebdon Rd., Grassington* ☎ *01756/751690* ⊕ *www. yorkshiredales.org.uk* ⊘ *Closed Jan. and weekdays Nov., Dec., Feb., and Mar.*

Skipton Castle
CASTLE/PALACE | Built by the Normans in 1090, and largely unaltered since the 17th century, Skipton Castle is one of the most complete and best-preserved medieval castles in Britain and still has its original kitchen, great hall, and main bedroom. Following the Battle of Marston Moor during the Civil War, it was the only remaining Royalist stronghold in the north of England, yielding in 1645 only after a three-year siege. So sturdy was the squat little fortification with its

rounded battlements (in some places the walls are 12 feet thick) that Oliver Cromwell ordered the removal of the castle roofs. The castle's owner, Lady Anne Clifford, was eventually allowed to replace the roofs, thanks to a special Act of Parliament, but only with the stipulation that they not be strong enough to withstand cannon fire. The Act was finally repealed in the 1970s to permit repairs at long last. A yew tree planted in the central Tudor courtyard more than 300 years ago by Lady Anne herself to mark the castle's recovery from its Civil War damage is still flourishing. ⊠ *The Bailey* ☎ *01756/792442* ⊕ *www.skiptoncastle. co.uk* ⊠ *£8.70.*

🍴 Restaurants

★ The Angel at Hetton

$$$ | MODERN BRITISH | Cars belonging to diners at this chef-owned country inn often fill the hidden away hamlet of Hetton five miles north of Skipton, such is the reputation of this highly regarded, Michelin-starred gastro-pub par excellence located in an early-18th-century building with contemporary decor and views across the Dales. Specializing in locally sourced seasonal food, such as beautifully prepared roast lamb, beef, and seafood, the restaurant features three-course fixed-price menus for lunch and a seven-course tasting menu for dinner, as well as à la carte options. **Known for:** exemplary food; vegetarian fine dining; good wine list. ⑤ *Average main: £28* ⊠ *Off B6265, Hetton* ☎ *01756/730263* ⊕ *www.angelhetton.co.uk* ⊗ *Closed Tues. and Wed.*

The Devonshire Grassington

$ | BRITISH | With its oak-paneled, candlelit dining room and open fires, this traditional inn is an inviting rural dining spot. Old favorites such as grilled steaks, smoked haddock fishcakes, and traditional Sunday roasts are served with fresh local vegetables (a gluten-free menu adds a contemporary note). **Known for:**

gluten-free options; good traditional pub food; welcoming atmosphere. ⑤ *Average main: £15* ⊠ *27 Main St., Grassington* ☎ *01756/752525* ⊕ *www.thedevonshire-grassington.co.uk.*

🛏 Hotels

Ashfield House

$ | B&B/INN | Three converted 17th-century stone cottages, once the homes of Grassington lead miners, make up this well-run small hotel off the main street. **Pros:** charming cottages; gorgeous gardens; warm service. **Cons:** design on the basic side; bathrooms quite small; cramped parking can be tricky. ⑤ *Rooms from: £67* ⊠ *3 Summers Fold, Grassington* ☎ *01756/752584* ⊕ *www. ashfieldhouse.co.uk* ⤳ *8 rooms* ⑩ *Free breakfast.*

The Devonshire Fell

$$ | B&B/INN | This more casual sister property of the Devonshire Arms down the road (guests have access to the larger property's spa and hiking trails) boasts outstanding views over a particularly lovely part of the Yorkshire Dales. **Pros:** lovely views; excellent location; tasty restaurant. **Cons:** skimpy complimentary breakfast; casual service; poor cell phone reception. ⑤ *Rooms from: £146* ⊠ *Burnsall Village, Burnsall* ✛ *Off B3160* ☎ *01756/729000* ⊕ *www.devonshirefell. co.uk* ⤳ *16 rooms* ⑩ *Free breakfast.*

Grassington Lodge

$ | B&B/INN | Light and airy, this Victorian house combines period charm with a contemporary ambience. **Pros:** lovely building; attentive hosts; good breakfasts. **Cons:** some rooms quite small; not a lot of amenities. ⑤ *Rooms from: £100* ⊠ *8 Wood La., Grassington* ☎ *01756/752518* ⊕ *www.grassingtonlodge.co.uk* ⤳ *12 rooms* ⑩ *Free breakfast.*

⚡ Activities

Avid summer hikers descend in droves on Malham, 12 miles northwest of Skipton, to tour the remarkable limestone formations. Malham Cove, a huge, 260-foot-high natural rock amphitheater, is a mile north of the village and provides the easiest local walk. Taking the 420 steps up to the top is a brutal climb, though you'll be rewarded by magnificent views.

At Gordale Scar, a deep natural chasm between overhanging limestone cliffs, the white waters of a moorland stream plunge 300 feet. It's a mile northeast of Malham by a lovely riverside path.

A walk of more than 3 miles north leads to Malham Tarn, an attractive lake on a slate bed in windswept isolation.

Malham National Park Centre
INFO CENTER | With informative displays, Malham's National Park Centre gives you some ideas for what to see and do, both in town and in Yorkshire Dales National Park. You can also get a list of bed-and-breakfasts and pub accommodations. ⊠ Malham National Park Centre, Chapel Gate, Malham ☎ 01729/833200 ⊕ www. yorkshiredales.org.uk ⊘ Closed Jan. and weekdays Nov., Dec., Feb., and Mar.

Hawes

30 miles north of Skipton.

The best time to visit the so-called cheesiest town in Yorkshire is on Tuesday, when farmers crowd into town for the weekly market. Crumbly, white Wensleydale cheese has been made in the valley for centuries, and it's sold in local stores and at the market. Allow time to explore the cobbled side streets, some of which are filled with antiques shops and tearooms.

GETTING HERE AND AROUND
Hawes is high in the moors on A684. To get here from Grassington, take the B6160 north for 23 miles. There's no train service, but buses travel from Leeds throughout the day on summer weekends.

👁 Sights

Dales Countryside Museum
MUSEUM | Located in the same former train station as the Hawes National Park Information Centre, this local museum traces life in the Dales past and present. A traditional rope-making shop opposite also welcomes visitors. ⊠ Station Yard, Burtersett Rd. ☎ 01969/666210 ⊕ www.dalescountrysidemuseum.org.uk ☜ £4.80 ⊘ Closed weekdays in Jan.

Wensleydale Creamery
MUSEUM VILLAGE | Sort of the cheese equivalent of a winery tour, this museum in a working dairy documents how the famed local cheese—so beloved by the popular animated characters Wallace and Gromit—developed over time. You can watch production (best seen between 10 am and 3 pm on weekdays) from the viewing gallery and then taste (and buy) over 20 varieties of the output in the excellent cheese shop. A restaurant serves plenty of samples—try Wensleydale smoked with ginger or with apple pie. ⊠ Gayle La. ☎ 01969/667664 ⊕ www.wensleydale.co.uk ☜ Tour £4.95.

Richmond

24 miles northeast of Hawes.

Tucked into a bend above the foaming River Swale, Richmond has a picturesque network of narrow Georgian streets and terraces opening onto a large cobbled marketplace that dates back to medieval times. The town's history can be traced to the late 11th century, when the Normans swept in, determined to subdue the local population and establish their rule in the north. They built the mighty castle whose massive keep still dominates the skyline.

GETTING HERE AND AROUND
East Coast Trains run regularly from Leeds and from London's King's Cross to the nearest station, Darlington. From here take the No. 27 bus that runs every 30 minutes. The journey from London takes around 2½ hours; from Leeds it takes about 1½ hours. By car, Richmond is on the rural B6274—follow signs off A1.

ESSENTIALS
VISITOR INFORMATION Richmond Tourist Information Centre. ⊠ *2 Queens Rd., Richmond* ☎ *01609/532980* ⊕ *www. richmond.org.*

 # Sights

★ Georgian Theatre Royal
ARTS VENUE | A jewel box built in 1788 and today an active community playhouse, this theater and museum is Britain's most complete Georgian playhouse still in its original form, retaining authentic features such as the wooden seating from which patrons watched 18th-century leading man David Garrick perform Shakespeare. You can see Britain's oldest painted scenery dating back to 1836 and try on theatrical costumes during the hourly tours, which run from Monday to Saturday between 10 and 4 mid-February through October. There's also an extensive theatrical archive that contains scripts, playbills, and images. ⊠ *Victoria Rd., Richmond* ☎ *01748/823710* ⊕ *www. georgiantheatreroyal.co.uk* ☛ *Tours £5.*

Richmond Castle
ARCHAEOLOGICAL SITE | One of the three oldest stone-built castles in England and considered to be one of Britain's finest examples of a Norman fortress, Richmond Castle sits in a commanding position 100 feet over the River Swale. If you climb the 130 steps to the top of the 12th-century great keep, you are rewarded with sweeping views over the Dales. Originally built around 1071 by the first Earl of Richmond to subdue the unruly inhabitants of the North, the castle retains much of its curtain wall as well as three chapels. There's also an even earlier, two-story structure known as Scolland's Hall, which was built in the 11th century and is believed to be the oldest great hall in England. During World War I, conscientious objectors were imprisoned in the castle, and you can still see the graffiti they inscribed. A path along the river leads to the ruins of golden-stone Easby Abbey. A historical note: when Henry Tudor (son of the Earl of Richmond) became Henry VII in 1485, he began calling his palace in southwest London after the site of his family seat, leading to that part of the city becoming known as Richmond. ⊠ *Riverside Rd., Richmond* ☎ *01748/822493* ⊕ *www.english-heritage.org.uk* ☛ *£6.90* ⊙ *Closed weekdays Nov.–Mar.*

🍴 Restaurants

The Black Bull Moulton
$$ | **BRITISH** | This handsome pub combines a cozy traditional wood-paneled bar with a restaurant in a contemporary glass-and-steel extension that specializes in traditional Yorkshire cooking. Using seasonal, locally sourced ingredients, options might include braised shoulder of venison with a bone marrow crumble; fish pie with Whitby-smoked haddock, Scottish salmon, king prawns, and scallops; or charcoal-grilled Yorkshire sirloin steak. **Known for:** excellent versions of local favorites; dishes from the cast-iron, charcoal-fired oven; attentive service. ⑤ *Average main: £18* ⊠ *Back La., Moulton* ☎ *01325/377556* ⊕ *www. theblackbullmoulton.com.*

The North York Moors and The North Yorkshire Coast

Shoulder of Mutton Inn

$ | **BRITISH** | This cozy inn in an 18th-century building on the outskirts of an unspoiled country village is traditional but not fussy, with open fireplaces, original oak beams, and windows that look out to panoramic views of the Dales. The food, which incorporates local ingredients whenever possible, offers similar traditional comforts. **Known for:** cozy, rural atmosphere; good value pub grub; excellent craft beer selection. $ *Average main: £15* ⊠ *Kirby Hill, Richmond* ☎ *01748/905011* ⊕ *www.shoulderofmutton.net* ☉ *Closed for food Mon. No lunch weekdays.*

🛏 Hotels

Frenchgate Restaurant and Hotel

$$ | **HOTEL** | This three-story Georgian town house on a quiet cobbled street has a secluded walled garden for summer days. **Pros:** lovely gardens; period atmosphere; luxurious bathrooms. **Cons:** some bedrooms not as nice as others; owner-manager can be a bit cranky; food uneven. $ *Rooms from: £198* ⊠ *59–61 Frenchgate, Richmond* ☎ *01748/822087* ⊕ *www.thefrenchgate.co.uk* ⌐ *9 rooms* ¶◯¶ *Free breakfast.*

★ Millgate House and Garden

$$ | **B&B/INN** | This 18th-century house in the center of Richmond has been beautifully restored, with a particularly elegant Regency dining room and sitting room. **Pros:** central location; elegant atmosphere with beautiful gardens; professional, generous hosts. **Cons:** rooms can be a bit chilly; focus on antique decor not for everyone; lots of steps and uneven footing in gardens. ⑤ *Rooms from: £145* ✉ *3 Millgate, Richmond* ☎ *01748/823571* ⊕ *www.millgatehouse.com* ↝ *6 rooms, 1 cottage* ◎ *Free breakfast.*

Danby

49 miles northeast of York, 15 miles west of Whitby.

The old stone village of Danby nestles in the green Esk Valley, a short walk from the summit of the moors. It's been settled since Viking times—Danby means "settlement of the Danes"—and these days it's home to the main information center for the Moors National Park. There's also a pub and a cozy bakery with a tearoom. Bring hiking boots, and within 10 minutes you can be surrounded by moorland looking down on the village below.

GETTING HERE AND AROUND

From York, take A64 to A169 and then follow the signs across the moor. Northern Rail travels to Danby station throughout the day from nearby towns. To get here from Whitby, take A171 west and turn north for Danby after 12 miles, after which it's a 3-mile drive over Danby Low Moor to the village.

Four community-funded Moorsbus routes run over the moors on Fridays, weekends, and holiday Mondays from May to September: one to Rievaulx Abbey and Helmsley; one to Ryedale; one to the Dalby Forest; and one to the North York Moors National Park and the Cleveland Way trail. A fifth service also operates on Saturday and goes all the way to York.

Ralph Cross ⊙

From Danby take the road due west for 2 miles to Castleton, and then turn south over the top of the moors toward Hutton-le-Hole. The narrow road has magnificent views over North York Moors National Park, especially at the old stone **Ralph Cross** (5 miles), which marks the park's highest point. Drive carefully, keeping your eye out for sheep in the road.

BUS CONTACTS Moorsbus.
☎ *01482/477216* ⊕ *www.moorsbus.org.*

⊙ Sights

Moors National Park Centre

INFO CENTER | **FAMILY** | This flagship visitor center of the North York Moors National Park sits on the banks of the River Esk, near Danby. There's an exhibition with interactive displays about the park's history, wildlife, and landscape, as well as a gallery with work by local artists and artisans. While parents relax in the café, children can scramble up the kids-only climbing wall or enjoy the beautiful outdoor play area. ✉ *Danby Lodge, Lodge La.* ☎ *01439/772737* ⊕ *www.northyorkmoors.org.uk* ⊙ *Closed weekdays Jan.–mid-Feb.*

Hutton-le-Hole

13 miles south of Danby.

Sleepy Hutton-le-Hole is a charming little place based around a wide village green, with woolly sheep snoozing in the shade of stone cottages. Unfortunately, it can be unbearably crowded in summer. You can always keep driving to either the charming nearby village of Thornton-le-Dale or to the medieval market towns of Helmsley or Pickering.

The ruins of Rievaulx Abbey, which was enormously wealthy in medieval times because of the wool trade, show how large the abbey was.

GETTING HERE AND AROUND

Hutton-le-Hole is on the moors off A170. It has no train station and is only accessible by bus May through September when the Moorsbus M6 travels between the area's small towns.

◉ Sights

Ryedale Folk Museum

MUSEUM VILLAGE | FAMILY | This excellent open-air folk museum explores the rural way of life from the Iron Age to the 1950s through more than 20 historic buildings (some restored, some reconstructed) including a medieval crofter's cottage, a Tudor manor house, a 16th-century glass kiln, a full-scale reconstructed Iron Age dwelling, and the oldest daylight photography studio in the country. There are opportunities to introduce kids to traditional farming techniques like threshing and winnowing (£6.50 extra charge) and activities like calligraphy and pottery. All entry is weather-permitting. ⊠ Off A170, Hutton le Hole ☎ 01751/417367 ⊕ www.ryedale-folkmuseum.co.uk ☞ £8.75 ⊗ Closed mid–Nov.–mid–Feb.

Helmsley

8 miles southwest of Hutton-le-Hole, 27 miles north of York.

The market town of Helmsley—with its flower-filled window boxes, stone cottages, churchyard, and streams crossed by arched bridges—is the perfect place to spend a relaxing afternoon. You can linger in its tea shops and tiny boutiques or explore the craggy remains of its Norman castle. Market day is Friday. Nearby are the impressive ruins of Rievaulx Abbey.

GETTING HERE AND AROUND

There's no train station in Helmsley, but it's served by bus from Scarborough. By car, Helmsley is on A170.

Visiting Yorkshire's Monastic Past 👁

The ruined abbeys of Fountains, Rievaulx, and Whitby, which vividly evoke the daily life of monks during the Middle Ages, are ideal for learning about the religious life and commercial activities of Yorkshire's great monasteries and the political machinations that destroyed them.

The sheer number of what were once richly decorated monastic buildings is a testament to the power of medieval Yorkshire's Catholic monastic orders. They became some of the richest in Europe by virtue of the international wool trade conducted from their vast estates with the help of lay workers. The buildings are now mostly romantic ruins, a result of the dissolution of the monasteries during the 16th century following Henry VIII's establishment of the Church of England (with himself as its head) in 1536. This was both a retaliation against the Catholic Church for denying him a divorce (and thus, in his view, a male heir) and a way of appropriating the monasteries' wealth. By 1540, no monasteries remained in England; the king confiscated all their property, redistributed their land, and destroyed or gave away many buildings.

👁 Sights

★ Rievaulx

ARCHAEOLOGICAL SITE | The perfect marriage of architecture and landscape, Rievaulx (pronounced ree- *voh*) Abbey sits in a dramatic setting two miles northwest of Helmsley, its soaring arches built to precisely frame the forested hillside rushing down to the River Rye. Founded in 1132 by a French Cistercian sect (there's a 13th century shrine containing the remains of the first abbot, William, at the entrance to the Chapter House), Rievaulx soon became one of the most powerful monasteries in Britain. By the end of the 13th century, the abbey was massively wealthy thanks to the monks involvement in the wool trade. The evocative ruins still give a good indication of how vast it once was, from the church's huge 13th-century presbytery (one of the finest examples of Early English architecture in northern England) to the imposing refectory (dining hall). You should also get a glimpse of the 12th-century cloisters with their (reconstructed) symmetrical columns.

By the time of the suppression of the monasteries in 1538 under Henry VIII, the abbey had shrunk dramatically, with only 23 monks still living there. The new owner, the Earl of Rutland, subsequently dismantled what was left of the abbey, sending off the roof leads and bells to the king and allowing villagers to cart away the abbey's stones to build their houses. What remains is a beautiful ghost of the magnificent building that once stood here. From Rievaulx Abbey it's a short climb or drive up the hill to Rievaulx Terrace, an 18th-century escarpment with a magnificent view of the abbey. At either end of the woodland walk are two mid-18th-century follies in the style of small Palladian temples. ✉ *Helmsley* ✛ *Off B1257* ☎ *01439/798228* ⊕ *www.english-heritage.org.uk* ✉ *£9.40* ⊘ *Closed weekdays Nov.–Feb.*

Shandy Hall

HOUSE | The Brontës aren't the only literary lions to have emerged from this part of Yorkshire. In his eccentric, satirical novel *Tristram Shandy*, Laurence Sterne experimented with the techniques of postmodern fiction in 1760, long before the traditional novel form had even emerged as a literary genre. Despite the book's often bawdy humor, Sterne was the local vicar, living and writing in this charming 15th-century house with 18th-century additions. Restored in the 1990s, it contains the world's largest collection of Sterne's work and memorabilia. Admission to the house is only by guided tour (2:45 and 3:45) or by appointment. There are also 2 acres of grounds, including a walled rose garden. ⊠ *Thirsk Bank, Coxwold* ✣ *Off A19* ☎ *01347/868465* ⊕ *www.laurencesternetrust.org.uk* ⌑ *House and garden £6; garden only £3* ⊗ *House closed Oct.–Apr. and Mon., Tues., Thurs., and Fri.; gardens closed Oct.–Apr. and Mon. May–Sept.*

🛏 Hotels

Black Swan Hotel
$$ | HOTEL | A splendid base for exploring the area, this ivy-covered property sits on the edge of Helmsley's market square. **Pros:** historic charm; great location; delicious food. **Cons:** design is a bit old-fashioned; bathrooms on small side; some spots need a face-lift. ⑤ *Rooms from: £155* ⊠ *Market Pl.* ☎ *01439/770466* ⊕ *www.blackswan-helmsley.co.uk* ⤴ *45 rooms* ⑩ *Free breakfast.*

🏃 Activities

Cleveland Way
HIKING/WALKING | Helmsley, on the southern edge of the moors, is the starting point of the long-distance moor-and-coastal footpath known as the Cleveland Way. Boots go on at the old cross in the market square, then it's 50 miles or so across the moors to the coast, followed by a similar distance south to Filey along the cliffs. The footpath is 110 miles long and takes around nine days start to finish. The trail passes close to Rievaulx Abbey, a few miles outside town. ⊠ *Helmsley* ⊕ *www.nationaltrail.co.uk.*

Hull

34 miles southeast of York; 45 miles southeast of Helmsley.

Strategically placed between the River Hull and the Humber Estuary, Hull is the gateway to the North of England and the third-busiest port in England (after London and Liverpool), though today the ships in the harbor are more likely to be carrying petroleum than the wool and whale blubber the town's fortune was built on. In the 1950s, it was one of the world's busiest fishing ports, but the trade has since declined. Hull's docks made it a magnet for German bombs during WWII, when it suffered terrible damage, becoming the second-most bombed city in England. However, traces of historic Hull can still be found in the Old Town, with its handsome Georgian houses built by 18th-century merchants on the original narrow medieval streets near the Market Place and the Church of the Holy Trinity, which dates back to the 14th century. Here you'll also find Wilberforce House, the birthplace of the antislavery campaigner William Wilberforce.

Hull suffered from the deindustrialization of the 1970s and '80s but has been revitalized since being named a European City of Culture in 2017, with a host of shops, galleries, and restaurants opening on Humber Street near the docks. The same year, the soaring Humber Bridge was given landmark status; when it opened in 1981, it was longest single-span suspension bridge in the world (a record it held for 16 years).

GETTING HERE AND AROUND
Trains leave London King's Cross for Hull every 40 minutes or so, and the journey takes between 3 and 3½ hours. From Leeds, trains run approximately hourly, and the trip takes an hour.

To drive from York, take the A1079 followed by the A63 (approximately 1¼ hours). From Leeds, the journey time is about the same—take motorways M1 and M62 to the A63.

TOURS
The Larkin Trail

SELF-GUIDED | The poet Philip Larkin, who moved to Hull in the early 1930s, spent the majority of his working life here and frequently wrote about the city, perfectly capturing modern life and its dissatisfactions. There are three options for exploring the 25 locations associated with Larkin's life and work: one focusing on Larkin-related sites in the city center; a second taking in the fringes of the city to include the university where he was employed as the librarian; and a third exploring the wider countryside celebrated in his writing. You can download a PDF map of the trail from the website or pick-up a hard copy at the tourist information center. ⌖ *Hull* ⊕ *www. thelarkintrail.co.uk.*

ESSENTIALS
VISITOR INFORMATION Hull Tourist Information Centre. ⌖ *Hull Paragon Interchange, Fernsway, Hull* ☎ *01482/228704* ⊕ *www.yorkshire.com.*

👁 Sights

The Deep

ZOO | **FAMILY** | Home to thousands of marine creatures including seven species of shark, the huge tanks of this iceberg-shaped aquarium are devoted to exhibits ranging from a lagoon featuring tropical fish to the 33-foot-deep Endless Oceans tank, where you descend via a glass elevator to view sharks, rays, loggerhead turtles, and other creatures. Penguin feedings (11:30 and 3:30 daily) and a hands-on exhibit where you can interact with small species like starfish and sea urchins are always popular. Be prepared to wait in line, especially during school holidays. Proceeds go toward worldwide marine conservation projects. ⌖ *Tower St., Hull* ☎ *01482/381100* ⊕ *www.thedeep.co.uk* 🎟 *£13.50.*

Ferens Art Gallery

MUSEUM | A grand neoclassical building dating back to 1927, the Ferens has a collection that ranges from Old Masters like Frans Hals, Canaletto, and Frederick Leighton to more modern artists like David Hockney, Henry Moore, and Stanley Spenser, as well as contemporary artists like Gillian Wearing, Helen Chadwick, and Nan Goldin. ⌖ *Queen Victoria Sq., Hull* ☎ *01482/300300* ⊕ *www. hcandl.co.uk/museums-and-galleries/ ferens.*

Hull Minster

RELIGIOUS SITE | With construction beginning in 1285 under Edward I, this is the only building of the original medieval "King's Town" to survive. For the first 700 of its existence it was known as the Church of the Holy Trinity until 2017 when it was granted Minster status. The nave, a superb example of the Perpendicular Gothic added in the mid-1300s, served as a model for other major churches of the period incuding Manchester and the original Coventry cathedral. As part of a Victorian-era restoration, the church acquired carved furniture by Robert "Mouseman" Thompson that incorporates seven of his trademark mice (there's a special find-the-mice tour for kids). Don't miss the Art Nouveau stained-glass windows, including two by the noted designer Walter Crane. Former worshippers here include antislavery campaigner William Wilberforce and the Restoration poet Andrew Marvell, whose statue stands in a square in front of the church. ⌖ *Market Pl., Hull* ☎ *01482/224460* ⊕ *www. hullminster.org* 🎟 *Guided tours £5* 🕒 *Closed Mon.*

★ Wilberforce House

MUSEUM | This small museum is dedicated to the politician and social reformer William Wilberforce (the building is also his actual birthplace). An MP for Hull, Wilberforce fought for 18 years to end Britain's slave trade until it was finally abolished in 1807, although it would be another 26 years before all the slaves in the British Empire were emancipated (Wilberforce heard the news on his deathbed). Galleries tell the history of the slave trade, its legacy, and the abolitionist movement, and include items related to West African culture as well as Wilberforce's journals and personal possessions. ⊠ *23–25 High St., Hull* ☎ *01482/613902* ⊕ *www.hcandl.co.uk/museums-and-galleries.*

🍴 Restaurants

Kardomah 94

$ | **CAFÉ** | More than just a restaurant, Kardomah is also a venue for theater, stand-up, music, dance, and spoken word performances. The all-day menu leans toward creative pizzas, wraps, and salads. **Known for:** generous portions; imaginative pizzas; group dining. ⑤ *Average main: £13* ⊠ *94 Alfred Gelder St., Hull* ☎ *01482/317941* ⊕ *www.kardomah94.com.*

🛏 Hotels

The Kingston Theatre Hotel

$ | **HOTEL** | This family-run hotel in an Old Town Victorian may not be the trendiest place you'll ever stay, but it's quiet, comfortable, and clean while offering warm Northern hospitality. **Pros:** welcoming staff; good value for money; excellent afternoon tea. **Cons:** decor can be tired; some noise between rooms; not great for the mobility-impaired. ⑤ *Rooms from: £85* ⊠ *1-2 Kingston Sq., Hull* ☎ *01482/225828* ⊕ *www.kingstontheatrehotel.com* ⇥ *28 rooms* ⦿ *Free breakfast.*

Scarborough

44 miles northeast of York.

There's no Scarborough Fair, and historians are divided on whether there ever was one, but don't let that stop you from heading to this classic English seaside resort on the North Sea. The liveliest tourist action is on South Bay, a riot of tacky arcades, ice-cream stands, and stores selling "rock" (luridly colored hard candy). Above the former spa are the lemon-hued Victorian and Regency terraces of the genteel South Cliff Promenade, with its views across Cayton Bay and a Victorian funicular linking it to the South Sands below. The South Bay and quieter North Bay are divided by a rocky headland on which sits the ruins of an 11th-century castle. The huddle of streets, alleyways, and red-roof cottages around the harbor gives an idea of what the town was like before it became a resort.

GETTING HERE AND AROUND

Scarborough is difficult to reach by public transportation. There are no direct trains from London, and a bus from London takes all day. Transpennine Express trains leave from York every hour or so; the journey takes just under an hour. The journey from Leeds by National Express bus takes about three hours. By car, Scarborough is on the coastal A165 road.

ESSENTIALS

TRAIN INFORMATION TransPennine Express. ☎ *0345/600–1671* ⊕ *www.tpexpress.co.uk.*

VISITOR INFORMATION Scarborough Tourist Information Centre. ⊠ *Stephen Joseph Theatre, Westborough* ☎ *01723/383636* ⊕ *www.discoveryorkshirecoast.com.*

◉ Sights

Rotunda Museum

MUSEUM | One of the country's first purpose-built museums, this extraordinary cylindrical building was constructed in 1829 to house Jurassic fossils and minerals collected nearby. Designed by William Smith, known as "the father of English geology," it now displays important archaeological finds, evidence of local dinosaurs, and a unique Bronze Age skeleton. Don't miss the frieze illustrating the geology of the nearby coastline. ⊠ Vernon Rd. ☎ 01723/353665 ⊕ www.scarboroughmuseumstrust.com/rotunda-museum ⊡ £3 ☉ Closed Mon.

Scarborough Castle

ARCHAEOLOGICAL SITE | There have been military structures on this promontory commanding a view of the North and South bays since prehistoric times. Digs have uncovered evidence of fortifications here dating back to 500 BC, and there is still some remaining stonework from a 4th-century Roman signaling station. In 1136, a cliff-top stone fortress was built by the Earl of Albemarle, and the massive keep that dominates the existing ruins was added by Henry II in 1158, along with the enormous curtain walls that made the castle virtually impregnable. It remained largely unscathed until Cromwell's cannons did their worst during the Civil War. Further demolition came in 1914 when German warships shelled the town, and in 2012 when local vandals significantly damaged the Roman stonework. ■TIP➔ **The castle has a spectacular panoramic view of the coast.** ⊠ Castle Rd. ☎ 01723/372451 ⊕ www.english-heritage.org.uk ⊡ £7.90 ☉ Closed Mon. and Tues.; closed weekdays Nov.–mid-Feb.

Sea Life Scarborough Aquarium

ZOO | FAMILY | This aquarium and marine sanctuary is a great—if rather expensive—way to entertain the kids for an afternoon. You can see marine habitats and creatures from around Britain and further afield: otters, penguins, jellyfish, loggerhead turtles, octopuses, and rescued seal pups are particularly popular. ⊠ Scalby Mills Rd., North Bay ☎ 01723/373414 ⊕ www.visitsealife.com ⊡ £16.50; £9.90 online.

St. Mary's with Holy Apostles

RELIGIOUS SITE | Most visitors to this small parish church near the castle are attracted by the churchyard's most famous occupant: Anne, the youngest Brontë sister. As a governess, Anne accompanied her employers to Scarborough for five summers, and she returned shortly before her death from tuberculosis in 1849 in the hope the sea air would stimulate a recovery. Her sister Charlotte decided to "lay the flower where it had fallen" and buried Anne above the bay she'd loved. The church itself was originally erected in 1150 and rebuilt in the 17th century. ⊠ Castle Rd. ☎ 01723/500541 ⊕ www.scarborough-st-marys.org.uk ☉ Closed Sat.

A Spa Is Born 🏃

In 1626, Elizabeth Farrow came upon a stream of acidic water running from a cliff south of Scarborough. This led to the town becoming a hugely popular spa on a par with Harrogate. By the 18th century, when icy sea bathing came into vogue, no beaches were busier than Scarborough's. Donkeys and horses drew wheeled cabins called bathing machines into the surf to enable ladies to change into swimming costumes while preserving their modesty. The city's prosperity manifested itself in the handsome Regency and early Victorian residences and hotels you see today.

A former smuggling center, the village of Robin's Hood Bay is known for its red-roofed cottages as well as its beach.

Restaurants

The Golden Grid

$ | SEAFOOD | Everyone visiting Scarborough has to have fish-and-chips at least once, and this harbor-front spot is a classic of its kind. Choose an upstairs window table for the view, and tuck into freshly fried, lightly battered cod or haddock. **Known for:** views over Scarborough Harbour; superfresh seafood; big crowds in a tight space. $ *Average main: £15* ✉ *4 Sandside* ☎ *01723/360922* ⊕ *www. goldengrid.co.uk.*

★ Lanterna

$$ | ITALIAN | This unpretentious family-run restaurant prides itself on *not* being trendy but nevertheless is regularly acclaimed as one of the best restaurants in Britain, let alone Yorkshire. With a constantly changing menu, it specializes in refined northern Italian dishes such as homemade ravioli with venison and spinach, as well as seafood specials using catches fresh off the boats in the harbor. **Known for:** authentic Piedmontese cuisine; fresh local seafood; small space that books up quickly. $ *Average main: £17* ✉ *33 Queen St.* ☎ *01723/363616* ⊕ *www. lanterna-ristorante.co.uk* ⊘ *Closed Sun. and Mon. No lunch.*

🛏 Hotels

Crown Spa Hotel

$ | HOTEL | The centerpiece of the Regency Esplanade, this grand hotel overlooking the South Bay was originally built in the 19th century to accommodate fashionable visitors. **Pros:** friendly staff; excellent sea views; free access to health club. **Cons:** housekeeping could be better; not all rooms have sea views; full breakfast is extra. $ *Rooms from: £117* ✉ *7–11 Esplanade, South Cliff* ☎ *01723/357400* ⊕ *www.crownspa-hotel.com* ⇥ *120 rooms* ⦿| *Free breakfast.*

🎭 Performing Arts

Stephen Joseph Theatre

ARTS CENTERS | Scarborough is firmly on Britain's theater map, largely thanks to the presence of noted playwright and local resident Alan Ayckbourn, who was for many years the artistic director of this theater and premiered most of his acclaimed plays here. His legacy lives on in the theater's commitment to new writing and its strong summer repertory season. There are two stages, plus a cinema, restaurant, and bar. ⊠ *Westborough* ☎ *01723/370541* ⊕ *www.sjt.uk.com.*

Robin Hood's Bay

15 miles northwest of Scarborough, 7 miles south of Whitby.

With red-roof cottages and cobbled roads squeezed into a narrow ravine, this tiny fishing village is considered by many to be the prettiest on the Yorkshire coast. Its winding stone staircases eventually bring you to the headland. Despite its name, the village has no connection to the famous medieval outlaw, beyond a historic association with illegal activity. It was once a smuggling center, with contraband passed up the streambed beneath cottages linked to one another by secret passages. The rocks exposed at low tide on the beach are a good hunting ground for Jurassic fossils. ■**TIP**➔ **Park in the pay lots at the top of the hill. Do not attempt to drive down the hill.**

GETTING HERE AND AROUND

Park in the public lots at the top of the hill. Robin Hood's Bay has no train station, but buses arrive from Scarborough and Whitby throughout the day.

👁 Sights

Robin Hood's Bay Beach

BEACH—SIGHT | Forget palm trees and white sand—this beach, part of the North York Moors National Park, is all about cliffs, dramatic views, and nature at its most powerful and elemental. It is scenic but deceptive—the tide rushes in quickly, so take care not to get cut off. Provided the tide is out, you can stroll for a couple of hours from the town along a rough stone shore full of rock pools, inlets, and sandy strands (a few are suitable for sunbathers) to the curiously named **Boggle Hole,** 3 miles to the south, where an old water mill nestles in a ravine. Farther south is **Ravenscar,** a Victorian village that consists of little more than a hotel. It can be reached by walking up the cliff along a hazardous but exhilarating path. **Amenities:** none. **Best for:** walking. ⊠ *Robin Hood's Bay* ☎ *01439/772700* ⊕ *www. northyorkmoors.org.uk.*

🍽 Restaurants

Bay Hotel

$ | **BRITISH** | Perfectly positioned at the bottom of the village, this friendly retreat dating to 1828 looks out from atop a seawall to dramatic views of the North Sea (if you can get a coveted window table) and has a warming open fireplace in winter. The reasonably priced menu leans towards well-prepared traditional pub grub and fresh seafood like Whitby scampi or crab and lemon salad. **Known for:** fresh seafood; dramatic views; good beer and service. ⑤ *Average main: £13* ⊠ *The Dock* ☎ *01947/880278* ⊕ *www. bayhotel.info.*

Hotels

Raven Hall Country House Hotel

$$ | RESORT | Set on 100 acres of landscaped grounds, this Georgian country-house hotel dramatically perched 600 feet above sea level on the North York Moors National Park's Ravenscar headlands has lovely views from most rooms, with the best enjoying outstanding vistas across Robin Hood's Bay. For an even more peaceful retreat with amazing views, stay in one of the eight eco-friendly luxury lodges. **Pros:** breathtaking coastal views; great for outdoorsy types; relaxing atmosphere. **Cons:** some areas tired; food variable; not much to do if you don't like the outdoors. ⑤ *Rooms from: £139* ✉ *The Avenue, off Station Rd., Ravenscar* ☎ *01723/870353* ⊕ *www. ravenhall.co.uk* ⇱ *55 rooms, 8 lodges* ⑩ *Free breakfast.*

🏃 Activities

Several superb long-distance walks start at, finish in, or run through Robin Hood's Bay.

Coast-to-Coast Walk

HIKING/WALKING | The village marks one end of the 190-mile Coast-to-Coast Walk; the other is at St. Bee's Head on the Irish Sea. Walkers finish at the Bay Hotel, overlooking the harbor. ✉ *Robin Hood's Bay.*

Lyke-Wake Walk

HIKING/WALKING | The 42-mile, east–west Lyke-Wake Walk across the moors starts at Osmotherley and finishes 3 miles from Robin Hood's Bay at Ravenscar. ✉ *Robin Hood's Bay* ⊕ *www.lykewake.org.*

Whitby

7 miles northwest of Robin Hood's Bay, 20 miles northeast of Pickering.

A fishing port whose connection to Bram Stoker has made it a magnet for goths (it draws hundreds to an annual Goth Weekend), Whitby is also a busy tourist hub. However, it handles the crowds so well you might not notice (except at dinnertime, when it's hard to get a seat in a restaurant). Climbing up a ravine at the mouth of the River Esk, the town's narrow streets rise from the curved harbor to cliffs surmounted by the dramatic ruins of a 13th-century abbey. Fine Georgian houses dominate the west side of the river (known as West Cliff). The smaller 17th-century buildings of the old town (known as East Cliff) are found on the other side of an Edwardian swing bridge. Its cobbled Church Street is packed in summer with people exploring the shop-lined alleyways.

Whitby came to prominence as a whaling port in the mid-18th century. Whaling brought wealth, and shipbuilding brought fame; it was from here that Captain James Cook (1728–79), explorer and navigator, departed on his first expedition in 1747, and all four of his subsequent world-exploring ships were built here. You can tour the coast around Whitby on a scaled-down replica of Cook's ship *Endeavour*.

GETTING HERE AND AROUND

A car is a must, as there are no direct buses or trains from London. National Express and Megabus serve the region, but you must change at least once, and the journey can take up to 10 hours. National Express trains from London's King's Cross Station go to Leeds, where you can change to a local train.

The ruins of Whitby Abbey rise above the pretty town of Whitby and the River Esk.

Alternatively, you can go from King's Cross to Middlesborough and from there take a scenic train ride to Whitby. The entire journey takes around nine hours.

Whitby has a small town center, and it's easily walkable. The train station is here, between the two cliffs. If you're looking for a taxi, they tend to line up outside the station.

ESSENTIALS

VISITOR INFORMATION Whitby Tourist Information Centre. ✉ *Langborne Rd.* ☎ *01723/383636* ⊕ *www.discoveryork-shirecoast.com.*

 Sights

Bark Endeavour

LOCAL INTEREST | FAMILY | This scaled-down replica of Captain Cook's ship was built by local craftspeople using original drawings and specifications, and it includes hard-wood decks, detailed rigging, and carved timber moldings. The ship runs half-hour tours of Whitby harbor and excursions along North Yorkshire's Jurassic coast

as far as Sandsend, accompanied by commentary on Cook's life and Whitby sights. Note that sometimes tours don't run in bad weather. ✉ *Fish Quay, Pier Rd.* ☎ *017881/004699* ⊕ *www.endeavour-whitby.com* ✈ *From £5.*

★ Captain Cook Memorial Museum

MUSEUM | This museum documenting the life of the famous mariner and those who sailed with him is located in the 17th-century house where he lodged as an apprentice seaman from 1746 to 1750. Exhibits devoted to Cook's epic expeditions display the legendary explorer's maps, diaries, and drawings. ✉ *Grape La.* ☎ *01947/601900* ⊕ *www.cookmuseum-whitby.co.uk* ✈ *£6.50* ⊗ *Closed Dec.–mid-Feb. and weekdays in Nov.*

Church of St. Mary the Virgin

RELIGIOUS SITE | Whitby's landmark church overlooks the town from the top of East Cliff, with the striking ruins of Whitby Abbey looming beyond. Bram Stoker lived in Whitby briefly and later said the image of pallbearers carrying coffins up the 199 stone steps that lead to the church inspired him to write *Dracula*. The oldest parts of St. Mary's (the quire and nave) are Norman, dating back to 1100, while the tower and transepts were added in the 12th and 13th centuries. The distinctive interior, notable for its enclosed box pews and triple-decker pulpit, is late-18th-century Georgian and most everything else you see today is the result of 19th- and 20th-century renovations. The churchyard, a setting in *Dracula*, is filled with the weather-beaten gravestones of former mariners and fishermen. ■TIP→ **Rather than walking, you can drive to the hilltop and park in the abbey's lot for a small fee. Otherwise, you can take the hourly Esk Valley Bus 97.** ⊠ *Abbey Plain, East Cliff* 🕾 *01947/603421* ⊕ *www.achurchnearyou.com/whitby-st-mary* 🖾 *Free; £1 suggested donation.*

Goathland

TOWN | This moorland village, 8 miles southwest of Whitby, has a charming 1865 train station that was the location for Hogsmeade Station, where students bound for Hogwarts disembarked in the film *Harry Potter and the Sorcerer's Stone*. While there, hop on the 18-mile-long **North Yorkshire Moors Railway,** which travels between Grosmont and Pickering, passing through picturesque towns and moorland. The route of the steam-powered trains extends to Whitby twice daily. ⊠ *Whitby* ⊕ *www.nymr.co.uk* 🖾 *Train from £11.40 one way* ⊙ *Closed Nov.–Mar.*

HM Bark Endeavour

LIGHTHOUSE | **FAMILY** | Whitby now has two replicas, under different ownership, of Captain Cook's ship the *Endeavour.* the original 40% scale model and this full-size version with 30-foot tall masts. Kids can visit a recreation of the captain's cabin where they can plot his journey on a magnetic map or learn how to tie nautical knots, as well as investigating what the ship's medical, sanitary, sailmaking, and disciplinary arrangements would have been. There's also a restaurant (not authentic) on-board.

⊠ *Endeavour Wharf* 🕾 *01947/600511* ⊕ *www.hmbarkendeavour.co.uk* 🖾 *£5.*

Whitby Abbey

ARCHAEOLOGICAL SITE | Set high on the East Cliff, the strikingly Gothic ruins of this once grand church are visible even from moorland hills miles away. The abbey, one of the very few founded by a woman (St. Hild in AD 657), was populated by a mixed community of monks and nuns. After the Vikings sacked it in the 9th century, it was refounded by the Benedictines in the 11th century and later enlarged (the headland is dominated by the shell of the abbey's 13th-century church), continuing to flourish until it was destroyed by Henry VIII. The excellent visitor center has exhibits on St. Hild and *Dracula* author Bram Stoker, Anglo-Saxon artifacts from the site, and interactive displays about the medieval abbey. ⊠ *Abbey La.* 🕾 *01947/603568* ⊕ *www.english-heritage.org.uk* 🖾 *£10* ⊙ *Closed weekdays Nov.–Feb. and Mon. and Tues. in Mar.*

Whitby Museum

MUSEUM | Exhibits in this quirky museum range from local geology and natural history to archaeology, whaling, and trade routes in Asia, plus an exceptional collection of marine fossils. It's notable for its old-school displays that use handwritten cards. ⊠ *Pannett Park* 🕾 *01947/602908* ⊕ *www.whitbymuseum.org.uk* 🖾 *£5* ⊙ *Closed Mon. Library and archive closed Jan.*

🍽 Restaurants

Ditto

$$ | **MODERN BRITISH** | With one serving a night and fixed-price menu options only, dining in this small (18-seat), family-run restaurant is more like eating in someone's home. If you get tired of Whitby's ubiquitous fish-and-chips, Ditto offers more fine-dining alternatives like steamed sea bass fillets with a creamy vegetable chowder and salmon gnocchi or slow-cooked pork belly in sour

718

cream with a mixed bean cassoulet. **Known for:** hearty, excellently prepared dishes; attentive service; lots of extras. ⑤ *Average main: £20* ✉ *26 Skinner St.* ☎ *01947/601404* ⊕ *www.ditto-restaurant. co.uk* ⊗ *Closed Sun.–Tues.*

★ Magpie Café

$ | **SEAFOOD** | Seafood is the draw here, and the long menu includes freshly caught salmon, haddock, halibut, and cod—all of which can be grilled or poached—plus Lindisfarne oysters. But the crowds come for the outstanding traditional fish-and-chips. **Known for:** fresh-off-the-boat seafood; perfect fish-and-chips; long waits. ⑤ *Average main: £14* ✉ *14 Pier Rd.* ☎ *01947/602058* ⊕ *www. magpiecafe.co.uk* ⊗ *Closed Jan.*

🛏 Hotels

Broom House

$$ | **B&B/INN** | This two-story stone house sits beneath forested hills in the tiny village of Egton Bridge, about five miles outside Whitby. **Pros:** gorgeous, peaceful setting; lovely rooms; friendly staff. **Cons:** far from Whitby; need a car to get around; breakfast not free. ⑤ *Rooms from: £130* ✉ *Broom House La.* ☎ *01947/895279* ⊕ *www.broom-house. co.uk* ⊗ *Closed Nov.–Feb.* ➾ *8 rooms* ⊚ *No meals.*

Dunsley Hall Country House Hotel

$ | **HOTEL** | Originally a shipping magnate's residence, this Victorian-era country house sits 4 miles west of Whitby on 4 acres of gardens and grounds, with views of the sea in the distance (the beach at Sandsend is a five-minute drive away). **Pros:** lovely gardens; attentive staff; good food. **Cons:** modern rooms not as charming; housekeeping could be better; decor is a bit tired. ⑤ *Rooms from: £120* ✉ *Dunsley Rd., Dunsley* ☎ *01947/893437* ⊕ *www.dunsleyhall. com* ➾ *26 rooms* ⊚ *Free breakfast.*

Shepherd's Purse

$ | **B&B/INN** | This charming little complex in the cobbled old town consists of shabby-chic guest rooms surrounding a courtyard. **Pros:** quirky, romantic style; comfortable rooms; nice location. **Cons:** some rooms are quite small; no breakfast; very feminine decor not for everyone. ⑤ *Rooms from: £80* ✉ *Sanders Yard, 95 Church St.* ☎ *01947/820228* ⊕ *www.theshepherdspurse.com* ➾ *6 rooms* ⊚ *No meals.*

White Horse and Griffin

$ | **HOTEL** | A 450-year-old former coaching inn at the base of the church steps, this hotel and restaurant once patronized by Charles Dickens is full of historic character, with open fireplaces, wood paneling, and exposed beams. **Pros:** comfortable, atmospheric rooms; historic building; friendly service. **Cons:** street noise in some rooms; steep stairs; parking can be difficult. ⑤ *Rooms from: £85* ✉ *87 Church St.* ☎ *01947/604857* ⊕ *www. whitehorseandgriffin.com* ➾ *10 rooms* ⊚ *Free breakfast.*

🎭 Performing Arts

Whitby Folk Week

CULTURAL FESTIVALS | Music, traditional dance, and storytelling fill the town during Whitby Folk Week, usually held the week before the late-August bank holiday. Pubs, halls, and sidewalks become venues for more than 600 traditional folk events by British performers. ✉ *Whitby* ☎ *01977/792205* ⊕ *www.whitbyfolk.co.uk.*

🏃 Activities

Whitby Regatta

FESTIVALS | Held each August since 1850, the Whitby Regatta is a three-day jamboree of rowing races, yacht racing, vintage car rallies, naval displays, military flybys, fireworks, music, and more. ✉ *Whitby* ☎ *07827/452753* ⊕ *www.whitbyregatta. co.uk.*

718

Chapter 14

HADRIAN'S WALL AND THE NORTHEAST

Updated by
Joseph Reaney

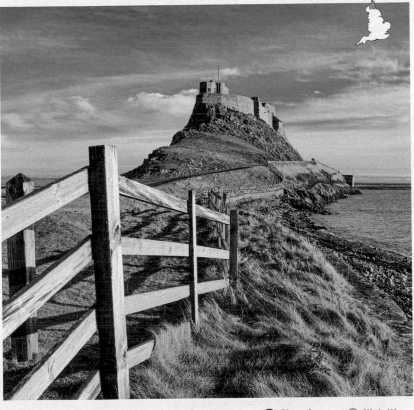

● Sights	🍴 Restaurants	🛏 Hotels	🛍 Shopping	🍸 Nightlife
★★★★☆	★★☆☆☆	★★☆☆☆	★★☆☆☆	★★☆☆☆

WELCOME TO HADRIAN'S WALL AND THE NORTHEAST

TOP REASONS TO GO

★ **Hadrian's Wall:** The ancient Roman wall is a wonder, as much for the wild countryside around it as for its stones and forts, such as Housesteads and Vindolanda.

★ **Castles, Castles, Castles:** Fought over by the Scots and the English, and prey to Viking raiders, the Northeast was heavily fortified. Barnard, Alnwick, and Dunstanburgh castles are spectacular remnants of this history.

★ **Medieval Durham:** A splendid Norman cathedral that dates back to the 11th century is just one of the city's charms. Take a stroll along its ancient winding streets.

★ **Lindisfarne (Holy Island):** To get to this remote, windswept island, visitors must drive across a causeway that floods at high tide. Island highlights include the ruins of a Norman priory.

The Northeast can be divided into four distinct sections. The southernmost part of the region is County Durham, which is centered around the beautiful and historic cathedral city of the same name. Farther north, the art-loving city of Newcastle upon Tyne and its southern neighbor Gateshead straddle the region's main river, the muddy Tyne. A third area to the west of Newcastle is Hadrian's Wall country, where the remains of the famous Roman fortification snake through rugged scenery. Finally, it's up to the Far Northeast, where towering castles and misty islands punctuate the stunning, final miles of England's eastern shoreline.

1 Barnard Castle. A pretty market town home to the substantial ruins of a medieval fortification.

2 Bishop Auckland. Named for the Bishops of Durham, this small town includes a well-preserved bishops' palace.

3 Durham. A historic city set on a rocky spur, home to one of England's most spectacular cathedrals.

4 Newcastle upon Tyne. A sprawling metropolis with a lively regional arts

scene and the Northeast's best nightlife.

5 Hadrian's Wall. The famous wall that once marked the northern border of the Roman Empire.

6 Hexham. This pretty town is a useful base for visiting Hadrian's Wall and the wild countryside surrounding it.

7 Greenhead. A town surrounded on all sides by Roman history, including the Housesteads Roman Fort.

8 Morpeth. A lively medieval market town and an ideal base for exploring historic Cragside and Brinkburn Priory.

9 Alnwick. A small town with some big sights, including a Harry Potter-featured castle and spectacular gardens.

10 Dunstanburgh Castle. An evocative castle tower ruin that silently stands guard over a windswept beach.

11 Bamburgh. Another stunning castle ruin on the Northumberland coast; best viewed from the Farne Islands.

12 Lindisfarne (Holy Island). This historic isle—only accessible at low tide—has a Christian history dating back to AD 635.

12 HOLY ISLAND

Lindisfarne

FARNE
ISLANDS

Cornhill-on-Tweed

Crookham

11 Bamburgh

Beadnell

Wooler

Belford

High-Newton
-by-the-Sea

SCOTLAND

Dunstanburgh Castle

10 Craster

Powburn

Alnwick Castle
and Gardens

Alnwick

9

Alnmouth

NORTHUMBERLAND

Warkworth

North
Sea

Longframlington

Rochester

Elishaw

0   10 mi

0   10 km

Northumberland
National Park

West
Woodburn

8

Morpeth

Blyth

Belsay

Hartley

Housesteads

5   Hadrian's Wall

Newcastle
upon Tyne

Wallsend

North Shields

7

Vindolanda

Greenhead   Henshaw

6   Hexham

Broomhaugh

Tyne

Wylam

4

South Shields

Gateshead

Sunniside

Sunderland

Chester-le-
Street

Washington

Castleside

Seaham

3

Durham

Ireshopeburn

Peterlee

Frosterley

Wear

Hartlepool

SCOTLAND

Bishop
Auckland

2

DURHAM

Staindrop

Stockton

Middlesbrough

1

Barnard
Castle

North York Moors
National Park

Darlington

HADRIAN'S WALL

The wall is a dramatic sight in the countryside.

Winding through the wild and windswept Northumberland countryside, Hadrian's Wall is Britain's most important Roman relic. It once formed the northern frontier of the Roman Empire—its most remote outpost and first line of defense against raiders from the north. Even today, as a ruin, the wall is an awe-inspiring structure.

One of the most surprising things about visiting the 73-mile-long wall is its openness and accessibility. Although many of the best-preserved sections are within managed tourist sites, Hadrian's Wall is also part of the landscape, cutting through open countryside. Signposted trails along the entire route allow you to hike or cycle along most of the wall for free. The area is also rich in archaeological treasures that paint a picture of a thriving, multicultural community. The soldiers and their families who were stationed here came from as far away as Spain and North Africa, and recent discoveries give us an insight into their daily lives.

POSTCARDS FROM THE PAST

"Oh, how much I want you at my birthday party. You'll make the day so much more fun. Good-bye, sister, my dearest soul."

"I have sent you two pairs of sandals and two pairs of underpants. Greet all your messmates, with whom I pray you live in the greatest good fortune."

—From 1st-century writing tablets unearthed at Vindolanda

SEEING THE WALL'S HIGHLIGHTS

Hadrian's Wall has a handful of Roman-era forts, the best of which are concentrated near Housesteads, Vindolanda, and Chesters. Housesteads is the most complete, although getting there involves a quarter-mile walk up a hill; Chesters and Vindolanda have excellent museums. The separate Roman Army Museum near Greenhead offers a good overview of the wall's history and is near one of the best sections in open countryside, at Walltown Crags.

GETTING AROUND BY CAR OR BUS

The tiny, winding B6318 road passes within a stone's throw of most of the forts. It's a true back road, so don't expect to get anywhere fast. Public transport is limited; the special AD 122 bus covers the highlights (but only during spring and summer), and several local buses follow parts of the same route.

EXPLORING BY FOOT OR BIKE

Hadrian's Wall Path meanders along the wall's entire length; it's a seven-day hike. Joining it for a mile or so is a great way to see the wall and stunning scenery. Try the section around Walltown, or near Corbridge, where the path goes by the remains of a Roman garrison town. Hadrian's Cycleway, for bicyclists, follows roughly the same route.

SIGHTSEEING RESPONSIBLY

The wall is accessible, but vulnerable. **Do not** climb on it, and **never** break off or remove anything. In muddy weather you're encouraged not to stand directly next to the wall, as over time this can make the soil unstable.

Roman writing tablet from Vindolanda

WALL TIMELINE

55 BC Julius Caesar invades what's now southern England, naming the island Britannia.

AD 122 Emperor Hadrian orders the construction of a defensive wall along the territory's northern border.

208 After the Romans make another disastrous attempt to invade Caledonia, Hadrian's Wall is expanded.

410 The Romans leave Britain. Local tribes maintain the wall for at least a century.

1700s Stones from the ruined wall are plundered for road building.

1830s A local philanthropist buys land around the wall to save it from further destruction.

1973 First Vindolanda tablets are found. More than 1300 will be excavated over the next 40 years.

1987 Hadrian's Wall becomes a UNESCO World Heritage Site.

Remains of a fort near Housesteads

For many Britons, the words "the Northeast" provoke a vision of near-Siberian isolation. Although there are wind-hammered, wide-open spaces and empty roads threading the wild high moorland, the Northeast also has simple fishing towns, small villages of remarkable charm, and historic abbeys and castles that are all the more romantic for their often-ruinous state.

This is also where you'll find two of England's most iconic sights: the medieval city of Durham and the stark remains of Hadrian's Wall.

Even the remoteness can be relative. Suddenly, around the next bend of a country road, you may come across an imposing church, a tall monastery, or a Victorian country house. The value found in the shops and accommodations, the uncrowded beaches ideal for walking, and the general friendliness of the people add to the appeal. Still, outside of a few key sights, the Northeast is off the well-trodden tourist path.

Mainly composed of the two large counties of Durham and Northumberland, the Northeast includes English villages adjacent to the Scottish border area, renowned in ballads and romantic literature for feuds, raids, and battles. Fittingly, Durham Cathedral, the seat of bishops for nearly 800 years, was once described as "half church of God, half castle 'gainst the Scot." Hadrian's Wall, which marked the northern limit of the Roman Empire, stretches across prehistoric remains and moorland.

Not far north of Hadrian's Wall are some of the most interesting parts of Northumberland National Park. Steel, coal, railroads, and shipbuilding created prosperous towns such as Newcastle upon Tyne, now one of the country's cultural centers.

The region's hundred or so miles of largely undeveloped coast is one of the least visited and most dramatic shorelines in all of Europe. Several outstanding castles perch on headlands and promontories along here, including Bamburgh, which according to legend was the site of Joyous Garde, the castle of Sir Lancelot of the Round Table.

MAJOR REGIONS

County Durham. Durham—the first major Northeastern town on the main road up from London—is by far the region's most interesting historic city. Its cobblestone streets and towering cathedral make it a charming place to visit. The city is surrounded on all sides by scenic countryside, ruined castles, and isolated villages.

Newcastle upon Tyne. Linked by seven bridges over the River Tyne, the city of Newcastle upon Tyne and the town of

Gateshead together form the region's largest, liveliest, and most cosmopolitan urban hub. It's also home to a number of art highlights, from outdoor sculptures to world-class indoor galleries.

Hadrian's Wall Country. A formidable line of Roman fortifications, Hadrian's Wall was the Romans' most ambitious construction in Britain. The land through which the old wall wanders is wild and inhospitable in places, but that only adds to the powerful sense of history it evokes. Museums and information centers along the wall make it possible to learn as much as you want about the Roman era, while nearby market towns like Hexham make a great base for exploration.

The Far Northeast. Extraordinary medieval fortresses and monasteries line the final 40 miles of the Northeast coast before England gives way to Scotland. Northumbria was an enclave where the flame of learning was kept alive during Europe's Dark Ages, most notably at Lindisfarne, home of saints and scholars. Castles abound, including the spectacularly sited Bamburgh and the desolate Dunstanburgh. The region also has some magnificent beaches, though because of the cold water and rough seas they're far better for walking than swimming. The three-mile walk from Seahouses to Bamburgh gives splendid views of the Farne Islands, and the two-mile hike from Craster to Dunstanburgh Castle is unforgettable. A bit inland are a few other pretty towns and castles.

Planning

When to Go

The best time to see the Northeast is in summer. This ensures that the museums—and the roads—will be open, and you can take advantage of the country-side walks that are one of the region's greatest pleasures. Rough seas and

inclement weather make it dangerous to swim at any of the beaches except in July and August; even then, don't expect warm water. Winter here isn't for the fainthearted. The weather can be terrible, but there are few places in England so beautiful and remote.

Planning Your Time

If you're interested in exploring Hadrian's Wall and the Roman ruins, you'll probably want to base yourself at a guest-house in or around Hexham. From there you can easily take in Housesteads and the other local landmarks. Anywhere in this area is within easy reach of Durham, with its lovely ancient buildings, or Newcastle, with its excellent museums. Romantics will want to spend a day or two driving up the coast to take in the incredible views.

Getting Here and Around

AIR
Newcastle's airport, which is a 15-minute drive from the city center, has regular flights from British and European cities.

CONTACTS Newcastle Airport. ⊠ Off A696, Woolsington ☎ 0871/882–1121 ⊕ www.newcastleairport.com.

BUS
National Express and Megabus travel to Durham and Newcastle and leave from London's Victoria Coach Station. The journey takes between six and eight hours, more than twice the time it takes by train, but it can be considerably cheaper, especially if you reserve in advance (book online to avoid premium telephone charges). Connecting services to other parts of the region leave from those cities; Traveline has more information and a journey planner. The Network One Explorer North East ticket (£10.90, or £20.60 for families of up to five) allows unlimited one-day travel on most local bus and Metro train

services in the Northeast. It's available from most bus and Metro stations or through the Go North East app.

CONTACTS Explorer Northeast Pass. ☎ *0191/276–3706* ⊕ *www. networkonetickets.co.uk.* **Megabus.** ☎ *0900/160–0900* ⊕ *uk.megabus.com.* **National Express.** ☎ *0871/781–8181* ⊕ *www.nationalexpress.com.* **Traveline.** ☎ *0871/200–2233* ⊕ *www.traveline.info.*

CAR

If you're headed to small villages, remote castles, or Hadrian's Wall, traveling by car is the best option. The A1 highway links London and Newcastle (five to six hours) and continues all the way up to Lindisfarne. In the Far Northeast, there are also two alternative scenic routes: the rural A697, which branches west off the A1 north of Morpeth; and the coastal B1340, which leaves the A1 at Alnwick and snakes up to Bamburgh.

TRAIN

Within England, the train is still the best way to reach the Northeast. London North Eastern Railway runs train services; the average travel time from London to Newcastle or Durham is three hours. From Newcastle, you can catch local trains to Hexham (30 minutes), Morpeth (15 minutes), and Alnmouth (for Alnwick, 25 minutes). National Rail Enquiries has more information and a journey planner.

CONTACTS London North Eastern Railway. ☎ *03457/225333* ⊕ *www.lner.co.uk.* **National Rail Enquiries.** ☎ *03457/484950* ⊕ *www.nationalrail.co.uk.*

Restaurants

The Northeast has some very fine local meats and produce. Look for restaurants that serve game from the Kielder Forest; local lamb from the hillsides; salmon and trout from the rivers; and shellfish, crab, and oysters from the coast. Outside the cities, the region lags somewhat behind other parts of England in terms of exceptional places to eat, although there are special spots to be found. Aside from the ubiquitous chains, the best bets are often small country pubs that serve the traditional, hearty fare associated with the region. Don't wait until too late to have dinner, though, as most places stop serving between 9 and 10 pm.

Hotels

The large hotel chains don't have much of a presence in the Northeast outside Durham and Newcastle. Instead, you can expect to find country houses converted into welcoming hotels, old coaching inns that still greet guests after 300 years, and cozy bed-and-breakfasts convenient to hiking trails. And if you've ever dreamed of staying in a castle, the Northeast delivers in spades.

Restaurant and hotel reviews have been shortened. For full information, visit Fodors.com. Restaurant prices are the average cost of a main course at dinner, or if dinner is not served, at lunch. Hotel prices are the lowest cost of a standard double room in high season, including 20% V.A.T.

WHAT IT COSTS in Pounds			
$	$$	$$$	$$$$
RESTAURANTS			
under £16	£1–£23	£24–£30	over £30
HOTELS			
under £125	£125–£225	£226–£350	over £350

Visitor Information

CONTACTS Durham Visitor Contact Center. ☎ *03000/262626* ⊕ *www.thisisdurham. com.* **NewcastleGateshead.** ⊕ *www. newcastlegateshead.com.* **Hadrian's Wall Country.** ☎ ⊕ *www.hadrianswallcountry. co.uk.*

Barnard Castle

245 miles north of London, 15 miles southwest of Bishop Auckland.

The handsome market town of Barnard Castle has sights of its own and can also serve as a base for venturing into the Teesdale Valley to the northwest. Its unusual butter market hall (known locally as Market Cross), surmounted by an old fire-alarm bell, marks the junction of the streets Thorngate, Newgate, and Market Place. Stores, pubs, and cafés line these thoroughfares. In 1838, Charles Dickens stayed at the **King's Head Inn** here while doing research for his novel *Nicholas Nickleby*. The local tourist office has a free "In the Footsteps of Charles Dickens" leaflet.

GETTING HERE AND AROUND

Barnard Castle is around a five-hour drive from London on the A1 (the last 13 miles are on the A66). You can also make the journey by train to Darlington, followed by local buses X75 or X76; this takes between three and four hours.

ESSENTIALS

VISITOR INFORMATION Barnard Castle Visitor Information Point. ⊠ *The Witham, 3 Horse Market* ☎ *01833/026–2626* ⊕ *www.thisisdurham.com.*

Sights

Barnard Castle

CASTLE/PALACE | The substantial ruins of Barnard Castle, which gave the town its name, cling to an aerie overlooking the River Tees. From the outside, it looks satisfyingly complete from the right angle; inside it's rather more ruined, though there are still plenty of interesting sights to see. Climb to the top of the cylindrical, 13th-century tower for stunning river views; stroll around the remains of the Great Hall, once the castle's communal dining hub; and learn about the Victorian hermit who squatted here and charged locals an entrance fee. When in the Inner Courtyard, keep an eye out for the figure of a carved boar above the oriel window—it was the family emblem of King Richard III (1452–85), placed there during his reign in honor of the elevated status he bestowed upon the castle. ⊠ *Scar Top* ⊹ *Off A67* ☎ *01833/638212* ⊕ *www.english-heritage.org.uk/barnard* 🖾 *£5.90* ⊘ *Closed weekdays Nov.–Mar.*

★ Bowes Museum

MUSEUM | This vast manor house, inspired by a French château, was built between 1862 and 1875. Highlights include paintings by Canaletto, El Greco, Francisco Goya, and François Boucher, in addition to beautiful collections of ceramics and glass, 18th-century French furniture, and 19th- and 20th-century fashion. Free tours are available daily at 11:30 am.
■ **TIP→ Don't miss the incredible 18th-century mechanical swan, which catches and swallows an articulated silver fish every day at 2 pm.** ⊠ *Newgate* ☎ *01833/690606* ⊕ *www.thebowesmuseum.org.uk* 🖾 *£14 (valid for a year).*

High Force

BODY OF WATER | The Upper Teesdale Valley's elemental nature shows its most volatile aspect in the sprays of England's highest waterfall. Located 15 miles northwest of Barnard Castle, the dramatic High Force cascade drops 69 feet into a plunge pool. From the roadside parking lot it's a 10-minute walk through woodland to the massive rocks over which the water tumbles. ⊠ *Off B6277* ☎ *01833/622336* ⊕ *www.raby.co.uk/high-force/waterfall* 🖾 *£2; parking £3* ⊘ *Closed in bad weather (often in winter).*

Bishop Auckland

15 miles northwest of Barnard Castle, 11 miles southwest of Durham.

For 700 years, between the 12th and 19th centuries, the powerful prince-bishops of Durham had their country residence in Auckland Castle, in the town of Bishop Auckland. When finally deprived of their powers in 1836, the bishops left Durham and made Bishop Auckland their official home.

GETTING HERE AND AROUND

Bishop Auckland is just off the A688 from Barnard Castle. Durham is accessible by continuing up the A688 to Spennymoor, where you change to the B6288 and A687. There's a train station in Bishop Auckland, but the line only runs east-to-west. Buses are the best option for going south-to-north; it's around 50 minutes by bus from Barnard Castle and 40 minutes to Durham.

ESSENTIALS

VISITOR INFORMATION Bishop Auckland Tourist Information Centre. ⊠ *Auckland Tower, Market Pl.* ☎ *01388/743750* ⊕ *www.aucklandproject.org/venues/auckland-tower.*

◉ Sights

Auckland Castle

CASTLE/PALACE | Arguably the greatest of the prince-bishops of Durham's properties is this Episcopal palace, which you enter through an elaborate stone arch. Much of what's on view today dates from the 16th century, although the limestone-and-marble chapel, with its dazzling stained-glass windows, was built in 1665 from the ruins of a 12th-century hall. The extraordinary paintings of Jacob and his 12 sons, by the 17th-century Spanish artist Francisco de Zurbarán, hang in the Long Dining Room. ⊠ *Off Market Pl.* ☎ *01388/743750* ⊕ *www.aucklandproject.org* ⊠ *£10* ⊙ *Closed Mon., Tues., and Jan.–mid-Feb.*

★ **Head of Steam**

MUSEUM | FAMILY | A family-friendly museum in nearby Darlington tells the story of the early days of rail travel. The town gained fame in 1825, when George Stephenson piloted his steam-powered *Locomotion No. 1* along newly laid tracks the few miles to nearby Stockton, thus kick-starting the railway age. Set in an abandoned 1842 train station, the museum has interactive exhibits and big steam trains that are great for kids; antique engines and scale models help bring history to life. There's also a café and children's activity room. Darlington is 13 miles southeast of Bishop Auckland, on the A68. There are also regular tain connections. ■**TIP→ A ticket for families with up to four kids costs £10.** ⊠ *North Road Station, Station Rd., Darlington* ☎ *01325/405060* ⊕ *www.head-of-steam. co.uk* ⊠ *£5.35.*

★ **Raby Castle**

CASTLE/PALACE | The stone battlements and turrets of moated Raby Castle, once the seat of the powerful Nevills and currently the home of the 11th Baron Barnard, stand amid a 200-acre deer park and ornamental gardens. Charles Nevill supported Mary, Queen of Scots in the 1569 uprising against Elizabeth I; when the Rising of the North failed, the estate was confiscated. Dating mostly from the 14th century (using stone plundered from Barnard Castle) and renovated in the 18th and 19th centuries, the luxuriously furnished castle has displays of art and other treasures. Rooms in wonderfully elaborate Gothic Revival, Regency, and Victorian styles are open for public viewing, as are the 18th century Walled Gardens and the Coach House, home to a collection of coaches and carriages dating back to the Georgian era. The castle is seven miles southwest of Bishop Auckland. ⊠ *Off A688, Staindrop* ☎ *01833/660202* ⊕ *www.raby.co.uk/ raby-castle* ⊠ *£13; park and gardens only £8* ⊙ *Closed Mon.–Tues. in Mar., June, and Sep.–Oct.; closed Mon. in July–Aug.; closed Nov.–Feb.*

Durham

11 miles northeast of Bishop Auckland, 18 miles south of Newcastle.

The great medieval city of Durham, seat of County Durham, stands dramatically on a rocky spur overlooking the countryside. Its cathedral and castle, a UNESCO World Heritage Site, rise together on a wooded peninsula almost entirely encircled by the River Wear (rhymes with "beer"). For centuries, these two ancient structures have dominated Durham, a thriving university town that's the Northeast's equivalent of Oxford or Cambridge. Steep, narrow streets overlooked by perilously angled medieval houses and 18th-century town houses make for fun exploring. In the most attractive part of the city, near the Palace Green and along the river, people go boating, anglers cast their lines, and strollers walk along the shaded paths. For great views, take a short stroll along the River Wear, and cross the 17th-century Prebends Footbridge. You can return to town via the 12th-century Framwellgate Bridge.

Despite the military advantages of its location, Durham was founded surprisingly late, probably in about the year 1000, growing up around a small Saxon church erected to house the remains of St. Cuthbert. It was the Normans, under William the Conqueror, who put Durham on the map, building the first defensive castle and beginning work on the cathedral. From here, Durham's prince-bishops, granted almost dictatorial local powers by William in 1072, kept a tight rein on the county, coining their own money and maintaining their own laws and courts. It wasn't until 1836 that these rights were restored to the English Crown.

GETTING HERE AND AROUND

East Coast trains from London's King's Cross Station arrive at the centrally located Durham Station once an hour during the day. The journey takes about three hours. There are even more regular non-direct trains via York, with a similar journey time. A handful of National Express and Megabus buses make the seven-hour trip from London daily. The Durham Cathedral Bus (Route 40) links parking lots and the train and bus stations with the cathedral, castle, and university. Between 10 am and 4 pm Monday through Saturday, cars are subject to a "congestion charge" of £2 (on top of parking charges) to enter the Palace Green area. You can pay the charge at the Parking Shop or over the phone. Payment must be made by 6 pm on the day of usage, or you'll be subject to a £50 fine.

ESSENTIALS

VISITOR INFORMATION World Heritage Site Visitor Centre. ⊠ *7 Owengate* ☎ *0191/334–3805* ⊕ *www.durhamworldheritagesite.com.* **The Parking Shop.** ⊠ *3-10 Old Pit Ln.* ☎ *0191/384–6633* ⊕ *www.durham.gov.uk.*

◉ Sights

★ Beamish, the Living Museum of the North

MUSEUM VILLAGE | FAMILY | Made up of buildings found on-site or moved from elsewhere in the region, this sprawling, award-winning complex—which celebrated its 50th year in 2020—explores the way people in the Northeast lived and worked from the early 1800s to the mid-1900s. A vintage bus and a streetcar take you around the site to various points of interest, including a farm estate; a pit village and colliery;

and an entire 1920s town complete with a bank, convenience store, and Masonic hall. Everything is staffed by workers in period costumes, and you can buy era-appropriate food and drinks in the pub, bakery, and "sweet shop" (candy store). As well as the permanent exhibits, there are special events year-round, from weekend-long festivals, where you're encouraged to come in old-style fancy dress, to traditional English celebrations such as May Day and Harvest Festival. Beamish is nine miles northwest of Durham. ■**TIP**➜ **You can spend at least half a day here, and tickets are valid for a whole year in case you want to return.** ⊠ *Off A693, Beamish* ☎ *0191/370–4000* ⊕ *www.beamish.org. uk* ≌ *£19.50* ⊗ *Closed Mon. and Fri. in mid-Jan.–mid-Feb.*

Durham Castle

CASTLE/PALACE | Facing the cathedral across Palace Green, Durham's stately, manorlike castle commands a strategic position above the River Wear. For almost 800 years the castle was the home of the enormously powerful prince-bishops; from here they ruled large tracts of the countryside and acted as the main line of defense against Scottish raiders from the north. Henry VIII was the first to curtail the bishops' autonomy, although it wasn't until the 19th century that they finally had their powers annulled. At that point, the castle was given over to the University of Durham, the third oldest university in England after Oxford and Cambridge (albeit more than 600 years younger; it was founded in 1832). The castle interior can only be seen on a 45-minute guided tour. These are usually available four times a day but are not held when the building is hired out for private events, so it's best to check the website or call ahead. ■**TIP**➜ **During university vacation times, the castle also offers bed-and-breakfast accommodations in the state rooms for around £200 per night; call or check the website for details.** ⊠ *Palace Green* ☎ *0191/334–2932* ⊕ *www.dur. ac.uk/durham.castle* ≌ *£5.*

Rounded arches and columns with zigzag patterns are hallmarks of the Romanesque style at Durham Cathedral.

★ Durham Cathedral

RELIGIOUS SITE | A Norman masterpiece in the heart of the city, Durham Cathedral is a vision of strength and fortitude, a far cry from the airy lightness of later Gothic cathedrals. Construction began about 1090, and the main body was finished around 1150. The round arches of the nave and the deep zigzag patterns carved into them typify the heavy, gaunt style of Norman, or Romanesque, building. The technology of Durham, however, was revolutionary; this was the first European cathedral to be given a stone, rather than a wooden, roof.

Note the enormous bronze **Sanctuary Knocker,** shaped like the head of a ferocious mythological beast, mounted on the massive northwestern door. By grasping the ring clenched in the animal's mouth, medieval felons could claim sanctuary; cathedral records show that 331 criminals sought this protection between 1464 and 1524. An unobtrusive tomb at the western end of the cathedral, in the Moorish-influenced **Galilee Chapel,** is the final resting place of the Venerable Bede, an 8th-century Northumbrian monk whose contemporary account of the English people made him the country's first reliable historian. In good weather, and if you're feeling up to it, you can climb the 325 steps up to the tower, which has spectacular views of Durham.

The impressive £10 million **Open Treasure** exhibition displays priceless artifacts from the cathedral's own collection. The exhibition also allows visitors to see parts of the cathedral that were previously closed to the public, including the **Monks Dormitory** and the **Great Kitchen,** with its breathtaking octagonal roof. Treasures on display include Anglo-Saxon art, gold and garnet crosses, elaborate vestments, illuminated manuscripts, and the original coffin of St. Cuthbert. Together it represents one of the most significant single collections of Anglo-Saxon artifacts in the world.

For a more modern take on this ancient monument, check out the elaborate LEGO model of Durham Cathedral, situated between the Undercroft Restaurant and shop. It's made up of more than 300,000 bricks.

Guided tours of the cathedral (one hour) are available Monday through Saturday at 10:30 am, 11 am, and 2 pm, though times can change if there's a special service going on. A choral evensong service takes place Tuesday through Saturday at 5:15 pm and Sunday at 3:30 pm. ⊠ Palace Green ☎ 0191/386–4266 ⊕ www.durhamcathedral.co.uk ⬛ Free (requested donation £3); Open Treasure £7.50; tower £5; guided tours £5; combined tour and Open Treasure £10 ⊘ No tours Sun.

Oriental Museum
MUSEUM | A 15-minute walk from the cathedral, this Durham University–owned museum displays fine art and craftwork from all parts of Asia and the Middle East. Galleries are ordered by culture, including Ancient Egypt, Japan, China, and Korea. Among the highlights are some exquisite Qing dynasty jade and lacquer ornaments, ancient tapestries and embroideries from the Himalayas, and a collection of Japanese woodblock prints from the Edo period. ⊠ Off Elvet Hill Rd. ☎ 0191/334–5691 ⊕ www.dur.ac.uk/oriental.museum ⬛ £1.50.

Prebends Footbridge
BRIDGE/TUNNEL | Delightful views are the reward of a short stroll along the River Wear's leafy banks, especially as you cross this 17th-century stone footbridge, reached from the southern end of Palace Green. J. M. W. Turner adored the view from here and painted a celebrated scene of Durham from the bridge. ⊠ S. Bailey.

🍴 Restaurants

Cafedral
$ | CAFÉ | FAMILY | Ignore the dad-joke pun—this is a really good, modern, vegetarian- and celiac-friendly café. Mismatched, shabby-chic furniture fills the cozy dining room, where you can enjoy delicious, fresh scones, cakes, gluten-free desserts, and tasty panini and wraps. **Known for:** fantastic gluten-free treats; vegetarian food; good coffee. ⑤ Average main: £6 ⊠ Owengate House, 1st fl., Owengate.

Finbarr's
$$ | EUROPEAN | Excellent seafood and indulgent desserts are the specialties at this popular bistro, but there are steaks and a few veggie options on the menu as well. Order the fishcakes with buttered spinach or the jumbo shrimp grilled Tandoori style (with a hint of Indian spice), and save room for the Knickerbocker Glory, an old-fashioned concoction of ice cream, sponge cake, fruit, and chocolate, served in a tall glass. **Known for:** intimate atmosphere; great seafood; heavenly desserts. ⑤ Average main: £20 ⊠ Aykley Heads House, Aykley Heads ☎ 0191/307–7033 ⊕ www.finbarrsrestaurant.co.uk.

Zen
$$ | THAI | This colorful and inviting restaurant, where diners are "shaded" indoors by a faux cherry blossom tree, mainly serves Thai food, but the menu is also scattered with Japanese, Chinese, and Indonesian dishes. A rather dizzying trip around Asia can take you from Thai green curry to sizzling Mongolian lamb to Japanese teriyaki beef, as well as some less familiar dishes like cod fillet wrapped in banana leaves and served with chili and lime. **Known for:** eclectic pan-Asian menu; buzzing atmosphere; tasty Thai curries. ⑤ Average main: £16 ⊠ Court Ln. ☎ 0191/384–9588 ⊕ www.zendurham.co.uk.

🛏 Hotels

Georgian Town House
$ | B&B/INN | At the top of a cobbled street overlooking the cathedral and castle, this family-run guesthouse has small, snug bedrooms with pleasant city views. **Pros:** great city center location; jovial owners; tasty pancakes right downstairs. **Cons:** most rooms are small; decor won't please everyone; some noise from nearby pubs. ⑤ Rooms from: £95 ⊠ 11

Crossgate ☎ 0191/386–8070 ⊕ www.thegeorgiantownhousedurham.co.uk ⇌ 8 rooms ❘◯❘ Free breakfast.

★ Lumley Castle Hotel

$$ | HOTEL | This is a real Norman castle, right down to the dungeons and maze of dark flagstone corridors—one room even has a bathroom hidden behind a bookcase. **Pros:** great for antiques lovers; gorgeous high-ceilinged restaurant; good value out of high season. **Cons:** easy to get lost among winding corridors; a little way out of Durham; (verily) ye banquet is cheesy. ⑤ *Rooms from: £190* ⊠ *Off B1284, Chester-le-Street* ☎ 0191/389–1111 ⊕ www.lumleycastle.com ⇌ 73 rooms ❘◯❘ No meals.

★ Seaham Hall

$$$ | B&B/INN | In 1815, Lord Byron married Annabella Milbanke in this foursquare mansion on a cliff top overlooking the sea; today, the sumptuous contemporary interior is a haven of luxury. **Pros:** pampering rooms; full of atmosphere; wonderful spa facilities. **Cons:** far outside town; high prices; you'll have to dress up for dinner. ⑤ *Rooms from: £305* ⊠ *Lord Byron's Walk, Seaham* ☎ 0191/516–1400 ⊕ www.seaham-hall.co.uk ⇌ 19 suites ❘◯❘ Free breakfast.

Victoria Inn

$ | B&B/INN | An authentically Victorian air pervades at this cozy pub near Durham Cathedral that also serves as a B&B. **Pros:** step-back-in-time atmosphere; lovely hosts; great value for city center. **Cons:** few amenities; pub doesn't serve full meals; some may find the decor a bit quaint. ⑤ *Rooms from: £95* ⊠ *86 Hallgarth St.* ☎ 0191/386–5269 ⊕ www.victoriainn-durhamcity.co.uk ⇌ 6 rooms ❘◯❘ Free breakfast.

▼ Nightlife

The Half Moon Inn

BARS/PUBS | This handsome old pub is popular for its excellent range of traditional ales, as well as for its old-school atmosphere that reminds you pubs like this are a dying breed. ⊠ *86 New Elvet* ☎ 0191/374–1918 ⊕ www.thehalfmoon-inndurham.co.uk.

Market Tavern

BARS/PUBS | Fans of real ales are drawn to the Market Tavern, which has been in business since the late 18th century. Today, it's a Greene King pub, serving a good range of drinks and decent pub food. ⊠ *27 Market Pl.* ☎ 0191/386–2069 ⊕ www.greeneking-pubs.co.uk.

🛍 Shopping

Bramwells Jewellers

JEWELRY/ACCESSORIES | The specialty here is a pendant copy of the gold-and-silver cross of St. Cuthbert. ⊠ *24 Elvet Bridge* ☎ 0191/386–8006 ⊕ www.bramwellsjewellers.co.uk.

Durham Indoor Market

SHOPPING CENTERS/MALLS | The food and bric-a-brac stalls in Durham Indoor Market, a Victorian arcade, are open Monday through Saturday, 9 am to 4:30 pm. An excellent farmers' market is held in Market Place on the third Thursday of every month. ⊠ *Market Pl.* ☎ 0191/384–6153 ⊕ www.durhammarkets.co.uk.

🏃 Activities

Browns Rowing Boats

BOATING | At this downtown boathouse, you can rent rowboats from mid-March through late September. There are also short river cruises available from here. ⊠ *The Boathouse , Elvet Bridge* ☎ 0191/386–3779 💷 £7; £20 for families.

Newcastle upon Tyne

18 miles north of Durham, 22 miles east of Hexham, 14 miles south of Morpeth.

Durham may have the glories of its castle, cathedral, and university, but the liveliest and most culture-crammed city in the Northeast is Newcastle upon

Tyne—along with its south-of-the-river neighbor Gateshead.

Settled since Roman times on the River Tyne, Newcastle made its fortune twice—first by exporting coal and later by shipbuilding. As a 19th-century industrial center, it had few equals in Britain, showing off its wealth in grand Victorian buildings lining the broad streets. Some of these remain, particularly on Grey Street, though it's the works of modern architecture that are most eye-catching today. The cluster of bridges (older and newer) crossing the Tyne is a quintessential city sight.

Much of the regeneration since the early 1990s has been based around the Quayside, particularly on the south bank in Gateshead. Here the Baltic Centre for Contemporary Art and the pedestrian-only Millennium Bridge—the world's first tilting bridge, which opens and shuts like an eyelid—have risen from industrial wasteland.

GETTING HERE AND AROUND

Newcastle Airport, a 15-minute drive from the city center, has flights from British and European cities. Metro trains connect to the center. The A1 highway links London and Newcastle (five to six hours).

East Coast trains from London's King's Cross take about three hours. National Express and Megabus have service from London's Victoria Coach Station several times a day; it's a six- to seven-hour trip.

Newcastle has a good public transportation system. Its Metro light-rail network is easy to use, well signposted, and has stops near most sights. Buses go to all the places the Metro doesn't reach.

ESSENTIALS

VISITOR INFORMATION NewcastleGateshead Tourist Information. ☎ ⊕ *www.newcastlegateshead.com.*

◉ Sights

★ Angel of the North

PUBLIC ART | South of Newcastle, near the junction of the A1 and A1(M) at Gateshead, stands England's largest—and one of its most popular—sculptures, the *Angel of the North.* Created by Antony Gormley in 1998, the rust-color steel sculpture is a sturdy, abstract human figure with airplane-like wings rather than arms. It stands 65 feet tall and has a horizontal wingspan of 175 feet. ■ **TIP→ Despite its size, the Angel is notoriously impossible to photograph properly from a car; if you want to see it up close, there's parking nearby, signposted on the A167.** ⊠ *A167, Gateshead* ⊕ *www.gateshead.gov.uk/article/3957/Angel-of-the-North* ⊠ *Free.*

Baltic Centre for Contemporary Art

ARTS VENUE | Formerly a grain warehouse and now the country's largest national gallery for contemporary art outside London, the BALTIC (as it's often styled) presents thought-provoking exhibitions by top names and emerging talents. There's no permanent collection, and the temporary installations change regularly, so check the website for details. There are also two great dining options here: the riverside café-bar BALTIC Kitchen and the rooftop restaurant Six. ⊠ *Gateshead Quays, S. Shore Rd., Gateshead* ☎ *0191/478–1810* ⊕ *www.baltic.art* ⊠ *Free.*

Discovery Museum

MUSEUM | **FAMILY** | Reconstructed streets and homes lead you from Roman times to the present day in this engaging museum. Kids will like its interactive approach to teaching Newcastle's history, and history buffs will be most thrilled by galleries showing off the town's maritime and industrial achievements, including the *Turbinia.* Built in 1894, it was once the fastest ship in the world and the first to be powered by steam turbines. ⊠ *Blandford Sq.* ☎ *0191/232–6789* ⊕ *www.discoverymuseum.org.uk* ⊠ *Free (donations welcome).*

★ Great North Museum: Hancock

MUSEUM | An amalgam of several collections belonging to Newcastle University and named for a Victorian founder of the Natural History Society of Northumberland, this beautifully renovated museum contains an impressive array of ancient archaeological finds, plus galleries on natural history and astronomy. Highlights include artifacts left behind by the Roman builders of Hadrian's Wall; ancient Egyptian mummies; and a reconstruction of the 1st-century Temple of Mithras at Carrawburgh. This place isn't designed for kids, but there's plenty here to amuse them, including a planetarium and a life-size model of a T. rex. ⊠ *Barras Bridge* ☎ *0191/208–6765* ⊕ *www.greatnorthmuseum.org.uk* 🔗 *Free (donations welcome).*

Laing Art Gallery

MUSEUM | One of the Northeast's finest art museums merits at least an hour's visit for its selection of 19th-century British art. The Pre-Raphaelites are on show, too, as are sculptures by Henry Moore. The new Northern Spirit gallery showcases some of the great artists from the region, including John Martin (1759–1854), who produced dramatic biblical landscapes, and siblings William and Mary Beilby, whose beautiful enameled-glass creations became highly prized in their 1770s heyday. ⊠ *New Bridge St.* ☎ *0191/232–7734* ⊕ *www.laingartgallery. org.uk* 🔗 *Free* ⊙ *Closed Sun.*

Life Science Centre

MUSEUM | FAMILY | Three high-tech shows and 60 kid-oriented exhibits bring science to life, with a number of themed "zones" highlighting everything from research on genes to travel to Mars. New for 2020 is the "Space Zone," which shows how space technology is now a part of people's everyday lives. The museum is interactive throughout but particularly in the "Experiment Zone," which is full of hands-on scientific gizmos, including fun experiments to demonstrate magnetism and chain reactions, that make scientific learning feel more like a trip to the playground. There are regular seasonal events, too, as well as an ice-skating rink in winter. ■ TIP➜ **Visiting as a family? Opt for the £31 family ticket for four.** ⊠ *Times Sq.* ☎ *0191/243–8210* ⊕ *www.life. org.uk* 🔗 *£12.*

Newcastle Castle

CASTLE/PALACE | Overlooking the Tyne River, the remains of the Norman castle recall the city's earlier status as a defensive stronghold. Built in 1080, this was the "new castle" that gave the city its name. The gatehouse and stone keep are all that remain; although the effect is somewhat diminished by the railroad viaduct that thoughtlessly separates the two. The "black gate" remains the point of entry, with a small exhibition on the surrounding area of Castle Garth, but the most interesting stuff—including the impressive Great Hall, the vaulted dungeon, and the rooftop views—are in the keep. ⊠ *Castle Garth, Off St. Nicholas St.* ☎ *0191/230–6300* ⊕ *www.newcastle-castle.co.uk* 🔗 *£8.50.*

Segedunum Roman Fort

MUSEUM | For a good introduction to Britain's Roman history, dip into this museum. It includes the remains of the substantial Roman fort of Segedunum, built around AD 125, as well as the easternmost section of the original Hadrian's Wall (there's a reason this part of town is called Wallsend) and a reconstructed Roman bath complex. Start your tour at the (unfortunately rather ugly) observation tower for a good overview of the site—as well as an exhibition on local shipbuilding—before heading down to ground level. The collection of artifacts covers the whole 300-year period of Roman occupation in the region, and it includes pieces of weaponry, armor, and a Roman stone toilet—the only one surviving in the country. ⊠ *Buddle St., Wallsend* ☎ *0191/278–4217* ⊕ *www. segedunumromanfort.org.uk* 🔗 *£6* ⊙ *Closed Sun. in Jan.–Mar.*

Sir Norman Foster designed the Sage Gateshead performance venue, an emblem of Newcastle's revival.

🍴 Restaurants

Peace & Loaf

$$$ | BRITISH | Aside from the labored pun-of-a-name, this fine restaurant, in the upscale suburb of Jesmond, hits all the right notes, with chef Dave Coulson serving up delicious, flavor-packed, and beautifully presented dishes. The interior is colorful and airy, and the waitstaff is friendly and attentive, though a little over-eager; you might struggle to catch your breath between servings of bread, drinks, endless amuse-bouches, and regular courses. **Known for:** rapid-fire service; good wines by the glass; triple-cooked chips with beef drippings. ⑤ *Average main: £25* ✉ *217 Jesmond Rd.* ☎ *0191/281–5222* ⊕ *www.peaceandloaf.co.uk.*

★ 21

$$ | MODERN BRITISH | A Newcastle classic, this sleek, modern bistro is a local favorite for romantic dinners as the warm wood, leather banquettes, and crisp white table linens lend a polished look. The menu focuses on contemporary, flavor-packed versions of classic British food, such as terrine of Northumbrian venison with celeriac and apple salad or fillet of smoked haddock with wholegrain mustard sauce. **Known for:** modern twists on traditional flavors; delicious desserts; romantic ambience. ⑤ *Average main: £23* ✉ *Trinity Gardens, Pandon* ☎ *0191/222–0755* ⊕ *www.21newcastle.co.uk.*

★ Ury

$ | INDIAN | This friendly, simply decorated Indian restaurant specializes in dishes from the Kerala region, with an outstanding vegetarian selection, as well as meaty dishes like *jagajili* (lightly battered and fried chicken cubes with spices and onions) and *vadakara*roast beef with ginger and garlic. A shared dosa (light-as-a-feather flatbreads stuffed with vegetables or curried potatoes) is the ideal way to mop up the last of those heavenly sauces. **Known for:** delicious Keralan specialties; freshly baked dosa; great vegetarian options. ⑤ *Average* *main: £10* ✉ *27 Queen St.* ☏ *0191/232–7799* ⊕ *www.uryrestaurants.com.*

Hotels

★ Jesmond Dene House

$$ | HOTEL | Occupying a sprawling 19th-century mansion in the northeastern part of the city, this attractive, independent boutique hotel is surrounded by beautiful manicured gardens and filled with polished oak floors, huge windows, and wandering staircases. **Pros:** stylish bathrooms with underfloor heating; delicious breakfasts; free private parking. **Cons:** restaurant can get booked up; 15 minutes by bus or tram to the center; "New House" rooms are less interesting. ⑤ *Rooms from: £195* ✉ *Jesmend Dene Rd.* ☏ *0191/212–3000* ⊕ *www.jesmonddenehouse.co.uk* ⇗ *40 rooms* ⦿❙ *Free breakfast.*

Malmaison

$$ | HOTEL | Converted from an old riverside warehouse, this glamorous, design-conscious hotel sits beside the pedestrian Millennium Bridge. **Pros:** spacious and soundproofed rooms; relaxing spa; good restaurant with river views. **Cons:** unreliable Wi-Fi; bordello chic decor not for everyone; lacks the intimacy of small hotels. ⑤ *Rooms from: £150* ✉ *104 Quayside* ☏ *0191/389–8627* ⊕ *www.malmaison.com* ⇗ *122 rooms* ⦿❙ *Breakfast; Some meals.*

ⓨ Nightlife

Madame Koo

DANCE CLUBS | This quirky cocktail bar and nightclub has a loose 1920s Oriental theme. The dance-floor music choices are eclectic, often switching between classic soul, indie, disco, and pop within a single set. ✉ *28-32 Collingwood St.* ☏ *0191/261–8271* ⊕ *www.madamekoo.co.uk.*

🏃 Activities

City Baths

SWIMMING | FAMILY | Back in 2020, after an eight-year-long, £7.5 million transformation, Newcastle's City Baths feature a 25-meter-long pool, sauna, and Turkish spa, all set within a historic building. The large gym hall is where the old pool used to be; you can see the outline on the floor. ✉ *Northumberland Rd.* ☏ *07815/619127* ⊕ *www.city-baths.co.uk.*

⬢ Performing Arts

Sage Gateshead

CONCERTS | The Sage Gateshead hosts concerts—jazz, world, pop, classical, folk, and rock—in a curving, silver building designed by Sir Norman Foster. ✉ *West St.* ☏ *0191/433–4661* ⊕ *www.sagegateshead.com.*

Theatre Royal

THEATER | The region's most established performing arts center, the Theatre Royal stages high-quality productions and is also a venue for touring musicals and dance. ✉ *100 Grey St.* ☏ *0844/811–2121* ⊕ *www.theatreroyal.co.uk.*

Hadrian's Wall

73 miles from Wallsend, north of Newcastle, to Bowness-on-Solway, beyond Carlisle.

The most important Roman relic in Britain extends across the countryside and can be accessed at many different points. Committed hikers can tackle the full, 73-mile-long Hadrian's Wall Path. The Sill National Landscape Discovery Centre, about a mile northwest of Vindolanda, reveals more about the local landscape.

GETTING HERE AND AROUND

The A69 roughly follows Hadrian's Wall, although sometimes it's a few miles in either direction. The best sections of the wall are near the narrower B6318, including Vindolanda, Housesteads Roman Fort, and Chesters Roman Fort. There's a small railway station at Hexham, with frequent trains from Newcastle.

The aptly named AD122 Hadrian's Wall Country bus runs between Newcastle and Carlisle during the summer months, stopping near all the major destinations along the way. A special "rover ticket" pass gives you unlimited travel on the route for one (£12.50), three (£25), or seven (£50) days. You can extend the tickets to cover any bus operating on the same route for a few extra pounds. Several other local buses depart from Newcastle and other towns in the region to various parts of the wall.

ESSENTIALS
VISITOR INFORMATION AD112 Hadrian's Wall Country Bus. ☎ ⊕ *www.hadrianswall-country.co.uk/travel/bus.*

◉ Sights

★ Hadrian's Wall
ARCHAEOLOGICAL SITE | Dedicated to the Roman god Terminus, the massive span of Hadrian's Wall once marked the northern frontier of the Roman Empire. Today, remnants of the wall wander across pastures and hills, stretching 73 miles from Wallsend in the east to Bowness-on-Solway in the west. The wall is a UNESCO World Heritage Site, and excavating, interpreting, repairing, and generally managing it remains a Northumbrian growth industry.

At Emperor Hadrian's command, three legions of soldiers began building the wall in AD 122 and finished it in four years. It was constructed by soldiers and masons after repeated invasions by Pictish tribes from what is now Scotland. During the Roman era it was the most heavily fortified wall in the world, with walls 15 feet high and 9 feet thick; behind it lay the vallum, a ditch about 20 feet wide and 10 feet deep. Spaced at 5-mile intervals along the wall were massive forts (such as those at Housesteads and Chesters), which could house up to 1,000 soldiers. Every mile was marked by a thick-walled milecastle (a fort that housed about 30 soldiers), and between each milecastle were two turrets, each lodging four men who kept watch. For more than 250 years the Roman army used the wall to control travel and trade and to fortify Roman Britain against the barbarians to the north.

During the Jacobite Rebellion of 1745, the English army dismantled much of the Roman wall and used the stones to pave what is now the B6318 highway. The most substantial stretches of the remaining wall are between Housesteads and Birdoswald (west of Greenhead). Running through the southern edge of Northumberland National Park and along the sheer escarpment of Whin Sill, this section is also an area of dramatic natural beauty. The ancient ruins, rugged cliffs, dramatic vistas, and spreading pastures make it a great area for hiking. ⊕ *www.hadrianswallcountry.co.uk.*

⚡ Activities

BIKING
Hadrian's Cycleways
BICYCLING | Between Tynemouth and Whitehaven, Hadrian's Cycleway follows the River Tyne from the east coast until Newcastle, where it traces the entire length of Hadrian's Wall. It then continues west to the Irish Sea. Maps and guides are available at the Tourist Information Centre in Newcastle. ⊕ *www.cyclenorthumberland.org.uk/listing/hadrians-cycleway.*

HIKING
Hadrian's Wall Path
HIKING/WALKING | One of Britain's national trails, Hadrian's Wall Path runs the entire 73-mile length of the wall. If you don't have time for it all, take one of the less-challenging circular routes. One of the most scenic (but also most difficult)

sections is the 12-mile western stretch between Sewingshields and Greenhead. ⊕ *www.nationaltrail.co.uk/hadrianswall.*

Hexham

22 miles west of Newcastle, 33 miles northwest of Durham.

The busy market town of Hexham is a popular base for visiting Hadrian's Wall. Just a few miles from the most significant remains, it's a bustling working town, but it has enough historic buildings and winding medieval streets to warrant a stop in its own right. First settled in the 7th century, around a Benedictine monastery, Hexham later became a byword for monastic learning, famous for its book painting, sculpture, and singing.

GETTING HERE AND AROUND
The A1 and A69 highways link London and the region (five to six hours). No major bus companies travel here, but the AD122 Hadrian's Wall Country Bus from Newcastle and Carlisle does. East Coast trains take about three hours to travel from London's King's Cross to Newcastle. From there, catch a local train.

Hexham is a small, walkable town. It has infrequent local bus service, but you're unlikely to need it. If you're driving, park in the lot by the tourism office and walk into town. The tourism office has free maps and will point you in the right direction.

ESSENTIALS
VISITOR INFORMATION Hexham Tourist Information Centre. ⊠ *Queens Hall, Beaumont St.* ☎ *01670/620450* ⊕ *www. visithexham.net.*

 Sights

Chesters Roman Fort
MILITARY SITE | In a wooded valley on the banks of the North Tyne River, 4 miles north of Hexham, this cavalry fort was known as Cilurnum in Roman times,

when it protected the point where Hadrian's Wall crossed the river. Although the setting is not as dramatic as the nearby Housesteads Roman Fort, this mazelike layout of surviving fortifications is said to be Britain's most complete Roman cavalry fort, while the military bathhouse by the river is the best-preserved Roman structure of its kind in the British Isles. The Museum of Roman Finds includes a fascinating array of artifacts including statues of river and water gods and Roman jewelry. ⊠ *B6318, Chollerford* ☎ *01434/681379* ⊕ *www.english-heritage.org.uk/chesters* ⊠ *£7.20* ⊗ *Closed weekdays in Nov.–Feb.; closed Mon.–Tues. in Mar.*

★ Corbridge Roman Town
ARCHAEOLOGICAL SITE | The foundations of this important Roman garrison town (the farthest north in the entire Roman Empire) are brought to life with a lively audio commentary, plus occasional reenactments during the summer. The recently renovated visitor center houses the Corbridge Hoard, a surprisingly well-preserved collection of tools and personal possessions left behind by Roman soldiers in the 2nd century, as well as other objects found in and around the site. In particular, look out for three items: the Corbridge Lion, a free-standing sandstone sculpture depicting a male lion on top of a deer; the Corbridge Lanx, a large silver dish intricately engraved with mythological scenes; and a gambling soldier's "cheat's dice," which on close inspection features two ones and no six. Corbridge Roman Town is around four miles east of Hexham. ⊠ *Corchester La., Corbridge* ☎ *01434/632349* ⊕ *www. english-heritage.org.uk* ⊠ *£7.90* ⊗ *Closed weekdays Nov.–Feb.*

★ Hexham Abbey
RELIGIOUS SITE | A site of Christian worship for more than 1,300 years, ancient Hexham Abbey forms one side of the town's main square. Most of the current building dates from the 12th and 13th centuries, and much of the stone, including that of the Anglo-Saxon crypt, was taken from

the nearby Roman fort at Corbridge. Inside, you can climb the 35 worn stone "night stairs," which once led from the main part of the abbey to the canon's dormitory, to overlook the whole ensemble—look out for the drop of lead on the sixth step, a remnant from when the roof was set alight by a Scottish army in 1286. Also of note inside are the portraits on the 16th-century wooden rood screen and the four panels from a 15th-century *Dance of Death* in the sanctuary. You can find out more about the history of the abbey in the free, interactive exhibition The Big Story. ⊠ *Beaumont St.* ☎ *01434/602031* ⊕ *www.hexhamabbey. org.uk* ⊠ *Free; requested donation £3.*

Hexham Market Place

PLAZA | Since 1239, this pretty square has been the site of a weekly market, held each Tuesday and Saturday. Crowded stalls are set out across the square under colored awnings, attracting serious shoppers and souvenir hunters year-round. A popular farmers' market takes over on the second and fourth Saturday of the month. Even when there's not an official market on, there's often one or two food stalls set up. ⊠ *Market Pl.* ☎ *01434/230605* ⊕ *www.hexhamfarmersmarket.co.uk.*

Old Gaol

MUSEUM | FAMILY | England's oldest purpose-built prison, dating from 1330, Hexham's Old Gaol houses fascinating exhibits about the history of the borderlands, including tales of the terrifying "reivers" and their bloodthirsty raids into Northumberland from Scotland during the 16th and 17th centuries. Photographs, weapons, and a reconstructed house interior give a full account of what the region was like in medieval times. A glass elevator takes you up and down four floors, including to the dungeon. ⊠ *Hallgate* ☎ *01670/624523* ⊕ *museumsnorthumberland.org.uk/hexham-old-gaol* ⊠ *£5* ⊗ *Closed Nov.—Mar.*

🍴 Restaurants

The Corbridge Larder

$ | DELI | Located near Corbridge Roman Town and the best deli for miles around, this place is filled with all manner of local produce, as well as specialty foods from small-time artisans across Europe. Try the delicious but alarmingly colored Delfts Blauw cheese from Holland; its almost fluorescent blue hue is entirely natural. **Known for:** local and international artisanal produce; lovely upstairs café; village-shop atmosphere. ⑤ *Average main: £10* ⊠ *18 Hill St., Corbridge* ☎ *01434/632948* ⊕ *www.corbridgelarder.co.uk.*

🛏 Hotels

Battlesteads Hotel

$$ | B&B/INN | 10 miles north of Hexham and "beyond the wall," this delightful old inn combines three virtues: good food, cozy rooms, and eco-friendly credentials, with a string of awards to prove it. **Pros:** secret walled garden; excellent Sunday roasts; green ethos. **Cons:** some rooms on the small side; no mobile phone reception; service slow when busy. ⑤ *Rooms from: £125* ⊠ *Hexham Rd., Wark* ☎ *01434/230209* ⊕ *www. battlesteads.com* ⤴ *22 rooms* ⌾ *Free breakfast.*

★ Langley Castle

$$ | HOTEL | Close your eyes and picture an English castle: you're probably seeing Langley, a lavish 14th-century fortification complete with turrets and battlements. **Pros:** romantic and historic setting; lavish afternoon tea; full movies and sports TV packages in rooms. **Cons:** breakfast hit or miss; decor a little tired in places; service can be slow. ⑤ *Rooms from: £175* ⊠ *Off A686* ☎ *01434/688888* ⊕ *www. langleycastle.co.uk* ⤴ *27 rooms* ⌾ *Free breakfast.*

Performing Arts

Queen's Hall Arts Centre

ARTS CENTERS | A wide range of theater, dance, and art exhibitions are on the bill at the Queen's Hall Arts Centre. ⊠ *1-2 Beaumont St.* ☎ *01434/652477* ⊕ *www. queenshall.co.uk.*

Activities

The Bike Place

This cycle-hire place in Kielder is the nearest to this part of Hadrian's Wall, despite being 34 miles northwest of Hexham. Still, it's a great excuse to head up into Northumberland National Park. Rental prices start at £30 per day, or £50 for e-bikes, and they can arrange delivery and collection for an extra fee. The main store is in Kielder village, though there's a second on Kielder Waterside, which is marginally closer. ⊠ *Kielder Cycle Centre, Station Garage, Kielder* ⊹ *Take A6079 from the main A69 road. The shop is signposted on the main road through the village* ☎ *01434/250457* ⊕ *www.thebike-place.co.uk.*

Greenhead

19 miles west of Hexham, 51 miles northwest of Durham.

Greenhead may be small, but it's a good base for exploring some of the Hadrian's Wall sites that lie farther west, including the Housesteads Roman Fort, the Roman Army Museum, and Vindolanda. In Northumberland National Park, around 6 miles northest of Greenhead, The Sill National Landscape Discovery Centre has informative displays about Hadrian's Wall and can advise about local walks.

GETTING HERE AND AROUND

Greenhead is on the A69 and B6318. The nearest train station is 3 miles east, in Haltwhistle.

ESSENTIALS

VISITOR INFORMATION The Sill National Landscape Discovery Centre. ⊠ *Northumberland National Park, Bardon Mill* ☎ *01434/341200* ⊕ *www.thesill.org.uk.*

Sights

Birdoswald Roman Fort

ARCHAEOLOGICAL SITE | Beside the longest unbroken stretch of Hadrian's Wall, Birdoswald Roman Fort reveals the remains of gatehouses, a granary, and a parade ground. You can also see the line of the original turf wall, later rebuilt in stone. Birdoswald has a unique historical footnote: unlike other Roman forts along the wall, it was maintained by local tribes long after being abandoned by the Romans. The small visitor center has artifacts discovered at the site, a full-scale model of the wall, and a good café. ⊠ *Wallace Dr.* ☎ *0370/333–1181* ⊕ *www. english-heritage.org.uk/birdoswald* 🎫 *£8.60* ☾ *Closed weekdays in Nov.– Feb.; closed Mon.–Tues. in Mar.*

★ **Housesteads Roman Fort**

MUSEUM | If you have time to visit only one Hadrian's Wall site, Housesteads Roman Fort is your best bet. Britain's most complete example of a Roman fort also features long sections of the wall, with an informative visitor center showcasing a collection of artifacts discovered at the site and computer-generated images of what the fort originally looked like. The site is a 10-minute walk uphill from the parking lot (not for those with mobility problems), but the effort is more than worth it to see the surprisingly extensive ruins, dating from around AD 125. Excavations have revealed the remains of granaries, gateways, barracks, a hospital, and the commandant's house. ■TIP→ **Come for the history, stay for the views: the northern tip of the fort offers sweeping vistas of Hadrian's Wall as it winds up and over distant hills and crags.** ⊠ *Off*

B6318, Haydon Bridge ☎ *01434/344363* ⊕ *www.english-heritage.org.uk/house-steads* ✉ *£8.10; parking £3.*

Roman Army Museum

MUSEUM | FAMILY | At the garrison fort of Carvoran, this museum makes an excellent introduction to Hadrian's Wall. Full-size models and excavations bring this remote outpost of the empire to life, with a host of historic artifacts including authentic Roman graffiti adorning the walls of an excavated barracks. There's also a flashy 3D film that puts it all into historical context. Opposite the museum, at Walltown Crags on the Pennine Way (one of Britain's long-distance national hiking trails), are 400 yards of the best-preserved section of the wall. The museum is 1 mile northeast of Greenhead. ✉ *Off B6318* ☎ *01697/747485* ⊕ *www.vindolanda.com* ✉ *£7.25; £12.60 combined with Vindolanda* ⊙ *Closed mid-Nov.–mid-Feb.*

★ Vindolanda

ARCHAEOLOGICAL SITE | About 8 miles east of Greenhead, this archaeological site—which celebrated its 50th anniversary in 2020—holds the remains of eight successive Roman forts and civilian settlements, providing an intriguing look into the daily life of a military compound. Most of the visible remains date from the 2nd and 3rd centuries, and new excavations are constantly under way. A reconstructed Roman temple, house, and shop provide context, and the museum displays rare artifacts, such as a handful of extraordinary wooden tablets with messages about everything from household chores to military movements. A full-size reproduction of a section of the wall gives a sense of its sheer scale. ✉ *Off B6318, Bardon Mill* ☎ *01434/344277* ⊕ *www.vindolanda.com* ✉ *£8.50; £12.60 combined with Roman Army Museum* ⊙ *Closed mid-Nov.–mid-Feb.*

🍴 Restaurants

Milecastle Inn

$ | BRITISH | The snug bar and restaurant of this remote, peaceful, 17th-century pub make an excellent place to dine. Fine local meat goes into its famous savory pies; take your pick from wild boar and duckling pie or maybe a plate of Whitby scampi with chips. **Known for:** tasty house specialty meat pies; traditional pub food; 17th-century building. $ *Average main: £12* ✉ *B6318, Haltwhistle* ☎ *01434/321372* ⊕ *www.milecastle-inn.co.uk.*

🛏 Hotels

Holmhead Guest House

$ | B&B/INN | Talk about a feel for history—this former farmhouse in open countryside, graced with stone arches and exposed beams, is not only built *on* Hadrian's Wall but also partly *from* it. **Pros:** full of atmosphere; close to Hadrian's Wall; reasonable rates. **Cons:** rooms are a bit of a squeeze; out of the action; you need a car to get around. $ *Rooms from: £72* ✉ *Off B6318* ☎ *01697/747402* ⊕ *bandb-hadrianswall.co.uk* ▭ *No credit cards* ⇆ *5 rooms* ▥ *Free breakfast.*

Morpeth

16 miles north of Newcastle, 22 miles south of Alnwick.

Surrounded by idyllic pastures and tiny lanes, the hilly medieval market town of Morpeth is the closest thing this part of Northumberland comes to bustling. It's an ideal base for exploring some of the region's more hidden-away sights to the north of Newcastle.

GETTING HERE AND AROUND

Just off the A1, Morpeth is easily reached by car. Trains leave Newcastle every hour and take less than 15 minutes. Buses X14, X15, X18, and 44 connect Newcastle and Morpeth, and the journey takes around 40 minutes.

ESSENTIALS

VISITOR INFORMATION Morpeth Tourist Information Centre. ✉ *The Chantry, Bridge St.* 🕾 *01670/623455* ⊕ *www.visitnorthumberland.com.*

Sights

Brinkburn Priory

RELIGIOUS SITE | A fine historical anecdote concerns this idyllic Augustinian priory, founded in the early 12th century. A group of Scottish "reivers" came looking for the place to raid and loot it, but because it was entirely hidden by forest, they were unable to find it and gave up. The monks were so happy that they sounded the bells in celebration, thus revealing the location—and the Scots promptly returned and sacked the place. Most of the beautiful, light-filled building is the result of a loving Victorian restoration, though the spirit of the original has been retained, along with a few physical elements. Highlights of the interior include the stunning stone-carved altar, the striking stained-glass windows, and the William Hill organ, regularly used for classical music concerts. On the same site is a mill and a 19th-century manor house, which incorporates the undercroft from the former monk's refectory. The house is said to be inhabited by the spirits of a monk and a nun, and several workmen have reported sightings in recent years. ■**TIP→ The walk from the car park takes 10 minutes, but it's a lovely way to first encounter the priory. Those with mobility problems can drive all the way down.** ✉ *Off B6344* 🕾 *01665/570628* ⊕ *www.english-heritage.org.uk* 🎫 *£5.20* 🕓 *Closed Mon.–Tues. in Apr.–Sep.; closed weekends in Oct.; closed Nov.–Mar.*

★ Cragside

HOUSE | **FAMILY** | The turrets and towers of Tudor-style Cragside, a Victorian country house, look out over the edge of a forested hillside. It was built between 1864 and 1895 by Lord Armstrong, an early electrical engineer and inventor, and designed by Richard Norman Shaw, a well-regarded architect. Among Armstrong's contemporaries, Cragside was called "the palace of a modern magician" because it contained so many of his inventions. This was the first house in the world to be lit by hydroelectricity; the grounds also hold an energy center with restored mid-Victorian machinery. There are Pre-Raphaelite paintings and an elaborate mock-Renaissance marble chimneypiece.

The grounds are as impressive as the house; they cover around 1,000 acres and include an enormous sandstone rock garden, a picture-perfect iron bridge, and 14 different waymarked paths and trails, which bloom with rhododendrons in June. There's also a children's adventure playground. If you come by car, don't miss the 6-mile Carriage Drive around the estate. There are some lovely viewpoints and picnic spots along the way, like at the gorgeous Nelly's Moss lake. ■**TIP→ Paths around the grounds are steep, and distances can be long, so wear comfortable shoes.**

✉ *Off B6341, Rothbury* 🕾 *01669/620333* ⊕ *www.nationaltrust.org.uk/cragside* 🎫 *Grounds and house £18; grounds only £13, in winter £7.50.*

🍴 Restaurants

Central Bean Coffee House

$ | **DELI** | There's a distinct Pacific Northwest vibe at this funky little independent eatery in central Morpeth. Locals flock to the place for fresh sandwiches, panini, cakes, or just a fine cup of joe. **Known for:** great coffee; quick breakfast spot; friendly staff. ⑤ *Average main: £5* ✉ *21 Sanderson Arcade* 🕾 *01670/512300* ⊕ *www.centralbean.co.uk* 🚫 *No credit cards* 🕓 *No dinner.*

Hotels

Macdonald Linden Hall

$$ | HOTEL | Built as a getaway for a wealthy banker in 1812, this charming country estate surrounded by 450 acres of private grounds is wonderfully secluded; it's a full five minutes' drive off the nearest public road. **Pros:** out-of-the-way escape; soothing spa; gorgeous original building. **Cons:** can get overrun by large tour groups; visiting spa means a trip outside; bedrooms not as well maintained as public areas. $ *Rooms from: £209* ⊠ *Off A697, Longhorsley* ☎ *0344/879–9084* ⊕ *www.macdonaldhotels.co.uk* 🗗 *50 rooms* ⦿ *Some meals.*

★ Thistleyhaugh

$ | B&B/INN | This ivy-covered stone farmhouse sits at the center of a 720-acre organic farm. **Pros:** idyllic farmhouse location; wonderful hosts; excellent breakfasts. **Cons:** isolated location not for everyone; you'll need a car; minimum two-night stay in summer. $ *Rooms from: £100* ⊠ *Off A697, Longframlington* ☎ *01665/570629* ⊕ *www.thistlyhaugh. co.uk* 🗗 *4 rooms* ⦿ *Free breakfast.*

Alnwick

22 miles north of Morpeth, 24 miles south of Lindisfarne.

Dominated by a grand castle, the little market town of Alnwick (pronounced *ahn*-ick) is the best base from which to explore the dramatic coast and countryside of northern Northumberland.

GETTING HERE AND AROUND

If you're driving, Alnwick is just off the A1. Buses X15 and X18 connect Alnwick with Newcastle, Morpeth, and Lindisfarne. The nearest train station is 4 miles away in Alnmouth (pronounced *alun*-mowth); trains travel between here and Newcastle roughly every hour and take 25 minutes.

VISITOR INFORMATION Alnwick Tourist Information Centre. ⊠ *The Playhouse, Bondgate Without* ☎ *01670/622152* ⊕ *www.visitalnwick.org.uk.*

Sights

Alnwick Castle

CASTLE/PALACE | FAMILY | Sometimes called the "Windsor of the North," the imposing Alnwick Castle will likely provoke cries of "Hogwarts!" from younger visitors as it comes into view over the hill; the grounds appear as the exterior of the famous School of Witchcraft and Wizardry in the *Harry Potter* movies. Older visitors might also recognize it as Brancaster Castle from the TV series *Downton Abbey*. In reality, the castle is the ancestral home to the dukes of Northumberland, whose family, the Percys, dominated in the Northeast for centuries.

Head inside to find family photos and other knickknacks scattered around the lavish staterooms, a subtle but pointed reminder that this is a family home rather than a museum. Highlights include the extraordinary gun room, lined with hundreds of antique pistols arranged in swirling patterns; the formal dining room, its table set as if guests are due at any minute; and the magnificent galleried library, containing 14,000 books in floor-to-ceiling cases.

There's plenty here for younger visitors: **Knights' Quest** lets kids dress up and complete interactive challenges; **Dragon's Quest** is a labyrinth designed to teach a bit of medieval history; and for the very young, there are Harry Potter–style events on certain dates, including **Broomstick Lessons** on the exact spot used in the movie (check the website for the schedule). Spooky ghost stories are told by costumed actors in the **Lost Cellars.** In addition, staff members hide a toy owl somewhere in each room of the castle, and kids get a

The romantic grounds of Alnwick Castle are filled with flowers and rolling fields.

certificate if they spot them all. Tickets are valid for one year, so you can come back if you don't see everything in a day. ⊠ Off B6431 ☎ 01665/511100 ⊕ www.alnwick-castle.com ✉ £16.75; combined ticket with Alnwick Gardens £28.70 ⊗ Closed Nov.–Mar.

★ Alnwick Garden

GARDEN | FAMILY | A marvelous flight of fancy, Alnwick Garden celebrated its 20-year anniversary at the turn of this decade and remains one of the area's most beautiful, unusual, and kid-friendly attractions. Alongside traditional features like perfectly manicured lawns, shaded woodland walks, and a charming rose garden are more unusual elements like the enormous Grand Cascade water feature, a Poison Garden with everything from hemlock to cannabis, and a laby-rinth of towering bamboo. The grounds are also home to the largest "Tai-haku" cherry orchard in the world, as well as a recently spruced up shop and a number of excellent dining and drinking options, including one of the area's most unique restaurants, the Treehouse. ■TIP➔ You can buy clippings of the unique varieties of roses in the shop. ⊠ Denwick La. ☎ 01665/511350 ⊕ www.alnwickgarden. com ✉ £14.30; combined ticket with Aln-wick Castle £28.70 ⊗ Closed Jan.; closed midweek mid-Nov.–mid-Dec.

🍴 Restaurants

★ The Treehouse

$ | MODERN BRITISH | The treetop location may sound gimmicky, but the effect at this extraordinary restaurant is quite magical and unexpectedly romantic, especially when the place is lit up at night. Here, an enormous complex of buildings spreads out over more than 550 square meters, with a roaring log fire at its center and furniture made from fallen branches. **Known for:** unique setting; Northeastern flavors and ingredients; inoffensive acoustic music on a loop. $ Average main: £15 ⊠ Alnwick Garden, Denwick La. ☎ 01665/660320 ⊕ www. alnwickgardenhospitality.com ⊗ No dinner Sun.

The Far
Northeast Coast

Berwick-upon-Tweed
Tweedmouth
Scremerston
A1
Lindisfarne
(Holy Island)

Farne Islands

Cornhill-on-Tweed
A698
Crookham
Milfield
Belford
Bamburgh
Kelso
B6353
Seahouses
Beadnell
A697
Wooler
A1
High-Newton
-by-the-Sea
Embleton
Dunstanburgh
Castle
SCOTLAND
B1340
Craster

Powburn
Alnwick
Alnmouth

NORTHUMBERLAND
A697
Birling
Warkworth
Catcleugh
Cragside
A1
A68
Longframlington
Radcliffe
Rochester
Brinkburn
Elishaw
Priory
Longhorsley
Northumberland
National Park
Raylees
A1068
West
Woodburn
A696
Ashington
Knowesgate
Morpeth
Kielder
Water
East Sleekburn
A68
Belsay
A1
Blyth

North Sea

SCOTLAND

0   6 mi
0   6 km

🛏 Hotels

★ The Cookie Jar

$$$ | HOTEL | With sumptuously appoint-
ed rooms, a popular bistro restaurant,
and convenient location right by the
castle, this historic convent-turned-bou-
tique-hotel is Alnwick's most luxurious
town-center stay. **Pros:** delicious cooked
breakfast; spacious and comfortable
rooms; homemade cookies in rooms.
Cons: superior rooms are expensive; no
dinner served midweek; unrelentingly
blue decor. ⑤ *Rooms from: £165* ✉ *12
Bailiffgate* ☎ *01665/510465* ⊕ *www.cook-
iejaralnwick.com* 🛏 *11 rooms* ⑩ *Free
breakfast.*

Dunstanburgh Castle

*8 miles northeast of Alnwick, 11 miles
south of Bamburgh.*

Dunstanburgh is as dramatic an old ruin
as they come and more than worth the
effort it takes to get here (this is not the
kind of place where you can just drive up
to the front gate).

GETTING HERE AND AROUND

The castle is accessible only by footpaths
from the villages of Craster or Embleton off the B1339 rural road. The X18
bus from Alnwick is the only practical
connection by public transportation; get
off in Craster and head to the main public
parking lot (the village is small enough

It's worth the scenic coastal walk to see the remote clifftop ruins of Dunstanburgh Castle.

that it's easy to find). The coastal path starts here and is clearly signposted. It's a beautiful route, but a bit of a hike at around 2½ miles there and back.

Sights

Dunstanburgh Castle

CASTLE/PALACE | Perched romantically on a cliff 100 feet above the shore, these castle ruins can be reached along a windy, mile-long coastal footpath that heads north from the tiny fishing village of Craster. Built in 1316 as a defense against the Scots, and later enlarged by John of Gaunt, the powerful Duke of Lancaster who virtually ruled England in the late 14th century, the castle is known to many from the popular paintings by 19th-century artist J. M. W. Turner. The castle is a signposted 1.3-mile walk from the nearest parking lot in Craster, on the outskirts of Alnwick. ■**TIP→ While Dunstanburgh is run by English Heritage, it's owned by the** National Trust, so a membership with either organization will get you in for free. ✉ *Dunstanburgh Rd., Alnwick* ☎ *01665/576231* ⊕ *www.english-heritage.org.uk/dunstanburgh* 🎫 *£5.70* ⊗ *Closed weekdays Nov.–Mar.*

🛏 Hotels

Doxford Hall Hotel

$$ | HOTEL | Around 6 miles east of Dunstanburgh Castle, halfway between Alnwick and Bamburgh, lies this 200-year-old country mansion—now a popular spa hotel. **Pros:** gorgeous Georgian property; fascinating "history of Northumberland" tapestry in hall; theraputic deep pressure massage. **Cons:** some rooms old fashioned; gym is small and a little tired; can get booked up with weddings. 🖫 *Rooms from: £220* ✉ *Off A1, Alnwick* ☎ *01665/589700* ⊕ *www.doxfordhall.com* ⇆ *36 rooms* ⑩ *Free breakfast.*

Bamburgh

16 miles north of Alnwick, 14 miles south of Lindisfarne.

Tiny Bamburgh has a splendid castle, and several beaches are just a few minutes' walk away.

GETTING HERE AND AROUND

Bamburgh can be reached by car on the B3140, B3141, or B3142. Buses X18 and 418 run from Alnwick to Bamburgh a few times per day. The nearest train station is in Chathill, about 7 miles away.

⊙ Sights

★ Bamburgh Castle

CASTLE/PALACE | You'll see Bamburgh Castle long before you reach it: a solid, weather-beaten, clifftop fortress that dominates the coastal view for miles around. A fortification of some kind has stood here since the 6th century, but the Norman castle was damaged during the 15th century, and the central tower is all that remains intact. Much of the structure—the home of the Armstrong family since 1894—was restored during the 18th and 19th centuries. The interior is mostly late Victorian (most impressively, the Great Hall), although a few rooms, such as the small but alarmingly well-stocked armory, have a more authentically medieval feel. The breathtaking view across the North Sea is worth the steep climb up from the main road; bring a picnic if the weather's good (or order to-go sandwiches at the café). ⊠ Off B1340 ☎ 01668/214515 ⊕ www.bamburghcastle.com ⊠ £11.75 ⊙ Closed weekdays Nov.–mid-Feb.

Farne Islands

ISLAND | Regular boat trips from the little village of Seahouses, 3 miles down the coast from Bamburgh, provide access to the Farne Islands with their impressive colonies of seabirds—including puffins, kittiwakes, terns, shags, and

Walking and Biking in the Northeast 🏃

Wide vistas, quiet roads, and fresh air make for excellent hikes and bike rides in the Northeast. Long-distance footpaths include the 90-mile Teesdale Way, which follows the River Tees through Barnard Castle and Middleton-in-Teesdale. Otherwise, the russet hills and dales of Northumberland National Park will please any serious walker. Bike routes to explore—in whole or in part—are the 220-mile Northumbria Cycling Kingdom loop and the 81-mile Coast and Castles cycle route.

guillemots—and barking groups of gray seals. Inner Farne, where St. Cuthbert, the great abbot of Lindisfarne, died in AD 687, has a tiny chapel. Look out for the ruined lighthouse beacons as you pass Brownsman Island. Four companies are currently licensed to make the trip to Farne and the other islands. Of these, **Billy Shiel's Boat Trips** (01665/720308 ⊕ www.farne-islands.com) has the most reliable advertised schedule; they cruise to Inner Farne every day April through October. There's always a 1 pm departure, as well as between two and five on-the-hour tours on either side of this; check the website for month-by-month schedules. They also visit the rocky Staple Island between May and July, daily at 10 am and 11 am. Cruises to each island cost £20 and take 2½ hours, including an hour's landfall (in good weather only). The other operators are **Golden Gate** (01665/721210 ⊕ www.farneislandsboattrips.co.uk), **Serenity** (01665/721667 ⊕ www.farneislandstours.co.uk), and **St. Cuthbert** (01665/720388 ⊕ www.farneislands.co.uk); call or check online for their daily schedules. All boat services leave from Seahouses harbor—look for

The Farne Island are home to a charming collection of seabirds, including a puffin colony.

the tiny booth selling tickets or the outlet in the main village parking lot. Each company offers a variety of other cruises, such as seal-spotting expeditions. Visit the individual websites to see what's on offer this season. ■TIP→ In addition to the cost of the boat trip, there's a National Trust landing fee of £11.60 (May through July) and £7.70 (in April, and August through November). ⊠ *Seahouses Harbour, Harbour Rd., Seahouses* ☏ *01289/389244 National Trust* ⊕ *www.nationaltrust. org.uk/farne-islands* ⛴ *Landing fees £7.70–£11.60.*

🍴 Restaurants

★ Grays Restaurant

$$ | BRITISH | Located on a quiet bay between Bamburgh and Lindisfarne and surrounded by 6 acres of woodland, this elegant, award-winning restaurant sits within the historic Waren House Hotel. The fixed-price dinners (one course for £22.50, two for £33.95, three for £42.50) feature local flavors, with options like the steamed Berwick white crab and apple

tian, Northumberland beef fillet with shallot confit, and Alnwick rum and chocolate ganache torte. **Known for:** picturesque surroundings; elegant, traditional menus; short serving time (from 6:30 pm to 8:30 pm). ⑤ *Average main: £22.50* ⊠ *Off B1342* ☏ *01668/214581* ⊕ *www.waren-househotel.co.uk.*

🛏 Hotels

Beadnell Towers

$$ | HOTEL | Five miles south of Bamburgh on the scenic coastal road, this chic boutique hotel combines 18th-century heritage and character with 21st-century luxury and comfort. **Pros:** delicious, locally sourced food; free parking for guests; a short walk to sandy Beadnell Bay. **Cons:** room decor varies wildly so pick carefully; restaurant gets busy on weekends; dogs can stay so barking may be heard. ⑤ *Rooms from: £159* ⊠ *The Wynding, Off B1340* ☏ *01665/721211* ⊕ *www.beadnelltowers.co.uk* ⇌ *18 rooms* ⦿ *Free breakfast.*

Lord Crewe Hotel

$ | **HOTEL** | This cozy, stone-walled inn with oak beams sits in the heart of the village and has simple, modern guest rooms decorated with pine furnishings; some of them date back to the 1600s. **Pros:** in the center of the village; good seafood restaurant; close to Bamburgh Castle. **Cons:** pub can get quite crowded; some uninspiring room decor; pet-friendly bar is ideal for dog lovers but not for allergy sufferers. ⑤ *Rooms from: £110* ✉ *Front St.* ☎ *01668/214243* ⊕ *www.lord-crewe. co.uk* ⌑ *7 rooms* ⦿| *Free breakfast.*

Lindisfarne (Holy Island)

14 miles north of Bamburgh, 24 miles north of Alnwick.

The cradle of northern England's Christianity and one-time home of St. Cuthbert, Lindisfarne (or Holy Island) has a religious history that dates from AD 635, when St. Aidan established a monastery here. Under its greatest abbot, the sainted Cuthbert, Lindisfarne became one of the foremost centers of learning in Christendom. Today, you can explore the atmospheric ruined priory and a castle.

GETTING HERE AND AROUND

By car, the island is reached from the mainland via a long drive on a causeway that floods at high tide, so check when crossing is safe. The tide schedule, which changes daily, is displayed at the causeway and printed in local newspapers. Traffic can be heavy; allow at least a half hour for your return trip. The only public transportation to Holy Island is run by Borders Buses. Bus 477 has limited service (a few buses per day and not every day) from Berwick-upon-Tweed railway station to the island.

ESSENTIALS

BUS CONTACTS Borders Buses.
☎ *01896/754350* ⊕ *www.bordersbuses. co.uk.*

⊙ Sights

Lindisfarne Castle

CASTLE/PALACE | Reached during low tide via a causeway from the mainland, this castle appears to grow out of the rocky pinnacle on which it was built 400 years ago, looking for all the world like a fairy-tale illustration. In 1903, architect Sir Edwin Lutyens converted the former Tudor fort into a private home that retains the original's ancient features. Across several fields from the castle is a walled garden designed by Gertrude Jekyll. Opening times are notoriously changeable—especially on Monday outside midsummer—and are always dependant on weather and tides, so it's best to call ahead. ✉ *Off Marygate, Lindisfarne* ☎ *01289/389244* ⊕ *www.nationaltrust. org.uk/lindisfarne-castle* ⊠ *£8.*

★ Lindisfarne Priory

RELIGIOUS SITE | In the year 875, Vikings destroyed the Lindisfarne community; only a few monks escaped, carrying with them Cuthbert's bones, which were reburied in Durham Cathedral. The sandstone Norman ruins of Lindisfarne Priory, reestablished in the 11th century, remain impressive and beautiful. A museum here displays Anglo-Saxon carvings. ✉ *Church Ln., Lindisfarne* ☎ *01289/389200* ⊕ *www.english-heritage.org.uk/lindisfarne* ⊠ *£7.20* ⊙ *Closed weekdays Nov.–Feb.*

Index

Photo Credits

Photo Credits

age fotostock (431). Britain on View/photolibrary.com (434-435). Martin Pettitt/Flickr, [CC BY-ND 2.0] (436). Britain On View/photolibrary.com (436). Look Die Bildagentur der Fotografen GmbH / Alamy (436). Andreas Tille/Wikimedia Commons, [CC BY 2.0] (436). John Glover / age fotostock (437). National Trust Photo Library/Britain On View/photolibrary.com (438). North Light Images / age fotostock (439). David Sellman/ Britain On View/photolibrary.com (439). Andy Williams / age fotostock (449). Simon Tranter / age fotostock (457). Chapter 9: Stratford-up- on-Avon and the Heart of England: trabantos/iStockphoto (459). Simon Reddy / Alamy (462). Monkey Business Images/Shutterstock (463). Foodpics/Shutterstock (463). Cotswolds Photo Library/Britain on View/photolibrary.com (469). Arenaphotouk/ Dreamstime (475). Travel Pix Collection / age fotostock (476). Tobias Grosskopf/Shutterstock (485). nPerspective/Shutterstock.com (500). A-Shropshire-Lad/iStockphoto (505). Ironbridge Gorge Museum Trust (508). Nadia/Flickr, [CC BY 2.0] (513). Corhob/Dreamstime (514). Chapter 10: Manchester, Liverpool, and the Peak District: Barcofigari/Dreamstime (517). Land of Lost Content / age fotostock (520). Jennifer Boyer/Flickr, [CC BY 2.0] (521). Havaska/Wikimedia Commons, [CC BY 2.0] (521). Pawel Libera/Britain on View/photolibrary.com (530). Chris Brink / age fotostock (536). Britain on View/photolibrary.com (542). Coleong/Dreamstime (556). Pat Scullion/Flickr, [CC BY 2.0] (561). Chapter 11: The Lake District: Rob Carter / Alamy (565). "Levens Hall & Gardens, photograph by Val Corbett (574). Simon Balson / Alamy (579). Alan Novelli/Britain On View/ photolibrary.com (588). Roy Shakespeare / age fotostock (589). Stewart Smith Photography/Shutterstock (590). Julius Honnor/Flickr, [CC BY 2.0] (591). Stewart Smith Photography/Shutterstock (591). Julius Honnor/Flickr, [CC BY 2.0] (591). Britain on View/photolibrary.com (592). Larra Jungle Princess/Flickr, [CC BY-ND 2.0] (593). Mike D Williams/Shutterstock (593). National Trust Photo Library/Britain on View/ photolibrary.com (597). Ashley Cooper / age fotostock (603). Atgimages/Dreamstime (607). Snake81/Dreamstime (611). Chapter 12: Cambridge and East Anglia: Alistair Laming / age fotostock (613). Shane W Thompson/Shutterstock (616). Roddy Paine / age fotostock (617). Monkey Business Images/Shutterstock (617). Quentin Bargate / age fotostock (623). Mark Sunderland / age fotostock (627). Vidler / age fotostock (638). David Calvert/Shutterstock (646). ëBurghley House Preservation Trustí (656). Durden Images/Shutterstock (658). Chapter 13: Yorkshire: Jason Friend / age fotostock (661). Alex Segre/Shutterstock (664). D. Pimborough/Shutterstock (665). Gervele/istockphoto (665). Peter Baker / age fotostock (675). Charlie Edward/Shutterstock (678). David Joyce/Flickr, [CC BY-ND 2.0] (679). Photolibrary.com (679). Convit/ Shutterstock (679). Photolibrary.com (680). Mattana/Wikimedia Commons, [CC BY 2.0] (680). joevare/Flickr, [CC BY-ND 2.0] (680). Charlie Edward/Shutterstock (681). Photolibrary.com (681). Photolibrary.com (682). Richard Croft/Wikimedia Commons, [CC BY 2.0] (682). travelllight/ Shutterstock (685). PrakichTreetasayuth/Shutterstock (688). Electropower/Dreamstime (691). Wojtek Buss / age fotostock (698). Dave Porter/ Britain on View/photolibrary.com (700). Emily_M_Wilson/iStockphoto (707). Khrizmo/iStockphoto (713 & 716). Chapter 14: Hadrian's Wall and the Northeast: Lee Frost / age fotostock (719). Ian McDonald/Shutterstock (722). Mark A. Wilson (Department of Geology, The College of Wooster)/Wikimedia Commons, [CC BY 2.0] (723). Michel wal/Wikimedia Commons, [CC BY 2.0] (723). Rod Edwards/Britain on View/ photolibrary.com (731). Alan Dawson / age fotostock (736). Romana photographer/shutterstock (745). coxy58/Shutterstock (747). gabrisigno/ Shutterstock (749). About Our Writers: All photos are courtesy of the writers.

Notes

Notes

Fodor's ESSENTIAL ENGLAND

Publisher: Stephen Horowitz, *General Manager*

Editorial: Douglas Stallings, *Editorial Director*; Jill Fergus, Jacinta O'Halloran, Amanda Sadlowski, *Senior Editors*; Kayla Becker, Alexis Kelly, *Editors*

Design: Tina Malaney, *Director of Design and Production*; Jessica Gonzalez, *Graphic Designer;* Mariana Tabares, *Design & Production Intern*

Production: Jennifer DePrima, *Editorial Production Manager*; Elyse Rozelle, *Senior Production Editor;* Monica White, *Production Editor*

Maps: Rebecca Baer, *Senior Map Editor*; David Lindroth and Mark Stroud (Moon Street Cartography), *Cartographers*

Photography: Viviane Teles, *Senior Photo Editor;* Namrata Aggarwal, Ashok Kumar, Carl Yu, *Photo Editors;* Rebecca Rimmer, *Photo Intern*

Business & Operations: Chuck Hoover, *Chief Marketing Officer*; Robert Ames, *Group General Manager*; Devin Duckworth, *Director of Print Publishing*; Victor Bernal, *Business Analyst*

Public Relations and Marketing: Joe Ewaskiw, *Senior Director Communications & Public Relations*

Fodors.com: Jeremy Tarr, *Editorial Director;* Rachael Levitt, *Managing Editor*

Technology: Jon Atkinson, *Director of Technology;* Rudresh Teotia, *Lead Developer*; Jacob Ashpis, *Content Operations Manager*

Writers: Robert Andrews, Jo Caird, Rhonda Carrier, Sally Coffey, Sophie Ibbotson, James O'Neill, Toby Orton, Joseph Reaney, Ellin Stein, Alex Wijeratna

Editors: Amanda Sadlowski, Cameron Todd

Production Editor: Monica White

2nd Edition

ISBN 978-1-64097-296-4

ISSN 2576–9294

SPECIAL SALES

This book is available at special discounts for bulk purchases for sales promotions or premiums. For more information, e-mail SpecialMarkets@fodors.com.

PRINTED IN THE UNITED STATES OF AMERICA

10 9 8 7 6 5 4 3 2 1

About Our Writers

Longtime contributor **Robert Andrews** loves warm beer and soggy moors but hates scavenging seagulls and the sort of weather when you're not sure if it's raining—all of which he found in abundance while updating the Cornwall and West Country chapter. He writes and revises other guidebooks and has penned his own guide to Devon and Cornwall.

Jo Caird is a travel and arts journalist who writes on theater, visual arts, film, literature, and food and drink, as well as cycling and scuba diving. For this edition, she worked on the Westminster and St. James, East London, and Greenwich sections in the London chapter.

A leading family travel expert, Manchester-based writer **Rhonda Carrier** writes for publications like *National Geographic Traveller*, the *Guardian*, and *Condé Nast Traveller*, as well as serving as comissioning editor for TaketheFamily.com. She updated the Manchester, Liverpool, and the Peak District chapter in this edition.

Sally Coffey is a journalist who specializes in British travel and tourism. She recently left her four-year editorship of *BRITAIN*—the official magazine of VisitBritain—and has been writing freelance travel articles for the *Guardian*, *Cruise International*, and *Discover Britain* as well as writing her own travel book on Scotland. Somehow she also managed to find time to update our Stratford-upon-Avon and the Heart of England chapter in this edition.

Sophie Ibbotson is a writer, entrepreneur, and lover of wild places, which means updating the Bath and the Cotswolds and the Lake District chapters was right up

her alley. Her travel writing has appeared in *Newsweek*, *Financial Times*, *Sunday Telegraph*, *City A.M.*, and *The Spectator*.

James O'Neill loves London and—as his work updating several neighborhood sections for this edition proves—loves rediscovering it, too. Although originally from Ireland, he's lived in London for almost 20 years—and still loves it just as much now as he did back then.

Having studied in London and never left—aside from a brief sojourn in Madrid—**Toby Orton** has experienced everything in the capital from Hackney to Notting Hill, Highgate to Peckham, and still finds it the most inspiring city in the world. He credits the bookshops, bars, galleries, clubs, and streets of London with making him the person he is today. He has written about travel, cycling, food, and drink for a range of websites and publications. For this edition, he updated several London neighborhoods and the Oxford and Thames Valley and Cambridge and East Anglia chapters.

Joseph Reaney is an experienced travel writer and editor born in England and based part-time in Scotland and part-time in the Czech Republic—and regularly writes about all three. He contributes to *National Geographic, Forbes Travel Guide*, and *USA Today*, among others, and runs his own travel content writing agency, World Words. When he has the time, he also writes and directs short films and comedy sketches. For this edition, he updated the Experience, Canterbury and the Southeast, and Hadrian's Wall and the Northeast chapters.

About Our Writers

Ellin Stein has written for publications on both sides of the Atlantic, including the *New York Times*, the *Times of London*, and *InStyle*. Her book *That's Not Funny, That's Sick: The National Lampoon and the Comedy Insurgents Who Captured the Mainstream*, was published by W. W. Norton & Co. in 2013. She has lived in London for two decades and is married to a native. For this edition, Ellin updated the South and Yorkshire chapters as well as Travel Smart England. Her territory also included several London neighborhoods.

London restaurant maven **Alex Wijeratna** is always amazed by the capital's rocket-fueled restaurant scene. He has written for publications including *The Times, Guardian,* and *Independent.* Alex updated the Soho and Covent Garden section in London.